# CRISIS INTERVENTION HANDBOOK

*Fourth Edition*

# CRISIS INTERVENTION HANDBOOK

## Assessment, Treatment, and Research

FOURTH EDITION

Edited by

Kenneth R. Yeager

Founding Editor

Albert R. Roberts

OXFORD
UNIVERSITY PRESS

# OXFORD
UNIVERSITY PRESS

Oxford University Press is a department of the University of
Oxford. It furthers the University's objective of excellence in research,
scholarship, and education by publishing worldwide.

Oxford   New York
Auckland   Cape Town   Dar es Salaam   Hong Kong   Karachi
Kuala Lumpur   Madrid   Melbourne   Mexico City   Nairobi
New Delhi   Shanghai   Taipei   Toronto

With offices in
Argentina   Austria   Brazil   Chile   Czech Republic   France   Greece
Guatemala   Hungary   Italy   Japan   Poland   Portugal   Singapore
South Korea   Switzerland   Thailand   Turkey   Ukraine   Vietnam

Published in the United States of America by
Oxford University Press
198 Madison Avenue, New York, NY 10016

Library of Congress Cataloging-in-Publication Data
Crisis intervention handbook: assessment, treatment and research / edited by
Kenneth R. Yeager, PhD. and Albert R. Roberts — Fourth edition.
   pages cm
Includes bibliographical references and index.
ISBN 978-0-19-020105-0 (alk. paper)
1. Crisis intervention (Mental health services)—Handbooks, manuals, etc.   2. Community
mental health services—Handbooks, manuals, etc.   I. Yeager, Kenneth, editor.
RC480.6.C744 2015
616.89'025—dc23
2014036614

9 8 7 6 5
Printed in the United States of America
on acid-free paper

# Contents

## Part VI:  Best Practice Outcomes

# Foreword

GRAYCE M. SILLS

This book belongs on the desk, and in the library, of every health professional regardless of discipline, background, experience, or training. By their very nature, human service professionals come in contact on a daily basis with more crisis than can be imagined. This book provides an authoritative, conceptually integrated paradigm for intervening in crisis situations. In this 21st century, with upheavals on the planet ranging from acts of war, to terrorism, to increasing numbers and kinds of natural disasters, all of us have in effect been put on permanent crisis alert. The conceptual model provided in this book, which presents Albert Roberts's approach combined with Kenneth Yeager's revisions, is the basis for what should be in every health professional's toolkit. Why is this not already so, and why is it a challenge for us to have a cadre of completely competent crisis intervention health service professionals available 24/7 in every community in America? In part this is so because American society in particular and, increasingly, modern societies worldwide like to see immediate results and instant satisfaction from nearly all activity.

We tend to learn the lessons of history but then forget them very quickly. Let us look back for a moment to World War II, when early on in the North African campaign we learned through a seminal paper by Roy Grinker and John Spiegel (1945) about the efficacy of an immediate intervention in response to a soldier's crisis in the trenches. This paper markedly influenced the treatment of World War II veterans at battlefield medic stations, where with short-term crisis intervention, essentially a replaying of the events that led to the crisis under conditions of significant social support, produced soldiers who were ready to return to the battlefield and not did not require treatment at the more remote military hospitals. These experiences led the foremost psychiatrists of the day to become politically active after they returned from the war. They advocated and were successful in getting Congress to pass the National Mental Health Act of 1946, which established community mental health centers that were to provide around-the-clock crisis intervention, thus applying what had been learned on the field of battle to increase the effectiveness of community programs.

However, problems persisted in terms of how to measure outcomes. How does one measure suicides averted or depression avoided? Without the metrics that were becoming increasingly important in the dynamics of health care, crisis intervention programs gave way to more intensive inpatient treatment. The lesson had been learned but was then forgotten, only to be discovered again in the aftermath of the Vietnam War. It was only when the US Veterans Administration began to establish drop-in centers in outpatient clinics that we rediscovered how important the element of time was in the treatment of crisis and how difficult it is to treat the effects of long-term crisis trauma. Now, once more, it seems as if we are on the cusp of relearning those important lessons first enumerated by Grinker and Spiegel (1945) and further elaborated by Lindeman's (1944) work on loss and grief as a response to crisis/trauma. With advances in technology, we are becoming able to measure the full impact of trauma and the impact of care when considering events avoided. Through years of technological development and innovation, science and clinical practice are now able to solidify into evidence informed practice approaches providing empirically informed approaches to care that are reflective of current best practices.

With this background in mind, what you will find in this newly revised book will be evidence-based best practices for a wide variety of types of crisis intervention. These chapters, with their case studies, offer clear maps for successful application of crisis intervention. I know of no other work that, once mastered, completely arms one to deal with crisis events. The chapters are written by nationally recognized content experts and are coordinated and pulled together masterfully by Dr. Kenneth Yeager. Dr. Yeager builds successfully on the work of his dear friend and colleague Albert R. Roberts. He crafts this work in a way that is both respectful to and reminiscent of the words and lifework of Dr. Roberts. In several of the chapters, you will see how the work of Dr. Roberts has been updated, yet the flavor and examples from the original work are maintained. Dr. Yeager's position over the past 10 years in the world of hospitals and healthcare has led to a depth of experience that is richly revealed in the pages of this work. This is played out in chapters regarding addiction, domestic violence, and a new chapter that reveals Dr. Yeager's important work in addressing crisis in healthcare providers. All the work presented in this book is based on day-to-day applications of crisis intervention processes and evidence. The important work spelled out in the pages of this text serves as both a foundation and a roadmap for future crisis intervention practices.

What of the future? Clearly, the results of the pioneering ACE study continue to show us a way for the creation of early intervention programs and also a way of mitigating trauma following adverse childhood events

(Felitti et al., 1998). Equally important as a guide for work in our future is the body of research devoted to the mind-body connection. The pioneering work of Kiecolt-Glaser and Newton (2001) has led to a certainty about the devastating physiological and physical effects that result from experiences with unresolved crisis. This begins to constitute the body of knowledge needed to demonstrate the efficacy of crisis intervention and crisis prevention strategies. While the future is always uncertain, what seems clear at this point in time is that the need for well-prepared, well-trained crisis intervenors will not lessen. Rather, one suspects that the need will continue to grow as the world becomes more connected. In that respect, it would seem that this textbook offers a roadmap for individual organizations communities and nation-states in this regard. In light of this, I would like to close this foreword with a quote from the late Abraham Kaplan (1973): "We have tasted the fruit of the tree of knowledge once for all. We have left Paradise forever behind us. But if we so choose, we can make use of that knowledge, not to make a heaven on earth, but so to dispose of the resources of the world around us even that the angels can look down and know something of a greatness of man's estate" (pp. 45–46).

REFERENCES

Felitti, M. D., Vincent, J., Anda, M. D., Robert, F., Nordenberg, M. D., Williamson, M. S.,... James, S. (1998). Relationship of childhood abuse and household dysfunction to many of the leading causes of death in adults: The Adverse Childhood Experiences (ACE) Study. *American Journal of Preventive Medicine, 14*(4), 245–258.

Grinker, R. S., & Spiegel, J. P. (1945). *War neuroses.* Philadelphia: Blakiston.

Kaplan, A. (1973). *Love and death: Talks on contemporary and perennial themes by Abraham Kaplan.* Ann Arbor: University of Michigan Press.

Kiecolt-Glaser, J. K., & Newton, T. L. (2001). Marriage and health: His and hers. *Psychological Bulletin, 127,* 472–503.

Lindeman, E. (1944). The symptomatology and management of acute grief. *American Journal of Psychiatry, 101,* 141–148.

# Acknowledgments

I want to express my sincere gratitude to the authors who contributed their expertise and original chapters to this book. This work could not have been completed without their hard work and dedication.

Grateful acknowledgment goes to my exceptional editor, Dana Bliss (Senior Editor, Academic and Professional Books at Oxford University Press), for his commitment to this fourth edition. His dedication to this body of work speaks volumes to his knowledge and respect for both the contributors and the contributions contained within this text, and to his efforts in bringing this revision to completion. A special thanks goes to Brianna Marron, Assistant Editor at Oxford University Press, for answering an endless litany of questions and always being available to help.

This book also owes a debt to Dr. Grayce Sills for completing the foreword to this work. My wife, Donna, deserves special thanks and appreciation for her patience with me for the lost weekends, but especially for the occasional pep talks as the hours required to complete the manuscript seemed to go on for a very long time. Thanks also to Caitlin Willet for her assistance with organizing and assembling the manuscript and her help through all phases of completing this revision. Finally, great appreciation goes to Dr. John Campo, Chairman of the Department of Psychiatry, of The Ohio State University, for his support of this endeavor.

I dedicate this book to the late Dr. Albert R. Roberts, who provided so much support and direction for young academicians throughout his tenure as a professor, mentor, editor, and friend. In completing this revision, I was struck by the numerous stories about him, all of which followed a similar storyline. Almost without exception, authors told of how Al provided them with the opportunity for their first publication. All spoke fondly of their interactions with Dr. Roberts and of his mentoring, support, guidance, and selflessness. Many indicated they would not be where they are today if it were not for the thought leadership offered by Al Roberts.

As I think back to my first telephone encounter with Dr. Roberts, I remember a brief introduction followed by nearly 90 minutes of conversation, resulting in my first publication. This also seems to be the case with many others. In a world where the pace is fast and the demands are great, the opportunity to interact with a person who thinks of others first is indeed an unusual experience. Yet, for so many, Al Roberts was the person who listened, guided, supported, and, most important, inspired.

## NATIONAL INTERNET RESOURCES AND 24-HOUR CRISIS INTERVENTION HOTLINES

*The National Suicide Prevention Lifeline* is a 24-hour, toll-free suicide prevention hotline. Persons in crisis can call 1-800-273-8255 and be connected to one of the 115 crisis centers in the NSPL network located in the city and state nearest to the caller's location. The national hotline network is administered through the Mental Health Association of New York City and is funded by the Substance Abuse and Mental Health Services Administration's Center for Mental Health Services of the US Department of Health and Human Services.

*The National Disaster Technical Assistance Center of the Substance Abuse and Mental Health Services Administration* (SAMHSA) in Bethesda, Maryland, provides resources and expertise to assist states, territories, and local communities that are preparing for or responding to the mental health needs of natural and human-made community disasters. Website: http://www.mentalhealth.samhsa.gov/dtac or phone: 1-800-308-3515. Resources are available online or by contacting SAMHSA by phone. These resources are extremely helpful to agencies, organizations, and communities to develop and implement disaster response plans.

# Contributors

## EDITOR

**Kenneth R. Yeager, PhD, LISW** is an Associate Professor, Clinical, in the College of Medicine, Department of Psychiatry and Behavioral Health of The Ohio State University; Director of Quality Improvement for OSU Harding Hospital; and Director of the Stress, Trauma and Resilience (STAR) Program. Dr. Yeager has numerous publications in the following areas: treating co-morbid substance abuse and mental illness; quality improvement and development quality metrics; and evidence-based practice, including the Oxford University Press book titled *Evidence-Based Practice Manual: Research and Outcome Measures in Health and Human Services.* He is a member of Oxford Bibliographies Online editorial board and a treating clinician for the National Football League Program for Substance Abuse.

## Contributors

Christopher D. Bowling,
  MSEd, CLEE
Commander, Patrol Zone Four
Crisis Intervention Team (CIT)
  Coordinator
Columbus, Ohio Division of Police
Columbus, Ohio

Ann Wolbert Burgess, RN,
  DNSc, FAAN
Professor of Psychiatric–Mental
  Health Nursing
School of Nursing
Boston College
Chestnut Hill, Massachusetts

Sophia F. Dziegielewski,
  PhD, LCSW
Professor
University of Central Florida
College of Health &
  Public Affairs
School of Social Work
Orlando, Florida

Yvonne Eaton-Stull,
  DSW, LCSW
Director of the Counseling
  Center
Allegheny College
Meadville, Pennsylvania

Brian Flynn, MSW, LCSW
Director of Admissions and
    Student Services
Department of Social Work
Binghamton University
Binghamton, New York

Gilbert J. Greene, PhD, LISW-S
Professor
College of Social Work
Ohio State University
Columbus, Ohio

Thomas K. Gregoire, PhD
Dean
College of Social Work
Ohio State University
Columbus, Ohio

Darcy Haag Granello, PhD, LPCC
Certified Wellness Counselor
Professor of Counselor Education
Project Director, OSU Suicide
    Prevention Program
Ohio State University
Columbus, Ohio

Vincent E. Henry, CPP, PhD
Professor and Director
Homeland Security Management
    Institute
Southampton College of Long
    Island University
Southampton, New York

Laura M. Hopson, PhD
Associate Professor
School of Social Work
The University of Alabama
Tuscaloosa, Alabama

George A. Jacinto, PhD, LCSW
Associate Professor
University of Central Florida
College of Health & Public Affairs
School of Social Work
Orlando, Florida

Laura K. Jones, PhD
Assistant Professor
Department of Applied
    Psychology & Counselor
    Education
College of Education and
    Behavioral Sciences
University of Northern
    Colorado
Greenley, Colorado

David P. Kasick, MD
Assistant Professor of Clinical
    Psychiatry
Director of Consultation-Liaison
    Psychiatry
Department of Psychiatry
Ohio State University Wexner
    Medical Center
Columbus, Ohio

Joshua Kirven, PhD
Assistant Professor
Cleveland State University
School of Social Work
Cleveland, Ohio

Karen S. Knox, PhD, LCSW
Professor and Field
    Coordinator
School of Social Work
Texas State University
San Marcos, Texas

Mo-Yee Lee, PhD
Professor
College of Social Work
The Ohio State University
Columbus, Ohio

Sarah J. Lewis, PhD
Associate Professor
School of Social Work
Barry University
Miami, Florida

Jan Ligon, PhD, LCSW
Associate Professor
Georgia State University
School of Social Work
Atlanta, Georgia

Gordon MacNeil, PhD
Associate Professor
School of Social Work
University of Alabama
Tuscaloosa, Alabama

Michelle Miller, MSW, LSW
Counselor
Allegheny College
Meadville, Pennsylvania

Scott Newgass, MSW, LCSW
Unit Coordinator, Connecticut
   State Department of Education
Professor
Department of Social Work
Southern Connecticut State
   University Connecticut State
   Department of Education
Hartford, Connecticut

Mary Sean O'Halloran, PhD
Professor
Department of Counseling
   Psychology
Director
Psychological Services Clinic
College of Education and
   Behavioral Sciences
University of Northern Colorado
Greeley, Colorado

Allen J. Ottens, PhD
Professor Emeritus
Department of Counseling
Adult and Higher Education
Northern Illinois University
DeKalb, Illinois

Debra A. Pender, PhD, LCPC
Associate Professor
Director Project Educare
Counseling, Adult and
   Higher Education
Northern Illinois
   University
DeKalb, Illinois

The late Albert R. Roberts,
   PhD, DABFE
Professor of Criminal Justice and
   Social Work
Faculty of Arts and Science
Rutgers University, Livingston
   College Campus
Piscataway, New Jersey

Beverly Schenkman Roberts, MEd
Health Advocate and Director
   Mainstreaming Medical
   Care Program
The Arc of New Jersey
North Brunswick,
   New Jersey

Donna Kirkpatrick Pinson, EdD,
   LCPC, NCC, NCSC
Assistant Professor of
   Counseling and Human
   Services
National Louis University
Elgin, Illinois

David J. Schonfeld, MD, FAAP
Director
National Center for School Crisis
   and Bereavement
Chair
Department of Pediatrics
Drexel University College of
   Medicine
Philadelphia, Pennsylvania

Norman M. Shulman, EdD
Clinical Assistant Professor
Department of Neuropsychiatry
and Behavioral Science
Texas Tech University School of
Medicine
Licensed Psychologist
Psychological Management
Services
Lubbock, Texas


Jonathan B. Singer, PhD, LCSW
Founder and Host of the Social
Work Podcast
Assistant Professor
School of Social Work
Temple University
Philadelphia, Pennsylvania

Janae R. Sones, BA
Doctoral Student in Counseling
Psychology
Department of Counseling
Psychology
College of Education and
Behavioral Sciences
University of Northern Colorado
Greenley, Colorado


Chris Stewart, PhD
Assistant Professor
School of Social Work
Texas A&M University-Commerce
Pittsburgh, Pennsylvania

# Introduction

The first edition of this book (published in 1990) and the second (published in 2000) were major successes, and the editor has kept the same framework with the five original parts. However, the third and some of the fourth edition is shaped by the events of September 11, 2001, and the attacks on the World Trade Center towers in New York City and the Pentagon in Washington, DC.

Since the publication of the first edition, crisis intervention practices and programs have changed considerably. In fact, since the third edition of this book, professional practice, evidence-based approaches, and the impact of technology have all driven remarkable changes in how we approach crisis intervention. Professional and public interest in crisis intervention, crisis response teams, crisis management, and crisis stabilization has grown tremendously in the past decade, partly due to the growing prevalence of acute crisis events impacting the lives of the general public. The focus of this book is on crisis intervention services for persons who are victims of natural disasters; school-based and home-based violence; violent crimes, such as homicide, aggravated assault, sexual assault, domestic violence, and date rape among college students; and personal or family crises.

Hundreds of thousands of persons in distress each year turn to healthcare, family counseling, and domestic violence and mental health facilities throughout the United States for help in resolving crisis situations. Many crises are triggered by a life-threatening event, such as acute cardiac arrest, attempted murder, criminal homicide, motor vehicle crashes, child custody battles, drug overdoses, psychiatric emergencies, sexual assaults, woman battering, suicide, and/or community disasters. For many, crisis events and situations become critical turning points in their life. A crisis can serve as a challenge and opportunity for rapid problem resolution and growth, or as a debilitating event leading to sudden disequilibrium, failed coping, and dysfunctional behavior patterns.

We are entering an unprecedented time of change within health and mental health service delivery. This is a time when "accountable care organizations" will be working to define and refine approaches to health and mental health care. Organizations will be challenged to act and think differently about how services are delivered and what services will receive reimbursement. This transformation in health and mental healthcare will move away from a traditional fee-for-service model to an outcome-based model. Within this model of care is the premise that moves healthcare providers from a reactive stance toward a proactive approach to care. Yet, within the day-to-day challenges we all face, there will be challenges that create the need for clinicians skilled in crisis intervention.

Many may say this transformation is tied to particular legislation, such as the Affordable Care Act of the Obama administration. Yet in reality the transformation of mental health is more than 50 years old, having begun with the Eisenhower Commission Report (1961) and the Community Mental Health Act of 1963. Both set the stage for the development of crisis intervention detailed in Chapter 1 of this book. The Rehabilitation Act of 1973 continued to support the work of crisis intervention even though the primary focus was populations with debilitating mental illness; this is so because those with chronic, debilitating mental illness at times require crisis intervention and stabilization. The President's New Freedom Commission on Mental Health of 2003 outlined the importance of principles of recovery. Key to this report is the realization that Americans understand that mental health is essential to overall health.

Let us remember, we are all only seconds away from being thrust into a crisis situation. Crisis is by nature sudden and devastating. It overwhelms individuals' coping mechanisms and has the potential to lead to devastating individual and family effects and consequences. This book is constructed around the reality that any of our lives can be shattered in a matter of seconds, and that the restoration of good health begins with the resolution of the crisis at hand. The intervention may be with an individual or a group. It may, and frequently does, require multiple interventions, requiring application of evidence-informed practices that have been empirically studied, tested, and at times standardized to provide optimal results.

In Chapter 1 and subsequent chapters, the authors focus on the extensive step-by-step, eclectic model of crisis intervention (interchangeable with the term *crisis counseling*). There remains much confusion among the general public regarding the definition of crisis intervention among mental health professionals in the aftermath of traumatic events, such as mass shootings, airplane disasters, and murders in the workplace. Front-line crisis workers and emergency services personnel are well trained and effective in rescuing survivors and defusing potentially disastrous situations. The average citizen is not aware of the vital work of crisis clinicians after the work of first responders/front-line crisis workers is completed. Because of a strong code of ethics and confidentiality safeguards, it would be a violation for social workers and psychologists to issue press releases or engage in interviews with journalists.

Controversy in the field of crisis intervention developed as a result of rigid adherence to a single model or approach rather than using an eclectic perspective that recognizes and accepts the most effective components of each model. *This is the first comprehensive handbook that prepares the crisis intervenor for rapid assessment and timely crisis intervention in the 21st century.* Emotional and psychological first aid can be effectively administered by trained volunteers, including emergency service workers. *However, crisis intervention or crisis counseling is much more extensive than critical incident debriefing and crisis stabilization, usually requiring considerably more time (usually 4 to 6 weeks) and graduate-level courses in a mental health discipline.* Because crisis intervention is a multidisciplinary field, the editor is more concerned with the graduate courses and training seminars completed, and the skills of the crisis intervenor, than with the particular academic discipline with which the crisis clinician is identified.

There are two primary phases to crisis intervention. The initial phase occurs either immediately after the acute crisis episode or disaster has occurred or within 48 hours of the event. This phase is generally referred to as *crisis stabilization, emotional first aid,* or *crisis management.* This phase is usually standard operating procedure for crisis response teams (who have been trained by the American Psychological Association disaster task force, the International Critical Incident Stress Foundation, and/or the American Red Cross), law enforcement agencies, hospitals and medical centers, and correctional agencies.

The specific nature of the intervention varies depending on the type of crisis event that has occurred. In the event of a crisis situation, the initial intervention revolves around providing emergency medical services if necessary, as well as crisis stabilization and emotional support for those impacted by the event, particularly those who were at the scene and witnessed the event. The first activity of the crisis team is to meet with the key people who are in charge at the site where the crisis event occurred to establish the plan of action. Next, the crisis team assembles the victims and observers to the crisis event (who have been medically stabilized) to provide a debriefing and to clarify the facts surrounding the event; identify postcrisis problems; provide an overview of what to expect emotionally in the aftermath of the crisis event; and describe where victims and observers can go for individual counseling and support. The team also facilitates individual and group discussions to help the parties involved to process the event as needed. Finally, the crisis team communicates with the leaders within the community or organization to help them understand how to identify and facilitate ongoing care for those impacted via referral to a licensed mental health professional.

Although the crisis team approach described here is the recommended response to an institutional or natural disaster, it is not always available and depends on the readiness and proactive stance of the community in which one lives and works. Every community should have access to trained crisis intervenors, either locally or through a consulting contract with a crisis team from a nearby city

The most popular model for individual crisis intervention is generally known as *crisis intervention* or *crisis counseling*, which takes place during the days and weeks immediately after the crisis event. This second phase or type of crisis intervention is commonly utilized by clinical social workers and psychologists in group private practices, crisis intervention units of community mental health centers, child and family counseling centers, and hospital settings. Various practice models have been developed to assist clinicians in working with persons in crisis, including the three-step model (assessment, boiling down the problem, coping alternatives). This book will consistently utilize Roberts's seven-stage crisis intervention model, which is applied as an intervention framework for providing crisis counseling. This thorough and sequential model can facilitate early identification of crisis precipitants, active listening, problem solving, effective coping skills, inner strengths and protective factors, and effective crisis resolution. The model consists of the following stages:

1. Assess lethality and mental health status.
2. Establish rapport and engage the client.
3. Identify major problems.
4. Deal with feelings.
5. Explore alternative coping methods and partial solutions.
6. Develop an action plan.
7. Develop a termination and follow-up protocol.

This handbook was written for front-line crisis workers, graduate students, and clinicians who work with individuals, families, and communities in crisis. Crisis theory and practice principles cut across several professions, including counseling, social work, psychology, psychiatric nursing, psychiatry, law enforcement, and victim assistance. Therefore, an interdisciplinary approach has been used in compiling and editing this book. This volume is a collaborative work, with original chapters written by prominent clinical social workers, health social workers, clinical nurse specialists, clinical psychologists, counseling psychologists, community psychologists, and victim advocates. Each practice chapter begins with one to three case studies or vignettes, followed by sections that present an introduction; the scope of the problem; and the research literature related to resilience and protective factors for specific high-risk groups (e.g., depressed adolescents, incest survivors, stressed-out college students, battered women, chemically dependent individuals). The main part of each chapter includes a framework for the practice of crisis intervention with a specific target group. Several detailed cases and case commentaries are included to demonstrate the steps in the operation of the seven-stage crisis intervention model. Also highlighted in each chapter are clinical issues, controversies, roles, and skills. Many of the chapters conclude with summaries and predictions for the future use of crisis intervention with a particular target group, such as callers to a 24-hour mobile crisis unit, college students in crisis, women with AIDS, adolescent suicide attempters, victims of violent crimes, victims of community disasters, and substance abusers.

Recognizing the necessity of having mental health professionals mobilized to respond quickly if a disaster occurred in their local community, the American Red Cross in the 1990s developed cooperative agreements with the American Counseling Association, the American Psychological Association, and the National Association of Social Workers to facilitate the development of mental health and crisis response teams to provide immediate intervention. As a result, within 24 hours of a major disaster in the United States (such as a plane crash or tornado) community crisis response teams are on the scene, providing crisis intervention services.

We cannot predict the psychological impact of crisis situations any more than we are able to predict the crisis situation itself. Each crisis has its basis in a unique and deeply set individualized response to the crisis event. Even those who experience the same crisis situation (e.g., a tornado or other natural disaster) will have an individualized response to the crisis. The best method for addressing crisis in the future begins with preparing ourselves as mental health professionals to develop the skills necessary for rapid acute lethality and clinical assessment, as well as training in evidence-based crisis intervention protocols, multicomponent critical incident stress management, trauma treatment methods, and other disaster mental health interventions.

This volume is intended to be a key resource for professionals who are called upon to intervene with individuals and groups in crisis. There is a very strong interest in the application of crisis theory and crisis intervention techniques among professionals practicing in school, family, health, mental health, victim assistance, and group private practice settings. This book has been designed primarily for front-line crisis workers (e.g., clinical psychologists and social workers at outpatient mental health centers, psychiatric–mental health nurses, social work case managers, and clinicians skilled in crisis management after a community disaster), clinicians in private practice, and graduate students who need to know the latest steps and methods for intervening effectively with persons in acute crisis. This book will also be useful as the primary text in courses on topics such as crisis intervention, crisis counseling, crisis intervention and brief treatment, social work practice II, and mental health practice, and as a supplementary text in health social work, introduction to human services, psychiatric nursing, and community psychology.

# I
## OVERVIEW

# 1

# Bridging the Past and Present to the Future of Crisis Intervention and Crisis Management

KENNETH R. YEAGER
ALBERT R. ROBERTS

This book is an interdisciplinary handbook, specially written by a team of over 30 esteemed crisis and trauma experts, to prepare crisis workers, crisis counselors, crisis therapists, emergency services workers, clergy, and graduate students for rapid lethality assessments, timely crisis intervention, and trauma treatment in the 21st century. It is the third edition of the *Crisis Intervention Handbook: Assessment, Treatment, and Research.*

We live in an era in which sudden and unpredictable crises and traumatic events have become the familiar subjects of everyday news. Millions of people are struck by potentially crisis-inducing events that they are not able to resolve on their own. They need immediate help from mental health professionals, crisis intervention workers, or their significant others. The up-to-date chapters in this book include thought-provoking case illustrations of acute crisis episodes, with a step-by-step crisis intervention protocol applied to each of the case histories discussed.

Recent events have exposed new and different forms of human-made crisis: The Virginia Polytechnic Institute shooting, which killed 32 and wounded 17 others; the Sandy Hook shooting, which took the lives of 20 students and 6 adults; the Colorado movie theater shooting, resulting in 12 fatalities; and the Boston Marathon bombings, which killed 3 and wounded an estimated 264 others.

The landscape of crisis intervention practices and services was forever altered on September 11, 2001, with the mass terrorist disasters at the World

Trade Center twin towers in New York City; the Pentagon in Arlington, Virginia; and United Airlines Flight 93, which crashed in Shanksville, Pennsylvania. As a result of this catastrophic terrorist attack, 2,973 lives were lost—the largest loss of life of US citizens, firefighters (343 fatalities, New York City Fire Department), and police (23 fatalities, New York City Police Department) on one day in our history. The impact of this attack spread far beyond New York and Washington, DC. All over the country, crisis intervention procedures were reviewed and updated.

The prevalence of social, psychological, criminal justice, and public health problems has increased dramatically in recent years. Most notable are these potentially crisis-inducing or trauma-provoking events:

Violent crimes (e.g., hostage situations, assaults, terrorist bombings, bioterrorism threats, domestic violence, muggings, sniper or drive-by shootings, sexual assaults, murders and attempted murders, violence in schools and the workplace, mass murders)

Traumatic stressors or crisis-prone situations (e.g., becoming divorced or separated from one's spouse, losing one's job, being hospitalized for a sudden heart attack, being diagnosed with cancer, being diagnosed with a sexually transmitted disease, having emergency surgery, watching a close family member die, sustaining serious injuries in a car accident, experiencing a near-fatal encounter)

Natural disasters (e.g., hurricanes, floods, tornadoes, earthquakes, volcanic eruptions)

Accidents (e.g., airplane crashes, train crashes, multiple motor vehicle and truck crashes, bus crashes, ferryboat crashes)

Transitional or developmental stressors or events (e.g., moving to a new city, changing schools in the middle of the year, divorce, unwanted pregnancy, having a baby with a disability, becoming physically disabled and placed in a nursing home)

The ever-present terrorist threat and risk for random acts of violence (e.g., mass shootings as reported by evening news) have created an ongoing state of anxious and panicky, hypervigilant response, which includes an intense fear of what might occur next and how it will impact one's loved ones. In addition to generalized fears about future terrorist attacks, there are numerous other scenarios that are potential triggers for a crisis:

The homicide rate in the United States in 2013 was higher than in virtually all other developed countries, according to the Federal Bureau of Investigation (http://www.fbi.gov/about-us/cjis/ucr/crime-in-the-u.s/2013/crime-in-the-u.s.-2013).

The Centers for Disease Control and Prevention reports that more than 38,000 people die annually from suicide, with suicide rates growing by more than 30% in the past 10 years. Suicides now surpass the number of persons killed in motor vehicle crashes per year. (see: http://www.cdc.gov/injury/wisqars/fatal_injury_reports.html)

Approximately one out of every five children and youths in the United States exhibits signs and symptoms of a psychiatric disorder each year.

Domestic violence is prevalent throughout the United States, with an estimated 8.7 million cases annually, with one in every four women experiencing domestic violence in her lifetime.

The Centers for Disease Control and Prevention reports that 331 persons die each day of the year from accidents (unintentional injuries).

The US Department of Health and Human Services reports that more than 4,500 new cases of cancer are diagnosed each day of the year.

The Centers for Disease Control and Prevention reports that 1,637 persons with heart disease die each day of the year.

All of these life-threatening or fatal events can produce acute crisis episodes and post-traumatic stress disorder (PTSD). Therefore, it is critically important for all mental health and public health professionals to provide early responses in the form of lethality assessments, crisis intervention, and trauma treatment (see Chapters 4, 5, 7, and 8 in this volume for an overview of interventions with disaster mental health strategies and for a discussion of first responders' and front-line crisis workers' application of the ACT model: assessment, crisis intervention, and trauma treatment).

The high physical and psychological costs of traumatic events, such as the ones listed earlier, are all too familiar to mental health and health care professionals. Chapter 8 presents a detailed discussion of the different weapons of mass destruction, how first responders should prepare for and respond to terrorist threats, and the vital work of the New York City Disaster Coalition of more than 300 licensed clinicians who have provided free and confidential treatment to survivors and their families after September 11.

Crisis intervention can lead to early resolution of acute stress disorders or crisis episodes, while providing a turning point so that the individual is strengthened by the experience. Crisis and traumatic events can provide a danger or warning signal, or an opportunity to sharply reduce emotional pain and vulnerability. The ultimate goal of crisis intervention is to bolster available coping methods or help individuals reestablish coping and problem-solving abilities while helping them to take concrete steps toward managing their feelings and developing an action plan. Crisis intervention can reinforce strengths and protective factors for those who feel overwhelmed by a traumatic event. In addition, it aims to reduce lethality and potentially harmful situations and provides referrals to community agencies.

When two people experience the same traumatic event, one may cope in a positive way and experience a manageable amount of stress, while the other person may experience a crisis state because of inadequate coping skills and a lack of crisis counseling. Two key factors in determining whether or not a person who experiences multiple stressors escalates into a crisis state are the individual's perception of the situation or event and the individual's ability to utilize traditional coping skills. Roberts and Dziegielewski (1995) have noted that crisis precipitants have different levels of intensity and duration; likewise, there are wide variations in different individuals' ability to cope. Some people are able to cope effectively and mobilize their inner strengths, despite their perceptions that the stressor or crisis precipitant is intense. However, many other individuals need to learn about new resources and acquire coping skills through skillful crisis intervention (Roberts, 1991, 2000). Professionals often confuse the meaning and operational definition of stressful life events, acute stress disorder, acute crisis episodes, and PTSD. Chapter 4 differentiates and clearly defines the differences between the four terms and also presents a paradigm with four different case studies: a person under stress, a person experiencing acute stress disorder, a person encountering an acute crisis episode, and a person suffering from PTSD. In Chapter 5, the six levels of the stress-crisis-trauma continuum are described, with case illustrations and treatment recommendations.

Counselors, social workers, psychiatric nurses, psychiatrists, psychologists, and emergency services personnel are working collaboratively to provide a new vision and clinical insights into crisis intervention and crisis response teams. Crisis intervention has become the most widely used time-limited treatment modality in the world. As a result of the crisis intervention and critical incident stress management movement, millions of persons in crisis situations have been helped in a cost-efficient and timely manner. Chapters 22 and 23 provide insight into methods to assist caregivers, both family members and professionals working within healthcare, in dealing with crisis, stress, compassion fatigue, and burnout. While it is vital to ensure that emergency responders have services available to help mitigate the consequences of disaster, emergency workers do not suffer alone. Families of responders cope with long absences and fears for their loved one's safety during the disaster event. They feel the aftershock as the emergency responder returns home having faced trauma and devastation. This work can be used by students and professionals in all the health and human service professions to further their understanding of crisis and its reduction and as a base for crisis intervention practice to increase their skills.

## CASE SCENARIOS

Some crisis situations are personal, such as the death of a loved one or being the victim of a rape, a robbery, or a severe battering incident; others are triggered by a sudden, community-wide traumatic event, such as an airplane crash, flood, hurricane, terrorist attack, or tornado. Both individual and community-wide traumatic events can cause widespread crisis for dozens, hundreds, or even many thousands of people.

---

### Secondary Victims in the Aftermath of the World Trade Center Terrorist Attack on September 11, 2001: A Retrospective Review

Shelley is a 20-year-old college junior whose uncle was one of the 343 brave New York City firefighters who died trying to rescue people trapped in the carnage of the twin towers at the World Trade Center on the morning of September 11, 2001. Shelley was very close to her uncle (her mother's brother) and grew up two blocks away from him and his family on Staten Island. Uncle Frank had three children, two at colleges in North Carolina and Massachusetts, and a third, Samantha, who was only 10 years old at the time. Samantha's father used to take her to work with him in the morning, where she would have breakfast with the other firefighters, and then her dad would drop her off at school, which was near the firehouse in Staten Island. After the attacks of 9/11, Shelley was very supportive of her mother, her widowed aunt, and her 10-year-old cousin and did her best to help with their immediate concrete and crisis needs.

Since returning to her classes at New York University in lower Manhattan, Shelley has had difficulty concentrating, has nightmares and gets only a few hours' sleep each night, and is anxious about her grades and graduation. Shelley speaks to her mother or aunt almost every day after her classes. She also attended her Uncle Frank's funeral and wake, as well as two memorial services. In addition, Shelley and other members of her immediate family watched the television coverage repeatedly after the terrorist attacks. Shelley seems to be overwhelmed emotionally by her grief-stricken aunt and young cousin, as well as the intrusive thoughts and nightmares she has of the television images of the collapse of the twin towers and the aftermath of the rescue efforts. Some days she cuts all classes and completely withdraws and isolates herself in her dorm room.

Shelley goes to the university counseling center on a referral from her academic adviser. However, she is very quiet and withdrawn due to her depressed mood and crisis reactions.

### Sudden Death of a Spouse and Child

Joe begins to barbecue the hamburgers for tonight's dinner. His wife and their two daughters are expected home in about 20 minutes. His older daughter had a track meet, and his wife and younger daughter went to watch her. The phone rings, and Joe is informed by a police officer that his wife and older daughter have been killed by a drunken driver who sped through a red light and smashed into their car two blocks from their house. His life will never be the same.

### Deaths and Injuries Related to Plane Crash

At 9:00 one morning, the pilot of a malfunctioning air force attack jet tried unsuccessfully to make an emergency landing. The out-of-control jet clipped the top of a bank building, then rammed into the lobby of a nearby hotel and exploded, killing 10 people and injuring several others. This tragic accident resulted in hundreds of persons in crisis: those injured in the explosion, the family members of the dead and injured, the guests and surviving employees at the hotel who witnessed the horror, and the employees and customers at the bank building that was struck by the plane, even though no one at the bank was physically hurt.

### Woman Battering

Judy B., a 27-year-old surgical nurse, was a survivor of wife battering. She and Ray had been married for 6 years, and they had two children. As Ray's drinking increased, so did his beatings. The final straw was a violent attack in which Ray punched Judy many times in her face. The day following this last assault, after looking at her swollen face in the mirror, Judy went to a gun store and purchased a handgun. As she drove home looking at the gun by her side, she finally decided to seek help. She called the battered women's shelter hotline and said, "I'm afraid that I'm going to kill my husband."

### Forcible Rape

Mary R. was a 22-year-old college senior when she was raped. At 11:00 one evening Mary had just left the health sciences library at the university and was walking the three long blocks to the parking lot where her car was parked. She recalls her reactions a week later: "I was sort of in shock and numb. It was a terrifying, painful, and degrading experience. It was something you don't expect to happen. But it could have been much worse. He held a knife to my throat while raping me. I thought he was going to kill me afterward. I'm glad to be alive."

### Robbery

John A., a 24-year-old blind male, was a victim of robbery. John was returning to his apartment in the Bronx following an afternoon appointment with his physician when he was robbed. John recalled what took place:

> A guy came up to me and pressed the cold barrel of his gun on my neck. He said if I don't give him what I got he would shoot me and the dog. I gave him the $21 I had. Nobody helped me. Everybody's afraid to intervene. They're afraid because they know the guy will get off or be put on probation and may come after them.

About a week after the robbery, I woke up sweating and had a serious asthma attack. I was hospitalized for a week. Now I try not to visit friends or my cousin in Manhattan. I go out a lot less. I stay home and listen to the radio or TV most of the time.

## Broken Romance, Depression, and Alcoholism

Liz, a 21-year-old college senior, is very depressed. She and her fiancé have just broken up, and she feels unable to cope. She cries most of the day, feels agitated, and isn't sleeping or eating normally. Since the beginning of the relationship a year ago, Liz has become socially isolated. Her family strongly dislikes her fiancé, and her fiancé discouraged her from spending time with her friends. Liz now doubts that she will find a job upon graduation in 3 months and is considering moving home. She comes from a large family, with parents who are very much involved with the other children. Thoughts of moving back home and losing her independence, as well as the broken romance and the lack of a support system, have immobilized Liz, who has cut all her classes for the past week. She has not talked with friends or family about the breakup, and she is "holed up" in her room in the dormitory, drinking herself into a stupor and refusing to eat or leave the building even for a walk.

---

Shelley, Joe, Judy, Mary, John, and Liz are experiencing crisis reactions in the aftermath of highly stressful hazardous events. The initial crisis reaction in the aftermath of the sudden death of a loved one or being the victim of a violent crime is usually a series of physiological and emotional reactions. Some common reactions and symptoms after traumatic and crisis events include overwhelming feelings of anxiety, despair, and hopelessness, guilt, intense fears, grief over sudden losses, confusion, difficulty concentrating, powerlessness, irritability, intrusive imagery, flashbacks, extreme suspiciousness of others, shame, disorientation, loss of appetite, binge drinking, sleep disturbances, helplessness, terror, exhaustion, losses or lapses of religious beliefs, and/or shattered assumptions about personal safety. Persons experiencing traumatic events or an accumulation of stressful life events usually attempt to understand and reduce their symptoms, to regain control of their environment, and to reach out to their support system (e.g., a significant other). Sometimes the person's internal and external coping methods are successful, and an acute crisis episode is averted; at other times vulnerable individuals and groups fail in their attempts to cope, and crisis episodes escalate.

Chapters 1 through 5 of this book link crisis theory to practice. The emphasis in the first five chapters is placed on the application of individual and group crisis intervention paradigms and models to facilitating crisis resolution. Chapter 1 links the past to the present state-of-the-art knowledge of conceptualizing crisis theory, crisis reactions, and crisis intervention practices. Chapter 2 focuses on how to conduct lethality/danger assessments and apply each of the seven stages of the crisis intervention model to three individuals with different degrees of suicide ideation presenting to a crisis center or psychiatric screening unit. Chapter 3 integrates Roberts's seven-stage crisis intervention model with solution-based therapy and a strengths perspective. Chapter 4 delineates and examines a stress, crisis, PTSD classification paradigm, which provides guidelines for practitioners to effectively assess the severity of the initial event, diagnostic symptoms, and treatment planning options. Chapter 5 develops a continuum of stress and crisis episodes ranging from low-level somatic distress to cumulative and catastrophic acute crisis episodes.

Chapters 7, 11, through 20 apply Roberts's seven-stage model of crisis assessment and intervention to particular high-risk groups and situations such as the following:

- Early adolescents who have experienced a significant loss
- Adolescents and adults with suicidal ideation and plans
- Child and adolescent psychiatric emergencies
- Crises on the college campus
- Battered women in crisis
- Crisis related to separation, divorce, and child custody
- HIV-positive women in crisis
- Persons experiencing psychiatric crises and coming to the local mental health center or emergency room
- A series of crises experienced by substance abusers
- People experiencing mental health–related crises and being helped by a front-line 24-hour mobile crisis team
- Persons in crisis as a result of the burden of caring for a terminally ill or disabled parent

This is the first comprehensive handbook to consistently apply a comprehensive seven-stage crisis intervention model to a wide range of clients in acute crisis.

## SCOPE OF THE PROBLEM AND PREVALENCE ESTIMATES

We live in an era in which traumatic events and acute crisis episodes have become far too prevalent. Each year, millions of people are confronted with traumatic crisis-producing events that they cannot resolve on their own, and they often turn for help to 24-hour telephone crisis hotlines; crisis units of community mental health centers; and outpatient, hospital-based programs.

During the past two decades, thousands of crisis intervention programs have been established throughout the United States and Canada. There are more than 1,400 grass-roots crisis centers and crisis units affiliated with the American Association of Suicidology or a local community mental health center. Altogether there are also more than 11,000 victim assistance programs, rape crisis programs, child sexual and physical abuse intervention programs, police-based crisis intervention programs, and battered women's shelters and hotlines. In addition, crisis services are provided at thousands of local hospital emergency rooms, hospital-based trauma centers and emergency psychiatric services, suicide prevention centers, and pastoral counseling services.

Crisis centers and hotlines provide information, crisis assessments, intervention, and referrals for callers with such problems as depression, suicide ideation, psychiatric emergencies, chemical dependency, AIDS, sexual dysfunction, woman battering, and crime victimization. Because of their 24-hour availability, they can provide immediate, though temporary, assistance. Some crisis victims do not have a caring friend or relative to whom they can turn; they often benefit from an empathetic, active listener. Even when significant others are available to aid the person in crisis, hotlines provide a valuable service by linking the caller to appropriate community resources.

The large number of documented calls to crisis hotlines—an estimated 4.3 million calls annually—indicates the importance of these programs (Roberts & Camasso, 1994). A Google search for "crisis hotlines in the United States" conducted in July 2014 produced more than 2 million hits, and this is just the tip of the iceberg. The number expands when one searches for suicide lines, rape crisis lines, and domestic violence lines. According to a Substance Abuse and Mental Health Services Administration media release from October 2011, the National Suicide Prevention Lifeline answered its 3 millionth call since its inception in 2005. This suicide prevention hotline now answers more than 2,200 calls per day (www.suicidepreventionlifeline.org).

The first national organizational survey of crisis units and centers yielded a response from 107 programs (Roberts, 1995). The researcher's summary findings indicated that a total of 578,793 crisis callers were handled by the crisis centers and programs in the 1-year period directly prior to receipt of the mailed questionnaire, or an annual average of 5,409 callers per crisis intervention program. In 1990, a total of 796 crisis intervention units and programs (affiliated with a community mental health center) were in operation throughout the United States, and the annual average number of callers received by each program was 5,409. As a result of multiplying the average number of callers by the number of programs, Roberts (1995) estimated the annual number of callers to be slightly more than 4.3 million. If we broaden our estimate to all national and local 24-hour crisis lines, including those for crime victims, survivors of terrorist attacks, battered women, sexual assault victims, troubled employees, adolescent runaways, and child abuse victims, as well as the crisis intervention units at mental health centers, the total estimate would be approximately 35 to 45 million crisis callers per year.

## CRISIS REACTIONS AND CRISIS INTERVENTION

A *crisis* can be defined as a period of psychological disequilibrium, experienced as a result of a hazardous event or situation that constitutes a significant problem that cannot be remedied by using familiar coping strategies. A crisis occurs when a person faces an obstacle to important life goals that generally seems insurmountable through the use of customary habits and coping patterns. The goal of crisis intervention is to resolve the most pressing problem within a 1- to 12-week period using focused and directed interventions aimed at helping the client develop new adaptive coping methods.

*Crisis reaction* refers to the acute stage, which usually occurs soon after the hazardous event (e.g., sexual assault, battering, suicide attempt). During this phase, the person's acute reaction may take various forms, including helplessness, confusion, anxiety, shock, disbelief, and anger. Low self-esteem and serious depression are often produced by the crisis state. The person in crisis may appear to be incoherent, disorganized, agitated, and volatile or calm, subdued, withdrawn, and apathetic. It is during this period that the individual is often most willing to seek help, and crisis intervention is usually more effective at this time (Golan, 1978).

Crisis intervention can provide a challenge, an opportunity, and a turning point within the individual's life. According to Roberts and Dziegielewski (1995), crisis clinicians have been encouraged to examine psychological and situational crises in terms of "both danger and opportunity" (p. 16). The aftermath of a crisis episode can result in either a highly positive or a highly negative change. Immediate and structured crisis intervention guided by Roberts's seven-stage model facilitates crisis resolution, cognitive mastery, and personal growth, rather than psychological harm.

A divorce, a robbery, a broken engagement, being the victim of a domestic assault, and being the close relative of a person killed in an automobile accident or a plane crash are all highly stressful occurrences that can result in an active crisis state. The persons involved may exhibit denial, intense anxiety, and confusion; they may express anger and fear, or grief and loss, but they can all survive. Crisis intervention can reduce immediate danger and fear, as well as provide support, hope, and alternative ways of coping and growing.

Persons in acute crisis have had similar reactions to traumatic events, from initial feelings of disruption and disorganization to the eventual readjustment of the self. During the impact phase, survivors of victimization and other crisis-producing events often feel numb, disoriented, shattered, fearful, vulnerable, helpless, and lonely. The survivors may seek help, consolation, and advice from friends or professionals within several hours or days after the traumatic or stressful life event.

Helping a person in crisis—in the aftermath of a violent crime, a suicide attempt, a drug overdose, a life-threatening illness, a natural disaster, a divorce, a broken romance, or an automobile crash—requires exceptional sensitivity, active listening skills, and empathy on the part of the crisis intervenor. If a hotline worker, crisis counselor, social worker, or psychologist is able to establish rapport with the person in crisis soon after the acute crisis episode, many hours of later treatment may be averted (Cutler, Yeager, & Nunley, 2013).

## DEFINING A CRISIS AND CRISIS CONCEPTS

Crisis may be viewed in various ways, but most definitions emphasize that it can be a turning point in a person's life. According to Bard and Ellison (1974), crisis is "a subjective reaction to a stressful life experience, one so affecting the stability of the individual that the ability to cope or function may be seriously compromised" (p. 68).

It has been established that a crisis can develop when an event, or a series of events, takes place in a person's life and the result is a hazardous situation. However, it is important to note that the crisis is not the situation itself (e.g., being victimized); rather, it is the person's *perception of and response to* the situation (Parad, 1971, p. 197).

The most important precipitant of a crisis is a stressful or hazardous event. But two other conditions are also necessary to have a crisis state: (a) the individual's perception that the stressful event will lead to considerable upset and/or disruption; and (b) the individual's inability to resolve the disruption by previously used coping methods (Cutler, Yeager, & Nunley, 2013).

*Crisis intervention* refers to a therapist entering into the life situation of an individual or family to alleviate the impact of a crisis to help mobilize the resources of those directly affected (Parad, 1965). In conceptualizing crisis theory, Parad and Caplan (1960) examine the fact that "crises have a peak or sudden turning point"; as the individual reaches this peak, tension increases and stimulates the mobilization of previously hidden strengths and capacities. They urge timely intervention to help individuals cope successfully with a crisis situation. Caplan (1961) states that "a relatively minor force, acting for a relatively short time, can switch the balance to one side or another, to the side of mental health or the side of mental ill health" (p. 293).

There is a general consensus among clinical social workers, counselors, psychologists, and emergency services workers that the following characterize a person in crisis:

1. Perceiving a precipitating event as being meaningful and threatening
2. Appearing unable to modify or lessen the impact of stressful events with traditional coping methods
3. Experiencing increased fear, tension, and/or confusion
4. Exhibiting a high level of subjective discomfort
5. Proceeding rapidly to an active state of crisis—a state of disequilibrium

The term *crisis* as it has been described here is applicable to most of the clients of the social workers, psychologists, emergency service workers, disaster mental health workers, and professional counselors who prepared chapters for this handbook. The definition of a crisis stated previously is particularly applicable to persons in acute crisis because these individuals usually seek help only after they have experienced a hazardous event and are in a vulnerable state, have failed to cope and lessen the crisis through customary coping methods, and want outside help.

## Foundation Assumptions and the Crisis Theory Framework

The conceptual framework for crisis intervention practice presented in this handbook incorporates the basic principles of crisis theory. The crisis intervention specialization is built on a basic knowledge of crisis theory and practice. Crisis theory includes a cluster of principles upon which crisis clinicians and researchers usually agree. In this book the prominent authorities on crisis intervention demonstrate the application of the crisis intervention process and practices to special groups at high risk of crisis. But first it will be helpful to summarize the foundation principles of crisis theory and to place them in a step-by-step crisis management framework.

## Basic Tenets of Crisis Theory

As mentioned earlier, a crisis state is a temporary upset, accompanied by some confusion and disorganization, and characterized by a person's inability to cope with a specific situation through the use of traditional problem-solving methods. According to Naomi Golan (1978), the heart of crisis theory and practice rests in a series of basic statements:

> Crisis situations can occur episodically during "the normal life span of individuals, families, groups, communities and nations" They are often initiated by a hazardous event. This may be a catastrophic event or a series of successive stressful blows which rapidly build up a cumulative effect.
>
> The impact of the hazardous event disturbs the individual's homeostatic balance and puts him in a vulnerable state ...
>
> If the problem continues and cannot be resolved, avoided, or redefined, tension rises to a peak, and a precipitating factor can bring about a turning point, during which self-righting devices no longer operate and the individual enters a state of a disequilibrium ... (an) active crisis. (p. 8)

## Duration of the Crisis

Persons cannot remain indefinitely in a state of psychological turmoil and survive. Caplan (1964) noted, and other clinical supervisors have concurred, that in a typical crisis state equilibrium will be restored in 4 to 6 weeks. However, the designation of 4 to 6 weeks has been confusing. Several authors note that crisis resolution can take from several weeks to several months. To clarify the confusion concerning this period, it is useful to explain the difference between restoring equilibrium and crisis resolution.

Disequilibrium, which is characterized by confusing emotions, somatic complaints, and erratic behavior, is reduced considerably within the first 6 weeks of crisis intervention. The severe emotional discomfort experienced by the person in crisis propels him or her toward action that will result in reducing the subjective discomfort. *Thus, equilibrium is restored*, and the disorganization is time limited.

Viney (1976) aptly describes *crisis resolution* as restoration of equilibrium, as well as cognitive mastery of the situation and the development of new coping methods. Fairchild (1986) refers to crisis resolution as an adaptive consequence of a crisis in which the person grows from the crisis experience through the discovery of new coping skills and resources to employ in the future. In this handbook, crisis intervention is viewed as the process of working through the crisis event so that the person is assisted in exploring the traumatic experience and his or her reaction to it. Emphasis is also placed on helping the individual do the following:

Make behavioral changes and interpersonal adjustments.

Mobilize internal and external resources and supports.

Reduce unpleasant or disturbing affects related to the crisis.

Integrate the event and its aftermath into the individual's other life experiences and markers.

The goal of effective crisis resolution is to remove vulnerabilities from the individual's past and bolster him or her with an increased repertoire of new coping skills to serve as a buffer against similar stressful situations in the future.

## HISTORICAL DEVELOPMENT

As far back as 400 B.C., physicians have stressed the significance of crisis as a hazardous life event. Hippocrates himself defined a crisis as a sudden state that gravely endangers life. But the development of a cohesive theory of crisis and approaches to crisis management had to await the twentieth century. The movement to help people in crisis began in 1906 with the establishment of the first suicide prevention center, the National Save-a-Life League in New York City. However, contemporary crisis intervention theory and practice were not formally elaborated until the 1940s, primarily by Erich Lindemann and Gerald Caplan.

Lindemann and his associates at Massachusetts General Hospital introduced the concepts of crisis intervention and time-limited treatment in 1943 in the aftermath of Boston's worst nightclub fire, at the Coconut Grove, in which 493 people perished. Lindemann (1944) based the crisis theory they developed on their observations of the acute and delayed reactions of survivors and grief-stricken relatives of victims. Their clinical work focused on the psychological symptoms of the survivors and on preventing unresolved grief among relatives of the persons who had died. They found that many individuals experiencing acute grief often had five related reactions:

1. Somatic distress
2. Preoccupation with the image of the deceased
3. Guilt
4. Hostile reactions
5. Loss of patterns of conduct

Furthermore, Lindemann concluded that the duration of a grief reaction appears to be dependent on the success with which the bereaved person does his or her mourning and "grief work." In general, this grief work involves achieving emancipation from the deceased, readjusting to the changes in the environment from which the loved one is missing, and developing new relationships. We learned from Lindemann that people need to be encouraged to permit themselves to have a period of mourning and eventual acceptance of the loss and adjustment to life without the parent, child, spouse, or sibling. If the normal process of grieving is delayed, negative outcomes of crises will develop. Lindemann's work was soon adapted to interventions with World War II veterans suffering from "combat neurosis" and bereaved family members.

Gerald Caplan, who was affiliated with Massachusetts General Hospital and the Harvard School of Public Health, expanded Lindemann's pioneering work in the 1940s and 1950s. Caplan studied various developmental crisis reactions, as in premature births, infancy, childhood, and adolescence, and accidental crises such as illness and death. He was the first psychiatrist to relate the concept of homeostasis to crisis intervention and to describe the stages of a crisis. According to Caplan (1961), a crisis is an upset of a steady state in which the individual encounters an obstacle (usually an obstacle to significant life goals) that cannot be overcome through traditional problem-solving activities. For each individual, a reasonably constant balance or steady state exists between affective and cognitive experience. When this homeostatic balance or stability in psychological functioning is threatened by physiological, psychological, or social forces, the individual engages in problem-solving methods designed to restore the balance. However, in a crisis situation, the person in distress faces a problem that seems to have no solution. Thus homeostatic balance is disrupted, or an upset of a steady state ensues.

Caplan (1964) explains this concept further by stating that the problem is one in which the individual faces "stimuli which signal danger to a fundamental need satisfaction ... and the circumstances are such that habitual problem-solving methods are unsuccessful within the time span of past expectations of success" (p. 39).

Caplan also described four stages of a crisis reaction. The first stage is the initial rise of tension that comes from the emotionally hazardous crisis-precipitating event. The second stage is characterized by an increased level of tension and disruption to daily living because the individual is unable to resolve the crisis quickly. As the person attempts and fails to resolve the crisis through emergency problem-solving mechanisms, tension increases to such an intense level that the individual may go into a depression. The person going through the final stage of Caplan's model may experience either a mental collapse or a breakdown, or may partly resolve the crisis by using new coping methods. J. S. Tyhurst (1957) studied transition states—migration, retirement, civilian disaster, and so on—in the lives of persons experiencing sudden changes. Based on his field studies on individual patterns of responses to community disaster, Tyhurst identified three overlapping phases, each with its own manifestations of stress and attempts at reducing it:

1. A period of impact
2. A period of recoil
3. A posttraumatic period of recovery

Tyhurst recommended stage-specific intervention. He concluded that persons in transitional crisis states should not be removed from their life situation, and that intervention should focus on bolstering the network of relationships.

In addition to building on the pioneering work of Lindemann and Caplan, Lydia Rapoport was one of the first practitioners to write about the linkage of modalities such as ego psychology, learning theory, and traditional social casework (Rapoport, 1967). In Rapoport's (1962) first article on crisis theory, she defined a crisis as "an upset of a steady state" (p. 212) that places the individual in a hazardous condition. She pointed out that a crisis situation results in a problem that can be perceived as a threat, a loss, or a challenge. She then stated that there are usually three interrelated factors that create a state of crisis:

1. A hazardous event
2. A threat to life goals
3. An inability to respond with adequate coping mechanisms

In their early works, Lindemann and Caplan briefly mentioned that a hazardous event produces a crisis, but it was Rapoport (1967) who most thoroughly described the nature of this crisis-precipitating event. She clearly conceptualized the content of crisis intervention practice, particularly the initial or study phase (assessment). She began by pointing out that in order to help persons in crisis, the client must have rapid access to the crisis worker. She stated: "A little help, rationally directed and purposefully focused at a strategic time, is more effective than more extensive help given at a period of less emotional accessibility" (Rapoport, 1967, p. 38).

This point was echoed by Naomi Golan (1978), who concluded that during the state of active crisis, when usual coping methods have proved inadequate and the individual and his or her family are suffering from pain and discomfort, a person is frequently more amenable to suggestions and change. Clearly, intensive, brief, appropriately focused treatment when the client is motivated can produce more effective change than long-term treatment when motivation and emotional accessibility are lacking.

Rapoport (1967) asserted that during the initial interview, the first task of the practitioner is to develop a preliminary diagnosis of the presenting problem. It is most critical during this first interview that the crisis therapist convey a sense of hope and optimism to the client concerning successful crisis resolution. Rapoport suggested that this sense of hope and enthusiasm can be properly conveyed to the client when the interview focuses on mutual exploration and problem solving, along with clearly delineated goals and tasks. The underlying message is that client and therapist will be working together to resolve the crisis.

## Seeking Help

In the late 1960s, the suicide prevention movement took hold, and suicide prevention centers were established across the United States. From the outset, the initial request for help was generally made via a telephone hotline, a practice that continues to the present day. Aided by funding from the National Institute of Mental Health's Center for Studies of Suicide Prevention, these centers grew from 28 in 1966 to almost 200 by 1972. They built on Caplan's crisis theory and the work of Edwin Schneidman and Norman Farberow at the Los Angeles Suicide Prevention Center (Roberts, 1975, 1979).

An enormous boost to the development of crisis intervention programs and units came about as a result of the community mental health movement. The availability of 24-hour crisis intervention and emergency services was considered a major component of any comprehensive community mental health center (CMHC). As a prerequisite to receiving federal funding under the Community Mental Health Centers Act of 1963, CMHCs were required to include an emergency services component in their system plan. During the 1970s, the number of CMHCs that contained crisis intervention units grew rapidly, more than doubling from 376 centers in 1969 to 796 as of 1980 (Foley & Sharfstein, 1983). The idea behind this development—which began in the late 1970s and continued into the early to mid-1980s—was to move crisis services as far into the natural environment as possible to prevent individuals in crisis from progressing into deeper levels of crisis by using the resources immediately available in their communities (Gerhard, Miles, & Dorgan, 1981). This model was conceptualized much earlier and implemented under then Georgia governor James Earl "Jimmy" Carter; the concept would later grow and form the basis of what eventually became the Joint Commission on Accreditation of Hospitals (JCAH) standards for community mental health centers in the 1970s and 1980s. Since this time, public mental health systems have evolved into increasingly sophisticated models for intervening with persons in acute crisis. Local mental health clinics and hospital emergency services provide staffed or on-call crisis service around the clock. Both specialized and generalist staff work to provide crisis management, emergency interventions, emergency involuntary holds, and civil commitments (Nunley, Nunley, Dentinger, McFarland, & Cutler, 2013).

What motivates people in crisis to seek help? Ripple, Alexander, and Polemis (1964) suggest that a balance of discomfort and hope is necessary to motivate a distressed person to seek help. *Hope*, as defined by Stotland (1969), is the perceived possibility of attaining a goal.

The crisis clinician knows that coping patterns differ for each of us. The crisis clinician also knows that for an individual to suffer and survive a crisis (such as losing a loved one, living through an earthquake or a tornado, attempting suicide, or being sexually assaulted), he or she must have a conscious purpose to live and grow. Each individual in crisis must define his or her own purpose. Persons in crisis need to ventilate, to be accepted, and to receive support, assistance, and encouragement to discover the paths to crisis resolution.

It is useful for the client to understand the specific personal meaning of the event and how it conflicts with his or her expectations, life goals, and belief system. Thoughts, feelings, and beliefs usually flow out freely when a client in crisis talks. The crisis clinician should listen carefully and note any cognitive errors or distortions (overgeneralizing, catastrophizing) or irrational beliefs. The clinician should avoid prematurely stating rational beliefs or reality-based cognitions for the client. Instead, he or she should help the client to recognize discrepancies, distortions, and irrational beliefs. This is best accomplished through carefully worded questions such as "How do you view yourself now that you realize that everyone with less than 5 years' seniority got laid off?" or "Have you ever asked your doctor whether he thinks you will die from cancer at a young age or what your actual risk of getting cancer is?"

## CRISIS INTERVENTION MODELS AND STRATEGIES

Several systematic practice models and techniques have been developed for crisis intervention work. The crisis intervention model applied in this book builds on and synthesizes those developed by Caplan (1964), Golan (1978), Parad (1965), Roberts (1991, 1998), and Roberts and Dziegielewski (1995). All of these practice models and techniques focus on resolving immediate problems and emotional conflicts through a minimum number of contacts. Crisis-oriented treatment is time limited and goal directed, in contrast to long-term psychotherapy, which can take several years to complete.

Crisis intervenors should "adopt a role which is active and directive without taking problem ownership" away from the individual in crisis prematurely (Fairchild, 1986, p. 6). The skilled crisis intervenor displays acceptance and hopefulness in order to communicate to persons in crisis that their intense emotional turmoil and threatening situations are not hopeless and that, in fact, they (like others in similar situations before them) will survive the crisis successfully and become better prepared for potentially hazardous life events in the future (Roberts & Yeager, 2009, pp. 40–47).

In order to become an effective crisis intervenor, it is important to gauge the stages and completeness of the intervention. The following seven-stage paradigm should be viewed as a guide, not as a rigid process, because with some clients the stages may overlap.

Roberts's (1991) seven-stage model of crisis intervention (Figure 1.1) has been utilized for helping persons in acute psychological crisis, acute situational crises, and acute stress disorders. The seven stages are as follows:

1. Plan and conduct a thorough assessment (including lethality, dangerousness to self or others, and immediate psychosocial needs).
2. Make psychological contact, establish rapport, and rapidly establish the relationship (conveying genuine respect for the client, acceptance, reassurance, and a nonjudgmental attitude).
3. Examine the dimensions of the problem in order to define it (including the last straw or precipitating event).
4. Encourage an exploration of feelings and emotions.
5. Generate, explore, and assess past coping attempts.
6. Restore cognitive functioning through implementation of action plan.
7. Follow up and leave the door open for booster sessions 3 and/or 6 months later.

1. *Plan and conduct a thorough psychosocial and lethality assessment.* In many cases, Stages 1 and 2 occur at the same time. However, first and foremost, basic information needs to be obtained to determine whether the caller is in imminent danger. Crisis clinicians are trained to perform an ongoing, rapid risk assessment with all clients in crisis. Crisis counselors, psychologists, and social workers encounter a full range of self-destructive individuals in crisis, including those who have taken potentially lethal drug overdoses, depressed and lonely callers who have attempted suicide, and impulsive acting-out adolescents threatening to injure someone. In cases of imminent

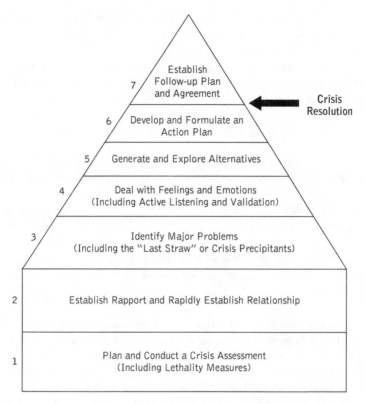

Figure 1.1   Roberts's Seven-Stage Crisis Intervention Model

danger, emergency medical or police intervention is often necessary. All suicide prevention and other 24-hour crisis hotlines have access to paramedics
and emergency medical technicians, poison control centers, the police, and
the emergency rescue squad. It is critically important for the crisis intervenor
to be in close contact with the crisis caller before, during, and after medical
stabilization and discharge.

In many other crisis situations, there is some potential for danger and
harm. As a result of potential danger to crisis callers with a history of reckless driving, binge drinking, chemical dependency, bipolar disorder, explosive anger, passive-aggressive behavior, schizophrenia, and/or preoccupation
with suicidal thoughts or fantasies, it is imperative that crisis intervenors use
Stages 1 through 7 of Roberts's model as a guide to crisis intervention.

Assessments of *imminent danger and potential lethality* should examine
the following factors:

- Determine whether the crisis caller needs medical attention (e.g., drug
  overdose, suicide attempt, or domestic violence).

- Is the crisis caller thinking about killing herself or himself? (Are these general thoughts, or does the caller have a specific suicide plan or pact, with the location, time, and method specified?)
- Determine whether the caller is a victim of domestic violence, sexual assault, and/or other violent crime. If the caller is a victim, ask whether the batterer is nearby or likely to return soon.
- Determine whether any children are in danger.
- Does the victim need emergency transportation to the hospital or a shelter?
- Is the crisis caller under the influence of alcohol or drugs?
- Is the caller about to injure herself or himself (e.g., self-injurious behaviors or self-mutilations)?
- Inquire whether there are any violent individuals living in the residence (e.g., assaultive boarders or perpetrators of elder abuse or sibling abuse).

If time permits, the risk assessment should include the following (recognize that a client who is in imminent danger needs to go immediately to a safe place):

- In domestic violence situations, determine the nature of the caller's previous efforts to protect herself or her children, in order to determine her ability to protect herself.
- In order to fully assess the perpetrator's threat in cases of domestic violence, inquire into the batterer's criminal history, physical abuse history, substance abuse history, destruction of property, impulsive acts, history of mental disorders, previous psychiatric diagnoses previous suicide threats or gestures, stalking behavior, and erratic employment or long periods of unemployment.
- If the caller is a victim of a violent crime, is there a history of prior visits to the hospital emergency room for physical abuse, drug overdose, or suicide attempts?
- Are there any guns or rifles in the home?
- Has anyone recently used a weapon against the caller?
- Has the caller received any terroristic threats, including death threats?
- Determine whether the caller is suffering from major depression, intense anxiety, phobic reactions, agitation, paranoid delusions, acute stress disorder, adjustment disorder, personality disorder, PTSD, and/or sleep disturbances.

2. *Make psychological contact and rapidly establish the relationship.* This second stage involves the initial contact between the crisis intervenor and the potential client. The main task for the clinician at this point is to establish rapport by conveying genuine respect for and acceptance of the client. The client also often needs reassurance that he or she can be helped and that this is the appropriate place to receive such help. For example, sufferers of

obsessive-compulsive disorders (OCDs) and phobias, such as agoraphobia, often believe that they will never get better. This is often the case when they have been misdiagnosed with a psychosis or personality disorder by a crisis clinician who has never seen patients with OCD or agoraphobia. If the crisis clinician has helped many other clients suffering from agoraphobia, he or she should describe the situation of a previous client, such as one who at one point could not even leave his room for a 4-month period and now is married and successfully working 5 days a week outside of his home.

3. *Examine the dimensions of the problem in order to define it.* It is useful to try to identify the following: (a) the "last straw," or the precipitating event that led the client to seek help; (b) previous coping methods; and (c) dangerousness or lethality. Crisis counselors should explore these dimensions through specific open-ended questions. The focus must be on *now* and *how* rather than on *then* and *why*. For example, key questions would be: "What situation or event led you to seek help at this time?" and "When did this event take place?"

4. *Encourage an exploration of feelings and emotions.* This step is closely related to examining and defining the dimensions of the problem, particularly the precipitating event. It is presented here as a separate step because some therapists overlook it in their attempt to make rapid assessment and find the precipitating event. It is extremely therapeutic for a client to ventilate and express feelings and emotions in an accepting, supportive, private, and nonjudgmental setting.

The primary technique for identifying a client's feelings and emotions is through *active listening*. This involves the crisis intervenor listening in an empathic and supportive way to both the client's reflection of what happened and how the client feels about the crisis event.

5. *Explore and assess past coping attempts.* Most youths and adults have developed several coping mechanisms—some adaptive, some less adaptive, and some inadequate—as responses to the crisis event. Basically, an emotionally hazardous event becomes an emotional crisis when the "usual homeostatic, direct problem-solving mechanisms do not work" (Caplan, 1964, p. 39). Thus, attempts to cope fail. One of the major foci of crisis intervention involves identifying and modifying the client's coping behaviors at both the preconscious and the conscious level. It is important for the crisis intervenor to attempt to bring to the conscious level the client's coping responses that now operate just below the surface, at the preconscious level, and then to educate the client in modifying maladaptive coping behaviors. Specifically, it is useful to ask the client how certain situations are handled, such as feelings of intense anger, loss of a loved one (a child or spouse), disappointment, or failure.

Solution-based therapy should be integrated into crisis intervention at this stage. This method emphasizes working with client strengths. The client is viewed as being very resourceful and having untapped resources or latent inner coping skills from which to draw upon. This approach utilizes specifically explicated clinical techniques (e.g., the miracle question, the partial miracle question, the scaling technique) appropriate for crisis intervention practice. Solution-focused therapy and the strengths perspective view the client as resilient. The resilient person generally has sufficiently high self-esteem, a social support network, and the necessary problem-solving skills to bounce back, cope with, and thrive in the aftermath of stressful life events or traumatic events.

Integrating strengths and solution-focused approaches involves jogging clients' memories so they recall the last time everything seemed to be going well, and they were in a good mood rather than depressed and/or successfully dealt with a previous crisis in their lives. These are some examples of components in a solution-focused approach:

- How would you have coped with the divorce or death of your parents when you were in a good mood?
- Write a letter to your parents, letting them know that you are setting a specific goal for yourself in order to make them proud of the values and ambition they instilled within you.
- If your deceased parents are in heaven looking down on you, what could you do to make them proud?

See Chapters 3, 6, and 19 for thorough applications of crisis intervention and brief solution-focused therapy with traumatized children and youth, as well as suicidal, abused, unemployed, and drug-addicted clients.

It is important to help the client to generate and explore alternatives and previously untried coping methods or partial solutions. If possible, this involves collaboration between the client and the crisis intervenor to generate alternatives. It is also important at this stage to explore the consequences and the client's feelings about each alternative. Most clients have some notion of what should be done to cope with the crisis situation, but they may well need assistance from the crisis clinician in order to define and conceptualize more adaptive coping responses. In cases where the client has little or no introspection or personal insights, the clinician needs to take the initiative and suggest more adaptive coping methods. Defining and conceptualizing more adaptive coping behaviors can be a highly productive component in helping the client resolve the crisis situation.

6. *Restore cognitive functioning through implementation of an action plan.* The basic premise underlying a cognitive approach to crisis resolution is that the ways in which external events and a person's cognitions of the events turn into personal crisis are based on cognitive factors. The crisis clinician who uses a cognitive approach helps the client focus on why a specific event leads to a crisis state (e.g., it violates a person's expectancies) and, simultaneously, what the client can do to effectively master the experience and be able to cope with similar events should they occur in the future. Cognitive mastery

involves three phases. First, the client needs to obtain a realistic understanding of what happened and what led to the crisis. In order to move beyond the crisis and get on with life, the client must understand what happened, why it happened, who was involved, and the final outcome (e.g., being locked out of one's house, a suicide attempt, death of an adolescent, a divorce, a child being battered).

Second, it is useful for the client to understand the event's specific meaning: how it conflicts with his or her expectations, life goals, and belief system. Thoughts and belief statements usually flow freely when a client in crisis talks. The crisis intervenor should listen carefully and note any cognitive errors or distortions (overgeneralizing, catastrophizing) or irrational beliefs. The clinician should avoid prematurely stating the rational beliefs or reality-based cognitions for the client. Instead, the clinician should help the client discover distortions and irrational beliefs. This can be facilitated through carefully worded questions such as "Do you still want to move out of state now that you know that the person who raped you and brutally killed his previous two victims will be executed today in the electric chair?" or "Have you ever asked your doctor whether he thinks you will die from a heart attack at a young age?"

The third and final part of cognitive mastery involves restructuring, rebuilding, or replacing irrational beliefs and erroneous cognitions with rational beliefs and new cognitions. This may involve providing new information through cognitive restructuring, homework assignments, or referral to others who have lived through and mastered a similar crisis (e.g., a support group for widows, for rape victims, or for students who have been confronted with school violence).

7. *Follow-up*. At the final session the client should be told that if at any time he or she needs to come back for another session, the door will be open and the clinician will be available. Sometimes clients cancel their second, third, or fourth appointment prior to resolving the crisis. For example, a client who was raped at knifepoint is up half the night prior to her appointment with her clinician. She mistakenly thinks her nightmares and insomnia are caused by the clinician. In actuality, she has not come to grips with her vulnerabilities and fears that the rapist will return. The clinician, knowing that victims of violent crimes often go into crisis on an anniversary of the crime (e.g., exactly 1 month or 1 year after the victimization), informs the client that she would like to see her again, and that as soon as she calls, she will be given an emergency appointment the same day.

## CRISIS INTERVENTION UNITS AND 24-HOUR HOTLINES

Where can persons in crisis turn for help? How do they find the phone number of the crisis intervention program in their area? Police officers, hospital emergency room staff, crisis workers, and psychiatric screeners are available 24 hours a day, 7 days a week. In fact, on weekends and at night they are often the only help available. The police or an information operator can give a person in crisis the name of a local hotline, a community crisis center, the crisis intervention unit at the local community mental health center, a rape crisis center, a battered women's shelter, or a family crisis intervention program that provides home-based crisis services. In addition, many large cities have information and referral networks funded by the United Way, the Community Service Society, or the American Red Cross. These information and referral (I and R) services give crisis callers the phone numbers of community agencies in their localities. Unfortunately, because of limited resources, some of these information and crisis lines are available only during regular business hours.

The information and referral services throughout the United States, which number in excess of 30,000, operate under different organizational auspices, including traditional social service agencies, community mental health centers, public libraries, police departments, shopping malls, women's centers, Travelers Aid centers, youth crisis centers, and area agencies on aging (R. Levinson, personal communication April 30, 2004). The goal of information and referral networks is to facilitate access to services and to overcome the many barriers that obstruct entry to needed resources (Levinson, 2003, p. 7). According to the United Way of America (1980), "I and R is a service which informs, guides, directs and links people in need to the appropriate human service which alleviates or eliminates the need" (p. 3).

Some information and referral networks are generic and provide information to the public on all community services, including crisis centers. Others are more specialized and focus on meeting the needs of callers such as those who are depressed and have suicide ideation, children and youths in crisis, women in crisis, survivors of violent crimes, runaways and homeless youths, or the elderly.

The *primary objective* of a crisis intervention program is to intervene at the earliest possible stage. Thus, given the immediacy and rapid response rate of telephone crisis counseling and referrals, 24-hour crisis lines generally meet their objective (Waters & Finn, 1995). With the development of crisis centers nationwide, there has been a considerable increase in the use of the telephone as a method of rapid crisis assessment and management. The 24-hour telephone crisis service maximizes the immediacy and availability of crisis intervention. It also provides anonymity to the caller while allowing the intervenor to assess the risk of suicide and imminent danger. The telephone crisis intervenor is trained to establish rapport with the caller, conduct a brief assessment, provide a sympathetic ear, help develop a crisis management plan, and/or refer the caller to an appropriate treatment program or service. In most cases effective crisis resolution can be facilitated by suicide prevention hotlines as long as they provide referral and follow-up services.

Waters and Finn (1995) identified and discussed the goals of the goals of the following types of hotlines types of crisis hotlines for special and high-risk groups:

- Career-oriented and job information hotlines
- Employee assistance hotlines
- Information and referral hotline for dementia caregivers
- Kidline (a hotline for children)
- Media call-ins
- Police emergency calls (911)
- Substance abuse crisis lines
- Suicide prevention hotlines
- Teen lines
- Telephone reassurance programs for the elderly
- Telephone crisis treatment for agoraphobia
- University-based counseling hotlines
- 24-hour availability for telephone therapy with one of the 300 licensed family therapists, psychologists, or social workers on call

## Suicide Prevention and Crisis Centers

Suicide prevention services began in London in 1906 when the Salvation Army opened an antisuicide bureau aimed at helping persons who had attempted suicide. At about the same time, the Reverend Harry M. Warren (a minister and pastoral counselor) opened the National Save-a-Life League in New York City. Over the years the league's 24-hour hotline has been answered by full-time staff, by trained volunteers, and, in a few instances, by consulting psychiatrists who have served on the agency's board of directors.

In the 1960s and early 1970s, federal funding was made available as a result of the Community Mental Health Centers Act of 1963 and by the National Institute of Mental Health (NIMH). Between 1968 and 1972, almost 200 suicide prevention centers were established (Roberts, 1979, p. 398). In the United States and Canada, that number now has increased more than sevenfold. In the past decade, a national network of suicide prevention crisis lines (the National Suicide Prevention Lifeline; www.suicidepreventionlifeline.org) has been established and is the key component of suicide prevention efforts across the United States (Gould & Kalafat, 2009; Gold, Munfakh, Kleinman, & Lake, 2012).

At about the same time that 24-hour suicide prevention centers were developing and expanding, crisis units of community mental health centers were also being established throughout the United States. The overriding goal of both types of crisis intervention programs was rapid assessment and early intervention for potentially suicidal callers. The challenges are great, and the numbers are very difficult to move in a positive direction. Caine (2013) identifies five challenges to moving the numbers: (a) inability to discriminate the relatively few true cases from large numbers of false positives; (b) a large number of false negative cases that escape prevention detection; (c) inability of clinical services to reach many individuals who have suicidal intent; (d) a continuing paucity of knowledge about fundamental biological, psychological, social, and cultural factors that contribute to apparent risk among diverse populations and groups; and (e) a lack of a coordinated approach to suicide prevention to deal effectively with the myriad local, regional, state, and national agencies and organizations approach to preventing suicide. See Chapters 2, 5, 6, 15, and 16 for detailed examinations of crisis intervention and follow-up treatment of depressed children, youth, and adults, and of persons with suicide ideation and prior suicide attempts (Caine, 2013, p. 823).

## National Domestic Violence Hotline

A 24-hour, toll-free, national domestic violence hotline became operational in February 1996. Operated by the Texas Council on Family Violence in Austin, this crisis phone line provides immediate crisis assessment and intervention, as well as referrals to emergency services and shelters throughout the United States. The national hotline received an initial $ 1 million grant from the US Department of Health and Human Services, and its annual budget is $1.2 million.

Table 1.1    Volume of Calls From the 15 States With the Highest and Lowest Utilization

| States | Number |
| --- | --- |
| *Highest Use* | |
| 1. California | 8,645 |
| 2. Texas | 7,151 |
| 3. New York | 4,433 |
| 4. Florida | 2,875 |
| 5. Pennsylvania | 2,353 |
| 6. Ohio | 2,268 |
| 7. New Jersey | 2,223 |
| *Lowest Use* | |
| 1. Virgin Islands | 21 |
| 2. Puerto Rico | 91 |
| 3. North Dakota | 104 |
| 4. Vermont | 107 |
| 5. South Dakota | 120 |
| 6. Alaska | 132 |
| 7. Wyoming | 150 |
| 8. Rhode Island | 150 |

In January 1997, the Center for Social Work Research at the School of Social Work of the University of Texas at Austin completed the first evaluation study of the National Domestic Violence Hotline (NDVH; Lewis, Danis, & McRoy, 1997). The high frequency of incoming calls to the NDVH—61,677 calls during its first 6 months of operation—is an important initial indicator of success. The volume of calls far exceeded expectations.

The NDVH reported receiving more than 230,000 calls in the year 2007, with an average volume of more than 19,500 calls per month. By the next year, in October 2008, it reported a 10 to 15% increase in call volume since the analysis of 2007. In 2007, the NDVH launched its "LoveIsRespect" web page (loveisrespect.org), a site targeting young people aged 13 to 24 that contains advice on developing dating skills, how to identify a good relationship, and how to recognize when one is a victim of abuse. This page, which utilizes both live chat and texting options and has a mobile-friendly design, has seen a remarkable volume of use since its inception, with more than 8,000 live chats monthly. A total of more than 90,000 chat conversations have occurred since 2011, with approximately 25% of them occurring on mobile devices. Customers report on average a 80% satisfaction rate for these live chat interactions.

## Child Abuse Hotlines and Referral Networks

Childhelp USA operates a national toll-free (1-800-4-A-Child) child abuse hotline dedicated to the prevention of physical and emotional abuse of children. It is staffed 24 hours a day with professional crisis counselors who, through interpreters, can provide assistance in 170 languages. This program, which utilizes a database of 55,000 resources, serves the United States, Canada, the US Virgin Islands, and Puerto Rico. Between its inception in 1982 and the end of 1999, it had received more than 2 million calls.

A number of states, cities, and counties have developed hotlines for reporting suspected cases of child abuse and neglect. Early case finding and rapid investigation and intervention can lead to resolving crisis situations and preventing further child maltreatment. Many communities have also developed parental stress hotline services, which provide immediate intervention for potentially abusive parents who are at risk of injuring their child. These crisis intervention hotlines offer supportive reassurance, advice, and nonjudgmental listening from trained volunteers and usually are available on a toll-free basis, 24 hours a day, 7 days a week.

Respite centers or crisis nurseries are available in most large cities to provide parents in crisis with temporary relief from child care. For example, New York City's Foundling Hospital has a crisis nursery that provides respite services, without judgment or questioning, for up to 21 days for parents or guardians of children aged birth to 10, with some exceptions for children up to the age of 12, who either are at risk of child abuse or neglect or are in a crisis due to lack of child care that may put the child at risk. The Fondling

Hospital also offers crisis social work services or emergency foster care placement for these families, and an aftercare worker provides follow-up services.

## Rape Crisis Programs

Programs for rape crisis have been developed by medical centers, community mental health centers, women's counseling centers, crisis clinics, and police departments. Social workers at rape crisis organizations provide crisis intervention, advocacy, support, education, and referral to community resources. Crisis intervention generally involves an initial visit or accompaniment by a social worker, crisis counselor, or nurse while the victim is being examined in the hospital emergency room. Although follow-up is often handled through telephone counseling, in-person counseling sessions may take place when the victim is in distress. In several parts of the country, rape crisis programs have begun support groups for sexual assault victims. See Chapter 11 for a comprehensive review of assessment and crisis intervention strategies for rape and incest survivors.

## Battered Women's Shelters and Hotlines

A number of state legislatures have enacted legislation that provides special grants, contracts, and city or county general revenue funding for hotlines and shelters for victims of domestic violence. Crisis intervention services for battered women and their children are available in every state and major metropolitan area in the country. The primary focus of these services is to ensure the women's safety, but many shelters have evolved into much more than just a place for safe lodging. Crisis intervention for battered women generally entails a 24-hour telephone hotline, safe and secure emergency shelter (the average length of stay being 3 to 4 weeks), an underground network of volunteer homes and shelters, and welfare and court advocacy by student interns and other volunteers (Roberts, 1998). Shelters also provide peer counseling, support groups, information on women's legal rights, and referral to social service agencies.

On September 15, 2010, 1,746 out of 1,920, or 91%, of identified local domestic violence programs in the United States and territories participated in the 2010 National Census of Domestic Violence Services. The following figures represent the information provided by the participating programs about services provided during the 24-hour survey period:

- 70,648 victims were served.
- 37,519 domestic violence victims found refuge in emergency shelters or transitional housing provided by local domestic violence programs.
- 33,129 adults and children received nonresidential assistance and services, including individual counseling, legal advocacy, and children's support groups.

- 23,522 hotline calls were answered. Domestic violence hotlines are a lifeline for victims in danger, providing support, information, safety planning, and resources. In the 24-hour survey period, local domestic violence programs answered 22,292 calls, and the NDVH answered 1,230 calls, or more than 16 hotline calls every minute.

More information about this survey can be found online (http://nnedv.org/downloads/Census/DVCounts2010/DVCounts10_Report_Color.pdf).

In some communities, emergency services for battered women have been expanded to include parenting education workshops, assistance in finding housing, employment counseling and job placement for the women, and group counseling for batterers. In the all-too-often neglected area of assessment and treatment for the children of battered women, a small but growing number of shelters provide either group counseling or referral to mental health centers, as needed. For a more complete discussion of crisis intervention practices with battered women and their children, see Chapter 16.

## Case Example

The Victim Services Agency in New York has a 24-hour crime victim and domestic violence hotline, staffed by 68 counselors and 20 volunteers, that responded to approximately 71,000 callers in 1998. The following is a case illustration of a battered woman who required many calls, hours of commitment from the crisis worker, and case coordination to resolve her life-threatening situational crisis.

---

### Jasmine

An emergency call was received at 8:00 one morning from Jasmine, the 15-year-old daughter of Serita, who begged the crisis worker to help her mom, frantically explaining, "My mom's live-in boyfriend is going to kill her." The crisis worker reported that the daughter described previous incidents of violence perpetrated by the boyfriend. Jasmine described a serious argument that had erupted at 6:00 that morning, with loud yelling from the boyfriend, who threatened to kill Serita with the gun he had recently obtained, while pointing it directly at her.

---

The crisis worker tried to build rapport with the terrified girl, asking where her mother was and whether she could be reached by phone. Jasmine replied that her mother had escaped temporarily to a neighbor's apartment as soon as the boyfriend stormed out of the apartment following a visit from the police, which had occurred a few minutes before Jasmine made her phone call to the Victim Services Agency.

Jasmine gave the worker the neighbor's phone number, and the worker called Serita there. The neighbor had called the police at 6:45 a.m. because of the yelling and fighting in the nearby apartment. The boyfriend had previously told Serita that if anyone ever called the police, he would kill her. After the police were called by the neighbor, Serita knew that her boyfriend's violent temper would become even worse. She was terrified to go to a local battered women's shelter, fearing that he would track her down and kill her.

Serita had a sister living in Georgia, who was willing to take her and Jasmine in on a temporary basis. The advantage of staying with her sister was that Serita had never talked to her boyfriend about where her sister lived, telling him just that it was "down South," and had never mentioned her sister's last name, which was different from Serita's. She believed he would never be able to find her if she traveled so far away from New York.

The worker needed to quickly coordinate plans with Travelers Aid to provide a bus ticket for Serita and her daughter to travel to Georgia that evening. Serita obtained an order of protection, and the police took the batterer's keys to the apartment. For a period of time during the afternoon, the batterer watched the apartment from across the street.

A taxicab (which had a special arrangement with Victim Services) was called to take Serita and Jasmine to Travelers Aid to pick up the bus ticket for her trip to Georgia. The driver needed to wait until the boyfriend had left the area before arriving at the apartment. The crisis worker felt that secrecy was necessary to avoid the inevitable confrontation that would have ensued if the boyfriend had seen Serita leaving the apartment with all her luggage.

Serita's escape from the batterer was handled flawlessly; she reached Georgia, with the batterer unaware of her plans or her intended destination. Serita and Jasmine stayed with Serita's sister until her Section 8 housing paperwork was transferred from New York to Georgia.

Chapter 3, by Gilbert Greene, Mo-Yee Lee, Rhonda Trask, and Judy Rheinscheld, demonstrates through case illustrations how to tap into and bolster clients' strengths in crisis intervention. The chapter demonstrates how to integrate Roberts's seven-stage crisis intervention model with solution-focused treatment in a stepwise manner. The crisis clinician utilizing this integrated strengths approach serves as a catalyst and facilitator for clients discovering their own resources and coping skills. Greene et al. systematically bolster their clients by emphasizing their resilience, inner strengths, and ability to bounce back and continue to grow emotionally. This highly practical overview chapter aptly applies the strengths-based approach to a diverse range of clients in crisis situations.

I firmly believe that crisis intervention that focuses on the client's inner strengths and resilience, and that seeks partial and full solutions, will become the short-term treatment of choice during the first quarter of the 21st century.

## SUMMARY

It is clear, in reviewing current progress in applying time-limited crisis intervention approaches to persons in acute crisis, that we have come a long way since it's inception. Crisis intervention is provided by several hundred voluntary crisis centers and crisis lines; by community mental health centers and their satellite programs; and by the majority of the victim assistance, child abuse, sexual assault, and battered women's programs available throughout the country. In addition, crisis services are provided at thousands of local hospital emergency rooms, hospital-based emergency psychiatric services, suicide prevention centers, crisis nurseries, local United Way–funded information lines, and pastoral counseling services. The crisis services that have proliferated in recent years are often directed toward particular groups, such as rape victims, battered women, adolescent suicide attemptors, victims of school violence as well as students who were in the building but were not directly harmed, separated and divorced individuals, victims of abusive parents, and victims of disasters. The increased development of crisis services and units reflects a growing awareness among public health and mental health administrators of the critical need for community crisis services.

This handbook provides an up-to-date, comprehensive examination of the crisis model and its application to persons suffering from an acute crisis. Most social workers, clinical psychologists, marital and family therapists, and counselors agree that crisis theory and the crisis intervention approach provide an extremely useful focus for handling all types of acute crisis. Almost every distressed person who calls or visits a community mental health center, victim assistance program, rape crisis unit or program, battered women's shelter, substance abuse treatment program, or suicide prevention program can be viewed as being in some form of crisis. By providing rapid assessments and timely responses, clinicians can formulate effective and economically feasible plans for time-limited crisis intervention.

REFERENCES

Bard, M., & Ellison, K. (1974, May). Crisis intervention and investigation of forcible rape. *Police Chief*, *41*, 68–73.

Bellak, L., & Siegel, H. (1983). *Handbook of intensive brief and emergency psychotherapy*. Larchmont, NY: CPS Inc.

Caine, E. D. (2013). Forging an agenda for suicide prevention in the United States. *American Journal of Public Health*, *103*, 822–829.

Caplan, G. (1961). *An approach to community mental health*. New York: Grune and Stratton.

Caplan, G. (1964). *Principles of preventive psychiatry*. New York: Basic Books.

Cutler, D. L., Yeager, K. R., & Nunley, W. (2013). Crisis intervention and support. K. R. Yeager, D. L. Cutler,

D. Svendsen, &
G. M. Sills (Eds.), *Modern
community mental Health: An
interdisciplinary approach*
(pp. 243–255). New York:
Oxford University Press.

Fairchild, T. N. (1986). *Crisis intervention strategies for school-based
helpers.* Springfield, IL: Charles
C. Thomas.

Foley, H. A., & Sharfstein, S. S.
(1983). *Madness and government: Who cares for the mentally
ill?* Washington, DC: American
Psychiatric Press.

Gerhard, R. J., Miles, D. G., &
Dorgan, R. E. (1981). *The bal-
anced service system: A model of
personal and social integration.*
Clinton, OK: Responsive Systems
Associates.

Golan, N. (1978). *Treatment in crisis
situations.* New York: Free Press.

Gould, M. S., & Kalafat, J. (2009).
Role of crisis hotlines in suicide
prevention. In D. Wasserman &
C. Wasserman (Eds.), *The Oxford
textbook of suicidology: The
five continents perspective* (pp.
459–462). Oxford: Oxford
University Press.

Gould, M. S., Munfakh, J. L.,
Kleinman, M., & Lake, A. M.
(2012). National suicide prevention
lifeline: Enhancing mental health
care for suicidal individuals and
other people in crisis. *Suicide and
Life-Threatening Behavior, 42,
1*, 22–35.

Levinson, R. W. (2003). *Information
and referral networks* (2nd ed.).
New York: Springer.

Lewis, C. M., Danis, F., & McRoy, R.
(1997). *Evaluation of the National
Domestic Violence Hotline.*
Austin: University of Texas at
Austin, Center for Social Work
Research.

Lindemann, E. (1944).
Symptomatology and management

of acute grief. *American Journal of
Psychiatry, 101,* 141–148.

Nunley, W., Nunley, B., Dentinger, J.,
McFarland, B. H., & Cutler, D. L.
(2013). Involuntary civil commitment: Applying evolving policy and
legal determination in community
mental health. In K. R. Yeager,
D. L. Cutler, D. Svendsen, &
G. M. Sills (Eds.), *Modern
community mental health: An
interdisciplinary approach* (pp.
49–61). New York: Oxford
University Press.

Parad, H. J. (1965). *Crisis inter-
vention: Selected readings.*
New York: Family Service
Association of America.

Parad, H. J. (1971). Crisis inter-
vention. In R. Morris (Ed.),
*Encyclopedia of social
work* (Vol. 1, pp. 196–202).
New York: National Association of
Social Workers.

Parad, H. J., & Caplan, G. (1960). A
framework for studying families in
crisis. *Social Work, 5*(3), 3–15.

Rapoport, L. (1962). The state of
crisis: Some theoretical considerations. *Social Service Review, 36,*
211–217.

Rapoport, L. (1967). Crisis-oriented
short-term casework. *Social Service
Review, 41,* 31–43.

Ripple, L., Alexander, E., &
Polemis, B. (1964). *Motivation,
capacity, and opportunity.*
Chicago: University of
Chicago Press.

Roberts, A. R. (1975). *Self-destructive
behavior.* Springfield, IL: Charles
C. Thomas.

Roberts, A. R. (1979). Organization
of suicide prevention agencies. In
L. D. Hankoff & B. Einsidler
(Eds.), *Suicide: Theory and clinical
aspects* (pp. 391–399). Littleton,
MA: PSG Publishing.

Roberts, A. R. (1991).
Conceptualizing crisis theory

and the crisis intervention model. In A. R. Roberts (Ed.), *Contemporary perspectives on crisis intervention and prevention* (pp. 3–17). Englewood Cliffs, NJ: Prentice-Hall.

Roberts, A. R. (1995). Crisis intervention units and centers in the United States: A national survey. In A. R. Roberts (Ed.), *Crisis intervention and time-limited cognitive treatment* (pp. 54–70). Thousand Oaks, CA: Sage.

Roberts, A. R. (1998). *Battered women and their families: Intervention strategies and treatment programs* (2nd ed.). New York: Springer.

Roberts, A. R. (2000). An overview of crisis theory and crisis intervention. In A. Roberts (Ed.), *Crisis intervention handbook* (2nd ed., pp. 3–30). New York: Oxford University Press.

Roberts, A. R., & Camasso, M. (1994). Staff turnover at crisis intervention units and programs: A national survey. *Crisis Intervention and Time-Limited Treatment, 1*(1), 1–9.

Roberts, A. R., & Dziegielewski, S. F. (1995). Foundation skills and applications of crisis intervention and cognitive therapy. In A. R. Roberts (Ed.), *Crisis*

*intervention and time-limited cognitive treatment* (pp. 3–27). Thousand Oaks, CA: Sage.

Roberts, A. R., & Yeager, K. R. (2009). *Pocket guide to crisis intervention*. New York: Oxford University Press.

Stotland, E. (1969). *The psychology of hope*. San Francisco: Jossey-Bass.

Tyhurst, J. S. (1957). The role of transition states—including disasters—in mental illness. In National Research council (Ed.), *Symposium on preventive and social psychiatry* (pp. 147–172). Government Printing Office, Washington DC.

United Way of America. (1980). *Information and referral: Programmed resource and training course*. Alexandria, VA: Author.

Viney, L. L. (1976). The concept of crisis: A tool for clinical psychologists. *Bulletin of the British Psychological Society, 29,* 387–395.

Waters, J., & Finn, E. (1995). Handling client crises effectively on the telephone. In A. R. Roberts (Ed.), *Crisis intervention and time-limited cognitive treatment* (pp. 251–289). Thousand Oaks, CA: Sage.

# 2

# *Lethality Assessment and Crisis Intervention With Persons Presenting With Suicidal Ideation*

KENNETH R. YEAGER
ALBERT R. ROBERTS

Every 13.7 minutes someone in this country commits suicide. This equates to 105 suicides every day throughout the United States. Crisis counselors and psychiatric screeners must make assessments, often under daunting conditions, that may determine life and death for thousands of people making calls to hotlines and appearing at emergency rooms across the country. In the following we recount three actual cases. How would you assess these situations, and how should the crisis intervention worker respond?

---

## Case 1 Synopsis: Maryann

Maryann has barricaded herself in her bedroom for the past 24 hours. She has called her cousin to offer him her favorite music collection. She has smashed her iPad and thrown her cell phone down the stairway. Her mother can hear her sobbing through the locked door. Knowing she has just broken up with her boyfriend and had taken an overdose of sleeping pills 8 months ago in a similar situation, Maryann's mother is worried. Making matters worse, Maryann lost her father within the past year. Maryann's mother calls the crisis intervention hotline.

## Case 2 Synopsis: Jeanette, Call Me "Jet"

Jeanette, who preferred to be called Jet, is a 27-year-old female who has suffered a traumatic event in conjunction with her heroin dependence. Jet presented to the treatment facility following an episode of physical and sexual abuse while under the influence of cocaine. While she was in treatment, Jet's withdrawal symptoms combined with her resistance to participate in programming led to her being considered noncompliant and resistant to treatment. Perceptions of Jet's treatment needs varied widely among staff. Unfortunately, her agitation led to an altercation with staff, resulting in an episode of physical restraint. During the restraint episode Jet, was retraumatized by the staff, as she was forced onto a bed in the restraint room by two male staff in a manner similar to the physical and sexual abuse she had experienced prior to her admission to the inpatient psychiatric facility. Jet reports dissociating during the restraint as she did during the sexual assault, and she is experiencing difficulty regaining her sense of her surroundings. Fortunately, she had not decompensated as she had previously.

### Case 3 Synopsis: Harvey

Harvey, a successful dentist, aged 53, has been suffering with bipolar disorder for 18 years. He entered a substance abuse treatment facility for alcohol dependence and was successfully undergoing treatment when he began exhibiting signs of major depressive disorder. Harvey confessed to his business partner that he planned to shoot himself. Staff reported that Harvey had a plan to end his life. Consequently, he was transferred to an inpatient psychiatric facility for stabilization. Harvey was remorseful and worked diligently on his treatment plan. He agreed not to harm himself, completing a safety plan for staff, who noted he had made plans for the future. He was returned to the substance abuse treatment facility, then to a halfway house, where, after 2 weeks, he was given a temporary leave to return home.

---

Were these three people in immediate danger of committing suicide? How will crisis counselors or psychiatric screeners determine the severity of the crisis and the most beneficial treatment? In this chapter we consider these important clinical issues and methods of suicide risk assessment. We review evidence-based findings concerning signs of acute suicidal behavior and present Roberts's seven-stage crisis intervention model, the most effective model for intervening quickly on behalf of persons with suicidal ideation. Readers will follow the process of each of the seven stages in the crisis intervention framework as it was applied to these three individuals. Finally, readers will find, perhaps to their surprise, what eventually happened to Maryann, Jet, and Harvey.

## SCOPE OF THE PROBLEM

Suicide and suicide attempts are a major social and public health problem in the United States. The scope of the problem is evidenced by national data indicating that in 2010, 38.364 people chose to end their life via suicide. This equates to nearly 105 people per day, or a death by suicide every 14 minutes. Suicide is now the 10th-leading cause of death in the United States, almost twice as common as homicide (CDC, 2012; Crosby, Han, Orgeta, Parks, & Gfoerer, 2011). In 2010, death by suicide surpassed motor vehicle deaths; in that year, there were 33,687 deaths from motor vehicle crashes and 38,364 suicides (CDC, 2012). Based on data examining suicides in 16 nonviolent death reporting system states in 2009, 33.3% of suicide decedents tested positive for alcohol, 23% for antidepressants, and 20.8% for opiates, including heroin and prescription painkillers.

Historically, suicide has been viewed as a problem of teenagers and the elderly; in recent years, however, there has been a surge in suicide rates among middle-aged Americans. From 1999 to 2010, the suicide rate among Americans aged 35 to 64 rose by nearly 30%, to 17.6 deaths per 100,000 people, up from 13.7. Although suicide rates are growing among both middle-aged men and women, far more men take their own lives. In 2012, the suicide rate for middle-aged men was 27.3 deaths per 100,000, while for women it was 8.1 deaths per 100,000. The most pronounced increases were seen among men in their 50s, a group in which suicide rates jumped by nearly 50%, to about 30 per 100,000. For women, the largest increase was seen in those aged 60 to 64, among whom rates increased by nearly 60%, to 7.0 per 100,000 (Reeves, Stuckler, McKee, Gunnell, Chang, & Basu, 2012). In all, the economic impact of completed suicides in the United States is estimated to be $34 billion annually. This cost to society results almost entirely from lost wages and work productivity (CDC, 2012).

Focusing on completed suicides exposes only the tip of the iceberg. Although no total count is kept of suicide attempts in the United States, it is estimated that each year approximately 1.1 million adults attempt suicide. This equates to a suicide attempt every 38 seconds (Crosby, Han, et al., 2011). And nearly 8.3 million people over the age of 18 report having seriously contemplated taking their own life. Among youth the numbers are equally devastating, with nearly 17% of high school students reporting contemplating suicide and approximately 8% reporting actual attempts during the same time frame. Of that population approximately 2.6% of the attempts were serious enough to require medical intervention (Crosby, Ortega, & National Center for Injury Prevention and control (US), Division of Violence Prevention, 2011; CDC 2012). These numbers do not take into account the nearly 200,000 individuals each year who are impacted by the suicide of a loved one (Eaton & Roberts, 2002).

Emergency departments, mental health centers, and crisis lines across the United States are the front line for addressing the risk of suicide. In 2011, a total of 487,700 people visited a hospital for injuries due to self-harm behaviors. This number indicates that for each person who takes his or her life, approximately 12 other people harm themselves, not all intending to end their life. Nonfatal, self-inflicted injuries result in an estimated $6.5 billion in combined medical costs and lost work costs (CDC, 2012).

On a busy night in the emergency department waiting area, a young psychiatric resident receives a page. A patient who was recently discharged from the inpatient unit asks a question: "I'm feeling funny. Could this be the medication?" The resident reads the page and accurately prioritizes to address the actively psychotic patient in the emergency waiting room. Twenty minutes later, there is another page from the same patient, pleading, "I'm feeling funny. . . . I need to speak with someone right now." The resident continues to address the needs of the four patients in acute distress in the emergency room. Another 20 minutes pass. The resident receives yet another page from the same patient: "I'm going to kill myself if I don't hear from someone in the next 10 minutes." With the acute issues addressed, the resident returns the patient's call. She asks the patient: "Are you currently suicidal?" The patient responds: "No, I knew that saying I was going to kill myself would get your attention. . . . I was tired of waiting for you to call back." Tired and frustrated, the psychiatric resident reprimands the patient: "The threat of suicide is not an appropriate way to have a question answered." The patient responds in frustration:

> You have no idea what I go through on a day-to-day basis and how often I consider taking my life, you don't know what I go through. . . . The effectiveness of the medication you are prescribing is disappointing at best, and the side effects are terrible. Three times this year you have hospitalized me when I'm trying my best by taking the medication you have prescribed. I just needed someone to talk to, and you act as if I mean absolutely nothing.

The patient arrives via a police car to the emergency department 7 hours later, having taken all of her prescribed antipsychotic medication.

Patients are facing remarkable barriers to treatment. Given the nature of their illness, persons with mental illness are challenged to access services. Community mental health centers as well as private psychiatric clinics are experiencing long waiting lists for services. Desperate and in an effort to have their voices heard, people at times take drastic steps to make a plea for services. The goal of mental health professionals is to assure that each individual voice is heard. No plea for service should go unanswered. However, dollars for services are shrinking. Mental health professionals are stretched beyond reasonable limits, and direct line staff are frequently reacting to the constraints of the treatment delivery system. This chapter presents a clear framework for providing effective crisis intervention within the current constraints of today's mental health practice environments.

## CRISIS INTERVENTION

Crisis intervention is a difficult task and is especially difficult to do well. As the acuity of mental health consumers increases and the service delivery system buckles under increasing pressure from those seeking services, specific and efficacious interventions and guidelines are clearly needed to keep the process flowing. Growing evidence indicates that the risk factors for suicide include a precipitating event such as multiple stressors or a traumatic event, major depression, increased substance abuse, deterioration in social or occupational functions, hopelessness, and verbal expressions of suicidal ideation (Roberts & Yeager, 2009; Weishaar, 2004). For some individuals, dealing with ambivalence (simultaneous thoughts of self-harm and thoughts of immediate gratification and satisfaction) is a day-to-day event. For others, the thought of suicide mistakenly appears to be an immediate fix to an emotionally painful or acutely embarrassing situation that seems insurmountable.

For the chemically dependent individual, suicide may be the easy way out of a cycle of use and withdrawal. Every person brought to local hospital emergency rooms or psychiatric screening centers is different. The scenarios are as endless and diverse as the population served. Therefore, it may be helpful to begin with a working definition of crisis:

> Crisis: An acute disruption of psychological homeostasis in which one's usual coping mechanisms fail and there exists evidence of distress and functional impairment. The subjective reaction to a stressful life experience that compromises the individual's stability and ability to cope or function. The main cause of a crisis is an intensely stressful, traumatic, or hazardous event, but two other conditions are also necessary: (1) the individual's perception of the event as the cause of considerable upset and/ or disruption; and (2) the individual's inability to resolve the disruption by previously used coping mechanisms. Crisis also refers to "an upset in the steady state." It often has five components: a hazardous or traumatic event, a vulnerable state, a precipitating factor, an active crisis state, and the resolution of the crisis. (Roberts, 2002, p. 516)

This definition is particularly applicable to persons in acute crisis because these individuals usually seek help only after they have experienced a hazardous or traumatic event and are in a vulnerable state, have failed to cope and lessen the crisis through customary coping methods, lack family or community social supports, and want outside help. Acute psychological or situational crisis episodes may be viewed in various ways, but the definition we are using emphasizes that a crisis can be a turning point in a person's life.

Crisis intervention generally occurs when a counselor or behavioral clinician enters into the life situation of an individual or family to alleviate the impact of a crisis episode by facilitating and mobilizing the resources of those directly affected. Rapid assessment and timely intervention on the part of crisis counselors, social workers, psychologists, or psychiatrists are of paramount importance.

Crisis intervenors should be active and directive while displaying a nonjudgmental, accepting, hopeful, and positive attitude. Crisis intervenors need to help clients to identify protective factors, inner strengths, psychological hardiness, and resiliency factors that can be utilized for ego bolstering. Effective crisis intervenors are able to gauge the seven stages of crisis intervention, while being flexible and realizing that several stages of intervention may overlap. Crisis intervention should culminate in a restoration of cognitive functioning, crisis resolution, and cognitive mastery (Roberts, 2000; Figure 2.1).

Practitioners addressing crisis frequently know the best approach to take; however, being in a stressful situation, they may revert to behaviors that are less than effective in treating the population presenting for crisis intervention. Therefore, we have included a quick reference list of Do's and Don'ts for crisis workers. Though these recommendations may seem obvious, it is important to keep them close as a reminder of effective tools or approaches to crisis intervention.

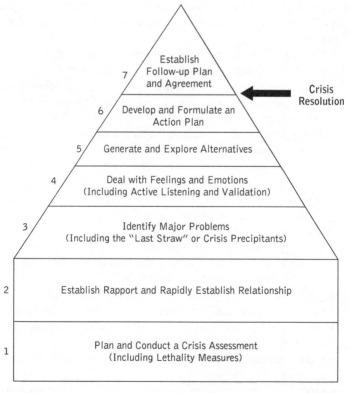

Figure 2.1    Roberts's Seven-Stage Crisis Intervention Model

Dos

- Treat every caller with respect: Speak and listen to the caller as you would like to be spoken and listened to.
- Help the caller to feel he or she did the right thing by calling. "I'm glad that you called."
- Assess in your own mind whether the call is an emergency:
  - Is the caller safe?
  - Is someone or something in immediate danger?
  - If so, act appropriately.
- Except in an emergency, at the beginning of the call concentrate on the caller's feelings and not on the situation.
- Make the caller feel heard. Be empathetic: "It sounds like you're feeling disappointed with your boyfriend."
- Allow the caller to vent his or her feelings.
- Be aware of your own feelings and how they may interfere with your handling of the call. For example, if you are having strong feelings about a divorce in your own life, you need to remind yourself to exclude these feelings when talking with a caller who is having problems with a divorce.
- Recognize that although you might feel you are not doing enough, just listening and "being there" may be extremely helpful and all that is necessary.
- If not obvious, ask what made the caller ask for help at this time.
- Help the caller to generate choices and make decisions.
- Help the caller establish a relationship with the agency rather than with you as an individual. You may not always be available when the caller is in need of help, but the agency can be.
- When ending a call, find out what the caller's plans are, what comes next, what tomorrow looks like. Offer to make a follow-up call.

Don'ts

- Do not minimize the caller's feelings. Do not say, "How can you feel that way? It's not as bad as you are imagining."
- Do not be judgmental, place blame, or take sides. There are usually more than enough people in the caller's life who fill these roles.
- Remain neutral, allowing the caller to solve his or her own problems.
- Do not preach, moralize, or diagnose.
- Do not offer solutions or tell the caller what you think he or she should do. Do not hide suggestions or statements in the form of questions, such as "Do you think it would be better to stay there and feel awful or go and talk it over with him?"
- Do not give compliments beyond reflecting the strengths illustrated in the caller's story.
- Do not ask the caller why he or she felt or behaved a certain way. The caller may not know why, may respond defensively, or both.

- Do not share your thoughts or theories with the caller. Share only your concern about the caller's well-being.
- Do not reveal to the caller whether another person has used the service.
- Do not have unrealistic expectations about what can be accomplished during a single call. If the caller's problems have developed over time, realizations and change will probably also take time.

## SUICIDE ASSESSMENT MEASURES, TOOLS, AND GUIDELINES

The critical first step in applying Roberts's seven-stage crisis intervention model (R-SSCIM) is conducting a lethality and biopsychosocial risk assessment. This involves a relatively quick assessment of the number and duration of risk factors, including imminent danger and availability of lethal weapons, verbalization of suicide or homicide risk, need for immediate medical attention, positive and negative coping strategies, lack of family or social supports, active psychiatric diagnosis, and current drug or alcohol use (Roberts & Yeager, 2009; Roberts, 2000).

Suicide risk assessments help elicit risk factors and protective factors. Risk and protective factors

- vary in presence and severity;
- may be modifiable or static;
- may contribute to risk in some individuals but not in others;
- include developmental, biomedical, psychopathological, psychodynamic, and psychosocial aspects of the patient's current presentation and history; and
- may be relevant only when they occur in combination with particular psychosocial stressors.

Suicide risk factors may be static or dynamic; it is important to consider both risk and protective factors, with attention to which factors are modifiable. The goal is to estimate the risk through a knowledgeable assessment with the focus on reducing risk, recognizing that risk factors alone do not determine predictability. Frequently, risk factors vary in severity, and they may only be relevant when they occur in combination. To decrease suicide risk, focus should be on attempting to mitigate risk factors and/or strengthen protective factors.

If possible, a medical assessment should include a brief summary of the presenting problem, any ongoing medical conditions, and current medications (names, dosages, and time of last dose). According to Roberts and Yeager (2009), if, during a suicide risk assessment, the person exhibits any of the following factors, it would seem prudent to call an ambulance; if the patient is already at the emergency room, he or she should be further evaluated by a psychiatric screener, psychiatric–mental health nurse, or psychiatric resident and hospitalized in a psychiatric crisis stabilization unit for 48 to 72 hours of observation and evaluation (Table 2.1):

- Patient expresses suicidal ideation: consider lethality and patient's expectations, history of attempts and lethality assessment, degree of ambivalence, wish to live and/or wish to die.
- Patient has a suicide plan: presence or absence of rescue possibility.
- Patient has access to lethal means and exhibits poor judgment.
- Patient has access to available means, especially firearms.
- Patient is agitated and exhibits imminent danger to self or others: assess for impulsivity, degree of desperation, agitation.
- Psychotic patient exhibits command hallucinations related to harming self or others.
- Patient is intoxicated or high on illegal drugs and acting in an impulsive manner.

Table 2.1    Decision Assistance for Level of Care Placement

| *Immediate safety risk, ONE* | *Potential safety risk, ONE* |
|---|---|
| _____ *DSM-IV-TR* Diagnosis | _____ *DSM-IV-TR* Diagnosis, ___ ___ ___ . ___ ___ |
| _____ *Command hallucinations with direction to harm self/others* | and *ONE* |
| _____ *Suicide/homicide attempt* | _____ Somatic symptoms |
| _____ *Suicide/homicide ideation, ONE* | _____ Behavioral symptoms |
| _____ Specific plan | _____ Psychological symptoms |
| _____ Nonspecific plan with means and no deterrents | _____ Suicidal/homicidal ideation. *ONE* |
| _____ Intent/potential to harm others | _____ Nonspecific plan |
|  | _____ Refusal to disclose plan |
| _____ *DSM-IV-TR diagnosis with associated symptoms and active substance abuse w/in past 24 hrs., ONE* | _____ Hx. of high lethality/intent pan year |
| _____ Suicide attempt within past year | _____ Active substance abuse w/in past 24 hrs./failed toxicology semen |
| _____ Hx. of high lethality/intent in past 6 mos. | _____ Substance dependence w/o withdrawal potential |
| _____ Current refusal to disclose plan | _____ Acute/debilitating medical condition with acceptable lab values /medical stability currently |
| _____ Self-mutilation and increase in intensity pattern | _____  Self-mutilation |
| _____ Psychiatric medication noncompliance/intensified symptoms characteristic of *DSM-IV-TR* diagnostic code ___ ___ ___ . ___ ___ |  |
| _____ Comorbid medical condition acute or debilitating illness | Continued Action Required: Select ONE from the Level of Care Indicators below |
| _____ *Delirium ONE* | • Severe impairment |
| _____ Unable to focus/sustain attention | • Moderate impairment |
| _____ Change in cognition | • Mild impairment |
| _____ Misinterpretations/illusions/ hallucinations |  |
| If any <u>one</u> criterion are met STOP . . . <u>Admit to Inpatient</u>. |  |
| If one criterion is not met continue to next section. |  |

(*continued*)

Table 2.1    Continued

| INPATIENT | PARTIAL HOSPITALIZATION/IOP | OUTPATIENT |
|---|---|---|
| *Patient, ONE*<br>\_\_GAF < 30<br>\_\_Unable/refuses to comply with treatment<br>\_\_Hx of inpatient admission w/in past 3 yrs.<br>\_\_Expected to comply with negotiation | *Patient agrees with treatment, ONE*<br>\_\_GAF 30 or below<br>\_\_Inconsistently compliant with treatment<br>\_\_Hx. of inpatient admission w/in past 3 yrs.<br>\_\_Expected to comply with continued negotiation | *Patient agrees with treatment*<br>\_\_GAF 30–50<br>\_\_Patient is expected to comply with tx. |
| *DLs, ONE*<br>\_\_Nonambulatory<br>\_\_Unable to attend to hygiene<br>\_\_Unable to nourish self<br>\_\_Unable to perform daily tasks/activities | *ADLs, ONE*<br>\_\_Ambulatory only with assistance<br>\_\_Maintains hygiene with frequent reminders<br>\_\_Declining unreliable nutritional status<br>\_\_Declining ability to perform daily tasks | *ADLs mild deterioration, ONE*<br>\_\_Ambulation<br>\_\_Hygiene<br>\_\_Nutrition<br>\_\_Daily tasks/activities |
| *Relationships, ONE*<br>\_\_Socially withdrawn<br>\_\_Nonverbal<br>\_\_Sexually inappropriate/abusive<br>\_\_Physical abuse<br>\_\_Terminated significant relationship(s)<br>\_\_Restraining order/hx. of domestic dispute | *Relationships, ONE*<br>\_\_Moderate conflict with significant others<br>\_\_Increasing verbal hostility/threatening<br>\_\_Socially isolated/alienated<br>\_\_Easily frustrated and exhibiting reckless or<br>\_\_Impulsive behavior or angry outbursts | *Relationship, ONE*<br>\_\_Significant other suggests/demands treatment<br>\_\_Increasing social isolation<br>\_\_Occasional arguments/avoidance of contact<br>\_\_Occasional verbal hostility |
| *Role Performance, ONE*<br>\_\_Absent > 5 days work/10 days (school)<br>\_\_Suspended/terminated/quit/expelled<br>\_\_Self-employed and unable to maintain business<br>\_\_Unemployed and unable to seek work<br>\_\_Unable to care for/neglect of dependent children/elders<br>\_\_Exposes dependent children/elders to physical abuse/sexual abuse<br>\_\_Removal from current living situation by authorities | *Role Performance*<br>\_\_Absent >3–4 days from work/> 5–9 days from school<br>\_\_Self-employed with significantly decreased productivity<br>\_\_Unemployed and job seeking 1–3 days/wk.<br>\_\_Formal warning/mandated employee assistance counseling<br>\_\_Ongoing academic difficulty/significant decreased productivity<br>\_\_Medical LOA due to psychiatric/substance abuse problem<br>\_\_Deterioration in care of children elders<br>Threatened removal of children/elders | *Role Performance, ONE*<br>\_\_Absent 1–2 days from work/1–4 days from school<br>\_\_Unemployed and job seeking > 4 days/wk.<br>\_\_Mild decrease in productivity at work/school<br>\_\_Informal warning about performance at work/school<br>\_\_Mild decrease in care for dependent children<br>\_\_Complaints registered with child/elder services/authorities |
| *Support System, ONE*<br>\_\_Unavailable<br>\_\_Unable to ensure safety<br>\_\_Intentional sabotage of treatment<br>\_\_Ongoing contact with perpetrator of abuse | *Support System, ONE*<br>\_\_Available weekends/nights only<br>\_\_Occasional visits/phone contact<br>\_\_Questionably competent/unable to manage symptoms | *Support System Consistent, supportive, competent, ONE*<br>\_\_Available 24 hrs/day<br>\_\_Available weekends/nights only<br>\_\_Occasional visits/phone contact<br>\_\_Able to manage intensity of symptoms |

- Family member reports on patient's suicidal thoughts: of family concern indicates potential risk.

Additional key elements of assessment to be considered include the following:

- Psychosocial stressors
- Support systems
- Actual or perceived interpersonal losses
- Financial difficulties or changes in socioeconomic status
- Employment status
- Cultural viewpoint
- Religious viewpoint
- Substance use—current and historical
- Psychiatric history/diagnosis

## TRIAGE ASSESSMENT

First responders, also known as crisis response team members or front-line crisis intervention workers, are called on to conduct an immediate debriefing under less than stable circumstances. Sometimes they may have to delay the crisis assessment until the patient has been stabilized and supported; in other disaster responses, an assessment can be completed simultaneously with the debriefing. According to many first responders, ideally (assessment, designated by the letter "A" precedes crisis intervention, designated by the letter "C," but in the midst of a disaster or acute crisis, this linear order is not always possible (see Chapter 7 in this book for a detailed discussion of the ACT integrative model).

In the immediate aftermath of a community disaster, the first type of assessment by disaster mental health specialists should be psychiatric triage. A triage or screening tool can be useful in gathering and recording information about the initial contact between a person experiencing crisis or trauma reactions and the mental health specialist. The triage form should include essential demographic information (name, address, phone number, e-mail address, etc.), perception of the magnitude of the traumatic event, coping methods, any presenting problem(s), safety issues, previous traumatic experiences, social support network, drug and alcohol use, preexisting psychiatric conditions, suicide risk, and homicide risk (Eaton & Roberts, 2002). Several hundred articles have examined emergency medical triage, but very few publications have discussed emergency psychiatric triage (Leise, 1995, pp. 48–49; Roberts, 2002). *Triage* has been defined as the medical "process of assigning patients to appropriate treatments depending on their medical conditions and available medical resources" (Liese, 1995, p. 48). Medical triage was first used in the military to respond quickly to the medical needs of soldiers wounded in war. Triage involves assigning physically ill or injured patients to different levels of care, ranging from "emergent" (i.e., immediate treatment required) to "nonemergent" (i.e., no medical treatment required).

Psychiatric or psychological triage assessment refers to the immediate decision-making process in which the mental health worker determines lethality and referral to one of the following alternatives:

- Emergency inpatient psychiatric hospitalization
- Outpatient treatment facility or private therapist
- Support group or social service agency
- No referral needed

The ACT intervention model refers to triage assessment, crisis intervention, and trauma treatment and referral to appropriate community resources. Concerning triage assessment, emergency psychiatric response should take place when the rapid assessment indicates that the individual is a danger to self or others or is exhibiting intense and acute psychiatric symptoms that may place him or her at risk. These survivors generally require short-term intervention, including support, therapy, and pharmacotherapy to protect themselves from self-harm (e.g., inability to care for themselves, suicide risk, and/or self-injurious behavior) or harm to other persons (e.g., murder and attempted murder). The small number of individuals needing emergency psychiatric treatment are generally diagnosed with moderate- to high-potential lethality (e.g., inability to care for self, suicidal ideation, and/or homicidal thoughts) and acute mental disorder. In the small percentage of cases where emergency psychiatric treatment is indicated, these persons are usually suffering from an accumulation of several previous traumatic events (Roberts & Yeager 2009; Burgess & Roberts, 2000).

Concerning the other categories of psychiatric triage, many individuals may be in a precrisis stage due to ineffective coping skills, a weak support system, or ambivalence about seeking mental health assistance. These same individuals may have no psychiatric symptoms and no suicide risk but may be experiencing psychological trauma and require psychological first aid, support, and observation.

Suicide prevention strategies as outlined by the Centers for Disease Control and Prevention, the US Department of Health and Human Services, and the National Institutes of Health depend on establishing the frequency and severity of suicidal behavior and identifying risk and protective factors as previously discussed (US Department of Health and Human Services, 2001; Crosby, Ortega, et al., 2011). Studies of risk factors used to predict suicide have consistently recommended that suicidal ideation and a history of suicide attempts are among the most important risk factors for suicide (Beck, Brown, Steer, Dahlsgaard, & Grishman, 1999; Brown, Beck, Steer, & Grisham 2000). It is important to note that a structured assessment of suicidal ideation and behavior significantly improves identification of high-risk patients relative to a routine clinical interview. Unfortunately, to date, no single standard measure has been identified to predict suicide. Accomplishment of accurate assessment requires crisis intervenors to employ valid and reliable assessment tools. It is recommend that every crisis counselor, psychiatric screener, medical social worker, psychiatric–mental health nurse, and psychiatrist be trained in the use of these suicide assessment measures. The measures include but are not limited to the following:

- Beck Hopelessness Scale
- Beck Depression Inventory
- Beck Scale for Suicide Ideation
- Columbia Suicide Severity Rating Scale
- Firestone Assessment of Self-Destructive Thoughts
- Modified Scale for Suicide Ideation
- Linehan Reasons for Living Scale
- Self-Monitoring Suicide Ideation Scale
- Scale for Suicide Ideation–Worst
- Lifetime Parasuicidal Count
- SADS Person Scale
- Suicide Potential Lethality Scale

Useful evidence-based measures of suicide risk include examination of the Beck Hopelessness Scale (BHS), the Columbia Suicide Severity Rating Scale, and the Scale for Suicide Ideation–Worst (SSI-W). The latter 19-item scale is an interviewer-administered rating scale that seems to accurately measure the magnitude of a patient's specific beliefs, behaviors, attitudes, and plans to commit suicide during the specific time period when he or she is at the highest risk of suicide. More specifically, interviewers asked patients to recall the approximate time frame and day when they had the most intense and strongest desire to kill themselves. Patients were then asked to keep this worst experience in mind while they answered and were rated on 19 items related to their wish to die, duration and frequency of suicide ideation, number of deterrents, actual amount of preparation for a contemplated attempt, and desire to make an active or passive suicide attempt (Beck, Brown, & Steer, 1997).

Retrospective longitudinal research of suicide ideation at its most severe point or worst point in time seems to be a valid predictor of eventual suicide among psychiatric outpatients within an average of 4 years from the initial assessment interview. This important study by Beck and associates (1999) was based on a large sample of 3,701 outpatients who sought psychiatric treatment at the University of Pennsylvania between 1979 and 1994. After follow-up on all patients 4 years after completion of treatment, it was found that only 30 of the former patients, or fewer than 1%, had committed suicide. All 3,701 patients were assessed on three scales: Scale for Suicidal Ideation–Current (SSI-C), SSI-W, and BHS. With regard to the findings related to the SSI-W: "Patients who scored in the higher risk category of SSI-W had a 14 times higher odds of committing suicide than patients who scored in the lower risk category" (p. 7). With regard to the BHS, patients who scored in the highest category for hopelessness had a 6 times higher odds of committing suicide than patients who scored in the lower-risk category.

One implication of the longitudinal study is that patients who present at outpatient clinics and community mental health centers may not be experiencing as much suicide ideation or hopelessness as they did in past days, weeks, or months. Therefore, it is critically important to determine suicide ideation at the worst point in time: when the person in crisis called a 24-hour crisis hotline, when the person asked a significant other to drive him or her to the hospital, or when the person arrived at the emergency room. It is also imperative to monitor risk of suicide at regular intervals throughout treatment.

The Columbia Suicide Severity Rating Scale is designed to distinguish the domains of suicidal ideation and suicidal behavior. To do so, four constructs are measured. The first is the severity of ideation, which is rated on a 5-point ordinal scale in which 1 = wish to be dead, 2 = nonspecific active suicidal thoughts, 3 = suicidal thoughts with methods, 4 = suicidal intent, and 5 = suicidal intent with plan. The second is the intensity of ideation subscale, which consists of five items, each rated on a 5-point ordinal scale: frequency, duration, controllability, deterrents, and reason for ideation. The third is the behavior subscale, which is rated on a nominal scale that includes actual, aborted, and interrupted attempts; preparatory behavior; and nonsuicidal self-injurious behavior. The fourth is the lethality subscale, which assesses actual attempts; actual lethality is rated on a 6-point ordinal scale, and if actual lethality is zero and potential lethality of attempts is rated on a 3-point ordinal scale. The Columbia Suicide Severity Rating Scale was designed to (a) provide definitions of suicidal ideation and behavior and nonsuicidal self-injurious behavior and corresponding probes; (b) quantify the full spectrum of suicidal ideation and suicidal behavior and determine their severity over specified periods of time; (c) distinguish suicidal behavior and nonsuicidal self-injurious behavior; and (d) employ a format that permits integration of information from multiple sources, such as patient interview and family and other interviews (Posner et al., 2011).

## TWO CAUTIONARY NOTES REGARDING SUICIDE LETHALITY ASSESSMENT

Unfortunately, two of the most frequently cited risk factors of high suicide intent—a history of one or more prior suicide attempts and a current suicide plan—are often misunderstood. It has been obvious to most clinicians and suicidologists that either having a history of a prior suicide attempt or having a specific suicide plan should result in a prediction of high suicide risk. However, it is critically important for crisis counselors and psychiatric screeners to be made aware that the research demonstrates that the absence of a prior suicide attempt should not be taken as an indication that the crisis caller will not commit suicide or make a very serious lethal attempt (Clark, 1998; Fawcett et al., 1990; Kleespies & Dettmer, 2000; Maris, 1992). Reviews of the suicide risk assessment literature indicate that 60% to 70% of suicide completers complete suicide on their first attempt and "had no known history of prior attempts" (Kleespies & Dettmer, 2000, p. 1120).

The second cautionary note relates to the fact that some patients may well be ambivalent about suicide, untrusting of the clinician or psychiatric screener, ashamed, or guarded and unwilling to share suicidal thoughts with a stranger such as a crisis clinician or psychiatric screener. In other cases, the suicidal individual may have a concrete and specific plan, including a location and a lethal method of suicide, but be unwilling to share his or her thoughts with anyone. Psychiatric screeners, intake workers, crisis counselors, psychiatric residents, and emergency room nurses and social workers should be vigilant and cautious in suicide risk assessments and should never assume that a crisis caller or patient is not at suicide risk because he or she reports no suicidal thoughts, wishes, or plans. In their research, Fawcett and associates (1990) found that a small group of depressed patients who committed suicide within 1 year of clinical suicide assessment were more likely to be those patients who said they had no suicidal thoughts or ideas. In sharp contrast, the large group of depressed patients who were still alive 5 years after initial assessment shared their suicidal thoughts and ideas with the clinician.

With regard to suicide risk estimates and lethality assessments, Rudd and Joiner (1998) have pointed out that individuals in the severe or imminent suicide risk category have predisposing factors, such as a long history of substance abuse, a family history of a parent or sibling who committed suicide, or a history of child physical or sexual abuse; multiple acute risk factors, such as a recent job loss due to substance abuse, depressed mood, or specific suicide plan with a lethal method available; and a lack of protective factors, such as a significant other or close family members and medication compliance.

In the current care environment, practitioners are required to determine imminent, moderate, and low suicide risk. In doing so, the individual practitioner is required to assign the patient to the most appropriate level of care. The implementation of Roberts's SSCIM provides appropriate interventions for resolution of moderate and low suicidal ideation immediately on the individual's seeking assistance. If the appropriate clinical pathway is followed during the initial assessment, application of the seven-stage model can provide insight in a nonthreatening manner to assist the patient in development of cognitive stabilization.

## EMERGING NEW TECHNOLOGY

As technology advances, so do opportunities in assessment and prevention of risk in persons with mental illness. While it is likely that the crisis intervention process will involve a clinical staff, there is no doubt that technology will impact the assessment and intervention process. The use of electronic medical records has grown tremendously in recent years, and the emergence of such records has been both a blessing and a curse. Although electronic records enhance legibility and streamline interprofessional communication and interconnectivity among multiple health systems using the same record platform, they can function as a barrier for workers who are not familiar or comfortable with the use of technology. Nevertheless, integration of technology into care is inevitable. In 2013, the Current Population Survey of the US Census Bureau indicated that 75.6% of households reported having "internet connectivity." Existing approaches to crisis outreach will evolve using web-based applications and increased numbers of self-help resources. Web-based outreach and prevention programs will be increasingly available to persons in crisis, providing access to supportive information at virtually any time. Community discussion forums, blogs posted by suicide prevention experts, and self-assessment tests that provide feedback and recommendations can all be integrated into web-based applications.

Social networking sites such as Facebook will ultimately permit users to communicate via posting, text, e-mail, and messaging. One key advantage of social networking sites for crisis intervention and outreach is that they facilitate social connections among peers with similar experiences. These sites have the potential to foster supportive interactions with others and to create a community among those who are coping with similar challenges.

Mobile devices and smartphones are capable of delivering evidence-based assessment tools and are appropriate for crisis intervention because they are carried on one's person and are accessible at all times of day. Apps (applications), which are programs designed for mobile devices, can be designed to help users self-assess, monitor psychiatric symptoms, and report needs and problems as they emerge. Users can personalize content while having the connectivity to access hotline links, psychological tools (e.g., relaxation exercises), and appointment reminders. Apps provide discreet and readily available modes of learning, communication processes and guidelines supporting the management of symptoms, which appear to be uniquely supportive of a confidential nonstigmatized approach to providing information and links to treatment.

Unfortunately, technology-based programs have limitations. Although many individuals have access to the Internet, technology-based programs must accommodate the communication habits, needs, and preferences of those seeking to use the technology. Not all technical platforms are compatible, which leads to barriers to access. Additionally, technology is always changing and evolving, in ways that rarely take into consideration user preference or culturally relevant or best communication methods for the end user. Other issues to consider are privacy concerns and clinical safety. Although the Internet can provide a sense of anonymity, fear of a potential breach of confidentiality may prevent individuals from full participation in programming. Issues of confidentiality, privacy, and privileged information exist for providers and vary from state to state with regard to the use of text and e-mail communication with patients.

Social networking sites and chat rooms can foster positive supportive interactions, but not all individuals who are seeking such interactions have good intentions. Consideration must be given for groups of vulnerable individuals regarding sharing of negative information that is not designed to protect the individual but rather can foster or support self-harm behaviors. A perfect example can be seen in groups that exist to discuss in great detail methods for completing suicide, such as use of a device known as the "helium hood kit." A related concern is the unregulated nature of online resources. Although established organizations such as the Crisis Call Center follow ethical guidelines and evidence-based approaches, many other sites do not follow available and accepted standard of care approaches. Further evaluation of technology-based programs will be important to identify best practices, to determine empirical support and evidence-based outcomes, as well as cost-benefit and patient outcome. Clearly, with appropriate innovations, research and evaluation technology can be applied in a positive and potentially life-saving approach.

## DISCUSSION OF SUICIDE IDEATION FLOW CHART AND INTERVENTION PROTOCOL

The operation of a crisis intervention program and a time-limited treatment program for persons with suicide ideation is depicted in Figure 2.2. This flow chart provides a general description of the different clinical pathways and the functions of mobile crisis intervention programs, emergency psychiatric units, inpatient treatment units, partial hospital programs, day treatment facilities, and other referral sources in the community.

Crisis intervention and suicide prevention programs usually maintain a 24-hour telephone crisis service that provides a lifeline as well as an entry point to behavioral health care for persons with major depression or suicidal thoughts and ideation. When the crisis worker answers the cry for help, his or her primary duty is to initiate crisis intervention, beginning with rapid lethality and triage assessment and establishing rapport. In essence, crisis

PERSON EXPRESSES SUICIDAL IDEATION

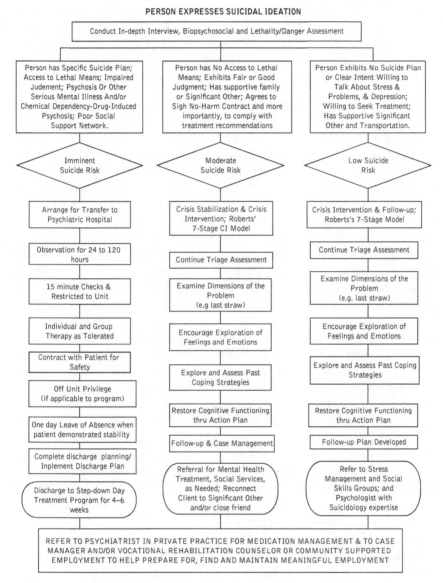

Figure 2.2   Person Expresses Suicidal Ideation

intervention and suicide prevention include the following primary steps in an attempt to prevent suicide:

1. Conduct a rapid lethality and biopsychosocial assessment.
2. Attempt to establish rapport and at the same time communicate a willingness to help the caller in crisis.

3. Help the caller in crisis to develop a plan of action that links him or her to community health care and mental health agencies. The most frequent outcome of depressed or suicidal callers is that they are transported to a psychiatric screening and intake, a behavioral health care facility, a hospital, or an addiction treatment program.

The crisis intervention worker assumes full responsibility for the case when he or she answers the phone. The caller cannot be rushed and handled simply by a referral to another agency. Crisis workers should follow the case until complete transfer of responsibility has been accomplished and some other agency has assumed responsibility. The crisis worker should complete the state-mandated mental health and psychiatric screening report, which makes an initial determination regarding whether or not the person is a danger to self or others. This report should be given to the transporting officer or ambulance driver and faxed/scanned and e-mailed (on a secure network) to the intake worker on duty at the receiving psychiatric unit or hospital. In other cases where the risk of suicide is low and a close family member or significant other is able and willing to take responsibility for the person in crisis, the client and the family member need telephone numbers to call in case of an emergency. The ultimate goal of all crisis and suicide prevention services is to relieve intense emotional pain and acute crisis episodes while helping the caller to find positive ways to cope with life.

It is imperative for all crisis clinicians to establish rapport with the person in crisis by listening in a patient, hopeful, self-assured, interested, and knowledgeable manner. The skilled crisis worker communicates that the person has done the right thing by calling and, furthermore, that the crisis worker is able to help. An empathetic ear is provided to the crisis caller to relieve his or her intense stress by active listening. The crisis worker should relate to the caller in a confidential, spontaneous, and noninstitutionalized manner (Roberts & Yeager 2009; Roberts, 2000; Yeager & Gregoire, 2000).

After listening to the story of the person in crisis and asking several key questions, the crisis worker makes a determination as to whether or not the caller has a high, moderate, or low suicide risk.

If the caller has a lethal method (e.g., a firearm) readily available and a specific plan for suicide, or has previously attempted suicide, he or she is considered to have a high suicide risk. Callers frequently evaluated as being at low risk for suicide still need help, but they are primarily depressed and sometimes expressing ambivalent thoughts about what it is like to be in heaven versus hell. They have not yet planned the specific details of suicide or shared a concrete plan with the crisis counselor. As discussed earlier, if the caller has predisposing factors (e.g., a possible copycat suicide, such as a teenager whose high school classmate, parent, or sibling has committed suicide), he or she may be at moderate to high risk of suicide. Other callers may be persons seeking information for themselves or a family member, social callers with personal problems such as loneliness, or callers needing emergency medical attention.

With regard to inpatient versus outpatient psychiatric treatment, the most important determinant should be imminent danger to self or others because of an inability to care for one's self or having a lethal means to commit suicide. It is also extremely important for crisis clinicians and intake psychiatric screeners to make a multiaxial differential diagnosis, which determines acute or chronic psychosocial stressors, dysfunctional relationships, decreased self-esteem or hopelessness, severe or unremitting anxiety, living alone without social support, intimate partner violence, personality disorders (particularly borderline personality disorders), major depressive disorders, bipolar disorders, and comorbidity (American Psychiatric Association, 2003).

## CASE STUDIES AND APPLICATION OF R-SSCIM

### Maryann

Maryann's mother reports that her 17-year-old daughter is barricaded in her bedroom and last night destroyed her iPad and threw her cell phone into the hallway. Maryann has not eaten for 24 hours. Her boyfriend broke up with her, and her mother has heard her crying for many hours. Maryann refuses to speak with her mother. The mother is very worried because 8 months earlier, Maryann had ingested a lot of sleeping pills and been rushed to the emergency room when she was distraught about the breakup with her previous boyfriend. A few hours ago, Maryann called her favorite first cousin and told him that she was giving him all of her music library. Maryann's father, with whom she was very close, passed away 12 months ago from cirrhosis of the liver. Her mother calls the psychiatric screening and crisis intervention hotline at one of New Jersey's large medical centers and indicates that she thinks her daughter is depressed and possibly suicidal.

### Suicide Risk Assessment

After reading Maryann's case synopsis and reviewing the suicide risk assessment flow chart (Figure 2.2), would your preliminary rapid assessment rate Maryann as at low, moderate, or high suicide risk?

It is important to keep in mind that although many persons at high risk of suicide have expressed or exhibited a specific suicide plan and availability of a lethal method (e.g., firearms or hanging), there are exceptions. There is a relatively small group of individuals who do not talk to anyone before making a lethal suicide attempt, but they do give clear clues of imminent suicide risk. For example, a college student fails a course for the first time and can't sleep, although he has never had a problem sleeping and has been an honor student for the past 3 years. Or a young adult who has never expressed paranoid delusions has now expressed irrational fears that a violent gang with 100 members is after him and will try to kill him tonight. These delusions are an outgrowth of a drug-induced psychosis. *Psychiatric screeners, crisis workers, counselors, social workers, family members, and close friends should be made aware of the fact that a critical clue to suicidal ideation and suicide attempts is a drastic change in behavior patterns, daily routine, or actions* (e.g., barricading oneself in a room for 24 hours and refusing to come out to eat or go to the bathroom, giving away prized possessions, having paranoid delusions or command hallucinations for the first time, talking about how wonderful it would be to go to heaven to be with one's recently deceased and loving father).

The psychiatric screener crisis worker who answered the phone determines that this Maryann seems to be at moderate to high risk of lethality and that the worker needs to go immediately to Maryann's home. The preliminary lethality assessment is based on the following seven high-risk factors:

1. This is the first time that Maryann has ever barricaded herself in her room.
2. She seems to be depressed, evidenced by not eating for 24 hours and crying for many hours.
3. She had a previous suicide attempt only 8 months ago.
4. She recently gave away prized possessions.
5. Her father, with whom she was close, died only 12 months ago.
6. She refuses to communicate with anyone.
7. She destroyed her iPad (property damage).

You are the crisis worker, and you are dispatched to the home. The following application focuses on what you should say and do when you arrive. We describe this crisis situation with specific details, statements, and questions related to each of the seven stages in the R-SSCIM. First, it is important to be aware that Stages 1 and 2 often take place simultaneously. However, in the case of life-threatening and high-risk suicide ideation, child abuse, sexual assault, or domestic violence, the emphasis is on rapid crisis, lethality, and triage assessment.

### Stage 1: Assess Lethality

The crisis worker needs to obtain background information quickly from the mother (rapid collateral assessment). Ask the mother if the daughter has been taking medications or if there have been any recent changes in medication. Then ask the mother if Maryann was ever prescribed an antidepressant medication. If yes, does she know what it is and whether Maryann has been taking it? Was it prescribed by a family doctor or a psychiatrist? Does Maryann currently have access to her medications or any other drugs? Ask the mother if anything about her daughter's situation has changed in the past 20 to 30 minutes (since her phone call). Next, give the mother something to do to engage her in the care process (e.g., ask her to call the ex-boyfriend or best girlfriend to obtain background data, especially whether Maryann has recently taken any illegal drugs). Assess Maryann's danger to herself and others (suicidal or homicidal thoughts), as well as substance abuse history and preexisting mental disorders. Ask questions about symptoms, traumatic events, stressful life events, future plans, suicidal ideation, previous suicide attempts, and mental illness. Ask about upcoming special events or birthday celebrations that the youth in crisis may be looking forward to, or recollections of happy events or celebrations in the past that may be repeated in the future (special events can instill hope for the future). Determine if Maryann needs immediate medical attention and whether there are any drugs, sleeping pills, or weapons in her room.

## Rapid Triage Assessment

1. The individual is a danger to herself or others and is exhibiting intense and acute psychiatric symptoms. These survivors generally require short-term emergency hospitalization and psychopharmacotherapy to protect themselves from self-harm or harm to other persons (Priority I: emergency medical treatment, ambulance or rescue transport, and psychiatric screening center).
2. The individual is in a precrisis stage due to ineffective coping skills, a weak support system, or ambivalence about seeking the help of a therapist. These individuals may have mild or no psychiatric symptoms or suicide risk. They may need one to three sessions of crisis counseling and referral to a support group.
3. The third type of client may have called a suicide prevention program or a 24-hour mobile crisis intervention unit for information because he or she is sad, anxious, lonely, or depressed.

It is important to determine whether the person in crisis needs the mobile crisis intervention team to respond quickly to the home or another place in the community. The caller may have just attempted suicide or is planning to attempt suicide shortly or may be experiencing command hallucinations of a violent nature (Priority I). The caller may be experiencing delusions and may be unable to leave the house (Priority II) or may be suffering from mood disturbance or depression and fleeting suicidal ideation, with no specific suicidal plan (Priority III, probably in need of an appointment with a caring counselor or therapist).

### Stage 2: Establish Rapport

It is very important to introduce yourself and speak in a calm and neutral manner. Crisis workers should do their best to make a psychological connection with the 17-year-old in a precrisis or acute crisis situation. Part of establishing rapport and putting the person at ease involves being nonjudgmental, listening actively, and demonstrating empathy. Establish a bridge, bond, or connection by asking Maryann about things she likes:

- "Do you have any posters on your wall right now?"
- "Do you have a favorite TV show?"
- "Do you have a favorite recording artist?"
- "What are your favorite foods or desserts?"

An alternative approach is brief self-disclosure, such as, "When I was 17 years old, my boyfriend broke up with me. I think I understand the emotional pain and sadness you are going through. I thought I loved my boyfriend very much. In fact, he was my first love. He broke up with me for another girl and I was very sad, just like you. But, about 2 months after the breakup, I met someone else, and we had a very enjoyable long-term relationship."

It is important to understand that many adolescents are impulsive and impatient; some may have escape fantasies, and others may be very sensitive and/or temperamental. It is important not to lecture, preach, or moralize. Make concise statements, be caring, display keen interest, and do not make disparaging or insulting statements of any kind or oversimplify your communication. Stages 3 and 4 sometimes take place simultaneously.

### Stage 3: Identify the Main Problem, Including Crisis Precipitants or Triggering Incidents

Ask questions to determine the final straw or precipitating event that led Maryann into her current situation. Focus on the problem or problems, and prioritize and focus on the worst problem first. Listen carefully for symptoms and clues of suicidal thoughts and intent. Make a direct inquiry about suicidal plans and about nonverbal gestures or other communications (e.g., diaries, poems, journals, school essays, paintings, or drawings). Because most adolescent suicides are impulsive and unplanned, it is important to determine whether the youth has easy access to a lethal weapon or drugs (including sleeping pills, methamphetamines, or barbiturates).

### Stage 4: Deal With Feelings and Emotions and Provide Support

Deal with the client's immediate feelings or fears. Allow Maryann to tell her story and say why she is feeling so bad. Provide preliminary empathy to the impact of Maryann's breakup with her boyfriend. Use active listening skills (e.g., paraphrasing, reflection of feelings, summarizing, reassurance, compliments, advice giving, reframing, and probes). Normalize the client's experiences. Validate and identify her emotions. Examine past coping methods. Encourage ventilation of mental and physical feelings.

### Stage 5: Explore Possible Alternatives

First, reestablish balance and homeostasis, also known as equilibrium: Ask Maryann what has helped in the past. For example, what did she do to cope with the loss and grief of losing a loved family member after her father passed away? Integrate solution-based therapy (e.g., full or partial miracle or exception questions). For example: what would your life today look like today if while you were sleeping a miracle happened and this problem didn't exist any longer? Ask her about bright spots from her past (e.g., hobbies, birthday celebrations, sports successes, academic successes, vacations). Mutually explore and suggest new coping options that build on previously identified strengths and alternatives. It is important for the crisis worker to jog the client's memories so she can verbalize the last time things seemed to be going well and she was in a good mood. Help the client find untapped resources.

### Stage 6: Help Client and Formulate an Action Plan

Provide the client with a specific phone number of a therapist.

### Stage 7: Follow-Up Phone Call, In-Person
### Appointment for Booster Session, or Home Visit

Let Maryann know that she can call you, and give her your beeper number. Let her know that the beeper is for an emergency. Depending on the crisis worker's assessment when leaving the home, it may be useful to schedule a follow-up with the therapist to whom Maryann is being referred, so that a team approach can be used.

Follow-up also may include a booster session with the crisis worker scheduled for 1 week or 30 days later.

## Jeanette

Jeanette introduced herself in the session by saying, "My name is Jeanette, but everyone calls me Jet." She is a 27-year-old female who presented to the hospital emergency department seeking treatment for a severe laceration above her right eye. In the process of triaging Jet, an astute medical student questioned if the cut was the result of physical abuse. Jet became tearful and reported that she had been beaten and sexually assaulted by two men while "semiconscious" at a house where there was "a party going on." Jet reported, "I was really high and almost passed out, when these two guys came in the room. I was too messed up to fight, it just happened. One of them was rough, he kept hitting me ... but I couldn't stop him, I was just too high to protect myself." As the assessment progressed, Jet reported current suicidal ideation as well as a past history of suicide attempts and substance abuse, including snorting and shooting heroin and drinking heavily for the past 3 years. Jet reports using as much as $400 worth of heroin, daily when available. Jet also drinks daily, reporting a tolerance of nearly two bottles of wine per day. During the admission interview, Jet reported that she feels there is no hope and that she would like to "end it all." She reported to staff that she knew that acetaminophen in a large enough dose would "do the trick." She reported a plan of picking up two large bottles on the way home, taking the drug with "heroin," and just not waking up. This report led to voluntary admission to the inpatient psychiatric unit for psychiatric stabilization and detoxification.

Following her admission to the inpatient unit, Jet slept for nearly 24 hours. On the third day of treatment (at approximately 9:00 a.m.), Jet lash out at her peers due to significant mood swings. At this time, she yelled at the nursing staff when she did not receive Motrin for her headache. As the day progressed, Jet experienced a variety of moods, ranging from relief to paralyzing anxiety. By noon she was involved in a confrontation with each nurse on duty. Jet reported severe cravings and feelings of uncertainty regarding her well-being and her ability to remain abstinent. By 2:00, staff reported that Jet was participating in treatment groups and integrating well into the community despite being quite ill. However, with the change of shift came a change of staff and new personality conflicts.

Jet was immediately confronted by the evening charge nurse for being late to treatment activities; there was a second confrontation regarding attendance at the evening 12-step meeting. Finally, at 10:00 p.m., Jet and the nurse were at the nursing station screaming at one another. Jet had requested a cup of coffee, and the charge nurse refused, stating, "You won't sleep taking a stimulant." At this, Jet lunged at the nurse and was immediately restrained by two male staff and given Haldol and Ativan. The effect of this restraint was similar to her feelings while being physically abused. Jet reports believing the two male staff were going to rape her. She began to fight, and the harder she fought, the worse her experience became. By 10:30, Jet was in five-point restraints, screaming and sobbing while reliving the trauma that had led to her admission to the psychiatric and detoxification unit.

## R-SSCIM Application

### Stage 1: Plan and Conduct a Crisis and Lethality Assessment

Stage 1 of the seven-stage crisis intervention model began with the night nurse speaking calmly with Jet and working to bring her to a rational state where the nurse could begin to assess the nature of the reaction Jet was displaying while restrained. The nurse accurately assessed that the restraints were a key part of the issue. Despite conflict between staff regarding Jet's actions, the night nurse began reducing Jet's distress by removing one restraint at a time, assuring Jet that the others would be removed as she demonstrated her ability to cooperate.

### Stage 2: Establish Rapport and Rapidly Establish Relationship

As Jet demonstrated her willingness to cooperate, the night nurse began the process of rapidly establishing rapport with her, as outlined in the seven-stage model. Establishing rapport began with a smile and quiet conversation. The nurse placed a cold compress on Jet's forehead and used another to wipe her face and arms. These simple acts of kindness would set the stage for further investigation, treatment, and stabilization.

Although establishing a relationship appears simple, it is frequently difficult to do well given the time constraints experienced in crisis stabilization. For example, in this case, the team was aware that Jet was experiencing withdrawal and mood swings characteristic of heroin dependence. For this reason, the night nurse began the process of assessing the physical distress related to withdrawal and began to approach Jet in a manner to address the physical and emotional aspect of her illness.

### Stage 3: Identify Major Problems (Including the Last Straw or Precipitants)

It is interesting to consider how each staff member responded to Jet as she progressed through the first day of treatment. Jet was labeled by staff as "depressed," "a danger to self and others," "noncompliant," and "drug seeking." As the team reviewed the case, they began to assume preferred philosophical and theoretical perspectives regarding this case and Jet's response to treatment. None considered the potential of retraumatization until the night nurse began to identify key components of the case.

While talking with Jet, the nurse utilized probing questions and active listening to facilitate Jet's expression of the "last straw" leading to her restraint. The probing questions were specifically designed to examine the dimensions of the problem in order to further define the problem. Jet reported:

> I began to remember the assault. When I was being assaulted, I was high, so the impact wasn't that bad ... but when those two big male staff held me down it all came rushing back in. I was there again. I kept trying to tell myself this wasn't real. But it was very real. I wasn't able to convince myself that they weren't going to hurt me. ... That's probably because they were hurting me. Not the same way, but it was the same in my mind at the time. I just remember not being able to move while they had their way with me.

### Stage 4: Deal With Feelings and Emotions

Dealing with the feelings and emotions that Jet experienced as a result of the retraumatization became a critical portion of the crisis intervention process. Having explored the dimensions of the problems as outlined by Jet, the crisis team once again utilized the strength of the positive rapport with the night nurse to address the feelings and emotions associated with this case. The crisis intervenor was able to offer assuring comments designed to reframe Jet's negative thoughts while at the same time validating accurate perceptions. The intervenor first explored concepts of fact as opposed to Jet's perceptions by asking clarifying questions:

> Intervenor: Jet, you said the abuse was your entire fault. What exactly do you feel you were doing wrong?
>
> Jet: I put myself in the position of being abused and shouldn't have. ... I shouldn't have used so much, I shouldn't have been at that party.
>
> Intervenor: No one deserves to experience what you have experienced, not at the party and not here in the hospital. What can we do today to begin to deal with this?
>
> Jet: Can you really help me to get sober? If you can, I'd like that. ... I don't ever want to be there again.
>
> Intervenor: I agree, that's a great start, and we can help with that, but you realize that at some point we will have to address the other issues?
>
> Jet: (tearful) Yes.

### Stage 5: Generate and Explore Alternatives

In this stage, Jet worked with the team to develop a plan for her ongoing problem-solving process. She and the social worker, having sorted through facts and perceptions, made a list of actions for Jet to engage in to facilitate psychiatric stabilization and to establish a program of recovery. Jet agreed that in addition to her withdrawal/maintenance protocol, she would begin taking an antidepressant (an SSRI) and that she would work with her social worker to address issues related to her abuse. Finally, Jet began to actively participate as a member of the women's recovery group.

### Stage 6: Develop and Formulate an Action Plan

Jet realized that she would need to establish a self-directed program of recovery. As time progressed, she was demonstrating clear thinking. She was able to formulate plans designed to distance herself from situations that led to her vulnerability, thus reducing fears that were previously driving her actions. Jet requested to speak with the second-shift charge nurse, the medical director, and staff involved in the restraint episode to discuss her experiences on the night she was restrained. She provided a powerful description of how staff had in fact engaged in actions that retraumatized her. In essence, Jet demonstrated restoration of cognitive functioning through the development of a self-directed plan of action.

### Stage 7: Establish Follow-Up Plan and Agreement

Given the moderate expression of suicidal ideation and the development of a plan of action designed to examine and explore the events leading to Jet's crisis admission and restraint episode, the staff now revisited Jet's case to determine the next most appropriate actions. With her plan in hand, Jet reported feeling stable enough to return to her home environment. Staff readministered the depression scale and the hopelessness scale that had been given at the beginning of the crisis intervention. Both scales had improved remarkably. More important, Jet was able to verbalize seeing a way out by being an active participant in her recovery plan. The plan consisted of 3 to 6 weeks of partial hospitalization to provide her with the necessary support and opportunity to implement her plan of action and to monitor her functioning as she progressed through the potentially stressful events contained in the plan of action.

Jet progressed well through her plan of action. She attended and actively participated in the partial hospitalization program. She attended a minimum of three 12-step support groups per week. During this time, she participated in group and individual sessions designed to increase her overall functionality.

One year later, Jet continues in her program of recovery. She is now the chairperson of the women's group that she attended on the first night of her admission. She is completing her first year of nursing school and plans to earn a master's degree as a psychiatric nurse practitioner.

### Harvey

Harvey is an extremely successful dentist practicing in the suburb of a Midwestern city. He is married with three children, aged 12, 15, and 18. Although extremely successful, Harvey has struggled with bipolar disorder since he was 33; he is currently 50. Harvey was referred to a substance abuse treatment facility for alcohol dependence. This referral came following three successive complaints to the state medical board stating that he smelled of alcohol. Harvey admitted his abuse of alcohol and that, on the days of the complaints, he had consumed drinks during lunch prior to returning to his practice in the afternoon.

Harvey had successfully completed detoxification and was in the 2nd week of his treatment when he demonstrated symptoms of major depressive disorder, severe. He expressed extreme feelings of despair and depressed mood nearly every day, loss of interest in almost all activities of the day, psychomotor agitation, fatigue, hypersomnia, and excessive guilt about being "sick." By the end of the 2nd week, he expressed suicidal ideation, including a plan to kill himself with a gun, which he had access to while on a therapeutic leave from the facility. This information was shared in a conversation with his business partner, who immediately called the treating facility to alert it to this issue.

The staff intervened, completing the first stage of Roberts's seven-stage model. In completing the lethality assessment, staff revealed a second, more pressing concern, which was that Harvey's actual plan was to hang himself in the bathroom of the halfway house that evening. As a result, Harvey was transferred to an inpatient psychiatric facility for a brief period of stabilization.

During this time, Harvey expressed remorse for his actions, stating, "I would never kill myself." He reported to staff that he had far too much to live for and simply would not waste his life. Harvey worked diligently on his treatment plan, participated in group and individual sessions, and completed goal work related to specific areas of needs, including family therapy and addiction treatment.

With regard to suicidal ideation, Harvey spoke openly in session with his family that he would not harm himself. Harvey agreed to complete a safety plan to protect against his suicidal ideation. He agreed to have his gun collection removed from the house and spoke openly of future plans. After 4 days, Harvey returned to the addiction treatment facility. He was admitted to the halfway house program. After 2 weeks in the halfway house, Harvey was granted a leave of absence.

Harvey's flight arrived in his hometown at 6:00 p.m. At 8:00, Harvey's wife contacted the treatment facility, expressing concern that he had not returned home. At 10:00 that evening Harvey's body was discovered at his office, the apparent victim of death by asphyxiation. He was found in the dental patient chair in his office with the nitrous oxide respirator on but without sufficient oxygen to support life. Although questions were raised related to the possibility of accidental death, the autopsy indicated the presence of sufficient lethal amounts of barbiturates in Harvey's system to facilitate overdose if asphyxiation had not occurred.

### R-SSCIM Application

In the case of Harvey, review of the clinical practice indicated that staff had completed all necessary steps to provide a treatment plan to protect the patient from self-harm. The psychiatric facility had followed the American Psychiatric Association's approved practice guideline for the management of depressive disorder. Family conferences had been completed. Harvey and family members agreed to have all of his guns removed from the house, and an additional safety sweep removed potentially mood-altering substances from the home environment.

Later, staff at the treatment facility indicated they believed that Harvey did not have a key to his office and that he had surrendered it to his wife when he was admitted to the addiction treatment center. Further, it was not clear to peers or family how or where Harvey had gained access to mood-altering substances. Discussions with Harvey's roommates provided no insight into potential risk for self-harm. Furthermore, everyone believed that Harvey was doing exceptionally well in his treatment.

Investigations were launched by the treating facility in an attempt to determine if there had been any discrepancies in Harvey's treatment that could have contributed to this event. Review of the case indicated that on numerous occasions there was clearly completed assessment of suicidal ideation. On each occasion, the patient denied suicidal ideation. In the record, numerous notes indicated discussion of his remorse for suicidal ideation and of his efforts to resolve issues that might lead to future suicidal ideation. Harvey was compliant with the treatment milieu, including group and individual sessions and medication, and was involved in family therapy.

The patient's discharge conference from the psychiatric facility summarized all progress made, including efforts to remove risk factors from the home. This documentation was compared with the halfway house documentation and demonstrated remarkable similarities in progress notes, which also described the patient's progress in management of his depressive symptoms and resolution of suicidal ideation. Although staff at the treatment center felt relieved with the knowledge the case had apparently not been mismanaged, concerns remained given the reality of the loss of this patient and how this could have happened.

In assessment of the case, some raised the question of whether it was possible that the patient could have made a decision to commit suicide but have chosen not to share this information with anyone. Was it possible for the patient to hide this from staff? A literature review found that Beck, Steer, Beck, and Newman (1993) had indicated that dealing with suicide by identifying intent only as a global concept is an oversimplification. Suicidal ideation and suicidal acts are complex patterns of behavior that require thorough analyses for better understanding. Furthermore, it is indicated that the decision to communicate suicidal ideation, plan, and intent is extremely personal. Although many individuals will discuss suicidal ideation prior to the attempt, some choose to communicate after the event with a note, and still others choose not to communicate at all.

In revisiting the subject, Beck and Lester (1976) conclude the following with regard to communication of suicidal ideation: There is no clear evidence that verbal communication, final acts, and previous suicide attempts are justifiably labeled together as ways of communicating suicidal intent. Prior verbalization of suicidal ideation or intent bears little relationship to the extent of the wish to die experienced at the time of the suicide attempt. Talking or not talking about suicidal plans may be a manifestation of personal style rather than an index of despair or hidden motives. It was believed, but of course not confirmed by those investigating Harvey's case, that the patient had indeed developed and carried out the plan without communication of his intent. In reality, this left staff of both facilities feeling helpless regarding their ability to predict potential for self-harm in this case.

## CONCLUSION

Due to the increasing demand for mental health professionals to work within time-limited and resource-limited environments with increasingly complex populations, straightforward, realistic approaches to crisis intervention are critically needed.

Our goal in this chapter has been to provide a realistic framework for crisis intervention, examining potential clinical pathways for patients presenting across the continuum of care need. Mental health practitioners working in crisis intervention and stabilization environments should consistently consider assessment strategies, the utility of instruments to assess and reassess patient status, the amount of time available, patient burden, cost, and the potential outcome of chosen interventions. Application of best practices based on evidence-based reviews and use of systematic approaches such as the R-SSCIM will assist practitioners by providing a stable framework for addressing crisis in a continuously changing care environment. It is the challenge of all mental health practitioners to develop their skills in rapid assessment and risk and rescue strategies, building on the strengths of the patient as outlined by the seven-stage model.

REFERENCES

American Psychiatric Association, Steering Committee on Practice Guidelines. (2003). *Practice guideline for the assessment and treatment of patients with suicidal behavior*. Washington, DC: American Psychiatric Association.

Beck, A. T., & Lester, D. (1976). Components of suicidal intent in completed and attempted suicides. *Journal of Psychology: Interdisciplinary and Applied*, 92(1), 35–38.

Beck, A. T., Brown, G., & Steer, R. (1997). Psychometric characteristics of the scale for suicide ideation with psychiatric outpatients. *Behavior Research and Therapy*, 11, 1039–1046.

Beck, A. T., Brown, G., Steer, R., Dahlsgaard, K., & Grisham, J. (1999). Suicide ideation at its worst point: A predictor of eventual suicide in psychiatric outpatients. *Suicide and Life-Threatening Behavior*, 29(1), 1–9.

Beck, A. T., Steer, R. A., Beck, J. S., & Newman, C. F. (1993). Hopelessness, depression, suicidal ideation, and clinical diagnosis of depression. *Suicide and Life-Threatening Behavior, 23,* 139–145.

Burgess, A. W., & Roberts, A. R. (2000). Crisis intervention for persons diagnosed with clinical disorders based on the stress-crisis continuum. In A. R. Roberts (Ed.), *Crisis intervention handbook: Assessment, treatment, and research* (2nd ed., pp. 56–76). New York: Oxford University Press.

Centers for Disease Control and Prevention. (2012). National Center for Injury Prevention and Control. Web-Based Injury Statistics Query and Reporting System (WISQARS) (2010). Retrieved from www.cdc.gov/injury/wisqars/indes

Clark, D. (1998). The evaluation and management of the suicidal patient. In P. M. Kleespies (Ed.), *Emergencies in mental health practice* (pp. 379–397). New York: Guilford Press.

Crosby, A. E., Han, B., Orgeta L. A. G., Parks, S. E., & Gfoerer J. (2011). Suicidal thoughts and behaviors among adults age ≥ 18 years—United States, 2008–2009. *Morbidity and Mortality Weekly Report, 60*(ss-13), 1–22.

Crosby, A. E., Ortega, L., Melanson, C., & National Center for Injury Prevention and Control (US)., Division of Violence Prevention. (2011). *Self-directed violence surveillance: Uniform definitions and recommended data elements. Centers for Disease Control and Prevention, National Center for Injury Prevention and Control, Division of Violence Prevention. Atlanta, Georgia.*

Eaton, Y., & Roberts, A. R. (2002). Frontline crisis intervention: Step-by-step practice guidelines with case applications. In A. R. Roberts & G. J. Greene (Eds.), *Social workers' desk reference* (pp. 89–96). New York: Oxford University Press.

Fawcett, J., Scheftner, W., Fogg, L., Clark, D. C., Young, M. A., Hedeker, D., & Gibbons, R. (1990). Time-related predictors of suicide in major affective disorder. *American Journal of Psychiatry, 147,* 1189–1194.

Kleespies, P. M., & Dettmer, E. L. (2000). An evidence-based approach to evaluating and managing suicidal emergencies. *Journal of Clinical Psychology, 56,* 1109–1130.

Leise, B. S. (1995). Integrating crisis intervention, cognitive therapy and triage. In A. R. Roberts (Ed.), *Crisis intervention and time-limited cognitive treatment* (pp. 28–51). Thousand Oaks, CA: Sage.

Maris, R. W., Berman, A. L., Maltsberger, J. T., & Yufit, R. I. (Eds.). (1992). *Assessment and prediction of suicide.* New York: Guilford Press.

Posner, K., Brown, G. K., Stanley, B., Brent, D. A., Yershova, K. V., Oquendo, M. A., ... Mann, J. J. (2011). The Columbia-suicide severity rating scale: Internal validity and internal consistency findings from three multisite studies with adolescents and adults. *American Journal of Psychiatry, 168,* 1266–1277.

Reeves, A., Stuckler, D., McKee, M., Gunnell, D., Chang, S. S., & Basu. S. (2012). Increase in state suicide rates in the USA during economic recession. *Lancet, 380*(9856), 1813–1814.

Roberts, A. R. (Ed.). (2000). *Crisis intervention handbook: Assessment, treatment, and research*. New York: Oxford University Press.

Roberts, A. R. (2002). Assessment, crisis intervention and trauma treatment: The integrative ACT intervention model. *Brief Treatment and Crisis Intervention, 2*(1), 1–21.

Roberts, A. R., & Yeager K. R. (2009). *Pocket guide to crisis intervention.* New York: Oxford University Press.

Rudd, M., & Joiner, T. (1998). The assessment, management, and treatment of suicidality: Toward clinically informed and balanced standards of care. *Clinical Psychology: Science and Practice, 5*, 135–150.

US Census Bureau. (2013). "Computer and Internet use in the United States." Current Population Survey Reports, P20-568. Washington, DC: Author.

US Department of Health and Human Services. (2001). *National strategy for suicide prevention: Goals and objectives for action.* Rockville, MD: Author.

Weishaar, M. E. (2004). A cognitive-behavioral approach to suicide risk reduction in crisis intervention. In A. R. Roberts & K. Yeager (Eds.), *Evidence-based practice manual: Research and outcome measures in health and human services* (pp. 749–757). New York: Oxford University Press.

Yeager, K. R., & Gregoire, T. K. (2000). Crisis intervention application of brief solution-focused therapy in addictions. In A. R. Roberts (Ed.), *Crisis intervention handbook: Assessment, treatment and research* (2nd ed., pp. 275–306). New York: Oxford University Press.

# 3

## *How to Work With Clients' Strengths in Crisis Intervention: A Solution-Focused Approach*

GILBERT J. GREENE
MO-YEE LEE

Through a review of literature, theory, and case examples, this chapter will address the following:

- How to use solution-focused therapy in working with the strengths of clients in crisis
- How to structure a solution-focused/strengths-based approach to crisis intervention in a stepwise manner
- How to consistently engage clients in "change talk" and not stay stuck in "problem talk"
- How to co-construct with clients outcome goals that include a future without the presenting problem
- How to develop a collaborative relationship and client change in ways consistent with enhancing client strengths

A *crisis* "is a period of psychological disequilibrium, experienced as a result of a hazardous event or situation that constitutes a significant problem that cannot be remedied by using familiar coping strategies" (Roberts, 1991, p. 4). The Chinese translation of the word *crisis* consists of two separate characters that literally mean "danger" and "opportunity." Crisis intervention views the provision of services to clients in crisis as an "opportunity" for clients to learn new coping skills. In fact, the literature has consistently stressed that clients need to develop new resources and coping skills in order for crisis interventions to be successful (Eaton & Roberts, 2009; James & Gilliland, 2013; Roberts, 1996; Roberts & Dziegielewski, 1995; Kanel, 1999). An assumption of crisis intervention is that the client's personal resources and coping mechanisms are inadequate to meet the challenge of the precipitating event. For successful crisis intervention, therefore, clients need to develop new resources and coping skills. This view of crisis intervention's focus emphasizes rectifying the client's "deficits."

People in crisis also have the "opportunity" to further identify, mobilize, and enhance the strengths (coping skills) they already have. Some scholars have stated that crisis intervenors should also identify and work with clients' strengths (Parad & Parad, 1990; Puryear, 1979; Roberts, 1991). Identifying and amplifying client strengths in the process of achieving goals and positive change have been increasingly emphasized in the literature (Greene & Lee, 2011). *Strength* has been defined as

> the capacity to cope with difficulties, to maintain functioning in the face of stress, to bounce back in the face of significant trauma, to use external challenges as a stimulus for growth, and to use social supports as a source of resilience. (McQuaide & Ehrenreich, 1997, p. 203)

Aspinwall and Staudinger (2002) state that strengths "primarily lie in the ability to flexibly apply as many different resources and skills as necessary to solve a problem or work toward a goal" (p. 13). Strength-based approaches have been successfully used for a wide variety of presenting problems in a wide variety of settings.

An assumption of strength-based approaches to change is that clients already have the resources and competencies to change but they are not using them, are underusing them, or have forgotten that they have them (Greene & Lee, 2011). Practitioners therefore should assess for and identify client strengths and work with clients to build on these strengths in the service of change. There is evidence in the literature that clients want practitioners to think positively of them (Bohart & Tallman, 2010; Gassman & Grawe, 2006; Kelly, 2000), and clients have negative reactions to practitioners who make "hostile, pejorative, critical, rejecting, or blaming" comments to them (Norcross, 2010, p. 130). Practitioners who emphasize client strengths rather than deficits can help facilitate engagement and the success of their work together (Bohart & Tallman, 2010; Friedlander, Escudero, & Heatherington, 2006; Sparks & Duncan, 2010; Walsh, 2006).

One approach to practice that emphasizes working with client strengths in crisis intervention is *solution-focused therapy* (DeJong & Berg, 2012; DeJong & Miller, 1995; Greene & Lee, 2011). There has been some discussion of using a solution-oriented/solution-focused approach to crisis intervention with various types of crises (Bakker, Bannink, & Macdonald, 2010; Berg, 1994; Berg & Miller, 1992b; Brown, Shiang, & Bongar, 2003; DeJong & Berg, 2008; Fiske, 2008; Hagen & Mitchell, 2001; Henden, 2008; Hopson & Kim, 2004; Johnson & Webster, 2002; Kondrat & Teater, 2012; Lipchik, 2002; McAllister, Zimmer-Gembeck, Moyle, & Billett, 2008; O'Hanlon & Bertolino, 1998; Rhodes & Jakes, 2002; Sharry, Darmody, & Madden, 2002, 2008; Softas-Nall & Francis, 1998a, 1998b; Wiger & Harowski, 2003; Yeager & Gregoire, 2005).

The solution-focused approach views clients as resilient. Resilience is a person's ability not only to cope with, survive, and bounce back from crisis and traumatic events but also to continue to grow and develop psychologically and emotionally (Walsh, 2006). In the crisis intervention literature, however, the emphasis has consistently been on helping people return only to their precrisis level of functioning, which is not consistent with clients being resilient. Fraser (1998) proposes that clinicians should consistently view a crisis as a catalyst for clients experiencing growth and development beyond precrisis homeostasis (second-order change). The solution-oriented approach provides a perspective and interventions that can be catalysts for such growth and development.

## CRISIS INTERVENTION AND SOLUTION-FOCUSED THERAPY

### Crisis Intervention

A crisis can result from situational stressors, transitional changes, or disasters (James & Gilliland, 2013; Parad & Parad, 1990). The degree to which an event is experienced as a crisis depends on how the person perceives it; a crisis for one person may not be a crisis for another (Roberts & Dziegielewski, 1995). A crisis occurs when a precipitating event disrupts an individual's or a family's usual ways of functioning, resulting in their experiencing a sense of disequilibrium (Roberts, 1991; Parad & Parad, 1990). When in this state, people experience a variety of strong feelings, such as vulnerability, anxiety, powerlessness, and hopelessness (Parad & Parad, 1990). At this point a person may resort to increasing the use of his or her usual coping strategies or trying some new strategies in a trial-and-error manner to attempt to deal with the crisis situation (Ewing, 1990). If these additional efforts are unsuccessful, the person might experience increasing tension and is at risk for major disorganization of his or her functioning (Caplan, 1964). After 4 to 6 weeks, clients will, with or without treatment, experience either a return to their previous equilibrium or a new equilibrium that may leave them coping better or worse than prior to the crisis (Parad & Parad, 1990). The primary purpose of crisis intervention is to accelerate the return to equilibrium and at least prevent individuals from stabilizing at a new, regressed level of equilibrium. There are various models of crisis intervention. One of the most complete models is the seven-stage approach developed by Roberts (1991): (1) assess lethality and safety needs; (2) establish rapport and communication; (3) identify the major problems; (4) deal with feelings and provide support; (5) explore possible alternatives; (6) assist in formulating an action plan; and (7) follow up.

Because of their disequilibrium and emotional distress, clients will often take steps that they otherwise might have resisted prior to the crisis and in the process develop new coping skills (Ewing, 1990; Parad & Parad, 1990; Roberts, 1991). Client change in crisis intervention is accomplished by various in-session and between-session activities. One clinician activity in the session involves challenging the client's negative self-talk or irrational beliefs by the use of "carefully worded questions" (Roberts, 1991, p. 8). The purpose of such questions is to get the client to replace the negative, irrational self-talk with positive, rational self-talk.

The clinician also works with the client to identify alternative courses of action for successfully dealing with the crisis. After various alternatives have been identified, the clinician and the client develop an action plan for implementing them. An action plan involves carrying out specific *tasks*, "primarily by the client, but also by the worker and significant others, designed to solve specific problems in the current life situation, to modify previous inadequate or inappropriate ways of functioning, and to learn new coping patterns" (Golan, 1986, p. 323). Tasks are specific actions that must be performed in order for the client to achieve his or her treatment goal (reestablish equilibrium; Fortune, 1985; Golan, 1986; Levy & Shelton, 1990). Most tasks are performed by the client in the form of between-session tasks (homework), but some are done within the treatment situation. Successfully performing therapeutic tasks should result in the client feeling, thinking, or behaving in new and different ways. In crisis intervention, clinicians should "encourage clients to think of alternative ideas, coping methods, and solutions" (Roberts, 1991, p. 12). However, when they are under the stress of helping clients deal with the crisis, clinicians are often tempted to jump in quickly to offer solutions and advice.

A clinician who offers advice to and generates solutions for a client may quicken crisis resolution but does not foster client empowerment. Clients often do not respond as quickly as clinicians would like. However, clients are more likely to generate their own solutions, and thus feel empowered, if clinicians show patience. Perhaps clinicians would be less likely to "rescue" (Friesen & Casella, 1982) clients and more likely to reinforce client strengths, even in a crisis, if they had a specific model to guide them in such situations. One therapeutic model that lends itself to working with client strengths in crisis situations is solution-focused therapy.

## Solution-Focused Therapy

Solution-focused therapy views change as inevitable and continuous (Greene & Lee, 2011; Kral & Kowalski, 1989). This approach presumes that there are fluctuations in the client's presenting problem such that it does not remain constant in severity and/or frequency; at times the problem is either not present or at least is less frequent or intense than at other times (Berg & Miller, 1992b). The task of a clinician using a solution-focused approach is to work collaboratively with the client to identify what she or he is already doing that contributes to the diminishing of the problem. Solution-focused therapy, therefore, emphasizes identifying and amplifying clients' strengths and resources used in solving or reducing the frequency and/or intensity of the presenting problem. This therapeutic approach assumes that clients ultimately possess the resources and capabilities to resolve their problems (de Shazer, 1985). Solution-focused therapy, therefore, is a nonpathologizing approach to working with clients (Greene & Lee, 2011).

In solution-focused therapy, the emphasis is on finding solutions rather than solving problems. The solution-focused therapist is a catalyst for the client to enlarge and increase the frequency of solution patterns rather than decreasing problem patterns; the focus is on "what is happening when things are going well" instead of "what is happening when the problem is present." Solution-focused therapy's emphasis on strengths and solutions helps build the expectation that change is going to happen (de Shazer et al., 1986). According to de Shazer et al. (1986), the more the therapeutic discourse concerns alternate futures and solutions, the more clients expect change to occur. The clinician's focus is on asking clients questions that achieve solutions through encouraging "change talk" (Weiner-Davis, 1993) or "solution talk" as opposed to "problem talk" (Walter & Peller, 1992). Change talk involves clients identifying either positive changes that have occurred in the problem or exceptions to the problem, or their no longer viewing the situation as problematic (Weiner-Davis, 1993). Gingerich, de Shazer, and Weiner-Davis (1988) found that when clinicians intentionally engage in change talk, clients are more than four times as likely to discuss change in their next speaking turn. This is in keeping with an assumption of solution-focused therapy that a small change is all that is necessary to elicit a larger change (O'Hanlon & Weiner-Davis, 1989; Walter & Peller, 1992), thus resulting in a positive self-fulfilling prophecy instead of a negative one (Greene & Lee, 2011).

Solution-focused therapy assumes that clients really do want to change rather than seeing them as resistant. Clients not changing is viewed as their way of letting the clinician know how to help them. Asking the client to do more of what he or she is already capable of doing can strengthen the therapeutic relationship because the clinician is not asking the client to do something unfamiliar (Molnar & de Shazer, 1987); the client is likely to get the message that he or she is OK and is not deficient or in need of "fixing." According to Berg and Jaya (1993), when clinicians focus on working with clients and respecting their way of solving problems, the clients will offer clinicians many opportunities to learn from them. Adaptation to the way clients see their situation not only is respectful but also promotes cooperation in therapy. It is the clinician's responsibility to be sensitive to the client's worldview (frame/frame of reference) and try to fit with it as closely as possible (Greene & Lee, 2011).

Solution-focused therapy is appropriate for use with clients in crisis because it is known to produce quick and dramatic changes. Solution-focused therapy is also especially useful with clients in crisis because the therapist usually begins in the present and focuses on quickly developing a collaborative relationship with the client and understanding the client's view of the problem. After the problem is defined as concretely and specifically as possible, the clinician moves the focus to discussion of solutions. A basic tenet of solution-focused therapy is that one does not need to know the cause or function of a problem in order to resolve it (O'Hanlon & Weiner-Davis, 1989). This is consistent with crisis intervention, in which a clinician does not have to know everything about the client's problem and the goal in order to successfully provide crisis intervention as soon as possible (James & Gilliland, 2013).

## A SOLUTION-FOCUSED APPROACH TO CRISIS INTERVENTION

The structure of a solution-focused approach to crisis intervention consists of the following steps: (1) developing a collaborative relationship with the client; (2) listening to the client's story and defining the primary presenting problem and identifying unsuccessful attempts to solve the problem (first-order change); (3) eliciting the client's definition of his or her desired outcome goals; (4) identifying and amplifying solution patterns (exceptions to the problem); (5) developing and implementing an action plan involving between-session tasks; and (6) terminating and following up. The solution-oriented crisis worker assesses lethality and safety needs from the very first contact with the client. Assessing lethality and safety needs, however, is not listed as a separate step here because it is done throughout the course of crisis. The solution-oriented crisis worker relies heavily on the use of questions during the interview to identify and amplify client strengths, competencies, successes, and solutions.

### Step 1: Developing a Collaborative Relationship With the Client

A dictionary definition of *collaborate* is "to work jointly with others." In collaborative relationships, "there is shared ownership for identifying and working toward solutions and goals" (Christenson & Sheridan, 2001, p. 97).

For collaboration to occur, the crisis clinician must use a number of skills, including empathy (identifying and reflecting the client's feelings), support, acceptance, tracking, matching and mirroring nonverbal communication, and learning and using the client's frame (frame of reference). Collaboration is done throughout the crisis intervention work but is especially important in the beginning. To facilitate collaboration, Berg (1994) recommends that the clinician should avoid confronting clients and provoking defensiveness, avoid getting into debates and arguments with clients, and, when appropriate, take a "one-down position" and see the client as the "expert" on her or his situation (p. 53). This step is comparable to Roberts's Stages 2 and 4.

In this step, the crisis worker also should immediately begin assessing the extent to which the client is a threat to him- or herself or to others or is being threatened by others. Such an assessment is certainly an initial focus and should continue throughout the crisis work. Ensuring client safety is analogous to Stage 1 (assessing lethality) of Roberts's model of crisis intervention. In the solution-focused crisis intervention model discussed here, assessing lethality, which includes ensuring client safety, is viewed not as a separate step but as a theme throughout the crisis work; the crisis worker performs these activities as the crisis work unfolds.

## Step 2: Listening to the Client's Story and Defining the Primary Presenting Problem and Identifying Unsuccessful Client's Attempts to Solve the Problem (First-Order Change)

Although the approach described in this chapter emphasizes "solutions," the first interview usually begins with the client describing the problem(s) that precipitated seeking crisis services. At this point the client may want to talk about the problematic situation and the accompanying painful feelings. Listening to and responding appropriately to the client's story is the vehicle for developing the collaborative relationship. The crisis worker can begin the interview by asking, "What kinds of concerns are you having now for you to want to see someone like myself?" Instead of using the word *problem*, the crisis worker may want to use *concern* or *issue* as a way to normalize the crisis event the client is experiencing. In this way, the crisis worker moves away from pathologizing the crisis and conveys the message that such an event can be a part of life, although mostly unexpected, that calls for extra effort to find a solution. A question many therapists use when beginning a first interview, which should be avoided, is: "What brings you here today?" This question can reinforce a sense of external locus of control, which most clients already are experiencing (Frank, 1982). Because all clinical work should be empowering to clients, we want to reinforce their having an internal locus of control; therefore, we need to be careful in the language we use and how we talk with them in the therapeutic conversation.

When the client mentions a number of problems, the crisis worker should ask the client to prioritize them. This prioritizing could be done by the worker saying the following: "You have mentioned several problems you are having now. I find it very helpful to work on one problem at a time, whenever possible. Which of the problems you just mentioned do you want to focus on first in our work together?" It is important for problems to be defined as specifically (concretely and behaviorally) as possible in terms of who, what, when, where, how, and how often.

Part of the client's story involves describing how he or she has already tried to resolve and cope with the difficult situation. As mentioned previously, before they talk with a crisis worker, clients often have tried different ways to resolve and cope with the crisis, but none have worked; this can result in clients feeling stuck in an unsuccessful vicious circle. Obtaining this information tells the crisis worker what not to try with the client because if it has not been successful for the client so far, it is very unlikely it will be successful at all. Clients are stuck in this vicious circle because they have been trying to resolve the crisis within their existing frames. Also, obtaining this information about the unsuccessful attempts to solve the problem helps to loosen up their existing frame so they will consider trying something different. Once the worker believes the client has defined the problem and the unsuccessful attempts to solve the crisis as clearly and concretely as possible, the worker should move on to asking the client to define his or her outcome goal(s). Some clients, however, have a greater desire to ventilate and may still want to keep focused on problem talk. When this occurs, it is best to not push clients to define goals and focus on solution talk until they are ready.

### Step 3: Eliciting the Client's Definition of Desire Outcome Goal(s)

In solution-focused therapy, more emphasis is placed on setting goals than on defining problems (de Shazer, 1985). A goal describes a desired future state for the client in terms of how she or he will be feeling, thinking, and behaving differently. Like problems, goals should be set by the client and defined as specifically as possible (de Shazer, 1988). Clients are much more likely to cooperate (not resist) in the clinical situation when the focus of the work is on their goals rather than on goals set by the clinician (Berg & Gallagher, 1991; Greene & Lee, 2011).

Often when clients are asked what their goal is, they might say something like: "I want to stop being depressed" or "I want to get rid of my depression." Goals, however, should be stated in the positive rather than the negative (the presence rather than the absence of something in terms of feeling, thinking, or behaving), such as, "What do you want to be feeling instead?" or "How do you want to be feeling differently?" (Walter & Peller, 1992). Goal setting involves clients representing to themselves a future reality that does not contain the presenting problem. The more they describe in detail how they want to be feeling, thinking, and behaving differently in the future, the more real these become (Walter & Peller, 1992). Consequently, the process of asking and answering the miracle question and the follow-up questions can be considered a form of unguided imagery (Greene & Lee, 2011).

### The Miracle Question and the Dream Question

Sometimes clients have trouble setting a goal with sufficient behavioral indicators and specificity. A clinician can use the *miracle question* or the *dream question* to facilitate such specificity. An example of the miracle question is the following:

> Suppose that after our meeting today you go home and go to bed. While you are sleeping, a miracle happens and your problem is suddenly solved, like magic. The problem is gone. Because you were sleeping, you don't know that a miracle happened, but when you wake up tomorrow morning, you will be different. How will you know a miracle has happened? What will be the first small sign that tells you that a miracle has happened and the problem is resolved? (Berg & Miller, 1992a, p. 359)

The *dream question*, which is an adaptation of the miracle question, is illustrated in the following:

> Suppose that tonight while you are sleeping you have a dream. In this dream you discover the answers and resources you need to solve the problem that you are concerned about right now. When you wake up tomorrow, you may or may not remember your dream, but you do notice you are different. As you go about starting your day, how will you know that you discovered or developed the skills and resources necessary to solve your problem? What will be the first small bit of evidence that you did this? (Greene, Lee, Mentzer, Pinnell, & Niles, 1998; Lee, Greene, Mentzer, Pinnell, & Niles, 2001)

These questions should be asked slowly, with short pauses between sentences. After asking the miracle or dream question, it is important for the clinician to follow up with questions to obtain a clear and specific description from the client of what the miracle picture will look like. The use of relationship questions is integral to obtaining such a description.

## Relationship Questions

Individuals never exist alone; all behavior is contextual, especially the interpersonal context. Besides asking clients to establish concrete, precise behavioral indicators of change through the use of the miracle question or the dream question, it is helpful to ask clients what their significant others might notice that is different about them and how they might respond differently after the imagined miracle (Greene & Lee, 2011). Establishing multiple indicators of change helps clients develop a clearer vision of a desired future appropriate to their real-life context. The following are examples of these kinds of questions:

- "In the morning after this miracle has happened, who will be the first person to notice that a miracle has happened?"
- "What will be the first thing people will notice that will tell them that a miracle has happened?"
- "How will people respond differently to you after this miracle?"
- "And how will you respond differently to them?"

To illustrate this process, the miracle question was adapted for use in the following cases.

---

### Domestic Violence

An anonymous woman called, and her voice was barely audible. She sounded exhausted, lethargic, hopeless, and depressed. She began the call by saying she lives with a man who is very abusive. He beat her up yesterday, claiming he must discipline her. He makes her write out her mistakes on paper 100 times, and then she must write him a formal apology promising not to do same mistakes again. When he goes to work, he locks all the doors, windows, cupboards, and the refrigerator. He allows her to eat only one meal a day and withholds that if she is being punished. After establishing a positive relationship with the client and having the client define the problem the worker then asked the client the following questions:

Worker: Suppose that while you are sleeping tonight a miracle happens and your problem is suddenly solved. Like magic, the problem is gone. Because you were sleeping, you don't know that a miracle happened, but when you wake up tomorrow, you will be different. How will you know a miracle happened? What will be the first small sign that tells you that a miracle has happened and the problem is resolved?

Client: He would be out of the house, and I would be here safe.

Worker: What would your being safe look like?

Client: I would be free to go about the house as I please and do what I want to do. I might even leave the house and walk to the store.

Worker: What would you do at the store once you were there?

Client: I might call my sister and talk to her, which I haven't done in months.

Worker: What would you talk to her about?

Client:   I'd probably tell her what a no-good SOB Bill is, and then she
          would help me figure out how to get out of the house for good.
Worker:   What would need to happen for even a small part of this mira-
          cle to happen?
Client:   Well, I'd have to have a plan. A plan that would let me sneak
          out of the house when Bill is at work.
Worker:   Have you ever done this before? (Questions on past successes)
Client:   Yes, a long time ago.
Worker:   How did you do that at that time?

---

## Harassment

An anonymous woman called feeling hopeless, helpless, and angry. She is a lesbian
who is being harassed and discriminated against by coworkers because of her
lesbianism. She feels trapped because she enjoys her work and does not want to
leave, but she is also sick of the harassment. Recently, someone has begun following her and driving by her house all night. She believes it is a coworker but has
no proof. The client reports feeling extremely fearful and has no idea what to do.

Worker:   Suppose that while you are sleeping tonight a miracle happens
          and your problem is suddenly solved, like magic. The problem
          is gone. Because you were sleeping, you don't know that a
          miracle happened, but when you wake up tomorrow, you will
          be different. How will you know a miracle happened? What
          will be the first small sign that tells you that a miracle has hap-
          pened and the problem is resolved?
Client:   I would be able to wake up, not in fear, and I would be able to
          go to work, enjoy my work and my coworkers, and I would
          be treated like any other normal decent human being, without
          being treated like some freak with the plague.
Worker:   That's a big miracle! What will be the first small sign that tells
          you a miracle has happened? (Focus on small, concrete behav-
          ior instead of the big, grandiose solutions)
Client:   Well, first, I'll wake up with no fear.
Worker:   What would your partner notice about you if you wake up
          with no fear?
Client:   Well, she'll probably feel that I am more relaxed ... umm,
          probably less tense.
Worker:   What will she notice you doing when you are more relaxed
          when you wake up in the morning?
Client:   Umm, I'll be in a good mood, maybe joke around a little bit,
          and get both of us a good breakfast (a smile on her face). Isn't
          that nice?
Worker:   What would it take for you to start acting as if you wake up
          with no fear?

Client:   I would need to know I was safe.
Worker:   What would you need to do in order to feel safe?
Client:   I would probably need to get the police involved. And maybe I could tighten up my security, you know, buy a deadbolt lock and a saber-toothed tiger (ha-ha!).
Worker:   See, you have some great ideas to help yourself! (Compliment) What will you do first? (Assisting client to develop a concrete plan to make her feel safe)

It is then helpful to follow up, defining the primary presenting problem and the corresponding outcome goal by asking the client to scale the problem and goal on a self-anchored scale of 0 to 10. Such scaling not only is helpful to further define problems and goals concretely and specifically but also can be useful in assessing client progress in treatment.

---

### Scaling Questions

Scaling questions allow for quantifying the client's problem and goal, which not only can be helpful in evaluating the client's situation and progress but also is an intervention itself (Greene, 1989). Scaling questions ask the client to rank the problem and goal on a scale of 0 to 10, with 0 as the worst the problem could possibly be and 10 as the most desirable outcome. The clinician usually begins each meeting by asking the client where he or she is on the 0 to 10 scale of the problem/goal continuum. When clients rank themselves higher on the scale in subsequent meetings, even slightly, the clinician asks what she or he has been doing to make this happen (Berg, 1994). This is a way to help the client identify what has been helpful, which may otherwise go unnoticed. The following case illustrates the use of scaling questions.

---

### Grief and Loss

A woman called saying she needed to talk. Her father died yesterday. The client is upset but goes on to say that her main problem is the fact that her divorce will be final any day. She was married for 3 years and has two children under the age of 3. Her husband left her with the children and has moved in with another woman. The client says she does not know how she will make it.

Worker:   I'm amazed that you've kept yourself going for the past 6 months.
Client:   Yeah, me too. I guess things have been worse.
Worker:   They've been worse than even now?
Client:   Yeah, when he first left I was at an all-time low.
Worker:   If I were to ask you to rate the way you're handling this situation on a scale of 0 to 10, with 0 being 6 months ago and 10

being where you want to get to, where would you say you're
at today?

Client:   I'd say I'm at a 3 or 4.

Worker:   Wow, that's pretty impressive given what you've been through.
How have you gotten yourself from a 0 to a 4?

Client:   Well, I decided I've got to keep myself going for the kids. I've
been taking classes to get my GED, even though I'm not very
good at math.

Worker:   Your kids give you energy to move on and to start planning for
your future.

Client:   Yes, I think so.

Worker:   What would need to happen in order for you to move from a
4 to a 5? (Using the scaling question to help the client identify
solutions)

Client:   Well, I haven't thought about that. . . . Maybe if I get support
from my own family. . . like if they babysit my babies when
I am preparing for the exam.

Worker:   Who in your family can possibly babysit your children? (Be
specific)

Client:   Maybe my sisters.

Worker:   How will they know that you need their help?

Client:   Well, maybe I need to talk to them. . . . We have pretty good
relationships with each other.

## Step 4: Identifying and Amplifying Solutions

After the client describes in detail a future without the problem(s), the crisis
worker can ask various questions to assist the client in identifying and amplifying solutions that can be conducive to realizing the envisioned future.

### Exception Questions

When clients first see a crisis clinician, they usually start talking about their
crisis situation and their corresponding feelings (the presenting problem). In
keeping with solution-focused therapy's assumption that there are fluctuations in how the client experiences the problem, the clinician asks questions
to learn when the problem does not exist or at least is less frequent or intense.
In regard to this, Kral and Kowalski (1989) state:

> The therapist's job is not to initiate change, but to punctuate the differences
> between the complaint pattern and the pattern of the exceptions (change)
> thereby making explicit the "naturally" occurring variations which are in
> the direction of the desired solution. (p. 73)

The assumption is that during these times the client is usually doing something to make things better, and the clinician asks further questions to discover what the client is doing. After "doing more of what works" comes "do more of the same," making the exception the rule (Kral & Kowalski, 1989). The next case provides an illustration of identifying exceptions.

---

### Maintaining Sobriety

Jane is extremely disappointed by and ashamed of her recent fall from sobriety. She had been sober for 19 months but yesterday got into a big argument with her ex-husband and spent the evening in a bar getting drunk.

Worker: You were able to stay sober for 19 months?

Client: Yeah, but what good is it? I wasn't sober last night!

Worker: It sounds like you felt drinking would be a way for you to deal with the stress of your ex-husband?

Client: Yeah, that's usually when I always got my drunkest, when he and I would get into one of those fights.

Worker: How many times during the last 19 months did you argue with your ex-husband and not drink?

Client: Well, there have been a few times.

Worker: How did you manage to not drink during those times?

Client: Well, one thing that kept me from drinking is going to my AA meetings. I really count on those people for support.

Worker: How did you know to go to an AA meeting when you had these arguments with your ex and you did not drink?

Client: I just told myself if I don't go to a meeting and talk to someone, I'm going to drink. And I got myself away from him.

Worker: That's very smart thinking on your part. Is this something you're willing to do again in the future?

Client: Well, I think I can, especially with the help of the program.

---

### Past Successes

Sometimes clients initially have difficulty identifying exceptions to their presenting problem in their current lives or their recent past. When this situation occurs, the clinician can ask about times in the past when the client successfully handled the same or similar situations and how she or he was able to do so (Berg & Gallagher, 1991). In regard to the presenting problem, the clinician can even ask the client about exceptions that occurred years earlier. If the client cannot come up with any exceptions, the clinician can ask about an exception to similar problems in the past. The idea is to find out what solutions have worked in the past and to apply them to the current crisis situation. The following case illustrates the use of identifying past successes.

---

## A Suicidal Client

The anonymous client was a 58-year-old woman who reported feeling depressed and suicidal. She began having these feelings at Christmas, when an argument developed between her sister and mother. The client stated that she had spent several years and much effort trying to mend these relationships, and she now fears it has all been for nothing. The argument also brought up many issues from her childhood, and now she finds it necessary to deal with these issues again. The client says she is so depressed that she is contemplating suicide.

Worker: Have you ever felt suicidal in the past?
Client: Yes, about 25 years ago.
Worker: Did you make a suicide attempt then?
Client: No, somehow I got out of it.
Worker: How did you do that?
Client: A doctor put me on antidepressants for a while. I also keep busy walking and exercising. Talking to friends also was very helpful.
Worker: How did you keep from thinking about those family problems?
Client: I just kept occupied.
Worker: Are you doing any of those things now that you did then?
Client: No, but I guess I could.
Worker: What is one small thing you could start with?

---

### Coping Questions

Oftentimes clients in crisis will state that nothing is going right, that they can find nothing positive in their lives, and that they are unable to identify any exceptions, either present or past. Such clients can feel hopeless about themselves and their future (Berg & Miller, 1992b). The crisis worker needs to recognize such negativity as a sign of great desperation and a signal for empathetic help. In such a situation, the client could perceive the clinician's focus on the positive as being artificial and imposing. The coping question can be quite effective with these clients in crisis who see little possibility for positive changes (Berg & Miller, 1992b). Coping questions can be an impetus for clients feeling a sense of empowerment because they start to become aware of resources they did not know they had or had forgotten (Berg, 1994). The following example illustrates the use of coping questions.

## The Desperate Single Mom

Loraine was a 26-year-old unemployed single mother with a 7-year-old, "impossible" boy, Teddy. According to Loraine, she had never been able to handle Teddy, who never listened and destroyed almost everything. Recently, Teddy set fire at the apartment and inappropriately touched a 5-year-old girl. Loraine claimed that she had a very bad relationship with Teddy, had not talked to him for a long time, and was on the verge of giving up. Loraine was very depressed and became agitated when the worker tried to get her to think about positive changes in the mother-child relationship, which seemed to be impossible to Loraine. The worker used the coping questions instead.

Worker: If I ask you to rank your relationship with Teddy on a scale of 0 to 10, with 1 as the worst scenario both of you can get to and 10 as the best possible relationship that both of you can have, how would you rank your relationship with Teddy now?

Client: I have to say it would be in the minus range.

Worker: Sounds like the situation is really bad. I just wonder what have you been doing to keep it from getting worse? You know, the situation can be much worse; how do you keep it from getting any worse?

Client: I do pay attention to him sometimes. I don't ignore him totally, even though sometimes I feel so depressed and overwhelmed it's all I can do to pay attention to what's going on with me.

Worker: So how are you able to do that—to take care of Teddy some of the time even though you are feeling so bad you don't feel like it?

Client: I just do it. I am his mother, and I do have responsibility for him. I really don't know how I do it. I let things go for a while, but eventually I just tell myself I've got to take care of Teddy, since no one else can. I know I should be doing a better job of being a mother, but right now I feel like I can barely take care of myself.

Worker: That's really something that you are able at times to get yourself to do what you have to do for Teddy even though you don't feel like it. Using the same 0 to 10 scale, with 1 meaning you don't want to take care of him at all and 10 meaning that you would do whatever you have to in order to take care of Teddy and keep him from getting into trouble, how would you rank yourself?

Client: I would say around 7.

Worker: That's pretty high. When was the last time you were able to take care of Teddy and keep him from getting into trouble? (Exception questions)

## Compliments

Many clients seeing a clinician for the first time expect to be judged and criticized, and they may be prepared to defend themselves (Wall, Kleckner, Amendt, & duRee Bryant, 1989). Complimenting clients is a way to enhance their cooperation rather than elicit defensiveness and resistance. Compliments do not have to be directly related to the presenting problem but can be related to whatever the client is doing that is good for him or her, that he or she is good at or aspires to (Berg & Gallagher, 1991, p. 101). Such compliments, therefore, are feedback to clients about strengths, successes, or exceptions. Clients are usually surprised, relieved, and pleased when they receive praise from the clinician. A consequence of therapeutic compliments is that clients are usually more willing to search for, identify, and amplify solution patterns. The following case provides an example of using compliments.

---

### Relationship Issues

Betty was hysterical when she called and asked for advice. She is a single mother of four children. Betty must work full-time to support her children and often feels guilty about the time she spends away from them. Betty's guilty feelings intensified today when she came home from work to find her 7-year-old daughter and 9-year-old son involved in "sexual play." She is feeling very inadequate as a parent.

Worker: Wow, this must feel terribly overwhelming for you. I want to commend you on your strength and courage in calling here today.

Client: Well, I don't know how strong I am. Look what a mess my kids are in. And it's all my fault. If I didn't have to work so much, this probably wouldn't be happening.

Worker: What have you said to your children about your working?

Client: They know I work to feed 'em, clothe 'em, and keep this shack over their heads.

Worker: That is a lot of responsibility: working, raising four children as a single parent, keeping food on the table, clothing on the children, and a home together. It takes a lot of energy, skill, and motivation to do that. I really admire you for being able to do all that.

---

Complimenting clients is helpful at any time during the interview but especially toward the end of a session as a preface to developing between-session tasks. However, clients in crisis often are overwhelmed by their problematic situations and tend to be pessimistic. The crisis worker has to be careful not to overcompliment, which the client may perceive as superficial and insincere. Compliments should be based on what clients have actually done or mentioned in the interview.

## Step 5: Developing and Implementing an Action Plan

Tasks assignments are also used in solution-focused therapy but in different ways than in other crisis intervention models (it should be pointed out that we prefer the use of the word *tasks* rather than *homework* because many clients have a negative association with the notion of "doing homework"). As mentioned earlier, solution-focused therapy assumes clients are already doing to some extent or are capable of doing whatever is needed for problem resolution and goal attainment. Therefore, tasks in solution-focused therapy involve the client identifying solutions and/or doing more of them (Walter & Peller, 1992). Solution-focused tasks are based on thoughts, feelings, and behaviors that the client has used in the past or is using in the present (Molnar & de Shazer, 1987).

The between-session tasks are delivered in the form of an end-of-session message. This message involves first complimenting the client, next providing a frame (also referred to as the *bridging statement*) in which the clinician provides a rationale for the task based on the client's frame of reference, and then the task itself. Using compliments has already been discussed earlier. The task frame and between-session task are discussed next.

The *task frame* is the part of the message that links the initial compliments to the concluding suggestions or tasks. As with compliments, any suggestions that the practitioner might offer must make sense to clients, or else they will be ignored. The content of the task frame is based on clients' frames of reference for their situation, which can be reflected in their language, values, beliefs, goals, exceptions, strengths, or perceptions. Commonly, the practitioner will begin the task frame by saying something like "I agree with you that ..." or "Because you believe ..." or "Since you want to. ..." When possible, it is also a good idea to incorporate the client's words and phrases in the task frame.

Tasks fall into two main categories: *observation tasks* and *behavioral tasks*. In an *observation task*, the practitioner suggests—on the basis of information gathered in the interview—that the client pay attention to a particular aspect of his or her life that is likely to prove useful in solution building. *Behavioral tasks* require the client to actually do something—to take certain actions that the practitioner believes will be useful to the client in constructing a solution. As with observation tasks, behavioral tasks are based on information gathered during the interview and should therefore make sense to the client within his or her frame of reference.

One consideration in deciding on a task is the client's level of *readiness to change*. The solution-focused approach considers three levels of readiness to change: *customer, complainant,* or *visitor.* A *customer* level is when someone recognizes that there is a problem and indicates a willingness to do something about it. A *complainant* level is when someone recognizes there is a problem but indicates he or she is not ready to do anything about it. And a *visitor* level is when someone does not recognize a problem and, of course, is not willing to anything about it. So throughout the work with the client, especially in the beginning, the clinician wants to assess for the client's level of *customership,* that is, "what is the client a customer for," and match the task with the client's level of readiness to change. For example, a client might be in crisis after a recent arrest for driving a car while drunk; the client may not see that he or she has a problem with drinking does want to "get the court off my back." The clinician should ask the client, "What do you have to do to get the court off your back?"

The following are some commonly used solution-focused tasks.

### Formula First Session Task

Between now and next the time we meet, we[I] would like you to observe, so that you can describe to us[me] next time, what happens in your [*pick one*: family, life, marriage, relationship] that you want to continue to have happen. (de Shazer, 1985, p. 137)

Clients in crisis situations often feel that nothing is going right for them and that they are losing control of their lives. This task helps refocus clients' attention to something they are doing *well* rather than problems or failures. This change of focus can lead to clients realizing that there still is something working in their lives, and thus they can have some sense of control of their life situation (Berg, 1994).

The name of this task comes from its successful use at the end of the first session with a wide variety of clients regardless of presenting problem (de Shazer et al., 1986). The formula first session task is especially useful with clients who present vaguely defined problems and are not responsive to the clinician's attempt to define them more concretely and specifically. In one follow-up survey on the use of the formula first session task, 89% of clients reported at the next session that they noticed things they wanted to continue, and 92% of these clients said that at least one was something "new or different" (de Shazer et al., 1986, p. 217).

### Keep Track of Current Successes

Identify the ways you are able to keep doing _____ (behaviors which are exceptions to the problem behavior). (Molnar & de Shazer, 1987, p. 356)

*or*

Pay attention to and keep track of what you do to overcome the temptation or urge to ... (perform the symptom or some behavior associated with the problem). (Berg & Gallagher, 1991, p. 101; Molnar & de Shazer, 1987, p. 356)

*or*

Between now and the next time we meet I would like for you to pay attention and notice when you have moved up one point on the 0 to 10 scale and what you did to get that to happen.

The purpose of this task is to help clients focus on what skills and abilities they have and use them to improve their situation. The more specific and detailed the clients are in making these descriptions, the more likely they are to incorporate such behaviors in their behavioral repertoire. Furthermore, the more they notice the connections between their behavior and positive outcomes, the more likely they are to have a sense of control over their problematic situation.

### Prediction Task

Oftentimes the client experiences the problem as outside her or his control. The client is able to identify exceptions but believes that she or he has no control over these occurrences. In the prediction task the client is asked to predict or rate something, such as, "First thing each morning rate the possibility of _____ (an exception behavior) happening before noon" (Molnar & de Shazer, 1987, p. 356). The purpose of this task is to help clients realize that the exception behaviors may be much more within their control than they think. Having a client keep a careful record of what he or she predicted and how the day actually turned out will produce important insights into the client's ability to make what appears to be a random or spontaneous exception into a deliberate one (Berg, 1994). The crisis worker can then encourage the client to do more of such deliberate exception, ultimately making the exception into the rule.

### Pretend the Miracle Has Happened

This task asks the client to pick a day on which to pretend that a miracle has happened and the problem or crisis that brought him or her for help is solved. The worker should encourage the client to do everything that he or she would do if the miracle had happened and to keep track of what seems different about him- or herself and how other people react to these differences (Berg, 1994). The purpose of this strategy is for clients to have a reason to have good feelings and successes in a way they otherwise would not. Clients do not need to wait for a miracle to happen before they can experience good feelings, thoughts, and behaviors that are associated with a problem-free situation. This task allows clients to learn that they can turn a desired "fantasy" into a reality.

Solution-focused tasks have been shown to be effective in a wide variety of problem situations. The important issue for the worker, however, is to find a good fit between the client's circumstances and strengths and the task assignment. The worker has to judge whether the task appears to make sense to the client and the client's readiness to engage in the specific task assignments.

## Step 6: Terminating and Following Up

A person in a crisis situation usually experiences significant disequilibrium. Crisis intervention attempts to prevent a person from stabilizing at a regressed level of functioning and preferably helps a person reestablish equilibrium with increased coping abilities. An important criterion for termination is for the client to return to the previous level of functioning, if not a higher one, rather than having all of his or her problems solved. In this regard, a solution-focused approach shares a philosophy with crisis intervention with respect to termination. A solution-focused approach perceives that life is full of problems to be solved, and it is simply not realistic for clients to solve all their problems before terminating the case. Instead, specific goal achievement is identified as the criterion for termination. Therefore, at termination, the worker assists clients to review their specific goals, assess their readiness for termination, and anticipate possible future setbacks. Scaling questions are frequently used in the process. The following examples illustrate the process.

---

### The Doubtful Single Father

John was a 37-year-old single father with a 9-year-old son, Justin, who has been diagnosed as having attention deficit hyperactivity disorder. The father has learning difficulties of his own and did not finish high school. John is separated from Susan, Justin's mother, who has some serious "mental problems" and "poor parenting skills." Justin chose to live with his father. In addition to the separation and the stresses of single parenting, John's mother died recently, and he became very depressed. Two months ago he got drunk, and the apartment caught on fire, apparently from a lighted cigarette. Luckily, no one got hurt. The Children Services Department got involved because of suspected child neglect. John had six sessions of crisis intervention and made tremendous improvement. Although John was still lacking confidence in his parenting, both John and the worker thought termination was in order at this time.

Worker:   John, suppose when we first started meeting, your ability to take care of Justin was at 1 and where you wanted your parenting ability to be was at 10. Where would you say you are at today between 0 and 10? (Evaluating progress)

Client:   I would say I am at maybe 6 or 7.

Worker:    That's a lot of progress. Looking back, what have you done to help yourself to be an adequate parent?

Client:    Well, I keep telling myself that I don't want to mess up the life of my son. Later on when I thought about it, I didn't dare to think about what would happen if I'd set the apartment on fire.

Worker:    So, you remind yourself a lot that you don't want that to happen again. What else have you been doing that's helpful?

Client:    Hey, the list that we came up with helps me a lot (client referred to a checklist that the worker developed with him about things that he should do regarding adequate parenting). I put it on the fridge so I can see it every day.

Worker:    I'm glad to hear that. What else have you been doing with Justin that's helpful? (Try to get a behavioral description of the interaction between father and son)

Client:    With Justin. . . . Oh, I guess I do more things with him. He really likes it.

Worker:    You know you have made terrific progress since we started. I just wonder on a scale of 0 to 10, with 10 meaning you have every confidence that you will keep up with your progress and 0 meaning you have no confidence at all to maintain the changes, where would you put yourself between 0 and 10 today? (Evaluating confidence to maintain the changes)

Client:    I don't know, maybe 5. Sometimes I have doubts about whether the situation would go back again.

Worker:    So, you're a little bit uncertain. What would it take for you to move from a 5 to a 6?

Client:    Maybe I just have to keep doing what I've been doing. Well, it's good to have someone reminding me, I guess.

Worker:    Who may be a good person to remind you?

Client:    Let me think. My sister is really concerned about Justin and me. She would probably like to help if I ask her.

Worker:    How easy would it be for you to talk to her about this?

Client:    Very easy; there should be no problem.

Worker:    I want to ask you a slightly different but very important question. What would be the earliest sign to you that you are starting to go backward? What would your sister notice about you that would tell her that you are beginning to slip?

---

The primary task at termination is for clients to evaluate and consolidate their progress. It is important for clients to know what is working for them so they can connect their own action to the successful outcomes. In this way, life is no longer a series of crises that are beyond their control. They can actively participate in creating solutions and enhance their skills and competencies as a result of the experience. The emphasis is no longer on deficits;

instead, clients' strengths are recognized and celebrated. The use of the compliment is especially important for clients who have successfully coped with a crisis. A general guideline is for clients to own and take full credit for their successes.

Besides evaluating and celebrating positive progress, it is important to assist clients to go beyond current successes and develop indicators that will tell them when they may need help in the future. A solution-focused approach views problems as both normal and inherent in human living. Therefore, helping clients to ameliorate all their problems is less realistic than helping clients to recognize times when they will need help again and/or giving them the skills for dealing with new problematic situations when they occur.

Sometime after termination of crisis intervention, the crisis worker, whenever possible, should contact the client to see how well she or he is doing (Roberts, 1991, 1996). The length of time between termination and follow-up will vary, but follow-up usually should occur within 1 month (Roberts, 1991, 1996). At termination the worker should inform the client that he or she will want to make a follow-up contact and seek permission to do so. Such a contact can help support and consolidate the client's continued successes, solutions, and strengths. In addition, during a follow-up contact the worker can make a referral for longer-term clinical work if the client requests it. Most therapeutic approaches do not make follow-up an explicit component, and solution-focused therapy is no exception. The authors of this chapter, however, agree with Roberts in this regard.

## SUMMARY AND CONCLUSION

Although crisis intervention and solution-focused therapy come from distinct therapeutic traditions, they do have commonalities. For instance, crisis intervention perceives most crises as self-limiting in that the state of disequilibrium usually lasts 4 to 6 weeks (Parad & Parad, 1990). Consequently, crisis work tends to be immediate, short-term, and intense. A solution-focused approach also emphasizes a rapid and brief response to clients' help-seeking efforts and is consistent with the 4- to 6-week time frame given that the average number of sessions regardless of presenting problem is between 3 and 5 (Macdonald, 2007).

Although a solution-focused approach assumes clients already have resources and strengths and that the purpose of intervention is to help clients successfully deal with their presenting problem(s) by utilizing what they bring with them to the treatment situation, it does not deny that at times a more direct approach may be necessary. A solution-focused approach encourages clients to look for exceptions to the problem and do more of the exception-maintaining patterns. A crisis event, however, may be so novel that new coping and problem-solving skills are needed. In a solution-focused approach, if no exceptions can be found, clients are encouraged to do something different. In fact, one of the basic tenets of solution-focused therapy is "If it works, do more of it. If it doesn't work, don't do it again, do something else" (de Shazer et al., 1986, p. 212). In addition, even a solution-oriented crisis worker may need to actively provide concrete services, practical support, information, and other interventions that will help alleviate clients' immediate disequilibrium in their life situations—actions that are not emphasized in a typical solution-focused approach. The authors of this chapter, however, encourage crisis workers, whenever possible, to not use a direct approach too quickly before trying a solution-focused approach. A more direct approach may quickly resolve the presenting crisis but may not leave the client with a greater sense of strength, competence, and empowerment.

Experience, skilled judgment, flexibility, and individualized treatment may best describe the wisdom required in using a solution-focused approach to crisis intervention. For many years now, the crisis intervention literature has recognized the "opportunity" inherent in a crisis situation: A person can experience notable personal growth if the situation is handled successfully (Caplan, 1964). This chapter adopts a strengths perspective operationalized by the use of solution-focused therapy integrated with crisis intervention. It is assumed that clients, in spite of their crisis situation, have a diverse repertoire of strengths and skills that they are not currently noticing. In solution-focused crisis intervention, clients are assisted in discovering and amplifying their strengths and resources—an intervention approach that envisions clients' new learning and strengths through the passages of life. This approach provides clinicians with a systematic way to work with clients' strengths and resilience to help them handle crises and experience personal growth and development.

There are numerous reports in the literature of successfully using solution-focused therapy with clients in crisis and difficult situations such as those who are suicidal (Kondrat & Teater, 2012; Sharry, Darmody, & Madden, 2002; Softas-Nall & Francis, 1998a, 1998b); those who have a serious mental disability (Hagen & Mitchell, 2001; Rhodes & Jakes, 2002; Rowan & O'Hanlon, 1999; Schott & Conyers, 2003) or are physically disabled (Johnson & Webster, 2002); those who have experienced child abuse or neglect (Berg & Kelly, 2000); those who are victims of domestic violence (Lee, Sebold, & Uken, 2002, 2003); those who have experienced trauma and PTSD (Bannink, 2014; Dolan, 1991; O'Hanlon & Bertolino, 1998; Tambling, 2012); and those who have inflicted self-harm (McAllister, et al., 2008; Selekman, 2002, 2009). The authors believe that a solution-focused approach to crisis intervention is the treatment of choice in the majority of crisis situations. In a review of the research on the effectiveness of solution-focused therapy, Gingerich and Peterson (2012) state: "We conclude there is strong evidence that solution-focused brief therapy is an effective treatment for a wide variety of behavioral and psychological outcomes and, in addition, it appears to be briefer and less costly than alternative approaches" (p. 281).

However, the studies of the effectiveness of solution-focused therapy have been done in clinical situations where the treatment was considered to be brief therapy of 10 or fewer sessions.

Because of ethical concerns, it is difficult if not impossible to conduct randomized controlled studies of the effectiveness of crisis intervention in briefer periods of time such as crisis emergencies. Currently, there are no well-designed studies that document the effectiveness of a solution-focused approach to crisis intervention. However, in a previous job at a crisis hotline, one of the authors documented that shortly after solution-focused techniques were introduced to the staff, the time spent on the telephone with chronic callers decreased from 1,000 minutes to 200 minutes in a 1-month period. Only future research can shed light on what this dramatic decrease means and whether it can be attributed to the use of a solution-focused approach.

To be consistent with the strengths-based orientation of solution-focused therapy, researchers have emphasized the importance of using instruments that have a strengths-based focus (Smock, 2012). Smock identifies and reviews several measures that could be effectively used in researching the effectiveness of solution-focused therapy in general. Many solution-focused clinicians are routinely using the Outcome Rating Scale (ORS) and the Session Rating Scale (SRS) to monitor the client's response to intervention and progress (Guterman, 2013; Murphy, 2008). The ORS and SRS, developed by Barry Duncan and Scott Miller and their colleagues (Miller, Duncan, Sorrell, & Brown, 2005), make up what Duncan and Miller have referred to at various times as the Partners for Change Outcome Management System (PCOMS), the Client-Directed Outcome Informed (CDOI) approach, or Feedback Informed Treatment (FIT). The ORS and the SRS each consist of four items using Likert scaling and have established validity and reliability. The client completes the ORS at the beginning of a session to find out how he or she is doing and then completes the SRS at the end of the session to find out his or her view on how the interview went. To monitor the client's response to treatment, the ORS and SRS are completed each time the client and clinician meet. The primary purpose of this process is to provide feedback to the clinician and client regarding how the client is responding to treatment. If the client is not making progress or even getting worse, the clinician needs to adjust his or her approach to the clinical work and do something different. Although the ORS and SRS can be used with any theoretical approach to treatment, using them is also now officially considered to be evidence based. That is, using them not only provides feedback on client progress but also significantly contributes to client improvement.

However, in a behavioral emergency there may not be time for a client to complete the ORS and SRS, and even if there is enough time, the client may not be interested in doing so. It has been the authors' experience that using the 0 to 10 scale can accomplish the same purpose as the ORS and SRS. Using the 0 to 10 scale not only can provide feedback on client progress but also is an intervention itself that can be used throughout the interview, not just at the beginning and end. Greene and Lee (2011) note that some studies have found that the 0 to 10 scale correlates well with other measures with established validity and reliability; however, more research needs to be done to further examine this.

ACKNOWLEDGMENTS   Portions of this chapter are adapted from G. J. Greene, M. Y. Lee, R. Trask, & J. Rheinscheld (1996), Client strengths and crisis intervention: A solution-focused approach, *Crisis Intervention and Time-Limited Treatment, 3*, 43–63.

REFERENCES

Aspinwall, L. G., & Staudinger, U. M. (2002). A psychology of human strengths: Some central issues of an emerging field. In L. G. Aspinwall & U. M. Staudinger (Eds.), *A psychology of human strengths: Fundamental questions and future directions for a positive psychology* (pp. 9–22). Washington, DC: American Psychological Association.

Bakker, J. M., Bannink, F. P., & Macdonald, A. (2010). Solution-focused psychiatry. *The Psychiatrist, 34,* 297–300.

Bannink, F. (2014). *Post traumatic success: Positive psychology and solution-focused strategies to help clients survive and thrive.* New York: Norton.

Berg, I. K. (1994). *Family based services: A solution-focused approach.* New York: Norton.

Berg, I. K., & Gallagher, D. (1991). Solution focused brief treatment with adolescent substance abusers. In T. C. Todd & M. D. Selekman (Eds.), *Family therapy approaches with adolescent substance abusers* (pp. 93–111). Boston: Allyn and Bacon.

Berg, I. K., & Jaya, A. (1993). Different and same: Family therapy with Asian-American families. *Journal of Marital and Family Therapy, 19,* 31–38.

Berg, I. K., & Kelly, S. (2000). *Building solutions in child protective services.* New York: Norton.

Berg, I. K., & Miller, S. D. (1992a, June). Working with Asian American clients: One person at a time. *Families in Society,* 356–363.

Berg, I. K., & Miller, S. D. (1992b). *Working with the problem drinker: A solution-focused approach.* New York: Norton.

Bohart, A. C., & Tallman, K. (2010). Clients: The neglected common factor in psychotherapy. In B. L. Duncan, S. D. Miller, B. E. Wampold, & M. A. Hubble (Eds.), *The heart and soul of change: Delivering what works in therapy* (2nd ed., pp. 83–111). Washington, DC: American Psychological Association.

Brown, L. M., Shiang, J., & Bongar, B. (2003). Crisis intervention. In G. Stricker & T. A. Widiger (Eds.), *Handbook of psychology: Clinical psychology* (vol. 8, pp. 431–453). New York: Wiley.

Caplan, G. (1964). *Principles of preventive psychiatry.* New York: Basic Books.

Christenson, S. L. & Sheridan, S. M. (2001). *Schools and families: Creating essential connections for learning.* New York: Guilford Press.

DeJong, P., & Berg, I. K. (2012). *Interviewing for solutions* (4th ed.). Pacific Grove, CA: Brooks/Cole.

DeJong, P., & Miller, S. D. (1995). How to interview for client strengths. *Social Work, 40,* 729–736.

de Shazer, S. (1985). *Keys to solution in brief therapy.* New York: Norton.

de Shazer, S. (1988). *Clues: Investigating solutions in brief therapy.* New York: Norton.

de Shazer, S., Berg, I. K., Lipchik, E. Nunnally, E., Molnar, A., Gingerich, W., & Weiner-Davis, M. (1986). Brief therapy: Focused solution development. *Family Process, 25,* 207–221.

Dolan, Y. (1991). *Resolving sexual abuse: Solution-focused and Ericksonian hypnosis for adult survivors.* New York: Norton.

Eaton, Y. M., & Roberts, A. R. (2009). Frontline crisis intervention. In A. R. Roberts (Eds.), *Social workers' desk reference* (2nd ed.) (pp. 207–215). New York: Oxford University Press.

Ewing, C. P. (1990). Crisis intervention as brief psychotherapy. In R. A. Wells & V. J. Giannetti (Eds.), *Handbook of the brief psychotherapies* (pp. 277–294). New York: Plenum Press.

Fiske, H. (2008). *Hope in action: Solution-focused conversations about suicide.* New York: Routledge.

Fortune, A. E. (1985). The task-centered model. In A. E. Fortune (Ed.), *Task-centered practice with families and groups* (pp. 1–30). New York: Springer.

Frank, J. D. (1982). Therapeutic components shared by all psychotherapies. In J. H. Harvey & M. M. Parks (Eds.), *Psychotherapy research and behavior change* (pp. 5–38). Washington, DC: American Psychological Association.

Fraser, J. S. (1998). A catalyst model: Guidelines for doing crisis intervention and brief therapy from a process view. *Crisis Intervention and Time-Limited Treatment, 4,* 159–177.

Friedlander, M. L., Escudero, V., & Heatherington, L. (2006). *Therapeutic alliances in couple and family therapy: An empirically-informed guide to practice.* Washington, DC: American Psychological Association.

Friesen, V. I., & Casella, N. T. (1982). The rescuing therapist: A duplication of the pathogenic family system. *American Journal of Family Therapy, 10,* 57–61.

Gassman, D., & Grawe, K. (2006). General change mechanisms: The relation between problem activation and resource activation in successful and unsuccessful therapeutic interactions. *Clinical Psychology and Psychotherapy, 13,* 1–11.

Gingerich, W. J. & Peterson, L. T. (2012). Effectiveness of solution-focused brief therapy: A systematic qualitative review of controlled outcome studies. *Research on Social Work Practice, 23,* 266–283.

Gingerich, W., de Shazer, S., & Weiner-Davis, M. (1988). Constructing change: A research view of interviewing. In E. Lipchik (Ed.), *Interviewing* (pp. 21–32). Rockville, MD: Aspen.

Golan, N. (1986). Crisis theory. In F. J. Turner (Ed.), *Social work treatment: Interlocking theoretical approaches* (pp. 296–340). New York: Free Press.

Greene, G. J. (1989). Using the written contract for evaluating and enhancing practice effectiveness. *Journal of Independent Social Work, 4,* 135–155.

Greene, G. J., & Lee, M. Y. (2011). *Solution-oriented social work practice: An integrative approach to working with client strengths.* New York: Oxford University Press.

Greene, G. J., Lee, M. Y., Mentzer, R. A., Pinnell, S. R., & Niles, D. (1998). Miracles, dreams, and empowerment: A brief therapy practice note. *Families in Society, 79,* 395–399.

Guterman, J. T. (2013). *Mastering the art of solution-focused counseling* (2nd ed.). Alexandria, VA: American Counseling Association.

Hagen, B. F., & Mitchell, D. L. (2001). Might within the madness: Solution-focused therapy and thought-disordered clients. *Archives of Psychiatric Nursing, 15*(2), 86–93.

Henden, J. (2008). *Preventing suicide: The solution focused approach.* New York: Wiley & Sons.

Hopson, L. M. & Kim, J. S. (2004). A solution-focused approach to crisis intervention with adolescents. *Journal of Evidence-Based Social Work, 1,* 93–110.

James, R. K., & Gilliland, B. E. (2013). *Crisis intervention strategies* (7th ed). Belmont, CA: Brooks/ Cole Cengage Learning.

Johnson, C., & Webster, D. (2002). *Re-crafting a life: Solutions for chronic pain and illness.* New York: Brunner-Routledge.

Kanel, K. (1999). *A guide to crisis intervention.* Pacific Grove, CA: Brooks/Cole.

Kelly, A. (2000). Helping clients construct desirable identities: A self-presentational view of psychotherapy. *Psychological Bulletin, 126,* 475–494.

Kondrat, D. C., & Teater, B. (2012). Solution-focused therapy in an emergency room setting: Increasing hope in persons presenting with suicidal ideation. *Journal of Social Work, 12,* 3–15.

Kral, R., & Kowalski, K. (1989). After the miracle: The second stage in solution focused therapy. *Journal of Strategic and Systemic Therapies, 8,* 73–76.

Lee, M. Y., Greene, G. J., Mentzer, R. A., Pinnell, S., & Niles, N. (2001). Solution-focused brief therapy and the treatment of depression: A pilot study. *Journal of Brief Therapy, 1*(1), 33–49.

Lee, M. Y., Sebold, J., & Uken, A. (2002). Brief solution-focused group treatment with domestic violence offenders: Listening to the narratives of participants and their partners. *Journal of Brief Therapy, 2*(1), 3–26.

Lee, M. Y., Sebold, J., & Uken, A. (2003). *Solution-focused treatment of domestic violence offenders: Accountability for change.* New York: Oxford University Press.

Levy, R. L., & Shelton, J. L. (1990). Tasks in brief therapy. In R. A. Wells & V. J. Gianetti (Eds.), *Handbook of the brief therapies* (pp. 145–163). New York: Plenum Press.

Lipchik, E. (2002). *Beyond technique in solution-focused therapy.* New York: Guilford Press.

Macdonald, A. (2007). *Solution-focused therapy: Theory, research and practice.* Thousand Oaks, CA: Sage.

McAllister, M., Zimmer-Gembeck, M., Moyle, W., & Billett, S. (2008). Working effectively with clients who self-injure. *International Emergency Nursing, 16,* 272–279.

McQuaide, S., & Ehrenrich, J. H. (1997). Assessing client strengths. *Families in Society, 78,* 201–212.

Miller, S. D., Duncan, B. L., Sorrell, R., & Brown, G. S. (2005). The Partners for Change Outcome Management System. *Journal of Clinical Psychology in Session, 61,* 199–208.

Molnar, A., & de Shazer, S. (1987). Solution focused therapy: Toward the identification of therapeutic tasks. *Journal of Marital and Family Therapy, 5,* 349–358.

Murphy, J. J. (2008). *Solution-focused counseling in schools* (2nd ed.). Alexandria, VA: American Counseling Association.

Norcross, J. C. (2010). The therapeutic relationship. In B. L. Duncan, S. D. Miller, B. E. Wampold, & M. A. Hubble (Eds.), *The heart and soul of change: Delivering what works in therapy* (2nd ed., pp. 113–141). Washington, DC: American Psychological Association.

O'Hanlon, B., & Bertolino, B. (1998). *Even from a broken web: Brief, respectful solution-oriented therapy for sexual abuse and trauma.* New York: Wiley.

O'Hanlon, W. H., & Weiner-Davis, M. (1989). *In search of solutions: A new direction in psychotherapy.* New York: Norton.

Parad, H. J., & Parad, L. G. (1990). Crisis intervention: An introductory overview. In H. J. Parad & L. G. Parad (Eds.), *Crisis intervention book 2: The practitioner's source-book for brief therapy* (pp. 3–68). Milwaukee, WI: Family Service America.

Puryear, D. A. (1979). *Helping people in crisis.* San Francisco: Jossey-Bass.

Rhodes, J., & Jakes, S. (2002). Using solution-focused therapy during a psychotic crisis: A case study. *Clinical Psychology and Psychotherapy, 9,* 139–148.

Roberts, A. R. (1991). Conceptualizing crisis theory and the crisis intervention model. In A. R. Roberts (Ed.), *Contemporary perspectives on crisis intervention and prevention* (pp. 3–17). Englewood Cliffs, NJ: Prentice-Hall.

Roberts, A. R. (1996). Epidemiology and definitions of acute crisis in American society. In A. R. Roberts (Ed.), *Crisis management and brief treatment: Theory, technique, and applications* (pp. 16–33). Chicago: Nelson-Hall.

Roberts, A. R., & Dziegielewski, S. F. (1995). Foundation skills and applications of crisis intervention and cognitive therapy. In A. R. Roberts (Ed.), *Crisis intervention and time-limited cognitive treatment* (pp. 3–27). Thousand Oaks, CA: Sage.

Rowan, T., & O'Hanlon, B. (1999). *Solution-oriented therapy for chronic and severe mental illness.* New York: Wiley.

Schott, S. A., & Conyers, L. M. (2003). A solution-focused approach to psychiatric rehabilitation. *Psychiatric Rehabilitation Journal, 27*(1), 43–50.

Selekman, M. D. (2002). *Living on the razor's edge: Solution-oriented brief family therapy with self-harming adolescents.* New York: Norton.

Selekman, M. D. (2009). *The adolescent and young adult self-harming treatment manual: A collaborative strengths-based brief therapy approach.* New York: Norton.

Sharry, J., Darmody, M., & Madden, B. (2002). A solution-focused approach to working with clients who are suicidal. *British Journal of Guidance and Counseling, 30,* 383–399.

Sharry, J., Darmody, M., & Madden, B. (2008). A solution-focused approach. In S. Palmer (Ed.), *Suicide: Strategies and interventions for reduction and prevention* (pp. 184–202). New York: Routledge.

Smock, S. A. (2012). A review of solution-focused, standardized outcome measures and other strengths-oriented outcome measures. In C. Franklin, T. S. Trepper, W. J. Gingerich, & E. E. McCollum (Eds.), *Solution-focused brief therapy: A handbook of evidence-based practice* (pp. 55–72). New York: Oxford University Press.

Softas-Nall, B. C., & Francis, P. C. (1998a). A solution-focused approach to a family with a suicidal member. *The Family Journal, 6*, 227–230.

Softas-Nall, B. C., & Francis, P. C. (1998b). A solution-focused approach to suicide assessment and intervention with families. *The Family Journal, 6*, 64–66.

Sparks, J. A., & Duncan, B. L. (2010). Common factors in couple and family therapy: Must all have prizes? In B. L. Duncan, S. D. Miller, B. E. Wampold, & M. A. Hubble (Eds.), *The heart and soul of change: Delivering what works in therapy* (2nd ed., pp. 357–391). Washington, DC: American Psychological Association.

Tambling, R. B. (2012). Solution-oriented therapy for survivors of sexual assault and their partners. *Contemporary Family Therapy, 34*, 391–401.

Wall, M. D., Kleckner, T., Amendt, J. H., & duRee Bryant, R. (1989). Therapeutic compliments: Setting the stage for successful therapy. *Journal of Marital and Family Therapy, 15*, 159–167.

Walsh, F. (2006). *Strengthening family resilience* (2nd ed.). New York: Guilford Press.

Walter, J. L., & Peller, J. E. (1992). *Becoming solution-focused in brief therapy*. New York: Brunner/Mazel.

Weiner-Davis, M. (1993). Pro-constructed realities. In S. Gilligan & R. Price (Eds.), *Therapeutic conversations* (pp. 149–160). New York: Norton.

Wiger, D. E., & Harowski, K. J. (2003). *Essentials of crisis counseling and intervention*. New York: Wiley.

Yeager, K. R. & Gregoire, T. K. (2005). Crisis application of brief solution-focused therapy in addictions. In A. Roberts (Ed.), *Crisis intervention handbook: Assessment, treatment, and research* (3rd ed.) (pp. 566–601). New York: Oxford University Press.

# 4

## Differentiating Among Stress, Acute Stress Disorder, Acute Crisis Episodes, Trauma, and PTSD: Paradigm and Treatment Goals

KENNETH R. YEAGER
ALBERT R. ROBERTS

Why focus on the distinguishing components among stressors, acute stress disorders, acute crisis episodes, and post-traumatic stress disorder (PTSD)? Can clear operational definitions and specific case illustrations clarify the parameters and differences among these four clinical concepts? What types of treatment goals are effective in treating the persons encountering the four events and disorders? What are the components of a diagnostic stress-crisis-trauma-PTSD paradigm? This chapter answers these vital questions. In addition, we thoroughly examine the clinical issues and controversies, diagnostic indicators, and treatment goals necessary for advancing mental health assessment, crisis intervention, and trauma treatment. We aim to enhance theory building, assessment, and practice skills in behavioral health and public health and medical settings.

There are few human conditions that are so diversely described as stress, crisis, and trauma. Many report that stress helps them to work productively and meet multiple deadlines; others report on the stressful burden of managing a professional career, parenting children, and caring for aging parents, launching the individual into a downward spiral that culminates in physical and emotional consequences of tremendous proportion. Then there is the term *crisis*, which some people use when they are having a bad day, as in "one crisis after another." In sharp contrast to stress and crisis perceptions, trauma reactions are frequently precipitated by a random, sudden, and arbitrary traumatic event, such as a natural disaster, terrorism and mass murder, violent sexual assault, or drive-by shootings (Roberts, 2002). One reason for the overuse of the words *stress, crisis,* and *trauma* is a lack of understanding of the true definitions and parameters of each term. Frequently in the academic literature, the definitions are overlapping.

Individuals do not respond to stress in the same manner. Responses are unique and often determined by each individual's personality and character, temperament, other stressors that day, protective factors and coping skills, adaptability to change and unexpected events, support system, and the intensity and duration of the stressor. Therefore, what is simple stress for one individual may result in the onset of a crisis episode or traumatic reaction for another (Corcoran & Roberts, 2000). At times, this confusion leads to denial or underestimation of stress and related conditions and a buildup of multiple stressors without effectively adapting and coping.

In a similar way, there has been dispute and confusion regarding PTSD since its introduction into the *Diagnostic and Statistic Manual of Mental Disorders (DSM-III)* in 1980. Historically, the *DSM-III-R* and *DSM-IV* PTSD committees implemented remarkable changes in the original *DSM-III* diagnostic criteria. Yet some continue to question the accuracy of this diagnosis or even the existence of an actual disorder beyond that of a social construct. Scott (1990), Summerfield (2001), Young (2004), and Jones and Wessely (2007) remarked that the diagnosis of PTSD at worst failed to consider or at best obscured the role of secondary gain in discussion of the phenomenon of failure to recover as associated with the disorder. Finally, McHugh and Treisman (2007) argued that the diagnosis of PTSD moved the field of mental health away from an understanding of the normal psychological response to trauma.

This chapter delineates and presents for discussion a trimodal approach to understanding and addressing stress, crisis, trauma, and PTSD. We define and compare each term, outlining similarities that contribute to confusion among mental health professionals. Case examples will demonstrate methodology to accurately delineate and discuss the degree and severity of the issue facing each individual, applying the solution-focused approach, crisis intervention, and a strengths perspective.

## HISTORICAL OVERVIEW, TERMS, AND CURRENT EVIDENCE

*Stress:* Any stimulus, internal state, situation, or event with an observable individual reaction, usually in the form of positively or negatively adapting to a new or different situation in one's environment. The concept generally refers to the nature of an experience, resulting from the person interacting in the context of his or her environment, through either physiological overarousal or underarousal, with an outcome of psychological or physiological distress (bad stress outcome) or eustress (good stress outcome). Stressors range from minor to major and can be positive or negative events. Generally, stressors are life events such as daily annoyances, pressures at home or on the job, marital discord and conflicts, emergencies, motor vehicle accidents, illness, and injury. Positive stressful life events and transitions include the birth of a child, a graduation ceremony, a family vacation, and a job promotion.

Mason (1975) developed one of the most inclusive operational definitions of stress, stressors, and stressful experiences. Mason delineated a conceptual framework and application of three different definitions of stress to unravel some of the confusion with general usage of the concept. Stress may be caused by (a) an internal state of the organism, also known as strain based on both the physiological and the psychological reactions; (b) an external event or stressor, such as combat trauma and natural disasters; major life events, such as marriage, divorce, and being laid off; noxious environmental stressors, such as air pollution and overcrowding; or role strain, such as a bad marriage; or (c) an experience that arises from a transaction between a person and his or her environment, particularly where there is a mismatch or poor fit between the individual's resources and the perceived challenge, threat, or need (Mason, 1975).

Hans Selye (1956) concluded from his influential physiological research, "Stress is part of life. It is a natural by-product of all our activities. ... The secret of life is the successful adjustment to ever-changing stress" (pp. 299–300). According to Selye's general adaptation syndrome, there are generally three stages in the human body's reaction to extreme stress. First is the alarm reaction, in which the body stirs its defense mechanisms—the glands, hormones, and nervous system—into action. Second is the adaptation stage, when the body fights back (e.g., the arteries can harden when the heart is under pressure). Third is the exhaustion stage, when the body's defenses seem to be unable to cope, and the individual becomes seriously ill and may die (Selye, 1956). Selye concludes that the best way to survive and thrive is to adapt and respond in positive ways to the stress of life.

Stressors frequently are characterized as ranging from minor to major and as negative or positive stimuli or events. They are inclusive of daily problems. Sometimes they appear as pressure; at other times, stressors are described as disturbing annoyances. Events such as intense marital strife or discord, physical illness of family members and friends, hospitalization of family members, caring for children and loved ones, accidents, emergencies, being responsible for a child with special needs or a terminally ill aging parent, job pressure to perform, financial difficulties, and even moving across town or severe weather can present as stressors. The challenges that are framed by stress, both positive and negative, provide defining structures for meaning in our day-to-day lives. The complete absence of stress can lead to boredom and lack of meaning in one's life. Too much stress, or a pileup of multiple stressors without effective coping, frequently can have a detrimental impact on an individual's physical and mental health.

Some careers, such as rescue work, emergency service work, surgical and emergency medicine, and law enforcement, are known to be highly stressful and physically demanding. In these high-stress jobs, people may thrive, be continually re-energized, and experience occupational growth, or they may encounter vicarious traumatization. Hans Selye, a Nobel laureate and founder of the International Institute of Stress in Montreal, in an interview with *Modern Maturity* magazine (Wixen, 1978), stated that he thrived on and derived considerable satisfaction from an extremely demanding schedule. Directly prior to the interview, Dr. Selye had spoken at a major medical conference in Europe, slept 4 hours, then traveled 2,500 miles to Houston and his next interview and conference speaking engagement. The next day he flew to Montreal and 2 days later began a 9-day speaking tour throughout Scandinavia. Dr. Selye never tried to avoid stress; instead, he indicated that stress gave him pleasure and a great degree of satisfaction (Wixen, 1978). In contrast, Regehr's (2001) recent article focuses on vicarious traumatization of the hidden victims of disaster and emergency rescue work and the positive and negative effects of group crisis intervention and critical incident stress debriefings with worker stress reactions and the symptoms of PTSD. Regehr systematically reviews the strengths and limitations of crisis debriefing groups.

When intensely stressful life events and well-documented physiological events are placed in motion, these physiological responses to stressors are best described as a chain of biochemical reactions that have the potential to impact all major organ systems. Stress begins in the brain. Reaction to perceived stressful or emergency events triggers what Walter Cannon (1927) described as the fight-or-flight response. In response to neurochemical messages, a complex chain reaction is triggered, impacting specifically serotonin, norepinephrine, and dopamine. Adrenal glands release adrenaline and other hormones. The immediate physiological responses are an increased heart rate and blood pressure, dilated pupils, and a heightened sense of alertness. These responses are linked to the survival mechanism of the human and have been present since the beginning of humankind (Chrousos & Gold, 1992; Haddy & Clover, 2001; McEwen, 1995).

Many have attempted to answer the question of the impact of stress. Simply put, how much stress is too much? There appears to be no definitive answer, as the same amount and type of stress may lead to negative consequences for one individual and have little to no impact on another. Thomas Holmes and Richard Rahe (1967) constructed a social readjustment rating scale after asking hundreds of people from a variety of backgrounds their response to changing life events and to rank the relative degree of adjustment necessary to address these life-change units (LCUs). For example, a child leaving for college = 28 LCUs; job promotion = 31 LCUs; marital separation = 56 LCUs; and death of a spouse = 100 LCUs. An accumulation of 200 or more LCUs in a single year increases the incidence of psychosomatic disorders.

Dohrenwend and Dohrenwend (1974) trace the relationship between stressful life events and physical illnesses as well as psychiatric disorders. Their review of the research indicates that a pileup of certain types of stressful life events is correlated with depression, heart disease, and attempted suicide. There is some research evidence that indicates specific types of stressful life events, such as marriage, marked trouble with your boss, being incarcerated, and death of a spouse, can play a significant role in the causation of several psychosomatic and psychiatric disorders (Dohrenwend & Dohrenwend, 1974). However, it should be noted that Dohrenwend and Dohrenwend document the methodological flaws and sampling biases in many of the early studies and aptly recommend greater use of prospective designs and controlled studies and development of reliable and measurable attributes of stressful life events and environmentally anchored measures.

*Specific psychic stress:* May be defined as a specific personality response or an unconscious conflict that causes a homeostatic disequilibrium contributing to the development of psychosomatic disorder. (Kaplan & Sadock, 1998, p. 826)

The changes that the body experiences in response to stress have long been thought to present a significant health threat. Franz Alexander (1950) hypothesized that unconscious conflicts are associated with certain psychosomatic disorders. For example, Friedman et al. (1984) identified the high-strung, so-called Type A personality as a stress response that predisposes a person to coronary disease. Clinical studies continue to confirm the connection between stress and vulnerability to illness, for instance, in decreased resistance to infection. There is remarkable evidence that persons under intense stress for long periods are more susceptible to the common cold. Recent research has demonstrated some of the impact of stress on the immune system's ability to fight illness. One such study demonstrated that women who scored highest on psychological stress scales had a shortage of cytokines, a set of proteins produced by the immune system to aid in the healing process. Despite recent advances, medical researchers are unable to explain the highly individualized response to stress. Many conclude that environmental factors combined with genetic makeup and innate coping skills are the best determinants of an individual's personal reaction to stress (Powell & Matthews, 2002; Cutler, Yeager, & Nunley, 2013).

*Crisis:* An acute disruption of psychological homeostasis in which one's usual coping mechanisms fail and there exists evidence of distress and functional impairment. The subjective reaction to a stressful life experience that compromises the individual's stability and ability to cope or function. The main cause of a crisis is an intensely stressful, traumatic, or hazardous event, but two other conditions are also necessary: (1) the individual's perception of the event as the cause of considerable upset and/or disruption; and (2) the individual's inability to resolve the disruption by previously used coping mechanisms. Crisis also refers to "an upset in the steady state." It often has five components: a hazardous or traumatic event, a vulnerable state, a precipitating factor, an active crisis state, and the resolution of the crisis. (Roberts, 2002, p. 1)

This definition of crisis is particularly applicable to persons in acute crisis because these individuals usually seek help only after they have experienced a hazardous or traumatic event and are in a vulnerable state, have failed to lessen the crisis through customary coping methods, lack family or community social supports, and want outside help. Acute psychological or situational crisis episodes may be viewed in various ways, but the definition we are using emphasizes that a crisis can be a turning point in a person's life. Crisis intervention occurs when a counselor, behavioral clinician, or therapist enters into the life situation of an individual or family to alleviate the impact of a crisis episode by facilitating and mobilizing the resources of those directly affected. Rapid assessment and timely intervention on the part of crisis counselors, social workers, psychologists, or child psychiatrists are of paramount importance. Crisis intervenors should be active and directive while displaying a nonjudgmental, accepting, hopeful, and positive attitude. Crisis intervenors need to help crisis clients to identify protective factors, inner strengths, psychological hardiness, or resiliency factors that can be utilized for ego bolstering. Effective crisis intervenors are able to gauge the seven stages of crisis intervention, while being flexible and realizing that several stages of intervention may overlap. Crisis intervention should culminate in a restoration of cognitive functioning, crisis resolution, and cognitive mastery (Roberts, 2000a).

*Acute stress disorder:* Acute stress disorder (ASD) is a common acute post-traumatic syndrome, which is strongly associated with the later development of post-traumatic stress disorder. ASD represents both an acute pathological reaction to trauma and the role of dissociative phenomena in both short-term and long-term reactions to trauma. The development of characteristic anxiety and dissociative and other symptoms that occurs within 1 month after exposure to an extreme traumatic stressor. As a response to the traumatic event, the individual develops dissociative symptoms. Individuals with ASD may have a decrease in emotional responsiveness, often finding it difficult or impossible to experience pleasure in previously enjoyable activities and frequently feeling guilty about pursuing usual life tasks. (American Psychiatric Association [APA], 2013)

The main difference between the *DSM-IV* and *DSM-5* is in the stressor criterion (Criterion A) for ASD. The criterion change requires specificity regarding whether the traumatic events were experienced directly, witnessed, or experienced indirectly. Additionally, the *DSM-IV* Criterion A2 addressing the subjective reaction to the traumatic event has been eliminated. This change builds on the evidence that acute post-traumatic reactions are heterogeneous and that *DSM-IV*'s previous emphasis on dissociative symptoms may have been overly restrictive; individuals may meet the diagnostic criteria in the *DSM-5* for ASD if they exhibit any 9 of 14 listed symptoms in the categories of intrusion, negative mood, dissociation, avoidance, and arousal (APA, 2013).

*Trauma:* Psychological trauma refers to human reactions to traumatic stress, violent crimes, infectious disease outbreaks, and other dangerous and life-threatening events. For psychological trauma to occur, the individual's adaptive pathways become shut off as a result of overexposure to stress hormones. Persistent hyperarousal mechanisms related to the traumatic event continually reoccur and are amplified by traumatic recollections stored in the brain. The victims of trauma find themselves rapidly alternating their mental states between relatively calm and peaceful to states of intense anxiety, agitation, anger, hypervigilance, and extreme arousal. (Roberts, 2000, pp. 2–3)

Psychological trauma, or the human trauma response, can take place soon after observing or being the victim of a traumatic stressor or event. This is usually the case in ASD. However, many times, individuals have a delayed reaction to a traumatic event; after a delay of several weeks to several months, the reaction usually surfaces in the form of symptoms of psychological trauma such as avoidance of familiar surroundings, intense fears, sudden breaking of appointments, social isolation, trancelike states, sleep disturbances and repeated nightmares, depressive episodes, and hyperarousal.

According to Terr (1994), there are two types of trauma among children. Type I refers to victims who have experienced and suffered from a single traumatic event. Type II trauma refers to victims who have experienced multiple traumatic events, such as ongoing and recurring incest, child abuse, or family violence; the exception is an extremely horrific single traumatic occurrence that is marked by multiple homicides and includes dehumanizing sights (e.g., dismembered bodies), piercing sounds, and strong odors (e.g., fire and smoke).

Personal impact in the aftermath of potentially stressful and crisis-producing events can be measured by the following:

- *Spatial dimensions:* The closer the person is to the center of the tragedy, the greater the stress. Similarly, the closer the person's relationship is to the victim, the greater the likelihood of entering into a crisis state.
- *Subjective crime clock:* The greater the duration (estimated length of time exposed and estimated length of exposure to sensory experiences, such as an odor of gasoline combined with the smell of a fire) that an individual is affected by the community disaster, violent crime, or other tragedy, the greater the stress.
- *Reoccurrence* (perceived): The greater the perceived likelihood that the tragedy will happen again, the greater the likelihood of intense fears, which contribute to an active crisis state on the part of the survivor (Young, 1995).

*Post-traumatic stress disorder:* A set of typical symptoms that develop after a person sees, is involved in, or hears of "an extreme traumatic stressor." PTSD is an acute, chronic, delayed, debilitating, and complex mental disorder. It includes altered awareness, detachment, dissociative states, ego fragmentation, personality changes, paranoid ideation, trigger events, and vivid intrusive traumatic recollections. PTSD is often comorbid with major depression, dysthymia, alcohol or substance abuse, and generalized anxiety disorder. The person reacts to this experience with fear and helplessness, sleep disturbances, hyperarousal and hypervigilance, persistently reliving the event through graphic and magnified horrific flashbacks and intrusive thoughts, and unsuccessful attempts to avoid being reminded of it. The symptoms must last for more than a month and must significantly affect important areas of life. (APA, 2013)

The *DSM-5* criteria for PTSD differ greatly from those in *DSM-IV*. As previously noted, the stressor criterion (Criterion A) is more specific regarding the individual experience of the traumatic events. Additionally, Criterion A2 (subjective reaction) has been removed, with focus on symptom clusters of re-experiencing, avoiding/numbing, and arousal have been expanded by separating avoidance and persistent negative alterations in cognitions and mood, which retains the majority of the *DSM-IV* numbing symptoms. Additional changes include the reconceptualized symptoms of persistent negative emotional states and alterations in arousal and reactivity, again maintaining the majority of the *DSM-IV* arousal symptoms. This also has been expanded to address irritability, aggression, recklessness, and self-destructive behaviors. Finally, PTSD is now sensitive to developmental stage for children and adolescents as diagnostic thresholds have been lowered, with separate criteria for children 6 years or younger with this disorder.

Some stressors are so severe that individuals may be more susceptible to the overwhelming effects of the experience. PTSD can arise from war experiences, torture, natural disasters, terrorism, rape, assault, or serious accidents.

The history of PTSD begins with Jacob DaCosta's paper "On Irritable Heart" (1871), which describes the symptoms of stress witnessed in Civil War soldiers. Initially the disorder was referred to as *traumatic neurosis*, reflecting the strong influence of psychoanalysis. This was replaced by the term *shell shock* during World War I, as psychiatrists hypothesized this was the impact of brain trauma resulting from the percussive blows of exploding bombshells. It was not until 1941, when the survivors of the Coconut Grove nightclub fire began to demonstrate symptoms of nervousness, nightmares, and graphic recollections of the tragedy that the definition was expanded to include operational fatigue, delayed grief, and combat neurosis. It was not until the return of Vietnam War veterans that the notion of post-traumatic disorder emerged in its current context. Throughout the history of this disorder, one inescapable fact has been present: The appearance of the disorder was roughly correlated with the severity of the exposure to stressors, with the most severe stressors resulting in the emergence of characteristic symptomatology in the victims. Currently, there is a growing body of evidence to demonstrate that traumatic experience can cause significant psychological difficulties for large numbers of people via situations such as natural disasters (Smith et al., 2014).

As previously stated, the critical feature of PTSD is the development of characteristic symptoms after exposure to an extreme traumatic stressor involving direct personal experience of an event or direct or threatened death or severe injury, threat to one's physical integrity or that of another person, or being witness to an unexpected violent death, serious harm, or threat of injury to self or another. In the DSM-5 this has been changed to be explicit as to whether the qualifying trauma events were experienced directly, witnessed, or experienced indirectly. Although many people demonstrate great resilience in the face of such adversity, demonstrating only short-lived or subacute stress reactions that diminish over time (Bonanno & Diminich, 2013), for others, a range of psychological difficulties may develop following trauma.

The 2000 National Comorbidity Survey–Replication (NCS-R) estimated lifetime prevalence of PTSD among trauma-exposed adults in the United States to be 6.8% (9.7% in women and 3.6% in men) and current (12-month) prevalence to be 3.6% (5.2% in women and 1.8% in men), or more than 7.7 million American adults per year (Kessler et al., 2005). Some demographic or occupational groups, such as police, fire/ EMS, healthcare workers, and military personnel, are at higher risk of PTSD because of higher rates of exposure to trauma (National Institutes of Mental Health, 2012).

Prevention, early identification, and management of PTSD can reduce significantly the burden of suffering experienced by the individual and the cost experienced by society. Two different prevention strategies have been used. The first strategy, universal prevention, is to deliver interventions to all people exposed to a trauma, regardless of symptoms or risk of developing PTSD. The second strategy is a targeted prevention intervention that is based on the assumption that while many people experience some symptoms of PTSD after trauma, only a relatively small percentage develop the psychiatric disorder of PTSD and its associated disability. Hence, the goal of a targeted approach to prevention is to identify, from the larger population exposed to a traumatic event, those who are at the greatest risk of developing the disorder of PTSD and then intervene only with those at high risk.

Interventions to prevent PTSD might involve a variety of psychological and pharmacological approaches, including but not limited to new and emerging interventions such as approaches from complementary and alternative medicine. These interventions are intended to be used both separately and in combination depending on individual need and preference (Agency for Healthcare Research and Quality, 2011). Despite evidence that some early interventions, such as certain forms of debriefing, are not effective for preventing PTSD or might even cause harm, these approaches are still widely used. One recent randomized control study concluded that although the use of debriefing did not prevent the onset of PTSD, it was effective in reducing harmful self-treatment approaches by the individual such as reducing harmful alcohol consumption/abuse (Tuckey & Scott, 2014). The continued application and evolution of debriefing indicate that advances in therapeutic approaches have improved debriefing processes. Despite continued uncertainty and controversy within the field regarding this intervention that intuitively seems as if it should help, prudence would dictate greater consideration should be given to scientific evidence when weighing all form of crisis intervention benefits and harms.

Currently, evidence supporting the efficacy of most interventions used to prevent PTSD is growing, but additional research will be required to determine best practices. We believe that developing a clinical prediction algorithm to identify those who are at high risk of developing PTSD after trauma exposure is perhaps a more crucial next step in the field of PTSD prevention than continuing to study which interventions are more effective than others. The ability to identify people most at risk for developing PTSD and then to evaluate the effectiveness of prevention interventions in those individuals should be the focus of ongoing clinical and research efforts (Cutler, Yeager, & Nunley, 2013).

To begin this process, we will address the need for a consolidated approach to individual and group psychological crisis intervention. Schnurr (2013) indicated that 89.6% of adults may experience a traumatic event over the course of their lifetime. Previous thought has linked the risk of exposure to trauma to specific occupational groups, including the military, firefighters, and law enforcement. However, recent events have expanded this scope to include educators, emergency medical personnel, and even innocent bystanders, as demonstrated after the September 11 terrorist attack in New York City.

The need for prompt intervention cannot be overestimated. More than a decade ago, Swanson and Carbon (1989) began writing on the need for prompt intervention in cases of stress, crisis, and trauma for the APA's task force on the treatment of psychiatric disorders. Concurrently, Roberts's seven-stage model of crisis intervention emerged, urging a systematic and eclectic approach to crisis intervention. There is an emergent need and strong argument for providing immediate aid and forming a treatment alliance with psychological trauma victims. The question is not whether to provide emergency psychological services but how to frame the interactions and diagnoses in a manner that provides accurate and consistent individualized care approaches.

## A CLINICAL FRAMEWORK

It is not difficult to understand the confusion experienced by practitioners surrounding the terms *stress, trauma*, and *crisis*, which are used to describe not only the event or situation but also an individual's response to the event and, at times, the diagnosis associated with that response. It is important to differentiate the severity of the event from patients' perceptions and their unique abilities to cope with the event. In doing so, the clinician will have a clearer picture of the appropriate diagnostic framework criteria and categories to be applied.

To utilize the diagram in Figure 4.1, the practitioner must first examine the severity of the event and its potential impact on the individual while accounting for individual personality and character, temperament, other stressors that day, protective factors and coping skills, adaptability to change and unexpected events, the individual's support system, and the intensity and duration of the stressor. Once the nature of the initial event is clearly understood, the practitioner can construct an accurate depiction of the individual's condition. Note: Accurate differentiation among stress, crisis, ASD, and PTSD should be accomplished through a multimeasurement, multidisciplinary approach: completion of an informational interview, examination of the social environment, application of scale measurement, and consultation with medical practitioners. This process leads to a greater understanding of the factors impacting the individual. Determinations made through this process are approximations, seeking to construct a framework to serve as a foundation for treatment planning and care delivery. This process is not a diagnostic criterion and is not intended to replace *DSM* classification.

The following section presents a series of case examples that differentiate among stress, crisis, ASD, and PTSD. Special emphasis is placed on the event, the individual's response to the event, the application of appropriate diagnostic criteria when warranted, resiliency factors, and treatment planning.

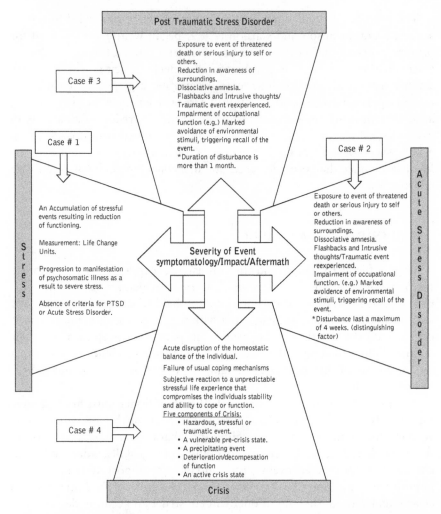

Figure 4.1   Stress, Crisis, Acute Stress Disorder, and PTSD
Classification Paradigm

## CASE ILLUSTRATIONS

### Case Example 1

Kevin is a manager in a large insurance corporation. He was brought in during a point of transition in the organization, replacing a manager who was less than effective but well liked. Kevin has held this position for 2 years. He has consistently found himself in the middle of critical and sensitive conflicts between department staff and administration. At this point in his life, Kevin is responsible for the care of his frail, elderly mother, who was diagnosed with terminal cancer 3 months earlier. He is a single parent with three children, of whom the eldest has recently left for college. Kevin is experiencing financial difficulties and may be facing foreclosure on his house. He presents for counseling to address job stress because he is fearful the company is looking at demoting him or terminating him from his position. On the positive side, Kevin reports that he has become involved in a significant new relationship, but he fears that this will end when "the wheels come off in his employment."

## Case Example 2

Jill is a nurse manager with 27 years of experience in critical care working in the transplant unit of a large metropolitan medical center. Two days prior to seeking assistance, her last living and favorite uncle was admitted to the medical center after having a mild heart attack. Jill reports that on the first day of her uncle's hospitalization, she assured him and his wife that they were in "the right place." Knowing the medical staff, Jill arranged for her uncle to be seen by the very best cardiologist and a group of nurses whom she personally knew and felt would do excellent work. Jill left the unit that day feeling very good about her work. When she returned to work the next day, she checked in on her uncle. A unit assistant told Jill that he had been moved to a critical care pod and that his condition had worsened over the last shift. Jill approached the critical care pod as her uncle experienced a major cardiac event. She remained present throughout the code, assisting the residents, cardiologist, and anesthesiologist. Unfortunately, her uncle did not survive the event. Still, Jill remained focused. She accompanied the cardiologist as he informed other family members of the unanticipated outcome. Jill contacted pastoral care to provide a private area for her aunt and cousins to grieve their loss. She was present until all arrangements had been made and her family had left the medical center. Realizing she could not work, Jill took the nearest stairwell to her unit to explain her absence. She was unable to proceed and was found by staff sitting on the stairs tearful and overwhelmed by the experience. Since that time she has relived the experience of the code, reporting vivid recollections of the death of her favorite uncle and the faces of her family members.

## Case Example 3

Thomas, a firefighter with Engine House 1 in a large metropolitan area, presents after the loss of three peers in a warehouse fire in the garment district. As Tom recounts, "This was the most intense fire I had ever seen. The smoke was extremely thick and very toxic. As time progressed, the heat was overwhelming." Tom notes that he and three peers were on the third floor of the warehouse when he heard a large explosion. "I knew it was bad. When you hear anything above the roar of the fire, it's got to be very big and very dangerous." At the time of the explosion, Tom had moved away from the team to secure equipment for advancement and to direct the reinforcement team. He reports:

> After the explosion, I turned around to see where my buddies were, but I didn't see 'em.... At first I thought it was the smoke, so I moved closer....

Then I saw what really happened. ... The floor had given way, it just fell out from under them. Two of my buddies were on the next floor down. I could hear them screaming, they were in the middle of the fire, there wasn't anything I could do for them. I just sat there and watched them thrash, kick, scream, and die. I didn't see Vince at first, then I saw him. He was hanging on a pipe about 4 feet below me. I reached down for him. I had a chance ... but when he reached up for my hand, all I grabbed was his glove. ... I still see his face as he fell. After I got out, I realized his glove was still in my hand. ... What I realized is ... Oh my God ... the flesh of his hand was still in the glove. I hadn't missed, there just was nothin' there to grab. Now I know what that look on his face was about. ... I can't seem to shake it. ... I haven't had a decent night's sleep for about 6 months. ... I was doing all I could to help. ... It haunts me. Sometimes it's not even a dream. I'm just thinking and there it is, boom ... right in my face, like I'm living it all over again. I'm just not sure how much more of this I can take. I don't know how I got out ... worse yet, I don't know why.

## Case Example 4

William is a 54-year-old information technology director for a large manufacturing firm. While working in the plant one afternoon, William was struck by a large piece of equipment that was being moved via overhead crane; this resulted in a closed-head trauma. Once he was physically stabilized, the true effects of William's injuries became apparent. William experienced moderate cognitive impairment, affecting his ability to concentrate and to consistently complete logical problem solving. The head trauma had also impacted William's ability to ambulate. It became apparent that his rehabilitation was going to be not only difficult and lengthy, but he would be challenged to learn to walk again. To further complicate matters, William was plagued by chronic pain in the form of migraine headaches, which would present without warning, often lasting for days. William is the sole support for his family and found that he had no short-term disability coverage and that his long-term disability income was only 60% of his regular income. He was faced with not only remarkable health issues but also remarkable financial stressors. William's wife and family were extremely supportive and actively participated in each phase of his rehabilitation. William was connected with a social worker to begin the process of establishing social, emotional, and vocational rehabilitation.

---

Clearly conceptualizing each of the cases provides the opportunity to examine the defining factors of stress, crisis, ASD, and PTSD. Figure 4.2 provides a roadmap for practitioners to process the nature of an individual's presenting problems and precipitating event and serves as a springboard for intervention based on the ACT intervention model (Roberts, 2002).

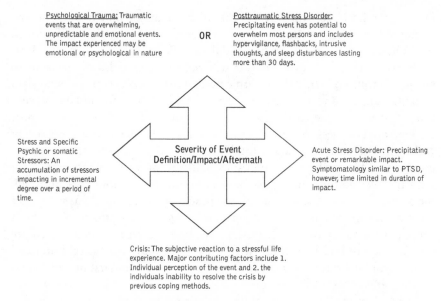

Figure 4.2   Five-Way Diagram of Trigger or Precipitating Event and Outcome

With the onset of crisis, stress, and trauma, the single common event is an episode that challenges or threatens the individual and his or her perception of the world. Based on the severity of the event and the individual's perception of the acute stressor, situational stressor, or accumulation of stressors, each person will progress in his or her response to the trigger/precipitating event.

## THE ACT INTERVENTION MODEL

A:  The "A" in the ACT intervention model refers to *assessment* of the presenting problem. This is inclusive of (a) triage assessment, emergency psychiatric response based on crisis assessment, and appraisal of immediate medical needs; and (b) trauma assessment, including the biopsychosocial and cultural assessment protocols.

C:  The "C" in the ACT intervention model refers to *connecting* to support groups, the delivery of social services, critical incident stress debriefing, and crisis intervention.

T:  The "T" in the ACT intervention model refers to *traumatic* reactions, sequelae, and posttraumatic stress disorders (Figure 4.3).

Immediate assessment of risk to self or others (e.g., suicide attempts, self-injurious behavior, and assessment of the individual's ability to care for self) or harm to others (e.g., potential for aggression toward others, attempted murder, murder) is the first step, the "A", of the ACT model. Individuals presenting with homicidal or suicidal ideation or the demonstrated inability to care for self will require a brief hospitalization to become stabilized. The primary objective of assessment is to provide data to better understand the nature of the event and the individual's perception of and response to the event, the extent of the individual's support system, effectiveness of coping mechanisms, and perceptions regarding willingness to seek assistance. Intake forms and rapid assessment instruments should be utilized to gather sufficiently accurate information to assist with the decision-making process. It is important to note that although the assessment is of the individual, the practitioner should always consider the person's immediate environment, including seeking information about supportive interpersonal relationships (Roberts & Lewis, 2002). Accurate assessment will lead to accurate diagnosis of the individual's condition and in turn will facilitate treatment interventions that are understandable, measurable, and accomplishable for the client.

The "C" in the ACT model addresses crisis intervention and connection to services. Although practitioners have training in a variety of theoretical approaches, this training is not easily applied to the nature of cases seen in actual practice in an emergency or crisis setting. The criteria for admission

**A** • Assessment/appraisal of immediate medical needs, threats to public safety and property damage

• Triage assessment, crisis assessment, trauma assessment and the biopsychosocial and cultural assessment protocols

**C** • Connecting to support groups, the delivery of disaster relief and social services, and critical incident stress debriefing (Mitchell & Everly's CISD model) implemented

• Crisis intervention (Robert's seven-stage model) implemented, through strengths perspective and coping attempts bolstered

**T** • Traumatic stress reactions, sequelae, and post-traumatic stress disorders (PTSDs)

• Ten step acute trauma and stress management protocol (Lerner & Shelton), trauma treatment plans and recovery strategies implemented

Figure 4.3    ACT Model

to inpatient psychiatric treatment require that patients be homicidal, suicidal, or unable to care for themselves. Although this is a very simplistic view of admission criteria, those working in psychiatry are acutely aware of the accuracy of these brief and overarching admission criteria. When trying to apply a clear, concise approach to crisis intervention regardless of diagnostic category or where the individual presents on the continuum of care need, practitioners are finding that traditional theoretical paradigms are not as effective as clear protocols. Roberts's (1991, 2000) seven-stage crisis intervention model provides practitioners with such a framework (Figure 4.4).

The "T" in the ACT model refers to trauma assessment and treatment. Traumatic events are overwhelming and highly emotionally charged experiences that remarkably impact the individual's ability to maintain psychological/psychiatric stability. Long-term exposure to a series of traumatic events (e.g., domestic violence) may lead to deterioration of psychological well-being. Furthermore, it is important to note that of those who experience traumatic events, only 3% to 5% develop PTSD.

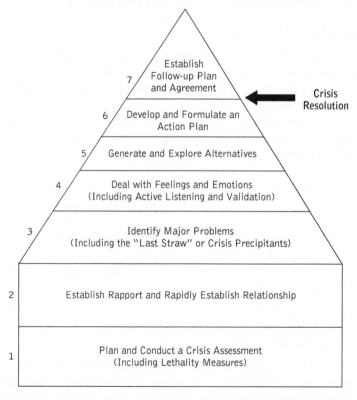

Figure 4.4    Roberts's Seven-Stage Crisis Intervention Model

Lerner and Shelton (2001) have developed a model of intervention that they believe is effective in intervening with traumatic stress and psychological trauma survivors to prevent escalation into PTSD:

1. Assess for danger/safety for self and others.
2. Consider the physical and perceptual mechanism of injury.
3. Evaluate the level of responsiveness.
4. Address medical needs.
5. Observe and identify each individual's signs of traumatic stress.
6. Introduce yourself, state your title and role, and begin to develop a connection.
7. Ground the individual by allowing him or her to tell his or her story.
8. Provide support through active and empathic listening.
9. Normalize, validate, and educate.
10. Bring the person to the present, describe future events, and provide referrals.

## APPLICATION OF ACT MODEL AND SEVEN-STAGE CRISIS INTERVENTION MODEL

### Case Example 1

Kevin presents with an accumulation of stress factors (Figure 4.5). On the LCU rating of common stressors, he has a cumulative stress score of 270. His psychosomatic symptoms are beginning to emerge as headaches and remarkable weight loss, accompanied by fleeting feelings of anxiety and hopelessness. After assessment of Kevin's situation, crisis intervention consisted of addressing the issues that he prioritized in the first session. These were addressed as follows:

Problem: Job stress.
Goal: Increased understanding of personal reaction to stress.
Methods:
1. List stressful situations experienced in order of severity (Stage 3 of Roberts's seven-stage model).
2. Consider alternatives to stress that have worked (Stage 5 of Roberts's seven-stage model).
3. List alternative actions for given stressful situations (Stage 6 of Roberts's seven-stage model).
4. Keep a log of activities and how these have impacted your stress level.

Initially, Kevin was reluctant to complete this task. In fact, his first list consisted of looking at the employment ads on a daily basis and finding a new position. It was noted that this would be helpful, but it would not resolve all of the problems Kevin was faced with. In subsequent sessions, Kevin did

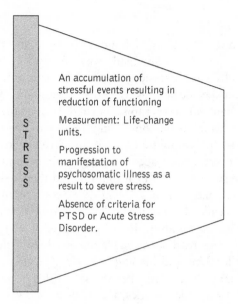

Figure 4.5    Associated Stress Symptoms

complete a list of stressors that encompassed each of those identified in the initial assessment. He acknowledged that he needed to take better care of himself. His list of activities included cutting back on caffeinated beverages and alcoholic beverages, improving his diet by staying away from fatty and fried foods, taking a walk each day on his lunch break, and making time after work to do something fun with his family and friends rather than focusing on the stressful daily events and how to "fix" them.

Kevin experienced an accumulation of stressors that were transitioning him into a state of specific psychic stress that was impacting his personal health. After accurate assessment, Kevin was able to work through the seven-stage crisis intervention model to address the stressors in his life. In Kevin's log was a statement that demonstrated his understanding of the impact of stress on his life: "I now understand that it is not my job or those around me that is causing my problems, it's all about what I do with what is given to me. If I focus on every little issue I will never be able to see my way out of the hole I am continually digging!"

The "T" in the ACT model was combined with the seventh step of Roberts's model, follow-up. Kevin indicated that the pending loss of his mother would be a remarkably difficult time for him. He was able to process his concerns about this with his group. He shared that of all his problems, this was the final remaining issue. In the closing session, Kevin shared a plan specifying who he will utilize for support and the actions he will take after the loss of his mother. He was reassured that should there be a need to come for additional sessions, there would be openings for him. Kevin agreed to do so if necessary.

*Case Autopsy*

Kevin attended a total of six 1-hour sessions that were based on a solution-focused approach combined with Roberts's seven-stage crisis intervention model. In each session, clear goals were outlined. Homework sessions focused on specific actions to be taken based on collaborative interaction between Kevin and his therapist. Kevin did not change jobs. Rather, he chose to maintain his focus on completing the day-to-day tasks and removing himself from the office politics. He ran his division strictly by the book and documented every action according to company policy. The therapist capitalized on the strengths of Kevin's family and their willingness to make changes to address pending issues. Kevin developed a plan to sell the home he was living in because his family no longer required such a large house. After speaking with his children, Kevin purchased a smaller house with a pool and a basement recreation room. He reports that this has been an excellent compromise for him and his children. Kevin was able to remove the majority of his financial stressors after the sale of his home. He was careful to remove himself from office politics, and while he was walking at lunch one day his boss was terminated. Kevin reports working to build a more positive rapport with his staff. In addition, Kevin displayed a number of resilience factors: supportive significant others or family, willingness to assess need for change, ability to enact changes, financial equity in his home to utilize for reduction of financial stressors, and consistent and steady full-time employment with good health benefits.

## Case Example 2

The unanticipated death of Jill's favorite uncle precipitated a situational crisis (Figure 4.6). Jill was quite skilled in dealing with stressful situations; however, this situation was more than the typical stressor faced in her work environment. Assessment of this case included application of the Beck Anxiety Scale. Jill's score reflected significant anxiety associated with this experience. Assessment of competencies of nursing practice indicated minimal impact; however, emotionally, Jill was not prepared to return to her work. There are many strong arguments for providing acute psychological counsel and forming a therapeutic rapport as early as possible following a traumatic event (Roberts, 2000b). Slaikeu (1984) argued that rapid intervention is essential to successful resolution of crisis. McGee (1974) cites "Hansel's law," indicating that the successful outcome for individuals addressing traumatic events increases directly as a function of the outcome's proximity in both time and place to the crisis event.

In Jill's case, the "C" and "T" of the ACT model took the form of brief, solution-focused intervention combined with Roberts's seven-stage crisis intervention model. This intervention was instituted within 48 hours of the

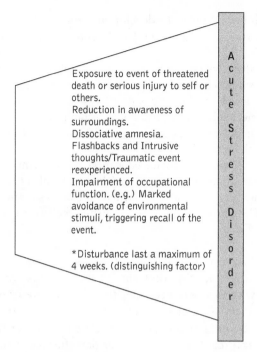

Exposure to event of threatened death or serious injury to self or others.
Reduction in awareness of surroundings.
Dissociative amnesia.
Flashbacks and Intrusive thoughts/Traumatic event reexperienced.
Impairment of occupational function. (e.g.) Marked avoidance of environmental stimuli, triggering recall of the event.

*Disturbance last a maximum of 4 weeks. (distinguishing factor)

Acute Stress Disorder

Figure 4.6   Symptoms of Acute Stress Disorder

trauma event. The intervention occurred in the psychiatry department associated with the hospital facility, thus providing proximity to the event. Jill's therapist provided support and assured her that the sessions would not be shared with her immediate supervisor and that they would work together as a team to develop her ongoing plan of care. Jill felt treatment in the institution of her employment was appropriate. These actions served to rapidly establish the therapeutic relationship between Jill and her therapist (Stage 2 of Roberts's seven-stage model).

The function of the debriefing was to "psychologically de-escalate" Jill, permitting the opportunity for her to explore and express feelings of guilt and her perception that she had not provided all of the assistance possible for her uncle (Stage 4 of Roberts's seven-stage model). As the debriefing continued, a pattern emerged of Jill's believing that she had a greater level of responsibility for her uncle's death than was warranted. Jill was experiencing remarkable difficulties sleeping and maintaining concentration, which ultimately resulted in significant distress in social and occupational functioning. Also, Jill was isolated from her primary support system, her family, as she felt that her failure to do all she could for her uncle made it impossible for her to seek assistance from them. Interventions associated with Jill's case utilized an integrated multicomponent approach, as debriefing as a stand-alone therapy has not been found to be as successful as a multicomponent approach.

Jill worked with her therapist to develop and formulate her treatment plan (Stage 6 of Roberts's seven-stage model). Interventions included:

1. Individual therapy sessions twice per week. Jill was encouraged to discuss the event and her subsequent reactions to the event.
2. Psychoeducational interventions to increase her awareness of a variety of coping mechanisms (e.g., relaxation techniques).
3. Pharmacotherapy, in this case sleep medication (zolpidem), was utilized to assist with her need for sleep.
4. A family conference to provide education and to permit cathartic ventilation in a manner that empowered family members to provide constructive support in the face of a demanding crisis situation.
5. Because Jill reported having strong spiritual beliefs, pastoral intervention was utilized.

Jill responded almost immediately to the support of her family, indicating that for the first time since the event, she felt that she was not alone. Within a week, Jill felt it was no longer necessary to utilize the prescribed medication. By the end of the second week of therapy, Jill asked to return to her unit and visit her friends. Soon after this visit, she related her belief in her ability to return to the workforce. Three weeks to the day after the traumatic event, Jill returned to work. It is important to note that Jill's experience met the diagnostic criteria for ASD (see Figure 4.6), specifically the time component. Her disturbance occurred within 4 weeks of the event and persisted for approximately 3 weeks, which is within the maximum 4-week duration (APA, 2013).

### Case Autopsy

Although Jill was no stranger to stressful experiences in the hospital setting, she was not prepared for the emotional trauma associated with the loss of her uncle in her work environment. Jill related during therapy that the resident reported to her later that he felt it strange that she was on the critical care unit on the day her uncle died; however, with the current nursing shortage, he assumed that Jill was covering an additional shift. In fact, none of the crisis team responding to the code had been aware that this was a relative. It was not until the cardiologist arrived that team members were aware of the true nature of the event. Jill reports that the cardiologist asked her in the hall while going to speak with the family if she was "all right." To this day, she is uncertain of her response.

Jill attended six follow-up sessions over a 4-month period and has not experienced significant symptoms associated with the traumatic event. The resilience factors she exhibited were pre-incident training and preparation, strong family support, support in her work environment, rapid response of debriefing and initiation of crisis intervention, spiritual beliefs, and cognitive abilities to apply a multicomponent approach.

## Case Example 3

Assessment of Tom indicated that he had been experiencing numerous diagnostic criteria for acute PTSD (Figure 4.7). Symptoms identified during the initial assessment included intense feelings of helplessness and horror associated with the event. Tom also reported recurrent distressing recollections of the event, specifically, images of his friend's face and the realization of why his friend was unable to hold on during his rescue efforts. Tom described intense feelings suggesting the presence of flashbacks related to the episode and said that he had been experiencing recurrent distressful dreams of the event that were uncharacteristically realistic. He also reported feeling estranged from his peer group. There was a remarkable tendency toward isolation and reduction of participation in significant activities. Most important, Tom began to avoid thoughts, feelings, and conversations associated with the traumatic event. Finally, Tom was experiencing sleep disturbance, including insomnia and early morning wakening, and difficulty concentrating and in the course of the assessment interview had demonstrated an exaggerated startle response.

As time progressed, Tom's condition began to deteriorate until he reached the point of suicidal ideation. He stated, "I can't deal with the torture of reliving this event every day. I don't understand why I had to survive. I should be dead." In this case, the "C" in the ACT model required admission to an inpatient psychiatric facility to facilitate psychiatric stabilization in a safe

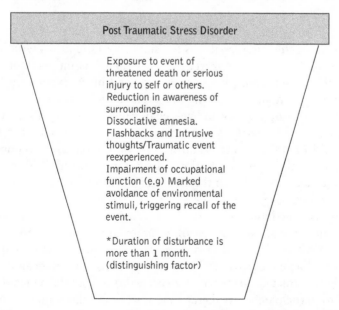

Figure 4.7   Symptoms of Post Traumatic Stress Disorder

environment. Pharmacotherapy for Tom consisted of a selective serotonin reuptake inhibitor (SSRI) and trazodone to assist with sleep.

Tom struggled to become involved in any form of therapy. He experienced remarkable difficulty relating to his peers on the unit. On two separate occasions, Tom experienced violent physical outbreaks. On one occasion, Tom was triggered by the unit fire alarm. This event was so severe that the crisis team was involved, and Tom was placed in seclusion to minimize stimuli. Haldol and Ativan were administered to minimize Tom's agitation and combative outbreak. On a second occasion, Tom became agitated after a verbal altercation with a peer. Tom worked with staff and on this occasion was able to respond to verbal de-escalation techniques.

Tom worked with the multidisciplinary treatment team to develop an integrated treatment plan. This was a slow process, initially focusing on integration into the community.

> Problem: Lack of participation in programming.
> Goal: Increased involvement in programming.
> Methods:
>    1. Tom will meet with Mary Ann Jones, LISW, each morning and pick three groups to participate in each day.
>    2. Tom will talk with Mary Ann Jones at the end of the day and relate how these groups helped.
>    3. Tom will eat dinner in the community room with at least two peers.
>    4. Tom will limit his time watching television to 1 hour per day.
>    5. Tom will sleep at least 8 hours per night, utilizing medication as needed for sleep.

The focus of the initial goal was to establish relationships with his peers and the staff (Stage 2 of Roberts's seven-stage crisis intervention model). As time progressed, Tom found art therapy and music therapy to be helpful in relaxing him and improving his interactions on the unit. He became more active in group therapy and was challenged to identify his major problems (Stage 3 of Roberts's seven-stage model). Tom shared that trusting again would be difficult. He began by sharing the recurrent thoughts and dreams, first in the form of questions, then in more detail. Within 3 weeks, he was beginning to deal with the feelings and emotions associated with the traumatic event.

Tom transitioned into the partial hospitalization program. One day while in group, he regressed as a result of an ambulance entering the emergency department with its lights and sirens on. However, he was able to utilize the group to explore alternatives to his natural response to isolate and relive his trauma. He contracted to stay with two peers throughout the remainder of the day and to participate in art therapy because he felt this would be relaxing.

Tom was able to build on his strengths and to utilize a solution-focused approach to develop a plan that functioned for that day.

### Case Autopsy

Tom's treatment has been lengthy. He continues to follow up in the outpatient clinic twice monthly for therapy and medication management. He has not been able to return to his work or the now empty site of the warehouse fire. Tom's treatment plan continues to be solution focused, primarily dealing with environmental triggers. He has applied for vocational rehabilitation and is interested in pursuing education in computers. Tom occasionally attends a community-based support group for persons with PTSD; however, he acknowledges his ambivalence regarding the effectiveness of this group. Tom continues on medication and participating in therapy. He reports better results from therapy because he does not like taking medication. He indicates now looking forward to his therapy sessions and that his growing resilience factors include a strong will to survive, willingness to learn, and discovery of the ability to express emotion through art, crafts, and music.

## Case Example 4

In the case of William, a series of neurocognitive testing indicated severe closed-head trauma. William was facing life-changing and lifelong adjustments secondary to his crisis event (Figure 4.8). Remarkably, he was open and willing to do whatever was necessary. Once medically stable, William was transferred to a long-term residential physical rehabilitation facility. Assessment indicated the need for physical strengthening and rehabilitation to establish optimal functioning capacity.

William and his family met with the team, consisting of a physician, neurologist, physical therapist, and social worker. William connected best with the social worker. Building on this strength, the treatment team selected the social worker to review and develop treatment planning with William. Initially, the treatment plan addressed physical strengthening and integration into a physical rehabilitation program. However, as time progressed, all team members became involved in assessment and reassessment of functioning. For example, 2 weeks into rehabilitation, William decided the process was too painful and that he could not continue. Rather than engaging in arguments with him, the team took the approach of establishing a treatment plan based on William's transitioning into an extended care facility rather than returning to his home as he had intended. The physician, physical therapist, and social worker met with William to discuss the nature of his extended care placement and the need to refocus attention on transition planning rather than on rehabilitation (Stage 5 of Roberts's seven-stage model).

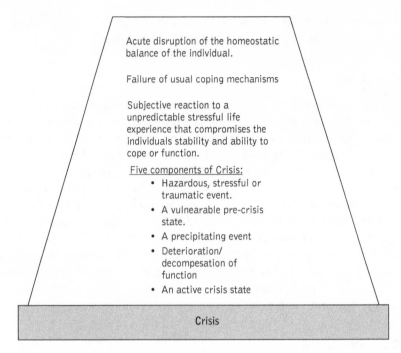

Figure 4.8    Associated Crisis Symptoms

This shift in planning evoked a remarkably emotional response. The team made time for William and listened to his complaints about their lack of caring, validated this feeling, and proceeded to rewrite his treatment plan to move in a more aggressive manner toward strength training and rehabilitation (Stage 6 of Roberts's seven-stage model). In solution-focused therapy, setting goals receives more emphasis than defining problems (de Shazer, 1985). In William's case, goal setting was based on a desired future state: how he perceived he would be acting, thinking, and feeling differently once the goal was accomplished. Without exception, William demonstrated willingness to work with the team and his family to successfully complete his rehabilitation (Yeager & Gregoire, 2000; Roberts & Yeager, 2009).

Resolving financial stressors was a remarkable issue in this case. Initially, William's wife assumed the responsibility for this process. However, the social worker arranged for a case conference with William's employer, William, his wife, and his attorney. Setting the process into motion led to a quick and fair settlement rather than a prolonged court hearing. Prior to this conference, William was asked with his family to establish concrete, precise indicators of changes for themselves. This process led to the ability to clearly articulate what their needs were and what concessions the family would be willing to make to facilitate the change process.

*Case Autopsy*

William was able to return to his home. Today he is able to walk with the assistance of support devices. He and his family are living a modest life. William is receiving disability income from his company based on agreements made in the rehabilitation facility. In this case, crisis intervention and solution-focused therapy integrated commonalities focusing on time-limited, intense interventions. Resistance was avoided through the presentation of alternative realities. William made his choice to continue in rehabilitation because this supported his perception of where he would like to be after being discharged from the facility. He demonstrated the following resilience factors: utilization of a multidisciplinary team approach, clear focus of ongoing living plans, a supportive family, integrated treatment planning, utilization of a problem-solving approach to address financial issues, and family cooperation.

## CONCLUSION

In each of the case examples, the critical components for completion of diagnosis and development of treatment planning were addressed. Diagrams outlining characteristic symptoms associated with each disorder were also provided for an integrated overview of the critical factors associated with accurate classification. More important, this chapter provided a paradigm to clarify critical components and operational definitions and demonstrated a method to examine parameters and differences both within and among stress, crisis, ASD, and PTSD.

REFERENCES

Agency for Healthcare Research and Quality. (2001, August). *Methods guide for effectiveness and comparative effectiveness reviews.* Rockville, MD. Retrieved from www.effectivehealthcare.ahrq.gov

Alexander, F. (1950). *Psychosomatic medicine.* New York: Norton.

American Psychiatric Association. (2013). *Diagnostic and statistical manual of mental disorders* (5th ed.). Arlington, VA: American Psychiatric Publishing.

Bonanno, G. A., & Diminich, E. D. (2013). Annual research review: Positive adjustment to adversity-trajectories of minimal-impact resilience and emergent resilience. *Journal of Child Psychology and Psychiatry, 54*, 378–401.

Cannon, W. B. (1927). *A laboratory course in physiology.* Cambridge, MA: Harvard University Press.

Chrousos, G. P., & Gold, P. W. (1992). The concepts of stress and stress system disorders: Overview of physical and behavioral homeostasis. *Journal of the American Medical Association, 267,* 1244–1252.

Corcoran J., & Roberts, A. R. (2000). Research on crisis intervention and recommendations for further research. In A. R. Roberts (Ed.), *Crisis intervention*

handbook: Assessment, treatment and research (2nd ed., pp.
453–486). New York: Oxford
University Press.

Cutler, D. L., Yeager, K. R., & Nunley,
W. (2013). Crisis intervention
and support. In K. R. Yeager,
D. L. Cutler, D. Svendsen, &
G. M. Sills (Eds.), Modern
Community Mental Health: An
interdisciplinary approach (pp.
243–255). New York. Oxford
University Press.

de Shazer, S. (1985). Keys to
solution in brief therapy.
New York: Norton.

Dohrenwend, B. S., & Dohrenwend,
B. P. (Eds.). (1974). Stressful life
events: Their nature and effects.
New York: Wiley.

Friedman, M., Thoresen, C. E., Gill,
J. J., Powell, L. H., Ulmer, D.,
Thompson, L., . . . & Bourg, E.
(1984). Alteration of type A behavior and reduction in cardiac recur-
rences in postmyocardial infarction
patients. American Heart Journal,
108, 237–248.

Haddy, R. I., & Clover, R. D. (2001).
The biological processes in psychological stress. Journal of
Collaborative Family Healthcare,
19, 291–299.

Holmes, T. H., & Rahe, R. H. (1967).
Social adjustment rating scale.
Journal of Psychosomatic Research,
11, 213–218.

Jones, E., & Wessely, S. (2007). A
paradigm shift in the conceptualization of psychological trauma in
the twentieth century. Journal of
Anxiety Disorders, 21, 164–175.

Kaplan, H. I., & Sadock, B. J. (1998).
Synopsis of psychiatry: Behavioral
sciences, clinical psychiatry
(8th ed.). New York: Lippincott
Williams and Wilkins.

Kessler, R. C., Berglund, P., Demler,
O., Jin, R., Merikangas, K. R., &
Walters, E. E. (January 01, 2005).

Lifetime prevalence and age-of-
onset distributions of DSM-IV disorders in the National Comorbidity
Survey Replication. Archives of
General Psychiatry, 62, 593–602.

Lerner, M. D., & Shelton, R. D.
(2001). Acute traumatic stress
management: Addressing emergent psychological needs during traumatic events. Commack,
NY: American Academy of Experts
in Traumatic Stress.

Lewis, S., & Roberts, A. R. (2002).
Crisis assessment tools: The good,
the bad and the available. Brief
Treatment and Crisis Intervention,
1, 17–28.

Mason, J. W. (1975). A historical
view of the stress field. Journal of
Human Stress, 1, 6–27.

McEwen, B. S. (1995). Stressful
experience, brain and emotions: Developmental, genetic
and hormonal influences. In M.
S. Gazzanga (Ed.), The cognitive
neurosciences (pp. 1117–1138).
Cambridge, MA: MIT Press.

McGee, R. K. (1974). Crisis intervention in the community.
Baltimore: University Park Press.

McHugh, P. R., & Treisman, G.
(2007). PTSD: A problematic diagnostic category. Journal of Anxiety
Disorders, 21, 211–222.

National Institutes of Mental Health.
(2012). The numbers count: Mental
disorders in America. Retrieved
from www.nimh.nih.gov/health/
publications/the-numbers-co
unt-mental-disorders-in america/
index.shtml

Powell, L. H., & Matthews, K. A.
(2002). New directions in understanding the link between stress
and health in women. International
Journal of Behavioral Medicine, 9,
173–175.

Regehr, C. (2001). Crisis debriefing
groups for emergency responders: Reviewing the evidence. Brief

*Treatment and Crisis Intervention,*
*1,* 87–100.

Roberts, A. (1991). *Contemporary perspectives on crisis intervention and prevention.* Englewood Cliffs, NJ: Prentice-Hall.

Roberts, A. R. (Ed.). (2000a). *Crisis intervention handbook: Assessment, treatment, and research* (2nd ed.). New York: Oxford University Press.

Roberts, A. R. (2000b). An overview of crisis theory and crisis intervention. In A. R. Roberts (Ed.), *Crisis intervention handbook: Assessment, treatment, and research* (2nd ed., pp. 3–30). New York: Oxford University Press.

Roberts, A. R. (2002). Assessment, crisis intervention and trauma treatment: The integrative ACT intervention model. *Brief Treatment and Crisis Intervention, 2,* 10.

Roberts, A. R., & Yeager, K. R. (2009). *Pocket guide to crisis intervention.* New York: Oxford University Press..

Schnurr, P. P. (2013). The changed face of PTSD diagnosis. *Journal of Traumatic Stress, 26,* 535–536.

Scott, W. (1990). PTSD in *DSM-III:* A case in the politics of diagnosis and disease. *Social Problems, 37,* 294–310.

Selye, H. (1956). *The stress of life.* New York: McGraw-Hill.

Slaikeu, K. A. (1984). *Crisis intervention: A handbook for practice and research.* Needham Heights, MA: Allyn and Bacon.

Smith, L. E., Bernal, D. R., Schwartz, B. S., Whitt, C. L., Christman, S. T., Donnelly, S., . . . Kobetz, E. (2014). Coping with vicarious trauma in the aftermath of a natural disaster. *Journal of Multicultural Counseling and Development, 42,* 1, 2–12.

Summerfield, D. (2001). The invention of post-traumatic stress disorder and the social usefulness of a psychiatric category. *British Medical Journal, 322,* 95–98.

Swanson, W. C., & Carbon, J. B. (1989). Crisis intervention: Theory and technique. In *Taskforce report of the American Psychiatric Association: Treatments of psychiatric disorders* (pp. 2520–2531). Washington, DC: American Psychiatric Association Press. 2520–2531.

Terr, L. (1994). *Unchained memories: True stories of traumatic memories, lost and found.* New York: Basic Books.

Tuckey, M. R., & Scott J. E. (2014). Group critical incident stress debriefing with emergency services personnel: A randomized control trial. *Anxiety Stress Coping,* 27(1),:38–54. doi:10.1080/106158 06.2013.809421

Wixen, H. (1978, October–November). Lesson in living. *Modern Maturity,* 8–10.

Yeager, K. R., & Gregiore, T. K. (2000). Crisis intervention application for brief solution-focused therapy in addictions. In A. R. Roberts (Ed.), *Crisis intervention handbook: Assessment, treatment and research* (2nd ed., pp. 275–306). New York: Oxford University Press.

Young, M. A. (1995). Crisis response teams in the aftermath of disasters. In A. R. Roberts (Ed.), *Crisis intervention and time-limited cognitive treatment* (pp. 151–187). Thousand Oaks, CA: Sage.

Young, A. (2004). When traumatic memory was a problem: On the historical antecedents of PTSD. In G. M. Rosen (Ed.), *Posttraumatic stress disorder: Issues and controversies* (pp. 127–146). Chichester, England: Wiley.

# 5

# Crisis Intervention for Persons Diagnosed With Clinical Disorders Based on the Stress-Crisis Continuum

KENNETH R. YEAGER
ANN WOLBERT BURGESS
ALBERT R. ROBERTS

All mental health professionals, including crisis clinicians, will benefit from applying the seven-level stress-crisis continuum. By determining the level and category that the person in crisis presents with, clinicians will be in an optimal position to determine whether crisis intervention, cognitive-behavioral therapy, medication, inpatient hospitalization, or other treatment modalities are appropriate. This chapter delineates and discusses a stress-crisis continuum consisting of seven levels to be used in conjunction with persons diagnosed with clinical disorders. Burgess and Roberts's first two levels are identified as somatic distress–crisis and transitional stress–crisis. In both, the stress symptomatology is usually reduced with brief crisis intervention and primary mental health care treatment. Levels 3, 4, and 5 seem to have occurred with increasing frequency during the 1990s. Individuals suffering from Level 3 (traumatic stress–crisis) benefit from individual and group crisis-oriented therapy; Level 4 (family crises) benefits from case management, and crisis treatment with forensic intervention; Level 5 (mentally ill persons in crisis) benefits from crisis intervention, case monitoring, and day treatment; Level 6 (psychiatric emergencies) benefits from crisis stabilization, hospitalization, and/or legal intervention; and Level 7 (catastrophic traumatic stress crises) involves multiple successive traumatic events in combination with a Level 4, 5, or

6 stressor and requires crisis stabilization, grief counseling, social support, and symptom resolution.

Healthcare and subsequently mental health are currently facing a transformation in service delivery. Some accounts estimate that the combined expanded Medicaid coverage and new health information exchange (HIE) insurance options will provide coverage for an additional 6 to 10 million people seeking treatment for mental health and substance use disorders. The implementation of new HIE insurance options will expand access to insurance to as many as 50 million Americans. Although this is necessary, it will not be sufficient to improve health and behavioral health outcomes. Improvement will not occur unless consumers are informed of how to access and use their health insurance benefits. For this new group of consumers, this could become a significant challenge. Without clearly articulated processes for how consumers of services will access benefits, many will be unable to enroll themselves in new insurance and Medicaid programs; we have seen challenges to date and are concerned that these may be just the tip of the iceberg. Additionally, once they are enrolled, consumers are likely to need help to access and utilize benefits within the expanded healthcare coverage plans. Consumers and their families will need help understanding exactly what reform can mean for them, how their benefits may change, and what new coverage options are available (Yeager, Cutler, Svendsen, & Sills, 2013). It is likely that the burden of helping these individuals to secure their benefits will once again fall on care providers; undoubtedly, this will further strain an already overtaxed workforce.

As we enter this new era of mental health reform, legislators, policy-makers, and healthcare administrators have an intensified interest in issues related to the quality of patient care, patterns of utilization of services, costs, and benefits. Every day, millions of individuals and families experience acute crisis episodes. These individuals are not able to resolve their crises on their own; as a result, many seek help from a mental health professional in their community.

We believe that to compete in the managed mental health care arena, crisis intervention will be a critical component. To practice crisis intervention requires a theoretical conceptualization of the stress-crisis continuum, the assessment and classification of levels of stress-crisis, and an empirical basis to the interventions.

There are questions that will need to be answered, such as: What will be the best model? Is a model of co-location of services more cost-effective than providing collaborative services? Choosing one model over another will eventually determine if the course of care remains task centered or returns to a person-centered model. Ultimately, legislation dictated that the final measure would be outcomes based. Thus, the question remains, What will provide the best outcome? In co-located care delivery systems, one can almost visualize an assembly line where hypertension is treated at one station and depression is treated at the next. This may be more efficient, but it certainly will not address the interactions of the illness. Collaborative care will address the interactions of the illness but may not provide a patient-centered approach that is holistic. Although it is possible to accomplish the same end, it is unclear which approach will be adopted, how it will be applied, and what the impact will be on healthcare systems as they develop fully. The good news is that grant funding will be included in the reform legislation and managed by Substance Abuse and Mental Health Services Administration to support the co-location of mental health and primary care providers. Additionally, seed dollars are earmarked to support new wellness and prevention programs, although the role of behavioral health in those programs has yet to be defined (Yeager, Cutler, Svendsen, & Sills, 2013). In any case, accountable care organizations (ACOs) are to be structured as a bundled risk model (under Medicare). In this model, providers create a care network that addresses the 80/20 effect of managing the 20% of the population that uses 80% of services provided. Providers will apply a proactive approach that seeks to manage care, improve quality, and reduce spending for "at-risk" patients. (ACOs typically involve hospitals or multispecialty physician practices working with additional outpatient providers to form a safety net for high-risk populations.) Therefore, the goal is to move from reactive to more proactive treatment approaches while reducing costs. In doing so, providers will need to have increased awareness and utilization of clearly structured models of assessment covering a wide range of healthcare needs.

This chapter presents a classification paradigm for assessing emotional stress and acute crisis episodes in terms of seven levels that fall along a stress-crisis continuum. This classification is an adaptation and expansion of Baldwin's (1978) crisis classification. The seven levels are somatic distress, transitional stress, traumatic stress–crisis, family crises, serious mental illness, psychiatric emergencies, and catastrophic/cumulative crises (see Baldwin's Table 2.1). With advancement from Level 1 to Level 7, the internal conflicts of the client become more serious and chronic.

For example, the closing case in this chapter illustrates cumulative levels of ongoing stress and crises that interact with a somatic distress and traumatic event: the diagnosis of HIV. The woman was an adopted child (transitional stress), and her sexual identity (transitional stress) was also an issue for her over the years. Much of her substance abuse and suicidal intent (psychiatric emergency) numbed her confusion over developmental issues, including her employment disruption (transitional stress) and physical assaults by female partners (transitional stress–crisis). The male patient assault (traumatic stress–crisis) precipitated her involvement in the legal system (transitional stress). Her HIV-positive status (somatic and traumatic event) remains her most immediate precursor to a series of acute crisis episodes.

Each of the seven types of crisis is presented with defining characteristics and suggested treatment modalities consistent with the managed mental health care objective of cost-effective and time-efficient clinical care. Cost-effectiveness measures of managed mental health and substance abuse services should be based on clearly delineated and measurable parameters. For example, what specific behavioral measures will indicate functional improvement of client groups receiving "x" number of crisis intervention sessions? Equally important from the insurance company's perspective is whether a client's improvement is predictable and within the guaranteed claim allowance or, ideally below, current claim costs.

## THEORETICAL FRAMEWORK

The clearest framework for the description of a psychological-biological stress continuum is the model reported by the Institute of Medicine study of stress and human health (Elliot & Eisdorfer, 1982). The model includes three primary elements, the activators/stressors, the reactions, and the consequences, which can be referred to as the "x-y-z sequence" (Elliot & Eisdorfer, 1982). Activators/stressors, which are the focus of this typology, may be internal or external events or conditions—such as depressive symptoms, a serious illness, death of a family member, violent crime victimization, child abuse, recurring psychosis, or a suicide attempt—that are sufficiently intense to evoke some change in the individual. Reactions include both biological and psychosocial responses to the activator/stressor. Consequences are the prolonged and cumulative effects of the reactions, such as physical and/or mental distress. The model attends to individual differences and variations throughout the sequence through its conceptualization of mediators, which are the filters and modifiers in the sequence (Elliot & Eisdorfer, 1982). Added to the model are interventions designed to reduce stress and symptomatology between reactions and consequences. This model suggests a dynamic, interactive process across the stress continuum between an individual and the environment (Lowery, 1987, p. 42).

Burgess and Roberts's (1995) stress-crisis continuum is an eclectic classification developed in 1995 and expanded from earlier models (Baldwin, 1978; Elliot & Eisdorfer, 1982).

## LEVEL 1: SOMATIC DISTRESS

---

### Case Example

Mrs. Gardner, a 30-year-old widow, was admitted to a psychiatric unit with numerous physical complaints, including urinary incontinence, nausea, generalized pain, and dizziness. The patient was about to be married for the second time and experienced severe symptoms while writing wedding invitations.

Her fiancé's brother had been killed suddenly in an automobile accident while working at his job on the railroad several weeks before the patient's admission. This death was similar to that of the patient's first husband, who was killed in an automobile accident 1 year after their marriage. As a child, the patient had enuresis frequently until age 7. Although the diagnosis of multiple sclerosis was ruled out at this admission, this diagnosis might still show up in later years.

Initially, Mrs. Gardner showed no distress over her symptoms. She was able to give up the catheter when other patients exerted negative reinforcement for this behavior. After this milieu intervention, Mrs. Gardner was able to control her own urine. She concurrently began to talk to the psychiatric nurse about her fear of losing her fiancé as she had lost her first husband, which was causing her to fear another marriage. The nurse helped the patient connect this dynamic understanding to the multiple somatic symptoms she experienced prior to admission, especially the urinary incontinence. Mrs. Gardner was discharged with no recurrence of the symptoms. She and her second husband continued attending couples counseling on an outpatient basis after their marriage.

---

Such crises are defined by somatic distress resulting from (a) a biomedical disease and/or (b) minor psychiatric symptoms. The mental health issue may or may not be clearly identified. Examples of this type of crisis precipitant include biomedical diagnoses such as cancer, stroke, diabetes, and lupus, as well as minor psychiatric states such as somatization, depression, and phobia or anxiety. The patient's response to this level of stress-crisis is generally anxiety and/ or depressive symptoms. The etiology of the crisis is biomedical, that is, there is generally an immune system suppression, a physical health disequilibrium, or, in minor psychiatric symptomatology, an unresolved dynamic issue.

Primary care providers generally see this type of somatic stress–crisis. Physical health symptoms bring the patient to a physician or nurse practitioner. A physical examination with laboratory testing can generally identify patients with a clear medical diagnosis. Those patients without a biomedical diagnosis may move into the first group at a later time with additional physical symptoms.

Patients without a confirmed medical diagnosis may report physical complaints ranging from a specific set of pain symptoms related to the head, back, abdomen, joints, or chest, or pain during menstruation or intercourse; gastrointestinal symptoms such as bloating, nausea, vomiting; sexual symptoms; and pseudoneurological symptoms such as body weakness, loss of sensation, fatigue, and impaired concentration (American Psychiatric Association [APA], 1994). In the case example, Mrs. Gardner had serious physical symptoms that were connected, in part, to an unresolved grief issue.

Patients both with and without a medical diagnosis can respond with minor psychiatric symptoms of anxiety and depression. Mechanic (1994) argues for a close connection between physical and mental health care in an integrated system in order to address the common comorbidities between physical and mental disorders. That is, a medical diagnosis of cancer or diabetes can easily increase a person's stress level, leading to the development of depressive symptoms.

## Research

Approximately half of all mental health care is provided by the general medical sector (Regier et al., 1993). Considerable evidence demonstrates a positive correlation between high-quality primary care and improved health outcomes (Starfield, Shi, & Macinko, 2005). In the United States, health outcomes are better in regions where the supply of primary care providers (PCPs) is highest (Shi et al., 2003). Other studies show a direct relationship between the quality of primary care and the outcomes of that care (Choudhry, Fletcher, & Soumerai, 2005). Studies indicate that utilization of primary care ambulatory services increases with patients who present with physical symptoms with underlying psychosocial issues. These studies suggest that 40% to 60% of all visits involve symptoms for which no biomedical disease can be detected (Barsky, 1981; Van der Gaag & Van de Ven, 1978). Bodily symptoms or negative mood may result from stress and/or psychosocial problems.

On the other hand, national studies estimate that, during a 1-year period, up to 30% of the US adult population meets criteria for one or more mental health problems, particularly mood (19%), anxiety (11%), and substance use (25%) disorders (Kessler, Chiu, et al., 2005). Mood and anxiety disorders are the most frequent disorders among primary care patients, occurring in approximately 20% to 25% of patients seen in clinics serving mixed-income populations and in as many as 50% of patients seen in clinics serving low-income populations. (Kessler, Demler, et al., 2005). Mental health problems are two to three times more common in patients with chronic medical illnesses such as diabetes, arthritis, chronic pain, headache, back and neck problems, and heart disease (Katon, 2003; Katon, Lin, & Kroenke, 2007). When undertreated or untreated, mental health problems are associated with poor adherence to treatment, adverse health behaviors that complicate physical health problems, and excess healthcare costs (Almeida & Pfaff, 2005; Kessler, Demler, et al., 2005; Kinnunen et al., 2006; Merikangas et al., 2007; Scott et al., 2009).

Untreated minor psychiatric symptoms can be costly for a primary care facility. When patients with negative laboratory results complain of vague somatic symptoms, they may be referred to as *somatizers*. Miranda and colleagues (1991) examined the prediction from Mechanic's (1994) attribution theory of somatization that somatizers who are under stress will overuse ambulatory medical services. As hypothesized, life stress interacted with somatization in predicting number of medical visits; somatizers who were under stress made more visits to the clinics than did nonsomatizers or somatizers who were not under stress. Although stress affected somatizers most, stress was predictive of increased medical utilization for all patients. These results suggest that psychological services intended to reduce overutilization of outpatient medical services might be best focused on stress reduction and be most beneficial to somatizers and persons with negative mood states.

The etiology of stress and medical illness is being studied in the stress–immune response research (Lowery, 1987). One program of research that addresses the stress-illness linkages by examining central arousal, immune changes, and clinical outcomes, albeit with different populations, is the work of Levy and colleagues. In a series of studies, Levy, Herberman, Lippman, and d'Angelo (1987) and Levy, Herberman, Whiteside, Kirkwood, and McFeeley (1990) found that breast cancer patients who were rated as less well adjusted to their illness, that is, expressing more distress, had lower levels of natural killer (NK) cell activity than did patients who were less distressed. Moreover, lower NK activity was associated with cancer spread to the axillary lymph nodes. In a sample of healthy individuals (Levy et al., 1990), younger subjects (18 to 29 years of age) who reported more perceived stress were more likely to have lower NK activity and lower levels of plasma beta endorphins, and they reported more infectious morbidity.

## Intervention

Patients with a defined medical illness will be treated with medical and nursing protocols appropriate to the illness. For patients without a clear medical diagnosis, the intervention strategy is symptom reduction, which requires the use of brief self-report assessment tools to first detect psychiatric symptomatology that is distressing but does not meet criteria for the *Diagnostic and Statistical Manual* (APA, 2013). The early treatment of psychiatric symptomatology has been shown to reduce symptoms and interrupt the progression to major psychiatric disorder (Miranda & Munoz, 1994).

An intervention of choice in Level 1 somatic distress–crisis is education. Teaching patients about their illness, symptoms, and subsequent healthcare has long been a priority in healthcare practice. The method of teaching may be self-tutorial, as in watching videotapes or reading written materials, or individually taught by a nurse or healthcare provider or through a group method of learning. One teaching method, described by Miranda and Munoz (1994), reports on an 8-week cognitive-behavioral course that was intended to teach patients to control negative moods. The course was similar to cognitive-behavioral therapy.

## LEVEL 2: TRANSITIONAL STRESS CRISIS

### Case Example

Mary, aged 8, is the only child of parents who have been married for 12 years. The mother indicated that it took 4 years for her to get pregnant with Mary. The pregnancy was complicated by a 69-pound weight gain, chronic indigestion, and a blood sugar level of 160 (the mother was told she had gestational diabetes). Mary was born at term; forceps were used because she was in the occiput-posterior head presentation (described by the mother as "sunny-side up"); the delivery was complicated by shoulder dystocia. Mary was large for gestational age, with a birth weight of 10 pounds, 13 ounces. At less than 24 hours of age, Mary had a generalized tonic-clonic seizure that lasted about 10 minutes. She continued to have intermittent seizures and was treated with Valium and phenobarbital. She became seizure free, and blood workups were negative. Skull films were negative except for bilateral hematomas from the forceps. Mary was continued on phenobarbital until 8 months of age. She was off anticonvulsants from 8 months until 15 months of age. Mary also had a heart murmur.

At age 8, neuropsychological testing revealed "a pattern of deficits consistent with right hemisphere atrophy and subsequent attention deficit disorder (ADD) with mild hyperactivity." Mary's primary ADD symptoms included visual distraction, slower processing speed, perceptual-motor disorganization, and impulsive response pattern. Both parent and teacher checklists reflect a high level of attentional problems, distractibility, impulsive behavior, and moderate behavior problems in both the home and the school settings. Mary's self-esteem is high; however, her ADD symptoms create considerable learning problems, and she is at continued risk for underachievement in the classroom. Her functioning was legally determined to be a result of neonatal head trauma.

---

Such crises reflect stressful events that are generally anticipated and reflect life transitions over which the child or adult may or may not have substantial control. Defining characteristics of transitional stresses are that there is disruption of the anticipated developmental event or role. The stressor is generally identified; the event is developmental in nature in that many people experience it. The transition is anticipated, and time is available to prepare for the changes that occur.

Transitional stresses include normative events around parenthood such as infertility or premature birth; childhood such as birth injury, hyperactivity, or illness; adolescence such as teen pregnancy or school problems; adulthood such as work disruption or chronic illness; and legal issues such as litigation. The individual's response is the development of personality trait rigidity and loss of personal flexibility. The etiology of the crisis is the failure to master developmental tasks.

The case example describes a medical problem in a normative life event of childbirth. The transitional stress results from interruption and delay in the normal neurobiological development of infancy into childhood. Mary's hyperactivity and academic problems are linked to a birth injury, something over which she and her mother had no control. Additionally, this injury has the capacity to compromise mastery of the developmental tasks of childhood, adolescence, and adulthood.

Erikson (1963) attributed a central or nuclear conflict to each of the eight developmental life issues. His theory further states that a relatively successful resolution of the basic conflicts associated with each level of development provides an important foundation for successful progression to the next stage. Whatever the resolution of these conflicts—mastery or failure—the result significantly influences personality development. Thus, in transitional stress, there is the potential to fail to master a developmental task.

J. S. Tyhurst (1957) studied transition states—migration and retirement—in the lives of persons experiencing sudden change during civilian disaster. Based on his field studies on individual patterns of responses to community disaster, Tyhurst identified three overlapping phases, each with its own manifestations of stress and attempts at reducing it: a period of impact, a period of recoil, and a post-traumatic period of recovery.

## Intervention

There are several useful interventions for transitional stress. The primary task of the crisis counselor during time-limited individual sessions is to educate the patient to an understanding of the changes that have taken or will take place and to explore any psychodynamic implications of these changes. Support is provided as needed, and anticipatory guidance is used to help the individual plan an adaptive coping response to problems that have resulted from the transition. Crisis intervention techniques are used if the event occurs without anticipatory information.

A second intervention is the use of group approaches. Following the brief individual therapy, the client is referred to self-help groups specific to the transition issue (e.g., parents without partners, parents of children with chronic illness). Self-help groups assist those experiencing a similar life transition (e.g., preretirement groups, childbirth preparation groups, group approaches to college orientation).

## LEVEL 3: TRAUMATIC STRESS CRISIS

---

### Case Example

Carol had been on maternity leave for 2 months and needed to return to work. She was a single parent who also had a 4-year-old boy and a 7-year-old girl, and she depended on the income she made as an assistant manager at a local restaurant, where she had worked for the past 5 years. Carol placed an ad for a baby-sitter in the newspaper. A woman called about the ad, set up an appointment, and the next day came to the house for an interview. Carol could not be there, so she had her mother come to the house to talk with the woman. The woman introduced herself to Carol's mother, who was holding the month-old baby. She seemed like a pleasant, competent woman and was well dressed. She said she didn't need the money but wanted to spend her time doing something she enjoyed. She said she had two teenage children of her own but missed taking care of an infant. Carol's mother wanted to see how she held a baby, so she handed the baby to the woman. At that moment the telephone rang, and Carol's mother went to the other room to answer it. As soon as she was out of sight, the woman left the house and drove off with the baby. When Carol's mother returned to the room, no one was there. She ran to the door just as the woman was driving away.

Carol's mother immediately called the police, who arrived within 5 minutes. Carol arrived shortly after and was told of her baby's kidnapping. She was devastated and at first blamed her mother. After this incident, Carol's mother began having nightmares and couldn't sleep. Carol, who could barely function, had to send the other children to their father's house to live temporarily.

The news media were immediately involved, and 4 days later the baby was recovered through a tip to a hotline. The abductor's husband's work associates had visited the baby and were suspicious when they noted it did not look like a newborn. They had heard the media announcement about the kidnapping and called the hotline. The abductor was a master's-prepared psychotherapist who had faked a pregnancy as a way to halt divorce proceedings. She pled guilty and spent 1 year in a psychiatric hospital plus 4 years on probation.

---

Such crises are precipitated by strong, externally imposed stresses. They involve experiencing, witnessing, or learning about a sudden, unexpected, and uncontrollable life-threatening event that overwhelms the individual. Other examples of traumatic crises include crime-related victimization of personal assault, rape, and sexual assault, arson, or hostage taking; victimization by natural disaster; being the victim of a serious vehicular accident or plane crash; sudden death of a partner or family member; accidents with physical dismemberment; and receiving a life-threatening medical diagnosis such as cancer. One traumatic stress–crises events occurred on April 19, 1995 when a terrorist truck bomb blew up outside of the federal office building in Oklahoma City in which 82 men, women, and children died. The trauma, stress, and crisis reactions of the hundreds of survivors and family members of the deceased will be remembered for years. The community was totally united, and hundreds of caring citizens came to the aid and support of the survivors. In addition, the FBI quickly mobilized and apprehended the two terrorists responsible for the bombing. However, a more deadly terroristic attack occurred on September 11, 2001 when 19 militants associated with the Islamic extremist group al-Qaeda hijacked four airliners and carried out suicide attacks against targets in the United States. Two of the planes were flown into the towers of the World Trade Center in New York City, a third plane hit the Pentagon just outside Washington, DC, and the fourth plane crashed in a field in Pennsylvania. Over 3,000 people were killed during the attacks in New York City and Washington, DC, including more than 400 police officers and firefighters.

The individual's response in the midst of a disaster or traumatic event is intense fear, helplessness, and behavior disorganization. Usual coping behaviors are rendered ineffective due to the sudden, unanticipated nature of the stress. There may be a refractory period during which the person experiences emotional paralysis and coping behaviors cannot be mobilized.

In the case example, the infant's grandmother directly experienced the abduction by offering the infant to the abductor to hold and then leaving the room to answer a telephone call. The infant's mother experienced the trauma by learning about the abduction when she returned home. The women were unable to process the information about the trauma, and thus the dysfunctional symptoms developed. Until the infant was returned, the mother and grandmother were unable to cope with daily activities.

## Research

Lindemann and his associates at Massachusetts General Hospital introduced the concepts of crisis intervention and time-limited treatment in 1943 in the aftermath of Boston's worst nightclub fire, at the Coconut Grove, in which 493 people perished. Lindemann (1944) and colleagues based their crisis theory on their observations of the acute and delayed reactions of survivors and grief-stricken relatives of victims. Their clinical work focused on the psychological symptoms of the survivors and on preventing unresolved grief among relatives of the persons who had died. They found that many individuals experiencing acute grief often had five related reactions: somatic distress, preoccupation with the image of the deceased, guilt, hostile reactions, and loss of patterns of conduct.

Furthermore, Lindemann and colleagues concluded that the duration of a grief reaction appears to be dependent on the success with which the bereaved person does his or her mourning and "grief work." In general, this grief work refers to achieving emancipation from the deceased, adjusting to the changes in the environment from which the loved one is missing, and developing new relationships. People need to be encouraged to permit themselves to have a period of mourning and eventual acceptance of the loss and adjustment to life without the deceased. If the normal process of grieving is delayed, negative outcomes will develop.

In the 1970s, the trauma of rape was introduced into the literature through the term *rape trauma syndrome* (Burgess & Holmstrom, 1974). Rape trauma consists of an acute phase of disorganization followed by a long-term phase of reorganization. A wide range of somatic, cognitive, psychological, and social symptoms are noted in both phases.

The trauma suffered by the victim affects her family, her social network, and the community. Recovery from rape is complex and influenced by many factors, including prior life stress, style of attack, relationship of victim and offender, number of assailants, preexisting psychiatric disorders, the amount of violence or the sexual acts demanded, and postrape factors of institutional response to the victim, social network response, and subsequent victimization. Clinicians should consider all these factors in assessing and identifying victims who are at high risk for slow recovery from rape and who will remain vulnerable to many life stresses for a long time.

The pioneering work of Charles R. Figley and members of the Consortium on Veteran Studies (Figley, 1978) provides insight into the Level 3 crisis of war combat. Figley suggests that combat includes four major elements that make it highly traumatic: a high degree of dangerousness, a sense of helplessness in preventing death, a sense of destruction and disruption, in both lives and property, and a sense of loss. Moreover, the long-term emotional adjustment to combat follows four stages: recovery, avoidance, reconsideration, and adjustment.

## Intervention

*Crisis reaction* refers to the acute stage, which usually occurs soon after the hazardous event and includes the neurobiology of trauma. During this phase, the person's acute reaction may take various forms, including helplessness, confusion, anxiety, shock, disbelief, and anger. Low self-esteem and serious depression are often produced by the crisis state. The person in crisis may appear to be incoherent, disorganized, agitated, and volatile or calm, subdued, withdrawn, and apathetic. It is during this period that the individual is often most willing to seek help, and crisis intervention is usually most effective at this time (Golan, 1978).

Tyhurst recommended a stage-specific intervention. He concluded that persons in a traumatic crisis state should not be removed from their life situation, and intervention should focus on bolstering the network of relationships. Cognitive-behavioral therapy to assist in the information processing of trauma (Burgess & Hartman, 1997) is a treatment recommended for rape-related post-traumatic stress disorder and depression. Also termed *cognitive processing therapy* (Resick & Mechanic, 1995), this treatment is time limited and effective. Other modalities to consider include pharmacotherapy with antianxiety medication to help with the long-term physiological symptoms of post-traumatic stress disorder. In addition and/or following individual trauma work, patients are referred for stress reduction/relaxation treatment, crisis or self-help groups, and psychoeducation groups.

Strategic solution-focused therapy (Quick, 1998) combines the principles and techniques of strategic therapy and solution-focused therapy. In this approach, the therapist clarifies problems, elaborates solutions, identifies and evaluates attempted solutions, and designs interventions that include validation, compliment, and suggestion components. The pragmatic principle of doing what works and changing what is not working is the goal for both the client and the therapist. See Chapter 3 for detailed information.

A therapeutic technique designed by Francine Shapiro, eye movement desensitization and reprocessing (EMDR), incorporates key aspects of many of the major therapeutic modalities. The basic underlying principles derive from an information-processing model that aims to directly access and process dysfunctional perceptions that were stored in memory at the time of the traumatic event. The state-dependent perceptions are considered primary to the development of post-traumatic stress symptoms. Additional, rigid thoughts are assumed to be caused by earlier life experiences that are dysfunctionally stored. The primary goal of EMDR is to release clients from the nonadaptive bonds of the past, thereby providing them with the ability to make positive and flexible choices in the present. Current research on EMDR substantiates its ability to rapidly and effectively process the targeted event and attendant traumatic information. The eight phases of treatment are considered necessary to resolve the trauma (Shapiro, 1998).

## LEVEL 4: FAMILY CRISIS

---

### Case Example

Meredith, aged 23, first met Willis, aged 29, when he came to the apartment she shared with a roommate hairdresser, to have a haircut. According to Willis, they felt an instant chemistry, and they began dating. From the beginning they isolated themselves from others, and when Meredith and her roommate parted, Willis asked Meredith to move in with him. Meredith ignored a nagging internal warning that this was not a good decision. For example, on their first date, Willis showed Meredith, a mental health counselor, his psychiatric record. She later said his diagnosis should have been a red flag to her: borderline personality disorder with antisocial, dependent, and passive-aggressive features. He also had an alcohol history.

Willis believed he had found his future marriage partner; Meredith did not. After several months, she met another man she wanted to date and told Willis, whose reaction was worse than she imagined. He became depressed and began cutting himself and leaving blood on tissues around the apartment and writing "I love you" in blood on the wall. He begged her not to leave.

As Meredith began dating her new boyfriend, Willis obtained his address and telephone number. He began to write threatening letters. The boyfriend ended the relationship by leaving town. Willis continued to mail Meredith notes and greeting cards, pleading with her and then berating her. Detectives told Willis they could not arrest him, since his letters had been written before the new state stalking law took effect. They suggested he enter a psychiatric hospital.

Meredith left town, but within months Willis located her. She found a balloon and a get-well card taped to her car and noticed two holes in the front windows of her apartment. When police arrested Willis, they found a stun gun, a rope, latex gloves, duct tape, and a pocketknife in his car. He pled no contest to his 16-month obsession with his ex-girlfriend.

---

Some emotional crises result from attempts to deal with primary interpersonal situations that develop within the family or social network (e.g., relational dysfunction). These relate back to developmental tasks and Level 2 transitional crisis. If unresolved, the family crises reflect a struggle with a deeper, but usually circumscribed, developmental issue that has not been resolved adaptively in the past and that represents an attempt to attain emotional maturity. These crises usually involve developmental issues such as dependency, value conflicts, sexual identity, emotional intimacy, power issues, or attaining self-discipline. Often a repeated pattern of specific relationship difficulties occurs over time in those presenting with this type of crisis (Baldwin, 1978). The crisis may be directed internally or externally, as in chronic abuse.

Examples of family crises include child abuse, the use of children in pornography, parental abductions, adolescent runaways, battering and rape, homelessness, and domestic homicide. The individual's response to this level of crisis is chronic fear, an inability to protect the self and others, and a type of learned helplessness. The etiology of the crisis relates to the neurobiology of chronic trauma. There is often undisclosed relationship abuse and divided family loyalty.

In the case example, the potential dangerousness of the male partner, Willis, is clearly noted. His psychiatric diagnosis of personality disorder suggests an unresolved developmental power issue as noted by his stalking.

## Research

It is important to note that every type of emotional crisis involves an interaction of an external stressor and a vulnerability of the individual. However, it is in Level 4 crisis that there is a shift from a primarily external locus of stress that produces the crisis to an internal locus determined by the psychodynamics of the individual and/or preexisting psychopathology that becomes manifest in problem situations. Child abuse and battering within a domestic violence context are prime examples of family crises. Both are interpersonal situations that exist around long-term relationships. See Chapter 17 for a review of the research on child abuse and crisis intervention.

## Intervention

In family violence, the goals of intervention in Level 4 crises are to help individuals restabilize their lives, strengthen their interpersonal relationships, and deter psychiatric symptomatology. First the crisis state, if there is one, must be resolved. All abuse must cease, and children and adults must be safe. The survivors must adapt to immediate losses and changes created by the disclosure of abuse and the protective response by others. The dysfunction in the family system must be addressed.

Roberts's (1995, 1996) seven-step crisis intervention model is implemented. This model offers an integrated problem-solving approach to crisis resolution. The steps include assessing lethality and safety needs; establishing rapport and communication; identifying the major problems; dealing with feelings and providing support; exploring possible alternatives; assisting in formulating an action plan; and conducting follow-up.

Recovery services are intended to aid survivors in resolving the long-term issues. Stress reduction interventions are of two types: (a) those designed to help the individual prevent or manage stress, and (b) those aimed at eliminating or reducing the potency of the stressor. Techniques to consider include physical activity to discharge repressed energy; nutrition therapy to enhance physiological recovery; spiritual support for persons who value religious beliefs to promote a sense of integrity with the natural world; relaxation to counter hypervigilance; pleasure activities to promote a sense of fun and humor; and expressive activities such as reading, art, and music.

A variety of psychoeducational and therapeutic interventions have been developed to change perpetrator behavior, many of which have produced an actual decrease in violent or exploitive behavior. Generally, interventions include components designed to increase the knowledge and skills of the perpetrator with regard to anger control, mediation, communication, and family roles.

Group models are often helpful. For example, narrative theory provides a useful framework for brief group treatment of persons in crisis because it proposes that understanding of experience is gained through social discourse. Groups offer persons in crisis a new context for attributing meaning to critical events (Laube, 1998).

## LEVEL 5: SERIOUS MENTAL ILLNESS

---

### Case Example

Mrs. Dee, aged 32, was referred to the mental health clinic by her case manager. When she arrived, clinging to her were her four children: Doddy (aged 2), Bryant (3), Katie (5), and Sally (6). The children were unkempt and waif-like. Mrs. Dee, chain-smoking cigarettes, stated that she wanted some Valium for her nerves. Mrs. Dee lives in a housing project with her husband, Jim. She and her family (namely, three sisters, a younger brother, father, and mother) have been known to the multiservice health center for more than 15 years. Mrs. Dee, upon questioning, revealed that she felt things were just getting to be too much this morning, and she decided to call her case manager. Although she did not describe herself as depressed, questioning revealed that she was hearing voices telling her not to eat because the food was poisoned. She had lost 20 pounds in the last month, and her sleeping was erratic because she felt the neighbors were able to see through her walls. She, as well as the children, looked emaciated. Although the children clung to their mother, she seemed to ignore them.

---

Three months earlier, Mrs. Dee had had a hysterectomy. She was upset with the home care she received after the surgery. She had been promised homemaker services, but when the homemakers came to the apartment, they quit the next day, which she attributed to the fact that they were Black and she was White Irish. A month later she got into a row with her father, who was an alcoholic. Her husband, who was out of work, was at home most of the day or out playing baseball. During this time, her three sisters were in and out of her apartment, as was her brother. All her siblings were on drugs or were drinking. Two sisters had children, and presently the state was stepping in to remove the children from their mothers because of neglect and multiple injuries that could not be accounted for.

Shortly after her return home from the hospital after the hysterectomy, Mrs. Dee slashed her wrists. She was taken to an emergency ward, where her wrists were stitched. She refused to talk to a psychiatrist. Homemaker help was sent to her house, but she refused to let the homemaker enter her house. She did develop a relationship with a nurse, and she recounted a life full of struggle. Her first child was born when she was 16. She married 2 years later and had another child, followed by a divorce, then marriage to her present husband and two more children. She had difficulty with her husband, who often beat her. During this time a social worker came to the house, and eventually all these children were placed in a foster home and later were given up for adoption. Thus, Mrs. Dee forbade any investigation into the records at this time for fear her present four children would be taken away. She claimed that she had been abused by the authorities and that her children were removed from her against her will. The current stressor of the hysterectomy and its unresolved meaning reactivated underlying psychotic symptoms and heightened the multiproblem nature of this family.

Such crises reflect serious mental illness in which preexisting problems have been instrumental in precipitating the crisis. Or the situation may involve a state in which the severity of the illness significantly impairs or complicates adaptive resolution. There is often an unidentified dynamic issue.

Other examples of serious mental illness include diagnoses of psychosis, dementia, bipolar depression, and schizophrenia. The patient response will be disorganized thinking and behavior. The etiology is neurobiological.

The case example indicates that Mrs. Dee was experiencing perceptual difficulties and paranoid thinking. An unresolved issue for her was related to the hysterectomy and the psychological meaning of the end to her childbearing.

## Intervention

The clinician needs to be able to diagnose the mental illness and adapt the intervention approach to include appreciation of the personality or characterological aspects of the patient. Persons with long-term and recurring severe mental illness require a mix of traditional medical and long-term treatments that are helpful in sustaining their function and role. Roberts's (1991, 1995, 1996) crisis intervention model may be used to reduce symptoms in an acute crisis.

The crisis therapist responds primarily in terms of the present problem of the patient, with an emphasis on problem-solving skills and environmental manipulation. The therapist gives support but is careful not to produce or reinforce dependency or regression by allowing the therapeutic process to become diffuse. The therapist acknowledges the deeper problems of the client and assesses them to the degree possible within the crisis intervention context, but does not attempt to resolve problems representing deep emotional conflict. Through the process of crisis intervention, the patient is helped to stabilize functioning to the fullest extent possible and is prepared for referral for other services once the process has been completed.

Case monitoring and management are indicated, as well as an assessment for inpatient hospitalization or sheltered care. Medication will be needed for psychotic thinking. Continuity of care is critical with this level of crisis and is generally accomplished through the case manager. Other services should include referral for vocational training and group work.

## LEVEL 6: PSYCHIATRIC EMERGENCIES

### Case Example

Mr. Mars, aged 65, was admitted to a psychiatric unit following a suicide attempt. According to his history, he had two older sisters and several older half siblings. His mother, who had glaucoma, died in her 90s of a cause unknown to the patient; his father died at age 66 of prostate cancer. Mr. Mars described himself as the "bully" in his family and said that he had always felt distant from his siblings and parents.

Mr. Mars enlisted in the Marine Corps after high school and served in World War II combat. After the war, he returned home and worked for 20 years as a truck driver, then for 8 years as a prison guard. He and his wife had no children. Prior to his diagnosis of diabetes, he drank beer regularly and enjoyed the company of his tavern friends. He had many interests prior to his work retirement, belonging to community groups, the Marine Corps League, and the VFW, and he was chairman of his church picnic.

Mr. Mars was first hospitalized at age 48 with complaints of an inability to sleep, no interest in work, suicide ideation, thoughts of wanting to hurt his wife, a peculiar preoccupation with numbers, lack of appetite, and weight loss. His recent diagnosis was diabetes mellitus, which was seen as a precipitant to the depression. He was diagnosed with psychotic depressive reaction and treated with Elavil, Trilafon, and group therapy and discharged after 6 weeks. Mr. Mars continued outpatient counseling and pharmacotherapy for a year. Counseling notes indicate he discussed his contemplated suicide at the time of hospitalization, displayed no insight into his condition, regretted not having children, always worked hard, had little communication with his wife, talked on a very superficial level, and had passive-aggressive behavior (e.g., waiting weeks to get even for a perceived wrong).

Mr. Mars's history of medical problems included diabetes, high blood pressure, and glaucoma. He had a transurethral resection of the prostate for a benign condition. His second psychiatric hospitalization occurred following the laceration of his left wrist and arm, which required surgical correction. On admission, he stated, "I wanted to end it all ... too many things in too little time." That evening he had eaten dinner around 6:00 p.m. and had a graham cracker snack at 10:00 p.m. While his wife was at choir practice, he cut his arm several times with a razor blade and "held it over the bathtub hoping to pass out and die." When nothing happened, he cut his arm several more times. He said that after retiring he "couldn't enjoy it like I wanted; I'm stuck in the house and bored." His stated goals for hospitalization were to "straighten out, get better and get the hell out of here."

Mrs. Mars stated her husband did not give her any indication he was depressed or was thinking of harming himself. She had gone to choir practice and when she returned found her husband over the bathtub with several deep lacerations; she called the ambulance. Mrs. Mars described her husband as selfish and self-serving, showing no consideration for others. She said they argued frequently and that he did not talk about his feelings. They had been married for 40 years. Mrs. Mars reported that when they argued, her husband would hold a grudge and not talk to her for days.

---

Psychiatric emergencies involve crisis situations in which general functioning has been severely impaired. The individual is rendered incompetent, unable to assume personal responsibility, and unable to exert control over feelings and actions that he or she experiences. *There is threat or actual harm to self and/or others.*

Examples of psychiatric emergencies include drug overdose, suicide attempts, stalking, personal assault, rape, and homicide. The individual presents with a loss of personal control. The patient's level of consciousness and orientation, rationality, rage, and anxiety all affect the level of cooperation during the immediate assessment of the need for emergency intervention.

The etiology of these crises focuses on the self-abusive component to suicide attempts and drug overdoses. Aggression toward others suggests a need for dominance, control, and sexualized aggression.

The case example illustrates serious suicidal intent on the part of Mr. Mars. Of interest is the denial by Mrs. Mars of any warning signs. By history it was learned that Mr. Mars was trying to dispense some of his money to a favorite niece when Mrs. Mars interceded. While in the hospital, he tried to run away from a group activity and into a river. Three weeks after admission, he successfully hung himself in a bathroom at 12:30 a.m., between 30-minute unit checks.

## Intervention

The clinician needs to be confident in his or her skills at managing a client's out-of-control behavior and/or must have adequate assistance available. When an emergency presents itself, with appropriate cooperation, questions need to be raised and answered regarding the location of the patient, exactly what the patient has done, and the availability of significant others. In the case of a suicide attempt, the clinician's immediate task, to assess the lethality of the act, is greatly aided by published lethality scales. Where medical-biological danger has been determined to exist or where sufficient data for that determination are not available, emergency medical attention is required. Dangerous and volatile situations should be handled by police and local rescue squads, which can provide rapid transportation to a hospital emergency room. Rapid medical evaluation is an essential first step in resolving a current and future suicidal crisis (Jobes & Berman, 1996).

Psychiatric emergencies are the most difficult type of crisis to manage because there may be incomplete information about the situation, the patient may be disruptive or minimally helpful, and there is an immediacy in understanding the situation in depth in order to initiate effective treatment. Patient assessment is greatly facilitated when informants with some knowledge of the precipitating events accompany the patient; in many instances they can be helpful in planning appropriate psychological and medical services (see Chapters 11, 18, 19, and 24).

The basic intervention strategy for Level 6 psychiatric crisis involves the following components: (a) rapidly assessing the patient's psychological and medical condition; (b) clarifying the situation that produced or led to the patient's condition; (c) mobilizing all mental health and/or medical resources necessary to effectively treat the patient; and (d) arranging for follow-up or coordination of services to ensure continuity of treatment as appropriate. It is in this type of psychiatric emergency that the skills of the crisis therapist are tested to the limit because he or she must be able to work effectively and quickly in highly charged situations and to intervene where there may be life-threatening implications of the patient's condition (Burgess & Baldwin, 1981; Burgess & Roberts, 1995).

Police or emergency medical technicians are often called to transport the patient to a hospital or jail. Medication, restraint, and/or legal intervention are all indicated for psychiatric emergencies.

## LEVEL 7: CATASTROPHIC CRISIS

---

### Case Example

A young bisexual woman in her mid-30s was admitted to a psychiatric hospital following a serious suicide attempt. A number of stressful events had occurred over a 3-month period. She began drinking heavily when her partner moved out of her apartment; she had a car accident during a snowstorm; later her car was stolen, and she began "drinking around the clock." She could not control herself and took a leave of absence from her computer analyst job. She was hospitalized briefly at the local psychiatric hospital. Three weeks after that hospitalization, one evening she was drinking with a man she met at a bar. He drove her home, and they continued drinking in her apartment. The man wanted sex, but she refused, and he forced the situation. After he left the apartment, she called a friend to take her to a local hospital, where a rape examination revealed vaginal lacerations. On returning home, the woman continued drinking and, while intoxicated, slashed her wrist with a broken glass. She again called her friend, who took her back to the hospital, where she received 10 sutures; later she was transferred to the psychiatric hospital.

The next day the woman requested discharge against medical advice. She returned to her apartment and went on an extended drinking bout for another 6 weeks, during which she was also very suicidal. About this time, she brought a legal suit against one of the male patients and the psychiatric hospital for simple assault, blood tests revealed that she was HIV-positive.

---

Level 7 has two or more Level 3 traumatic crises in combination with Level 4, 5, or 6 stressors. Classifying an individual into one of the preceding levels of crisis is dependent upon the nature, duration, and intensity of the stressful life event(s) and one's perception of being unable to cope and lessen the crisis. Sometimes a crisis is temporary and quickly resolved; at other times it can be life-threatening and extremely difficult to accept and resolve (e.g., having AIDS or a multiple personality disorder, or losing all family members due to a disaster).

## SUMMARY

The lack of an up-to-date classification model for determining levels of emotional crises has resulted in a significant gap to advancing the development of crisis theory. The revised and expanded Baldwin (1978) crisis typology is presented to increase communication between therapists and other crisis care providers in clinical assessment, treatment planning, and continuity of healthcare within a managed care context.

REFERENCES

Almeida, O. P., & Pfaff, J. J. (2005). Depression and smoking amongst older general practice patients. *Journal of Affect Disorders, 86,* 317–321.

American Psychiatric Association. (1994). *Diagnostic and statistical manual of mental disorders* (4th ed.). Washington, DC: Author.

American Psychiatric Association. (2013). *Diagnostic and statistical manual of mental disorders: DSM-5.* Washington, DC: Author.

Baldwin, B. A. (1978). A paradigm for the classification of emotional crises: Implications for crisis intervention. *American Journal of Orthopsychiatry, 48,* 538–551.

Barsky, A. J. (1981). Hidden reasons some patients visit doctors. *Annals of Internal Medicine, 94,* 492.

Burgess, A. W., & Baldwin, B. A. (1981). *Crisis intervention theory and practice.* Englewood Cliffs, NJ: Prentice-Hall.

Burgess, A. W., & Hartman, C. R. (1997). Victims of sexual assault. In A. W. Burgess (Ed.), *Psychiatric nursing: Promoting mental health* (pp. 425–437). Stamford, CT: Appleton and Lange.

Burgess, A. W., & Holmstrom, L. L. (1974). Rape trauma syndrome. *American Journal of Psychiatry, 131,* 981–986.

Burgess, A. W., & Roberts, A. R. (1995). The stress-crisis continuum. *Crisis Intervention and Time-Limited Treatment, 2* (1), 31–47.

Choudhry, N. K., Fletcher, R. H., & Soumerai, S. B. (January 1, 2005). Systematic review: The relationship between clinical experience and quality of health care. *Annals of Internal Medicine, 142,* 260–273.

Elliott, G. R., & Eisdorfer, C. (1982). *Stress and human health.* New York: Springer.

Erikson, E. H. (1963). *Childhood and society* (2nd ed.). New York: Norton.

Figley, C. (1978). *Stress disorders among Vietnam veterans: Theory, research and treatment implications.* New York: Brunner/Mazel.

Golan, N. (1978). *Treatment in crisis situations.* New York: Free Press.

Jobes, D. A., & Berman A. L. (1996). Crisis assessment and time-limited intervention with high-risk suicidal youth. In A. R. Roberts (Ed.), *Crisis management and brief treatment: Theory, practice and research* (pp. 53–69). Chicago: Nelson-Hall.

Katon, W. J. (2004). Clinical and health services relationships between major depression, depressive symptoms, and general medical illness. *Biological Psychiatry, 54,* 216–226.

Katon, W., Lin, E., & Kroenke, K. (2007). The association of depression and anxiety with medical symptom burden in patients with chronic medical illness. *General Hospital Psychiatry, 29,* 147–155.

Kessler, R. C., Chiu, W. T., Demler, O., Merikangas, K. R., & Walters, E. E. (2005). Prevalence, severity, and comorbidity of twelve-month

*DSM-IV* disorders in the National Comorbidity Survey Replication (NCS-R). *Archives of General Psychiatry, 62,* 617–627.

Kessler, R., Demler, O., Frank, R., Olfson, M., Pincus, H. A., Walters, E. E., ... Zaslavsky, A. M. (2005). Prevalence and treatment of mental disorders, 1990 to 2003. *New England Journal of Medicine, 352* (24):2515–2523.

Kinnunen, T., Haukkala, A., Korhonen, T., Quiles, Z. N., Spiro, A., & Garvey, A. J. (2006). Depression and smoking across 25 years of the Normative Aging Study. *International Journal of Psychiatry in Medicine, 36,* 413–426.

Laube, J. J. (1998). Crisis-oriented narrative group therapy. *Crisis Intervention and Time-Limited Treatment, 4,* 215–226.

Levy, S. M., Herberman, R. B., Whiteside, T., Kirkwood, J., & McFeeley, S. (1990). Perceived social support and tumor estrogen/progesterone receptor status as predictors of natural killer cell activity in breast cancer cell patients. *Psychosomatic Medicine, 52,* 73–85.

Levy, S. M., Herberman, R. B., Lippman, M., & d'Angelo, T. (1987). Correlation of stress factors with sustained depression of natural killer cell activity and predicted prognosis in patients with breast cancer. (1987). *Journal of Clinical Oncology, 5,* 348–353.

Lindemann, E. (1944). Symptomatology and management of acute grief. *American Journal of Psychiatry, 101,* 141–148.

Lowery, B. (1987). Stress research: Some theoretical and methodological issues. *Image, 19*(1), 42–46.

Mechanic, D. (1994). Integrating mental health into a general health care system. *Hospital and Community Psychiatry, 45,* 893–897.

Merikangas, K. R., Ames, M., Cui, L., Stang, P. E., Ustun, T. B., Von Korff, M., & Kessler, R. C. (2007). The impact of comorbidity of mental and physical conditions on role disability in the U.S. household population. *Archives General Psychiatry, 64,* 1180–1188.

Miranda, J., & Munoz, R. (1994). Intervention for minor depression in primary care patients. *Psychosomatic Medicine, 56,* 136–142.

Miranda, J., Perez-Stable, E., Munoz, R. F., Hargreaves W., & Henke C. J. (1991). Somatization, psychiatric disorder, and stress in utilization of ambulatory medical services. *Health Psychology, 10*(1), 46–51.

Quick, E. K. (1998). Strategic solution focused therapy: Doing what works in crisis intervention. *Crisis Intervention and Time-Limited Intervention, 4,* 197–214.

Regier, D. A., Narrow, W. E., Rae, D. S., Manderscheid, R. W., Locke, B. Z., Goodwin, F. K. (1993). The de facto US mental and addictive disorders service system: Epidemiologic Catchment Area prospective 1-year prevalence rates of disorders and services. *Archives of General Psychiatry, 50,* 85–94.

Resick, P., & Mechanic, M. (1995). Cognitive processing therapy with rape victims. In A. R. Roberts (Ed.), *Crisis intervention and time-limited cognitive treatment* (pp. 182–198). Thousand Oaks, CA: Sage.

Roberts, A. R. (Ed.). (1991). *Contemporary perspectives on crisis intervention and prevention.* Englewood Cliffs, NJ: Prentice-Hall.

Roberts, A. R. (Ed.). (1995). *Crisis intervention and time-limited cognitive treatment.* Thousand Oaks, CA: Sage.

Roberts, A. R. (1996). The epidemiology of acute crisis in American society. In A. R. Roberts (Ed.), *Crisis management and brief treatment* (pp. 13–28). Chicago: Nelson-Hall.

Scott, K., Von Korff, M., Alonso, J., Angermeyer, M. C., Bromet, E., Fayyad, J., . . . Williams, D. (2009). Mental-physical co-morbidity and its relationship to disability: Results from the World Mental Health Surveys. *Psychological Medicine, 39*(1), 33–43.

Shapiro, F. (1998). Eye movement de-sensitization and reprocessing (EMDR): Accelerated information processing and affect-driven constructions. *Crisis Intervention and Time-Limited Interventions, 4,* 145–157.

Shi, L., J. Macinko, B. Starfield, J. Wulu, J. Regan, & R. Politzer. (2003). The relationship between primary care, income inequality, and mortality in the United States, 1980–1995. *Journal of the American Board of Family Practice, 16,* 412–422.

Starfield, B., Shi, L., & Macinko, J. (2005). Contribution of primary care to health systems and health. *Milbank Quarterly, 83,* 457–502.

Tyhurst, J. S. (1957). The role of transition states—including disasters—in mental illness. In The National Research Council (Ed.), *Symposium on social and preventive psychiatry* (pp. 149–172). Washington, DC: Walter Reed Army Institute of Research.

Van der Gaag, J., & Van de Ven, W. (1978). The demand for primary health care. *Medical Care, 16,* 299.

Yeager, K., Cutler, D. L., Svendsen, D., & Sills, G. M. (2013). *Modern community mental health: An interdisciplinary approach.* New York: Oxford University Press.

# 6

# Suicide Crisis Intervention

DARCY HAAG GRANELLO

Suicide crisis intervention occurs within a variety of organizational frame-works, such as domestic violence shelters, 24-hour hotlines, hospitals, home-less shelters, outpatient settings, and crisis intervention units of community mental health centers. Each year, millions of individuals become so distressed or overwhelmed by their life situations or traumatic events that they expe-rience acute crises. These crisis situations can often be the critical turning points in a person's life. According to Roberts (2005), "They can serve as a challenge or opportunity for rapid problem resolution and growth, or as a debilitating event leading to sudden disequilibrium, failed coping, and dys-functional behavior patterns" (p. 3). For some people, the crises can lead to suicidal thoughts, attempts, or completions.

Working with individuals in suicide crisis is one of the most difficult and challenging aspects of crisis intervention work. Every day, crisis intervention specialists and screeners must make suicide risk assessments and determine appropriate intervention strategies for the people they serve. These often life-and-death decisions are typically made with limited time and often with incomplete information, and many of these workers have inadequate train-ing in working with suicidal individuals or insufficient resources to support their work. Suicide crisis interventionists often work with children and adults who have serious mental illnesses or emotional disorders who lead lives char-acterized by recurrent, significant crises and chaos. Many such individuals experience a cascade of crisis events, leading to multiple encounters with differing aspects of the mental health crisis system. For these individuals, the suicide crisis is not the inevitable consequence of the mental disability but the combined impact of multiple, significant factors, including lack of access to mental healthcare, poverty, unstable housing, coexisting substance use, co-occurring health problems, discrimination, and victimization (Substance Abuse and Mental Health Services Administration [SAMHSA], 2009a). It is within this context that some of the most critical and demanding work occurs within the field of crisis intervention.

What is perhaps most surprising—and encouraging—is that in spite of these challenges, there is evidence that suicide crisis intervention helps prevent suicide. Empirical studies across different types of settings and with different types of interventions have demonstrated reduced suicidality among those who make use of the services, although many of the studies have significant design flaws, such as the lack of a control group, that make it difficult to make definitive statements about effectiveness. Although the results of these studies are not universally consistent, most researchers and clinicians would agree with the assessment of the World Health Organization that brief crisis intervention serves an important role in suicide prevention efforts (Fleischmann et al., 2008).

## MAGNITUDE OF THE PROBLEM

Each year in the United States, more than 39,000 people take their own lives, which equates to more than 108 people a day, or a person lost to suicide every 13 minutes (McIntosh & Drapeau, 2014). In the United States, suicide is more than three times as common as homicide (Federal Bureau of Investigation, 2014). Over the past decade, the suicide rate in the United States has been steadily increasing. In 2011 (the latest year for which numbers are available), the suicide rate was 12.7 per 100,000, up from 10.4 per 100,000 in the year 2000 (Suicide.org).

As alarming as these numbers are, focusing only on completed suicides belies the true magnitude of the problem. Each year, an estimated 1.1 million adults have a suicide attempt, translating to an attempt every 38 seconds. Greater still is the number of Americans who seriously consider suicide. In 2008, a national study of suicide risk found that 8.3 million American adults aged 18 or older (3.7% of the population) seriously considered suicide in the past year, and 2.3 million (1% of the population) made a suicide plan (Crosby, Han, Ortega, Parks, & Gfroerer, 2011). Among youth, 17% of high school students reported that they had seriously considered suicide in the past year, and more than 8% reported that they had actually attempted suicide during the same period, with 2.6% having an attempt that required medical attention (Eaton et al., 2007). A 2006 study of college students found that 1 in 10 said that they had "seriously considered suicide" during the past year (American College Health Association, 2007).

Although all races and ages and both genders are affected by suicide, some groups are at higher risk. Males are four times more likely than females to die by suicide, representing 78.8% of all suicide deaths.

However, women are three times more likely than men to attempt suicide, with approximately 59 attempts for every completion (compared with 8 attempts for every completion in men). Whites/Caucasians have suicide rates that are higher than those of any other racial or ethnic group. The Caucasian rate of 15.1 per 100,000 is higher than the rates for Hispanics (5.2 per 100,000), Blacks/African Americans (5.2 per 100,000), American Indians/Alaskan Natives (11.9 per 100,000), or Asian/Pacific Islanders (5.8 per 100,000; Crosby et al., 2011).

Suicide risk differs by age. Among those aged 25 to 34, suicide is the second leading cause of death (behind accidents). Suicides represent the third leading cause of death among 15- to 24-year-olds (nearly 13% of all deaths annually). In addition, young people are significantly more likely to engage in suicide attempts. For every completed suicide in the 15 to 24 age group, it is estimated that there are up to 200 suicide attempts (Arias, Anderson, Kung, Murphy, & Kochanek 2003), compared with between 2 and 4 attempts for every completion in adults older than 65 (Miller, Segal, & Coolidge, 2000).

There are significant gender differences in suicide risk based on age. For example, suicide rates for women peak between the ages of 45 and 54. For men, suicide rates rise with age, with the highest rates occurring after age 65. Suicide rates for males older than 65 are approximately 40 per 100,000, compared with 6 per 100,000 for females. The highest suicide rate for any age group, however, is for Caucasian males older than 85. Their rate of nearly 70 per 100,000 makes this group, by far, the most likely of any demographic group to complete suicide (Granello & Granello, 2007).

Clearly, suicide affects every demographic segment of society, and professionals who work in crisis intervention settings will encounter suicidal individuals regardless of the demographics of the specific segment of the population they serve. No group is immune from the effects of the national burden of suicide.

## CORE PRINCIPLES FOR RESPONDING TO SUICIDE CRISES

In 2009, the Substance Abuse Mental Health Services Administration (2009a) developed practice guidelines for anyone interacting with persons in suicide crisis. Because of the multiple professionals and paraprofessionals who intervene and try to assist, it is important that there be some broad-based crisis standards to ensure that every person in suicide crisis receives intervention that is guided by standards that are consistent with recovery and resilience. The standards have 10 essential values at their core, which are appropriate for suicide crisis intervention, regardless of the specific situation, setting, population, or the credentials of the person offering assistance.

### Standard 1: Avoid Harm

Individuals in suicide crisis can place their own safety, as well as that of crisis responders or others, at risk. Appropriate suicide crisis response establishes both physical and psychological safety for everyone involved. Although physical restraints may sometimes be necessary, these are employed only when there is an urgent need to establish physical safety and there are few viable alternatives to address the immediate risk of significant physical harm.

### Standard 2: Intervene in Person-Centered Ways

Even though working with suicidal individuals may become routine in some settings (e.g., hotlines, emergency rooms), appropriate crisis assistance avoids rote interventions based on diagnosis or institutional historical practices. According to SAMHSA (2009a), "Appropriate interventions seek to understand the individual, his or her unique circumstances and how that individual's personal preferences and goals can be maximally incorporated into the crisis response" (p. 5).

### Standard 3: Share Responsibility

When individuals are in suicide crisis, they often feel out of control and helpless. Interventions that are done *to* the person, rather than *with* him or her, can reinforce these feelings of helplessness. According to SAMHSA (2009a), "An appropriate crisis response seeks to assist the individual in regaining control by considering the individual an active partner in—rather than a passive recipient of—services" (p. 5).

### Standard 4: Address Trauma

All crises, including suicide crises, are intrinsically traumatic events. Further, some aspects of the intervention (e.g., transports in police car, physical restraints, involuntary hospitalization) may impose further trauma. For many people in crises, these ordeals are compounded by a history of trauma, crisis, and chaos. According to SAMHSA, once safety is established, crisis interventionists must address any harm resulting from the crisis or crisis response. In addition, crisis responders should "seek out and incorporate [relevant trauma history] into their approaches" (SAMHSA, 2009a, p. 6).

### Standard 5: Establish Feelings of Personal Safety

People in suicide crises have an urgent need to feel safe. Often their actions, which may seem hostile or agitated to others, stem from attempts at self-protection (Chiles & Strosahl, 2005). According to SAMHSA (2009a), "Assisting the individual in attaining the subjective goal of personal safety requires an understanding of what is needed for that person to experience a sense of security ... and what interventions increase feelings of vulnerability" (p. 6).

## Standard 6: Use a Strengths-Based Approach

All individuals, even those in suicide crises, have personal strengths that can be used to foster a sense of competence. Unfortunately, crisis intervention often focuses almost exclusively on the problems and difficulties in the person's life. According to SAMHSA (2009a), "An appropriate crisis response seeks to identify and reinforce the resources on which an individual can draw, not only to recover from the crisis event, but also help protect against further occurrences" (p. 6).

## Standard 7: Consider the Whole Person

When people are in suicide crisis, they can become defined by their situation or their psychiatric diagnosis. It is important to remember that this crisis is just one aspect of a complex person. People in suicide crisis may have other psychiatric, medical, or social welfare needs, and the services they receive are often compartmentalized, with little connection or communication between providers. They also may have real-world concerns about what is happening to their homes, families, pets, or jobs during their absence or when they are unable to function. Crisis interventionists are reminded to try to gain a more complete understanding of the person in order to help make connections between providers and services that will assist the individual through the crisis period.

## Standard 8: Treat the Person Seeking Assistance as a Credible Source

Because people in suicide crisis can have difficulty providing accurate information about sequencing of events or the specifics of their symptoms, it may be tempting for crisis workers to be skeptical about the information provided, particularly when stories include obvious delusional thoughts or are not well grounded in reality. As a consequence, legitimate complaints and concerns may be disregarded. However, even when the facts are in question, the telling of one's story is an important step in crisis resolution, and it is important not to be dismissive of the person as a credible source of both factual and emotional information (SAMHSA, 2009a).

## Standard 9: Focus on Recovery, Resilience, and Natural Supports

Because suicide crisis intervention, by definition, is time limited and occurs during acute crises and in high-stress situations, it is easy to focus exclusively on the crisis. However, according to the SAMHSA (2009a), standards, "An appropriate crisis response contributes to the individual's larger journey toward recovery and resilience and incorporates these values. ... interventions should preserve dignity, foster a sense of hope, and promote engagement with formal systems and informal resources" (p. 7).

## Standard 10: Move From a Reactive to a Preventative Approach

Although suicide crisis intervention is by necessity reactive, anything that can be done to help put measures in place to reduce the likelihood of recurrence is an important component of the crisis response process. This includes assessing for factors that contributed to the current crisis and addressing any unmet needs that could contribute to a relapse.

The proactive, preventative, self-directed, and holistic aspects of these 10 standards are consistent with the standards developed by advocacy groups to help people in crisis manage the behavioral healthcare system (e.g., National Consensus Statement on Mental Health Recovery). For suicidal individuals, these standards not only promote client safety and welfare but also help focus all interactions on restoring hope, which has been identified as a critical component of suicide crisis intervention (Joiner, 2005). When clients in crisis receive the message that they can survive the crisis and go on to lead meaningful lives, they are significantly more likely to participate in outpatient services after their contact with crisis intervention services (Asarnow et al., 2011; Millstein, 2010).

## SUICIDE RISK ASSESSMENT

As critical as it is for individuals in suicide crisis to receive appropriate, timely, and effective interventions, no effective treatment can begin until a proper suicide risk assessment is completed. However, assessing an individual to determine level of suicide risk is one of the most difficult and challenging experiences a mental health professional can face. Accurate suicide risk assessment is essential to identify acute, modifiable, and treatable risk factors and to help healthcare professionals recognize when clients need more specific interventions to help them manage their lives (Granello, 2010a). Suicide risk assessment is the most critical component of any interaction with suicidal individuals (Chiles & Strosahl, 2005). Given the high prevalence of suicidal behavior in crisis settings, the essential nature of accurate risk assessment, and the impact of suicidal behavior on the mental health treatment community, it is vital that crisis intervention specialists and screeners have access to state-of-the-art information regarding assessment of suicide risk.

Suicide risk assessment requires a complex set of skills, including knowledge, training, and experience. In general, the determination of suicide risk is based on a comprehensive assessment of individual risk factors and warning signs, as well as a careful appraisal of protective factors that can work to help mitigate the risk. Crisis intervention specialists who engage in suicide assessment often rely on formal (structured) and/or informal (unstructured) tests and interview protocols. There are dozens of commercially available assessments for children, adolescents, and adults, as well as assessments for a variety of special populations. In addition, countless informal checklists and interview protocols are readily available. The content and methods used for suicide assessment have been the subject of many books, articles, and websites. Some of the most commonly used suicide risk assessment strategies are discussed in the following pages. However, it is important to note that suicide risk assessment is extremely complex, and individuals who engage in this type of assessment require training and supervision that are beyond the scope of any single text to provide. Thus, this review is intended only as a first step in understanding the role of suicide risk assessment in suicide crisis intervention.

## THE KEY PRINCIPLES OF SUICIDE RISK ASSESSMENT

Before a discussion of the specific content to be included in suicide risk assessment, it is useful to step back to the big picture and consider the principles that guide the process of this type of assessment. Because the nature of suicide risk assessment encourages the assessor to focus on the specific content, details, and minutiae and to ask concrete, direct questions, these core principles are a reminder to draw attention back to the bigger picture, to provide the context for assessment, and a reminder to crisis intervention workers of the foundational principles that will best serve their clients during suicidal crises. These core principles do not override the importance of ascertaining specific risk factors or replace the specific content or method of the assessment. Rather, the two components, content and process, are complementary, and they come together to form a comprehensive risk assessment (Granello & Granello, 2007).

The 12 process principles, or clinical aphorisms, outlined here are based on a comprehensive review of the research and literature, as well as clinical experience, and were first articulated in a text by Granello and Granello (2007) and further described in a subsequent article (Granello, 2010a). The list is not intended to be exhaustive; clinicians may further the discussion by adding more process elements as they become apparent. Further, the ordering of the list is not intended to be hierarchical. In general, the list is intended to bring the discussion back to the core principles that undergird a suicide risk assessment.

## Principle 1: Suicide Risk Assessment of Each Person Is Unique

Assessing a person for suicide risk always includes a comprehensive analysis of risk factors and warning signs. Risk factors can be demographic (e.g., male, over 65, Caucasian), psychological (e.g., untreated mood disorder, personality disorder, substance abuse), cognitive (e.g., rigid cognitive structures, poor problem-solving ability, impulsivity), and/or environmental/situational (e.g., loss of job, breakup of significant relationship, incarceration). They can be proximal (e.g., a sudden crisis or loss) or distal (e.g., an ongoing stressor, such as illness or poverty).

There are more than 100 identified suicide risk factors in the research and literature. Warning signs (e.g., giving away prized possessions, developing a plan, withdrawing from others) also can help determine risk. These risk factors are based on aggregate data. They tell us who in the population is at highest risk. In general, the more warning signs and risk factors an individual has, the higher the risk (Schwartz & Rogers, 2004). Thus, learning these warning signs and risk factors is an essential component of suicide risk assessment training.

The risk factors and warning signs, however, do not give clinicians the whole picture when they are faced with a suicidal individual. For example, it is not particularly helpful to know that, statistically, middle-aged African American females are very unlikely to complete suicide when the middle-aged African American female sitting in front of us has just made an attempt. Persons who do not "fit" the profile can, in reality, be at imminent risk, and two persons with similar risk profiles can be at very different levels of risk. Suicide risk manifests itself differently in different people, and all of the checklists and formal and informal assessments cannot ever take into account the uniqueness of the person and his or her risk profile. It is for this reason that when conducting suicide risk assessments, it is vitally important to learn as much as possible about the individual, from as many sources of information as possible, to determine how the risk factors, warning signs, and protective factors come together in a unique way for that person and how they manifest themselves in an individual level of risk.

## Principle 2: Suicide Risk Assessment Is Complex and Challenging

Persons who are suicidal typically do not want to die; they simply want their pain to end (Granello & Granello, 2007). Problem-solving and coping are compromised by cognitive rigidity and strong emotions until the only option to stop the pain appears to be suicide. The fact that most suicidal people feel ambiguous about suicide and death makes suicide assessment incredibly difficult. However, the ambiguity also is the best hope for survival because it is what allows intervention to occur.

When people feel suicidal, they often cannot say for certain whether they are going to kill themselves. When asked, they may not be able to say whether or not they will be able to stay safe from self-harm. Even if they do know this with certainty, those feelings are likely to change from day to day and from moment to moment. Thus, anyone trying to assess for suicide attempts to predict risk from what are often vague and tumultuous emotional states and irrational cognitions *that even the suicidal individual does not fully understand.* The complexity of this task is enormous. Suicide risk assessment is successful only to the degree that suicide is foreseeable, and all of these features make predicting suicide risk extraordinarily challenging.

## Principle 3: Suicide Risk Assessment Is an Ongoing Process

Suicide risk is not fixed, and suicide risk assessment is a process, not an event (Simon, 2002). Suicidal thoughts and behaviors are highly unstable, and completed suicide assessments quickly can become obsolete. Even among clients who are not considered to be at elevated risk, suicide risk assessment is an important component of treatment, especially at times of impending transition, heightened stress, or changes in environmental supports (Berman, Jobes, & Silverman, 2006). It is a commonly held myth that asking someone about suicide will cause him or her to consider suicide. The reality, however, is that it is important to begin the discussion of suicide with all clients, and asking about suicide does not elevate risk (Schwartz & Rogers, 2004). In fact, randomized studies have demonstrated that talking about suicide to high-risk teenagers actually lowers their distress (Gould et al., 2005).

Frequent risk assessment also is useful in differentiating between immediate and ongoing risk. It is not unusual to encounter clients in crisis settings who are at continual low-level risk for suicide. However, for most individuals, an acute suicide crisis tends to be a relatively time-limited event. When assessing suicide, it may be helpful to ask, "Did you feel suicidal this morning? Yesterday? Last week?" to help uncover whether suicidal thoughts are ongoing or acute.

## Principle 4: Suicide Risk Assessment Errs on the Side of Caution

Perhaps this principle is so obvious that it does not bear inclusion. Or perhaps it may get overlooked in the process of assessment precisely because it is so obvious. There are two types of potential errors to be made in suicide risk assessment. A false positive in this context is when a person is judged to be suicidal when he or she is not. False positives are relatively common in wide-scale screening efforts, and individual and more careful assessment is required of those who come up positive in a general screening (Sher, 2004). False positives exact a burden in time and resources and should not be taken lightly. The second type of error that can be made is a false negative (e.g., believing someone is not suicidal when he or she is), and this represents a very dangerous possibility. It is impossible to know the rate of false negatives in general screenings, but one study found that a screening instrument failed to identify 14% of actively suicidal individuals in a veteran population (Herman, 2006). Ultimately, the consequences for a false negative error can be fatal.

## Principle 5: Suicide Risk Assessment Is Collaborative

Suicide risk assessment uses a team approach whenever possible. Multiple perspectives enrich the assessment and provide the best standard of care. They help reduce the possibility that a single crisis worker will miss an important piece of information or make a wrong decision. There are three important components of the team approach: collaboration, corroboration, and consultation.

*Collaboration* is the act of working together with a sense of urgency and commitment, for a shared objective, in this case safety from self-harm. Collaboration can occur with a wide variety of people and agencies, including other treatment professionals, school personnel, families, and community organizations. The key is that clinicians recognize that keeping someone safe is a responsibility that works best when shared and when information flows freely among all who can help. It is important to note that client safety concerns override issues of confidentiality, although it is therapeutically important, whenever possible, to have clients agree to the collaborative approach. If confidentiality must be broken, appropriate documentation should be made (Shea, 2002).

*Corroboration* of suicide risk with friends and family can be extremely important to understand the level of risk, particularly in settings where the clinician has limited interaction with the client and does not have a history against which to judge current functioning. For example, in emergency room settings, family may be able to provide information on changes in mood or behavior or availability of means. Inconsistencies between the client's self-report and the report of corroborating sources can highlight or clarify risk (Shea, 2002).

*Consultation* with professional colleagues is common practice in suicide assessment and is always advised when treating suicidal individuals (Packman & Harris, 1998). Edwin Shneidman (1981), often called the father of suicidology, cautioned that there is no instance in a therapist's professional life when consultation with a colleague is more important than in the case of a highly suicidal person. Consultation enhances both therapeutic care and legal protection. Consultation must be well documented in order for it to be legally recognized (Shea, 2002). Supervision is a more formalized and structured type of consultation, and clinicians with limited experience in suicide assessment should always make use of supervision from a more experienced colleague when faced with a potentially suicidal client (Shea, 2002).

## Principle 6: Suicide Risk Assessment Relies on Clinical Judgment

Countless formal and informal tests, checklists, and interview protocols for suicide exist, but none has yet been found to accurately determine whether or not a person will attempt or complete suicide. Uncertainty is an inevitable part of suicide assessment (Simon, 2006). Training and experience can help crisis intervention workers develop clinical judgment to master—or at least manage—that uncertainty. Clinical judgment allows clinicians to interpret all of the existing data and information against the backdrop of their training, experience, and knowledge (Silverman, Berman, Bongar, Litman, & Maris, 1998). Clinicians with limited experience in suicide assessment should never rely on their own clinical judgment but instead should seek consultation and supervision from more experienced therapists. Nevertheless, even clinicians with years of experience in the assessment of suicidal persons at times question whether they have made the right choices or done all they could (e.g., Meichenbaum, 2005), again highlighting the need for ongoing consultation.

## Principle 7: Suicide Assessment Takes All Threats, Warning Signs, and Risk Factors Seriously

Individuals who attempt or complete suicide often express their intent to others. In fact, more than 90% of adolescents who complete suicide give clues (either verbal or other warning signs) before they attempt. About one third of people who attempt suicide will make another attempt within the year, and about 10% to 12% of those who threaten or attempt go on to complete suicide, typically within 5 to 10 years of the first attempt (Runeson, 2001). As many as 20% of calls to suicide hotlines are from friends and family members who are concerned about what to do when someone they love threatens suicide (Mishara, 1995). In spite of these numbers, it is sometimes challenging to convince others, even mental health professionals, to take threats and attempts seriously. Suicide threats and attempts are often associated with tremendous consequences in terms of personal suffering, the anguish of family and friends, and economic costs of hospitalization and treatment (DeQuincy,

2006). Perhaps it is not surprising, then, that family and friends may want to minimize the threat (Samy, 1995).

Nevertheless, it is essential that crisis interventionists take every threat or warning sign seriously and complete a more comprehensive risk assessment whenever there is reason for concern. Farberow and Shneidman (1961) conceptualized all suicide threats and attempts as a cry for help, likening them to a drowning person waving his or her hands in the air and needing immediate assistance. It may be tempting to minimize these threats, particularly with those who make frequent attempts or threats, are frequent callers to hotlines or users of emergency services, or who engage in self-harm (Comtois, 2002). These suicidal threats may be dismissed as manipulative (Dear, Thomson, & Hills, 2000). However, what is clear is that people who threaten suicide do so because they are desperately trying to seek the attention of someone who can help, and dismissing these threats as manipulative only encourages them to engage in more harmful behaviors in order to receive the assistance they need (Granello, 2010a).

## Principle 8: Suicide Risk Assessment Asks the Tough Questions

Sometimes, when people are considering suicide, they will speak in euphemisms or veiled threats, such as "They won't have me to kick around anymore" or "They'll be happier when I'm gone." It is important that clinicians not imitate this approach but instead ask direct and specific questions, and use words such as *suicide* and *death*. This not only limits the possibility of miscommunication but also sends a powerful message that it is okay to talk about suicidal thoughts with the clinician. Shea (2002) argued that talking about suicide and death in a calm, frank way can be a relief for people who recognize that there is one safe place where their "horrible secret" can be shared (p. 120). The American Psychiatric Association guidelines highlight the importance of direct inquiry into suicidal thoughts, plans, and behaviors (Jacobs & Brewer, 2006). The recommended approach is asking straightforward questions with the stated goal of trying to understand the individual in order to help relieve his or her suffering (Schwartz & Rogers, 2004). Open-ended questions that allow for complexity and ambiguity in the answers also are important, as many suicidal persons do not unequivocally want to die and therefore may answer "no" to a closed-ended question. For example, the question "How do you feel about living and dying?" is typically more productive than "Do you intend to kill yourself?" (International Association for Suicide Prevention, 2006). Finally, it is important to note that the use of just one "gatekeeping" question on intake—such as "Have you ever felt suicidal?" or "Do you feel suicidal now?"—may not be sufficient. As many as 44% of persons with past histories of suicide attempts answer "no" to a general gatekeeping question regarding past attempts and therefore may be missed for follow-up questioning (Barber, Marzuk, Leon, & Portera, 2001). Multiple questions are needed, and inconsistencies between self-report and presentation may provide a clue that further investigation or collateral information is required (Jacobs & Brewer, 2006).

## Principle 9: Suicide Risk Assessment Is Treatment

The moment a crisis intervention worker begins to assess someone for suicide, treatment has begun. Assessment, when done correctly, begins to identify themes, patterns, and problems that will become the basis for intervention. Even the process of assessment itself can begin the healing and start suicidal individuals on the path of change. A major part of suicide assessment is emotional ventilation, or allowing people to tell their stories and feel heard and understood (Westefeld et al., 2000). Yalom (1975) noted that the telling of one's story in and of itself is curative. Feeling heard and understood, experiencing empathy from another human being, and feeling valued (unconditional positive regard) are cornerstones of Carl Rogers's client-centered therapy, and most clinicians would agree that although they may not be sufficient conditions for change, they are valuable nonetheless. Many people tell stories of having their suicidal thoughts or feelings negated, ridiculed, or minimized by well-intentioned others (e.g., "Don't be ridiculous, you have so much to live for!" or "There's other fish in the sea. He's not worth it"). Clinicians who help those at suicide risk feel heard and understood through active listening help foster a therapeutic relationship that is the cornerstone of effective treatment. In fact, research has found that one of the most significant factors in assessing suicide risk and determining the prognosis for success of suicide interventions is the quality of the therapeutic relationship (Bongar, 2002). The therapeutic relationship plays a major role in determining a client's willingness to seek help, and clients indicate that a strong alliance with a helping professional has a significant impact on helping them through a serious emotional crisis.

## Principle 10: Suicide Risk Assessment Tries to Uncover the Underlying Message

There are as many reasons for suicide as there are suicidal individuals. This is part of what makes assessment so complicated and why the risk factors can provide only general information. However, each suicide has an underlying message, and a completed suicide means that the message was not received (Portes, Sandhu, & Longwell-Grice, 2002). Uncovering the message is an important component of suicide risk assessment because the message will determine, in large part, the intervention. Although there are many explanations for what brings a person to the brink of death, most can be summed up in three major categories: communication, control, or avoidance.

For some individuals, suicidal threats and attempts are a form of *communication*, providing a way to tell others just how unbearable their psychological pain has become (Nock & Kessler, 2006). Sometimes people who are suicidal are unable to express their pain in direct ways, and their interactions may come across as angry, hostile, sarcastic, or withdrawn. Others express their pain in very direct ways yet do not receive the assistance they need to help them manage the pain. Still others find that as conventional methods of communication become less effective and others no longer respond to verbal cries for help, suicidal threats and behaviors increase (Bonnar & McGee, 1977).

*Control* can be a powerful motivator, and suicide can be used as a method to control one's own fate or the actions of others. At the moment of completing suicide, individuals may have a sense that they are in control of their own world, have control over their own destiny, and may even believe they can influence the destiny of others. Attempting or threatening suicide to make others respond in a particular way or to seize control when the world seems chaotic and unsafe are examples of suicidal messages of control.

*Avoidance* of enduring or impending physical or emotional pain or suffering is a third motivating factor. Persons who contemplate or attempt suicide typically do so when their other strategies for solving a problem have been exhausted and they have no more ideas for how to alleviate their unbearable psychological pain. The common link among people who kill themselves for avoidance is the belief that suicide is the only solution to a set of overwhelming feelings or anticipated pain. The attraction of suicide is that it will finally end these intolerable feelings.

## Principle 11: Suicide Risk Assessment Is Done in a Cultural Context

Statistically, suicide in the United States remains primarily a Caucasian male phenomenon. However, there is much diversity within the Caucasian male population, and it would be unwise to assume a homogeneity that does not exist. In addition, it is extremely dangerous and ill-advised to ignore the suicide risk in other cultural or ethnic groups. Suicide rates are high in several ethnic minority groups and are increasing dramatically in others. Other groups (e.g., Latina women) have low rates of completion but high rates of attempts (Granello & Granello, 2007). When assessing risk, there are cultural differences in suicide attitudes, levels of acceptability, and appropriate intervention strategies (Range et al., 1999). Some cultures have strong cultural and/or religious injunctions against suicide. Although this can be a protective factor, it also can prevent individuals from reaching out and seeking help. Other cultures have strong beliefs about the mental health system and, in general, underutilize available services.

Although extremely little is known from a research perspective about culturally appropriate suicide assessment, it is clear that it is important to understand the specific cultural group or subgroup with which the client identifies, how this group views suicide, and the degree to which the individual has internalized these beliefs. Without clear multicultural guidelines for suicide assessment, what remains clear is that culturally sensitive risk assessment relies on cultural empathy and cultural sensitivity (Wendler & Matthews, 2006).

## Principle 12: Suicide Risk Assessment Is Documented

Client suicides are among the most frequent malpractice claims against mental health professionals, and the single most important thing clinicians can do to protect themselves against litigation is to document their work (Simon, 2002). Courts recognize that not all suicides are preventable, and they typically support clinicians who make consistent and systematic efforts to keep their clients safe. The only way for the legal system to determine these efforts (or lack thereof) is through documentation. According to the law, a suicide risk assessment that is not documented did not happen.

## THE CONTENT OF SUICIDE RISK ASSESSMENT

Describing the content of what should be included in a suicide risk assessment is a more difficult task than outlining the underlying principles. That is because more than 100 risk factors have been identified in the research and literature, and there is no universally agreed-upon format in place for the content of what should be included in a suicide risk assessment. Clearly, there are critical differences based on both setting and client demographics. Several models for determining content of suicide risk assessments are presented here, with the caution that crisis intervention specialists must always seek training, experience, and supervision before implementing any suicide risk assessment.

The risk factors that have the most empirical support include the following:

- Male
- Single
- Widowed
- Divorced/separated
- Elderly
- Psychiatric illness
  o Depression*

o Schizophrenia
o Alcoholism*
o Drug addiction*
o Personality disorder (especially with lability of mood), impulsivity, aggression
o Anxiety disorders
• Psychosis*
• Hopelessness/helplessness*
• Previous suicide attempt(s)/self-harm*
• Social isolation*/rejection by others
• Physical illness (life-threatening/chronic/debilitating)*
• Unemployed/retired
• Family history of affective disorder, alcoholism, or suicide*
• Bereavement/loss (recent); preoccupation with anniversary or traumatic loss*
• Childhood bereavement
• Social classes at the extremes (either the poorest or the wealthiest)
• Family destabilization due to loss, personal abuse, violence, sexual abuse*
• Recent trauma (physical/psychological)*
• Specific suicide plan formulated*
• Exhibits one or more uncharacteristic intense negative emotions*
• Preoccupation with earlier abuse*

Warning signs
• Giving away prized possessions/putting personal affairs in order*
• Radical changes in characteristic behaviors or moods*

*It has been suggested by Gilliland and James (1997) that individuals should be treated as high-risk if four to five or more of the factors shown with an asterisk are manifested. Clinicians are reminded to always use clinical judgment in assessing risk.

In general, a suicide risk assessment uses an interview format that does more than just ask a few simple questions. At a minimum, clients are led through a series of topic areas that include the following (Granello & Granello, 2007):

• Suicidal intent—present/recent thoughts about killing oneself. Level of intent is more predictive of suicide attempt/completion than the specific lethality of the plan.
• Details of the suicide plan—the more specific, the more dangerous.
• The means by which the person plans to complete suicide (gun, hanging, overdose, etc.). Be sure to consider the lethality of the means (a gun is more lethal than ingesting several over-the-counter aspirin). However, the person's belief about the lethality of the method is more important

than the actual lethality. If the person believes that aspirin will be lethal, and doesn't die, he or she may try again using a more lethal method.

- Accessibility of those means to the suicidal person (how easy it is for the person to obtain the means). In other words, the person's threatening to shoot him- or herself is less of an immediate threat if he or she does not have access to a gun, versus someone who says, "I will shoot myself using my dad's pistol, which is in his dresser drawer, and the bullets that are in the garage."
- History of suicidal thoughts and attempts (including self-harm).
- Stability of the current mood (e.g., did the person feel suicidal yesterday? Last week? This morning?).
- Family history of suicide attempts or completions as well as family history of mental disorders.
- Client's mental state, including cognitive rigidity, concentration problems, agitation, anger, and impulsivity.
- Assessment of warning signs and specific risk factors.
- Willingness/ability to comply with emergency/safety procedures.

In addition to these specific topic areas, it may be useful to assess the level of psychological pain the person is enduring, as well as the self-hatred or self-loathing that makes choosing to live difficult. Most clinicians agree that understanding the level of *hopelessness* is critical to understanding risk because individuals in severe psychological pain who have no reason to believe their lives will ever improve are at high risk for suicide.

## American Association of Suicidology

The American Association for Suicidology (AAS) model for assessing suicide risk uses the mnemonic "IS PATH WARM" (2006). This phrase is intended to remind anyone working with a potentially suicidal individual to assess the critical areas of risk, including the following:

- Ideation—threatened or communicated
- Substance abuse—excessive or increased
- Purposelessness—no reason for living
- Anxiety—agitation, insomnia
- Trapped—feeling there is no way out
- Hopelessness
- Withdrawing—from friends, family, society
- Anger (uncontrolled)—rage, seeking revenge
- Recklessness—risky acts, unthinking
- Mood changes (dramatic)

As is the case with all suicide mnemonics and scales, the purpose of "IS PATH WARM" is to augment clinical judgment. In other words, no matter the outcome or prescribed intervention noted by any suicide assessment aid, including this one, it is up to the clinician to ensure his or her client's safety (Juhnke, Granello, & Lebrón-Striker, 2007).

## American Psychiatric Association

The American Psychiatric Association ([APA] 2003) developed practice guidelines for assessing suicide risk, including a sequence of questions that might be used within each broad category (see the APA guidelines for a complete listing of these questions). In general, APA recommends assessment of the following:

- Current presentation of suicidality
  o Suicidal thoughts, plans, behaviors, and intent
  o Mental state, including hopelessness, impulsivity, anhedonia, panic, or anxiety
  o Substance use/abuse
  o Thoughts, plans, or intentions of violence toward others
  o Reasons for living/plans for the future
- Psychiatric illnesses (current or past)
  o In particular, mood disorders, schizophrenia, anxiety disorders, personality disorders, and substance use
- History
  o Previous attempts or other self-harm
  o Current or past medical diagnoses
  o Family history of suicide attempts or mental illness
- Psychosocial situation
  o Acute or chronic psychosocial stressors or crises
  o Difficulties with employment, living situation, social supports
  o Cultural or religious beliefs about death or suicide
  o Individual strengths or vulnerabilities
- Coping skills
  o Personality traits
  o Past responses to stress
  o Capacity for reality testing
  o Ability to tolerate psychological pain and satisfy psychological needs

## Substance Abuse and Mental Health Services Administration

SAMHSA (2009b) also uses a mnemonic to help emergency personnel engage in a five-step triage for suicide risk assessment. Called the SAFE-T (Suicide Assessment, Five-Step Evaluation, and Triage), this model is more global than simply looking for risk factors; it reminds those who work with suicidal individuals of the steps in the process of assessment:

1. Identify risk factors, including those that can be modified to reduce risk.
2. Identify protective factors, including those that can be enhanced.
3. Conduct suicide inquiry, including suicidal thoughts, plans, behaviors, and intent.
4. Determine risk/intervention level, including appropriate intervention to address and reduce risk.
5. Document the assessment of risk, rationale, intervention, and follow-up.

In general, the point of all of these risk assessments is to remind those who work with potentially suicidal individuals to complete—and document—a suicide risk assessment with all of their clients. Although no specific risk assessment strategy has been found to be superior to others in identifying persons who will attempt or complete suicide, the large overlap of key content areas in each of these models highlights the need for risk assessment strategies that include these essential areas of inquiry. Crisis intervention specialists who work in settings with specific clientele (e.g., children, adolescents, LGBT individuals, veterans, persons with disabilities) may find that there are population-specific categories of risk that should be incorporated in addition to those highlighted in the models included here.

## BRIEF INTERVENTIONS
## WITH INDIVIDUALS IN SUICIDE CRISIS

There is a widely held belief among suicidologists that most suicidal individuals do not want to die but simply cannot imagine continuing to live in their current state of psychological turmoil (Granello & Granello, 2007). In fact, suicidal crises are typically the result of a temporary, reversible, and ambivalent state, and interventions with suicidal clients are based on the premise that the suicidal crisis, if successfully navigated, need not be fatal (Granello, 2010b). Individuals who receive appropriate treatment for mental disorders have the best likelihood of recovery (Bongar, 2002).

Although there are ongoing attempts to develop evidence-based best practice models for assessment and intervention, at present, validated assessment and intervention strategies are limited, particularly in crisis intervention settings. In general, working with clients in suicidal crisis includes many levels of care, including inpatient, short- and long-term outpatient, day treatment, hotline or electronic communication, and emergency intervention. Models and algorithms are available to assist clinicians in determining appropriate levels of care. These models vary, but they generally include (a) conducting meaningful assessments, (b) developing treatment plans, (c) determining levels of care, (d) engaging in psychiatric evaluations for medications, (e) increasing access to treatment, (f) developing risk management plans, (g) managing clinician liability, and (h) assessing outcomes. (For more information on determining levels of care, see Bongar, 2002.)

In general, interventions with suicidal clients are based on a two-tier approach. The first tier is short-term stabilization, which is the focus of crisis intervention work. Crisis interventionists working with clients in suicidal crises use very specific acute management strategies to keep clients alive and invested in counseling long enough to move to further treatment that allows them to explore the core problems underlying suicidality. The goal of the first tier of intervention is to prevent death or injury and restore the client to a state of equilibrium. The second tier of intervention addresses the client's underlying psychological vulnerability, mental disorders, stressors, and risk factors, which is typically done through longer-term outpatient counseling. However, it is not until clients are stabilized using crisis intervention strategies that the ongoing work of counseling can begin (Granello, 2010b).

## CRISIS STABILIZATION

The goals of immediate intervention with suicidal intervention are based on models of crisis intervention (e.g., Aguilera, 1998; Greenstone & Leviton, 2002; James & Gilliland, 2001), with specific strategies and techniques that are unique to this population. In general, an expanded version of Roberts and Ottens's (2005) seven-step model for crisis intervention is recommended (Granello & Granello, 2007). This model has crisis theory as the theoretical foundation and research and practice from the field of suicidology to ground the specific intervention strategies offered within each step. Thus, the seven-step model provides an overall strategy for counselors in their work with suicidal clients, and most mental health counselors who have worked in crisis intervention will recognize this general approach. The overall model is provided here; details and examples of specific strategies developed for each stage of the model can be found in an article by Granello (2010b).

The overall suicide crisis intervention model is broad enough to fit with many types of individuals in many different settings. However, these strategies are intended only as a guide, and the needs of any individual may vary significantly from the steps or interventions discussed herein. For example, specific developmental, multicultural, or cognitive limitations of clients may shape the implementation of these strategies. Further, although these steps in the process are presented in a linear fashion, as with all stage models, the reality of implementation often means that there is much overlap and movement between the steps. Importantly, these steps *do not replace existing models and algorithms for suicide assessment and intervention* but are intended to provide specific strategies to help implement traditional intervention guidelines.

## Step 1: Assess Lethality

The first and most important step in working with suicidal persons is accurate assessment. Although this assessment may occur slowly, over the course of the entire discussion, with more information becoming apparent as the person tells his or her story, a general understanding of level of lethality will be important information for guiding the process. Suicide risk assessment protocols are used to help understand lethality. An individual in suicide emergency, for example, has a clear intent to die whenever the opportunity first presents itself (Sommers-Flanagan & Sommers-Flanagan, 1995). As a general stipulation, crisis interventionists should approach all situations of suicide risk as a potential suicide emergency until they obtain sufficient information to be convinced otherwise (Kleespies, Deleppo, Gallagher, & Niles, 1999). Included within this step are the need to ensure safety (of the suicidal person as well as others) and to employ the agency's existing suicide emergency plans, when appropriate.

## Step 2: Establish Rapport

Research has demonstrated that one of the most significant factors in assessing suicide risk and determining prognosis for success of suicide interventions is the quality of the therapeutic relationship (Bongar, 2002). Paulson and Everall (2003) found that suicidal adolescents stated that the quality of the therapeutic relationship was one of the most helpful aspects of treatment. Conversely, research also has found that a *lack of a therapeutic relationship* actually has a negative impact on outcomes for clients in suicidal crises (Maltsberger, 1986). Basic counseling skills and the Rogerian core conditions help convey a genuine, caring, and nonjudgmental therapeutic stance (Chiles & Strosahl, 2005). Specific strategies in this step include staying with the client, managing countertransference, normalizing the topic, conveying calm, moving from an authoritarian to a collaborative approach, and supporting the decision for help-seeking.

## Step 3: Listen to the Story

Individuals who are suicidal may have tried to express their suicidal thoughts and behaviors to others. In fact, research shows that as many as 70% of individuals who died by suicide communicated their suicidal intent to someone else in the week prior to their death. That number is even higher for adolescents and young adults, perhaps as high as 85% (US Department of Health and Human Services, 2004). Yet research clearly demonstrates that most suicidal statements are met with less than helpful responses, most commonly silence, ridicule, or judgment (Suicide Prevention Resource Center, 2005). Allowing suicidal individuals to tell their stories and fully explore what led to their suicide risk is, in and of itself, therapeutic (Yalom, 1975). Williams and Morgan (1994) noted that the skilled clinician will recognize "the immense value of reaching out and listening to resolve a suicidal crisis, no matter how complex and apparently insoluble the individual's problems might seem" (p. 16). Specific strategies in this step include listening, understanding, and validating; slowing things down; creating a therapeutic window; categorizing the problems; and identifying the message.

## Step 4: Manage the Feelings

People who are in suicidal crisis often feel overwhelmed by their emotions. Because of the ambiguity that is frequently part of the crisis (e.g., not wanting to die but wanting the pain to end), it is not unusual for many different emotions to occur simultaneously. Some common themes have been identified regarding the state of mind of suicidal persons (Shneidman, 1981). These include acute perturbation or an exacerbation of the already-troubled state of mind; increased negative emotions, such as self-loathing, guilt, or shame; cognitive restriction, or the inability to engage in problem-solving; and focused attention on the thought of suicide as a way to end the emotional pain. To help individuals in suicide crisis manage their feelings, specific strategies include encouraging emotional ventilation, acknowledging the psych-ache, and teaching tolerance of negative emotions.

## Step 5: Explore Alternatives

There is much evidence that people in suicidal crisis have diminished problem-solving skills. During a suicidal crisis, people engage in *selective abstraction*, using a set of filters to make negative generalizations about the world and about themselves (Granello & Granello, 2007). People who are suicidal often fail to recognize the reasons they have for living or the potential alternatives to their current situation. Exploring alternatives is *not the same thing* as providing advice or answers. Included in this step are the strategies of minimizing the power struggle; establishing a problem-solving framework; engaging the social support system, as appropriate; restoring hope; and assisting the individual to envision possibilities and develop resilience.

Exploring alternatives is critical, but it is also critical that this not be done too early in the process. In other words, if a clinician moves the person in crisis too quickly to this stage, before a relationship is fully established and before the person has a chance to tell his or her story or express emotions, he or she may feel minimized, rushed, and not yet ready to engage in problem-solving. Timing is important.

## Step 6: Use Behavioral Strategies

There is clearly a continuum of risk with people in suicidal crisis, and a comprehensive suicide risk assessment will help determine risk level and necessary level of care. The key is to develop and implement an individualized comprehensive plan. For example, if there is to be ongoing risk assessment, how often and by whom will this be done? Is there a need for a psychiatric evaluation to help treat an underlying mental disorder? If the treatment is to be done in an outpatient setting, should the number of types of treatment sessions be increased? All these questions and more must be addressed in a comprehensive action plan.

In general, the development of a short-term positive action plan and a safety plan are the recommended strategies. These plans are generally preferred over the more traditional no-suicide contracts, which have no empirical evidence to support their use. Safety plans provide suicidal individuals with specific, detailed, and individualized strategies for what they should do if they become suicidal in the future (see Stanley & Brown, 2012, for a more detailed discussion of the use of safety plans in emergency departments).

## Step 7: Follow-Up

The type of follow-up needed will depend on the level of risk and the action plan implemented. In general, all individuals at increased risk for suicide require aggressive and frequent follow-up care (Macdonald, Pelling, & Granello, 2009). Research has shown that during a suicidal crisis, persons in the low to moderate risk category benefit most from (a) intensive follow-up, including case management, telephone contacts, and possibly home visits; (b) a clear safety plan for the individual to follow if the risk escalates; and (c) short-term cognitive-behavioral therapy to improve problem-solving and reduce suicidal ideation (although this has not been demonstrated as effective for long-term risk reduction).

Multiple studies have investigated the effectiveness of follow-up contact after brief interventions during suicide crises. Intensive case management is the general recommended approach, and outreach after the crisis has been demonstrated to lessen subsequent suicide risk (Leitner, Barr, & Hobby, 2008). Telephone calls (e.g., De Leo & Heller, 2007), follow-up home visits (e.g., Roberts & Everly, 2006), and postcards (Carter, Clover, Whyte, Dawson, & D'Este, 2005) have all been demonstrated to be effective methods to decrease suicide ideation and improve compliance with follow-up care. More recently, post–acute care text messaging was used in a pilot study with positive results. Individuals who received four text messages in the days following discharge believed that the strategy had a positive effect on their overall health, and most people in the sample believed it reduced their suicidal ideation (Berrrouiguet, Gravey, Le Galudec, Alavi, & Walter, 2014).

Regardless of contact mechanism, it is clear that follow-up is a critical component of –post–crisis intervention care for suicidal individuals.

Finally, at the conclusion of the suicide crisis (or periodically in settings or agencies that have frequent encounters with suicidal individuals), it is important for staff to assess the strategies employed to determine if changes to existing protocols need to be made. A candid after-the-fact assessment can provide an excellent opportunity to improve future interventions.

## CURRENT STATE OF THE RESEARCH AND NEXT STEPS

Working with individuals in suicide crisis is difficult and challenging, and there are significant barriers to overcome when providing this type of care. Nevertheless, there is evidence that these types of interventions show promise for managing individuals in acute crisis. In several large-scale studies, suicide hotlines have been demonstrated to be a cost-effective strategy to help reduce suicide risk. In one study, callers to suicide hotlines reported that they believed the contact had an immediate positive effect, and the interaction left them feeling less suicidal, alone, afraid, and anxious and more hopeful, supported, and wanting to live (Coveney, Pollock, Armstrong, & Moore, 2012). Another study found that callers had significant reductions in negative affect and intent to die, which persisted at follow-up. Importantly, this same study found that among seriously suicidal individuals (e.g., those who had a prior attempt or a plan when they called), 11.6% reported at follow-up that the call prevented them from harming or killing themselves (Gould, Kalafat, Munfakh, & Kleinman, 2007). In another study, 100 taped calls to an adolescent suicide hotline found significant decreases in suicidality and significant improvements in the mental states of the callers over the course of the call (King, Nurcombe, Bickman, Hides, & Reid, 2003).

The results of studies of suicide crisis intervention in emergency departments are less consistent. Nevertheless, several studies show great promise for short-term interventions in this setting. Several studies have demonstrated the value of these types of interventions for increasing compliance with aftercare for suicidal adolescents (see Brent et al., 2013, for a review), and at least one pilot study demonstrated positive results with a single-session family-based crisis intervention program (Wharff, Ginnis, & Ross, 2012).

According to the SAMHSA (2009a) guidelines for working with individuals in suicide crisis, the most critical and immediate next step is the development of organizational infrastructures, across emergency departments, psychiatric programs, foster care, and community agencies and resources, that allow people in suicide crisis to receive the best possible care. The recommendations include the following:

- Staff that is appropriately training and has demonstrated competence with the population served
- Staff and staff leadership that understand, accept, and promote concepts of recovery and resilience and the balance between protection from harm and personal dignity
- Staff that has timely access to critical information, through effective access to reliable records, about the individual in crisis, including health and psychiatric history, advance directives, or crisis/safety plans
- Staff that is afforded the flexibility and resources, including time, to establish truly individualized, person-centered plans to address the immediate crisis and beyond
- Staff that is empowered to work in partnership with the individual being served and is encouraged to implement novel solutions
- An organizational culture that does not isolate its programs or staff from the surrounding community
- Coordinated services with outside services and active collaboration with referral organizations
- Rigorous performance-improvement programs that use data in meaningful ways to refine the crisis care and programs provided to individuals at suicide risk

Crises are part of the life experience of many individuals, and for the more than 1 million adults in the United States who have a suicide attempt each year, contact with suicide crisis intervention may be part of the lived experience as well. Although this work is clearly complex and challenging, it also has great potential to be incredibly effective and extremely rewarding. When a person is moved from a suicide crisis back to a stable life in the community, the positive effects are enormous, for the individual, the family, and the community at large. As much as 7% of the US population (approximately 22 million people) state that they have been exposed to a suicide death within the last year, with 1.1% of the sample in a large national study stating that they have lost an immediate family member to suicide within the last year (Crosby & Sacks, 2002). Clearly, the important work that occurs in suicide crisis intervention has the potential to ripple outward, beyond the individuals directly involved, and into the larger community.

REFERENCES

Aguilera, D. C. (1998). *Crisis intervention: Theory and methodology* (8th ed.). St Louis: Mosby.

American Association of Suicidology. (2006). *IS PATH WARM?* Retrieved from http://www.suicidology. org/c/document_library/get_ file?folderId=232&name=DLFE-31. pdf

American College Health Association. (2007). *American College Health Association—National College*

Health Assessment: Reference group data report—fall 2006. Baltimore, MD: Author.

American Psychiatric Association. (2003). Practice guideline for the assessment and treatment of patients with suicidal behaviors. Arlington, VA: American Psychiatric Publishing.

Arias, E., Anderson, R. N., Kung, H. C., Murphy, S. L., & Kochanek, K. D. (2003). Deaths: Final data for 2001. National Vital Statistics Reports, 52(3). Hyattsville MD: National Center for Health Statistics.

Asarnow, J. R., Baraff, L. J., Berk, M., Grob, C. S., Devich-Navarro, M., Suddath, R., . . . Tang, L. (2011). An emergency department intervention for linking pediatric suicidal patients to follow-up mental health treatment. Psychiatric Services, 62, 1303–1309. doi:10.1176/appi.ps.62.11.1303

Barber, M. E., Marzuk, P. M., Leon, A. C., & Portera, L. (2001). Gate questions in psychiatric interviewing: The case of suicide assessment. Journal of Psychiatric Research, 35, 67–69.

Berman, A. L., Jobes, D. A., & Silverman, M. M. (2006). Adolescent suicide: Assessment and intervention (2nd ed.). Washington, DC: American Psychological Association.

Berrrouiguet, S., Gravey, M., Le Galudec, M., Alavi, Z., & Walter, M. (2014). Post-acute text messaging outcome for suicide prevention: A pilot study. Psychiatry Research, 217, 154–157. doi:10.1016/j.psychres.2014.02.034

Bongar, B. (2002). Risk management: Prevention and postvention. In B. Bongar (Ed)., The suicidal patient: Clinical and legal standards of care (2nd ed., pp. 213–261). Washington, DC: American Psychological Association.

Bonnar, J. W., & McGee, R. K. (1977). Suicidal behavior as a form of communication in married couples. Suicide and Life-Threatening Behavior, 7, 7–16.

Brent, D. A., McMakin, D. L., Kennard, B. D., Goldstein, T. R., Mayes, T. L., & Douaihy, A. B. (2013). Protecting adolescents from self-harm: A critical review of intervention studies. Journal of the American Academy of Child and Adolescent Psychiatry, 52, 1260–1271.

Carter, G. L., Clover, K., Whyte, I. M., Dawson, A. H., & D'Este, C. (2005). Postcards from the EDge project: Randomised controlled trial of an intervention using postcards to reduce repetition of hospital treated deliberate self poisoning. British Medical Journal, 331 (7520), 805.

Chiles, J. A., & Strosahl, K. D. (2005). Clinical manual for the assessment and treatment of suicidal patients. Washington, DC: American Psychiatric Association.

Comtois, K. A. (2002). A review of interventions to reduce the prevalence of parasuicide. Psychiatric Services, 53, 1138–1144.

Coveney, C. M., Pollock, K., Armstrong, S., & Moore, J. (2012). Callers' experiences of contacting a national suicide prevention helpline: Report of an online survey. Crisis, 33, 313–324. doi:10.1027/0227-5910/a000151

Crosby, A. E., Han, B., Ortega, L. A. G., Parks, S. E., & Gfroerer, J. (2011). Suicidal thoughts and behaviors among adults aged > 18 years—United States, 2008-2009. Morbidity and Mortality Weekly Report, 60 (SS-13), 1–22.

Crosby, A. E., & Sacks, J. J. (2002). Exposure to suicide: Incidence and association with suicidal ideation and behavior. *Suicide and Life-Threatening Behavior, 32,* 321–328.

Dear, G. E., Thomson, D. M., & Hills, A. M. (2000). Self-harm in prison: Manipulators can also be suicide attempters. *Criminal Justice and Behavior, 27,* 160–175.

De Leo, D., & Heller, T. (2007). Intensive case management for suicide attempters following discharge from inpatient psychiatric care. *Australian Journal of Primary Health, 13*(3), 49–58.

DeQuincy, L.. (2006). Out of options: A cognitive model of adolescent suicide and risk-taking. *Journal of Child and Family Studies, 15,* 253–254.

Eaton, D. K., Kann, L., Kinchen, S. A, Ross, J. G., Hawkins, J., & Harris W. A. (2007). Youth risk behavior surveillance—U.S. 2005. *Morbidity and Mortality Weekly Report, 55,* (No. 2 SS-5), 1–108.

Farberow, N. L., & Shneidman, E. S. (Eds.). (1961). *The cry for help.* New York: McGraw-Hill.

Federal Bureau of Investigation. (2014). *Crime in the United States 2011.* Retrieved from http://www.fbi.gov/about-us/cjis/ucr/crime-in-the-u.s/2011/crime-in-the-u.s.-2011/tables/expanded-homicide-data-table-8

Fleischmann, A., Bertolote, J. M., Wasserman, D., DeLeo, D., Bolhari, J., Botega, N. J., … Thanh, H. T. (2008). Effectiveness of brief intervention and contact for suicide attempters: A randomized controlled trial in five countries. *Bulletin of the World Health Organization, 86,* 703–709.

Gilliland, B. E., & James, R. K. (1997). *Crisis intervention strategies* (3rd ed.). Pacific Grove, CA: Brooks/Cole.

Gould, M. S., Kalafat, J., Munfakh, J. L. H., & Kleinman, M. (2007). An evaluation of crisis hotline outcomes, Part II: Suicidal callers. *Suicide and Life-Threatening Behavior, 37,* 338–352.

Gould, M. S., Marrocco, F. A., Kleinman, M., Thomas, J. G., Mostkoff, K., Cote, J., & Davies, M. (2005). Evaluating iatrogenic risk of youth suicide screening programs: A randomized controlled trial. *Journal of the American Medical Association, 293,* 1635–1643.

Granello, D. H. (2010a). The process of suicide risk assessment: Twelve core principles. *Journal of Counseling and Development, 88,* 363–371.

Granello, D. H. (2010b). A suicide crisis intervention model with 25 practical strategies for implementation. *Journal of Mental Health Counseling, 32,* 218–235.

Granello, D. H., & Granello, P. F. (2007). *Suicide: An essential guide for helping professionals and educators.* Boston: Allyn and Bacon.

Greenstone, J. L., & Leviton, S. C. (2002). *Elements of crisis intervention: Crises and how to respond to them.* Springfield, IL: Charles C. Thomas.

Herman, S. M. (2006). Is the SADPERSONS Scale accurate for the Veteran Affairs population? *Psychological Services, 3,* 137–141.

International Association for Suicide Prevention. (2006). *IASP guidelines for suicide prevention.* Retrieved from http://www.med.uio.no/iasp/english/guidelines.html

Jacobs, D. G., & Brewer, M. L. (2006). Application of the APA practice guidelines on suicide to clinical practice. *CNS Spectrums, 11,* 447–454.

James, R. K., & Gilliland, B. E. (2001). *Crisis intervention strategies* (4th ed.). Belmont, CA: Brooks/Cole.

Joiner, T. E., Jr. (2005). *Why people die by suicide.* Cambridge, MA: Harvard University Press.

Juhnke, J. A., Granello, P. F., & Lebron-Striker, M. (2007). *IS PATH WARM? A suicide assessment mnemonic for counselors.* Alexandria, VA: American Counseling Association.

Kleespies, P. M., Deleppo, J. D., Gallagher, P. L., & Niles, B. L. (1999). Managing suicidal emergencies: Recommendations for the practitioner. *Professional Psychology: Research and Practice, 30,* 454–463.

King, R., Nurcombe, R., Bickman, L. Hides, L., & Reid, W. (2003). Telephone counseling for adolescent suicide prevention: Changes in suicidality and mental state from beginning to end of a counseling session. *Suicide and Life-Threatening Behavior, 33,* 400–411.

Leitner, M., Barr, W., & Hobby, L. (2008). Effectiveness of interventions to prevent suicide and suicidal behavior: A systematic review. Edinburgh: Scottish Government Social Research.

Macdonald, L., Pelling, N., & Granello, D. H. (2009). Suicide: A biopsychosocial approach. *Psychotherapy in Australia, 15*(2), 62–72.

Maltsberger, J. T. (1986). *Suicide risk: The formulation of clinical judgment.* New York: New York University Press.

McIntosh, J. L., & Drapeau, C. W. (for the American Association of Suicidology). (2014). *U.S.A. suicide 2011: Official final data.* Washington, DC: American Association of Suicidology.

Retrieved from http://www.suicidology.org

Meichenbaum, D. (2005). 35 years of working with suicidal patients: Lessons learned. *Canadian Psychology, 46,* 64–72.

Miller, J. S., Segal, D. L., & Coolidge, F. L. (2000). A comparison of suicidal thoughts and reasons for living among younger and older adults. *Death Studies, 25,* 257–265.

Millstein, D. L. (2010). Predictors of caller feedback evaluations following crisis and suicide hotline calls. *Dissertation Abstracts International: Section B. Sciences and Engineering, 71*(5-B), 3362.

Mishara, B. L. (1995). How family members and friends react to suicide threats. In B. L. Mishara (Ed.), *The impact of suicide* (pp. 73–81). New York: Springer.

Nock, M. K., & Kessler, R. C. (2006). Prevalence of and risk factors for suicide attempts versus suicide gestures: Analysis of the National Comorbidity Survey. *Journal of Abnormal Psychology, 115,* 616–623.

Packman, W. L., & Harris, E. A. (1998). Legal issues and risk management in suicidal patients. In B. Bonger, A. L. Berman, R. W. Maris, M. M. Silverman, E. A. Harris, & W. L. Packman (Eds.), *Risk management with suicidal patients* (pp. 150–186). New York: Guilford Press.

Paulson, B. L., & Everall, R. D. (2003). Suicidal adolescents: Helpful aspects of psychotherapy. *Archives of Suicide Research, 7,* 309–321.

Portes, P. R., Sandhu, D. S., & Longwell-Grice, R. (2002). Understanding adolescent suicide: A psychosocial interpretation of developmental and contextual factors. *Adolescence, 37,* 805–817.

Range, L. M., Leach, M. M., McIntrye, D., Posey-Deters, P. B., Marion, M. S., Kovac, S. H., Baños, J. H., & Vigil, J. (1999). Multicultural perspectives on suicide. *Aggression and Violent Behavior, 4,* 413–430.

Roberts, A. R. (2005). Bridging the past and present to the future of crisis intervention and crisis managements. In A. R. Roberts (Ed.), *Crisis intervention handbook: Assessment, treatment, and research* (3rd ed., pp. 3–33). New York: Oxford University Press.

Roberts, A. R., & Everly, G. S. (2006). A meta-analysis of 36 crisis intervention studies. *Brief Treatment and Crisis Intervention, 6,* 10–21.

Roberts, A. R., & Ottens, A. J. (2005). The seven stage crisis intervention model: A road map to goal attainment, problem solving, and crisis resolution. *Brief Treatment and Crisis Intervention, 5,* 329–339.

Runeson, B. (2001). Parasuicides without follow-up. *Nordic Journal of Psychiatry, 55,* 319–323.

Samy, M. H. (1995). Parental unresolved ambivalence and adolescent suicide: A psychoanalytic perspective. In B. L. Mishara (Ed.), *The impact of suicide* (pp. 40–51). New York: Springer.

Schwartz, R. C., & Rogers, J. R. (2004). Suicide assessment and evaluation strategies: A primer for the counselling psychologist. *Counselling Psychology Quarterly, 17,* 89–97.

Shea, S. (2002). *The practical art of suicide assessment. A guide for mental health professionals and substance abuse counselors.* Hoboken, NJ: Wiley.

Sher, L. (2004). Preventing suicide. *QJM: An International Journal of Medicine, 97,* 677–680.

Shneidman, E. S. (1981). Psychotherapy with suicidal patients. *Suicide and Life-Threatening Behavior, 11,* 341–359.

Silverman, M. M., Berman, A. L., Bongar, B., Litman, R. E., & Maris, R. W. (1998). Inpatient standards of care and the suicidal patient: Part II. An integration with clinical risk management. In B. Bongar, A. L. Berman, R. W. Maris, M. M. Silverman, & E. A. Harris (Eds.), *Risk management with suicidal patients* (pp. 84–109). New York: Guilford Press.

Simon, R. I. (2002). Suicide risk assessment: What is the standard of care? *Journal of the American Academy of Psychiatry and the Law, 30,* 340–344.

Simon, R. I. (2006). Patient safety versus freedom of movement: Coping with uncertainty. In H. Hendin (Ed.), *The American Psychiatric Publishing textbook of suicide assessment and management* (pp. 423–439). Washington, DC: American Psychiatric Publishing.

Sommers-Flanagan, J., & Sommers-Flanagan, R. (1995). Intake interviewing with suicidal patients: A systematic approach. *Professional Psychology: Research and Practice, 26,* 41–47.

Stanley, B., & Brown, G. K. (2012). Safety planning intervention: A brief intervention to mitigate suicide risk. *Cognitive and Behavioral Practice, 19,* 256–264.

Substance Abuse and Mental Health Services Administration. (2009a). *Practice guidelines: Core elements for responding to mental health crises.* HHS Publication No. SMA-09-4427. Rockville, MD: Center for Mental Health Services.

Substance Abuse and Mental Health Services Administration.

(2009b). *SAFE-T*. US DHHS Publication No. (SMA) 09-4432 • CMHS-NSP-0193. Retrieved from http://store.samhsa.gov/product/Suicide-Assessment-Five-Step-Evaluation-and-Triage-SAFE-T-/SMA09-4432

Suicide.org. (2014). Suicide statistics. Retrieved from http://www.suicide.org/suicide-statistics.html#death-rates

Suicide Prevention Resource Center. (2005). Best practices registry. Retrieved from http://www.sprc.org/featured_resources/

US Department of Health and Human Services. (2004). *National consensus statement on mental health recovery*. Retrieved from http://mentalhealth.samhsa.gov/publications/allpubs/sma05-4129/

Wendler, S., & Matthews, D. (2006). Cultural competence in suicide risk assessment. In R. I. Simon &

R. E. Hales (Eds)., *The American Psychiatric Publishing textbook of suicide assessment and management* (pp. 159–176). Washington, DC: American Psychiatric Publishing.

Westefeld, J. S., Range, L. M., Rogers, J. R., Maples, M. R., Bromley, J. L., & Alcorn, J. (2000). Suicide: An overview. *Counseling Psychologist*, *28*, 445–510.

Wharff, E. A., Ginnis, K. B., & Ross, A. M. (2012). Family based crisis intervention with suicidal adolescents in the emergency room: A pilot study. *Social Work*. *57*(2), 133–143.

Williams, R., & Morgan, H. G. (1994). *Suicide prevention—the challenge confronted*. London: NHS Health Advisory Service.

Yalom, I. D. (1975). *The theory and practice of group psychotherapy*. New York: Basic Books.

# II

CRISIS INTERVENTION: DISASTER
AND TRAUMA

# 7

# The ACT Model: Assessment, Crisis Intervention, and Trauma Treatment in the Aftermath of Community Disasters

KENNETH R. YEAGER
ALBERT R. ROBERTS

Professionals working in the area of crisis intervention know all too well the feelings that accompany being notified that a crisis or community disaster has occurred. For some the feeling is exhilaration; for others it is a sinking feeling, one of contemplating loss and sorrow; for some it is a spiritual calling; and for still others it is a call to duty or a willingness to do whatever is necessary to make a difference and contribute to the healing process. For all it is a very personal process that is hard to define, encompassing a variety of emotions both positive and negative. It is a task that requires preparation. Even with heightened efforts since the third edition of this text, health and mental health professionals continue to be less than well equipped to deal with the many thousands of persons encountering psychological trauma and acute crisis episodes. Although most health professions are anxious to help those presenting after catastrophic events and/or traumatic experiences, victims continue to experience shock, fear, somatic stress, trauma, anxiety, and grief in varying degrees, with few if any comprehensive models for assessment, crisis intervention, or trauma treatment integrated into current practice models. Very real threats of natural disasters, crime, motor vehicle accidents, and mental health or financial crisis, to name a few, highlight the need for crisis-oriented intervention plans. For all communities across the nation, the risk remains high. The need exists for greater integration of effective models of crisis intervention across all intervention points that will work to improve the function of those who experience psychological trauma.

This chapter presents a conceptual three-stage framework and intervention model that should be useful in helping mental health professionals provide acute crisis and trauma treatment services. The assessment, crisis intervention, and trauma treatment (ACT) model may be thought of as a sequential set of assessments and intervention strategies. This model integrates various assessment and triage protocols with three primary crisis-oriented intervention strategies: the seven-stage crisis intervention model, psychological debriefing, and trauma support services.

## OVERVIEW

This part of the fourth edition of the *Crisis Intervention Handbook* was prepared to provide administrators, clinicians, crisis counselors, trainers, researchers, and mental health consultants with the latest theories and best crisis intervention strategies and trauma treatment practices currently available. This knowledge base should assist all clinicians whose clients may be in a precrisis or crisis state; experts in crisis intervention or trauma treatment were invited to write or cowrite chapters for this part of the *Handbook*.

Since the publication of the third edition of this book, which focused on the terrorist attacks of September 11, the nature of the crises we face has continued to evolve. Although a fear of terrorism remains in the wake of the Boston Marathon bombing, the attack on Sandy Hook Elementary, the shootings at a Colorado movie multiplex, and the 2011 attack on US representative Gabrielle Giffords all present evolving and different types of threats. The suddenness and extreme severity of the recent seemingly unprovoked attacks, combined with the fear of new and emerging violence that may lie ahead, serve as both a challenge and a wake-up call for all mental health professionals as we expand and coordinate interagency crisis response teams, crisis intervention programs, and trauma treatment resources.

Those who witness violence in the community are vulnerable to higher rates of anxiety, fear, hopelessness, and depression, which have been common in adolescents exposed to violence (Kelly, 2010; DuRant, Treiber, Goodman, & Woods, 1996; Becker, 2006; Williams 2006). For quite some time, researchers have recognized the harmful effects of exposure to violence, and numerous studies exploring the potential consequences of community violence on mental health have been published. Reviews of this literature demonstrate a significant positive correlation between exposure and psychological symptoms, including externalizing symptoms, anxiety, depression, post-traumatic stress disorder (PTSD), and other internalizing behaviors (Buka, Stichick, Birdthistle, & Earls, 2001; Gorman-Smith, Henry, & Tolan, 2004). At this time, the strength of this relationship varies between outcomes and between studies, confusing the pattern of findings. Differences in methodologies and the presence of moderating factors, such as subtypes of community violence or different age groups, may account for a portion of this variation.

Natural disasters present an ongoing threat of monumental proportions. Recent events include the April 28, 2011, outbreak of 358 tornadoes, with one of the deadliest in Tuscaloosa and Birmingham, Alabama, in which 324 tornadic deaths occurred, along with another 24 weather-related deaths. Past research on natural disasters has broadly demonstrated a consistent link between the experience of such events and the presence of psychopathology, which is not always clearly defined or always agreed upon by researchers. However, several studies (Davis, Tarcza, & Munson 2009; DiMaggio, Galea, & Richardson, 2007; Kessler et al., 2008) have demonstrated a link between natural disasters and the presence of trauma. The severity of the disaster has a significant impact, with the severity of the disaster correlated to the severity of the psychological impact as reported by victims (Toukmanian, Jadaa, & Lawless, 2000; Sattler & Hoge, 2006). Additionally, the destruction of personal property and exposure to stressful postdisaster events have been reported to affect psychopathology and to serve as potential risk factors for increased difficulties in the period after the disaster. Conversely, a greater level of social and professional support and the establishment of effective coping behaviors appear to serve as protective factors after traumatic events, yet the influence of such factors appears to be complex, difficult to define, and highly individualized.

This chapter presents a theoretical framework and intervention model that may be useful for mental health professionals who provide crisis and trauma services. It is built on two premises, the first being that counselors, psychologists, nurses, and social workers should have a conceptual framework, also known as a planning and intervention model, to streamline and improve the delivery of services for persons in a precrisis or traumatic state. The second premise is that mental health professionals need an organizing framework to determine which assessment and intervention strategies to use first, second, and third. Albert R. Roberts developed this three-part conceptual framework as a foundation model to initiate, implement, evaluate, and modify a well-coordinated crisis intervention and trauma treatment programs.

Severe crisis situations are sudden, unexpected, dangerous, and potentially life-threatening. Many of them affect large groups of people, and some impact smaller groups. Nevertheless, crisis situations are overwhelming to human adaptation and our basic coping skills. One constant throughout time is that a seemingly overwhelming variety of crisis situations exist. Undoubtedly, there will continue to be a need for crisis response. It is imperative that all emergency services personnel and crisis workers be trained to respond immediately and appropriately. In the aftermath of catastrophic events, and regardless of the nature of the event, there will be a need for crisis stabilization for some involved. Many of those who experience potentially traumatic events will return to functioning normally, but others will not. After a crisis, people will experience a variety of symptoms, including surprise, shock, denial, numbness, fear, anger, adrenal surges, isolation, loneliness, arousal, attentiveness, vigilance, irritability, sadness, and exhaustion (Cutler, Yeager, & Nunley, 2013).

A crisis can be viewed as either an opportunity or a dangerous and potentially life-threatening event, depending on the situation or individual perception at a given point in time. Stressful or traumatic events can and frequently do combine with life stage issues and lead to a crisis reaction representative of a turning point in the individual's life. When an individual can be assisted in mobilizing individual untapped strengths or unidentified protective factors or capabilities, he or she may be able to derive new meaning from the crisis event and be set on a positive trajectory. The crisis can result in personal growth and be seen as a meaningful and life-changing process. When support is not present, the opposite occurs, and the individual is at risk to proceed on a course of personal or psychosocial destruction. Negative coping, such as by consuming alcohol, can lead to professional and personal problems. The impact of a crisis on the individual is also based on the perception of the events that created considerable upset or a disruption in the individual's coping abilities; with the right social support mechanisms over time, however, the individual's coping equilibrium can be re-established (Cutler, Yeager, & Nunley, 2013).

The individual's inability to resolve the disruption through his or her innate coping mechanisms may lead to greater reliance on negative coping (e.g., avoidance, procrastination, anger, isolation, consumption of alcohol or other mood-altering substances). The following factors should be considered when addressing a crisis:

- Each person will at some point in his or her life experience an acute or traumatic stress that is not necessarily harmful or emotionally toxic. It is the overall context of the event in the person's life that determines his or her ability to overcome the acute distress and to manage the crisis.
- Homeostasis is a natural state of equilibrium that all people seek. An individual is more amenable to intervention when in a state of disequilibrium that is the end result of an acute crisis. This state usually occurs when individual attempts to resolve the crisis by usual coping mechanisms have failed or been less than effective.
- Each person possesses untapped resources or new coping responses that can be accessed and used to deal with a traumatic event, and the event itself can serve as the catalyst for the development of new coping strategies to be applied to address both immediate and future coping needs.

- The dearth of prior experiences in overcoming adversity can be used as a positive in address emerging crisis situations. Similarly, prior experiences with crisis situations will create anxiety, which can be used to build resolve to apply greater individual resources to resolution of emerging challenges.
- The duration of any crisis situation is limited, depending on the precipitating event, the response of the individual, and available resources.
- Certain affective, cognitive, and behavioral tasks must be mastered through a series of identifiable and predictable stages of crisis stabilization (Roberts & Yeager, 2009; Cutler, Yeager, & Nunley, 2013).

It is important that crisis workers understand processes and evidence-informed approaches associated with crisis intervention. Like many of the "pure concepts" in mental health, at times evidence is lacking, and pathways and clinical guidelines will carry the crisis intervenor only so far. Yet crisis intervention has a long history in mental health care and has a rich tradition of both process and evidence for workers to rely on in the skill-building process.

This overview chapter and the later chapters in this part examine the different definitions of acute stress, crisis, and psychological trauma, as well as disaster mental health and crisis intervention strategies. Allen Ottens and Donna Pender examine the growing challenges of crisis intervention for caregivers, specifically the psychological and physical health effects of the caregiver burden. They walk readers through processes in addressing the challenges that caregivers face and explain approaches for meeting needs for respite, confronting emerging family conflict, addressing the growing and challenging aspects of caring for loved ones, and restoring balance in the lives of caregivers whose focus often is solely on the care recipient to the exclusion of themselves.

David Kasick and Christopher Bowling outline the growth of the crisis intervention team (CIT) model that has evolved out of a 25-year partnership between front-line patrol officers within law enforcement and mental health professionals to allow officers to better understand the behavioral manifestations of mental illness and their potential impact on law enforcement encounters with those with mental health issues within the community. The authors provide an overview of the development of CIT and the evolution of this program, detailing how the program is designed, implemented, and accepted in communities across the United States. This chapter reviews the influence and outcomes of the CIT program, as well as structured support interventions for individuals who frequently experience crisis situations within the community.

Vincent Henry (currently a professor of criminal justice and Director of Long Island University's Homeland Security Management Institute) was a first responder to the World Trade Center attacks and participated in the rescue and recovery activities there. In the weeks immediately after the September 11 attacks and near the end of his 21-year career as an New York City police officer and detective, he served as the commanding officer of a sniper unit on top of St. Vincent's Hospital in lower Manhattan, protecting injured survivors and watching for terrorists. His chapter provides an overview of specific types of weapons of mass destruction and the type of response protocols utilized by police, fire departments, emergency medical services, and disaster mental health coalitions. He examines some of the psychological crises and traumas experienced by first responders to terrorist attacks and describes a successful clinical service consisting of more than 300 specially trained clinical volunteers, the New York Disaster Counseling Coalition. This counseling and psychotherapy group provides free, confidential treatment services to all first responders and their family members who request services. The volunteer clinicians have offices throughout the New York metropolitan area, northern New Jersey, southern Connecticut, and parts of Pennsylvania.

Scott Newgass and David Schonfeld, in their chapter addressing school crisis intervention, crisis prevention, and crisis response, illustrate the importance of having a preexisting comprehensive crisis response plan designed to assist schools in anticipating and meeting the needs of their students, staff, and the larger community in the critical hours after a crisis. Such a plan provides critical knowledge on the processes, levels of intervention, and notification and communication steps providing clearly outlined tasks and processes for all crisis team members.

Sophia Dziegielewski and Joshua Kirven's timely chapter focuses on the nature and extent of bioterrorism threats in the United States and an application of the seven-stage crisis intervention model to reduce fear, stress, crisis, and trauma among the survivors of bioterrorist attacks.

According to Lenore Terr (1994), a professor of psychiatry, there are two types of trauma among children. Type I refers to child victims who have experienced a single traumatic event, such as the 26 children from Chowchilla, California, who were kidnapped in 1976 and buried alive in their school bus for almost 27 hours. Type II trauma refers to child victims who have experienced multiple traumatic events, such as ongoing incest or child abuse. Research has demonstrated that most children experiencing a single isolated traumatic event had detailed memories of the event but no dissociation, personality disorders, or memory loss. In sharp contrast, child survivors experiencing multiple or repetitious incest and/or child sexual abuse trauma (Type II trauma) exhibited dissociative disorders (also known as multiple personality disorders) or borderline personality disorder (BPD), recurring trancelike states, depression, suicidal ideation and/or suicide attempts, sleep disturbances, and, to a lesser degree, self-mutilation and PTSD (Terr, 1994; Valentine, 2000). The age of the incest victim frequently mediates the coping strategies of adult survivors who face crisis and trauma.

Research has indicated that when the childhood incest was prolonged and severe, an adult diagnosis of BPD, disassociative disorder, panic disorder, alcohol abuse or dependency, and/or PTSD occurs with greater frequency (Valentine, 2000). The exception to the low incidence of long-lasting mental disorders among victims of a Type I trauma is an extremely horrific, single traumatic occurrence that is marked by multiple homicides and includes dehumanizing sights (e.g., dismembered bodies), piercing sounds, and strong odors (e.g., fire and smoke). The long-lasting psychological impact of the September 11 mass disasters will not be known for at least another decade, at which time prospective and retrospective longitudinal research studies will have been completed.

The American Academy of Experts in Traumatic Stress (AAETS) is a multidisciplinary network of professionals dedicated to formulating and extending the use of traumatic stress reduction protocols with emergency responders (e.g., police, fire, emergency medical services personnel, nurses, disaster response personnel, psychologists, social workers, funeral directors, and clergy). Dr. Mark D. Lerner, a clinical psychologist and president of ATSM, and Dr. Raymond D. Shelton, director of emergency medical training at the Nassau County (New Jersey) Police Training Academy and director of professional development for ATSM, provide the following guidance for addressing psychological trauma quickly during traumatic events:

> Crisis intervention and trauma treatment specialists are in agreement that before intervening, a full assessment of the situation and the individual must take place. By reaching people early, during traumatic exposure, we may ultimately prevent acute traumatic stress reactions from becoming chronic stress disorders. The first three steps of Acute Traumatic Stress Management (ATSM) are: (1) assess for danger/safety for self and others; (2) consider the type and extent of property damage and/or physical injury and the way the injury was sustained; and (3) evaluate the level of responsiveness—is the individual alert, in pain, aware of what has occurred, or in emotional shock or under the influence of drugs? (Lerner & Shelton, 2001, pp. 31–32)

Personal impact in the aftermath of potentially stressful and crisis-producing events can be measured by the following:

- *Spatial dimensions:* The closer the person is to the center of the tragedy, the greater the stress. Similarly, the closer the person's relationship is to the victim, the greater the likelihood of entering into a crisis state.
- *Subjective crime clock:* The greater the duration (estimated length of time exposed and estimated length of exposure to sensory experiences, e.g., an odor of gasoline combined with the smell of a fire) that an individual is affected by the community disaster, violent crime, or other tragedy, the greater the stress.

- *Reoccurrence* (perceived): The greater the perceived likelihood that the tragedy will happen again, the greater the likelihood of intense fears, which contribute to an active crisis state on the part of the survivor (Young, 1995).

## THE ACT INTERVENTION MODEL OF CRISIS AND TRAUMA ASSESSMENT AND TREATMENT

Somatic stress, crisis, and psychological trauma frequently take place in the wake of potentially traumatizing events. Unfortunately, most individuals have little or no preparation for traumatic events, leaving them feeling ill equipped to address the crisis situation at hand. Most are not aware of the skills they bring to the table; few, if any, understand the steps required to overcome the precipitating event. When entering into a crisis intervention situation, the important first step is determining the immediate psychosocial needs of all those impacted by the crisis situation. Thus, the focus of this section is to examine the "A" (assessment) component of the ACT intervention model for acute crisis and trauma treatment (Figure 7.1). First, we provide a brief discussion of psychiatric triage assessment and the different types of assessment protocols. Second, we examine the components of a crisis

---

**A** • Assessment/appraisal of immediate medical needs, threats to public safety and property damage

• Triage assessment, crisis assessment, trauma assessment and the biopsychosocial and cultural assessment protocols

---

**C** • Connecting to support groups, the delivery of disaster relief and social services, and critical incident stress debriefing ( Mitchell & Everly's CISD model) implemented

• Crisis intervention ( Robert's seven-stage model) implemented, through strengths perspective and coping attempts bolstered

---

**T** • Traumatic stress reactions, sequelae, and post-traumatic stress disorders (PTSDs)

• Ten step acute trauma and stress management protocol (Lerner & Shelton), trauma treatment plans and recovery strategies implemented

---

Figure 7.1   ACT Model

assessment. Third, we discuss and review dimensions of the biopsychosocial and cultural assessment. Finally, we provide a brief overview of the types of rapid assessment instruments and scales used in mental health, crisis, and trauma assessments.

## Triage Assessment

First responders, or crisis response team members, also known as front-line crisis intervention workers, are called on to conduct an immediate debriefing under less than stable circumstances and sometimes have to delay the crisis assessment until right after immediate stabilization and support. With other disaster responses, an assessment can be completed simultaneously with the offering of psychological support. According to many crisis intervention specialists, the "A" (assessment) precedes "C" (crisis intervention), but in the rough and tumble of the disaster or acute crisis, the sequence is not always that linear.

In the immediate aftermath of a community disaster, the first type of assessment by disaster mental health specialists should be psychiatric triage. A triage/screening tool can be useful in gathering and recording information about the initial contact between a person experiencing crisis or trauma reactions and the mental health specialist. The triage form should include essential demographic information (name, address, phone number, e-mail address, etc.), perception of the magnitude of the traumatic event, coping methods, any presenting problems, safety issues, previous traumatic experiences, social support network, drug and alcohol use, preexisting psychiatric conditions, suicide risk, and homicide risk (Eaton & Roberts, 2002; Roberts & Yeager, 2009). *Triage* has been defined as the medical "process of assigning patients to appropriate treatments depending on their medical conditions and available medical resources" (Leise, 1995, p. 48). Medical triage was first used in the military to respond quickly to the medical needs of wounded soldiers. Triage involves assigning physically ill or injured patients to different levels of care, ranging from "emergent" (i.e., immediate treatment required) to "nonemergent" (i.e., no medical treatment required).

Psychiatric or psychological triage assessment refers to the immediate decision-making process in which the mental health worker determines lethality, overall functioning, and the most appropriate next level of care, including referral to one of the following alternatives:

- Emergency inpatient hospitalization
- Outpatient treatment facility or private therapist
- Support group or social service agency
- No referral needed

The "A" in Roberts's ACT intervention model refers to triage, crisis, and trauma assessments and referral to appropriate community resources.

With regard to triage assessment, emergency psychiatric response should take place when the rapid assessment indicates that the individual is a danger to self or others and is exhibiting intense and acute psychiatric symptoms that would require care in an environment designed to provide supportive factors to facilitate psychiatric stabilization. These survivors generally require short-term hospitalization and stabilization processes specifically designed to protect them from self-harm (e.g., inability to care for self, potential for self-harm and/or self-injurious behavior) or harm to other persons. The very small number of individuals needing emergency psychiatric treatment generally are diagnosed with moderate- to high-potential risk for potential harm. Many of these will present with a history of mental illness. Thus, those who were unstable at the time of the crisis may become destabilized and present with issues of lethality (e.g., suicidal ideation and/or homicidal thoughts) and acute mental disorders. In the small percentage of cases where emergency psychiatric treatment is indicated, these persons usually are suffering from an accumulation of several previous traumatic events (Burgess & Roberts, 2000; Cutler, Yeager, & Nunley, 2013).

With regard to the other categories of psychiatric triage, many individuals may be in a precrisis stage due to ineffective coping skills, a weak support system, or ambivalence about seeking mental health assistance. These same individuals may have no psychiatric symptoms and no suicide risk. However, because of the catastrophic nature of the crisis event or natural disaster, persons who have suddenly lost a loved one and have no previous experience coping with sudden death may be particularly vulnerable to acute crisis or traumatic stress. Therefore, it is imperative that all mental health professionals become knowledgeable about timely crisis and trauma assessments.

## Crisis Assessment

The primary role of the crisis counselor and other clinical staff in conducting an assessment is to gather information that can help to resolve the "C" (crisis). Of course, it makes sense to build the individual assessment around the nature of the crisis with an eye toward identifying key contributing factors associated with the crisis. Intake forms and rapid assessment instruments help the crisis clinician or mental health counselor to make better-informed decisions on the type and duration of treatment recommended. Although crisis assessment is oriented to the individual, it must always include an assessment of the person's immediate environment and interpersonal relationships. As Gitterman (2002) eloquently points out in *The Life Model*:

> The purpose of social work is improving the level of fit between people and their environments, especially between people's needs and their

environmental resources. ... [The professional function of social work is] to help people mobilize and draw on personal and environmental resources for effective coping to alleviate life stressors and the associated stress. (p. 106)

Crisis assessment is specifically formulated to facilitate treatment planning and decision making. The ultimate goal of crisis assessment is, first, to provide a systematic method of organizing client information related to personal characteristics, parameters of the crisis episode, and the intensity and duration of the crisis, and, second, utilizing these data to develop effective treatment plans. In the words of Lewis and Roberts (2001):

Most intake workers have failed to distinguish between stressful life events, traumatic events, coping skills and other mediators of a crisis, and an active crisis state. Most crisis episodes are preceded by one or more stressful, hazardous, and/or traumatic events. However, not all stressed or traumatized individuals move into a crisis state. Every day thousands of individuals completely avert a crisis, while many other thousands of individuals quickly escalate into a crisis state. (p. 20)

Thus, it is extremely important to assess and measure whether a person is in a crisis state so that individual treatment goals and an appropriate crisis intervention protocol can be implemented. (For a detailed discussion of crisis-specific measurement tools and crisis-oriented rapid assessment instruments, see Lewis & Roberts, 2001; Roberts & Yeager, 2009, pp. 14–23.)

## Biopsychosocial and Cultural Assessments

There are different methods of assessment designed to measure clients' situation, stress level, presenting problems, and acute crisis episode: monitoring and observing, client logs, semistructured interviews, individualized rating scales, goal attainment scales, behavioral observations, self-reports, cognitive measures, and diagnostic systems and codes (LeCroy & Okamoto, 2002; Pike, 2002).

Although there is broad agreement that each element of the extensive general evaluation be sufficiently detailed to paint an accurate description of the presenting or ongoing problem, the specific elements of the assessment will vary according to its purpose and the individualized needs of the patient.

- Reason for the evaluation
- Physical and mental health history
- History of substance use
- Developmental, psychosocial, and sociocultural status.

Vandiver and Corcoran (2002) aptly identify and discuss the biopsychosocial-cultural model of assessment as the first step in the clinical interview aimed at providing the necessary information to "establish treatment goals and an effective treatment plan" (p. 297). It is important for individual assessments to gather information on the following:

1. Current health status and history (e.g., hypertension) and past health status (e.g., diabetes) or injuries (e.g., brain injury); current medication use and health and lifestyle behaviors (e.g., fitness exercises, nutrition, sleep patterns, substance abuse).
2. The psychological status of the client, including mental status, appearance and behavior, speech and language, thought process and content, mood and affect, cognitive functioning, concentration, memory, and insight and general intelligence. An additional critical area of assessment is the determination of suicidal or homicidal risk and possible need for an immediate referral.
3. Substance use and abuse history, age of first use, frequency of use, amount of substances used over what time frame.
4. The sociocultural experiences and cultural background of the client, including ethnicity, language, assimilation, acculturation, spiritual beliefs, environmental connections (e.g., community ties, neighborhood, economic conditions, availability of food and shelter), social networks and relationships (e.g., family, friends, coworkers).
5. Occupational and military history of the client, including current employment and type of work, perception of support within the work environment.
6. Legal history, including exploration of any current or remote legal issues and the potential impact of current legal issues on functioning or return to baseline functioning.
7. Spiritual history and belief system, the degree to which the individual relies on his or her spiritual belief system and method of accessing systems of support.

The assessment process should provide a step-by-step method for exploring, identifying, describing, measuring, classifying, diagnosing, and coding health or mental health problems, environmental conditions, resilience and protective factors, positive lifestyle behaviors, and level of functioning. Austrian (2002) delineates the 10 basic components of a biopsychosocial assessment as follows:

1. Demographic data
2. Current and previous agency contacts
3. Medical, psychiatric, and substance abuse history
4. Brief history of client and significant others
5. Summary of client's current situation

6. Presenting request
7. Presenting problem as defined by client and counselor
8. Contract agreed on by client and counselor
9. Intervention plan
10. Intervention goals

For mental health professionals, the diagnostic gold standard is the *Diagnostic and Statistical Manual-IV-TR* (*DSM-IV-TR*; American Psychiatric Association, 2000; Munson, 2002; Williams, 2002). Although most payer sources are using the *Diagnostic and Statistical Manual-5* (*DSM-5*; APA, 2013), many continue to accept the *DSM-IV-TR*.

For classification of diseases, functioning, and disability, the International Classification of Diseases ICD-9 (ICD-10) of the Centers for Disease Control and Prevention is the widely accepted method. Additional information can be found at http://www.cdc.gov/nchs/icd.htm.

Rapid assessment instruments include the following:

- Depression, Anxiety and Stress Scales (DASS; Lovibond & Lovibond, 1995)
- Person-in-Environment system (Karls, 2002)
- Impact of Events Scale—Revised (IES-R; Weiss & Marmar, 1997)
- Traumatic Exposure Severity Scale (TESS; Elal & Slade, 2005)
- Goal attainment scales (Pike, 2002)

Additional listings of mental health screening and assessment tools for child and adolescent primary care settings can be found at http://www.heardalliance.org/wp-content/uploads/2011/04/Mental-Health-Assessment.pdf.

## CRISIS INTERVENTION STRATEGIES

It is imperative for all communities throughout the United States and Canada to have a multidisciplinary and comprehensive crisis response and crisis intervention plan ready for systematic implementation and mobilizations in the aftermath of a major disaster. Crisis intervention models and techniques provide guidelines for practitioners to resolve clients' presenting problems, stress and psychological trauma, and emotional conflicts with a minimum number of contacts. Crisis-oriented treatment is time limited and goal directed, in contrast to long-term psychotherapy, which can take 1 to 3 years to complete (Roberts, 2000).

There is a growing need to provide a structured, systematic approach to identification and treatment of emerging crisis in individuals through a multitiered approach involving primary healthcare workers, who can conduct accurate assessment and provide linkage for those in crisis to the most appropriate level of care. Walker, Tucker, Lunch, and Druss (2014) proposed that mental health interventions in complex contexts, including emergencies, have to be based at the community health level in order to optimize effectiveness in linking with ongoing care and in providing affordable approaches with access to services and culturally valid approaches to care, in a manner that is most beneficial to communities while meeting individuals' needs at the most appropriate level of care (Yeager & Minkoff, 2013).

The promotion of psychosocial interventions that focus on supporting and educating families must be made a community service priority in order to intervene early in emerging complex mental health problems as a consequence of crisis and/or trauma. This, in conjunction with access to services via primary care networks, provides the most cost-effective access point of services within the healthcare system. Although they have not been formally tested, primary healthcare workers providing nonjudgmental services and providing linkage and medication when necessary have been found to be valuable and helpful to many local communities (Seelig & Kayton, 2008). Finally, there is a need for public education to increase awareness both of the socioeconomic conditions and family environmental conditions associated with crisis and trauma and of the long-term mental health impact. Public education programs should not only increase awareness of the emotional needs of those in crisis but also increase awareness of the circumstances in which psychosocial problems are more likely to occur, and the need for empathic response to distress, while "depathologizing" normal responses to human-made and natural disasters. The media are also influential in retraumatizing individuals through repeated showing of images of disasters and recounting of disturbing experiences. Yet it should be noted that there is a public benefit in responsible reporting, including unspectacular coverage that focuses on challenges, individuals' needs, and information about new and restored community resources after natural and human-made disasters (Cutler, Yeager, & Nunley, 2013).

## Roberts's Seven-Stage Crisis Intervention Model

Although counselors, psychologists, and social workers have been trained in a variety of theoretical models, very little graduate coursework has provided them with a crisis intervention protocol and guidelines to follow in dealing with crises. Roberts's (1991, 2000) seven-stage crisis intervention model begins to provide practitioners with this useful framework.

---

### Case Example

The 24-hour crisis intervention unit of a New Jersey mental health center received a call from the mother of a 22-year-old college senior whose father (who had worked on the 95th floor of the World Trade Center) was killed on September 11. The college student had barricaded himself in his bedroom. His mother indicated that she had overheard a phone conversation between her depressed son, Jonathan, and his cousin. Jonathan told his 19-year-old female cousin that he needed her to come over immediately because he was giving her his Super Nintendo set and all of his games. The mother was concerned about possible suicidal behavior because her son had never given away any of his prized possessions before. In addition, during the past 2 weeks he had been eating very little, was sleeping 12 to 15 hours each day, was refusing to return to college, and had been mentioning that heaven would be a nice place to live. His mother also overhead him asking his cousin if she thought there were basketball hoops in heaven so that he and his father could play basketball again.

---

Roberts's (1996) seven-stage crisis intervention model (Figure 7.2) was initiated.

*Stage 1: Assess lethality.* The mother who phoned crisis services had some information about the current mental status of the client. She indicated that

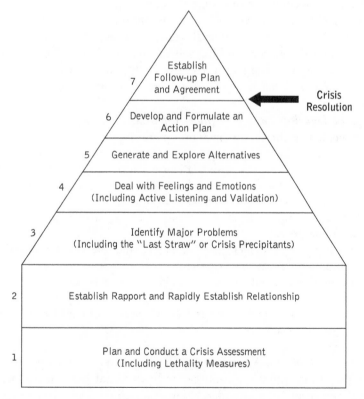

Figure 7.2   Roberts's Seven-Stage Crisis Intervention Model

she could hear her son speak very softly in a muffled voice through the locked and barricaded bedroom door. The mother further indicated that her son has stayed in his bedroom for about 12 hours since he telephoned his cousin and put his CDs and Super Nintendo game on the front porch. Crisis services immediately dispatched a worker to the residence.

*Stage 2: Establish rapport.* Showing understanding and offering support were two essential skills utilized by the crisis worker to establish a working relationship with the client. Immediately requesting that he open his bedroom door would not have been a helpful intervention. Workers need to begin where the client is. Through attentive listening, paraphrasing, and the use of open-ended questions, the worker eventually got Jonathan to agree to let him in his room so they could hear each other better.

*Stage 3: Identify problems.* Luckily, Jonathan had not yet done anything to harm himself, but he was contemplating suicide. He had a vague plan of overdosing but no available method. He expressed his major problem as the sudden death of his father.

*Stage 4: Deal with feelings.* The crisis worker allowed Jonathan to tell his story about why he was feeling so bad. The worker was able to validate and identify Jonathan's emotions. They then began to explore together more effective ways of coping with his upsetting feelings.

*Stage 5: Explore alternatives.* Various options were discussed, including inpatient and outpatient mental health services. The client allowed his mother to join the worker and himself during this stage. The mother provided a lot of support and encouragement to the client as well. At this stage, Jonathan indicated that he was feeling better and would not "do anything stupid."

*Stage 6: Develop an action plan.* Jonathan, his mother, and the crisis worker decided on the following action plan:

1. A contract for safety was signed by the client (this is a written agreement that the client agrees to call crisis services for help before he will act on any thought to harm himself or others).
2. A release of information was obtained by the worker to contact an outpatient provider.
3. An outpatient provider was contacted, and the client received an appointment for the next afternoon.
4. The mother hid all medications on the recommendation of crisis services.
5. Both Jonathan and his mother were given a crisis card to call if any additional concerns or issues arose.

*Stage 7: Follow up.* A follow-up phone call was made to the residence the next evening. Jonathan's mother indicated that her son was in good spirits that day and had attended his first appointment with the therapist.

Jonathan told the crisis worker that he was doing great, he thought his therapist was "really cool," and he had plans to "go bowling with friends on Saturday."

Effective crisis intervenors should be active, directive, focused, and hopeful. It is critically important that the crisis worker gauge the stages and completeness of the intervention. Roberts's seven-stage crisis intervention paradigm "should be viewed as a guide, not as a rigid process, since with some clients stages may overlap. Roberts'... model of crisis intervention has been utilized for helping persons in acute psychological crisis, acute situational crises, and acute stress disorders" (Roberts, 2000, p. 15). The seven stages of crisis intervention combined with a strengths perspective will now be discussed.

## Roberts's Model From a Strengths Perspective

### Stage 1

Plan and conduct a thorough biopsychosocial and crisis assessment. This involves a quick assessment of risk and dangerousness, including suicide and homicide/violence risk assessment, need for medical attention, positive and negative coping strategies, and current drug or alcohol use (Eaton & Ertl, 2000; Roberts, 2000). If possible, a medical assessment should include a brief summary of the presenting problem, any medical conditions, current medications (names, dosages, and most recent dose), and allergies. This medical information is essential to relay to emergency medical responders who are attempting to treat problems such as overdoses.

A drug or alcohol assessment should include information about drugs used, amount used, time of last use, and any withdrawal symptoms the client is experiencing. Any knowledge of angel dust, methamphetamine, or PCP ingestion should always precipitate a team crisis response with the police, due to the likelihood of violent and bizarre behavior.

The initial crisis assessment should examine resilience and protective factors, internal and external coping methods and resources, and the degree of extended family and informal support network. Many individuals in a precrisis or crisis situation socially isolate themselves and are unaware of and lack insight into which persons would be most supportive in their efforts at crisis resolution and recovery. The crisis clinician can facilitate and bolster clients' resilience by encouraging them to telephone or write a letter to persons who may well support their efforts at recovery. Seeking advice on how best to cope with a crisis related to self-destructive patterns such as polydrug abuse, binge drinking, self-injurious behavior, or depression can lead to overwhelming support, suggestions, advice, and encouragement from one's support network (Yeager & Gregoire, 2000).

## Stage 2

Rapidly establish rapport and the therapeutic relationship (this often occurs simultaneously with Stage 1). Conveying respect and acceptance is a key step in this stage. Crisis workers must meet clients where they are; for example, if the client begins a conversation talking about his dog or parakeet, this is where we should begin (Roberts, 2000). We also must display a neutral and nonjudgmental attitude, ensuring that our personal opinions and values are not apparent or stated. Poise, maintaining a calm demeanor, and appearing to be in control are essential skills in crisis work (Belkin, 1984).

## Stage 3

Identify the issues pertinent to the client and any precipitants to the client's crisis contact. Use open-ended questions in asking clients to explain and describe their problem and to tell their story in their own words (Roberts, 2000). This provides the crisis worker with valuable insights into the nature of the presenting problem. It is important for clients to feel that the worker is truly interested in them and understands them; this also helps build rapport and trust. Also helpful during both Stage 2 and Stage 3 is using the questions of solution-focused therapy (SFT) to identify clients' strengths and resources, which includes discerning their effective past coping skills (Greene, Lee, Trask, & Rheinscheld, 2000; also see Yeager & Gregoire, 2000). Some of the SFT questions that would be helpful are:

- Exception question (identifying times when the problematic situation is not present or is just a little bit better and what is different about those times compared with the present crisis situation)
- Coping question
- Questions for identifying past success

Identifying client strengths and resources should also help in developing rapport and trust, as clients tend to develop comfort more quickly with someone who is not focusing only on their shortcomings (deficits, dysfunction, and failures; Greene, Lee, Trask, & Rheinscheld, 2000).

## Stage 4

Deal with feelings and emotions by effectively using active listening skills. Show the client that you are listening to what he or she is saying by responding with encouraging phrases, such as "Uh-huh" and "Oh." This type of verbal feedback is especially important when providing telephone intervention. Additional skills include reflection, paraphrasing, and emotion labeling (Bolton, 1984). Reflection involves restating the words, feelings, and ideas of the client; paraphrasing involves restating the meaning of the client's words in the worker's own language; and emotion labeling involves the worker summarizing the emotions that seem to underlie the client's message, for example, "You sound very angry" (Eaton & Roberts, 2002, p. 73).

## Stage 5

Generate and explore alternatives by identifying the client's strengths and previous successful coping mechanisms. Ideally, the ability of the worker and the client to work collaboratively during this stage should yield the widest array of potential resources and alternatives. According to Roberts (2000), the person in crisis is viewed as resourceful and resilient

> and having untapped resources or latent inner coping skills from which to draw upon.... Integrating strengths and solution-focused approaches involves jogging clients' memories so they recall the last time everything seemed to be going well, and they were in a good mood rather than depressed and/or successfully dealt with a previous crisis in their lives. (p. 19)

Aguilera and Messick (1982) state that the ability to be creative and flexible, adapting ideas to individual situations, is a key skill in effective workers.

## Stage 6

Implement the action plan. The crisis worker should assist the client in the least restrictive manner, enabling the client to feel empowered. Important steps in this stage include identifying persons and referral sources to be contacted and providing coping mechanisms (Roberts & Roberts, 2000). Crisis workers at Community Integration, Inc. Crisis Services utilize carbon forms to record the plan developed by worker and client. This is a useful mechanism to provide clients with phone numbers and specifics of the plan to follow, and it also provides the necessary documentation for other crisis workers to know what to encourage and reinforce on subsequent contacts with the client (Eaton & Ertl, 2000).

## Stage 7

Establish a follow-up plan and agreement. Crisis workers should follow up with the client after the initial intervention to ensure that the crisis has been resolved and to determine the postcrisis status of the client and the situation. This can be accomplished via telephone or face-to-face contact. In a team setting, when someone other than the original crisis worker will be conducting follow-ups, the utilization of a dry erase board can be a good organizational tool. At a glance, all workers can view the list of cases needing follow-up, when follow-up was requested, and items to address during follow-up contact. Of course, documentation in the client's chart would be more detailed and specific (Eaton & Roberts, 2002).

## CRISIS VERSUS TRAUMA REACTIONS

For the most part, individuals function in their daily lives in a state of emotional balance. Occasionally, intensely stressful life events will stretch a person's sense of well-being and equilibrium. However, even stressful life events are frequently predictable within a person's ordinary routines, and he or she is able to mobilize effective coping methods to handle the stress. In sharp contrast, traumatic events lift people out of their usual realm of equilibrium and make it difficult to re-establish a sense of balance. Trauma reactions are often precipitated by a sudden, random, and arbitrary traumatic event. The most common types of trauma-inducing stressors are violent crimes, acts of terrorism, and natural disasters (Young, 1995).

### Trauma Assessment and Treatment

Traumatic events are overwhelming, unpredictable, and emotionally shocking experiences. The potentially traumatizing event may be a large-scale disaster, such as an earthquake, Hurricane Bonnie's devastation in southern Florida, or the bombing of the Oklahoma City Federal Office Building. These were all disasters that occurred at one point in time. Traumas may also build up from a series of traumatic events that may repeat themselves many times over months and years, such as domestic violence, incest, and war. The impact of the traumatic event(s) may be both physical and psychological. Nevertheless, it is important to note that the majority of individuals who are exposed to a traumatic event experience psychological trauma symptoms but never develop PTSD.

Working with survivors and secondary victims of mass murders poses special issues and problems for mental health professionals and requires specialized knowledge, skills, and training. For example, clients suffering from PTSD may need emergency appointments with little notice, or they may need to see their trauma therapist the morning after a night of intense nightmares and flashbacks. As a result of upsetting memories and insomnia after the nightmares, clients may have angry outbursts in the clinician's office. In addition, mental health practitioners working in outpatient and inpatient settings need to recognize that for some survivors of disaster-induced trauma, stress and grief reactions will last for 10 to 60 days and then totally subside. For others, there may be delayed acute crisis reactions at the 1-month and 1-year anniversaries of the disastrous event. Still others will develop full-blown PTSD, evidenced by their chronic intrusive thoughts, avoidance behavior, flashbacks, nightmares, and hypervigilance, which may persist for years. The traumatic memories keep intruding during the day and in the middle of the night until they become unbearable.

Research has indicated that the effects of community disasters on levels of psychological distress, transient stress reactions, acute stress disorder, generalized anxiety disorder, death anxiety, and PTSD vary from one study to the next (Blair, 2000; Chantarujikapong et al., 2001; Cheung-Chung, Chung, & Easthope, 2000; Fukuda, Morimoto, Mure, & Maruyama, 2000; Hasanovic, Sinanovic, Selimbasic, Pajevic, & Avdibegovic, 2006; Kohrt et al., 2008). PTSD and high levels of psychological distress seem to be dependent factors such as: age, gender, personal resources and living arrangements, and quality of life after the traumatic event. Lev-wiesel's (2000) retrospective study of 170 Holocaust survivors 55 years posttrauma found that the most significant mediating factor in preventing PTSD was the child survivor's living arrangements at the end of the war. The study findings indicate that the most traumatic stress and PTSD were experienced by child survivors who had been placed in foster homes, and the lowest traumatic stress was found in survivors who were sheltered by the partisans and/or hid in the woods (Lev-wiesel, 2000). With regard to the influence of age and gender on the severity of depressive symptoms among 1,015 adults 1 year after the Armenian earthquake, the following was found: "Persons between the ages of 31–55 reported significantly higher depressive ratings than individuals who were 17–30," and women had much higher scores on the Beck Depression Inventory than the men in the study (Toukmanian, Jadaa, & Lawless, 2000, p. 296). Research demonstrates that resilience, personal resources, and social supports are important variables in mediating and mitigating the development of PTSD (Fukuda et al., 2000; Gold et al., 2000; Lev-wiesel, 2000). In addition, although depressive symptomatology seems to be comorbid with PTSD, in studies of prisoners of war, higher educational levels and social support were associated with lower depressive symptoms and trauma (Gold et al., 2000; Solomon, Mikulciner, & Avitzur, 1989).

Several studies have examined whether there is an association between trauma exposure during traumatic events and death anxiety after witnessing or experiencing life-threatening or near-death encounters associated with a plane crash. For example, Cheung-Chung, Chung, and Easthope (2000) found that in the aftermath of an airline crash in Coventry, England, in which the plane crashed near 150 private homes (no residents were killed, although multiple fires spread throughout the neighborhood as a result of the crash), 40% of the witnesses had intrusive thoughts, 30% found that other things kept making them think about the disaster, 36% had trouble falling or staying asleep, and 33% had pictures of the disaster popping into their minds. In sharp contrast, 70% reported that they either rarely or never had any dreams about the crash. With regard to death anxiety or fear of death, close to one in three persons (29%) expressed fears or anxiety about death. This study indicates the different responses of individuals who have witnessed an aircraft disaster. Unfortunately, these types of studies rarely conduct a psychiatric or biopsychosocial history to determine the relationship between preexisting psychiatric disorders or physical illnesses and the development of partial or full-blown PTSD.

Post-traumatic stress reactions are a pattern of conscious and subconscious expressions of behavior and emotional responses related to handling recollections of the environmental stressors of the traumatic or catastrophic event and the immediate aftermath. First and foremost, public safety must be maintained. In other words, police, firefighters, and emergency services personnel should make sure that all survivors are transported to a safe place and that there is no further danger at the disaster site. Only after all survivors are in a safe place should group grief counseling, and mental health referrals begin. In the weeks and months after the disaster, mental health professionals and crisis intervenors need to be ready to conduct crisis and trauma assessments. Only mental health professionals experienced in crisis and trauma work should conduct the assessments and interventions. Rushed assessments by inexperienced professionals or volunteers and use of standardized mental health intake rating forms have resulted in the false labeling of clients with post-traumatic stress reactions as having personality disorders.

In the months after a community disaster, trauma therapists should be available and on call for follow-up work. Once the traumatized person is referred to an experienced trauma therapist, the following should take place:

1. A comprehensive biopsychosocial, crisis, and trauma assessment should be completed.
2. Specific treatment goals and a treatment plan should be developed.
3. An agreed number of sessions, specified in a formal or informal contract, should be determined.
4. Both directive and nondirective counseling techniques should be utilized, applying empirically tested and evidence-supported approaches to trauma.
5. An open-door policy should be maintained so that clients can return periodically for booster sessions or follow-up treatment when needed.

## Acute Stress Management

The American Academy of Experts in Traumatic Stress is an interdisciplinary network of professionals providing emergency responses and timely intervention for survivors of traumatic events. Drs. Mark D. Lerner and Raymond D. Shelton (2001) have written a monograph that includes their detailed traumatic stress response protocol. The following is a summary of

Lerner and Shelton's 10 stages of acute stress management provides useful guideposts for all first responders (i.e., emergency service personnel, crisis response team members, and disaster mental health workers) in the direct aftermath of a community disaster:

1. Assess for danger/safety for self and others.
2. Consider the physical and perceptual mechanism of injury.
3. Evaluate the level of responsiveness.
4. Address medical needs.
5. Observe and identify each individual's signs of traumatic stress.
6. Introduce yourself, state your title and role, and begin to develop a connection.
7. Ground the individual by allowing him or her to tell his or her story.
8. Provide support through active and empathic listening.
9. Normalize, validate, and educate.
10. Bring the person to the present, describe future events, and provide referrals.

## Eye Movement Desensitization and Reprocessing

Another trauma treatment model that has had some degree of success, although it is viewed as controversial by many practitioners, is eye movement desensitization and reprocessing (EMDR). This time-limited eight-stage treatment method is utilized after a therapeutic bond has been established with the patient. A growing amount of evidence indicates that EMDR is effective with patients who have had one specific traumatic experience when the treatment is implemented by an experienced therapist with extensive formal training in EMDR. The EMDR protocol includes eight phases, with specific steps in each phase (Shapiro, 1995). EMDR integrates cognitive-behavioral strategies, such as desensitization, imaginal exposure, and cognitive restructuring, and systematic bilateral stimulation and relaxation techniques. A number of studies, including a meta-analysis, have documented the efficacy of EMDR in treating PTSD. This approach has shown significant positive effects when compared with other treatment modalities or pharmacotherapy for PTSD and other trauma-induced problems (Rubin, 2002; Van Etten & Taylor, 1998). Rubin has reviewed controlled randomized studies that found positive effects, particularly with regard to reducing trauma symptoms in children who were suffering from a single trauma and/ or loss of a loved one. (See the article by Karen Knox [2002] for a relevant case application of EMDR with a young adult family member who lost a loved one in the World Trade Center terrorist attack.) It should be noted that the research has shown that EMDR has not been effective in reducing psychiatric sequelae of agoraphobia, social phobia, and generalized anxiety disorder (Rubin, 2002).

## Cognitive Processing Therapy

Cognitive processing therapy (CPT) is a time-limited therapy that has been found to be effective for PTSD and other corollary symptoms after traumatic events (Monson et al., 2006; Resick et al., 2002). Although the original research on CPT focused primarily on rape victims, CPT has since been applied in a structured, sequenced approach to address the unique needs of patients suffering from PTSD and/or depression. Specifically, CPT is a short-term treatment that may work in as few as 12 treatment sessions. Of course, treatment may be provided for longer periods depending on each individual's needs. Sessions address the following issues:

- Educating patients about PTSD and explaining the nature of their symptoms
- Helping patients explore how traumatic events have affected their lives
- Learning about connections between trauma-related thoughts, feelings, and behaviors
- Remembering the traumatic event and experiencing the emotions associated with it
- Increasing patients' ability to challenge maladaptive thoughts about the trauma
- Helping patients increase their understanding of unhelpful thinking patterns and learn new, healthier ways of thinking
- Facilitating patients' exploration of how each of five core themes has been affected by their traumatic experiences.

CPT is like cognitive therapy in that it is based in the idea that PTSD symptoms stem from a conflict between pretrauma beliefs about the self and the world (e.g., the belief in the just-world concept, that is, if I work hard and do things right, good things will happen to me) and posttrauma information (e.g., the trauma as evidence that the world is not a safe place). These conflicts are identified through therapy and are thought of as "stuck points," which are addressed through writing about the trauma. During CPT, the patient is asked to write about his or her traumatic event in detail. The patient is then instructed to read the story aloud repeatedly, both in and outside of the session. The therapist helps the client identify and address stuck points and errors in thinking via "cognitive restructuring." Errors in thinking may include thoughts such as "I am a bad person" or "I did something to deserve this." The therapeutic process aids the patient in examining and addressing these errors or stuck points by examining evidence for and against those thoughts and developing new thoughts to replace the errors in thinking.

CPT is appropriate for patients who have experienced a traumatic event and are suffering from PTSD and/or depression. It probably is not appropriate for patients who are currently a danger to themselves or others, or who are in imminent danger due to their involvement in an abusive relationship (or due to being stalked). Also, if a patient is so dissociative or has such severe panic attacks that he or she cannot discuss the trauma at all, then other therapy may need to precede the onset of CPT.

## Crisis Worker Self-Care

One cannot discuss working with populations affected by crisis and trauma without discussing the crisis counselor or social worker as well. An overlooked element of crisis work is the responsibility of the mental health professional to engage in appropriate self-care. Crisis intervenors are not immune to stress and stress responses. Each individual will respond differently to different situations depending on the severity of the crisis and the meaning the crisis represents to the intervenor, family friends, or organizations, yet there are certain signs and symptoms that are associated with a maladaptive stress response. Symptoms are more likely to be identified in newer crisis intervenors than in seasoned professionals who have worked many hours under stressful conditions and have developed and refined coping mechanisms to respond to stressful situations.

Factors associated with maladaptive stress response include the duration and severity of the event. The intensity of the event experienced by the crisis worker should be considered as a contributing factor to the development of stress reactions. This factor is highly subjective because not all persons will respond the same to any given event. Finally, in any situation that has compromised the crisis worker's ability to function within the home, work, or social environment, intrusive thoughts related to a crisis may be reflective of an emerging anxiety disorder. Individuals reporting such symptoms should be considered for mental health assistance and referral and respite from direct crisis work until this issue is resolved. For a list of common psychological, emotional, cognitive, behavioral, and physical responses associated with maladaptive stress reactions, see Roberts and Yeager (2009, pp. 189–192).

## CONCLUSION

The attacks of September 11, 2001, resulted in huge personal, psychological, and financial traumas. Such community disasters can overload our traditional coping methods. Mental health professionals and emergency responders are always ready and eager to aid persons in crisis. However, prior to September 11, no one had anticipated that the United States would be victimized in an assault of the magnitude that occurred; therefore, the health care and mental health organizations were not prepared with an interagency coordinated disaster mental health response. Since September 11, there have been numerous human-initiated and natural disasters. Because of the threat of terrorist activity in the future, both in the United States and throughout the world, mental health educators and practitioners must develop the following: training and certification programs for crisis intervenors and trauma specialists; systematic and empirically tested procedures and protocols for crisis response, crisis intervention, and trauma treatment in the event of a future mass disaster or terrorist attack; and coordinated interagency disaster mental health teams on call and ready for rapid deployment to community disasters in their respective regions.

Behavioral clinicians, mental health counselors, and social workers are increasingly being expected to respond quickly and efficiently to individuals and groups who are in need of crisis intervention and time-limited, trauma-focused treatment. This overview has presented the ACT conceptual model to help communities respond to survivors of disasters and prepare for the future. Concerns about the growing threat of violence in corporations, manufacturing facilities, hospitals, and educational institutions are resulting in organizational pressure being placed on practitioners to be skilled in effectively assessing risks and unmet needs and providing rapid intervention. Roberts's (1991, 2000) seven-stage crisis intervention model provides clinicians with a useful framework to follow. Lerner and Shelton's (2001) 10-step trauma assessment and intervention model also provides a useful framework to facilitate the recovery of survivors of traumatic events. These conceptual models will assist practitioners in facilitating effective crisis resolution and trauma reduction.

A number of studies and a meta-analysis have demonstrated that certain population groups benefit from crisis intervention programs. Females aged 15 to 24 and 55 to 64 benefited the most from suicide prevention and crisis intervention programs (J. Corcoran & Roberts, 2000). The research on the effectiveness of crisis intervention programs with people presenting with psychiatric emergencies also shows positive outcomes; however, those clients with preexisting severe personality disorders usually benefited from crisis intervention only when it was augmented with short-term inpatient treatment followed by twice-a-week outpatient treatment and medication management (J. Corcoran & Roberts, 2000). The research on the effectiveness of crisis intervention after the September 11 terrorist attacks has yet to be completed. Therefore, it is recommended that future studies should be strengthened by including standardized crisis assessments at pretest, posttest, and follow-ups, along with determining preexisting psychiatric conditions. In addition, whenever possible, matched naturally occurring comparison groups or quasi-control groups (no crisis intervention) should be created. Most important, longitudinal follow-up studies, whether through face-to-face or telephone contact, should be administered at uniform intervals (e.g., 1 month, 3 months, 6 months, 12 months, 24 months, 36 months, 5 years, and 10 years after the initial crisis intervention). Independent evaluators or researchers or university-based researchers should be hired or contracted with by crisis intervention units of local community mental health centers, victim assistance programs, and outpatient hospital clinics. The call to action is clear, and the need is clearly defined. The task of addressing the ever-changing face of crisis is a growing and daunting challenge that is ever present. In this time of healthcare and mental health transformation, it is important that legislators, first responders, care providers, and academicians work together to determine effective approaches to crisis in a consolidated effort to manage the ever-growing challenges of crisis intervention.

REFERENCES

Aguilera, D., & Messick, J. (1982). *Crisis intervention: Theory and methodology* (4th ed.). St. Louis: Mosby.

American Psychiatric Association. (2013). *Diagnostic and statistical manual of mental disorders: DSM-5*. Washington, DC: Author.

Austrian, S. (2002). Biopsychosocial assessment. In A. R. Roberts & G. J. Greene (Eds.), *Social workers' desk reference* (pp. 204–208). New York: Oxford University Press.

Becker, S. M. (2006). Psychosocial care for adult and child survivors of the 2004 tsunami disaster in India. *American Journal of Public Health, 96,* 1397–1398.

Belkin, G. (1984). *Introduction to counseling* (2nd ed.). Dubuque, IA: William C. Brown.

Blair, R. (2000). Risk factors associated with PTSD and major depression among Cambodian refugees in Utah. *Health and Social Work, 25,* 23–30.

Bolton, R. (1984). *People skills*. Englewood Cliffs, NJ: Prentice-Hall.

Buka, S. L., Stichick, T. L., Birdthistle, I., & Earls, F. J. (2001). Youth exposure to violence: Prevalence, risks, and consequences. *American Journal of Orthopsychiatry, 71,* 298–310.

Burgess, A. W., & Roberts, A. R. (2000). Crisis intervention for persons diagnosed with clinical disorders based on the stress-crisis continuum. In A. R. Roberts (Ed.), *Crisis intervention handbook: Assessment, treatment, and research* (2nd ed., pp. 56–76). New York: Oxford University Press.

Chantarujikapong, S. I., Scherrer, J. F., Xian, H., Eisen, S. A., Lyons, M. J., Goldberg, J., et al. (2001). A twin study of generalized anxiety disorder symptoms, panic disorder symptoms and post-traumatic stress disorder in men. *Psychiatry Research, 103,* 133–145.

Cheung-Chung, M. C., Chung, C., & Easthope, Y. (2000). Traumatic stress and death anxiety among community residents exposed to an aircraft crash. *Death Studies, 24*, 689–704.

Corcoran, J., & Roberts, A. R. (2000). Research on crisis intervention and recommendations for future research. In A. R. Roberts (Ed.), *Crisis intervention handbook: Assessment, treatment, and research* (2nd ed., pp. 453–486). New York: Oxford University Press.

Cutler, D. L., Yeager, K. R., & Nunley, W. (2013). Crisis intervention and support. In K. R. Yeager, D. L. Cutler, D. Svendsen, & G. M. Sills (Eds.), *Modern community mental health: an interdisciplinary approach* (pp. 243–255). New York: Oxford University Press.

Davis, T. E., III, Tarcza, E., & Munson, M. (2009). The psychological impact of hurricanes and storms on adults. In K. Cherry (Ed.), *Lifespan perspectives on natural disasters: Coping with Katrina, Rita, and other storms* (pp. 97–112). New York: Springer Science and Business Media.

DiMaggio, C., Galea, S., & Richardson, L. D. (2007). Emergency department visits for behavioral and mental health care after a terrorist attack. *Annals of Emergency Medicine, 50*, 327–34.

DuRant, R. H., Treiber, F., Goodman, E., & Woods, E. R. (1996). Intentions to use violence among young adolescent. *Pediatrics, 98*, 1104–1108.

Eaton, Y., & Ertl, B. (2000). The comprehensive crisis intervention model of Community Integration, Inc. Crisis Services. In A. R. Roberts (Ed.), *Crisis intervention handbook: Assessment, treatment, and research* (2nd ed., pp. 373–387). New York: Oxford University Press.

Eaton, Y., & Roberts, A. R. (2002). Frontline crisis intervention: Step-by-step practice guidelines with case applications. In A. R. Roberts & G. J. Greene (Eds.), *Social workers' desk reference* (pp. 89–96). New York: Oxford University Press.

Elal, G., & Slade, P. (2005). Traumatic Exposure Severity Scale (TESS): A measure of exposure to major disasters. *Journal of Traumatic Stress, 18*, 213–220.

Fukuda, S., Morimoto, K., Mure, K., & Maruyama, S. (2000). Effect of the Hanshin-Awaji earthquake on posttraumatic stress, lifestyle changes, and cortisol levels of victims. *Archives of Environmental Health, 55*, 121–125.

Gitterman, A. (2002). The life model. In A. R. Roberts & G. J. Greene (Eds.), *Social workers' desk reference* (pp. 105–107). New York: Oxford University Press.

Gold, P. B., Engdahl, B. E., Eberly, R. E., Blake, R. J., Page, W. F., & Frueh, B. C. (2000). Trauma exposure, resilience, social support, and PTSD construct validity among former prisoners of war. *Social Psychiatry and Psychiatric Epidemiology, 35*, 36–42.

Gorman-Smith, D., Henry, D. B., & Tolan, P. H. (2004). Exposure to community violence and violence perpetration: The protective effects of family functioning. *Journal of Clinical Child and Adolescent Psychology, 33*, 439–449.

Greene, G. J., Lee, M. L., Trask, R., & Rheinscheld, J. (2000). How to work with clients' strengths in crisis intervention: A solution-focused approach. In A. R. Roberts (Ed.), *Crisis intervention handbook: Assessment, treatment, and research* (2nd ed., pp. 31–55). New York: Oxford University Press.

Hasanovic, M., Sinanovic, O., Selimbasic, Z., Pajevic, I., & Avdibegovic, E. (2006) Psychological disturbances of war-traumatized children from different foster and family settings in Bosnia and Herzegovina. *Croatian Medical Journal, 47*, 85–94.

Karls, J. M. (2002). Person-in-environment system: Its essence and applications. In A. R. Roberts & G. J. Greene (Eds.), *Social workers' desk reference* (pp. 194–198). New York: Oxford University Press.

Kasick, D. P., & Bowling C. D. (2013). Crisis intervention teams: A boundary-spanning collaboration between the law enforcement and mental health communities. In K. R. Yeager, D. Cutler, D. Svendsen, & G. M. Sills (Eds.), *Modern community mental health: An interdisciplinary approach* (pp. 304–315). New York: Oxford University Press.

Kelly, S. (2010). The psychological consequences to adolescents of exposure to gang violence in the community: An integrated review of the literature. *Journal of Child and Adolescent Psychiatric Nursing, 23*(2), 61–73.

Kessler, R. C., Galea, S., Gruber, M. J., Sampson, N. A., Ursano, R. J., & Wessely, S. (2008). Trends in mental illness and suicidality after Hurricane Katrina. *Molecular Psychiatry, 13*, 374–384.

Kohrt, B. A., Jordans, M. J. D., Tol, W. A., Speckman, R. A., Maharjan, S. M., Worthman, C. M., & Komproe, I. H. (2008) Comparison of mental health between former child soldiers and children never conscripted by armed groups in Nepal.

*Journal of the American Medical Association, 300*, 691–702.

LeCroy, C., & Okamoto, S. (2002). Guidelines for selecting and using assessment tools with children. In A. R. Roberts & G. J. Greene (Eds.), *Social workers' desk reference* (pp. 213–216). New York: Oxford University Press.

Leise, B. S. (1995). Integrating crisis intervention, cognitive therapy and triage. In A. R. Roberts (Ed.), *Crisis intervention and time-limited cognitive treatment* (pp. 28–51). Thousand Oaks, CA: Sage.

Lev-wiesel, R. (2000). Posttraumatic stress disorder symptoms, psychological distress, personal resources, and quality of life. *Family Process, 39*, 445–460.

Leise, B.S., (1995). Integrating crisis intervention, cognitive therapy and triage. In A. R. Roberts (Ed.), *Crisis intervention and time-limited cognitive treatment* (pp. 28–51). Thousand Oaks, CA: Sage.

Lewis, S., & Roberts, A. R. (2001). Crisis assessment tools. In A. R. Roberts & G. J. Greene (Eds.), *Social workers' desk reference* (pp. 208–212). New York: Oxford University Press.

Lovibond, S. H., & Lovibond, P. F. (1995). Manual for the Depression Anxiety Stress Scales (2nd ed.) Sydney: Psychology Foundation.

Monson, C. M., Schnurr, P. P., Resick, P. A., Friedman, M. J., Young-Xu, & Stevens, S. P. (2006). Cognitive processing therapy for veterans with military-related posttraumatic stress disorder. *Journal of Consulting and Clinical Psychology, 74*, 898–907.

Munson, C. (2002). Guidelines for the *Diagnostic and Statistical Manual*

(*DSM-IV-TR*) *multiaxial system diagnosis.* In A. R. Roberts & G. J. Greene (Eds.), *Social workers' desk reference* (pp. 181–189). New York: Oxford University Press.

Pike, C. K. (2002). Developing client-focused measures. In A. R. Roberts & G. J. Greene (Eds.), *Social workers' desk reference* (pp. 189–193). New York: Oxford University Press.

Resick, P. A., Nisith, P., Weaver, T. L., Astin, M. C., & Feuer, C. A. (2002). A comparison of cognitive processing therapy, prolonged exposure and a waiting condition for the treatment of posttraumatic stress disorder in female rape victims. *Journal of Consulting and Clinical Psychological, 70,* 867–879.

Roberts, A. R. (1991). Conceptualizing crisis theory and the crisis intervention model. In A. R. Roberts (Ed.), *Contemporary perspectives on crisis intervention and prevention* (pp. 3–17). Englewood Cliffs, NJ: Prentice-Hall.

Roberts, A. R. (1996). Epidemiology and definitions of acute crisis episodes. In A. R. Roberts (Ed.), *Crisis management and brief treatment.* Chicago: Nelson-Hall.

Roberts, A. R. (2000). An overview of crisis theory and crisis intervention. In A. R. Roberts (Ed.), *Crisis intervention handbook: Assessment, treatment, and research* (2nd ed., pp. 3–30). New York: Oxford University Press.

Roberts, A. R., & Roberts, B. S. (2000). A comprehensive model for crisis intervention with battered women and their children. In A. R. Roberts (Ed.), *Crisis intervention handbook: Assessment, treatment, and research* (2nd ed.,

pp. 177–207). New York: Oxford University Press.

Roberts, A. R., & Yeager, K. R. (2009). *Pocket guide to crisis intervention.* New York: Oxford University Press.

Rubin, A. (2002). Eye movement de-sensitization and reprocessing. In A. R. Roberts & G. J. Greene (Eds.), *Social workers' desk reference* (pp. 412–417). New York: Oxford University Press.

Sattler, J. M., & Hoge, R. D. (2006). *Assessment of children: Behavioral, social, and clinical foundations.* San Diego: J. M. Sattler.

Seelig, M. D., & Kayton, W. (2008). Gaps in depression care: Why primary care physicians should hone their depression screening, diagnosis and management skills. *Journal of Occupational & Environmental Medicine, 50,* 451–458.

Shapiro, F. (1995). *Eye movement de-sensitization and reprocessing: Basic principles, protocols, and procedures.* New York: Guilford Press.

Solomon, Z., Mikulciner, M., & Avitzur, E. (1989). Coping, locus of control, social support, and combat-related posttraumatic stress disorder: A prospective study. *Journal of Personality and Social Psychology, 55,* 279–285.

Terr, L. (1994). *Unchained memories: True stories of traumatic memories, lost and found.* New York: Basic Books.

Toukmanian, S. G., Jadaa, D., & Lawless, D. (2000). A cross-cultural study of depression in the aftermath of a natural disaster. *Anxiety, Stress, and Coping, 13,* 289–307.

Valentine, P. (2000). An application of crisis intervention to situational crises frequently experienced by adult survivors of incest. In A. R. Roberts (Ed.), *Crisis intervention handbook: Assessment, treatment, and research* (2nd ed., pp. 250–271). New York: Oxford University Press.

Vandiver, V. L., & Corcoran, K. (2002). Guidelines for establishing treatment goals and treatment plans with Axis I disorders: Sample treatment plan for generalized anxiety disorder. In A. R. Roberts & G. J. Greene (Eds.), *Social workers' desk reference* (pp. 297–304). New York: Oxford University Press.

Van Etten, M., & Taylor, S. (1998). Comparative efficacy of treatments for post-traumatic stress disorder: A meta-analysis. *Clinical Psychology and Psychotherapy, 5*, 126–145.

Walker, E. R., Tucker, S. J., Lynch, J., & Druss, B. J. (2014). Physical healthcare and mental healthcare. In K. R. Yeager, D. Cutler, D. Svendsen, & G. M. Sills (Eds.), *Modern community mental health: An interdisciplinary approach* (pp. 217–227). New York: Oxford University Press.

Weiss, D., & Marmar, C. (2007). The Impact of Event Scale—Revised. In J. Wilson & T. Keane (Eds.), *Assessing psychological trauma and PTSD* (pp. 219–238). New York: Guilford Press.

Williams, J. B. W. (2002). Using the *Diagnostic and Statistical Manual for Mental Disorders*, 4th ed., text revision (*DSM-IV-TR*). In A. R. Roberts & G. J. Greene (Eds.), *Social workers' desk reference* (pp. 171–180). New York: Oxford University Press.

Yeager, K. R., & Minkoff, K. (2013). Establishing a comprehensive, continuous, integrated system of care for persons with co-occurring conditions. In K. R. Yeager, D. Cutler, D. Svendsen, & G. M. Sills (Eds.), *Modern community mental health: An interdisciplinary approach* (pp. 497–515). New York: Oxford University Press.

Williams, R. (2006). The psychosocial consequences for children and young people who are exposed to terrorism, war, conflict and natural disasters. *Current Opinion in Psychiatry, 19*, 337–349.

Yeager, K. R., & Gregoire, T. K. (2000). Crisis intervention application of brief solution-focused therapy in addictions. In A. R. Roberts (Ed.), *Crisis intervention handbook: Assessment, treatment, and research* (2nd ed., pp. 275–306). New York: Oxford University Press.

Young, M. A. (1995). Crisis response teams in the aftermath of disasters. In A. R. Roberts (Ed.), *Crisis intervention and time-limited cognitive treatment* (pp. 151–187). Thousand Oaks, CA: Sage.

# 8

## Crisis Intervention and First Responders to Events Involving Terrorism and Weapons of Mass Destruction

VINCENT E. HENRY

July Fourth was a beautiful day in Veterans Memorial Park, and Central City police officers Pedro (Pete) Bernal and Dennis O'Loughlin were happy to be assigned to the Park Car that day. The thousand-acre park was full of people strolling, cycling, and rollerblading; a band was playing at the gazebo; and families spread their picnic blankets on the lawns and barbecued at the small beach at the edge of MacArthur Lake. "It doesn't get much better than this," Officer Bernal said to his partner as they cruised slowly past the playground filled with laughing children, "and it sure beats answering jobs all day in Sector Charlie. It's too bad every day can't be as nice and relaxed as today. A day like today makes you glad to be alive. Good country, America."

"It sure is. What should we do for lunch?" O'Loughlin replied, savoring the aromas of various ethnic foods emanating from all the pushcarts in the park. "It's almost one o'clock and I'm starving." After some discussion, they settled on a Cuban sandwich for Dennis and two hot dogs with mustard, relish, onions, and sauerkraut for Pete. The call came just as they were getting back in their cruiser.

"Park Car One on the air?"

"Park Car One. Go ahead, Central."

"Park One, we have multiple aided calls in the vicinity of the gazebo on the Great Lawn. Callers state several people are having seizures. An ambulance is on the way. Please check and advise."

Dennis and Pete looked at each other. Both were experienced and well-trained cops, and the implications of the call were readily apparent to them. Just this week the precinct's intelligence liaison officer, Lieutenant Kennedy, had briefed the outgoing roll call to be especially on guard for potential terrorist events during the holiday weekend. Based on information received at the weekly regional Terrorstat meeting, Kennedy related that credible but unspecified threats—"intelligence chatter"—had been received by the FBI and passed on to local agencies. Although the information was not specific, and although the nation and the city remained at Threat Condition Yellow, officers should be especially attentive when responding to unusual events.

"Ten-four, Central. Please try the callback numbers and determine the number of victims and if there are any other symptoms. Have the ambulance stand by at the south entrance to the park and have Park Two stand by near the boathouse until we check and advise."

Dennis and Pete regretfully put aside their food, started up their cruiser, and headed slowly toward the Great Lawn. They had been partners for almost 10 years and were experienced enough to know that they should not rush in to a situation like this, but instead respond carefully and gather as much information as possible on their way to the scene. A great many things had changed in police work during their 10 years as partners, not the least of which was the strategic and tactical approach they now took to calls that might involve a terrorist act. The terrorist attacks on the World Trade Center and the Pentagon in 2001, as well as the Boston Marathon bombing of 2013 and more than 60 foiled terrorist plots since the 9/11 attacks, required cops across the nation to adopt a new and very different orientation to the way they worked, and the possibility that even the most mundane and seemingly ordinary call for service might have some terrorist connection was always in the back of their minds. So far, Central City had escaped the realities of terrorism, but Bernal and O'Loughlin and their entire department were well prepared and well trained to handle terrorist incidents.

Perhaps because Bernal and O'Loughlin were so well trained and so well prepared, they were also terribly frightened by the prospect of a terrorist attack, especially one involving weapons of mass destruction (WMDs). Everyone, it seems, was affected by the September 11 terrorist attacks, and in that respect these police officers were no different: Like many others, they had been riveted by media accounts of the attacks, and for days and weeks afterward they followed the frightening and terrible events closely in the news. As police officers, though, Bernal and O'Loughlin had a particularly strong interest in the September 11 attacks. Because they were experienced cops, they could very easily relate to the challenges and struggles faced by the police, fire, and other rescue personnel who responded to the World Trade Center or the Pentagon, and they felt great empathy for them. Similarly, they were affected by the Madrid train bombings of 2004; by the terrorist attacks on London's Underground subway system and an iconic London double-decker bus in 2005; by the multiple coordinated terrorist attacks in Mumbai in November 2008; by the mass shootings at Fort Hood, in Columbine and Aurora, Colorado, and at the Sandy Hook Elementary school; and by various other bombings and mass shootings. They had great empathy for the victims, as well as for the police who responded to these attacks. These events resonated with O'Loughlin and Bernal, and as cops are wont to do, they often proposed and discussed the types of scenarios they might encounter and debated their own tactical response should they ever encounter similar events. Today would prove that the time they spent discussing and debating tactical responses had not been wasted.

As experienced cops, O'Loughlin and Bernal could well understand the extent of the human tragedy resulting from these and other terrorist attacks: the anguish of thousands of families torn apart, the sorrow of thousands of friends of those who lost their lives, the pain and suffering of all those who were injured, the economic impact on those who lost their jobs and whose families lost a source of income. Bernal and O'Loughlin understood all this, and because they understood it so well—and because they were such good cops—they prepared themselves as thoroughly as they could for the possibility that such an event might take place in their city. Their department provided excellent training, but like many other cops, they sought out additional knowledge and skills that might become important if a terrorist attack occurred.

Bernal and O'Loughlin knew a great deal about terrorism and WMDs, and what they knew frightened them. They were frightened now, but they could not afford to let their fear become immobilizing: they had a job to do and responsibilities to fulfill. The public needed protection, and it was their role as police officers to provide that protection. Beyond the cognitive knowledge and skills they had acquired, the two cops had prepared themselves physically, emotionally, and psychologically for this day. Later, they would both talk about how frightened they were, but their overall preparation had steeled them emotionally and psychologically, and they were able to put their fear aside to fulfill both the public's expectations of them and their own profound and personal expectations of themselves. Both would later say that although they were afraid, they were also focused on the task required of them, and their fear had a somewhat distant or abstract quality. There was a job to do, and they refused to permit the substantial fear they felt to prevent them from doing what needed to be done.

Despite the warmth of the day, they rolled up the cruiser's windows and turned off the air conditioner; if the situation turned out the way they hoped it wouldn't, at least they would be partially protected from airborne contaminants that might be drawn in through the ventilation system. Pete rummaged in the gear bags on the cruiser's back seat, pulling out two pairs of binoculars, a small radiation detector, and a copy of the department's field guide to hazardous materials and WMDs.

On the way to the scene, they carefully watched the holiday crowds for anything unusual or out of the ordinary. No one they passed appeared to be ill, and no one seemed to be in a particular hurry to leave the area. Dennis stopped the cruiser at the edge of the woods surrounding the Great Lawn, about a quarter mile from the gazebo.

Pete scanned the area with his binoculars, first looking at the commotion near the gazebo and then scanning the trees at the edge of the lawn. Dennis also scanned the scene with his binoculars. The band had stopped playing, and highly excited people were milling around, trampling the picnic blankets and turning over barbecue grills. Some civilians lay prone or rolled on the ground as others tired to administer aid; others gathered their children and tried to flee the chaotic scene. Some fell to the ground as they ran, and others fell to their knees to vomit. Dennis and Pete could hear frenzied shouting, and several civilians, spotting the cruiser, ran toward the cops.

"No birds. I don't see any birds in the trees. And there's a mist or cloud hanging over the area. It could be barbecue smoke, but I don't know. There's a dog having some kind of seizure, too. What have you got?" Dennis said to his partner. "Rats. Look at the rats crossing the road. The rats are running away. The wind is blowing toward the west, spreading the cloud. Move the car up the hill to the east roadway, but don't get any closer to the gazebo. I think I see dead pigeons at the verge of the woods. I get nothing on the radiation detector for now, but we may be too far away."

The first civilian, a highly distraught man with a flushed face, streaming tears, and vomit on his shirt, reached the cruiser and shouted frantically at the cops to help. Pete and Dennis both knew that time, distance, and shielding were the keys to their self-preservation, just as they both knew that they would become liabilities rather than assets if they became contaminated or affected by whatever substance was making these people sick. Time, distance, and shielding were the keys to their survival as well as the survival of the victims. Pete used the loudspeaker to order the man to back off from the police car: the civilian could potentially be a vector to spread whatever chemical or biological agent was afflicting the crowd, and the two cops would be of no help to anyone if they became affected by it. They would later say that one of the hardest things about the situation was resisting the urge to rush in to immediately render aid; it is, after all, the natural tendency of cops and rescue workers to run toward trouble in order to help. But the very fact that they lived to discuss the incident was evidence that they acted wisely and according to the way they'd been trained.

Still, they would later be troubled by an amorphous sense of guilt—a sense of guilt that was, they knew, quite irrational because the reality was that they had performed superbly in every respect. The nagging thoughts remained, though: Perhaps they could have done more. Perhaps more lives could have been saved if only they had done something differently. If only they hadn't stopped for lunch. If only they responded more quickly. If only...

The guilt was just one lasting outcome of their experience, however. The horrible images and associations connected with their experiences on that day and on the days and weeks that followed would stay with them, always near the forefront of consciousness and seemingly ready to re-emerge at the slightest provocation. One of the most difficult things was that no one, other than those who were also at the park that day, really seemed to understand how different the world—their world—had become. No one seemed to understand what they had seen and felt and smelled and touched, how it changed their psychological world. They, along with the others who responded, were lauded as heroes, a label that was at first intoxicating but which they quickly came to resent. They, along with the others who responded, became the toast of the town after the attack—everyone, it seemed, wanted to be seen with these heroes and to bask in the reflected power of the horrible things they had come to know. They became suspicious that the expressions of support, encouragement, and thanks offered by others after the attack were hollow and counterfeit. It made them angry that no one else seemed to understand them, or that nothing would ever be the same.

Pete communicated with the man using the loudspeaker, learning more about what had gone on near the gazebo as the first victims fell ill and taking notes about the symptoms. He learned there was a faint odor, like the smell of newly cut grass, at the time the first people fell ill.

Dennis picked up the radio and spoke calmly:

Park Car One to Central. Be advised we have a likely mass chemical or biological event on the Great Lawn. Numerous civilians down. There is a crowd of several hundred people, and we'll be moving them away from the scene to the east side of the park near the boathouse. Notify the Emergency Response Unit. Notify Midtown Hospital, Saint Mary's, and all the other hospitals to expect casualties. Notify the patrol supervisor that we'll set up a temporary emergency headquarters in the Parks Department office north of the Lawn pending his arrival. Notify the chief and the Fire Department. Have all available PD units respond to seal the park entrances, exits, and perimeter, and have a unit respond to the Broadway bus station to prevent further contamination from people leaving the park. Have the ambulances respond to the boathouse area to set up an aid station. Central, caution the responding units not to approach the gazebo or the Great Lawn itself until we have further information about the contaminant and its effects. Also, caution the responding units to be aware of secondary devices or events. Here are the symptoms, Central...

The threat of terrorist events involving WMDs is real, and the futuristic scenario described here is not at all far-fetched.

The September 11, 2001, terrorist attacks on the World Trade Center and the Pentagon changed the United States forever, ushering in a host of new and unprecedented realities for the American people, for the intelligence and national security communities, for medical personnel, for private security entities, and perhaps especially for police, fire, and emergency medical personnel. In particular, police, fire, and emergency medical service personnel—the agencies and individuals most likely to be the first responders to possible terrorist attacks—faced compelling demands to develop and adopt new strategies and tactics, to undertake new training, and to view their roles and their work in an entirely different way. As first responders, police, fire, and emergency medical service personnel are the first line of defense in case of terrorist attack, but the enormity and complexity of the challenges they face make it abundantly clear that they alone cannot bear the responsibility for ensuring public safety. Although first responders play a critical role in homeland security, emergency and disaster management, and domestic preparedness, and although a great deal of attention and resources have already been allocated to counter the terrorist threat, much more needs to be done. As new threats, methods, and tactics of terrorist actions evolve, so too must the strategies and tactics employed to counter them.

Perhaps most important, the realistic potential that American people, towns, and cities may again come under attack from terrorists demands that significant systemic changes continue to evolve across the broad spectrum of public agencies and private entities charged with the responsibility for ensuring public safety. We must develop and implement a broader, more coordinated, more cohesive, and more focused approach to terrorism and to WMDs, and that approach must necessarily entail new relationships among all these public agencies and private entities.

The actions necessary to bring about these changes are extensive, and they lie well beyond the scope of this chapter to fully describe or explore. This chapter focuses more narrowly on the issue of WMDs in the hands of terrorist groups, on the danger they pose to the American people and our nation as a whole, and on the steps necessary to create a more viable system to counter the threat. The importance of adequate preparation for potential future terrorist acts involving WMDs is illuminated by the more than 60 terrorist plots foiled since 9/11 (Zuckerman, Bucci, & Carafano, 2013), by the Boston Marathon and Fort Hood terrorist attacks, and by the consensus among knowledgeable experts that additional future acts of terrorism are a practical inevitability. It is not a matter of whether such incidents will occur, but when they will occur (Shenon & Stout, 2002).

In the first section of this chapter, I define WMDs in general and provide an overview of specific types of WMDs as a way of understanding the nature of the threat they pose. I then examine, in a general way, the type of response protocols that police, fire, emergency medical service, and other agencies have employed in relation to a mass terrorist attack, highlighting some of the problems and issues that are likely to emerge. I then explore some of the psychological consequences that are likely to become manifest among first responders to terrorist and WMD events, finally describing an innovative and successful approach to providing first responders with the type and quality of clinical services they may need.

Largely because I had a professional involvement as a first responder to the World Trade Center attacks of September 11, 2001 and the rescue and recovery activities that took place in the ensuing months, this chapter draws many examples and insights from those experiences. The events surrounding the World Trade Center attacks serve as a useful model from which a variety of guiding principles and insights can be distilled, including insights into the range and quality of psychological consequences that are likely to affect first responders to terrorist events.

By no means, however, does this chapter present or represent an exhaustive exploration of the threats, the consequences, or the short- or long-term outcomes of a terrorist attack involving WMDs.

## WEAPONS OF MASS DESTRUCTION: AN OVERVIEW

Weapons of mass destruction are devices, biological organisms, or chemical substances that, when successfully detonated or dispersed, are readily capable of causing massive casualties. WMDs have been defined in various ways. The Department of Defense (Henneberry, 2001), for example, defines them as "weapons that are capable of a high order of destruction and/or of being used in such a manner as to destroy large numbers of people." The definition goes on to note that these can include nuclear, chemical, biological, and radiological weapons. For legal purposes, Title 18 of the US Code (18 USC 113B) incorporates specific mention of various types of firearms and other weapons in its definition of WMDs, but it goes on to include

> any weapon designed or intended to cause death or serious bodily injury
> through the release, dissemination, or impact of toxic or poisonous chemi-
> cals, or their precursors; any weapon involving a disease organism; or
> any weapon that is designed to release radiation or radioactivity at a level
> dangerous to human life. (18 USC 113B)

The Federal Emergency Management Agency ([FEMA], 2002, p. 9) defines WMDs as "any weapon that is designed or intended to cause death or serious bodily injury through the release, dissemination, or impact of toxic or poisonous chemicals; disease organisms; radiation or radioactivity; or explosion or fire." The FEMA definition goes on to point out that WMDs are distinguished from other types of terrorist tools because they may not be immediately obvious, because it may be difficult to determine when and where they have been released, and because of the danger they pose to first responders and medical personnel. Although a great deal of research has taken place on battlefield exposure to WMDs, scientists have a more limited understanding of how such weapons might affect civilian populations, particularly those in densely populated urban environments.

Another difficulty is that of attribution. The nature of many WMDs, especially biological agents, is such that quickly or immediately determining the individual or group responsible for their use may not be possible. In the absence of credible claims of responsibility, the attribution necessary to focus the investigation, to apprehend those responsible, to interdict future attacks, or to respond with military force or law enforcement action may be greatly delayed.

Examples of WMDs include nuclear devices (ranging from nuclear bombs to smaller and more easily constructed "dirty bombs" that spread deadly radiation in a relatively small area), biological devices (such as anthrax, smallpox, ricin, and other deadly toxins), and chemical agents (such as nerve agents and gaseous poisons). These three categories of weapons are often referred to collectively as nuclear, biological, and chemical (NBC) weapons. It should also be recognized that the hijacked airliners used in the September 11 terrorist attacks on the Pentagon and the World Trade Center clearly conform to the FEMA definition of a WMD: They were high-powered explosive devices loaded with highly flammable fuel that caused a tremendous number of casualties, they were not immediately obvious as weapons, and they posed an exceptionally high degree of danger to first responders and medical personnel as well as to the general public.

The improvised explosive devices (IEDs) contained in pressure cookers and concealed in backpacks that were used in the Boston Marathon bombing, like the IEDs used in the 2004 Madrid train bombings and the 2005 London bombings, could easily have been converted to "dirty bombs" that spread radiological materials by including a sufficient quantity of low-grade nuclear materials found in X-ray machines and other medical equipment as well as in many university research laboratories. Indeed, the acquisition in July 2014 of nearly 90 pounds of reportedly "low-grade" uranium from a Mosul University research laboratory by the terrorist group Islamic State in Iraq and Syria (ISIS) alerted the United States Homeland Security community to the potential threat of dirty bomb attacks here, despite statements by International Atomic Energy Commission officials that the material was not suitable for a nuclear device (Cowell, 2014).

## Biological and Chemical Agents in Warfare and Terrorism

Chemical and biological agents have been used in warfare between nations for many years, and they have been extremely effective weapons in terms of causing casualties and death, as well as in spreading fear and panic among an enemy's soldiers. More recently, they have become highly valued and sought-after weapons of choice for terrorists and extremist groups for essentially the same reasons, as well as the fact that they are rather easily manufactured and deployed. The first modern wartime use of chemical weapons of war occurred during World War I, when German forces used chlorine gas against Allied forces in April 1915 during the Second Battle of Ypres. British forces retaliated in September of that year, firing artillery shells containing chlorine gas against the German forces at Loos. Poison gas was a fairly successful but nevertheless imperfect battle-field weapon: French and Algerian troops fled in a panic when they confronted chlorine gas at Ypres, but shifting winds during the British action at Loos also caused numerous casualties among the British forces employing these weapons (Duffy, 2002). The fact that the spread and effect of poison gases and of some biological agents can be so easily affected by wind and other environmental factors makes them particularly unpredictable and especially dangerous to first responders, to rescue personnel, and to civilians in densely populated urban areas.

Fear of contamination and concerns that toxic residue from these substances may remain in and around a location where they have been employed or on objects within the area may result in public avoidance of the location and its environs. Particularly if dispersal of a chemical or biological agent takes place in a business or commercial district, a transportation facility, a shopping mall, or another public space, the dispersal could have profound economic consequences as well.

The development and use of poison gases continued throughout World War I. Phosgene gas was used by both sides in the conflict; ironically, it was seen as an improved weapon because it caused less choking and coughing than chlorine gas and was therefore more likely to be inhaled. Phosgene also had a delayed effect in which soldiers might suddenly die up to 48 hours after their exposure. Mustard gas, an almost odorless chemical, was developed by Germany and first used against Russian troops at Riga in 1917. The strategic advantages of mustard gas (also known as Yperite) included inflicting painful blisters, the fact that it was more difficult to protect against than chlorine or phosgene, and the fact that it could remain potent in the soil for weeks, making it dangerous to recapture contaminated trenches or territory lest additional casualties occur (Duffy, 2002). The use of chlorine, phosgene, and mustard gas continued throughout World War I, resulting in a terrible casualty rate. According to one estimate, there were almost 1,240,000 casualties from poison gas during World War I, including more than 90,000 deaths. Russia alone suffered nearly 420,000 gas casualties (Duffy, 2002).

The decades following World War I saw continued development of poison gases as well as some use on the battlefield. During the 1920s, British forces used chemical weapons against Kurdish rebels in Iraq; in the 1930s, Italy used mustard gas in its campaign to conquer Ethiopia, and Japan made use of chemical weapons in its invasion of China. The first nerve agent, tabun, was developed in Germany in 1938.

In the United States and throughout the world, water supply systems have proved to be a very attractive and frequently used vector for planned, attempted, and successful biological attacks by terrorists upon civilian populations. Gleik (2006) provides an extensive list of criminal and terrorist attacks involving the water supply, an infrastructure sector that has been exploited in attempts or plots by both domestic and international terrorist groups to disseminate toxic substances—including biological agents and poisons—in the United States.

In 1970, for example, the Weathermen, a radical domestic terrorist group whose members bombed police stations, courts, the Pentagon, and the US Capitol, reportedly sought biological agents to introduce into civilian water supplies in major American cities to protest the Vietnam War and American foreign policy (Gleik, 2006). In 1972, members of a right-wing neo-Nazi group known as the Order of the Rising Sun were arrested in possession of up to 40 kilograms of typhoid bacteria they planned to spread throughout the water supplies of several Midwestern American cities that included Chicago and St. Louis (Gleik, 2006; Sachs, 2002, p. 3). In 1975, members of the survivalist/fundamentalist group Covenant, Sword, and Arm of God were charged with possessing 30 gallons of potassium cyanide that they intended to introduce into the water supplies of New York City, Chicago, and Washington, DC. The group reportedly sought to hasten the coming of the Messiah by poisoning "sinners" in American cities, although, as Gleik (2006) notes, the quantity of poison in their possession was insufficient to achieve their goal. In 2003, al-Qaeda operatives in Saudi Arabia issued generic threats against the water supply infrastructure of American cities (Gleik, 2006, p. 482).

Indeed, it was in recognition of the significant threat that the introduction of biological and/or chemical agents into its water supply posed—as well as the inherent vulnerability of an extensive and widely distributed system of reservoirs, dams, and viaducts that had previously been virtually unprotected from such threats—that New York City began to harden potential water supply infrastructure in the months following the 9/11 attacks. The new policies and strategies included increased surveillance and patrols of key watershed resources and, for the first time, attempts to effectively limit or restrict public access to watershed areas: among other measures, the City of New York began to require proof of identity before issuing hunting and fishing permits for reservoir and watershed lands. Another bioterrorism event—one involving a more direct and low-tech distribution vector—occurred in the United States in 1984, when members of a religious cult known as Rajneeshee infected an estimated 751 people in Oregon with salmonella bacteria (Torok et al., 1997). Cult members grew the bacteria from cultures they purchased from a medical supply company and disseminated the bacteria by spraying it on restaurant salad bars. Their goal was to influence the results of an upcoming local election by making a large number of voters too sick to vote on election day (McDade & Franz, 1988; Sachs, 2002, pp. 4–5). Investigators considered the possibility of bioterrorism when the outbreak occurred, but that was deemed unlikely; the source of the contamination only became apparent when the FBI subsequently investigated the cult for other criminal violations. This incident highlighted the difficulties of distinguishing a bioterrorist attack from a naturally occurring infectious disease outbreak (McDade & Franz, 1988).

The series of anthrax attacks that took place across the United States in 2001 were a type of terrorist attack, spreading tremendous alarm and fear throughout the population. In these incidents, anthrax spores were distributed, perhaps at random, through the US Postal Service to individuals, corporations, and political figures, and at least 10 cases of anthrax infection were documented by health officials (Jernigan et al., 2001; Traeger et al., 2001). Despite an intensive and lengthy FBI investigation, the identity and motivation of the person or persons responsible for these attacks have never been completely determined and remain a matter of debate.

Former Iraqi dictator Saddam Hussein used both chemical weapons (nerve agents) and biological weapons (anthrax) on Iranian forces during the 1980–1988 war between Iran and Iraq, and he also used cyanide against Iraqi Kurds in 1987 and 1988. In 1995, members of the Aum Shinrikyo (or Supreme Truth) cult dispersed deadly sarin gas on the Tokyo subway system, killing a dozen people and injuring more than 5,500 others (Lifton, 1999).

The Aum Shinrikyo subway attack in Tokyo, which represents the first known successful use of poison gas or other WMD by terrorists, had a tremendous impact on Japan's government and on Japanese society because it spread such fear and alarm among members of the public. The Japanese people, like the rest of the world community, were not well prepared for the possibility that a fairly small and relatively obscure religious cult would carry out such an attack, nor were they prepared for the possibility that a fairly small cult *could* carry out this type of attack. The fact that such a small group marshaled the resources necessary to kill and injure large numbers of people and spread panic across an entire nation had repercussions throughout the world, demonstrating just how easily terrorists or extremist groups can manufacture and disseminate deadly WMDs.

Aum Shinrikyo was a doomsday cult centered around leader Shoko Asahara's apocalyptic philosophy and his twisted notion that only the true believers belonging to the cult would be saved when the world ended. Asahara's goal in undertaking the attack was to hasten the end of the world. The cult, which accumulated immense wealth from its members, recruited young scientists as members and put them to work producing biological and chemical weapons. It also began to stockpile hundreds of tons of deadly chemicals and acquired a helicopter to help distribute the gas over densely populated Japanese cities (Kristof, 1995; Lifton, 1999).

Aum Shinrikyo's terrorist attack was unusual to the extent that the plot was successfully executed and that it used poison gas to cause a large number of deaths, but the apocalyptic philosophy and worldview the group embraced are not all that rare. Rather, the notion of destroying the world or a large part of the world's population as the means to hasten an apocalyptic event that would bring on a new world order—typically a purer world order untainted by evil—is a common theme among fundamentalist religious extremists (Lifton, 1999; Strozier, 2002).

Sarin, an exceptionally toxic nerve agent that is several hundred times more toxic than cyanide, was first developed by Nazi scientists in the 1930s. Also known as GB, sarin is a fairly complex chemical compound that can take either liquid or gaseous form, and although its manufacture requires a fairly high level of skill, training, and knowledge of chemistry, it is made from common chemicals that are readily available to the public. Once Aum Shinrikyo cult members manufactured a quantity of sarin, they employed a rather simple and unobtrusive method to disseminate it: Liquid sarin was sealed in paint cans and other containers that cult members carried into subway stations in shopping bags. They simply put down the bags, casually punctured the containers with the tips of their umbrellas, and walked away while the liquid evaporated into a gas and spread through the area. Experts concur that the 1995 subway attack was, like the cult's lesser-known and less deadly 1994 Matsumoto attack also carried out with sarin gas in Nagano Prefecture, was simply a test, a dry run in anticipation of and preparation for a much larger and much more deadly attack. Experts also concur that many more lives would have been lost and many more people would have been injured if Aum Shinrikyo had been able to manufacture a purer form of sarin, had manufactured a larger quantity of it, or had distributed it more effectively (Kristof, 1995; Lifton, 1999).

Perhaps one of the most frightening aspects of Aum Shinrikyo's attack on the Tokyo subway system was the relative ease with which the group obtained the necessary precursor chemicals to manufacture large quantities of deadly sarin. Many other biological and chemical agents also are relatively easy to obtain, manufacture, and disseminate, making them very attractive to terrorist organizations. Depending on the particular chemical or biological agent involved, a relatively small and easily transportable amount of the substance can spread throughout an area and contaminate or infect people who come in contact with it. Especially when toxic biological substances with a prolonged incubation period are involved, signs of illness may not be immediately apparent. Individuals infected with the toxic substance may then act as vectors, spreading the substance to others with whom they have contact. Because days or even weeks might elapse before the first infected individuals become noticeably ill, they can spread the infection to literally hundreds or thousands of other people, many of whom will in turn become vectors spreading the disease.

A chemical event, in contrast, is likely to immediately produce dozens of victims, and first responders who lack adequate personal protection equipment may also become victims. All exposed victims must be decontaminated before leaving the scene because hospital emergency rooms will not accept the victims of a biological or chemical incident until they have been properly decontaminated.

Chemical agents can enter the body in various ways. Some agents are disseminated as aerosols or gases and enter the body through the respiratory tract; others are disseminated in a liquid form and enter the body through contact with the skin. Because the eyes and mucous membranes are particularly sensitive to many toxic agents, irritated eyes and nasal passages often indicate exposure. Although other chemical agents can be ingested via contaminated food or liquid, inhalation and skin contact are the primary hazard for victims and emergency responders.

There are three basic categories of chemical agents: nerve agents, blister or vesicant agents, and choking agents.

### Nerve Agents

Nerve agents, which include the substances tabun (GA), soman (GD), sarin (GB), and methylphosphonothioic acid (VX), are an especially toxic class of chemical weapon that act on the body by interrupting the central nervous system to prevent the transmission of nerve impulses. Exposure to nerve agents initially results in twitches and spasms and ultimately leads to the permanent impairment of the central nervous system or, with sufficient exposure, to death. Other symptoms of exposure to nerve agents typically include dilation of pupils (pinpoint pupils), runny nose and lacrimation (tearing of eyes), salivation (drooling), difficulty breathing, muscle twitches and spasms, involuntary defecation or urination, and nausea and vomiting.

Depending on their purity, nerve agents generally take the form of colorless liquids, although some may have a slight yellowish tinge if impurities are present. Tabun and sarin may have a slightly fruity odor, soman may have a slight odor of camphor, and methylphosphonothioic acid smells like sulfur. Nerve agents evaporate fairly quickly and can be absorbed into the body through either inhalation or absorption through the skin. Nerve agents vary a bit in terms of their toxicity and the amount of exposure necessary to bring on symptoms or cause death, but all are exceptionally deadly at exceptionally low dosages. Exposure to a fatal dose of a nerve agent, if untreated, will typically cause death in a matter of minutes. The typical treatment for nerve agents is an injection of atropine.

### Blister or Vesicant Agents

Blister or vesicant agents act by producing burns or blisters on the skin or any other body part they come in contact with, and they can be fatal. They act quickly on the eyes, lungs, skin, and mucous membranes, inflicting severe damage on the lungs and respiratory tract when inhaled and resulting in vomiting and diarrhea when ingested.

Blister agents include mustard gas (also known as Yperite or sulfur mustard), nitrogen mustard (HN), lewisite (L), and phosgene oxime (CX). Mustard gas and lewisite are particularly dangerous because they produce severe injuries for which there is no known antidote or therapy; a single drop of liquid mustard on the skin can cause serious damage and itching in only a few minutes, and exposure to even a slight amount of mustard in its gaseous state can cause painful blistering, tearing, and lesions of the eyes. Depending on weather conditions and on the extent and duration of exposure, the effects of mustard gas can be delayed for up to a day. Several hours after the exposure, respiratory effects become apparent in the form of severe burning pain in the throat, trachea, and lungs. Although most mustard gas victims survive, severe pulmonary edema or swelling of the lungs may result in death. The only effective form of protection against mustard gas is the use of a full-body protective suit (Level I protection) and the use of a gas mask or respirator.

Although gas masks, respirators, and full-body protective suits may be available to first responders, but they are not routinely carried by first responders, and significant time may elapse before this equipment reaches the scene of a chemical incident. This type of protective gear is not, however, typically available to members of the public who may be in close proximity to a chemical event. Safe response to a chemical incident presumes that first responders have forewarning that an attack is imminent or underway, that protective gear is readily available, and that first responders are sufficiently trained and sufficiently informed about the indicators of a poison gas attack to take the necessary protective steps before venturing into a location where it is present.

Lewisite, which is typically colorless and odorless in its liquid state but as a gas may emit a faint scent of geraniums, causes symptoms that are generally similar to those caused by mustard gas but that also include a decrease in both blood pressure and body temperature. Inhalation of lewisite in high concentrations can lead to death in a few minutes, and in order to be effective, the antidote (dimercaprol) for skin blistering must be applied before the actual blistering begins to take place.

Phosgene oxime, which has a sharp and penetrating odor, can exist as a white powder or, when mixed with water or other solvents, in a liquid state. Contact with this agent is extremely painful, and it quickly irritates the skin, the respiratory system, and the eyes, leading to lesions of the eye, blindness, and respiratory edema. Contact with the skin immediately produces an area of white surrounded by reddened skin and swelling. Because phosgene oxime is heavier than air, it can remain in low-lying areas for quite some time, thus posing a particular danger for rescue workers.

### Choking Agents

These agents enter the body via the respiratory tract and often cause severe pulmonary edema. Because these agents are most effectively deployed as gases, they are typically stored and transported in bottles or cylinders prior to being disseminated into the air. As their name implies, choking agents quickly attack and cause severe damage to the lungs and respiratory system, and they can cause pulmonary edema and death. Choking agents include phosgene (CG), diphosgene (DP), and chlorine (CL) in liquid or gaseous form. It should be noted that although phosgene and phosgene oxime are similarly named, they are chemically different substances that have different properties and symptoms. Symptoms include severe coughing, choking, nausea, lacrimation, difficulty breathing, and vomiting. The initial symptoms may subside for a period of up to a day, but the symptoms typically return when pulmonary edema develops, and individuals exposed to choking agents may go into shock as their blood pressure and heart rate drop precipitously.

## Biological Agents

Biological agents share some characteristics with chemical agents, but important differences distinguish this class of WMDs from chemical agents. Although chemical agents typically produce symptoms relatively quickly, biological agents may not produce symptoms during incubation periods that may last up to several weeks. As a result, there may be no early warning signs of a bioterrorist event, and first responders may not easily or immediately recognize that they have been exposed. In contrast to the three classes of chemical agents, biological agents do not typically produce immediately apparent symptoms on the skin or in the respiratory system. Many biological agents are living organisms, and because these bacteria or viruses cannot be detected by any of our senses, because exposure can take place without warning, because symptoms may not be immediately apparent, and because the scientific devices used to detect and identify them are complex and difficult to use, proper diagnosis and treatment may be delayed. Detection of a biological event generally occurs only after an incubation period has elapsed and the infected person or persons become ill.

Biological agents, which include anthrax, tularemia, cholera, plague, botulism, and smallpox, can be disseminated through a population in several ways. Although some biotoxins (such as anthrax) may be spread through contact with the skin (either through direct contact or through cuts and lacerations), in terms of WMDs and the terrorist goals of causing widespread casualties, the most effective means of dissemination are to aerosolize the biological agent into a fine mist or powder that is unknowingly inhaled or to contaminate food or water that members of the public will ingest.

The three classes of biological agents are bacteria, viruses, and toxins. Bacteria and viruses are living organisms that require a host organism in order to survive and reproduce. After entering the body (usually through inhalation or ingestion), the organism establishes itself within the host, begins to replicate, and produces toxins that cause severe and often fatal illnesses.

The difficulties involved in detecting and diagnosing biological WMD attacks can be especially pronounced when the biological agents result in a slowly developing community health crisis or an epidemic of some sort, or when the exposed population becomes geographically dispersed after exposure. Because a prolonged incubation period often precedes the appearance of symptoms, bioterrorist attacks may be difficult to trace back to their source and may not be easily recognized as part of a terrorist act. The implicit challenges of detecting, diagnosing, and tracing back an infected population that has become geographically dispersed makes the threat scenario of a mass biological exposure in a transportation facility or conveyance—such as an international airport or an international airline flight—particularly attractive to terrorists. The difficulties involved in detecting and diagnosing cases of anthrax infection across the nation in the fall of 2001 provide another example.

Although a more focused direct attack, such as the rapid release of a large quantity of a fast-acting biological toxin in an office building or a mass transportation center, would probably be recognized and dealt with more quickly, both forms of attack can have a potent psychological impact on the public as well as on first responders. Beyond the deaths and illnesses that may occur, such attacks suit the needs and objectives of terrorists because they can generate substantial fear and public alarm. Substantial economic impact can also be achieved if the public begins to avoid the type of location or facility—such as mass transit hubs—where such attacks are known to have taken place. Transportation facilities, shopping malls, movie theaters, and other facilities where the pubic congregates are particularly attractive targets for terrorist attacks involving chemical or biological WMDs.

## Terrorism and the Use of Nuclear Material

Although the likelihood is small that a terrorist organization could obtain or manufacture a high-grade nuclear device capable of destroying a large area, much less transport it to the United States and detonate it, there is a much greater potential for terrorists to construct an improvised nuclear device (IND) or "dirty bomb." Such an improvised weapon, while inflicting far less property damage than a conventional nuclear device, would nevertheless have a devastating physical and psychological impact by spreading radioactive contamination throughout a densely populated urban area.

A dirty bomb is essentially a conventional explosive device surrounded by radioactive materials that, on detonation, spreads radioactive material within a relatively small fallout zone. Depending on the size of the device and the type and amount of radioactive material involved, the immediate area surrounding the detonation might be uninhabitable for a long time, and those directly exposed to the radioactive fallout are likely to suffer radiation sickness. The possibility also exists that exposed victims might eventually develop cancer, leukemia, or other diseases related to radiation exposure.

The possibility that INDs or dirty bombs might be detonated in urban areas is particularly alarming because the materials required for such devices can be obtained fairly easily, because large amounts of radioactive material are not required for an effective device, and because radiation cannot be detected by human senses. A seemingly "ordinary" small explosion in or near a large crowd of people could spread nuclear contaminants through the crowd, with no immediately apparent symptoms. The low-grade nuclear materials required to construct such a device are used, transported, and stored in various locations, including hospitals and medical facilities, research laboratories, and industrial manufacturing facilities across the nation. Although these materials are more carefully guarded today than they were in the past, it is probably not beyond the capacity of a determined terrorist organization to obtain them.

As previously described, the acquisition of nearly 90 pounds of nuclear material from an Iraqi university's research laboratory by the (ISIS terrorist group illuminates the relative ease with which these materials can be acquired, as well as this (and, likely, other) terrorist organization's interest in constructing and employing an IND.

## FIRST RESPONDER SAFETY: TIME, DISTANCE, AND SHIELDING

Generally speaking, the police, fire, and emergency workers who might be called on to respond initially to a nuclear, biological, or chemical event are not adequately trained to deal effectively with those events. This is not to say that most police and emergency workers lack *any* training in this area, but that they lack the highly specific training and special expertise required to recognize and deal with many of the complex and unique threats posed by such events. As described here, it is an exceptionally complicated matter for first responders to identify the specific type of chemical or biological agents used in a bombing, and the related challenge of developing an immediate tactical response that accounts for all the complex variables at play while ensuring a safe response is equally difficult. At present, many first responders are not equipped with the special tools, gear, and protective equipment these events may require, nor are they adequately trained to recognize and respond safely to chemical, biological, or nuclear events. Patrol officers, firefighters, and emergency medical service personnel who initially respond to an event involving WMDs should not be expected to undertake the specific duties and responsibilities that are more properly performed by well-equipped and more highly trained specialists. Rather, their primary role should be to recognize the threat, to minimize additional exposure to chemical or biological agents, to ensure the safety of victims, to safeguard the scene, and to report their findings to those more competent to deal with these issues.

Another primary responsibility of first responders is that of minimizing their own contact with the chemical or biological agent and collecting and communicating as much relevant information as possible to supervisory authorities to ensure the safety and effectiveness of other responding units. First responders who rush in to a WMD event not only risk death or serious injury from secondary devices that may have been placed at or near the scene with the specific intent to disable or kill rescuers but also may become a significant liability to other victims as well as to other responders if they become contaminated themselves. The first responder who rushes in and becomes a victim may exacerbate the overall problem, consuming precious time and resources. The would-be rescuer who approaches or enters a contaminated scene too precipitously can easily become an additional casualty.

As Gordon M. Sachs (2002) points out, responders must make some tough choices and difficult decisions:

> The first instinct for emergency responders at any incident is always to rush in and save as many people as possible; however, in a terrorist-related incident there are many factors to consider. Can the victims be saved? Will responders become targets? Was an agent of some type released? If it was, will responders have the means to detect it? Will their gear provide adequate protection? These are but a few of the questions that we must become accustomed to asking when responding to terrorist-related incidents. There is no reason to allow civilians to suffer needlessly; neither can there be any reason to send responders haphazardly into unknown and dangerous environments. (pp. vii–vii)

Four types or levels of protective gear may be used by emergency workers during WMD events. *Level A* protection is a chemical-resistant suit that entirely encapsulates the emergency worker; it includes a self-contained breathing apparatus (SCBA) or an independent air supply so that workers are not exposed to fumes, biological agents, or other toxic substances that may be present in the environment. This level of protection provides maximum respiratory and skin protection and is typically used when the situation involves a high potential for liquid splashes or vapor hazards or when the chemical agent is unidentified. Generally speaking, this level of protection is used by highly trained specialists who enter the "hot zone," or the area closest to the WMD's point of dispersal.

*Level B* protection is a chemical-resistant suit, including gloves, that does not entirely encapsulate the rescue worker, but it does include an SCBA or an independent air supply. This type of gear provides a high level of respiratory protection but less protection against liquids and gases that may affect the skin or be absorbed through the skin. This type of gear provides the minimum amount of protection one should use in the "hot zone" and is not recommended for prolonged exposure or use in that zone.

*Level C* protection is provided by hooded chemical-resistant clothing and gloves and is equipped with an air-purifying respirator or gas mask. It is generally utilized when there is minimal or no hazard posed by the potential for liquid splashes or direct contact.

*Level D* protection is the type most police, fire, and emergency medical workers typically have available to them: their uniforms and clothing. This type of protective gear provides minimal protection from chemical, biological, or nuclear hazards and should not be worn in or near the primary contamination zone.

Perhaps the most important tools available to ensure the safety of first responders, though, have nothing to do with equipment or gear. They are the concepts of *time, distance,* and *shielding*, which, when properly applied, can be the key to the first responders' self-preservation. In terms of *time*, emergency responders should keep the time they spend in the vicinity of the incident to an absolute minimum. Minimizing the time spent in proximity to a nuclear, biological, or chemical substance generally reduces one's chance of illness or injury by minimizing one's exposure to the toxic substance. If emergency workers absolutely need to approach the scene of a suspicious detonation or dispersal to rescue someone or to inspect it more closely, they should not remain there a moment longer than necessary. They should also be aware that if they do approach the scene, they may inadvertently become a vector to spread the substance, and they should take appropriate steps to decontaminate as quickly as possible. First responders who come in proximity to the scene should promptly notify their supervisors and medical personnel to ensure a proper decontamination, and until decontamination occurs, they should avoid contact with others.

Preventive or prophylactic decontamination—typically involving a "wash-down" with copious amounts of water—may be indicated until the substance is identified. As a precautionary measure, and in recognition of the fact that unknown contaminants might have been dispersed, many of the first responders to the 9/11 attacks on the World Trade Center were decontaminated, had their uniforms "bagged," and were issued new clothing before they were permitted to enter police facilities or mix with personnel who had not been present at the scene (Henry, 2001, 2004a).

Similarly, emergency workers should maintain a safe and appropriate *distance* from the hazard, and they should try to move uphill from the source if possible in order to avoid exposure to heavier-than-air gasses that might collect in lower areas. In terms of distance, emergency responders must also bear in mind that many substances can be spread by wind currents, and they should consider the direction and velocity of the wind in determining a safe location. Various charts and tables are available to first responders to help them determine the proper interval of safety between them and a particular type, source, and quantity of toxic substance, but the likelihood that a responder will access, consult, and rely on these documents' guidance in the midst of an emergency response may be questionable. Police, fire, and emergency workers should prepare themselves for the possibility of a WMD attack by obtaining these tables, becoming generally familiar with the guidance they provide, and consulting them again before approaching the scene. For example, the *North American Emergency Response Guide*, developed jointly by the US Department of Transportation, Transport Canada, and the Secretariat of Communications and Transportation of Mexico for use by first responders to transportation incidents involving hazardous materials, permits users to quickly identify the type of substance involved in the incident and to protect both themselves and the public during the initial response phase. That guide is available to first responders in the form of a smartphone or tablet computer "app."

First responders should also bear in mind that these charts and tables provide general guidelines, and that qualified experts who subsequently arrive at the scene are likely to evaluate the situation and adjust the distances of the hot, warm, and cold zones. In establishing the initial zones, first responders should remain flexible and, if necessary, should err on the side of safety to extend the distance. In terms of distance, first responders must also bear in mind that secondary devices or booby traps designed to injure and disable rescuers may be in the area, and they should proceed cautiously. The secondary devices might be as powerful as or perhaps more powerful than the primary device.

*Shielding* refers to any object that can be used to protect the first responder from a specific hazard and can include buildings, vehicles, and any personal protective equipment available. The type of shielding responders should use is determined by a number of factors, including weather, the physical environment, the geography, and the topography of the area; buildings in urban areas may, for example, provide shielding (as well as a better vantage point) that is not available in a more rural area, where a hill or elevation may fulfill the same functions. Simply rolling up the windows of a police car, turning off the air conditioner, and putting on gloves can provide some degree of safety and protection to police officers approaching the scene of a potentially toxic event. If an officer's department does not furnish personal protective gear (as it should), he or she would be well advised to purchase an inexpensive and lightweight Tyvek jumpsuit and make it a standard piece of equipment in the responder's gear bag.

The most critical concerns for first responders must be their own safety and protection, and they must avoid the compelling urge to rush into a situation to render help. It can be exceptionally difficult for a dedicated police officer, firefighter, or emergency medical worker to resist the impulse to render aid to someone in need because this impulse is often a key feature of the responder's professional and personal identity and has likely been reinforced over the course of his or her career through training, experience, and internalization of the occupational culture's norms and values. Nevertheless, training and common sense must prevail. As noted throughout this chapter, the rescuer who becomes a victim exacerbates and complicates the situation that other responders must confront.

## THE PRIVATE SECTOR'S ROLE

The problems associated with preventing, deterring, responding to, and investigating terrorist attacks involving WMDs are enormously difficult and complex, and they require solutions that are equally complex. We must recognize that the threat posed by a terrorist WMD attack involves much more than simply developing effective first-response capabilities and that an actual attack will have resounding impacts and repercussions throughout the local (and possibly the national) economy, the healthcare system, the corporate and business communities, public utilities, and government operations at every level. We must also recognize that depending on the type, the quality, and the extent of a WMD attack, literally hundreds of public agencies and private sector entities may be called on to participate in the initial response, in rescue and recovery, and in ongoing rebuilding efforts. We need look no further than the 9/11 World Trade Center attacks in New York to realize that hundreds of organizations become involved in the overall recovery effort. Although police, fire, and emergency medical personnel handled most of the first-responder duties in the early minutes and hours following the attack, they were very quickly joined at the scene by personnel from a host of other organizations. These included the American Red Cross and other relief organizations; the telecommunications, gas, and electric utilities operating in New York City; federal law enforcement agencies (the FBI, BATF, Secret Service, and US Customs, to name a few); law enforcement from other states and jurisdictions (the New York State Police, the New Jersey State Police, and practically every local municipality in the region immediately dispatched officers to the scene); FEMA; every branch of the US military; the National Guard; and a raft of others. Personnel from all these organizations quickly converged on the scene, and although they were willing and to a large extent able to help out, the lack of central direction and focus created enormous confusion and duplication of efforts. Without for a moment reducing the commitment and bravery displayed by these individuals, the area that became known as Ground Zero quickly degenerated to a state of near chaos as everyone tried to pitch in and help (Henry, 2004a, 2004b).

Immediately after the attack, hospital emergency rooms within a 100-mile radius of New York City were mobilized and put on alert. Off-duty medical personnel were called in to hospitals and medical facilities, and medical personnel in private practices showed up to volunteer at hospitals. Private ambulance services were mobilized for the transport of casualties, and buses from the city's Transit Authority were commandeered to bring police and other rescuers to the scene. Corporate facilities, office buildings, and college campuses went into a high-security mode, often deploying their security personnel to evacuate and lock down their facilities. The city's transportation infrastructure—public transportation, subways and buses, bridges and tunnels, roads and highways—quickly became overwhelmed by the effort to evacuate tens of thousands of people from Lower Manhattan.

Communications systems were overwhelmed. Most cell phone service throughout Lower Manhattan ended when the World Trade Center towers fell and cellular repeaters were destroyed, and a main switching station for the city's hard-wire telephone system flooded when water pipes burst, interrupting most service in the area. There was little or no interoperability between the police and fire radio communication systems to begin with, and the loss of radio repeaters made radio communications even more difficult.

In the days after the attack, help poured in from across the nation in the form of personnel, equipment, food, and medical supplies, and a complex logistical system of depots and distribution points had to be established and implemented. Within a few days, responders from as far away as California were on the scene at Ground Zero. The work went on 24 hours a day for months, and workers required food, medical attention, and places to rest and recuperate between shifts. Heavy construction equipment was rushed to New York to aid in the removal of debris, and thousands of construction workers were deployed to make the area safe. The rescue and recovery phase of operations continued for several weeks in the futile hope that additional survivors would be located, and fires burned at the World Trade Center site for 99 days. The fires and smoke, along with the airborne hazardous materials they contained, prompted public health officials to monitor air quality throughout the Lower Manhattan area. As bodies and body parts were recovered, they were removed to a medical examiner's facility for DNA testing in hopes of identifying the dead and bringing closure to surviving family and friends. Canine rescue teams were brought in to aid in the search for victims, and the animals required extensive and specialized veterinary care. Psychologists, psychiatrists, and mental health workers arrived to provide crisis intervention and therapy for those traumatized by the event, and a special center for family and friends of victims was established to help them deal with their loss and with the legal, financial, and personal consequences.

Even before the rescue and recovery phase ended, the process of removing millions of tons of debris via truck and barge to a site on Staten Island commenced. The debris would be sifted by hand by NYPD detectives and other law enforcement officers to locate body parts as well as any personal effects or crime scene evidence that might be recovered, and all recovered items had to be logged, vouchered, and forwarded to the morgue or to temporary storage facilities. Complicating the entire operation was the fact that the World Trade Center site became the world's largest and most difficult crime scene, and all the precautions ordinarily undertaken to discover and preserve evidence were put in place. Providing security for the site was a monumental task.

The list of actions and activities that took place in the aftermath of this horrific and devastating attack goes on and on, and without belaboring the point, it should suffice to say that this was the largest and most complicated enterprise ever undertaken as the result of a terrorist WMD attack. Tens of thousands of individuals, hundreds of public agencies, and dozens of private sector entities played a role in the initial response, in the rescue and recovery, or in the removal operations phases.

## THE TRAUMATIC IMPACT ON FIRST RESPONDERS

The psychological repercussions of the September 11 terrorist attacks were far-ranging and consequential, as individuals across the nation and around the world felt the traumatic impact of the events and their aftermath. Indeed, the consequences and repercussions of the terrorist attacks continue to resonate in public discourse, in the political sphere, and in our individual and collective social and psychological worlds. Without minimizing the traumatic impact the attacks had on any individual or group, it should be pointed out that as individuals and as a group, first responders to the World Trade Center, many of whom witnessed the devastation firsthand, encountered profound sensory images of death and destruction and were in close proximity to the alien landscape of Ground Zero for a protracted period, were certainly among the most traumatized. These first responders are, in Robert Jay Lifton's (1980) definition, survivors: They have come in close physical and psychological contact with death but remained alive, and their postexposure lives and experiences can be understood in terms of Lifton's (1967, 1974, 1980, 1983) "psychology of survival" perspective. The psychology of survival is a natural, adaptive, and universal human psychological response to an entirely unnatural experience involving profound death trauma, and as an adaptive and protective response it permits the individual to physically and psychologically survive the traumatic experience.

First responders to the World Trade Center attacks clearly manifest the five themes and features of Lifton's psychology of survival, a psychological perspective that was developed from extensive studies of other death-immersed groups. Among the groups Lifton studied were survivors of the Hiroshima atomic bombing (1967, 1970) and of natural disasters (Lifton & Olsen, 1976) and Vietnam veterans (1973). Lifton also developed and refined this perspective in studies of Nazi doctors and the medicalization of killing (1986), the psychology of genocide (1986, 1990), the threat of nuclear extinction (1982, 1987, 1990), and the process of "thought reform" in the development of cults (1963). Given the breadth and scope of Lifton's research on traumatized individuals and groups and the fact that it has been successfully applied in the area of police psychology (Henry, 1995, 2001, 2004a, 2004b), his model seems particularly appropriate to understand the experience of first responders to terrorist events. The post–September 11 lives of first responders are characterized by lasting features of psychic numbing, death guilt, suspicion of various forms of nurturance they perceive as counterfeit, a lasting death imprint or indelible psychic image of death trauma, and a powerful quest to make coherent meaning of their absurd and painful experience (Henry, 2001, 2004a, 2004b).

Many first responders, particularly the police officers, firefighters, and emergency medical service personnel who were physically present during the actual attack as well as those involved in the rescue and recovery efforts following the World Trade Center's collapse, were deeply traumatized by their experience. In the days and weeks following the attacks, those who worked at Ground Zero experienced a complete immersion in profound sensory images of death and destruction, and many experienced a deep and penetrating grief for lost friends, peers, and coworkers. Although each individual experienced and interpreted the event differently, many or most first responders were exposed to the traumatic sights and smells of death on a massive and unprecedented scale. Many experienced the trauma of body handling as they dug through the rubble in search of survivors and, ultimately, victims. They experienced, probably to a far greater extent than the average person physically distant from the site, an overarching sense of fear that a subsequent attack would imperil their safety. They were exposed to choking clouds of smoke rising from the rubble, and many understood or supposed

238 Crisis Intervention: Disaster and Trauma

that the noxious fumes they breathed contained all sorts of carcinogenic and poisonous chemical compounds likely to affect their future health. Many rescuers worked seemingly endless hours in and around the pile of rubble, and along with the stress and the lack of sufficient sleep and food, their physical exertion led quickly to an overall exhaustion. Many were physically and emotionally isolated from their families as they worked almost continuously for weeks on end. Their depletion, isolation, and absence in a time of great public fear often engendered resentment and anger among family members—perhaps especially among children—who interpreted the responder's absence as evidence that the responder's priorities placed professional duties above family responsibilities. This introduced tremendous (and often enduring) strains to their most intimate relationships—the very relationships that are critical in providing the kind of ongoing sustenance and support traumatized individuals require. The specific (and quite complex) dimensions and features of the trauma experienced by first responders have been described at length elsewhere, as have many of the social and psychological outcomes and repercussions of that traumatic exposure (Henry, 2004a, 2004b).

It seems unnecessary to belabor the point further in the context of this chapter. It should be pointed out, however, that in addition to manifesting the features of survivor psychology, many first responders to the World Trade Center attacks as well as to the attacks on the Pentagon and the crash site in Shanksville, Pennsylvania can be expected to eventually manifest the symptoms of post-traumatic stress disorder (PTSD) or other traumatic syndromes. To a greater or lesser extent, all the first responders to these events carry the psychological baggage of having been suddenly immersed in this profound and unprecedented imagery of death and destruction in social, psychological, and physical environments that served to compound and magnify the traumatic impact of that imagery. Although many continue to experience psychological difficulties, there remain few adequate sources of available treatment. Where resources are available, many first responders generally are resistant to accessing and utilizing them. Seeking help and acknowledging one's own vulnerability or victimhood can be anathema to the responder's personal and professional identity.

Generally speaking, members of the police and firefighter occupational cultures have traditionally been reluctant to seek assistance or treatment for the psychological difficulties they may encounter as a result of their work. Although this widely recognized dynamic is often simplistically attributed to the "macho" features of their tight-knit and insular cultures—cultures that are often characterized as suspicious of outsiders and that place great value on ideals of personal courage and stoic self-sufficiency—it must be recognized that the reality of organizational life in police and fire agencies can also operate synergistically with these cultural features to actively discourage members from acknowledging difficulties and seeking help for them.

This seems especially true of police agencies, whose formal and informal policies may in fact operate to effectively penalize officers who seek help. At the very least, policies can easily create the perception that negative career consequences will accrue to officers who come forward to admit they are having psychological difficulties.

It must be recognized that although many police, fire, and emergency medical service agencies provide employee assistance programs or other counseling services to their members, the advent of these services is a relatively recent phenomenon, and they are not central to the agencies' larger organizational goals. Perhaps especially in the context of police agencies, a larger overriding organizational goal is that of liability abatement, and this goal impacts the provision of psychological services in important ways. Stated succinctly, officers who step forward to acknowledge their psychological difficulties pose a distinct problem for police agencies in terms of liability: By acknowledging difficulties, they implicitly increase the agency's potential liability if those officers subsequently become involved in, for example, an incident involving physical or deadly physical force. The legal issue of the officer's fitness for duty will inevitably arise in these and other cases, and the agency will have to prove that it performed due diligence in evaluating the officer before he or she was returned to full enforcement duties. Agencies that encourage members to come forward with their problems concomitantly increase their potential liability for the on- or off-duty actions those members take or fail to take.

Perhaps especially in police agencies (where liability may be greater), members who acknowledge difficulties may find themselves removed from active duty, stripped of their weapons and enforcement powers, and relegated to desk duty for a prolonged period pending treatment, fitness evaluation, and administrative resolution of their case. Such reassignment becomes public knowledge throughout the member's workgroup and inevitably involves both a stigma and a significant loss of privacy. Because such reassignment involves an undoing of the officer's professional identity and a loss of the symbols of office, it may actually exacerbate his or her troubles. Further compounding the problem is the fact that many police officers, firefighters, and emergency medical service personnel have little trust in the abilities of agency therapists or in their assurances of confidentiality. These therapists are, after all, in the agency's employ, and they represent the agency's interests, so the inherent perception of a conflict of interest may be magnified in the perspective of an already mistrustful officer. As members of tight-knit and insular occupational cultures whose features are not well understood by "outsiders," they often have little faith in the capacity of civilian therapists to understand the unique realities of their occupational and social worlds, the depth and dimension of the trauma and human suffering they frequently witness, the physical and emotional hazards they regularly face, or the particular worldview that sets them apart from the larger culture. Many police officers, firefighters, and emergency medical service personnel are under-standably suspicious of the bureaucracies and distrustful of their agencies' employee assistance policies, and many simply do not seek help for fear they will be stigmatized, penalized, or misunderstood (see, generally, Henry, 2001, 2004a, 2004b).

An upshot of this complex dynamic is that although many police officers, firefighters, and emergency medical service personnel who participated in rescue and recovery efforts at Ground Zero, the Pentagon, and the crash site in Shanksville were traumatized by their experience, they generally resist any impulse to acknowledge and seek help for their troubles. The answer to the empirical question of precisely how many first responders demonstrate clinical symptoms of traumatic disorders remains uncertain and may not be known for some time, but some early research indicates the number is sub-stantial (Centers for Disease Control and Prevention, 2002a, 2002b, 2002c, 2002d; Galea et al., 2002; Goode, 2001; Schuster, 2001). Given their over-all reluctance to seek help and the fact that stress-related symptoms often emerge long after the traumatic exposure, the extent of traumatic syndromes among rescue workers may not be known for years, if ever. But although a clear causal link to the effects of trauma related to September 11 cannot be entirely established, anecdotal evidence documents a dramatic increase in the number and severity of drug- and alcohol-related incidents (both on and off duty) among FDNY firefighters (see, e.g., Celona, 2004; Hu, 2004).

## THE NEW YORK DISASTER COUNSELING COALITION

Fortunately for first responders in New York City, there existed an organi-zation that provided an array of necessary psychological services to police, firefighters, emergency medical service personnel, and their families, an organization whose structure, goals, and orientation offered a viable and attractive alternative to agency-based resources and helped to overcome a great deal of the traditional reluctance to seek assistance. The New York Disaster Counseling Coalition (NYDCC) was founded on September 12, 2001, by a group of concerned clinicians and psychotherapists who rec-ognized the traumatic impact the World Trade Center attacks would have on first responders and their families. They also recognized and, in terms of formulating NYDCC's structure, policies, and operational protocols, accounted for many of the organizational and cultural impediments that deter first responders from officially seeking help.

The NYDCC, chartered as a nonprofit organization, quickly grew into a network of almost 300 fully licensed, fully insured, fully credentialed clini-cians with terminal degrees in their respective fields. These clinicians, repre-senting a broad array of specializations and treatment approaches, including psychologists, psychiatrists, and clinical social workers, committed to voluntarily provide a minimum of 1 hour of pro bono treatment services each week to a first responder or his or her family member who was affected by the September 11 attacks. Importantly, the commitment these mental health professionals made to their first responder and family member clients was open-ended and reflective of the motto of NYDCC: they agreed to provide their services "for as long as it takes." Depending on the individual circumstances of each referral, treatment for a first responder client or family member might consist of a few sessions, or it might continue for years. At no time, however, was the first responder or family member client charged a fee of any kind. Consistent with the canons of ethical practice and availing law, principles of client-clinician confidentiality applied, and clinicians did not notify the client's agency that he or she was receiving treatment.

The NYDCC model is unique in the nation, and its highly innovative and effective approach clearly addresses the specific needs of the first responder community. NYDCC's operational protocols were designed to assure confidentiality and privacy. Following a brief telephone intake interview (conducted by a trained psychotherapist) aimed at evaluating the scope and dimensions of the particular issues the client faced, he or she was provided with names and contact information for three volunteer clinicians with appropriate credentials or areas of specialization in the client's local area of residence. Almost 300 volunteer clinicians became members of the NYDCC referral network, with offices that were widely distributed throughout the New York metropolitan area and a region that included northern New Jersey, southern Connecticut, and parts of Pennsylvania. Consistent with NYDCC's pledge of complete confidentiality, no personally identifying data were recorded during the intake interview. The information retained at NYDCC was collected solely for statistical purposes and consisted of the caller's agency, age, gender, and county of residence. The individual clinicians typically maintained their own confidential clinical treatment notes, but they did not submit health insurance reimbursement claims, and there was no paper trail the agency might trace back to the responder to indicate he or she sought or received treatment.

As a nonprofit entity, the NYDCC was entirely supported by contributions and funding from philanthropic foundations. All the volunteer therapists in the NYDCC referral network were thoroughly vetted and required to submit proof of licensure and malpractice insurance as well as a curriculum vita and two professional reference letters from colleagues who had known them for a minimum of 2 years. NYDCC staff regularly updated records proving continued licensure and valid malpractice insurance, and the volunteers had the opportunity to attend an array of ongoing training sessions to help them understand and treat the unique constellation of difficulties first responders confront. These sessions addressed such topics as understanding the occupational cultures of police and firefighters, domestic violence in law enforcement families, the socialization and training of police, and a number of other issues uniquely affecting members of the first responder community and their families. Given the number of participating mental health professionals who volunteered 1 hour each week and the number of clients referred, NYDCC estimated it provided the equivalent of more than $1.4 million in treatment services each year to first responders and their families. The cost-effectiveness of the NYDCC model is clearly evident in the fact that this figure represents approximately six times NYDCC's total operating costs, including rent, utilities, the salaries of two employees, and all outreach expenses.

One of the supreme ironies affecting the provision of services to all of those affected by the September 11 attacks is that federal, state, and private philanthropic funding sources originally devoted to psychological treatment were rather quickly depleted, and sufficient additional funds to maintain NYDCC's operations became unavailable. Without this funding, NYDCC was forced to end its operations in 2005. One element of this irony arises from the fact that the psychological features resulting from traumatic exposure often do not begin to manifest themselves until years after the traumatic event, and this appears to be particularly true among first responders, who may resist acknowledging or reporting their difficulties. Whether due to delayed manifestation of symptoms, to resistance to seek treatment on the part of first responders, or to some combination of both, NYDCC referral statistics revealed steadily increasing rates and numbers of referrals for clinical services among first responders and their families with the passage of time.

Another ironic element is the fact that NYDCC (and other not-for-profit or volunteer entities that do not charge a fee for services) was ineligible under current federal rules to receive funding under FEMA or other federal agencies' mental health counseling grant programs. If NYDCC clinicians charged their full fees for treatment services and submitted health insurance claims—that is, if they created the very paper trail that makes first responders reluctant to access those services—the organization would have been eligible for federal support. Federal regulations, however, did not permit volunteer organizations to receive funds to provide clinical services.

Beyond providing free, high-quality, and confidential mental health services to first responders and their families, NYDCC also engaged in a range of initiatives aimed at supporting police, firefighters, and emergency medical service personnel (and their families) and remediating the stress resulting from the physical and emotional dangers they deal with on a daily basis. These initiatives included a series of seminars designed to educate retiring first responders about their pension benefits, employment opportunities, and life after retirement, and the success and demand for these seminars gave rise to the Retirement Services Division within NYDCC. The Retirement Services Division consisted of retired first responders who are available to confer with prospective retirees about these and other issues and to fulfill an important peer support function. Privately sourced grant funding also permitted NYDCC to conduct several weekend-long seminars to help nearly 200 first responders and their spouses or significant others to develop more resilient relationships.

Another NYDCC initiative was the "DCC in a Box" Replication Project, an effort to formally memorialize the experience of NYDCC and record the lessons learned from developing a concept first conceived in the immediate aftermath of September 11 into a fully functioning entity that provided free and confidential clinical treatment services to hundreds of first responders and their families. The goal of the Replication Project was to make these nuts-and-bolts lessons available to other cities so that similar disaster counseling coalitions can be created prior to a disaster, allowing cities to quickly mobilize the necessary personnel and resources in the event of an attack or disaster. Clearly, NYDCC represents a unique and viable model to provide first responders and their families with the broad range of clinical and other services they require as the result of their traumatic exposures. The model is based on an altruistic appreciation for the needs and concerns of first responders, and it is an exceptionally cost-effective model that accounts for and overcomes many of the factors that inhibit police officers, firefighters, and emergency medical services personnel from going to their agencies for help.

## CONCLUSION

The new realities of terrorism and WMDs demand an entirely new set of policies, practices, and relationships among a host of entities and institutions charged with ensuring public safety. As illustrated by the experiences and lessons of the September 11 attacks on the World Trade Center and the Pentagon, police, fire, and emergency medical services face unprecedented challenges in the future, and similar challenges confront virtually every institution in the United States.

This chapter has outlined some of the issues, problems, and threats posed by the specter of terrorism and terrorists' use of WMDs and has identified the compelling need for highly coordinated response and recovery planning that integrates resources, skills, personnel, and capabilities of a range of public sector agencies and private sector organizations. No plan can pretend to be perfect; there are simply too many unforeseen issues and exigencies that arise in specific events, and the planning must therefore be crafted for flexibility and adaptability. This involves nothing less than a new mindset that accepts, accounts for, and takes up the challenges posed by the realities of our world.

Recent history reveals the extent and dimension of the threat posed by WMDs, their availability to terrorists and extremist groups, and the massive casualties they can inflict on public safety personnel and members of the public. These threats are not likely to subside and in fact may increase as terrorist groups continue to strengthen, grow, and expand their capabilities. Concurrent with that expansion and the evolution of new terrorist tactics and capabilities, the threat to the American homeland, to the American people, and to the way of life we enjoy continues to grow and mature. There is a compelling need for more and better training for the first responders to such events so that they can recognize events involving WMDs and so that they can operate safely to minimize deaths, injuries, and damage. Similarly, there is a pressing need for more and better equipment to help first responders achieve their goals. But here again we see the need for a new mindset among emergency workers, a mindset of safety and preparedness that infiltrates all their duties and activities. Beyond the essential role played by first responders, the issues of better training, better equipment, and better coordination apply as well to the broad array of secondary responders and institutions that will be called on once the immediate crisis has passed.

Terrorism and the use of WMDs pose a particularly significant threat to first responders: the police officers, firefighters, and emergency medical service personnel who are our first line of defense against such attacks and are typically among the first individuals and groups to enter the sites where attacks have taken place. By the nature of their work, first responders to terrorist and WMD events are exposed to a range of traumatic experiences, and many inevitably suffer the lasting physical, social, and psychological consequences of that exposure.

For a variety of complex and interrelated reasons, first responders who experience psychological difficulties are typically reluctant to seek help from their agencies' employee assistance programs. First responders are often distrustful of their agencies' motivations in offering help, they are often suspicious of an inherent conflict of interest they perceive among therapists employed by their agency, and they often lack faith that their problems will be treated with sensitivity and confidentiality. Many believe that by coming forward to acknowledge a difficulty and to seek help for it they place their reputation and their career in jeopardy. As a result, first responders as a group are generally reluctant to seek the kind of help they often need.

The New York Disaster Counseling Coalition provided an innovative model for treatment that overcame or minimized many or all of the factors contributing to first responders' resistance. Created in recognition of the fact that many first responders to the World Trade Center attacks would suffer lasting psychological consequences and cognizant of the factors that encourage resistance, the NYDCC's referral and treatment protocols illuminated the kind of organization first responders need. The NYDCC model, which can easily be adapted and implemented in other venues in preparation for terrorist attacks or other forms of trauma-producing disasters, is a highly cost-effective means of providing high-quality psychological services to first responders and their families. The realities of our world are such that organizations like NYDCC and the crisis intervention and relief services they provide must become part of an integrated and intelligent national response to the threat of terrorism and WMDs.

REFERENCES

Celona, L. (2004, August 16). 28th Firefighter booze bust. *New York Post*, p. 7.

Centers for Disease Control and Prevention. (2002a, September 11). Impact of September 11 attacks on workers in the vicinity of the World Trade Center: New York City. *Morbidity and Mortality Weekly Report*, 51(35), 781–783.

Centers for Disease Control and Prevention. (2002b, September 11). Injuries and illnesses among New York City Fire Department rescue workers after responding to the World Trade Center attacks [Special issue]. *Morbidity and Mortality Weekly Report*, 51.

Centers for Disease Control and Prevention. (2002c, September 11). Psychological and emotional effects of the September 11 attacks on the World Trade Center: Connecticut, New Jersey and New York, 2001. *Morbidity and Mortality Weekly Report*, 51(35), 784–786.

Centers for Disease Control and Prevention. (2002d, January 11). Rapid assessment of injuries among survivors of the terrorist attack on the World Trade Center: New York City, September 2001. *Morbidity and Mortality Weekly Report*, 51(1), 1–5.

Cowell, A. (2014, July 10) 'Low-grade' nuclear material is seized by rebels in Iraq, U.N. Says. *New York Times*. Retrieved From: http://www.nytimes.com/2014/07/11/world/middleeast/iraq.html

Duffy, M. (2002, May 5). Weapons of war: Poison gas. Retrieved from http://www.firstworldwar.com/weaponry/gas.htm

Federal Emergency Management Agency. (2002, July). *Managing the emergency consequences of terrorist incidents: Interim planning guide for state and local governments*. Washington, DC: Author. Retrieved from http://http://www.fema.gov/pdf/plan/managingemerconseq.pdf

Galea, S., Ahern, J., Resnick, H., Kilpatrick, D., Bucuvalas, M., Gold, J., & Vlahov, D. (2002). Psychological sequelae of the September 11 terrorist attacks in New York City. *New England Journal of Medicine*, 346(13), 982–987.

Gleik, P. H. (2006). Water and terrorism. *Water Policy*, 8, 481–503.

Goode, E. (2001, September 25). Therapists hear survivors' refrain: "If only." *New York Times*, p. F1.

Henneberry, O. (2001, December 5). *Bioterrorism information resources*. Paper presented at the New Jersey Hospital Association conference "Thinking the Unthinkable: Biochemical Terrorism and Disasters: Information Resources for Medical Librarians."

Princeton, NJ. Retrieved from http://www.njha.com/ep/pdf/bio-cdchandout

Henry, V. E. (2001). *The police officer as survivor: The psychological impact of exposure to death in contemporary urban policing* (Unpublished doctoral dissertation). Graduate School and University Center of the City University of New York.

Henry, V. E. (2004a). *Death work: Police, trauma, and the psychology of survival.* New York: Oxford University Press.

Henry, V. E. (2004b). Police, the World Trade Center attacks and the psychology of survival: Implications for clinical practice [Special issue: Dialogues on Terror: Patients and Their Psychoanalysts, Part 2]. *Psychoanalysis and Psychotherapy.*

Hu, W. (2004, February 29). Firefighter in crash took cocaine, city says. *New York Times*, p. B1.

Jernigan J. A., Stephens D. S., Ashford D. A., Omenaca C., Topiel M. S., Galbraith M., Tapper M., . . . Anthrax Bioterrorism Investigation Team. (2001, November–December). Bioterrorism-related inhalational anthrax: The first 10 cases reported in the United States. *Emerging Infectious Diseases*, 7(6). Retrieved from http://www.cdc.gov/ncidod/eid/v017n06/jernigan.html

Kristof, N. D. (1995, March 25). Police find more chemicals tied to sect. *New York Times.*

Lifton, R. J. (1967). *Death in life: Survivors of Hiroshima.* New York: Basic Books.

Lifton, R. J. (1970). *History and human survival.* New York: Random House.

Lifton, R. J. (1973). *Home from the war: Vietnam veterans: Neither victims nor executioners.* New York: Basic Books.

Lifton, R. J. (1974). The sense of immortality: On death and the continuity of life. In R. J. Lifton & E. Olson (Eds.), *Explorations in psychohistory: The Wellfleet papers* (pp. 271–287). New York: Simon and Schuster.

Lifton, R. J. (1976). *The life of the self: Toward a new psychology.* New York: Simon and Schuster.

Lifton, R. J., & Olsen, E. (1976). The human meaning of total disaster: The Buffalo Creek experience. *Psychiatry*, 39(1), 1–18.

Lifton, R. J. (1980). The concept of the survivor. In J. E. Dimsdale (Ed.), *Survivors, victims, and perpetrators: Essays on the Nazi Holocaust* (pp. 113–126). New York: Hemisphere.

Lifton, R. J. (1983). *The broken connection: On death and the continuity of life.* New York: Basic Books. (Original work published 1979)

Lifton, R. J. (1986). *The Nazi doctors: Medical killing and the psychology of genocide.* New York: Basic Books.

Lifton, R. J. (1999). *Destroying the world to save it: Aum Shinrikyo, apocalyptic violence, and the new global terrorism.* New York: Henry Holt.

McDade, J. E., & Franz, D. (1988, July–September). Bioterrorism as a public health threat. *Emerging Infectious Diseases*, 4(3). Retrieved from http://www.cdc.gov/ncidod/eid/v014n03/mcdade.htm

Sachs, G. M. (2002). *Terrorism emergency response: A workbook for responders.* Upper Saddle River, NJ: Prentice-Hall.

Schuster, M. A., Stein, B. D.,

Jaycox, L. H., Collins, R. L., Marshall, G. N., Elliott, M. N., ... Berry, S. H. (2001, November 15). A national survey of stress reactions after the September 11, 2001, terrorist attacks. *New England Journal of Medicine, 345*(20), 1507–1512.

Shenon, P., & Stout, D. (2002, May 21). Rumsfeld says terrorists will use weapons of mass destruction. *New York Times*, p. A1.

Strozier, Charles B. (2002). *Apocalypse: On the psychology of fundamentalism in America.* New York: Wipf and Stock.

Török, T. J., Tauxe, R. V., Wise, R. P., Livengood, J. R., Sokolow, R., Mauvais, S., ... Foster, L. R., (1997, August 6). A large community outbreak of salmonellosis caused by intentional contamination of restaurant salad bars. *Journal of the American Medical Association, 278*(5), 389–395.

Traeger, M. S., Wiersma, S. T., Rosenstein, N. E., Malecki, J. M., Shepard, C. W. Raghunathan, P. L., ... Florida Investigation Team. (2002, October). First case of bioterrorism-related inhalational anthrax in the United States, Palm Beach, Florida, 2001. *Emerging Infectious Diseases, 8*(10). Retrieved from http://www.cdc.gov/ncidod/EID/v018n010/02–0354.htm

United States Code, 18 USC 113B.

Zuckerman, J., Bucci, S., & Carafano, J. J. (2013, July 22). *60 Terrorist plots since 9/11: Continued lessons in domestic counterterrorism.* Washington, DC: Heritage Foundation Special Report No. 137. Retrieved from http://www.heritage.org/research/reports/2013/07/60-terrorist-plots-since-911-continued-lessons-in-domestic-counterterrorism

# 9

## An Examination of the US Response to Bioterrorism: Handling the Threat and Aftermath Through Crisis Intervention

SOPHIA F. DZIEGIELEWSKI

JOSHUA KIRVEN

The world is changing rapidly as we become a global community. But as we evolve, the question is, are we safer? The United States, which once may have felt immune from these horrific acts, is repeatedly finding out it is just as vulnerable as other nations throughout the world. The United States had never seen terrorist attacks such as those experienced on September 11, 2001. Following those attacks, many individuals have struggled with how to best address the vulnerabilities of American society relating to terrorist activity, causing for many a sense of hyperalertness. It seems the America that we knew has changed forever as we look at public health and criminal justice, simultaneously (Potter & Rosky, 2013).

The United States, along with the rest of the world, was shocked and stunned when the terrorist attacks of September 11, 2001, unfolded. Following the attacks, debates relating to terrorist activity within the United States and the vulnerabilities inherent in American society emerged. The issues of extensive borders and the relative ease with which immigrants can disappear into American society, and the global and open nature of lifestyles Americans have come to depend on, leave the society susceptible to terrorist threats and attacks. Furthermore, the threat of biological warfare and fears of a new type of war abound.

This chapter identifies several issues that have affected the previous open nature of the American lifestyle with impending threats of biological warfare. This turbulent environmental context has caused the American people to experience a level of stress and fear they have never before known.

The purpose of this chapter is to present a brief overview of enhanced US policy on terrorism, stressing the application of Roberts's (1991) seven-stage model of crisis intervention as one means to address the growing fears of the American public. All helping professionals, regardless of whether they work directly with a crisis survivor, need to be aware of basic crisis intervention techniques and how exposure to crisis impacts public health. Application of this model is stressed as one way to provide education in this area while highlighting how to best help individuals cope when faced with the continual threat of a new type of war that is often hard to detect. Recommendations for therapeutic content are made within the current time-limited practice setting that require a proactive joining of law enforcement, public health centers, government agencies, community organizers, and professional practitioners to assess potential threats within the United States and to address the growing fears of Americans in regard to safety and security.

## TERRORISM AND THE UNITED STATES

*Terrorism* is defined by the Department of Defense as "the calculated use of violence or the threat of violence to inoculate fear; intended to coerce or to intimidate governments or societies in the pursuit of goals that are generally political, religious or ideological" (Terrorism Research Center, 2005). Terrorism is a crime that targets innocent and unsuspecting victims, and its purpose is to heighten public anxiety, fear, and sense of being unsafe. Although acts of terrorism may seem random, they are planned by the perpetrators, whose main objective is to publicize their attacks. Acts of terrorism and fear in the United States and its allied nations are becoming more common (Graham, 2011). The growing threat of terrorism and terrorist activity is expanding across the United States, and success in combating it will require agencies to implement proactive approaches and strategies (Terrorism Research Center, 2000, 2005). According to McVey (1997):

It is time to recognize certain events that are currently occurring in society as potential forewarning. Disregarding them may result in tragic consequences. History clearly shows that those law enforcement agencies caught behind the operational curve of [terrorist] campaigns have a harder time controlling them and reducing their societal disruption than those that are properly prepared. (p. 7)

## The Ultimate Price of Secrecy

The value of an individual life has been brought into question, and for some the extremist views that disregard one's own safety has become second to fighting for a social or political cause. This wanton disregard for self-safety in pursuing the destruction of others continues to gain increased attention in modern terrorist activity. Threats are becoming more prevalent where extremist devout followers are willing to complete suicide missions. These new martyrs, as described by Bunker and Flaherty (2013), are known as body cavity bombers and have developed a new culture of terror. The counterterrorism strategy is further challenged by the threat of murderously enhanced "mules" carrying secreted drugs in their bodies to escape detection by customs and police (Flaherty, 2008, 2012, 2014). Today's terrorists now have the capability to surgically implant explosives in body cavities, thus becoming a new type of suicide bomber and security risk.

## Terrorism Trends

The current trends in terrorism and terrorist activity make the need for a proactive approach critical:

1. Terrorism is becoming an increasingly frequent war strategy, causing present and future concern.
2. Terrorists are becoming more sophisticated and proficient at using technology.
3. The targets of terrorists' attacks will advance from buildings and airplanes to chemical plants, citywide water systems and utility companies, economic systems, and countries.
4. Traditional weapons will become obsolete against technologically advanced terrorists.
5. The United States will continue to be a target of terrorism (Bowman, 1994; Levy & Sidel, 2003; McCormick & Whitney, 2013).
6. More human beings will be using themselves as suicide bombers as a form of sacrifice, commitment, and martyrdom (Flaherty, 2012; Terrorism Research Center, 2005).

Since the 1980s, the United States has had a policy relating to counterterrorism; however, it is largely reactive in nature and lacks preemptive capabilities. This four-pillar policy states that (a) the United States makes no concessions to terrorists and strikes no deals; (b) the United States uses a "full-court press" to isolate terrorists and to apply pressure on state sponsors of terrorism to force them to change their behavior; (c) rules of law are followed to bring terrorists to justice; and (d) the United States seeks international support to increase counterterrorism capabilities (Badolata, 2001; Nordin, Kasimow, Levitt, & Goodman, 2008).

# US VULNERABILITIES: OPEN BOUNDARIES

Examining the vulnerabilities inherent in the United States further supports the need for a preemptive approach to combating terrorists and terrorism. First, the United States has extensive borders that are extremely easy to penetrate. Millions of legal and illegal immigrants enter the country each year. Second, the security measures at airports and other ports of entry are weak, and resources are stretched thin; in most cases, undertrained and ill-equipped personnel secure ports of entry. Third, the structure of law enforcement in the United States can also be seen as a vulnerability because communication between federal, state, and local agencies is often lacking, and in cases where jurisdictions and charters overlap, friction between the agencies often occurs. Fourth, inconsistencies and practices within the Transportation Security Administration (TSA) rest in concerns such as airport size, time of year of travel, traffic volume of passengers, and work satisfaction of TSA officers (Edwards, 2013; Ramsay, Cutrer, & Raffel, 2010). Finally, the infrastructure of the United States has been centralized, allowing for large concentrations of people to inhabit relatively small areas. These large population areas capture the attention of terrorists because they allow for more casualties and a more public arena for attacks (Terrorism Research Center, 2000, 2005).

Since the September 11 terrorist attacks, government and law enforcement agencies have begun to implement strategies to counter these vulnerabilities; however, the openness of US borders, which is the most critical area in need of change, is the most difficult vulnerability to effectively control. The current influx of immigrants highlights the necessity of an effective system that can scan and monitor individuals who are entering the United States.

## Immigration Policies and Potential for Exploitation

Knowledgeable Americans have come to understand that our welcoming immigration policies are easily exploited by terrorists and that porous borders and lax immigration enforcement are no longer an option. With at least 8 million illegal aliens living in the United States and nearly 1 million new aliens arriving each year, the potential for terrorists entering the United States undetected is high (Camarota, Beck, Kirkorian, & Wattenberg, 2007).

There are many reasons to examine the nation's immigrant population. First, the more than 50 million immigrants and their minor children now constitute one sixth of US residents, so how they are faring is vitally important to the United States. Moreover, understanding how immigrants are doing is the best way to evaluate the effects of immigration policy. Absent a change in policy, between 12 and 15 million new immigrants (legal and illegal) will likely settle in the United States in the next decade, and perhaps 30 million new immigrants will arrive in the next 20 years. Immigration policy determines the number allowed in, the selection criteria used, and the level of resources devoted to controlling illegal immigration. The future, of course, is not set, and when decisions on immigration policy are made, it is critically important to know what impact the immigration flow has had in recent decades (Camarota, 2012).

Using the latest Census Bureau data from 2010 and 2011 provides a detailed picture of the more than 50 million immigrants (legal and illegal) and their US-born children (under 18) in the United States by country of birth, state, and legal status. One of the most important findings is that immigration has dramatically increased the size of the nation's low-income population; however, there is great variation among immigrants by sending country and region. Moreover, many immigrants make significant progress the longer they live in the country. But even with this progress, immigrants who have been in the United States for 20 years are much more likely to live in poverty, to lack health insurance, and to access the welfare system than are native-born Americans. The large share of immigrants arriving as adults with relatively little education partly explains this phenomenon.

Currently, the estimated number of illegal immigrants in the United States is roughly 5 million, with an estimated increase of about 275,000 persons per year. Those who enter legally at various ports of entry and then overstay their visas and disappear into society represent the bulk of illegal immigrants. It is possible for illegal immigrants to disappear, move, or use different names, making location and deportation extremely inefficient (see Table 9.1).

## BIOTERRORISM: THREATS OF ANTHRAX AND SMALLPOX

*Bioterrorism* is defined as "the overt or covert dispensing of disease pathogens by individuals, groups, or governments for the expressed purpose of causing harm for ideological, political, or financial gain" (Texas Department of Health, 2001). Further, *biological weapons* are defined as "any infectious agent such as a bacteria or virus, when used intentionally to inflict harm upon others" (Texas Department of Health, 2001). Since the September 11 attacks, the fear of bioterrorism has escalated in the United States. In addition, previous cases and the continued threat of anthrax infections have exposed America's vulnerabilities to biological agents, highlighting the need for greater security measures to protect against bioterrorism attacks.

Table 9.1    Key Facts

**Does Immigration Have a Role to Play?**

- The number of immigrants (legal and illegal) in the country hit a new record of 40 million in 2010, a 28% increase over the total in 2000.
- Of top sending countries, the largest percentage increase in the last decade was for immigrants from Honduras (an increase of 85%), India (74%), Guatemala (73%), Peru (54%), El Salvador (49%), Ecuador (48%), and China (43%).
- New immigration (legal and illegal) plus births to immigrants added 22.5 million residents to the country over the last decade, equal to 80% of total US population growth.
- Recent immigration has had only a tiny impact on the nation's age structure. If the nearly 14 million immigrants who arrived in 2000 or later are excluded from calculations, the average age in the United States as of 2010 shows an increase from 37.4 years to 37.6 years—roughly 2 months (Camarota, 2012).

## Bioterrorism Possibilities

According to the Centers for Disease Control and Prevention (CDC, 2014a), biological agents can create a risk to national security because they are easily disseminated through air, water, or food. Furthermore, bioterrorism can lead to high mortality, impacting public health systems and causing panic and social disruption, leading to special action and funding to increase public preparedness (Ellis, 2014). Bioterrorism mirrors conventional terrorism in that it is designed to affect a large number of people, it can be implemented with little or no warning, and it instills panic and fear in the population. However, several other aspects of bioterrorism must be examined. First, the vast number of methods that can be used to spread biological agents into an environment are a concern. Airborne dissemination, pharmaceutical contamination, food or drink contamination, injection or direct contact, and water contamination can all be used by terrorists attempting to unleash biological agents (Levy & Sidel, 2003; Texas Department of State Health Services, 2013). Other considerations include the vast number of biological agents that exist that could be used in a bioterrorism attack, the ability of terrorists to acquire such biological agents, and the massive casualties that could result if a bioterrorism attack occurs.

## Anthrax and Smallpox

The biological agent that has gained primary attention since the September 11 attacks is anthrax, which was spread through contaminated letters at several US post offices to postal workers and the offices of two US senators (Ellis, 2014; Levy & Sidel, 2003). According to the CDC (2014b; see also Ellis, 2014; Levy & Sidel, 2003), anthrax is an infectious disease that is caused by the spore-forming bacterium *Bacillus anthracis*, also known as anthrax spores. Humans can contract anthrax through inhalation and through breaks in the skin; it is not contagious. If anthrax is contracted through inhalation, the incubation period is generally 2 to 5 days, and the symptoms mirror those of the flu: fever, muscle aches, nausea, and cough. More serious symptoms include difficulty breathing, high fever, and shock. Inhalation anthrax is almost always fatal once symptoms appear. If the disease is contracted through the skin, the incubation period is generally 1 to 2 days. Symptoms of skin exposure to anthrax begin as a small, itchy bump followed by a rash. Left untreated, the lesions fill with fluid and eventually turn black as the tissue begins to die. About 20% of untreated cases of infection through the skin result in death (CDC, 2014b). Although potentially fatal, anthrax can be treated effectively through antibiotics if treatment is initiated early (CDC, 2014b).

A second biological agent that has gained attention as a possible bioterrorism tool is smallpox. According to the American Medical Association (CDC, 2014c), when used as a biological weapon, smallpox represents a serious threat because of its fatality rate of 30% or more among unvaccinated persons. Smallpox has long been feared as the most devastating of all infectious diseases, and its potential for devastation today is far greater than at any previous time. Routine vaccination throughout the United States ceased more than 25 years ago. In a now highly susceptible, mobile population, smallpox would be able to spread widely and rapidly throughout this country and the world (CDC, 2014c).

According to the CDC (2014c), the smallpox virus has an incubation period of 12 days after exposure. Initial symptoms include high fever, fatigue, headache, and backache, which are then followed by a rash on the face, arms, and legs. The rash progresses into lesions that become filled with pus, turn into scabs, and eventually fall off. Smallpox is highly contagious and is spread by infected saliva droplets. Although many individuals with smallpox recover, death occurs in up to 30% of cases. There is no proven treatment for smallpox; however, a vaccine can lessen the severity of or prevent illness if given within 4 days of exposure.

## IS THE UNITED STATES PREPARED FOR A BIOTERRORISM ATTACK?

On June 22–23, 2001, the Johns Hopkins Center for Civilian Biodefense Studies, in conjunction with the Center for Strategic and International Studies, the ANSER Institute for Homeland Security, and the Oklahoma National Memorial Institute for the Prevention of Terrorism, held an exercise at Andrews Air Force Base in Washington, DC, named "Dark Winter." The first such exercise of its kind, Dark Winter was constructed as a series of mock National Security Council meetings in reaction to a fictional, covert smallpox attack in the United States (O'Toole & Inglesby, 2001).

The result of the drill highlighted several areas of concern with regard to governmental preparedness against bioterrorism attacks. First, there was a basic lack of understanding by leaders on the subject of bioterrorism. Second, early responses to the mock attack were slow to determine how many persons were exposed and how many trained medical personal would be needed. Also, the drill highlighted that the US health care system lacks the ability to deal with mass casualties, and there is a shortage of necessary vaccines and medicines. Finally, the Dark Winter drill highlighted that conflicts between different levels of federal and state government and uncertainty in authority hampered responses ("Avoiding Dark Winter," 2001, pp. 29–30).

Due to the results of the drill and the September 11 attacks, lawmakers are trying to increase funding for various agencies to counter bioterrorism and its effects. In an effort to increase support, the fiscal 2002 spending bill for the Departments of Labor, Health and Human Services, and Education (HR 3061-H Rept 107-229) included $393 million for measures to defend against biological or chemical attacks, an increase of $100 million in this area. Furthermore, the 2002 Senate bill (S 1536-S Rept 107-84) allocated $338 million, and the House and Senate Armed Services Committees also greatly expanded biological defense and research efforts. The House's fiscal 2002 defense authorization bill (HR 2586-H Rept 107-194) funded chemical and biological defense procurement at $361.7 million. The House bill cut the administration's request for chemical and biological weapons research and development by $5 million, to $502.7 million, but it increased spending for the Defense Advanced Research Projects Agency's biological warfare defense program by $10 million, to $150 million. The Senate's defense authorization bill (S 1416-S Rept 107-62) included similar increases for chemical and biological weapons programs as part of an overall boost of more than $600 million to deal with "nontraditional threats" such as terrorism and cyberattacks. The Senate bill also directed the Defense Department to build a new facility to produce vaccines against anthrax and other biological agents (McCutcheon, 2001).

## Psychological Implications of Terrorism

A central aspect of terrorism that should be examined is the psychological effect on the American people caused by acts of terrorism. Research on natural and human-caused disasters suggests that psychological reactions to terrorism are more intense and more prolonged than psychological reactions following natural types of disaster (Myers & Oaks, 2001). Terrorist attacks, by their very nature, are designed to instill fear, anxiety, and uncertainty in a population.

Several characteristics of terrorism can increase the magnitude and severity of psychological effects. First, terrorist attacks occur without warning, which produces a disruption to society and people's way of life. A lack of warning also prevents individuals from taking protective action, both physical and psychological. Terrorist attacks become more horrifying for individuals because there is usually a sudden change in reality and surroundings. For example, the New York City skyline changed in a matter of hours when the World Trade Center buildings collapsed and only a pile of smoking debris was left. Another psychological effect of terrorism is the threat to personal safety and security for both citizens and responders. Individuals need to feel safe and secure in their surroundings while building safe relationships (Goelitz & Stewart-Kahn, 2013). Areas that were previously believed to be safe suddenly become unsafe, and this feeling of insecurity can be maintained in an individual for an extended period. Acts of terrorism can also be traumatic in the scope of their destruction: the exposure by citizens, survivors, and responders to gruesome situations; the anger caused by the intentional human causalities; and the degree of uncertainty, lack of control, and social disruption that a society is exposed to (Myers & Oaks, 2001).

The September 11 attacks were different from other terrorist acts because of the magnitude and suddenness of the tragedy; the vast loss of life on American soil; the ability of citizens to follow the events of the attack through extensive media coverage; and the method of using airplanes, considered to be a common and safe mode of transportation, as a means of destruction (Dyer, 2001).

Although every person who experiences a traumatic event responds to that event in a unique way, there are many feelings and reactions that are common in the aftermath of a tragedy. These include sadness, anger, rage, fear, numbness, stress, feelings of helplessness, feeling jumpy or jittery, moodiness or irritability, change in appetite, difficulty sleeping, nightmares, avoidance of situations that are reminders of the trauma, inability to concentrate, and guilt because of survival or lack of harm during the event (Dyer, 2001). These reactions are especially pronounced for a parent in the aftermath of a child's death (Feigelman, Jordan, McIntosh, & Feigelman, 2012).

According to the National Center for Post-Traumatic Stress Disorder (2001), there are several steps that individuals can take in the wake of a disaster to reduce symptoms of stress and readjust to some sense of normalcy. First, following a tragedy, an individual should find a quiet place to relax and attempt to sleep at least briefly. Next, individuals need to re-establish priorities so that a sense of purpose and hope can be regained. Using the natural support of others such as friends, family, coworkers, and other survivors is necessary to establish a sense of togetherness and to help reduce stress. Individuals should also try to engage in positive activities that can serve as a distraction from traumatic memories of or reactions to the event. Finally, a person should seek out the advice of a doctor or counselor for help in treating symptoms of depression or post-traumatic stress disorder (PTSD; National Center for Post-Traumatic Stress Disorder, 2001).

Studies of the psychological implications of terrorist attacks in the United States (Canetti-Nism, Halperin, Sharvit, & Hobfoll, 2009; Schuster et al. 2001; Silver, Holman, McIntosh, Poulin, Gil-Rivas, 2002), Spain (Miguel-Tobal et al., 2006), and Israel (Bleich, Gelkopf, & Solomon 2003; Shalev and Freedman 2005) have pointed to PTSD as one of the most prominent and prevalent expressions of psychological distress following such severe attacks. This condition develops in response to witnessing or experiencing a threatening or harmful event that elicits fear, helplessness, or horror. Other than exposure to a traumatic event, the criteria for diagnosis of PTSD include persistent re-experiencing of the trauma (e.g., intrusive memories and nightmares), active avoidance of reminders of the trauma and general numbing, and symptoms of hyperarousal (e.g., anger, sleep disturbance, hypervigilance). Furthermore, at least six symptoms must be present for at least 1 month and cause clinically significant distress or impairment in functioning (American Psychiatric Association, 2013). Because of the multiple criteria for diagnosis, many individuals may not be diagnosed as suffering PTSD yet still display related symptoms and experience considerable psychological distress. According to the American Psychological Association (1994), individuals who have experienced or witnessed a terrorist attack develop a state of acute stress reaction and may exhibit one or all of these symptoms:

- Recurring thoughts of the incident
- Becoming afraid of everything, not leaving the house, or isolating oneself
- Stopping usual functioning, no longer maintaining daily routines
- Experiencing survivor guilt (thinking, "Why did I survive?" or I should have done something more")
- Feeling a tremendous sense of loss
- Being reluctant to express feelings, losing a sense of control over one's life

## APPLICATION OF ROBERTS'S SEVEN-STAGE CRISIS INTERVENTION MODEL AS AN ACUTE POST-TRAUMATIC INTERVENTION

Effective intervention with survivors of trauma precipitated by a crisis of this nature requires a careful assessment of individual, family, and environmental factors. According to Roberts (1991), a *crisis* is by definition short-term and overwhelming, and the response will involve an emotionally taxing change. In a terrorist attack, the crisis event has caused a senseless disruption in the individual's normal and stable state. It makes sense that the individual's usual methods of coping will not work, and a quiet place must be established to allow the individual to think and regroup.

According to Roberts (1991), there are seven stages of working through crisis:

1. Assessing lethality and safety needs
2. Establishing rapport and communication
3. Identifying the major problems
4. Dealing with feelings and providing support
5. Exploring possible alternatives
6. Formulating an action plan
7. Providing follow-up

This model and support for development of the subsequent stages of adjustment can help the individual begin to prepare for the long journey of recovery to follow. Assisting the individual in crisis as early as possible to begin this process can help create a better, healthier adjustment for all involved. In addition, it is important for helping professionals to remember that both pleasure and pain remain a necessary part of growth, change, and adaption. Individuals who have suffered a crisis need to be allowed to experience both pleasure and pain and to realize that both emotions can coexist as well as wax and wane throughout the healing process.

In applying this model, the following assumptions are made: (a) All strategy will follow a "here and now" orientation utilizing a strengths-based perspective (Jones-Smith, 2014); (b) most of the interventions provided should be given as close to the actual crisis event as possible (Raphael & Dobson, 2001; Simon, 1999); (c) the intervention period will be both intensive and time limited (typically 6 to 12 meetings; Roberts, 1991); (d) the adult survivor's behavior is viewed as an understandable (rather than a pathological) reaction to stress (Roberts & Dziegielewski, 1995); (e) the crisis counselor will assume an active and directive role in assisting the survivor in the adjustment process (Parsons & Zhang, 2014); and (f) all intervention efforts are designed to increase the survivor's remobilization and return to the previous level of functioning.

## Stage 1: Assessing Lethality

The unpredictability of terrorist attacks and the fear of further attacks make recovery from this type of acute trauma particularly problematic. Also, other events that happen in the environment are more likely to be emotionally linked to terrorist activity, regardless of actual cause, making it even more difficult for the survivor to progress past the active danger phase toward assuring safety. Listed here are some of the hazardous events or circumstances that can be linked to the recognition or reliving of terrorist traumatic events. Again, these events, although they may be unrelated to terrorist activity, can still trigger anxious responses from individuals:

1. Growing public awareness of the prevalence of the traumatic event or similar traumatic events (i.e., an accidental plane crash with subsequent loss of human life or incidents related to bioterrorism in the environment)
2. Acknowledgment by a loved one or someone else that the client respects that he or she has also been a victim (often termed a *survivor*)
3. A seemingly unrelated act of violence against the individual or a loved one, such as rape or sexual assault
4. The changing of family or relationship support issues
5. The sights, sounds, or smells that trigger events from the client's past (these can be highly specific to individuals and the trauma experienced)

Thus, when dealing with trauma, the sensitivity thresholds and the memories associated with the individual's interpretation process can vary (Wilson, Freidman, & Lindy, 2001).

## Immediate Danger

With the seriousness and unpredictability related to terrorist acts, any intervention efforts will require careful assessment of suicidal ideation. In addition, initial and subsequent hospitalization and medication may be required to help deal with serious episodes of anxious or depressed feelings surrounding the crisis event. Although no individual wants to experience pain, some professionals believe that some degree of pain is needed to facilitate the healing process. Therefore, medications should be used only by individuals with the most severe cases or as adjuncts to intervention, rather than as a crutch to simply avoid dealing with uncomfortable feelings (Dziegielewski, 2013a, 2013b).

When addressing the potential for suicidal behavior, questions to elicit signs and symptoms of suicidal ideation or intent should be direct in nature. The client should be asked about feelings of depression, anxiety, difficulties in eating or sleeping, psychological numbing, self-mutilation, flashbacks, panic attacks or panic-like feelings, and increased substance use. After carefully identifying the degree of loss experienced by the individual and based on the age and the circumstances of the trauma experienced, the individual's living situation needs to be assessed. Helping the client to identify members of his or her support system not only will help to assure that the client is not still in danger but also will remind the client of the level and types of support that remain immediately accessible.

The first few contacts the crisis worker has with the individual in crisis should be individualized, structured, and goal oriented to help the individual move past the traumatic event. It is critical for the crisis counselor to help the individual to generate understanding that what happened in regard to the traumatic event was beyond his or her personal control. A dialogue needs to be created in which the individual is free to share his or her experiences and in response the counselor responds in a nonjudgmental way (Derezotes, 2014).

In these initial meetings (meetings 1–3), the goal of the therapeutic intervention is to recognize the hazardous event and help the survivor to acknowledge what has actually happened. In addition, when dealing specifically with terrorism, the individual needs to be made aware that other, seemingly unrelated events may also trigger a similar panic-like response. Once the individual is aware that panic symptoms may reoccur, specific preparation needs to be made to handle these occurrences and the feelings they elicit. Because the survivor of trauma is currently being subjected to periods of stress that disturb his or her sense of equilibrium, counselors should attempt to restore homeostatic balance.

Individuals should also be made aware that a crisis situation can be so overwhelming that the survivor may choose to focus on events other than the crisis event. For crisis counselors, it is essential to help the survivor get to the root of the problem (i.e., the event that precipitated the crisis or the reason for the visit). During these initial meetings, the survivor becomes aware of and acknowledges the fact that the crisis or trauma has occurred. Once this is realized, the survivor enters into a vulnerable state (Roberts & Dziegielewski, 1995). The impact of the traumatic event is so horrific that it disturbs the survivor and his or her ability to utilize traditional problem-solving and coping methods. When these usual methods are found to be ineffective, tension and anxiety continue to rise, and the individual becomes unable to function effectively.

In the initial meetings, the assessment of the survivor's past and present coping behaviors is important; however, the focus of intervention must remain on the here and now. The crisis counselor must make every effort to stay away from past or unresolved issues unless they relate directly to the handling of the traumatic event.

## Stage 2: Establishing Rapport and Communication

Many times, the devastating events that surround the immediate and unforeseeable loss of a loved one leave survivors feeling as though family and friends have abandoned them, or that they are being punished for something they did. Crisis counselors need to be prepared for the possibility that these types of unrealistic interpretations may result in the survivor having feelings of overwhelming guilt. Feelings of self-blame may impair the individual's capacity for trust, and this may be reflected in a negative self-image and poor self-esteem. A low self-image and poor self-esteem may increase the individual's fear of further victimization. Many times, survivors of trauma question their own vulnerability and know that revictimization remains a possibility. Regardless of the type of therapy, this makes the role of the counselor in establishing rapport with the client essential (Parsons & Zhang, 2014).

When possible, the crisis counselor should progress slowly and try to let the survivor set the pace for all attempts at intervention because the survivor may have a history of being coerced, and forcing a confrontation on issues may not be helpful. Allowing the survivor to determine the pace creates a trusting atmosphere that gives the message "The event has ended, you have survived, and you will not be hurt here." Survivors often need to be reminded that their symptoms are a healthy response to an unhealthy environment (Vazquez & Rosa, 2011). They need to recognize that they have survived heinous circumstances and continue to live and cope. Trauma victims may require a positive future orientation, looking toward aspirations and dreams based on living on in honor of the loved one and building happy, satisfactory tomorrows (Call, Pfefferbaum, Jenuwine, & Flynn, 2012). Restoring a feeling of hope that change can occur is crucial to the survivor's well-being.

Perhaps more than anything else, throughout each of the meetings, these survivors need unconditional support and positive regard. These factors are especially crucial to the working relationship because a history of lack of support, blaming, and breaches of loyalty is common. The therapeutic relationship is a vehicle for continued growth and development of coping skills and the ability to move beyond the traumatic event (Call et al., 2012).

## Stage 3: Identify the Major Problems

Terrorist attacks can be multifaceted, and once the major problems relevant to the particular event are identified and addressed, determining how to best provide support becomes essential. Once a survivor has been given individual attention, he or she may be ready for group participation. In crisis work, emphasis always needs to be placed on teaching relaxation techniques, encouraging physical exercise, and creating an atmosphere in which the survivor gains an understanding that self-care is at the root of all healing, providing the basis for future coping and stabilizing efforts.

In these next few meetings (meetings 4–6), the crisis counselor needs to assume a very active role. First, the major problems to be dealt with and addressed must be identified. These problems must be related directly to how responses and actions will affect the present situation. Awareness through education regarding the effects and consequences of terrorism is discussed. Discussing the event can be very painful for the individual; simply re-acknowledging what happened can push the individual into a state of active crisis marked by disequilibrium, disorganization, and immobility (e.g., the last straw). Although this process may be painful, once the survivor enters full acknowledgment, new energy for problem solving will be generated. This challenge stimulates a moderate degree of anxiety plus a kindling of hope and expectation. The actual state of disequilibrium can vary, but it is not uncommon for individuals who have suffered severe trauma to remain in this state for 4 to 8 weeks or until some type of adaptive or maladaptive solution is found.

## Stage 4: Dealing With Feelings and Providing Support

The energy generated from the survivor's personal feelings, experiences, and perceptions drives the therapeutic process (Kira, 2010). It is critical that the counselor demonstrate empathy and an anchored understanding of the survivor's worldview that moves from fear and pathology to resiliency and strength. One effective practice method for a survivor of loss or trauma is being able to reflect and narrate happy memories. Another practice strategy can be continuing a loved one's legacy through goal setting and spiritual connection creating an optimal frame of reference that is based on internal strengths and inner validation (Kirven, 2014). The symptoms the survivor is experiencing are to be viewed as functional and as a means of avoiding further pain. Even severe symptoms such as dissociative reactions should be viewed as a constructive method of removing oneself from a harmful situation and exploring alternative coping mechanisms. Survivors' experiences should be normalized so that they can recognize that being a victim is not their fault. Reframing symptoms are coping techniques that can be helpful. In this stage (meetings 7–8), the survivor begins to reintegrate and gradually becomes ready to reach a new state of equilibrium. Each particular crisis situation (type and duration of incest, rape, etc.) may follow a sequence of stages, which can generally be predicted and mapped out. One positive result from generating the crisis state in Stage 3 is that in treatment, after reaching active crisis, survivors seem particularly amenable to help. They can be most free to share their concerns and create a dialogue when they feel that they are being understood (Derezotes, 2014).

Once the crisis situation has been acknowledged, distorted ideas and perceptions regarding what has happened need to be corrected and information updated so that clients can better understand what they have experienced. Survivors eventually need to confront their pain and anger so that they can develop better strategies for coping. Furthermore, normal responses can include contradictory feelings that fluctuate between anger and love or fear and rage, all of which are considered a normal part of the response. Focusing on a strengths-based approach, throughout the counseling process there must be recognition of the client's continued courage in facing and dealing with these issues (Jones-Smith, 2014).

With the increasing diversity of the US population, there is a growing demand for practitioners to provide culturally appropriate assessment, treatment, and preventive services (Paniagua, 2014; Vazquez & Rosa, 2011). Practitioners need to be attuned to recognizing the role that culture can play in both expectations and actions. This is especially important in assessing and treating sexual dysfunction because culture can influence not only cognition and individual experiences but also the behavior that results (Dziegielewski, 2015). In addition, media images and a lack of education can produce unrealistic expectations of performance and prowess that may clearly affect not only the relationship but also what the client is willing to share.

## Stage 5: Exploring Possible Alternatives

Moving forward requires traveling through a mourning process (generally in meetings 9–10). Sadness and grief at one's loss need to be experienced. Grief expressions surrounding betrayal and lack of protection permit the victim to open to an entire spectrum of feelings that have been numbed. Now, acceptance, letting go, and making peace with the past begins (Vazquez & Rosa, 2011).

## Stage 6: Formulating an Action Plan

Here the crisis worker must be very active in helping the survivor to establish how the goals of the therapeutic intervention will be completed. Practice, modeling, and other techniques such as behavioral rehearsal, role-play, and writing down one's feelings and an action plan become essential in addressing intervention planning (Dziegielewski, 2013a). Often, survivors have realized that they are not at fault or to blame. What their role was and what part they played become more clear, and self-blame becomes less pronounced. Survivors begin to acknowledge that they did not have the power to help themselves or to change things. Often, however, these realizations are coupled with anger at the helplessness they feel at not being able to control what has happened to them. The role of the mental health professional becomes essential here in helping clients to look at the long-range consequences of acting on their anger and in planning an appropriate course of action. The main goal of these last few sessions (meetings 11–12) is to help individuals reintegrate the information learned and processed into a homeostatic balance that allows them to function adequately once again. Referrals for additional therapy should be considered and discussed at this time (i.e., additional individual therapy, group therapy, couples therapy, family therapy).

Table 9.2    Adoption of ALICE

---

**ALERT. Use Plain and Specific Language. Avoid Code Words.**

The purpose of the ALERT is to inform as many people as possible within the danger zone that a potentially life-threatening situation exists. Communication is essential and can be facilitated via many different methods (PA, text, e-mail, personal senses). No matter the method of delivery, the objective should be a conveyance of information, not telling a person what must be done or issuing a command.

The use of plain language, delivered through as many delivery channels as possible, is the best way to ensure awareness within the danger zone. It will empower as many as possible with the ability to make an informed decision as to their best option that will maximize survival chances.

ALICE, along with the Department of Homeland Security (DHS) and the Federal Emergency Management Agency (FEMA), recommends plain and specific language. ALICE training discusses methods for clearly conveying warnings and the ways various communication technologies can facilitate those messages.

**LOCKDOWN. Barricade the Room. Silence Mobile Devices. Prepare to EVACUATE or COUNTER If Needed.**

Lockdown is an important response in the event of an active shooter or violent intruder, but there has to be a semi-secure starting point from which survival decisions should be made.

The ALICE training program explains scenarios where lockdown is the preferable option and dispels myths about traditional lockdown procedures. Relying on lockdown alone will significantly endanger occupants in a violent intruder situation. Traditional lockdown creates readily identifiable targets and makes a shooter's mission easier, whether in a hospital, a school, a church, or a business.

ALICE trainers instruct on practical techniques for how to better barricade a room, what to do with mobile and electronic devices, how and when to communicate with police, and how to use your time in lockdown to prepare to use other strategies (i.e., Counter or Evacuate) that might come into play should the active shooter gain entrance.

**INFORM. Communicate the Shooter's Location in Real Time.**

Inform is a continuation of Alert and uses any means necessary to pass on real-time information. Video surveillance, 911 calls, and PA announcements are just a few of the channels that may be used by school employees, safety officers, and other personnel.

An emergency response plan should have clear methods outlined for informing school employees, hospital workers, or any other employees of the whereabouts of a violent intruder. No one wants to have to deploy such methods, but in the horrible event that an armed intruder would enter a facility, emergency preparedness training could take over.

Information should always be clear and direct. As much as possible, communicate the whereabouts of the intruder. Effective information can keep the shooter off balance, giving people in the school more time to further lock down or evacuate to safety.

Active shooters work alone 98% of the time. If the shooter is known to be in an isolated section of a building, occupants in other wards can safely evacuate while those in direct danger can lockdown and prepare to counter. Knowledge is the key to survival.

**COUNTER. Create Noise, Movement, Distance, and Distraction With the Intent of Reducing the Shooter's Ability to Shoot Accurately.**

ALICE training does not believe that actively confronting a violent intruder is the best method for ensuring the safety of all involved, whether in a school, a hospital, a business, or a church.

(continued)

Table 9.2  (Continued)

Counter focuses on actions that create noise, movement, distance, and distraction with the intent of reducing the shooter's ability to shoot accurately. Creating a dynamic environment decreases the shooter's chance of hitting a target and can provide the precious seconds needed in order to evacuate.

ALICE does not endorse civilians fighting an active shooter unless confronted directly in a life-and-death situation. Counter is a last-ditch and worst-case scenario option.

If an active shooter makes his or her way into a school, hospital, church, or business, there are steps that can be taken as an effort to survive an attack. With workplace violence as a rising trend across the United States, this method is not limited to preventing a school shooting. The ALICE training program provides examples for real, effective ways to counter an active shooter, when there is no other option left.

Counter is about survival, the last barrier between a shooter and a potential victim, and anything a person can to do to gain control is acceptable. It's the opposite of being a sitting duck, and every action taken is a step toward survival.

*EVACUATE*. When Safe to Do So, Remove Yourself From the Danger Zone.

Our human instinct in the face of danger is to remove ourselves from that threat. ALICE training provides techniques for safer and more strategic evacuations.

An active shooter in a building presents a situation like no other. Evacuating to a safe area takes people out of harm's way and hopefully prevents civilians from having to come into any contact with the shooter. By evacuating, citizens can avoid having to employ the techniques learned in ALICE training for how best to counter an active shooter.

Did you know that you should break a window from the top corner as opposed to the center? Many useful techniques that civilians do not know exist and can save your life. ALICE trainers teach strategies for evacuating through windows, from higher floors, and under extreme duress.

ALICE trainers also give instructions on what to do at rally points, including communicating with law enforcement and administering first aid. Evacuation is the number one goal.

Hopefully, evacuating a school, workplace, or church is always an option in the event of an active shooter. The ALICE Training Program provides lessons and information for all facets of a violent intruder gaining access to a building. Safety is our primary focus for this program, and we do not endorse risking lives of students or employees (ALICE Training Institute, 2014).

## Stage 7: Follow-Up Measures

Follow-up is very important for intervention in general, but it is almost always neglected. In the successful therapeutic exchange, significant changes have been made in the survivor in regard to his or her previous level of functioning and coping. Measures to determine whether these results have remained consistent are essential. Often, follow-up can be as simple as a phone call to discuss how things are going. Follow-up within 1 month of termination of the sessions is important. It may also be helpful to suggest debriefing or intervention to help the survivor reach a higher level of adjustment (Raphael & Dobson, 2001). It is important not to push individuals before they are ready; sometimes a survivor needs time to self-recover, and once this is done, he or she will open up to further intervention.

Other measures of follow-up are available but require more advanced planning. A pretest-posttest design can be added, as outlined in Chapter 27, can be used by simply using a standardized scale at the beginning of treatment and again at the end. Scales to measure the signs and symptoms of psychological trauma are readily available. See Fischer and Corcoran (2007a, 2007b) for a thorough listing of measurement scales that can be used in the behavioral sciences.

Finally, it is important to realize that when dealing with this type of stress reaction, the determination of the course and type of intervention will always rest with the survivor. At follow-up, many survivors may need additional therapeutic help yet be unable to express the request for a debriefing session, whereas others, after having initially adapted to the crisis and learned to function and cope, may find that they want more. After all, supporting the survivor as he or she progresses through the crisis period remains the ultimate goal of any helping intervention. Whether or not the survivor requests additional services, the crisis counselor should be prepared to help the client become aware of the options available for continued therapy and emotional growth. If additional intervention is requested, referrals for group therapy with other survivors of similar trauma, individual growth-directed therapy, couples therapy to include a significant other, and family therapy should be considered.

One model that has attracted interest as a plan for addressing and preparing for a terrorist threat is referred to as ALICE (with the letters representing steps designated as "alert," "lock down," "inform," "counter," and "evacuate"). See Table 9.2 for a description of the steps involved in utilizing this model (ALICE Training Institute, 2014). The basic purpose in implementing ALICE is to use every available technology to alert as many individuals as possible that they could be either in or close to a danger zone and to suggest ways to diminish the threat and bring the individuals to safety. This awareness is designed to empower individuals to move forward and take responsibility for the self as well as helping others to seek safety.

## CULTURAL SENSITIVITY

As outlined in the application of Roberts's seven-stage model, addressing cultural sensitivity needs to be enhanced at every stage of the intervention. As a result of the growing population of immigrants and misperceptions related to the potential for terrorism, the need for cultural sensitivity has never been greater. It should come as no surprise that with the increasing diversity of the US population, there is a greater demand for practitioners to provide culturally appropriate assessment, treatment, and preventive services (Dziegielewski, 2014; Paniagua, 2014).

## FUTURE DIRECTIONS

The tragic events of September 11, 2001, are often viewed as having forever changed the way we look at terrorism in the United States. Terrorism in its various forms has exposed, on a national scale, the need for tighter security at the nation's borders, as well as continued efforts to ensure protection from biological warfare (Levy & Sidel, 2003). Questions remain, such as: How were the hijackers of September 11 able to get past airport security even though many of them were on an FBI watch list (McGeary & Van Biema, 2001, p. 29)? And, with threats of terrorism against the United States on the rise, how can Americans once again feel safe? Whether directly exposed to terrorist activity or not, everyone can be affected by the fear of terrorism, and addressing these fears has led to heightened security and changes especially at our airports that will never return to earlier, more lax policies. One only has to take a trip to the local airport and engage in domestic or international travel to see the most basic effects this tragic event has had on our society.

With so many people being directly affected by terrorism and many more suffering the byproducts of living in an unpredictable environment, the issue of crisis counseling to address stress and coping has gained significant attention. This increased attention has led to a rapid increase in many theoretical, empirical, and applied studies and provides much of the impetus for this updated text. Recent events have led some researchers to claim that coping with trauma and stress has become a sociocultural phenomenon, which might result in higher self-reported stress levels due to the proliferation of information about stress in the popular culture.

Historically, three types of stress have been identified: systemic or physiological, psychological, and social (Levy & Sidel, 2003). However, the recent experiences of terrorism and the ways for coping with the resulting trauma and stress remain diverse. The levels of stress that these survivors experience, the sources of stress, stress related to self-esteem and self-perception, stress and coping skills, and how to best handle stressful situations are just a few of the many issues that need to be researched further.

The violence caused by the recent turn of events starting with the attacks of September 11, 2001 was unprecedented in US history. The American people have traditionally been expected to adjust to new social environments, maintain good personal and occupational standing, and face pressures related to supporting friends and family. In treatment, what cannot be underestimated is the need to be sure that the people being served are not made to feel disenfranchised, worthless, invisible, betrayed, and marginalized. When this happens, they can fall into a negative mental status of anger and hopelessness, where an impulse to do harm to others or country can increase. Therefore, it is important that as practitioners we keep in mind the following, which can be thought of as the "three V's" (referring to "value," "validate," and "visible"):

- *Value:* Help all individuals feel that they have value and are able to make a contribution to their community and country.
- *Validate*: Despite individuals' current status or appearance, validate them and their experience from their perspective. Be nonjudgmental and attentive in promoting an optimal worldview and hope for the future.
- *Visible: Never disregard or ignore anyone!* Acknowledge all people with dignity regardless of their current status or appearance. Use eye contact, small talk, kind words, friendly gestures, and positive hand movements, and take a few seconds out of your day to validate their existence.

In the future, practitioners who are assessing individuals related to terrorism need to be aware of vulnerable populations such as the homeless, the mentally disabled, re-entry ex-offenders, trauma survivors, estranged parents from their children, and people who have recently lost their job. All of these characteristics and situations can result in severe stress for individuals, and listening and being sensitive to the concerns they voice may assist greatly to reduce frustration and prevent traumatic-level retaliation.

In addition, the survivors of trauma need to continue to develop new roles and modify old ones in response to the developmental tasks they face. When an individual is pressured by these multiple demands, he or she can experience role strain, role overload, and role ambiguity, which often result in intense feelings of stress. More attention needs to be given to understanding crisis and the responses that will occur initially and those that will continue to resurface after the initial phase of the trauma has passed. The threats of terrorist attacks can have considerable psychological effects, from immediate responses to those that are more prolonged or delayed (DiGiovanni, 1999). Also, more information is needed regarding the most effective time to address a stressful event (Raphael & Dobson, 2001). Coping and stress management techniques can help individuals return to a previous level of functioning, where healthy individuals who have been exposed to extreme trauma can receive the health and support needed.

ACKNOWLEDGMENT Special thanks to Kristy Sumner for her contributions to the previous version of this chapter.

## REFERENCES

ALICE Training Institute. (2014). *How to respond to an active shooting event.* Retrieved from http://www. alicetraining.com/what-we-do/ respond-active-shooter-event/

American Psychiatric Association. (2013). *Diagnostic and statistical manual of mental disorders* (5th ed.). Washington, DC: Author.

Avoiding dark winter. (2001). *The Economist, 361*(8245), 29–30.

Badolata, E. (2001). How to combat terrorism: Review of United States terrorism policy. *World and I, 16*(8), 50–54.

Bleich A., Gelkopf, M., & Solomon, Z. (2003). Exposure to terrorism, stress-related mental health symptoms, and coping behaviors among a nationally representative sample in Israel. *Journal of the American Medical Association, 290,* 612–620.

Bowman, S. (1994). *When the eagle screams.* New York: Birch Lane Press.

Bunker, R. J., & Flaherty, C. (2013). *Body cavity bombers: The new martyrs.* Bloomington, IN: iUniverse, Inc.

Call, J. A., Pfefferbaum, B., Jenuwine, M. J., & Flynn, B. W. (2012). Practical legal and ethical considerations for the provision of acute disaster mental health services. *Psychiatry, 75,* 305–322.

Camarota, S. A. (2012). *Immigrants in the United States, 2010: A profile of America's foreign-born population.* Center for Immigration Studies. Retrieved from http://cis.org/2012-profile-of-americas-foreign-born-population.

Camarota, S. A., Beck, R., Kirkorian, M, & Wattenberg, B. (2007, August). 100 Million more: Projecting the impact of the US population from 2007 to 2060. Center for Immigration Studies. Retrieved from: http://cis.org/articles/2007/back707transcript.html

Canetti-Nisim, D., Halperin, E., Sharvit, K., & Hobfoll, S. E. (2009). A new stress-based model of political extremism. *Journal of Conflict Resolution, 53,* 363–389. doi:10.1177/0022002709333296

Centers for Disease Control and Prevention [CDC]. (2014a). Emergency preparedness and response. Bioterrorism overview. Retrieved from http://emergency. cdc.gov/bioterrorism/overview.asp

Centers for Disease Control and Prevention [CDC]. (2014b). Anthrax. Retrieved from: http:// www.cdc.gov/anthrax/

Centers for Disease Control and Prevention [CDC]. (2014c). Smallpox basics. Retrieved from: http://emergency.cdc.gov/ agent/smallpox/disease/

Derezotes, D. S. (2014). *Transforming historical trauma through dialogue.* Thousand Oaks, CA: Sage.

DiGiovanni, C. J. (1999). Domestic terrorism with chemical or biological agents: Psychiatric aspects. *American Journal of Psychiatry, 156,* 1500–1505.

Dyer, K. (2001). What is different about this incident? Retrieved from www.kirstimd.com/911_ health.htm

Dziegielewski, S. F. (2015). *DSM-5™ in action.* Hoboken, NJ: Wiley.

Dziegielewski, S. F. (2013a). *The changing face of health care social work: Opportunities and challenges for professional practice* (3rd ed.). New York: Springer.

Dziegielewski, S. F. (2013b). *Social work practice and psychopharmacology: A person and environment approach.* New York: Springer.

Dziegielewski, S. F. (2014). *DSM-IV-TR™ in action* (2nd ed.-*DSM-5* Update). Hoboken, NJ: Wiley.

Edwards, C. (2013). Privatizing the Transportation Security Administration. *Policy Analysis, 742*, 1–16.

Ellis, R. (2014). Creating a secure network: The 2001 anthrax attacks and transformation of postal security. *Sociological Review, 62*, 161–182. doi:10.1111/1467-954X.12128

Feigelman, W., Jordan, J. R., McIntosh, J. L., & Feigelman, B. (2012). *Devastating losses: How parents cope with the death of a child to suicide or drugs.* New York: Springer.

Fischer, J., & Corcoran, K. (2007a). *Measures of clinical practice: A sourcebook: Vol. 1. Couples, Families and Children* (4th ed.). New York: Free Press.

Fischer, J., & Corcoran, K. (2007b). *Measures of clinical practice: A sourcebook: Vol. 2. Adults* (4th ed.). New York: Free Press.

Flaherty, C. (2008). 3D Tactics and information deception. *Journal of Information Warfare, 2*(7), 49–58.

Flaherty, C. (2012) *Dangerous Minds: A Monograph on the Relationship Between Beliefs—Behaviours—Tactics.* Published by OODA LOOP (September 7, 2012). Retrieved from: http://www.oodaloop.com/security/2012/09/07/dangerous-minds-the-relationship-between-beliefs-behaviors-and-tactics/

Flaherty, C. (2014). 3D vulnerability analysis solution to the problem of military energy security and interposing tactics. *Journal of Information Warfare, (13)*1, 33–41.

Goelitz, A., & Stewart-Kahn, A. (2013). *From trauma to healing: A social worker's guide to working with survivors.* New York: Routledge.

Graham, S. (2011). *Cities under siege: The new military urbanism.* New York: Verso.

Jones-Smith, E. (2014). *Strengths-based therapy: Connecting theory, practice, and skills.* Thousand Oaks, CA: Sage.

Kira, I. A. (2010). Etiology and treatment of post-cumulative traumatic stress disorders in different cultures. *Traumatology, 16*(4), 128–141. doi:10.1177/1534765610365914

Kirven, J. (2014). The reality and responsibility of pregnancy provides a new meaning to life for teenage fathers. *International Journal of Choice Theory and Reality Therapy, 33*(2), 23–30.

Levy, B. S., & Sidel, V. W. (2003). *Terrorism and public health.* New York: Oxford University Press.

McCormick, S., & Whitney, K. (2013). The making of public health emergencies: West Nile virus in New York City. *Sociology of Health and Illness, 35*, 268–279. doi:10.1111/1467.9566.12002

McCutcheon, C. (2001). From "what-ifs" to reality. *Congressional Quarterly Weekly, 59*, 2463–2464.

McGeary, J., & Van Biena, D. (2001). The new breed of terrorist. *Time, 158*(13), 29–39.

McVey, P. (1997). *Terrorism and local law enforcement.* Springfield, IL: Charles C. Thomas.

Miguel-Tobal, J. J., Cano-Vindel, A., Gonzalez-Ordi, H., Iruarrizaga, I., Rudenstine, S., Vlahov, D., & Sandro, G. (2006). PTSD and depression after the Madrid March 11 train bombings.

Journal of Traumatic Stress,
19(1), 69–80.

Myers, D., & Oaks, N. (2001, August). *Weapons of mass destruction and terrorism.* Presented at the Weapons of Mass Destruction/Terrorism Orientation Pilot Program. Pine Bluff, AR: Clara Barton Center of Domestic Preparedness.

National Center for Post-Traumatic Stress Disorder. (2001). Self-care and self-help following disaster. Retrieved from www.ncptsd.org/facts/disasters. html

Nordin, J. D., Kasimow, S., Levitt, M. J., & Goodman, M. J. (2008). Bioterrorism surveillance and privacy: Intersection of HIPAA, the common rule, and public health law. *American Journal of Public Health, 98,* 802–807.

O'Toole, T., & Inglesby, T. (2001). *Shining a light on dark winter. Johns Hopkins Center for Civilian Biodefense Studies.* Retrieved from www.hopkins_biodefense. org

Paniagua, F. A. (2014). *Assessing and treating culturally diverse clients: A practice guide* (4th ed.). Thousand Oaks, CA: Sage.

Parsons, R. D., & Zhang, N. (2014). *Becoming a skilled counselor.* Thousand Oaks, CA: Sage.

Potter, R. H., & Rosky, J. W. (2013). The iron fist in the latex glove: The intersection of public health and criminal justice. *American Journal of Criminal Justice, 38,* 276–288. doi:10.1007/s12103-012-9173-3

Ramsay, J. D., Cutrer, D., & Raffel, R. (2010). Development of an outcomes-based undergraduate curriculum in homeland security. *Homeland Security Affairs,* 6(2), 1–20.

Raphael, B., & Dobson, M. (2001). Acute posttraumatic interventions. In J. P. Wilson, M. J. Friedman, & J. D. Lindy

(Eds.), *Treating psychological trauma and stress* (pp. 139–157). New York: Guilford Press.

Roberts, A. R. (1991). *Contemporary perspectives on crisis intervention and prevention.* Englewood Cliffs, NJ: Prentice Hall.

Roberts, A. R., & Dziegielewski, S. F. (1995). Foundations and applications of crisis intervention and time-limited cognitive therapy. In A. R. Roberts (Ed.), *Crisis intervention and time-limited cognitive treatment* (pp. 13–27). Newbury Park, CA: Sage.

Schuster, M. A., Stein, B. D., Jaycox, L. H., Collins, R. L., Marshall, G. N., Elliott, M. N.,... Berry, S. H. (2001). A national survey of stress reactions after the September 11, 2001, terrorist attacks. *New England Journal of Medicine, 345,* 1507–1512.

Shalev, A. Y., & Freedman, S. (2005). PTSD following terrorist attacks: A prospective evaluation. *American Journal of Psychiatry, 162,* 1188–1191.

Silver, R. C., Holman, A. E., McIntosh, D. N., Poulin, M., & Gil-Rivas, V. (2002). Nationwide longitudinal study of psychological responses to September 11. *Journal of the American Medical Association, 288,* 1235–1244.

Simon, J. D. (1999). Nuclear, biological, and chemical terrorism: Understanding the threat and designing responses. *International Journal of Emergency Mental Health,* 1(2), 81–89.

Terrorism Research Center. (2000). Combating terrorism. In *U.S. Army field manual.* Retrieved from www.terrorism.com.index. html

Terrorism Research Center. (2005). Combating terrorism. In *Utilizing terrorism early warning groups to meet the national preparedness goal*. Retrieved from www. terrorism.com.index. html

Texas Department of Health. (2001). Bioterrorism FAQs. Retrieved from www.tdh.state.tx.us/bioterrorism/ default.htm

Texas Department of State Health Services. (2013). Bioterrorism pre- paredness. Retrieved from https:// www.dshs.state.tx.us/prepared- ness/chem_pros.shtm

Vazquez, C. I., & Rosa, D. (2011). *Grief therapy with Latinos: Integrating culture for clinicians*. New York: Springe.

Wilson, J. P., Friedman, M. J., & Lindy, J. D. (2001). Treatment goals for PTSD. In J. P. Wilson, M. J. Friedman, & J. D. Lindy (Eds.), *Treating psychological trauma and stress* (pp. 3–27). New York: Guilford Press.

# 10

## Crisis Intervention Teams: Police-Based First Response for Individuals in Mental Health Crisis

DAVID P. KASICK
CHRISTOPHER D. BOWLING

---

### Case Example

Shortly after sunset on a cool fall evening, a young woman calls 911 to report that her boyfriend may be suicidal. She describes to the police dispatcher that he has become increasingly despondent over the past month since his mother died 2 months ago after being diagnosed earlier that spring with terminal cancer. She describes that he has had ongoing struggles with unemployment since his recent graduation from college, a recent diagnosis of depression from his family doctor, and a prescription for an antidepressant medication that she does not believe he is taking. She describes a recent increase in alcohol consumption and an increase in verbal conflict about trivial matters. Earlier that evening, she reports, he left their apartment after an argument about a cable television bill. He made a provocative comment about being dead the next time she saw him, and he has not been responding to phone calls or text messages for more than an hour. She is frightened, and is concerned that he could have access to a firearm. She provides a description of the vehicle he was driving to the police dispatcher.

Within 30 minutes, patrol officers from the police department's crisis intervention team (CIT) located the man sitting at a picnic table next to his car in a secluded area of a local park. He was sitting still and was noted to be despondent and tearful. Although he was found to be unarmed, he was initially irritable and terse with the officers. They observed him looking through a childhood photo album of pictures of his mother and engaged him in a discussion about how he had been coping recently. The officers asked about his girlfriend's concerns and took careful note of his description of a decline in functioning, as they recognized multiple signs and symptoms of depression they had learned about during their CIT training. Over the course of their discussion, the officers listened intently and noted an emerging sense of relief and calmness, with the man later disclosing that he had purchased a bottle of an over-the-counter pain medication shortly before their arrival, with thoughts of overdosing in the park. He recounted some of his struggles and losses to the officers and described the argument with his girlfriend from earlier in the evening. Recognizing the signs and symptoms of a decompensated mental illness, the officers discussed going to the local mental health crisis facility with the man and encouraged him to make use of their crisis services to pursue further mental health evaluation and intervention. He was agreeable to being transported there by police. Upon arrival at the crisis facility, officers conveyed the incident details as well as their observations of the man's behavior to the crisis workers. Following further triage care at the crisis facility, he was admitted to a psychiatric hospital for ongoing inpatient care.

---

## INTRODUCTION

The CIT model has grown over the past 25 years to become known as a best practice framework for developing and guiding law enforcement response to individuals experiencing a mental health crisis. Forged from a collaborative partnership of community and professional partners, active CIT programs train and maintain a cadre of front-line patrol officers within a law enforcement agency who have received additional training in identifying, assessing, de-escalating, and resolving situations in which law enforcement officers encounter an at-risk individual with a mental illness. CIT-trained officers are selected to respond when calls to law enforcement/public safety agency dispatchers are thought to involve a person experiencing a mental health crisis. These first responders become both generalists and specialists in that they continue to perform general policing duties but are also sent as policing specialists to service calls involving persons in a mental health crisis. Linking officers who have the most training and expertise in working with at-risk consumers was designed to have a positive impact on the safety and outcomes of such encounters.

Contact with law enforcement is often an inevitable reality for many individuals with an acute or chronic mental illness in the post-deinstitutionalization era. By training officers to better understand the behavioral manifestations of mental illness and their potential impact on law enforcement encounters, CIT aims to simultaneously improve attention to the needs of the mentally ill, without compromising the goals of public safety (Morrissey, Fagan, & Cocozza, 2009). Through improving integration of roles and relationships between the criminal justice and mental health communities, law enforcement officers are able to more effectively and safely intervene through their role as de facto gatekeepers at the front doors of both the mental health and the criminal justice system. CIT programs aim to improve the safety of the officer and subject, reduce use of force, and increase referral of individuals to mental health services while diverting them from the criminal justice system when appropriate to do so (Compton et al., 2014a, 2014b).

After initial conceptualization and success of CIT in Memphis, Tennessee, the "Memphis model" has since been repeatedly adapted and replicated by individual communities, leading to a national and international network of CIT programs. The opportunity for local communities to organize CIT programs, develop training sessions, and maintain active program coordination strengthens partnerships between law enforcement and several key community stakeholders. The platform of CIT provides a forum for law enforcement officers, mental health consumers and families, mental health advocacy groups, and local mental health treatment providers to learn about each other's culture, viewpoints, and needs from a better-informed perspective, diminishing some of the mistrust or misinformation that may have overshadowed past interactions between these groups. As a joint stakeholder model, CIT provides an opportunity to impact individual outcomes following law enforcement contact as well as a way to better organize community resources around coordination of mental health crisis treatment. This mutually beneficial transcendence of the traditional boundaries between the criminal justice and mental health communities impacts individual outcomes as well as improves system-wide communication as local communities work to maintain effective coordination of community mental health crisis treatment.

CIT is now regarded as a law enforcement best practice and is building an academic evidence base to support the benefits perceived by early stakeholders (Watson & Fulambarker, 2012; Thompson & Borum, 2006). Beyond the perceived benefits noted by early program adopters, further academic study in the era of evidence-based practice has revealed an emerging evidence base which supports that CIT has contributed to improving mutually safe and effective outcomes for individuals in crisis and the law enforcement officers encountering them. New opportunities for maintaining and growing the grass-roots network of CIT programs may lie in the landscape of social media and electronic educational and research technology.

## The Evolution and Spread of CIT

The law enforcement crisis intervention team model traces its roots to the first program developed by the Memphis, Tennessee, Police Department in 1988. In September 1987, Memphis police officers were involved in the fatal shooting of a mentally ill individual who, after cutting himself with a knife while possibly suicidal, was threatening officers and did not comply with their instructions. Although review of the incident did not find the officers guilty of any criminal wrongdoing, public outcry drove the formation of a community task force comprising law enforcement, mental health providers, and mental health advocates to analyze the factors surrounding the incident and develop a better model of training and response. From their collaborative efforts, the framework for the first CIT program emerged.

Law enforcement agencies have long recognized the likelihood that their personnel will find themselves in situations involving individuals displaying aberrant behaviors driven by active, severe mental illnesses (Bittner, 1967). In 1996, a survey of larger urban police departments suggested that the proportion of police contacts and investigations thought to involve an individual with a mental illness was approximately 7% (Deane, Steadman, Borum, Veysey, & Morrissey, 1999). At that time, fewer than half of the survey respondents indicated that their department had any type of specialized mental health response for such situations. These situations commonly require the officer to exercise significant discretion in deciding how to resolve the encounter, balancing the need to protect the welfare of the larger community with the need to protect citizens with mental illness who cannot care for themselves (Lamb Weinberger, & DeCuir, 2002).

Prior to the late 1980s and the development of the CIT model, standard basic academy training for law enforcement officers to interact with individuals with mental illness was highly variable and often sparse. Academy classroom hours were generally devoted to core topics such as response to and management of criminal activity and disorder, police professionalism, understanding and application of criminal and traffic laws, legal issues, use of weapons, driving skills, and defensive tactics. These core elements often overshadowed more in-depth exploration of understanding individuals with characteristics that could lead to a wide range of behaviors potentially warranting the assistance or attention of law enforcement officers in the community. For example, in 2006, the minimum standard in the state of Ohio for training peace officers was 16 hours of training (out of 582 total hours) for dealing with "special populations," which included individuals with mental illness, developmental and physical disabilities, and physical handicaps. Beyond these minimum requirements for training at the basic academy level, the growth of the CIT model has thus provided a continuing educational framework for additional peace officer training and skill development.

The population of individuals with serious mental illness in the United States has both grown and shifted from residential hospital to outpatient community settings over the past 40 years, followed by subsequent funding and service shortfalls, the closure of inpatient psychiatric treatment beds, and circumstances in which many mentally ill individuals are receiving significantly less support than in previous decades (Lamb & Weinberger, 2005). Instead of being treated in asylums or hospitals as was the case a generation earlier, growing numbers of seriously mentally ill individuals are being housed and treated in jails and other correctional settings. When coupled with the added vulnerabilities of homelessness and addictive disorders, the opportunity for mentally ill individuals to have street-level contact with law enforcement increased, leading to law enforcement officers becoming a primary referral source for psychiatric emergency facilities (Borum, Deane, Steadman, & Morrisey, 1998). As the growing, unintended consequences of the deinstitutionalization movement took shape, and individuals with serious behavioral pathology transitioned from the protection of the inpatient mental health treatment system to the street and more frequent interactions with the criminal justice system, law enforcement officers increasingly recognized the complexities of calls involving people with mental illnesses. Noting the diverse and changing needs of the population, officers found that they needed to work in partnership with mental health specialists and other social agencies to transition the law enforcement response from makeshift interventions to comprehensive policies reflecting professional systemic collaboration (Chappell & O'Brien, 2014). Not surprisingly, the CIT model has flourished in an era of growing community-oriented policing approaches.

Similarly, as communities recognize the overrepresentation of individuals with mental illnesses in correctional environments, interest in CIT as a mechanism for facilitating jail diversion has also grown. In many instances, law enforcement officers have a significant amount of discretion about how to resolve calls with individuals in crisis. Outcomes of such encounters could include criminal arrest, often on misdemeanor charges stemming from behaviors driven by undertreated mental illness. For situations where treatment is more appropriate than further criminalization of individuals with behaviors driven by active mental illness, CIT has been conceptualized as a pre-arrest diversion program, and as one of a series of sequential intercept interventions that can prevent further penetration of the individual deeper into the legal system (Munetz & Griffin, 2006). De-escalation, a core training element in the CIT model, may also be critical to jail diversion because it may help diminish impulsive or emotionally charged responses to perceived police provocation (Compton et al., 2014a). Heightened officer awareness of local mental health referral and treatment options for individuals in crisis may help diminish the need for "mercy booking" during instances where officers believe that some subjects would receive better mental health services in jail than if left on their own in the community.

In addition to widespread growth across the United States, the CIT model has been adapted internationally, including programs across Canada and abroad in Australia (Chapell & O'Brien, 2014). The need for such a specialized police mental health response in Australia arose from similar officer-involved shooting situations as transpired previously in Memphis, with similar subsequent identification of the need for further officer training. Modifications in Australia have been made to adapt the core CIT concepts to large, state-run agencies that serve both urban and vast rural areas. Building on current models like the Memphis CIT model, the Canadian Mental Health Commission has proposed the TEMPO model to serve as

a national-level, multilevel learning strategy for Canadian police personnel, adding additional emphasis to lifelong learning and variable adult
learning methods beyond didactic instruction (Coleman & Cotton, 2014).
Mclean and Marshall (2010) report that police officers in Scotland, who
lack a model for mental health crisis response similar to CIT, have reported
ongoing frustrations in the face of inefficiency, poor access to mental health
crisis services and the lack of a collaborative care model to improve crisis
outcomes.

## CIT CURRICULAR MODELS AND
## BEST PRACTICES

Following the success of the initial crisis intervention team in Memphis,
other communities and law enforcement agencies across the country began
developing their own versions of crisis intervention teams. Many of these
programs were founded on grass-roots efforts at the local level to capture
the unique needs of the local law enforcement agency, the local mental
health system, and the specific population of the community being served.
Conversely, other agencies participated as members of statewide programs
(in the state of Georgia, for example) driven by a centralized, top-down
approach with a common curriculum and administrative structure (Oliva &
Compton, 2008).

As the various curricula were adapted to meet the goals of the stakeholders, many agencies continue to refer to the elements and structure first
conceptualized in Memphis, leading to the concept of the "Memphis model"
(Dupont, Cochran, & Pillsbury, 2007). The goals of this model emphasize
CIT programs as being "more than just training," with a focus on improving officer and consumer safety and redirecting mentally ill individuals from
the criminal justice system to the healthcare system (Dupont et al., 2007).
Individual programs continue to pragmatically weave the core ongoing,
operational, and sustaining elements suggested by the Memphis model into
their programs to meet the unique and dynamic needs of their communities.

Ongoing program elements emphasized in the Memphis model include
active partnerships between leadership of law enforcement agencies—for
example, police departments and sheriff's offices, members of the judiciary,
and corrections agencies—with members of the advocacy community and
mental health professionals. Coordinators from each group are identified and
act as liaisons to each of the other key stakeholder groups. Joining the individuals who interact on the front lines through encountering, de-escalating,
transport and disposition, risk assessment, and care provision, with advocates who are able to humanize and promote the interests of consumers is
considered critical in the planning and implementation of policies guiding

the development of local CIT programs. The mutual benefits of education, training, and shared community ownership in crisis situations are difficult to capitalize upon without the existence of such partnerships (Dupont et al., 2007).

Operational elements set forth in the Memphis model center around policies and procedures within law enforcement and mental health agencies considered necessary to effectively handle each crisis situation (Dupont et al., 2007). Adequate numbers of law enforcement officers assigned to the patrol function, ideally 20% to 25% of a department's patrol officers, should be trained to have around-the-clock availability. Accordingly, all law enforcement/public safety dispatchers should also be trained to properly identify a mental health crisis and route the nearest CIT officer to the scene. Ideally, a range of inpatient and outpatient referral options should be available to officers, with specific policies in place to facilitate easily accessible, immediate mental health care when necessary. Turnaround time for CIT officers transporting an individual to mental health care settings should be minimal and not exceed the time needed to process a criminal arrest, so as to remove the potential for jail booking to be preferred as a less time-intensive option.

Patrol officer CIT training under the Memphis model focuses on building crisis de-escalation skills through experience, ideas, and information from a variety of individuals from the mental health, law enforcement, and advocacy communities (Dupont et al., 2007). Volunteer officers apply for training and are selected for a 40-hour course.

Based on a review of training schedules for programs around the United States, CIT core curricula typically consist of the following major categories: mental illnesses and their treatments, co-occurring disorders such as substance use disorders and personality disorders, interaction with family members and consumers, legal issues, the local community mental health system, and de-escalation skills.

Program curricula vary in the organization of content; for example, mental illness diagnostic terminology or psychotropic medications and their effects may be presented in an aggregate fashion or be broken into blocks corresponding to major diagnostic categories. Some programs include specific blocks on suicide risk assessment and child/adolescent mental health issues. Substance use disorders are the most commonly presented co-occurring disorder. Programs may also provide training and education on those who have either independent or co-occurring mental illnesses and developmental disabilities, helping law enforcement officers understand the differences between these conditions and the entities that provide services to these persons.

CIT core training curricula provide methods for law enforcement officers to interact with family members of those who have a mental illness and with consumers of mental health services. These methods include panel discussions, facility visits, and riding in the field with mental health case managers. Panel discussions are held in the classroom, and consumers and family members have distinct times to present their information to the law enforcement officers in the class. When resources permit, law enforcement officers ride in the community with case managers from mental health service–providing agencies or engage in site visits with agencies that provide mental health services. The goal for riding with case managers is to let law enforcement officers observe case manager interaction with clients to provide a context for the de-escalation skills to be taught and to allow law enforcement officers to observe persons with mental illnesses when they are not in crisis. Interacting with persons with a mental illness who are not in crisis provides an additional perspective to law enforcement officers, as officers are typically called when a crisis state exists. Officers learn about effective communication skills by listening to consumer perspectives and by observing the communication and interaction methods that case managers use with clients.

The legal aspects of local civil commitment laws are part of the core training curriculum. Topical matter includes a review of the state's statutes and methods for taking a person into emergency custody to have him or her evaluated by a medical professional, any procedures that have been codified by the state to take a person into emergency custody, and client rights. Law enforcement officers learn how to write effective probable cause statements and how to take a person into custody and deliver that person to a place of care and safety. During this part of the curriculum officers also learn about court decisions at the local, state, and federal levels that regulate when and how they can take a person into custody and how any force used to take a person into custody will be evaluated.

The final large block of training consists of training officers in the use of de-escalation skills and then having the officers demonstrate those skills in a practicum. Verbal de-escalation patterns and communication methodologies are provided during core training sessions and are taught either as part of an action-response framework or independently. Additional framing can be used to help law enforcement officers tailor their responses based on their observations of the subject's mood, thoughts, anxiety, and personality at the scene of a call for service. Once law enforcement officers receive the designed de-escalation training, a practicum is often utilized to allow them to apply the newly learned skills in a practical setting. The practicum method most often used is role-play. Role-play scenarios are built with guidelines and rule sets for role-players so that law enforcement officers experience success when they use the taught de-escalation skills. CIT programs use a variety of role-players, to include mental health professionals, medical actors, experienced CIT officers, family members, or consumers. The role-plays differ from program to program and in design. Some scenarios are designed to allow a specified team of law enforcement officers to complete a single role-play scenario; others allow multiple teams of officers to complete a single scenario, switching when the allotted time has expired. When the role-play is completed, debriefing of the scenario takes place and permits direct learning for participants and vicarious learning for those who were observing the role-play.

Reciprocal training for the course faculty is also recommended under the Memphis model, including a patrol ride-along "in order to fully understand the complexities and differences that exist between mental health care and law enforcement" (Dupont et al., 2007). Graduating officers from many programs receive a special CIT uniform pin, which elevates awareness of the CIT program and signifies their CIT training status to fellow officers, consumers, and the general public.

## CURRENT STATE OF CIT PROGRAMS

The rapid spread of CIT programs has been profound, with estimates of 400 law enforcement agencies with active CIT programs across the United States in 2006 to as many as 2,700 active programs by 2013 (Watson, Morabito, Draine, & Ottati, 2008; Compton et al., 2014a). Although the common goals of improving safety, outcomes, and jail diversion may exist across agencies, the specific policies, needs, and challenges surrounding sustaining individual CIT programs may vary widely. CIT programs exist in small rural sheriff's offices, large urban metropolitan police departments, suburban police departments, and university and airport police departments. Each setting brings significant variation in the diversity of population, the community resources available, and the number and density of officers working in a given area at any given time. Accordingly, providing adequate training to the number of officers and dispatchers required to provide 24/7 CIT availability can present hardships in small departments needing to provide coverage for staff attending 40 hours of training (Compton et al., 2010). Implementation in areas without access to a psychiatric emergency receiving facility with a "no refusal" policy, or in rural areas with limited proximal mental health resources, can lead to challenges in sustaining functional CIT programs (Compton et al., 2010).

However, CIT implementation and training have been successfully adapted to meet the needs of unique patrol settings, emphasizing special problems and overcoming implementation obstacles in rural areas. Focus group research conducted by McGriff and colleagues (2010) reviewed unique needs for CIT officers operating in a large international airport setting. Compared with other urban or suburban patrol settings, airport officers face numerous unique challenges, including a high concentration of homeless and transient individuals using the airport for shelter or as a place to obtain food or perform self-care activities; the need to assess psychiatric symptoms among travelers who are tense, anxious, and frustrated by airport delays; the need for careful and efficient de-escalation given ubiquitous video surveillance; and the density of public onlookers surrounding encounters with individuals they contact.

Skubby and colleagues (2013) recently analyzed focus group interviews of law enforcement officers and mental health professionals who have overcome implementation obstacles in rural Ohio communities. In rural areas, similar to urban implementation, stakeholders acknowledged different ways of thinking about the mentally ill and had misperceptions about each other's professional culture and duties; this changed significantly following CIT development, which facilitated communication and greater cooperation derived from a sense of shared collaboration that came from working together. Some rural areas with small departments decided to train all officers in order to maintain continuous CIT officer availability, despite the hardship of covering patrol duties for officers attending week-long training or the need for part-time officers to use vacation days from their other jobs to attend training. Diminished resources in rural areas, including the closure of state hospitals and the lack of a consistently available drop-off mental health evaluation site, continue to challenge program sustainability. Training grants from the National Alliance on Mental Illness (NAMI) and increased community support have been helpful in facilitating training sessions. Methods for further data collection, program evaluation, effectiveness targets, and academic collaborations are still evolving in rural areas.

Other examples of collaborative response to mental health crises exist outside of the CIT police-based, police officer response model. Non-sworn law enforcement–based mental health employees have been used in some locales to provide on-scene and telephone consultations to sworn law enforcement officers, as have mobile mental health crisis teams deployed independently through the local community health system (Borum et al., 1998). Despite the growing popularity of the CIT model, more study is needed to clarify the precise advantages or disadvantages it may confer in comparison to other modes of crisis response.

## CIT INFLUENCE AND OUTCOMES

CIT programs appear to have the potential to positively impact community mental health work and facilitate boundary-spanning partnerships among program stakeholders, and they are beginning to demonstrate supporting data around officer-level outcomes, now regarded by some as a law enforcement best practice (Compton et al., 2014a; Watson & Fulambarker, 2012). Over the past 10 years, the academic community has begun to accumulate an evidence base that supports the benefits of CIT, lends support to the justification for establishing and maintaining CIT programs, and further delineates aspects of CIT program organization and training that hold potential for being evidence-based practices. Research partnerships between local police departments in Memphis, Tennessee; Akron, Ohio; Chicago, Illinois; as well as at the state level in Georgia and Florida, in concert with respective local university faculty, have led to the collection and examination of data that more precisely illustrate the impact and promising value of CIT training. Initial reports and anecdotal perceptions of program success in Memphis and among other early CIT adopters are now being investigated more rigorously, with attempts at replication in departments in urban and rural settings. The expanding deployment of CIT continues to occur as a beneficent response to community needs and as a model with supporting evidence that is worthy of sustaining financial support.

Programs and their stakeholders have organized at the national and international levels, with yearly conferences since 2005 that have disseminated innovations in teaching techniques and tactical practices. Further study of CIT program outcomes related to training differences, community differences, disposition of interactions, costs, and benefits of law enforcement and community safety all appear to be viable avenues of outcomes-oriented research (Morrissey et al., 2009). Similarly, the CIT stakeholder interface appears to represent an opportunity for collaborative research between community- and university-based mental health professionals.

Compton and colleagues (2008) conducted a systematic review of the available research on CIT, noting that in spite of the enthusiasm surrounding the opportunity for collaboration between stakeholders, as well as the resources being devoted to CIT training, relatively limited outcomes research is available. Much of the current research has been done by authors from mental health backgrounds rather than by criminologists or social scientists. Of the available studies, Compton suggests that CIT may have positive effects ranging from officers' attitudes and training, to jail diversion and improved consumer outcomes. Among the current studies, officer-level and system-level outcomes such as dispositions of police calls eliciting a CIT response and prebooking jail diversion are better represented than patient-level outcomes. Officer-level outcomes continue to be a focus of current research, suggesting complexities of capturing data among consumers and system-level providers.

Critics of the rapid spread of the CIT concept across the United States have cited a lack of rigorous outcomes data beyond descriptive evidence, as well as the lack of universal access to adequate receiving facilities serving as a transport destination for officers considering jail alternatives, which is thought to be a key to the initial success in Memphis (Geller 2008). Follow-up studies regarding long-term utility, more diverse and controlled study samples, the impact of proactive, continuous contact from specialized teams, specific research examining the precise amount and type of specialized training needed, and the generalizability of the original Memphis model remain areas of ongoing research need (Tucker, Van Hesselt, & Russell, 2008). More specific measures of the strength of collaborations between stakeholder groups may help to better understand factors that contribute to program success.

More research is also needed into how CIT may affect the operation of local mental health systems. For example, officers may be aware that they are interacting with a mentally ill individual but may perceive barriers that lead to the belief that criminal arrest is a more reliable disposition. Such barriers could include long waits to access mental health emergency services, more rigid mental health criteria for holding individuals, and problems with information exchange between officers and mental health crisis workers that could lead to quick release (Lamb et al., 2002). Through uniting and facilitating regular communication among stakeholders, CIT could plausibly impact the coordination of solutions for these and other common problems officers report when accessing local emergency mental health resources.

## CIT OFFICER-LEVEL OUTCOMES

The unofficial role of law enforcement officers as "street corner psychiatrists" has long been recognized, derived from an era with fewer organized law enforcement responses to persons with mental illnesses (Teplin & Pruett, 1992). Now, CIT training has led to improvements in training and resources to address the challenges law enforcement officers face in managing situations with individuals in crisis. Having exposure to CIT training led Memphis officers to perceive that they were more effective at meeting the needs of mentally ill individuals in crisis, keeping the mentally ill out of jail, and minimizing the amount of officer downtime while dealing with mental health crisis calls, all while maintaining community safety (Borum et al., 1998). The Memphis CIT program had low arrest rates, high officer availability and rapid response time, and frequent referrals and transport for mental health evaluation in comparison to other police-based diversion models (Steadman, Deane, Borum, & Morrissey 2000). The strength of community partnerships and the availability of a psychiatric triage center were considered key factors in the success of the Memphis model.

Law enforcement officers have several options for how to resolve dispatched calls or triage encounters with individuals possibly experiencing the effects of a mental illness, including leaving the individual at the scene, transporting them to a hospital or treatment facility, or transporting them to jail. At times, legal obligations do not preclude officer discretion (e.g., "must arrest" situations). Ritter, Teller, Marcussen, Munetz, and Teasdale (2011) examined the role that both dispatcher call coding and CIT training appeared to have in Akron, Ohio, on the disposition of each encounter, finding that both dispatch codes and officers' on-scene assessments had an impact on transport decisions. Specifically, calls dispatched as a "suspected suicide" or "mental disturbance" were more likely to result in transport to treatment than were calls dispatched as "needing assistance," "disturbance," "suspicious person," "assault," "suspicion of a crime," and "meet a citizen." Ritter and colleagues also found that CIT officer recognition of specific signs and symptoms of mental or physical illness emphasized in CIT training, or other issues such as substance abuse and nonadherence to medication, led to increased rates of transport to treatment, regardless of how the call was dispatched. Their study underscored the importance of dispatcher training as a component of CIT training, as well as support for the concept that CIT officers are more likely to consider treatment options over other potential outcomes.

Other studies have similarly concluded that CIT has led to improvement in officers' beliefs about and understanding of specific mental illnesses, and has led to increased referrals to psychiatric services (Broussard, McGriff, Demir Neubert, D'Orio, & Compton, 2010; Compton, Esterberg, McGee, Kotwicki, & Oliva, 2006; Demir, Broussard, Goulding, & Compton, 2009, Dupont & Cochran, 2000). CIT training is also thought to have increased the safety of both officers and individuals through a reduction of officer injuries, and it may lead to a reduction in the use of force between officers and individuals with mental illness (Compton et al., 2011; Dupont & Cochran, 2000).

Georgia CIT-trained officers have suggested that their training curriculum enhances the self-efficacy of police officers in interacting with, interviewing, de-escalating, and referring individuals with depression, schizophrenia, and alcohol and cocaine dependence (Bahora, Hanafi, Chien, & Compton, 2008). Similarly, this study also revealed a correlation between CIT training and a reduction of the need for social distance, for example, living near, working with, or being friends with an individual with mental illness. The extent to which these changes in perceived confidence or stigma would affect interactions or officer decision-making was not evaluated.

Further research by Compton and colleagues (2014) of a large cohort of Georgia officers with and without CIT training (586 total officers) demonstrated that officers with CIT training performed better on measures of knowledge about mental illnesses, diverse attitudes about mental illnesses and their treatments, self-efficacy, social distance stigma, de-escalation skills, and referral decisions. Among the officers studied, a median of 22 months had elapsed between training and research assessment, supporting that earlier reports of improvements of officer knowledge, attitudes, stigma, and self-efficacy persist beyond the immediate effects of training. This suggestion that the intended impact on the training audience is sizable and persisting is an important development, supporting the concept that CIT may lead to important transformational change in officers' ability to effectively manage encounters with mentally ill people. Potential limitations to this and many officer-level studies include the validity of the officers' self-reported perceptions and whether responses to posttraining interpretations of vignette-based assessments consistently translate to behavioral changes in the field.

CIT also appears to have benefits that can be replicated in large, urban police departments. CIT training in the Chicago Police Department has been successfully implemented, as evidenced by application of skills from training to actual cases, police collaboration with community service providers, diversion to mental health services, voluntary officer response to mental health calls, and community requests for CIT-trained officers (Canada, Angell, & Watson, 2010). Watson and colleagues (2010) also found that CIT training in Chicago appeared to have a more substantial impact on the decision-making of officers who had a personal familiarity with mental illness or who had positive perceptions of mental health services in their area. However, in Chicago, CIT training has shown less clear benefit in reducing injury during encounters (Kerr, Morabito, & Watson, 2010).

Further research by Bonfine, Ritter, and Munetz (2014) about how CIT impacts individual officers in Ohio found that CIT training was perceived to positively impact perceptions of officer, community, and individual safety and additionally led to improvements in officer confidence, abilities, and preparedness of response during calls to individuals in crisis. Further improvements in perceptions of the effectiveness of their police department were also noted by CIT officers, which also were associated with improved levels of perceived confidence in non-CIT officers, suggesting a possible diffusion effect of CIT concepts through police departments. Attitudes about safety and departmental effectiveness also increased with more frequent personal contact with individuals with mental illnesses. Perceived helpfulness of the mental health system also improved the officers' perception of police department effectiveness.

## CIT IMPACT ON THE MENTAL HEALTH SYSTEM

CIT has provided an opportunity for mental health care providers to strengthen alliances with the law enforcement community through serving as a mechanism for fostering stakeholder interaction. While these two professional cultures have presumably had past interactions, as well as curiosity about each other through the common ground of assisting consumers in crisis, misperceptions and unrealistic expectations may have more readily persisted prior to such a partnership. In comparison to officer-level outcomes, less has been written to date examining the impact of CIT training on the attitudes and perceptions of mental health professionals, although their beliefs and attitudes toward the role of law enforcement officers are important to consider. The accessibility, responsiveness, and perceived helpfulness of mental health emergency services appeared to have an impact on the perceptions of officers and could have an impact on the disposition of police interventions (Borum et al., 1998). Accordingly, the attitudes toward, beliefs about, and understanding of law enforcement culture by mental health workers are likely to play a substantive role in shaping these relationships and spanning previous boundaries.

Further study could investigate how the collaboration necessary to develop and implement CIT programs may lead to improved communication, reduction of systemic friction, and more appropriate understanding of the limitations of each side of the intervention continuum. Aside from the opportunity to develop academic research, clinicians may find involvement in the implementation and teaching of CIT programs to be an important conduit for community involvement and helpful in reducing burnout; perhaps it could even improve a sense of workplace safety though officer presence at crisis facilities. The opportunity to collaborate with other professional agencies through involvement with CIT programs could also appeal to students considering a career as mental health professionals. Exposure to and involvement with CIT training programs may also be an important tool for elevating the awareness of trainees (physicians, nurses, social workers, counselors) to the network of community resources as well as challenges facing consumers and providers outside of traditional treatment settings.

## CIT IMPACT ON CONSUMERS, FAMILIES, AND ADVOCATES

From a consumer advocacy perspective, CIT programs provide an opportunity to achieve positive outcomes for individuals with mental illness following contact with law enforcement officers. Among these advocacy-oriented goals, the ability to facilitate treatment for consumers in crisis, when indicated, in lieu of incarceration or no intervention, is key. However, perhaps even more important is the ability to be understood by an empathic responding officer, who may have a better understanding and appreciation of common problems facing consumers derived from ongoing work as a CIT officer. While much of the current CIT research focuses on officer-level outcomes, data supporting the outcomes of CIT as it impacts consumers are emerging.

The appropriateness of CIT referrals to psychiatric emergency services has been examined by two studies that reviewed patient-focused outcomes. Broussard et al. (2010) examined whether CIT training leads to excessive or inappropriate referrals by examining the characteristics of patients brought to treatment settings by CIT-trained officers in comparison with those brought by non-CIT-trained officers or family members. Their findings suggested that patient characteristics of CIT-trained officer referrals are similar to the characteristics of patients referred by nontrained officers. This suggests that CIT training does not lead to a narrower (referring only severely ill individuals) or broader (referring individuals not needing emergency services) view of patients needing emergency services based on severity of illness.

An earlier study by Strauss et al. (2005) in Louisville, Kentucky, revealed similar findings and concluded that CIT officers were able to adequately identify patients requiring emergency care, although a higher proportion of patients with schizophrenia were referred by CIT-trained officers. Strauss and colleagues suggest that CIT programs may reduce psychiatric morbidity by referring severely ill individuals to the appropriate level of treatment earlier than might occur otherwise.

Consumers in crisis appear to have been positively impacted by the development of the CIT model through increased linkage to treatment. In data collected from the Akron, Ohio, Police Department, CIT-trained officers appear to transport individuals experiencing mental health crises to treatment at a higher rate than do non-CIT-trained officers (Teller, Munetz, Gil, & Ritter, 2006). Additionally, a greater proportion of individuals were transported to treatment voluntarily for both CIT-trained and nontrained officers, possibly due to a diffusion of training techniques or the referral of more challenging situations to CIT officers. Since the inception of the Akron program, the number and proportion of calls to police dispatch involving the possibly mentally ill have increased. Teller and colleagues theorized that this could be related both to increased dispatcher assessment and awareness of mental health emergencies, and possibly to increased consumer comfort in calling police to identify mental health crises due to awareness of the program. This study did not find a reduction in the arrest rate between trained and nontrained officers, perhaps attributable to a referral bias of more difficult cases or CIT officer awareness of the Akron Mental Health Court post-arrest diversion program (Teller et al., 2006).

Similarly, data from the Chicago Police Department suggest that the department's CIT officers have a higher likelihood of directing persons with mental illness to the mental health system (Watson et al., 2010). In examining the effects of CIT training, this study revealed that direction of individuals to the mental health system and reduction in "contact only" encounters were most robust among officers who had a positive view of mental health resource availability and among officers with prior familiarity with mental illness. As in Akron, the Chicago study did not demonstrate a reduction in arrests, although the Memphis program has reported low rates of arrests (Teller et al., 2006; Watson et al., 2010; Dupont & Cochran, 2000; Steadman, Deane, Borum, & Morrisey, 2000). Among the limitations noted in studying the effects of CIT were a lack of pretraining controls, nonrandomization of officers to CIT, lack of independent verification of mental illness in subjects encountered by trained and nontrained officers, and a possible lack of recognition or documentation of mental illness in subjects encountered by non-CIT-trained officers (Watson et al., 2010).

Compton and colleagues (2014) have continued to demonstrate consumer-level benefits, reiterating the potential impact for CIT to shift dispositional decisions in situations when arrest is not mandatory. Among a group of CIT and non-CIT officers in Georgia, CIT-trained officers had a decreased likelihood of arresting an individual they believed to be suffering from a behavioral disorder, including a serious mental illness, a drug or alcohol problem, or a developmental disability. In this study, there was no overall difference in use of force attributed to CIT training, although CIT officers were less likely to use force as behavior became more resistant. A higher percentage of CIT officers used verbal engagement or negotiation as their highest level of force, in comparison to non-CIT officers, suggesting the enhanced use of verbal de-escalation skills that may be strengthened by CIT training. Similar to other studies, transport to a treatment facility was significantly more likely than by nontrained officers, including when CIT officers reverted to using force.

Among the benefits of CIT in rural areas noted by Skubby and colleagues (2013), support from families who recognize the benefit of more organized and effective de-escalation responses has been demonstrated by being more willing to proactively call law enforcement to prevent escalation of a family member in crisis. Quieter and more private de-escalation with proactive hospital transport was viewed by focus group members to be much more beneficial for families and consumers than the broad community awareness in rural areas when large numbers of officers are called out for escalating crises. The advocacy reach of NAMI in rural areas where there was diminished availability of well-resourced or academic stakeholders was also viewed as critical in helping to facilitate program organization and training.

## FUTURE OPPORTUNITIES AND CHALLENGES FACING CIT

### Succession Planning

As CIT programs are organized, established, and evolve within individual communities, many factors are critical in maintaining and sustaining the success of local programs. CIT programs continually rely on the energy of dedicated officers, professional volunteers, advocates, consumers, and coordinators who continue to value the benefits of collaborative work. The first generation of program organizers and coordinators, who developed relationships in the context of building programs, have witnessed the transformational impact that such a program can have on a community. CIT officers are promoted, transfer out of patrol assignments, and retire, just as mental health professionals follow career path changes. More than a job title or assigned responsibility by virtue of position or rank, thoughtful leadership and coordinator succession planning are key in ensuring that the lines of communication, collaborative spirit, and shared sense of purpose that united and propelled the founding stakeholders are carried forward as program leadership changes hands. Mental health CIT program coordinators require dedication, the ability to understand their own systems' strengths and weaknesses, and constant pursuit of the resources to perpetuate CIT programs. Law enforcement CIT program coordinators require similar enthusiasm and commitment and ideally have volunteered after previous CIT officer core training and experience as a CIT officer. While the law enforcement chain of command can be set up to support CIT, the coordinator has to be involved and willing to take on the various issues that law enforcement faces in working with mental health service providers, as well as with advocates and consumers.

## Structured Support Interventions for Individuals in Frequent Crisis

Some individuals in the community are frequent utilizers of crisis services or calls for CIT officers and would benefit from additional proactive or follow-up interventions beyond repeated calls to emergency dispatchers. The Houston, Texas, Police Department created a Mental Health Division that coordinates the activities of the CIT with other behind-the-scenes support elements (http://www.houstoncit.org). One program is the Crisis Intervention Response Team (CIRT), which pairs a CIT officer and a licensed professional clinician from the county service board. They are removed from taking calls for service and instead respond to help out on the most serious calls along with conducting proactive and follow-up CIT investigations. Other CIT support functions include teams of mental health professionals and sworn officers who perform homeless outreach, sworn officers who inspect boarding houses, and case manager/sworn officer teams that are dedicated to the care needs of chronic consumers.

## Fostering Growth Into Current Unserved Areas of Need

CIT officers find the demand for their specialized skills to be growing as the complex behavioral needs of the population are increasingly recognized, a role consistent with law enforcement expectations of the US Department of Justice and the Americans With Disabilities Act. Because CITs often have personnel who are known to be receptive to working with populations with diverse behavioral needs, officers now find themselves expanding their role with individuals with intellectual and developmental disabilities, military veterans, persons with traumatic brain injuries, and persons with primary substance addiction issues such as opiate addictions to avoid overdoses and other forms of premature death. In addition, stakeholder groups representing those with autism spectrum disorders and dementia syndromes are reaching out to law enforcement to ensure that officer training reflects the specialized needs unique to these individuals. Understanding the experiences of local CIT officers may also be especially helpful in attempting to analyze the root causes of community behavioral needs and could help stakeholders prioritize community behavioral services and resources.

## Advanced Training

Ongoing training for experienced CIT officers is needed as medical practice and legal standards evolve, communities change, and policies and procedures are modified. However, the content, means, and facilitators of such training have not been consistently defined or applied. Identifying individual CIT officer needs, in the context of their experiences in their local community, may help inform advanced training curriculum development curricula as officers self-identify their weaknesses in certain areas.

## Potential CIT Educational and Training Innovations in the Digital Era

Since the Memphis CIT core curricular concepts were conceptualized more than 25 years ago, online and blended learning models have gained prominence in the world of business and secondary education. Although the Memphis model emphasizes the experiential and empathy-building value of a live 40-hour training course, the optimal techniques for facilitating teaching for a new generation of officers have not been studied. Younger officers may arrive to CIT training with very different educational and learning experiences than preceding generations, favoring active learning methods over a traditional didactic classroom format (Freeman et al., 2014).

Participating in online learning before attending a CIT course could address didactic lecture content and would shorten the time necessary for the remainder of the core training course. Self-paced learning in an online format could replace some of the core training courses for CIT or could be a preferred model for advanced training for experienced CIT officers. Experiential training and application would still be conducted face to face following an initial module review. Such a blended model could reduce the burden of law enforcement agencies needing to release their personnel for an entire week and reduce time demands for instructors, who could be available as subject matter experts to address pre-reviewed material. Online testing and program data collection could also be facilitated, and larger training consortiums could share the expense of developing and maintaining online learning and software platforms. Reduced costs of classroom training could help extend elements of online training to agencies that may not otherwise be able to support CIT training.

Social media also have the potential to facilitate content learning and retention, data collection, and continuing CIT education for a younger generation of officers who are adept at using these methods. Social media could be used for CIT information exchange provided that users would feel free to engage in synchronous or asynchronous conversations within a preestablished framework, being mindful that not all speech of a public servant is appreciated or protected.

Use of personal devices could also help to create maximum performance for CIT. Because of their accessibility during routine patrol functions, such devices can facilitate communication with CIT instructors and classmates, as well as augment retention of content. Mobile or tablet applications, dedicated web-based wikis, or a CIT officer virtual community of practice site with question-and-answer message forums could all improve dissemination of CIT knowledge and skills. Virtual classroom training focused on specific informational needs could be especially useful for advanced skill training and to facilitate interaction between students and CIT subject matter experts.

An electronic performance support system (EPSS) could also facilitate active learning, curriculum outcomes research, and program feedback through capturing the behavior changes and degree of knowledge application from what has been learned by officers once they are back on the streets. Additional testing could be conducted at time intervals to gauge the level of retention by those who have completed a core course or advanced CIT training courses; this could also more easily facilitate surveys of trained versus nontrained officers. EPSS platforms could be created to be accessible from mobile devices to help officers remember de-escalation frameworks, to provide information on medications and their uses, and to provide a listing of available services. Some of this material could be quickly reviewed by responding officers on the scene when the situation is stabilized and assessment and outcome decisions must be made. Risk assessment instruments could also be part of this EPSS and could serve as digitized versions of pocket flip books carried by various professionals.

### Adjusting to a Changing Healthcare Environment

Mental health work in modern communities requires an understanding of the goals and needs of multiple stakeholders and subcultures, and of the dynamic availability and delivery of mental health services. Law enforcement officer adjustment to the accountability, flexibility, and communication skills taught in CIT training has been positive and supported by research, although less is known about the impact of the rapid proliferation of CIT programs on fixed mental health services or their ability to manage the potential influx of referrals. The availably of a central drop-off location with minimal officer turnaround time has been thought to have been a key component of the initial success in Memphis. Locales with less centralized or continuously available mental health services, or with a more complex or decentralized system of triaging individuals with complex medical or addiction presentations, or officer drop-off of individuals who lack treatment benefits may complicate the efficiency or fidelity of the model. Similarly, wider access to mental health insurance benefits through the Affordable Care Act of 2013 could increase the demand for mental health crisis services. Larger numbers of individuals seeking crisis services could impact CIT officer experiences in ways that are not yet known, but have the potential to strain crisis center capacity or impact CIT officer availability or turnaround time. Optimistically, CIT programs have already facilitated important partnerships and professional networks across local systems that will afford the opportunity to more efficiently assess and process the system-level impact of these important healthcare delivery changes.

## SUMMARY

Modern law enforcement response to persons in mental health crisis has evolved through the influence of the CIT model. Aligning the needs and goals of law enforcement agencies, mental health treatment providers, and individual consumers to produce organized, safe, and effective policies and practices for crisis responses has been both popular and successful in the United States and is now growing abroad. Over the past 25 years, CIT programs have been instrumental in facilitating stakeholder communication and opportunities for learning and development, and they serve as a forum for continuous improvement. The resources and methods needed to sustain and optimize CIT programs in an era of economic efficiency and evidence-based practice will be further informed and optimized by ongoing research dedicated to understanding the impact of the key program elements. Opportunities to use educational technologies and social media may also support the first responders who bridge the gap between the street and the front door of the mental health care system. The multidisciplinary boundary-spanning professional partnerships that have been established to support CIT programs are well positioned to continue to strengthen communities and need to be carefully maintained.

REFERENCES

Bahora, M., Hanafi, S., Chien, V. H., & Compton, M. T. (2008). Preliminary evidence of effects of crisis intervention team training on self-efficacy and social distance. *Administration and Policy in Mental Health and Mental Health Services Research, 35*, 159–167.

Bittner, E. (1967). Police discretion in emergency apprehension of mentally ill persons. *Social Problems, 14*, 278–292.

Bonfine, N., Ritter, C., & Munetz, M. (2014). Police officer perceptions of the impact of crisis intervention team (CIT) programs. *International Journal of Law and Psychiatry, 37*, 341–350.

Borum, R., Deane, M., Steadman, H., & Morrisey, J. (1998). Police perspectives on responding to mentally ill people in crisis: Perceptions of program effectiveness. *Behavioral Sciences and the Law, 16*, 393–405.

Broussard, B., McGriff, J. A., Demir Neubert, B. N., D'Orio, B., & Compton, M. T. (2010). Characteristics of patients referred to psychiatric emergency services by crisis intervention team police officers. *Community Mental Health Journal, 46*, 579–584.

Canada, K. E., Angell, B., & Watson, A. C. (2010). Crisis intervention teams in Chicago: Successes on the ground. *Journal of Police Crisis Negotiations, 10*(1–2): 86–100.

Chappell, D., & O'Brien, A. (2014). Police responses to persons with a mental illness: International perspectives. *International Journal of Law and Psychiatry, 37,* 321–324.

Coleman, T., & Cotton, D. (2014). TEMPO: A contemporary model for police education and training about mental illness. *International Journal of Law and Psychiatry, 37*, 325–333.

Compton, M. T., Bahora, M., Watson, A. C., & Oliva, J. R. (2008). A comprehensive review of extant research on crisis intervention team programs. *Journal of the American Academy of Psychiatry and the Law, 36*, 47–55.

Compton, M. T., Bakeman, R., Broussard, B., Hankerson-Dyson, D., Husbands, L, Krishan, S., . . . & Watson, A. C. (2014a). The police-based crisis intervention team (CIT) model: I. Effects on officers' knowledge, attitudes, and skills. *Psychiatric Services 65*, 517–522.

Compton, M. T., Bakeman, R., Broussard, B., Hankerson-Dyson, D., Husbands, L, Krishan, S.,. . . & Watson, A. C. (2014b). The police-based crisis intervention team (CIT) model: II. Effects on level of force and resolution, referral, and arrest *Psychiatric Services, 65*, 523–529.

Compton, M. T., Broussard, B., Hankerson-Dyson, D., Krishan, S., Stewart, T., Oliva, J. R., & Watson, A. C. (2010). System- and policy-level challenges to full implementation of the crisis intervention team (CIT) model. *Journal of Police Crisis Negotiations, 10*(1–2), 72–85.

Compton, M., Demir Neubert, B., Broussard, B., McGriff, J., Morgan, R., & Oliva, J. (2011). Use of force preferences and perceived effectiveness of actions among crisis intervention team (CIT) police officers and non-CIT officers in an escalating psychiatric crisis involving a subject with schizophrenia. *Schizophrenia Bulletin, 37*, 737–745.

Compton, M. T., Esterberg, M. L., McGee, R., Kotwicki, R. J., &

Crisis Intervention Teams   295

Oliva, J. R. (2006). Crisis intervention team training: Changes in knowledge, attitudes, and stigma related to schizophrenia. *Psychiatric Services 57*, 1199–1202.

Deane, M. W., Steadman, H. J., Borum, R., Veysey, B., & Morrissey, J. (1999). Emerging partnerships between mental health and law enforcement. *Psychiatric Services, 50*(1), 99–101.

Demir, B., Broussard, B., Goulding, S., & Compton, M. (2009). Beliefs about causes of schizophrenia among police officers before and after crisis intervention team training. *Community Mental Health Journal, 45*, 385–392.

Dupont, R., & Cochran, S. (2000). Police response to mental health emergencies—barriers to change. *Journal of the American Academy of Psychiatry and the Law, 28*, 338–344.

Dupont, R., Cochran, S., & Pillsbury, S. (2007). Crisis intervention team core elements. University of Memphis School of Urban Affairs and Public Policy, Department of Criminology and Criminal Justice, CIT Center. Retrieved from http://cit.memphis.edu/pdf/CoreElements.pdf

Freeman, S., Eddy, S. L., McDonough, M., Smith, M. K., Okoroafor, N., Jordt, H., & Wenderoth, M. P. (2014). Active learning increases student performance in science, engineering, and mathematics. *Proceedings of the National Academy of Sciences of the United States of America, 111*, 8410–8415.

Geller, J. L. (2008). Commentary: Is CIT today's lobotomy? *Journal of the American Academy of Psychiatry and the Law, 36*, 56–58.

Kerr, A. N., Morabito, M., & Watson, A. C. (2010). Police encounters, mental illness and injury: An exploratory investigation. *Journal of Police Crisis Negotiations, 1*(10), 116–132.

Lamb, H. R., & Weinberger, L. E. (2005). The shift of psychiatric inpatient care from hospitals to jails and prisons. *Journal of the American Academy of Psychiatry and the Law, 33*, 529–534.

Lamb, H. R., Weinberger, L. E., & DeCuir, W. J. (2002). The police and mental health. *Psychiatric Services, 53*, 1266–1271.

McGriff, J. A., Broussard, B., Demir Neubert, B. N., Thompson, N. J., & Compton, M. T. (2010). Implementing a crisis intervention team (CIT) police presence in a large international airport setting. *Journal of Police Crisis Negotiations, 10*, 153–165.

Mclean, N., & Marshall, L. A. (2010). A front line police perspective of mental health issues and services. *Criminal Behavior and Mental Health, 20*, 62–71.

Morrissey, J. P., Fagan, J. A., & Cocozza, J. J. (2009). New models of collaboration between criminal justice and mental health systems. *American Journal of Psychiatry, 166*, 1211–1214.

Munetz, M. R., & Griffin, P. A. (2006). Use of the sequential intercept model as an approach to decriminalization of people with serious mental illness. *Psychiatric Services, 57*, 544–549.

Oliva, J. R., & Compton, M. T. (2008). A statewide crisis intervention team (CIT) initiative: Evolution of the Georgia CIT program. *Journal of the American Academy of Psychiatry and the Law, 36*, 38–46.

Ritter, C., Teller, J. L., Marcussen, K., Munetz, M., & Teasdale, B.

(2011). Crisis intervention team officer dispatch, assessment, and disposition: Interactions with individuals with severe mental illness. *International Journal of Law and Psychiatry 34*, 30–38.

Skubby, D., Bonfine, N., Novisky, M., Munetz, M., & Ritter, C. (2013). Crisis intervention team (CIT) programs in rural communities: a focus group study. *Community Mental Health Journal, 49*, 756–764.

Steadman, H., Deane, M., Borum, R., & Morrisey, J. (2000). Comparing outcomes of major models of police responses to mental health emergencies. *Psychiatric Services, 51*, 645–649.

Strauss, G., Glenn, M., Reddi, P., Afaq, I., Podolskaya, A., Rybakova, T.,... El-Mallakh, R. S. (2005). Psychiatric disposition of patients brought in by crisis intervention team police officers. *Community Mental Health Journal, 41*, 223–228.

Teller, J. L., Munetz, M. R., Gil, K., & Ritter, C. (2006). Crisis intervention team training for police officers responding to mental disturbance calls. *Psychiatric Services, 57*, 232–237.

Teplin, L., & Pruett, N. (1992). Police as street-corner psychiatrist: Managing the mentally ill. *International Journal of Law and Psychiatry. 15*, 139–156.

Thompson, L. E., & Borum, R. (2006). Crisis intervention teams (CIT): Considerations for knowledge transfer. *Law Enforcement Executive Forum, 6*(3), 25–36.

Tucker, A. S., Van Hesselt, V. B., & Russell, S. A. (2008). Law enforcement response to the mentally ill: An evaluative review. *Brief Treatment and Crisis Intervention, 8*, 236–250.

Watson, A. C., & Fulambarker, A. J. (2012). The crisis intervention team model of police response to mental health crises: A primer for mental health practitioners. *Best Practices in Mental Health, 8*(2), 71–81.

Watson, A. C., Morabito, M. S., Draine, J., & Ottati, V. (2008). Improving police response to persons with mental illness: A multi-level conceptualization of CIT. *International Journal of Law and Psychiatry, 31*, 359–368.

Watson, A. C., Ottati, V. C., Morabito, M., Draine, J., Kerr, A., & Angell, B. (2010). Outcomes of police contacts with persons with mental illness: The impact of CIT. *Administration and Policy in Mental Health, 37*, 302–317.

# III

CRISIS INTERVENTION WITH
CHILDREN, ADOLESCENTS, AND
YOUNG ADULTS

# 11

## Child and Adolescent Psychiatric Emergencies: Mobile Crisis Response

JONATHAN B. SINGER

This chapter describes the application of Roberts's (2005) seven-stage crisis intervention model (R-SSCIM) and Myer's (2001) triage assessment model to youth experiencing a psychiatric crisis, defined as a suicidal, homicidal, or actively psychotic episode. Although most children have their first contact with mental health services during a crisis (Burns, Hoagwood, & Mrazek, 1999), there is relatively little research on crisis intervention, and almost nothing written on mobile crisis response for children and adolescents (Singer, 2006). This chapter is an effort to bridge that gap by presenting three case studies of youth experiencing suicidal, homicidal, or psychosis-driven crises. This chapter provides a realistic description of crisis intervention over the phone, in schools, at home, in the hospital, and in a youth homeless shelter. The chapter includes a review diagnostic criteria from the *Diagnostic and Statistical Manual of Mental Disorders* (*DSM-5*; American Psychiatric Association, 2013) for three disorders that are commonly found in youth experiencing psychiatric crises: depression, bipolar, and schizophrenia spectrum disorders. Throughout the chapter, dialogue is used to illustrate crisis assessment and behavioral and solution-focused intervention techniques.

## CASE STUDIES

### Nikki: Suicidal Youth with Bipolar Disorder

On Tuesday morning, Mr. Anderson, a school counselor at a local elementary school, called the Child and Adolescent Psychiatric Emergency (CAPE) team to request a suicide assessment. Nikki, an 8-year-old female, had drawn a picture of herself with knives cutting large pieces out of her body; blood was spurting everywhere, and a man was standing to the side, laughing. The counselor reported that Nikki was well known in the principal's office because of her frequent outbursts and fights with other children. According to Mr. Anderson, there were two previous incidents that caused concern for Nikki's well-being.

The first crisis occurred 3 months earlier. Mr. Anderson reports that during recess, Nikki was screaming at her classmates and stomping on the ground and refused to comply with the teacher's requests. Nikki reportedly picked up a rock and threw it at one of her classmates, grazing the student's shoulder. The school responded as follows: Nikki was restrained by school administrators and removed from the playground. Her classmates were taken back to the classroom, and the wounded student received first aid. The parents of both Nikki and the wounded classmate were called. School administrators had separate conversations with both parents. The school counselor was brought into the classroom to debrief the students. The zero-tolerance policy at Nikki's school required her to be temporarily expelled to the alternative elementary school. Although by law the school is not allowed to recommend mental health services to the parents, the school counselor mentioned that many children with anger problems benefit from counseling and provided the phone number for some local service providers. After a disruptive first week at the alternative school, Nikki's behavior improved somewhat due to individualized attention, structured classes, a no-talking policy, and weekly visits with the on-campus psychologist. Upon Nikki's return to her home school, the counselor again visited the classroom and provided a presentation to the students on what it means to be a friend. Nikki's behavior was somewhat difficult that first day, but the remainder of the week was without incident.

The second crisis occurred 2 weeks prior to the current crisis. Nikki reportedly refused to come in after recess. Her behavior escalated rapidly, going from arguing, to yelling, to stomping her feet on the ground, to biting her arm. At the first sign of self-injurious behavior, Nikki's teacher called for backup and restrained Nikki. During the restraint, Nikki smashed the back of her head into her teacher's face, bruising the teacher's jaw and enraging Nikki even more. Nikki was in restraints for approximately 10 minutes before her mother arrived. According to Mr. Anderson, Nikki's mother was "furious" with Nikki and screamed at her to "quit actin' a fool." Nikki's behavior de-escalated rapidly. She was suspended for 2 days and taken home. The school followed a similar protocol for dealing with Nikki's classmates: The school counselor provided an in-service presentation, the teacher discussed the importance of listening to teachers, and Nikki's mother was again reminded that some children receive therapy services for this type of behavior.

Today's crisis appeared to be different from the previous two in that Nikki was not acting inappropriately. After confirming that Nikki's parent had been contacted and was on the way, a crisis worker drove out to the school to do a crisis and suicide assessment.

Later in the chapter I will describe an application of Roberts's seven-stage model of crisis intervention, including issues of building rapport, compliance with medication, relapse, and developmental issues.

---

### Rolando: Actively Psychotic and Homicidal Youth

At 8:55 p.m. the phone rang in the offices of the CAPE team. "Don't answer it," I said to my coworker, Kim. "The on-call shift starts in 5 minutes. If you pick up, we might be here for hours. Let the on-call person take it." Kim reminded me that she was the on-call worker for the night. I agreed to stick around and help out if needed. Kim had done the same for me many times; that was part of the deal when working as a team. The call was from Lupe, a mother who was well known to the CAPE team staff. Her 16-year-old son, Rolando, had been diagnosed with schizophrenia after his first hospitalization 2 years earlier. Tonight would begin the family's third involvement with mobile crisis services.

The two previous hospitalizations were very similar to each other. Prior to each hospitalization, Rolando stopped taking his medication, decompensated, threatened to kill his brother, and was brought to the hospital by the mental health deputies from the sheriff's department. Because of funding restrictions, Rolando stayed 6 days for his first hospitalization and 4 days for the second. Both times he was admitted to the adolescent unit, placed in an observation room for 24 hours, and screened for suicide every 15 minutes. After 24 hours without indicating harm to himself or others, he was placed in a private room with 15-minute checks. He participated in group therapy on the fourth, fifth, and sixth days.

According to hospital records, Rolando described an increase in auditory and tactile hallucinations starting at age 13. He reported that they started to bother him when he was 14, but he knew they were not real, and therefore he did not mention them to anyone. His tactile hallucinations were relatively infrequent, but when present, they consisted of feeling small insects trapped under his skin. The voices (outside of his head, unrecognizable, and neither male nor female) told him to kill his brother. Occasionally he would hear people laughing at him. He reported difficulty concentrating in class, getting into fights with classmates, and being easily overwhelmed. After the sixth day at the hospital, despite continued reports of hearing voices, he was discharged to the CAPE team and the care of the agency's psychiatrist.

Tonight Lupe reported that Rolando and his 13-year-old brother were arguing and pushing each other. Lupe was afraid that the violence might escalate. For the past 2 days, Rolando has been tormented by command hallucinations telling him to kill his brother. Rolando and Hector got into a fist-fight on the previous night. Today Rolando stayed home from school. Lupe threatened to call the police if Rolando did not return to school tomorrow. Rolando trashed his room and told Lupe that he hoped she died. Soon after that, Hector threw a pillow at Rolando and told him to shut up. According to the client record, two to three times a year Rolando becomes actively psychotic and attempts to kill his brother. It sounded like tonight was turning into another one of those nights, but potentially worse. According to Lupe, Rolando was accusing everyone in the house of trying to kill him. Lupe reported that she did not remember Rolando ever being convinced of his paranoia before.

---

Rolando's case provides an opportunity to illustrate Roberts's seven-stage model of crisis intervention (2006) and Myer's triage assessment model (2001). The case study will illustrate and discuss treatment in a hospital setting and in the home. The case will also address challenges and rewards of working with highly conflictual families. Solution-focused techniques will be integrated with family-centered treatment. Finally, cultural issues will be presented and integrated into the case study.

---

## Brandon: Runaway Youth With Depression

On Sunday afternoon, the 24-hour crisis hotline received a call from staff at the local youth shelter. A 15-year-old male named Brandon had checked in to the shelter that morning after a 4-day, 30-hour bus ride from California. He told the staff that if they called the police, he would run away and did not care if he lived or died. The shelter supervisor stated that homeless youth were allowed to stay 24 hours before the police were called, unless parental consent could be obtained. Based on Brandon's statements, the supervisor requested a suicide assessment.

Although this was the first time Brandon had run away from home, he and his mother were homeless until he was 11 years old. During those years, his mother would find temporary housing with men whom she would befriend. Some of these men physically and/or sexually abused Brandon. Brandon attended 40 schools before dropping out in the eighth grade. He was often popular in school but never sustained friendships as a result of frequent moves.

The CAPE team and the youth shelter had a symbiotic relationship. The CAPE team would provide crisis assessments for youth at the shelter who were suicidal or psychotic. In return, the shelter provided respite for youth who presented at the CAPE team in crisis primarily due to conflict in the home. If the child was between the ages of 14 and 17, a low risk for suicide outside of the home but high risk for suicide in the home, the shelter would agree to provide temporary respite (up to a week) with signed parental consent. The shelter accessed CAPE services approximately twice a month, and CAPE used the shelter three to four times a year. The collaboration between the two agencies created a safety net for adolescents who were not appropriate for hospitalization but whose families lacked the coping skills to prevent an escalation of violence. The respite enabled the CAPE team to provide crisis intervention to the family and adolescent in the shelter.

---

The case example of Brandon illustrates the complexity of working with a runaway adolescent. According to 1800runaway.org (National Runaway Safeline, 2014), on any given night there are 1.3 million runaway or homeless youth in the United States. Like Brandon, nearly 1 in 6 homeless youth report a history of sexual assault prior to leaving home, and 75% of homeless youth have dropped out or will drop out of school (National Runaway Safeline, 2014). The case application will highlight challenges to building rapport with youth who are in crisis in part because they have poor relationships with adults. This case study will also highlight the role of technology and social media in crisis work.

Although the details of Brandon's crisis differ from Rolando's and Nikki's, all three of these cases illustrate how R-SSCIM (Roberts & Ottens, 2005) can help the crisis worker provide effective and timely crisis intervention. For the youth in the case studies, failure to provide timely crisis intervention could result in death. Spoiler alert: Because this is a textbook, no one dies. But not all youth in crisis are fortunate enough to be case examples in a crisis intervention handbook. Before they were cases in a textbook, Nikki, Rolando, and Brandon were youth on the author's caseload. The interventions and techniques are drawn from the author's experiences. Rationales for what to do and why, as well as illustrative dialogue, are provided.

Roberts (2005) defines crisis as "a period of psychological disequilibrium, experienced as a result of a hazardous event or situation that constitutes a significant problem that cannot be remedied by using familiar coping strategies" (p. 11). The role of a *mobile crisis unit* is to provide crisis assessment and intervention to people out in the community. The goal of a *crisis assessment* is to identify the event or situation that precipitated or triggered the crisis. The goal of *crisis intervention* is to restore clients (either individual or family) to their precrisis state of functioning. Some have argued that effective crisis resolution can have as its goal to leave the client in a *better* place than prior to the onset of the crisis (see Chapter 3 in this volume). But what if precrisis functioning was barely functioning at all? What if, prior to the precipitating event, the client experienced hallucinations, delusions of grandeur, chronic low-risk suicidal ideation, or homicidal ideation? In these situations, crisis intervention needs to first resolve the immediate crisis and then plan for ongoing treatment of the underlying psychopathology (Singer, 2006). The presence of a serious mental illness can make crisis intervention more complicated. An effective crisis worker should be familiar with the symptoms and typical presentation of psychiatric disorders that can increase vulnerability to crisis, such as depressive, bipolar, and schizophrenia spectrum disorders (American Psychiatric Association, 2013). These diagnoses are briefly reviewed so that the crisis worker can have a superficial understanding of the symptoms and be aware of what factors must be considered when making referrals for postcrisis treatment.

In this chapter, I look at mobile crisis intervention with the 20% of youth who have a serious mental illness, defined as any emotional, behavioral, or mental disorder that severely disrupts the youth's daily functioning at home, at school, or in the community (Merikangas et al., 2010). The chapter moves from an overview of the structure of mobile crisis intervention and agency considerations, to a review of youth psychopathology and the state of the literature on outpatient crisis intervention services for youth. Following a brief explanation of R-SSCIM and Myer's (2001) triage assessment model, three case studies are used to illustrate the application of the models.

## AGENCY CONSIDERATIONS

Although various model programs exist (e.g., Eaton & Ertl, 2000), the organization and structure of mobile crisis services will change depending on state and local requirements. In Austin, Texas, mobile crisis services were provided through the local community mental health agency, where the author was employed between 1996 and 2002. From 1996 to 1999, the author provided mobile crisis response services to approximately 250 children and families per year and averaged five crisis assessments per week. Children were eligible for services if they were under the age of 18 and either had no insurance or received Medicaid or coverage under the Children's Health Insurance Plan (CHIP) and were in crisis. A child was said to be in crisis if he or she was suicidal, homicidal, or actively psychotic. Children covered under private insurance were triaged over the phone and then referred to their insurance provider or told to call 911 if risk was emergent.

Mobile crisis intervention is one of a number of services that make up the social service safety net. Services range in intensity from least restrictive (outpatient specialty mental health services such as those discussed in this chapter) to most restrictive (inpatient hospitals and residential treatment centers; (Schoenwald, Ward, Henggeler, & Rowland, 2000; Wilmshurst, 2002). Table 11.1 provides an example of the *continuum of care* that was available to children and families in Austin, Texas, when the youth described in this chapter were receiving services. If the purpose of crisis intervention is to restore functioning, then there must be services beyond crisis intervention to maintain that functioning. For children and families in crisis, a single session or episode of crisis intervention will not result in long-term change. Longer-term services are needed to address the dynamics that produced the crisis. Unfortunately, in 2010, fewer than half (45%) of youth who met criteria for a *DSM-IV* disorder in the past year used mental health services (Green et al., 2013), and surprisingly, youth with more severe symptoms were not more likely to use services (Merikangas et al., 2010). According to the Substance Abuse and Mental Health Services Administration (2010), in 2009, 2.9 million (12%) youth aged 12 to 17 received specialty mental health

Table 11.1  Continuum of Care at Children's Mental Health Services in Austin, Texas

| Program | Population | Services | Duration | |
|---|---|---|---|---|
| **CAPE Team** (Child and Adolescent Psychiatric Emergency) | Children who were suicidal, homicidal, or actively psychotic | Crisis intervention, IT*, FT**, service coordination; office- and community-based | As many hours per day as needed, up to 30 days | Most Intensive |
| **FPP** (Family Preservation Program) | Children who were engaged in activities that put them at risk for removal from their home or school | Crisis intervention, IT, FT, service coordination; community-based | 6–8 hours per week, up to 120 days | |
| **DPRS Program** (Department of Protective and Regulatory Services) | Children with open cases with the DPRS due to confirmed cases of parental neglect or abuse | Provided traditional office-based therapy and skills training to children; protective parenting classes to parents; made recommendations for or against reunification | 1–2 two hours per week, up to 2 years | |
| **DayGlo** | Children with *DSM-IV* diagnoses | IT, FT, GT***. Office-based | 1 hour per week, up to 3 years | |
| **Zilker Park Program** | Children with *DSM-IV* diagnoses | Outdoor, experiential therapy program for children aged 7–11 | 4 hours per week, 6 months to 3 years | Least Intensive |
| **Intake** | Children under 18, except for those presenting in crisis | Intake assessment, diagnosis, referral to appropriate program | Up to 2 hours | |
| **Service Coordination** | Children and families participating in the DPRS, DayGlo, or Zilker Park program. CAPE and FPP provide service coordination | Coordinate medication checks, psychiatric evaluations, connect with community resources, including rent assistance, utilities, food | 1–2 hours per month for the duration of services | |
| **Medication Services** | All children with biologically based diagnoses | Medication checks, psychiatric evaluations | As long as needed | |

*IT: Individual treatment.
**FT: Family treatment.
***GT: Group treatment.

treatment or counseling for emotional or behavioral problems. The most likely reason for receiving services in the past year was feeling depressed (46.0%), followed by having problems with home or family (27.8%), breaking rules and "acting out" (26.1%), and thinking about or attempting suicide (20.7%). Additionally, 2.9 million (12%) youth received mental health services in an education setting, as did 603,000 youth (2.5%) in a general medical setting and 109,000 youth (0.4%) in a juvenile justice setting.

Within the author's agency, the two programs that worked most closely together were the CAPE team and the Family Preservation Program (FPP). After the CAPE team provided intensive crisis stabilization services, FPP would provide slightly less intensive community-based family-centered services. FPP workers would provide services wherever the client and family would most benefit: homes, schools, juvenile detention facilities, or hospitals. Evans et al. (2003) report success using an intensive in-home crisis service similar to the FPP. They report that more than 75% of children enrolled in their programs were maintained in the community. This is significant because, by definition, children entering FPP programs are at risk for removal from the home. Because the purpose of the mobile crisis unit was to provide crisis intervention with the intention of keeping children out of the hospital and in their homes, the availability of a local FPP provided a logical referral along the continuum of care.

The continuum of care extended to programs outside of the agency. Mobile crisis workers for children and adolescents had regular contact with a number of agencies. Some agencies were service recipients, others were services providers, and some were both recipients and providers. Recipient agencies included the local homeless shelter for youth, the school system, and the juvenile detention facility. Provider agencies were law enforcement and emergency medical assistance. Developing a working relationship with law enforcement is mandatory whenever involuntary hospitalizations are part of the job. Both the Austin Police Department and the Travis County Sheriff's Department had mental health units staffed by officers who were specifically trained in mental health issues. Hospitals both received and provided services: They provided most-restrictive environments for clients who were unable to be safe in the community, and they received services through a special agreement. In the latter, agency workers would provide co-therapy with the hospital staff, attend discharge staffings, and coordinate services between the hospital and the client's family.

## PSYCHIATRIC DISORDERS

One of the cornerstones of crisis theory is that crisis is universal; anyone can be in a situation that overwhelms his or her usual coping strategy (Lindemann, 1944). Although the experience of crisis might be universal, the diathesis-stress model suggests that people who start out with fewer coping strategies (because of emotional or behavioral problems, for example) are more likely to have a poorer response to stressful situations and are therefore more vulnerable to going into crisis (Coyne & Downey, 1991). Crisis workers need to evaluate the precrisis mental health of the youth so that appropriate modifications to the crisis intervention can be made. Familiarity with the most common psychiatric disorders will better prepare crisis workers to meet the needs of children and adolescents with a preexisting psychiatric disorder. We briefly review depressive, bipolar, and schizophrenia spectrum disorders, three disorders that play a part in the lives of the children in the case studies. The reader should note that although our review is based on *DSM-5* criteria, the youth in this chapter were diagnosed under the previous edition of the *DSM* (APA, 2000). For a more thorough discussion of these disorders, the reader is encouraged to consult the current version of the *Diagnostic and Statistical Manual of Mental Disorders* (American Psychiatric Association, 2013) or a current abnormal psychology textbook (e.g. Barlow & Durand, 2014).

## Depressive Disorders

Mood disorders are present in 80% of adolescents who attempt suicide and in 60% of adolescents who die by suicide (Brent, Poling, & Goldstein, 2011). Approximately 11% of adolescents will experience persistent depressive disorder (dysthymia; [*DSM-5* code: 300.4]) or a major depressive episode before adulthood, with girls reporting depressive symptoms nearly three times as often as boys (12.4% vs. 4.3%; Merikangas et al., 2010). Rates of major depressive disorder [*DSM-5* code: 296.xx] increase significantly between the ages of 13 and 16, from 4% to 11.6%, respectively (Substance Abuse and Mental Health Services Administration, 2010). Youth with significant depressive symptomology are more likely to engage in self-harming behaviors such as cutting and burning (also called nonsuicidal self-injury), have difficulty developing and maintaining prosocial interpersonal relationships, are more likely to perform poorly in academic and work settings, and are more likely to abuse illicit substances. Approximately 40% of youth meet criteria for more than one class of disorder (i.e., anxiety, behavior, mood, or substance use disorder; Merikangas et al., 2010). Comorbid depression and substance use increase risk for high-lethality suicide attempts among youth both with (Jenkins, Singer, Conner, Calhoun, & Diamond, 2014) and without (O'Brien & Berzin, 2012) a history of nonsuicidal self-injury.

### Bipolar Disorder

Prior to *DSM-5*, bipolar disorder was considered a type of depressive disorder. However, bipolar disorder is a stand-alone category in *DSM-5*

(American Psychiatric Association, 2013), in part due to research that found that the presence of manic symptoms among people with depression is not always synonymous with bipolar disorder. This is particularly true among children, for whom rapid mood swings and extremely high levels of energy can be attributed to causes other than mania. Bipolar disorder is characterized by episodes of both mania and depression. Bipolar I disorder [(*DSM-5* code: 296.xx) requires a major depressive episode and a manic episode with elation/euphoric or irritable mood and persistently increased activity or energy levels. Bipolar II disorder (*DSM-5* code: 296.89) requires a major depressive episode and a less severe form of mania called *hypomania*. Although bipolar II was originally thought of as a less severe form of bipolar disorder, people now recognize that the presence of longer-term mild mania with depression causes a similar degree of functional impairment as bipolar I. Furthermore, a recent study suggested that the new *DSM-5* criteria will result in rates of diagnosis for bipolar II that are similar to those for bipolar I (Phillips & Kupfer, 2013).

Approximately 3% of youth meet criteria for lifetime prevalence of bipolar I or II disorder (Merikangas et al., 2010). Rates more than double between age 13 (1.9%) and 17 (4.3%). Females are slightly more likely to meet criteria (3.3%) than males (2.6%). Risk for developing bipolar disorder is primarily genetic. Youth with a parent or sibling who has bipolar disorder are up to six times as likely to develop the disorder as are youth with no family history of bipolar disorder (Nurnberger & Foroud, 2000). Half of all cases of bipolar disorder start before age 25 (Kessler et al., 2005).

## Schizophrenia Spectrum Disorder

Approximately 1% of people worldwide meet criteria for schizophrenia (*DSM-5* code: 295.90), but rates for schizophrenia in youth have not been established (McClellan, Stock, & American Academy of Child and Adolescent Psychiatry [AACAP] Committee on Quality Issues [CQI]), 2013). The first psychotic episode for most males is in their early- to mid-20s, and for females in their late 20s (APA, 2013). According to the American Academy of Child and Adolescent Psychiatry (McClellan et al., 2013) practice parameters, providers should use *DSM-5* adult criteria to diagnose and guide treatment for youth who meet criteria for schizophrenia. Structured diagnostic interviews are recommended. When interviewing children younger than 12, providers should assess for psychotic symptoms within a developmental context. Specifically, providers should clarify that "bizarre thinking" or accounts of seeing or hearing things that others do not see or hear are different from developmentally appropriate fantasy or difficulty distinguishing inner voices from distressing hallucinations. Individuals experiencing true psychosis typically report symptoms as confusing, distressing, and beyond their control. Criterion A symptoms are the same in *DSM-IV-TR* as in *DSM-IV* (delusions, hallucinations, disorganized speech, grossly disorganized or catatonic behavior, and negative symptoms). In *DSM-5*, however, at least two of the five symptoms must be present for at least 1 month (rather than just one in *DSM-IV-TR*), and one of the two must be delusions, hallucinations, or disorganized speech (APA, 2013). Youth-specific criteria include a rule out of autism spectrum disorder and the acknowledgment that youth might never have achieved an age-appropriate level of functioning prior to onset of symptoms. Treatment of schizophrenia requires a multimodal approach, including case management, crisis intervention, skills training, antipsychotic medication, educational support, social support, and family therapy (McClellan, Stock, & American Academy of Child and Adolescent Psychiatry Committee on Quality Issues, 2013; Roth & Fonagy, 2005; Schimmelmann, Schmidt, Carbon, & Correll, 2013). In this chapter, the acute psychotic episode is synonymous with a crisis state (although the reverse is not true). The necessity for medication as a primary means of crisis stabilization differentiates an acute psychotic episode from the traditional definition of a crisis state.

The authors of *DSM-5* rightly point out that people with schizophrenia are more frequently victimized than individuals in the general population. That said, crisis workers often come into contact with people with schizophrenia when there is risk of violence (toward self or others). The case study of Rolando presented in this chapter is an example of risk for violence. People with schizophrenia disorders are at high risk for suicide, with the suicide rate among people with schizophrenia being approximately 44.5 times the national suicide rate (579 vs. 13 per 100,000; Hor & Taylor, 2010; Drapeau & McIntosh, 2014). To place this number in context, the leading cause of death in the United States is heart disease, with a rate of 191 per 100,000 (Drapeau & McIntosh, 2014). Bennett and colleagues (2011) found that people with schizophrenia "are significantly more likely than those in the general community to commit homicide offences" (p. 226). A recent meta-analysis found that 38.5% of all homicides committed by people with psychosis were committed by people in their first episode, prior to treatment (Nielssen & Large, 2010). Researchers have consistently found that when people with schizophrenia disorders commit homicide offenses, the most likely victim is a family member, specifically a family member who lives in the home (Estroff, Swanson, Lachicotte, Swartz, & Bolduc, 1998; Joyal, Putkonen, Paavola, & Tiihonen, 2004; Nordström & Kullgren, 2003). Family members are at particular risk of violence because they are the primary caregivers of people with serious mental illness, including schizophrenia disorders (Solomon, Cavanaugh, & Gelles, 2005). Furthermore, "A [family's] lack of knowledge and ability to manage violent behaviors may exacerbate aggressive incidents, putting the safety of the entire family unit at risk" (Solomon et al., 2005, p. 41). In sum, people with schizophrenia spectrum disorders are more likely to be violent during a first episode of psychosis and are more likely to kill a family member than anyone else. Consequently, mobile crisis workers have an ethical and professional obligation to assess for both suicide and homicide risk and to provide family members with safety plans and referrals whenever symptoms of schizophrenia are present, even when there person in crisis does not display enough symptoms to meet criteria for diagnosis.

## RESILIENCE AND PROTECTIVE FACTORS

Although it is necessary for crisis workers to be aware of the symptoms and presentation of psychopathology, any successful psychosocial intervention identifies and builds on client strengths and resources. This is particularly true of crisis intervention. Crisis episodes are by definition time limited. The support that a crisis worker provides is temporary, but the strengths and resources that clients bring to the table become the building blocks for regaining precrisis functioning. Although anyone can experience a crisis, people who move out of crisis states quickly can be thought of as resilient. *Resilience* was originally conceptualized as something internal to the individual. Masten, Best, and Garmezy (1990) give an "individual" definition of resilience as "the process of, capacity for, or outcome of successful adaptation despite challenging or threatening circumstances" (p. 425). They identify three circumstances that can demonstrate resilience: (a) overcoming the odds, (b) sustained competence under adversity, and (c) recovery from trauma. More recently, resilience has been understood as resulting from both internal/individual and environmental factors. Michael Ungar (2012) defines resilience as "a set of behaviors over time that reflect the interactions between individuals and their environments, in particular the opportunities for personal growth that are available and accessible" (p. 14). Behaviors that reduce risk for harm are considered *protective factors* (King, Foster, & Rogalski, 2013).

### Technology, Psychiatric Assessment, and Crisis Intervention

Accurate identification of psychiatric disorders in youth typically requires a clinical interview, observation, and information from family members and collateral contacts such as teachers and probation officers to provide data on symptoms and functional impairment. Self-report measures, and screening and diagnostic tools are helpful but not sufficient to accurately identify psychiatric disorders (Eack, Singer, & Greeno, 2008). Given that noncrisis outpatient mental health providers rarely have the time or training to assess for and identify the variety of psychiatric disorders that are present in people who access community mental health, it is unreasonable to expect mobile crisis workers to conduct a thorough diagnostic assessment while simultaneously providing crisis response. And yet, knowing if a person has a history of emotional or behavioral disorders can help a crisis worker figure out if temporary deficits in coping skills are due to the current crisis or are a function of prior long-term deficits. There are several technology solutions that can improve data collection for mobile crisis workers.

Web-based applications and mobile devices such as smartphones, tablets, and laptops make it possible for mobile crisis workers to travel with advanced diagnostic tools in a way that was impossible only a few years ago. One example of a web-based self-report screening tool for youth that holds promise for mobile crisis response is the Behavioral Health Screen (BHS; G. Diamond et al., 2010). The BHS identifies current and past-year symptoms of several disorders, including trauma, anxiety, depression, and substance use, as well as behaviors such as suicidal ideation and attempt and nonsuicidal self-injury. The database automatically generates a report for the provider of significant symptoms and areas of concern. There are several versions of the tool, but the one that is most relevant for crisis workers was developed for emergency departments (BHS-ED; Fein et al., 2010). When the feasibility and effects of the BHS-ED were evaluated in a busy urban emergency department, researchers found that youth completed the BHS-ED in approximately 10 minutes and that identification of psychiatric problems increased significantly (Fein et al., 2010).

Technologies such as computerized assessments and mobile applications (apps), widely available secure high-speed Internet connections, and affordable hardware have started to change the delivery and use of healthcare services (Barak & Grohol, 2011; Singer & Sage, 2015). The use of technology can be unintentional, such as texting clients or using online maps to identify local resources (Mishna, Bogo, Root, Sawyer, & Khoury-Kassabri, 2012). There are also intentional telehealth and mHealth initiatives, such as remote supervision and consultation and use of mobile apps to track psychiatric symptoms, and self-guided computerized therapy to reduce depressive and anxiety symptoms and improve mental health at a population level (Elias, Fogger, McGuinness, & D'Alessandro, 2014; Okuboyejo & Eyesan, 2014; Powell et al., 2013).

As the availability and use of mobile technology increase, so will the possibilities for more comprehensive crisis assessment and intervention. For example, although not designed for mobile crisis workers, the BHS, described earlier, could be used in the following way: A crisis worker could travel with a tablet, connect to the BHS online through a secure data connection, have the youth fill out the BHS online, and then read the report. The data could then be used as part of the crisis assessment and intervention, or as part of the planning process for postcrisis discharge and referrals. In addition to standardized assessments, the crisis worker could use a suicide prevention app like MY3 (my3app.org) to identify and mobilize a suicidal youth's support network or could help clients address trauma symptoms using the US government's prolonged exposure therapy app (PE-Coach; www.t2.health.mil/apps/pe-coach; Aguirre, McCoy, & Roan, 2013; Elias et al., 2014). As discussed later in the chapter, technology use is widespread even among runaway and homeless youth (Rice, Kurzban, & Ray, 2012; Wenzel et al., 2012). A study conducted in 2010 found that 62% of homeless youth owned a cell phone, and 41% used their phones to communicate with friends and family weekly (Rice et al., 2012). Mobile crisis workers can use the technology that most youth have in their pockets—the mobile phone—to encourage texting, accessing healthy social networks, and connection with others. Youth who use online social networks to connect with friends and family at home are significantly less depressed and anxious than youth whose primary social connections are with other homeless and runaway youth (Rice et al., 2012). For a more detailed review of technology and social services, see Singer and Sage (2015) and Barak and Grohol (2011).

## CLINICAL PRESENTATION: ISSUES, CONTROVERSIES, ROLES, AND SKILLS

Although mobile crisis intervention provides essential therapeutic services to suicidal, homicidal, or psychotic youth (Evans, Boothroyd, & Armstrong, 1997; Greenfield, Hechtman, & Tremblay, 1995; Gutstein, Rudd, Graham, & Rayha, 1988; Henggeler et al., 1999) and has demonstrated significant financial savings by diverting youth from in-patient settings (Evans et al., 2001; Evans et al., 2003; Schoenwald et al., 2000), there is surprisingly little research on what works and what does not work in youth psychiatric emergency services. Research on pediatric mental health has increasingly focused on the integration of mental and physical healthcare services and on the influence of parental psychopathology on youth mental health (Hoagwood et al., 2012). Research on how to best work with youth in a suicidal crisis has focused primarily on interventions in an emergency department (Ginnis, White, Ross, & Wharff, 2013; Sobolewski, Richey, Kowatch, & Grupp-Phelan, 2013) or a clinical lab setting (G. S. Diamond et al., 2010; Esposito-Smythers, Spirito, Kahler, Hunt, & Monti, 2011). Outpatient research has focused almost entirely on adults (Salkever, Gibbons, & Ran, 2014) or on youth with substance use problems (Dembo, Gulledge, Robinson, & Winters, 2011). As a result, the recommendations in this chapter derive from the author's experience, unless otherwise cited.

## Roberts's Seven-Stage Model

R-SSCIM provides an excellent framework for organizing information gathered during a crisis assessment. Four benefits to using Roberts's model are (a) it provides a structure within which to organize data; (b) it reminds the practitioner which important areas to cover; (c) it allows practitioners to spend their time and energy making decisions about techniques, strategies, and skills they will use; and (4) it can be validated and critiqued for efficacy. When crisis workers follow clear, defined protocols, there is less room for individual error and greater continuity of services over time (e.g., during a shift change or with the use of relief workers).

## Myer's Triage Assessment Model

Myer's (2001; Myer, Williams, Ottens, & Schmidt, 1992) triage assessment model is a useful framework for rapid assessment of three domains of functioning: affective (emotional), cognitive (thinking), and behavioral (actions). Each domain is assessed and rated on a 10-point scale, where 1 = no impairment and 10 = severe impairment. The three scores are added together to provide an overall severity rating. The higher the rating, the more impaired the client. In the affective domain, the crisis worker assesses the client's emotional reaction to the crisis based on three pairs of emotions: anger/hostility, anxiety/fear, and sadness/melancholy. If more than one pair of emotions is present, the crisis worker rates the emotions as primary, secondary, or tertiary. Accurate assessment of the primary emotion and the severity of impairment is invaluable in successful application of Roberts's fourth stage: dealing with feelings and providing support. For the cognitive domain, the crisis worker assesses the client's perception of how the crisis has affected, is affecting, or will affect his or her physical, psychological, social, and moral/spiritual life. For the behavioral domain, the crisis worker assesses the client's behavioral reaction to the crisis. Myer (2001) asserts that clients will use one of three behaviors: approach, avoidance, or immobility. Each can move the client toward or away from successful crisis resolution. According to Meyer (2001), "Approach behaviors are either overt or covert attempts to resolve the crisis. Avoidance behaviors ignore, evade, or escape the crisis event. Immobility refers to behaviors that are nonproductive, disorganized, or self-defeating attempts to cope with the crisis" (p. 30).

## CASE STUDY 1: NIKKI

### Stage 1: Assessing Lethality

When assessing for lethality, a crisis worker gathers data to determine whether the person in crisis is at risk for harm. Failure to assess for lethality is both a legal liability and a failure to provide a professional service (Bongar & Sullivan, 2013). Accurate assessment of lethality provides the crisis worker with a solid base from which to move forward with the crisis intervention. A professional assessment instills a sense of confidence in the client. There are three parts of the lethality assessment, although they are not sequential and, depending on the situation, are not equally weighted. The assessment of self-harm is also known as a suicide assessment. The crisis worker must determine if there is *ideation* (thoughts about killing oneself), *intent* (desire to kill oneself), and *plan* (when and how to kill oneself, including access to the means). During the assessment of self-harm, the crisis worker must be careful to avoid mentioning "harm" and "hurt" when assessing for suicide. The difference between "I want to hurt myself" and "I want to kill myself" is important. One suggests the infliction of pain to a sustained life; the other suggests the infliction of pain to end a life. The crisis worker who asks, "Have you had thoughts of hurting yourself?" might elicit the verbalized "no" and the nonverbalized "I have no intention of hurting any more than I already do. I want to end my pain and I plan on ending it by killing myself." The crisis worker could instead ask, "During all that has happened in the past 24 hours, have you found yourself thinking that you would be better off dead?" In situations where rapport would be lost with the immediate questioning of suicide (e.g., assessment of grief), it is appropriate to ease into the suicide assessment. The following brief example demonstrates one way of moving from "harm" to "kill":

Crisis Worker:   Have you had thoughts of hurting yourself?
Client:   No.
Crisis Worker:   Have you thought of dying?
Client:   Yes.
Crisis Worker:   Have you thought of killing yourself?
Client:   Yes.
Crisis Worker:   When?
Client:   This morning.

Precise questions result in accurate data. Determining suicide risk is possible only with accurate data (Shea, 2002).

In many parts of the United States, mobile crisis units provide assessment and intervention services to youth in schools, but most school mental health professionals report feeling ill-equipped to handle youth experiencing psychiatric crises (Allen et al., 2002; Erbacher, Singer, & Poland, 2015; Slovak & Singer, 2011). Because schools are the most important service site for the identification, referral, and provision of mental health services to school-age youth in the United States (Green et al., 2013), mobile crisis units can ensure that youth get the clinical attention they need, regardless of school personnel training or resources.

Working with children requires the crisis worker to use simple language and concepts, as in this example:

| | |
|---|---|
| Crisis Worker: | Hi, Nikki, my name is Jonathan. You know what I do all day? I talk with kids who say they are thinking of killing themselves. Some kids want to hurt or kill someone else. Others kids hear or see things that nobody else can hear or see. |
| Nikki: | I ain't crazy like that. |
| Crisis Worker: | Oh. So maybe I'm in the wrong place. How embarrassing (smile). Why do you think I'm here, then? |
| Nikki: | (smiles) Because I drew that picture. |
| Crisis Worker: | You know, Nikki, I think you're absolutely right about that. Before you tell me about the picture, I want to let you know that you can tell me almost anything and I won't tell anyone else. They will be just between you and me. There are some things I have to tell your mom, or Mr. Anderson. Can you guess what they are? |

The caseworker's tone is playful, but the content is serious. By turning the review of confidentiality ("There are some things I have to tell your mom") into a game, the caseworker demonstrates to Nikki that he is speaking her language, the language of play (Gil, 1991). Because play is the main form of treatment for children under the age of 12, a bag of art supplies (large sheets of paper, markers, crayons, colored pencils) is an invaluable tool for the mobile crisis worker. The caseworker takes out some sheets of construction paper and markers. Nikki and the caseworker draw pictures as they talk.

Nikki reported that she had thoughts of killing herself while drawing the picture in the classroom but did not have them at that moment. Her plan was to stab herself to death with a knife from her kitchen, as she had depicted in the drawing. She was unclear when she might kill herself: "Maybe I'll do it after Shante's birthday party [next month]." Although suicidal ideation must be taken seriously, Nikki's time frame (next month) provided an important window of opportunity for intervention. She denied homicidal ideation and stated that she did not hear voices or see things that were not there.

The assessment of lethality in a family requires the assessment of both the parent and the child. Rudd, Joiner, and Rajab (2001) recommend evaluating the parent's ability to fulfill essential functions (e.g., provision of resources, maintenance of a safe and nonabusive home) and parenting functions (e.g., limit setting, healthy communication, and positive role modeling). The overall suicide risk will go up or down depending on how well the parent can fulfill essential and parenting functions. Based on Nikki's reports of ideation without plan or intent, she was at low risk for suicide. Interviewing Nikki's mom, Mrs. D, would provide important information about her ability to fulfill her essential and parenting functions. The lethality assessment with Mrs. D. is described in Stage 2 in order to reinforce the idea that "it is critically important to establish rapport while assessing lethality and determining the precipitating events/situations" (Roberts & Ottens, 2005, p. 331).

## Stage 2: Establishing Rapport and Communication

Rapport is a short way of saying that the practitioner and the client are comfortable with each other (Kanel, 2013). Developing rapport might have started during Stage 1, as the client began to feel safer in his or her external environment. Rapport building continues throughout the intervention process as the worker develops a deeper understanding of what will best help the client to resolve the crisis. During the initial rapport-building stage, the crisis worker assures the client that he or she made the right decision by seeking help and that the crisis worker will provide some assistance to the problem. Kanel (2013, p. 60) identifies five basic attending skills that are used in developing rapport in crisis situations: attending behavior (eye contact, warmth, body posture, vocal style, verbal following, and overall empathy); questioning (open- and closed-ended); paraphrasing (restatement, clarifying); reflection of feelings (painful, positive, ambivalent, nonverbal); and summarization (tying together the precipitating event, the subjective distress, and other cognitive elements). These attending skills can be used throughout the crisis intervention process. The following is the beginning of a 30-minute interview:

Crisis Worker: Mrs. D., I'm glad you could come to the school so quickly.

Mrs. D: (frowning) Uh, yeah. That's all right.

Crisis Worker: It sounds like you are not surprised that you were called to the school.

Mrs. D: (angry) Do I look surprised? The office people don't even have to look up my phone number. It is like I'm on speed dial with a prerecorded message that says, "We're afraid Nikki might hurt herself."

Crisis Worker: What usually happens once you get up here?

Mrs. D: Do you have kids?

Crisis Worker: No, I don't.

Mrs. D: Well, if you did, you wouldn't be asking foolish questions.

Crisis Worker: Sometimes we have to ask questions that seem foolish, Mrs. D. What usually happens when you get here?

Mrs. D:      The principal gets all up in my face about teaching her
             manners.
Crisis Worker:  And when you get home?
Mrs. D:      (smiling) Nothing. It is all over by then. I'm not going
             to let her behavior ruin my day.

This brief interaction suggested that Mrs. D. did not believe that Nikki's suicidal statements were legitimate. This reaction is common among parents whose children have repeated or chronic suicidal ideation (Slovak & Singer, 2012). The interview with Mrs. D. suggested a number of things. First, rapport building will be crucial in engaging her in treatment. Second, as per Rudd, Joiner, and Rajab (2001), she was partially fulfilling essential functions of providing basic needs such as shelter and transportation but not parenting functions such as nurturing and emotional validation; specifically, she had been aware of Nikki's suicidal ideation for a couple of years but had never pursued treatment. She reported that "limit setting doesn't work." At the end of the interview, the caseworker had doubts about Mrs. D's ability to keep Nikki safe or to provide an environment that was relatively free of emotional triggers. In any situation where lethality is an issue, consultation with a supervisor is advised. Because the mother's evaluation raised the risk of lethality, the caseworker contacted his supervisor, who recommended that the family come in for an emergency evaluation with the psychiatrist. Mrs. D reluctantly agreed to travel with the caseworker back to the offices.

## Stage 3: Identifying Major Problems

Nikki and her mother met the caseworker in the CAPE team office to complete a more thorough psychosocial assessment in preparation for the appointment with the psychiatrist. A useful technique in family assessment is to speak with each member separately and then together as a family (G. S. Diamond, Diamond, & Levy, 2013). This can be challenging for office-based providers whose agency policies prohibit at-risk youth from being alone in the waiting room (Singer & Greeno, 2013), and in this situation another CAPE team worker stayed with Nikki while the caseworker and Mrs. D identified the major problems in their family. Mrs. D reported that she receives psychotherapy and medication for bipolar disorder. According to her, Nikki's rage and anger were the biggest problem. As a result of her ongoing tantrums, their landlord had served them an eviction notice before they left for school today.

Mrs. D:      Right in front of Nikki he says that *she* has 30 days
             to stop breaking things and disturbing the neighbors
             or else she's going to have to find a new place to sleep.

I was *so* angry with her. I told her she'd better get her act together and not get us kicked out.

Crisis Worker: It sounds like both you and the landlord were angry with Nikki. When you said that she'd better get her act together, did you let her know what exactly you meant by that and what her consequences would be if she didn't?

Mrs. D: (suspiciously) Well, you know, she knows that I just mean not to be so loud and bothering the neighbors. I don't really give consequences.

Thirty minutes into the interview, it was clear that Mrs. D. was angry at Nikki and felt that her daughter's behavior put an undue burden on her. Nikki, for her part, internalized her mother's harsh and critical response. Youth suicidal behavior can serve a variety of functions within a family. One function is to express behaviorally what cannot be communicated verbally. When Nikki was overwhelmed by her mother's anger, she acted out because it was unsafe to tell her mother how she felt. Another function of a suicidal crisis is to force a parent who is emotionally unstable to "get her act together" and care for the child. More assessment and contact with the family was needed to determine if either dynamic was at play. These dynamics are examples of bidirectional family influence.

Mrs. D also shared information about Nikki's behavior at home, indicating that Nikki would go through rapid cycles of feeling happy and being violent and rageful (like this morning). Mrs. D stated that she did not think Nikki was bipolar because Nikki's behavior was very different from her own experience of bipolar disorder.

The caseworker met with Nikki and determined that the precipitating event was the landlord's signing the eviction notice. When a precipitating event is so specific, it is valuable to spend time in Stage 4: dealing with feelings and processing the thoughts and feelings that were triggered by the event. To continue identifying problems, the family agreed to speak with the psychiatrist about Nikki's anger and her suicidal ideation. The psychiatrist reviewed the intake assessment and determined that Nikki met criteria for bipolar disorder. She did not believe that Nikki posed a threat to herself at that time and therefore did not meet criteria for hospitalization. A safety plan was written down, and a copy was given to Mrs. D. The family was instructed to contact 911 in case of an imminent threat to safety, or the 24-hour hotline if Nikki felt suicidal. The caseworker agreed to call the family that night to check in. The psychiatrist prescribed a mood stabilizer and twice-weekly therapy with a CAPE team caseworker. Because Mrs. D takes the bus to work, the caseworker agreed to meet after school at their house.

## Stage 4: Dealing With Feelings and Providing Support

The plan was to discuss Nikki's suicidal ideation, explore feelings, and provide psychoeducation about bipolar disorder. Regular assessment of suicidal ideation is vital during a suicidal crisis. The caseworker is advised to ask the basic questions at every session, such as: "Have you had thoughts of killing yourself today? If so, how and when? How important is it that you succeed?" Proper documentation of this routine assessment will provide excellent continuity of care when the case is transferred, and it will reduce the risk of a lawsuit in the event of a completed suicide (see Bongar & Sullivan, 2013).

There is a simple yet elegant tool for helping individuals and families better identify emotions. The "How Are You Feeling Today?" chart illustrates dozens of common emotions. A laminated version can be used for circling emotions with a dry-erase marker and for playing checkers. In a game of "Feelings" checkers, checkers are placed on images of faces that represent specific feelings. As players move their checkers to a new feeling, they (a) identify the emotion, (b) talk about a time when they had that emotion, or (c) discuss a situation in which they think they might have that emotion. With children of Nikki's age, a popular variation of the game requires players to imitate the feeling face they land on.

During school visits, Nikki and the caseworker discussed bipolar disorder and explored emotions. For the first 2 weeks of services, however, Mrs. D refused to allow the caseworker to come into the house for the prearranged appointments. She also declined the caseworker's offer to meet at the school.

By the end of the 2nd week, there was no indication that either Mrs. D or Nikki was taking her medication. Mrs. D refused to sign a release of information so that Nikki's caseworker could coordinate services with Mrs. D's caseworker. In a more traditional therapy model, it is standard practice to ultimately refuse to provide services if the client is legally preventing the therapist from adequately doing his or her job. Services to crisis clients preclude the option of refusing services.

## Stage 5: Exploring Possible Alternatives

During a typical Stage 5, clients explore alternative solutions to the problem. Because Mrs. D was refusing to participate in services, the caseworker decided to explore possible solutions for engaging the family. There is one reframe that, on occasion, has been successful in developing a therapeutic alliance with nonparticipating parents. The following dialogue illustrates the concept of "It's not you, it's them":

Crisis Worker:   I'm wondering if you've noticed a change in Nikki's behavior.

| | |
|---|---|
| Mrs. D: | I wish, but no. |
| Crisis Worker: | I've been thinking about this a lot. My job is to help you two develop some new coping skills, and I'm failing you. As far as I can tell, things are as bad now as they were when I first met you. |
| Mrs. D: | (skeptical) Mmm hmm. |
| Crisis Worker: | Tell me if this is true: Your parenting style would work really well with a different kid. |
| Mrs. D: | My 10-year-old nephew listens to me; I don't see why she don't. |
| Crisis Worker: | Exactly. So here's my thought. Your parenting is not the problem. The problem is that Nikki's behavior requires a different approach to parenting. |
| Mrs. D: | Well, ain't that the truth. |
| Crisis Worker: | I'm wondering if you can remember a time when you did something different that made a difference in the way you got along? |
| Mrs. D: | One night I was so tired, instead of yellin' at her to sit down, I just let her run around the apartment. We didn't fight once that night. |

There are a number of components that make this a successful intervention. The first is the caseworker's taking responsibility for the family's problems. It is as if he is temporarily holding a heavy bag that the family has lugged around for years. The second component is externalizing the problem: "It's not you, it's them." The third component is the use of the exception question. This helped Mrs. D to step back into the role of successful mother, even if for but a minute.

After this dialogue, Mrs. D opened her door to treatment again. Nikki started taking her meds regularly, and the caseworker brought over the "Feelings" checkerboard. The school reported that Nikki's behavior became more stable in the classroom. Due to the family's progress, the caseworker discussed transferring them to FPP for home-based services.

Four weeks after the initial call, the weekend on-call worker was paged to Mrs. D's house. Nikki had cut herself with a dull knife. She was transported to the emergency room and later was released with the recommendation that she "get some sleep." After consulting with the agency's on-call psychiatrist, the recommendation was made that she remain in the city, but that she live temporarily with her grandmother, with whom she has a close and loving relationship.

The caseworker implemented Stages 1 and 2 again. In Stage 3, he and Nikki explored the precipitating event for the recent suicide attempt. According to Nikki, on the day she tried to kill herself, she had seen the landlord put a piece of paper under her mother's door. She assumed it was the eviction notice they had been threatened with 4 weeks earlier. It is very important to be aware of anniversary or trigger dates. The caseworker missed it, but Nikki remembered.

Because Nikki was temporarily living with her grandmother, the caseworker had an opportunity to gather new information about the family, including confirmation of Mrs. D's drug addiction and history of prostitution. With the new information, the caseworker invited Mrs. D to join the discussion about family problems, possible solutions, and the formulation of a new action plan.

## Stage 6: Formulating an Action Plan

The action plan for the family after the second round of the seven-stage model included the following:

1. Weekly house meetings to discuss family issues and watch a movie together
2. Taking medication regularly as directed
3. Regular appointments for Mrs. D with her psychiatrist
4. Regular attendance at Narcotics Anonymous meetings
5. Transition to the Family Preservation Program

## Stage 7: Follow-Up

The traditional term for the end of services with a client is *termination* (Hepworth, Rooney, Rooney, & Strom-Gottfried, 2013). Because of the brief but intense nature of crisis intervention, which almost always results in the client's moving on to another service, the term *transition* is a better fit (Singer, 2005). At the end of the 2nd month, the caseworker met the family and their new FPP therapist for a transition session. The family discussed what they had learned during the course of the services. The caseworker shared his impressions of the family's strengths. Nikki had made no suicidal statements since the second crisis, and she was no longer considered a risk to herself or others. The family was told that they could always contact crisis services in the future if they needed to. The complexities of this case were easier to navigate through the application of Roberts's framework.

## CASE STUDY 2: ROLANDO

Another type of crisis encountered by mobile crisis responders is the psychotic or homicidal client. The following case study presents the use of R-SSCIM with a 16-year-old Latino male, diagnosed with schizophrenia, who is in a homicidal crisis. This case study illustrates phone-based triage, services in the home and hospital, and the use of pharmacotherapy and family therapy in the resolution of the crisis. The use of Spanish words throughout the case study emphasizes the importance of linguistic competency and culturally relevant services.

## Stage 1: Assessing Lethality

Assessment of harm to self was illustrated in the first case example. The second area of lethality, addressed in this case example, is the assessment of harm to others: What is the likelihood that the client will hurt someone (including the crisis worker)? Whereas the suicidal client might turn on him- or herself to deal with overwhelming hurt, anger, fear, and frustration, the homicidal client turns on others. As with the suicide assessment, the crisis worker should assess for ideation, intent, and plan to harm others. Except for the rare occasion when the client clearly verbalizes homicidal ideation, the crisis worker needs to do an explicit lethality assessment. Some areas to assess include the following:

1. Does the person have a history of violence against others? (If law enforcement knows the person by name, there is a good chance that there is a history of violence.)
2. Is the person taking responsibility for his or her actions, or is he or she blaming others for the current situation?
3. Is he or she talking about "getting back" at someone for what has happened?
4. Are there lethal weapons in the immediate area? The crisis worker should check the surroundings for weapons (knives or guns) or possible weapons (heavy ashtrays, broken bottles, scraps of wood).

Once the crisis worker has enough information to assess the client's response, he or she needs to ask specific questions about whether or not the client has thoughts of, an intention of, or a plan for harming others.

According to Roberts (2005), most initial contact in a crisis happens over the phone. As a crisis worker, the author found a number of specific benefits to providing crisis intervention over the phone:

1. Reading from a risk assessment checklist without fear of breaking eye contact
2. Being able to write notes during the assessment
3. Communicating with other crisis team members during the phone call
4. Coordinating services with other agencies, such as supervisors, psychiatrists, and law enforcement.

The assessment of lethality is urgent in Rolando's situation. Lupe's stated reason for contacting the CAPE team was that she was fearful that Rolando would harm his brother. His medical records indicate a history of violence. For maximum safety of everyone involved (crisis workers included), we continued our intervention over the phone. In the following dialogue, Kim uses strengths-based language, open- and closed-ended questions to gather descriptions and specific information, and reflection of feeling to maintain rapport.

| | |
|---|---|
| Crisis Worker: | Lupe, what are you doing to keep yourself safe right now? |
| Lupe: | (voice trembling) I took the phone into the bathroom. |
| Crisis Worker: | I'm glad you're safe. Where are Rolando and his brother right now? |
| Lupe: | Yellin' at each other in the other room. |
| Crisis Worker: | Does Rolando have access to any knives or other weapons? |
| Lupe: | The knives have been locked up since the last time. I don't think there is anything else in the house. |
| Crisis Worker: | I'm glad to hear that. You take your family's safety seriously. What started all of this? |
| Lupe: | I don't know. I think Hector was teasing Rolando. I'm kinda worried; Rolando's been acting real funny today, though. |
| Crisis Worker: | You're worried about the way Rolando has been acting. Has he been taking his medication? Can you check his bottle? You're in the bathroom, right? |
| Lupe: | *Ay no!* Kim, it looks like he hasn't taken his meds in at least a week. *¿Que vamos a hacer* [What are we going to do]? I'm afraid to leave the bathroom. |
| Crisis Worker: | *No te preocupas* [Don't worry]. I hear the fear in your voice. You've been doing great so far tonight. I see no reason why that will change. |

One of the challenges of crisis intervention is that, at any given time, the intervention can go in a number of directions. Without Roberts's framework to remind us that we have not finished our assessment of lethality, we might focus on Lupe's escalating anxiety and proceed with exploring emotions and providing support (Stage 4). Rather than ignore Lupe's experience, we use it to further our assessment of lethality. Lupe's statements provide us with valuable data about her own assessment of safety and her parental authority in the situation. As noted earlier, crisis workers should assess both the youth's level of risk and the parent's capacity and ability to protect (Rudd, Joiner, & Rajab, 2001).

Myer's (2001) triage assessment model assists in assessing Lupe's capacity to function. Lower scores on affect, behavior, and cognition suggest higher functioning. When the crisis worker assessed Lupe, her primary emotion was anxiety or fear, based on her use of the word *fear*. Given the potential for violence in the situation, her affect is appropriate to the situation, with a brief escalation of emotions. On the affective severity scale, she rates a 3 out of 10. Her cognitive domain is future oriented and focused on safety: "What are we *going* to do?" She believes something terrible will happen because Rolando is not taking his medications. She demonstrates some difficulties with problem solving and making decisions. Her fears about the future are not without basis. On the cognitive severity scale, she rates a 5 out of 10. Behaviorally she is immobile: She is unable to leave the bathroom to address the situation. Her behavior is exacerbating the situation; the longer she stays in the bathroom, the more chance there is that violence could occur. On the behavioral severity scale, she rates an 8 out of 10. Myer's model helps us to interpret the data. By identifying the most severely impaired domain, we can prioritize our interventions. Based on our assessment, we determine that Lupe cannot be considered a protective factor in the current crisis.

Rapid response is a hallmark of crisis intervention. Like Kim, crisis workers need to be able to think on their feet. Recognizing Lupe's crisis state, Kim writes a note to me: "Should we call the police?" I write, "Ask Lupe if she's comfortable with the police coming. If so, tell her I'd like to speak with Rolando." Involving Lupe in the decision to call the police addressed her cognitive domain: we affirmed her authority as a parent and provided her the opportunity to make a decision. Asking her to leave the bathroom and hand the phone to Rolando addresses her immobility. There are three purposes in talking to Rolando. The first is to remove him from the offending environment (his brother and the living room). The second is to gather more information about his mental state, to involve him in the intervention, and to determine if he can contract for safety. Third, if Rolando is assessed to be a danger to others, he will not be in the living room when the police arrive.

I assessed Rolando's current functioning and mental status. He confirmed that he had stopped taking his meds, had been sleeping poorly, and had no appetite. He denied use of alcohol or other drugs. He reported that he had no thoughts of killing himself and stated that he would only hurt his brother, not kill him. He refused to contract for safety. The dialogue that follows indicated that the situation was not safe, and it was appropriate for Kim to call the police.

|               |                                                      |
|---------------|------------------------------------------------------|
| Rolando:      | Hector won't stop talking about me. All the time, yo. He and his friends are always saying things about me behind my back. He needs to stop, dawg. |
| Crisis Worker:| How do you know they are talking about you?          |
| Rolando:      | I know. What, you don't believe me? (laughs, then becomes angry) I know what you're thinking. I know |

what they're all thinking. Even when they don't speak
out loud, I hear them.

Crisis Worker:  I can understand how you'd be angry if you thought
your brother and his friends were talking about you. If
you're willing, I'm going to help you so that he doesn't
talk about you anymore. Are we cool?

Rolando presents with delusions of reference, thought broadcasting,
and paranoia, all clear indications of psychosis. The extent to which his
paranoia is based on actual events or delusional thinking is unclear; medical records note that Hector takes pleasure in teasing Rolando for being
"crazy." Rolando's presentation of psychosis, his stated intention to harm
his brother, and his prior history of violence when not taking medication
place him at a high potential for lethality. Using the Community Integration,
Inc. Intervention Priority Scale (Roberts, 2002), we rate the call a Priority
I because of the threat of imminent violence. Priority I requires the mobilization of emergency services to stabilize the situation. I write a note to Kim to
page the on-call psychiatrist for a consultation and call the police. The psychiatrist confirms that children will start to decompensate after a week or
two of being off their meds. The psychiatrist recommends hospitalization to
stabilize Rolando on his medications, stating that the last time he was hospitalized, it took approximately a week for the antipsychotics to reduce both
negative and positive symptoms associated with his psychosis. The police
agree to meet us at the house. Police involvement was crucial for three reasons: (a) Police involvement increases the safety for the family and the crisis
workers. (b) At age 16, Rolando was old enough to sign himself in and out
of treatment in the state of Texas. The only way to comply with the psychiatrist's recommendations was to have a police officer sign an emergency psychiatric commitment order. If this crisis had occurred in September 2003,
rather than 1999, Rolando's mother would have been able to sign him into
the hospital because by that time the age of consent had been raised to 18.
(c) The police officer could safely transport Rolando to the hospital.

Rolando stays on the phone with us as we travel to his house. With the
police present, he agrees to be transported to the hospital. The psychiatrist
on call admits him to the adolescent unit and starts him on his meds. At
Rolando's request and with the permission of the hospital, I agree to return
for visits.

## Stage 2: Establishing Rapport and Communication

The second stage in Roberts's seven-stage model is establishing rapport and
communication. CAPE team workers had established rapport with Rolando

and his family over the course of their involvement with the team 2 years earlier, after Rolando's first hospitalization. During the first meeting at the hospital since Rolando has been stabilized on his meds, the family shared with the caseworkers some of the elements that facilitated rapport building. The first two comments speak to the value of language and the importance of cultural competence in developing a working relationship (Clark, 2002; Fernandez et al., 2004):

| | |
|---|---|
| Rolando: | Man, you know what's cool? You [addressing the CAPE team caseworker] speak Spanish with my mom. None of the staff at the hospital can do that. |
| Lupe: | Yeah, that's really nice. *¿Sabes que* [Do you know what]? I also like that you have *personalismo* [a warm and familiar way of relating to people]. |
| Rolando: | The best thing, dawg, is that you don't mind when I talk about some of the crazy thoughts I have. I know my world ain't like yours, but you cool with that. |
| Crisis Worker: | I appreciate you saying all of those things. What's true is that one of your strengths as individuals and a family is that you have a great capacity to trust others. |

Rolando's reference to his "world" is a common way for people with psychotic disorders to identify their experience (Roth & Fonagy, 2005). The caseworker's willingness to discuss Rolando's "crazy thoughts" is more important in developing and maintaining rapport than it is in providing relief from his auditory hallucinations.

The caseworker continued to provide co-therapy with the hospital staff for another week, at which time Rolando was discharged back to the community. He was no longer suffering from hallucinations or delusions. His focus was improved, and he appeared more relaxed. Because his psychotic symptomology was managed, Rolando was able to address the psychodynamic issues that preceded the crisis.

### Stages 3 and 4: Identifying Major Problems and Dealing With Feelings

The higher the level of family conflict, the more important it is to deal with feelings while identifying major problems. The identification of the precipitating event can bring up feelings as family members try to blame each other for the crisis. The crisis worker can use strengths-based techniques to normalize feelings and reconceptualize individual blame as group responsibility.

The following dialogue illustrates the use of strengths-based language as the crisis worker facilitates a conversation among the three family members:

Crisis Worker:  Who would like to share their thoughts as to what kicked off this last round of stress?

Lupe:  If Rolando would just take his medicine, this wouldn't keep happening.

Rolando:  Mom, you say it like this was all my fault. What about Hector?

Hector:  What about me? I didn't do anything.

Crisis Worker:  One of the amazing things about families is that everyone can be in the same room, see and hear the same things, and have completely different memories of it. None of them are wrong, they are just different. Rather than talk about what happened before Lupe called the office last week, perhaps we can talk about what the family has been doing to keep things going well these past 7 months.

Hoff, Hallisey, and Hoff (2009) caution crisis workers to avoid identifying one family member as the problem. She recommends identifying the entire family as the client. In this case, the client is no longer Rolando, and the problem is no longer Rolando's schizophrenia. It is now a systemic issue with the whole family. This does not mean that Rolando's contribution to the family crisis should not be ignored. Indeed, Rolando's psychotic episode (which is synonymous with an acute crisis state), likely precipitated the family crisis (Hoff, Hallisey, & Hoff, 2009). The discussion of major problems allowed each member of the family to take responsibility for his or her role in the crisis. The caseworker's responsibility was to ensure that people felt safe. A safe environment is an environment where family members acknowledge each other's share, take responsibility in front of others, praise each other, and agree to work toward solutions.

Mediating conflict is important in maintaining a safe environment. When working with people with a diagnosis of schizophrenia, maintaining a calm and emotionally safe environment is crucial. People with schizophrenia often have deficits in their ability to understand and manage their own and others' emotions (Eack, 2012). Some treatments, such as cognitive enhancement therapy (Eack, Hogarty, Greenwald, Hogarty, & Keshavan, 2007), explicitly address these deficits, and others, such as art therapy, create low-stimulation environments and encourage nonverbal expressions. Family art therapy is an expressive therapy that is well suited for families with a youth who has schizophrenia (Kwiatkowska, 2001). The components of art therapy (focused kinesthetic work expressing ideas) address the treatment goals of schizophrenia: developing social skills to reduce family conflict and increasing client participation in family activities. For a person with schizophrenia, creative or representational drawing can be a normalizing activity.

The caseworker asked family members to draw a picture of (a) the family, (b) how they are feeling right now, (c) how they were feeling the night of the crisis, and (d) how they would like to feel. The caseworker set up ground rules for discussing the activity. According to Lupe, this was the first time in months that the family had laughed together; drawing is one of the few activities where criticism is seen as laughable (e.g., "Dude, you call that a sun? It looks Mom's *barbacoa*."). While Rolando had a much more difficult time creating a recognizable picture of the family, his drawings of feelings were remarkable. His brother and mother had difficulty representing abstract concepts as well as he did. Rolando's pride in his accomplishments was a steppingstone to increased self-confidence.

## Stage 5: Exploring Possible Alternatives

The family identified one precipitating factor and three main problems that they would like to work on. The precipitating factor was Rolando's yelling at his mom to say that Hector had hidden his medication. When the family processed the precipitating factor, they were able to see the part that each played in the crisis. As an alternative to blaming, arguing, and escalating emotions, the family stated they would like to improve relationships between family members, reduce conflict between the brothers, and reduce the stimulation in the house. Korkeila et al. (2004) report a positive correlation between optimism in adulthood and reports of positive parent-child relationships. The clinical importance of working with families to develop positive parent-child relationships cannot be overemphasized. The development of optimism begins with a strong parent-child relationship. In addition to the family's suggestions, the caseworker recommended a fourth goal. Although this is not typical in traditional outpatient therapy, taking an active approach is appropriate in crisis intervention. The goal was to eliminate threats to family members. The caseworker explained that there could be no progress on the other goals until the family believed that they would all be safe. The family agreed to the goals.

The caseworker met with Rolando individually. The purpose was not to single him out as a problem but to provide extra support given that he was transitioning from a most restrictive to a least restrictive environment. He discussed his frustration at having no close friends. Rather than having a long discussion about the issue, which can be challenging for people who have difficulty processing information, the caseworker helped Rolando draw a sociogram. The sociogram is a genogram (McGoldrick, Gerson, & Petry, 2008) that represents a person's social rather than familial world. Through this exercise, Rolando was able to identify friends with whom he could spend more time. Addressing social concerns is significant for people with schizophrenia. Youth with serious mental illness often need concentrated efforts to help them participate in social activities that are crucial for their psychosocial development.

## Stage 6: Formulating an Action Plan

One challenge to crisis work with families is the programmatic limitation of 30 days per family. One of the goals of this family was to strengthen relationships. The caseworker recognized that to support that goal, the family would benefit most from longer-term services. The solution came in the form of a referral to the FPP. Similar to the crisis unit, FPP is mobile and provides services in people's homes. The difference is that the FPP services are somewhat less intensive (twice a week instead of daily), but they are more long term. FPP provided individual and family therapy to address the ongoing concerns of the family.

Solution-focused therapy is well suited for Stage 6. One of the classic solution-focused techniques for setting goals is the miracle question (Berg & Miller, 1992):

> Suppose that after our meeting today you... go to bed. While you are sleeping a miracle happens and your problem is solved, like magic. The problem is gone. Because you were sleeping, you don't know that a miracle happened, but when you wake up tomorrow morning, you will be different. How will you know a miracle has happened? What will be the first small sign that tells you that a miracle has happened and that the problem is resolved? (p. 359)

The responses were as follows:

|  |  |
|---|---|
| Lupe: | I wouldn't have to yell, "*Mijo*, get out of bed. You're going to be late to school." |
| Rolando: | Hector and I wouldn't yell at each other. |
| Crisis Worker: | Instead of yelling, what do imagine doing differently? |
| Rolando: | I don't know. Say nothing? |
| Hector: | Rolando would be nice to me like he used to be. |

The miracle question proves the crisis worker with some concrete behavioral indicators of what might be different when the current problem is no longer a problem. This idea would be incorporated into longer term treatment, rather than crisis intervention. The final step in the action plan was to have Lupe join the local chapter of the National Alliance on Mental Illness (NAMI), an organization that provides social support and has an educational function that can reduce stress and increase knowledge of disorders.

## Stage 7: Follow-Up

The final stage of Roberts's model is follow-up. The final two sessions were very important in bringing closure to the crisis. The penultimate session reviewed the progress made by the family. The following dialogue illustrates termination work with the family:

Crisis Worker:  What was one of the most important things you learned about yourself and the family as a result of this experience?

Lupe:  My house is much more calm if I am calm. I never knew how important I was. I know that sounds silly, but it is true.

Rolando:  I'm the most important person in the family! Nah, just kidding, dawg. For real, my brother is a nice guy.

Hector:  When Rolando takes his meds and Mom goes to her meetings, I don't get so mad. I don't know why, but I just don't.

Crisis Worker:  It sounds like all of you have learned a great deal in the last 4 weeks. I have one more question for you: Let's say you met a family that was going through the same things as you were going through when you first started CAPE services. What advice would have for them?

Rolando:  I would tell them to take their meds. That's real important.

Lupe:  I would tell the mom to do whatever she could to have the family involved with crisis services.

Hector:  I'd tell them not to get in this situation in the first place. (everyone laughs)

The family was successful at meeting their goals and the goals of the program. There were no incidents of violence for the duration of the services. Lupe was able to build a new support network. Rolando stabilized on his meds and successfully increased his social circle. Hector demonstrated improved functioning both at school and at home. When we met with the FPP, the goal was to maintain Rolando in the community by engaging the family in communication skills training and cognitive behavioral therapy. Hector's vision of Rolando being nice to him would form the basis of a goal the family could get on board with and work toward. The crisis that had been so powerful and vivid 4 weeks earlier was a foundation on which the family had built a new way of interacting and being together as a family.

## CASE STUDY 3: BRANDON

## Stages 1 and 2: Assessing Lethality and Establishing Rapport

The third area of lethality is the assessment of whether the client is in danger of being harmed by those around him or her. The crisis worker can think about the connection between Stages 1 and 2 in the following way: In Stage 1, the crisis worker helps clients believe that their external world is safe (safe from harm to self or others or harm by others); in Stage 2, a feeling of safety is established between the crisis worker and the client. Once both external safety and interpersonal safety have been established, the crisis worker and client can work through the remaining stages to re-establish the client's internal safety. As with all of Roberts's stages, the assessment of lethality should be revisited if the crisis worker believes that the client's initial reports have changed or were not accurate to begin with.

Traveling to the shelter, the crisis worker wondered what threats to harm might be present with Brandon. The most recent statistics suggest that between 16% and 50% of homeless youth have attempted suicide (Votta & Manion, 2004; Walls & Bell, 2011). The mortality rate for street-involved youth is estimated at 921 per 100,000, which is approximately 20 times greater than the rate for youth in the general population (50 per 100,000; Murphy, Xu, & Kochanek, 2013; Roy et al., 2004). Rates of sexual and physical abuse range from 35% to 45% (Votta & Manion, 2004), and between 10% and 28% of street youth have reported exchanging sex for shelter, food, drugs, or other subsistence needs (survival sex; Walls & Bell, 2011). Violence toward homeless youth is also greater than for nonhomeless youth (Kidd, 2003). Any psychosocial assessment of street-involved youth should cover these mentioned areas, and a referral for a full medical evaluation should be made (Elliott & Canadian Paediatric Society, Adolescent Health Committee, 2013). A simple way for crisis workers to assess basic information about history of abuse, survival sex, and so forth is to create a checklist that youth can fill out, giving them an opportunity to disclose information without having to talk about it. The tone of the items on the checklist should be respectful and nonblaming. The following is an example of possible wording for the introduction to such a checklist:

> Youth who are no longer living at home sometimes find themselves thinking, feeling, or doing things they would never had thought, felt, or done before leaving home. Youth often report a history of abuse, current substance use, survival sex, suicidal and homicidal ideation, etc.

Then the young person completing the checklist would have the option to respond to questions on a scale of 1 to 5, where 1 = none of the time and 5 = nearly all of the time. Examples of questions include: "Have you ever exchanged sex for food, clothing, shelter, or drugs? Have you had thoughts of killing yourself in the past week?" The case worker can review the checklist and follow up with any concerning items.

Assessing these sensitive topics is impossible without establishing rapport. However, because most runaway youth leave home because of a problem with the adult caretaker, there is a built-in distrust of adults and authority. Lambie (2004) suggests that adolescents' distrust of adults is often expressed by displays of defiance and hostility when first meeting counselors. A strengths perspective reframes their defiance as a protective factor: Living on the street requires a healthy skepticism. Rapport building with adolescents is simplified when the crisis worker is familiar with adolescent culture (movies, music, stars, hobbies, etc.). Humor is similarly important. The crisis worker considered all of these factors as he drove to the shelter.

The following are some basic rules for working with adolescents in crisis and traditional counseling:

1. Let them know you are willing to listen, without interruption, to their story.
2. Reflect and restate more than question.
3. Empathize with their situation.
4. Provide them opportunities to take responsibility in the session and in their life.
5. Be honest when you think they are telling you what they think you want to hear. (Peterson, 1995)

In this initial meeting's dialogue, the crisis worker is careful to let the client know he is not going to be biased against him for being a teenager:

| | |
|---|---|
| Crisis Worker: | Hey, Brandon, my name is Jonathan. I work with kids who want to kill themselves, kill other people, or who are actively psychotic. Am I in the right place? (smile) |
| Brandon: | (not smiling) I didn't ask you to come. |
| Crisis Worker: | Yeah, the shelter supervisor called and said you threatened to run if the police were called and that you didn't care if you lived or died. |
| Brandon: | (visibly agitated) Man, I hate it when adults talk for me! |
| Crisis Worker: | You and me both. Tell me if this sounds about right: Adults think they have to be in charge, so they are always telling teenagers how to live. People like me have to listen to adults talk about how kids don't act right, when the adults were the ones who told the kids how to act in the first place. |

Brandon:    (holding back a smile).

Crisis Worker:    I'd much rather hear your side of the story. Since I'm here, why don't you tell what's going on.


In this dialogue, the crisis worker anticipates and addresses objections before they arise. In this situation, the objection would be "Why should I talk to you? You're an adult and you just don't understand."

After using basic attentive skills and explaining confidentiality, the crisis worker conducted a suicide assessment. Brandon expressed morbid nonsuicidal ideation: "Life would be so much better if I woke up dead." He had no thoughts of ending his own life, even though he thought about death, and he had no intent and no plan. He did have dozens of old scars on his arms and legs. When asked about them, he said that he used to cut in order to deal with his feelings of anger and frustration, but not with the intention of ending his life. Such self-injury without suicidal intent, or *nonsuicidal self-injury* (NSSI), was rare 30 years ago, but today as many as 20% of youth report having engaged in at least one episode of NSSI (Muehlenkamp, Claes, Havertape, & Plener, 2012). Reasons for engaging in NSSI include the desire to manage intolerable emotions, to relieve stress or pressure, to deal with frustration or anger, and to feel something (Muehlenkamp, Brausch, Quigley, & Whitlock, 2013; Singer, 2012). Only a small percentage of youth who engage in NSSI are also at risk for suicidal ideation or attempts. Risk factors for suicidal behavior among youth who engage in NSSI include multiple, repeated self-injury over a period of time, self-injury to punish others, and moderate to high depression and substance use (Jenkins et al., 2014; Whitlock et al., 2013). Through the lethality assessment, the crisis worker was learning that Brandon was not at risk for suicide and had a history of, but not current, NSSI.

The next part of the lethality assessment was to assess the risk of Brandon harming someone else:

Crisis Worker:    Is there anyone you are planning on harming?

Brandon:    Not here.

Crisis Worker:    Tell me more.


Brandon explains that he would "do anything" to make his mom's boyfriend suffer. He reports that he left California because of ongoing abuse and humiliation at the hands of his mother's boyfriend. Even though Brandon's reports suggested risk of harm to others, the fact that he was in Austin and the potential victim was in California meant that the risk was low. If Brandon stated that he had a plan to return to California and hurt the boyfriend, then risk would be moderate to high. In most states, the caseworker would have a duty to warn the boyfriend of the potential for harm.

However, at the time of the assessment Brandon was considered at low risk for suicide and violence toward others.

## Stage 3: Identifying Major Problems

The crisis worker is interested in finding the precipitating event, or the straw that broke the camel's back. Stage 3 is all about exploring what has happened in the past couple of days that precipitated the current crisis. With Brandon, identifying the precipitating event required a careful review of recent events in his life. Because homeless youth experience so many challenges to their basic functioning (physical and sexual abuse, survival sex, substance use, street violence, hunger, etc.), the crisis worker has to be careful not to assume that one of those areas was the precipitating event. Brandon was reluctant to talk about the events leading up to his leaving California. The crisis worker uses the "I don't know" technique (G. Maddox, personal communication, April 4, 1997) to maintain rapport and encourage Brandon to share:

Crisis Worker:   What happened that made you want to leave?
Brandon:   Dunno.
Crisis Worker:   Is it that you really don't know, or you just don't want to tell me? If you don't know, I can help you figure it out. On the other hand, if you don't want to tell me, let me know. I respect you and wouldn't ask you to tell me anything you are not comfortable with. I just ask that you respect me by being honest.
Brandon:   Okay. I don't want to tell you.

This dialogue makes it clear that Brandon knew what happened. It was not necessary that the case worker knew. We explored the severity of the event using negative scaling questions (Selekman, 2002). This variation of the solution-focused technique of scaling questions is useful when discussing something horrible. In the author's experience, teenagers respond well to these questions.

Crisis Worker:   On a scale from –1 to –10, with –1 being bad to –10 being the worst ever, what would you rate the event?
Brandon:   –7.
Crisis Worker:   Wow. What would be a –10?
Brandon:   If he kills my mom.
Crisis Worker:   (lengthy silence, looking at Brandon) That would be a –10, wouldn't it?

When asked, Brandon said he did not think his mother was in danger, nor did he think her safety depended on him being at home. For many homeless youth, returning to their home places them in greater danger than if they remain on the street (Kidd, 2003). One example of Brandon's resilience is his decision to leave a dangerous situation. Many street kids can be seen as survivors who took their future into their own hands.

Exploration of the precipitating event led to a discussion of current problems. These primarily involved meeting his basic needs: food, shelter, and clothing. Now that problems had been identified and rapport was firmly established, we were in a good position to begin addressing feelings.

## Stage 4: Dealing With Feelings and Providing Support

People in crisis tend to experience things in extremes: They feel too little or too much; they are overly focused on a single idea, or they are overwhelmed by a constant barrage of ideas; they are incapable of action, or they cannot control their behaviors. Youth in crisis often feel either detached and numb or constantly emotionally overwhelmed. The simple acts of labeling feelings and validating the person's emotional state help the person feel less overwhelmed and more in control, opening the door to problem-solving. Adolescents, especially those with highly conflictual parent-child relationships, are not used to adults acknowledging and understanding their feelings. Doing so improves rapport and the adolescent's sense that he or she is with a safe adult.

Roberts's model does not contain a stage for dealing with cognitive and behavioral elements of a crisis. Myer's (2001) triage assessment model is a useful framework for assessing cognitive and behavioral domains. The following dialogue provides insight into how the caseworker assessed Brandon's affective, behavioral, and cognitive functioning, and he validated Brandon's experience:

Crisis Worker:   Brandon, I've been asking you a lot of question for the past 2 hours. Here you are, in a homeless shelter, thousands of miles away from your mother, and uncertain of your future. How are you feeling? Are you happy, scared, angry, sad, or something in between?

Brandon:   (clenched fists, tight jaw, furrowed brow) I'll tell you how I feel. I feel like I can't go home anymore. My mom is probably disowning me because her boyfriend is convincing her that I'm no good. I don't have any friends. Not that it matters. I'm outta here soon.

Brandon's nonverbal cues suggested that he was feeling anger and frustration. The fact that he followed the phrase "I feel like..." with cognitive rather than affective content (the belief that he can no longer go home, rather than expressions of sadness, anger, or frustration) suggested that either he lacked the words to express his emotions or that he was uncomfortable being vulnerable in front of the crisis worker.

> Crisis Worker:  Brandon, I can totally understand why the thought of
> your mom's boyfriend turning her against you would
> make you so angry.
> Brandon:  (softer) Damn right.

The crisis worker suggests an emotion (anger) and validates Brandon's rationale for his feelings. Note that the crisis worker did not say Brandon was right. It is possible that Brandon is completely wrong about his mother and her boyfriend. Validating feelings simply means acknowledging how the person feels and the reason the person might feel that way.

Brandon's statement "I'm outta here soon" provided insight into his behavioral functioning. Myer (2001) suggested that in crisis situations behaviors can be thought of as either approach (i.e., action—fight or flight) or avoidance (i.e., no action—freeze). Brandon's behavioral response to the current crisis is best described as approach: He left California, he threatened to leave the shelter if it called the cops, and he just told the crisis worker that he was "outta here." The crisis worker needs to determine if the approach behaviors will intensify the crisis or if they will help to resolve them. If Brandon stated that he was traveling back to California to resolve issues with his mother and her boyfriend, then those approach behaviors could be seen as crisis resolving. Leaving the shelter with no safe destination and no plan for finding stable housing is an example of crisis perpetuating approach behaviors. In the problem-solving stage, the crisis worker could include an exploration of what might happen if Brandon left and what options exist for crisis resolution.

Brandon's statements about loss provided a great deal of information about his cognitive state. He believes that he *lost* his home when he left (past). He believes that he *will* lose his relationship with his mom (future). He *has* no friends (present). The goal for the crisis worker would be to help Brandon think more expansively and less rigidly about his present and future. Basic cognitive therapy techniques would be effective here.

In the following dialogue, the caseworker validates and supports Brandon. In doing so, he opens the door to exploring possible alternatives (Roberts's Stage 5):

> Crisis Worker:  One of the things I'm really impressed by, Brandon, is
> your approach to solving problems: You got yourself

|   |   |
|---|---|
| | out of a bad situation in California. You found the shelter in Austin. You agreed to talk with me. All of those things are real strengths. |
| Brandon: | (silent, eyes moving around nervously) |
| Crisis Worker: | (recognizing Brandon's discomfort with praise, reframes the silence) I also appreciate you letting me say some of these things without interruption. That's a skill that not many people have. |
| Brandon: | Thanks. |
| Crisis Worker: | I also know that you are concerned about having to leave the shelter. I have the same questions you do: Where will I go? Will I be safe? How will I survive? *If* you are willing, I'd be happy to talk about some possible solutions to these problems. |
| Brandon: | Okay. |

## Stage 5: Exploring Possible Alternatives

Most adults know how to problem-solve even if they cannot name the steps. Many youth have not yet learned these steps. People in crisis have difficulty remembering and focusing. I found that writing the problem-solving steps on a piece of paper provided a structured activity during the session and increased the likelihood that the steps would be followed. Additionally, using the solution-focused technique of identifying past successes was very helpful during the brainstorming step.

|   |   |
|---|---|
| Crisis Worker: | Now that we have identified the problem as "I don't have a place to live," we brainstorm solutions. Tell me whatever comes to mind, as strange as they might sound, and we'll write them down. When we're done, we'll go back and evaluate which alternative would be the best solution. |
| Brandon: | You could give me a thousand dollars. My mom could get rid of her boyfriend and come get me. The shelter could let me stay. I could hitchhike to the next town and stay in their shelter until they kick me out. . . . I can't think of any others. |
| Crisis Worker: | I'm impressed with how quickly you came up with that list. You mentioned that you and your mom were homeless when you were a kid. Did you ever stay with someone that was safe and protected you? |
| Brandon: | A couple of times Mom and I went and stayed at her cousin's house. |
| Crisis Worker: | Great! So another alternative is to contact your relatives and see if you could stay with them. |

Brandon's behavioral coping style, approach, is reflected by his choice of possibilities. If a client is sufficiently cognitively impaired, the crisis worker will have to be more active in providing alternatives. Stage 5 can be an exciting and rewarding stage if the previous stages have been adequately addressed. If the crisis worker has difficulty engaging the client in exploring alternatives, it will be necessary to either re-examine the problem or address affect, cognitions, or behaviors that get in the way of looking forward. In addition to housing, Brandon identified problems with his cell phone, feeling disconnected from his friends at home, and dislike of the other kids in the shelter. During the action plan stage, we focused on his housing and cell phone.

## Stage 6: Formulating an Action Plan

The creation of an action plan based on the alternatives generated in Stage 5 is a two-part process. First, support the client to develop specific actions based on the alternatives. Second, ensure that the steps are realistic and measurable and have built-in support. The question "How will you know when you have achieved your goal?" is useful in evaluating the action steps. The following is Brandon's action plan:

1. *Problem*: I have nowhere to live.
   *Solution*: Call Aunt Emerson in North Carolina and ask if I can stay with her.
   *Support*: The caseworker will text tonight to see if I have gotten in touch with my aunt.
2. *Problem*: I don't know what is going on with my mom. I can't text her because my phone is out of juice.
   *Solution*: Charge the phone, text mom.
   *Support*: Shelter staff will lend me a charger and agree to keep my phone in the office so that it can charge safely.
3. *Strength*: I am good at solving my problems.
   *Plan*: When I get stuck, I will sit down with a pen and paper and write out all the possible alternatives to my problem.
   *Support*: If I'm on the street, I'll call the National Runaway Safeline (1800runaway.org) or use their chat line over my phone or at a computer in the library (Singer, 2011).

## Stage 7: Follow-Up

The last stage of Roberts's model is follow-up. In all clinical relationships, closure is important. It is a time when the crisis worker can provide final feedback about progress and the client can provide feedback about what has changed in his or her life. For many clients, closure is one of the few times when a close relationship has had a formal ending. The process of getting closure allows the client to look forward without regret or a sense of loss. The experience is just as valid a therapeutic tool as any implemented in the previous six stages.

Brandon's text to the crisis worker said that the aunt was happy to have him come to North Carolina. She bought a train ticket for him online. The shelter staff agreed to let Brandon print out the ticket in their office. The next day the crisis worker met Brandon at the train station and gave him a phone charger that had been left at the office. The crisis worker bought Brandon an ice cream cone at McDonald's, and they talked Brandon's experiences in services and what his plan was for the next 24 hours. The crisis worker stated that he would check in with Brandon, and Brandon agreed that he would call or text the crisis worker when he arrived in North Carolina or if there were any issues after he arrived.

## SUMMARY AND CONCLUSION

The information presented in this chapter was intended to provide a practical view of pediatric mobile crisis intervention. The assessment techniques and interventions were based more in practice wisdom than empirical knowledge. This is in part because almost nothing has been written about outpatient crisis intervention for youth. As if to highlight this gap in the knowledge base, crisis intervention as a treatment modality was omitted in a recent comprehensive review of outpatient mental health services for youth (Garland et al., 2013).

The empirical literature is not the only place where information on crisis intervention is missing. Graduate students routinely report having little or no training in working with people experiencing psychiatric emergencies (Debski, Spadafore, Jacob, Poole, & Hixson, 2007; Singer & Slovak, 2011). Even if graduate education were available, it is difficult to acquire the skills and knowledge necessary to be an effective crisis intervention worker without having field experience. If you find yourself overwhelmed by the amount of information presented, I encourage you to take a deep breath. Part of learning how to deal with crises involves increasing your own coping skills as a professional (Singer & Dewane, 2010): Be yourself; stay current with the literature; seek supervision whenever possible; listen to episodes of the Social Work Podcast (www.socialworkpodcast.com); and allow yourself to take in the amazing gift of watching persons in crisis rediscover themselves.

REFERENCES

Aguirre, R. T. P., McCoy, M. K., & Roan, M. (2013). Development guidelines from a study of suicide prevention mobile applications (apps). *Journal of Technology in Human Services, 31,* 269–293. doi:10.1080/15228835.2013.814750

Allen, M., Burt, K., Bryan, E., Carter, D., Orsi, R., & Durkan, L. (2002). School counselors' preparation for and participation in crisis intervention. *Professional School Counseling, 6,* 96–102.

American Psychiatric Association. (2000). *Diagnostic and statistical manual of mental disorders, text revision: DSM-IV-TR* (4th ed.). Washington, DC: Author.

American Psychiatric Association. (2013). *Diagnostic and statistical manual of mental disorders* (5th ed.). Washington, DC: Author.

Barak, A., & Grohol, J. M. (2011). Current and future trends in Internet-supported mental health interventions. *Journal of Technology in Human Services, 29,* 155–196. doi:10.1080/152288 35.2011.616939

Barlow, D. H., & Durand, V. M. (2014). *Abnormal psychology: An integrative approach* (7th ed.). Belmont, CA: Cengage Learning.

Bennett, D. J., Ogloff, J. R. P., Mullen, P. E., Thomas, S. D. M., Wallace, C., & Short, T. (2011). Schizophrenia disorders, substance abuse and prior offending in a sequential series of 435 homicides. *Acta Psychiatrica Scandinavica, 124,* 226–233. doi:10.1111/ j.1600-0447.2011.01731.x

Berg, I. K., & Miller, S. D. (1992). *Working with the problem drinker: A solution-focused approach.* New York: Norton.

Bongar, B. M., & Sullivan, G. (2013). *The suicidal patient: Clinical and legal standards of care* (3rd ed.). Washington, DC: American Psychological Association.

Brent, D. A., Poling, K. D., & Goldstein, T. R. (2011). *Treating depressed and suicidal adolescents: A clinician's guide.* New York: Guilford Press.

Burns, B., Hoagwood, K., & Mrazek, P. (1999). Effective treatment for mental disorders in children and adolescents. *Clinical Child and Family Psychology Review, 2,* 199–252.

Clark, L. (2002). Mexican-origin mothers. *Western Journal of Nursing Research, 24,* 159–180.

Coyne, J. C., & Downey, G. A. (1991). Social factors and psychopathology: Stress, social support, and coping processes. *Annual Review of Psychology, 42,* 401–425. doi:10.1146/annurev. ps.42.020191.002153

Debski, J., Spadafore, C. D., Jacob, S., Poole, D. A., & Hixson, M. D. (2007). Suicide intervention: Training, roles, and knowledge of school psychologists. *Psychology in the Schools, 44,* 157–170. doi:10.1002/pits.20213

Dembo, R., Gulledge, L., Robinson, R. B., & Winters, K. C. (2011). Enrolling and engaging high-risk youths and families in community-based, brief intervention services. *Journal of Child and Adolescent Substance Abuse, 20,* 330–350. doi:10.1080/10678 28X.2011.598837

Diamond, G. S., Diamond, G. M., & Levy, S. A. (2013). *Attachment-based family therapy for depressed adolescents.* Washington, DC: American Psychological Association.

Diamond, G., Levy, S., Bevans, K. B., Fein, J. A., Wintersteen, M. B.,

Tien, A., & Creed, T. (2010). Development, validation, and utility of Internet-based, behavioral health screen for adolescents. *Pediatrics, 126*(1), e163–170. doi:10.1542/peds.2009-3272

Diamond, G. S., Wintersteen, M. B., Brown, G. K., Diamond, G. M., Gallop, R., Shelef, K., & Levy, S. (2010). Attachment-based family therapy for adolescents with suicidal ideation: A randomized controlled trial. *Journal of the American Academy of Child and Adolescent Psychiatry, 49*, 122–131.

Drapeau, C. W., & McIntosh, J. L. (2014). *U.S.A. suicide: 2012 official final data.* Washington, DC: American Association of Suicidology. Retrieved from http://www.suicidology.org

Eack, S. M. (2012). Cognitive remediation: A new generation of psychosocial interventions for people with schizophrenia. *Social Work, 57*, 235–246.

Eack, S. M., Hogarty, G. E., Greenwald, D. P., Hogarty, S. S., & Keshavan, M. S. (2007). Cognitive enhancement therapy improves emotional intelligence in early course schizophrenia: Preliminary effects. *Schizophrenia Research, 89*, 308–311. doi:10.1016/j.schres.2006.08.018

Eack, S. M., Singer, J. B., & Greeno, C. G. (2008). Screening for anxiety and depression in community mental health: The Beck Anxiety and Depression Inventories. *Community Mental Health Journal, 44*, 465–474. doi:10.1007/s10597-008-9150-y

Eaton, Y. M., & Ertl, B. (2000). The comprehensive crisis intervention model of Community Integration, Inc. Crisis Services. In A. R. Roberts (Ed.), *Crisis intervention handbook* (pp. 31–55). New York: Oxford University Press.

Elias, B. L., Fogger, S. A., McGuinness, T. M., & D'Alessandro, K. R. (2014). Mobile apps for psychiatric nurses. *Journal of Psychosocial Nursing and Mental Health Services, 52*(4), 42–47. doi:10.3928/02793695-20131126-07

Elliott, A. S., & Canadian Paediatric Society, Adolescent Health Committee. (2013). Meeting the health care needs of street-involved youth. *Paediatrics and Child Health, 18*(6), 317–326.

Erbacher, T. A., Singer, J. B., & Poland, S. (2015). *Suicide in schools: A practitioner's guide to multi-level prevention, assessment, intervention, and postvention.* New York: Routledge.

Esposito-Smythers, C., Spirito, A., Kahler, C. W., Hunt, J., & Monti, P. (2011). Treatment of co-occurring substance abuse and suicidality among adolescents: A randomized trial. *Journal of Consulting and Clinical Psychology, 79*, 728–739. doi:10.1037/a0026074

Estroff, S. E., Swanson, J. W., Lachicotte, W. S., Swartz, M., & Bolduc, M. (1998). Risk reconsidered: Targets of violence in the social networks of people with serious psychiatric disorders. *Social Psychiatry and Psychiatric Epidemiology, 33*(suppl. 1), S95–S101.

Evans, M. E., Boothroyd, R. A., & Armstrong, M. I. (1997). Development and implementation of an experimental study of the effectiveness of intensive in-home crisis services for children and their families. *Journal of Emotional and Behavioral Disorders, 5*(2), 93–105.

Evans, M. E., Boothroyd, R. A., Greenbaum, P. E., Brown, E. C., Armstrong, M. I., & Kuppinger, A. D. (2001). Outcomes associated with clinical profiles of children in psychiatric crisis enrolled in intensive, in-home interventions. *Mental Health Services Research*, 3(1), 35–44.

Evans, M. E., Boothroyd, R. A., Armstrong, M. I., Greenbaum, P. E., Brown, E. C., & Kuppinger, A. D. (2003). An experimental study of the effectiveness of intensive in-home crisis services for children and their families: Program outcomes. *Journal of Emotional and Behavioral Disorders*, 11(2), 92–102, 121.

Fein, J. A., Pailler, M. E., Barg, F. K., Wintersteen, M. B., Hayes, K., Tien, A. Y., & Diamond, G. S. (2010). Feasibility and effects of a Web-based adolescent psychiatric assessment administered by clinical staff in the pediatric emergency department. *Archives of Pediatrics and Adolescent Medicine*, 164, 1112–1117. doi:10.1001/archpediatrics.2010.213

Fernandez, A., Schillinger D., Grumbach K., Rosenthal, A., Stewart, A. L., Wang, F., & Pérez-Stable, E. J. (2004). Physician language ability and cultural competence: An exploratory study of communication with Spanish-speaking patients. *Journal of General Internal Medicine*, 19, 167–174.

Garland, A. F., Haine-Schlagel, R., Brookman-Frazee, L., Baker-Ericzen, M., Trask, E., & Fawley-King, K. (2013). Improving community-based mental health care for children: Translating knowledge into action. *Administration and Policy in Mental Health and Mental Health Services Research*, 40(1), 6–22. doi:10.1007/s10488-012-0450-8

Gil, E. (1991). *The healing power of play: Working with abused children*. New York: Guilford Press.

Ginnis, K. B., White, E. M., Ross, A. M., & Wharff, E. A. (2013). Family-based crisis intervention in the emergency department: A new model of care. *Journal of Child and Family Studies*. doi:10.1007/s10826-013-9823-1

Green, J. G., McLaughlin, K. A., Alegría, M., Costello, E. J., Gruber, M. J., Hoagwood, K., . . . Kessler, R. C. (2013). School mental health resources and adolescent mental health service use. *Journal of the American Academy of Child and Adolescent Psychiatry*, 52, 501–510. doi:10.1016/j.jaac.2013.03.002

Greene, G., Lee, M., Trask, R., & Rheinscheld, J. (2005). How to work with clients' strengths in crisis intervention: A solution-focused approach. In A. R. Roberts (Ed.), *Crisis intervention handbook: Assessment, treatment, and research* (3rd ed., pp. 64–89). New York: Oxford University Press.

Greenfield, B., Hechtman, L., & Tremblay, C. (1995). Short-term efficacy of interventions by a youth crisis team. *Canadian Journal of Psychiatry*, 40, 320–324.

Gutstein, S. E., Rudd, M. D., Graham, J. C., & Rayha, L. L. (1988). Systemic crisis intervention as a response to adolescent crisis: An outcome study. *Family Process*, 27, 201–211.

Henggeler, S. W., Rowland, M. D., Randall, J., Ward, D. M., Pickrel, S. G., Cunningham, P. B., . . . Santos, A. B. (1999). Home-based multisystemic therapy as an alternative to the hospitalization of youths in psychiatric crisis: clinical outcomes. *Journal of the American Academy of Child* and *Adolescent Psychiatry, 38,* 1331–1339.

Hepworth, D. H., Rooney, R. H., Rooney, G. D., & Strom-Gottfried, K. (Eds.). (2013). *Direct social work practice: Theory and skills* (9th ed.). Belmont, CA: Brooks/Cole, Cengage Learning.

Hoagwood, K. E., Jensen, P. S., Acri, M. C., Olin, S. S., Lewandowski, R. E., & Herman, R. J. (2012). Outcome domains in child mental health research since 1996: Have they changed and why does it matter? *Journal of the American Academy of Child and Adolescent Psychiatry, 51,* 1241–1260.e2. doi:10.1016/j.jaac.2012.09.004

Hoff, L. A., Hallisey, B. J., & Hoff, M. (2009). *People in crisis: clinical and diversity perspectives* (6th ed.). New York: Routledge.

Hor, K., & Taylor, M. (2010). Suicide and schizophrenia: A systematic review of rates and risk factors. *Journal of Psychopharmacology, 24*(4 suppl.), 81–90. doi:10.1177/1359786810385490

Jenkins, A. L., Singer, J. B., Conner, B. T., Calhoun, S., & Diamond, G. (2014). Risk for suicidal ideation and attempt among a primary care sample of adolescents engaging in nonsuicidal self-injury. *Suicide and Life-Threatening Behavior,* n/a–n/a. doi:10.1111/sltb.12094

Joyal, C. C., Putkonen, A., Paavola, P., & Tiihonen, J. (2004). Characteristics and circumstances of homicidal acts committed by offenders with schizophrenia. *Psychological Medicine, 34,* 433–442.

Kanel, K. (2013). *A Guide to crisis intervention* (5th Ed.). Belmont, CA: Cengage Learning.

Kessler, R. C., Berglund, P., Demler, O., Jin, R., Merikangas, K. R., & Walters, E. E. (2005). Lifetime prevalence and age-of-onset distributions of *DSM-IV* disorders in the National Comorbidity Survey Replication. *Archives of General Psychiatry, 62,* 593–602. doi:10.1001/archpsyc.62.6.593

Kidd, S. A. (2003). Street youth: Coping and interventions. *Child Adolescent Social Work Journal, 20,* 235–261.

King, C. A., Foster, C. E., & Rogalski, K. M. (2013). *Teen suicide risk: A practitioner guide to screening, assessment, and management.* New York: Guilford Press.

Korkeila, K., Kivela, S.-L., Suominen, S., Vahtera, J., Kivimaki, M., Sundell, J., ... Koskenvuo, M. (2004). Childhood adversities, parent-child relationships and dispositional optimism in adulthood. *Social Psychiatry and Psychiatric Epidemiology, 39,* 286–292.

Kwiatkowska, H. Y. (2001). Family art therapy: Experiments with a new technique. *American Journal of Art Therapy, 40*(1), 27–40.

Lambie, G. W. (2004). Motivational enhancement therapy: A tool for professional school counselors working with adolescents. *Professional School Counseling, 7,* 268–277.

Lindemann, E. (1944). Symptomatology and management of acute grief. *American Journal of Psychiatry, 101,* 141–148.

Masten, C. A., Best, K., & Garmezy, N. (1990). Resilience and development: Contributions from the study of children who overcome adversity. *Development and Psychopathology, 2,* 425–444.

McClellan, J., Stock, S., & American Academy of Child and Adolescent Psychiatry (AACAP) Committee on Quality Issues (CQI). (2013). Practice parameter for the assessment and treatment of children and adolescents with schizophrenia. *Journal of the American Academy of Child and Adolescent Psychiatry, 52,* 976–990. doi:10.1016/j.jaac.2013.02.008

McGoldrick, M., Gerson, R., & Petry, S. S. (2008). *Genograms: Assessment and intervention* (3rd ed.). New York: Norton.

Merikangas, K. R., He, J.-P., Burstein, M., Swanson, S. A., Avenevoli, S., Cui, L., . . . Swendsen, J. (2010). Lifetime prevalence of mental disorders in U.S. adolescents: Results from the National Comorbidity Survey Replication—Adolescent Supplement (NCS-A). *Journal of the American Academy of Child and Adolescent Psychiatry, 49,* 980–989. doi:10.1016/j.jaac.2010.05.017

Mishna, F., Bogo, M., Root, J., Sawyer, J.-L., & Khoury-Kassabri, M. (2012). "It just crept in": The digital age and implications for social work practice. *Clinical Social Work Journal, 40,* 277–286. doi:10.1007/s10615-012-0383-4

Muehlenkamp, J. J., Brausch, A., Quigley, K., & Whitlock, J. (2013). Interpersonal features and functions of nonsuicidal self-injury. *Suicide and Life-Threatening Behavior, 43*(1), 67–80. doi:10.1111/j.1943-278X.2012.00128.x

Muehlenkamp, J. J., Claes, L., Havertape, L., & Plener, P. L. (2012). International prevalence of adolescent non-suicidal self-injury and deliberate self-harm. *Child and Adolescent Psychiatry and Mental Health, 6*(1), 10. doi:10.1186/1753-2000-6-10

Murphy, S., Xu, J., & Kochanek, K. (2013). Deaths: Final data for 2010. *National Vital Statistics Reports, 61*(4), 1–117.

Myer, R. A. (2001). *Assessment for crisis intervention: A triage assessment model.* Pacific Grove, CA: Brooks/Cole.

Myer, R. A., Williams, R. C., Ottens, A. J., & Schmidt, A. E. (1992). Crisis assessment: A three-dimensional model for triage. *Journal of Mental Health Counseling, 14,* 137–148.

National Runaway Safeline. (2014). NRS statistics on runaways. Retrieved from http://www.1800runaway.org/learn/research/third_party/

Nielssen, O., & Large, M. (2010). Rates of homicide during the first episode of psychosis and after treatment: A systematic review and meta-analysis. *Schizophrenia Bulletin, 36,* 702–712. doi:10.1093/schbul/sbn144

Nordström, A., & Kullgren, G. (2003). Victim relations and victim gender in violent crimes committed by offenders with schizophrenia. *Social Psychiatry and Psychiatric Epidemiology, 38,* 326–330. doi:10.1007/s00127-003-0640-5

Nurnberger, J. I., Jr., & Foroud, T. (2000). Genetics of bipolar affective disorder. *Current Psychiatry Reports, 2,* 147–157.

O'Brien, K. H. M., & Berzin, S. C. (2012). Examining the impact of psychiatric diagnosis and comorbidity on the medical lethality of adolescent suicide attempts. *Suicide and Life-Threatening Behavior, 42,* 437–444. doi:10.1111/j.1943-278X.2012.00102.x

Okuboyejo, S., & Eyesan, O. (2014). mHealth: Using mobile technology to support healthcare. *Online Journal of Public Health Informatics, 5,* 233. doi:10.5210/ojphi.v5i3.4865

Phillips, M. L., & Kupfer, D. J. (2013). Bipolar disorder

diagnosis: Challenges and future directions. *Lancet, 381*(9878), 1663–1671. doi:10.1016/ S0140-6736(13)60989-7

Powell, J., Hamborg, T., Stallard, N., Burls, A., McSorley, J., Bennett, K., . . . Christensen, H. (2013). Effectiveness of a web-based cognitive-behavioral tool to improve mental well-being in the general population: Randomized controlled trial. *Journal of Medical Internet Research, 15*(1), e2. doi:10.2196/jmir.2240

Peterson, E. (1995) Communication barriers: 14 tips on teens. The National Parenting Center. Retrieved from http:// www. tnpc.com/parentalk/ adolescence/ teens49.html

Rice, E., Kurzban, S., & Ray, D. (2012). Homeless but connected: The role of heterogeneous social network ties and social networking technology in the mental health outcomes of street-living adolescents. *Community Mental Health Journal, 48,* 692–698. doi:10.1007/s10597-011-9462-1

Roberts, A. R. (2002). Assessment, crisis intervention, and trauma treatment: The integrative ACT intervention model. *Brief Treatment and Crisis Intervention,* 2, 1–22.

Roberts, A. R. (2005). Bridging the past and present to the future of crisis intervention and crisis management. In A. R. Roberts (Ed.), *Crisis intervention handbook: Assessment, treatment, and research* (3rd ed., pp. 3–34). New York: Oxford University Press.

Roberts, A. R., & Ottens, A. J. (2005). The seven-stage crisis intervention model: A road map to goal attainment, problem solving, and crisis resolution. *Brief Treatment and Crisis Intervention,*

5, 329–339. doi:10.1093/ brief-treatment/mhi030

Roth, A., & Fonagy, P. (2005). *What works for whom? A critical review of psychotherapy research* (2nd ed.). New York: Guilford Press.

Roy, E., Haley, N., Leclerc, P., Sochanski, B., Boudreau, J.-F., & Boivin, J.-F. (2004). Mortality in a cohort of street youth in Montreal. *Journal of the American Medical Association, 292,* 569–574. doi:10.1001/jama.292.5.569

Rudd, D. M, Joiner, T., & Rajab, H. M. (2001). *Treating suicidal behavior: An effective, time-limited approach.* New York: Guilford Press.

Salkever, D., Gibbons, B., & Ran, X. (2014). Do comprehensive, coordinated, recovery-oriented services alter the pattern of use of treatment services? Mental health treatment study impacts on SSDI beneficiaries' use of inpatient, emergency, and crisis services. *Journal of Behavioral Health Services and Research, 41,* 434–446.

Schimmelmann, B. G., Schmidt, S. J., Carbon, M., & Correll, C. U. (2013). Treatment of adolescents with early-onset schizophrenia spectrum disorders: In search of a rational, evidence-informed approach. *Current Opinion in Psychiatry, 26,* 219–230. doi:10.1097/ YCO.0b013e32835dcc2a

Schoenwald, S. K., Ward, D. M., Henggeler, S. W., & Rowland, M. D. (2000). Multisystemic therapy versus hospitalization for crisis stabilization of youth: placement outcomes 4 months postreferral. *Mental Health Services Research,* 2(1), 3–12.

Selekman, M. D. (2002). *Living on the razor's edge: Solution-oriented brief family therapy with self-harming adolescents.* New York: Norton.

Shea, S. C. (2002). *The practical art of suicide assessment: A guide for mental health professionals and substance abuse counselors.* Lexington, KY: Mental Health Presses.

Singer, J. B. (2005). Adolescent Latino males with schizophrenia: Mobile crisis response. *Brief Treatment and Crisis Intervention,* 5, 35–55. doi:10.1093/brief-treatment/mhi002

Singer, J. B. (2006). Making stone soup: Evidence-based practice for a suicidal youth with comorbid attention-deficit/hyperactivity disorder and major depressive disorder. *Brief Treatment and Crisis Intervention,* 6, 234–247. doi:10.1093/brief-treatment/mhl004

Singer, J. B. (Producer). (2011, May 19). #67 – National Runaway Switchboard: Interview with Maureen Blaha [Episode 67]. *Social Work Podcast* [Audio podcast]. Retrieved December 12, 2014 from http://www.socialworkpodcast.com/2011/05/national-runaway-switchboard-interview.html

Singer, J. B. (Producer). (2012, August 10). #73 - Non-suicidal self-injury (NSSI): Interview with Jennifer Muehlenkamp, Ph.D. [Episode 73]. *Social Work Podcast* [Audio podcast]. Retrieved December 12, 2014 from http://www.socialworkpodcast.com/2012/08/non-suicidal-self-injury-nssi-interview.html

Singer, J. B., & Dewane, C. (2010). Treating new social worker anxiety syndrome (NSWAS). *New Social Worker,* Summer. Retrieved from http://www.socialworker.com/feature-articles/career-jobs/Treating_New_Social_Worker_Anxiety_Syndrome_%28NSWAS%29/

Singer, J. B., & Greeno, C. M. (2013). When Bambi meets Godzilla: A practitioner's experience adopting and implementing a manualized treatment in a community mental health setting. *Best Practices in Mental Health,* 9(1), 99–115.

Singer, J. B., & Sage, M. (2015). Technology and social work practice: Micro, mezzo, and macro applications. In K. Corcoran (Ed.), *Social workers' desk reference* (3rd ed.). New York: Oxford University Press.

Singer, J. B., & Slovak, K. (2011). School social workers' experiences with youth suicidal behavior: An exploratory study. *Children and Schools,* 33, 215–228. doi:10.1093/cs/33.4.215

Slovak, K., & Singer, J. B. (2011). School social workers' perceptions of cyberbullying. *Children and Schools,* 33, 5–16. doi:10.1093/cs/33.1.5

Slovak, K., & Singer, J. B. (2012). Engaging parents of suicidal youth in a rural environment. *Child and Family Social Work,* 17, 212–221. doi:10.1111/j.1365-2206.2012.00826.x

Sobolewski, B., Richey, L., Kowatch, R. A., & Grupp-Phelan, J. (2013). Mental health follow-up among adolescents with suicidal behaviors after emergency department discharge. *Archives of Suicide Research,* 17, 323–334. doi:10.1080/13811118.2013.801807

Solomon, P. L., Cavanaugh, M. M., & Gelles, R. J. (2005). Family violence among adults with severe mental illness: A neglected area of research. *Trauma, Violence and Abuse,* 6(1), 40–54. doi:10.1177/1524838004272464

Substance Abuse and Mental Health Services Administration. (2010). *Results from the 2009 National Survey on Drug Use and Health: Mental health findings*. HHS Publication No. SMA 10-4609. Rockville, MD: Office of Applied Studies.

Ungar, M. (2012). Social ecologies and their contribution to resilience. In M. Ungar (Ed.), *The social ecology of resilience: A handbook of theory and practice* (pp. 13–32). New York: Springer.

Votta, E., & Manion, I. (2004). Suicide, high-risk behaviors, and coping style in homeless adolescent males' adjustment. *Journal of Adolescent Health* 34, 237–243. doi:10.1016/j.jadohealth.2003.06.002

Walls, N. E., & Bell, S. (2011). Correlates of engaging in survival sex among homeless youth and young adults. *Journal of Sex Research, 48,* 423–436. doi:10.1080/00224499.2010.501916

Wenzel, S., Holloway, I., Golinelli, D., Ewing, B., Bowman, R., & Tucker, J. (2012). Social networks of homeless youth in emerging adulthood. *Journal of Youth and Adolescence, 41,* 561–571. doi:10.1007/s10964-011-9709-8

Whitlock, J., Muehlenkamp, J. J., Eckenrode, J., Purington, A., Baral Abrams, G., Barreira, P., & Kress, V. (2013). Nonsuicidal self-injury as a gateway to suicide in young adults. *Journal of Adolescent Health, 52,* 486–492. doi:10.1016/j.jadohealth.2012.09.010

Wilmshurst, L. A. (2002). Treatment programs for youth with emotional and behavioral disorders: An outcome study of two alternate approaches. *Mental Health Services Research, 4*(2), 85–96.

# 12

# Crisis Intervention With Early Adolescents Who Have Suffered a Significant Loss

MARY SEAN O'HALLORAN

JANAE R. SONES

LAURA K. JONES

This chapter uses three examples to examine crisis intervention with early adolescents. We identify important developmental considerations in assessment, planning, intervention, and outcome evaluation and apply Roberts's (2005) seven-stage crisis intervention model in working with significant losses in the lives of youth. The losses include the death of loved ones, divorce, and the impact of exposure to violence outside the home; however, the issues we address can be generalized to other types of crises.

Adolescence is a time of significant physical, social, neurological, and psychological change (Anthony, Williams, & LeCroy, 2014; Busso, 2014). Because change is occurring rapidly during this period of life, writers in the field of adolescent development often divide this time into three periods: early adolescence, from about the age of 10 to 14; middle adolescence, from about 15 to 17; and late adolescence, roughly from 18 through 23 (Hooyman & Kramer, 2006). We focus on the first of these, early adolescence.

Adolescence has been characterized as a critical period in neurophysiological development (Marco, Macri, & Laviola, 2011). During this stage of development, the early adolescent brain not only faces structural modifications but also experiences significant synaptic refinement, regional integration, and hormonal and neurochemical surges particularly in relation to areas of the brain underlying cognitive control, emotional reactivity and regulation, motivation, risk taking, and social cognition (Blakemore, 2012b; Brenhouse & Andersen, 2011; Sturman & Moghaddam, 2011). For example, the prefrontal cortex of the brain (i.e., the area just behind the forehead) is critically important to cognitive control, regulation of emotional behaviors, and decision-making) and is among the last structures of the human brain to fully develop and establish sound connections with other key brain areas such as the limbic system (i.e., the key emotional center of the brain; Rahdar & Galván, 2014). Additionally, across adolescence peaks and functional shifts in the expression of specific dopamine receptors occurs in various brain areas, patterns that may underlie increased sensitivity to rewards and perhaps sensation-seeking behaviors (Blakemore & Robbins, 2012; Casey & Jones, 2010; Casey, Jones, & Hare, 2008). Such brain and physiological changes serve as the basis for many of the fundamental developmental tasks of adolescence, such as developing a sense of identity and autonomy, including clarification of values and a sense of purpose; increased decision-making abilities (Blakemore & Robbins, 2012); and relationship skills (Blakemore, 2012a; Burnett, Sebastian, Cohen, Kadosh, & Blakemore, 2011).

Erik Erikson (1959, 1963, 1968) wrote extensively on adolescent identity, and the reader is referred to his work on the eight stages of psychosocial development. Furthermore, Steinberg and Lerner (2004) referred to the shift in the field of developmental psychology to thinking of adolescence as a period "characterized by dramatic changes in the context, and not simply the content, of development" (p. 49), emphasizing that conflict with parents and siblings, mood disruptions, and engaging in risky behaviors are common to many, though certainly not all, adolescents (Steinberg & Sheffield Morris, 2001). During this time of already rapid change, the adolescent who is facing a crisis may be more seriously impacted than a person at a different developmental stage. Authors have concluded that given the significant structural, functional, and neurochemical shifts occurring during adolescence, the adolescent brain, much like the brain during early prenatal and early infancy periods, is maximally sensitive to environmental stress and trauma (Marco, Macri, & Laviola, 2011; Rahdar & Galván, 2014). For example, in summarizing a comprehensive body of literature, Eiland and Romeo (2013) indicate that the amygdala, prefrontal cortex, and hippocampus (i.e., a corticolimbic brain structure used in memory consolidation), which are still developing well into adolescence, are also among the most reactive and vulnerable to acute and pervasive stress and can undergo potentially long-lasting morphological and functional maladaptive changes as a result. Supporting such notions are findings that numerous mental health disorders have an onset during adolescence, which may be perpetuated by such stress sensitivity (Blakemore, 2012b; Spear, 2009). Findings such as this and an awareness of the distinct cognitive, social, and neurobiological capacities of this age group are critical for anyone doing crisis intervention in order to employ relevant, developmentally appropriate, and effective interventions.

We include, where pertinent, discussions of techniques drawn from brief therapies. Fosha (2004) states that in brief therapy, the belief is "work as if there were no next session" (p. 66); indeed, crisis intervention focuses on quickly helping a person in crisis to return to normal functioning. Given the nature of crisis situations and the effectiveness of short-term crisis modalities (e.g., Meir, Slone, Levis, Reina, & Livni, 2012; Vernberg et al., 2008), such approaches are preferable in crisis contexts.

As part of the increasing focus on evidence-based research (Lambert, 2013), the past decade has seen growing support for particular treatments for children and adolescents exposed to trauma and those who are dealing with grief and loss. These include specific interventions designed for children and adolescents with particular concerns, such as trauma-focused cognitive-behavioral therapy or grief-focused cognitive-behavioral therapy (Cohen, Mannarino, & Deblinger, 2006; Spuij, van Londen-Huiberts, & Boelen, 2013). Overall, most studies on grieving children and adolescents utilize a cognitive-behavioral framework, which has shown to be effective with other forms of trauma and useful when post-traumatic stress disorder (PTSD) symptoms are present with grief (Cohen et al., 2006).

The 2004 National Institute of Mental Health (NIMH) Workgroup on Child and Adolescent Mental Health Intervention Development and Deployment recommended that research focus on single disorders as opposed to assuming generalizability of treatment strategies across disorders (National Institute of Mental Health [NIMH], 2004). Recent research specifically addressing grief has examined spirituality and loss (Muselman & Wiggins, 2012), differences in bereavement and depressive symptomology following a parental death (Cerel, Fristad, Verducci, Weller, & Weller, 2006), the impact of a peer death (Malone, 2012), and complicated grief presentation following a parent's death (Melhem, Moritz, Walker, Shear, & Brent, 2007) as well as sibling death (Dickens, 2014). Moreover, Haine, Ayers, Sandler, and Wolchik (2008) outline evidence-based best practices for working with children and adolescents who have been parentally bereaved. Their review summarized several factors that impact a child's response to grief and suggestions for practitioners. Many studies do not specifically address early adolescents; commonly, the age range of participants is from 6 to 18 (e.g., Cerel et al., 2006) or includes high school–aged adolescents (aged 15–18; e.g., Malone, 2012).

We illustrate how Roberts's model can be applied to early adolescents using three cases, detailed in the following.

---

### Jenny

Jenny, a 13-year-old White girl, has suffered a series of significant losses. This past year her parents divorced, following several years of progressive deterioration of her father's health due to alcoholism, and, most recently, her beloved grandmother died. Jenny has become increasingly withdrawn from friends and family, less active in school, and more worried about her appearance; she has lost nearly 10 pounds. Her brothers notice that Jenny spends more time alone in her room online, playing video games and checking her Facebook account, and has stopped going to their baseball games. Feeling that relationships end in tragedy and that there is little she can control, Jenny avoids closeness and seeks to control her life through rigorous diet and exercise. The model discussed by Roberts (2005) to help intervene in a crisis situation demonstrates how brief therapies are helpful in assisting an early adolescent who is forced to cope after a series of losses.

## Esperanza

The case of Esperanza demonstrates the utility of Roberts's model in stabilizing an adolescent in crisis after a serious loss, the death of a beloved parent. Esperanza is a Mexican-American girl of 12. Five months ago, her parents were snowmobiling in the mountains when the vehicle spun out of control and they were thrown off. Her mother was hurt but recovered within a month;, however, her father broke his neck and died. Since then, Esperanza has had great difficulty sleeping and concentrating. The academic work she once took great pride in has suffered, and her grades have dropped so precipitously that she may not pass seventh grade. She is very depressed and posted on Facebook that she wants to die.

In this case, special attention was paid to Esperanza's lethality. A lethality assessment, the first step in Roberts's model, was combined with the second step of relationship building. This case demonstrates how the application of Roberts's model provides a heuristic and sensible approach to assisting an adolescent after a tragedy.

## Peter

The case of Peter allows us to examine the utility of Roberts's model following a tragic and catastrophic event where the early adolescent does not perceive that he can ask for help until a later date.

It appeared to be a routine Tuesday morning at Franklin Middle School. Yet, shortly before noon, a call came to the principal's office from the school district superintendent concerning an "incident" at the nearby high school. The high school was put on lockdown as it became clear that several students had been shot. Administrators told Mr. Hernandez, the middle school principal, that they would provide directions for how they would like middle school children and their families to be informed. The school district administrators worked quickly to develop a statement and contact parents of high school students, aware that word would quickly spread via social networking sites. Mr. Hernandez asked the lead school counselor, Ms. Lee, to be prepared to meet with any middle school students who might be at risk or closely impacted due to having siblings at the high school. Mr. Hernandez, learning that word had already spread among his students, called Peter and three other students whose siblings were rumored to have been shot to meet with Ms. Lee and to help facilitate reunions with the children's parents.

In these cases the counselor needs to convey genuine respect for and acceptance of the client in order to offer reassurance (Stanley, Small, Owen, & Burke, 2012).

---

## CRISIS IN THE LIVES OF EARLY ADOLESCENTS

Crises impact the lives of children and adolescents as a result of experiences as close to home as child abuse and divorce and as far away, for some, as Hurricane Sandy, the massacres at Sandy Hook Elementary School and an Aurora, Colorado movie theater, the terrorist attacks of September 11, 2001, and wars throughout the world. Natural and human-made events precipitate crises; we are exposed to these events daily, either personally or through the media. Crises are typically distinguished in two ways: a one-time, acute crisis or a more chronic state of crisis. Many authors use different language for this distinction. For example, Terr (1990) used the terms *Type I crisis* (an acute single event) and *Type II crisis* (the result of seemingly unremitting and prolonged events). Now, although these terms are not included in the *Diagnostic and Statistical Manual of Mental Disorders* (American Psychiatric Association, 2013), this distinction is commonly made using Herman's (1992) phrase "complex trauma," to describe repeated instances or forms of trauma (e.g., Ford & Courtois, 2013). Most discussions of crisis intervention focus on a single experience of trauma, which Roberts (1996) refers to as an "acute situational crisis":

> A sudden and unpredictable event takes place... the individual or family members perceive the event as an imminent threat to their life, psychological well-being, or social functioning; the individual tries to cope, escape the dangerous situation, gain necessary support from a significant other or close relative or friend, and/or adapt by changing one's lifestyle or environment; coping attempts fail and the person's severe emotional state of imbalance escalates into a full-blown crisis. (p. 17)

We discuss immediate, short-term responses to difficult, acute, and intense events (Roberts, 2005). Unlike longer-term psychotherapy, crisis intervention is aimed at helping clients regain psychological homeostasis and return to their usual level of functioning and does not focus on treatment of long-standing psychopathology (Yeager & Roberts, 2005). In many cases, crisis intervention is precisely what is needed to assist an adolescent in crisis, but it is important to remember that, in other situations, more intensive therapy or ongoing support will be needed. It is essential to assess each individual's specific needs carefully and to remember that access to longer-term psychotherapy—such as trauma-focused cognitive-behavioral therapy (Cohen et al., 2006) or an adolescent grief and loss group (Malone, 2012)—may be especially important for individuals who have experienced prolonged and repeated crises. Crisis intervention may be very useful when an early adolescent has experienced a violent event, if such an event has happened to someone close to him or her, or if the early adolescent has faced personal loss through the death of a loved one or divorce.

## Scope of the Problem and Clinical Considerations

Among early adolescents, crises can take many forms, and the impact of these can vary greatly among individuals. Particular vulnerabilities and risk factors are discussed later; here, it is important to note that no adolescent is protected from the effects of a crisis by gender, culture, or socioeconomic status. Our examples focus on crises brought on by the impact of violence outside the home, loss due to the death of a loved one, and the divorce of parents.

Violence is all too common in the lives of youth, whether by direct exposure in their communities, homes, or schools, or through indirect exposure from media or online social networking. Violence claimed the lives of more than 8,000 young people in the United States in 2010 (Heron, 2013). In addition, the top three leading causes of death for adolescents were all related to violence: accidents, homicide, and suicide (Heron, 2013). Daily, seven young people under the age of 19 are killed by firearms (Children's Defense Fund [CDF], 2013). Violence is pervasive in school settings as well. In 2011, almost 8% of high school students reported being threatened or injured with a weapon on school property (US Census Bureau, 2012). In 2010, 828,000 students aged 12 to 18 reported being victims of nonfatal crimes on school property (US Census Bureau, 2012). Tragically, there has been a dramatic increase in deadly violence in schools, such as the shooting at Sandy Hook Elementary School in Newtown, Connecticut, in December 2012 (Fox & DeLateur, 2014) and the mass stabbing at Franklin Regional Senior High School in Murrysville, Pennsylvania, in April 2014 (Mandak, 2014).

Other crises are common in the lives of early adolescents. In the United States in 2009, more than 1.1 million children and adolescents were growing up in homes where divorce had occurred in the past year (US Census, 2009). Divorce, though often considered a family crisis, may also be seen as an opportunity for positive change and growth (Cui, Fincham, & Durtschi, 2011). Amato and Anthony (2014) utilized national data sets to determine the effects of divorce on children and adolescents. They found that divorce and, to a lesser extent, other family disruptions (i.e., military deployment) were associated with consistent decreases in child and adolescent well-being. Specifically, parental divorce resulted in lowered self-control and reading and math achievement, as well as increased externalizing behavior. Yet, these trends were different for parental relationships with more risk factors for divorce, such as lowered socioeconomic status. For example, children whose parents had a lower propensity for divorce actually had increased reading achievement and self-control following parental divorce (Amato & Anthony, 2014). Research such as this helps practitioners provide treatment with greater specificity and develop prevention efforts that are more effective and relevant to their community.

The death of a parent or caregiver is one of the most significant and serious losses, especially for an early adolescent who is still dependent on the adult's care and support. The bonds of attachment at this age can be very strong; such writers as Bowlby (1980) and Worden (1996) have explored the impact of parental death on children and adolescents in depth. Neurophysiological research also suggests that the release of gonadal hormones during adolescence (e.g., estrogen) is strongly correlated with an increased expression of oxytocin, a hormone related to social attachment and pair-bonding that can lead to an increased sensitivity to social stimuli and memory for social information (Steinberg, 2008).

Data indicate that 4% of youths under age 18 in the United States live with a widowed parent; the numbers are significantly lower for those who live with a surviving father than for those who live with a surviving mother (US Census Bureau, 2012). In addition to those who will lose a parent or caregiver to death, many early adolescents will experience the loss of a sibling, peer, or grandparent. In a study with more than 2,000 adolescents, only 7% had not experienced a death of either a family member, a friend, or a pet (Harrison & Harrington, 2001). Recent work has emphasized that parental loss may further complicate early adolescent developmental tasks and determined four areas that are commonly impacted by both: identity, relationships with external friends and family, bodily preoccupation, and abandonment and exclusion (Keenan, 2014). Additionally, Brent, Melhem, Masten, Porta, and Payne (2012) found that adolescents struggling with parental bereavement can experience long-term developmental competency deficits in work, career planning, peer attachment, and future educational aspirations. Other researchers have explored the impact of sibling and peer death (e.g., Dickens, 2014; Malone, 2012; Webb, 2010).

Complicated grief, or grief lasting more than 15 months that is characterized by an inability to accept the grief, high levels of emotional and/or behavioral problems, and difficulty returning to a normal state of functioning (Auman, 2007), is particularly difficult to treat and leads to poor wellness outcomes in adolescents. Risk factors for complicated grief include traumatic deaths, high emotional reaction by caregiver, type of relationship with deceased, inadequate emotional support from caregivers, and poor family communication (Dickens, 2014). Warning signs indicating complicated grief in adolescents include anger, guilt, somatic concerns, social withdrawal, feeling forgotten by their family, and problems with school performance (Dickens, 2014).

## ASSESSMENT: VULNERABILITIES, RISK FACTORS, AND COPING

It is difficult to predict how an early adolescent will react to a crisis. As an adolescent develops, the path of his or her life is marked by thousands of events that vary in the magnitude, duration, and meaning they have for the person. Individuals react quite differently to similar life events, so understanding that variability is at the heart of stress research is critical to identifying how individuals will react to a crisis situation. Furthermore, during this period of neurological, behavioral, social, and contextual transition, an early adolescent must cope with many biological and environmental stressors, including puberty, new experiences, increased responsibilities, and developing future plans and goals. Adding financial hardship of the family, educational challenges, societal prejudice, illness, and other external acute stressors increases an early adolescent's vulnerability to a crisis event.

Adolescents cope with stressors in many different ways, and identifying risk factors that predispose individuals to maladaptive coping after a crisis is an important domain of research. Initially, research focused mostly on internal cognitive or biological factors, indicating that expectations about the world and attributions about the causes of events are particularly important in determining responses to acute stressors. Early adolescents' coping processes and subsequent adjustment are dependent on how they appraise a stressful situation and what attributions they make concerning who is responsible for the outcome (Seligman, 2007). Rueger and Malecki (2011) found that young adolescents with more pessimistic attributional styles and low levels of parental support were more vulnerable to developing symptoms of depression during extreme times of stress. Finally, Young, LaMontagne, Dietrich, and Wells (2012) completed a study with early adolescents on the association between negative life events and cognitive vulnerabilities (e.g., dysfunctional attitudes) in the development of depressive symptoms. A ruminative response style, or focusing a negative emotional state without taking action to change, was strongly associated with negative life events and consequently more symptoms of depression.

Specific neurobiological and physiological correlates of susceptibility to crisis responses have also been identified. For example, in a classic monozygotic twin study, the volume of the hippocampus contributed to adverse psychological consequences following traumatic events (Gilbertson et al., 2002). Other authors highlight the complex interaction between intrinsic factors (e.g., temperament, biological predisposition) and extrinsic factors (e.g., social support) in the capacity to cope with stressful or crisis situations (Keller & Feeny, 2014). Furthermore, differences in symmetry of frontal lobe activation have been noted in response to stress and threat in the environment; specifically, higher right frontal lobe activation in children has been shown to be indicative of fearful, anxious, and negative responses (Pérez-Edgar, Kujawa, Nelson, Cole, & Zapp, 2013; Ishikawa et al., 2014). Other styles more reflective of temperament (such as a depressive, stress-reactive, or psychosomatic style) may also reflect the potential for a negative outcome following a crisis event. In a recent meta-analysis examining the effects of personality factors on responses to stress, Jakšić, Brajković, Ivezić, Topić, and Jakovljević (2012) found a direct relationship between negative emotionality, neuroticism, harm avoidance, trait hostility, and trait anxiety, as well as lower levels of extraversion, and conscientiousness with adverse outcomes.

Research has also focused on the sociocultural and familial factors that increase risk for maladaptive coping. In 2005, Miller and Townsend highlighted the reliance on middle-class, White participants to understand adolescent stressors, thus limiting our knowledge of the experience of adolescents from other backgrounds and cultures. From the adult literature, we know that racial and ethnic minority groups in the United States experience more stress symptoms than do individuals of European descent (Pole, Gone, & Kulkarni, 2008) and that these groups experience more stress related to perceived discrimination or microaggressions (Sue & Sue, 2013). Poverty and socioeconomic status (SES) must be considered important factors in understanding levels of coping. For example, Reiss (2013) conducted a meta-analysis evaluating the effects of SES on general mental health outcomes for children and adolescents. She identified an inverted relationship between at least one aspect of SES (e.g., parental unemployment, parent education, household income) and mental health, with children and adolescents having a two to three times greater risk for mental health concerns if they came from a socioeconomically challenged family. Region of residence may also be an important factor in determining risk. In a seminal study looking at these differences, Atav and Spencer (2002) compared the health risk behaviors between rural, suburban, and urban adolescents; rural students were at significantly higher risk for smoking, drinking, drug use, teen pregnancy, and carrying a weapon. These findings have been replicated consistently over the years (e.g., Curtis, Waters, & Brindis, 2011), highlighting the paucity of resources and the often lower SES of rural communities as compounding risks for poorer health outcomes. Furthermore, Hackman, Farah, and Meaney (2010) detailed the influence of SES on brain development, particularly areas responsible for language and executive function, and highlighted the mediating roles of prenatal factors, parental care, and cognitive stimulation in such effects. This points to the need for family-based interventions, considering the critical impact of external risk factors on early adolescents, an important emphasis we demonstrate through the three case studies presented in this chapter.

Finally, at least some aspects of risk factors can vary with gender, although the research on this is inconclusive. Using a longitudinal design, Werner and Smith (2001) found that in childhood, boys seem to have more mental health problems, with the trend reversing during adolescence, with girls encountering more problems, which are directly related to stressful life events. Additionally, specific vulnerabilities are correlated with gender. Males tended to have increased vulnerability related to parental psycho-pathology and with substance abuse issues, whereas females seemed more vulnerable to lasting effects of childhood and adolescent illnesses and problems in relationships with their families, mothers in particular. Gerson and Rappaport (2013) report that girls may be more impacted by earlier trauma than boys. In a recent meta-analysis of 64 empirical studies, Trickey, Siddaway, Meiser-Stedman, Serpell, and Fields (2012) found support for earlier research indicating that being female was a significant risk factor for developing PTSD, especially in the context of intentional, human-caused traumatic events. It is important to note, however, that some research has found discrepancies in the magnitude of gender differences when comparing early, middle, and late adolescence (Young et al., 2012).

With changes in the United States healthcare model, assessing the outcome of crisis intervention (e.g., coping or changes in symptomology) is important. Outcome measures usually consist of symptom severity checklists, such as the Impact of Events Scale (Chasson, Vincent, & Harris, 2008) or the Oregon Mental Health Referral Checklists (Corcoran, 2005). A comprehensive, self-report checklist often used in research (e.g., Goldstein et al., 2011) to assess PTSD symptoms in children is the Trauma Symptom Checklist for Children (TSCC; Briere, 1996), a 54-item checklist assessing anxiety, depression, post-traumatic stress, anger, dissociation, and sexual concerns. Self-report measures may be difficult for early adolescents to complete, so some experts recommend structured clinical interviews, such as the Clinician Administered PTSD Scale for Children and Adolescents (Nader et al., 1996), as the "gold standard" in PTSD assessment (Rosner, Arnold, Groh, & Hagl, 2012). Importantly, research suggests that using subscales on the Child Behavior Checklist, a broad symptom assessment, is not effective for assessing PTSD; instead, specific PTSD measures are recommended (Rosner et al., 2012).

## RESILIENCE AND PROTECTIVE FACTORS

Although research on what makes an individual respond in a maladaptive manner to an acute stressor is important for understanding what makes some individuals more susceptible to crisis than others, by itself this research offers a limited view. Instead, in the past decade, research on how people maintain mental health in the face of crises has gained prominence. Researchers have increasingly studied resilient persons who grew up in aversive environments yet became productive, caring adults. Resilience has been described as the ability to bounce back from trauma (Davidson et al., 2005), adaptive coping, and creation of positive outcomes after experiencing adversity (Bonanno, Galea, Bucciarelli, & Vlahov, 2007). Mash and Dozois (2003) defined the resilient child as one who manages to avoid negative outcomes and/or achieve positive outcomes despite being at significant risk for the development of psychopathology, who displays sustained competence under stress, and who shows recovery from trauma.

Internal psychological and external social or familial forces that contribute to resilience have been identified. Following Wekerle and Wolfe's (2003) work discussing the importance of one's mood and ability to regulate mood states, Davis and Humphrey (2012) found that adolescents with higher emotional intelligence (understanding and regulation of emotions) experienced lower symptomology when they did not have a complex trauma history, like the three adolescents in our case studies.

Additionally, Braun-Lewensohn et al. (2009) conducted a study examining the most effective coping strategies of adolescents (aged 12–18) following a traumatic event. Results indicated that problem-focused coping (e.g., "Work at solving the problem to the best of my ability," p. 592) was the most weakly associated strategy with post-traumatic stress symptoms, followed by reference to others (e.g., "Talk to other people about my concern," p. 592) and nonproductive coping (e.g., "Worry about what will happen to me," p. 592) and indicated better well-being. Considering that crisis intervention typically follows a short-term, problem-solving model for coping, these findings have marked implications for crisis intervention and provide support for its usage.

Other protective factors that contribute to resilience include developing a cultural and racial identity, adequate support from an adult figure, a sense of curiosity, and involvement in organized activities that promote wellness (Zimmerman et al., 2013). The specific factors that may be most important for a given individual vary. For example, Singh (2013) examined resiliency factors with transgender youth (aged 15–23) of color, a population that appears through early research to be at higher risk for relational and environmental stressors. Similarly to other research, developing a racial/gender identity and social support in the LGBTQQ community were important for resilience; uniquely, use of social media to establish identity was also important. Future research could determine if the use of social media (i.e., Facebook, Twitter, Instagram) for other adolescents may also be key to fostering resilience.

The ultimate goal in the study of resilience is to design interventions that further reduce risk factors and/or increase protective factors, and such interventions may have implications for crisis intervention. Preventative interventions are less documented in reference to crisis intervention; there is much more research in the context of depression and substance use, and in a school setting or primary care setting (Green et al., 2013; Knapp & Foy, 2012). Some of the work on attributional and problem-solving style already mentioned provides promising solutions to this. In addition, Elliott, Kaliski, Burrus, and Roberts (2013) synthesized current research on resilience and provide a "blueprint" to foster and build resilience in adolescents, including modeling, positive reinforcement, and creating positive self-evaluations.

Finally, the study of post-traumatic growth (PTG) in children and adolescents is gaining more attention. PTG emphasizes gaining strength or a positive outlook *after* a traumatic event, including making positive changes to self and increased life satisfaction (Levine, Laufer, Stein, Hamama-Raz, & Solomon, 2009). Wolchik, Coxe, Tein, Sandler, and Ayers (2008) followed parentally bereaved adolescents over 6 years and found that intrapersonal coping, interpersonal coping, and seeking support from another parent or guardian had a significant positive effect on certain factors of PTG. Developmental stage can also change PTG; for example, young adolescents have more flexible worldviews and thus may be more prone to view the world as one extreme following trauma (e.g., the world is a wholly dangerous place; Kilmer, 2006).

## CASE EXAMPLES

We now examine three case studies in light of Roberts's (2005) seven-stage model of intervention: (1) assess psychosocial needs, especially lethality, (2) establish rapport, (3) identify major problems, (4) deal with feelings, (5) explore alternatives, (6) generate an action plan to put these alternatives into practice, and (7) follow up.

### Jenny: Parental Divorce, Paternal Alcoholism, and Death of Grandmother

Jenny is a 13-year-old, White, middle-class American girl whose parents, Bill and Emily, both aged 40, divorced a year ago following several years of progressive deterioration of her father's health and increased absences from home due to alcoholism. She is the eldest child, with two younger brothers, aged 10 and 8. For the past 2 years, her mother has become increasingly involved in her work as an administrator for a health care network and is the sole contributor to family finances. Jenny and her family have less contact with Bill. He moved to a nearby town, where he owns an apartment complex.

Prior to the separation, when her father's health was worsening, Jenny could talk to her mother and grandmother about her sadness for and anger toward her father. He had been through several treatment programs but never followed through with aftercare. After the last treatment failure, Emily filed for divorce. Although Jenny tried to talk to her mother, Emily had grown bitter and responded, "Your father can't or won't get beyond his problems, but we can do better than that. It is time to move on." Jenny felt sad that she could not talk to her mother and turned to her grandmother, Margaret, who provided significant emotional support and comfort.

However, 2 months ago, Jenny's beloved grandmother died. Jenny became increasingly withdrawn from friends and family. Although she became quieter and seemed mostly sad, she had several angry outbursts at her mother and her brothers. She frequently woke at night crying and complained to her mother that she was afraid to go back to sleep for fear her nightmares would return. She frequently dreamed that she was hiking up a mountain with family and friends. Whenever she turned around, someone had gotten lost and she could not find them. As darkness fell, she was alone on the mountain with the cold night approaching.

Over the past month, Jenny had become increasingly worried about her appearance and had lost nearly 10 pounds. Her mother worried that Jenny was eating less and spending more time running and swimming than was healthy. She noticed Jenny's online search history included phrases such as "How to lose weight fast" and "diet secrets," which she found concerning. Jenny's brothers noticed that Jenny spent more time alone in her room online and playing video games and had stopped going to their baseball games.

## Crisis Intervention: Application of Roberts's Seven-Stage Model

Jenny's mother was worried, and at the recommendation of the school counselor, she set up an appointment for herself and her daughter with a counselor in the community. Early in crisis intervention it is essential to assess lethality and establish rapport with a client (Roberts, 2005). Although the counselor, Lena, encouraged both Emily and Jenny to talk, Jenny was hesitant to disclose her feelings, saying that there was nothing anyone could do because her grandmother was gone and her dad was too sick to care. Lena was able to establish a relationship with Jenny by respecting and acknowledging her feeling of hopelessness that anything would change regarding the death of her grandmother, her father's alcoholism, and her parents' divorce. She affirmed the myriad feelings Jenny's losses engendered, such as sadness, anger, guilt, and anxiety, and pointed out that sometimes people feel sick and tired and may act out (Worden, 2008), but that these feelings can be common for preadolescents under similar circumstances. Lena encouraged Jenny by stating that teens often find it helpful to talk about losses in counseling. She conveyed that she could help Jenny develop new ways to cope with and manage her feelings. She mentioned that she had worked with other teens who suffered losses and that, although each person is different, people have some similar experiences when bad things happen. Jenny cried as she told Lena that her grandmother was "the one person who believed in me, no matter what. My dad left and has not done much with us the last couple of years. Now my mom has to work so much. I know she loves us, but has too much to do and Gram was always there for me." Jenny feared that the people she loved would leave her through illness or death and thought that maybe it was better to be alone and not depend on people. She reasoned, "Everyone leaves for some reason, and if I don't need people too much, I won't be so sad if something bad happens." Lena accurately understood Jenny's concerns and, using open-ended questions, probed further and discovered that Jenny's fear of losing people was part of the reason she had withdrawn from friends.

Jenny disclosed that sometimes she wished she could be with her grandmother. The counselor inquired further, and Jenny stated that if she were dead, she would be with her grandmother. Lena asked if Jenny had thought about suicide, and Jenny said she had, but that she would never do it because she knew how sad it would make her mother. Lena conducted a brief suicide assessment, asking Jenny about ways she had thought of killing herself. Jenny was vague, saying, "I don't know, maybe a lot of aspirin." The counselor asked Jenny to scale her suicidal thoughts from 1 to 10, with 1 being "not at all" and 10 being "very serious" (see Berman, Jobes, & Silverman, 2006, for more on adolescent suicide risk assessment). Jenny responded, "It's 1. I could never do that to my family and my Gram would not like that." Lena reflected back that even in death, Jenny's grandmother's opinion was very important.

Although the reason for seeking services was primarily Jenny's response to her grandmother's death, Lena was also aware of the divorce and wanted to explore that as well. Kaufman and Kaufman (2005) note that in situations of grief with multiple losses like Jenny's, stresses that are superimposed on one another will affect each person differently, but the combined impact of multiple stressors is more likely to lead to greater problems, such as fragmentation of coping abilities.

In the third stage of the crisis intervention model, therapists work to develop a focus for intervention. Jenny's counselor examined the number and significance of the recent losses Jenny had experienced and noted that her grandmother's death was the most recent in a series of losses. Roberts (2005) discusses the importance of identifying the precipitating event that leads a client to seek help; this may be the "last straw," but if many events led to the crisis, problems must be prioritized so that a central focus can be developed. Jenny's counselor asked her to identify the important events she thought led to her being in counseling. Jenny expressed anger that she has had too much to deal with and is tired of so many bad things happening. Lena asked an open-ended question: "What are the losses you are thinking of right now?" Jenny explained about her father's increasing withdrawal from home, the nights spent away from his family, her mother becoming so busy with work, her parents' divorce, and the humiliation of her family having to move into a smaller house due to financial problems.

Lena acknowledged and further explored Jenny's feelings. Jenny agreed that the divorce was hard on her because her mom was so sad, but that her father had been "missing" for a long time, and it was better than staying married. She had not discussed the divorce much, except with her grandmother, and she still found it hard to believe her parents were divorced: "I had such a great childhood, and I kept thinking if Daddy could find the right hospital he would be better and things could be like they were." With such a long list of events, Roberts (2005) suggests it may be helpful to rank them by priority to clarify a focus. Jenny identified her grandmother's death and her parents' divorce as most concerning to her.

After major problems have been identified, the therapist should prioritize encouraging and exploring feelings, which is the focus of the fourth intervention stage. Throughout counseling, Lena used active listening and other foundational counseling skills to develop a relationship and to encourage Jenny to express her feelings. Lena consistently linked past experiences with the present through use of such skills as paraphrasing, reflection, and open-ended questions. Although conversation was the most common vehicle for expression, Jenny loved to paint and write poetry; creative outlets allowed her to better access and explore her feelings. The literature is replete with useful strategies for helping children of different ages work through grief (see Silverman, 2000; Webb, 2010; Worden, 2008).

Jenny angrily admitted that she had closed herself off to her father because he yelled a lot and was mean; to feel better, she had chosen to spend more time with people who were "good" to her, such as her grandmother and friends. Her feelings about moving to a smaller house included embarrassment at having to move from "a big house with a pool table in the basement where my friends could hang out to a small house with so few rooms that my brothers have to share a room. Even though it was hard to move, it is better than leaving my school and friends." Jenny had also spent time writing in her journal and doing artwork, which she found relaxing. Although those activities helped her to cope, now she worried that she was "too sad" and that her friends would not want to be around her anymore.

Lena mentioned that sometimes when people are distressed and things feel out of control they try to control what is within their own reach, such as their weight. Jenny mentioned that her cheerleading coach, trying to be helpful, suggested that exercise was helpful in improving her own mood; thus Jenny, searching for ways to feel better, began to exercise more and more. Some friends noticed that she looked thinner and complimented her on it, whereupon Jenny thought maybe dieting and cutting out sweets might help her lose the few pounds she had gained over the winter.

Although the fourth stage of the crisis intervention model focuses on exploring and expressing feelings, it is important to note that such exploration occurs in most stages of intervention. Throughout the counseling process it is imperative that a counselor stay attuned to the child's needs and respond in an empathic way. In the fifth stage, emphasis is placed on assessing past coping attempts, developing alternatives, and designing specific solutions. While listening to Jenny, Lena was particularly attentive to ways Jenny coped effectively so she could reinforce adaptive behaviors and cognitions. With Lena's help, Jenny explored how she had handled past stressors such as her parents' divorce, moving, and her father's alcoholism. As noted earlier, Jenny found it helpful to spend more time with people who were good to her, such as friends and her grandmother. She had also reframed the move to a smaller house as not so bad because it was better than having to leave her school, and she often journalled. Although these activities had helped in the past, Jenny complained that they were not working now, and, furthermore, she had lost one of her strongest supporters. Roberts (2005) notes that clinicians may need to take the initiative when clients have little insight or are emotionally distressed. Jenny felt disappointed that former coping strategies either were unavailable or that she could not seem to use them effectively.

It is sometimes helpful to learn about what others have done to cope (Supiano, 2012); thus, Lena asked if Jenny would like to hear about how some of her other clients managed when they experienced losses. Because Jenny seemed interested, Lena told her about a boy whose favorite uncle had died. The boy talked about feelings, as Jenny did, and then created a way to let go of some of his problems. One technique was to imagine inhaling his anger and pain deep into his lungs and then exhaling those feelings into a balloon, then taking the balloon outside and letting the feelings go by releasing the balloon into the air. He also wrote a letter to his uncle about the wonderful things they had done together and read this to his counselor. Afterward, they explored how he felt doing this and what he found helpful.

Lena asked Jenny to imagine she was a counselor; what coping strategies would she recommend to a 13- or 14-year-old who was dealing with so many losses? Jenny laughed and insisted on sitting in Lena's chair as she assumed the role of an expert. Jenny had a plethora of ideas: spending time with close friends and family, writing feelings on sticky-notes and then sticking the notes on a wall to create a poem, painting feelings, cutting images and words from magazines and creating a collage, engaging in relaxing activities, taking bubble baths, watching funny movies, and exercising.

One coping strategy Lena wanted to address was Jenny's exercise behavior and weight loss. She conveyed her concern that this could exacerbate problems. Jenny felt good about losing weight; she argued that she been a little overweight and that exercise was healthy. Lena also worked with clients who had eating disorders and was aware of the futility in arguing about weight. Instead, she focused on the effectiveness, or lack thereof, of Jenny's using diet and excessive exercise to feel better about herself. Jenny admitted she felt tired and had problems concentrating if she did not eat enough and that, although she enjoyed exercise, it was starting to feel all-consuming to her.

> Lena: On a scale of 1 to 10, with 1 being tired and 10 being very energetic, where are you?
>
> Jenny: I'd like to say 8, but I feel like a 4 today.
>
> Lena: Okay, what would it take to move that to a 5 or 6?
>
> Jenny: Get some sleep!
>
> Lena: How can you do that today?
>
> Jenny: Hmm. I woke up hungry, so if I ate more and exercised a little less, I think I would have more energy.
>
> Lena: What are you willing to do today to move in that direction?
>
> Lena: I will eat dinner and just go for a short bike ride instead of for an hour. Then I will have time to relax before bedtime.

The focus shifted from weight and food to helping Jenny feel more energetic. Reframing the problem encouraged Jenny to see she had solutions for her problems. Jenny and Lena spoke openly about Jenny's parents' divorce and about her depression, eating disorder loss, and grief. Jenny also explored helpful and healthy websites and blogs from teens who had dealt with similar concerns. Through talking, artwork, and writing poetry, Jenny began to understand that many of her feelings of loneliness, anger, sadness, and depression were rooted in the multiple losses she experienced and that it was normal to have problems when such events occurred. Jenny talked about her feelings in counseling and thought up ways to reconnect with people who were important to her, especially those she said "believed in" her. Jenny decided to spend more time with her mom's younger sister Jane, a favorite aunt, and to see her friends more often.

In a group meeting Jenny and Lena spoke with Emily, Jane, and the school counselor; all agreed that Jenny had suffered many losses and needed their support. Jane arranged her schedule to have weekly "dates" with Jenny. They took hikes, went to movies, and had dinner. Emily shifted responsibilities so she would have fewer evening meetings and could spend more time with her children. Emily was also more sensitive to her daughter's feelings and created opportunities for Jenny to share her thoughts and feelings. The school counselor suggested that Jenny speak to one or two of her closest friends so they would know what had been going on. Jenny practiced what to say, talked with her friends, and found that they had been worried about her and were eager to help. The school counselor, apprised of the cheerleading coach's recommendation, considered ways he could consult with school staff to help children cope more effectively with loss and grief.

In the sixth stage of the crisis intervention model, a critical step requires moving from generating ideas to developing and implementing an action plan. As Jenny began to feel better, was listened to, and had more energy, she felt capable of taking more action. She began to create artwork to better express, understand, and manage her feelings. Some of her collages expressed anger and sadness, but others expressed hope and a future orientation. She created a poem about loss and change that was later published in a collection by young authors. She felt proud for turning her grief and anger into hope and a published work.

In the follow-up stage of crisis intervention, at both 1 month and 2 months after counseling was formally terminated, Jenny was functioning well and was satisfied that counseling had helped her through a difficult period of her life.

## Esperanza: Parental Death

Esperanza is a 12-year-old Mexican American girl. She lives on a small ranch with her family, who raise llamas and horses. She has three older sisters (aged 18, 16, and 15), a younger brother (aged 10), and a horse named Cookie. Her mother, Ana, is 41 and co-owns an insurance business in a small town with her brother. Her father, Michael, ran the family business until his tragic death 5 months ago. Ana and Michael were snowmobiling in the mountains when the vehicle spun out of control and they were thrown off. Her mother broke her leg and had other minor injuries. Her father broke his neck and died.

In the first few months after their father's death, Esperanza and her siblings openly mourned his loss and took great care of their mother, who alternated between weeping and openly worrying for her children. Due to her injuries, the children took care of the cleaning, cooking, and ranch work. The eldest, Camille, who was just beginning college, took a semester off to help. She ran the home smoothly and was efficient in helping the other children get ready for school and complete their homework and chores. The other sisters, Luisa and Margaret, although devastated by their father's death, spent much time together and began a project gathering together family photos and making a digital photo album to dedicate to their father's memory. The youngest, Martin, although very often distracted and sad, spent a lot of time with his cousins at his aunt and uncle's house a few miles from home.

After her father's death, Esperanza had difficulty sleeping and concentrating. She complained of stomachaches to her older sister, Luisa, who gave her teas to soothe her stomach and told Esperanza not to bother their mother. Her academic work, in which she once took great pride, suffered; her grades dropped so precipitously that she was in danger of failing seventh grade. She was alternately very passive or aggressive at school. She posted on Facebook that she wanted to die. She thought the rest of her family was "managing" better than she. Esperanza told Luisa she felt responsible for their father's death and that their mother must be very angry with her.

One of the cousins who was in Esperanza's class reported to Ana what she had seen on Facebook. Ana immediately went to Esperanza, who denied feeling suicidal and said she did not mean what she had posted. However, Esperanza cried for hours after this and kept repeating that it was her fault her father died. Ana, who is devoutly Catholic, contacted her parish priest, a warm and thoughtful man with a reputation for being available during times of crisis. He came to the house and spoke with all of the family to see how they were doing; finally, he spoke with Esperanza in the presence of her mother. Esperanza was inconsolable and wailed that she wanted to be with her father and that her father might forgive her if she could be with him. No one could figure out why Esperanza felt so responsible. At last Father Romero recommended that Ana call a counselor he knew who was helpful in working with grieving children. Esperanza and Ana made an appointment and the following week met with the counselor, whose office was 30 minutes away.

## Crisis Intervention: Application of Roberts's Seven-Stage Model

Given the concern expressed by those close to Esperanza (that she was considering suicide and seemingly inconsolable), it was essential for her counselor to quickly establish a relationship with her. This required, empathy, respect, and genuineness (Joiner, Orden, Witte, & Rudd, 2009; Roberts, 2000; Rogers, 1965). It was also critical to assess her lethality. Esperanza is 12 years old and is probably in the third stage of cognitive development, the formal operational stage (Piaget, 1968). At this stage, thinking is logical and children are able to understand abstractions. Of particular relevance here, children of this age can understand that death is not a reversible process (Webb, 2010), and thus her wish to die had to be treated very seriously. Webb also notes that although it is uncommon for children to express suicidal ideation when a parent dies, their threats must be taken very seriously.

Many writers, including Worden (2008), indicate that family members may hesitate in asking about suicidal ideation, fearing that they may suggest ideas to the child. Worden recommends a gentle inquiry to initiate the discussion. Following Roberts (2005), the first stage in crisis intervention is to assess lethality, which includes an assessment of danger to self and others and attending to immediate psychosocial needs. Stage 2 of this model focuses on establishing rapport and rapidly building the relationship. Both steps were attended to in the first half of the counseling session when the counselor, Sara, made it clear to Esperanza that she knew why those who loved her had referred her to counseling. Sensitive to Esperanza's acute sense of loss, the counselor began an assessment of lethality after exploring Esperanza's feelings about being referred to counseling. Utilizing a suicide assessment can help counselors accurately evaluate and track clients' lethality risk. Maheshwari and Joshi (2012) identify three psychometrically sound measures of suicide risk that are suitable for this age: the Modified Scale of Suicidal Ideation; the Suicidal Ideation Questionnaire-Junior; and the Columbia–Suicide Severity Rating Scale. Joiner and Ribeiro (2011) also identify helpful outcome measures for suicide assessment. Bertolino (2003) stresses the importance of counselors working *with* adolescent clients to keep them involved in choosing the direction of therapy and to make it a collaborative venture. Explaining the role of the counselor and the participation of parent and child in planning treatment will do much to demystify the process of counseling and give the child and parent a sense of control. This is important with clients like Esperanza because bereaved children may feel they have less control over events than nonbereaved children (Silverman, 2000). To the extent possible, a counselor should help children feel they have some control and choice in counseling.

In the second half of the first session, Sara met with the entire family, except for Martin, who was on a trip with his cousins. Each member of the family was asked what they were most concerned about at the present time. All emphasized their worry for Esperanza and her talk of suicide. It surprised the family that the basis for Esperanza's desire to die was related to her certainty that her mother was angry with her and blamed Esperanza for the death of her husband. Ana expressed shock that Esperanza felt responsible, and she reassured Esperanza that she was not. Ana was able to correct Esperanza's misperception that it was she who "made" her parents go snowmobiling on the fateful day.

Ana told her family that on the morning of the snowmobiling accident her father had been reluctant to go because he had "so much work to do." Ezperanza teased him about the work and said she would feed the llamas and clean the barns if he promised to bring back snowballs for her. Their relationship was marked by humor and playfulness. Her father relented and agreed to go on the trip. She wailed that if only she had not "made" him go, he would still be alive. Ana and her sisters tried clearing up this misperception. Although this did not lessen Esperanza's agony over her father's death, it helped her to feel that she was not responsible. It was helpful to have the family gathered because they were able to provide the support that was essential in helping Esperanza through this crisis. Esperanza admitted she had wanted to die to get away from her painful feelings, but she did not have a specific plan for killing herself. The counselor then initiated safety planning with Esperanza, identifying multiple people she could reach out to for support, activities to distract herself when she was experiencing suicidal ideation, and community resources, including a national suicide hotline (Joiner & Ribeiro, 2011). After sharing this plan with her family and ensuring she did not have a plan or specific means of committing suicide, the session ended with scheduling an appointment to meet again in a few days. Esperanza's plan included many strategies, including letting one of her sisters, her mom, her aunt or uncle know how she was feeling, drawing or writing in her journal, going for a walk, riding her horse, cooking, or listening to music on her iPod.

In the next session, after another suicide assessment, Sara began to accomplish the tasks set forth in the third stage of Roberts's model. This stage focuses primarily on identifying the major problem or event that precipitated the crisis. In some cases, it may be helpful to identify problems and to rank them by priority to clarify a focus and address potentially harmful aspects of the problem. However, Esperanza made it clear that her crisis was about one problem and one problem only: her father's death.

Discussion about this loss led naturally into the fourth stage: expression of feelings. Sara helped Esperanza explore her feelings using active and empathic listening, reflecting her feelings and also using gentle confrontation when she observed incongruencies. For example, at one point, Esperanza said, "Everyone is handling this better than me. My sisters don't miss him at all." Saying this, she laughed, while at the same time tears fell from her eyes. Sara gently addressed the discrepancy between Esperanza's tears and her laughter. Esperanza clarified that she did not believe her sisters were managing as well as they seemed, but their concentration on a project to memorialize their father made Esperanza feel "left out."

Techniques designed to help children express their feelings about loss are discussed in the works of many writers (e.g., Silverman, 2000; Webb, 1999, 2004, 2010; Worden, 2008). Techniques that Esperanza found helpful included writing a letter to her father and reading it in session while exploring her feelings, going to the site of the accident and planting a small tree in her father's memory, and looking at photographs of her family, especially a few special ones of times she spent with her father on the ranch and at county fairs. Esperanza likes art, and she wanted to create a collage with color copies of the photographs. She began working on this with Sara's encouragement during part of their sessions. Esperanza did not want to take the collage home, fearing that it might make her mother cry. In a subsequent session with Esperanza and her mother, Sara helped both of them talk about their loss. Both felt closer to each other as they were able to talk about how the loss impacted them. Ana asked Esperanza to bring the project home so they could work on it together, and Esperanza was excited to be doing something special with her mother.

This collage project is an example of what Roberts recommends in the fifth stage of his model, which focuses on generating and exploring adaptive coping strategies during a crisis. Very often, a client is too distressed to develop good coping strategies; initially, this was the case with Esperanza. Geldard and Geldard (1999) and Raftopoulos and Bates (2011) note that the adolescent who feels suicidal finds coping difficult and is emotionally strained, to the point that suicide seems like a way to cope. Using the foundational counseling skills noted earlier, Sara discussed the fact that many young people who have suffered the death of a parent may go through a time when they cry, feel sad, and have trouble concentrating. Worden (2008) cautions against labeling these symptoms "depression" because they are normal in the first year following parental death and often lessen by the first anniversary; we need to exercise caution in using the term *depression* to describe a normal response.

Sara helped her to see that her responses were normal, but that it was very important to either develop new coping resources or find a way to use the resources that had helped her in the past. Sara asked Esperanza to describe how she had coped during a time in her past when nothing seemed to be going right or when something bad had happened. Esperanza recalled that when her cousin's parents divorced, it was a hard time for her, too, because she felt very close to her aunt and uncle. She prayed to God to help her through this time and spent a lot of time with her cousin, who was very sad, and she rode horses and cleaned the barn. With her Sara's assistance, Esperanza generated three coping lists: (a) helping myself on the inside, (b) helping myself by being with others, and (c) helping myself by doing things. Sara and Esperanza brainstormed about items for each category. Esperanza decided to post three large sheets of paper on the walls around the room, and using different-colored markers, she wrote ideas as they emerged. Under the heading "Helping myself on the inside," Esperanza wrote "pray." She had prayed since her father's death, but initially it was for God to make him well, then for God to take her to her father. Now she wrote, "pray to God to help me through this hard time" and "to give me strength." Her counselor suggested "listening to the relaxation DVD," which she had made at Esperanza's request because it helped her stomach pains go away. Esperanza added "drawing and painting in my journal" because she enjoyed artistic expression. The second list ("Helping myself by being with others") included numerous items, such as spending more time playing video games with her little brother, helping her sisters cook, arranging outings with friends or cousins, and staying with her godparents overnight. Sara interpreted it as a very positive indicator of her progress that Esperanza was willing to spend time with others because, since her father's death, she had been very isolated and withdrawn from those who could offer support. It was the collage of her family and remembering special times with her father that Esperanza put under the heading for the last coping category ("Helping myself by doing things").

It was in the sixth step of Roberts's model, developing an action plan, that Esperanza became stuck. Having ideas, as Esperanza did, is essential, but these ideas need to be planned and executed to help to restore functioning (Roberts, 2005). Initially, Esperanza was excited to begin taking steps in her categories. She had no trouble creating goals and developing intermediate steps, but when Sara asked which one she would work on this week, Esperanza became indecisive. Outside of counseling, Esperanza sought advice from her mother and sisters, but she did not take their suggestions and became surly when encouraged to follow her own plans. In counseling, Esperanza pushed Sara to choose for her. When Sara declined, Esperanza became annoyed and said people were not helping her, and why should she try if everyone else was giving up? Her change in mood was remarkable.

Sara recalled a client she had worked with long ago whose brother had died in an accident. This girl similarly went through a time of indecision and inaction. Esperanza was curious to hear that this girl had found it hard to accept that she had the right to be happy and move on with her life after her brother died. Esperanza was afraid that if she went on with her life and was happy, it might seem like she was betraying her father's memory. As Roberts (2005) notes, it can be helpful for clients to know that we have worked with others who have had difficulty in executing plans, and it is equally helpful for them to know that these clients ultimately succeeded in overcoming their self-imposed obstacles.

Esperanza worried that she would begin to forget details from her life with her father, and she sometimes still blamed herself for "making" her father go on the trip. After further clarifying and expressing her feelings, Esperanza decided to focus on completing the collage so that her fear about forgetting her father could be laid to rest. She also said she would pray more often for God to give her strength to believe she had nothing to do with the accident. Thus, after exploring the difficulty in implementing plans, Esperanza was ready to continue with a course of action.

The last stage of crisis intervention is follow-up. Likely, Sara would include an outcome measure of Esperanza's suicidal ideation as noted earlier and a measure of trauma symptoms, such as the TSCC (Briere, 1996) or Clinician Administered PTSD Scale for Children and Adolescents (Nader et al., 1996) to determine the outcome of treatment and Esperanza's overall psychological functioning. Worden and his colleagues on the Child Bereavement Project (Worden, 2008; Worden & Silverman, 1996; McClatchy & Wimmer, 2012) found that recently bereaved children were no more or less disturbed than the matched nonbereaved controls on a variety of psychological measures. However, when the data were examined 1 and 2 years after the death of a parent, there were significant differences between bereaved children and the control group of nonbereaved children. In particular, adolescent boys (aged 12 to 18) who did not show much difference at 1 year after the death of a parent did indicate that they were more withdrawn and had slightly more social problems than controls. The preadolescent girls had no more problems than the nonbereaved control group at

1 year past the parental death, but there were significant changes by 2 years, including more anxiety and depression. This research has implications for mental health professionals and others who work with children. We must be aware of the long-term effects of losing a parent and that problems may not appear until 1 or 2 years after the death.

Esperanza made very good progress in therapy, and after 4 months of working together, she and Sara mutually decided to terminate their regular sessions and moved to periodic check-ins. Sara met with Esperanza five times over the next 2 years and also met with the entire family three times to keep apprised of how everyone else was doing. Nearly 14 months after her father's death, Camille, the eldest, began to develop insomnia and frequent periods of sadness. Having anticipated that one of the other children in the family might later experience more grief over the father's death, Sara encouraged Camille to meet with a counselor at the university Camille attended.

At 2 years and 4 months after her father's death, Esperanza felt that she was functioning well. She had good support from family and friends, was performing very well in school, and had won several statewide equestrian events, of which she was proud. She told Sara that in the future she might want to come back to counseling, but right now she was too busy having a full and satisfying life, and even periodic follow-up no longer seemed necessary.

## Peter: Tragic Death of a Sibling

Peter is a biracial Asian American 12-year-old from an urban family who are actively involved in their local and church communities. Peter lives with his parents, Judy and Paul, aged 43 and 44, respectively, and his older sister, Cheryl, aged 16. Judy is part owner of a landscape architecture company, serves on the city council in her community, and volunteers for Habitat for Humanity. Paul is a civil engineer, and a volunteer firefighter. Three grandparents live in the same city. Peter's maternal grandmother died 3 years ago following surgical complications.

The week following spring break, Peter was on his way to history class at Timbercrest Middle School. He noticed a group of kids in the hall talking loudly about a shooting at Southridge High School that morning. The news spread like wildfire via texts and Facebook. Peter instantly thought of his sister, Cheryl, a Southridge student, and texted her. He headed to class but was distracted and continued to text Cheryl and his parents. Peter checked Facebook and Twitter to look for updates. Apparently, three students had brought weapons into the high school and began firing indiscriminately shortly before noon. Midway through the history class, Peter and three other students were called to the counselor's office. All of these students had siblings at the high school who were known to be wounded or unaccounted for.

Ms. Lee met with the students, who were all very upset and agitated after hearing rumors about the shootings, and provided what limited information she had while reassuring the students that their parents were on their way. Peter was surprised to see his father enter Ms. Lee's office, and before he was able to react, his father led Peter away with Mr. Hernandez, the principal, close behind. Peter sat baffled in Mr. Hernandez's office as his father told him that Cheryl had been shot and was in critical condition. Peter did not ask any questions. He simply said that he wanted to go home.

Cheryl would not recover from the shooting and passed away within days. Two weeks after her tragic death, Peter's parents provided support for Peter as best they could, but they seemed to be in a daze. To family friends and relatives, Peter appeared to be coping well, and after a 7-day absence from school, he returned to classes. Extended family, friends, and neighbors still dropped by the house with small gifts, food, and offers of assistance. Peter avoided visitors and spent any free time with his maternal grandfather, Clay.

Media attention remained consistent for several months after the Southridge shooting. The scale of the tragedy (6 students died, and 10 were seriously injured) led to national and international news coverage, to which Peter was exposed daily as he scrolled through his Facebook and Twitter feeds. Funds were made available for mental health counseling for the students, teachers, and families affected by the shootings. A month before school ended for the year, Ms. Lee encouraged Judy and Paul to take Peter to see a grief counselor at the local hospice center. Peter seemed to need further support, particularly because his grades were suffering and he was avoiding his friends and after-school club events. Peter resisted yet later consented to counseling to please his parents. The hospice counselor, Andrew, met with Peter for three sessions. He was very kind and helped Peter understand that his reactions to the tragedy (difficulty sleeping, being sad, frequently thinking about his sister, and not wanting to see friends) were normal. He encouraged Peter to join a grief group, but after one session Peter denied any concerns and told his grandfather, who drove him to the group, that he did not want to return to counseling. Clay conveyed Peter's struggles to Judy and Paul, and counseling was terminated at the end of the school year.

Two months passed, with Judy and Paul experiencing the benefits of grief support group counseling. As they rebounded, Paul returned to recreational activities, such as golfing; Judy increased her work hours and returned to city council meetings. She decided to travel for a business trip for a few days. When Peter learned that his mother was leaving, he lashed out and slammed a door, causing an expensive vase to fall and break. Peter was sick the next day with a fever. Judy rescheduled her trip for the following month and at that time left town without further incident from Peter.

Peter began reporting somatic concerns and a fear of ghosts to his grandfather. He was certain that another tragedy was soon to happen. When Clay scheduled an appointment with his doctor for a blood pressure problem,

Peter became anxious and inconsolable. Judy and Paul encouraged Peter to return to counseling with Andrew.

## Crisis Intervention: Application of Roberts's Seven-Stage Model

Peter's presenting concerns in counseling were related to worries about his grandfather's medical problems. He appeared sad and angry, and he cried briefly. He stated that what was happening to his grandfather was "not fair." Andrew simply allowed Peter to talk. A consistent message was that his grandfather "has been there for me through everything." After listening attentively and empathically to Peter's concerns, Andrew spoke generally about "problems people have little control over." He acknowledged that Peter was courageous to return to counseling and that it might help Peter talk about things that he could and could not control.

After Andrew conveyed genuine respect for and acceptance of Peter (Roberts, 2005), the boy relaxed in sessions. Peter's increased acceptance of the counseling process enabled Andrew to begin examining the dimensions of the tragedy and the subsequent problems. They began to discuss the time Peter lashed out over the summer. Peter related that he was mad at his mother for leaving and saddened by his grandfather's medical condition. When Andrew asked if Peter was afraid, he simply said "Maybe" and asked, "Why does God make it so hard for people?" This led to further exploration of his spirituality, and Peter seemed to relax more as the counselor openly encouraged him to discuss his beliefs. Andrew is aware that many problems faced by clients have a spiritual aspect, especially grief and loss issues. Having a counselor who is willing to explore spirituality can facilitate trust in the therapeutic relationship for religious or spiritual clients (Post & Wade, 2009).

The discussion of God opened the door for Andrew to explore Peter's loss and to assess if Peter was at risk for self-harm or suicidal ideation. Peter looked away sadly and said, "My sister is with God." They discussed how she had died, and Andrew asked very directly if Peter would like to be "with God." Peter spontaneously declared, "Death is awful and kids shouldn't die" and began to cry. Andrew facilitated Peter's emotional expression with a respectful silence and reflection of feelings. Peter wiped at his tears and stated, "I can't do anything about it anyway," then said he did not want to talk about it anymore.

Andrew sensed that Peter was pulling away emotionally and shifted the conversation back to Peter's grandfather, which was a safer subject. They ended the session by briefly talking about Clay and how Peter could talk to his grandfather to express his worries to him.

Two sessions later, Peter, now 13 years old, had started eighth grade. Judy called Andrew before the next session to explain that Peter was experiencing a difficult start to the school year and was struggling with completing his homework on time. On the second day of school, he was sent home for fighting. In the session, Peter readily admitted that he fought with another boy in his class who was making mean jokes about blondes. He began to cry and said that his grandfather had to "go back for more testing. It is just not fair. Why us?" He was anxious and agitated. He changed the subject to ask why someone at his sister's funeral said that "God works in strange ways." Peter was encouraged to explore his feelings, and he wondered aloud whether or not he wanted to believe in a God who allows such awful things to happen.

Andrew encouraged Peter to explore the role that God played in his life. This discussion enabled Peter to talk about his grandmother's death due to illness, his sister's tragic death, and his grandfather's problems. Peter's eyes were wet as he discussed his grandmother, whom he recalled was a lot of fun, and his sister, whom he used to tease with jokes. After a smile came to his face, Peter stated that maybe he was ready to talk about his sister. He began to relate the events of the previous spring as the counselor listened in an empathic and supportive manner.

Andrew examined the coping attempts that had worked for Peter in the past and identified ones that may be adaptive in the future. Peter said that he used to be a good problem solver, he believed in God, he liked music, and he made friends easily. Over the summer, however, he spent a lot of time alone, playing video games and listening to music. He recalled that, following his sister's death, he did not know what to do and felt numb and helpless. He related a recent story about a moment of silence at his school to mark the 6-month anniversary of the shootings at Southridge High and how he wanted to talk to another student whose brother was murdered that tragic day. He felt sad that the boy appeared very isolated, yet Peter remembered how he felt last summer and realized that he had made a choice not to be so isolated. Peter said he still found it hard to talk about sad things because two of his favorite people to talk with are now dead. Andrew reflected his sadness concerning the intensity of grief Peter experienced at such a young age.

Peter spent two sessions talking about Cheryl and the shootings at Southridge High. Andrew encouraged Peter to explore the story and his feelings more deeply each session. Peter's parents were becoming more open to discussions with Peter and Clay, who visited the house regularly. Andrew decided that Peter was ready for Stage 5, generating and exploring adaptive coping strategies.

Peter gained insight into his thoughts and feelings concerning Cheryl's death, and he discussed the ebb and flow of his emotions: "One moment I am fine, and the next I am sad." Peter still sometimes found it a challenge to concentrate in school and sometimes had trouble sleeping. He was aware of his intrusive thoughts, bothered by his mother's business trips, and worried about his grandfather's health. To manage and cope better, he asked his mother to check in more often when she was out of town and asked his grandfather to be honest about his failing health. Peter was now willing to admit his fear of events he cannot control. He still wanted God "to make it all right." The youth director at his church helped Peter to see that God may want Peter to focus on making himself well. Peter admitted he was doing just that by talking to his counselor, making new friends, and spending less time playing video games. Although he did not like some of the kids in school, he conceded that fighting was not helpful.

Exploring fears, denial, isolation, worries, and events he could not control enabled Peter to move to Stage 6, developing an action plan. He began to understand the difference between external events he could not control and steps he could take to develop more realistic plans. He thought doing homework was something he could complete daily and that doing this helped him gain a greater sense of control.

Following the 1-year anniversary of Cheryl's death, Judy and Paul turned her room into a guest room. Several of her photos decorated the walls, and Peter decided to "take his grieving" there. He related that about once a week he went into the room. He noted that sometimes he went there to cry but left with a smile as he looked over photo albums and DVDs of his childhood with Cheryl. Peter decided to become a member of the confirmation class at church. He renewed his interest in soccer and began to play on weekends with a team. Peter made the decision to re-engage in life.

The final session of crisis intervention found Peter feeling successful because he was able to mediate a school conflict and could work on homework for extended periods of time and enjoy his involvement in sports. Through his volunteer work in the community with children who have disabilities, he became more grateful for his life. He realized that tragedies and losses change everyone in the community. He understood that his grief for Cheryl would not end in the near future, yet he was ready to terminate counseling.

A year and a half after counseling ended, Peter was ready to enter high school, and he decided to attend Southridge, even though he had been given other options. Although he no longer sees Andrew, he now feels able to reach out to the school counselor as needed. He reported that he misses his sister and, at times, still grieves her death.

## Special Considerations

There are many considerations to bear in mind in working with early adolescents who have suffered a serious loss. Each child is unique, and counselors should expect to find significant individual differences in personality style and temperament that can alter responses to acute stressors. It is important to understand further that all responses are affected by biopsychosocial, cultural, and familial influences. It is not within the scope of this chapter to explore each of these influences in depth, but we wish to highlight the importance of developmental stages, cultural issues, and the differences between youths coping with single episodes and with a series of crises, as well as ethical considerations in working with youth.

First, as noted earlier, adolescence can be divided into three periods. However, the developmental characteristics representative of each period are not always completely consistent with a child's chronological age. For example, a 13-year-old early adolescent eldest child whose parent died may "grow up quickly" as he or she is required to take on additional responsibilities in the home. This child may seem more similar to an older adolescent of 15 or 16 years. Likewise, a child who has suffered a crisis may regress and seem younger than his or her chronological age. Intervention in such cases may include using approaches designed for older or younger children, respectively. For the latter, play therapy may prove beneficial. In the tech age, interventions that incorporate social media, texting, or video games may prove fruitful and engage adolescents in a new way. Although there is limited research on the use of technology in crisis intervention, web-based interventions for the prevention of depression have been pilot tested, but reported results are limited by small sample sizes (Landback et al., 2009; Saulsberry et al., 2013). Boydell and colleagues (2014) provide a thorough description of using technology to provide mental health services to adolescents and their families in Ontario, an interesting prototype for other communities looking to increasing telehealth services for adolescents. Finally, successful interventions need to include a careful assessment of each individual's stage of cognitive and emotional development and to design and apply specific techniques in response to this assessment. Outcome measures that help to track symptomology and inform best areas of treatment assist with developmental assessment.

Second, cultural differences, which influence myriad behaviors, attitudes, values, and family structures, must also be taken into consideration in working with early adolescents. For example, in our second case, it was clear that Esperanza and Martin's godparents played an important role in their support systems, but this will not be true in all families. In many cases, we must assess, early on, culturally variable definitions of family membership and use the client's definition of family in choosing whom to treat and whom to include in any intervention. It may also be the case that the values of the client's culture conflict with those of the counselor. For example, many counselors might view Camille's choice to stay home as being "codependent" or "enmeshed"; such a counselor might have suggested that she should return to college to resume her studies rather than take off a semester. However, Camille's family and community do not share this view. They value maintenance of the family and the individual's commitment to the family above avoiding a temporary delay in an individual's education. Furthermore, grieving and views on death and dying are culturally contextualized, creating another point in these case studies where cultural competence in particularly important. Note that our point is *not* that the counselor should assume a homogeneous, stereotypic set of culturally determined values for any group of people; there is great variation within all groups. Rather, we stress that it is essential to examine one's own cultural assumptions and remain open to the likelihood that these are not appropriate for all people. This will often be particularly important during Roberts's Stages 5 and 6, when counselor and client are working to frame goals and develop plans to implement these goals. The complexity and importance of this issue warrant special consideration by the reader, and we strongly recommend examining the literature focusing more extensively on the relations among adolescents, family, and culture (Goldstein et al., 2011; McGoldrick, Giordano, & Garcia-Preto, 2005; Myer et al., 2014; Ponterotto, Casas, Suzuki, & Alexander, 2010; Rueger & Malecki, 2011; Stone & Conley, 2004; Suzuki, Ponterotto, & Meller, 2008; Walsh, 2012).

As discussed earlier, it is also important to acknowledge the differences between clients who present with a single crisis episode, such as Esperanza, and those who present with a series of crises, such as Jenny. In *Helping Bereaved Children*, Webb (2010) discusses a case of two children dealing with the dual loss of parents, as well as with the death of a beloved godfather. In complicated bereavement cases such as these, Dickens (2014) notes that expressions of grief are similar following divorce and death, but that there are some differences that can lead to complex reactions. One difference is the intense anger a child may feel about the divorce, coupled with self-blame for the failed marriage and often with a hope that parents will reunite (Webb, 2010). When someone dies, grief reactions will vary greatly, in part related to the degree of closeness one felt with the person who died. In Jenny's case, she was very close to her grandmother and openly grieved more for her than she did when her parents divorced. However, her reaction was complex, perhaps due in part to mixed feelings about her parents' divorce. Worden (1996) also noted that children may feel they need to hide their mourning in a divorce situation because of conflict between parents. This was certainly the case with Jenny, whose mother was not very supportive of her grieving the divorce but was much more attentive when Jenny's grandmother died.

Finally, there are ethical and legal issues specific to work with minor children that must be in the forefront of the counselor's mind. In many cases, minor children are not legally able to give informed consent for treatment (Knapp, Younggren, VandeCreek, Harris, & Martin, 2013). Informed consent implies that individuals understand the options available to them, can competently make a decision regarding those options, and agree to the option they choose. The age at which children are considered competent to give informed consent varies by state, but in most cases children need the permission and signatures of caregivers, depending upon the unique nature of the parental relationship. In divorce situations, this can be complicated by the fact that, if parents have shared custody, both parents must grant permission for the minor child to receive therapy. Thus, the child's ability to receive needed services may be compromised if either parent is unwilling to permit psychological treatment. It is vital for counselors to know who the custodial caregivers are and to obtain proof of the right to consent to treatment for the child (Thompson & Henderson, 2007). There is also the issue of willingness to participate on the part of the minor child, which can be seriously impacted by the stresses and conflicts that are typical of early adolescent development. For example, an adolescent child (such as Peter) may be referred to therapy but may not want services and may be resentful about being "forced" into counseling. Furthermore, early in therapy, there must be an explicit discussion among all parties regarding confidentiality, including such issues as what a counselor must report to parents even when a minor is adamant that he or she does not want a parent to be informed (i.e., abuse or a child threatening to do harm to him- or herself or another person). There must also be a discussion with parents about permitting a counselor or child to not disclose information to them about counseling sessions. Counselors must be aware of their professional code of ethics and the laws in their state regarding the age of consent, exceptions to consent, the rights and limits to confidentiality, and the rights to privacy (Corey, Corey, & Callanan, 2011). The earlier these issues are addressed, the better for all parties concerned. Addressing these issues early on in an intervention is important not just for ensuring a counselor's compliance with ethical and legal requirements but also for establishing rapport and trust during the early stages of intervention. Adolescents are particularly likely to view unexpected (from their perspective) exposure of information as a fundamental violation of trust, which can compromise any form of intervention.

## CONCLUSION

Crisis intervention is a critical and necessary resource for early adolescents. The counselor skilled in crisis intervention can assist in stabilization and intervention to prevent immediate crises from becoming long-standing problems. Crisis intervention is a more cost-effective and time-effective way of dealing with problems than long-term therapy, although it is clear that there are cases in which such therapy is necessary.

Counselors working with early adolescents in crisis need to be especially aware of the impacts of developmental issues on individual responses to acute stressors. Individuals in this age group vary widely, although it must be assumed that all are struggling with complex and pervasive neurophysiological, behavioral, social, and contextual changes. An awareness of this struggle must be built into any approach to crisis intervention. One important force that influences the course of early adolescent change is an individual's cultural context, and counselors need to be aware of this and of their own cultural preconceptions. Applying Roberts's model of intervention, keeping considerations like these in mind, has the potential for successful outcomes in many, and perhaps most, instances.

REFERENCES

Amato, P. R., & Anthony, C. J. (2014). Estimating the effects of parental divorce and death with fixed effects models. *Journal of Marriage and Family, 76,* 370–386. doi:10.1111/jomf.12100

American Psychiatric Association. (2013). *Diagnostic and statistical manual of mental disorders* (5th ed.). Arlington, VA: Author.

Anthony, E. K., Williams, L. R., & LeCroy, C. W. (2014). Trends in adolescent development impacting practice: How can we catch up? *Journal of Human Behavior in the Social Environment, 24,* 487–498. doi:10.1080/10911359.2013.849220

Atav, S., & Spencer, G. A. (2002). Health risk behaviors among adolescents attending rural, suburban, and urban schools. *Family Community Health, 25*(2), 53–64.

Auman, M. (2007). Bereavement support for children. *Journal of School Nursing, 23,* 34–39.

Berman, A. L., Jobes, D. A., & Silverman, M. M. (2006). *Adolescent suicide: Assessment and intervention* (2nd ed.). Washington, DC: American Psychological Association.

Bertolino, B. (2003). *Change-oriented therapy with adolescents and young adults.* New York: Norton.

Blakemore, S. J. (2012a). Development of the social brain in adolescence. *Journal of the Royal Society of Medicine, 105*(3), 111–116. doi:10.1258/jrsm.2011.110221

Blakemore, S. J. (2012b). Imaging brain development: The adolescent brain. *Neuroimage, 61,* 397–406. doi:10.1016/j.neuroimage.2011.11.080

Blakemore, S. J., & Robbins, T. W. (2012). Decision-making in the adolescent brain. *Nature Neuroscience, 15,* 1184–1191.

Bonanno, G. A., Galea, S., Bucciarelli, A., & Vlahov, D. (2007). What predicts psychological resilience after disaster? The role of demographics, resources and life stress. *Journal of Consulting and Clinical Psychology, 75,* 671–682.

Bowlby, J. (1980). *Attachment and loss: Volume 3. Loss.* New York: Basic.

Boydell, K. M., Hodgins, M., Pignatiello, A., Edwards, H., Teshima, J., & Willis, D. (2014). Using technology to deliver mental health services to children and youth in Ontario: A scoping review. *Journal of the Canadian of Child and Adolescent Psychiatry, 23,* 87–99.

Braun-Lewensohn, O., Celestin-Westreich, S., Celestin, L. P., Verleye, G., Verté, D., & Ponjaert-Kristoffersen, I. (2009). Coping styles as moderating the relationships between terrorist attacks and well-being outcomes. *Journal of Adolescence, 32,* 585–599. doi:10.1016/j.adolescence.2008.06.003

Brenhouse, H. C., & Andersen, S. L. (2011). Developmental trajectories during adolescence in males and females: A cross-species understanding of underlying brain changes. *Neuroscience and Biobehavioral Reviews, 35*, 1687–1703.

Brent, D. A., Melhem, N. M., Masten, A. S., Porta, G., & Payne, M. W. (2012). Longitudinal effects of parental bereavement on adolescent developmental competence. *Journal of Clinical Child and Adolescent Psychology, 41*, 778–791.

Briere, J. (1996). *Trauma symptom checklist for children (TSCC) professional manual.* Odessa, TX: Psychological Assessment Resources.

Burnett, S., Sebastian, C., Cohen Kadosh, K., & Blakemore, S. J. (2011). The social brain in adolescence: Evidence from functional magnetic resonance imaging and behavioural studies. *Neuroscience and Biobehavioral Reviews, 35*, 1654–1664. doi:10.1016/j.neubiorev.2010.10.011

Busso, D. S. (2014). Neurobiological processes of risk and resilience in adolescence: Implications for policy and prevention science. *Mind, Brain, and Education, 8*, 34–43. doi:10.1111/mbe.12042

Casey, B. J., & Jones, R. M. (2010). Neurobiology of the adolescent brain and behavior: Implications for substance use disorders. *Journal of the American Academy of Child and Adolescent Psychiatry, 49*, 1189–1201.

Casey, B. J., Jones, R. M., & Hare, T. A. (2008). The adolescent brain. *Annals of the New York Academy of Sciences, 1124*, 111–126.

Cerel, J., Fristad, M. A., Verducci, J., Weller, R. A., & Weller, E. B. (2006). Childhood bereavement: Psychopathology in 2 years postparental death. *Journal of the American Academy of Child and Adolescent Psychiatry, 45*, 681–690. doi:10.1097/01.chi.0000215327.58799.05

Chasson, G. S., Vincent, J. P., & Harris, G. E. (2008). The use of symptom severity measured just before termination to predict child treatment dropout. *Journal of Clinical Psychology, 64*, 891–904. doi:10.1002/jclp.20494

Children's Defense Fund. (2013). *Protect children, not guns: Key facts.* Washington, DC: Author.

Cohen, J. A., Mannarino, A. P., & Deblinger, E. (2006). *Treating trauma and traumatic grief in children and adolescents.* New York: Guilford Press.

Corcoran, K. (2005). The Oregon Mental Health Referral Checklists: Concept mapping the mental health needs of youth in the juvenile justice system. *Brief Treatment and Crisis Intervention, 5*, 9–18. doi:10.1093/brief-treatment/mhi003

Corey, G., Corey, M. S., & Callanan, P. (2011). *Issues and ethics in the helping professions* (8th ed.). Belmont, CA: Cengage Learning.

Cui, M., Fincham, F. D., & Durtschi, J. A. (2011). The effect of parental divorce on young adults' romantic relationship dissolution: What makes a difference? *Personal Relationships, 18*, 410–426. doi:10.1111/j.1475-6811.2010.01306.x

Curtis, A. C., Waters, C. M., & Brindis, C. (2011). Rural adolescent health: The importance of prevention services in the rural community. *Journal of Rural Health, 27*, 61–70. doi:10.1111/j.1748-0361.2010.00319.x

Davidson, J. R. T., Payne, V. M.,
Connor, K. M., Foa, E. B.,
Rothbaum, B. O., & Hertzberg,
M. A. (2005). Trauma, resilience,
and saliostasis: Effects of treat-
ment in post-traumatic stress
disorder. *International Clinical
Psychopharmacology, 20*, 43–48.

Davis, S. K., & Humphrey, N. (2012).
Emotional intelligence as a moderator of stressor–mental health
relations in adolescence: Evidence
for specificity. *Personality
and Individual Differences,
52*, 100–105. doi:10.1016/
j.paid.2011.09.006

Dickens, N. (2014). Prevalence
of complicated grief and post-
traumatic stress disorder in
children and adolescents following sibling death. *Family
Journal, 22*, 119–126.
doi:10.1177/1066480713505066

Eiland, L., & Romeo, R. D. (2013).
Stress and the developing adolescent brain. *Neuroscience,
249*, 162–171. doi:10.1016/j.
neuroscience.2012.10.048

Elliott, D. C., Kaliski, P., Burrus,
J., & Roberts, R. D. (2013).
Exploring adolescent resilience through the lens of
core self-evaluations. In S.
Prince-Embury & D. H. Saklofske
(Eds.), *Resilience in children, adolescents, and adults: Translating
research into practice* (pp.
199–212). New York: Springer.

Erikson, E. (1959). Identity and the
life cycle. *Psychological Issues,
1*, 1–171.

Erikson. E. (1963). *Childhood and
society*. New York: Norton.

Erikson, E. (1968). *Identity: Youth
and crisis*. New York:
Norton.

Ford, J. D., & Courtois, C. A. (2013).
*Treating complex traumatic stress
disorders in children and adolescents: Scientific foundations
and therapeutic models*.
New York: Guilford Press.

Fosha, D. (2004). Brief integrative
therapy comes of age: A commentary. *Journal of Psychotherapy
Integration, 14*(1), 66–92.

Fox, J. A., & DeLateur, M. J.
(2014). Mass shootings in
America: Moving beyond Newton.
*Homicide Studies, 18*, 125–145.
doi:10.1177/1088767913510297

Geldard, K., & Geldard, D. (1999).
*Counseling adolescents: The pro-
active approach*. Thousand Oaks,
CA: Sage.

Gerson, R., & Rappaport, N.
(2013). Traumatic stress and
posttraumatic stress disorder in
youth: Recent research findings on
clinical impact, assessment, and
treatment. *Journal of Adolescent
Health, 52*, 137–143.

Gilbertson, M. W., Shenton, M. E.,
Ciszewski, A., Kasai, K., Lasko,
N. B., Orr, S. P., & Pitman,
R. K. (2002). Smaller hippocam-
pal volume predicts pathologic
vulnerability to psychological
trauma. *Nature Neuroscience, 5*,
1242–1247.

Goldstein, A. L., Wekerle, C.,
Tonmyr, L., Thornton, T.,
Waechter, R., Pereira, J.,…
MAP Research Team. (2011).
The relationship between
post-traumatic stress symptoms
and substance use among adolescents involved with child welfare: Implications for emerging
adulthood. *International Journal
of Mental Health Addiction,
9*, 507–524. doi:10.1007/
s11469-011-9331-8

Green, J. G., McLaughlin, K. A.,
Alegría, M., Costello, E. J.,
Gruber, M. J., Hoagwood, K.,…
Kessler, R. C. (2013). School mental health resources and adolescent
mental health service use. *Journal
of the American Academy of*

*Child and Adolescent Psychiatry*, *52*, 510–510.

Hackman, D. A., Farah, M. J., & Meaney, M. J. (2010). Socioeconomic status and the brain: Mechanistic insights from human and animal research. *Nature Reviews Neuroscience*, *11*, 651–659.

Haine, R. A., Ayers, T. S., Sandler, I. N., & Wolchik, S. A. (2008). Evidence-based practices for parentally bereaved children and their families. *Professional Psychology: Research and Practice*, *39*, 113–121. doi:10.1037/0735-7028.39.2.113

Harrison, L., & Harrington, R. (2001). Adolescents' bereavement experiences: Prevalence, association with depressive symptoms, and use of services. *Journal of Adolescence*, *24*, 159–169.

Herman, J. L. (1992). *Trauma and recovery: The aftermath of violence from domestic violence to political terrorism*. New York: Guilford Press.

Heron, M. (2013). Deaths: Leading causes for 2010. *National Vital Statistics Reports*, *62*, 1–96.

Hooyman, N. R., & Kramer, B. J. (2006). *Living through loss: Interventions across the lifespan*. New York: Columbia University Press.

Ishikawa, W., Sato, M., Fukuda, Y., Matsumoto, T., Takemura, N., & Sakatani, K. (2014). Correlation between asymmetry of spontaneous oscillation of hemodynamic changes in the prefrontal cortex and anxiety levels: A near-infrared spectroscopy study. *Journal of Biomedical Optics*, *19* (2), 027005-1-027005-7.

Jakšić, N., Brajković, L., Ivezić, E., Topić, R., & Jakovljević, M. (2012). The role of personality traits in posttraumatic stress disorder (PTSD). *Psychiatria Danubina*, *24*, 256–266.

Joiner, T. R., Orden, K., Witte, T. K., & Rudd, M. (2009). *The interpersonal theory of suicide: Guidance for working with suicidal clients*. Washington, DC: American Psychological Association.

Joiner, T. R., & Ribeiro, J. D. (2011). Assessment and management of suicidal behavior in children and adolescents. *Pediatric Annals*, *40*, 319–324.

Kaufman, K. R., & Kaufman, N. D. (2005). Childhood mourning: Prospective case analysis of multiple losses. *Death Studies*, *29*, 237–249.

Keenan, A. (2014). Parental loss in early adolescence and its subsequent impact on adolescent development. *Journal of Child Psychotherapy*, *40*(1), 20–35. doi:10.1080/0075417X.2014.883130

Keller, S. M., & Feeny, N. C. (2014). Posttraumatic stress disorder in children and adolescents. In M. Lewis & K. Rudolf (Eds.), *Handbook of developmental psychopathology* (pp. 743–759). New York: Springer.

Kilmer, R. P. (2006). Resilience and posttraumatic growth in children. In L. G. Calhoun & R. G. Tedeschi (Eds.), *Handbook of posttraumatic growth: Research and practice* (pp. 265–288). Mahwah, NJ: Erlbaum.

Knapp, P. K., & Foy, J. M. (2012). Integrating mental health care into pediatric primary care settings. *Journal of the American Academy of Child and Adolescent Psychiatry*, *51*, 982–984.

Knapp, S., Younggre, J. N., VandeCreek, L., Harris, E., & Martin, J. N. (2013). *Assessing and managing risk in psychological practice: An individualized approach* (2nd ed.). Rockville, MD: American Psychological Association Insurance Trust.

Lambert, M. J. (Ed.). (2013). *Bergin and Garfields's handbook of psychotherapy and behavior change* (6th ed.). Hoboken, NJ: Wiley.

Landback, J., Prochaska, M., Ellis, J., Dmochowska, K., Kuwabara, S. A., Gladstone, T.,... Van Voorhees, B. W. (2009). From prototype to product: Development of a primary care/Internet based depression prevention intervention for adolescents (CATCH-IT). *Community Mental Health Journal, 45*, 349–354. doi:10.1007/s10597-009-9226-3

Levine, S. Z., Laufer, A., Stein, E., Hamama-Raz, Y., & Solomon, Z. (2009). Examining the relationship between resilience and posttraumatic growth. *Journal of Traumatic Stress, 22*, 282–286. doi:10.1002/jts.20409

Maheshwari, R., & Joshi, P. (2012). Assessment, referral, and treatment of suicidal adolescents. *Pediatric Annals, 41*, 516–521. doi:10.3928/00904481-20121126-13

Malone, P. A. (2012). The impact of peer death on adolescent girls: An efficacy study of the adolescent grief and loss group. *Social Work with Groups, 35*, 35–49. doi:10.1080/01609513.2011.561423

Mandak, J. (2014, April 16). Classes resume a week after mass stabbing at Franklin Regional High School. *Huffington Post.* Retrieved from http://www.huffingtonpost.com/2014/04/16/classes-to-resume-mass-stabbing-franklin_n_5158663.html

Marco, E. M., Macrì, S., & Laviola, G. (2011). Critical age windows for neurodevelopmental psychiatric disorders: Evidence from animal models. *Neurotoxicity Research, 19*, 286–307. doi:10.1007/s12640-010-9205-z

Mash, E. J., & Dozois, D. J. (2003). Child psychopathology: A developmental-systems perspective. In E. J. Mash & R. A. Barkley (Eds.), *Child psychopathology* (2nd ed., pp. 3–71). New York: Guilford Press.

McClatchey, I. S. & Wimmer, J. S. (2012). Healing components of bereavement camp: Children and adolescents give voice to their experiences. *Omega-Journal of Death and Dying. 65*, 11–32.

McGoldrick, M., Giordano, J., & Garcia-Preto, N. (2005). *Ethnicity and family therapy* (3rd ed.). New York: Guilford Press.

Meir, Y., Slone, M., Levis, M., Reina, L., & Livni, Y. B. D. (2012). Crisis intervention with children of illegal migrant workers threatened with deportation. *Professional Psychology: Research and Practice, 43*, 298–305. doi:10.1037/a0027760

Melhem, N. M., Moritz, G., Walker, M., Shear, M. K., & Brent, D. (2007). Phenomenology and correlates of complicated grief in children and adolescents. *Journal of American Academy of Child and Adolescent Psychiatry, 46*, 493–499. doi:10.1097/chi.0b013e31803062a9

Miller, D. B. & Townsend, A. (2005). Urban hassles as chronic stressors and adolescent mental health: The Urban Hassles Index. *Brief Treatment and Crisis Intervention, 5*, 85–94. doi:10.1093/brief-treatment/mhi004

Muselman, D. M. & Wiggins, M. I. (2012). Spirituality and loss: Approaches for counseling grieving adolescents. *Counseling and Values, 57*, 229–240.

Myer, R. A., Williams, C., Haley, M., Brownfield, J., McNicols, K. B., & Pribozie, N. (2014). Crisis intervention with families: Assessing changes in family characteristics. *Family Journal, 22*, 179–185. doi:10.1177/1066480713513551

Nader, K., Kriegler, J. A., Blake, D. D., Pynoos, R. S., Newman, E., & Weathers, F. W. (1996). Clinician Administered PTSD Scale, Child and Adolescent Version. White River Junction, VT: National Center for PTSD.

National Institute of Mental Health. (2004). *The National Advisory Mental Health Council Workgroup on Child and Adolescent Mental Health Intervention Development and Deployment blueprint for change: Research on child and adolescent mental health.* Washington, DC: Government Printing Office.

Pérez-Edgar, K., Kujawa, A., Nelson, S. K., Cole, C., & Zapp, D. J. (2013). The relation between electroencephalogram asymmetry and attention biases to threat at baseline and under stress. *Brain and Cognition, 82*, 337–343.

Piaget, J. (1968). *Six psychological studies.* New York: Vintage Books.

Pole, N., Gone, J. P., & Kulkarni, M. (2008). Posttraumatic stress disorder among ethnoracial minorities in the United States. *Clinical Psychology: Science and Practice, 15*, 35–61. doi:10.1111/j.1468-2850.2008.00109.x

Ponterotto, J. G., Casas, J. M., Suzuki, L. A., & Alexander, C. M. (Eds.). (2010). *Handbook of multicultural counseling* (3rd ed.). Thousand Oaks, CA: Sage.

Post, B. C., & Wade, N. G. (2009). Religion and spirituality in psychotherapy: A practice-friendly review of research. *Journal of Clinical Psychology, 65*, 131–146.

Raftopoulos, M., & Bates, G. (2011). "It's knowing that you are not alone": The role of spirituality in adolescent resilience. *International Journal of Children's Spirituality, 16*, 151–167.

Rahdar, A., & Galván, A. (2014). The cognitive and neurobiological effects of daily stress in adolescents. *NeuroImage, 92*, 267–273. doi:10.1016/j.neuroimage.2014.02.007

Reiss, F. (2013). Socioeconomic inequalities and mental health problems in children and adolescents: A systematic review. *Social Science and Medicine, 90*, 24–31.

Roberts, A. R. (1996). Epidemiology and definitions of acute crisis in American society. In A. R. Roberts (Ed.), *Crisis management and brief treatment* (pp. 16–35). Chicago: Nelson-Hall.

Roberts, A. R. (2000). An overview of crisis theory and crisis intervention. In A. R. Roberts (Ed.), *Crisis intervention handbook: Assessment, treatment, and research* (2nd ed., pp. 3–30). New York: Oxford University Press.

Roberts, A. R. (2005). Bridging the past and present to the future of crisis intervention and crisis management. In A. R. Roberts (Ed.), *Crisis intervention handbook: Assessment, treatment and research* (3rd ed., pp. 3–33). New York: Oxford University Press.

Rogers, C. (1965). *Client-centered therapy: Its current practice, implications, and theory.* Boston: Houghton Mifflin.

Rosner, R., Arnold, J., Groh, E., & Hagl, M. (2012). Predicting PTSD from the Child Behavior Checklist: Data from a field

study with children and adolescents in foster care. *Children
and Youth Services Review,*
34, 1689–1694. doi:10.1016/j.
childyouth.2012.04.019

Rueger, S. Y., & Malecki, C. K.
(2011). Effects of stress, attributional style, and perceived parental
support on depressive symptoms
in early adolescence: A prospective
analysis. *Journal of Clinical Child
and Adolescent Psychology,* 40,
347–359.

Saulsberry, A., Corden, M. E.,
Taylor-Crawford, K., Crawford,
T. J., Johnson, M., Froemel, J.,. . .
Van Voorhees, B. W. (2013).
Chicago urban resiliency building (CURB): An Internet-based
depression-prevention intervention for urban African-American
and Latino adolescents. *Journal
of Child and Family Studies,*
22, 150–160. doi:10.1007/
s10826-012-9627-8

Seligman, M. E. P. (2007). *The optimistic child.* Boston: Houghton
Mifflin.

Silverman, P. R. (2000). *Never too
young to know: Death in children's lives.* New York: Oxford
University Press.

Singh, A. A. (2013). Transgender
youth of color and resil-
ience: Negotiating oppression
and finding support. *Sex Roles,*
68, 690–702. doi:10.1007/
s11199-012-0149-z

Spear, L. P. (2009). Heightened
stress responsivity and emotional
reactivity during pubertal matu-
ration: Implications for psychopathology. *Development and
Psychopathology,* 21(1), 87–97.

Spuij, M., van Londen-Huiberts,
A., & Boelen, P. A. (2013).
Cognitive-behavioral therapy
for prolonged grief in children: Feasibility and multiple
baseline study. *Cognitive and
Behavioral Practice,* 20,
349–361.

Stanley, P. H., Small, R., Owen,
S. S., & Burke, T. W. (2012).
Humanistic perspectives on
addressing school violence. In
M. B. Scholl, A. S. McGowan, &
J. T. Hansen (Eds.), *Humanistic
perspectives on contemporary
counseling issues* (pp. 167–190).
New York: Taylor and
Francis Group.

Steinberg, L. (2008). A social neuroscience perspective on adolescent risk-taking. *Developmental
Review,* 28(1), 78–106.

Steinberg, L., & Lerner, R. M.
(2004). The scientific study of
adolescence: A brief history.
*Journal of Early Adolescence,*
24(1), 45–54.

Steinberg, L., & Sheffield Morris, A.
(2001). Adolescent development.
*Annual Review of Psychology,* 52,
83–110.

Stone, D. A., & Conley, J. A. (2004).
A partnership between Roberts'
crisis intervention model and the
multicultural competencies. *Brief
Treatment and Crisis Intervention,*
4, 367–375. doi:10.1093/
brief-treatment/mhh030

Sturman, D. A., & Moghaddam,
B. (2011). The neurobiology of
adolescence: Changes in brain
architecture, functional dynamics, and behavioral tendencies.
*Neuroscience and Biobehavioral
Reviews,* 35, 1704–1712.

Sue, D. W., & Sue, D. (2013).
*Counseling the culturally diverse*
(6th ed.). Hoboken, NJ: Wiley.

Supiano, K. P. (2012). Sense-making
in suicide survivorship: A qualitative study of the effect of grief support group participation. *Journal
of Loss and Trauma,* 17, 489–507.

Suzuki, L. A., Ponterotto,
J. G., & Meller, P. J. (Eds.).
(2008). *Handbook of

*multicultural assessment* (3rd ed.). San Francisco: Wiley.

Terr, L. (1990). *Too scared to cry.* New York: HarperCollins.

Thompson, C. L., & Henderson, D. A. (2007). *Counseling children* (7th ed.). Belmont, CA: Brooks/Cole.

Trickey, D., Siddaway, A. P., Meiser-Stedman, R., Serpell, L., & Field, A. P. (2012). A meta-analysis of risk factors for post-traumatic stress disorder in children and adolescents. *Clinical Psychology Review, 32,* 122–138.

US Census Bureau. (2009). *Marital events of Americans: 2009.* Washington, DC: Author.

US Census Bureau. (2012). *America's families and living arrangements: 2012.* Washington, DC: Author.

Vernberg, E. M., Steinberg, A. M., Jacobs, A. K., Brymer, M. J., Watson, P. J., Osofsky, J. D., &... Ruzek, J. I. (2008). Innovations in disaster mental health: Psychological first aid. *Professional Psychology: Research and Practice, 39,* 381–388. doi:10.1037/a0012663

Walsh, F. (Ed.). (2012). *Normal family process: Growing diversity and complexity* (4th ed.). New York: Guilford Press.

Webb, N. B. (Ed.). (1999). *Play therapy with children in crisis* (2nd ed.). New York: Guilford Press.

Webb, N. B. (Ed.). (2004). *Mass trauma and violence: Helping families and children cope.* New York: Guilford Press.

Webb, N. B. (Ed.). (2010). *Helping bereaved children: A handbook for practitioners* (3rd ed.). New York: Guilford Press.

Wekerle, C., & Wolfe, D. A. (2003). Child maltreatment. In E. J. Mash & R. A. Barkley (Eds.), *Child psychopathology* (2nd ed., pp. 632–684). New York: Guilford Press.

Werner, E. E., & Smith, R. S. (2001). *Journeys from childhood to midlife: Risk, resilience, and recovery.* Ithaca, NY: Cornell University.

Wolchik, S. A., Coxe, S., Tein, J. T., Sandler, I. N., & Ayers, T. S. (2008). Six-year longitudinal predictors of posttraumatic growth in parentally bereaved adolescents and young adults. *Omega: Journal of Death and Dying, 58,* 107–128.

Worden, J. W. (1996). *Children and grief.* New York: Guilford Press.

Worden, J. W. (2008). *Grief counseling and grief therapy: A handbook for the mental health practitioner* (4th ed.). New York: Springer.

Worden, J. W., & Silverman, P. R. (1996). Parental death and the adjustment of school-age children. *Omega: Journal of Death and Dying, 33,* 91–102.

Yeager, K. R., & Roberts, A. R. (2005). Differentiating among stress, acute stress disorder, acute crisis episodes, trauma, and PTSD: Paradigm and treatment goals. In A. R. Roberts (Ed.), *Crisis intervention handbook: Assessment, treatment, and research* (3rd ed., pp. 90–119). New York: Oxford University Press.

Young, C. C., LaMontagne, L. L., Dietrich, M. S., & Wells, N. (2012). Cognitive vulnerabilities, negative life events, and depressive symptoms in young adolescents. *Archives of Psychiatric Nursing, 26*(1), 9–20. doi:10.1016/j.apnu.2011.04.008

Zimmerman, M. A., Stoddard, S. A., Eisman, A. B., Caldwell, C. H., Aiyer, S. M., & Miller, A. (2013). Adolescent resilience: Promotive factors that inform prevention. *Child Development Perspectives, 7,* 215–220. doi:10.1111/cdep.12042

# 13

## Crisis Intervention at College Counseling Centers

ALLEN J. OTTENS
DEBRA A. PENDER

This chapter's focus is on the application of Roberts's (1996; 2005, pp. 20–25) seven-stage crisis intervention model to the delivery of crisis intervention services at college and university counseling centers. Roberts's model is especially relevant, given several compelling reasons for providing crisis intervention as a therapeutic modality in this setting and with this particular clientele. First, traditional-age (18–24 years old) college students often encounter crises—death of a parent or friend (Balk, 2008), dating violence (Lawyer, Resnick, Bakanic, Burkett, & Kilpatrick, 2010), suicidality (Schwartz & Friedman, 2009), crushing financial debt in the face of a tight job market (Case, 2013; Institute for College Access & Success, 2011), and a myriad of threats to academic performance, to name a few—that pose a risk to their accomplishing critical developmental tasks. These tasks include managing emotions, developing intellectual competence, achieving independence, and developing mature relationships (Chickering & Reisser, 1993).

Second, there is evidence that college counseling centers are being challenged by increasing numbers of students (Watkins, Hunt, & Eisenberg, 2011) who present with more severe psychological issues. In a recent survey of college counseling center directors, they estimated that about 20% of the clients presented with severe treatment concerns, 16% with suicidal thoughts/behaviors, and 36% with depression (Mistler, Reetz, Krylowicz, & Barr, 2012; see http://files.cmcglobal.com/AUCCCD_Monograph_Public_2013.pdf). Benton, Robertson, Tseng, Newton, and Benton (2003), after seeing a significant increase in the severity of clients' problems over a 13-year span, suggested that crisis intervention and trauma debriefing will be important areas of professional development for all facets of college counseling centers. In fact, counseling services at many colleges have changed their focus from the provision of personal counseling to crisis management (Kadison & DiGeronimo, 2004).

Furthermore, Ottens and Fisher-McCanne (1990) point out that crisis intervention as a form of brief therapy is highly compatible with both college students' characteristics and realities of the academic setting. According to Fukuyama (2001), time-limited therapy or brief therapy models fit naturally within the quarter or semester structure of most colleges and universities. Furthermore, most clients at college counseling centers meet the criteria suited to brief therapeutic interventions: acute problem onset, previous good adjustment, ability to relate, and high initial motivation (Butcher & Koss, 1978). From an institutional standpoint, crisis intervention, with its brief duration (typically 3 to 13 weeks), makes sense as counseling centers face lengthening waiting lists and set limits on the number of sessions available.

The chapter is organized around two composite case examples of relatively common types of crises encountered by college counselors. We discuss the particulars of each case and present clinical information relevant to the crisis issues. Finally, using the case examples as templates, we guide the reader through the seven stages of the Roberts model, demonstrating how the model can be adapted for brief, crisis-oriented therapy in the college context.

## THE IMPOSTER PHENOMENON

### Megan, the "Imposter"

Megan (not her real name) is a 20-year-old second-semester sophomore who attends a large public university. She is enrolled in a prelaw curriculum. A serious, high-achieving student (GPA of 3.9 on a 4.0 scale), Megan has set her sights on one day becoming a partner in a top-notch corporate law firm.

Megan presents herself as a walk-in client at her university counseling center. She is in obvious distress, expressing worry that she will fail an important midterm exam. This, in turn, has left her calling into serious question whether she has the ability to eventually perform as a lawyer. When the on-call counselor inquires about how it follows that a low grade on this test will cancel out her law career, Megan responds:

> I've been worrying about this big macroeconomics exam next week and how I'll mess it up. It covers complicated material where it's not enough just to know the principles but you've got to be able to apply them. That got me thinking. Next year I'll be taking all upper-level courses—no more

common core fluff—taught by some of the top professors. I mean, you won't be able to "b.s." them, which is basically what I've been doing all along with the TAs who teach the introductory classes. I won't be able to keep getting A grades by just regurgitating what the instructor wants back onto the test. Then all this thinking started to snowball into "If I can't handle this normal academic pressure, how will I make it as a corporate lawyer?"

After disclosing (a) the conviction that her academic accomplishments are due mostly to taking easy courses and an ability to dupe instructors, (b) the fear that her academic charade will soon be found out, and (c) the terrible disappointment that her glittering future is slipping away, Megan slumps in her chair and sobs quietly. Existentially speaking, she must feel as if she is no longer standing on solid ground. She says she has not been sleeping well for the past week in anticipation of this exam; additionally, her racing thoughts seem to have a mind of their own. Because she believes that her academic situation and emotional state are out of her control, she remarks that she does not know if she can continue living this way.

She considers a host of impulsive coping options: changing majors, dropping out of school, avoiding her few friends on campus, and hatching plans to deceive her parents. Interspersed among Megan's pressured descriptions of these ill-conceived plans are numerous self-deprecating statements, such as "I can't continue fooling myself and others like this" and "I knew eventually others would see the real me."

## Definitions and Clinical Considerations

What Megan is experiencing is a syndrome originally described by Clance and Imes (1978) as an internal experience of intellectual phoniness prevalent among a select group of women in clinical and college settings, which they named the *imposter phenomenon* (IP). According to Clance and Imes, there are three primary features of imposterism. First, there is the belief that others have an inflated sense of one's actual abilities. Second, there is a fear that one will be uncovered as a phony, as not measuring up. Third, the imposter is convinced that her success has been due to luck or external factors—or, in Megan's case, to easy classes and easily duped teaching assistants. The emergence of this syndrome s has been described as follows: "When self and/or other imposed perfectionism becomes exaggerated, the normally expected, transient self-doubt that most college students face can become an imposter syndrome such that students feel like imposters at risk for exposure as frauds at any moment" (Girard, 2010, p. 190). The imposter experience persists despite independent, objective, and tangible evidence to the contrary.

Clance and O'Toole (1988) describe the female imposter experience as cyclical. The cycle begins when the student faces an exam, project, or task that involves external evaluation. The individual experiences great self-doubt and fear that, as in Megan's case, may be expressed as generalized anxiety, psychosomatic complaints, or sleep disturbance. It is important for the university crisis counselor to keep in mind that "imposters" are actually high achievers who may attempt to cope by overpreparing or by procrastinating, only to end up in a frenzied rush to catch up. The cycle ends with the imposter likely to have successfully completed the test or project. When she is praised or rewarded for her success, she discounts the recognition, which further feeds into her self-doubt and belief that suffering leads to success. And so the cycle repeats itself because there is always the lurking fear that one will not be able to maintain one's success (Langford & Clance, 1993).

Imposters tend to be introverted and feel terrorized by failure. The intellectual inauthenticity these women describe often leads to the fear of being publicly unmasked as a fake (Jarrett, 2010). This fear led to Megan's choosing impulsive and dysfunctional coping methods.

## Scope of the Problem

The failure to internalize success was initially viewed as unique to females (Clance & Imes, 1978). Subsequent research has been equivocal with regard to gender differences in the expression and prevalence of IP (Thompson, Davis, & Davidson, 1998). King and Cooley (1995), in a study of 127 undergraduates, found that higher levels of IP for females were associated with greater family achievement orientation, higher grade point averages, and more time spent on academic endeavors. However, these results need to be interpreted with caution because of the use of imprecise measures of academic achievement (e.g., GPA) and achievement orientation. The college counselor should bear in mind that when a study uncovers a greater prevalence of IP among females, it may be an artifact of gender-role stereotyping or parental messages regarding scores (King & Cooley, 1995). In their review of IP research, Langford and Clance (1993) stated that research has failed to uncover any differences between men and women with regard to imposter feelings.

Thompson et al. (1998) compared imposters and nonimposters from within a sample of 164 undergraduates. The imposters evidenced higher levels of anxiety, lower self-esteem, and a greater need for perfectionism. One finding of particular relevance for college counselors from this study is the tendency of imposters to overgeneralize, that is, to equate academic failure with failure as a person. Earlier, Carver and Ganellen (1983) reported this tendency to overgeneralize to be a powerful predictor of depression in college students. Returning to the vignette, if the college counselor has not already assessed for it, he or she should be sure to ask Megan about depressive symptomatology.

## Major Vulnerabilities and Risk Factors

Clance and Imes (1978) and Matthews and Clance (1985) suggested that IP develops in the dynamic interactions of the family of origin. Clance (1985) hypothesized that the family context may provide four essential elements in the development of IP. First, in childhood, the imposter believes that her abilities are unique and atypical in her family. Second, the feedback she receives from outside the family system conflicts with feedback from within the system. Third, she is not recognized or praised for accomplishments by family members. Finally, family members communicate that success and intelligence should come with little effort.

The crisis counselor needs to be mindful of the role assigned to the IP sufferer within the family and how that role impacts current thoughts and feelings. Clance and O'Toole (1988) suggested that the IP sufferer has received either of two messages from her family: You are not the bright one, or you are the bright one and success will come easily to you. King and Cooley (1995) considered it possible that IP females in their study received parental messages that implied academic achievement was due to effort rather than talent. Such messages might impress on females that they inherently have less intellect to help them get by. Clance, Dingman, Reviere, & Stober (1995) found that IP appears to be correlated with parents' selective valuation of certain of the child's characteristics over others—attractiveness and sociability, for example, over intelligence. Hence, the child comes to understand that self-concept is based on virtues that are more valued by parents. Sonnak and Towell (2001) investigated IP in British university students. They found that students who reported parents as more controlling and protective had higher scores on a measure of IP.

King and Cooley (1995) presented data that support the hypothesis that a family environment that emphasizes achievement is associated with higher levels of IP. They recommended obtaining students' perceptions of the importance of achievement in their families of origin. Miller and Kastburg (1995) interviewed six women employed in higher education settings who came from blue-collar family backgrounds. Although IP was not an issue for all six, for some of the women IP dogged them as a "lifelong charade." This is very preliminary evidence suggesting that socioeconomic status (SES) might impact the degree of IP present.

Crisis counselors should be mindful and inquire about the IP sufferers' perceptions of achievement orientation in their families of origin and recollections of parental messages about achievement and ability. A gauge of the families' SES level might also fill out the clinical picture, as well as ascertaining whether the IP client is the first in the family to attend college.

In addition to the family of origin discussion, a three-pronged study conducted by Leary, Patton, Orlando, and Funk (2000) with college undergraduates strongly suggests that the behavior of imposters possesses a notable

392 Children, Adolescents, and Young Adults

self-presentation element. For example, those research participants who scored high on imposterism and were not likely to be "found out" by audiences were not likely to belittle their accomplishments to the same extent as those who believed their shortcomings may become public. Therefore, the implication for counselors is that one must carefully examine the relationship between an imposter's private self-perception and his or her public self-presentation (Leary et al., 2000). More recent research has called into question some of the hallmarks that characterize IP. McElwee and Yurak (2007), for example, found that an IP sufferer may feel inadequate but not fraudulent. Moreover, rather than regarding IP as a trait, McElwee and Yurak suggested it may be regarded as a self-presentation strategy. Thus, presenting oneself as an imposter might lower expectations for a performance and reduce the pressure one might feel to do well. Perhaps this might be akin to the procrastinator who can always attribute a lower grade to lack of time rather than to a lack of intellect. We await further research in this area.

## Resilience and Protective Factors

Megan's request for assistance and support should be viewed by the college crisis worker as an invitation to intervene in the IP cycle. Typically, imposter feelings are not presented in a forthright manner by the client. Persons suffering from IP usually do not seek assistance due to the potential for shame and the embarrassment of being found out. Therefore, it is critical to establish an empathic, nonauthoritarian, therapeutic alliance (Clance & O'Toole, 1988) that allows for identification and emergence of these feelings.

Megan presented at the counseling center with feelings of intense anxiety and a sense of dread prior to her exam. This is significant because the IP sufferer customarily moves away from others who could help. Clance and O'Toole (1988) described this movement away as an attempt to isolate oneself in order to deal with the fear and shame that accompany IP. The alert counselor begins by establishing a supportive and inclusive relationship. The nonjudgmental, accepting relationship reduces Megan's tendency to isolate herself. This relationship may provide the basis for a later referral into a support group. Because the counselor will want to avoid delving in too deeply and quickly with a client like Megan, he or she will rely heavily on a personal characteristic required of effective crisis workers: cognitive dexterity and flexibility necessary for making do with only fragmentary knowledge of the client's complex personal-social-emotional-cultural background (Ottens, Pender, & Nyhof, 2009).

A crisis counselor is probably less likely to delve into an exploration of the client's family background and elucidation of parenting behavior that might have led to the client becoming so intent on winning others' approval. This excursion into the past is likely to dredge up feelings of anger and hurt that are better dealt with after the crisis is attenuated.

If future research corroborates the findings on McElwee and Yurak—that IP is a self-presentation strategy that protects against too high expectations—it would be unwise for the counselor to attack such a defense without helping the client to understand how he or she is using it to cope and what might be more adaptive coping choices.

## CRISIS INTERVENTION: APPLICATION OF THE MODEL (MEGAN)

### Stage 1: Establish Rapport and Relationship

Megan, a prelaw student, is a walk-in client at her university's counseling center. She is panicking over an upcoming exam. She describes her symptoms, which include an inability to concentrate and spiraling anxiety. "I've got to do well on this test," she repeats, while emphasizing the importance of grades, given her career ambition of becoming a corporate lawyer. During this initial contact, the counselor communicates her concern about Megan's fear of failing by intermittent eye contact, voice tone, and physical proximity. Establishing rapport is crucial, as the counselor surmises that Megan, like other IP clients, may be ashamed to ask for help—an act tantamount to admitting failure. Instead of weakness, the counselor strives to frame Megan's help seeking in terms of hopefulness and strength of character:

> Counselor: I'm optimistic about your ability to prevent events from getting out of control. In fact, coming here to talk to someone suggests that you knew this was the right thing to do.
>
> Megan: Well, I felt like I had nowhere else to turn. I can't keep living this way.
>
> Counselor: But isn't there always the option of "toughing it out" in isolated silence? Instead, you seem to be making a more proactive choice.

### Stage 2: Conduct a Thorough Assessment, Including Immediate Psychosocial Needs

The event triggering Megan's panic was the thought that she might not possess the necessary self-confidence for a law career, especially if such a thing as an exam could disquiet her so. She then connected this thought to a realization that there was nothing of intellectual substance to her. She had gotten stellar grades in common core courses because she is a good "con": She could give back on exams and papers exactly what the instructor wanted to see. However, she fears that when she takes more advanced courses from respected professors, they will see right through her game. With this information, the counselor establishes the initial clinical impression that Megan presents with the imposter phenomenon. It becomes evident to the counselor that Megan's modal coping style is to overachieve and motivate herself through worrying. Through probes and brief history taking, the counselor defines the scope and duration of the problem. Actually, feeling phony is a long-standing concern for Megan, but it appears now in bold relief given the stressor of the big exam. The nature of IP is such that Megan is likely to struggle to acknowledge previous success and personal strengths despite evidence to the contrary.

The Clance Impostor Phenomenon Scale (CIPS; Clance, 1985) is available online (www.paulineroseclance.com/impostor_phenomenon.html) and may be used with permission. It consists of 20 items on a 5-point Likert scale. A score of 40 or more is suggestive of IP having some degree of impact on one's life. In Megan's case, the counselor used some of her responses to items to facilitate rapport building and brief history taking, especially those items that tap into feelings of being an intellectual fraud and success being attributable to external factors.

The counselor also took note of an indirect message communicated by Megan. Was it indicative of some self-harm ideation?

| | |
|---|---|
| Counselor: | Megan, a few minutes ago you said that you didn't know if you can continue living this way. Is that an expression of just how out of control this situation has gotten? |
| Megan: | Absolutely. If this is what important exams are going to do to me, I don't want any more of it. I mean, I can't continue to freak out over every test. |
| Counselor: | I want to be sure I understand exactly what you mean. Are you saying to me that your approach to taking tests has to change—that you don't want to continue freaking out whenever there's a test? |
| Megan: | Yes, that's what I mean. |
| Counselor: | As opposed to saying, "I can't continue living this way" when somebody has plans to hurt themselves? |
| Megan: | You mean suicide? (Face reddens.) Oh, no, that's not anything I'm even thinking about. |

## Stage 3: Identify Major Problems

In this case, the precipitating event, the upcoming exam, was quickly established. The problems needing to be addressed were intertwined: how to attenuate the symptoms of anxiety and effectively prepare for the exam.

During this stage, Megan is allowed to express her feelings, which are a mix of catastrophizing about the test outcome and self-doubting personal criticisms. Besides the raw feelings, the counselor also listens for Megan's beliefs about her intellect, work ethic, and attributions for her previous successes. Knowing that IP may have a familial component, the counselor "tunes into" any disclosures about parent-driven perfectionism, parental expectations for Megan's academic accomplishments, or parental definitions of what counts as success.

## Stage 4: Deal With Feelings and Emotions

There are two distinct aspects to this component of the crisis intervention model. The counselor strives to allow Megan to freely express her feelings, to experience catharsis, and to tell the story about her current crisis situation. To this end, the counselor relies on standard active listening and therapeutic responding skills: accurate paraphrasing, minimal encouragers, reflecting feelings, summarizing, and reassurances (Egan, 2014). These complementary counselor responses not only allow the client's dysfunctional style to unfold but also are the basis for establishing a working alliance (Kiesler, 1988). Very cautiously, the counselor at this stage will work "anticomplementary" responses into her dialogue with Megan. Anticomplementary responses include advice giving, interpretations, reframes, and probes. Such responses are designed to begin the process of challenging the client's maladaptive cognitive and behavioral choices (Kiesler, 1988). Such confrontational interventions loosen Megan's maladaptive schemas, help her consider behavioral options, and question her attributions of failure and success. The judicious blending of complementary (supporting or bonding) responses and anticomplementary (challenging or frustrating) responses is thought to constitute an interplay that is fundamental to the therapy process (Hanna & Ottens, 1995). The following is a probing response typical of this stage:

Megan:      (emphatically) I can't afford to take this test lightly. I'll try psyching myself up—"You've got to prove yourself on this test! You *can't* screw it up! What if you fail?"

Counselor:  Consider this for a moment: Will your success on the test be *because of* or *in spite of* that kind of self-talk?

## Stage 5: Generate and Explore Alternatives

The crisis counselor must deal with the immediate concern of how Megan will cope with the upcoming test. Beyond that, the larger questions of dealing with the distorted view of her personal competency and possible familial dynamics may be issues for later counseling work. The counselor is aware that IP clients devalue their opinions and overvalue those of the "authority." Hence, a collaborative approach is used to brainstorm ways to handle the exam. All options are fair game. Eventually, three options are seriously discussed that are the opposite of Megan's initial avoidant, impulsive choices: (a) Join a study group with some laid-back friends; (b) provide tutoring for her roommate who is struggling in a Spanish class, because this will give Megan a chance to display an expertise that cannot easily be disaffirmed; and (c) practice a rapid relaxation technique (Ottens, 1991) to lower anxious arousal while studying.

## Stage 6: Develop and Formulate an Action Plan

For the short term, that is, to manage the crisis of the upcoming exam, the counselor and Megan adopt a three-pronged approach. First, they draw up a behavioral contract that includes the three coping choices outlined previously. Second, they identify the types of sabotaging self-talk Megan might use to negate the contract (e.g., "Why waste my time helping my roommate?" "This won't work!"). Third, the counselor makes an explicit commitment to be there to help: "Megan, I want you to know that as long as you are committed to working on this contract, I will do all I can to help and support you. This truly is a 50-50 effort on both of our parts."

There are also longer-term considerations, because for the IP client there will always be another test, term paper, or important evaluation that will be cause for self-doubt. Even if Megan excels on the big exam, it will be easy for her to discount her success or to attribute it to external factors. Hence, continued intervention is recommended to target her beliefs around themes of negative self-efficacy, perfectionism, and the use of worry as a self-motivator. She also believes that others can somehow see into her and spot her as a phony. In subsequent sessions, the counselor will address these issues, as well as familial achievement expectations. Group counseling is an option, especially if the group is composed of other women who share these IP beliefs.

## Stage 7: Conduct Follow-Up

Brief, crisis-oriented therapy in this case consisted of 10 individual counseling sessions. Megan elected not to join a group at this time but kept this idea in mind as a later option. The counselor and Megan agreed to schedule a follow-up session during the 2nd week of the next semester.

At that follow-up session, the counselor must note whether Megan has fallen back into the IP cycle. The counselor will want to (a) assess the fluidity or rigidity of Megan's cognitions, (b) discuss future stressors, (c) inquire into how she is rehearsing to handle those stressors, (d) assess her relationships with peers, and (e) learn what evidence she now uses for gauging performance.

## CAMPUS-TARGETED VIOLENCE/CRISIS INTERVENTION

### The Case of Thomas

Thomas, a 20-year-old White male, was one of the hundreds of people attending a candlelight vigil on the campus of Northern Illinois University (NIU) on Friday, February, 15, 2008. It was the night after the tragic fatal shootings that had occurred on campus. The day before, at 3:05 p.m., a lone gunman had entered a lecture hall class in Cole Hall and opened fire on the instructor and students. Chaos reigned as many students tried to run, hide, or call 911. Others were immobile, frozen in their seats, unable to comprehend the scene of carnage (Northern Illinois University, 2008).

This evening the throng of mourners endured temperatures only 2 degrees above zero—with a much lower wind chill factor. As professor of counselor education, director of the Counseling Lab training center, and a licensed clinical professional counselor, I (D.P.) had been volunteering my services to the stunned, numbed members of the campus community. By this time I had been providing crisis assistance nonstop for almost 24 hours. Wearily, I told my spouse, "I've done all I can for now. I have to go home."

As we walked to our car, I reflected on what I had witnessed over those 24 hours. Had fate somehow designed me to be at this place at this point in time? Was I being called upon, so to speak, to use my crisis intervention skills at this extreme moment? I've hardly ever felt more needed—and more grateful for the crisis intervention training that I had received over the years. My reverie was interrupted by a young man who had split off from the crowd in order to sidle up to me. He struck up a conversation by asking if I had a son or daughter on campus. When I said no, he asked if I were a student. I stifled a giggle at the implausible assumption he had made and replied, "No, I'm a professor." With just that one bit of self-disclosure, he became instantly greatly distressed and animated. "I *have* to talk to a professor! Right now! *Tonight!*"

His agitation caught me off guard, but his urgency to make contact aroused my crisis response instincts. "Might we step inside that building right over there?" I suggested. My husband followed but at a considerate enough distance that he was beyond earshot. Then I realized that Thomas's friends had also respectfully dropped back as he had come forward toward me.

Now with some privacy and ample space so that he would not fill crowded, I ventured to ask, "What do you need?" Thomas replied—pleaded really—"I need you to promise me to carry a gun to class. Get professors to carry guns to protect the students. You've got to make it so that this place is safe for me to graduate from!" As his narrative tumbled out, he began to place a context around this incongruous request. During his freshman year, he had been distressed by threats and even open displays of violence. He had seen students carrying knives and was witness to some serious fighting during homecoming and rush week. As a sophomore, he actually saw a knife attack on Fraternity Row and the attacker arrested by university police. Now a junior, he was present for what, in his scheme of things, must have been the next most logical escalation in a progression of campus violence. A sinister coincidence brought Thomas and the gunman together in that lecture room—gunman in front on the stage, Thomas in one of the farthest rows back. On this day, his habit of sitting as far as possible from the instructor's gaze paid off. He was one of the first out the door when the shooting started. Thomas escaped, and like every other survivor on the NIU campus and in the DeKalb community, he was discovering that the worst can happen here.

What I also learned from Thomas in our 30-minute encounter was that he had come to NIU to escape the violence of his own family and neighborhood. Attending, and graduating from, the university was a way to create the life he wanted to live, not the life he had experienced so far. He had constructed a worldview of college as a safe place. Tragedy could not follow him there. Thomas was very clear: He felt defenseless, unsafe, and in need of promises, not just reassurances—especially the promise that I would advocate for my fellow professors to carry guns to classes. *Would I do that for him?*

A rule of effective crisis intervention is to be genuine, to not lie. So, I gently told him what I believed my mission on campus to be. It was to prepare a new generation of adults to become counselors who would be on the "front lines," skilled in recognizing when people are suffering with mental illness and may be a risk to harm others. I then shifted the narrative to how I am one of those absent-minded professors everybody hears about. You can almost bet that I will lose my keys nearly every class. Imagine if I left a firearm lying around. "Carrying a gun," I confessed to Thomas, "just isn't in my make-up. But, I'm determined to work very, very hard on trying to stop the violence through words and healing."

Thomas had begun to calm significantly at this point, so I started to ask the crisis assessment questions to draw essential information from him. After all, this young man was mostly a blank slate to me, having picked me, a total stranger, to pour out all the fears, rage, and hopelessness he had inside. I asked whether he was alone. "No," he said. "I've got my friends with me. We're all going back to the dorm to eat pizza and play video guitar games." By now the campus was mostly deserted. For those students who couldn't or wouldn't leave, the university was providing free pizzas.

When I asked him about making contact with his parents, he became agitated again. He was so adamant that he was in "no way going to call or even attempt to see them" that he started to take leave from me. I backed off from this topic, reassuring him, "It's OK. You clearly know what you want to do." That brought a smile to his lips and a confirmation that I had handled this idea properly. "You're good at your job," he said.

We discussed risk of suicide and his plans for the weekend. It was clear he had no ideation toward self-harm; moreover, he had a plan that involved connecting with his friends and others in the dorms. I could see by his body language that he was feeling it was time for leave-taking. He nodded toward his friends and said they were getting hungry and so was he. He mentioned that the pizza was donated by local restaurants, so they wanted to get to it before the good slices were gone. I made a contract for follow-up contact, handing him both the official "here's who to call card" and my own card with my personal number on it. We ended by talking a little about things he might want to do to increase his overall feelings of safety, including seeing a counselor for a while. He thanked me and rejoined his friends, and they all disappeared down an icy path between the residence halls.

## CRISIS INTERVENTION: APPLICATION OF THE MODEL (THOMAS)

### Stage 1: Establish Rapport and Relationship

In today's world of instant media coverage of tragedy, especially when an act of targeted violence is committed on a college campus (see http://www2.ed.gov/admins/lead/safety/campus-attacks.pdf), crisis counselors are often called to action immediately. This call to serve means being able to adapt to rapidly changing situations as details emerge about what has or has not happened and to be able to provide psychological first aid (supportive listening at the same time as active assessment of the client's stability, emotional regulation, and ability to engage in problem solving; Vernberg et al., 2008).

Thomas had approached the counselor without even being aware he was talking to one. He was in a state of crisis when he introduced himself, as exhibited by his approaching a total stranger, the sound of pleading in his voice, his distraught appearance, and his inability to make eye contact. All of these symptoms are consistent with a person who has witnessed loss of life (American Psychiatric Association, 2013). He was talking rapidly and seemed desperate to find someone to listen, yet he had not approached any of the on-scene counselors who were wearing armbands for easy identification. I had removed mine moments before, when I had decided to leave the scene.

The first step in establishing rapport was introducing myself as a professional counselor and as one of the crisis support people there at the vigil. The second step was to quickly assess both his safety and my own. We decided to go into a nearby building to find a spot that allowed for privacy and yet was open enough that his friends and my husband could monitor without hearing what was being spoken. Thomas was able to vent for several minutes and shared his frustration about his expectation that NIU should be a safe place, but that yesterday, it was not. Pacing with him, keeping a soft and quiet tone, and slowing him down were some of the interventions I used.

## Stage 2: Conduct a Thorough Assessment, Including Immediate Psychosocial Needs

Thomas was at risk for the development of a post-traumatic exposure reaction or even a disorder. Roberts (2005) suggested assessing personal safety and the client's immediate psychosocial needs. I made Thomas aware of the bounds of confidentiality, and then we discussed whether he felt suicidal. He did not. His fears were about the external world and seeking safety from others. His fears were both immediate and longer term (family of origin), but we agreed to focus on the concerns about the shooting and ways to feel safe on the campus. I was concerned about his degree of isolation and refusal to connect with family, but with further assessment, I discovered he had a strong peer network. He and his friends were going to remain on campus during the week of healing. He was seeking help and was receptive after we met, disclosing issues that were deep-seated (family trauma, estrangement), as well as more current exposures to campus violence. He made it abundantly clear that he did not feel safe on campus. Psychological first aid (PFA; Ruzek et al., 2007) is designed for on-scene and field support efforts after any kind of disaster or trauma. Certainly, witnessing loss of life is one such situation. The priorities are listening, support, and assessment for safety, which dovetail with the goals of the first two stages of the Roberts model.

## Stage 3: Identify Major Problems

For Thomas, the university campus was now a place of high risk and danger, and this reality clashed with his longer-held assumption of the campus as a safe, nurturing oasis. These incompatible perceptions propelled the angst and upset he was experiencing. Thomas had constructed a plan to escape from the "drama and trauma" of his earlier life by going to college and succeeding there. The shooting in his Cole Hall classroom had culminated in a shattering of primary world assumptions around fairness, safety, and mastery. At this moment, Thomas did not regard life as fair, but he still believed that life is worth living, despite doubts that he could master whatever life puts in front of him (Janoff-Bulman, 1992).

Thomas's reaction—albeit a natural one to an abnormal event—to witnessing the shooting and the resulting chaos, coupled with the subsequent reliving of the moments as he thought of them and told friends (and even me) about them, served as a potential early warning sign of post-traumatic stress disorder reactions in the weeks to come. Other vulnerabilities for Thomas, included (a) potential isolation (refusal to connect with family), (b) his "accidental" help-seeking behavior (reaching out and happening to find a crisis specialist), and (c) his belief system that he needed "someone out there" to be responsible for his safety.

## Stage 4: Deal With Feelings and Emotions

The purposes of an on-scene psychological intervention are to support, assess, and stabilize. So even though there were ample issues to pursue, the essential aims were to affect a calming influence, explore Thomas's social network connections, and see if he could regulate his emotions. I also checked on the appropriateness of his decision-making capacity for the near future and established that he was going to be safe from self-harm.

Thomas's greatest need was to vent his urgent feelings about the shooting and being unsafe. A turning point in our brief encounter hinged on some genuine self-disclosures I shared with him. After I shared my personal limitations with firearms—how I was not "psychologically wired" to be comfortable around them—and my ideas about counseling, helping people, and trying to make a difference before people harmed others, he was open to new thinking and began to move away from his original stance.

## Stage 5: Generate and Explore Alternatives

It is important to reduce isolation and restore naturally occurring social networks. After the shooting tragedy, many of the students living on campus had already left or were in the process of returning home for the recess week of healing time. Thomas was very clear that returning home or even calling his parents was not an option. He did generate a plan of safety and connectedness for the coming week.

## Stage 6: Develop and Formulate an Action Plan

Thomas's willingness to engage in the psychological first aid counseling and to open up about his life was a definite protective factor. It was important to follow his rules about topics, especially that of family life, so he was aware of and maintaining his own personal boundaries during the conversation. Once he was presented with the idea that there could be more than one way of providing safety, including trying to help people prior to, during, and after a shooting, his state of agitation was calmed significantly. Although I was not promising him that I would carry a weapon, nor promising to advocate that all professors should, I was simply and genuinely sharing with him another path within my life and skill set. Thomas opened up, calmed down, and began to share more about the other acts of violence he had seen in his 3 years at the university.

Resilience during crisis may be underrecognized by many students. For example:

> Student reports of emotion states were collected both before and after the on-campus Valentine's Day, 2008 shootings at Northern Illinois University (NIU). A separate group of students not on campus when the shootings occurred provided emotion state reports and predictions of the emotions they would expect to experience 2 weeks after a shooting occurred. Examination of these data suggests that: (1) emotion states of NIU students reflected resilience, and (2) students made affective forecasting errors indicating that this resilience was unexpected. (Hartnett & Skowronski, 2008, p. 275)

So, part of the work of the session with Thomas was to do the assessment and then point out to him the self-identified resiliencies that he had not known were present.

## Stage 7: Conduct Follow-Up

Thomas was a young man with a specific and short-term need to ventilate about the tragedy he had witnessed. He was hesitant to agree to make an appointment with me for follow-up, but he was willing to take my business card and the official referral card in case he wanted to talk some more. His friends signaled that they were ready and hungry, and he left with them.

## CONCLUSION

Several themes emerge from the vignettes of Megan and Thomas. First, the concerns facing both of them need to be addressed by the counselor in a sensitive, knowledgeable, and culturally aware manner that demonstrates an understanding of the potential impact that gender, trauma, and family history can have on the presentation and maintenance of symptoms. Second, the crisis worker in a college counseling center should be cognizant of the personal context in which these symptoms emerge (e.g., client's potential for self-blame, desire for perfection, academic expectations, and assumptive world). Third, the potential for students to isolate from those who could help them needs to be understood in terms of students' developmental needs for autonomy, personal competency, and self-definition. In both vignettes, the potential for isolation was high. The availability of a caring professional allowed each client to engage in a process of stabilization that was facilitated by following the crisis intervention model (Roberts, 1996). Finally, there is the need for ongoing training and education so that counselors can keep abreast of issues facing today's college population. This training builds competency into the counseling staff and makes for more effective service delivery.

Crisis-oriented interventions are a critical and valuable resource for college students. By definition, the college crisis counselor is the initial contact person and stabilization resource who can serve as the conduit to myriad campus and community services. Appropriate crisis intervention and follow-up on the college campus support a student's efforts to balance the academic and emotional demands of college, as well as allowing the counselor an effective strategy to manage a burgeoning caseload.

REFERENCES

American Psychiatric Association. (2013). *Diagnostic and statistical manual of mental disorders* (5th ed.). Arlington, VA: Author.

Balk, D. E. (2008). Grieving: 22 to 30 percent of all college students. In H. L. Servaty-Seib & D. J. Taub (Eds.), *Assisting bereaved college students* (pp. 5–14). San Francisco: Jossey-Bass.

Benton, S. A., Robertson, J. M., Tseng, W-C., Newton, F. B., & Benton, S. L. (2003). Changes in counseling center client problems across 13 years. *Professional Psychology: Research and Practice, 34*, 66–72.

Butcher, J. N., & Koss, M. P. (1978). Research on brief and crisis-oriented therapies. In S. L. Garfield & A. E. Bergin (Eds.), *Handbook of psychotherapy and behavior change* (2nd ed., pp. 725–767). New York: Wiley.

Carver, C. S., & Ganellen, R. J. (1983). Depression and components of self-punitiveness: High standards, self-criticism, and over-generalisation. *Journal of Personality and Social Psychology, 48*, 1097–1111.

Case, J. P. (2013). Implications of financial aid: What college counselors should know. *Journal of College Student Psychotherapy, 27*, 159–173.

Chickering, A. W., & Reisser, L. (1993). *Education and identity* (2nd ed.). San Francisco: Jossey-Bass.

Clance, P. R. (1985). *The impostor phenomenon: When success makes you feel like a fake.* Toronto, ON: Bantam.

Clance, P. R., Dingman, D., Reviere, S. L., & Stober, D. R. (1995). Impostor phenomenon in an interpersonal/social context: Origins and treatment. *Women and Therapy, 16*, 79–96.

Clance, P. R., & Imes, S. A. (1978). The imposter phenomenon in high-achieving women: Dynamics and therapeutic intervention. *Psychotherapy: Theory, Research, and Practice, 15,* 241–247.

Clance, P. R., & O'Toole, M. A. (1988). The imposter phenomenon: An internal barrier to empowerment and achievement. *Women and Therapy, 6,* 51–64.

Egan, G. (2014). *The skilled helper* (10th ed.). Belmont, CA: Brooks/ Cole.

Fukuyama, M. A. (2001). Counseling in colleges and universities. In D. C. Locke, J. E. Myers, & E. L. Herr (Eds.), *The handbook of counseling* (pp. 319–341). Thousand Oaks, CA: Sage.

Girard, K. A. (2010). Working with parents and families of young adults. In J. Kay & V. Schwartz (Eds.), *Mental health care in the college community* (pp. 179–202). Hoboken, NJ: Wiley-Blackwell.

Hanna, F. J., & Ottens, A. J. (1995). The role of wisdom in psychotherapy. *Journal of Psychotherapy Integration, 5,* 195–219.

Hartnett, J. L., & Skowronski, J. J. (2010). Affective forecasts and the Valentine's Day shootings at NIU: People are resilient, but unaware of it. *Journal of Positive Psychology, 5,* 275–280.

Institute for College Access and Success. (2011, October). *Student debt and the class of 2011.* Oakland, CA: Author.

Janoff-Bulman, R. (1992). *Shattered assumptions: Towards a new psychology of trauma.* New York: Free Press.

Jarrett, C. (2010). Feeling like a fraud. *The Psychologist, 23,* 380–383.

Kadison, R. D., & DiGeronimo, T. F. (2004). *College of the overwhelmed: The campus mental health crisis and what to do about it.* San Francisco: Jossey-Bass.

Kiesler, D. J. (1988). *Therapeutic metacommunication.* Palo Alto, CA: Consulting Psychologists Press.

King, J. E., & Cooley, E. L. (1995). Achievement orientation and the imposter phenomenon among college students. *Contemporary Educational Psychology, 20,* 304–312.

Langford, J., & Clance, P. R. (1993). The imposter phenomenon: Recent research findings regarding dynamics, personality and family patterns and their implications for treatment. *Psychotherapy, 30,* 495–501.

Lawyer, S., Resnick, H., Bakanic, V., Burkett, T., & Kilpatrick, D. (2010). Forcible, drug-facilitated, and incapacitated rape and sexual assault among undergraduate women. *Journal of American College Health, 58,* 453–460.

Leary, M. R., Patton, K. M., Orlando, A. E., & Funk, W. W. (2000). The imposter phenomenon: Self-perceptions, reflected appraisals, and interpersonal strategies. *Journal of Personality, 68,* 725–756.

McElwee, R. O., & Yurak, T. J. (2007). Feeling versus acting like an impostor: Real feelings of fraudulence or self-presentation? *Individual Difference Research, 5,* 201–220.

Mistler, B. J., Reetz, D. R., Krylowicz, B., & Barr, V. (2012). *The Association for University and College Counseling Center Directors annual survey: Reporting period September 1, 2011 through August 31, 2012.*

Northern Illinois University. (2008). *Report of the February 14, 2008, shootings, Northern Illinois*

*University*. Retrieved from http://www.niu.edu/feb14report/Feb14report.pdf

Ottens, A. J. (1991). *Coping with academic anxiety* (2nd ed.). New York: Rosen.

Ottens, A. J., & Fisher-McCanne, L. (1990). Crisis intervention at the college campus counseling center. In A. R. Roberts (Ed.), *Crisis intervention handbook: Assessment, treatment, and response* (pp. 78–100). Belmont, CA: Wadsworth.

Ottens, A. J., Pender, D., & Nyhof, D. (2009). Essential personhood: A review of counselor characteristics needed for effective crisis intervention work. *International Journal of Emergency Mental Health*, *11*(1), 43–52.

Roberts, A. R. (1996). Epidemiology and definitions of acute crisis in American society. In A. R. Roberts (Ed.), *Crisis management and brief treatment: Theory, technique, and applications* (pp. 16–33). Chicago: Nelson-Hall.

Roberts, A. R. (2005). Bridging the past and present to the future of crisis intervention and crisis management. In A. R. Roberts (Ed.), *Crisis intervention handbook: Assessment, treatment, and research* (3rd ed., pp. 3–34). New York: Oxford University Press.

Ruzek, J. I., Brymer, M. J., Jacobs, A. K., Layne, C. M., Vernberg, E. M., & Watson, P. J. (2007). Psychological first aid. *Journal of Mental Health Counseling*, *29*(1), 17–49.

Schwartz, L. J., & Friedman, H. A. (2009). College student suicide. *Journal of College Student Psychotherapy*, *23*, 78–102.

Sonnak, C., & Towell, T. (2001). The imposter phenomenon in British university students: Relationships between self-esteem, mental health, parenting rearing style and socioeconomic status. *Personality and Individual Differences*, *31*, 863–874.

Thompson, T., Davis, H., & Davidson, J. (1998). Attributional and affective responses of impostors to academic success and failure outcomes. *Personality and Individual Differences*, *25*, 381–396.

Vernberg, E. M., Steinberg, A. M., Jacobs, A. K., Brymer, M. J., Watson, P. J., Osofsky, J. D.,... Ruzek, J. I. (2008). Innovations in disaster mental health: Psychological first aid. *Professional Psychology: Research and Practice*, *39*, 381–388.

Watkins, D. C., Hunt, J., & Eisenberg, D. (2011). Increased demand for mental health services on college campuses: Perspectives from administrators. *Qualitative Social Work*, *11*, 319–337.

# 14

## School Crisis Intervention, Crisis Prevention, and Crisis Response

SCOTT NEWGASS
DAVID J. SCHONFELD

### Vignette 1

A fourth-grade boy is fatally wounded by his cousin while playing with a gun that they find at home. Uncomfortable with addressing the child's death, the school administrators decide not to discuss it with the boy's classmates until after finding someone who can advise them on how to handle such a situation. Several days later, they identify a consultant who can visit the class.

Over the phone, the administrators request that the consultant meet during the upcoming visit with the student who had pulled the trigger to advise them on whether referral for mental health counseling is indicated. They inform the consultant that since the death, the other students have been calling him "murderer," and the school has therefore transferred the boy to another school. Given this limited information, the consultant advises over the phone that referral to mental health counseling is appropriate given the circumstances and suggests that it is not necessary to wait until the visit in a few days in order to assess the child directly.

The consultant arrives at the school about a week after the death has occurred. The child's desk remains unchanged. When the consultant meets several of the students as they return from recess, they explain that they do not wish to discuss what happened and are reluctant to carry on any conversation. Several students begin crying loudly as the consultant is introduced. With some difficulty, the students are encouraged to begin discussing their classmate's death and their reactions to it.

### Vignette 2

A school staff member working late on Friday afternoon is notified by a parent that one of the school's third-grade students has just been injured by a gunshot wound to the face. The child's brother, who is in the fourth grade at the school, had been playing with a handgun that accidentally discharged. The principal is notified, and he immediately contacts the other members of the crisis team. The crisis team talks over the phone for the rest of the evening and begins making plans while the principal and the school social worker go to the hospital to offer support to the family. Using the school crisis telephone tree, the entire school staff is contacted over the weekend and notified about an emergency staff meeting on Monday morning prior to the start of the school day.

On Monday morning, the crisis team meets early and discusses its plans; it is joined by consultants from the Regional School Crisis Prevention and Response Program. A staff meeting is held immediately after this meeting, just before the children's arrival. Staff members are encouraged to talk about their reactions to the recent events and are provided advice on how to facilitate discussions within their classrooms. Notification announcements are distributed, and all teachers agree to read the announcement during the homeroom period.

Several children arrive at school with copies of the local newspaper that carries a banner headline story about the tragedy. Rumors are already beginning to surface among the youngsters. Many of the children are just hearing about the situation from their peers as they arrive at school.

At a predetermined time during the homeroom period, each class is informed of the incident by its teacher, who then facilitates a discussion. Mental health staff join the teacher in leading the discussions in the English and Spanish classes of the two children who were involved in the event. The children are encouraged to express their thoughts and feelings; misinformation is corrected (e.g., according to one rumor, the child intentionally shot his sister over a minor disagreement) and concerns answered (e.g., several students volunteer that their parents have advised them to avoid their classmate because he has a gun and may try to kill them). Ultimately, most of the classes decide that they want to do something to show their support for the family. Students begin working on cards, banners, and letters to send to the student in the hospital, as well as cards of support for the student who fired the gun.

Several parents arrive at the school throughout the course of the day because of the impact that this accident has had on the community. A number of these parents do not speak English as their native language. Bilingual staff are available to provide direct support or translation services. A room is identified for parents to come and meet with others so that they have an opportunity to express their upset and concern, as well as to receive some direction on how they can contribute to their children's adjustment during this time. The Child Development–Community Policing Program holds a community meeting at the school to discuss handgun violence.

Over the next several weeks, many staff members talk about their own distress—some because of the recent events, some because the crisis has triggered memories of prior losses. The staff form a mutual support group that continues for several weeks after the crisis. The crisis team provides ongoing evaluation of the needs of students, staff, and parents. The boy who pulled the trigger returns to class the following week and is welcomed back by his classmates. His sister subsequently recovers and is also welcomed back to school. On follow-up, the school staff report that the management of the crisis has led to increased respect for the new principal and has brought them closer as a school community.

## Vignette 3

A 14-year-old girl is the unintended victim of a shooting outside her house. One month later, a classmate commits suicide during the school day. Another month passes, and another classmate kills himself during a 3-day weekend.

The first incident presented several obstacles to the school's attempts to provide services; the death took place at the beginning of a week's vacation, and the student, recently transferred into the school, had developed only a small network of friends and acquaintances. When the students returned to school the following week, the staff made announcements in each classroom and offered support services for any students wanting to discuss their reactions to the news or the circumstances of community violence.

When the second student died, several hundred students utilized the support room services over the course of several days. Multiple staff members were assigned from other schools by the coordinator of counseling services of the district crisis team to assist with the interventions. While interventions took place in classrooms and the support rooms, a group within the school initiated by the crisis team began to plan how to reach out to parents in the community in an attempt to prevent further suicides. The media coordinator accepted all calls from the press and provided complete information about the interventions taking place, including information on warning signs of suicidality and suggestions for parents on how to discuss this situation with their children. Students began leaving graffiti messages on the locker of the student who had recently died, as well as on the locker of the student who had died a month previously. After discussion with the crisis team about memorialization, the principal announced that messages left on the two students' lockers would be allowed to remain until the following weekend, at which time they would be removed. Parents of children who utilized support room services were contacted directly by telephone concerning the level of intervention their child received and whether or not follow-up with an outside agency for ongoing therapy might be helpful.

After the third death, another suicide, the school again provided support room services and began to delegate mental health staff to assist in the classroom interventions. Several parents called the school asking that their child be evaluated because of concern about their youngster's suspected suicidality. Only a few students were referred for emergent evaluation off-site, and the parents of students requiring that level of evaluation were asked to come to the school and transport their child. School personnel helped families with inadequate insurance to identify mental health services willing to see their children for evaluation and treatment. A meeting was held after the first day of intervention to provide classroom staff with helpful information about screening for suicidal ideation and risk. The press was again contacted to reiterate the suggestions for parents that had been published after the first suicide. A community meeting was scheduled for parents and interested community members to hear from experts in crisis intervention, at-risk behaviors among teenagers, and suicide. More than 400 parents attended.

---

As comparison of the preceding vignettes illustrates, the presence of a preexisting comprehensive crisis response plan will assist a school in anticipating and meeting the needs of its students, staff, and the larger community at the time of crisis. Although crisis can be disruptive to the educational process and be associated with short- and long-term psychological effects, these consequences can often be ameliorated if adequate support is provided at the time of crisis (Kline, Schonfeld, & Lichtenstein, 1995). These support services are more likely to be provided at school if a systematic school crisis response plan is already in place.

Schools have as their principal focus educational goals. Whereas schools are required to have a fire evacuation plan and to conduct regular fire drills, they less commonly have developed and implemented a plan for attending to the psychological and emotional needs of students and staff at the time of crisis. Some personnel within schools (as well as many professionals outside of school systems) view these latter concerns as clinical issues that fall outside the realm of an educational institution. As a result, many schools remain unprepared for a crisis and fail to mobilize optimally the clinical and support resources both within the school and within the broader community to support students and staff when a crisis occurs.

Although schools may attempt to assemble an ad hoc crisis team to address an acute episode, at the time of the crisis many staff members respond to the event in ways that do not allow them to take a thoughtful, broad, and long-term view of the needs of students and staff (Klingman, 1988). An effective crisis response requires prior preparedness and a systematic organizational response that is both flexible enough to be applicable to a broad range of crisis situations and specific enough to provide guidance at the time of a particular crisis.

The plan should address three broad areas: safety and security; obtaining, verifying, and disseminating accurate information to staff, students, parents, and the general public (when appropriate); and the emotional and psychological needs of those involved. All three domains must be addressed concurrently, or none will be addressed effectively. This is unlikely to occur in the absence of an organizational school crisis response plan, prior training of school staff, and dedicated response staff and resources within the school.

With the emerging and hard-won knowledge proceeding from the experiences of responders to school and community crises including shootings at Red Lake, Minnesota; Virginia Tech; a movie theater in Aurora, Colorado;

and Sandy Hook Elementary in Newtown, Connecticut, schools and first responders have added to the structural components and procedural aspects of responding to victim needs along with those of the wider community. For instance, in situations where a number of individuals have been victimized, rapid and accurate identification becomes a priority. To avoid using already traumatized staff familiar with the students killed at Sandy Hook Elementary to identify the victims, the district was able to use class photographs to accomplish this task. Schools should consider scheduling class photographs as early in the school year as possible to be prepared for such a need should it arise. It is also essential for schools and their districts to identify potential sites for relocation, both temporary and for the long term if the circumstances require, as was necessary for Sandy Hook Elementary. Likewise, it is becoming increasingly necessary that schools and their staff be familiar with the protocols associated with the Incident Command System (ICS) and the National Management Incident System (NIMS). Online training in core competencies is available through the FEMA Emergency Management Institute at http://training.fema.gov/IS/crslist.aspx. These training curricula will assist school staff in providing crisis supports in collaboration with local, state, and (sometimes) federal first responders and support agencies. The State of Connecticut recently passed legislation requiring that all school staff receive an overview of ICS and NIMS at the beginning of each school year and work toward becoming NIMS compliant through training offered by FEMA. Connecticut also requires each public school to participate in a crisis drill at least every 3 months. Although each school should familiarize its staff and students with the procedures of a "lockdown," schools are encouraged to simulate a variety of scenarios to test their response capabilities. Each school and district is also required to develop an All Hazards Safety and Security Plan in conjunction with their local first responder agencies and consistent with the Local Emergency Operations Plan and to submit these plans to the state Division of Emergency Management and Homeland Security.

An effective response should validate typical reactions to traumatic events and provide the mechanisms for students and staff to express and begin to resolve their personal reactions to the event. An organizational plan for systematic school crisis preparedness and response allows schools to remain proactive and ahead of unfolding crises by anticipating needs, assessing developing hazards, and identifying the resources available to respond to a crisis, as well as any service gaps that should be addressed. Relying exclusively on external resources to address a crisis may result in a sense of disempowerment among the staff, may contribute to the public's misperception of the capacity of school personnel to address the psychological and emotional needs of students, and may lead to a failure to anticipate and meet the long-term needs of students and staff subsequent to the initial intervention that may be provided by an external response team. While mental health resources from the community play a vital role in assisting a school in its response to a crisis, primary interventions should be provided by school staff whenever possible because they already have some history with their students, and they will continue to be with the students—and the school—long after the crisis is over.

## THE SCHOOL CRISIS RESPONSE INITIATIVE

In 1991, the School Crisis Response Initiative was formed to address how schools might best prepare for crises. The organizing group, representing the fields of education, pediatric medicine, psychiatry, psychology, social work, and police, included members from Yale University School of Medicine, Department of Pediatrics and Child Study Center, and the Consultation Center; four area school systems; and the New Haven Police Department.

The group set three initial goals: (a) to develop a systematic organizational protocol (Schonfeld, Kline, & Members of the Crisis Intervention Committee, 1994; Schonfeld, Lichtenstein, Kline Pruett, & Speese-Linehan, 2002) that would define and anticipate the types of crises that may impact the student body and the local community, identify interventions that would be most effective in reducing long-term trauma, and create a structure to ensure a rapid, reliable, and replicable response mechanism with preliminary definition of personnel and responsibilities; (b) to provide the necessary training to prepare school staff in delivering services based upon the model; and (c) to increase the collaborative relationships between schools and community mental health and social service providers. To date, personnel associated with the program's development have trained more than 40,000 school and community staff in the use of the model, consulted to more than 3,000 district- and school-level crisis response teams, and provided technical assistance to schools during more than 400 crisis situations. In 2003, the Office of Victims of Crime published a bulletin describing the basic structure of the program elements (Schonfeld & Newgass, 2003; http://www.ovc.gov/ publications/bulletins/schoolcrisis/welcome.html). Although the initiative ended in 2005, the concepts have continued to be provided nationally and internationally through training and consultation, and statewide replication was initiated in Connecticut during the 2006–2007 school year.

In the early hours of September 11, 2001, schools throughout the United States were confronted with the overwhelming tasks of assessing risk, managing accessibility to graphic images made available in real time by electronic media, ensuring the safety of their students and staff, providing a stabilizing environment, and assuring parents during those moments of doubt and fear that the school was still safe for their children. Despite widespread chaos and confusion during the initial hours of that autumn morning, schools throughout the country accomplished those tasks with heroic capacity. In the subsequent weeks and months, the perceived need for increased safeguards and preparedness was a focus of resolution, legislation, and program development. Of particular concern was ensuring that an infrastructure for providing security and mobilized response be developed to meet the physical and mechanical needs that arise during a crisis.

With an inexperienced and vulnerable population to serve, schools especially need to develop systems of safety and response to ensure considered and flexible interventions addressing the dangers that they may be exposed to. As a significant component to any crisis plan, schools must also address the psychological and emotional implications of a crisis in their community. Developing the ability to respond to commonly encountered challenges to a school community's sense of well-being allows staff to identify and improve their response capacities, as opposed to preparing only for those most challenging circumstances. This chapter describes a systematic program developed to prepare school personnel to meet the multiple needs arising out of a crisis with a minimum of stress on the individuals involved in the response.

On September 11, the entire country looked to New York City schools with a sense of awe and appreciation due to the remarkable efforts and the professionalism exhibited by all the staff through the long day and into the late night, ensuring that every student returned safely to their homes. The New York City Department of Education developed a citywide plan for its 1,200 schools that would provide the mechanisms for a coordinated response. The emotional and physical safety of its students and their families was a significant goal of this plan. In December 2001, the School Crisis Response Initiative began the process of providing integrated training to school-based crisis teams throughout the city of New York. Over the subsequent 2 years, more than 10,000 school staff members and more than 1,000 school and district crisis teams were provided with training in crisis preparedness and response practices. The elements provided through these trainings are discussed in this chapter.

## CRISES BENEFITING FROM A TEAM RESPONSE

Not all crises affecting school children require or benefit from a team response. Generally, circumstances involving issues of privacy and confidentiality, such as child abuse in the home or a sexual assault, are better handled through student assistance teams, unless information about these events has become widely known and generated considerable concern among many members of the school community. Crises that involve significant numbers of students or school staff that typically benefit from a team response include situations involving loss and grief (e.g., the death of a student or staff member); when there is a perceived threat to personal safety (e.g., a school bus accident, an abduction, or a fire); environmental crisis (e.g., a hurricane, a chemical spill on a nearby road, or a gas leak in the school); and when there is a perceived threat to emotional well-being (e.g., a bomb threat, hate-crime graffiti left at the school, or public disclosure of sexual misconduct of staff or students). The organizational model as outlined in this chapter provides a general response plan that is applicable across specific crisis contexts. In special situations, such as suicide postvention (Brent, Etkind, & Carr, 1992; Davidson, Rosenberg, Mercy, Franklin, & Simmons, 1989; Schonfeld et al., 1994), adaptations of the model are indicated in order to address their unique contingencies.

## LEVELS OF INTERVENTION

The Regional School Crisis Prevention and Response Program developed its protocols within a hierarchical framework built upon multiple levels of proficiency, skill sets, and access to student, staff and family needs. A regional or state-level resource team made up of representatives from mental health, police, academic, school administration, and support agencies should meet on a quarterly basis to review program activities, improve mechanisms for training school staff, address service deficits in target areas, and provide support and technical assistance to representatives from the district-level teams. The regional or state-level team also operates as an information clearinghouse on school crisis prevention and response and related topics, providing technical assistance and supports to districts encountering crises.

The next level within the hierarchy is the district-level team, which provides crisis response oversight for the individual school system. This team is generally composed of central office administrators and mental health staff. It establishes relevant district-wide policies and oversees resource allocation, staff training and supervision, and technical assistance directed toward schools within the district at the time of crisis.

The third level in the hierarchy is that of the school-based team, which is generally composed of the school's administrator(s); nursing, social work, psychology, and guidance/counseling staff; classroom staff; and others. Some schools may include a parent representative to assist in contacting parents more rapidly and to provide a liaison between the school and parents. This team is most capable of anticipating the reactions and needs of the students and staff and is therefore most suited to provide the direct services to students and families at the time of crisis. This team can draw upon additional resources through the district-level team, such as supplemental counseling staff from other schools. Because school-level teams will provide the most direct services to students, they will also experience the greatest level of stress. These teams in particular must have a proactive plan to address the needs of staff providers who may experience vicarious traumatization or compassion fatigue. Because schools provide the first level of support and intervention to students, staff, and the families in their community, it is important for them to do so within the context and structure of the ICS. Doing so will relieve school staff and administration of many of the decisions that may need to be made concerning deployment of resources and personnel, and facility use and access.

The organizational model utilizes a structure with seven roles. Although each role has its own set of tasks and responsibilities, each member of the team should be cross-trained in anticipation of absences. The roles include crisis team chair, assistant team chair, coordinator of counseling services, media coordinator, staff notification coordinator, communication coordinator, and crowd management coordinator (Schonfeld et al., 1994; Schonfeld et al., 2002). Table 14.1 outlines specific responsibilities for each role.

## NOTIFICATION/COMMUNICATION

A team member who is notified of a crisis involving one of its students should immediately notify the chair of the crisis team and inform him or her of what is known to date and whether or not the information has been confirmed. It is preferable that confirmation not be obtained from the family of the victim; rather, the purpose of contact with the family should be to offer condolences and support. Liaison with the local or regional police facilitates timely and accurate confirmation of crisis events, as well as assisting in the coordination of services. A contact person within emergency services, when indicated, should be established to assure that the school system is updated as the event unfolds. The chair will assure that the remaining members of the school and district crisis teams are notified when indicated and decide whether to contact the rest of the school staff before the next school day. The staff notification coordinator will facilitate the contact with all school personnel through the use of a preestablished telephone tree. Before contact is made with the general staff, the crisis team should meet or consult by telephone to determine what initial steps will be taken to meet anticipated needs and will make this information available to the staff notification coordinator. The crisis team chair or designee will make contact with the victim and/ or family to offer support and assistance.

Following notification of a crisis, staff should meet, either at the end of the day or prior to the beginning of the next school day, depending on the circumstances and timing. Table 14.2 outlines a sample agenda for this meeting. The crisis team needs to ensure that all information pertinent to the crisis is obtained and disseminated to students and staff in a fashion

Table 14.1   Roles of Crisis Team Members

| Members | Role |
| --- | --- |
| Crisis team chair | Chair all meetings of the crisis team and oversee the broad and specific functioning of the team and its members. |
| Assistant team chair | Assist the chair in all functions and substitute in the event of the unavailability of the chair. |
| Coordinator of counseling | Determine the extent and nature of counseling services indicated by a particular crisis and (along with counterpart on District Team) mobilize community resources as needed. Oversee training and supervision of staff providing counseling services. Identify and maintain ongoing liaison with community resources. |
| Media coordinator | Serve as the sole contact person (along with counterpart on District Team) for all media inquiries. Prepare a brief press release, if indicated, and appropriate statements, in collaboration with other members of the team, for staff, student, and parent notification. |
| Staff notification coordinator | Establish, coordinate, and initiate a telephone tree for notification of team members and other school staff after school hours. |
| Communication coordinator | Oversee all direct in-house communication. Screen incoming calls and maintain a log of phone calls related to the crisis. Assist the staff notification coordinator and help maintain an accurate phone directory of community resources and district-level staff. |
| Crowd management coordinator | In collaboration with local police and fire departments, plan mechanisms for crowd management in the event of various potential crises and directly supervise the movement of students and staff in the event such plans are initiated. A crowd control plan must include arrangements to cordon off areas with physical evidence, to assemble students and faculty for presentations, and, in the event of an actual threat to the physical safety of students, to assure the safe and organized movement of students in order to minimize the risk of harm. |

*Source:* Adapted with permission from Schonfeld, D., Kline, M., & Members of the Crisis Intervention Committee. (1994). School-based crisis intervention: An organizational model. *Crisis Intervention and Time-Limited Treatment, 1,* 158.


Table 14.2   Emergency Staff Meeting Agenda

- Share all current information about the crisis event and response, as well as any memorial plans that have already been established.
- Provide a forum for teachers and other staff to ask questions, share their own personal reactions or concerns, and offer feedback about reactions they anticipate or have noticed among the student body.
- Distribute notification announcements and finalize plans for notifying students and contacting parents (when appropriate).
- Inform staff of specific activities to support students, staff, and parents.

that facilitates their processing the information and their reactions in the most meaningful way. The school should identify those students closest to the victim(s) and arrange for them to be notified in a quiet and supportive location where their grief can be expressed in private. For the remainder of the student body, announcements should be structured to provide the information to all classes at approximately the same time, thereby reducing the potential problems that may arise should students with different amounts of information meet and compare notes. Rumors and speculation should be corrected as quickly as possible. In general, public address announcements should be avoided because of their depersonalized and disaffected quality and because they cannot anticipate or respond to students' reactions. If it is a staff member who has died, it is best to use a classroom teacher who is already known to the students and has an established relationship with them to cover the class on a short-term basis. A substitute can be used for this second class but would face enormous challenges if assigned to the grieving classroom.

Notification of parents is usually addressed through printed material sent home with students on the day of notification. In addition to providing information about the crisis event, written material can offer guidance on how parents can help their children deal with their reactions to the crisis and provide information on community mental health resources. Handouts providing suggestions on how to help children of different developmental levels deal with grief, bereavement (Schonfeld, 1993), trauma, or loss, and outlining typical and atypical reactions, as well as guidelines for when to seek additional mental health services, should be prepared prior to any crisis event and placed on file within the school or school district. For those children who are provided individual counseling or services within the support room, contact should be made directly with parents, usually by phone.

If it is likely that media attention will be generated by the event, the media coordinator should contact media representatives and provide them with the appropriate information by way of a press release. Suggestions concerning how the media can best help, and be least disruptive to the students and staff, should be offered. Interviews should be discouraged on school grounds, except those provided by the media coordinator.

## MEMORIALIZATION

Teams will need to address both the content and the timing of memorialization. Often, questions regarding memorial activities will be raised within hours of notification of the crisis event. This may divert attention from addressing the acute emotional and psychological needs of the students and staff. The team may need to address early on how best to handle graffiti tags, posters, signs, buttons or T-shirts with a picture of the deceased, and quasi-sanctified memorial areas that draw numbers of students. In some situations, early discussion of memorialization may prompt premature closure of the crisis response.

Spontaneous public displays in hallway shadow boxes or bulletin boards should be discouraged. Rather, students and staff should be given the opportunity to understand and express their needs through more thoughtful interventions. Using school resources and facilities to make multiple copies of newspaper articles, generating buttons commemorating the victim, or other activities that create semipermanent reminders that may persist in the community long after the initial trauma has worn off should be avoided. For longer-term memorial projects, schools should consider that the special acknowledgments of naming permanent objects after the person or dedicating a yearbook may set a precedent that will then be expected when another member of the school community dies. Memorial responses are more successful if they involve an assembled acknowledgment with some ritual content, such as a moment of silence or the lighting of a single candle. When a death involves suicide or another cause of death that bears a stigma (e.g., death by automobile accident while under the influence of alcohol), staff will need to help students acknowledge the loss of the individual student or staff member while taking care not to glamorize the means of death (Schonfeld et al., 1994; Brent et al., 1992).

The team should address how to handle the deceased's desk, locker, personal possessions, assignments hung up for display, and so forth. The team should anticipate that the deceased's locker may be utilized by other students as an informal memorial site, where they will post messages, place flowers, or otherwise acknowledge the loss. These spontaneous expressions should be monitored regularly to detect any unexpected reactions. The team can work with the student's class to help them identify how they would like to deal with the child's empty desk.

The team should remember that it is not the content of the memorial activities that is most important; rather, it is the process of engaging the members of the school community in the planning of a meaningful event. While raising money for a permanent memorial (such as a tree or plaque) may provide staff and students a means of "doing something" to show they care, it is far more helpful to facilitate an ongoing discussion among members of the school community about *how* they care about the deceased and for the survivors and what would be the most meaningful way(s) to express that concern prior to (or in place of) raising such funds.

Major crises that draw the extended attention of national and international media often result in an overabundance of donations and overwhelming numbers of cards and letters offering encouragement and support. Schools should consider including in their protocols steps that might be taken to process and address the contributions coming in at a time when resources may already be stretched. Much like the need to assess the potential contributions of volunteers offering assistance, schools will need to prioritize what contributions need to be dealt with immediately, such as food donations, and what can be left to a later time. It may even become necessary to identify an off-site location not connected with the school or district to receive these materials.

## SUPPORT ROOMS

The school should consider when it is appropriate to set up support rooms for those students who require more intensive intervention than can be provided by teacher-directed class discussions. The crisis response plan should specify the staffing and location (e.g., in areas without heavy traffic) of support rooms. Support rooms are best for handling limited numbers of students who generally are sharing similar reactions and symptoms. Homogeneous groups of 3 to 6 participants work well; larger groups of 7 to 10 can generally tolerate more variety in the reactions of participants. When several groups are manifesting different reactions, the school should consider using separate support rooms to meet the distinctive needs of each group. If a number of large groups seek services within the support room(s), more staffing may be required; the coordinator of counseling services should draw on counseling staff from other schools within the district, as well as community mental health resources, if appropriate. He or she should also determine if on-site assistance from community service providers will be necessary or if a direct referral system would work best. In many ways, large groups (i.e., more than eight or nine participants) function similarly to classroom groups. If many groups of this size seek assistance through the support rooms, this may indicate that the interventions provided in the classrooms did not sufficiently meet the needs of many students, highlighting the need for further training and support of classroom teachers.

The support room staff, under the guidance of the coordinator of counseling services, should perform an initial assessment, following the principles of mental health triage, of students seeking to utilize the services offered in the support room. Those students with emergent mental health needs demanding immediate action should be referred directly to the appropriate community resources. Extensive evaluations and counseling services in the school setting prior to referral of these students should be avoided. Referring large groups of students to hospital emergency rooms to rule out suicidal risk is not an effective response plan and may only weaken the collaborative relationships between school and community mental health staff. Therefore, the crisis team needs to identify appropriate emergency services in the community that can respond immediately if needed at the time of crisis, as well as urgent services that can be provided within 48 hours for this purpose. Identifying students with needs requiring emergency treatment, such as those assessed as potentially suicidal, is a critical role of the counseling staff. Mental health staff in the support room should be identified as being available for specific, individualized tasks (e.g., one person may have the best assessment skills for suicidality and can be assigned for that purpose, whereas another may have advanced skills around grief work). Evaluations should be brief and goal specific, with the intention of screening students for the most appropriate level of service. The counseling staff should defer more lengthy evaluations and services until a later time, such as the next school day. Youngsters assessed as not requiring emergent mental health services should be offered limited immediate interventions, perhaps in a group setting. Support groups, which might continue to meet on an ongoing basis, may be a useful outcome of the support rooms (Schonfeld et al., 2002).

Many students who might benefit from additional evaluation and intervention may not request, nor present themselves to support rooms for, these services. School staff may identify students as requiring further evaluation because of the circumstances of the crisis (e.g., if the student was a witness to the crisis or was a close friend of the victim) or by their reactions upon notification (e.g., if the student has an extreme or atypical response). As a result, the general classroom staff will need to be able to determine who within their classrooms may be at risk and have a mechanism through which to refer these individuals for additional evaluation and intervention. Table 14.3 outlines risk factors that increase the likelihood that students will require additional services after a crisis event. These factors involve the nature and extent of the student's relationships with the victim, the quality of the student's coping with prior challenges, as well as the current crisis event, and the presence of predisposing factors and concurrent life stressors. Those staff who are part of early identification and intervention programs within the school (e.g., student assistance teams, mental health teams, child study teams) should be brought into the crisis response assessment and planning so that they are able to share their prior knowledge of those students who were experiencing difficulties before the crisis.

Individual services should, except on rare occasions, be directed either toward alleviating the dominant features or symptoms that prompted the need for individual attention or toward preliminary assessment regarding the need for referral to community mental health services (e.g., for students with severe suicidal ideation or profound decompensation). Although mental health resources within individual school districts vary greatly in the amount, extent, and nature of counseling services their staff can provide, all school districts need to establish relationships with local community services to provide supplemental or specialized mental health services for crisis situations.

School-based crisis intervention planning and response cannot occur in isolation from the community. A critical component of crisis preparedness planning involves identifying community resources, as well as service gaps, for

Table 14.3   Risk Factors for Students

**Group affiliation with the victim**
School staff should make themselves aware of the formal and informal social networks and
the activities that the victim shared with other students: academic, shop, and special
classes; after-school clubs, teams, and extracurricular activities; community and social
activities engaged in off-site; the victim's residential neighborhood.
A staff member should consider following the victim's schedule of classes for the first day(s).
The crisis team should reach out to the external sites to offer support and guidance to the
nonprofessionals who might have regular contact with peers (e.g., the Scout leader, Little
League coach, or dance instructor).

**Shared characteristics, interests, or attributes with the victim**
Students who perceive themselves as sharing characteristics, interests, or attributes with the
victim may be more inclined to have increased anxiety and distress.

**Students with prior demonstration of poor coping**
Social isolation
History of suicidal ideation/attempts
Prior history of arrests, acting-out behaviors, aggression, or drug/alcohol abuse

**Students exhibiting extreme or atypical reactions**
Students with grief reactions surpassing those of the general student body that would not be
explained by close affiliation with the victim
Students with close relationships with the deceased who exhibit very little reaction to the news

**Students with personal history related to the trauma**
Former victims of crime or violence
Students who have threatened or acted violently in the past

**Students with concurrent adverse personal situations**
Family problems
Health problems
Psychiatric history
Significant peer conflicts

addressing the emergent mental health needs of students and staff at the time of
a crisis. Specific staff should be identified within community social service and
mental health agencies to serve as liaisons with the school system. Through
effective collaboration between schools and community mental health providers, solutions can be developed to increase the community's capacity to address
mental health needs in a timely and effective manner at the time of crisis. Such
collaboration and community planning to improve the mental health infrastructure will have clear benefit for members of the school community even
outside the context of a crisis event (e.g., when making referrals for students
who have non-crisis-related issues that may require ongoing counseling).

   Schools must also consider the unique needs of students that have identified special education needs, mental health issues, or behavioral disorders. This is especially important when the perpetrator of a violent act is
rumored or known to suffer from or have suffered from a psychological
or developmental disability, as has been discussed quite publicly concerning the perpetrator of the Newtown tragedy. Students with disability may
become an unwarranted target of concern for students and their parents,

but with compassionate and proactive effort on the part of school staff, the individuals themselves can have their needs addressed while the larger school community can be provided with appropriate contextual information that does not violate privacy. Parents are important collaborators with schools in meeting the continuum of issues arising within the student body during and after a crisis. Parents can provide essential healing to their children, especially when they are given appropriate developmental information and are encouraged to share their own understanding of the child's needs. Schools with students who are at risk due to disabling developmental, psychological, or behavioral health issues should work with parents to ensure that each student's needs are met during any crisis response (Newgass & Gurwitz, 2009).

## CLASSROOM INTERVENTIONS

To meet the emerging needs of students during a school's response to crisis, interventions can be offered in classrooms. Classroom activities will reduce the demands on individual counseling resources, allowing them to target those students who require more intensive intervention.

Additional in-service training is required to prepare teachers to provide this service. The training should be general enough in nature (e.g., children's developmental understanding of death and their responses to loss; Schonfeld, 1993) that it is clear to teachers (and administrators) that the skills learned can be applied more broadly than just at the time of major crisis events. Teachers may also need additional support and backup by school counseling staff in order to be able to provide this service within their classrooms. A crisis often awakens feelings related to a prior (or concurrent) crisis that may assume a primary focus for a particular child. At these times of stress, given an appropriate opportunity, children may be inclined to disclose a wide range of personal crises (e.g., prior deaths, unresolved issues regarding parent conflict or divorce). Teachers need timely access to appropriate backup services to address these "incidental" concerns (Schonfeld, 1989).

At the time of a crisis, teachers may benefit from additional briefing regarding the types of reactions that they may anticipate in their classrooms and some of the specific behavioral changes that are common after a crisis. Particularly when people are experiencing difficulty in identifying and expressing their feelings, teachers need to be attentive to nonverbal communication. Eye contact, posture, and energy levels may contribute valuable information for directing the flow of the discussion and determining whether a student's needs are being met through classroom interventions.

There are three general categories of classroom activities that can contribute to children's expression of their feelings and thoughts: discussions, written efforts, and art projects. Teachers will be most familiar with the developmental capabilities of their students, as well as their methods for coping with prior stressful situations, and should select the modalities that provide the best match.

Discussions are most effective when led by the teacher. However, if due to his or her personal connection with the crisis event the teacher feels unable to direct the classroom activity, it may be necessary for another staff person to guide the discussion initially while the teacher is allowed to observe and participate. Discussions should attempt to demystify the event and address any magical thinking that may be influencing the students' perceptions through efforts to correct rumors, provide logical explanations of what has transpired wherever possible, and draw out the impressions that students are forming so as to be able to reinforce accurate understanding and redirect mistaken impressions (Newgass & Schonfeld, 1996). Graphic details describing injuries and attendant imagery should be avoided; consideration of the developmental needs and capacities of students can guide how much information they need to process the experience without overwhelming their defensive structures (Yussen & Santrock, 1982).

During these discussions, teachers should not attempt to hide their own feelings and reactions but instead should be encouraged to model meaningful and compassionate ways to talk about feelings. Students will need assistance in focusing on their feelings, as opposed to behaviors or sensations, during these discussions. Teachers should consciously take time for themselves to become aware of their feelings and reactions. Opportunities should be provided for teachers to talk with their peers about how they are reacting to the incident and to their discussions with students.

Written activities are often used as a way of allowing students to express their angst and sorrow. If they are used excessively, or indiscriminately, their impact may be diluted. Entire classes are often assigned the "task" of writing a note or some other exercise, such as a poem or a recollection of a joyful time spent with the victim. However, this activity does not acknowledge the unique relationships that individual students may have or may have had with the victim of a trauma. Whereas some students may have very deep and meaningful relationships with the victim, others' relationships may be more distant or conflicted. An assignment that assumes all relationships are equivalent may reduce the effectiveness for those very students most in need of expressing their loss.

Written activities are most beneficial for students with better-developed writing skills and capacity for abstraction. Regardless of the assignment and its purpose (i.e., to be shared within the class, to be sent to the family in an effort to extend emotional support, or as an aid to individual processing of the event), all written assignments associated with responding to a crisis should be reviewed to identify any signs of extreme emotional distress or inappropriate content.

After the third death at the school mentioned in Vignette 3, several staff worked together with groups of students to produce a notebook of poetry and reflections that might be presented to the parents of the child. When a number of students submitted contributions that reflected their confusion, hurt, and sorrow expressed in a way that may have been painful for the victim's family to read (e.g., "it was cruel of you to do this to us... you left us behind with the pain, while you get to escape it"), the staff guided students toward forming themselves into small peer review groups to read and reread each other's work and offer suggestions on alternate ways to express the intended emotional message. As one student commented, "Because we did this, I've found new ways to describe how I feel."

Art projects and manipulatives can also be used to facilitate emotional expression in a classroom setting. These generally take the form of pictures, banners, and temporary memorials. This intervention may be especially helpful for younger children, but all age groups can use art-related activities to express their inner state. The benefits may expand as multiple sensory experiences are permitted through use of the medium; many students may benefit from finger painting because it employs multiple sensations (i.e., visual, tactile, and olfactory). Whatever the approach, it is important that the activity be used to elicit emotional responses and not to "diagnose" the students because of the content or structure of their artwork.

In one of the classrooms at the school responding to the crisis in Vignette 3, the art teacher invited students to draw a picture of their feelings. Several media were available for the students' use, including pencils, crayons, tempera, and charcoal. After the students had completed their drawings, the teacher asked each student to come forward and describe how the images on the paper illustrated their feelings. Several students became emotional as they talked, and the group spontaneously offered support, encouragement, and validating comments to one another. Several students commented that they were encouraged to hear others describe feelings that they themselves held but hesitated to share.

In adapting these interventions to special education classes, it may be helpful to allow additional "quiet time" and/or to alternate rest with physical activity (Axline, 1983). Music may help students relax so that they are better able to attend to their emotional reaction to a crisis. For some students, concrete methods that provide a framework are most effective, such as the use of a "feelings identification chart" to assist them in better identifying their feelings. Storytelling can also be used. The stories that may be most helpful depend upon the individual class and students. One technique is to tell a story in "rounds," wherein the teacher begins the story and the students take turns contributing elements, while the teacher offers modifications, if necessary. The teacher ultimately brings the story to a close with a straightforward solution that is reality based yet hopeful.

In one classroom at the school that responded to the crisis in Vignette 2, the individual leading the discussion asked if anyone could think of a story that would show how people can respond to tragedies. One youngster suggested starting the story with "A kid got shot." The facilitator added, "But she went to the hospital, where they are helping her to get better." Another child added, "She nearly died," and the facilitator contributed, "But everyone is pretty sure that she'll be all right in a few weeks." He went on to repeat the story as it had developed to that point: "A kid got shot, but she went to the hospital, where they are helping her to get better. She nearly died, but everyone is pretty sure that she'll be all right in a few weeks." He then asked if anyone wanted to add the next line, to which a girl replied, "And then she'll be able to come back to school." He once again repeated the story, now with a concluding sentence, and was able to use this as a means to examine the children's fears about the violence associated with guns, concerns of death, anxiety about hospitals, and their longing for the girl's return to school. This led to a more directed discussion about the students' worries and techniques to facilitate coping.

## FOLLOW-UP AND STAFF SUPPORT

Children and adults grieve and respond to a crisis over time, and long-term reactions to significant events should be expected. Mechanisms need to be in place for referring students and staff for additional counseling outside of the school, if this proves to be necessary. A list of local community agencies, pediatricians, and private mental health providers should be available to staff and parents.

The staff members' responsibility to provide services to students at the time of crisis does not relieve them from experiencing their own reactions to the event. Acute reactions to crisis events among staff members should not be overlooked or discounted; rather, attempts should be made to normalize the distressing reactions that many will experience and provide opportunities for additional support. Unfortunately, mental health services and Employee Assistance Programs (EAPs) may bear a stigma in the minds of some staff. As part of their crisis protocol, schools should proactively identify any EAP contacts, along with necessary phone numbers and contact names, at the very beginning of a response and encourage staff to make use of their services. Frequent reminders about the service and the guarantee of confidentiality should be given throughout the time that crisis intervention services are offered. Although EAP services may be an appropriate locus for services, they are only in place to provide brief treatment and preliminary assessment, typically three to five sessions before referral to other services is necessary. If a staff member has a particularly adverse reaction, distinct from and greater than that of most other staff members, the administration might instead consider direct referral to a mental health provider who will be able to continue providing services beyond the short term so as to ensure continuity of services. After a crisis, a school system should contact the EAP to see if its services were adequate to meet the needs of the staff; underutilization of the service may suggest the need for identifying an alternate means of providing staff support at the time of crisis. Given that it is not unusual to be overwhelmed by the experiences associated with a major crisis, use of these services should not be considered abnormal in any way, and any information concerning the delivery of services should be obtained in aggregate so that individual privacy is maintained.

Debriefing, a review of activities that has the goal of gaining a better understanding of a team's capacity, should be offered after the team has emerged from the response cycle. Whereas debriefing is intended to focus on the team's activities in executing the crisis plan, there is also an opportunity for team members to express their personal reactions to the event and to identify steps that might relieve stress during future crisis responses. In some cases, a debriefing session may include staff members outside of the crisis team, such as for a teacher whose classroom was most directly impacted by the crisis. The debriefing session will also allow the team to develop plans to evaluate and address ongoing issues, such as the possibility of post-traumatic and anniversary reactions among students and staff.

## TRAINING AND TECHNICAL ASSISTANCE

Training of crisis response teams is most effective if it includes all members of the team, which often requires considerable planning. In addition to being most convenient for the trainer (thereby facilitating the involvement of outside consultants), the primary advantage is that team building will develop more predictably when all parties receive training together.

Training for a school crisis team should provide background knowledge on crisis theory and children's developmental understanding of and reactions to death (Schonfeld, 1993); introduce and familiarize the participants with the organizational model (Schonfeld et al., 1994); provide information on classroom interventions; and employ team-building activities. The importance of recognizing and addressing staff needs should be underscored throughout the training.

A vignette activity, wherein team members adopt roles from the model in order to address a school crisis situation, should be used to help the newly developing teams experience the manner of problem solving and decision-making that will confront them in a crisis. This vignette should provide the amount of information that might be available to schools at the time of an actual crisis. The subsequent processing of the experience with teams should clarify that there is no "right way" to respond. Rather, the training facilitators should elicit their reasons for making the structural decisions and draw out their rationale for intervention (Gallessich, 1990). The goal is to help the group learn how best to function as a team, and to appreciate both the complexity of responding to a crisis and how an organizational plan can help anticipate many of the issues and provide a mechanism for responding effectively.

It is often helpful to bring together several teams for training off-site (to minimize interruptions that may distract or remove participants from the training) in a full-day (i.e., 5- to 6-hour) workshop. The trainer/consultant can then follow up with individual teams to adapt the practices to the unique issues associated with each team's school. While providing the technical assistance, it is important that the unique cultural, economic, and environmental aspects of the school and its population be considered and that the plan be adapted to meet these unique circumstances. The individual providing technical assistance can also help identify unique vulnerabilities for a school. For example, a school serving a marginalized immigrant population should anticipate the need for increased translation and outreach services at the time of a crisis. Psychological vulnerabilities can also be considered, such as decreased support at home in communities with a high percentage of single-adult-headed households, or increased baseline stressors and decreased resources in disadvantaged communities.

## CONCLUSION

A school-based crisis intervention team composed predominantly of school-based staff is ideally suited to coordinate crisis prevention activities and to provide intervention services to students at the time of a crisis. This chapter has discussed a systematic crisis intervention model to organize the activities of this team and has highlighted issues to consider in establishing and training school-based crisis teams. If representatives of community social service and mental health agencies are involved in the planning process, it is more likely that their services can be accessed at the time of a crisis for the mutual benefit of the students and the community. Planning for possible contingencies will facilitate optimal performance of the team while ameliorating the negative consequences impacting the students and the service providers, who, as members of the school community, will likely be reacting to the crisis themselves.

ACKNOWLEDGMENTS    The authors would like to acknowledge the contributions of the members of the Regional School Crisis Prevention and Response Program, including representatives of the public school systems of East Haven, New Haven, North Haven, and West Haven, Connecticut. We gratefully acknowledge the support of our program from the Community Foundation for Greater New Haven, the William Caspar Graustein Memorial Fund, the State of Connecticut (Office of Policy and Management), ACES (Area Cooperative Educational Services, Hamden, Connecticut), and the Office for Victims of Crime.

REFERENCES

Axline, V. (1983). *Play therapy.* New York: Ballantine.

Brent, D., Etkind, S., & Carr, W. (1992). Psychiatric effects of exposure to suicide among the friends and acquaintances of adolescent suicide victims. *Journal of the American Academy of Child and Adolescent Psychiatry, 31,* 629–640.

Davidson, L., Rosenberg, M., Mercy, J., Franklin, J., & Simmons, J. (1989). An epidemiologic study of risk factors in two teenage suicide clusters. *Journal of the American Academy of Child and Adolescent Psychiatry, 262,* 2687–2692.

Gallessich, J. (1990). *The profession and practice of consultation.* San Francisco: Jossey-Bass.

Kline, M., Schonfeld, D., & Lichtenstein, R. (1995). Benefits and challenges of school-based crisis response teams. *Journal of School Health, 65,* 245–249.

Klingman, A. (1988). School community in disaster: Planning for intervention. *Journal of Community Psychology, 16,* 205–216.

Newgass, S., & Gurwitz, R. (2009, Summer). Crisis and the individual with autism. *Autism Spectrum Quarterly,* 8–10.

Newgass, S., & Schonfeld, D. (1996). A crisis in the class: Anticipating and responding to students' needs. *Educational Horizons, 74,* 124–129.

Schonfeld, D. (1989). Crisis intervention for bereavement support: A model of intervention in the children's school. *Clinical Pediatrics, 28,* 27–33.

Schonfeld, D. (1993). Talking with children about death. *Journal of Pediatric Health Care, 7,* 269–274.

Schonfeld, D., Kline, M., & Members of the Crisis Intervention Committee. (1994). School-based crisis intervention: An organizational model. *Crisis Intervention and Time-Limited Treatment, 1,* 155–166.

Schonfeld, D., Lichtenstein, R., Kline Pruett, M., & Speese-Linehan, D. (2002). *How to prepare for and respond to a crisis*. Alexandria, VA: Association for Supervision and Curriculum Development.

Schonfeld, D., & Newgass, S. (2003). *School Crisis Response Initiative*. Washington, DC: US Department of Justice, Office for Victims of Crime.

Yussen, S., & Santrock, J. (1982). *Child development: An introduction*. Dubuque, IA: Wm. C. Brown.

# 15

# Crisis Intervention With Chronic School Violence and Volatile Situations

LAURA M. HOPSON
GORDON MACNEIL
CHRIS STEWART

## Case Studies

John Hanson is a 17-year-old Asian American male. He attends Boca Vista High School, where he is a junior. John is a good student, with an overall grade point average of 3.6. John has had little trouble at school. His greatest transgression was when he was caught skipping school to attend a concert. He plans to attend college and become an engineer. He has a supportive family and has good relationships with both parents and his younger sister. John is a witness to a tragic event at school. Two days ago a fellow student, whom John did not know personally but recognized from several shared classes, shot several students and a teacher before committing suicide. One of the students was a close friend of John. John is experiencing extreme grief and does not feel able to speak with his parents about his feelings.

Jack Fraser is a 13-year-old white male attending Prairie View Middle School. Jack has reasonable grades, with an average of 2.5 in all subjects. Jack is small for his age. His parents have been divorced for 3 years, and he currently lives with a supportive mother. He has been the victim of an ongoing campaign by some other students. Several of the school athletes have been bullying Jack for several months because he is a member of the drama club. These students post derogatory comments online, calling him a "fag." They also continue the bullying at school. Last week, the boys beat Jack, causing moderate harm, though no bones were broken.

Aretha Jackson is a 16-year-old African American female. She attends Andrew Jackson High School, where she is a sophomore. She attends school regularly and has earned a grade point average of 3.0. She lives with her mother and grandmother. She has one younger brother and one older brother. She receives good support from both her mother and grandmother.

Her father left her mother when Aretha was very young, and she has no recollection of him. Aretha has experienced a violent episode when changing classes. Another girl threatened her with a box cutter. Aretha had, unknowingly, trespassed into an area that "belonged" to the girl and her friends. Aretha escaped without injury but is upset about the event and fears it may happen again.

---

## INTRODUCTION

In this chapter we discuss two principle forms of school violence: the first form includes acts of violence ranging from bullying, robbery, and simple assaults to homicide; the second form includes those catastrophic outbursts against schoolmates and school personnel typified by the shootings in Colorado, Arkansas, and Kentucky. These catastrophic school violence events have a powerful impact on the communities in which they occur. However, the more common form of violence, while not garnering the media attention of catastrophic events, may be of greater concern for schools due to the chronicity and frequency of these violent acts and the greater numbers of students, teachers, parents, and other school personnel directly impacted by these violent acts daily in schools nationwide. Both forms of school violence require intervention by human service personnel (or trained school personnel). In particular, comprehensive crisis intervention services should be readily available for those victimized by the violence or exposed to it. This chapter presents a crisis intervention strategy targeting survivors of school violence that employs Roberts's crisis intervention model (Roberts, 1991, 1996) in combination with cognitive therapy.

In writing this chapter, we address school violence in a general sense; we do not identify interventions for specific violent acts (such as rape or aggravated assault). We purposefully neglected two areas of violence: We have limited our discussion to violence against persons, thus omitting aggression toward property such as vandalism, arson, and bombing of school buildings. Because the focus of this text is crisis intervention, we do not provide a detailed discussion of prevention interventions but, rather, interventions that are useful in responding to incidents of school violence.

## DEFINITION OF THE PROBLEM

The term *school violence* encompasses a wide array of behaviors ranging from verbally abusing a peer to mass shootings. Despite the diversity of these acts, they are all overt, aggressive acts that result in physical or psychological pain, injury, or death (Fredrick, Middleton, & Butler, 1995). The Centers for Disease Control and Prevention (CDC) defines youth violence as "the intentional use of physical force or power, against another person, group, or community, with the behavior likely to cause physical or psychological harm." School violence is a subset of youth violence that occurs at school, on the way to or from school, and during or on the way to a school-sponsored event (CDC, 2012).

Astor (1998) suggests that social workers adopt a similarly broad definition of violence, as presented by Straus, Gelles, and Steinmetz (1980): Violence is "an act carried out with the intention, or a perceived intention, of causing physical pain or injury to another person. The physical pain can range from a slight pain such as a slap, to murder" (p. 20). Astor promotes this definition because it includes milder forms of aggression that are common in elementary schools. He contends that lax rules about aggression or tolerance for milder forms of aggression in lower grades fosters more severe aggressive acts in later grades. For our discussion we ascribe to the operational definition that school violence is any intentional verbal or physical act that produces pain in the recipient of that act while the recipient is under the supervision of the school.

Much of the research literature related to school violence in recent years has focused on bullying (Dake, Price, & Telljohann, 2003). Based on the pioneering work of Olweus (1978), *bullying* is defined as repeated aggressive behavior intentionally meant to harm another person (Smith, 2000). Incidents of bullying included name-calling, rumors, threats of physical injury, coercion to do things students did not want to do, purposeful exclusion from activities, destruction of property on purpose, pushing, tripping, or being spit on (US Department of Education, 2013).

Research indicates that many students fear going to school each day because of bullying. Consequences of bullying for victims include anxiety, depression, absences from school, substance use, violent behavior, and suicidal behavior (Litwiller & Brausch, 2013). These consequences extend to bystanders, as well. Students who are not directly involved but who witness bullying report levels of anxiety and depression that sometimes exceed levels reported by victims (Cohen & Geier, 2010; Rivers, Poteat, Noret, & Ashurst, 2009).

Although research on cyberbullying is relatively new, a growing number of studies indicate its harmful consequences for bullies, victims, and bystanders. Students targeted by cyberbullying report feeling sad and anxious (Beran & Li, 2005). Incidents of cyberbullying included posting hurtful information on the Internet; sending harassing text messages, instant messages, or e-mails; having private information purposefully shared on the Internet; and being excluded online (US Department of Education, 2013). Students victimized by cyberbullying are more likely to report skipping school and carrying a weapon to school than students who were not bullied online (Ybarra, Diener-West, & Leaf, 2007).

## SCOPE OF THE PROBLEM

Tragic, catastrophic events have served as vehicles for the popular press to identify school violence as a critical issue. Highly publicized incidents of school shootings have dramatically increased concern nationwide about the perceived level of violence in schools (Schildkraut & Hernandez, 2014). However, violent deaths in schools are relatively rare. Less than 2% of youth homicides occur at school, a percentage that has been stable for the past decade (CDC, 2012). Although these acts of violence involve relatively small numbers of youths and adults in schools, they have had devastating impacts on communities. They have also been important influences on policy at the local, state, district, and national levels (Schildkraut & Hernandez, 2014).

Although deaths due to violence on school property may have decreased in recent years, other forms of school violence are, unfortunately, all too common. The percentage of schools reporting one or more incidents of violence, theft, or other crimes hovers around 85% and has remained stable (US Department of Education, 2013).

Bullying in school continues to present serious problems to school safety. According to a recent survey, 12% of students reported being in a physical fight, and 20% reported being bullied on school property during the past year (CDC, 2012). In 2011, about 28% of middle and high school students reported being bullied at school, and 9% reported being cyberbullied. The majority of students who experience bullying do not tell their parents or teachers about the bullying behavior, which makes it difficult to identify those in need of intervention (Bonanno & Hymel, 2013). However, the percentage of students who report bullying incidents has increased during the past decade from approximately 26% to 40% (US Department of Education, 2013).

## RISK AND PROTECTIVE FACTORS

Many researchers in the area of school violence suggest that the situation is best described from a social-ecological perspective (Espelage & Swearer, 2003). From this perspective, individual, family, school, and societal factors all have some influence on creating a violent situation. The school violence literature generally prescribes multifactorial, transactional models to explain violent incidents (Espelage & Swearer, 2003; Verlinden, Hersen, & Thomas, 2000). These ecological systems models delineate multiple factors interacting on multiple levels through various developmental stages to explain and maintain violent behavior. So, it is possible to have individual characteristics operating in varying family, school, and community environments interacting to create an infinite number of behavioral outcomes.

One group of risk factors includes biological and psychosocial characteristics such as an adolescent's degree of impulse control (Fishbein et al., 2006; Pardini, Lochman, & Wells, 2004), psychological and emotional problems, an adolescent's family history regarding alcoholism, and genetic factors (Osofsky & Osofsky, 2001; Verlinden, Hersen, & Thomas, 2000). For example, children with a genetic predisposition toward sensitivity to stress may exhibit more aggressive behavior when exposed to stressors in their environment (Wolff, Santiago, & Wadsworth, 2009). In addition, youths' capacity for self-control influences their behavior.

Also important are adolescents' interpersonal relationships with peers and adults. These factors include peer involvement in drug use and delinquent behavior and their engagement in school (Dake, Price, & Telljohann, 2003). Support from prosocial peers and adults in their homes, neighborhoods, and schools tends to protect youth from aggressive and violent behavior (Bowen, Hopson, Rose, & Glennie, 2011). Youths from low-income families who are exposed to more stressors in their home and neighborhood environments are more likely to behave aggressively in school (Lochman, Wells, Qu, & Chen, 2012).

In addition, many low-income families live in disadvantaged neighborhoods in which children are exposed to violence (Lochman, Wells, Qu, & Chen, 2012). Exposure to neighborhood violence increases tendencies toward aggressive behaviors (e.g., Barry, Lochman, Fite, Wells, & Colder, 2012). Neighborhood problems may also have an adverse effect on parenting (Gutman, McLoyd, & Tokoyawa, 2005), further increasing children's risk for aggressive behavior (Brody et al., 2003).

The social environment of the school can also increase or mitigate risk for aggressive and violent behavior. Schools tend to have fewer problems with aggressive behavior when there are positive relationships among adults within the school and positive student-teacher relationships (Crosnoe, 2004; McNeely, Nonnemaker, & Blum, 2002; Powers, Bowen, & Rose, 2005; Whitlock, 2006). School climates that foster a sense of safety and fairness in disciplinary practices also tend to have less aggressive behavior (Cohen & Geier, 2010).

## INTERVENTIONS

Most of the literature related to school violence interventions focuses on prevention efforts. Prevention is easier, cheaper, and more effective than reducing the impact of violence after if occurs (Rich, 1992). A number of reviews of school violence prevention programs have been published (see Allen-Meares, Washington, & Welsh, 1996; Dryfoos, 1998; Goldstein & Conoley, 1997), and we encourage readers attempting to prevent or avert school violence in their communities to become familiar with the multitude of prevention program options available. The Olweus Bullying Prevention Program is perhaps the most widely researched prevention program and has demonstrated effectiveness in reducing bullying incidents and improving the social climate of the school (Limber, Nation, Tracy, Melton, & Flerx, 2004). Another program is the Stop Bullying Now! campaign sponsored by the US Department of Health and Human Services (www.stopbullyingnow.hrsa. gov). This program provides information for both parents and adolescents to deal with current problems and help prevent future bullying. However, because this chapter focuses on crisis intervention, we do not discuss prevention programs in detail. Instead, we focus on interventions pertinent to individual victims of violence.

## CRISIS INTERVENTION APPLICATION

School settings provide unique environments for conflict among students. Because the student population in most schools is reasonably small, individuals commonly interact with the same peers repeatedly throughout the day. This familiarity has positive aspects, but it can exacerbate tensions between individuals because some may not be able to avoid those with whom they are having difficulty. Crisis intervention plans necessarily have to address this issue.

Youth in middle and high schools experience intense developmental changes. Not least of these is their creation of a self-identity. During middle school and high school years, youth commonly affiliate with subgroups (such as "brains," "jocks," and "stoners"). The labeling associated with these groups can lead to stigmatization, and individual identity is sometimes subsumed by group identity (Scherr, 2012). There is often tremendous peer pressure to adhere to group norms, and members commonly become intolerant of those who do not share their values or beliefs. Consequently, crisis intervention efforts need to assess the victim's self-identify and degree of subgroup assimilation to produce changes consistent with the individual's values. Proposed changes that conflict with the norms of the client's group need to be evaluated with regard to the client's willingness to challenge those norms.

Another factor that can contribute to difficulty in using a crisis intervention model is the common imposition of authority by school faculty and personnel through the use of fear and force. Strict rules and degrading experiences have been associated with violence against teachers as well as school

property (Espelage et al., 2013). It is widely held that adolescents are distrustful of adults. A reckless imposition of authority can result in the youth's
unwillingness to take advantage of services provided by adults (Curcio &
First, 1993).

Although some trainers or educators adhere to a specific therapeutic model
for intervening with crises, the diversity of acts constituting school violence
indicates that an array of therapeutic models be considered. Roberts's (1996,
2005) seven-step crisis intervention model has garnered wide acceptance in
the social work and social service practice community. It is applicable to a
broad spectrum of populations and problems. Other chapters of this text
present the model in detail, so we direct the reader to those chapters rather
than restating its general principles.

It has been our experience that Roberts's crisis intervention model is most
useful as an organizing structure or overriding framework in combination
with a supplemental therapeutic intervention. Specifically, youth experiencing initial trauma reactions to victimization respond well to behavioral interventions followed by cognitive therapy (Jaycox, Kataoka, Stein, Langley, &
Wong, 2012; Langley, Nadeem, Kataoka, Stein, & Jaycox, 2010). Cognitive
therapy is one of the most widely used intervention methods in social work
practice (Hepworth, Rooney, Rooney, & Strom-Gottfried, 2012). It is often
used in conjunction with other interventions such as assertiveness training
and desensitization (Hepworth et al., 2012). The following provides a brief
description of the basic principles of cognitive therapy and an illustrative
application of the method within the overarching structure of Roberts's crisis intervention model with one of the cases presented at the beginning of
the chapter. Included is a brief discussion of special concerns and considerations practitioners should note when applying Roberts's model to victims
of school violence.

## COGNITIVE THERAPY

Judith Beck (2011) presents a set of 10 principles on which cognitive therapy
is based;

### Principle 1

Cognitive therapy is based on an ever-evolving formulation of clients and
their problems in cognitive terms. The worker is reminded that current
thinking is of paramount importance, as it is the present that can be altered.
Although precipitating factors and historical developmental events are tremendously important, particularly in the context of school violence, their

primary importance is in maintaining thoughts that impede the client from full functioning.

### Principle 2

Cognitive therapy requires a sound therapeutic alliance. Consistent with training texts in most social service professions, the therapist-client relationship is of primary importance. Demonstrating empathetic interpersonal skills and requesting feedback concerning the relationship are encouraged. There may be difficulties in establishing a positive alliance due to the role differences between the worker and the adolescent, but our experience suggests that those who are truly in crisis quickly dismiss their attitudes when they are physically moved from their peers, who can serve as an audience, and when the worker is able to accurately identify their emotional and cognitive state.

### Principle 3

Cognitive therapy emphasizes collaboration and active participation by both the worker and the client. Consistent with Principle 6, the therapist may be more active and directive in the initial stages of therapy and allow more freedom and exploration by the client as therapy progresses.

### Principle 4

Cognitive therapy is goal oriented and problem focused. Many victims of school violence are overwhelmed by the traumatic experience and unable to identify their problem. Using a cognitive approach in conjunction with the crisis intervention model can provide tremendous opportunity to enhance clarity for our clients. Depending on clients' ability to problem-solve, they may need little more assistance than identifying their problem. This is particularly the case when the client identifies a goal of ceasing to ruminate about the event.

### Principle 5

Cognitive therapy initially emphasizes the present. Although a significant transgression creates difficulty for clients responding to particular acts of school violence, it is the cognitive processing of those events that serves as an enduring problem.

### Principle 6

Cognitive therapy is educative, aims to teach clients to be their own therapist, and emphasizes relapse prevention. In educating clients about the cognitive model, the therapist provides clients a means of helping themselves. Consistent with crisis intervention values, clients are empowered to help themselves rather than becoming dependent on the therapist.

## Principle 7

Cognitive therapy aims to be time limited and posits several goals that are consistent with this aim: Provide symptom relief, facilitate a remission of the disorder, help clients resolve their most pressing problems, and teach them tools so that they can help themselves in the future. Given that the precipitating problem for the client is external (interpersonal), cognitive therapy tends to be effective and efficient in relieving distress in adolescent clients. This time-limited structure is congruent with the overarching structure of Roberts's crisis intervention model.

## Principle 8

Cognitive therapy sessions are structured. Reviewing the client's progress since the previous meeting, setting an agenda for the session, getting feedback from any homework, discussing agenda items, giving new homework assignments, and summarizing the session are common tasks used in cognitive therapy sessions.

## Principle 9

Cognitive therapy teaches patients to identify, evaluate, and respond to their dysfunctional thoughts and beliefs. Through Socratic questioning or guided discovery, therapist and client discover irrational or dysfunctional thoughts that maintain behaviors serving to impede the client from full functioning. By identifying these thoughts and critically evaluating their validity and usefulness, the client is taught to create new schemas that lead to healthier, adaptive behaviors.

## Principle 10

Cognitive therapy uses a variety of techniques to change thinking, mood, and behavior. Although Socratic questioning and guided discovery are central tools for cognitive therapy, techniques from other therapeutic approaches are employed as well.

These principles are applied through a process in which the therapist assists clients in (a) accepting that their self-statements, assumptions, and beliefs largely mediate their emotional reactions to the precipitating event; (b) identifying dysfunctional beliefs and patterns of thoughts that underlie their problems; (c) identifying situations that engender dysfunctional cognitions; (d) substituting functional self-statements for self-defeating cognitions; and (e) rewarding themselves for successful coping efforts (Hepworth et al., 2012).

In the case of survivors of school violence, some of the client's thoughts may be rational: There may be real threats of subsequent violence. There may be times when life really is so hard that an appropriate response is to become clinically depressed or anxious. In fact, such a response may be part of a natural grieving process (Benbenishty & Astor, 2005). In either event, a primary problem may be that clients, finding that they are unable to carry out tasks in the same way they had previously, give up and do little more than retreat from life. They generalize their lack of control about one part of their life to all areas of their life. Reversing this pattern becomes the primary goal of cognitive therapy and the crisis intervention. In achieving this goal, the therapist allows the client to accept the negative thoughts (e.g., "When I am around those people I may be in danger"), but either challenges the negative *automatic* thoughts of the client (e.g., "I automatically think that whenever I see them I am in danger. But maybe that isn't so, maybe I'm just worried that I might be in a situation where they could jump me again") or develops strategies to facilitate the client's distracting him- or herself from the negative thoughts and challenging their implications (Beck, 2011).

## APPLICATION OF ROBERTS'S CRISIS INTERVENTION MODEL WITH COGNITIVE THERAPY

### Assessing Lethality

In assessing the case of Aretha Jackson presented at the beginning of the chapter, we would be concerned that she is safe from further threats of violence. Crisis intervention for persons victimized by school violence should begin with a comprehensive assessment of the incident and persons involved. Ensuring that the victim is safe is of paramount importance. Although the specific perpetrator of the violence may be removed from the scene, members of that person's subgroup may be cause for concern. We would need to know if the girl who threatened Aretha still poses a threat to her. For instance, we would need to find out if she continues to bring a weapon to school. In the case of box-cutters or other weapons, simply disarming the perpetrator of violence may not be sufficient because the weapon can be easily replaced.

Determining if Aretha is a member of an organized group or gang would be important. It is also important to determine if she is a member of any informal groups (geeks, brains, etc.). We might make these inquiries by asking Aretha who she associates with, if we are familiar with most of the student population. We also need to assess the client's degree of assimilation into the group at the outset of the first interview.

The client's accounting of pertinent events preceding the altercation should be carefully noted. If possible, the therapist should obtain school information specific to individual students because intervening after violent events is enhanced by knowledge of the participants, their family situations, specific stressors and strengths, social supports, and so on (Jaycox, Kataoka, Stein, Langley, & Wong, 2012). In Aretha's case, we would try to access her school records prior to meeting with her. Although we value her accounting of the violent event, we also try to gather background information so that we can contextualize her comments.

We are concerned with three aspects of potential lethality in Aretha's case. First, how likely is it that she will commit harm to herself as a result of the victimization? Many adolescents are concerned with "saving face" and not losing the respect of their peers. If the individual fears that he or she will be humiliated or disgraced by being victimized, the threat of lethality is increased. We are more concerned with older adolescents in this regard than with early adolescents or younger children. In Aretha's case, we do not think this risk is great, as she readily came for help. Second, what is the likelihood that Aretha will think about personally redressing the wrong done to her? The common inability of adolescents to think temporally beyond today and to delay gratification can often increase the possibility that they will react to "even the score." Aretha's fear that the threat will be repeated suggests that this risk is not great. The third aspect of lethality the therapist should assess is the degree to which there is a viable threat of recrimination by the perpetrator's subgroup. In Aretha's case, we are indeed concerned and will employ the school's administration and security personnel to intervene on her behalf. We will also work with her to identify potential dangerous situations she should avoid.

## Establishing Rapport and Communication

As noted, many adolescents have a general distrust of adults. The victim may think that he or she can handle the situation without adult interference. However, it has been our experience that students are willing to trust persons in positions of authority when they are in crisis situations.

We will pay attention to our use of effective interviewing microskills (attentive listening, body language, paraphrasing, etc.) and strive to project an aura of professionalism without being authoritarian with Aretha. Although it does not appear to be the case with Aretha Jackson, it is often the case that the victim played an active part in creating the situation that resulted in violence. Nonetheless, the worker should view the client in the victim role for the purposes of crisis intervention. Assuming an authoritarian role will certainly undermine any rapport that has been established between the worker and the client. As noted by Maercker and Muller (2004), de-emphasizing the term *victim* and instilling the idea that the client is a *survivor* may be helpful.

## Identifying Major Problems

Precipitating events must be identified if the client is to successfully process the violent event. This information may be difficult to obtain, particularly if the violent act was an indiscriminate, aggressive act against a representative of a group rather than a specific individual. Many times, the individual unknowingly provokes the attack. In these instances, it is fruitful for therapists to use their professional knowledge to help identify possible causes of the attack. It appears that Aretha unknowingly or unintentionally provoked the threat against her. Helping her understand why the other girl reacted the way she did will help Aretha process the meaning of the threat. If we are unaware of this meaning, we sometimes contact school security personnel or administrators to get their perception of the interaction. Although it may be possible to get this information from the perpetrator directly, we have found that the school personnel may have already done so.

A second reason for gathering additional information about the violent act is that adolescents, even when not engaged in a crisis situation, are not known to be particularly good witnesses or reporters of events to which they are a part, so working to gather other views of the event may be helpful in assisting the client to understand what really happened. This understanding may help the client identify or reframe his or her actual problems.

Many violent events are the culmination of a series of negative encounters between the victim and the perpetrator. These bullying situations are similar to a person's being stalked, as the victim may have taken all known steps to avoid an altercation to no avail. As Roberts and Roberts (1990, 2005) state, when these steps fail, the client is likely to enter an active crisis state. Although the client is likely to desire answers to the question of why he or she has been targeted, the therapist should remain focused on the nature of the interpersonal behavior pattern, as that is the client's problem.

Entering this active crisis state can provoke a sense of disequilibrium or disorganization, but it also is indicative of the client's generating resources to begin overcoming the crisis-provoking event (Roberts & Roberts, 2005). It is at this point that cognitive therapy can be applied because the victim has begun to make self-statements that may be interfering with normal behaviors. Aretha may be considering her role in the violent interaction as something she should have known about or something she did herself. Her fears may be causing her to become overly cautious.

During the first couple of sessions with Aretha, we will work to make sure she is not ruminating about the past event. We will work to identify those problems that impede her ability to function as she did prior to the violence. Specifically, we will help her understand that it is her cognitive responses that restrict her after the violent event.

## Dealing With Feelings and Providing Support

Social service providers need to be attentive to social withdrawal of children exposed to traumatic violent events, as inhibition of their normal activity can serve as an indicator of their degree of stress. Children's grief responses are often more delayed than adult responses. Still, noting that children are being quiet and polite "angels" may indicate that they are having difficulty adjusting to the aftermath of the precipitating event (Jimerson, Stein, & Rime, 2012; Ursano, Fullerton, & Norwood, 1995).

Students typically feel fear, anger, frustration, powerlessness, embarrassment, and shame when they have been victimized by violent aggressors. If they are witness to another's victimization, they may also feel guilt that they did not respond more assertively or effectively. Providing attentive, nonjudgmental support allows clients to work through their emotional responses to the event. Normalizing the client's experience facilitates this process. Reconciling the mixture of feelings resulting from being victimized allows clients to move toward applying energy to actively engaging in problem solving.

We will work with Aretha to help her understand that her fearful reaction to being threatened is normal and reasonable. If her emotional vocabulary is limited, we may try to help her broaden it so that she does not fall prey to the common problem of youngsters reporting being only "angry" or "sad" because they have not identified other emotions.

## Exploring Possible Alternatives

Once the client's level of emotional distress has been reduced, he or she can begin to generate alternative solutions to the problem(s). Therapists can help clients develop a list of viable alternative responses that will achieve the clients' goals. It is important when working with adolescents to prod them to persist and brainstorm possibilities rather than accepting the first idea that comes to mind.

It is at this stage that we begin to help clients challenge their irrational cognitions or mediate their emotional reactions to the precipitating event. We work with them to explore if their perceptions are accurate reflections of what is going on in the external world. While we acknowledge the protective function of these thoughts, we help the youth see that there are other ways of thinking about the current situation and that the past is the past. Translating these concepts so they can be understood by young children is sometimes quite challenging, and we often remind ourselves that patience is indeed a virtue.

## Formulating an Action Plan

In this step, goals should be clearly formulated. The goals should be concrete, specific, and measurable (Hepworth et al., 2012). Also, if they are not collaboratively established, there is a risk that the client will not be invested in achieving the stated goals. Providing a mechanism for the client to actively direct treatment goal setting can provide a model for subsequent self-empowerment activity (Roberts, 2005).

The therapist is cautioned to remember that school students may lack the cognitive or emotional maturity (or the verbal acumen) to identify the steps necessary to carry out a plan that will achieve their identified goals. We have found that employing a problem-solving model such as the task-centered model (see Behrman & Reid, 2005) can provide a structure for articulating this plan. Cognitive-behavioral interventions are compatible with the task-centered model, and the time-limited nature of the model has been amenable to using it in school settings.

Although we have, by this time, already begun our cognitive intervention by challenging the client's self-talk and beliefs, we use this step to direct the client to demonstrate behavioral tasks that indicate that she is achieving her goals. In Aretha's case, we will make sure that she is again doing things that she avoided in the wake of the violent threat. We are very supportive of all efforts (no matter how small) that indicate she is making progress toward overcoming whatever impediments she had immediately following the violent event. We are particularly concerned that Aretha reward herself for her progress, as school victims are often reluctant to acknowledge their progress. We want them to be aware of their progress and how they have overcome their own problems. If our cognitive intervention is to be educational, Aretha needs to be aware of her progress in order to replicate it later.

## Follow-Up Measures

As in other interventions, the active phase of treatment can vary in duration. By definition, a crisis is time-bound, and there comes a point at which the crisis aspect of the problem diminishes; then, either the intervention has been effective and the client will terminate services, or continued services need to be contracted. Our cognitive intervention, embedded in Roberts's crisis intervention model, typically focuses on only one or two dysfunctional beliefs or thoughts that are constricting the client from full functioning.

However, we recognize that many clients have cognitive or emotional difficulties prior to their victimization that may impede their full recovery. Although successful treatment in crisis intervention is typically defined as the client's return to previous levels of functioning (Roberts, 2005), the trauma of being victimized by or exposed to school violence may require treatment beyond the intervention necessary to address the crisis aspect of the problem. In these cases, the client should be referred to service providers for this help. Ethical practice standards indicate that after terminating with the client, the therapist should follow up to ensure that the client is maintaining satisfactory mental health.

Our work with Aretha continued for 3 weeks while she responded to being threatened by her peer. During that time she overcame her irrational fear of other girls in her school who belonged to organized gangs. Although she respected the potential for violence that these girls presented, Aretha also recognized that she was not being singled out as a target for aggression. She no longer avoided public areas of the school. She was able to identify irrational self-talk and challenge these thoughts. As a consequence, Aretha was pleased that she was able to address her own fears and conduct her social activities in the same way she had prior to her violent altercation with her peer. We should note that the perpetrator of the violence had been suspended from school for 1 week, and that school security personnel had been vigilant in their surveillance of the girls the perpetrator had been hanging out with.

## CATASTROPHIC EVENTS

Although, as noted earlier, the number of catastrophic events is small in the context of all school violence, the devastating effects of homicides on entire communities has galvanized the media's attention on this phenomena. The media's unwavering attention to the catastrophic homicidal school violence events of the past few years provides a profusion of anecdotal information about the perpetrators, victims, and societal responses to these events, but no systematic research has been presented that provides an understanding of this phenomenon. As in the previous section, our discussion is limited to the crisis intervention aspects of this phenomenon, focusing on the victims of the event rather than the perpetrators. Further, our discussion is limited to post-occurrence interventions. These emanate from literature on disaster relief, but they provide the best information relative to treating survivors of these devastating events.

### Assessment/Risk Factors

A primary goal in helping survivors of catastrophic school violence is restoring and promoting normative cognitive, emotional, and interpersonal functioning to those adversely affected by trauma and grief (Murphy, Pynoos, & James, 1997). In doing so, service providers should remember that individuals differ in their capacity to adjust to catastrophic events.

Freedy, Resnick, and Kilpatrick (1992) have developed a risk factor model for disaster adjustment. They suggest that workers perform short clinical assessments of factors thought to predict adjustment difficulties in the days and weeks following the disaster. Their identified risk factors include those who have experienced high numbers of negative life events within the past year and individuals with mental health problems prior to the disaster. Experiences during the phenomenon that indicate high risk for poor adjustment include threats of personal injury (including death), personal injury, exposure to grotesque sights, and the loss of a family member or loved one (witnessed or not). Ursano and colleagues (1995) suggest that the single best predictor of the probability and frequency of postdisaster psychiatric problems is the severity of the disaster, as indicated by the number of injured and the types of their injuries. Having effective cognitive coping skills and a social support network that promotes personal control and competence prior to the disaster are thought to be protective factors that can mediate the risk for poor adjustment to disasters (Freedy et al., 1992).

## Post-Occurrence Interventions

We are proponents of an integrated model combining Roberts's crisis intervention model and cognitive therapy. However, we recognize that catastrophic events require additional consideration. For instance, the needs of individuals following a disaster can be considered in the context of Maslow's (1968) hierarchy of needs, suggesting that initial intervention efforts focus on establishing safety and physical health. Social and psychological interventions should follow. A crucial intervention component should be to educate members of the community about "normal responses to abnormal events" (Ursano et al., 1995). These responses are physical, cognitive, and emotional in nature. Physical responses usually begin with a sense of shock and disorientation. This commonly triggers a "fight or flight" response, which manifests with increased heart rate and breathing and increased sensory perception. Because this intense response cannot be maintained for long periods of time, exhaustion follows (Young, 1991, 1995).

Cognitive and emotional responses are similar to the physical responses, with shock and disbelief manifesting initially, perhaps including denial and a sense of suspension of reality. This shock is followed by emotional turmoil as the individual engages emotions such as anger, frustration, guilt, and grief in responding to the losses resulting from the crisis (Young, 1991, 1995). It may take the individual weeks or months to proceed through the shock and emotional turmoil responses, leaving the person mentally and emotionally exhausted. This emotional exhaustion commonly leaves the individual feeling as though he or she is on an emotional roller coaster: at one moment overwhelmed by emotion, and the next moment devoid of emotion. Some persons erect defenses to this phenomenon by constricting their range of emotional involvement in the external world around them (Young, 1991). The goal of crisis intervention can be seen as facilitating the client's journey through this process until he or she emerges as a "fully-responsive, fully-involved" person. It is often appropriate to include family members or friends in counseling sessions because they can reinforce messages and provide ongoing support. This is the case even if those family members or friends have been traumatized by the event themselves. Peer support groups also provide a valued forum for support in the aftermath of catastrophic events (Young, 1991).

The National Organization of Victim Assistance (NOVA) has been responding to catastrophic school violence events for almost two decades (Young, 1991, 1995). Those administering post-event services will welcome NOVA's expertise, particularly the group debriefing process it employs. This intervention provides an important mechanism for moving groups of survivors through Stages 3 and 4 of Roberts's crisis intervention model (identifying major problems, and dealing with feelings and providing support).

NOVA's intervention addresses the complicating factor of a whole community's being overwhelmed by the catastrophic event. In these instances it becomes important for survivors and their service providers to form a protective barrier against intrusive external forces, including media personnel. Using adults as buffers against external forces is appropriate, provided the adults are not overwhelmed by the trauma themselves. One method of accomplishing this is to facilitate crisis intervention with the adults so that they can then attend to their children. As noted earlier, the grief response in children is typically delayed (in comparison with adult reactions). This period of shock or denial can be problematic if it lasts for extended periods of time, but it does provide a window of time when attention can be focused on adult care providers. Note that we are not suggesting that needed crisis intervention services be withheld from children, and we acknowledge that adults' ability to provide care for their children while they are in the midst of a trauma response should be assessed as well.

In addition to the trauma experienced by those directly exposed to the violent event, the social networks of these victims are also affected by the violence. In particular, parents and siblings of youth are at risk for secondary trauma responses. Social service workers need to be aware of potential interpersonal difficulties manifesting in families exposed to school violence in the weeks and months following the occurrence. Distributing literature offering supportive services can be helpful to those who are not educated about the symptoms of secondary stress reactions, or who have minimized their psychological or social problems subsequent to the violent event.

Finally, social workers and other crisis intervention providers are reminded that persons providing relief services may need psychiatric help as well, particularly police, medical personnel, hotline workers, insurance claims settlers, and community leaders. Special attention should be paid to "heroes," as there is often tremendous pressure to serve as spokespersons for the survivors or relief workers. These heroes may experience conflicting feelings of guilt, satisfaction, and anxiety that their actions do not justify their "hero" status.

The case of John Hanson exemplifies the need for crisis intervention in a catastrophic event. The assessment of John's situation is of critical importance. The length of time John was exposed to traumatic events and the nature of the events he witnessed will help determine the type and length of his treatment. Those students who witnessed shootings and might have been placed in hostage situations will need special consideration and are more likely to exhibit chronic symptomology than those who were present or witnessed peripheral events.

The need for involvement from NOVA would be stressed, as well as the need for a group debriefing. Because this event affects the entire community, it would be important to include John's parents and close friends to empower them to help in the healing process. Educating John's parents and other support network members about normal reactions to abnormal situations would be a primary goal because those closest to John would need to be prepared for these reactions. In working with John directly, we would use a cognitive intervention similar to that described in treating Aretha Jackson. Emphasizing John's fears about his lack of control in the violent situation, and the possibility of repeated catastrophic events would require his addressing irrational thoughts that impede his post-traumatic event functioning. While we work with him to address his cognitive distortions, we also remain supportive of his emotional recovery. Through these interventions it is likely that John will learn to cope with the catastrophic situation.

## POLICY INTERVENTIONS

In response to acts of school violence, most schools (at least 75%) have enacted zero-tolerance discipline policies, which dictate that students be suspended for behaviors ranging from disrespectful language to carrying a weapon at school. These policies mandate that a predetermined consequence, usually a severe penalty of suspension, be automatically applied to a list of behaviors, regardless of their severity or the context (American Psychological Association Zero Tolerance Task Force, 2008). A review of 20 years of research provides little evidence of the effectiveness of these policies in improving the social climate of the school or making schools safer. In fact, they appear to be harmful by resulting in the disproportionate use of suspensions with students of color and students with disabilities (American Psychological Association Zero Tolerance Task Force, 2008). Recommendations for improving schools' responses to violent behavior include the following:

- Be flexible in applying zero-tolerance policies, allowing more behaviors to be addressed in the classroom, when appropriate.
- Improve communication between teachers and parents about behavioral problems in the classroom.
- Clearly define behaviors that are infractions and provide training to teachers and staff in addressing problem behaviors at school.
- Evaluate strategies to improve behavior to ensure that they are effective. (American Psychological Association Zero Tolerance Task Force, 2008)

A range of federal policies have been proposed as ways of responding to incidents of mass shootings and suicides in schools and preventing future incidents. These include harsher penalties for juveniles committing violent offenses and stricter gun control policies, including background checks for individuals wanting to purchase guns. Following the school shootings at Columbine in 1999, more than 800 bills related to gun control were introduced, but only 10% were passed (Schildkraut & Hernandez, 2014). More recently, incidents of school violence have prompted federal initiatives aimed at increasing the numbers of mental health providers in schools (Klein, 2013). The question remains whether these policy interventions are effective in reducing the number or severity of these catastrophic events (Schildkraut & Hernandez, 2014).

## Culturally Competent Intervention

Although there appears to be little relationship between special populations or specific demographic characteristics and acute, catastrophic school violence, there is some research on more chronic violence or bullying. Generally, extant research suggests that no single demographic factor may predispose an individual to bullying, including membership in or identification with a typically oppressed or vulnerable population (www.stopbullying.gov). There appear to be gender differences in bullying behavior, but there does not appear to be meaningful variation in the rate of bullying based on gender (Silva, Pereira, Mendonca, Nunes, & Olivera, 2013; Wimmer, 2009).

The impact of ethnicity is less clear, with Vervoort, Scholte, and Overbeek (2010) noting that some research findings present evidence of ethnically based bullying, and other studies suggest that ethnicity may be only one of several factors contributing to harassment. Still other evidence suggests that race or ethnicity plays little role in bullying (Seals & Young, 2003).

Although there are conflicting findings regarding the role of race and ethnicity in bullying, the influence of sexual orientation is clearer. One study (Bochenek & Brown, 2001) suggests that most LGBT youth experience bullying based on their sexual orientation. Other research indicates that LGBT youth not only are more likely to be victims of bullying but also are more likely to suffer from mental health issues, such as post-traumatic stress disorder and depressive symptomology, as a result of bullying (Rivers, 2001, 2004).

Although the research is mixed on the influence of demographic characteristics on bullying, practitioners are reminded that intervening with clients belonging to minority populations warrants keen sensitivity to cultural considerations. There are numerous cultural considerations that impact one's ability to successfully engage clients. Cultural norms and values can profoundly affect a child's response to a violent incident and his or her long-term adjustment (Silva & Klotz, 2006). Because an individual's gender, race, socioeconomic status, sexual orientation, and other aspects of his or her identity could be the focus of incidents of school violence and bullying, it is critical that responses to these incidents be culturally informed. In the prevention literature, researchers call for interventions that educate school communities about valuing differences. These efforts could also be important to emphasize in the school's response to violent incidents.

Because of their professional development and code of ethics centered on issues of social justice, social workers are well prepared to call attention to school policies or interventions that marginalize subgroups of students based on any personal characteristic or their socioeconomic status. They can advocate for culturally responsive interactions among students, between students and school personnel, and with students' families (Banks & Banks, 2010). Kumpfer, Pinyuchon, Texixeira de Melo, and Whiteside (2008) offer steps for making interventions culturally relevant. She advocates for matching any intervention to the needs of the target population and its characteristics, including age, ethnicity, and language (Eggert, Seyl, & Nicholas, 1990; Hooven, Herting, & Snedker, 2010). There are also resources to guide social workers in intervening with students from particular cultural groups (see Cauce et al., 2002; Griner & Smith, 2006; Cartledge & Johnson, 1997; Castillo, 1997; McGoldrick, Giordano, Pearce, & Giordano, 1996).

## Secondary Trauma

A growing area of concern regards secondary trauma responses on the part of service providers, school personnel, and even parents. Literature emanating from research on post-traumatic stress disorder indicates that those who are vicariously exposed to traumatic events are susceptible to experiencing trauma themselves (Figley, 1995; Hudnall, 1996). The risk of secondary trauma is higher for those who are repeatedly exposed to persons who have experienced trauma. Therefore, workers providing crisis intervention services need to take steps to ensure their own health (see Figley, 1995; Hudnall, 1996).

In response to the prevalence of secondary trauma in service providers, Sandra Bloom, MD, Joseph Foderaro, MSW, and Ruth Ann Ryan, RN, developed the Sanctuary Model. The Sanctuary Model is a trauma-informed approach to creating an organizational culture that supports healing from traumatic experiences (National Child Traumatic Stress Network, 2008; Rivard, Bloom, McCorkle, & Abramovitz, 2005). The Sanctuary Model aims to create an emotionally and physically safe environment for traumatized individuals and their service providers. Although more rigorous evaluation of the Sanctuary Model is needed, the emerging research demonstrates that it is a promising approach for creating a healthy environment that promotes emotional health and well-being for agency personnel and the clients they serve. The model has been used primarily in health and mental health settings, but it is currently being applied to school settings as well (Esaki et al., 2013; Stanwood & Doolittle, 2004).

## CONCLUSION AND POLICY RECOMMENDATIONS

Although continued efforts and resources need to be devoted to prevention programs, there will always be a need for crisis intervention programs. In addition to violence between individuals, tensions between student subgroups in schools have always resulted in aggression between these groups, and crisis interventions with individuals are appropriate for dealing with these skirmishes or transgressions. If these tensions escalate, they can lead to devastating events that traumatize whole schools, if not whole communities. In these instances, disaster-relief models of crisis intervention are most appropriate. School district administrators, as well as social service agency administrators, would be well advised to establish both prevention and post-occurrence plans addressing the issue of school violence.

REFERENCES

Allen-Meares, P., Washington, R. O., & Welsh, B. L. (1996). *Social work services in schools* (2nd ed.). Boston: Allyn and Bacon.
American Psychological Association Zero Tolerance Task Force. (2008). Are zero tolerance policies effective in the schools? An evidentiary review and recommendations. *American Psychologist, 63,* 852–862.

Astor, R. A. (1998). School violence: A blueprint for elementary school interventions. In E. M. Freeman, C. G. Franklin, R. Fong, G. L. Shaffer, & E. M. Timberlake (Eds.), *Multisystem skills and interventions in school social work practice* (pp. 281–295). Washington, DC: National Association of Social Workers Press.

Banks, J. A., & Banks, C. A. M. (2010). *Multicultural education: Issues and perspectives* (7th ed.). Hoboken, NJ: Wiley.

Barry, T. D., Lochman, J. E., Fite, P. J., Wells, K. C., & Colder, C. R. (2012). The influence of neighborhood characteristics and parenting practices on academic problems and aggression outcomes among moderately to highly aggressive children. *Journal of Community Psychology, 40,* 372–379.

Beck, J. S. (2011). *Cognitive therapy: Basics and beyond* (2nd ed.). New York: Guilford Press.

Behrman, G., & Reid, W. J. (2005). Posttrauma intervention: Basic tasks. In A. R. Roberts (Ed.), *Crisis intervention handbook: Assessment, treatment, and research* (3rd ed., pp. 291–302). New York: Oxford University Press.

Benbenishty, R., & Astor, R. A. (2005). *School violence in context: Culture, neighborhood, family, school, and gender.* New York: Oxford University Press.

Beran, T., & Li, Q. (2005). Cyber-harassment: A new method for an old behavior. *Journal of Educational Computing Research, 32,* 265–277.

Bochenek, M., & Brown, A. W. (2001). *Hatred in the hallways: Violence and discrimination against lesbian, gay, bisexual, and transgender students in US schools.* New York: Human Rights Watch.

Bonanno, R. A., & Hymel, S. (2013). Cyber bullying and internalizing difficulties: Above and beyond the impact of traditional forms of bullying. *Journal of Youth and Adolescence, 42,* 685–697. doi:10.1007/s10964-013-9937-1

Bowen, G. L., Hopson, L. M., Rose, R. A., & Glennie, E. J. (2012). Students' perceived parental school behavior expectations and their academic performance: A longitudinal analysis. *Family Relations, 61*(2), 175–191.

Brody, G. H., Ge, X., Kim, S. Y., Murry, V. M., Simons, R. L., Gibbons, F. X., ... Conger, R. D. (2003). Neighborhood disadvantage moderates associations of parenting and older sibling problem attitudes and behavior with conduct disorders in African American children. *Journal of Consulting and Clinical Psychology, 71,* 211–222.

Cartledge, G., & Johnson, C. T. (1997). School violence and cultural diversity. In A. P. Goldstein and J. C. Conoley (Eds.), *School violence intervention: Practical handbook* (pp. 391–425). New York: Guildford.

Castillo, R. J. (1997). *Culture and mental illness: A client-centered approach.* Pacific Grove, CA: Brooks/Cole.

Cauce, A. M., Domenech-Rodríguez, M., Paradise, M., Cochran, B. N., Shea, J. M., Srebnik, D., & Baydar, N. (2002). Cultural and contextual influences in mental health help seeking: A focus on ethnic minority youth. *Journal of Consulting and Clinical Psychology, 70*(1), 44–55.

Centers for Disease Control and Prevention. (2012). School violence

fact sheet. Retrieved from http://
www.cdc.gov/violenceprevention/
pdf/schoolviolence_factsheet-a.pdf

Cohen, J., & Geier, V. K. (2010).
*School climate research summary,
January 2010.* Retrieved from
www.schoolclimate.org/climate/
research.php

Crosnoe, R. (2004). Social capital
and the interplay of families and
schools. *Journal of Marriage and
Family, 66,* 267–280.

Curcio, J. L., & First, P. F. (1993).
*Violence in the schools: How to
proactively prevent and defuse it.*
Newbury Park, CA: Sage.

Dake, J., Price, J., & Telljohann, S.
(2003). The nature and extent
of bullying at school. *Journal of
School Health, 73*(5), 173–181.

Dryfoos, J. (1998). *Safe passage: Making it through
adolescence in a risky society.* New York: Oxford
University Press.

Eggert, L., Seyl, C., & Nicholas, L.
(1990). Effects of a school-based
prevention program for potential
high school dropouts and drug
abusers. *International Journal of
the Addictions, 25,* 773–801.

Esaki, N., Benamati, J., Yanosy, S.,
Middleton, J., Hopson, L. M.,
Hummer, V., & Bloom, S. (2013).
The Sanctuary Model®: A theo-
retical framework. *Families in
Society, 94*(2), 87–95.

Espelage, D., Anderman, E. M.,
Brown, V. E., Jones, A., Lane,
K. L., McMahon, S. D., . . .
Reynolds, C. R. (2013).
Understanding and preventing
violence directed against teach-
ers. *American Psychologist,
68*(2), 75–87.

Espelage, D., & Swearer, S. (2003).
Research on school bullying and
victimization: What have we
learned and where do we go from
here? *School Psychology Review,
32,* 365–384.

Figley, C. R. (1995). *Compassion
fatigue: Coping with secondary traumatic stress disorder in
those who treat the traumatized.*
New York: Brunner/Mazel.

Fishbein, D. H., Hydeb, C., Eldreth,
D., Paschall, M. J., Hubal, R.,
Dasa, A., . . . Yung, B. (2006).
Neurocognitive skills moder-
ate urban male adolescents'
responses to preventive interven-
tion materials. *Drug and Alcohol
Dependence, 82,* 47–60.

Frederick, A. D., Middleton, E. J., &
Butler, D. (1995). Identification of
various levels of school violence.
In R. Duhon-Sells (Ed.), *Dealing
with youth violence: What
schools and communities need to
know* (pp. 26–31). Bloomington,
IN: National Educational Service.

Freedy, J. R., Resnick, H. S., &
Kilpatrick, D. G. (1992).
Conceptual framework for evalu-
ating disaster impact: Implications
for clinical intervention. In
L. S. Austin (Ed.), *Responding
to disaster: A guide for mental
health professionals* (pp. 3–24).
Washington, DC: American
Psychiatric Press.

Goldstein, A. P., & Conoley,
J. C. (1997). Student aggression: Current status. In
A. P. Goldstein and J. C. Conoley
(Eds.), *School violence intervention: A practical handbook* (pp.
3–22). New York: Guilford Press.

Griner, D., & Smith, T. B. (2006).
Culturally adapted mental health
intervention: A meta-analytic
review. *Psychotherapy: Theory,
Research, Practice, Training, 43,*
531–548.

Gutman, L. M., McLoyd,
V. C., & Tokoyawa, T. (2005).
Financial strain, neighbor-
hood stress, parenting behaviors

and adolescent adjustment in urban African-American families. *Journal of Research on Adolescence, 15*, 425–449.

Hepworth, D. H., Rooney, R. H., Rooney, G. D., & Strom-Gottfried, K. (2012). *Direct social work practice: Theory and skills* (9th ed.). Belmont, CA: Brooks/Cole.

Hooven, C., Herting, J., & Snedker, K. (2010). Long-term outcomes for the Promoting CARE suicide prevention program. *American Journal of Health Behavior, 34*, 721–736.

Hudnall, B. (1996). *Secondary traumatic stress: Self-care issues for clinicians, researchers, and educators.* Lutherville, MD: Sidran Press.

Jaycox, L. H., Kataoka, S. H., Stein, B. D., Langley, A., & Wong, M. (2012). Cognitive behavioral intervention for trauma in schools. *Journal of Applied School Psychology, 28*, 239–255).

Jimerson, S. R., Stein, R., & Rime, J. (2012). Developmental considerations regarding psychological trauma and grief. In S. Brock and S. Jimerson (Eds.), *Best practices in school crisis prevention and intervention* (2nd ed., pp 377–400). Bethesda, MD: National Association of School Psychologists Press.

Klein, A. (2013). Obama presses school safety: Mental health initiatives. *Education Week, 32*(18), 12.

Kumpfer, K. L., Pinyuchon, M., Texixeira de Melo, A., & Whiteside. H. O. (2008). Cultural adaptation process for international dissemination of the Strengthening Families program. *Evaluation in the Health Professions, 31*, 226–239. doi:10.1177/0163278708315926

Langley, A. K., Nadeem, E., Kataoka, S. H., Stein, B. D., & Jaycox, L. H. (2010). Evidence-based mental health programs in schools: Barriers and facilitators of successful implementation. *School Mental Health, 2*, 105–113.

Limber, S. P., Nation, M., Tracy, A. J., Melton, G. B., & Flerx, V. (2004). Implementation of the Olweus Bullying Prevention Programme in the southeastern United States. In P. K. Smith, D. Pepler, & K. Rigby (Eds.), *Bullying in schools: How successful can interventions be?* (pp. 55–79). Cambridge: Cambridge University Press.

Litwiller, B. J., & Brausch, A. M. (2013). Cyber bullying and physical bullying in adolescent suicide: The role of violent behavior and substance use. *Journal of Youth and Adolescence, 42*, 675–684. doi:10.1007/s10964-013-9925

Lochman, J. E., Wells, K. C., Qu, L., & Chen, L. (2012). Three year follow-up of Coping Power intervention effects: Evidence of neighborhood moderation? *Prevention Science, 14*, 364–376. doi:10.1007/s11121-012-0295-0

Maercker, A., & Muller, J. (2004). Social acknowledgement as a victim or survivor: A scale to measure a recovery factor of PTSD. *Journal of Traumatic Stress, 17*, 345–351.

Maslow, A. H. (1968). *Toward a psychology of being.* New York: Van Nostrand Reinhold.

McGoldrick, M., Giordano, J., Pearce, J. K., & Giordano, J. (1996). *Ethnicity and family therapy* (2nd ed.). New York: Guilford Press.

McNeely, C. A., Nonnemaker, J. M., & Blum, R. W. (2002). Promoting student connectedness to school: Evidence from the national longitudinal study of ado-lescent health. *Journal of School Health, 72,* 138–146.

Murphy, L., Pynoos, R. S., & James, C. B. (1997). The trauma/grief focused group psycho-therapy module of an elementary school-based violence preven-tion/intervention program. In J. D. Osofsky (Ed.), *Children in a violent society* (pp. 223–255). New York: Guilford Press.

National Child Traumatic Stress Network. (2008). Trauma-informed interventions. Sanctuary Model: General infor-mation. Retrieved from http://www.nctsnet.org/nctsn_assets/pdfs/promising_practices/Sanctuary_General.pdf

Olweus, D. (1978). *Aggression in the schools: Bullies and whipping boys.* Oxford: Blackwell.

Osofsky, H., & Osofsky, J. (2001). Violent and aggressive behaviors in youth: A mental health and prevention perspective. *Psychiatry, 64,* 285–295.

Pardini, D., Lochman, J. E., & Wells, K. C. (2004). Negative emo-tions and alcohol use initiation in high-risk boys: The moderating effect of good inhibitory con-trol. *Journal of Abnormal Child Psychology, 32,* 505–518.

Powers, J. D., Bowen, G. L., & Rose, R. A. (2005). Using social environ-ment assets to identify intervention strategies for promoting school success. *Children and Schools, 27,* 177–187.

Regoli, R. M., & Hewitt, J. D. (1994). *Delinquency in society: A child-centered approach.* New York: McGraw-Hill.

Rich, J. (1992). Predicting and controlling school violence. *Contemporary Education, 64*(1), 35–39.

Rivard, J. C., Bloom, S. L., McCorkle, D., & Abramovitz, R. (2005). Preliminary results of a study examining the implemen-tation and effects of a trauma recovery framework for youths in residential treatment. *Therapeutic Community: The International Journal for Therapeutic and Supportive Organizations, 26*(1), 83–96.

Rivers, I. (2001). Retrospective reports of school bullying: Stability of recall and its implications for research. *British Journal of Developmental Psychology, 19*(1), 129–141.

Rivers, I. (2004). Recollections of bullying at school and their long-term implications for les-bians, gay men, and bisexuals. *Crisis: The Journal of Crisis Intervention and Suicide Prevention, 25*(4), 169–175.

Rivers, I., Poteat, V. P., Noret, N., & Ashurst, N. (2009). Observing bullying at school: The mental health implications of witness sta-tus. *School Psychology Quarterly, 24,* 211–223.

Roberts, A. R. (1991). Conceptualizing crisis theory and the crisis intervention model. In A. R. Roberts (Ed.), *Contemporary perspectives on crisis intervention and preven-tion* (pp. 3–17). Englewood Cliffs, NJ: Prentice-Hall.

Roberts, A. R. (2005). Bridging the past and present to the future of crisis intervention and crisis management. In A. R. Roberts (Ed.), *Crisis intervention handbook: Assessment, treat-ment, and research* (3rd ed., pp. 3–34). New York: Oxford University Press.

Roberts, A. R., & Roberts, B. (1990). A comprehensive model for cri-sis intervention with battered women and their children. In A. R. Roberts (Ed.), *Crisis intervention handbook: Assessment, treatment, and research* (pp. 106–123). Belmont, CA: Wadsworth.

Roberts, A. R., & Roberts, B. S. (2005). A comprehensive model for crisis intervention with battered women and their children. In A. R. Roberts (Ed.), *Crisis intervention handbook: Assessment, treatment, and research* (3rd ed., pp. 441–482). New York: Oxford University Press.

Scherr, T. G. (2012). Addressing the needs of marginalized youth at school. In S. Jimerson, A. Nickerson, M. Mayer & M. Furlong (Eds.), *Handbook of school violence and school safety* (2nd ed., pp. 106–116). New York: Routledge.

Schildkraut, J., & Hernandez, T. C. (2014). Laws that bit the bullet: A review of legislative responses to school shootings. *American Journal of Criminal Justice, 39,* 358–374.

Seals, D., & Young, J. (2003). Bullying and victimization: Prevalence and relationship to gender, grade level, ethnicity, self-esteem, and depression. *Adolescence, 38,* 735–747.

Silva, A., & Klotz, M. B. (2006). Culturally competent crisis response. Retrieved from http://www.nasponline.org/resources/culturalcompetence/cc_crisis.aspx

Silva, M., Pereira, B., Mendonca, D., Nunes, B., & Olivera, W. (2013). The involvement of girls and boys with bullying: An analysis of gender differences. *International Journal of Environmental Research and Public Health, 10,* 6820–6831.

Smith, P. (2000). Bullying and harassment in schools and the rights of children. *Children and Society, 14,* 294–303.

Stanwood, H. M., and Doolittle, G. (2004). Schools as sanctuaries. *Reclaiming Children and Youth, 13,* 169–172.

Stopbullying.gov.(2014, December 2). Risk factors. Washington, DC: US Department of Health and Human Services. Retrieved from http://www.stopbullying.gov/at-risk/factors/index.html

Straus, M., Gelles, R., & Steinmetz, S. K. (1980). *Behind closed doors: Violence in the American family.* New York: Anchor Press/Doubleday.

Ursano, R. J., Fullerton, C. S., & Norwood, A. E. (1995). Psychiatric dimensions of disaster: Patient care, community consultation and preventive medicine. *Harvard Review of Psychiatry, 3,* 196–209.

US Department of Education, National Center for Education Statistics. (2013). Fast facts: School crime. Retrieved from http://nces.ed.gov/fastfacts/display.asp?id=49

Verlinden, S., Hersen, M., & Thomas, J. (2000). Risk factors in school shootings. *Clinical Psychology Review, 20*(1), 3–56.

Vervoort, M. H., Scholte, R. H., & Overbeek, G. (2010). Bullying and victimization among adolescents: The role of ethnicity and ethnic composition of school class. *Journal of Youth and Adolescence, 39*(1), 1–11.

Whitlock, J. L. (2006). Youth perceptions of life in school: Contextual correlates of school connectedness in adolescence. *Applied Developmental Science, 10,* 13–29.

Wimmer, S. (2009). Views on gender differences in bullying in relation to language and gender role socialisation. *Griffith Working Papers in Pragmatics and Intercultural Communication, 2*(1), 18–26.

Wolff, B. C., Santiago, C. D., & Wadsworth, M. E. (2009). Poverty and involuntary engagement stress responses: Examining the link to anxiety and aggression within low-income families. *Anxiety, Stress, and Coping, 22,* 309–325.

Ybarra, M., Diener-West, M., & Leaf, P. J. (2007). Examining the overlap in Internet harassment and school bullying: Implications for school intervention. *Journal of Adolescent Health, 41,* S42–S50.

Young, M. A. (1991). Crisis intervention and the aftermath of disaster. In A. R. Roberts (Ed.), *Contemporary perspectives on crisis intervention and prevention* (pp. 83–103). Englewood Cliffs, NJ: Prentice-Hall.

Young, M. A. (1995). Crisis response teams in the aftermath of disasters. In A. R. Roberts (Ed.), *Crisis intervention and time-limited cognitive treatment* (pp. 151–187). Newbury Park, CA: Sage.

# IV

## VULNERABLE POPULATIONS

# 16

# A Comprehensive Model for Crisis Intervention With Battered Women and Their Children

KENNETH R. YEAGER
ALBERT R. ROBERTS
BEVERLY SCHENKMAN ROBERTS

Intimate partner violence (IPV) affects millions of women who are being or have been assaulted by intimate partners and ex-partners across their life span (Black et al., 2011). Without a better understanding of what constitutes effective crisis intervention, without better-trained personnel staffing 24-hour domestic violence hotlines, and without a much more comprehensive social service delivery system put in place, too many of these women will end up as a statistic in either hospital or homicide records or, at the very least, living out lives ruined by emotional pain, suffering, or permanent injuries. This chapter presents the all too sobering facts about battered women and their children and suggests the most effective models for crisis intervention, police-based domestic violence units, 24-hour crisis hotlines, and service delivery systems.

## Case Scenarios

Sonia was a 20-year-old college student at the time of the interview. She had met Brad the summer after she graduated from high school. Brad was her first boyfriend to take her to expensive restaurants and college fraternity parties. He was very polite to her parents and younger sister when he visited her home to take her on dates. Sonia thought she was very much in love with Brad.

Although Sonia was a virgin, 6 months into the relationship, they had sexual intercourse for the first time. Sonia indicated that Brad was very romantic, and the wine she drank that night put her in the mood. Shortly thereafter, Brad thought that Sonia was looking at his friend Tony, and Brad was so jealous that he slapped her for the first time. The next day, Brad apologized, brought Sonia flowers, and blamed his slapping her on the liquor and his love for her. She forgave him. Sonia was completely unprepared for the rapid escalation in violence several months later, when Brad became furiously jealous and violent because of a practical joke from a male coworker of Sonia's. Sonia's lips were bleeding, the insides of her gums were torn up, and she had a swollen face. Sonia indicated that she was in a state of shock and questioned whether she would be able to trust another boyfriend in the future. She obtained a temporary restraining order with the help of her parents. She reported that the police were very helpful by taking photographs of her bruised face and asking her to write down what had happened and to sign the police report. The police then went to Brad's house and served him with the restraining order, prohibiting him from having any contact with Sonia or harassing her in any way.

Christy, a 24-year-old college graduate who now manages a restaurant, was physically abused and stalked by a former boyfriend when she was 18, during her freshman year at college. Christy reported that she still has nightmares from time to time in which a current boyfriend (after the batterer) becomes violent toward her. She wonders if the nightmares and lethargy will ever go away. Christy enjoys her job and career and feels that what was most useful to her was the crisis counseling she received soon after the abuse.

Pamela, a 29-year-old teacher and devout Catholic with two young children, initially thought the emotional and physical abuse from her husband was due to the enormous stress associated with his being a medical student. Pamela convinced herself that the abuse would end as soon as her husband completed his residency and had his own medical practice. Pamela endured several years of abuse even years after her husband was established as a respected physician. She permanently left and divorced her husband as a result of the good advice from her priest, crisis intervention, and social support at a group for formerly battered women at the local women's resource center and shelter. Pamela does volunteer work at the local shelter.

Do you know what some women get for their birthdays? A black eye, a punch in the ribs, or a few teeth knocked out. It's so frightening because it doesn't just happen on their birthday. It may be every month, every week, or even every day. It's so frightening because sometimes the man abuses the kids, too. Or maybe she's pregnant, and he kicks her in the stomach in the same spot where, just a few minutes earlier, she felt the baby moving. It's so frightening because the woman doesn't know what to do. She feels so helpless. He's in control. She prays he'll come to his senses and stop. He never does. She prays he won't hurt their kids. He threatens to. She prays he won't kill her. He promises he will (Haag, n.d.).

We were married 13 years. It was OK until the past 5 years, when he started to hit me to hurt me. He was doing drugs. He was usually high, or when he couldn't get drugs, he'd hit me 'cause he couldn't have it. We'd get in an argument because he'd want money, and I'd say no, and that's how it would start. He punched and kicked me. Usually I had a black eye and black and blue marks on my legs. He used to steal my money—he stole my Christmas money and my food stamps. He tried to say someone broke into the house, but I knew he had it.

My ex-husband drank every day, especially in the summer. He is very violent. I fear for my life that one day he will get me alone and kill me. He hated my little dog because I spoiled him. He would tell me that he was going to drop-kick him (he weighed only 4 pounds). I had to give my dog away because I didn't want him to hurt it. I had to give up my family and friends for the same reason. He broke my nose without even thinking twice. He also tried to strangle me a couple of times, and he didn't let go until I faked passing out. I've had to fake a blackout, and that is the only reason I am alive. For all he knew, I could have been dead when he left me lying there on the floor.

---

The description of the fear, anguish, and physical injuries to which battered women are repeatedly subjected comes from the late Albert Roberts's research files. Case illustrations are included in this chapter to acquaint crisis intervenors, social workers, nurses, psychologists, and counselors with the painful history of the women they will be counseling and assisting. Increasingly, battered women are turning to emergency shelters, telephone crisis intervention services, mental health centers, and support groups for help. Recognition of the need for and actual establishment of crisis intervention services for victims of the battering syndrome has increased dramatically since the 1970s.

The most promising short-term interventions with battered women include 24-hour crisis hotlines, crisis-oriented support groups, shelters for battered women, and/or therapy. Despite the growing and pervasive negative effects of IPV on societies, there are few controlled trials of interventions for IPV in health care settings. In fact, there is a clear lack of quantitative data on how different types and severity of abuse relate to women's health, quality of life, and service use and to effective approaches to care (e.g., Straus et al., 2009; Wuest et al., 2010). Difficulties around clarification are complicated because most measures of IPV do not characterize the severity or type of abuse, even though studies have demonstrated that such categorization is associated with higher levels of depression, anxiety, post-traumatic stress, and chronic pain and lower levels of quality of life (Dutton, Kaltman, Goodman, Weinfurt, & Vankos, 2005; Straus et al., 2009; Wuest et al., 2010). Although only a small number of research studies have been conducted on the effectiveness of different types of crisis services for battered women, one research article that analyzed 12 outcome studies demonstrated positive outcomes. Tutty, Bidgood, and

Rothery (1993) studied outcomes of 76 formerly battered women in Canada after completion of a 10- to 12-session support group and found significant improvements in self-esteem and locus of control and decreases in stress and physical abuse 6 months after treatment. Gordon (1996) examined 12 outcome studies on the effectiveness of intervention by community social services, crisis hotlines, women's groups, police, clergy, physicians, psychotherapists, and lawyers. In summary, it seems that battered women consistently found crisis hotlines, women's groups, social workers, and psychotherapists to be very helpful. In sharp contrast, the battered women respondents reported that usually police, clergy, and lawyers are *not* helpful to different types of abused women (Gordon, 1996). In all, the availability of resources appears to be a greater predictor of whether survivors progress to using active help-seeking strategies to cope with violence. Zosky (2011) found that survivors of violence who could identify a range of available resources they could access for help were more likely to use active means of engagement as opposed to passive means of disengagement (e.g., avoidance or tension reduction to cope with violence; see also Taft, Resick, Panuzio, Vogt, & Mechanic, 2007).

This chapter will examine the alarming prevalence of woman battering, risk factors and vulnerabilities, precursors to crisis episodes, and resilience and protective factors. In addition, the following types of crisis intervention programs will be discussed: early intervention by police-based crisis teams and victim assistance units; assessment and detection in the hospital emergency room; electronic technology to protect battered women in imminent danger; specific intervention techniques used by crisis hotlines and battered women's shelters; and short-term treatment for the victim's children. The chapter will also discuss the importance of referrals.

## SCOPE OF THE PROBLEM

Intimate partner abuse is one of the most harmful, traumatic, and life-threatening criminal justice and public health problems in American society. Since the 1970s, when domestic violence was first identified (Walker, 1984), IPV has continued to grow in significance as a social issue. It is estimated that 25% of women will be victims of IPV at least once in their lifetimes, and 1.5 million women a year in the United States will be victimized by their partners (Tjaden & Thoennes, 2000). Intimate partner abuse continues to be the single greatest health threat to American women between the ages of 15 and 50. More women sustain injuries as a result of intimate partner abuse than from the combined total of muggings and accidents. The statistics are overwhelming:

- More than 22 million women in the United States have been raped in their lifetime. (Black et al., 2011, pp. 19–24)

- In the United States, 18.3% of women have survived a completed or attempted rape. (Black et al., 2011)
- Of the 18.3% of women who have survived rape or attempted rape, 12.3% were younger than age 12 when they were first raped, and 29.9% were between the ages of 11 and 17. (Black et al., 2011)
- Every 90 seconds, somewhere in America, someone is sexually assaulted. (calculation based on 2012 National Crime Victimization Survey, Bureau of Justice Statistics) (Turman, Langton, & Planty, 2012)
- One out of every five American women has been the victim of an attempted or completed rape in her lifetime. (Black et al., 2011)
- Approximately 1,270,000 women are raped each year. Another 6,646,000 are victims of other sexual crimes, including sexual coercion, unwanted sexual contact, or unwanted sexual experiences. (Truman, 2011)
- Fifteen percent of sexual assault and rape victims are under age 12; 29% are aged 12 to 17; 44% are under age 18; 80% are under age 30. The highest-risk years are ages 12 to 34. (Truman, 2011)
- Girls aged 16 to 19 are four times more likely than the general population to be victims of rape, attempted rape, or sexual assault. (Truman, 2011)
- Most female victims are raped before the age of 25, and almost half of female victims are under the age of 18. (Black et al., 2011).
- More than 75% of female victims were raped or sexually assaulted before age 25. (Black et al., 2011)
- Almost two thirds of all rapes are committed by someone who is known to the victim. Seventy-three percent of sexual assaults were perpetrated by a nonstranger (48% of perpetrators were a friend or acquaintance of the victim, 17% were an intimate, and 8% were another relative). (Black et al., 2011)
- Almost 64% of women who reported being raped, physically assaulted, and/or stalked since age 18 were victimized by a current or former husband, cohabiting partner, boyfriend, or date. (Black et al., 2011)
- Of female rape or sexual assault victims in 2010, 25% were assaulted by a stranger, 48% by friends or acquaintances, and 17% by were intimate partners. (Black et al., 2011)
- Almost 10% of high school students are victims of dating violence each year. (Eaton et al., 2010)
- Ninety-three percent of juvenile sexual assault victims know their attacker; 34.2% of attackers were family members, and 58.7% were acquaintances (Snyder, 2000)
- The Campus Sexual Assault Study estimated that between 1 in 4 and 1 in 5 college women experience completed or attempted rape during their college years. (Krebs, Lindquist, Warner, Fisher, & Martin, 2007)
- About one third of female murder victims aged 12 or older are killed by an intimate partner. (Truman, 2011)

- It is estimated that 43% of lesbian and bisexual women and 30% of gay and bisexual men have experienced at least one form of sexual assault during their lifetimes. (Rothman, 2011)
- About 67.9% of rape victims are White, 11.9% are Black, 14% are Hispanic, and 6% are of other races. (Black et al., 2011)
- An estimated 17,500 women and children are trafficked into the United States annually for sexual exploitation or forced labor. (US Department of State, http://www.state.gov/documents/organization/192587.pdf)
- Offenders have been reported to be armed with a gun, knife, or other weapon in 11% of rape or sexual assault victimizations. (Truman, 2011)

The most accurate statistics on the lifetime prevalence of IPV come from the National Violence Against Women Survey conducted by Professors Patricia Tjaden and Nancy Thoennes with grants from the National Institute of Justice and the Centers for Disease Control and Prevention (CDC). This study, which was based on telephone interviews with a nationally representative sample of 8,000 men and 8,000 women, indicated that 25% of the women and 7.6% of the men stated that they had been physically battered and/or raped by a spouse, cohabiting partner, or date during their lifetime. These national figures document the high prevalence and consequences of intimate partner abuse. In actuality, however, some women are at much greater risk of becoming victims of IPV than others. The women who are at the highest risk of encountering violence from dates and steady boyfriends are high school and college students (Roberts, 1998, 2002).

Date abuse, binge drinking, club drugs, and drug-facilitated sexual assault have been escalating on college campuses and at bars and rave parties frequented by high school students and young adults who are not in school. Female college students, particularly those who are living away from their families during the first year or two of college, are at heightened risk of becoming victims of dating violence because of the peer pressures to drink or do drugs combined with the lack of supervision and protection often provided by their families (Roberts & Roberts, 2005).

Woman battering is one of the most life-threatening, traumatic, and harmful public health and social problems in American society. Recent estimates indicate that each year approximately 8.7 million women have been victims of some form of assault by their partner (Roberts, 1998; Straus & Gelles, 1991; Tjaden & Thoennes, 1998; Tjaden & Thoennes, 2006). Partner violence continues to be the single greatest health threat to American women under the age of 50. On an annual basis, more women sustain injuries as a result of domestic violence than from the combined total of muggings and accidents (Nurius, Hilfrink, & Rafino, 1996; Truman, 2011; Black et al., 2011).

Women who suffer the most severe injuries require treatment in hospital emergency rooms and hospital trauma centers. In the United States, it is estimated that 35% of emergency room visits are made by women who need emergency medical care as a result of domestic violence–related injuries (Valentine, Roberts, & Burgess, 1998; Duterte et al., 2008; Truman, 2011).

The frequency and duration of violence range from women who are hit once or twice (and make a decision to end the relationship immediately) to women who remain in the relationship and are beaten with increasing frequency for an extended period, which may last for many years (Roberts & Burman, 1998; Lutenbacher, Cohen, & Mitzel, 2003). Petretic-Jackson and Jackson (1996) and Walker (1985) found a strong correlation between women who had suffered chronic abuse and the onset of bipolar disorder, anxiety disorder, post-traumatic stress disorder (PTSD), panic disorder, and/or depression with suicide ideation. Additionally, D. M. Johnson and Zlotnick (2006) point out that unlike other PTSD victims, victims of IPA face very real and ongoing threats; therefore, treatments that incorporate exposure are contraindicated, as habituation to feared stimuli may increase their risk for further victimization.

Although there were only 7 emergency shelters for battered women in 1974 (Roberts, 1981), by 1998 there were more than 2,000 shelters and crisis intervention services coast-to-coast for battered women and their children (Roberts, 1998). Through crisis intervention, many women are able to regain control of their lives by identifying current options and goals and by working to attain those goals. The children of battered women may also be in crisis, but their plight has sometimes been overlooked as domestic violence programs focused their efforts on emergency intervention for the women. Progressive programs now incorporate crisis intervention for children (as well as for the mothers) in the treatment plan.

Battered women are usually subjected to a prolonged pattern of abuse coupled with a recent severe attack; by the time the victim makes contact with a shelter, she is generally in need of both individual crisis intervention and a crisis-oriented support group. Abused women are subjected to an extended period of stress and trauma that results in a continual loss of energy. The woman is in a vulnerable position, and when a particularly severe beating takes place or when other factors occur (e.g., the abuser begins to hurt the children), the woman may be thrust into a state of crisis (Young, 1995).

Effective treatment for battered women and their children in crisis requires an understanding of crisis theory and the techniques of crisis intervention. According to Caplan (1964), Janosik (1984), and Roberts (1996b), a crisis state can occur rapidly when the following four things happen:

1. The victim experiences a precipitating or hazardous incident.
2. The incident is perceived by the woman as threatening to her or her children's safety, and as a result tension and distress intensify.
3. The battered woman attempts to resolve the situation by using customary coping methods and fails.

4. The emotional discomfort and turmoil worsen, and the victim feels that the pain or anguish is unbearable.

At this point of maximum discomfort, when the woman perceives the pain and torment as unbearable, she is in an active crisis state. During this time there is an opportunity for change and growth, and some women are mobilized to seek help from a 24-hour telephone crisis intervention service, the police, a hospital emergency room, or a shelter for battered women.

The emphasis in crisis assessment is on identifying the nature of the precipitating event and the woman's cognitive and affective reaction to it. The five most common precipitating events that lead battered women in crisis to seek the help of a domestic violence program are (a) an acute battering incident resulting in serious physical injury; (b) a major escalation in the degree of violence, for example, from shoving and slapping to attempted strangulation or stab wounds; (c) an impairment in the woman's hearing, sight, or thought process as a direct result of severe batterment; (d) a high-profile story in the news media about a woman who was brutally murdered by her partner after suffering in silence for many years; and (e) a serious abusive injury inflicted on the woman's child. Often the precipitating event is perceived by the woman in crisis as being the final incident, or "last straw," in a long history of violence (L. Edington, personal communication, February 19, 1987; R. Podhorin, personal communication, February 12, 1987; Roberts, 1998; Schiller-Ramirez, 1995; Goodyear-Smith, Arrol, & Coupe 2009).

Crisis intervention with battered women needs to be done in an orderly, structured, and humanistic manner. The process is the same for victims of other violent crimes, but it is particularly important to respond quickly to abused women because they may continue to be in danger as long as they remain in a place where the batterer can locate them. Crisis intervention activities can result in the woman either returning to her precrisis state or growing from the crisis intervention so that she learns new coping skills to use in the future (Roberts, 1998).

## ZERO TOLERANCE

*In a dating, cohabiting, or marital relationship, there is never an excuse, justification, or rationalization that allows a man (or adolescent boy) to hit a woman (or an adolescent girl).* The professional literature on domestic violence is replete with citations of the horrendous problems that ensue when women have become involved in long-term relationships in which they are assaulted on a frequent basis. The purpose of this chapter is to educate counselors, social workers, young women, and their families and friends regarding the full spectrum of violent relationships, with the goal of helping them to prevent the likely progression, over time, from the initial incident of being slapped to becoming the victim of severe beatings later on.

One 20-year-old woman who has benefited from a good therapeutic relationship with a psychologist (following her having been hit by a boyfriend when she was 17) now makes it a practice to tell all men she starts to date that she has *zero tolerance* for violence in her dating relationships. She explains that she was slapped around by her first boyfriend, and she will not allow herself to go through that type of disrespect and trauma again. Thus far, her boyfriends have been sensitive to her previous victimization, and she has not been abused again. But her attitude is this: "I need to set forth these boundaries right up front, on the very first date, to reinforce to every guy I date that this isn't going to happen to me ever again. And if, in the future, I meet a guy who is put off by my dating ground rules, then good riddance to him!"

## BATTERED WOMEN AT HIGH RISK OF CRISIS EPISODES

For some women, the effects of partner abuse can be short-term, with a quick recovery, whereas for others the result is chronic dysfunction and mental health disorders. Domestic violence researchers have found that among women who are battered for many years, those who receive the most severe forms of injury seem to have the highest risk for the following difficulties: nightmares and other sleep disturbances, re-enactment of trauma, major depression, post-traumatic stress symptoms, substance abuse, self-destructive behavior, psychosexual dysfunction, and/or generalized anxiety disorder. Research studies indicate that, in general, these women's mental health problems were not present early in the relationship but developed as a result of the repeated acts of violence (Gleason, 1993; Woods & Campbell, 1993; Liang, Goodman, Tummala-Narra, & Weintraub, 2005).

PTSD may occur when an individual perceives an event as life-threatening to herself or significant others. Characteristic features of PTSD identified in the clinical literature are as follows:

1. Integration of the traumatic experience by re-experiencing the traumatic event (through recurrent and/or intrusive thoughts, flashbacks, nightmares, or other intense reactions)
2. Management of subsequent stress (increased arousal and hypervigilance)
3. Facilitation of affective expression
4. Determination of the meaning of victimization (Petretic-Jackson & Jackson, 1996, p. 210)

As a result of one or more severe battering incidents, some battered women have had their cognitive schemas or mental maps altered. According to Valentine, Roberts and Burress (1998), under extreme duress, the battered woman's schema is imprinted strongly with a survival message that guides the victim even after the crisis has passed. Victims are then left with the chore of either assimilating that event into their previously existing schemas or altering their schemas to incorporate this terrifying event. PTSD symptoms consist of intrusive thoughts [nightmares], hypervigilance [i.e., startle responses], and avoidance [i.e., blunted affect to avert all reminders of the incident] (see Chapter 4 in this volume).

Crisis intervention and time-limited treatment with battered women must be approached with empathy, sensitivity, and caution. When an abused woman is suffering from PTSD, if the crisis intervenor asks the woman to "re-experience" the violent event, the counselor may inadvertently precipitate a retraumatization rather than the intended therapeutic opportunity (Petretic-Jackson & Jackson, 1996; Zosky, 2011). Before crisis intervention is initiated, it is critically important to create a safe, highly flexible, empowering environment where symptom relief strategies are emphasized. If avoidance, startle overreactions, and nightmares are the primary presenting problems, the crisis intervenor may well facilitate the narrative and storytelling process by utilizing experiential techniques, art therapy, poetry, photographs, and/or police reports.

Stress management techniques can build on the battered woman's inner strengths and potential for positive growth. Examples of these techniques are progressive relaxation, guided imagery, refocusing one's attention on external reality, good nutrition, developing a support system, and using "dosing"—"a technique in which attention is alternately shifted toward and away from the traumatic experience" (Petretic-Jackson & Jackson, 1996, p. 210). Many battered women seem to have developed very limited affective expression as a result of suppressing their emotions. In addition, because battered women generally suppress feelings of anger, they may suddenly express rage a year or two after leaving the batterer.

Many battered women who experienced three or more traumatic and severe battering incidents often take a long time to gain a sense of control of their environment. Their self-esteem, trust in men, and cognitive assumptions are often shattered. The survivor's low self-esteem, weak decision-making skills, intrusive thoughts, and flashbacks often result in a series of acute crisis episodes. The crisis intervenor or counselor needs to help the woman build trust while bolstering her self-esteem. This is done through modeling, reframing, stress inoculation, relaxation techniques, exercise, thought stopping, encouraging journal entries, solution-based therapy, and cognitive restructuring.

## TRAUMATIC BATTERING EVENTS, LEGAL ACTION, MEDICAL INJURIES, AND SLEEP DISTURBANCES AS PRECURSORS TO CRISIS EPISODES

Several types of traumatic, life-threatening mental health and legal events or situations often can precipitate a crisis. These include the following:

- A battered woman sustains a life-threatening injury (e.g., a concussion, multiple stab wounds, a miscarriage, or strangulation).
- A child is severely physically or psychologically harmed by the batterer.
- The victim obtains a restraining order or files for divorce, and her taking legal action enrages the batterer, resulting in stalking, terroristic threats, and/or a rapid escalation of the battering incidents.
- A battered woman encounters explicit kidnapping or terroristic death threats against herself, her children, and/or her elderly parents.
- The batterer has already made explicit death threats against the formerly battered woman, and he is soon to be released from prison or a residential drug treatment program.

In Roberts's (1996a) study of 210 battered women, the majority of the participants interviewed had experienced one or more severe beatings. The outcomes of these beatings were manifested in anxiety, depression, sleep disturbances, panic attacks, and intrusive thoughts. The following are illustrations of sleep disturbances:

Somebody chases me or is trying to kill me. I can't remember the last pleasant dream I had.

I have nightmares about him burning up the house. I keep dreaming that the kids and I were trapped in the house with flames all around us and we couldn't get out. I would see his face in the flames, with him pointing at us and laughing while we are crying and in pain.

I have the same nightmare a few times a week. I see this guy who looks like my former boyfriend (drug dealer who was shot 3 years ago by the Newark police). He is raising up out of the casket, and he said he loved me and is coming back to stab me to death so I can join him in hell. I wake up screaming, shaking, and sweating. A lot of times I can't fall asleep even though I'm mentally and physically exhausted. The next day at work I'm very jumpy and afraid to talk to any of the men in the office. When my supervisor asks me something, I get this flashback and am reminded of my nightmare and I start crying. I go into the ladies room sometimes for an hour and cry and cry, and then leave work early. I go home and try to calm down by smoking cigarettes and talking with my daughter.

In crisis intervention work with battered women, clinicians must be prepared to understand a range of potential precipitants and precursors. Crisis clinicians need to be aware of the aftermath of traumatic events, common triggering incidents, and precursors to crisis episodes in order to provide battered women with the most appropriate interventions.

## RESILIENCE AND PROTECTIVE FACTORS

The previous section examined high-risk groups and trauma, sleep disturbances, and other precursors to crisis episodes. Those groups of individuals with preexisting risk factors and trauma histories have difficulty recovering. In sharp contrast, some abused women have significant inner strengths, also known as *resilience* and *protective factors*, that have been found to mediate and lessen the impact of stress related to battering. The most common protective factors include high self-esteem, a social support network, and cognitive coping skills. One of the most important components of maximizing a battered woman's recovery is accomplished through believing in the client and helping her to realize her strengths. Many battered women feel trapped, socially isolated, and overwhelmed by the physical and emotional pain they have endured. Crisis intervenors and counselors can help the woman to recognize alternative coping strategies.

During the past decade, a growing number of crisis intervenors, counselors, social workers, and psychologists have recognized that a strengths perspective that builds on the resilience of individuals is much more fruitful to helping clients grow and change in positive directions than the previous 50 years of emphasis on pathologizing the client (Saleebey, 1997; Black, 2003). The strengths perspective of crisis intervention utilizes empowerment, resilience, healing and wholeness, collaboration, and suspension of disbelief. *Empowerment strategies* create opportunities for individuals and communities (Roberts & Burman, 1998). *Resilience* focuses on accelerating growth and identifying inner capabilities, knowledge, and personal insights. *Healing* refers to the ability of the body and mind to resist disease and chaos. The resilience literature incorporates a strong belief that individuals have self-righting tendencies and a spontaneous inclination toward healing and survival (Saleebey, 1997; Weil, 1995; Black, 2003). *Collaboration* refers to clients, counselors, crisis intervenors, and family members all working together to help strengthen the client. *Suspension of disbelief* refers to the ending of pessimism and cynicism and the affirmation of belief, learned optimism, self-protective strategies, a sense of humor, and commitment to change.

An integrated approach to crisis intervention combines Roberts's (1996b) seven-step crisis intervention practice model with solution-based therapy. Chapter 3 of this book provides a detailed discussion with several case applications of an integrated model of solution-based therapy. This practice model emphasizes building on and bolstering one's inner strengths, protective factors, latent coping skills, and positive attributes. It systematically reinforces the importance of realistic goal setting, identifying and explicating the positive exceptions in situations or behavior patterns, and the importance of the dream and miracle questions. We firmly believe that crisis intervention based on enhancing positive coping skills, rediscovering the exceptions and positive alternatives to crisis situations, building on and optimizing the client's bright spots and inner strengths, and seeking partial and full solutions will become common practice during the twenty-first century.

Tedeschi and Calhoun (1995) interviewed more than 600 college students who had recently experienced significant stressful life events, including a parent's death, being the victim of a crime, or receiving an accidental injury. The goal of their research was to determine which personality factors might lead to personal growth when an individual is confronted with a crisis situation. The researchers identified the characteristics of extroversion, openness, agreeableness, conscientiousness, and having an "internal locus of control" as benefiting persons in crisis by allowing them to find some positive outcome connected to what might otherwise be viewed as a devastating circumstance. For instance, those who indicated growth from the traumatic experience were more likely to report that they had experienced positive change (i.e., developing a new area of interest, forming a new relationship, or enhancing one's spiritual beliefs).

Some battered women develop positive coping strategies, whereas others develop negative and potentially self-destructive coping strategies. Examples of positive coping strategies include using formal and informal social support networks, seeking informational support, and requesting help from a shelter for battered women. Examples of negative coping mechanisms are dependence on alcohol or drugs and suicide attempts.

Positive coping strategies help women to facilitate their own survival and expedited recovery. The core focus of Lazarus and Folkman's (1984) conceptualization and application of the coping process is based on how an individual makes an appraisal of the stressful event. Appraisal takes place when an individual experiences an event and determines that it is "excessive relative to resources." There are two levels of appraisal related to coping responses:

1. Primary appraisal is viewed as the first level, wherein a person evaluates whether the event has the potential to cause harm (i.e., physical injury), to instill fear, or to interfere with a goal. More specifically, the individual decides whether a particular situation is at risk. The outcome reflects the individual's assessment of the stressful life event and the significance of the event for that individual's well-being.

2. When the event is perceived as harmful or threatening, the individual enters into secondary appraisal, wherein the available resources for coping are examined. When a person is confronted with a circumstance that is perceived as threatening or harmful, the person "enters into secondary appraisal" when she makes efforts to cope with the event (e.g., leaving the violent home immediately and living with a relative or at a shelter). (Lazarus & Folkman, 1984)

Battered women in crisis who are contemplating leaving the violent relationship are confronted by both internal and external barriers. Recent legislation, policy reforms, and federal funding initiatives have resulted in increased funding for transitional housing, job training, and concrete services for battered women. These societal and community-wide changes have empowered and improved the economic status of some battered women who were trapped by poverty, limited welfare checks and food vouchers, no employment skills, a lack of affordable housing, and no affordable child care. However, these policy changes and reforms are not enough.

As noted by Carlson (1997), the following four internal barriers often keep the battered woman trapped in a recurring pattern of acute crisis episodes: "low self-esteem; shame and self-blame for the abuse; poor coping skills; and passivity, depression, and learned helplessness" (p. 292). Carlson (1997) proposed an intervention model grounded in both an ecological perspective and Lazarus and Folkman's (1984) stress and coping paradigm. This practice model should be used by licensed mental health clinicians who are also trained in domestic violence (Carlson, 1997). The intervention is summarized as follows:

• Practice orientation: nonjudgmental acceptance, confidentiality, and a belief in self-determination of the client
• Engagement and developing a collaborative relationship
• Assessment (based on Petretic-Jackson and Jackson [1996], as discussed earlier in this chapter)
• Intervention: development of a safety plan, increasing information, enhancement of coping, enhancement of problem-solving and decision-making skills, and reducing isolation by increasing social support

Unfortunately, although it is important to study the correlation between coping methods in facilitating crisis resolution among battered women, there is a dearth of research in this area. A thorough review of the research related to crime victimization and the connection between cognitive appraisal, attributions, and coping mechanisms indicates no conclusive findings (Wyatt, Notgrass, & Newcomb, 1990; Frieze & Bookwala, 1996; Frazier & Burnett, 1994; K. Johnson, 1997; Straus et al., 2009; Wuest et al,

2010). Examples of specific strengths are high self-esteem, having a devoted mother, conscientious performance at work or in a job training program, or having a social support network.

Much of the professional literature on this topic focuses on the cognitive resources individuals employ when coping with unexpected, stressful life events (Lazarus & Folkman, 1984; Folkman & Lazarus, 1985). Coping has been defined by Folkman (1984) as "cognitive and behavioral efforts to master, reduce, or tolerate the internal and/or external demands that are created by the stressful transaction" (p. 843). These demands include perceptions of potential loss and/or harm, at which time the individual evaluates choices for coping via problem-focused and emotion-focused strategies. Problem-focused strategies are based on the use of problem-solving and action plans, whereas emotion-focused strategies utilize the control of negative or distressing emotions.

Kubany and colleagues (2003, 2004) conducted one of the first recognized clinical trials of a cognitive trauma therapy tailored specifically for IPV survivors suffering from PTSD. Their treatment approach, called Cognitive Trauma Therapy for Battered Women (CTT-BW), was designed in collaboration with advocates and survivors. This model included standard modalities such as psychoeducation about PTSD and stress management and exposure (e.g., talking about the trauma, homework, watching domestic violence in television programs or movies). This approach was also specifically designed to mitigate four areas of concern identified as critical issues to be addressed in the treatment of abuse survivors. These included:

- Trauma-related guilt that many survivors reported (guilt about failed marriage, effects on children, decisions to stay or leave)
- Histories of other traumatic experiences
- Likelihood of ongoing stressful contact with the abuser in relation to parenting
- Risk for subsequent revictimization

Modules were specifically designed to address these concerns, while examining and reframing negative cognitive distortions about the self and inaccurate cognitions that function to support and exacerbate trauma symptoms. At the same time, treatment provided assertiveness and self-advocacy skills training; strategies for managing contact with former partners particularly around custody and visitation; and strategies for identifying and avoiding potential perpetrators in the future. Therapy was provided in an individual format in eight to eleven 90-minute sessions for most clients (Kubany et al., 2003).

To be eligible for participation in the study, individuals had to meet the following requirements: must have been out of the relationship for at least 30 days. must verbalize no desire to reconcile, plus have no physical or sexual victimization for a minimum of 30 days; must have a history of partner-abuse related abuse related PTSD; must demonstrate moderate or higher abuse-related guilt; must not be actively abusing alcohol or drugs; and must not have an active diagnosis of schizophrenia or bipolar disorder. This study involved 37 ethnically diverse IPV survivors who were randomly assigned to receive either immediate or delayed treatment. Five women (14%) dropped out of treatment. Due to the small sample size of this feasibility study, the researchers were not able to test possible group differences between women who received treatment initially and those in the delayed treatment group. Within-group improvements, however, were promising.

IPV survivors improved on PTSD symptoms posttreatment, and these improvements were maintained for 3 months (retention rate = 68%). This outcome stands, regardless of whether the investigators included only women who completed treatment or all women.

D. M. Johnson, Zlotnick, and Perez (2011) designed a program for women living in domestic violence shelters, which they named Helping to Overcome PTSD Through Empowerment (HOPE). This approach involves nine to twelve 60- to 90-minute individual sessions conducted twice weekly over a maximum of 8 weeks. This approach to care was based heavily on Herman's (1992) multistage model, which involves three stages of recovery: (a) re-establishing safety and a sense of self-care; (b) remembering and mourning; and (c) reconnection. Herman's approach prioritizes women's safety needs; this approach does not include exposure therapy but, rather, focuses heavily on women's empowerment.

In Johnson's model, therapists focus on women's individual needs and choices and help them develop the necessary skills to reach their goals. Once sufficient progress had been demonstrated, sessions focus on building cognitive and behavioral skills to address PTSD symptoms and triggers; optional modules are available to address common co-occurring issues such as substance abuse and managing grief. One aspect of Johnson's approach that distinguishes it from other clinical trials of cognitive-behavioral therapy's effect on PTSD is that participants were eligible for this study if they met subthreshold PTSD criteria (e.g., meeting the re-experiencing criteria and either the avoidance or arousal criteria of PTSD). Individuals were not included in the study if they had a diagnosis of bipolar disorder or psychosis. Participants were required to be stable if taking psychotropic medications for the prior 30 days; and free of significant suicidal ideation or risk.

Seventy IPV survivors were randomized to receive HOPE or to continue receiving standard shelter services and were then interviewed again 1 week, 3 months, and 6 months after they left the shelter. Compared with women in the control condition, those in the HOPE condition were less likely to experience abuse 6 months after leaving the shelter. Additionally, participants receiving at least five sessions of HOPE were 12 times less likely to experience re-abuse than were women who received shelter services without

HOPE counseling. Measures of PTSD symptoms demonstrated no signifi-cant condition differences with one exception: Women who received HOPE reported less emotional numbing. Participants randomized to receive HOPE showed significant improvement over time on depression severity, empower-ment, and social support compared with women in the "services as usual" group. Additionally, satisfaction with the treatment was high, and engage-ment in treatment while in the shelter was also high. There were two par-ticipants who dropped out of this study. In all, 34 of the 35 women assigned to receive HOPE participated in at least 1 session, and 63% attended at least 5 sessions (26% attended all 12 sessions). Sixty-nine percent of the women did not complete all 12 sessions because they left the shelter prior to completing HOPE.

## SPECIALIZED DOMESTIC VIOLENCE UNITS

In addition to changes in arrest policies and customary practices in domestic cases, many police departments have created specialized domestic violence units to follow up on all domestic-related complaints. Specialized units have the ability to further investigate domestic crimes, make appropriate referrals and arrests, and ensure victim safety long after the patrol officer has left the scene. In some cases, unit members serve as the first responders to domes-tic calls for service. Units are generally staffed with police investigators or detectives and are often linked with specialized units in a prosecutor's office. They offer an opportunity for personnel to develop specialized knowledge and expertise regarding the investigation and prosecution of domestic crimes. In theory, units create the infrastructure necessary for aggressive, proactive responses to domestic violence rather than the traditional reactive policing approach.

These units also provide an opportunity to link police services with shelter, victim/witness, and batterer programming. Multidisciplinary approaches that integrate the need for both legal and social service interventions are likely to be the most effective in terms of protecting victim safety and ensur-ing offender accountability. Several police departments in the United States provide illustrations of the modern police response to domestic violence.

The first is the Domestic Violence Enforcement Team within the Ann Arbor Police Department in Ann Arbor, Michigan, which partners with the local battered women's advocacy program. The Enforcement Team was strategically placed in a building adjacent to the SAFE House in an effort to break down the barriers between the police and victim advocacy services and to improve the outcomes for victims. The police unit is able to track the status of cases, cutting through bureaucratic red tape and expediting the serving of bench warrants. Police attend every defendant arraignment and are able to take all domestic cases seriously. Police link with SAFE House staff after an arrest has been made, bringing immediate in-person services to the victim (Littel, Malefyt, Walker, Tucker, & Buel, 1998).

The Austin/Travis County Family Violence Protection Team within the Austin Police Department in Travis County, Texas, is another example of a collaborative, community response to family violence that provides multiple services in one location. Leading the community in a zero-tolerance policy toward family violence, the team (consisting of members of the Austin Police Department, the Travis County Sheriff's Office, SafePlace [formerly the Center for Battered Women and Rape Crisis Center], Legal Aid of Central Texas, the Women's Advocacy Project [attorneys], and the Travis County Attorney's Office) collaborates to investigate, prosecute, and provide legal and social services for victims. Investigations center around cases of assault, kidnapping, stalking, and protective order violations. Legal services streamline the process for obtaining emergency or long-term protective orders. The majority of cases are processed by the county attorney's office, and felonies are handled by the district attorney's office. Victim services are provided by victim service counselors from SafePlace, the Austin Police Department, and the Travis County Sheriff's Department. The Austin Child Guidance Center is also available to provide free counseling for children. The team has been in operation since 1997, funded by the Violence Against Women Grants Office (Austin City Connection, 2000).

The final example is provided by the Domestic Violence Impact Unit in the Longview, Washington, Police Department. This six-member team consists of a sergeant, police officers, civilian investigator, legal coordinator, crime analyst, and administrative specialist. The unit works to coordinate law enforcement, prosecution, probation, and victim services in domestic violence cases. It provides education and training to police officers, advocates, prosecutors, probation officers, and other community and criminal justice partners. An automated case management system assists the team in tracking offenders and their activities as they are processed through the system.

Not unlike the departments highlighted here, specialized units provide departments with the opportunity to thoroughly investigate misdemeanor-level domestic crimes, a function that in the past has been lost to other felony crimes. Following up on high-risk cases is critical to breaking the cycle of violence before it escalates to the felony level. Creating dialogue between police units, victims' programs, and victims promotes the protection of victims and the opportunity to prevent future acts of violence.

The Waterloo, Iowa, Police Department has dedicated officers and the Domestic Abuse Response Team (DART), which handles more than 450 domestic violence cases a year. In October 2011, the Waterloo Police Department was recognized by Verizon Wireless for its efforts in working in conjunction with the Black Hawk County Attorney's Office to actively intervene in cases of domestic violence. In 1995, prior to implementation of the

DART team, approximately one third of Waterloo's 493 domestic violence cases were dismissed due to the inability to successfully prosecute them. Through a nonprofit organization, Seeds of Hope, serving Black Hawk, Grundy, and Hardin Counties, residents have been provided with quality education and comprehensive services, including individual and child advocacy, legal advocacy, support groups, safe homes, transitional housing, transportation, and emergency cell phones, as well as a 24-hour crisis line for victims of domestic violence.

Police departments frequently organize their functions through the creation of specialized departments or units. Division of labor into smaller subunits has been an effective tool for contemporary police departments to manage the variety of tasks required of them. For example, police departments may have investigative units or squads for narcotics, sex crimes, juvenile crimes, fraud, special weapons, arson, and so on. Generally organized around specific crime types, specialized units have afforded police departments the opportunity to attend to the specific dynamics of particular crimes.

Although there are inherent challenges in the specialization of police functions, Peak (1998) identifies several advantages to such specialization. Specialized units place the responsibility for certain tasks with specific individuals, ensuring that the work is completed. This is especially true in the case of domestic violence. Historically, police investigators followed up only on domestic cases that involved felony-level assaults or homicides. Therefore, the majority of battering incidents were addressed only by patrol officers at the scene, with only the most severe cases of abuse being transferred to an investigative bureau. Specialized units also provide for the development of expertise and training that ultimately lead to increased efficiency, effectiveness, staff cohesion, and improved morale.

Although the potential is great for specialized units, Susan T. Krumholz (2001) argues that there may be a disjuncture between the image of a domestic violence unit and the reality that some units merely serve a symbolic role. Her research with 169 police departments in Massachusetts revealed a number of issues of concern. First, only 8% of the police departments with domestic violence units reported being supported from a line item in the department's budget, and 11% received partial funding by line item. The majority of departments acknowledge that they were funded solely by grants. This raises serious questions about the stability of such units after the grant period has ended. Krumholz also found that departments with such units required on average only 2 more hours of training per year than police departments without such units. Additionally, she found that the average unit was staffed by two full-time officers, and the majority of units were in operation only during normal business hours.

Further research is needed before we can fully understand the impact of specialized units in the creation of a local community environment where victims can be protected and abusers can be held accountable. Because many police departments find that the majority of their calls for service involve domestic incidents, specialized units may provide the most prudent organizational strategy to taking domestic assault seriously.

## THE ROLE OF TECHNOLOGY IN A COORDINATED COMMUNITY RESPONSE

Technology continues to revolutionize the police industry. Advanced photographic techniques, computers, DNA profiling, innovations in fingerprinting and forensic techniques, automated crime analysis, computer-aided investigations, computer-aided dispatch, case management systems, simulated training tools, nonlethal weapons, and surveillance technologies are but a few of the many examples of innovative crime-fighting tools. As police become more skilled in using such technologies and communities agree to invest resources in them, police departments are likely to apply such these advances to combat domestic violence in a broad way.

We see the potential for technology in protecting battered women from their abusive partners and deterring violent batterers from repeating their abusive and brutal acts. Cellular phones, electronic monitoring systems, and online police services are just a few of the applications of modern technology to policing domestic violence. Internet resources provide helpful tips for victims of domestic violence; for example, the website for the National Network to End Domestic Violence (2014) provides a variety of helpful tips for protecting privacy and data of victims and survivors. For a summary of technology and safety planning, see http://nnedv.org/resources/safetynet-docs.html (NNEDV, 2014).

### Cellular Phones

A national campaign to donate cellular phones for victims of domestic violence is currently underway. Sponsored by the Wireless Foundation (2004), a philanthropic organization dedicated to utilizing wireless communication for the public good, the Call to Protect program to date has received 30,606 donated cellular phones to provide links to emergency services for victims and their advocates. Established by the Cellular Telecommunications Industry Association (CTIA), the Wireless Foundation coordinates Call to Protect, a national donate-a-phone campaign. CTIA members Motorola, Brightpoint, Inc., in partnership with the National Coalition Against Domestic Violence (NCADV), provide free wireless phones and airtime. The phones are preprogrammed to notify authorities at the push of a button. Call to Protect was started by the Wireless Foundation, Motorola, and the National Coalition Against Domestic Violence. As a result of this national program combined with numerous other statewide and citywide programs across the United States have collected more than 2 million cell phones to help victims of domestic violence.

Verizon Wireless has continued to support the fight against IPV by sponsoring the HopeLine from Verizon, a program that connects survivors of domestic violence to resources and funds organizations nationwide. This program began in 1995 when the company Bell Atlantic Mobile introduced the HopeLine concept. Since 2001, Verizon has collected more than 10.8 million phones and accessories, turning them into support mechanisms for victims of domestic violence. The HopeLine program supplies refurbished phones that are equipped with 3,000 anytime minutes of airtime and texting capabilities. HopeLine phones are available to survivors affiliated with participating domestic violence agencies. Verizon also provides a HopeLine app for smartphones and tablets that provides access to domestic violence resources. Within this app (which is available for download at http://www.verizonwireless.com/aboutus/hopeline/index.html), a button connects callers directly to the National Network to End Domestic Violence for crisis intervention, information, or referrals. Additionally, Verizon has provided more than $21 million in grants to domestic violence organizations since 2001 (Verizon Wireless, 2014).

## Electronic Monitoring

Recent developments in electronic monitors, computerized tracking of offenders and victims, and video surveillance all function to enhance crime investigations and crime prevention efforts, with the overarching goal being to reduce and eventually eliminate violent crime by controlling the physical environment. Since 2000, 21 states and the District of Columbia have enacted legislation mandating or recommending that justice agencies employ GPS to protect victims of domestic violence during the pretrial period; several other states are in the process of considering such legislation.

When used for domestic violence offenses, GPS is typically assigned during the pretrial period, an identified high-risk time period, interventions begin with arrest and continue through the pretrial and trial period concluding with case disposition. This highly volatile time often is characterized by heightened danger to the victim and attempts by the accused to dissuade the victim from participating in the prosecution of the case. It is extremely important that programs are based on an understanding of the dynamics of domestic violence rather than utilizing the GPS program as a way of handling problems unrelated to domestic violence (e.g., jail overcrowding). Effective and efficient communication between the agency and victims is paramount for all GPS for domestic violence/IPV programs. As a cautionary note, programs should carefully monitor victims' expectations for program performance and the program's actual capabilities and practices to identify potential gaps in services. A lack of programming to meet expectations can lead to a sense of frustration, fear, and loss of confidence in the system. It is important to remember that victims of violence avoid direct communication and frequently experience difficulty trusting large organizations. Thus, providing accurate information to victims about the capabilities and limitations of the GPS platform in use is critical for victim welfare and safety.

Victims who are correctly informed about the absence of protection may not feel safe, but their actual safety will be enhanced when victim feedback about agency standards and practices is incorporated in the programming policy and planning for improving effectiveness, especially during the victims early learning phase. Incorporating victims' feedback empowers them to share individualized concerns, transforming victim input into a catalyst for agency innovation.

Quality and performance improvement includes learning from mistakes, misunderstandings, blind spots, and limitations. Process improvement is critical to a program's continued progress in effective intervention. Challenges for technology-based programming include staying abreast of technological innovations, becoming familiar with the situations of defendants and victims, and developing supervised innovative approaches to address identified gaps in technology, services, and policy.

Given the nature of domestic violence/IPV, it is not always possible to provide victims with the resources they should optimally have, and training victims on how to do safety planning is essential. It is important that victims are informed of how to develop and to modify their safety plan. This requires the victims to provide communication to all assisting parties to facilitate clear and accurate coordination among all relevant stakeholders (e.g., monitoring agency personnel, judges, victim advocates, attorneys, shelter workers, and police).

Promoting greater understanding among all stakeholders within the local justice system of the purpose and value of GPS for domestic violence/IPV programs may ultimately spearhead community efforts to develop a coordinated response to domestic violence, with GPS being integrated into standardized approaches to high-risk domestic violence/IPV cases.

It is important to note concerns regarding misuse of monitoring as a tool. When initially conceptualized, GPS was designed to function as a "prosocial" tool providing a method to monitor and provide positive support. However, at least 39 states require monitoring, with the tool being used nearly exclusively to document rule violations; with well over 250,000 individuals being monitored for a variety of offenses, the tool may have morphed into something very different. The question remains: Is this a prosocial support tool, a monitoring tool, or a means of control and punishment? The answer to this question remains in the control of those using this tool.

## Online Information and Apps

Police departments nationwide use the Internet as a tool to communicate with the community regarding crime issues. Through their mobile apps and web pages, police departments have created a vehicle through which information about domestic violence issues can be disseminated to the public at large. Police department electronic tools can provide community members with critical information regarding the dynamics of domestic violence, what to do if you are a victim, and where to access community resources.

If you have a iPhone or an Android, go to the app store and look for available applications to use to support and protect victims of domestic violence/IPV. When searching my phone, I found 34 related applications for domestic violence. One of the most interesting is an app labeled "Aspire News," which is disguised to look like a normal news app but actually is a tool to help people in domestic violence situations. The "Help" section contains several useful tools to help people exit a dangerous situation or survive a life-threatening one. Once the app is downloaded, the user can use this section to set up a "trusted contacts" list; the user can then create a message that will be sent to the trusted contacts in the case of an emergency. When the user is in a dangerous situation, this app enables him or her to discreetly call for help by opening the app and tapping the screen three times. The phone will immediately send out a message to each of the trusted contacts, including the physical location of the phone and the pre-typed message. The phone then automatically begins recording audio that will be sent to the trusted contacts. As an additional protection, the app contains an "emergency exit" feature designed to keep the user safe. All the user needs to do is tap a large "X" in the top corner of the screen, the app quickly closes the domestic violence–related page and brings up the news section. For more information on how to use technology to protect against domestic violence and to enhance personal safety, see resources supplied by the National Network to End Domestic Violence (http://nnedv. org/resources/safetynetdocs.html).

## CRISIS INTERVENTION BY POLICE-BASED CRISIS TEAMS AND VICTIM ASSISTANCE UNITS

Surveys of police departments around the United States indicate that approximately 80% to 90% of officers' time is spent on service calls, also known as order maintenance activities, for assaults among family members, neighbor disputes, bar fights, traffic accidents, and incidents involving individuals who are drunk and disorderly. The police may have the skills to intervene and resolve a dispute among neighbors, a bar fight, or a traffic accident, but they are rarely skilled in providing crisis intervention and follow-up counseling with victims of domestic violence (Roberts, 1990, 1996a).

In recognition of the large amount of time police spend responding to repeat family violence calls and their lack of clinical skills, a growing number of police departments have developed crisis intervention teams staffed by professional crisis clinicians and/or trained volunteers. Victims often turn to their local city, county, or township police department when confronted with the unpredictable injuries or life-threatening danger posed by domestic violence. As a result of the *Thurman* case (in which a battered woman was awarded $2.3 million in her lawsuit against the Torrington, Connecticut, police department for its failure to protect her from her violent husband), more police departments have been responsive to calls from domestic violence victims. Police can respond quickly to domestic violence calls and can transport the victim to the local hospital emergency room or a battered women's shelter. In some cities, police receive backup from the crisis team, which arrives at the home or police department shortly after the police transport the victim to police headquarters. The first such crisis team began in 1975 at the Pima County District Attorney's Office in Tucson, Arizona. The acceptance of and growing reliance on this program by the Tucson Police Department are revealed by the significantly increased number of police referrals to the crisis team—there were a total of 840 police referrals in 1977, compared with 4,734 referrals in 1984. It should be noted that these figures reflect referrals for all types of crime victims, but most referrals are for domestic violence cases. Because violence in the home accounts for a considerable percentage of police calls, abused women are frequent beneficiaries of this innovative system.

During the mid-1980s through the 1990s, a small but growing number of police departments developed programs to provide immediate crisis counseling to victims of domestic violence, as well as victims of other violent crimes such as rape. The crisis intervention team provides the following services: crisis counseling, advocacy, transportation to and from medical centers and shelters, and referrals to social service agencies. The majority of clients, over the years, have been battered women.

The crisis intervention team staff are civilian employees, trained volunteers from the community, or clinical social workers (e.g., New York City collaborative programs between Victim Services and the New York Police Department; Austin, Dallas, and Houston Police Departments; Plainfield, New Jersey, Police Department). A crisis team (always consisting of two individuals) is notified of a crisis situation via the police radio, and the crisis counselors usually meet the police at the crime scene. The police, after determining that the counselors will not be in danger, may leave the home. The clinicians utilize a basic crisis intervention model of assessing the situation, discussing the options, forming a plan of action, and aiding the victim in implementing the plan. The New York and Texas programs have between

3 and 18 full-time staff members and two to four graduate student interns each semester, as well as trained volunteer workers.

By 1998, similar programs had been developed under the auspices of the police departments in many cities, including South Phoenix, Arizona; Santa Ana, San Diego, and Stockton, California; Indianapolis, Indiana; Detroit, Michigan; Omaha, Nebraska; Las Vegas, Nevada; East Windsor, Plainsboro, South Brunswick, and South River, New Jersey; Rochester, New York; Memphis, Tennessee; and Salt Lake City, Utah. However, there are still many communities that have not initiated this type of program. It is hoped that the success of these 24-hour crisis intervention programs will encourage other localities to establish a similar type of service.

In 2004, Dr. Jacquelyn Campbell of the Johns Hopkins University School of Nursing developed the Lethality Assessment Program (LAP), currently a program for first responders. The goal of the LAP is to prevent domestic violence homicides, serious injury, and re-assault by encouraging more victims to utilize the support and shelter services of domestic violence programs. The LAP is a two-pronged intervention process using a research-based lethality screening tool and protocol for referral that provides direction for officers to initiate appropriate action based on the results of the screening process. Officers arriving at the scene of a domestic violence call assess the situation; if the standards that indicate danger are met, the officer will ask the victim to answer a series of 11 questions from the lethality screening tool.

If the victim's response to the questions indicates risk for homicide, the officer initiates a protocol referral by privately telling the victim he or she is in danger and that in situations similar to the victim's, people have been killed. The officer makes a phone call to a domestic violence hotline and proceeds with one of two responses to address the immediate safety.

Response 1: The victim chooses not to speak with the hotline counselor. The officer reviews the factors that are predictive of death to inform and protect the victim so he or she can be on the lookout for known risk factors, encourages the victim to contact the domestic violence program, provides the victim with referral information, and may follow other protocol measures designed to address the victim's safety and well-being.

Response 2: The victim chooses to speak with the hotline counselor. The officer responds to the outcome of the telephone conversation between the victim and the counselor. The officer or law enforcement agency may participate in coordinated safety planning with the victim and the counselor. After having spoken to a hotline counselor at a local domestic violence services program, the victim may or may not seek further assistance.

To the best of our knowledge, the LAP is the first lethality assessment program in the nation that makes use of a research-based screening tool and accompanying referral protocol, which takes a sophisticated approach to risk assessment for lethality in domestic violence situations (Dixon, 2008).

## VOCATIONAL TRAINING FOR BATTERED WOMEN

Thousands of battered women in large urban areas have been trapped in an intergenerational cycle of poverty, violence, and a dearth of marketable job skills. As part of President Bill Clinton's welfare-to-work initiative, battered women's programs in some cities have developed job training programs specifically for women who were previously abused by their partner. For example, Victim Services in New York City initiated two innovative employment skills training programs. Victim Services' first welfare-to-work training program, Project RISE, began in New York City in late 1997 to help victims of domestic violence who have been recipients of welfare enter the workforce with good-paying jobs. Project RISE provides 6-month training programs to teach formerly battered women word-processing computer skills (specifically, Microsoft Word and Excel). The second innovative program, Project Superwomen, assists domestic violence survivors to obtain nontraditional employment in blue-collar positions (which traditionally were held solely by men) that offer a stable income and benefits but do not require advanced training. The women receive 3 months of training to prepare them to work in building maintenance positions, which have the advantage of flexible hours and, often, rent-free housing. The women learn such skills as replacing broken locks; handling light plumbing repairs; and spackling, sanding, and painting apartment walls.

## ASSESSMENT AND INTERVENTION IN THE EMERGENCY ROOM

A visit to the emergency room may provide the initial opportunity for some victims to recognize the life-threatening nature of the violent relationship and to begin making important plans to change their situations. At a growing number of large hospitals in urban areas, crisis assessment and intervention are being provided to battered women by emergency room staff.

A recommended way for emergency rooms to handle detection and assessment of batterment is through an adult abuse protocol. Two of the pioneers in the development of these protocols are Karil Klingbeil and Vicky Boyd of Seattle, who in 1976 initiated plans for emergency room intervention with abused women. The social work department of the Harborview Medical Center in Seattle developed an adult abuse protocol that provides specific information on the assessment to be made by the involved staff—the triage nurse, the physician, and the crisis clinician. Using a protocol serves two purposes: First, it alerts the involved hospital staff to provide the appropriate clinical care; second, it documents the violent incident so that if the woman decides to file a legal complaint, "reliable, court-admissible evidence" (including photographs) is available (Klingbeil & Boyd, 1984).

Although this protocol was developed for use by emergency room crisis clinicians, it can easily be adapted for use by other health care personnel. The following case example describes how the adult abuse protocol has been successfully used.

---

### Case Example

Mrs. J was admitted to the emergency room accompanied by her sister. This was the second visit within the month for Mrs. J and the emergency room triage nurse and social worker realized that her physical injuries were much more severe on this second visit. Mrs. J was crying, appeared frightened, and in spite of the pain, she constantly glanced over her shoulder. She indicated that her husband would follow her to the emergency room and that she feared for her life. The social worker immediately notified Security.

Mrs. J indicated that she just wanted to rest briefly and then leave through another entrance. She was four months pregnant and concerned about her unborn child. She reported that this had been the first time Mr. J had struck her in the abdomen. The social worker spent considerable time calming Mrs. J in order to obtain a history of the assaultive event. Consent for photography was obtained and Mrs. J indicated that she *would* press charges. "The attack on my child" seemed to be a turning point in her perception of the gravity of her situation, even though Mr. J had beaten her at least a dozen times over the previous two years.

While the social worker assisted in the history taking, a physician provided emergency medical care: several sutures over the right eye.

With Mrs. J's permission, an interview was conducted with her sister who agreed to let Mrs. J stay with her and also agreed to participate in the police reporting. When Mrs. J felt able, the social worker and sister helped her complete necessary forms for the police who had been called to the emergency room.

Although the physician had carefully explained the procedures and rationale to Mrs. J, the social worker repeated this information and also informed her of the lethality of the battering, tracing from her chart her last three emergency room visits. Mrs. J was quick to minimize the assaults but when the social worker showed her photographs from those visits, documenting bruises around her face and neck, she shook her head and said, "No more, not any more." Her sister provided excellent support and additional family members were on their way to the emergency room to be with Mrs. J. When the police arrived Mrs. J was able to give an accurate report of the day's events. . . . She realized there would be difficult decisions to make and readily accepted a follow-up counseling appointment for a Battered Women's group. (Klingbeil & Boyd, 1984, pp. 16–24)

---

It should be noted that not all cases are handled as easily as this one. The two aspects of Mrs. J's situation that led to a positive resolution were (a) the immediate involvement of emergency room staff and their discussion with the patient of her history and injuries, and (b) the availability of supportive relatives.

Before the woman leaves the emergency room, the crisis clinician should talk with her about whether to return home or to seek refuge with friends, with family, or at a shelter for abused women. The emergency room staff should be able to provide names and phone numbers of referral sources. It is helpful if the pertinent information is printed on a small business card (which is easy to tuck away in a pocket or purse) and given to all abuse victims, as well as to suspected victims (Klingbeil & Boyd, 1984). Even if a woman refuses to acknowledge that her current bruises are the result of batterment, she may decide to keep the card for future use.

Merely having an adult abuse protocol does not ensure that it will be used. A study conducted by Flaherty (1985) at four Philadelphia hospitals found that the protocol was used selectively, mainly for victims who volunteered that they had been battered. The medical staff thus ignored the opportunity to help batterment victims who were not able to volunteer the information. The researchers cited the following reasons for underutilization of the protocol:

1. Some physicians and nurses did not regard battering as a medical problem.
2. Some of the emergency room staff believed that it would be an invasion of privacy to ask a woman questions about how she was injured.
3. Many viewed completing the protocol as an additional burden when they were already overworked.

Of those medical personnel who did recognize batterment as a legitimate problem, the most frequently used intervention technique was the tear-off list of referral sources, which was printed at the bottom of the protocol.

There is a crucial difference between Flaherty's (1985) Philadelphia study and the procedures described previously by Klingbeil and Boyd (1984) in Seattle. The Philadelphia study requested the cooperation of nurses and physicians but did not involve medical crisis clinicians. In contrast, the Harborview Medical Center protocol was created and implemented by the hospital's social work department. It emphasized a multidisciplinary team approach, with the social workers taking the lead role in conducting screening and assessment, often talking to the victim while the physician provided medical treatment. This trend has continued, according to Dr. Karin Rhodes and colleagues (2011) from the University of Pennsylvania. The researchers examined all emergency department visits and IPV-related police events over a 4-year period (1999–2002). The study took place within eight emergency departments, 12 police jurisdictions, and the prosecuting attorney's office in a semirural Midwestern county in the United States.

A total of 993 female victims of domestic violence generated 3,246 related police incidents over the 4-year period. Approximately 80% went to emergency departments after the date of the documented incident. Nearly 80% of them came with medical complaints, and 72% were never identified as victims of abuse, even though, on average, these women visited the emergency department seven times over the study period. Women who had filed a police complaint that day or been taken to the hospital by the police, those who self-disclosed domestic assault, and those who had mental health and substance abuse issues were more likely to be identified as victims of IPV.

When victims were identified, the emergency department response included legally useful documentation 86% of the time, police contact 50% of the time, and a social worker 45% of the time. Unfortunately, only 33% of the time did providers assess whether the victim had a safe place to go, and only 25% of identified victims were referred to domestic violence services.

The authors conclude: "Our work shows that the majority of police-identified intimate partner violence victims frequently use the emergency department for health care, but they are unlikely to be identified or receive any intervention in that setting. Current screening practices for intimate partner violence victims are ineffective and policy-driven interventions for identified victims are, at best, erratically implemented." (Rhodes, Kothari, Dichter, Cerulli, Wiley, & Marcus, 2011, pp. 97–98)

## INTERVENTION TECHNIQUES USED BY TELEPHONE HOTLINES AND BATTERED WOMEN'S SHELTERS

Battered women in crisis may reach out for help in any number of ways. The initial contact is generally by telephone, making the phone a lifeline for many women. Violence often occurs late in the evening, on weekends, or on holidays, and shelter staff are usually available 24 hours a day to respond to a crisis call. But a woman in crisis who has just been brutally beaten probably does not know the name or phone number of the local shelter. A frequent scenario is that of a woman and her children hastily escaping from home late in the evening and fleeing to a neighbor's home to make an emergency call for help. Not having the number of the local shelter, these women generally contact the police, a toll-free statewide domestic violence hotline, or the citywide or community-wide crisis hotline (which aids people in all types of crisis). If the woman contacts the community-wide hotline, there is generally a brief delay while the worker gathers some basic information and then gives the caller the phone number of the closest shelter. An alternative is for the crisis intervenor to take the caller's phone number and have the shelter worker call her back.

When a battered woman in crisis calls a hotline, it is essential that she be able to talk immediately to a trained crisis clinician—not be put on hold or confronted with an answering machine or voice mail. If she is not able to talk to a caring and knowledgeable crisis intervenor, she may just give up, and a valuable opportunity for intervening in the cycle of violence will have been lost. In these situations time is of the essence; if the violent male is still on the rampage, he is likely to search for her, thereby endangering not only his mate but the neighbor as well.

Hotline workers distinguish between a *crisis call*—one in which the woman is in imminent danger or has just been beaten—and other types of calls in which the individual is not in immediate danger but is anxious or distressed and is seeking information or someone to talk to. The overriding goal of crisis intervention is ensuring the safety of the woman and her children. To determine whether the call is a crisis call, the worker asks questions such as the following:

- Are you or your children in danger now?
- Is the abuser there now?
- Do you want me to call the police?
- Do you want to leave, and can you do so safely?
- Do you need medical attention?

Programs have different policies regarding transporting women who need refuge but have no way to get there. Although some shelters will send staff to pick up the woman at her home, it is more common for shelter policy to prohibit staff from doing so because of the possibility of the staff member being attacked by the abuser. In cities that have a crisis intervention team affiliated with the police department (e.g., New York City, or Plainsboro and East Windsor, New Jersey), the shelter staff can contact the police, who investigate the situation and radio for the victim advocate or crisis counselor to transport the victim and her children to the shelter. Many times the police themselves are prevailed upon to provide the transportation. Another alternative is for the victim advocate from the shelter to meet the battered woman at the local hospital emergency room.

Once the urgent issues pertaining to the woman's physical safety have been resolved, the crisis intervenor can begin to help the victim talk about her situation and discuss possible courses of action. Throughout this process it is important for the crisis intervenor to remember that he or she can present different alternatives, but the client must make her own final decisions in order to be empowered.

The following is a step-by-step guide to intervention with battered women (originally developed by Jones, 1968), which is included in the training manual prepared by the Abuse Counseling and Treatment (ACT) program in Fort Myers, Florida. It is referred to as the A-B-C process of crisis management—the "A" referring to "achieving contact," the "B" to "boiling down the problem," and the "C" to "coping with the problem."

A. *Achieving contact*
1. Introduce yourself: name, role, and purpose.
2. If a phone call, ask the client if she is safe and protected now.
3. Ask the client how she would like to be addressed: first name, surname, or nickname; this helps the client regain control.
4. Collect client data; this breaks the ice and allows the client and clinician to get to know each other and develop trust.
5. Ask the client if she has a clinician or if she is taking any medication.
6. Identify the client's feelings and ask for a perception check.

B. *Boiling down the problem*
1. Ask the client to describe briefly what has just happened.
2. Encourage the client to talk about the here and now.
3. Ask the client what is the most pressing problem.
4. Ask the client if it were not for said problem, would she feel better right now?
5. Ask the client if she has been confronted with a similar type of problem before, and if so, how she handled it then. What worked and what didn't?
6. Review with the client what you heard as the primary problem.

C. *Coping with the problem*
1. What does the client want to happen?
2. What is the most important need—the bottom line?
3. Explore what the client feels is the best solution.
4. Find out what the client is willing to do to meet her needs.
5. Help the client formulate a plan of action: resources, activities, time.
6. Arrange follow-up contact with the client.

Careful recruitment and thorough training of crisis intervention staff are essential to a program's success. It is also necessary for an experienced clinician to be on call at all times for consultation in difficult cases. In addition to knowing what to say, clinicians need to learn about the tone of voice and attitude to be used while handling crisis calls. Crisis clinicians are advised to speak in a steady, calm voice, to ask open-ended questions, and to refrain from being judgmental.

A shelter's policies and procedures manual should include guidelines for crisis staff. For example, the ACT program in Fort Myers, Florida, has developed a 45-page training manual, which includes sections on shelter policies and procedures, referral procedures, and background information on domestic violence that discusses both the victims and the abusers. The ACT manual explains the wide variation in the emotional reactions of the women who call for help. The client's speaking style may be "fast, slow, hesitant, loud, barely audible, rambling, loss of words, [or] normal." Her emotional reaction may be "angry, highly upset, hysterical, withdrawn, laughing, calm, icy, guilty, or a combination of these" (Houston, 1987, p. 5). No matter what characteristics the caller exhibits, the crisis clinician's task is to try to help the victim cope with the immediate situation. However, the guidelines also advise crisis clinicians to avoid the pitfall of believing they need to provide the caller with immediate, expert solutions to her problems. Crisis clinicians should not subject themselves to guilt feelings if they cannot help an abused woman resolve her situation. If the clinician suspects child abuse or neglect, he or she is required to notify the supervisor and then report the suspected abuse to the appropriate agency (Houston, 1987).

Shelter staff are confronted with a dilemma when the caller is an abused woman who is under the influence of drugs or alcohol or who has psychiatric symptoms. Although such women are victims of batterment, they also have a significant problem that the staff are not trained to treat. Shelter policy generally requires crisis intervenors to screen out battered women who are under the influence of alcohol or drugs, but there are exceptions. At Womanspace (in central New Jersey), women with drug or alcohol problems are accepted provided they are simultaneously enrolled in a drug or alcohol treatment program. Likewise, it is the crisis clinician's responsibility to determine whether a woman's behavior is excessively irrational or bizarre or whether she is likely to be a danger to herself or others. If a woman is suspected of having psychiatric problems, she is generally referred to the psychiatric screening unit of a local hospital or to a mental health center for an evaluation.

## ART THERAPY

Art therapy has been used effectively with women as well as children who have been subjected to domestic violence. As part of a comprehensive treatment approach in shelters for battered women and their children, art therapy can help victims (including young children) communicate their painful experiences in a nonverbal manner that is less threatening than traditional talk therapy. The goal of art therapy is to deal with the violence that took place while also empowering the mother and enhancing her parenting skills. It is helpful in initiating the healing process for the mother and her children to have the opportunity to communicate what has occurred through their drawings (Riley, 1994).

Art therapy is also helpful when working with young children who have limited verbal ability. The following illustration shows how art therapy was used in a family session with a battered 23-year-old mother and her 4-year-old son:

Although this child was not able to draw complete figures and fully describe the reason that brought him to the shelter, he was able to tell a story about the images he created. He said that the figure on the upper right was sneaking up on the smaller round circle directly to the left of it, which he identified as a "rock star." He said that the first figure bit the rock star in the leg. This very young boy was able to articulate the same story theme that his mother expressed in more detail. His mother explained through her picture that the four-year-old had bitten the abuser's leg when the abuser last attacked the mother. (McGloughlin, 1999, p. 53)

## INDIVIDUALIZED TREATMENT FOR CHILDREN

Battered women who seek temporary shelter to escape from the violence at home generally have children who come to the shelter with them. The children often feel confused, afraid, and angry. They miss their father and do not know if or when they will see him again. It is not uncommon for children to be misinformed or uninformed about the reason they were suddenly uprooted from their home, leaving their personal possessions, friends, and school to stay at a crowded shelter. Similarly, the children may not realize that all of the other children have come to the shelter for the same reason.

Moreover, according to Prelipp (personal communication, February 13, 1987) large numbers of these children have at one time or another also been victims of physical abuse. The 1986 annual report from the Family Violence Center in Green Bay, Wisconsin, provided data on child abuse committed by the batterer. The center found that close to half (73) of the 148 abusers of the women had on one or more occasions also beaten their children).

The following is a true story written by Lisa, a 10-year-old girl who came to a shelter after her father's violent attack on her mother.

---

### My Life, by Lisa

One day around two months ago my mom and dad got into a fight. First, my mom and I come home from the mall. We had a really nice time there. But, when we came home our nice time got to be terrible. I knew they were going to get into a fight so I went into my bedroom and did my homework. I knew he was going to talk to her about something, but I didn't know what. Then I heard my mom start screaming and I went to the door and asked what was wrong. My dad said, "Oh, nothing is wrong. Go do your homework." But I knew something was wrong so I went and prayed to God. My dad was really mean that night. I hated him so bad. My mom did not deserve to get hurt. I love her more than anything else in the entire world. Then I heard my mom scream something but I didn't understand what she said because my dad covered her mouth with his hand. Afterward she told me she said call the cops. Anyway, I went back to the door by the bedroom and told my mom I needed help on my homework, but I didn't. I just wanted my mom to come out of the bedroom because I was afraid. Then they both came out. And I hugged my mom and went to bed. Then my dad started to strangle my mom. So I went out and told my dad to stop. He told me to go back to the bedroom and go to sleep. So, I did. But I was so stupid. Then I heard my mom screaming. So I went back into the living room and he was kicking my mom. He wouldn't stop, he kept kicking her in her arm and legs. I told him to stop. He told me to go back to bed but I said, No! Then he took his guitar and was gonna hit her over the head. But I went on top of my mother. He told me to get off. But I said, No. So he put down the guitar, then he got her ice for her arm. Then I went to sleep crying. The next morning I didn't go to school and she didn't go to work. Then he called up the house and talked to her for a while. He threatened to kill her. So we left to go to the shelter. And here I am *now.* (Arbour, 1986)

---

This girl was fortunate in that her mother brought her to the Jersey Battered Women's Service in northern New Jersey, which has a carefully developed counseling program for battered mothers and their children. Sadly, however, there are still a number of shelters that offer only basic child care services; they do not provide the art therapy and crisis counseling needed to help children deal with the turmoil of recent events (Alessi & Hearn, 1998).

Nevertheless, innovative techniques for helping children have been incorporated into the programs of the more progressive shelters. St. Martha's Hall, a shelter in St. Louis, Missouri, provides counseling for the children, and also requires mothers to participate in parenting classes and to meet with the coordinator of the children's program about establishing family goals and meeting the child's individual needs. The program also provides opportunities for the mother and child to participate jointly in relaxing recreational activities (Schiller-Ramirez, 1995).

Two other types of intervention—coloring books and groups for children—are used at some shelters.

## Coloring Books as Part of an Individualized Treatment Approach

Some shelters utilize specially designed coloring books that discuss domestic violence in terms children can understand. Laura Prato of the Jersey Battered Women's Service in Morristown, New Jersey, has created two coloring books (Prato, n.d.), one for children aged 3 to 5 entitled *What Is a Shelter?* and another for 6- to 11-year-olds called *Let's Talk It Over.* In addition to the children's books, Prato has written two manuals for shelter workers that serve as a discussion guide for counselors. The books contain realistic, sensitive illustrations that depict the confused, sad, and angry emotions the children are feeling. They are illustrated in black and white so that the children can color the pictures if they wish. Funding for preparation and printing of the books and manuals came from the New Jersey Division of Youth and Family Services. The purpose of the coloring books and the way in which they are to be used are explained in the introduction to the counselors' manuals. The manuals state that the books are used as part of the intake and orientation process for all children who stay at the shelter. The stated objectives of the books are as follows:

- To provide assurances of the child's continued care and safety
- To encourage children to identify and express their feelings
- To provide information needed for children to understand what is happening in their families
- To provide information that will improve each child's ability to adapt to the shelter setting
- To begin to assess the individual child's needs and concerns

The clinicians' manuals stress the importance of how the book is presented to the child, as shown in the following passage:

> The process surrounding the use of the orientation books is extremely important. It is likely to be the initial contact between the counselor and the newly arrived family and one that will set the tone for future interactions. Consistent with the JBWS Children's Program philosophy, this initial meeting communicates respect for mother and child and acceptance of their feelings. (Prato, n.d.)

Before meeting with the child, the clinician meets privately with the mother to show her the book, explain its purpose, and ask for her permission to read the book to her child. The clinicians are advised to read any available intake information prior to meeting with the child so that they are better able to "anticipate the individual child's special concerns and place the child's responses in a meaningful context" (Prato, n.d.). The books have been prepared in a way that encourages the child's active participation. Throughout both books there are several places where the child can write his or her thoughts on the page. For example, one of the pages in *Let's Talk It Over* focuses on a child staying at a shelter who misses her father. The caption under the picture states:

> Many children at the shelter think a lot about their fathers, and that's okay. You may not see your father for a while until everyone in your family has a chance to think about things carefully. The little girl in the picture is wondering about her father.... What questions do you think she is asking?

There is a place on that page for the child's response to the question. The response could be written by the child or dictated to the counselor, who would write it in the book. On the next page is a large blank space and a caption that reads, "You may use this page to draw a picture of your father." Books such as those developed by the Jersey Battered Women's Service are very appropriate in helping children cope with the crisis that has led to their staying at the shelter.

## REFERRAL

Knowledge of referral sources is essential when intervening on behalf of abused women in crisis situations. It is just as important for the police, hospitals, and human service agencies to know about and refer to programs helping battered women and their children as it is for staff at domestic violence treatment programs to refer clients to appropriate community resources.

It is frequently determined that the battered woman needs a variety of services, such as job training and placement, low-cost transitional housing, day care, and ongoing counseling; therefore, referral should be made to the appropriate service providers. In its 1995 year-end report, St. Martha's Hall in St. Louis itemized the agencies to which its clients had been referred (Schiller-Ramirez, 1995). Most women were referred to three or more agencies, and several clients were given nine or more referrals, depending on their individual needs. The most frequently used referral sources were as follows:

Legal aid
Medical care
Job bank
Day care programs
Women in Need (WIN), long-term housing for single women
Alcoholics Anonymous
Women's Self-Help Center, providing counseling and support groups
St. Pat's, a Catholic social service agency that finds low-cost housing and
    provides classes in budgeting money and other life skills

Examples of other, less frequently used, referral sources were

| | |
|---|---|
| A shelter in another state | Dental care |
| Alateen | GED program |
| Al-Anon | Crisis nursery |
| Literacy Council | Victim Services |
| Big Brothers Big Sisters | Red Cross |

There are two ways in which programs providing crisis intervention services can facilitate the referral process: (a) by publicizing their services to the population at large and to other service providers, and (b) by becoming knowledgeable about community services needed by their clients and in some instances accompanying them to the appropriate agencies.

*Publicize the program through the following methods*:

1. Print brochures that describe the program's services, and have business cards that provide the program's name and phone number. These materials should be made available in large quantity to police officers, emergency room staff, and other potential sources of referral to the program.
2. Participate in interdisciplinary workshops and seminars on family violence so that the program can become widely known. In addition, this enables the staff to learn about appropriate programs to which their clients can be referred.
3. Attend in-service training programs for police officers, countywide hotline staff, emergency room staff, and others to discuss referral of abused women and to resolve any problems in the referral process that may have occurred.
4. Alert the public through newspaper articles and public service announcements on radio and television, with the program's phone number prominently mentioned.

*Become familiar with community resources.* Information for crisis clinicians on appropriate referral sources should be available in several ways:

1. The phone number of the most urgently needed agencies—such as the police, victim assistance program, drug or alcohol treatment programs, and psychiatric screening unit—should be readily available, preferably printed on each intake sheet or telephone log form.
2. The program's training manual should contain a section on the most frequently used referral sources. For example, the manual of the ACT program in Fort Myers, Florida, contains eight pages of often-used referral sources, which list the address, phone number, office hours, and services provided for each source.
3. Most major metropolitan areas have a comprehensive resource guide (published by the local United Way or an affiliate such as Call for Action) that provides a comprehensive listing of all of the community services in that area. All programs serving abused women and their children should have a copy of and be familiar with their community's resources handbook.

The way in which referrals are made is extremely important because it may affect the outcome. All too often, victims in crisis do not follow through in making the initial contact with the referral agency. Clinicians and advocates at St. Martha's Hall and other shelters provide support by accompanying the client to the agency in order to demonstrate how to obtain services. This is viewed as a positive alternative to the often intimidating and frustrating experience encountered by women who are given a referral but are expected to fend for themselves.

## SUMMARY AND CONCLUSION

A number of important issues and techniques related to crisis intervention with battered women and their children have been examined in this chapter. Specific methods for crisis intervention in different settings have also been discussed. As increased numbers of women in acute crisis seek help, crisis clinicians and victim advocates must be prepared to respond without delay. Crisis intervention for battered women and their children may do much to alleviate the emotional distress and anguish experienced by those exposed to the trauma of domestic violence. Because of their experience and specialized training, crisis clinicians and medical social workers can play a vital role in assisting women and children in crisis.

Law enforcement officers, victim advocates, hospital emergency room staff, and clinicians at citywide crisis lines and battered women's shelters often come in contact with abused women who are experiencing a crisis. Effective crisis intervention requires an understanding by these service providers of the value and methods of crisis intervention, as well as the community resources to which referrals should be made. Battered women are often motivated to change their lifestyle only during the crisis or postcrisis period. Therefore, it is important for service providers at community agencies to offer immediate assistance to battered women in crisis. With an estimated 8 million couples involved in battering episodes annually, policymakers and program developers should give priority to expanding urgently needed crisis-oriented and follow-up services for battered women and their children.

REFERENCES

Alessi, J. J., & Hearn, K. (1984). Group treatment of children in shelters for battered women. In A. R. Roberts (Ed.), *Battered women and their families* (pp. 49–61). New York: Springer.

Arbour, D. (1986, December). *Disabuse Newsletter.* Morristown, NJ: Jersey Battered Women's Service.

Austin City Connection. (2000). Austin Police Department: formal name? Family Violence Protection Team. Retrieved from www.ci.austin.tx.us/police/afvpt

Black, C. J. (2003). Translating principles into practice: Implementing the feminist and strengths perspectives in work with battered women. *Affilia, 18*, 332–349.

Black, M. C., Basile, K. C., Breiding, M. J., Smith, S. G., Walters, M. L., Merrick, M. T., ... Stevens, M. R. (2011). *The National Intimate Partner and Sexual Violence Survey (NISVS): 2010 summary report.* Atlanta, GA: Centers for Disease Control and Prevention, National Center for Injury Prevention and Control.

Caplan, G. (1964). *Principles of preventive psychiatry.* New York: Basic Books.

Carlson, B. E. (1997). A stress and coping approach to intervention with abused women. *Family Relations, 46*, 291–298.

Dixon, T. (2008, January 11). New move against domestic abuse: Police trained to give assessments, refer counselors. *Baltimore Sun*, final edition, B01.

Duterte, E. E., Bonomi, A. E., Kernic, M. A., Schiff, M. A., Thompson, R. S., & Rivara, F. P. (2008). Correlates of medical and legal help seeking among women reporting intimate partner violence. *Journal of Women's Health, 17*(1), 85–95.

Dutton, M. A., Kaltman, S., Goodman, L. A., Weinfurt, K., & Vankos, N. (2005). Patterns of intimate partner violence: Correlates and outcomes. *Violence and Victims, 20*, 483–497.

Eaton, D. K., Kann, L., Kinchen, S., Shanklin, S., Ross, J., Hawkins, J., ... Centers for Disease Control and Prevention (CDC). (2010, January 1). Youth risk behavior surveillance—United States, 2009. *Morbidity and Mortality Weekly Report Surveillance Summaries, 59*(5), 1–142.

Flaherty, E. W. (1985, February). *Identification and intervention with battered women in the hospital emergency department: Final report.* Philadelphia: Philadelphia Health Management Corp.

Folkman, S. (1984). Personal control, and stress and coping processes: A theoretical analysis. *Journal of Personality and Social Psychology, 46*, 839–852.

Folkman, S., & Lazarus, R. S. (1985). If it changes it must be a process: Study of emotion and coping during three stages of college examination. *Journal of Personality and Social Psychology, 48*, 150–170.

Frazier, P. A., & Burnett, J. W. (1994). Immediate coping strategies among rape victims. *Journal of Counseling and Development, 72*, 633–639.

Frieze, I., & Bookwala, J. (1996). Coping with unusual stressors: Criminal victimization. In M. Zeidner & N. S. Endler (Eds.), *Handbook of coping: Theory, research and applications* (pp. 303–321). New York: Wiley.

Gleason, W. J. (1993). Mental disorders in battered women: An empirical study. *Violence and Victims, 8*, 53–68.

Goodyear-Smith, F. Arroll, B., & Coupe, N. (2009). Asking for help is helpful: Validation of a brief lifestyle and mood assessment tool in primary health care. *Annals of Family Medicine, 7*, 239–244.

Gordon, J. (1996). Community services available to abused women in crisis: A review of perceived usefulness and efficacy. *Journal of Family Violence, 11*, 315–329.

Haag, R. (n.d.). The birthday letter. In S. A. Prelipp (Ed.), *Family Violence Center, Inc. training manual.* Green Bay, WI: mimeographed.

Herman, J. L. (1992). *Trauma and recovery.* New York: Basic Books.

Houston, S. (1987). *Abuse Counseling and Treatment, Inc. (ACT) Manual.* Fort Myers, FL: ACT.

Janosik, E. H. (1984). *Crisis counseling.* Belmont, CA: Wadsworth.

Johnson, D. M., & Zlotnick, C. (2006). A cognitive-behavioral treatment for battered women with PTSD in shelters: Findings from a pilot study. *Journal of Traumatic Stress, 19, 559–564.*

Johnson, D. M., Zlotnick, C., & Perez, S. (2011). Cognitive behavioral treatment of PTSD in residents of battered women's shelters: Results of a randomized clinical trial. *Journal of Consulting and Clinical Psychology, 79, 542–551.*

Johnson, K. (1997). Professional help and crime victims. *Social Service Review, 71, 89–109.*

Jones, W. A. (1968). The A-B-C method of crisis management. *Mental Hygiene, 52, 87–89.*

Klingbeil, K. S., & Boyd, V. D. (1984). Emergency room intervention: Detection, assessment and treatment. In A. R. Roberts (Ed.), *Battered women and their families: Intervention strategies and treatment programs* (pp. 7–32). New York: Springer.

Krebs, C. P., Lindquist, C. H., Warner, T. D., Fisher, B. S., & Martin, S. L. (2007). *The campus sexual assault (CSA) study.* U.S. Department of Justice. National Institute of Justice, Washington, DC.

Krumholz, S. T. (2001, June). *Domestic violence units: Effective management or political expedience?* Paper presented at the annual meeting of the Academy of Criminal Justice Sciences, Washington, DC.

Kubany, E. S., Hill, E. E., & Owens, J. A. (2003). Cognitive Trauma Therapy for Battered Women with PTSD: Preliminary findings. *Journal of Traumatic Stress, 16* (1), 81–91.

Kubany, E. S., Hill, E. E., Owens, J. A., Iannce-Spencer, C., McCaig, M. A., Tremayne, K. J., & Williams, P. L. (January 01, 2004). Cognitive trauma therapy for battered women with PTSD (CTT-BW). *Journal of Consulting and Clinical Psychology,* 72(1), 3–18.

Lazarus, R. S., & Folkman, S. (1984). *Stress, appraisal and coping.* New York: Springer.

Liang, B., Goodman, L., Tummala-Narra, P., & Weintraub, S. (2005). A theoretical framework for understanding help-seeking processes among survivors of intimate partner violence. *American Journal of Community Psychology,* 36(1–2), 71–84.

Littel, K., Malefyt, M. B., Walker, A., Tucker, D. D., & Buel, S. M. (1998). *Assessing justice system response to violence against women: A tool for law enforcement, prosecution and the courts to use in developing effective responses.* Violence Against Women Online Resources, Department of Justice, Office of Justice Programs. Retrieved from www.vaw.umn.edu

Lutenbacher, M., Cohen, A., & Mitzel, J. (2003). Do we really help? Perspectives of abused women. *Public Health Nursing,* 20(1), 56–64.

McGloughlin, M. (1999). *Art therapy with battered women and their children.* M.A. thesis, Eastern Virginia Medical School, Norfolk, Virginia.

National Network to End Domestic Violence. (2014). Web page Retrieved from http://nnedv.org/resources/safetynetdocs.html

Nurius, P., Hilfrink, M., & Rafino, R. (1996). The single greatest health threat to women: Their partners. In P. Raffoul & C. A. McNeece (Eds.), *Future issues in social work practice* (pp. 159–171). Boston: Allyn and Bacon.

Peak, K. (1998). *Justice administration*. Englewood Cliffs, NJ: Prentice-Hall.

Petretic-Jackson, P., & Jackson, T. (1996). Mental health interventions with battered women. In A. R. Roberts (Ed.), *Helping battered women: New perspectives and remedies* (pp. 188–221). New York: Oxford University Press.

Prato, L, (Undated). *What is a shelter? Lets talk it over; What is a shelter? A shelter worker's manual; Let's talk it over: A shelter workers manual.* Morristown, NJ: Jersey Battered Women's Service.

Rhodes, K. V., Kothari, C. L., Dichter, M., Cerulli, C., Wiley, J., & Marcus, S. (January 01, 2011). Intimate partner violence identification and response: time for a change in strategy. *Journal of General Internal Medicine, 26*(8), 894–899.

Riley, S. (1994). *Integrative approaches to family art therapy.* Chicago: Magnolia Street Publishers.

Roberts, A. R. (1981). *Sheltering battered women: A national study and service guide.* New York: Springer.

Roberts, A. R. (1990). *Helping crime victims.* Newbury Park, CA: Sage.

Roberts, A. R. (1996a). A comparative analysis of incarcerated battered women and a community sample of battered women. In A. R. Roberts (Ed.), *Helping battered women: New perspectives and remedies* (pp. 31–43). New York: Oxford University Press.

Roberts, A. R. (1996b). Epidemiology and definitions of acute crisis in American society. In A. R. Roberts (Ed.). *Crisis management and brief treatment: Theory, technique and applications* (pp. 16–33). Chicago: Nelson-Hall.

Roberts, A. R. (1998). *Battered women and their families* (2nd ed.). New York: Springer.

Roberts, A. R. (2002). Myths, facts, and realities regarding battered women and their children: An overview. In A. R. Roberts (Ed.), *Handbook of domestic violence intervention strategies: Policies, programs, and legal remedies* (pp. 3–22). New York: Oxford University Press.

Roberts, A. R., & Burman, S. (1998). Crisis intervention and cognitive problem-solving therapy with battered women: A national survey and practice model. In A. R. Roberts (Ed.), *Battered women and their families: Intervention strategies and treatment programs* (2nd ed., pp. 3–28). New York: Springer.

Roberts, A. R., & Roberts, B. S. (2005). *Ending intimate abuse: Practical guidelines and survival strategies.* New York: Oxford University Press.

Rothman, E. F., Exner, D., Baughman, A. L. (2011). The prevalence of sexual assault against people who identify as gay, lesbian, or bisexual in the United States: a systematic review. *Trauma, Violence, & Abuse,*12(2), 55.

Saleebey, D. (1997). *The strengths perspective in social work practice* (2nd ed.). White Plains, NY: Longman.

Schiller-Ramirez, M. (1995). *St. Martha's Hall year end report 1994.* St. Louis, MO: St. Martha's Hall.

Snyder, H. (2000). Sexual assault of young children as reported to law enforcement: Victim, incident, and offender characteristics. National Center for Juvenile Justice, NCJ 182990.

Straus, H., Cerulli, C., McNutt, L. A., Rhodes, K. V., Conner, K. R., Kemball, R. S., & Houry, D. (2009). Intimate partner violence and functional health status: Associations with severity, danger, and self-advocacy behaviors. *Journal of Women's Health, 18,* 625–631.

Straus, M., & Gelles, R. (1991). *Physical violence in American families.* New Brunswick, NJ: Transaction Books.

Taft, C. T., Resick, P. A., Panuzio, J., Vogt, D. S., & Mechanic, M. B. (2007). Examining the correlates of engagement and disengagement coping among help-seeking battered women. *Violence and Victims, 22,* 3–17.

Tedeschi, R. G., & Calhoun, L. G. (1995). *Trauma and transformation growing in the aftermath of suffering.* Thousand Oaks, CA: Sage.

Thurman v. City of Torrington, 595 F. Supp. 1521 (D. Conn. 1985).

Tjaden, P., & Thoennes, N. (1998). Battering in America: Findings from the National Violence Against Women Survey. *Research in Brief* (pp. 60–66). Washington, DC: National Institute of Justice, US Department of Justice.

Tjaden, P. N. T. (2000). Prevalence and consequences of male-to-female and female-to-male intimate partner violence as measured by the National Violence Against Women Survey. Sage Family Studies Abstracts, 22, 2.

Tjaden, P. G., Thoennes, N., United States, & National Institute of Justice (US). (2006). *Extent, nature, and consequences of rape victimization: Findings from the National Violence Against Women Survey.* Washington, DC: US Department of Justice, Office of Justice Programs, National Institute of Justice.

Truman, J. L (2011, September). *National Crime Victimization Survey: Criminal victimization, 2010* (NCJ Report No. 235508). US Department of Justice, Office of Justice Programs Bureau of Justice Statistics, NCJ 235508.

Turman, J. L., Langton, L., & Planty, M. (2012). Criminal Victimization, 2012. US Department of Justice, Office of Justice Statistics. *Bulletin.* October 2013. NCJ 243389. http://www.bjs.gov/content/pub/pdf/cv12.pdf

Tutty, L., Bidgood, B., & Rothery, M. (1993). Support groups for battered women: Research on their efficacy. *Journal of Family Violence, 8,* 325–343.

US Bureau of Justice Statistics (2000). *Sexual assault of young children as reported to law enforcement 2000.* Retrieved from http://www.bjs.gov/index.cfm?ty=pbdetail&iid=1147

US Department of State. (2012, January 1). *The promise of freedom.* The 2012 Trafficking in Persons Report. Washington, DC: Author.

Valentine, P. V., Roberts, A. R., & Burgess, A. W. (1998). The stress-crisis continuum: Its application to domestic violence. In A. R. Roberts (Ed.), *Battered women and their families* (2nd ed., pp. 29–57). New York: Springer.

Verizon Wireless. (2014). HopeLine from Verizon. Retrieved from http://www.verizonwireless.com/aboutus/hopeline/index.html

Walker, L. E. (1985). Psychological impact of the criminalization of domestic violence on victims. *Victimology: An International Journal, 10*, 281–300.

Weil, A. (1995). *Spontaneous healing.* New York: Knopf.

Wireless Foundation. (2004). Donate a wireless phone, help protect domestic violence victims and save lives. Retrieved from www.wirelessfoundation.org

Woods, S. J., & Campbell, J. C. (1993). Posttraumatic stress in battered women: Does the diagnosis fit? *Issues in Mental Health Nursing, 14*, 173–186.

Wuest, J., Ford-Gilboe, M., Merritt-Gray, M., Wilk, P., Campbell, J. C., Lent, B., . . . Smye, V. (2010). Pathways of chronic pain in survivors of intimate partner violence. *Journal of Women's Health, 19*, 1665–1674.

Wyatt, G. E., Notgrass, C. M., & Newcomb, M. (1990). Internal and external mediators of women's rape experiences. *Psychology of Women Quarterly, 14*, 153–176.

Young, M. A. (1995). Crisis response teams in the aftermath of disasters. In A. R. Roberts (Ed.), *Crisis intervention and time-limited cognitive treatment* (pp. 151–187). Thousand Oaks, CA: Sage.

Zosky, D. (2011). A matter of life and death: The voices of domestic violence survivors. *Affilia, 26*, 201–212.

# 17

# *Crisis Intervention With Stalking Victims*

KAREN S. KNOX
ALBERT R. ROBERTS

## Case Scenario

For the past 6 months, Barbara, who is a 20-year-old university junior, has been harassed and cyberstalked by a former coworker. Although she knew he had a "crush" on her, she was very careful to maintain a professional working relationship and appropriate boundaries with him at work. When he asked her out for coffee, she made it clear that she was not interested in dating him and stated that their employer would not approve either.

Two months later, Barbara quit that job and was relieved to not be around this man anymore, since he always seemed to be staring at her or trying to be near her at work. Barbara was not aware that he had already started cyberstalking her through her social networking and e-mail accounts. He was able to get her online passwords to her school and personal e-mail accounts, and she also found out that he was accessing several university organization websites and blogs in order to find out more about her and her friends. She notified her friends about his actions, changed her passwords, and called him to ask him to stop harassing her. She hoped that this would make him stop, but the opposite happened, and he started sending her threatening e-mails, posting hateful comments, and spreading rumors about her to classmates and several campus organizations.

In the past 2 weeks, she has been worried that the former coworker is now following her. Barbara is not sure what to do at this point because she does not have any proof that he is stalking her, and she is reluctant to contact the campus police in fear that he will continue to escalate. Barbara is having problems sleeping and focusing on her studies. Her grades have dropped, and she has been cutting classes. She has begun to limit her activities and stay home a lot because she is afraid he may hurt her. Barbara is considering dropping out of school or moving to get away from him, but she feels so overwhelmed that she avoids talking to her parents or friends about her fears.

Last night, he sent an e-mail threatening to rape her. It scared her so much that she called a friend, who advised Barbara to go to the university counseling center and offered to pick her up and go with her.

---

Over the past two decades, antistalking legislation and research on stalking have increased awareness about the prevalence and impacts of these crimes for victims. Legal and clinical responses to stalking victims and perpetrators emerged with the first stalking law that was passed in 1990 in California, and all of the states, the federal government, the District of Columbia, and US Territories have passed laws making stalking a criminal act. However, legal definitions and punishment for stalking crimes vary across jurisdictions. Many states base their laws on the guidelines set forth by the Model Antistalking Code, which requires repeated, purposeful conduct that would cause fear of bodily injury or death to self or an immediate family member (Cass, 2011). The element of fear ranges from the victim having emotional distress or being frightened to fear of bodily harm or death, and the victim's emotional reactions can have an impact on reporting, investigating, and prosecuting stalking offenders (Baum, Catalano, Rand, & Rose, 2009). Several countries, including Australia, New Zealand, England, and Wales, do not require the element of victim fear for stalking crimes, and many other countries have antistalking laws, including the Netherlands, Italy, Germany, Japan, Canada, and Israel (Cass, 2011; McEwan, Mullen, & MacKenzie, 2007). However, there are other countries that still do not have criminal laws against stalking, such as France, Greece, Spain, Iran, and Pakistan, and although India and Taiwan have laws against cyberstalking, they do not have antistalking laws (Office on Violence Against Women, 2012).

As reported in two national studies conducted by the US Department of Justice (Baum et al., 2009) and the Centers for Disease Control and Prevention (Office on Violence Against Women, 2012), the prevalence of stalking during a 12-month period in the United States is estimated at 3.4 million people aged 18 or older, and 1 in 6 females and 1 in 19 males report being stalked at some point in their life. Reports indicate that females are three times more at risk for being stalked than men, and that young adults had the highest rates of stalking victimization, with more than half of female victims and one third of male victims being stalked before the age of 25 (Office on Violence Against Women, 2012). Three out of 4 stalking victims knew their offender in some way, and 66% of female victims and 41% of male victims are stalked by a current or former intimate partner (Office on Violence Against Women, 2012). More than 1 in 4 victims of stalking also report being victims of cyberstalking, and more than 40% of undergraduates report experiencing cyberstalking (Baum et al., 2009; Reyns, Henson, & Fisher, 2012).

These statistics point out the growing need for interventions at both the macro and micro levels for stalking victims. Stalking victims need effective responses from the criminal justice system and counseling professionals to ensure their safety and well-being—physically, psychologically, and emotionally. Crisis intervention with stalking victims and survivors is primarily found in the fields of victim services, sexual assault, and domestic violence because the majority of victims are women who have been acquainted with or had a relationship with their stalker. These fields of practice use crisis intervention and brief time-limited therapy to address the immediate needs of the stalking survivors. However, many survivors continue treatment with support groups or individual therapy.

This chapter provides an overview of the complex problem of stalking, its impacts on victims, and victims' treatment needs. Definitions of stalking and the major types of stalkers and stalking behaviors are discussed. Empirical studies and measurement tools that support best practices for working with stalking survivors are presented, and an overview of crisis intervention with stalking survivors is presented and applied to the case scenario as a model of treatment.

## OVERVIEW OF STALKING

### Definitions of Stalking

One concern about defining stalking is the requirement that the victim have a specific emotional reaction to the crime, which places some responsibility on the victim, rather than focusing on the offender's conduct in legal decisions about investigation and prosecution. Definitions of stalking require repetitive behaviors, not just a single act, which can also create problems in legal decisions. How many times are sufficient to establish a repeated pattern? This requirement places the burden on the victim or law enforcement to document and show proof of repeated stalking behaviors. The purpose of legal definitions is to identify and prosecute criminal behavior, and although they may vary across jurisdictions, legal definitions historically have included three elements:

1. There is a pattern of willful, malicious, and repeated behavioral intrusion on another person (the target) that is clearly unwanted and unwelcome.
2. There is an implicit or explicit threat that is evidenced in those behavioral intrusions.
3. As a result of those behavioral intrusions, the person who is threatened (the target) experiences reasonable fear. (Meloy, 1998; Tjaden & Thoennes, 1998)

Clinical definitions differ from legal ones in purpose and scope, and they tend to be more easily operationalized and measurable for clinical understanding and research purposes (Meloy, 1998). These definitions focus on specific types of behaviors and actions that are perceived as harassment by the victim, including unwanted pursuit, threats, surveillance, and intrusive actions. Clinical definitions may include actions or behaviors that are not considered criminal offenses but can still be intrusive and distressing. For example, sending gifts, asking the victim out on dates, and attempting to pursue or reconcile a relationship are not typically stalking until the repeated patterns and unwanted attention are established. An attempt to create a definition of stalking by analyzing perceptions of stalking-like behaviors among participants in one research study found two major clusters, one composed of classic stalking behaviors and the other composed of primarily threatening stalking behaviors (Cass, 2011; Sheridan, Davies, & Boon (2001):

*Classic Stalking Behaviors*
- Constantly watching/spying on/following the target
- Standing and staring at the target's home or workplace or loitering in the neighborhood
- Driving by the target's home or workplace and purposefully visiting places the target frequents
- Telephoning, mailing, sending unwanted gifts after expressly being told not to do so

*Threatening Stalking Behaviors*
- Taking and collecting photographs without the target's knowledge
- Making death threats and threatening suicide
- Causing criminal damage or vandalism to the target's home or workplace
- Refusing to accept that a prior relationship with the target is over
- Sending bizarre or sinister items to the target's home or workplace
- Confining the target against her or his will

## Gender and Diversity Factors

Clinical definitions also include assessment and diagnosis of any emotional or psychiatric symptoms caused as a result of the stalking, such as anxiety, depression, acute stress, or post-traumatic stress. Self-medication and substance abuse should be assessed, as these are common treatment issues for these mental health diagnoses. There is a lack of research on cultural and ethnicity factors in this field of practice, and the majority of research sample participants are White. One study references a link between unrequited love and jealousy in Chinese, Maori, and Japanese cultural folklore and novels (Davis, Swan, & Gambone, 2012). Kulkarni, Racine, and Ramos (2012) examine Latinas' perception of domestic violence, and their findings indicate that although more than 75% of their sample ($n$ = 93) perceived physical aggression by males as domestic violence, only 60% viewed stalking as domestic violence. Latinas who have not been abused in their sample identify stalking as domestic violence more than those who have been abused (Kulkarni et al., 2012).

Clinical assessment of the survivor's perceptions of the stalking behaviors is necessary because factors such as gender and prior relationship with the offender may influence those perceptions. Several studies report that males and females do not define and understand stalking behavior in the same way (Dennison & Thomson, 2002; Yanowitz, 2006). Another study reports that men exhibit more victim-blaming tendencies than women and that men endorse more stalking myths than women (Sinclair, 2010). However, a recent study reports no differences in the perceptions of male and female participants but also espouses that definitions varied considerably, with no collective definition of stalking (Cass, 2011). This study did find that a prior relationship influences perceptions, with cases involving strangers and acquaintances being significantly more identified as stalking than cases between ex-intimates, as some behaviors by the latter were seen as attempts at closure or reconciliation (Cass, 2011).

Research indicates that definitions of stalking affect reporting rates, with only 41% of female victimizations and 37% of male victimizations being reported to the police (Baum et al., 2009). The most common reasons for not reporting are that it was considered a private or personal matter or that it was a minor incident (Baum et al., 2009). This same study reports that only 54% of individuals who met the criteria for stalking labeled the incident as stalking, suggesting that unacknowledged victimization rates may be high (Baum et al., 2009). Another study reports that males are more likely to acknowledge stalking victimization when they have been physically attacked, experience cyberstalking, are spied on, or have stalkers show up at places the victim frequents (Englebrecht & Reyns, 2011). Females are more likely to acknowledge stalking if the stalker enters their home or car, if they lose time at work, if they are cyberstalked, or if the stalker shows up spontaneously to see them (Englebrecht & Reyns, 2011). It is apparent that defining stalking is a complex matter that has multiple factors and conditions to consider.

## Typologies of Stalkers

Typologies of stalkers generally include factors such as the type of relationship with the victim, types of behaviors, motivations, and prevalence of psychiatric disorders. The RECON typology (relationship and context-based; Mohandie, Meloy, McGowan, & Williams, 2006) focuses exclusively on the type of previous relationship and identifies two types of stalkers:

- Type I stalkers are those who have had a romantic relationship or who have been friends or acquaintances with the victim
- Type II stalkers are those who have not known, or only slightly know, their victims and celebrity stalkers.

The Multiaxial Classification of Stalkers (Dressing, Foerster, & Gass, 2010) includes motivations and mental disorders, and although the majority of stalkers do not suffer from a mental disorder, psychotic stalking can occur as a symptom of schizophrenia or erotomania:

| | |
|---|---|
| 1. Psychopathological | a. psychotic stalker |
| | b. progressive psychopathological development |
| | c. no relevant psychiatric disorder |
| 2. Relationship | a. victim is ex-partner |
| | b. victim is a prominent individual in public life |
| | c. acquaintance, professional contact, stranger |
| 3. Motivation | a. positive feelings (love, affection, reconciliation) |
| | b. negative feelings (revenge, anger, jealousy, power) |

Empirical evidence indicates that most stalkers are former intimate partners, with 48% of women being stalked by ex-boyfriends, 10.9% being stalked by current husbands, and 33.7% being stalked by former or separated husbands (Tjaden & Thoennes, 2002; Norris, Huss, & Palarea, 2011). The link between stalking and intimate partner violence is evident, with 66.7% of sample participants experiencing at least one stalking behavior using the Risk Assessment Inventory for Stalking (RAIS; Palarea, Scalora, & Langhinrichsen-Rohling, 1999). This 36-item self-report measure assesses a range of stalking behaviors, their severity, and their impact on the victim, and includes four subscales:

- Distant Contact: unwanted phone calls
- Proximate Contact: unwanted visits
- Threat Behaviors: threatening to kill or commit suicide
- Harm Behaviors: violence against pets or property

The strongest relationships are found between stalking-related behaviors and psychological and sexual aggression, suggesting the motivation to re-establish control of the relationship and the victim (Norris et al., 2011). Obsessive relational intrusion (ORI) is stalking that emerges from a desired or previous relationship with attempts to initiate or re-establish the relationship despite opposition and other attempts on the target's part to disengage from unwanted pursuit behaviors. Nguyen, Spitzberg, and Lee (2012) categorize unwanted pursuit behaviors into the following types:

- *Hyperintimacy* behaviors to be involved in a relationship with the target
- *Mediated contacts* and cyberstalking

- *Pursuit, proximity, and surveillance* to follow or check on the target
- *Invasion* strategies of a victim's property, space, or privacy
- *Proxy* tactics to engage or be involved with the target's social network or employment
- *Harassment and intimidation* to frighten, pressure, or control the target
- *Coercion and constraint* to control by isolating, restraining, or kidnapping
- *Aggression* or violence and physical harm or death

The Obsessive Relational Intrusion scale developed by Cupach and Spitzberg (2004) is a 28-item measure of these unwanted pursuit behaviors and was one of the instruments used in the study by Nguyen et al. (2012) that identified several important relationships between gender, coping, and social support. Females tend to see unwanted pursuit as more threatening than males, and male pursuers are seen as more threatening than female pursuers. As ORI pursuit behaviors escalate or increase, females tend to rate their social support as less adequate; however, social support is not a significant coping strategy for males. And, as ORI pursuit behaviors increase, victims tend to increase their coping strategies; if these fail to be effective, however, then stress and frustration also increase (Nguyen et al., 2012). Because stalking and unwanted ORI pursuit behaviors are excessive and repetitive and can escalate over time, victims may not have the resilience and coping skills to deal effectively without both legal and clinical intervention. Even with legal intervention, future unwanted pursuit behaviors are possible when the offender gets out of jail or is on probation or parole.

Studies show that almost half of convicted stalkers recidivate, and 80% did so within 1 year after conviction (Rosenfeld, 2004; Malasch, Keijser, & Debets, 2011). Additionally, stalking is not the only crime that stalkers are convicted of, with robbery, burglary, destruction of property, forgery, theft, and rape convictions also being reported (Malsch et al., 2011). Few studies have examined cultural or gender differences in stalkers, but one study of female stalkers indicates elevated rates of moderate violence, but no gender differences for severe violence (Thompson, Dennison, & Stewart, 2012). This study's findings suggest support for the sociocultural belief that female-perpetrated violence is less damaging and more justifiable than male-perpetrated violence, and indicate that victims may not report female-perpetrated moderate violence incidents to police, resulting in underreporting of incidents of stalking by females (Thompson et al., 2012).

A more recent and prevalent type of stalking involves the Internet and social networking sites. *Cyberstalking* refers to repeated threats or harassment through e-mails or other computer-based communications. Certain factors about e-mail and the Internet facilitate this type of stalking, such as anonymity, which allows the stalker to fantasize and be deceptive without the accompanying social anxiety of face-to-face interactions. Hazelwood and Koon-Magnin (2013) examine cyberstalking legislation in the United States and identify several themes present in the statutes, including intent, anonymity, alarm/fear/distress, prior contact with the criminal justice system, jurisdiction, and reference to minors. Goodno (2007) identifies five important differences between cyberstalking and traditional stalking behaviors:

1. A message sent online can be sent to anyone with Internet access, is present immediately, and cannot be taken back or deleted.
2. The stalker can be anywhere in the world.
3. The stalker can remain anonymous.
4. The stalker can impersonate another person.
5. The stalker can use a third party to contact or communicate with the victim.

A recent study indicates that prior attachment, jealousy, and violence issues in relationships are significant predictors of cyberstalking behaviors, and females admitted greater frequency of cyberstalking than males (Strawhun, Adams, & Huss, 2013). Two measurement instruments for assessing cyberstalking are the Electronic Use Pursuit Behavioral Index (EUPBI; Strawhun et al., 2013) and Cyber Pursuit (Spitzberg & Cupach, 1998). These instruments record the frequency and intensity of cyberstalking and whether participants have been either perpetrators or victims of cyberstalking. Some cyberstalking behaviors include flooding an e-mail account with unwanted or threatening messages, posting negative comments on a blog, spreading rumors through bulletin boards, tracing another person's Internet activity, continuing to "friend" someone on Facebook after an initial rejection, revealing someone's private information online, and intentionally harming someone's computer through a virus (Strawhun et al., 2013). Another study reports that a larger percentage of females (46.3%) were cyberstalked than males (32.1%), and 48% of non-White respondents versus 39.8% of White respondents experienced some form of electronic pursuit (Reyns et al., 2012).

## Theories of Stalking

The theoretical knowledge base on stalking focuses on four main theories that attempt to identify and explain how their concepts and hypotheses are evidenced in stalking. The first theory is *coercive control* (Dutton & Goodman, 2005; Davis et al., 2012), which involves surveillance, demands, threats of harm, delivery of threats/harm, continued control of the target's social environment, including isolating and restricting access to social supports and financial resources. The second theory is *self-regulation* (Davis et al., 2012;

DeWall, Baumeister, Stillman, & Gailliot, 2007; Kring & Sloan, 2010), which is associated with antisocial, addictive, and impulsive behaviors. The third theory is *relational goal pursuit theory* (Cupach & Spitzberg, 2004; Davis et al., 2012; Spitzberg, Cupach, Hannawa, & Crowley, 2008), which includes self-regulatory failure and cognitive distortions concerning the significance of the stalking behaviors and the reactions and impacts for targets (Davis et al., 2012). Cupach and Spitzberg (2004) espouse that individuals who are jealous, possessive, and desperate and have insecure attachment and intense attraction styles are more likely to engage in stalking behaviors and obsessive relational intrusions. The fourth theory is *attachment theory*, which predicts that anxiously attached individuals are more likely to exhibit jealousy, angry temperament, and a controlling style and are more likely to engage in psychological and physical abuse (Davis et al., 2012; DeSmet, Loeys, & Buysse, 2012; Dutton & Winstead, 2006; Dye & Davis, 2003; Follingstad, Bradley, & Helf, 2002; Wigman, Grahma-Kevan, & Archer, 2008). There are no longitudinal studies on attachment theory, prediction of stalking behaviors, or persistent pursuit, and Davis et al. (2012) recommend more longitudinal studies and research examining how attachment theory, coercive control theory, relational goal pursuit theory, and self-regulation theory are related.

## Impacts of Stalking Victimization

Victims of stalking over months or even years experience psychological terrorism, with pervasive fear, anger, and distress at not being able to control their privacy (Davis & Frieze, 2000). The National Violence Against Women Survey reports that 30% of the women and 20% of the men victims sought counseling, 68% felt their personal safety had gotten worse, 42% were very concerned for their personal safety, and 45% carried something to protect themselves (Tjaden & Thoennes, 1998). Stalking that is accompanied by assaults and verbal threats is strongly connected to serious emotional consequences for victims (Davis & Frieze, 2000). Although many stalkers are not physically violent, 81% of women stalked by an ex-husband were physically assaulted, and 31% were sexually assaulted (Tjaden & Thoennes, 1998). Both male and female stalking victims report significantly more problems with poor health, depression, illness, injury, and substance abuse (Davis, Coker, & Sanderson, 2002; Logan & Walker, 2010).

Stalking victims experience psychological trauma and post-traumatic stress disorder (PTSD) symptoms, including recurrent nightmares, problems with sleeping, intrusive thoughts, depression, anxiety, and feeling overwhelmed and vulnerable. Many stalking victims resort to the same strategies that battered women have used to escape the terror: moving or relocating, quitting jobs, changing their names and appearance, going underground and leaving friends and family behind, and becoming more isolated and less trusting. Many survivors still live in fear years after the stalking has ended, afraid that the stalker will reappear, will find them, or will be released from prison to return and continue stalking.

Social and economic costs for stalking survivors include changing or losing a job or school; relocation; restricting activities and staying home; losing social connections and support systems; changing routines; changing e-mail addresses, phone numbers, and social networking sites; vandalism; property loss; and medical, legal, and counseling expenses (Sheridan & Lyndon, 2012). Spitzberg and Cupach, 2002, 2007) group victim behavioral coping actions into five categories:

- Moving inward: denial, meditation, drugs
- Moving outward: contacting others for support or protection
- Moving toward or with: negotiating or reasoning with the stalker
- Moving against: threatening or harming the stalker
- Moving away: attempting to escape the stalker or relocation

Studies indicate that many stalking victims are not satisfied with responses from law enforcement and do not feel that the police took them seriously or that sufficient steps had been taken (Van der Aa & Groenen, 2011). Logan and Walker (2010) report that both criminal justice and victim service representatives overwhelmingly recommend reporting stalking to the police, and 44.8% of victims services representatives would advise the victim to document the stalking behaviors versus only 20.8% of criminal justice representatives. Another significant difference between criminal justice (40.3%) and victim services (73.3%) representatives is evident in advising victims to protect themselves and develop a safety plan (Logan & Walker, 2010).

Treatment involves interventions that are aimed at symptom reduction of the impact issues, as well as practical issues associated with personal safety and legal responses. Specific theoretical models used with stalking victims include crisis intervention, relaxation training, cognitive-behavioral therapy, solution-focused therapy, and eye movement desensitization and reprocessing. This chapter focuses on the use of crisis intervention with stalking survivors.

## OVERVIEW OF CRISIS INTERVENTION

### Theory and Principles

Crisis intervention is an action-oriented model that is present focused, with the target(s) for intervention being specific to the hazardous event, situation, or problem that precipitated the state of crisis. Therefore, this model focuses on problems in the here and now and addresses past history and psychopathology only as they are relevant to the current conditions (Knox & Roberts, 2007).

Crisis theory postulates that most crisis situations are limited to a period of 4 to 6 weeks. Crisis intervention is time limited in that the goal is to help the client mobilize needed support, resources, and adaptive coping skills to resolve or minimize the disequilibrium experienced by the precipitating event. Once the client has returned to her or his precrisis level of functioning and homeostasis, any further supportive or supplemental services are usually referred to appropriate community agencies and service providers (Knox & Roberts, 2007).

For example, a stalking victim may receive emergency crisis intervention services from a combination of agencies and programs over a period of time. Victim advocates and crisis counselors in law enforcement may work with the client through the aftermath of the stalking incidents, assist in the reporting and initial investigation, and provide short-term crisis intervention. Medical social workers may provide crisis counseling during a medical examination, and in the case of rape, sexual assault crisis programs typically have emergency response services for intervention at the hospital and will follow up with counseling and support services afterward. Most rape crisis centers and domestic violence shelters provide short-term individual counseling services and time-limited groups, along with basic needs services, shelter, and relocation assistance. Any further long-term therapy needs would then be referred to other clinical practitioners, support groups, or counseling programs.

Time frames for crisis intervention vary depending on several factors, including the agency mission and services, the client's needs and resources, and the type of crisis or trauma. Crisis intervention can be as brief as one client contact or may require several contacts over a few days of brief treatment; others may provide ongoing and follow-up services for up to 8 weeks. Additional crisis intervention booster sessions may well be needed in the future. For stalking survivors, another critical time for crisis reactions is experienced when any court proceedings are conducted. This may require client involvement or court testimony that triggers memories and feelings about the stalking incidents that can produce crisis reactions and retraumatization.

Individuals experiencing trauma and crisis need immediate relief and assistance, and the helping process must be adapted to meet those needs as efficiently and effectively as possible. However, clients in an active state of crisis are more amenable to the helping process, and this can facilitate completion of such tasks to meet the rapid response time frame. With a stalking survivor, medical needs must be assessed and intervention initiated immediately. After this, safety issues are addressed. The victim may not feel safe at home if the stalking incident occurred there or if there is concern that the stalker will not be arrested and can find the person there.

Crisis intervention counseling should be implemented simultaneously while addressing these other needs, with the police and/or medical social worker providing multiple crisis services during this first contact. This process could take several hours, depending on the response time by law enforcement and medical professionals and the client's coping skills, level of support, and resources. The crisis worker will need to follow through until the client has stabilized or been contacted by another collateral provider of crisis services.

The crisis worker must be knowledgeable about the appropriate strategies, resources, and other collateral services to initiate timely intervention strategies and meet the goals of treatment. For example, crisis intervention with stalking victims of family violence requires education and training on the dynamics and cycle of battering and abuse, familiarity with the community agencies providing services to this client population, and knowledge about the legal options available to victims.

Another characteristic of crisis intervention models is the use of tasks as a primary change effort. Concrete, basic needs services such as emergency safety, medical care, food, clothing, and shelter are the first priority in crisis intervention. Mobilizing needed resources may require more direct activity by the social worker in advocating, networking, and brokering for clients, who may not have the knowledge, skills, or capacity to follow through with referrals and collateral contacts at the time of active crisis.

Of course, the emotional and psychological traumas experienced by the client and significant others are important components for intervention. Ventilation of feelings and reactions to the crisis are essential to the healing process, and the practice skills of reflective communication, active listening, and establishing rapport are essential in developing a relationship and providing supportive counseling for the client.

## CRISIS INTERVENTION MODEL AND CASE APPLICATION

Roberts's (2000) seven-stage crisis intervention model can be used with a broad range of crises and can facilitate the assessment and helping process for effective crisis intervention across diverse types of clients and trauma situations. This model can be especially useful in working with stalking survivors because such varied types of relationships, behaviors, and actions are involved. A discussion and summary of the clinical interventions and goals for each of the seven stages is presented next to allow the reader to understand how crisis intervention can be applied to the stalking case scenario with Barbara.

### Stage 1: Assessing Lethality

Assessment in this model is ongoing and critical to effective intervention at all stages, beginning with an assessment of the lethality and safety issues for the client. With stalking survivors, it is critical to assess the risk for attempts, plans, or means to harm by the stalker, particularly if the offender is not in legal custody.

It is important to assess whether the client is in any current danger and to consider future safety concerns in treatment planning. For example, if the stalker is arrested, bail can bring release; if the stalker is incarcerated, the stalking survivor needs to be informed about release dates. In addition to determining lethality and the need for emergency intervention, it is crucial to maintain active communication with the client, either by phone or in person, while emergency procedures are being initiated (Roberts, 2000).

To plan and conduct a thorough assessment, the social worker also needs to evaluate the severity of the stalking incident, along with the client's current emotional state and immediate psychosocial needs. The client's current coping skills, support systems, and resources are also important in assessment and intervention planning. In the initial contact, assessment of the client's past or precrisis level of functioning and coping skills is useful; however, past history should not be a focus of assessment unless it is related directly to the immediate traumatic event. In stalking cases, the relationship is an important factor in the behaviors and actions of the stalker, so gathering this information is useful.

The goals of this stage are assessing and identifying critical areas of intervention, while also recognizing the hazardous event or trauma and acknowledging what has happened. At the same time, the stalking survivor becomes aware of his or her state of vulnerability and initial reactions to the crisis event. It is important that the crisis worker begin to establish a relationship based on respect for and acceptance of the client while also offering support, empathy, reassurance, and reinforcement that the client has survived and that help is available (Roberts, 2000).

As Barbara and the social worker at the university counseling center begin the first session, it is important that the stalking incidents be identified and assessed for lethality concerns. Because the stalking behavior has escalated after she tried to mediate and the stalker has threatened to sexually assault her, the clinical assessment should be a high risk for threat of harm for Barbara. It is obvious from Barbara's emotional state and the impacts she describes that there is a need for immediate intervention at the legal and counseling levels. The social worker's tasks in this stage are to assess the level of risk and validate Barbara's fears and the impacts she is experiencing due to the stalking incidents.

## Stage 2: Establishing Rapport and Communication

Survivors of stalking may question their own safety and vulnerability, and trust may be difficult for them to establish at this time. Therefore, active listening and empathic communication skills are essential to establishing rapport with and engagement of the client. Even though the need for rapid engagement is essential, the crisis worker should try to let the client set the pace of treatment. Many stalking victims feel out of control or powerless and should not be coerced, confronted, or forced into action; once they have stabilized and dealt with the initial trauma reactions, they will be better able to take action (Knox & Roberts, 2007).

Trauma survivors may require a positive future orientation, with an understanding that they can overcome current problems and hope that change can occur. During this stage, clients need unconditional support, positive regard, concern, and genuineness. Empathic communication skills such as minimal encouragers, reflection of thoughts and feelings, and active listening can reassure the client and help establish trust and rapport. The crisis worker needs to be attentive to the tone and level of the verbal communications to help the client calm down or de-escalate from the initial trauma reactions (Knox & Roberts, 2007).

While Barbara is telling the social worker about the stalking incidents, the social worker is not only assessing lethality but also engaging Barbara in the therapeutic relationship and allowing her to ventilate and express her feelings about what has been happening. Using active listening skills and empathic communication assists Barbara and the social worker in identifying the major issues and problems that have been caused by the stalker, and will aid in Barbara's recognition of the seriousness of the stalking and her vulnerability and risk so that she will be motivated to take steps to deal with the situation effectively and safely.

The social worker must also pay attention to his or her body language and facial expressions because stalking survivors may have been violated physically and be hypersensitive to physical space and body movements, which can frighten or startle them. Being observant of the survivor's physical and facial reactions can provide cues to the worker's level of engagement with the client, as well as a gauge to the client's current emotional state. It is also important to remember that delayed reactions or flat affect are common with trauma victims; social workers should not assume that these types of reactions mean that the survivor is not in crisis (Knox & Roberts, 2007).

## Stage 3: Identifying the Major Problems

The social worker helps Barbara prioritize the most important problems or impacts by identifying these problems in terms of how they affect her current status. Encouraging the client to ventilate about the stalking incidents can lead to problem identification, and some clients have an overwhelming need to talk about the specifics of the stalking situation. This process enables the client to figure out the sequence and context of the event(s), which can facilitate emotional ventilation while providing information to assess and identify major problems to work on. In some stalking cases, the victim may not be aware of the entire sequence of behaviors or actions until the most recent incident, which can precipitate a flood of reactions and emotions when the extent of the stalking is revealed. As Barbara discusses the stalking incidents with the social worker, she begins to realize the extent of the life changes she has been experiencing and starts to get angry and place responsibility for her problems on the stalker. The social worker assesses this change from feeling overwhelmed as a positive step that can aid in intervention planning.

Although Barbara has not confided in her family or friends, they may be important to intervention planning in supportive roles or to ensure the client's safety. However, they may experience their own reactions to the crisis situation, and this should be taken into consideration in contracting and implementing the intervention plan. The social worker must ensure that the client system is not overwhelmed during this stage; the focus should be on the most immediate and important problems needing intervention at this time. The first priority in this stage is meeting the basic needs of emotional and physical health and safety. After these have stabilized, other problems can then be addressed.

## Stage 4: Dealing With Feelings and Providing Support

It is critical that the social worker demonstrate empathy and an anchored understanding of Barbara's experiences so that her symptoms and reactions are normalized and can be viewed as functional strategies for survival. Many survivors blame themselves, and it is important to help them accept that being a victim is not their fault. Many stalking victims blame themselves for being in the relationship or for not being able to predict this type of behavior. Validation and reassurance are especially useful in this stage because survivors may be experiencing confusing and conflicting feelings.

Many clients follow the grief process when expressing and ventilating their emotions. First, survivors may be in denial about the extent of their emotional reactions and may try to avoid dealing with them in hopes that they will subside. They may be in shock and not be able to access their feelings immediately. However, significant delays in expression and ventilation of feelings can be harmful to the client in processing and resolving the trauma (Roberts, 2000).

Some survivors may express anger and rage about the situation and its effects, which can be healthy as long as these feelings do not escalate out of control. Helping the client calm down and attend to physiological reactions is important in this situation. Other clients may express their grief and sadness, and the crisis worker needs to allow time and space for this reaction without pressuring the client to move along too quickly.

Catharsis and ventilation are critical to healthy coping, and throughout this process, the crisis worker must recognize and support the survivor's courage in facing and dealing with these emotional reactions and issues. The social worker must also be aware of his or her own emotional reactions and level of comfort in helping the client through this stage (Roberts, 2000). Because Barbara is appropriately expressing her emotional and situational needs, the social worker can proceed to the next stage of taking action.

## Stage 5: Exploring Possible Alternatives

In this stage, the social worker can facilitate healthy coping skills by identifying Barbara's strengths and resources. Many survivors feel they do not have a lot of choices, and the social worker needs to be familiar with both formal and informal community services to provide referrals. The social worker may need to be more active and directive in this stage if the client has unrealistic expectations or inappropriate coping skills and strategies. Remember that clients are still distressed and in disequilibrium at this stage, and professional expertise and guidance may be necessary to produce positive, realistic alternatives for them. In stalking cases, several areas of the survivor's life can be affected that entail major changes in lifestyle or residence, and effective safety and treatment plans need to be implemented quickly, which requires professional input and experience. Barbara is currently experiencing disturbances in her physical (problems with sleeping and self-care), emotional (feeling afraid and overwhelmed), educational (cutting classes and not focusing on her studies), and social areas (restricting activities and staying home). Barbara has many strengths, including her ability to be successful in school and at work, her determination and self-sufficiency, her friends and family, and her motivation to not let her stalker continue to control her life. She is intelligent, has good self-esteem and adaptive coping skills, and is able to express her feelings and thoughts about the main issues and problems appropriately.

## Stage 6: Formulating an Action Plan

In this stage, the social worker must take an active role; however, the success of any intervention plan depends on the client's level of involvement, participation, and commitment. In planning an intervention, the social worker must help Barbara look at both the short-term and the long-range impacts. The main goals are to assist Barbara in achieving an appropriate level of functioning and maintain adaptive coping skills and resources. It is important to have a manageable treatment plan so that the Barbara can follow through and be successful. The client should not be overwhelmed with too many tasks or strategies, which may set him or her up for failure (Knox & Roberts, 2007).

Clients must also feel a sense of ownership in the action plan so that they can increase the level of control and autonomy in their lives and to ensure that they do not become dependent on other support persons or resources. Using a mutual process in intervention planning can maximize obtaining a commitment from the client to follow through with the action plan and any referrals. Ongoing assessment and evaluation are essential to determine whether the intervention plan is appropriate and effective in minimizing or resolving the client's identified problems. During this stage, clients should be processing and reintegrating the crisis impacts to achieve homeostasis and equilibrium in their life.

The social worker discusses Barbara's legal options and encourages her to report her stalker to the police so they can intervene and assist her by arresting and filing charges against him. Barbara can also apply for a restraining order to keep her stalker from contacting her or being physically near her. The victim services counselor at the police department can assist her through the investigation process and provide additional support, referrals, and crisis intervention services. As the case proceeds through the legal system, a victim advocate can provide services through the court proceedings and notify Barbara of any victim's compensation program services and benefits that she may be eligible for, including financial assistance for counseling, medical services, or safety and relocation expenses that arise as a result of the crimes. The social worker also recommends that Barbara confide in her friends and family so they can provide additional support and assistance through the legal proceedings and her daily activities or any changes she may need to accomplish as a result of the stalking. The social worker points out that her friend has already helped Barbara take the most important step in alleviating her situation by bringing her to the counseling center and providing emotional support.

The social worker recommends that Barbara continue individual counseling provided through the university counseling center and group therapy, which is helpful for survivors to get additional support from their peers who also have experienced stalking incidents. Termination should begin when the client has achieved the goals of the action plan or has been referred for additional services through other treatment providers. It is important to realize that many stalking survivors may need longer-term therapeutic help in working toward crisis resolution. Stalking sometimes continues over significant time periods, with the average case occurring over 1.8 years (Tjaden & Thoennes, 1998). These survivors may experience PTSD symptoms requiring long-term treatment.

## Stage 7: Follow-Up Measures

Hopefully, the sixth stage has resulted in significant changes and resolution for the client in regard to his or her postcrisis level of functioning and coping. This last stage should help determine whether these results have been maintained, or if further work remains to be done. Typically, follow-up contacts should be made within 4 to 6 weeks after termination. The social worker at the university counseling center and the court victim advocate will need to be available for Barbara to evaluate and provide any further counseling or safety needs when her stalker gets out of jail, during any legal proceedings, which can be a lengthy process taking many months, or when her stalker is placed on probation. It is important to remember that final crisis resolution may take many months or years to achieve, and survivors should be aware that certain events, places, or dates can trigger emotional and physical reactions to the previous trauma. For example, a critical time is at the first anniversary of a crisis event, when clients may re-experience old fears, reactions, or thoughts. This is a normal part of the recovery process, and clients should be prepared to have contingency plans or supportive help through these difficult periods.

REFERENCES

Baum, K., Catalano, S., Rand, M., & Rose, K. (2009). *Stalking victimization in the United States* (NCJ Report No. NCJ 224527). Washington, DC: US Department of Justice, Bureau of Justice Statistics.

Cass, A. I. (2011). Defining stalking: The influence of legal factors, extralegal factors, and particular actions on judgments of college students. *Western Criminology Review*, 12(1), 1–14. http://wcr.sonoma.edu/v12n1/Cass.pdf

Cupach, W. R., & Spitzberg, B. H. (2004). *The dark side of relationship pursuit: From attraction to obsession and stalking.* Mahwah, NJ: Erlbaum.

Davis, K. E., Coker, A. L., & Sanderson, M. (2002). Physical and mental health effects of being stalked for men and women. *Violence and Victims, 17,* 429–443.

Davis, K. E., & Frieze, I. H. (2000). Research on stalking: What do we know and where do we go? *Violence and Victims, 15,* 473–487.

Davis, K. E., Swan, S. C., & Gambone, L. J. (2012). Why doesn't he just leave me alone: Persistent pursuit: A critical review of theories and evidence. *Sex Roles, 66,* 328–339.

Dennison, S., & Thomson, D. (2002). Identifying stalking: The relevance of intent in commonsense reasoning. *Law and Human Behavior, 26,* 543–561.

De Smet, O., Loeys, T., & Buysse, A. (2012). Post-breakup unwanted pursuit: A refined analysis of the role of romantic relationship characteristics. *Journal of Family Violence, 27,* 437–452.

DeWall, C. N., Baumeister, R. F., Stillman, T. F., & Gailliot, M. T. (2007). Violence restrained: Effects of self-regulation and its depletion on aggression. *Journal of Experimental Social Psychology, 43*, 62–76.

Dressing, H., Foerster, K., & Gass, P. (2010). Are stalkers disordered or criminal? Thoughts on the psychopathology of stalking. *Psychopathology, 44*, 277–282. doi:10.1159/000325060

Dutton, M. A., & Goodman, L. A. (2005). Coercion in intimate partner violence: Toward a new conceptualization. *Sex Roles, 52*, 743–756.

Dutton, M. A., & Winstead, B. A. (2006). Predicting unwanted pursuit: Attachment, relationship satisfaction, relationship alternatives, and break-up distress. *Journal of Social and Personal Relationships, 23*, 565–586.

Dye, M. L., & Davis, K. E. (2003). Stalking and psychological abuse: Common factors and relationship-specific characteristics. *Violence and Victims, 18*, 163–180.

Englebrecht, C. M., & Reyns, B. W. (2011). Gender differences in acknowledgement of stalking victimization: Results from the NCVS stalking supplement. *Violence and Victims, 26*, 560–579.

Follingstad, D. R., Bradley, R. G., & Helf, C. M. (2002). A model for predicting dating violence in college students: Anxious attachment, angry temperament, and need for control. *Violence and Victims, 17*, 35–47.

Goodno, N. H. (2007). Cyberstalking, a new crime: Evaluating the effectiveness of current state and federal laws. *Missouri Law Review, 72*, 125–197.

Hazelwood, S. D., & Koon-Magnin, S. (2013). Cyber stalking and cyber harassment legislation in the UnitedStates: A qualitative analysis. *International Journal of Cyber Criminology, 7*, 155–168.

Knox, K., & Roberts, A. R. (2007). The crisis intervention model. In P. Lehmann & N. Coady (Eds.), *Theoretical perspectives for direct social work practice: A generalist-eclectic approach* (pp. 249–274). New York: Springer.

Kring, A. M., & Sloan, D. M. (Eds.). (2010). *Emotional regulation and psychopathology.* New York: Guilford.

Kulkarni, S. J., Racine, E. F., & Ramos, B. (2012). Examining the relationship between Latinas' perceptions about what constitutes domestic violence and domestic violence victimization. *Violence and Victims, 27*, 182–193.

Logan, T. K., & Walker, R. (2010). Toward a deeper understanding of the harms caused by partner stalking. *Violence and Victims, 25*, 440–453.

Malasch, M., Keijser, J. W., & Debets, S. E. C. (2011). Are stalkers recidivists? Repeated offending by convicted stalkers. *Violence and Women, 26*(1), 3–15. doi:10.1891/0886-6708.26.1.3

McEwan, T. E., Mullen, P. E., & MacKenzie, R. (2007). Anti-stalking legislation in practice: Are we meeting community needs? *Psychiatry, Psychology and Law, 14*, 207–217. Retrieved from https://www.stalkingrisk-profile.com/what-is-stalking/stalking-legislation

Meloy, J. R. (1998). The psychology of stalking. In J. R. Meloy (Ed.), *The psychology of stalking: Clinical and forensic perspectives* (pp. 2–27). San Diego, CA: Academic Press.

Mohandie, K., Meloy, J. R., McGowan, M. G., & Williams, J. (2006). The RECON typology of stalking: Reliability and validity based upon a large sample of North American stalkers. *Journal of Forensic Sciences, 51*(1), 147–155.

Nguyen, L. K., Spitzberg, B. H., & Lee, C. M. (2012). Coping with obsessive relational intrusion and stalking: The role of social support and coping strategies. *Violence and Victims, 27,* 414–433.

Norris, S. M., Huss, M. T., & Palarea, R. E. (2011). A pattern of violence: Analyzing the relationship between intimate partner violence and stalking. *Violence and Women, 25*(1), 103–115. doi:10.1891/0886-6708.26.1.103

Office on Violence Against Women. (2012). *Grant funds used to address stalking: 2012 report to Congress.* Retrieved from www.ovw. usdoj.gov/docs/bjs-stalking-rpt. pdf-229k-2012-08-15

Palarea, R. E., Scalora, M. J., & Langhinrichsen-Rohling, J. (1999). *Risk assessment inventory for stalking.* Unpublished measure.

Reyns, B. W., Henson, B., & Fisher, B. S. (2012). Stalking in the twilight zone: Extent of cyberstalking victimization and offending among college students. *Deviant Behavior, 33,* 1–25. doi:10.1080/0 1639625.2010.538364

Roberts, A. R. (2000). An introduction and overview. In A. R. Roberts (Ed.), *Crisis intervention handbook: Assessment, treatment and research* (2nd ed., pp. 3–21). New York: Oxford University Press.

Rosenfeld, B. (2004). Violence risk factors in stalking and obsessional harassment: A review and preliminary meta-analysis. *Criminal Justice and Behavior, 31*(1), 9–36.*

Sheridan, L., Davies, G., & Boon, J. (2001). Stalking: Perceptions and prevalence. *Journal of Interpersonal Violence, 16,* 151–167.

Sheridan, L., & Lyndon, A. E. (2012). The influence of prior relationship, gender, and fear on the consequences of stalking victimization. *Sex Roles, 66,* 340–350.

Sinclair, H. C. (2010). Stalking myth-attributions: Examining the role of individual and contextual variables on attributions in unwanted pursuit scenarios. *Sex Roles, 66,* 378–391. doi:10.1007/ s11199-010-9853-8

Spitzberg, B. H., & Cupach, W. R. (1998). *The dark side of close relationships.* Mahwah, NJ: Erlbaum.

Spitzberg, B. H., & Cupach, W. R. (2007). The state of the art of stalking: Taking stock of the emerging literature. *Aggression and Violent Behavior, 12,* 64–86.

Spitzberg, B. H., Cupach, W. R., Hannawa, A. F., & Crowley, J. (July 17–20, 2008). *Testing a relational goal pursuit theory of obsessive relational intrusion and stalking.* Poster presented at the International Association for Relationship Research Conference, Providence, Rhode Island.

Strawhun, J., Adams, N., & Huss, M. T. (2013). The assessment of cyberstalking: An expanded examination including social networking, attachment, jealousy, and anger in relation to violence and abuse. *Violence and Victims, 28,* 715–730. http://dx.doi. org/10.1891/0886-6708.11-00145

Thompson, C. M., Dennison, S. M., & Stewart, A. (2012). Are female stalkers more violent than male stalkers? Understanding gender differences in stalking violence using contemporary sociocultural beliefs. *Sex Roles, 66,* 351–365. doi:10.1007/s11199-010-9911-2

Tjaden, P., & Thoennes, N. (1998). *Stalking in America: Findings from the National Violence Against Women Survey* (NCJ Report No. 169592). Washington, DC: National Institute of Justice and Centers for Disease Control and Prevention.

Tjaden, P., & Thoennes, N. (2002). The role of stalking in domestic violence crime reports generated by the Colorado Springs Police Department. In K. E. Davis, I. H. Frieze, & R. D. Maiuro (Eds.), *Stalking: Perspectives on victims and perpetrators* (pp. 9–30). New York: Springer.

Van der Aa, S., & Groenen, A. (2011). Identifying the needs of stalking victims and the responsiveness of the criminal justice system: A qualitative study in Belgium and the Netherlands. *Victims and Offenders, 6,* 19–37.

Wigman, S. A., Grahma-Kevan, N., & Archer, J. (2008). Investigating sub-groups of harassers: The roles of attachment, dependency, jealousy, and aggression. *Journal of Family Violence, 23,* 557–568.

Yanowitz, K. (2006). Influence of gender and experience on college students' stalking schemas. *Violence and Victims, 21,* 91–99.

# 18

# Crisis Intervention Application of Brief Solution-Focused Therapy in Addictions

KENNETH R. YEAGER
THOMAS K. GREGOIRE

This chapter describes the application of Roberts's seven-stage crisis intervention model in substance dependence treatment, combined with a strengths perspective and brief solution-focused therapy. Additionally, it discusses factors of resilience and methods to capitalize on potential resilience factors within the framework of solution-focused approaches. Application of crisis intervention in addictions encompasses three cases from a direct practice viewpoint, integrating key factors into concise case autopsies utilizing this approach. Finally, the chapter provides a brief discussion of evidence-based practice in the field of addiction treatment.

The examples that follow provide a brief outline of the case examples to be detailed throughout this chapter:

## Case 1

Dennis is a 41-year-old White male who progresses rapidly through crack cocaine dependence. Consumed by overwhelming cravings for cocaine, Dennis abandons his wife, children, business, and responsibilities. As he seeks comfort in crack cocaine and sex, he progresses into a repetitive cycle of craving, use, and pornography. Having lost all that is important in his life, Dennis presents seeking stabilization from his addiction.

This case demonstrates practical application of Roberts's model as a method to stabilize the individual and how this model can be utilized to develop effective treatment planning within the time constraints of a managed care treatment climate.

The second case of Susan examines Roberts's model in combination with the strengths perspective in addressing opioid addiction in the chronic pain client.

---

### Case 2

Susan's pain is the result of several automobile accidents. Her chronic pain serves as the backdrop for compulsive behaviors rooted in her preoccupation with minimizing her pain while at the same time feeding her addiction. Susan presents in crisis, fearing legal consequences and being cut off from her supply of pain medications.

---

In this case application, Roberts's model demonstrates effective methods for brief interventions building on the strengths of the addicted chronic pain patient. Application in this case deflects the client's natural defense structures, assisting her to build on her supports rather than remaining entrenched in the agony of her injuries.

---

### Case 3

Scott is a 20-year-old polysubstance-dependent individual who presents in acute withdrawal from several substances, including cocaine, heroin, and methamphetamine. Scott's use began at age 12 and has progressed to complete loss of control. At this point Scott has been asked to leave the university he has been attending and not to return to his parents' home after stealing a large amount of money from his parents. Scott presents in active withdrawal to the treatment center accompanied by his grandfather, who hopes the center can assist his grandson in reclaiming all aspects of his life through the process of recovery.

---

This case demonstrates how Roberts's model is combined with solution-focused theory to lead the client toward a greater assumption of self-responsibility in the development of a self-directed program of recovery. It demonstrates application of the miracle and exception questions in day-to-day practice as Scott moves through the stages of crisis intervention. Scott's story illustrates the effectiveness of combined solution-focused theory and Roberts's crisis intervention model in addressing issues that reach beyond the issue of dependence to move the patient through the process of recovery.

## CRISIS OVERVIEW

The experience of crisis is an inescapable reality. For some, crisis may occur only infrequently. For others, crisis occurs frequently, with one crisis leading to another. Just as crises occur at varying intervals for individuals, there are variances in an individual's ability to cope with crisis (Roberts & Dziegielewski, 1995). Some are able to "work through" their perceptions and reactions to the event with little intervention. For many, however, successful resolution of a crisis event requires skillful intervention to clarify the individual's response to the event (Roberts, 1990).

Crisis intervention consistently occurs when one is addressing substance dependence. Persons presenting for substance dependence treatment frequently find themselves seeking assistance following a crisis or possibly a series of crises. Psychiatrists, psychologists, and social workers functioning within the managed care delivery system have been challenged to provide cost-effective treatment within the least restrictive environment. Professionals practicing in addiction treatments are finding that crisis intervention skills combined with brief solution-focused intervention strategies are effective when applied in today's abbreviated lengths of stay; the same skills will be equally important, if not more important, as substance abuse treatment transitions to a new venue with physician offices working together with treatment facilities to provide care for those with substance use disorders. The challenges will be great as this emerging model experiences growing pains. However, in this transition, substance abuse treatment will become closely aligned with primary care and will be focused more on screening and early intervention. Substance abuse treatment will be considered an "essential service," meaning health plans are required to provide it, providing the opportunity to treat the full spectrum of the disorder, including people who are in the early stages of substance abuse, rather than waiting until the disorder has destroyed lives prior to engaging in treatment services.

In past decades, managed care hastened a fundamental shift in substance abuse treatment delivery. Today the Affordable Care Act (2010) continues to shape the treatment landscape. The Affordable Care Act will provide one of the largest expansions of mental health and substance use disorder coverage in a generation. Beginning in 2014, under the law, all new small-group and individual market plans are required to cover 10 essential health benefit categories, including mental health and substance use disorder services, and will be required to cover them at parity with medical and surgical benefits. These new protections will build on the Mental Health Parity and Addiction Equity Act (2008) to expand mental health and substance use disorder benefits and federal parity protections for behavioral health to 62 million Americans. Currently, just 2.3 million Americans receive any type of substance abuse treatment, which is less than 1% of the estimated total population of people who are affected by the most serious of the substance use disorders. While almost all large-group plans and most small-group plans include coverage for some mental health and substance use disorder services, there are limitations to benefits or coverage, leading to significant gaps in care for many people. Additionally, some plans offer very limited or no coverage for substance use disorders. The final rule implementing the essential health benefits directs nongrandfathered health plans in the individual and small-group markets to cover mental health and substance use disorder services, as well as to comply with the federal parity law requirements beginning in 2014 (Garfield, Lave, & Donahue, 2010; Congressional Budget Office, 2013).

Currently, federal programs, such as Medicaid and Medicare, focus on inpatient services, like detox programs, but do not cover office visits for substance abuse treatments. However, by the end of 2014, under the Affordable Care Act, coverage of substance use disorders is likely to be comparable to that for other chronic illnesses, such as hypertension, asthma, and diabetes. Government insurers (Medicare and Medicaid) will cover physician office visits (with an emphasis placed on preventative services such as screening, brief intervention, assessment, evaluation, and medication), clinic visits, home health visits, family counseling, alcohol and drug testing, four maintenance and anticraving medications, monitoring , and smoking cessation. This shift is significant because it provides access to care for thousands of individuals while at the same time adding general practitioners to a very limited pool of addiction treatment providers.

## ESTIMATES OF THE SUBSTANCE DEPENDENCE PROBLEM IN AMERICA

Substance abuse and dependence treatment as a profession continues to adapt to emerging data and facts associated with current prevalence and trends in the United States. A major source of information on substance use patterns among Americans aged 12 and older has been the annual National Survey on Drug Use and Health (NSDUH) produced by the Substance Abuse and Mental Health Services Administration (SAMHSA) in 2013, which provides the most recent data available at the time of publication of this text, referencing use patterns in 2012.

### Alcohol

In the 2012 NSDUH report, drinking by underage persons has declined. Current rates of alcohol use by individuals aged 12 to 20 have declined from

28.8% to 24.3%; additionally, binge-drinking rates declined from 19.3% to 15.3%. The same decreasing trend is present for the rate of heavy drinking in the age group of 12 and older, with rates for heavy drinking episodes decreasing from 6.2% to 4.3%. As in previous years, binge drinking and heavy drinking remain more prevalent in men than in women. In 2012, 30.4% of men and 16.0% of women aged 12 or older reported binge drinking (five or more drinks on the same occasion) in the past month, and 9.9% of men and 3.4% of women reported heavy alcohol use (binge drinking on at least 5 separate days within a 1-month period; SAMHSA, 2013).

Estimates for driving under the influence of alcohol have also demonstrated a significant decline. In 2012, an estimated 29.1 million people, or 11.2% of persons aged 12 or older, had driven under the influence of alcohol at least once in the past year; this number is down from 14.2% in 2002. Although this decline in driving while under the influence is encouraging, concerns remain because there is no acceptable or safe number of impaired drivers.

## Drugs

In 2012, an estimated 23.9 million Americans aged 12 or older were current illicit drug users, meaning they had used an illicit drug during the month prior to the survey interview. This estimate represents 9.2% of the population aged 12 years or older.

Marijuana is the most commonly used illicit drug in America, and the number of users has been increasing. In 2012, it is estimated that marijuana was used by 18.9 million current (past month) users, which equates to approximately 7.3% of people aged 12 or older; this represents a significant increase from 14.4 million (5.8%) of the population in 2007. More than half of new illicit drug users begin with marijuana. Within the 2.9 million individuals reported initial use of illicit drugs, 65.6% report using marijuana as their first drug. The next most common were prescription pain relievers, followed by inhalants, which are most commonly abused among younger teens (SAMHSA, 2013).

With the exception of opiates, the use of most other drugs of abuse has not changed remarkably or has declined in recent years. In 2012, 6.8 million Americans aged 12 or older (or 2.6%) had used psychotherapeutic prescription drugs nonmedically (without a prescription or in a manner or for a purpose not prescribed) in the past month. Additionally, 1.1 million Americans (0.4%) had used hallucinogens (a category that includes Ecstasy and LSD) in the past month (SAMHSA, 2013).

Cocaine use has decreased in recent years. From 2007 to 2012, the number of current users aged 12 or older dropped from 2.1 million to 1.7 million. Methamphetamine use has also declined slightly from 530,000 current users in 2007 to 440,000 in 2012 (SAMHSA, 2013).

Heroin dependence continues to grow in the United States. According to the NSDUH, in 2012, about 669,000 Americans reported using heroin in the past year, a number that has been on the rise since 2007. This trend appears to be driven largely by young adults aged 18 to 25, among whom there have been the greatest increases. The number of people using heroin for the first time is remarkably high, with 156,000 people starting heroin use in 2012, nearly double the number in 2006 (90,000) (SAMHSA, 2013). It is no surprise that with opiate use on the rise, more people are experiencing negative health effects associated with repeated use of opiates. The total number of drug-related emergency department visits increased by 81% from 2004 (2.5 million visits) to 2009 (4.6 million visits). Emergency department visits involving nonmedical use of pharmaceuticals increased by 98.4% over the same period, from 627,291 visits to 1,244,679 visits.

The largest pharmaceutical increases were observed for oxycodone products (242.2% increase), alprazolam (148.3% increase), and hydrocodone products (124.5%) (SAMHSA, 2013).

The number of people meeting criteria for dependence or abuse of heroin according to the fourth edition of the *Diagnostic and Statistical Manual of Mental Disorders (DSM-IV)* doubled from 214,000 in 2002 to 467,000 in 2012 (SAMHSA, 2013). The recently released *DSM-V* no longer separates substance abuse from dependence but instead provides criteria for opioid use disorders that range from mild to severe, depending on the number of symptoms a person has (American Psychological Association, 2013, pp. 540–550).

## Treatment Delivery Gap

In 2012, 23.1 million Americans in the United States aged 12 or older needed treatment for an illicit drug or alcohol use problem (8.9% of persons aged 12 or older). The number in 2012 was similar to the number in each year from 2002 to 2010 (ranging from 22.2 million to 23.6 million), but it was higher than the number in 2011 (21.6 million). In 2012, 2.5 million persons (1.0% of persons aged 12 or older and 10.8% of those who needed treatment) received treatment at a specialty facility. The rate and the number in 2012 were not different from the rates and numbers in 2002 and in each year from 2004 through 2011 (SAMHSA, 2013), indicating efforts to improve access to substance abuse treatment have been limited in effectiveness against a growing population of those needing treatment.

Among persons in 2012 who received their most recent substance use treatment at a specialty facility in the past year, 50.2% reported using their "own savings or earnings" as a source of payment for their most recent specialty treatment, 41.0% reported using private health insurance, 30.2% reported using public assistance other than Medicaid, 28.7% reported using

Medicaid, 24.7% reported using funds from family members, and 24.1% reported using Medicare.

Of the 20.6 million persons aged 12 or older in 2012, 1.1 million persons (5.4%) reported that they perceived a need for treatment for their illicit drug or alcohol use problem but did not receive treatment at a specialty facility. Of these 1.1 million persons, 347,000 (31.3%) reported that they made an effort to get treatment, and 760,000 (68.7%) reported making no effort to get treatment. Based on combined data from 2009 through 2012 (SAMHSA, 2012), among persons aged 12 or older who needed but did not receive treatment for illicit drug or alcohol use (although they made an effort to receive it), the most frequently reported reasons for not receiving treatment were as follows:

1. No health coverage and could not afford cost (38.2%)
2. Not ready to stop using (26.3%)
3. Had health coverage, but it did not cover treatment or did not cover cost (10.1%)
4. Getting treatment might have negative effect on job (9.5%)
5. Did not know where to go for treatment (8.9%)
6. No transportation or inconvenient (8.2%)
7. Might cause neighbors/community to have a negative opinion (7.9%)
8. Did not have time for treatment (7.1%)

## Prevalence of Severe Mental Illness

In 2012, 34.1 million persons aged 18 or older (14.5% of this population) had received mental health treatment or counseling during the past 12 months. The use of mental health services in the past year varied by age for adults. Percentages for those who used mental health services were higher among adults aged 26 to 49 (15.2%) and those aged 50 or older (14.8%) than among those aged 18 to 25 (12.0%; SAMHSA, 2013).

In 2012, the types of mental health services most commonly used by adults in the past year were as follows:

Prescription medication management (12.4%, or 29.0 million adults)

Outpatient clinical services (6.6%, or 15.5 million adults)

Inpatient mental health services (0.8%, or 1.9 million adults)

Although the numbers have tended to fluctuate moderately from year to year, the use of mental health services has remained similar for the past decade. It should be noted that respondents could report using more than one type of mental health care (SAMHSA, 2013).

Among adults aged 18 or older in 2012 who reported using mental health services in the past year, the following service utilization trends presented: 66.7% used one type of care (inpatient, outpatient, or prescription medication), 30.7% used two types of care, and 2.6% used all three types of care.

Among adults aged 18 or older in 2012 who used outpatient mental health services in the past year, several types of locations were reported where services were received. These were the office of a private therapist, psychologist, psychiatrist, social worker, or counselor who was not part of a clinic (55.1%); an outpatient mental health clinic or center (23.5%); a doctor's office that was not part of a clinic (20.1%); and an outpatient medical clinic (6.6%).

Among adults with severe mental illness (SMI) in 2012, the rate of mental health service use was lower among adults aged 18 to 25 (53.1%) than that among adults aged 26 to 49 (63.5%) and those aged 50 or older (66.3%). In 2012, among all adults aged 18 or older with past–year any mental illness (AMI), 35.3% used prescription medication, 22.4% used outpatient services, and 3.0% used inpatient services for a mental health problem in the past year.

The percentages of adults with past-year SMI who used prescription medication, outpatient services, and inpatient services were 57.8%, 39.0%, and 6.2%, respectively (respondents could report that they used more than one type of service). Among the 17.9 million adults aged 18 or older in 2012 with past-year AMI who reported receiving mental health services in the past year, 56.2% received one type of care (inpatient, outpatient, or prescription medication), 39.3% received two types of care, and 4.5% received all three types of care.

Among the 6.0 million adults aged 18 or older in 2012 with past-year SMI who reported receiving mental health services in the past year, 43.5% received one type of care (inpatient, outpatient, or prescription medication), 49.3% received two types of care, and 7.2% received all three types of care.

In 2012, there were 11.5 million adults aged 18 or older (4.9% of all adults) who reported an unmet need for mental health care in the past year. These included 5.4 million adults who did not receive any mental health services in the past year. Among adults who did receive some type of mental health service in the past year, 17.8% (6.1 million) reported an unmet need for mental health care. (Unmet need among adults who received mental health services may reflect a delay in care or a perception of insufficient care.) Among the 5.4 million adults aged 18 or older in 2012 who reported an unmet need for mental health care and did not receive mental health services in the past year, several reasons were indicated for not receiving mental health care. These included an inability to afford the cost of care (45.7%), believing at the time that the problem could be handled without treatment (28.2%), not knowing where to go for services (22.8%), and not having the time to go for care (14.3%).

## DEFINITIONS OF DEPENDENCE, ACUTE
## STRESSORS, AND CRISIS EVENT

Crisis events within the substance-dependent population vary somewhat from traditional models of crisis, yet there remains one overwhelming similarity. This is the failure of an individual's coping strategies to ameliorate a current crisis. Frequently, within the substance-dependent population, physiological factors work to precipitate crisis as the individual experiences loss of control over his or her use.

Crisis events within the substance-dependent population vary somewhat from the experience of crisis in other disciplines. Persons with addiction problems are highly motivated to maintain the status quo, at least with respect to their substance use. Addicts often make excessive use of denial and other defense mechanisms to avoid crisis and protect their lifestyle. Consequently, practitioners often see clients only in extreme distress and may experience a brief window in which to engage the client. It is at this time that the individual's temporary loss of control creates a willingness to engage in new behaviors to address the crisis event. The applications of brief crisis models, such as that described here, are very advantageous in assisting individuals with an alcohol or other drug problem (Ewing, 1990; Parad & Parad, 1990; Norman, Turner, & Zunz, 1994; "Embedded Crisis Workers," 2014).

Definitions of substance dependence have varied over the years. For many, the "disease concept" of substance dependence is the primary diagnostic tool. Two examples of diagnostic definitions for substance dependence are those of the World Health Organization and the American Psychiatric Association, which to this day remain the primary diagnostic criteria for substance dependence:

- According to the World Health Organization (1974), substance dependence is a state, psychic and sometimes also physical, resulting from the interaction between a living organism and a drug, characterized by behavioral and other responses that always include a compulsion to take the drug on a continuous or periodic basis in order to experience its psychic effects, and sometimes to avoid the discomfort of its absence.
- The *DSM-IV* (American Psychiatric Association, 1994), the accepted diagnostic tool for the profession of social work, defines substance abuse and dependency with varying criteria for each category. It is of interest to note that the *DSM-IV* separates dependence with physical dependence from substance dependence without physical dependence. This distinction is an addition to the criteria of dependence. This is likely because of the prevalence of crack cocaine and the recent re-emergence of hallucinogenic drugs that do not appear to cause physical dependence. Two components separate abuse from dependence.

A simplistic definition of *substance dependence* is: "If alcohol/drugs are causing problems in your life... then you likely have a problem with alcohol/ drugs." This is the case when approaching addiction from a crisis intervention perspective. Persons entering treatment frequently report that the coping mechanisms they used in the past are not working. If the individual could "control" her or his use or life circumstances, there would be no need to seek assistance. Wallace's (1983, 1989) biopsychosocial model of addiction highlights the pervasiveness of alcohol and other drug problems. Crisis for persons with this disorder is just as likely to be precipitated by intrapsychic discomfort, social conflict, or the physiological consequences of continued substance use. Effective evaluation of the crisis mandates that practitioners attend to each area.

## APPLICATION OF ROBERTS'S SEVEN-STAGE CRISIS INTERVENTION MODEL AND ANALYSIS OF RISK AND PROTECTIVE FACTORS

Within Roberts's crisis intervention model applied to substance dependence, the social worker must be aware of the delicate balance between stabilization and removal of motivation for treatment. Chemical-dependent persons use maladaptive defense structures combined with numerous irrational beliefs to minimize the extent and severity of their dependence. Crisis intervention often involves addressing the individual's rationalizations, justifications, catastrophizing, and use of negative self-talk to work his or her way out of treatment (Roberts, 1990; Dattilio & Freeman, 1994; Greene, Lee, & Trask, 1996; Yeager, 2000).

To this end, there are differences between the substance-dependent population and the general population seeking assistance. Roberts initially reported the seven-stage model, which identified establishment of rapport as the first stage. In a review of Roberts's work as applied by professionals in clinical practice, one can see the ongoing development of this model. Subsequent publications by Roberts recommend interchanging assessment of lethality (Stage 2) with establishment of rapport (Stage 1), depending on the presenting problem(s) of the patient (Roberts, 1996).

This is particularly true of cocaine-dependent persons, who experience tremendously intense crises in short periods of time, yet because there is little withdrawal, cocaine-dependent persons may mistake crisis stabilization as an all-clear to resume use (Yeager, 1999). The inertia of the recovery environment is extremely powerful; when combined with the powerful cravings frequently associated with crack cocaine, the equation is complete for the relapse process. Second, special emphasis must be placed on examination of

Table 18.1   Roberts's Seven-Stage Model and Solution-Focused Applications

| Stage | Application |
| --- | --- |
| Make psychological contact. | Acceptance, support, empathy, mirroring nonverbal communication. |
| Examine the dimensions of the problem in order to define it. | Scaling, examination of resilience factors, empowering the patient, assess support factors. |
| Encourage exploration of feelings and emotions. | Acceptance, support, empathy. |
| Explore and assess past coping attempts. | Exception question, scaling question, past success. |
| Generate and explore alternatives and specific solutions. | Miracle question, exception question, past success, prediction task, track current success. |
| Restore cognitive functioning through implementation of action plan. | Scaling, empowerment, exception question, past success tracking, track current success. |
| Follow up. | Scaling in the form of outcome studies. |

*Note:* This table is a representation of techniques to use with each stage of Roberts's model. The absence of assessment of lethality as presented in additional publications by Roberts is due to the use of solution-focused therapy as persons progress through the process of recovery. This is not indicative that patients presenting for substance dependence may not experience lethality issues. Work with persons who are substance dependent requires ongoing mental status assessment.

the dimensions of the problem (Stage 2), exploration of feelings and emotions (Stage 3), and exploration of past coping attempts. Emphasis on these stages will assure the substance-dependent individuals of remaining connected with treatment. The following example of crisis intervention with a cocaine-addicted individual demonstrates this process (Roberts, 1990). Table 18.1 provides an overview of Roberts's seven-stage model and compatible solution[focused interventions.

## CASE STUDY 1: DENNIS

### Dennis E., Cocaine Dependent

Dennis is a 41-year-old self-employed chemical researcher who presented following "binge pattern" episode of cocaine use. Dennis reported being sober for a 10-year period following treatment for alcohol dependence. Dennis eventually began to taper off his attendance of 12-step support meetings as his family and business grew. Dennis is married with two children, aged 8 and 11. His younger daughter was diagnosed with leukemia 1 year ago. Dennis reports being very close to his daughters, stating that he reads to them every evening and never misses a doctor's appointment with his younger daughter. Dennis is extremely successful in his work. He reports having secured government contracts for the next 5 years that total millions of dollars of profits for his company. He reports that at this time last year he was receiving an award for "researcher of the year." His plan was to celebrate with a glass of wine.

After this event, there were no apparent consequences. Approximately 1 week later, Dennis drank again, this time at a ball game, to the point of intoxication. Again, there were no consequences. The next day he was extremely tired and was faced with deadlines in his work. He purchased a gram of cocaine, worked 27 hours straight, and completed two projects, including a million-dollar grant application.

Dennis believed he had successfully found the "old Dennis," the one who could work for hours with no breaks. Dennis states that his relapse was "a major memory event." He reports his thinking instantly reverted to where his thoughts were in his previous addiction to alcohol. His use of cocaine rapidly increased. Within a 1-month period, he was using 3 grams of cocaine daily. In an attempt to save money, he began to smoke crack cocaine.

The introduction of crack cocaine led to isolative patterns of use. Dennis recalls the panic he felt at 3:00 a.m. when he realized that his staff would be returning to work in a few hours, knowing that he would not be able to continue to use cocaine within the confines of his office. Acting on impulse, Dennis removed his computer from his office and drove to a motel, taking with him cocaine worth approximately $3,000. With nothing to do in the motel, Dennis began visiting pornographic sites on the Internet. He reports becoming preoccupied with these sites. Caught in a cycle of crack cocaine use, he found that sexual fantasy, paranoia, and isolation began to dominate and control his behaviors. He was particularly occupied with an interactive triple-X-rated site; he reports engaging in fantasy, substituting acquaintances for the persons with whom he was interacting. It was not until the supply of cocaine was depleted that the cycle was broken.

Dennis was missing for 4 days before returning home. He had missed two doctor's appointments with his daughter and reports pending separation between him and his wife. Dennis identifies the separation as the precipitating event for seeking treatment. Within the initial contact, he acknowledged hoping his heart would explode so he would not have to face the disappointment of his family following his relapse. He quickly added that death would have been easier to face than having to look at the sadness in his daughter's eyes.

---

Seeking to understand the severity of Dennis's situation, fears, and feelings led to the rapid establishment of a working relationship (Roberts, 1990). Making psychological contact with Dennis consisted of showing a genuine interest in and respect for him and offering hope. Dennis, like many cocaine addicts, found it easy to share where he had been. What is difficult for many in early recovery is the ability to see a way out of the insanity associated with their cocaine dependence. Letting Dennis know that he was not the first to present with this problem simply did not reduce his anxiety. He needed to hear that there are common symptoms associated with cocaine dependence, including physical, mental, and emotional preoccupations with the drug. Although this discussion was helpful, Dennis continued to experience remarkable anxiety. There was no significant reduction in tension until discussion of sexual preoccupation occurred. At this point, it became clear that cocaine use had taken Dennis to a place he had not anticipated. Avoiding pushing Dennis away by discussing this issue in detail, the therapist assured him that many authors had discussed the concurrent sexual component with cocaine dependence (Hser et al., 1999; Balsheim, Oxman, Van Rooyen, & Girod, 1992: Wang et al, 2012). Offering to provide Dennis with information related to this topic, and connecting him with a cocaine-specific group to address this issue seemed to provide a combination of understanding and awareness of resources. This minimized the anxiety that Dennis had carried into the initial session.

Stage 2 in crisis intervention as outlined by Roberts (2000) is "examining the dimensions of the problem in order to define it" (p. 18). In this area, a couple of issues required further examination. First was gaining a greater degree of insight into the precipitating event that led Dennis to the treatment center on this date. The therapist used probing questions to expand the information provided initially.

Q:  Dennis, you said the pending separation was what led you to seeking help. Can you tell me more about what happened?

A:  When I did finally go home, there weren't any questions of "Where were you?" "Are you all right?" or "Thank God you're home!" There was only silence and sadness. When the silence was broken, it was by the sobs of Tiffany. She was trying hard not to... but there was no way she could hold back. I knew she was torn between her mother's instructions and her wanting to make sure I was O.K. God just knowing that my daughter... after all she had been through... was worried about me, she was a victim of my use... I just couldn't take it. I asked Donna to take me to treatment. There was no answer. Instead, she handed me separation papers and said, "We had an agreement. If you use, you have to leave." I knew she was right, so I got in the car and drove myself. I can't bear the thought of living my life without them.

This account provided much more information and understanding than the previous answer of pending separation. There was greater understanding of the pain Dennis and his family were experiencing. It also provided information surrounding Donna's willingness to do what was best for herself and the children. Dennis knew this was what needed to happen, but he acknowledged that this did not make it any less painful (Roberts, 1990; DeJong & Miller, 1995).

Contained within the information provided by Dennis is Stage 3 of Roberts's seven-stage crisis model; while examining the dimensions of the problem, Dennis was encouraged to express his feelings and emotions. Dennis clearly expressed the pain associated with the realization that his wife and children had become the victims of his addiction. Further exploration of this issue at this time was not necessary. Dennis had experienced the impact of the feeling, and it was important to encourage him to move beyond it. Dennis noted that it was important for him to stand still and feel this hurt because it will be necessary to remember this pain when he experiences cravings to use in the future (Roberts, 1990).

Dennis reports that "only the pain associated with the consequences of use is powerful enough to thwart relapse." A basic tenet of solution-focused therapy when applied in crisis intervention is that one does not need to know the cause or function of the problem in order to resolve it (O'Hanlon & Weiner-Davis, 1989). In this case, recognizing that Dennis knew best how to cope with his cravings provided a powerful tool for treating his cravings. Because of the respect between the counselor and the patient, and the counselor's willingness to listen, Dennis taught his counselor how to address cravings (Berg & Jaya, 1993).

### Clinical Issues/Interventions/Special Considerations

Because Dennis has been sober previously, Stage 4 of Roberts's model, exploring and assessing past coping attempts, became a vital part of the ongoing recovery plan. Assigning specific tasks for Dennis to complete assisted in re-establishing equilibrium. Dennis was given the assignment to list the right and the wrong ways he had treated his disease in the past. For example, his alarm going off in the morning had provided the opportunity to hit the snooze button four or five times, waking up late and rushing to work. Alternatively, he could get up, fix a healthy breakfast, read his morning meditation books, and begin the day with a plan for recovery. Giving Dennis a clear-cut way to measure coping strategies provided him with a tool to build upon his strengths and to work toward a solution (Fortune, 1985; Levy & Shelton, 1990; Roberts, 1990).

Upon completing the assignment, Dennis identified any specific areas that presented within his recovery environment as high risk. Identifying the reciprocal processes between an individual and his or her recovery environment is crucial for understanding how a patient uses environmental resources in the problem-solving process and how the environment creates challenges for the individual (Pillari, 1998; Zastrow, 1996; Newman & Newman, 1995). Dennis was able to identify three primary areas. First was payday: "It's a very simple equation for me: *Time plus money equal cocaine*." The second area he identified was Internet pornography, and the third were his uncontrollable mood swings.

Dennis was asked to rank the three high-risk situations on a scale of 1 to 10, with 10 being remarkable cravings and 1 being no cravings at all. Scaling provides a clear measure of the problem at hand when working to resolve a crisis (Saleebey, 1996). Dennis rated having money as a 10; his rationale is that there was not a time when he did not experience remarkable cravings when he had money. He rated his Internet pornographic fixation as a 7, stating, "I don't always have to be high to go there." When asked if he felt this required further addressing, Dennis replied, "Absolutely. It's still a very real trigger for my addiction." The third area of mood swings posed more of a problem. Initially Dennis rated this as a 5; after a few minutes of thought, however, he changed it to a 9, reporting, "I never know when it's going to hit. Sometimes it's nothing, other times I'm a raging lunatic." For the sake of argument, it was agreed upon that this would remain a 9. Dennis agreed to address the potential for rage at the worst possible level so as not to minimize the extent and severity of the mood swings.

Following the discussion, the therapist instructed Dennis to list alternatives or possible solution-oriented actions he could take to minimize the impact of each high-risk situation. This took situations previously seen as negative out of the control of the patient and provided the opportunity to assume an active role in minimizing the impact of these issues (Berg, 1994).

### Special Considerations of Treatment Planning

Dennis returned with a plan that was simple and applicable in each area. In an effort to control money as a trigger, he agreed to relinquish control of his finances to his business partner. Dennis had contacted this person, who agreed to take over his checkbook and to manage his finances. Dennis and his partner agreed that he would receive an allowance of $10 per day for lunch and incidentals. A company or bank check would be used for larger transactions.

The issue of the Internet was a bit more complicated because Dennis completed a great deal of his research online. Two changes were agreed upon. First, Dennis was to move his computer into the main lab, an area that was public and provided sufficient observation to minimize his accessing of Internet sites that contained pornographic material. The second was utilization of a "Net nanny" program that blocked access to pornographic sites. However, all quickly agreed that Dennis was smart enough to work around this if he wanted. The last agreed-upon change was that Dennis would work between the hours of 8:00 a.m. and 6:00 p.m. because there was no real reason for him to be spending excess time in the office. He agreed that the evenings required his focusing on recovery.

The area of mood swings was more abstract and thus required different planning skills. Dennis presented a list of recovering persons whom he agreed to contact daily to minimize the possible occurrences of mood swings. He further agreed to keep this list with him at all times and to contact these persons if he began to experience a mood swing. Dennis noted the need for ongoing treatment and agreed to attend the intensive outpatient program four evenings per week, including a specialized cocaine group one evening per week. Dennis then stated he felt it would be in his best interest to enter a sober living house rather than seeking an apartment on his own, acknowledging that his mood swings occurred primarily when he was alone. Again, the emphasis was placed on the importance of addressing triggers in the person's recovery environment (Pillari, 1998).

In approximately 2½ days, Dennis had stabilized. He developed a plan of action to address the major threats to his recovery and agreed to participate in ongoing outpatient treatment and to move into a sober living arrangement. Treatment had capitalized on Dennis's strengths. He developed the treatment plan and agreed that he was now ready to move ahead with his plan. When asked to report on his level of comfort as scaled on his treatment plan, Dennis reported being extremely comfortable with his recovery plan; he felt ready to move to an intensive outpatient level of care.

### Analysis of Risk and Protective Factors (Dennis)

The recovery dimensions outlined by the American Society of Addiction Medicine (Hoffman, Halikas, Mee-Lee, & Weedman, 1991) represent a useful framework for analyzing this case. Such an approach requires the clinician to consider risk and protective factors in each area. Biomedical risks include family history and physical health factors. Relapse potential responses are closely tied to craving or cue reactivity, which are the physiological responses addicts experience when exposed to prior cues for using. The issue of cue reactivity is particularly important when working with persons addicted to cocaine because cues to resume use have been described as stronger than many other drugs (Chiauzzi, 1994). In this case, it would appear that overwork and compensating for becoming intoxicated served as cues for Dennis's resumption of cocaine use. Fueled partly by a need to compensate for the physical consequences of his intoxication, and in an effort to increase his energy level, Dennis quickly reverted to a destructive pattern of use.

Psychological or emotional behavioral risk factors include the role of expectations with regard to the perceived positive consequences of further drug use, a lack of effective coping skills, and the presence of psychopathology (Chiauzzi, 1991). Clearly, Dennis approached his first use of cocaine with positive expectations, which initially were rewarded with an increase in his productivity. In describing intrapersonal relapse risk factors, Cummings, Gordon, and Marlatt (1980) noted that both extreme negative and positive emotions might contribute to relapse. Both were operating in Dennis's case. Dennis had been tremendously successful in the workplace, with a growing business that had high profits. In fact, his initial use of alcohol occurred in response to receiving a recognition award. Chiauzzi (1994) noted that the assessment of relapse risk often overlooks the contribution of positive emotions. Just as in extreme negative experiences, extreme highs contribute to upsetting one's equilibrium, often a precipitating event in a crisis. At the same time, Dennis's younger daughter suffered from a potentially fatal illness. By the time Dennis sought help, the paranoia and isolation created by cocaine use and his shame at relapsing had exacerbated his crisis.

Persons in crisis and those in relapse share many characteristics (Chiauzzi, 1994; Degenhardt et al., 2011). These include the general loss of equilibrium brought on by extreme emotions, and the consequent compression of one's coping repertoire. At the time of initial consultation, Dennis's ability to contemplate a way out of his crisis was limited to hoping for his own death. However, his affect and mood swings represented an additional psychological risk factor. At presentation, Dennis was extremely depressed. Addressing these mood symptoms was essential to ensuring his ability to remain drug free. Brown et al. (1998) found higher levels of depressive symptoms associated with greater urge to use cocaine, alcohol, and other drugs in high-risk situations.

Social risk factors requiring inquiry included the stability of family relationships, the presence of negative life events, and a lack of supportive social contact (Chiauzzi, 1991). The recent binge by Dennis had led his wife to threaten him with separation. In addition, although he had been tremendously successful at work, his recent crisis had created substantial problems in that setting. The presence of employment and family problems accounts for a significant amount of variance in posttreatment adjustment (McClellan et al., 1994; Degenhardt et al., 2011). In choosing to taper off his attendance at self-help group meetings, Dennis had reduced his contact with the appropriate social support. Havassy, Hall, and Wasserman (1991) found that a lack of social support for a continuing goal of abstinence predicted subsequent relapse.

### Case Autopsy: Follow-Up (Dennis)

As planned, Dennis transitioned into a sober living arrangement. He successfully completed a 6-week intensive outpatient treatment consisting of 3 hours of education and group therapy four evenings per week. Dennis again became active in the fellowships of Alcoholics Anonymous (AA) and Cocaine Anonymous (CA). Dennis and his family did reunite; however, his daughter died shortly after his first-year anniversary of recovery. Dennis was able to cope with her death without using mood-altering substances. He reported that the support from his friends in the "program" was tremendous during the time of his loss.

Dennis did experience one relapse after 18 months of remaining clean. At the time, he reported drinking approximately 24 beers at a concert. He reported that being overconfident and eliminating the majority of 12-step support meetings from his schedule contributed to his relapse. Following this use, Dennis presented for one individual session, where he reviewed the plan he had developed to re-establish his recovery. In this session, Dennis worked on Stages 2 through 6 of Roberts's model without prompting from the therapist. Using the skills he had learned in previous treatments, Dennis examined the dimensions of the problem; he explored his feelings and emotions and discussed what he needed to "get back to his program of recovery." Dennis discussed several alternatives and specific plans to resolve issues with Donna should she not accept him back into the home. Upon leaving, he successfully implemented this plan. Because of this single self-directed intervention, Dennis was able to limit this relapse to a single-use episode. At this time, Dennis has been clean for more than 2 years. He was elected businessman of the year last year and reports that he is hopeful that he will not return to use.

## CASE STUDY 2: SUSAN

### Susan C., Opioid Dependent

Almost 6 years ago to the day, Susan C. had brought her brother-in-law to the center for treatment for his cocaine dependence. She was disgusted by his antics, including how he had given up all responsibilities and had placed his family at risk by taking illegal drugs. On this date, Susan C. was brought to treatment by the same brother-in-law, who is now 4 years clean and sober. The onetime schoolteacher sat in the assessment office, a mere shadow of herself.

Susan explained: "I was in four car wrecks in a little over 3 years. I have two compressed discs in my spine, which cause a great deal of pain. Initially my physician prescribed Darvocet and Percodan. These worked well for a while. But little by little the pain came back; it always comes back. It may have been the result of sleeping wrong or jerking while stepping down a step; there always seems to be something to aggravate the pain. For a while I was able to tolerate the pain. Now I can't seem to cope with it. My use of medication has steadily increased. Now I'm using oxycodone and Oxycotin along with Ultram, Tylenol 3, Percocet, and Darvocet to tolerate the pain.

"I've been seeing other doctors and getting prescriptions from them too. It all started out somewhat innocently when I was seeking a second opinion for the pain. I discovered that if I didn't tell them the visit was for a second opinion, they would prescribe the same or similar medications. The next thing I know I'm seeing five or six doctors and all are prescribing similar medications. I used to save them just in case I needed them... you know for vacations or whatever. As time progressed, I needed more and more pills.

Now I'm taking all that are prescribed. It's become a nightmare. I'm having trouble keeping straight in my head what prescription goes with what doctor and what pharmacy. I think my insurance company and the pharmacy are on to me.

"Yesterday, one pharmacist refused to fill my prescription without consulting my physician first. He wasn't going to give the prescription back. I raised so much hell he reluctantly gave it to me. I immediately went to another pharmacy in the same chain, and they did fill it. Now I'm scared. I wonder what happens to the prescriptions when they have been filled? Where do they go? Do they go back to the doctor? If they do, I'm in deep trouble. You see, I was so afraid that I wouldn't get the prescription filled that I changed the number from 20 to 50. I know it wasn't right, but I was desperate.

"My pain is real... and the medication I take comes from doctors. I know I need this medication. If I don't have it, the pain becomes too great to deal with. After all, it was the physicians who got me hooked on them. What I really need is a doctor who will give me something strong enough to deal with the pain I'm experiencing. It's not like I'm some sort of a street bum. I'm not some rumdum who is just crawling out from under a bridge. I have a genuine problem with pain! They can't send me to jail because I have a legitimate health problem... can they?"

---

Susan's was not an uncommon problem; one study found just fewer than 28% of a pain clinic's patients met three or more criteria for substance abuse (Chabal, Erjavec, Jacobson, Mariano, & Chaney, 1997; Degenhardt et al., 2011). Women often use more socially acceptable substances, such as prescription drugs, and often abuse them in medicinal ways (Nichols, 1985). This case will demonstrate the effectiveness of combining Roberts's crisis intervention model and the strengths perspective approach. In working with Susan, the establishment of psychological contact takes the form of genuine respect for her chronic pain issues, combined with acknowledgment of the need to develop new coping skills to address her pain (Saleebey, 1996; Sullivan & Rapp, 1991; S. D. Miller & Berg, 1995). Roberts's first stage in crisis intervention and the strengths perspective fit nicely together because they both work to maintain the dignity and integrity of the patient. Both approaches recognize the individual's innate ability to establish recovery and seek to build on previous effective coping skills (Roberts, 1990; Saleebey, 1992, 1996; Harris, Smock, & Tabor, 2011).

In this case, the therapist could assure Susan of the program's ability to address her pain issues. However, there was also the need to caution her that seeking several prescriptions from several different physicians was not legal and that there could be consequences associated with doing this. With that proviso, the therapist assured Susan that the action she was now taking was the single best step she could take to minimize any potential legal consequences.

When combining Roberts's model and the strengths perspective, the initial question was not "Do you believe or think that you might have a drug problem?" Instead, it became "You have been functioning up to now under some very difficult circumstances. What are you doing that has helped you to keep going despite the pain?" This approach moves the client toward an approach that focuses on today rather than on yesterday and all the pain of the past (Roberts, 1990; C. A. Rapp, 1992; Saleebey, 1996; Harris et al., 2011).

The initial interview should focus on the patient's strengths. For example, instead of asking "What brought you to treatment today," the question becomes "What is it that gave you the courage to ask for help today?" In the case of chronic pain, focusing on pain will only serve to keep the client focused on the perceived need to medicate his or her pain. A focus on what life could be like if the pain was minimized will eventually lead the client to seek alternative methods for addressing the pain.

Providing the client with an opportunity to examine both coping skills and environmental supports, when combined with the client's strengths, becomes a viable approach within Roberts's second and fourth stages of crisis intervention. The goal was to capitalize on the client's view of her problem as a medical issue rather than as an addiction, which eliminated resistance to entering the recovery process. The desired outcome was to assist the patient in minimizing her dependence on pain medication rather than to force the admission of addiction.

Helpers should assure clients who are entering detoxification from pain medications that they are expected to participate in activities that support pain management through methods other than medication. They should also be informed that medication is given only in response to withdrawal symptoms—for example, elevated pulse, temperature, and blood pressure.

In addition to the limits placed on the client in relation to the use of medication to address pain issues, the therapist asked Susan to develop her personal plan of alternative solutions, Stage 5 of Roberts's crisis intervention model. When possible, the client should be encouraged to collaborate with persons in her recovery environment whom she has identified as supportive (Mclaughlin, Irby, & Langman, 1994: Shorey, Stuart, Anderson, & Strong, 2013). Susan identified several persons as supportive; however, she had little insight regarding how these persons could help. In addition, Susan neglected to identify several important persons. To address this, the helper asked Susan to identify persons she may have omitted from her support person list and asked her to describe her rationale for omissions from the previous list. There were several false starts before completion of this assignment. Susan's list grew to include her mechanic, plumber, paperboy, and garbage collector; however, her physicians, employer, and recovering brother-in-law did not make several of the revised lists. Eventually, Susan resolved to add her physicians, pharmacists, and even her brother-in-law to the list. The list included one brief explanation for the omissions; it read, "OK, OK, I now understand how I am trying to hold on to my old ways!"

Once this task had been completed, Susan was asked to compose a letter to each person on her list, seeking their support for her efforts and requesting suggestions on how she might cope with pain by methods other than medication. Given the possible legal issues involved, the helper cautioned her to provide only vague information related to what prompted this call for assistance. Susan completed 15 letters and agreed to mail 3 per day. The goal was to amplify the patient's individual resilience by increasing awareness of informal networks of support and encouragement (Benard, 1994; Berg & Miller, 1992, Shorey et al., 2013).

The response was overwhelming. As each letter, card, bouquet of flowers, and telephone call arrived, Susan became less and less defensive. She began to acknowledge how her reliance on the medication as her solitary coping mechanism had led to isolation from the very persons who were the most willing to help her. In addition, Susan became increasingly aware of the sadness, frustration, anger, and fear she was experiencing. Exploration of these feelings, Roberts's Stage 3, led her to becoming the person she felt she was before the accidents and the onset of her problems (Roberts, 1990).

Using the suggestions provided to Susan by her strengths-based support group led to the development of her action plan. Susan incorporated each suggestion into (a) a daily plan for recovery, (b) a list of actions to be taken in high-risk situations, and (c) a medical management plan developed with the assistance of her primary physician and the physician who supervised her detoxification.

With this plan in place and demonstration of medical stability, Susan was discharged from the detoxification program 5 days after her initial presentation. She received a prescription for decreasing amounts of Klonopin to ensure successful completion of her detoxification on an outpatient basis and weekly follow-up individual appointments with her counselor on the detoxification unit.

### Analysis of Risk and Protective Factors (Susan)

In assessing Susan's case, it was important to recognize that physical dependence and tolerance were an expected component of her long-term opioid use for pain. Sees and Clark (1993) noted that determining the existence of dysfunctional behavior is the salient point in the diagnosis of addiction. However, as this case demonstrated, the need for continued pain medication can occur independently of the physical health problem. Ultimately, Susan discovered that much of her pain was unrelated to her long-standing injury. This was consistent with Robinson's (1985) suggestion that for some persons pain continues to exist after the physiological process has ameliorated because of the continued reinforcement provided by drug use.

Accessing Susan's social network represented a step toward engaging an important protective factor. Women with addiction problems commonly have fewer social supports than men (Kaufmann, Dore, & Nelson-Zlupko, 1995) and are often more likely to use in isolation. Kail and Litwak (1989) suggested engagement of relatives and friends contributed to reducing the likelihood of prescription medicine abuse. Other authors have empirically demonstrated the important role of social support in maintaining the benefits of treatment (Bell, Richard, & Feltz, 1996; Havassy et al., 1991).

Perhaps partly because of her brother-in-law's experience, Susan was ambivalent about characterizing her use of drugs as addictive. A strengths-based approach represented an effective mechanism for overcoming the initial denial that might have impeded engagement in substance abuse treatment (R. Rapp, Kelliher, Fisher, & Hall, 1994). The choice to eschew pressuring Susan to label herself as addicted also contributed to the therapist's ability to create a collaborative relationship. William Miller (1995) observed that self-labeling was not an important determinant of subsequent outcomes. Instead, the goal of the initial interview is to "create a salient dissonance or discrepancy between the person's current behavior and important personal goals" (W. Miller, 1995, p. 95).

### Case Autopsy: Follow-Up (Susan)

Following discharge, Susan maintained weekly appointments for a 1-month period. She then began biweekly sessions for a 2-month period and finally finished the remainder of the year with sessions once per month. As time progressed, Susan acknowledged that the symptoms of pain she had experienced were most likely related to withdrawal from the medication. She noted that she had not used mood-altering substances to address her pain, finding that the nonsteroidal anti-inflammatory medications work extremely well for her.

Following her first drug-free year, with a level of pain that was expected and seen to be reasonable, Susan returned to work. Three years after the crisis, Susan has completed a master's degree in education and is a principal in an inner-city high school. She is an extremely strong advocate of prevention programming to keep teens away from drugs. To this day, Susan reports she is not certain if she is an "addict"; however, she quickly acknowledges that her use of medication was the basis of her problems.

## CASE STUDY 3: SCOTT

### Scott S., Polysubstance Dependence

Scott presented at the treatment facility accompanied by his grandfather, who reported seeking substance-dependence treatment at this facility 20 years earlier and had remained abstinent from all mood-altering chemicals since that time. Scott related to the interviewer that he felt he was "at the end of his rope." His parents have disowned him after he took approximately $4,500 from their business and spent it on a week-long binge.

Scott reported using intravenous heroin, alcohol, and cocaine for the past 14 days. His recent binge began when the university he had been attending refused to admit him to classes. Scott returned to campus for the January term only to find he had been placed on academic suspension after not meeting the requirements of academic probation from the previous semester. Scott remained on campus with friends rather than returning home to his parents.

Scott's first experience with mood-altering substances was with LSD, which he first took at approximately age 12. He remembered being asked if "he wanted to take something that would make him giggle and laugh all night long." He began to smoke pot shortly after this use. Scott reported being an avid "head" throughout high school, having used cannabis daily since age 13. He began to use alcohol on a regular basis at age 14, drinking up to six beers per day in conjunction with an eighth of an ounce of cannabis per day.

Scott said he can best be described as a "garbage head," explaining, "That's a person who has taken about everything." Scott has experimented with sedative hypnotics, amphetamine, and inhalants. His favorites are LSD, cocaine, heroin, and alcohol. Scott had experienced more than 200 acid trips, using LSD and other hallucinogens. The majority of this use occurred between the ages of 14 and 17.

At age 16, Scott began to use powder cocaine. His initial use was limited to weekends; however, it progressed rapidly to near-daily use following graduation from high school. His peak tolerance was $300 per day of intravenous cocaine combined with up to a fifth of alcohol (whiskey). Scott felt his use was out of control, and he wanted to stop the cocaine use. Also during this time Scott was using crystal methamphetamine. He said, "Now that's a drug that will steal your soul." Scott stated this was the only time that he became fearful when he was using. He reported a period when he became extremely violent and out of control as a result of his crank use.

Scott said, "The high is so intense, it never seems to end. Once in a while you get a chance to catch your breath, but this doesn't last very long." Scott noted it was during this time that he became involved in stealing and "boosting" in order to support his habit. He indicated that when he was using this drug, he just did not care: "The stuff makes you feel invincible. There are a lot of violent and crazy people out there, and the worst are doing crank!"

A friend introduced Scott to heroin when Scott was following the band Phish. His initial use was intranasal, but he quickly progressed to IV use. Scott noted that his use has progressed to three $65 bags per day. His liver enzyme tests were all elevated to approximately 10 times normal, indicating possible hepatitis. Scott noted that his alcohol consumption had decreased to two 40-ounce beers daily.

He was currently facing legal consequences for writing "bad checks" and shoplifting. Scott did not expect to be readmitted to the university, which he reported is particularly frustrating to his father, since both he and Scott's grandfather graduated from the school. Scott stated he is becoming "dope sick" and really doesn't care about the stupid college. He has tried to stop on his own and has failed each time, as the "jones" (withdrawal) becomes more intense.

Scott noted that while driving to the hospital he had seen at least three places where he could cop. He felt that if he was not admitted quickly, he would likely leave and find some dope. He reported that he is not craving, but needs to have something to keep the sickness away or he will find and use heroin. Scott is angry and frustrated that his grandfather has to pay for his admission; however, he acquiesced following his grandfather's insistence that he get help today or walk away from all of the family. The grandfather also reminded Scott that he may well be Scott's last advocate. Scott acknowledged that he has tried everything he knows to establish recovery and has failed. Feeling that he had no other options, Scott agreed to be admitted to the treatment program.

---

Scott's pattern of use was not atypical of young adults. Use of heroin by American teenagers has increased dramatically in recent years. The pattern of Scott's substance use presented a number of risk factors. Polydependence on alcohol and cocaine has been linked to more acute dependence, an increase in the likelihood of leaving treatment early, and poorer long-term outcomes (Brady, Sonne, Randall, Adinoff, & Malcolm, 1995; Troncale, 2004). Scott's family history of alcoholism and his early age of first use also placed him in a high-risk group for greater psychopathology, increased recidivism, and continued negative consequences (Barbor, Korner, Wilbur, & Good, 1987; Penick et al., 1987; Troncale, 2004).

Scott was not a person who trusted very easily. Therefore, the worker emphasized the process of gaining psychological contact with Scott during assessment. When the worker asked Scott to decide if his grandfather would be involved in the assessment process, Scott chose to "do this on his own." The assessing clinician sought to establish a positive relationship, beginning by examining Scott's resilience factors rather than his problems; resilience factors include skills, abilities, knowledge, and insight into what needs to occur to develop a plan for mitigating the crisis (Roberts, 1990). In doing so, the assessor established a relationship with Scott, which led him to feeling a part of the recovery process rather than having a process thrust upon him. Scott requested medication to help with the physical withdrawal he had experienced in the past, but he did not want to take anything that might continue his dependence. He reported a previous methadone detoxification and stated he felt one drug was a substitute for another. Scott asked if any other form of drug detoxification was available that could minimize the physical symptoms without maintaining his dependence. He was assured that detoxification could be accomplished with a combination of clonidine used as a patch and orally; Buprenex to minimize cravings and withdrawal symptoms; Bentyl to minimize cramping associated with opioid withdrawal; Motrin to address aches and pains; and Imodium to address diarrhea (Ginther, 1999).

While not pretending to understand the detoxification process, Scott agreed that it seemed to him that his request would be granted, and he entered detoxification with the stipulation that if he felt like a zombie he would leave. Program staff respected and agreed with this requirement.

In individual meetings with Scott, his social worker sought to further define and examine the parameters of the problem (Roberts, 1990) by eliciting Scott's definition of it. The goal in this case was to enhance Scott's awareness of the tensions and conflicts that were present in his life by providing acceptance and empathy and by mirroring nonverbal communication in an environment free from confrontation (Greene et al., 1996). When defining the problem, it is important to allow the patient to explore her or his feelings and emotions surrounding the issues, which is Roberts's Stage 3 (Roberts, 1990).

In this case, Scott quickly identified feeling oppressed by his parents, believing that they were trying to force him into a role that he did not want. He spoke of feeling like an abused child:

> Not in the classic sense of abuse. It's like they never listen to my wants and needs, they believe if they give me everything they think I should have, then I will be happy. In all honesty, they could have kept all of the shit they gave me and just listened for a few minutes. That would have really made me happy. Instead they keep throwing things at me, the right clothes, the right club memberships, the right college, that make me what they think I should be instead of hearing what I really want to be!

Scott shared that as he progressed through school toward a business degree, he felt as though he was "selling out" and was being forced to become everything that he hated. He reported feeling conflict between being relieved that he did not have to continue in his classes and the fear of telling his father about his expulsion from school.

Roberts's fourth stage of crisis intervention, exploring past coping attempts (Roberts, 1990), addresses the fine line between solution-focused treatment and sustaining motivation without providing the client with justification for his or her illness. This stage merges well with solution-focused theory because it provides the opportunity to apply the exception question (Koslowski & Ferrence, 1990; Greene et al., 1996). In this case, the worker asked Scott to examine the right and wrong ways he has treated his disease in the past. This is an inventory of what worked for Scott and what did not when he had attempted to stay sober in the past. Scott was encouraged to develop his list of behaviors that supported his previous attempts at abstinence.

By this point, Scott had progressed into the second day of his detoxification and was quite agitated. He was frustrated and was resistant to examination of strengths or weaknesses. This provided an opportunity to apply scaling questions with the exception questions. The worker used the scaling question to provide Scott with a mechanism to mark his progress. This question asked the client to rank the problem he was experiencing on a scale of 1 to 10, with 10 being the most desirable state and 1 being the least desirable outcome (De Jong & Miller, 1995; S. D. Miller & Berg, 1995).

At times it is possible to use the scaling question in combination with the exception question or the miracle question (DeShazer, 1988; De Jong & Miller, 1995; Greene et al., 1996). For example, when meeting in medical rounds, the physician asked Scott:

Physician: On a scale of 1 to 10 [as described above,] how do you feel today?

Scott: I feel like shit.... I'm sick, my head is pounding, my stomach is cramped, my nose is running, I'm either hot or cold and sweating all the time. It could be a little worse, so I'll say I'm about a 3 today.

Physician: When is the last time you felt this lousy and didn't use?

Scott: [Silence] Never!

Physician: You must be doing detox exactly right. If you have never made it beyond this point without using before, you are definitely doing something right! Your addiction is real angry with you, and it is attempting to get you to self-medicate. Just keep doing what you are doing, and we will get you through the worst of the detoxification.

This supportive interaction provided Scott with an opportunity to notice progress that otherwise would have been overlooked. He was also encouraged to learn that, despite feeling poorly, he was doing his detoxification exactly right. Each subsequent interaction with the physician began with the scaling question and follow-up supportive feedback. Roberts's Stage 5, exploring alternatives and specific solutions, provided a format for the miracle question. The miracle question directed Scott to set new and previously unimagined goals for his recovery (DeShazer, 1988). For example, his social worker asked Scott: "Suppose after this meeting you fell asleep, and while you were sleeping a miracle happened and your problems were suddenly resolved. Because you were asleep, you are not aware that the miracle has happened. What will be the signs that tell you the miracle has occurred?"

From this question, Scott identified three clear indicators. First, "I wouldn't be dope sick. Second, I really wouldn't give a damn what my parents said or did. And, third, I would be living my life clean, accomplishing the goals I really wanted." Follow-up questioning attempted to develop a clearer understanding of coping mechanisms and alternative behaviors Scott might apply. Scott indicated that if his parents permitted him to seek education in an area of interest, he would not likely be failing school. If he were not failing and was studying what he wanted, he would be making progress toward his life dream of becoming a marine biologist. From this discussion Scott developed the following goals:

1. Doing whatever he needs to do to finish his detox
2. Telling his parents that he was leaving the school he was attending
3. Making independent living arrangements
4. Enrolling in a college other than where he had been and completing his basic education requirements
5. Seeking acceptance into the University of Florida Marine Biology Program

Using the miracle question to define Scott's goals provided the format for the development and implementation of recovery-specific goals. Shortly after discussing this with his social worker, Scott became an active member in groups. He seemed to have a greater interest in the recovery process. Scott selected a sponsor in the 12-step fellowship of Narcotics Anonymous (NA). He began seeking permission to attend additional NA meetings and to spend time with his sponsor. Scott wrote a letter to his parents explaining his removal from the university. This generated an angry yet predictable response from his father; nevertheless, Scott used his growing sober support system to work his way through this problem. Because of these interactions, over a 4-day period Scott requested placement with a long-term halfway house facility where he could practice independent living skills and from where he could apply to the university.

Scott was now involved in Stage 6 of Roberts's model, the restoration of cognitive functioning. Scott had actively examined the events that had contributed to the crisis. He was in the process of developing a clear understanding of the process of addiction and its progression over time. Scott began to verbalize awareness of the overgeneralizations, "shoulds," projections, catastrophizing, and self-defeating behaviors that led to his maladaptive dependence on mood-altering substances.

Finally, Scott was replacing his irrational beliefs with new recovery-supported cognitions, using his sponsor and support group to think through his thoughts before turning them into action. Scott reported using the sober support group to increase his awareness of the behaviors that will be required to support his recovery and to facilitate the development of a self-directed program of recovery.

Following a 6-day detoxification and medical stabilization, Scott made the transition to a 3- to 6-month halfway house program. He was developing and implementing his plan for recovery. Scott was "cautiously optimistic" when he left the detoxification center, saying, "This is the first time I've taken the risk to do something out of the shadow of my family. It feels great!"

### Analysis of Risk and Protective Factors (Scott)

Among the factors that contributed to Scott's current crisis were the fear of his parents' reaction to his school failure and his general conflict with them over his educational goals. To some extent, Scott's crisis was exacerbated by his need to be emancipated from his parents. Paradoxically, his drug and alcohol addiction only further delayed development, including the task of developing his own agenda for his future. Bentler (1992) empirically demonstrated that drug and alcohol use by young people impedes many of their important developmental tasks (Wang et al., 2012).

The therapist's attention to Scott's cognitive function and negative thought patterns was an important step in helping Scott on the road to recovery. Carroll, Rounsaville, and Gawin (1991) demonstrated that cognitive treatment was highly effective with cocaine-dependent persons and was particularly beneficial among the more severe cases. Benefits gained from cognitive treatment are maintained over a long time (O'Malley et al., 1994).

Scott's willingness to embrace 12-step groups was a very positive step toward resolving his crisis. The literature is replete with the benefits of these approaches. Weiss et al. (1996) reported a positive association between self-help participation and short-term outcomes among cocaine-dependent patients. Other authors have published similar findings on the general efficacy of 12-step groups when working with alcohol and other drug-dependent clients (Stevens-Smith & Smith, 1998; Johnsen & Herringer, 1993). In fact, Humpreys and Moos (1996) found no significant differences among health outcomes at 1 or 3 years for persons who participated in AA groups only versus those who received outpatient treatment. The benefits of participation in self-help groups seem to have a long-term effect. One study found that ongoing participation in self-help groups was associated with better outcomes even after 3 years (Longabaugh, Wirtz, Zweben, & Stout, 1998; Laudet, 2007).

Participation in self-help groups has also been associated with improvements in other life areas. In addition to finding that participation predicted better posttreatment substance use outcomes, Morgenstern, Labouvie, McCrady, Kahler, and Frey (1997) determined that 12-step participation was positively associated with increased self-efficacy, motivation to change, and improved coping ability.

Involvement in self-help groups has the potential to influence the social domain as well. Persons who participated in 12-step groups were found to have more close friends, as well as fewer friends who were using alcohol and other drugs (Humphreys & Noke, 1997). Persons participating in an after-care program had significant reductions in job absenteeism, inpatient hospitalizations, and arrest rates (N. Miller, Ninonuevo, Klamen, Hoffmann, & Smith, 1997).

### Case Autopsy: Follow-Up (Scott)

Scott was discharged from the detoxification level of care and moved into the partial hospitalization program for 10 additional days. During this time, he worked to solidify his self-diagnosis while building his sober support network. Scott developed concrete plans to address high-risk situations, including arranging to enter a sober house near the university. Scott left the treatment center after a total of 16 days in the hospital. He continued his treatment in the intensive outpatient program for 6 weeks, after which he received aftercare for 3 additional months.

Scott's awareness of the provoking nature of his relationship with his family led to the development of what he called his "family of choice" within the recovery community. He was extremely proud of his involvement in the local recovery fellowships, which provided the opportunity to realize and use his assets and abilities. The input he provided to his peer group complemented his awareness of the need for peer input into his recovery. Scott notes, "My thinking for myself stinks, but my ability to give others feedback is great. I can see exactly what they need. Just as they can see exactly what I need. As a collective, we are doing great things in recovery." Working within the recovery community provided for exponential growth for Scott's recovery from addiction and in his development of mature problem-solving strategies.

Scott applied for, and was accepted into, a marine biology program. He obtained grants and student loans to facilitate his transition. Approximately 6 months after entering detoxification, Scott had realized his goal of studying marine biology. He had also become active in the student union, providing guidance to students who are experiencing problems with substance abuse and dependence. Scott has now been sober for nearly 3 years. Every year Scott visits the treatment center, and last year he and his grandfather attended the 24th anniversary of the treatment center. He continues to communicate with his counselor and peers in recovery by telephone and e-mail.

## THE ROLE OF EVIDENCE-BASED PRACTICE
## IN SUBSTANCE DEPENDENCE TREATMENT

In the early 1990s, a worldwide movement began promoting the adoption of evidence-based practice in medicine. This movement emphasized evaluation and utilization of research in decision making as applied to the direct care arenas. The origins of evidence-based practice can be traced to the early 1900s with the work of Mary Richmond and Richard Cabot and may be defined as "the conscientious, explicit and judicious use of current best evidence in making decisions about the care of individual patients" (Roberts & Yeager, 2004, pp. 6, 11).

Evidence-based addiction medicine (EBAM) involves combining clinical expertise with the best available evidence collected from a variety of external sources. The practitioner applying evidence-based approaches seeks to answer questions frequently asked by managed care entities addressing issues of (a) the origin of the treatment approach, (b) the validity of the treatment approach, and (c) the nature of the proposed treatment approach and how the clinician is applying best practice principles. The clinician answers critical questions posed by the managed care entity and provides the highest-quality care as applied to the individual seeking substance dependence treatment.

Challenges arise for practitioners when there is an attempt to weigh the relative effectiveness of the research presented in a manner that tailors the research to an individual treatment need. Unfortunately, scientific research, by nature, does not prove anything. Nor will all scientific research apply to each individual treated. However, there is an increasing desire to provide the highest quality of care, which requires the application of valid research and clinical evidence for decision support (Roberts & Yeager, 2004).

Frequently, medical research is biased, written in the form of persuasive communication with the goal of swaying the reader to accept the thinking, research, and findings presented. At the very least, treatment providers are responsible for reviewing and verifying research with a critical eye and need to be skillful in ranking the order of research by the strength of the evidence provided.

In general, the decision-making using evidence-based methods is achieved in a series of steps (Gibbs & Gambrill, 2002; Hayward, Wilson, Tunis, & Bass, 1995). The first step is to evaluate the problem to be addressed and formulate answerable questions: What is the best way of assisting an individual with these characteristics who suffers from dependence? Which group treatment method is most effective in reducing recidivism of those addicted to opiates?

The next step is to gather and critically evaluate the evidence available. Evidence is generally ranked hierarchically according to its scientific strength. It is understood that various types of intervention will have been

Table 18.2   Levels of Evidence

| |
|---|
| Level 1   Meta-analysis or replicated randomized controlled treatment (RCT) that includes a placebo condition/control trial or from well-designed cohort or case control analytic study, preferably from more than one center or research group or national consensus panel recommendations based on controlled, randomized studies. |
| Level 2   At least one RCT with placebo or active comparison condition, evidence obtained from multiple time series with or without intervention, or national consensus panel recommendations based on uncontrolled studies with positive outcomes or based on studies showing dramatic effects of an intervention. |
| Level 3   Uncontrolled trial with 10 or more subjects, opinions of respected authorities, based on clinical experiences, descriptive studies, or reports of expert consensus. |
| Level 4   Anecdotal case reports and case studies. |

evaluated more frequently and rigorously by virtue of the length of time they have been used and the settings in which they are used. Thus, for newer treatments, only Level 4 evidence may be available (Table 18.2). In such cases, practitioners should use the method with caution, continue to search for evidence of efficacy, and be prepared to evaluate the efficacy of the method in their own practice. The final steps involve applying the results of the appraisal to practice or policy and then continuously monitoring the outcome (Roberts & Yeager, 2004).

The bottom line is demonstrating an impact on clinical outcome, rating the relative effectiveness or ineffectiveness of a particular approach to treatment, and then asking questions such as, How does this approach compare to other, more traditional approaches to treatment? How many patients will achieve better outcomes with this approach?

Critical thinking provides the potential for critical analysis of the evidence and its impact on the individual's treatment. It is important to note that this is not an exact science. Currently, it is an unfortunate truth that there are few randomized controlled studies in the area of addiction treatment. Additionally, there is a need for a greater number of studies supporting evidence-based approaches in addiction treatment. There is a need for the development of stronger levels of evidence, higher-quality research, and research studies reflective of the principles of evidence-based practice and practice-based research.

Those working in the addictions field can support this through application of evidence-based practice and subscribing to evidence-based approaches. Direct care providers can support those entities providing research through adoption of clinical practice guidelines based on high-quality research and by challenging approaches presented in the popular press that lack an evidence-based approach.

Finally, there are always questions pertaining to the best approach for any given patient on any given day. However, as substance dependence treatment grows in sophistication and professionalism, the application of an evidence-based approach will function as a strong foundation for the development of the next generation of research in the treatment of addiction. In doing so, practitioners will be facilitating a transition toward a rational, sensible, clinically complex approach to care of the individual and improving the quality of care provided, as well as providing a clinically complex approach to care based on increasingly relevant clinical evidence.

## CONCLUSION

The challenge facing social workers in substance-dependence treatment is to balance cost against quality. A completely new dimension of substance-dependence treatment is emerging. This dimension is crisis intervention and brief treatment, designed to stabilize patients as quickly and effectively as possible (Edmunds et al., 1997; Azzone, Frank, Normand, & Burnam, 2011).

Roberts's crisis intervention model, combined with brief solution-focused therapy and a strengths perspective, provides extremely flexible, practical approaches to intervention with substance-dependent individuals in crisis. The established routes of Roberts's model provide clear guidelines for intervention and progression through detoxification and into a meaningful recovery process. This approach facilitates the development of a self-directed plan of recovery that capitalizes on the individual's strengths rather than taking the approach of more familiar problem-focused models utilized by traditional substance-dependence programs (Day, 1998).

As a result of using the crisis intervention/solution-focused approach, patients experienced rapid normalization and return to their recovery environment. Crisis response in this format sought to place substance-dependent individuals in their environment as soon as they are medically stable. The goal was to facilitate greater utilization of the system of community support and relationships that are present in day-to-day life. Keeping the substance-dependent individual in contact with his or her community while participating in outpatient programming provided greater opportunity to address relapse traps and triggers as they occurred.

Links between the crisis and the patient's life history were identified and examined in a manner that maintained the patient's historical and existential continuity. The focus on community supports provided patients the opportunity to reframe what once was perceived as a using environment to an environment where sober support was found. The end result is a treatment process that allows patients to pass through the crisis event while maintaining their dignity, sense of strength, pride, trust, spirituality, and personal identity.

Substance-dependence treatment has traditionally placed a great deal of emphasis on outcome. Meaningful outcome studies have been undertaken to evaluate the effectiveness of treatment modalities for more than 25 years. Employing crisis intervention in combination with solution-focused therapy outcomes will need to be examined for its efficacy. It will be important to identify the outcomes that this type of treatment can be expected to bring about, in both short- and long-term goals (e.g., detoxification and stabilization versus maintenance of established recovery goals over extended periods of time). Examination of outcomes within the solution-focused crisis intervention approach will be important for several reasons.

First, emphasis on customer-driven quality improvement may provide the opportunity to respond to what consumers and their families desire in the treatment of substance dependence. Substance dependence, by nature, is disempowering. Many of the systems established for the treatment of substance dependence have resulted in patients experiencing further disempowerment (Day, 1998). It will be important to fully understand how a solution-focused crisis intervention approach impacts outcome.

Second, this model is consistent with policy development and behavioral health care management systems that have been established over the past decade. This model is designed to incorporate individualized treatment planning, utilization of community support, capitalization on consumer strengths, and consumer choice. This model can provide a framework to examine the effectiveness of brief intervention within the recovery environment.

Finally, the model has the potential to accomplish the goals not only of the consumer but also of the payers and system administrators within the public and private sectors. That goal is to reduce the risk and exposure to unplanned increases in costs. Application of the crisis intervention solution-focused approach at this time appears to meet this challenge by (a) reducing hospital days, (b) reducing use of emergency services, (c) increasing utilization of community support, and (d) reducing relapse potential.

This chapter is not intended to present Roberts's seven-stage model as a replacement for traditional approaches to substance-dependence treatment. The intention is to provide an alternative framework that can be applied within the substance-dependence treatment setting. We hope that this approach will be considered, applied, refined, and researched as a viable alternative when social workers are faced with increasingly complex cases combined with reduced resources.

REFERENCES

American Psychiatric Association. (1994). *Diagnostic and statistical* *manual of mental disorders* (4th ed.). Washington, DC: Author.

American Psychiatric Association. (2013). *Diagnostic and statistical manual of mental disorders* (5th ed.). Washington, DC: Author.

Azzone, V., Frank, R. G., Normand, S. L., & Burnam, M. A. (2011). Effect of insurance parity on substance abuse treatment. *Psychiatric Services, 62*, 129–124.

Balsheim, K., Oxman, M., Van Rooyen, G., & Girod, D. (1992). Syphilis, sex and crack cocaine: Images of risk and mortality. *Social Science and Medicine, 31*, 147–160.

Barbor, T. F., Korner, P., Wilbur, P., & Good, F. (1987). Screening and early intervention strategies for harmful drinkers: Initial lessons learned from the Amethyst Project. *Australian Drug and Alcohol Review, 6*, 325–339.

Beinecke, R., Callahan, J., Shepard, D., Cavanaugh, D., & Larson, M. (1997). The Massachusetts Mental Health/Substance Abuse Managed Care Program: The provider's view. *Administration and Policy in Mental Health, 23*, 379–391.

Bell, D., Richard, A., & Feltz, L. (1996). Mediators of drug treatment outcomes. *Addictive Behaviors, 21*, 597–613.

Bentler, P. (1992). Etiologies and consequences of adolescent drug use: Implications for prevention. *Journal of Addictive Diseases, 11*(3), 47–61.

Berg, I. K. (1994). *Family-based services: A solution-focused approach*. New York: Norton.

Berg, I. K., & Jaya, A. (1993). Different and same: Family therapy with Asian-American families. *Journal of Marital and Family Therapy, 19*, 31–38.

Berg, I. K., & Miller, S. D. (1992). *Working with the problem drinker: A solution-focused approach*. New York: Norton.

Brady, K., Sonne, E., Randall, C., Adinoff, B., & Malcolm, R. (1995). Features of cocaine dependence with concurrent alcohol abuse. *Drug and Alcohol Dependence, 39*, 69–71.

Brown, R., Monti, P., Myers, M., Martin, R., Rivinus, T., Dubreuil, M., & Rohsenow, D. (1998). Depression among cocaine abusers in treatment: Relation to cocaine and alcohol use and treatment outcome. *American Journal of Psychiatry, 155*, 220–225.

Carroll, K., Rounsaville, B., & Gawin, F. (1991). A comparative trial of psychotherapies for ambulatory cocaine abusers: Relapse prevention and interpersonal psychotherapy. *American Journal of Drug and Alcohol Abuse, 17*, 229–247.

Chabal C., Erjavec, M., Jacobson, L., Mariano, A., & Chaney, E. (1997). Prescription opiate abuse in chronic pain patients: Clinical criteria, incidence, and predictors. *Clinical Journal of Pain, 13*, 150–155.

Chiauzzi, E. (1991). *Preventing relapse in the addictions: A biopsychosocial approach*. New York: Pergamon Press.

Chiauzzi, E. (1994). Turning points: Relapse prevention as crisis intervention. *Crisis Intervention, 1*, 141–154.

Congressional Budget Office. (2013). *Effects of the Affordable Care Act on health insurance coverage—February 2013 baseline*. Retrieved from https://www.cbo.gov/publication/43900

Cummings, G., Gordon, J., & Marlatt, G. (1980). Relapse: Prevention and prediction. In W. Miller (Ed.), *Addictive behaviors: Treatment of alcoholism, drug abuse, smoking, and obesity* (pp. 291–321).

Oxford: Pergamon Press.

Dattilio, F., & Freeman, A. (1994). *Cognitive-behavioral strategies in crisis intervention.* New York: Guilford Press.

Day, S. L. (1998). Toward consumer focused outcome and performance measurement. In K. M. Coughlin, A. Moore, B. Cooper, & D. Beck (Eds.) *Behavioral outcomes and guidelines sourcebook 1998: A practical guide to measuring, managing and standardizing mental health and substance abuse treatment* (pp. 179–185). New York: Fulkner and Gray.

Degenhardt, L., Bucello, C., Mathers, B., Briegleb, C., Ali, H., Hickman, M., & McLaren, J. (2011). Mortality among regular or dependent users of heroin and other opioids: A systematic review and meta-analysis of cohort studies. *Addiction, 106,* 32–51.

DeJong, P., & Miller, S. D. (1995). How to interview for client strengths. *Social Work, 40,* 729–736.

DeShazer, S. (1988). *Clues: Investigating solutions in brief therapy.* New York: Norton.

Edmunds, M., Frank, R., Hogan, M., McCarty, D., Robinson-Beale, R., & Weisner, C. (1997). Managing managed care: Quality improvement in behavioral health. In K. M. Coughlin, A. Moore, B. Cooper, & D. Beck (Eds.), *Behavioral outcomes and guidelines sourcebook 1998: A practical guide to measuring, managing and standardizing mental health and substance abuse treatment* (pp. 134–143). New York: Fulkner and Gray.

Embedded Crisis Workers help to decompress ED, connect mental health and addiction medicine patients with needed resources. (2014). *ED Management: The Monthly Update on Emergency Department Management, 26*(2), 13–7.

Ewing, C. P. (1990). Crisis intervention as brief psychotherapy. In R. A. Wells & V. J. Giannetti (Eds.), *Handbook of brief psychotherapies* (pp. 277–294). New York: Plenum.

Fortune, A. E. (1985). The task-centered model. In A. E. Fortune (Ed.), *Task-centered practice with families and groups* (pp. 1–30). New York: Springer.

Garfield, R. L., Lave, J. R., & Donahue, J. M. (2010). Health reform and the scope of benefits for mental health and substance use disorder services. *Psychiatric Services, 61,* 1081–1086.

Ginther, C. (1999, April). Schuckit addresses state-of-the-art addiction treatments. Special report: Addictive disorders. *Psychiatric Times,* 55–57.

Greene, G. J., Lee, Mo-Yee, & Trask, R. In addition, Rheinscheld, J. (1996). Client strengths and crisis intervention: A solution-focused approach. *Crisis Intervention, 3,* 43–63.

Harris, K., Smock, S., & Tabor, W. M. K. (2011). Relapse resilience: A process model of addiction and recovery. *Journal of Family Psychotherapy, 22,* 265–274.

Havassy, B., Hall, S., & Wasserman, D. (1991). Social support and relapse: Commonalties among alcoholics, opiate users, and cigarette smokers. *Addictive Behaviors, 16,* 235–246.

Hoffman, N., Halikas, J., Mee-Lee, D., & Weedman, R. (1991). *Patient placement criteria for the treatment of psychoactive substance use disorders.* Chevy Chase, MD: American Society of Addiction Medicine.

Hser, D., Chou, Yihling, Hoffman, Chih-Ping, & Anglin, V. (1999). Cocaine use and high-risk behavior among STD clinic patients. *Sexually Transmitted Diseases*, 26, 82–86.

Humphreys, K., & Noke, J. (1997). The influence of post-treatment mutual help group participation on the friendship networks of substance abuse patients. *American Journal of Community Psychology*, 25, 1–16.

Kail, B., & Litwak, E. (1989). Family, friends and neighbors: The role of primary groups in preventing the misuse of drugs. *Journal of Drug Issues*, 19, 261–281.

Kaufmann, E., Dore, M., & Nelson-Zlupko, L. (1995). The role of women's therapy groups in the treatment of chemical dependence. *American Journal of Orthopsychiatry*, 65, 355–363.

Koslowski, L. T., & Ferrence, R. G. (1990). Statistical control in research on alcohol and tobacco: An example from research on alcohol and mortality. *British Journal of Addiction*, 85, 271–278.

Koslowski, L. T., Henningfield, R. M., Keenan, R. M., Lei, H., Leigh, G., Jelinek, L. C., ... Haertzen, C. A. (1993). Patterns of alcohol, cigarette, and caffeine and other drug use in two drug abusing populations. *Journal of Substance Abuse Treatment*, 10, 171–170.

Laudet, A., Stanick, V., & Sands, B. (2007). An exploration of the effect of on-site 12-step meetings on post-treatment outcomes among polysubstance-dependent outpatient clients. *Evaluation Review*, 31, 613–646.

Levy, R. L., & Shelton, J. L. (1990). Tasks in brief therapy. In R.

A. Wells & V. J. Giannetti (Eds.), *Handbook of the brief therapies* (pp. 145–163). New York: Plenum.

Longabaugh, R., Wirtz, P., Zweben, A., & Stout, R. (1998). Network support for drinking, Alcoholics Anonymous and long-term matching effects. *Addiction*, 93, 1313–1333.

McClellan, A., Alterman, A., Metzger, D., Grisson, G., Woody, G., Luborsky, L., & O'Brien, C. (1994). Similarity of outcome predictors across opiate, cocaine, and alcohol treatment: Role of treatment services. *Journal of Consulting and Clinical Psychology*, 62, 1141–1158.

Miller, N., Ninonuevo, F., Klamen, D., Hoffmann, N., & Smith, D. (1997). Integration of treatment and post-treatment variables in predicting results of abstinence-based outpatient treatment after one year. *Journal of Psychoactive Drugs*, 29, 239–248.

Miller, S. D., & Berg, I. K. (1995). *The miracle method: A radically new approach to problem drinking.* New York: Norton.

Miller, W. (1995). Increasing motivation for change. In R. Hester & W. Miller (Eds.), *Handbook of alcoholism treatment approaches: Effective alternatives* (2nd ed., pp. 89–104). Boston: Allyn and Bacon.

Morgenstern, J., Labouvie, E., McCrady, B., Kahler, C., & Frey, R. (1997). Affiliation with Alcoholics Anonymous after treatment: A study of its therapeutic effects and mechanisms of action. *Journal of Consulting and Clinical Psychology*, 65, 768–777.

Newman, B. M., & Newman P. R. (1995). *Development through life: A psychological approach* (6th ed.). Pacific Grove, CA: Brooks/

Cole.

Nichols, M. (1985). Theoretical concerns in the clinical treatment of substance-abusing women: A feminist analysis. *Alcoholism Treatment Quarterly, 2,* 79–90.

Norman, E., Turner, S., & Zunz, S. (1994). *Substance abuse prevention: A review of the literature.* New York: State Office of Alcohol and Substances Abuse Services.

O'Hanlon, W. H., & Weiner-Davis, M. (1989). *In search of solutions: A new direction in psychotherapy.* New York: Norton.

O'Malley, S., Jaffe, A., Chang, G., Rode, S., Shottenfeld, R., Meyer, R., & Rounsaville, B. (1994). Six-month follow-up of naltrexone and coping skills therapy for alcohol dependence. *Archives of General Psychiatry, 53,* 217–224.

Parad, H. J., & Parad, L. G. (1990). Crisis intervention: An introductory overview. In J. J. Parad & L. G. Parad (Eds.), *Crisis intervention book 2: The practitioner's source-book for brief therapy* (pp. 3–68). Milwaukee, WI: Family Service America.

Penick, E., Powell, B., Bingham, S., Liskow, V., Miller, M., & Read, M. (1987). A comparative study of familial alcoholism. *Journal of Studies on Alcoholism, 48,* 136–146.

Pillari, V. (1998). *Human behavior in the social environment.* Pacific Grove, CA: Brooks/Cole.

Rapp, C. A. (1992). The strengths perspective of case management with persons suffering from severe mental illness. In D. Saleebey (Ed.), *The strengths perspective in social work practice* (pp. 45–48). New York: Longman.

Rapp, R., Kelliher, C., Fisher, J., & Hall, F. (1994). Strengths-based case management: A role in addressing denial in substance abuse treatment. *Journal of Case Management, 3,* 139–144.

Roberts, A., R. (2000). An overview of crisis theory and crisis intervention. In A. R. Roberts (Ed.), *Crisis intervention handbook: assessment, treatment, and research,* 2nd Edition. New York: Oxford University Press.

Roberts, A. R. (1990). Overview of crisis theory and crisis intervention. In A. R. Roberts (Ed.), *Crisis intervention handbook: Assessment, treatment, and research* (pp. 3–16). Belmont, CA: Wadsworth.

Roberts, A. R. & Yeager, K. R. (Eds.) (2004). *Evidence Based Practice Manual: research and outcome measures in health and human services.* New York: The Oxford University Press.

Roberts, A. R., & Yeager, K. (2009). *Pocket guide to crisis intervention.* Oxford: Oxford University Press.

Roberts, A. R. (1996). Battered women who kill: A comparative study of incarcerated participants with a community sample of battered women. *Journal of Family Violence, 5,* 291–304.

Roberts, A. R., & Dziegielewski, S. F. (1995). Foundation skills and applications of crisis intervention and cognitive therapy. In A. R. Roberts (Ed.), *Crisis intervention and time-limited treatment* (pp. 3–27). Thousand Oaks, CA: Sage.

Robinson, J. (1985). Prescribing practices for pain in drug dependence: A lesson in ignorance. *Advances in Alcohol and Substance Abuse, 5,* 135–162.

Saleebey, D. (1992). Introduction: Power in the people. In D. Saleebey (Ed.), *The strengths perspective in social work practice* (pp. 3–17). New York: Longman.

Saleebey, D. (1996). The strengths perspective in social work practice: Extensions and cautions. *Social Work, 41,* 296–305.

Shorey, R. C., Stuart, G. L., Anderson, S., & Strong, D. R. (2013). Changes in early maladaptive schemas after residential treatment for substance use. *Journal of Clinical Psychology, 69,* 912–922.

Sees, K., & Clark, H. (1993). Opioid use in the treatment of chronic pain: Assessment of addiction. *Journal of Pain and Symptom Management, 8,* 257–264.

Stevens-Smith, P., & Smith, R. L. (1998). *Substance abuse counseling: Theory and practice.* Upper Saddle River, NJ: Merrill.

Substance Abuse and Mental Health Services Administration. (2002). *Results from the 2001 National Household Survey on Drug Abuse: Volume 1. Summary of national findings* (DHHS Publication No. SMA 02-3758, NHSDA Series: H-17). Rockville, MD: Author.

Substance Abuse and Mental Health Services Administration (2013). *Results from the 2012 National Survey on Drug Use and Health: Summary of national findings,* NSDUH Series H-46 (HHS Publication No. SMA 13-4795). Rockville, MD: Author.

Sullivan, W. P., & Rapp, C. A. (1991). Improving clients outcomes: The Kansas technical assistance consultation project.

*Community Mental Health Journal, 27,* 327–336.

Troncale, J. A. (2004). Understanding the dynamics of polysubstance dependence. *Addiction Professional, 2,* 3.

Wallace, J. (1983). Alcoholism: Is a shift in paradigm necessary? *Journal of Psychiatric Treatment and Evaluation, 5,* 479–485.

Wallace, J. (1989). A biopsychosocial model of alcoholism. *Social Casework, 70,* 325–332.

Wang, X., Li, B., Zhou, X., Liao, Y., Tang, J., Liu, T., . . . Hao, W. (2012). Changes in brain gray matter in abstinent heroin addicts. *Drug and Alcohol Dependence 126,* 304–308.

Weiss, R., Griffin, M., Najavits, L., Hufford, C., Kogan, J., Thompson, H., . . . Siqueland, L. (1996). Self-help activities in cocaine dependent patients entering treatment: Results from NIDA Collaborative Cocaine Treatment Study. *Drug and Alcohol Dependence, 43,* 79–86.

World Health Organization Expert Committee on Drug Dependence. (1974). *Twentieth report* (Technical Report Series No. 5(51)). Geneva: Author.

Yeager, K. R. (2000). The role of intermittent crisis intervention in early recovery from cocaine addiction. *Journal of Crisis Intervention and Time-Limited Treatment, 45*(5), 179–197.

Zastrow, C. (1996). *Introduction to social work and social welfare* (6th ed.). Pacific Grove, CA: Brooks/Cole.

# 19

## Mobile Crisis Units: Front-Line Community Mental Health Services

JAN LIGON

### Gloria

Late Friday afternoon, a caseworker from the outpatient mental health center received a call from Gloria, a long-standing client. Gloria was to see the worker and psychiatrist that morning but never came. She was very agitated on the telephone and told her caseworker that she did not intend to return to the mental health center, stating, "Don't call me anymore or you might be sorry you did." Gloria's diagnosis is schizophrenia, and she has been hospitalized many times over the years when her symptoms would exacerbate, usually because she had stopped taking her medications. She lives alone in an apartment and receives health benefits, monthly income, rent supplements, and reduced-rate passes for public transportation. The outpatient office was closing for the weekend, so the caseworker called the crisis center to convey what Gloria had said. All clients have access to the crisis center, and caseworkers often call to relate concerns they have about clients who may call or need services after hours. Gloria did call the crisis center about 10:00 that night and told the hotline worker, "I'm telling all of you that if you don't leave me alone, somebody's going to get hurt." The hotline worker immediately contacted the mobile crisis unit (MCU) by cellular telephone to relate the details of the call and to provide information maintained on the computer about the client, including her diagnosis, medications, and treatment history. The MCU proceeded to Gloria's apartment, the last of five calls it would make on that shift.

### Cindy

It was a hot, humid summer night, when tempers often run short. The MCU received a radio call from the county police to advise about a domestic disturbance on an isolated road in the county. The police stated that Cindy, aged 19, had shot a high-caliber gun into the ceiling of her grandmother's house. The grandmother ran to a neighbor's and called the police. Cindy and her father live in another county. She had not been following curfew rules, and he told her, "You can just go to your grandmother's because I'm done with you here." After a few days with her grandmother, Cindy began to call her father to try to work things out, but he reinforced that he had reached his limit with her. That night, after he hung up on Cindy, she became very upset, grabbed a gun in the house, and shot it into the ceiling several times. The police contacted the MCU for assistance, and on arrival there were five police cars and numerous neighbors who had walked over from their modest houses along the road. Cindy's father had been contacted and would arrive soon. Computer records had no previous history to report.

### Michael

This evening had been a quiet one for the MCU when a radio communication came in from the county police SWAT team. The team had received a call from Amanda, who advised that her husband, Michael, was in the house with her, armed and threatening to kill himself. Upon arrival, the SWAT team learned that the man had a painful and debilitating physical condition that had become worse. He was very despondent and wanted to die. Amanda stated, "I've talked him down from these states before, but this time things are much worse. He wants to die, but he doesn't want me to be left alone. Our parents are deceased, and we have no children. We're really all each other has." Although the SWAT team was requesting a backup consultation from the MCU, the scene quickly became one that required negotiation not only with the client but also with the intervening teams.

---

As behavioral health services for mental and substance abuse problems have shifted from institutional and inpatient settings to community services and programs, methods for dealing with crisis episodes are changing. In the past, many crisis episodes were addressed by involuntarily transporting clients to an emergency receiving facility such as a psychiatric hospital. However, with the declining influence of institutional inpatient facilities and the growing impact of evolving behavioral health care models and systems, it is becoming increasingly likely that crises will now be addressed at the community level. One promising approach to crisis intervention, the MCU, has been utilized in a number of communities to intervene at the local level, often in the client's home.

## OVERVIEW OF THE PROBLEM

In 2011, more than 41 million US adults (18%) experienced a mental health problem, and 20 million (8%) had a problem with substance abuse

(SAMHSA, 2013). The Centers for Disease Control and Prevention (CDC, 2012) reports that about 8 million adults have suicidal thoughts annually, with suicide ranking as the 10th most frequent cause of death for all persons over the age of 10 in the United States.

As SAMHSA (2012) reports, "By 2020, mental and substance use disorders will surpass all physical diseases as a major cause of disability worldwide" at a cost to society of more than $500 billion for substance abuse alone.

Despite the prevalence of behavioral health problems across the life span, the amount of funding to prevent and treat these problems has declined as a proportion of all health care expenditures. Funding for services is heavily dependent on the public sector, which supports almost two thirds of the services provided (SAMHSA, 2013).

## EXPANSION OF COMMUNITY CRISIS SERVICES

Reding and Raphelson (1995) note that as early as the 1920s psychiatrists in Amsterdam provided home-based psychiatric services with the belief that the care was more effective than that received in an inpatient hospital ward. During that same period, emergency psychiatric services began to appear in the emergency wards of general hospitals as "essentially an on-the-spot adjustment to situational exigencies" (Wellin, Slesinger, & Hollister, 1987, p. 476). Emergency services in urban psychiatric hospitals were begun in the 1930s, followed by community-based services in the 1950s. As documented by Yeager and Roberts in the overview chapter of this book describing how crisis services became available in the community following passage of the Community Mental Health Center (CMHC) Act of 1963, which required that all centers receiving federal funds offer 24-hour crisis and emergency services as one of five mandated categories of services.

The CMHC Act focused on moving mental health services from institutional settings to the community, and early intervention was an important component of these programs. With ongoing federal support, these services continued to expand in the 1970s, and the total number of community mental health centers offering emergency services expanded 69% from 1976 to 1981 (Wellin et al., 1987). Between 1969 and 1992, the number of mental health episodes per year doubled, the number of admissions to outpatient and partial care facilities tripled, and the rate of inpatient admissions remained constant. The number of admissions to state and county mental hospitals declined by 45% from 1975 to 1992, and the number of admissions to substance abuse treatment facilities receiving public funds remained constant from 1993 to 1996. More than 50% of the funding for substance abuse treatment is from public sources, and 90% of treatment is outpatient

(Rouse, 1998). In recent years funding has come from state authorities focusing on specific high-risk areas. In 2014 California announced the approval of 75.3 million in grants to support 28 countries with a fleet of three dozen vehicles and five dozen staff members for mobile support teams. Minnesota provided an additional six million dollars in funding to support mental health crisis teams.

As an increasing number of clients become covered by various forms of managed care, it is likely that the trend to utilize outpatient and community-based services will expand even further. Community-based crisis intervention presents a unique challenge to both practitioners and administrators of behavioral health services. The need for crisis services continues to grow, while inpatient and institutional supports continue to decline. Therefore, it is essential that community programs develop and implement services that are congruent with community needs. Georgia is one example of a state in which mental health services have been reformed based on legislation that was primarily driven by consumers of services and their families.

## MENTAL HEALTH REFORM IN GEORGIA

In 1993, the Georgia General Assembly passed House Bill 100 (HB100) to reorganize mental health, mental retardation, and substance abuse services in the state into 28 community service boards. The community boards were originally overseen by 19 regional boards; however, the number of regional boards has now been reduced to 13. The law requires that a minimum of 50% of all board members must be consumers of services or their families. The 13 regional boards receive funding, determine needs, contract for the provision of services, and monitor the outcomes of services provided. Additional details about the Georgia reform are available elsewhere (Elliott, 1996). Since the 1993 reform in Georgia, services for residents of DeKalb County, located in metropolitan Atlanta, are now provided by the DeKalb Community Service Board (DCSB), based in Decatur, Georgia. DCSB provides a wide range of services to more than 10,000 of the county's 600,000 residents. The county has a long history of commitment to and advocacy for addressing mental health, mental retardation, and substance abuse issues. Services had previously been provided through outpatient programs, and inpatient treatment was provided through one of the state's seven psychiatric hospitals.

## CRISIS SERVICES

Following the passage of HB100, DeKalb County began to offer inpatient services for crisis stabilization in the community. This was consistent with the wishes of consumers and their families that services be provided in the community so that the need for hospitalization could be reduced. The facility's interdisciplinary team of physicians, psychiatrists, nurses, social workers, paraprofessional health workers, dietary workers, and volunteers provide around-the-clock access to assessments, physical examinations, medication, treatment, and case management services. Treatment approaches include individual therapy, 12-step groups, and education groups. In addition, many clients are transported to specialized community programs such as day treatment programs or residential programs in the community. The crisis facility also serves as the base of operation for the county's crisis telephone service. In addition, since 1994 an MCU has been in continuous service and provides essential intervention and support services that were not available prior to its inception.

## DEVELOPMENT OF MOBILE CRISIS UNITS

*Mobile crisis units* (MCUs) can be broadly defined as a community-based program, staffed by trained professionals who may be summoned to any location to deliver services. A number of programs have been previously documented in the literature, and early efforts focused on in-home psychiatric services (Chiu & Primeau, 1991). Other programs were specifically intended to avoid hospital admissions (Bengelsdorf & Alden, 1987; Henderson, 1976) and for providing training to psychiatric residents (Zealberg et al., 1990). More recent efforts have included programs that target the homeless mentally ill (Slagg, Lyons, Cook, Wasmer, & Ruth, 1994), with the ability to offer "medications that would otherwise be administered by court order in a hospital" (Reding & Raphelson, 1995, p. 181).

Although the specific features of MCUs vary, Zealberg, Santos, and Fisher (1993) identify a number of advantages offered by MCUs, including increased accessibility of services, the benefit of assessing in the "patient's native environment" (p. 16), and the ability to intervene without delay, to avoid unnecessary arrests or hospitalizations, and to offer crisis training opportunities to mental health professionals. Because police officers are often the first source of contact and response to community crises, the authors also note that MCUs offer the opportunity to collaborate with the law enforcement system.

## ROLE OF LAW ENFORCEMENT

Police activities related to mental health and substance abuse are particularly problematic for law enforcement because these calls can be very time-consuming and frequently are not perceived as "real police work" (Olivero & Hansen, 1994, p. 217) compared with activity associated with criminal behavior. Zealberg et al. (1993) note that police officers have little training in mental health issues, and "techniques that were developed for use with criminals are often not applicable to nor successful with psychotic patients" (p. 17). This is a significant concern to law enforcement, with Hails and Borum (2003) noting that 7% to 10% of all police calls are related to mental health issues.

Law enforcement agencies and behavioral health care services are systems that may be prone to clash (Kneebone, Roberts, & Hainer, 1995). For example, in the past law enforcement was integrally involved in providing assistance for the involuntary admissions of mental health and substance abuse patients to psychiatric hospitals. However, the current system has become more restrictive concerning involuntary commitments (Olivero & Hansen, 1994) while favoring community-based interventions. Efforts to support community treatment and avoid psychiatric hospitalizations are congruent with the intent of deinstitutionalization. However, there has been a corresponding increase in the number of persons with a history of mental problems who are jailed rather than hospitalized, a systemic shift that has been referred to as "transinstitutionalization" (Olivero & Hansen, 1994, p. 217). As noted by Zealberg et al. (1993), "Mobile crisis teams can alleviate the anxiety of law enforcement personnel and can prevent police overreaction" (p. 17). Such was the case in Memphis, when the development of a crisis intervention team came about after the shooting of a mentally ill person by a police officer (Cochran, Deane, & Borum, 2000). The authors note that partnerships between law enforcement and mental health services can be of great benefit in "managing crisis calls in an effective, expedient, and sensitive manner" (p. 1315).

## DIFFERENCES IN MCU STAFFING AND SERVICE DELIVERY

MCUs have varied greatly in staffing and service delivery approaches. Gaynor and Hargreaves (1980) note that some mobile units were more likely to use mental health professionals, with psychiatrists available on a consultant basis, whereas Chiu and Primeau (1991) describe a team approach that includes a psychiatrist, a registered nurse, and a social worker. Some MCUs have been positioned as support and consultant services, which are called for assistance by the law enforcement or mental health systems (Bengelsdorf & Alden, 1987; Henderson, 1976; Zealberg, Christie, Puckett, McAlhany, & Durban, 1992). Other programs have been based in vans or other vehicles and offer outreach services to targeted populations (Chiu & Primeau, 1991; Slagg et al., 1994).

Community MCUs differ with respect to staffing and objectives, and the role of law enforcement in these programs also varies. Programs have been described that are designed to increase the knowledge and effectiveness of police officers when working with mental health issues (Dodson-Chaneske, 1988; Teese & Van Wormer, 1975), as a collaboration with police and psychiatric services (Zealberg et al., 1992), or as a team consisting of police officers and mental health professionals (Lamb, Shaner, Elliott, DeCuir, & Foltz, 1995). On the other hand, many programs have focused on the delivery of services without law enforcement collaboration (Bengelsdorf & Alden, 1987; Chiu & Primeau, 1991; Slagg et al., 1994). Deane, Steadman, Borum, Veysey, and Morrissey (1999) surveyed urban police departments concerning their method of response to situations involving mental health issues and found no significant differences in four approaches to the calls.

## MOBILE CRISIS SERVICES IN DEKALB COUNTY, GEORGIA

Prior to 1994, many crises involving mental health and substance abuse problems in DeKalb County were addressed by police officers who responded to these calls. If necessary, individuals could be arrested, or they could be transported involuntarily by the sheriff's department to the state psychiatric hospital. Community residents, family members, and mental health advocates were very vocal about their displeasure with this arrangement for several reasons. First, the opportunity to resolve the situation at the location of the incident was limited by the expertise of the officer who responded. Second, many arrests and incarcerations were for behavior that was directly related to a mental health issue and were potentially avoidable. Finally, when clients were assessed at the psychiatric hospital, it was not uncommon for the facility to make decisions that conflicted with the judgment and opinions of community providers and family members. With the consumer and family focus of the reform in Georgia, it was now possible for county residents to secure services that were desired, including the MCU.

The MCU operates from 3:00 to 10:30 p.m., 7 days per week, and pairs a uniformed police officer with a mental health professional who operate from a regular marked police car. Each team works 4 days per week, with the operations based at the county's mental health and substance abuse crisis center, which includes the 24-hour crisis telephone service, walk-in services, and inpatient crisis stabilization and detoxification unit. About half of the referrals to the MCU are made by police dispatchers or other officers through the police radio communications system. The other half of the referrals come from the crisis unit or other mental health workers via cellular telephone and pager. Police officers have continuous access to field supervisors, and the mental health worker has direct access to consultation, including administration and staff psychiatrists. In addition, client histories are available through both the law enforcement and the mental health information system. The MCU responds to a wide range of calls that occur in homes, public places, and schools. About half of the calls involve a psychotic episode, one fourth are related to suicidal individuals, and about one fourth include a substance abuse problem as well. About six calls are completed per shift, which includes a combination of crisis calls and prearranged client and family follow-up calls.

## APPLICATIONS OF ROBERTS'S SEVEN-STAGE MODEL

Roberts (1991) provides a highly practical approach to crisis intervention that is consistent with the needs of members of mobile crisis teams. It is important to address each of the seven stages in the model, beginning with Stage 1, assessing lethality and safety needs, followed by Stage 2, establishing rapport and communication. Stage 3 involves identifying the major problems, followed by Stage 4, dealing with feelings and providing support. Possible alternatives are explored in Stage 5, followed by the formulation of a plan in Stage 6 and follow-up during Stage 7. Roberts (1991) aptly stresses the importance of using sound judgment in sequencing the model's stages. For example, an MCU call involving a frightened mental health client could begin with Stage 2 to establish rapport, whereas a call concerning an actively suicidal client would begin with assessing lethality, Stage 1.

### Case Application: Gloria

In the case of Gloria, assessing the lethality of her threats is consistent with Stage 1 and began with contacts to the outpatient case manager and the telephone crisis worker. These were both excellent resources to determine from their experience and case records if any history of violence toward self or others was evident. In Stage 2, the telephone crisis worker had already spoken with Gloria at her apartment, as well as to her neighbor, who was with her and was considered a supportive person. In Stage 3, it was determined that Gloria's threats were consistent with her not being properly medicated. In the past, this usually resulted in her being transported to the psychiatric hospital and involuntarily admitted.

On this call, the team consisted of a uniformed officer and a licensed master's-level social worker, who proceeded to the apartment. In Stage 4, the crisis telephone worker had begun the process of offering support to Gloria and her neighbor and provided an opportunity to express feelings. However, given Gloria's level of hostility, this dialogue was of limited benefit, and her neighbor was relieved to know that the MCU was en route. As the MCU team entered her apartment, Gloria became very fearful about the presence of a uniformed officer. It was now important to go back to Stage 1 to specifically make sure there were no weapons in the apartment and to assess Gloria's intent to harm herself or someone else. Although a full discussion of assessing suicidal and homicidal intent is beyond the scope of this chapter, a more thorough review of risk factors and assessment techniques is available elsewhere (Sommers-Flanagan & Sommers-Flanagan, 1995).

Continuing to Stages 2, 3, and 4, Gloria was calmed by the team and encouraged to relate to it the details of her missing her usual appointment, the status of her medications, her recent appetite and sleep patterns, and any recent events or circumstances that may have impacted her mental status. In Stages 5 and 6, it was important to consider the input of both Gloria and her neighbor, as well as the previous feedback from the case manager and telephone worker. The team was able to acquire her trust, and she provided helpful input in developing a plan. Gloria had not stopped taking her medications, but she was running low on her supply and was attempting to stretch what she had, which led to her decompensation. Although one option was to transport her to the crisis center for further evaluation, her neighbor was willing to stay with her for the night. If there were any difficulties, she could contact the telephone crisis line. In Stage 7, the neighbor was willing to bring Gloria to the outpatient mental health center for a walk-in meeting with her case worker and the psychiatrist and to replenish her medications at the center pharmacy.

This case illustrates several benefits of the MCU. First, the combination of a law enforcement officer and a mental health worker is of tremendous benefit in assessing safety and providing the option of involuntary transportation, if needed. Second, the appearance of a uniformed officer and a plainclothes worker has the effect of balancing the need for authority and empathic support in crisis work. This is not always possible if an officer is working solo and may have to move swiftly to an arrest that could have been avoided. By the same token, it may not be safe for a mental health professional to attempt such a call alone. Finally, there was significant benefit in addressing the crisis from a contextual perspective in Gloria's home. This includes her physical environment and also makes it possible to more accurately assess the viability of her neighbor as an action plan alternative. There was no further contact until the next morning, when Gloria arrived with her neighbor at the mental health center.

## Case Application: Cindy

In the case of Cindy, the assessment of lethality in Stage 1 had been addressed by law enforcement officers prior to the arrival. In many cases the MCU is not the first responder to police calls but is summoned by officers when appropriate. The MCU was contacted by officers on the scene via police radio. On this shift, the mental health worker was a licensed clinical social worker who had the authority to sign, if necessary, an involuntary order to transport the woman to the psychiatric emergency receiving facility. Although the objective is not to arrest or hospitalize individuals, it is beneficial for the authority to initiate an involuntary intervention to be present. In Stage 2, because Cindy's father had arrived, team members met separately with him and with Cindy, and in Stages 3 and 4 both felt comfortable sharing their feelings and relating their views of the problems. Options in Stage 5 included arrest, involuntary transportation to the psychiatric hospital, or transportation to the crisis center, which is a voluntary status facility. It was agreed that the client would go to the crisis center for further evaluation. Given her age and the lack of any client history, she was admitted for overnight observation, was re-evaluated the next morning, and was referred to the outpatient mental health division for both individual and family therapy. For Stage 7, a telephone call was placed to the father; it was determined that Cindy had returned home, and she and her father did follow-up with outpatient services.

This case description illustrates several benefits of MCUs reported by Zealberg and colleagues (1993). First, the ability to observe and interview on-site "allows for the most complete assessment with the least trauma to the patient" (p. 16). In this case, it was also possible to interview Cindy and her father individually and to then combine the information obtained from them to identify similarities and differences. Second, mobile units can respond quickly, prevent situations from escalating, and avoid unnecessary arrests or hospitalizations. Third, a well-executed mobile crisis call "allows for better public education about mental health issues and resources" (p. 17). Fourth, potential cost savings to the county include not only the avoidance of unnecessary arrests or hospitalizations but also the opportunity for "officers to return to duty more quickly" (p. 17).

## Case Application: Michael

This evening had been a quiet one for the MCU when a radio communication came in from the county police SWAT team. It had received a call from Amanda, who advised that her husband, Michael, was in the house with her, armed and threatening to kill himself. Upon arrival, the SWAT team learned that the man had a painful and debilitating physical condition that had become worse. He was very despondent and wanted to die. Amanda stated, "I've talked him down from these states before, but this time things are much worse. He wants to die, but he doesn't want me to be left alone. Our parents are deceased, and we have no children. We're really all each other has." Although the SWAT team was requesting a backup consultation from the MCU, the scene quickly became one that required negotiation not only with the client but also with the intervening teams.

The case of Michael points out the importance of Stage 1 in assessing both lethality and past experiences with coping behaviors. Although his wife was not being held hostage, this case presented an element of extreme risk and danger to Michael and Amanda and required the use of negotiation skills (Strentz, 1995). On this evening, the team consisted of the uniformed police officer and a registered nurse, and computer records found no criminal or mental health information on Michael. After consultation with the SWAT team, it was agreed that the nurse would, consistent with Stage 2, attempt to first establish rapport with Amanda and use her alliance to connect with Michael. The problems (Stage 3) were clear, so the predominant effort on this call was to connote empathy and provide support (Stage 4). Given the severity of Michael's physical and mental conditions, the only option in Stages 5 and 6 would be to arrange for his hospitalization. The dialogue between the MCU nurse and the couple went extremely well, and Michael voluntarily surrendered the gun and agreed to go with the MCU to the hospital. A follow-up call to the hospital for Stage 7 confirmed that Michael was safe and stabilizing in the hospital.

Although the outcome of this case was positive, it was important to note the difference between this call and others handled by the MCU and SWAT teams. A follow-up meeting was held with the SWAT team and a mobile crisis worker to review the call. The SWAT team members expressed the need for additional training around mental health and substance abuse issues, which was subsequently provided. As noted by Strentz (1995), "The element of danger coexists with the opportunity for successful resolution and personal growth" (p. 147). Therefore, it is also essential to provide cross-training about SWAT team interventions to team members of MCUs.

## OUTCOMES OF MCUS

Outcome information about MCUs is limited, and Geller, Fisher, and McDermeit (1995) note that "beliefs about mobile crisis services far outnumber facts" (p. 896). Although Reding and Raphelson (1995) reported a 40% reduction in hospital admissions during a 6-month period, a study by Fisher, Geller, and Wirth-Cauchon (1990) did not "support the numerous claims regarding the ability of mobile crisis intervention to reduce the use of hospitalization" (p. 249). However, Fisher et al. (1990) report that "some mobile crisis teams may be very effective in reducing hospitalizations because they function as part of a system which has other key services available for treatment and diversion" (p. 250).

In addition, Fisher et al. (1990) note that these units often reach people in need of hospitalization, so "that the unnecessary hospitalizations prevented by mobile crisis units are offset by the admission of individuals needing inpatient care who are discovered" (p. 251). Another problem is that "large numbers of persons who have committed minor crimes are taken to jails instead of to hospitals or other psychiatric treatment facilities" (Lamb et al., 1995, p. 1267). Lamb et al. (1995) conducted a follow-up study in Los Angeles of clients having a history of criminal and mental problems who had received outreach services from a police–mental health team and found that "remarkably, only two percent of the group were taken to jail" (p. 1269). A study of mental health response models in three law enforcement jurisdictions provides further support that collaborations between police and mental health services can reduce arrests and unnecessary incarcerations of people who have mental health problems (Steadman, Deane, Borum, & Morrissey, 2000).

Dyches, Biegel, Johnsen, Guo, and Min (2002) conducted a matched samples study of those who received mobile crisis services with those receiving services from a hospital. The authors found that consumers were 17% "more likely to receive community-based mental health services after the crisis event than a consumer from the hospital-based intervention cohort" (p. 743). With respect to those who did not have a previous history of mental health services, the authors found that "the hospital-based cohort's likelihood of receiving postcrisis mental health services was 48% less than that of the mobile crisis cohort" (p. 744). Ligon and Thyer (2000) assessed client satisfaction with mobile crisis services in Georgia and found that both mental health clients and their family members reported levels of satisfaction comparable to those for other outpatient services.

Simakhodskaya, Haddad, Quintero, & Malavade (2009) note that mobile crisis outreach services in conjunction with emergency room (ER) based crisis services has the potential to reduce ER visits and improve compliance with recommendations for follow-up care. Kisely et al. (2010), found that a mobile crisis partnership between police and mental health professionals in Nova Scotia resulted in a significant reduction in the involvement of officers' time, better engagement with clients, and an increase in outpatient contacts for services.

## INITIATING AND SUSTAINING MCUS

The future of MCUs is dependent on the ability of multiple systems to recognize their value and to then collaborate in a manner that will assure quality services that can be sustained in the community. Although it is impossible to document how many MCUs have opened and closed over the years, a number of factors can influence these programs. First, crisis work can be dangerous when interventions occur in neighborhoods and homes with persons who may exhibit or have histories of violent behavior (Zealberg et al., 1993). Second, the behavioral health and law enforcement systems are rife with conflicts between the two systems (Dodson-Chaneske, 1988; Teese & Van Wormer, 1975), so "constant attention must be given to such collaboration" (Zealberg et al., 1992, p. 614). Finally, the larger political and turf factors that exist in any community can, unfortunately, lead to premature cuts despite a program's efficacy (Diamond, 1995; Reding & Raphelson, 1995). Indeed, Hails and Borum (2003) found that only 8% of 84 medium-sized and large law enforcement agencies had access to an MCU in their jurisdictions.

The political and organizational environments in which these units operate will no doubt present both obstacles and opportunities. It is also essential to work closely with law enforcement and to include ongoing supervision and training opportunities for police officers and mental health workers. In addition, consumers of services and their families must be involved in the development and refinement of MCUs. The support of mental health advocacy groups at the national, state, and local levels is also beneficial in the further development of MCUs.

## FUTURE OPPORTUNITIES

Although the application and outcomes of MCUs are encouraging, there are a number of opportunities to improve these services and to expand their availability. Zealberg, Hardesty, Meisler, and Santos (1997) identify several key areas of concern that include medical issues and the need for technology to support these units. The authors note that "one of the more frustrating aspects of mobile crisis work involves patients whose presenting symptoms include medical as well as psychiatric diagnoses" (p. 272). Ambulance and EMS services can assist with medical problems, but collaboration with these operations may be problematic due to multiple providers of these services in communities or poor communication capability with MCUs. Because MCUs often address issues related to physical health and medications, the DeKalb unit has found that coupling psychiatrically trained registered nurses with the police officer can be very beneficial. In addition, the DeKalb MCU added a limited number of antipsychotic and side effects medications, which are carried onboard, ordered by the unit psychiatrist, and administered by the onboard nurse.

Technology offers immense opportunities to improve mobile crisis services. First, equipment is increasingly portable and more affordable, and it is feasible to equip MCUs with computers, cellular telephones, and other useful technology. Second, the ability to merge sources of information is improving, and it is possible for MCUs to determine any criminal and mental health history on clients quickly and efficiently. Finally, technology enables team members of MCUs to enter data and update records without burdensome paperwork and forms. This can include outcome data, new client information, and instructions for other services concerning follow-ups.

Virtually all the MCUs that have been documented are based in urban areas, which is understandable given the concentration of population and availability of resources. However, rural areas are extremely underserved; 21% of all rural counties have no mental health services, compared with only 4% in urban counties. The situation is much worse if overnight care is required; 78% of rural counties have no overnight services, compared with 27% in urban counties (Rouse, 1998). Coupled with the lack of public transportation in rural areas, MCUs offer the potential not only to provide services where needed but also to initiate any follow-up services that may be required. Indeed, crisis response initiatives in rural areas have the potential to reduce the use of costly inpatient treatment and retain those who need services in the community (Boynge, Lee, & Thurber, 2005).

Although the costs of operating MCUs are a significant concern to communities, Zealberg et al. (1997) note that indirect cost savings must be considered, including the reduced loss of time for police officers, court costs that are avoided when situations are resolved without arrests, and avoidance of high-cost inpatient care in many cases. In addition, behavioral health care is increasingly provided under managed care models. Therefore, managed care organizations are also in a position to gain from such cost savings as avoiding hospitalizations and need to partner with the public sector in developing and supporting MCUs.

MCUs operate across a wide range of geography and sites and encounter very diverse populations. Based on the experience of an MCU based in New York City, Chiu (1994) provides case examples and suggestions on working with Asian, Hispanic, African American, and other diverse groups. In addition, Lyons, Cook, Ruth, Karver, and Slagg (1996) note that the inclusion of consumers of mental health services on MCU teams may be beneficial when responding to calls across a variety of settings, including homes and public places. For example, the authors found that "consumer staff were more likely to do street outreach than were non-consumer staff" (p. 38); they go on to note that consumer experience "can be an advantage for mobile crisis assessment with persons with problems of mental illness and housing instability" (p. 40).

MCUs can be of tremendous benefit to communities when they are carefully staffed and supported by all stakeholders, including consumers of services and their families, law enforcement, and both public and private providers of behavioral health services. However, more research needs to be conducted to determine what combinations of staffing, services, technology, and intervention techniques are most effective and in what settings. It is also important to learn more about working with diverse populations and to investigate the benefits to rural residents through the implementation and evaluation of programs in these underserved areas.

Also promising is the expansion of crisis intervention teams (CITs), covered in Chapter 10 of this volume. Although CIT models vary, the use of partnerships that involve interdisciplinary behavioral health professionals, law enforcement officers, and emergency response services can be very useful in both urban (Franza & Borum, 2011) and rural (Skubby, Bonfine, Novisky, Munetz, & Ritter, 2013; Tyuse, 2012) communities in the United States and worldwide (Watson & Fulambarker, 2013).

REFERENCES

Bengelsdorf, H., & Alden, D. C. (1987). A mobile crisis unit in the psychiatric emergency room. *Hospital and Community Psychiatry, 38*, 662–665.

Boynge, E. R., Lee, R. G., & Thurber, S. (2005). A profile of mental health crisis response in a rural setting. *Community Mental Health Journal, 41*, 675–685.

Centers for Disease Control and Prevention. (2012). Suicide. Retrieved from http://www.cdc.gov/violenceprevention/pdf/Suicide-DataSheet-a.pdf

Chiu, T. L. (1994). The unique challenges faced by psychiatrists and other mental health professionals working in a multicultural setting. *International Journal of Social Psychiatry, 40*, 61–74.

Chiu, T. L., & Primeau, C. (1991). A psychiatric mobile crisis unit in New York City: Description and assessment, with implications for mental health care in the 1990s. *International Journal of Social Psychiatry, 37*, 251–258.

Cochran, S., Deane, M. W., & Borum, R. (2000). Improving police response to mentally ill people. *Psychiatric Services, 51*, 1315–1316.

Deane, M. W., Steadman, H. J., Borum, R., Veysey, B. M., & Morrissey, J. P. (1999). Emerging partnerships between mental health and law enforcement. *Psychiatric Services, 50*, 99–101.

Diamond, R. J. (1995). Some thoughts on: "Around-the-clock mobile psychiatric crisis intervention." *Community Mental Health Journal, 31*, 189–190.

Dodson-Chaneske, D. (1988). Mental health consultation to a police department. *Journal of Human Behavior and Learning, 5*, 35–38.

Dyches, H., Biegel, D., Johnson, J., Guo, S., & Min, M. (2002). The impact of mobile crisis services on the use of community-based mental health services. *Research on Social Work Practice, 12*, 731–751.

Elliott, R. L. (1996). Mental health reform in Georgia, 1992–1996. *Psychiatric Services, 47*, 1205–1211.

Fisher, W. H., Geller, J. L., & Wirth-Cauchon, J. (1990). Empirically assessing the impact of mobile crisis capacity on state hospital admissions. *Community Mental Health Journal, 26*, 245–253.

Franza, S., & Borum, R. (2011). Crisis intervention teams may prevent arrests of people with mental illness. *Police Practice and Research, 12*, 265–272.

Gaynor, J., & Hargreaves, W. A. (1980). "Emergency room" and "mobile response" models of emergency psychiatric services. *Community Mental Health Journal, 16*, 283–292.

Geller, J. L., Fisher, W. H., & McDermeit, M. (1995). A national survey of mobile crisis services and their evaluation. *Psychiatric Services, 46*, 893–897.

Hails, J., & Borum, R. (2003). Police training and specialized approaches to respond to people with mental illnesses. *Crime and Delinquency, 49*, 52–61.

Henderson, H. E. (1976). Helping families in crisis: Police and social work intervention. *Social Work, 21*, 314–315.

Kisely, S., Campbell, L. A., Peddle, S., Hare, S., Pyche, M., Spicer, D., & Moore, B. (2010). A controlled before-and-after evaluation of a mobile crisis partnership between mental health and police in Nova Scotia. *Canadian Journal of Psychiatry, 55*, 662–668.

Kneebone, P., Roberts, J., & Hainer, R. J. (1995). Characteristics of police referrals to a psychiatric unit in Australia. *Psychiatric Services, 46*, 620–622.

Lamb, H. R., Shaner, R., Elliott, D. M., DeCuir, W. J., & Foltz, J. T. (1995). Outcome for psychiatric emergency patients seen by an outreach police–mental health team. *Psychiatric Services, 46*, 1267–1271.

Ligon, J., & Thyer, B. A. (2000). Client and family satisfaction with brief community mental health, substance abuse, and mobile crisis services in an urban setting. *Crisis Intervention, 6*, 93–99.

Lyons, J. S., Cook, J. A., Ruth, A. R., Karver, M., & Slagg, N. B. (1996). Service delivery using consumer staff in a mobile crisis assessment program. *Community Mental Health Journal, 32*, 33–40.

Olivero, J. M., & Hansen, R. (1994). Linkage agreements between mental health and law: Managing suicidal persons. *Administration and Policy in Mental Health, 21*, 217–225.

Reding, G. R., & Raphelson, M. (1995). Around-the-clock mobile psychiatric crisis intervention: Another effective alternative to psychiatric hospitalization. *Community Mental Health Journal, 31*, 179–187.

Roberts, A. R. (1991). Conceptualizing crisis theory and the crisis intervention model. In A. R. Roberts (Ed.), *Contemporary perspectives on crisis intervention and prevention* (pp. 3–17). Englewood Cliffs, NJ: Prentice-Hall.

Simakhodskaya, Z., Haddad, F., Quintero, M., & Malavade, K. (2009). Innovative use of crisis intervention services with psychiatric emergency room patients. *Primary Psychiatry, 16*, 60–65.

Skubby, D., Bonfine, N., Novisky, M., Munetz, M. R., & Ritter, C. (2013). Crisis intervention team (CIT) programs in rural communities: A focus group study. *Community Mental Health Journal, 49*, 756–764.

Slagg, N. B., Lyons, J. S., Cook, J. A., Wasmer, D. J., & Ruth, A. (1994). A profile of clients served by a mobile outreach program for homeless mentally ill persons. *Hospital and Community Psychiatry, 45*, 1139–1141.

Sommers-Flanagan, J., & Sommers-Flanagan, R. (1995). Intake interviewing with suicidal patients: A systematic approach. *Professional Psychology: Research and Practice, 26*, 41–47.

Steadman, H. J., Deane, M. W., Borum, R., & Morrissey, J. P. (2000). Comparing outcomes of major models of police responses to mental health emergencies. *Psychiatric Services, 51*, 645–649.

Strentz, T. (1995). Crisis intervention and survival strategies for victims of hostage situations. In

A. R. Roberts (Ed.), *Crisis intervention and time-limited cognitive treatment* (pp. 127–147). Thousand Oaks, CA: Sage.

Substance Abuse and Mental Health Services Administration (SAMHSA). (2012). *A behavioral health lens for prevention.* Retrieved from http://captus.samhsa.gov/sites/default/files/capt_resource/capt_behavioral_health_fact_sheets_2012_0.pdf

Substance Abuse and Mental Health Services Administration (SAMHSA). (2013). *Behavioral Health, United States, 2012.* HHS Publication No. SMA 13–4797. Rockville, MD: Author.

Teese, C. P., & Van Wormer, J. (1975). Mental health training and consultation with suburban police. *Community Mental Health Journal, 11,* 115–121.

Tyuse, T. (2012). A crisis intervention team: Four year outcomes. *Social Work in Mental Health, 10,* 464–477.

Watson, A. C., & Fulambarker, A. J. (2013). The crisis intervention team model of police response to mental health crises: A primer for mental health practitioners. *Best Practices in Mental Health, 8*(2), 71–83.

Wellin, E., Slesinger, D. P., & Hollister, C. D. (1987). Psychiatric emergency services: Evolution, adaptation, and proliferation. *Social Science and Medicine, 24,* 475–482.

Zealberg, J. J., Christie, S. D., Puckett, J. A., McAlhany, D., & Durban, M. (1992). A mobile crisis program: Collaboration between emergency psychiatric services and police. *Hospital and Community Psychiatry, 43,* 612–615.

Zealberg, J. J., Hardesty, S. J., Meisler, N., & Santos, A. B. (1997). Mobile psychiatric emergency medical services. In S. W. Henggeler & A. B. Santos (Eds.), *Innovative approaches for difficult-to-treat populations* (pp. 263–274). Washington, DC: American Psychiatric Press.

Zealberg, J. J., Santos, A. B., & Fisher, R. K. (1993). Benefits of mobile crisis programs. *Hospital and Community Psychiatry, 44,* 16–17.

Zealberg, J. J., Santos, A. B., Hiers, T. G., Ballenger, J. C., Puckett, J. A., & Christie, S. D. (1990). From the benches to the trenches: Training residents to provide emergency outreach services: A public/academic project. *Academic Psychiatry, 14,* 211–217.

# 20

## Crisis Intervention With HIV-Positive Women

SARAH J. LEWIS

This chapter is intended to provide an overview of crisis intervention with women who have been diagnosed with the human immunodeficiency virus (HIV) and the many factors that must be considered when working with this population. In order to provide stabilization during a time of crisis, it is necessary to have an understanding of not only the emotional and social implications of being HIV positive but the physical consequences as well. Because HIV is most prevalent in minority communities, it is imperative that clinicians understand cultural ramifications and coping strategies. Clinicians must also be ready to address other co-occurring morbidities such as substance abuse, interpersonal violence, and health disparities.

In 2010, an estimated 47,500 people became newly infected with HIV in the United States (Centers for Disease Control and Prevention, 2010). Although the number of cases of acquired immunodeficiency syndrome (AIDS) has steadily declined, the rate of HIV infection has remained relatively stable since the early 1990s. In 2011, there were 10,257 reported cases of women with HIV in the United States. There are disproportionately higher rates of infection per 100,000 among African Americans (48.6), Latinas (7.9), and multiple races (7.5) compared with Whites (2.0; Centers for Disease Control and Prevention, 2011). The data showed an encouraging decreasing trend in HIV infections among Black women (a 21% decrease between 2008 and 2010); however, it will take years of data to confirm the estimates.

Women living within inner cities who are most affected by poverty and crime are hardest hit by the AIDS crisis (see Table 20.1) (Frieden, 2011; Watkins-Hayes, Pittman-Gay, & Beaman, 2012). Because of the

Table 20.1    Diagnoses of HIV Infection Among Adult and
Adolescent Females by Race/Ethnicity

| Race/Ethnicity | No. | Rate |
|---|---|---|
| American Indian/Alaska Native | 51 | 5.5 |
| Asian | 153 | 2.3 |
| Black/African American | 6,595 | 40.0 |
| Hispanic/Latino | 1,530 | 7.9 |
| Native Hawaiian/other Pacific Islander | 8 | 3.9 |
| White | 1,776 | 2.0 |
| Multiple races | 144 | 7.5 |
| Total | 10,257 | 7.7 |

*Source*: Centers for Disease Control and Prevention, 2011.

heterogeneity of the female HIV-positive population, it is important to consider the cultural health beliefs as well as historical racism and sexism with which these women have been plagued. Many of the crises associated with HIV are related not to illness but to contextual factors in which HIV flourishes and the social and developmental consequences of HIV, a stigmatized disease (Burke, Thieman, Gielen, O'Campo, & McDonnell, 2005; Larios, Davis, Gallo, Heinrich, & Talavera, 2009; Lillie-Blanton et al., 2010).

Clients with HIV often are affected by the "SAVA syndemic," which is the synergistic impact of substance abuse, violence, and AIDS. According to a review of the literature, the SAVA syndemic has a negative impact on HIV-related risk taking, mental health, health care utilization, and adherence to antiretroviral medication (Meyer, Springer, & Altice, 2011). Social workers and other care providers must be able to assess and address the individual and synergistic effects of these issues in context.

In 2011, there were fewer than 150 cases of HIV that had been parentally transmitted (Dowshen & D'Angelo, 2011). This is due to interventions to test and treat pregnant women with prophylactic and therapeutic antiretrovirals during pregnancy, labor, and immediately after labor, as well as to provide alternatives to breastfeeding. However, because of the advent of powerful combination therapies, the infants who were born HIV positive generations ago are now in their teens and 20s and face extraordinary developmental challenges. Many people take for granted the luxury of everyday decisions such as going out on a date or on a spur-of-the-moment getaway, eating whatever their heart desires, sharing secrets with a friend, and planning a family; these adolescents and young adults often have to struggle with these and many other decisions due to the consequences of the virus.

## CASE VIGNETTES

The following cases are typical of those that face social workers working within a community-based AIDS organization that provides case management.

---

### Case 1

Mary was a 30-year-old African American woman who came into the HIV testing center very upset after finding her live-in boyfriend's HIV medications. Linda was an active substance abuser and prior to moving in with this boyfriend, had been in jail for 6 months, and had been homeless for a few days. Linda claimed that she had tested HIV negative while she was in jail, and even though she had been physically assaulted while she was homeless, she was not raped. Her boyfriend, James, had saved her from the street. She knew that he was very possessive and could get mean at times, but overall he was good to her and let her live at his house. Mary believed that there was good in everyone and that is what someone should look for—not the bad. She claimed that even though she lived the life of a sinner, she loved God like a saint.

When Mary was cleaning, she found some pill bottles in James's drawer and looked up the names of the medications on the Internet. When she found out the pills were for HIV, she was shocked because even though James could be cruel, she still believed that he would have told her if he was HIV positive. It was difficult to tell what was worse, telling James that she looked in his drawer and found his medications, or being HIV positive. She had no idea what James was going to do now that she knew about his HIV status. Even though he was the one who was HIV positive and could have passed the virus to her, she was afraid that he was going to be angry and have a violent outburst because he had beaten her before for less; or even worse, in her eyes, he might throw her out of the house. She knew that she could press charges against him for exposing her to the virus with prior knowledge of his status, but she had no intention of doing that. Like many women in Mary's predicament, she used drugs with James regularly, and he provided her with a place to stay and financial security.

### Case 2

Maria was a 25-year-old Hispanic female who had known of her HIV-positive status for 5 years. She went for testing after receiving an e-mail from a website that delivers anonymous partner notifications that said, "I'm sorry, I didn't know I had an STD when we had sex, you need to be tested." At first she thought it was a joke, but after a few days she decided that it wouldn't hurt to get tested anyway because in the last 6 months she had had unprotected sex with two different men and didn't want to take any chances. When she discovered that she was positive, she thought that it was the end of the world, but with the help of a support group she worked through her initial shock. Although Maria was close to her family of origin, she had never shared her HIV status with them, and since being diagnosed with HIV, she had never been in a sexual relationship.

At first Maria was very good about taking her medication, claiming that she never missed a dose. However, her viral load recently went well beyond the detectable level, and her CD4 level had fallen below 200. When a person's CD4 falls below 200 it is a sign that his or her immune system is severely compromised and is an indicator of AIDS. When first asked, Mary claimed that every now and again she would forget to take her medication, stating that she tried to remember, but sometimes she would get busy. Upon further probing, it was discovered that Maria's insurance had changed, and all the HIV medications were put on the highest tier in the formulary, meaning she had to pay all of her deductible before the insurance would pay for any of the medication. Because Maria did not have enough money to cover the cost of her medication, she was taking only half of her prescribed dose. Maria was a very proud woman and had never asked for a handout, and she was ashamed to admit that even though she worked and paid insurance premiums, she still could not afford her medications. Ever since Maria had run into financial difficulties, she stopped going to the support group because she liked to be "the woman with the answers, not the woman with the problems." She stated that she had started to become isolated from her family and was becoming "more and more depressed by the minute."

---

## DEFINITION OF CRISIS

*Crisis* is defined as the perception or experience of an event or situation as an intolerable difficulty that exceeds one's current resources and coping mechanisms. Although a stressful or hazardous event precipitates the crisis, it is the appraisal of the event and the individual's inability to cope with the perceived consequences of the event using previous coping traits or learned behaviors that designate a crisis (Berjot & Gillet, 2011; Folkman, Lazarus, Dunkel-Schetter, DeLongis, & Gruen, 1986; Folkman, Lazarus, Gruen, & DeLongis, 1986). These coping traits or learned behaviors can be adaptive or maladaptive depending on the short- and or long-term mental consequences. A defining characteristic of a crisis is that it is time limited; however, a situational crisis can evolve into an acute stress disorder if it meets all criteria for post-traumatic stress according to the *Diagnostic and Statistical Manual of Mental Disorders* with a duration lasting from 3 days to 1 month (American Psychiatric Association, 2013).

One of the most significant predictors of stress in the HIV-positive population is being female (McIntosh & Rosselli, 2012). This stress consists of compounded events that are more than mere hassles of daily living but are true impediments to psychosocial functioning. Socioeconomic stressors such as financial burden, unemployment, child care, domestic violence, substance abuse, racism, and sexism all contribute to the depletion of coping resources and have an impact on psychosocial as well as health outcomes. HIV-positive individuals also suffer from external and internalized stigma that hinders everyday living. Several studies have shown that stressful life events predict progression to AIDS and health care utilization (Pence et al., 2007; Whetten et al., 2006; Wyatt et al., 2011). This may be due to adherence to medication and other primary care due to psychological effects of stressors and past and present traumas, or to the physical effects of stress, which are known to compromise the immune system response through a cascade of adrenal and sympathetic nervous system activity (McIntosh & Rosselli, 2012).

Discrimination and stigma continuue to be acute and chronic stressors, which can contribute to a crisis state. Unfortunately, HIV triggers most of society's negative "isms." Individuals with HIV face a level of discrimination that is far worse than that experienced by individuals with other chronic or terminal diseases (Colbert, Kim, Sereika, & Erlen, 2010; Vanable, Carey, Blair, & Littlewood, 2006; Wagner et al., 2010). Even when one does not disclose one's HIV status, one can still be impacted by internalized stigma. Internalized stigma does not require overt mistreatment; it can occur simply by accepting perceived societal judgment and threat of rejection.

## SCOPE OF THE PROBLEM AND PSYCHOSOCIAL VARIABLES

Much has changed in the last three decades since the beginning of the AIDS crisis, but unfortunately some things have stayed the same. Both pre- and post-exposure prophylaxis for HIV are now available that have been found to be effective for high-risk populations; there are interventions for infected pregnant mothers that have virtually wiped out vertical transmission of HIV; and there are medications that help people live longer, healthier lives. But there is still an HIV epidemic. There were an estimated 216,966 women living with diagnosed HIV in the United States in 2010 (Centers for Disease Control and Prevention, 2011). In addition, there are thousands of women who do not know their HIV status.

Most people know that HIV is transmitted through bodily fluids such as blood, semen, vaginal secretions, and breast milk and that it leads to suppression of the immune system. Clinicians should familiarize themselves, however, with disease progression, surveillance case reporting, and advances in the field such as pre- and post-prophylaxis for HIV. When working with individuals with HIV, clinicians must be willing and able to discuss both psychosocial issues and the chronic medical issues that their clients may be facing.

When an individual is first exposed to HIV, she usually will experience flulike symptoms, which can include swollen glands, fever, muscle aches, pains, fatigue, and headache (Selik et al., 2014). This is the body's natural response to a foreign "invader" and is called acute viral syndrome (ARS) or primary HIV infection. At this time, a large amount of the virus is being produced in the body because there are no antibodies to ward off infection. As a result, at this stage of the infection, CD4 counts fall dramatically. While an individual is in the acute stage of infection, she is particularly infectious because of a high viral load. As the body begins to develop antibodies, the viral load decreases, which is called the *viral set point*, and the CD4 count increases. Current recommendations are to initiate antiretroviral therapy (ART) at this point in the disease trajectory.

The next stage is considered to be the latency stage (Selik et al., 2014). In the stage, the body continues to make the virus; however, there are few if any symptoms. Individuals taking ART may remain in the latency stage for decades with no HIV-related symptoms. The goal of ART is to reduce the viral burden to undetectable levels. This is not to say that the individual does not have the virus, but instead that the level of viral RNA in the person's blood is lower than the threshold needed for detection on the test being used. In this stage, a person is less contagious, and an undetectable viral load is even considered to be a transmission risk reduction strategy (Hall, Holtgrave, Tang, & Rhodes, 2013; Selik et al., 2014).

The final stage of progression is AIDS, which occurs when one becomes vulnerable to opportunistic infections due to the lack of immune system response. In order to be considered in this stage, an individual must have a CD4 lymphocyte count of 200 or below or have been diagnosed with an opportunistic infection. There are more than 20 opportunistic infections due to HIV, with some of the most common ones being candidiasis, invasive cervical cancer, cryptococcosis, cytomegalovirus, Kaposi's sarcoma, tuberculosis, *Pneumocystis carinii* pneumonia, recurrent pneumonia, and wasting syndrome (Selik et al., 2014).

Viral suppression and quality of life are dependent on adherence to ART. Unlike with other chronic illnesses in which regimens can be resumed after a lapse of missed doses, HIV often builds a resistance to medications without strict adherence. Decreased immune system response as a result of the depletion of the CD4 count is another possible result of nonadherence, as is increased risk of transmission of the virus due to an increased viral load. There are several barriers to adherence, and females have a significantly higher risk of nonadherence than do men (Puskas et al., 2011). The factors that may contribute to these findings are depression, reduced disclosure of HIV status, lack of support, and a greater likelihood that a woman will be lost in follow-up medical care.

At the end of 2010 there were an estimated 888,921 adults and adolescents diagnosed with HIV infections living in the United States and six dependent areas (Centers for Disease Control and Prevention, 2011). This number does not take into account all the cases that are not diagnosed. There were 223,045 females living with diagnosed HIV; 60% of these women were Black/African American, 19% were White, and 18% were Hispanic/Latino. Approximately 2% of the women were of multiple races, 1% were Asian, and less than 1% were American Indian/Alaska Native and Native Hawaiian/Other Pacific Islander.

There were 10,512 reported HIV infections in adolescent and adult females in 2011, 86% of which were contracted through heterosexual contact, 14% through injection drug use, and less than 1% through other types of transmission (Centers for Disease Control and Prevention, 2011). These data include persons at any stage of disease and are based on estimates resulting from adjustment for reporting delays and missing transmission category. During the years 2008 through 2011, the largest percentage of diagnosed cases of HIV for both men and women was for Blacks/African Americans, wherein the percentages were 46% for Black/African American, 28% for Whites, 22% for Hispanic/Latinos, 2% each for Asians and persons of multiple races, and less than 1% each for American Indians/Alaska Natives and Native Hawaiians/other Pacific Islanders.

Among the 10,512 HIV infections in 2011 in women, 63% were among Blacks/African Americans, 17% were among Hispanics/Latinos, and 17% were among Whites. Approximately 1% each were among Asians and individuals of multiple races, and less than 1% were among American Indians/ Alaska Natives and Native Hawaiians/other Pacific Islanders. The rate (per 100,000 population) of diagnoses of HIV infection among Black/African American females (.40) was 20 times higher than the rate for Whites (2.0) and approximately 5 times that for Hispanics/Latinos (7.9; Centers for Disease Control and Prevention., 2011).

The AIDS diagnosis rate of individuals with HIV peaked in 1992 through 1993 and has dramatically decreased since then due to increasingly effective medication regimes. Decreases, however, are not consistent across races. Blacks/ African Americans surpassed Whites for the first time in AIDS diagnoses in 1994, and their rate has remained higher since that time (Centers for Disease Control and Prevention, 2011). The percentage of people classified as living with AIDS in 2011 were 49% Black/African American, 26% White, 21% Hispanic/ Latino, 2% were multiple races, 2% were Asian, less than 1% each were American Indian/Alaska Native and Native Hawaiian/other Pacific Islander.

## Intimate Partner Violence, Substance Abuse, and HIV

Other chapters in this text address domestic violence, but it is important to discuss the intersection of HIV and domestic violence and the compounding effect of that intersection. The chances of experiencing physical or sexual intimate partner violence (IPV) are significantly associated with having a partner at high risk for HIV (Burke et al., 2005; Gielen, McDonnell, O'Campo, & Burke, 2005; Siemieniuk et al., 2013). Conversely, the estimated rate for IPV among women who are HIV positive is more than double the national rate. Women who have experienced IPV have been found to be less likely to exhibit high levels of self-efficacy for HIV prevention due to the inability to negotiate condom use, high-risk sex before the current violent relationship, and substance abuse (El-Bassel et al., 1998; Siemieniuk et al., 2013). High risk due to multiple sex partners is also associated with abuse-related psychological distress (Andrinopoulos et al., 2011). Women who are HIV positive also have higher prevalence rates than the general population for recent post-traumatic stress disorder (PTSD; 30%), childhood sexual abuse (39.3%), childhood physical abuse (42.7%), childhood abuse (58.2%), lifetime sexual abuse (61.1%), lifetime physical abuse (72.1%), and lifetime abuse (71.6%; Machtinger, Wilson, Haberer, & Weiss, 2012) (see Table 20.2).

Substance abuse is a factor that can be examined on its own, but the synergistic effects of substance abuse with IPV are devastating. This problem is considered to be one of epidemic proportions and even has acquired its own moniker: the SAVA syndemic. Substance abuse and violence are mutually reinforcing health and social problems. In 2011, Meyer, Springer, and Altice completed a literature review that consisted of 45 articles related to

Table 20.2    Meta-Analytic Prevalence Rates of Traumatic Events and PTSD in HIV-Positive Women)

| Categories | No. of Studies | Pooled $n$ | Prevalence[a] | 95% CI | Prevalence[b] |
|---|---|---|---|---|---|
| Recent PTSD | 6 | 499 | 30 | 18.8–42.7 | 5.2 |
| IPV | 8 | 2,285 | 55.3 | 36.1–73.8 | 24.8 |
| Adult sexual abuse | 8 | 2,237 | 35.2 | 20.1–51.4 | –[c] |
| Adult physical abuse | 5 | 1,791 | 53.9 | 30.2–76.8 | –[c] |
| Adult abuse | 2 | 532 | 65 | 58.9–70.8 | –[c] |
| Childhood sexual abuse | 7 | 3,013 | 39.3 | 33.9–44.8 | 16.2 |
| Childhood physical abuse | 6 | 1,582 | 42.7 | 31.5–54.4 | 22.9 |
| Childhood abuse | 2 | 232 | 58.2 | 36.0–78.8 | 31.9 |
| Lifetime sexual abuse | 8 | 1,182 | 61.1 | 47.7–73.8 | 12.0 |
| Lifetime physical abuse | 6 | 878 | 7.1 | 60.1–8.1 | -[c] |
| Lifetime abuse unspecified | 6 | 1,065 | 71.6 | 61.0–81.1 | 39 |

[a] Pooled prevalence from random-effects model (DerSimonian-Laird).
[b] National samples of US women.
[c] Data from a national sample not available or national samples report conflicting rates.
Source: Machtinger, Wilson, Haberer, & Weiss, 2012, p. 2097.

(a) HIV-associated risk-taking behaviors, (b) mental health, (c) healthcare utilization and medication adherence, and (d) the bidirectional relationship between violence and HIV status; they confirmed that not only does the additive effect of substance abuse increase risk behavior, but it also lead to poor decision-making and negative health consequences. These risks are particularly high in poor urban women.

Substance abuse was identified as a primary risk factor from the beginning of the HIV/AIDS crisis. Intravenous drug use is a direct pathway to infection; however, other methods of delivery also increase exposure to the virus. Drugs generally associated with high-risk behavior are heroin, methamphetamines, crack, and "club drugs" like Ecstasy, ketamine, GHB, and poppers. Alcohol has also been shown to be a high-risk factor for HIV exposure.

Drug abuse, IPV, and mental health issues that may or may not be a result of abuse must be considered throughout any intervention. It is important that substance abuse and mental illness treatment be advised and offered concomitantly with medical treatment. If substance abuse and/or psychiatric illness are not addressed initially, sabotage of the medical intervention as well as client-worker relationships is likely. Although there are several reasons for addressing these concurrent problems, possibly the most important are the severe individual and societal consequences associated with nonadherence to drug regimens.

## Adherence to Medication

Nonadherence to antiretrovirals is directly related to the development of antiretroviral drug resistance. Poor adherence can be a problem with any chronic illness; however, as early as 1996, the issue of nonadherence was recognized as a potential disaster with protease inhibitors in the treatment of HIV (Lewis & Abell, 2002). HIV replicates hundreds of millions of times a day, creating approximately 10 billion viral particles. Every replication is a potential for a mutation that is drug resistant (Richman, 2004). When no antiretroviral is being used, these mutations are mostly random natural accidents and make no meaningful difference. When doses are missed, as is the case with nonadherence, or "drug holidays," the mutations become systematic because the particles that are most drug susceptible are killed when the medication is taken, leaving only drug-resistant particles to replicate.

In the past it was said that 95% adherence was required for sustained viral suppression; however, now studies show that although it is not optimal, viral suppression can happen with as low as 73% adherence to protease inhibitors and 54% adherence to the more powerful nonnucleoside reverse-transcriptase inhibitors (NNRTIs) combined with dual nucleoside analogues (Bangsberg, 2006). The lower threshold is good news given that the average adherence rate for most individuals was found to be 75%, but it does not diminish the importance of adherence; the lower the adherence rate, the higher the likelihood of medication resistance. Sustained viral suppression is the goal of HIV treatment; it means greater quality of life and a reduced risk of transmission of the virus to others.

## RESILIENCE AND PROTECTIVE FACTORS

In 2013, Cantisano, Rimé, and Muñoz-Sastre found that on a questionnaire that assessed illness-related emotions, social sharing of emotion, and emotional inhibition, women with HIV scored significantly higher in guilt and shame than women with diabetes and cancer. They also found that women who were HIV positive were concerned about reflecting a negative image of themselves when talking about their illness and shared their disease status with fewer people than did the cancer and diabetes patients. Several studies have shown that when social support is increased, women with HIV have better health outcomes and a higher quality of life (Dyer, Stein, Rice, & Rotheram-Borus, 2012; Smith, Rossetto, & Peterson, 2008; Vanable et al., 2006; Vyavaharkar et al., 2010). Optimism, religiosity, and finding meaning have also been found to be factors that are related to resiliency in women who are HIV positive.

Most AIDS service organizations (ASOs) that provide case management, as well as clinicians independent of ASOs, serve clients who are currently facing crisis events; they also attempt to prepare clients for possible future events in order to prevent a crisis situation. During intake, myths are dispelled by educating the client about the disease spectrum, constitutional symptoms, what to do and what not to do to stay healthy, and strategies for safer sex. Suggestions for keeping the immune system healthy usually include topics such as nutritional facts, information on support groups, hotlines, counselors for stress management and other mental health issues, medication adherence issues, and spiritual support. Useful Internet sites are available to help clients and clinicians keep up with new clinical trials and news briefs, as well as providing simple lay information such as at www.thebody.com and www.poz.com.

## ROBERTS'S SEVEN-STAGE CRISIS INTERVENTION MODEL

Roberts's seven-stage model of crisis intervention provides an excellent framework for working with HIV-positive individuals who are experiencing a crisis state (Roberts & Ottens, 2005). The seven stages of intervention are as follows:

- Assessing lethality and safety needs
- Establishing rapport and communication
- Identifying the major problems
- Dealing with feelings and providing support
- Exploring possible alternatives
- Formulating an action plan
- Providing follow-up

It is important for the clinician to remember that what separates a crisis from a difficult situation is the lack of tools and the perception of danger. For example, when a person gets a flat tire on his or her car, if one has the tools, a spare tire, and a safe place to change the tire, the flat is a mere inconvenience. However, if that person is alone on a dark, deserted highway and has no lug wrench, a feeling of crisis begins to stir. The event, the flat tire, is not the crisis. The feeling aroused by the perception of danger generated by the context in which the event is taking place and the lack of tools to ameliorate the situation are the crux of the crisis. The clinician's acknowledgment and assessment of the perceived danger are the starting point for crisis intervention. Roberts's seven-stage model is meant to be a flexible framework for practice, providing guidelines for crisis intervention without rigidity.

## Lethality Assessment and Building Rapport

Suicide has been linked to chronic illness, substance abuse, previous suicide, and family history of suicide (Davis, Koch, Mbugua, & Johnson, 2011; World Health Organization, 2006). Along with the chronic illness, each of the other factors is higher in the HIV population than in the general population (Davis et al., 2011). Rates of mental health disorders, including depression and anxiety, are higher in individuals with HIV, which may be a result of, or be exacerbated by, stigma, discrimination, and health concerns. Some medications are associated with side effects such as unipolar or bipolar mood disorders. It is important that every counselor be cognizant of the increased suicide risk for this population and screen accordingly. The World Health Organization (2006, p. 14) suggests the following when doing a suicide assessment in a crisis state:

- Be calm and supportive.
- Be nonjudgmental.
- Encourage self-disclosure.
- Acknowledge suicide is a choice, but don't normalize the choice.
- Actively listen and positively reinforce self-care.

- Keep the counseling process in the here and now.
- Avoid in-depth counseling until the crisis abates.
- Call upon others to help assess the potential for self-harm.
- Ask questions about lethality.
- Remove lethal means.

Clinicians can find free suicide screening tools on the Internet for free such as the Columbia Suicide Severity Rating Scale (C-SSRS); Suicide Assessment Five Step Evaluation and Triage (SAFE-T), and; the Suicide Behaviors Questionnaire (SBQ-R; SAMHSA-HRSA Center for Integrated Health Solutions, 2013). All agencies and private practitioners should have protocols on safety procedures in place before ever being faced with a suicidal client. If the potential for self-harm is suspected, the clinician must follow through with the aforementioned protocols.

Crisis intervention with HIV-positive women begins with rapport building or relationship building. The tools or assets that the clinician needs in this stage are a nonjudgmental attitude, the ability to understand verbal and nonverbal communication, sincerity, objectivity, and an appropriate sense of humor.

When attempting to build rapport, it is important for the clinician to remember the stigma that is associated with having an HIV-positive status. The clinician will be asking the client to reveal very personal parts of her life that are not customarily talked about with anyone, let alone a stranger. After working with the HIV-positive population for a while, it is easy to forget the discomfort associated with topics such as sex and drug use. These topics become a part of the everyday experience of the practitioner; however, the discomfort may remain for the client. The practitioner must provide a safe and respectful atmosphere for such disclosures; this can be done through modeling a level of comfort with sensitive material that is often considered taboo.

It is during this stage of assessment that most information gathering will be done. Most agencies have a routine intake form consisting of several pages of questions. These questions are generally used to collect demographic information (place of residence, family size, income, etc.), possible HIV exposure routes, method of payment for medical services, some medical information, and information about the client's family system or other avenues of support. A succession of rapid-fire questions can severely hinder the attempt to build a mutually respectful relationship because there is no give and take between parties: The client is doing all the giving. Such one-way communication sets up a dynamic in which the clinician is the one with all the power, diminishing the client.

When clinicians are familiar with the intake and assessment process, it is much easier to guide the client to tell his or her story as opposed to giving one-sentence answers to a series of questions. This storytelling provides both a more relaxed atmosphere for the client and an opportunity for the clinician to assess cognitive functioning. A moderately scheduled interview guide is used to assure the collection of all needed information. This guide allows provides structure, but also gives the clinician flexibility so that rapport can be built with the client. The guide does not have to be an actual form (although that may be helpful in the beginning) but instead a way of thinking or arranging the interview. The format of the guide is funnel shaped, meaning the interview starts with very open questions that lead to more direct questions such as:

- Maria, what brings you in to see me today?
- Walk me through your pill-taking regimen.
- Let's talk about your viral load.

Each question in the preceding sequence gets more focused. There may or may not be several questions between these questions, depending on the depth and breadth of Mary's responses. The guide is moderately scheduled because it gives an outline, not the exact questions or timing of the questions. All the information needed by the agency must be gathered, but it can be gathered in a time frame agreed upon by both the client and the clinician. Depending on the circumstances, another option might be to use the Cultural Formation Interview, a tool developed by the American Psychiatric Association (2013) that can be used to have the client identify issues in her own cultural framework.

## Assessment of the Problem

The primary challenge for clinicians working with HIV-positive individuals is resisting the urge to become enthralled by the crisis. Because death is so embedded in societal consciousness as the ultimate negative consequence of danger, it is hard to recognize that death is not a crisis. A sign on the wall of the employee lounge in one AIDS service organization reads: "There is no such thing as a crisis." This is to remind clinicians that no matter what the circumstance, when individuals have the tools they need, there is no crisis. The questions and issues that the practitioner needs to identify and assess related to HIV for each of the two cases illustrations are shown in Table 20.3.

When working with HIV-positive clients, it is important to always consider possible cognitive impairment of a physiological nature. This is not to imply that the social service clinician should attempt to medically diagnose a client with HIV brain involvement; however, the clinician should be able to recognize telltale signs in order to make immediate medical referrals. These signs may include, but not be limited to, memory impairment, illogical or disorganized thinking, severe headaches, blurred vision, a change in speech, or a change in gait.

Table 20.3   Type of Danger and Coping Strategies

| Aspect of Current Crisis Related to HIV | Positive and Negative Coping Strategies |
| --- | --- |
| Perceived danger | Past positive/negative coping strategies |
| Mary: HIV exposure/domestic violence. | Mary: drugs and belief in God |
| Maria: Financial | Maria: social support and self-reliance. |
| Is the danger physical or emotional or contextual? | Action |
| | Mary: HIV testing; medical supervision; domestic violence counseling |
| Mary: Physical | |
| Maria: Contextual/physical | Maria: Financial aid; AIDS Drug Assistance Program |

Because of the heterogeneity of the HIV-positive population, practitioners should take every opportunity to learn about the cultures and customs of the people they serve. For example, research has shown that spirituality and religious involvement play a role in the health beliefs and well-being of African American women (Boyd-Franklin, 2010; Dalmida, 2006; Figueroa, Davis, Baker, & Bunch, 2006). Not all cultures place the same importance on life events, and it is important to consider the presenting crisis within the context of the client's cultural identity.

The clinician must assist the client to rank order or prioritize the major problems, as well as the perceived danger that these problems evoke. The clinician may prioritize the presenting problems differently from the client; however, it is the client who is feeling the distress. If the practitioner believes that groundwork must be laid before tackling the prioritized problem, he or she is obligated to work through these issues with the client.

For example, Mary identified her main problems as possible exposure to HIV and potential violence and/or homelessness. If Mary tests HIV negative, she needs to be referred to a physician who will potentially prescribe a pre-exposure prophylaxis (PrEP), which is a special course of HIV treatment that aims to prevent people from becoming infected with HIV. It is also important in this case to do a thorough domestic violence assessment.

In the case of Maria, she needed to get financial assistance for her medication. She was very proud and was even willing to let her health suffer rather than accept what she perceived to be welfare, but she was unaware of the dire the consequences of nonadherence. The lack of social support combined with internalized stigma was directly impacting her mental health. The clinician's role in this case is was to assist Maria in acquiring her medication and educate her about adherence as well as help her to re-engage with social support.

## Exploration of Feelings

Women who have been diagnosed with HIV could be experiencing one or more of many feelings:

- Shame: "I caught this disease through drug use or sex."
- Betrayal: "I can't believe that he was cheating on me."
- Anger: "That no good so-and-so gave this to me."
- Loss: "I won't be able to have sex—or a baby—ever again."
- Fear: "My partner will kill me if I tell him I have HIV."
- Guilt: "I may have given HIV to someone else."

Throughout this chapter, perceptions and thoughts have been discussed as the driving force behind crisis. Emotions, according to cognitive theorists, are also driven by cognitions. A primary objective in crisis intervention, therefore, is to provide information to correct distorted ideas and provide better understanding of the precipitating event. This is not to be done in an emotionless vacuum but instead in a supportive environment that emphasizes the client's strengths.

The clinician must actively listen during this cathartic phase and gently keep the client on track by asking open-ended questions. The clinician's job at this point is not only to actively listen to the client but also to see the client within her system. This will provide tools for the next stage, in which solutions are explored. In order to see the larger client system, the practitioner must constantly keep in mind five things: (a) the stage of development of the client (e.g., Ericson or some other developmental theorist); (b) the stage of disease; (c) the client's place in a family or support system; (d) cultural norms; and (e) strategies that have worked in the past in similar situations.

In the first case illustration, Mary had several issues to contend with that primarily dealt with fear: She was a 27-year-old female who had already spent some time in jail and on the street. She stated that her boyfriend "took good care of her" and that even though he was abusive, she was safer there than on the street. She did not know whether or not she was positive but suspected that because he was positive, she must be too because they did not practice safe sex. Mary had no support system other than James. She was very loyal to him because she felt she owed him, and she knew that the way to handle this situation was to just keep the peace. She would get tested and take care of things herself. She believed that after everything she had been though, that "if she was willing to walk it, God would show her the way."

Maria, in contrast, was dealing with shame. She felt the internalized stigma of having HIV, which was compounded by the importance she placed on taking care of herself. For her, having to ask for help was a crushing blow on multiple levels. Maria did not value money for its own sake but because it provided her with a sense of security and control. When she perceived that she could not take care of herself because the medication cost too much, that was her sign that the disease had gotten the better of her.

## Exploration of Alternatives and Action Plan

Throughout the assessment process, information is gathered in order to explore possible solutions. By this point in the intervention, the clinician has determined whether the client is suicidal or homicidal, has established rapport, has investigated the major problem(s), and has explored feelings and thoughts the client is experiencing as a result of the problem(s). Finding a workable solution and developing an action plan are the next two steps. The solution must be generated with the client and must take into account the tools with which she has to work.

When finding a workable solution, the clinician often has to take the role of an active guide. As a result of the crisis, the client is experiencing disequilibrium and may be unable to identify tactics or skills to alleviate the situation. The client may not recognize that she has overcome similar or more difficult hurdles in the past, and it is the role of the practitioner to point out these strengths and accomplishments.

The action plan should contain identifiable steps. It is a good idea to take out a piece of paper and write down each step with the client. Draw a line vertically down the paper, and on one side of the line write down the objective or task, and on the other side write down who is to accomplish the task and the time frame in which it is to be accomplished. The client may only be able to make one phone call a day. This may not seem like much of an accomplishment, but it starts a momentum toward the goal.

In the case of Mary, there were a few issues that needed to be addressed simultaneously. Mary needed to get tested for HIV, but regardless of her HIV status, she needed to have access to a physician who could evaluate her either for HIV treatment or for PrEP. In the meantime, however, Mary needed to make some decisions about her relationship. She did not want to leave James, so a plan had to be devised for how she was going to discuss HIV with him and remain safe from harm. It was important that she find a safe place in case James became violent. Mary and James often went for a walk in the park after James got home from work, and because it was a public space with some areas to speak in private, Mary and the clinician felt that would be a good place to have the conversation. She decided with the counselor that she would get tested before she talked to him so that she could tell him her status and let him know that she loved him and wanted to stay with him, whether or not she was HIV positive. Role plays were done to prepare for different situations, and the counselor and Mary agreed that no drug or alcohol should be used before the difficult discussion.

The counselor gave her information about the PrEP so that she could explain it to James if he wanted information. Mary was also given some information that was printed from a website regarding rapid testing; the syndemic of HIV, domestic violence, and substance abuse; and safety information and plans for domestic violence. The counselor then sent Mary to the health department for rapid testing and asked her to follow up the next day.

Maria had a completely different set of needs and different skills with which to work. She needed financial assistance to secure her medications, but along with that she needed to reconnect with her support group. Maria also needed to get her viral load under control again, but she could not do that until she garnered funding for her medication. She made too much money for the AIDS Drug Assistance Program (ADAP), so she had to apply directly to the drug companies for assistance. Next the counselor worked with Maria to set up an account on www.thebody.com to send daily text reminders about taking her medications once she got them in order to assist her with adherence. Maria also set up accounts for two different online support groups. Both Maria and the counselor agreed that the online groups were not there to take the place of face-to-face meetings but that they were a good supplement.

## Follow Up

The last step of every action plan should be some form of follow-up with the crisis intervention counselor. A set appointment or follow-up contact with the clinician both gives the client an incentive to accomplish each task on the objective list and provides assurance that she does not have to do it all on her own. During the follow-up contact, the problem and steps taken to overcome the problem are reviewed. If the problem still exists, additional possible solutions are investigated. If the problem has been resolved, it is important for the clinician to affirm the client's accomplishment. This affirmation will help to anchor these newfound coping strategies for future use.

## CONCLUSION

Even though the number of deaths from AIDS-related illnesses have decreased in the recent past, the number of new HIV infections has not slowed. Minority women, who are often already marginalized, are disproportionately affected and infected by HIV and AIDS. Due to the nature of the virus and the stigma that is associated with it, these women may face serial crises.

When working with HIV-positive women, clinicians must be alert to domestic and other forms of violence, as well as drug abuse, all of which are confounding variables. It is also important to be sensitive to cultural norms, including the roles that women play within each culture. The crisis intervention assessment should be within a cultural context that considers the client's system of support. It is important to recognize the client's strengths and successful coping strategies that have been utilized in the past. A plethora of resources are available for social workers, nurses, and other individuals who provide care to individuals who are HIV positive. New information and interventions are made available frequently, and it is important that workers stay up to date in order to give clients the most accurate information.

REFERENCES

American Psychiatric Association. (2013). *Diagnostic and statistical manual of mental disorders* (5th ed.). Arlington, VA: American Psychiatric Publishing.

Andrinopoulos, K., Clum, G., Murphy, D. A., Harper, G., Perez, L., Xu, J., . . . Ellen, J. M. (2011). Health related quality of life and psychosocial correlates among HIV-infected adolescent and young adult women in the US. *AIDS Education and Prevention : Official Publication of the International Society for AIDS Education, 23,* 367–381. Retrieved from http://www.pubmedcentral.nih.gov/articlerender.fcgi?artid=3287350&tool=pmcentrez&rendertype=abstract

Bangsberg, D. R. (2006). Less than 95% adherence to nonnucleoside reverse-transcriptase inhibitor therapy can lead to viral suppression. *Clinical Infectious Diseases : An Official Publication of the Infectious Diseases Society of America, 43,* 939–941. doi:10.1086/507526

Berjot, S., & Gillet, N. (2011). Stress and coping with discrimination and stigmatization. *Frontiers in Psychology, 2,* 33. doi:10.3389/fpsyg.2011.00033

Boyd-Franklin, N. (2010). Incorporating spirituality and religion into the treatment of African American clients. *Counseling Psychologist, 38*(7), 97–1000. doi:10.1177/0011000010374881

Burke, J. G., Thieman, L. K., Gielen, A. C., O'Campo, P., & McDonnell, K. A. (2005). Intimate partner violence, substance use, and HIV among low-income women: Taking a closer look. *Violence Against Women, 11,* 1140–1161. doi:10.1177/1077801205276943

Cantisano, N., Rimé, B., & Muñoz-Sastre, M. T. (2013). The social sharing of emotions in HIV/AIDS: A comparative study of HIV/AIDS, diabetic and cancer patients. *Journal of Health Psychology, 18,* 1255–1267. doi:10.1177/1359105312462436

Centers for Disease Control and Prevention. (2010). HIV/AIDS surveillance report. *HIV Surveillance Report, 2010, 22,* 1–79.

Centers for Disease Control and Prevention. (2011). *HIV surveillance report, 23.* Retrieved from http://www.cdc.gov/hiv/topics/surveillance/resources/reports/

Colbert, A. M., Kim, K. H., Sereika, S. M., & Erlen, J. A. (2010). An examination of the relationships among gender, health status, social support, and HIV-related stigma. *Journal of the Association of Nurses in AIDS Care, 21*, 302–313. doi:10.1016/j.jana.2009.11.004

Dalmida, S. G. (2006). Spirituality, mental health, physical health, and health-related quality of life among women with HIV/AIDS: Integrating spirituality into mental health care. *Issues in Mental Health Nursing, 27*, 185–198. doi:10.1080/01612840500436958

Davis, S. J., Koch, D. S., Mbugua, A., & Johnson, A. (2011). Recognizing suicide risk in consumers with HIV/AIDS. *Journal of Rehabilitation, 77*, 14–19. Retrieved from http://ezproxy.library.wisc.edu/login?url=http://search.ebscohost.com/login.aspx?direct=true&db=aph&AN=58200255&site=ehost-live

Dowshen, N., & D'Angelo, L. (2011). Health care transition for youth living with HIV/AIDS. *Pediatrics, 128*, 762–771. doi:10.1542/peds.2011-0068

Dyer, T. P., Stein, J. A., Rice, E., & Rotheram-Borus, M. J. (2012). Predicting depression in mothers with and without HIV: The role of social support and family dynamics. *AIDS and Behavior, 16*, 2198–2208. doi:10.1007/s10461-012-0149-6

El-Bassel, N., Gilbert, L., Krishnan, S., Schilling, R., Gaeta, T., Purpura, S., & Witte, S. S. (1998). Partner violence and sexual HIV-risk behaviors among women in an inner-city emergency department. *Violence and Victims, 13*, 377–393.

Figueroa, L. R., Davis, B., Baker, S., & Bunch, J. B. (2006). The influence of spirituality on health care-seeking behaviors among African Americans. *ABNF Journal : Official Journal of the Association of Black Nursing Faculty in Higher Education, Inc, 17*, 82–88.

Folkman, S., Lazarus, R. S., Dunkel-Schetter, C., DeLongis, A., & Gruen, R. J. (1986). Dynamics of a stressful encounter: Cognitive appraisal, coping, and encounter outcomes. *Journal of Personality and Social Psychology, 50*, 992–1003. doi:10.1037/0022-3514.50.5.992

Folkman, S., Lazarus, R. S., Gruen, R. J., & DeLongis, A. (1986). Appraisal, coping, health status, and psychological symptoms. *Journal of Personality and Social Psychology, 50*, 571–579. doi:10.1037/0022-3514.50.3.571

Frieden, T. R. (2011). Foreward: CDC Health Disparities and Inequalities Report—United States, 2011. *Morbidity and Mortality Weekly Report, Surveillance Summaries / Centers for Disease Control, 60*(suppl.), 1–2.

Gielen, A. C., McDonnell, K. A., O'Campo, P. J., & Burke, J. G. (2005). Suicide risk and mental health indicators: Do they differ by abuse and HIV status? *Women's Health Issues, 15*, 89–95. doi:10.1016/j.whi.2004.12.004

Hall, H. I., Holtgrave, D. R., Tang, T., & Rhodes, P. (2013). HIV transmission in the United States: Considerations of viral load, risk behavior, and health disparities. *AIDS and Behavior, 17*, 1632–1636. doi:10.1007/s10461-013-0426-z

Larios, S. E., Davis, J. N., Gallo, L. C., Heinrich, J., & Talavera, G. (2009). Concerns about stigma, social support and quality of life in low-income HIV-positive Hispanics. *Ethnicity and Disease, 19*, 65–70.

Lewis, S. J., & Abell, N. (2002). Development and evaluation of the Adherence Attitude Inventory. *Research on Social Work Practice, 12*(1), 107–123. doi:10.1177/104973150201200108

Lillie-Blanton, M., Stone, V. E., Snow Jones, A., Levi, J., Golub, E. T., Cohen, M. H., . . . Wilson, T. E. (2010). Association of race, substance abuse, and health insurance coverage with use of highly active antiretroviral therapy among HIV-infected women, 2005. *American Journal of Public Health, 100*, 1493–1499. doi:AJPH.2008.158949 [pii] 10.2105/AJPH.2008.158949 [doi]

Machtinger, E. L., Wilson, T. C., Haberer, J. E., & Weiss, D. S. (2012). Psychological trauma and PTSD in HIV-positive women: A meta-analysis. *AIDS and Behavior, 16*, 2091–2100. doi:10.1007/s10461-011-0127-4

McIntosh, R. C., & Rosselli, M. (2012). Stress and coping in women living with HIV: A meta-analytic review. *AIDS and Behavior, 16*(8), 2144–2159. doi:10.1007/ s10461-012-0166-5

Meyer, J. P., Springer, S. A., & Altice, F. L. (2011). Substance abuse, violence, and HIV in women: A literature review of the syndemic. *Journal of Women's Health, 20*, 991–1006. doi:10.1089/ jwh.2010.2328

Pence, B. W., Reif, S., Whetten, K., Leserman, J., Stangl, D., Swartz, M., . . . Mugavero, M. J. (2007). Minorities, the poor, and survivors of abuse: HIV-infected patients in the US Deep South. *Southern Medical Journal, 100*,

1114–1122. doi:10.1097/01. smj.0000286756.54607.9f

Puskas, C. M., Forrest, J. I., Parashar, S., Salters, K. A., Cescon, A. M., Kaida, A.,. . . Hogg, R. S. (2011). Women and vulnerability to HAART non-adherence: A literature review of treatment adherence by gender from 2000 to 2011. *Current HIV/ AIDS Reports, 8*(4), 277–287. doi:10.1007/s11904-011-0098-0

Richman, D. D. (2004). HIV drug resistance. *New England Journal of Medicine, 350*, 1065–1071. Retrieved from http://www. pubmedcentral.nih.gov/articlerender.fcgi?artid=2652074&tool=pmc entrez&rendertype=abstract

Roberts, A. R., & Ottens, A. J. (2005). The seven-stage crisis intervention model: A road map to goal attainment, problem solving, and crisis resolution. *Brief Treatment and Crisis Intervention, 5*, 329–339. doi:10.1093/ brief-treatment/mhi030

SAMHSA-HRSA Center for Integrated Health Solutions. (2013). Suicide prevention in primary care. *e-solutions newsletter*. Retrieved from http:// www.integration.samhsa.gov/ about-us/esolutions-newsletter/ suicide-prevention-in-primary-care

Selik, R. M., Mokotoff, E. D., Branson, B., Owen, S. M., Whitmore, S., & Hall, H. I. (2014). Revised surveillance case definition for HIV infection—United States, 2014. *Morbidity and Mortality Weekly Report, Recommendations and Reports / Centers for Disease Control, 63*, 1–10. Retrieved from http://www.ncbi.nlm.nih.gov/ pubmed/24717910

Siemieniuk, R. C., Krentz, H. B., Miller, P., Woodman, K., Ko,

K., & Gill, M. J. (2013). The clinical implications of high rates of intimate partner violence against HIV-positive women. *Journal of Acquired Immune Deficiency Syndromes, 64*, 32–38. doi:10.1097/QAI.0b013e31829bb007

Smith, R., Rossetto, K., & Peterson, B. L. (2008). A meta-analysis of disclosure of one's HIV-positive status, stigma and social support. *AIDS Care, 20,* 1266–1275. doi:10.1080/09540120801926977

Vanable, P. A., Carey, M. P., Blair, D. C., & Littlewood, R. A. (2006). Impact of HIV-related stigma on health behaviors and psychological adjustment among HIV-positive men and women. *AIDS and Behavior, 10,* 473–482. doi:10.1007/s10461-006-9099-1

Vyavaharkar, M., Moneyham, L., Corwin, S., Saunders, R., Annang, L., & Tavakoli, A. (2010). Relationships between stigma, social support, and depression in HIV-infected African American women living in the rural southeastern United States. *Journal of the Association of Nurses in AIDS Care, 21,* 144–152. doi:10.1016/j.jana.2009.07.008

Wagner, A. C., Hart, T. A., Mohammed, S., Ivanova, E., Wong, J., & Loutfy, M. R. (2010). Correlates of HIV stigma in HIV-positive women. *Archives of Women's Mental Health, 13,* 207–214. doi:10.1007/s00737-010-0158-2

Watkins-Hayes, C., Pittman-Gay, L., & Beaman, J. (2012). "Dying from" to "living with": Framing institutions and the coping processes of African American women living with HIV/AIDS. *Social Science and Medicine, 74,* 2028–2036. doi:10.1016/j.socscimed.2012.02.001

Whetten, K., Leserman, J., Lowe, K., Stangl, D., Thielman, N., Swartz, M., ... Van Scoyoc, L. (2006). Prevalence of childhood sexual abuse and physical trauma in an HIV-positive sample from the Deep South. *American Journal of Public Health, 96,* 1028–1030. doi:10.2105/AJPH.2005.063263

World Health Organization. (2006). *Preventing suicide: A resource guide for dounsellors.* Geneva: Author Retrieved from http://whqlibdoc.who.int/publications/2006/9241594314_eng.pdf

Wyatt, G. E., Hamilton, A. B., Myers, H. F., Ullman, J. B., Chin, D., Sumner, L. A., ... Liu, H. (2011). Violence prevention among HIV-positive women with histories of violence: Healing women in their communities. *Women's Health Issues, 21.* doi:10.1016/j.whi.2011.07.007

# 21

# Animal-Assisted Crisis Response

YVONNE EATON-STULL
BRIAN FLYNN

The mudslides in Oso, Washington, the shootings at the Washington, DC, Navy Yard, and Hurricane Sandy are all examples of disasters that still resonate in the national psyche. Footage of these recent crises and disasters has inundated our living rooms as we watch the survivors and responders as they attempt to cope, respond, and recover from these traumatic events.

When a disaster occurs, its impact touches both the individual and the community. Whether the incident is naturally occurring or is human-made, the reactions of stress and grief often experienced after a disaster are normal responses to abnormal situations. Most individuals do not see themselves as needing mental health support after the disaster and will not seek out services. This often leads to an intensification of symptoms and the possibility of longer-term mental health struggles. By providing emotional support at the impact of a disaster or shortly thereafter, these reactions may be lessened. The NATO Joint Medical Committee (2008) defines *recovery* as "the psychosocial care that describes the dynamic, continuing interactional processes that include strengths and vulnerabilities, resources available, and positive aspects of the environment" (p. 40). The question is, What strategies and techniques are most valuable in facilitating recovery from traumatic events?

At an international expert consensus workshop in 2002, six federal agencies conducted an extensive review of the disaster intervention literature, and three follow-up roundtables occurred. They recommended the following empirically supported intervention principles: promoting sense of safety, calming, a sense of self-efficacy and community efficacy, connectedness, and hope (Watson, Brymer, & Bonanno, 2011). The individual, informal intervention of psychological first aid (PFA) was determined to meet these standards (Kaul & Welzant, 2005). Following the expert consensus recommendations, the PFA field operations guide was developed by the National Child Traumatic Stress Network (NCTSN) and the National Center for PTSD (NCPTSD) (Brymer et al., 2006) as an evidence-informed approach to helping people in the immediate aftermath of disaster. In addition to the support from these reputable, reliable organizations, PFA is also endorsed by NATO as the evidence-informed approach to decreasing distress and fostering adaptive functioning and coping (NATO Joint Medical Committee, 2008).

Animal-assisted crisis response (AACR) offers the addition of a certified crisis response dog to crisis responders as an effective way to provide PFA and help people affected by crises and disasters. To increase knowledge of this specialized form of crisis intervention, a review of a few key terms is essential. *Therapy dog* is used to describe a dog that has been evaluated for its temperament and obedience and is registered with an organization, not "certified." However, there are just about as many therapy dog organizations as there are breeds of dogs; thus, the types of evaluations vary. For example, some may evaluate these dogs only once whereas others may require periodic re-evaluations. Pet Partners is a national organization that provides training in addition to conducting regular screenings and evaluations of the handler and the dog (Pet Partners, 2012). Information about Pet Partners can be accessed at http://petpartners.org/. Although many therapy dogs may be well suited to respond to crises and disasters, many may not. So what do we do? Assure that responding teams have animal-assisted crisis response (AACR) certification.

AACR teams are specially screened dog and handler teams that have been evaluated and extensively trained to be able to respond to chaotic, unpredictable environments and interact effectively with individuals who are expressing intense emotions. These crisis response dogs are utilized to provide comfort and support following crises and disasters (HOPE AACR, n.d.). These teams must demonstrate prior and current animal-assisted experience with various populations and pass an intense evaluation to determine aptitude to engage in AACR work. Certification training includes didactic information on crisis intervention, incident command, stress management, self-care, and canine behavior. Additional experiential training prepares these teams to respond effectively in emotionally charged and chaotic environments. Responders can obtain more information about AACR at http://www.hopeaacr.org and request certified teams to assist them when responding to crises.

Much like other emergency service professionals, these AACR teams are required to obtain continuing education. In 2010, national standards were developed that outline the requirements for AACR teams. These requirements are vital to the delivery of safe and professional services (National Standards Committee for AACR, 2010). Two national organizations, HOPE AACR and National AACR, meet these standards, which include minimum training, such as incident command system, crisis intervention, self-care, as

Table 21.1    Difference Between Therapy Dog Visits and AACR Response

|  | Therapy Dog | AACR |
|---|---|---|
| Visits/response | Scheduled in advance | Crises often come without warning |
| Mode of travel | Usually by car | May be by air, bus, boat, train, emergency vehicle |
| Working environment | Routine, predictable, familiar | Unpredictable, chaotic, unfamiliar |
| Clientele | Often 1:1 visits or small groups | Often very large groups, crowds |
| Emotional stimuli | Often low-key emotions | Intense emotions, high stress, grief |
| Support from others | Often have support and assistance from agency staff | Must be self-sufficient, not a burden to other responders |
| Length of visit/response | Typically ½-hr to 1½-hr visits | Several hours to several days |
| Mode of visit/response | Often work alone | Work with other teams |
| Demand | Not too demanding, often indoor | Physically demanding, long time periods, may be outdoors |
| Animal | Can use dogs, cats, horses, other small animals | Only dogs are recommended due to acceptance of them as "helpers" |

*Source*: HOPE AACR, 2008.

well as canine behavior and stress management. These AACR organizations monitor and evaluate teams on an ongoing basis and require active participation and involvement in crisis and disaster response. These certified teams demonstrate professionalism and follow a standard of conduct. Table 21.1 summarizes the differences between a therapy dog visit and an AACR crisis callout. This distinction further demonstrates the need to make sure you have the right type of dog for the job.

Responders who provide crisis intervention are now realizing the benefits of our four-legged canine friends in providing positive PFA interventions. Positive intervention strategies should focus on ways to decrease physiological arousal, offer emotional comfort and support, and encourage social contact and communication (Orner, Kent, Pfefferbaum, Raphael, & Watson, 2006). AACR offers an innovative way to meet these early intervention goals by providing various physiological, emotional, and social benefits.

## PHYSIOLOGICAL BENEFITS

Exposure to crises and disasters causes physiological arousal, but touch, proximity, and animal-assisted interventions can lead to stress reduction and trauma recovery (Yorke, 2010). In a large meta-analysis of 69 studies, Beetz, Uvnas-Moberg, Julius, and Kotrschal (2012) determined that there are well-documented physical benefits following animal interaction. This valuable intervention has the potential to lessen or prevent more serious effects. Many specific factors contribute to the development of post-traumatic stress disorder (PTSD), but one known predictor is elevated heart rate (Bryant, Creamer, O'Donnell, Silove, & McFarlane, 2008; DeYoung, Kenardy, & Spence, 2007; Kassam-Adams, Garcia-Espana, Fein, & Winston, 2005; Kuhn, Blanchard, Fuse, Hickling, & Broderick, 2006). Interaction with dogs has been shown to decrease one's heart rate (Barker, Knisely, McCain, Schubert, & Pandurangi, 2010; Kaminski, Pellino, & Wish, 2002; Morrison, 2007). Thus, the utilization of AACR in the aftermath of a crisis can have a preventative mental health benefit for the survivors.

Several studies have also found that cortisol, a stress hormone, decreases following interaction with animals (Barker et al., 2010; Kaminski et al., 2002; Odendaal, 2000; Viau, Arsenault-Lapierre, Fecteau, Champagne, Walker, & Lupien, 2010). Decreases in blood pressure are also supported in the literature (Barker et al., 2010; Odendaal, 2000). The use of AACR to reduce stress hormones (cortisol), heart rate, or blood pressure offers innovative, nonpharmacologic ways to decrease physiological arousal and promote recovery.

## EMOTIONAL BENEFITS

The emotional impact of crises and disasters can be overwhelming. Two of the most common reactions include fear and anxiety (National Center for PTSD, 2010). Interventions that focus on strategies to lessen these responses are certainly indicated. Experienced disaster responders offer valuable insights into the impact of AACR. Greenbaum (2006), based on her experience during the events surrounding the attacks of 9/11, asserts that dogs' nonjudgmental, supportive nature was a natural calming agent. Graham (2009), a disaster responder to fires and tornadoes, felt these teams create a compassionate presence for those impacted by disasters. These dogs offer a sense of security and reassurance by offering unconditional love and acceptance. In fact, Chandler (2008) states that during Hurricane Katrina, they were much more effective than other interventions in providing nurturance and alleviating anxiety for survivors.

Research in the mental health field also lends support to the benefits of animal intervention in decreasing anxiety. Cutting-edge research is being conducted at the Virginia Commonwealth University Center for Human Animal Interaction, and readers are encouraged to visit its website at http:// chai.vcu.edu/. Several studies with various populations have found that anxiety reduction occurs after interaction with animals (Barker & Dawson,

1998; Hoffman et al., 2009; Jasperson, 2010; Lang, Jansen, Wertenauer, Gallinat, & Rapp, 2010; Sockalingam et al., 2008). Additionally, responders are well aware of the personal impact that disaster and crisis work may have on them as well. Rossetti, DeFabiis, and Belpedio (2008) found that the presence and utilization of dogs in the workplace also decreased the stress of staff.

## SOCIAL BENEFITS

AACR teams work collaboratively with various professionals who respond to crises and disasters. Responders have a critical role in identifying those in need of further services and supports, so any strategies to assist in making these beneficial connections should be considered. After the crash of Continental Flight 3407 in 2009, canine teams were a great supplement to the work of mental health providers (Homish, Frazer, McCartan, & Billittier, 2010). In her qualitative research with AACR handlers, Bua (2013) found that AACR dogs provide a medium between survivors and practitioners acting as extensions of crisis counselors. In an extensive review of 69 studies on human-animal interactions, Beetz and colleagues (2012) found well-documented benefits for social attention, social behavior, and interpersonal interactions; making social connections is an essential postcrisis role (Wells, 2009).

## THEORETICAL SUPPORT

Human-animal interactions offer a valuable healing form of crisis intervention. According to the biophilia hypothesis, "Animals signal safety, security, and well-being; therefore, encounters with animals are significant and can activate experiences that lead to change" (Schaefer, 2002, pp. 4–5). Disasters and crises can shatter one's belief that the world is a safe place. Dogs offer a sense of stability and security, enhancing feelings of safety and hope. A related theory, the social support theory, "provides additional backing that animal companionship helps buffer stress" (Halm, 2008, p. 373). Immediately after crises, victims tend to seek social connections and support. Animals can provide this form of unconditional love and encouragement. Practitioners can facilitate these interactions to improve recovery from disasters and crises.

Previous research supports physiological benefits, such as decreased blood pressure, heart rate, and cortisol levels. Physical changes created by the human-animal interaction not only may protect survivors from the negative effects of stress but also may prevent serious long-term consequences like PTSD. Emotional assistance is also well supported in the research.

Table 21.2   How AACR Complements PFA

| PFA Action | How AACR Complements PFA |
| --- | --- |
| Make contact/engage with survivors | Offers nonjudgmental, unconditional acceptance |
| Enhance safety and comfort | Provides physical comfort, support, and grounding |
| Calm and stabilize survivors | Acts as a calming agent, decreases anxiety |
| Gather information | Increases comfort, which helps people open up |
| Connect with social supports | Social catalyst function, helps engage people |
| Give information on coping | Conveys information via a comfortable source |
| Link with collaborative services | Builds therapeutic bridges |

Source: Brymer et al., 2006.

Interaction with animals alleviates anxiety, reduces fear, induces relaxation, and improves mood. Finally, social advantages are well documented. The social benefits of animal interaction include increased interactions, decreased isolation, and enhanced engagement with responders. Disasters and crises can be devastating and life changing; thus, it is essential to continue to utilize and develop interventions that positively impact survivors' recovery.

Based on the foregoing research, the manner in which the AACR teams accomplish PFA is summarized in Table 21.2.

The therapeutic benefits of AACR to those experiencing the psychological impact of disaster and trauma are clearly demonstrated. AACR offers an invaluable tool for PFA providers and disaster responders. Future goals should include spreading awareness of AACR and increasing the number of trained and certified teams that can respond to incidents when they occur.

REFERENCES

Barker, S. B., & Dawson, K. S. (1998). The effects of animal-assisted therapy on anxiety ratings of hospitalized psychiatric patients. *Psychiatric Services, 49,* 797–801.

Barker, S. B., Knisely, J. S., McCain, N. L., Schubert, C. M., & Pandurangi, A. K. (2010). Exploratory study of stress-buffering response patterns from interaction with a therapy dog. *Anthrozoos, 23,* 79–91. doi:10.2752/1753037 10X12627079939341

Beetz, A., Uvnas-Moberg, K., Julius, H., & Kotrschal, K. (2012). Psychosocial and psychophysiological effects of human-animal interactions: The possible role of oxytocin. *Frontiers in Psychology, 3,* 234. doi:10.3389/ fpsyg.2012.00234

Bryant, R. A., Creamer, M., O'Donnell, M., Silove, D., & McFarlane, A. C. (2008). A multi-site study of initial respiration rate and heart rate as predictors of post-traumatic stress disorder. *Journal of Clinical Psychiatry, 69,* 1694–1701.

Brymer, M., Jacobs, A., Layne, C., Pynoos, R., Ruzek, J., Steinberg, A., Vernberg, E., & Watson, P. (NCTSN, and NCPTSD). (2006). *Psychological first aid: Field operations guide*, 2nd edition. Available at www.nctsn.org and www.ncptsd.va.gov

Bua, F. (2013). *A qualitative investigation into dogs serving on animal assisted crisis response (AACR) teams: Advances in crisis counseling* (Doctoral dissertation). Retrieved from http://hdl.handle.net/1959.9/279067

Chandler, C. K. (2008, March). *Animal assisted therapy with Hurricane Katrina survivors.* Based on a program presented at the annual conference and exhibition of the American Counseling Association, Honolulu, HI. Retrieved from http://counseling-outfitters.com/vistas/vistas08/Chandler.htm

DeYoung, A. C., Kenardy, J. A., & Spence, S. H. (2007). Elevated heart rate as a predictor of PTSD six months following accidental pediatric injury. *Journal of Traumatic Stress, 20*, 751–756.

Graham, L. B. (2009). Dogs bringing comfort in the midst of a national disaster. *Reflections, 15*(1), 76–84.

Greenbaum, S. D. (2006). Introduction to working with animal assisted crisis response animal handler teams. *International Journal of Emergency Mental Health, 8*(1), 49–64.

Halm, M. A. (2008). The healing power of the human-animal connection. *American Journal of Critical Care, 17*, 373–376.

Hoffman, A., Lee, A. H., Wertenauer, F., Ricken, R., Jansen, J. J., Gallinat, J., & Lang, U. (2009). Dog-assisted intervention significantly reduces anxiety in hospitalized patients with major depression. *European Journal of Integrative Medicine, 1*, 145–148. doi:10.1016/j.eujim.2009.08.002

Homish, G. G., Frazer, B. S., McCartan, D. P., & Billittier, A. J. (2010). Emergency mental health: Lessons learned from Flight 3407. *Concepts in Disaster Medicine, 4*, 326–331.

HOPE AACR. (2008). *Comfort in times of crisis* [Brochure]. Retrieved from http: www.hopeaacr.org

HOPE AACR. (n.d.). Frequently asked questions. Retrieved from http://hopeaacr.org/frequently-asked-questions/#2

Jasperson, R. A. (2010). Animal-assisted therapy with female inmates with mental illness: A case example from a pilot program. *Journal of Offender Rehabilitation, 49*, 417–433. doi:10.1080/10509674.2010.499056

Kaminski, M., Pellino, T., & Wish, J. (2002). Play and pets: The physical and emotional impact of child-life and pet therapy on hospitalized children. *Children's Health Care, 31*, 321–335. doi:10.1207/S15326888ChC3104_5j

Kassam-Adams, N., Garcia-Espana, J. F., Fein, J. A., & Winston, F. K. (2005). Heart rate and posttraumatic stress in injured children. *Archives General Psychiatry, 62*, 335–340.

Kaul, R. E., & Welzant, V. (2005). Disaster mental health: A discussion of best practices as applied after the Pentagon attack. In A. R. Roberts (Ed.) *Crisis intervention handbook: Assessment, treatment, and research* (pp. 200–220). New York: Oxford University Press.

Kuhn, E., Blanchard, E. B., Fuse, T., Hickling, E. J., & Broderick, J. (2006). Heart rate of motor vehicle accident survivors in the emergency department, peritraumatic psychological reactions, ASD, and PTSD severity: A 6-month prospective study. *Journal of Traumatic Stress, 19,* 735–740.

Lang, U. E., Jansen, J. B., Wertenauer, F., Gallinat, J., & Rapp, M. A. (2010). Reduced anxiety during dog assisted interviews in acute schizophrenic patients. *European Journal of Integrative Medicine, 2,* 123–127. doi:10.1016/j.eujim.2010.07.002

Morrison, M. (2007). Health benefits of animal-assisted interventions. *Complementary Health Practice Review, 12*(1), 51–62. doi:10.1177/1533210107302397

National Center for PTSD. (2010). Mental health reactions after disaster. Retreived from http://www.ptsd.va.gov/professional/pages/helping-survivors-after-disaster.asp

National Standards Committee. (2010). Animal-Assisted Crisis Response National Standards. Retrieved from http://hopeaacr.org/wp-content/uploads/2010/03/AACRNationalStandards7Mar10.pdf

NATO Joint Medical Committee. (2008). *Psychosocial care for people affected by disasters and major incidents: A model for designing, delivering and managing psychosocial services for people involved in major incidents, conflict, disasters and terrorism.* NATO: Retrieved from http: www.healthplanning.co.uk/nato/

Odendaal, J. S. J. (2000). Animal-assisted therapy—magic or medicine? *Journal of Psychosomatic Research, 49,* 275–280.

Orner, R. J., Kent, A. T., Pfefferbaum, B. J., Raphael, B., & Watson, P. J. (2006). The context of providing immediate postevent intervention. In E. C. Ritchie, P. J. Watson, & M.

J. Friedman (Eds.), *Interventions following mass violence and disasters* (pp. 121–133). New York: Guilford Press.

Rossetti, J., DeFabiis, S., & Belpedio, C. (2008). Behavioral health staff's perceptions of pet-assisted therapy: An exploratory study. *Journal of Psychosocial Nursing, 46*(9), 28–33.

Schaefer, K. (2002). Human-animal interactions as a therapeutic intervention. *Counseling and Human Development, 34*(5), 1–18.

Sockalingam, S., Li, M., Krishnadev, U., Hanson, K., Balaban, K., Pacione, L.R., & Bhalerao, S. (2008). Use of animal-assisted therapy in the rehabilitation of an assault victim with a concurrent mood disorder. *Issues in Mental Health Nursing, 29,* 73–84. doi:10.1080/01612840701748847

Viau, R., Arsenault-Lapierre, G., Fecteau, S., Champagne, N., Walker, C., & Lupien, S. (2010). Effect of service dogs on salivary cortisol secretion in autistic children. *Psychoneuroendocrinology, 35,* 1187–1193. doi:10.1016/j.psyneuen.2010.02.004

Watson, P. J., Brymer, M. J., & Bonanno, G. A. (2011). Postdisaster psychological intervention since 9/11. *American Psychologist, 66,* 482–494. doi:10.1037/a0024806

Wells, D. L. (2009). The effects of animals on human health and well-being. *Journal of Social Issues, 65,* 523–543.

Yorke, J. (2010). The significance of human-animal relationships as modulators of trauma effects in children: A developmental neurobiological perspective. *Early Child Development and Care, 180,* 559–570. doi:10.1080/03004430802181189

# V

## CRISIS INTERVENTION IN HEALTHCARE SETTINGS

# 22

## Trauma Support Services for Healthcare Workers: The Stress, Trauma and Resilience (STAR) Program

KENNETH R. YEAGER

## INTRODUCTION

On a sunny Monday afternoon, you find three registered nurses tearfully watching a vital sign monitor. One quickly reaches forward and hits the computer keyboard to silence a critical alarm. In a nearby critical care pod, you find a physician, two additional nurses, and a family circled around the bedside of an elderly woman as life supports are being removed. As the lines on the monitor go flat, tears of sadness continue to flow. All healthcare workers are seasoned professionals, so what makes this case different? Why are these healthcare professionals at risk for psychological trauma?

Early the next morning, a resident is alone crying in the resident office. A code has just occurred, and a young patient has died. The patient, a college student, was admitted the prior afternoon in acute respiratory distress. Despite heroic efforts by staff, this patient could not be saved.

In a third case, an operating team begins a routine procedure. During the initial incision, however, the laser scalpel malfunctions and sparks, the alcohol prep based dressings immediately catch fire, and the surgeon and team work quickly, realizing the imminent risk of a fire in an oxygen-rich environment. The surgeon grabs draping material to smother the fire, and immediate medical assistance is provided to the patient. After the event, the surgeon goes to the shower to clean up. He realizes that his hands are burned, the hair on the left side of his head is singed, and his left eyebrow is nearly burned away. Although no harm came to anyone in the operating room, and the patient was not harmed, the surgeon is unable to leave the prep room. He is sitting on a wooden bench, staring blankly into space, when his peers enter the room.

Each day in the United States, people experiencing healthcare crises place their lives in the hands of capable healthcare providers. These healthcare providers are highly skilled and educated women and men who provide care in complex and at times chaotic care environments. The question is, Who takes of the emotional well-being of these healthcare providers? How do these providers process the things they see and the things they do that by their very nature are emotionally traumatic?

## BACKGROUND

Traumatic events often have a profound and lasting effect on everyone who is directly and indirectly involved. These concerns are all too common, given that a majority of the US population will experience a trauma within their lifetime, and some will experience multiple traumas firsthand (Kessler, Sonnega, Bromet, & Nelson, 1997). Healthcare providers are just one professional group that is exposed to multiple traumas as they extend care to patients facing life-threatening conditions. The continued contact with a traumatized population brings to light the issue of secondary traumatization, that is, traumatization through indirect exposure to a traumatic event (Peebles-Kleiger, 2000; Balch, Shanafelt, Sloan, Satele, & Kerer, 2011).

Secondary traumatization has recently received attention within the mental health literature (Bride, 2007, Figley, 2002a; Ortlepp & Friedman, 2002; Sabin-Farrell & Turpin, 2003; Salston & Figley, 2003). A growing literature has examined the impact of secondary traumatization on healthcare providers (e.g., nurses, medical providers, and chaplains); several hypotheses stemming from this research suggest that caregivers who are in continuous exposure to difficult care situations may be impacted by compassion fatigue. Meadors and Lamson (2008) found that higher levels of personal stressors were positively correlated with higher levels of clinical stress among intensive care providers.

## STRESS AND BURNOUT PREVALENCE IN HEALTHCARE

It has been reported that close to 7% of professionals who work with traumatized individuals demonstrate emotional reactions that are similar to symptoms of post-traumatic stress disorder (PTSD; Thomas & Wilson, 2004). According to the American Psychological Association (2002, 2013), these symptoms are grouped into three categories: re-experiencing the traumatic event; increased arousal; and persistent avoidance and numbing of general thoughts associated with related stimuli. A growing body of evidence documents the impact of compassion fatigue on healthcare providers. This has been evidenced via research linking compassion fatigue with healthcare providers (Balch et al., 2011; Clark & Gioro, 1998; Dyrbye, Shanafelt, Thomas, & Durning, 2009; Maytum, Heiman, & Garwick, 2004; Peebles-Kleiger, 2000; Pfifferling & Gilley, 2000; Sabo, 2006; Schwam, 1998; White, 2006, Worley, 2005). Additionally, Shanafelt et al. (2012) assessed physicians for burnout and satisfaction with work-life balance, using the Maslach Burnout Inventory; in this study, 45.8% of physicians reported at least one symptom of burnout. Shanafelt notes substantial differences in burnout were observed by specialty, with the highest rates occurring in physicians at the front line of care access (e.g., family medicine, general internal medicine, and emergency medicine).

## Clearing the Definitional Air

*Secondary traumatic stress* references the distress and emotional disruption associated with continued contact with individuals who have experienced a primary traumatization (Bride, 2007). Figley (2002b) has defined it as the "natural consequence behaviors and emotions resulting from knowing about a traumatizing event experienced by a significant other." In early significant publications, Bride (2007, p. 88) suggested that an individual who has indirectly experienced a trauma may exhibit symptoms of arousal, intrusion, and avoidance similar to what was previously associated with PTSD. It is likely that many healthcare providers who have cared for traumatized patients have struggled with secondary traumatic stress at some point in their careers. Sometimes healthcare providers are forced to overcome symptoms related to trauma, given real or pseudo-beliefs about their ability to go from patient to patient with little or no emotional connection (Clark & Gioro, 1998).

The notion of *compassion fatigue* was first introduced by Joinson (1992) in reference to nurses who were burning out due to the everyday rigors of their duties in the emergency department. Although Figley (2002b) has indicated that the terms *compassion fatigue* and *secondary traumatic stress* may be used interchangeably, he has also described compassion fatigue as a consequence of working with a significant number of traumatized individuals in combination with a strong empathic orientation.

*Burnout* has been found to overlap with the previously discussed concepts of compassion fatigue and secondary traumatic stress (Baird & Kracen, 2006; Figley, 2002b; Jenkins & Baird, 2002). Burnout is conceptualized as a multidimensional construct, or *meta*-construct, with three distinct domains: emotional exhaustion, depersonalization, and a reduced sense of personal accomplishment (Maslach & Leiter, 1997). It is viewed as "a defensive response to prolonged occupational exposure to demanding interpersonal situations that produce psychological strain and provide inadequate support" (Jenkins & Baird, 2002, p. 424).

## PREVALENCE OF DEPRESSION

Nearly 1 in 5 hospital nurses is wrestling with depression, creating wellness and productivity concerns for their employers, according to Letvak, Ruhm and McCoy (2012), who surveyed nearly 1,200 hospital RNs and found that 18% of them were depressed—or twice the rate of the national population. These researchers concluded that higher depression scores were linked with higher body mass index, a higher number of health problems, and job satisfaction; they also reported that hospital-based nurses have difficulty concentrating and are prone to higher medical error rates.. The researchers found that pain and depression were significantly linked with presenteeism, which in turn accounted for medication errors, patient falls, and perceived quality of care.

More than 70% of the nurses surveyed by Letvak et al. (2012) reported working with some pain or health problem that negatively affected their productivity in the past 2 weeks. These researchers concluded that "high-stress environments are likely to contribute to more health problems for nurses, including mental health issues" (Letvak, 2012, p. 180), and that mental health issues are less likely to be disclosed to employers than physical problems. The study recommended devoting more attention to depression screening for nurses and early treatment.

## PHYSICIAN BURNOUT

With regard to physician burnout, *Archives of Internal Medicine*, shanafelt et al. (2012) surveyed 7,288 physicians on key burnout measures. Participants completed a 22-item Maslach Burnout Inventory to assess emotional exhaustion, depersonalization, and a low sense of personal accomplishment; 45.8% of respondents reported at least one of these burnout symptoms. The researchers also compared physicians' responses with those from 3,400 individuals in other professions, finding that 38% of physicians had burnout symptoms, compared with 28% of the other individuals. Although previous studies by Shanafelt have indicated that surgical specialists would be at highest risk of burnout, Shanafelt et al. (2012) study found that physicians working in emergency medicine, general internal medicine, neurology, and family medicine had the highest burnout rates. In 2011, West, Shanafelt, and Kolars assessed 16,294 internal medicine residents using data collected from 2008 and 2009 Internal Medicine In-Training Examination Scores

(IM-ITE) and the 2008 IM-ITE survey. Overall burnout and high levels of emotional exhaustion and depersonalization were reported by 8,343 of 1,692 (51.5%); by 7,394 of 16,154 (45.1%); and by 4,541 of 15,737 (28.9%) responding residents, respectively. Quality of life was rated as "as bad as it can be" or "somewhat bad" by 2,402 of 16,178 responding residents. These numbers demonstrate higher than previously expected scores on factors related to burnout in internal medicine residents.

## NURSING BURNOUT

The rates of stress and burnout among nurses have been found to be higher than those among other healthcare professionals, with approximately 40% of hospital nurses having burnout levels that are higher than the norm for healthcare workers (Aiken et al., 2001). Many studies have indicated that the prevalence of burnout is higher among nurses who work in especially stressful settings, such as oncology, mental health, emergency medicine, and critical care. However, an early study found no difference in burnout rates for nurses in acquired immunodeficiency syndrome (AIDS) units, oncology units, intensive care units, and general medical-surgical units (van Servellen & Leake, 1993).

### Cost of Nursing Turnover

Nurse burnout—a result of working in high-stress environments—is bad for patient care and expensive for hospitals. A conservative estimate of the price of hiring a new nurse totals $10,000 in direct recruitment costs. For a hospital with 400 RNs on staff, as many as 80 new nurses may need to be recruited and trained every year, with costs adding up to $800,000 annually—and that covers just the direct costs. The potential replacement cost could range between $42,000 for a medical-surgical nurse and $64,000 for a specialty nurse. Jones and Gates (2007) place an even higher price tag on nurse turnover: $47,403 for a medical-surgical nurse and $85,197 for a specialty nurse. For the hypothetical 400-nurse hospital, the cost of replacing just 80 nurses annually could total $4 million in direct and hidden costs.

## STRATEGIES FOR MANAGING STRESS AND AVOIDING BURNOUT

There are two primary approaches to preventing and/or coping with work-related stress and burnout. Given that the most significant factors in stress and burnout are related to the work environment, modifying the environment to eliminate the factors has the potential for the most success.

However, it is often difficult to change an organizational structure, which means that individuals must make changes themselves.

The primary goal in any setting is to stop the burnout cycle early by preventing the accumulation of stress. When implemented appropriately, preventing burnout is easier and more cost-effective than resolving it once it has occurred (Maslach & Leiter, 1997). Burnout that is addressed in later stages may take months or years to resolve fully (Lyckholm, 2001). Thus, stress management techniques and other interventions to ensure psychosocial well-being should be a priority for both individuals and institutions/ organizations, with a goal of preventing stress and managing it in its early stages.

Attention to personal and professional lifestyle habits is essential for individuals to prevent and manage stress effectively. Self-care, time management, and strong interpersonal relationships are key elements for maintaining physical and psychosocial well-being. In addition, care must be taken to protect an individual's professional lifestyle. Many healthcare facilities provide some form of staff support, most frequently in the form of peer support or staff debriefing. Although psychological debriefing represents the most common form of early intervention for recently traumatized people, there is little evidence supporting its continued use with individuals who experience potentially traumatizing events (Rose, Bisson, Churchill, & Wessely, 2002). There are clearly articulated humanitarian reasons to provide mental health interventions to people soon after exposure to trauma, yet there is growing consensus that early intervention for psychological trauma, generically called *psychological debriefing*, does not prevent subsequent psychological pathology or protect against burnout. In fact, there is some evidence that psychological debriefing may exacerbate subsequent symptoms (for reviews, see McNally, Bryant, & Ehlers, 2003; Rose et al., 2002).

Even with this knowledge one time psychological debriefing is not effective and at times may be harmful programs are growing nationally to provide support for healthcare workers using this approach. This should not be surprising given the demand for efficient management of the extensive individual, corporate, and societal costs associated with healthcare provider burnout. Few in healthcare would argue that providing support for staff who on a daily basis "see things people should not have to see" and "do things that people should not have to do" is a bad thing. The important question to answer is, What is the best, most efficient way to shape organizational approaches to healthcare provider stress, trauma, and burnout? The remainder of this chapter is dedicated to defining and outlining a promising process to mitigate the harmful effects of stress, trauma, and burnout among healthcare providers (Hobfoll, Spielberger, Figley, & van der Kolk, 2001; Wilson, Raphael, Meldrum, Bedosky, & Sigman, 2000).

## Risk Factors

The premise that exposure to trauma is a risk factor for or precursor to the development of burnout, and eventually more serious disorders such as acute stress disorder (ASD) or even PTSD, has been the driving factor underlying most models of psychological debriefing. However, this assumption has resulted in intervention efforts typically failing to address the role of other risk factors in disturbing or arresting adjustment after exposure to potentially traumatizing events. For this reason, the "standardized" approach fails to acknowledge the personal and social resources that, in many cases, facilitate the recovery process. In healthcare, certain factors should be identified in the event of exposure to potentially traumatizing events. Potential trigger factors for burnout, ASD, or PTSD vary among individuals and specific situations. The following discussion is not exhaustive but provides some common examples.

### *Professional Closeness or Distance*

In the first example presented in this chapter, nurses involved in the withdrawal of care are impacted to a greater degree because they have come to know the family of the patient. They have connected with the patient's husband over an extended period, hearing about how the couple met, became high school sweethearts, and remained together for nearly 50 years. They have observed his daily visitations and vigilance and have received small gifts in expression of his gratitude for the care provided. All of this has served to shorten the distance between the professional and the individual. This case epitomizes how the very drives that bring a person to healthcare (e.g., a desire to provide care, to assist others, and to make a difference in other people's lives) set the individual up to be at greater risk for traumatization. When people connect, professional distance is lessened, and the potential for psychological distress is greater. One may conclude that the best way to prevent this traumatization is to not connect; this may work for some healthcare providers, but it is not always possible and is not conducive to compassionate care. We recommend simply recognizing the potential for traumatization, acknowledging the potential impact, preparing staff in advance, and providing support prior to difficult situations. Although this may not be possible in every case, it can be very effective in mitigating the risk of psychological traumatization.

### *Similarity to Self, Family, and Peers*

In the second case, the resident is impacted by the sudden loss of a college student under her care. This case was difficult for a number of reasons, including that the student was very young, with much of his life still ahead of him. The resident was able to relate to this patient's potential and also experienced the emotional distress of the family at the loss of their son. She was further impacted by the fact her younger brother is of a similar age and has a similar appearance. She reports, "It could have been my little brother . . . and there was nothing I could do to save him." This realization brings an awareness of the fragility of life uncomfortably close. The resident struggles to cope by compartmentalizing this information because she is aware that she must move forward with her other cases and has little time to process.

### Potential Risk or Harm to Self

The third case presented in this chapter highlights one of the key characteristics of ASD and PTSD (APA, 2013). The surgeon in this case is acutely aware of the risks posed by the situation that has occurred. He is struck by this only after the event when he notices that the hair on his face has been burned away and realizes the potential for much greater danger to him and the others in the room. He is less able to separate from the experience because of the acute awareness of potential risk and because of the reminder each time he looks in the mirror. It is important to note that in this type of case, it is not the actual outcome but the potential outcomes that create distress. For this reason, a single debriefing will unlikely be sufficient to process the thoughts associated with the incident. Brief intervention of three to five sessions of cognitive-behavioral therapy (CBT), to process the event, examining thoughts and feelings experienced with emphasis on cognitive reframing, has shown great improvement in outcomes in stabilizing individuals after such events (Litz, Gray, Bryant, & Adler, 2002; Cougle, Resnick, & Kilpatrick, 2009).

Additional factors to take into account when considering the most appropriate type of intervention for psychological trauma are age (because younger persons are found to be more vulnerable to risk) and gender (because females have been shown to be at higher risk of developing ASD and PTSD). Intelligence is another risk indicator that is mentioned in the literature, but it is difficult to think of a scenario in which this factor would influence the decision to provide support. It is important to understand the history of prior trauma experiences, specifically with the presence of hyperarousal because this may indicate some lingering impact of prior trauma, that could complicate intervention (Green et al., 2000; Nishith, Mechanic, & Resnick, 2000; Cougle et al., 2009).

The strength and number of social supports of the individual(s) involved and the potential loss of support are factors to be considered when addressing potentially traumatizing events (Rama-Maceiras, Parente, & Kranke, 2012). For example, healthcare providers typically respond to events as part of a team; because of this environmental fact, the individual's response to the event may be very public, which may need to be factored in to the support process. In other cases, communication with team members after a significant event can assist with individual re-entry to the unit where care was provided. An individual's recovery from trauma is predicated on the presence and quality of positive supports, combined with the individual's inclination to access support and to disclose accounts of the traumatic event (Halpern, Maunder, Schwartz, & Gurevich, 2012). After most events in healthcare, the individual will want to provide his or her side of the story to the unit's authority figure. This is extremely important because it serves as the opportunity to preserve personal integrity, through sharing personal perceptions of timing, individual interactions, and series of events contributing to the event outcome. To date, early psychological interventions have not taken into account the importance of social factors in healthcare providers' ability to recover from the trauma (Martin, Rosen, Durand, Knudson, & Stretch, 2000).

In addition, preexisting conflict in significant relationships could negatively impact the ability to recover from a potentially traumatizing event, especially for those motivated to use others as supports in the recovery process. As previously stated, the desire to express one's side of the event may be impacted by the team nature of many events. For some, the process of restoring equilibrium and coherence may rely heavily on the support of peers in the work environment. For others, this process may require respite from the demands of the work environment, yet with access to discuss the events. Conflicts within significant relationships may impact the effectiveness of restoration of equilibrium if one does not have consistent support from peers or an opportunity to disengage and gather one's sense of self and security prior to returning to the work environment. It is important to consider individual needs and match all intervention to specifically assessed individual need (Halpern et al., 2012).

In all, it is important to consider multiple personal and environmental factors because the presence or absence of resources becomes an important factor in considering the amount of support needed to assure the best opportunity to attain or maintain resources necessary to sustain functioning. These resources can include life conditions (e.g., marriage, family, peer support), personal resources (e.g., self-esteem, professional skill sets/competencies), and professional resources (e.g., occupation, professional licenses and credentials). Within the healthcare setting, trauma survivors face a different set of stressors than those who have experienced the trauma of a natural disaster. Healthcare professionals have concerns regarding the impact of the trauma on their professional standing, which in turn may have significant professional, financial, and social implications that could spiral into deeper personal issues. Thus, stress is driven by threatened or actual loss of professional resources; those in immediate debriefing situations may not be able to attend to interventions designed to address psychological variables of anxiety and affective symptoms when there are broader legitimate concerns regarding professional consequences. The question becomes, What is the

most appropriate approach when working with healthcare providers immediately after potentially traumatizing events?

Let us first acknowledge that determination of the most appropriate type
of early intervention for post-trauma problems and the type of individual
or group who can benefit from early intervention are empirical questions
that have yet to be fully answered. However, let us assume that the most
appropriate and defensible approach is one that establishes a clear process
for assessing those who have experienced a potentially traumatizing event,
and that, once the assessment has been completed and indicates which individuals require intensive intervention, those persons should be provided
with immediate brief emotional support, followed by multisession interventions that have demonstrated empirically supported approaches to treating
trauma.

## A FRAMEWORK FOR
## TRAUMA SUPPORT SERVICES

To this point we have examined what is important to understand prior to
determining intervention processes. The framework for brief emotional supportive therapy (BEST) to be applied is Roberts's seven-stage crisis intervention model. This model lends itself very well to brief psychological supportive
services to staff following potentially traumatizing events within the work
environment (Figure 22.1).

In Stages 1 and 2 or Roberts's Seven Stage Model the critical first step in
applying this model is to plan and conduct a crisis assessment. When working with healthcare providers, it is important to gather as much information
as possible regarding the event prior to arrival on the unit. The information may be communicated by a nurse manager or another individual in
an administrative role on the unit, or it may come as a request from direct
care staff involved in the event. When providing BEST it is important to
understand the nature of the event, its location, the number and types of
staff involved, critical elements of the event, and reason for the call if not
clearly articulated, and type of setting for initial interactions. Establishing
and communicating a central meeting place for staff who are involved is the
final step prior to interactions on the unit. At times of crisis, communication can be difficult. Assigning a specific staff member to communicate the
time and location of BEST or crisis intervention is key to the success of the
intervention (Roberts, 1991, 2000; Roberts & Yeager, 2009).

Once the trauma support services team is on the unit, initial interactions
continue the process of gathering information for completion of the crisis
assessment. Because gaining the trust of staff on the unit is essential, attention is given to rapidly establishing relationships and rapport.

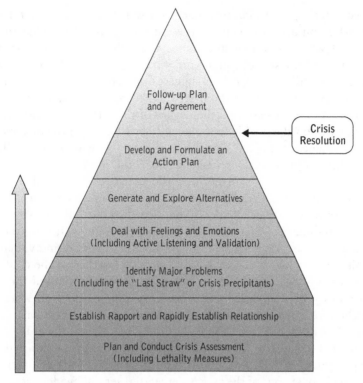

Figure 22.1    Roberts's Seven Stage Model Outlined as the Framework for Trauma Support Services

We recommend that prior to potentially traumatizing events, the trauma support staff become familiar with unit staff; frequent visits to high risk areas. We refer to this as rounding on the units, providing information about the programming, and getting to know unit staff, their roles and work histories, and their interests within and outside of the work environment are all helpful in accomplishing this. Precrisis rounding processes are extremely important because they serve to introduce the unit staff to the support team, which in turn increases staff willingness to invite the support team into their work environment at the time of crisis.

At the time of initial entry to the unit after a potentially traumatizing event, proceed to the preestablished location for the initial crisis session using BEST. Along the way, observe staff responses, assure that there is sufficient coverage for the unit, and note which staff are working on the floor, observing their outward emotional functioning. After the initial meeting, make rounds, touching base with staff working the unit if possible to assure there are not unresolved stress issues or questions that need to be addressed for staff members who were not directly involved in the incident.

When entering the room, introduce yourself, providing a brief description of who you are, why you are present on the unit, and what the process is and why it is important. There is much discussion of timing of intervention. Many suggest intervening as soon as possible after an event (Campfield & Hills, 2001); others suggest that debriefing can occur as long as days or even weeks later (Foa, Hearst-Ikeda, & Perry, 1995). Timing of the intervention is based on the nature of the interaction with staff. In the initial session the goal is to gather information and provide education and psychological support. This involves interacting with the staff, permitting staff to provide their perceptions of the event and of the timing of the incidents as they evolved, and the potential emotional impact of these events on staff. You will frequently hear comments such as "I'm not exactly sure what happened ... it all happened so fast." Remember, this is not a fact-finding mission or a risk management inquiry. It is a process of gathering initial information to inform your assessment of individual staff and unit functioning. It is all right and normal for there to be confusion. The details will be ironed out in the administrative review of the event. The task of the debriefing team is to hear and support the staff where they are at the moment of the initial intervention. Critical events are critical because they do not neatly fit into the frame of reference held by staff at the time of the incident. Many will ask: "How could something like this happen on our unit?" Exploring this type of question leads to understanding exactly how far out of the staff's perceptual set the incident actually is; typically, the further from their realm of understanding, the harder it will be for staff to clarify in their minds what has occurred and to place this into a frame of reference they are able to process. Thus, active, supportive listening to the stories as presented by staff and facilitating interactions between staff members while hearing their accounts of the event all serve to stabilize and make sense of situations that frequently do not make sense to staff on the unit.

Listen to staff as they describe what occurred: Hear the tone of their voices; observe their body language; determine, when possible, naturally occurring supports between staff members as well as potential conflict points. Listen for potential assignment of blame to either individuals or the administration. Remind staff that this is not a process of assigning blame and redirect the conversation back to staff and their immediate needs. Listen for intrusive thoughts staff are having, such as "All I can think of is the sound of ..." or "I keep seeing the expression on her face ..." These are potential "stuck points," or issues staff may need assistance in dealing with. Frequently, these initially identified stuck points become the focus of later BEST intervention using a cognitive-behavioral approach to process the thoughts, feelings, and subsequent behaviors related to these thoughts.

Observe staff as they interact. Are there participants who are relying on repressive coping process or who are particularly reserved, guarded, shut down, or tearful? Be aware that initial BEST interventions provide and gather information and are educational and supportive. Although it may be tempting to focus on or target the emotions of a particularly upset staff member, this may not be in the best interest of staff. If in the intervention process a staff person who is distraught over events is unwilling to share his or her perceptions, provide support but be careful to not push this person too far in initial meetings. Numerous studies have demonstrated the potentially damaging effects of interventions when they are not done properly. The best approach is to include individualized coping strategies of each participant, consider who is in the greatest need for intervention, and determine what intervention or learning method best meets the individual's needs and will be the most helpful to the person in the long run.

It is important to understand that BEST interventions are voluntary and that no one should be forced to participate in this initial group intervention. Forced interventions can retraumatize staff; for example, demanding that a person participate in psychological debriefing may be perceived as a sign of distrust, or thinking the person is not able to process difficult situations on his or her own. Be aware that how staff are approached at a time of crisis may be perceived as a threat to the individual's integrity or professionalism.

Providing education is the next step in the BEST intervention. As previously stated, persons involved in the BEST intervention are not always going to have a frame of reference for what just happened. Similarly, they are not going to have a frame of reference for what happens next. At this point, providing information becomes important in the restoration of "sensemaking." Albert Wu (2000) coined the phrase "second victim" in his landmark work at Johns Hopkins University working with physicians involved in potentially traumatizing events. In this work, Wu indicates six stages of functioning within the process of second victim syndrome (Figure 22.2). When articulating these stages, Wu also provided

| Pre Incident Peer Support Team Development | | | | | | | |
|---|---|---|---|---|---|---|---|
| Stage 1-3 Impact Realization | | | Stage 4 Enduring the Administrative Review Process | Stage 5 Obtaining Emotional Psychological Support | Stage 6 Building Resilience | | |
| Chaos Incident Response | Intrusive Thoughts | Restoring Personal Integrity | | | Isolating Dropping Out | Surviving | Thriving |
| Triage First Aid Support Resources (Peer and Manager Based) | | | Stabilization Resilience Building | | | | |

Figure 22.2

a reasonably accurate and predictable roadmap for staff of what to expect after a potentially traumatizing event.

In Stages 1 through 3, Wu (2000) describes the process of impact and realization experienced by healthcare providers as (a) the chaos of incident response, (b) intrusive thoughts, and (c) restoring personal integrity. In the initial visit, providing this roadmap functions as the basis for discussion or psychoeducation for staff, explaining what they have experienced (and why this is normal and expected) and what they might be experiencing. As described earlier, many may experience intrusive thoughts regarding a particular sound or other sensory perception within the event. Others may have an overwhelming need to describe what they did and the rationale for a particular course of action as a way of telling their side of the story in an effort to preserve or restore personal integrity. Others respond to the chaos of the event by attempting to construct an individualized frame of reference for what has occurred. The education function within Roberts's seven-stage crisis intervention model delivered as BEST interventions then seeks to further inform participants of the next steps.

By nature, systems function to retraumatize those who have been involved in potentially traumatizing events. Wu describes the fourth stage of the second victim syndrome as "enduring the administrative review process" Fortunately, critical events, although not uncommon in healthcare as a whole, are relatively rare in individual areas or units of healthcare. Healthcare staff are for the most part unaware of administrative, legal, and risk management processes. Because of this, providing education to staff on what to expect during the administrative review process is an important preparatory task and should include the following:

- Risk management processes (e.g., interviews with the institution's legal and risk management team)
- Describing quality improvement inquiries, development of root cause analysis, and development of event-related action plans to mitigate or eliminate future similar foreseeable events
- Providing support for staff when completing interviews or when completing police reports in the event of forensic cases or assaults on staff within healthcare settings
- Being present and providing support for depositions
- Providing preparation and support for media reporting of difficult or high-profile cases

In general, providing preemptive education helps staff to understand and process where they are and where they might be headed as they work to adapt to the aftermath of a critical and potentially traumatizing event.

When designing trauma support services for healthcare staff, be certain to align the program with hospital administration, hospital legal support, risk management, and quality and safety programming. This aids in understanding processes that have the potential to be retraumatizing to staff and aids in linking the trauma support services program with staff involved in critical and potentially traumatizing events.

The third step of the BEST aspect of crisis intervention during Stages 1 and 2 of crisis intervention involves providing assistance with accessing ongoing emotional and psychological support. Most adults have a network of social and emotional resources. Spend time with the group or individual to determine what aspects of their lives will serve as supports for stabilization. Ask members how they take care of themselves. It is important early in the intervention to begin the process of working toward the solution, and building upon individual strengths is the foundation of crisis intervention, BEST intervention, and trauma support services. Each individual has an inherent skill set that can be applied when facing potentially traumatizing events. It is important to frame this stage of intervention as examining knowledge that will bring forward opportunities to problem solving. Such problem-solving opportunities include, but are not limited to:

• Practical problem-solving skills, more frequently referred to as common sense
• Emotional capacity for understanding and acceptance
• Establishment of realistic expectations for recovery processes
• Ability to comprehend and follow instructions
• Ability to access potential support systems

Timing is an important consideration in the establishment of support services for staff. Because of the critical nature of healthcare, there will be competing priorities that will force workers to pursue practical needs versus attending to their own emotional or psychological needs (Roberts & Yeager, 2009). Avoidance is a key symptom of traumatization, with the option of focusing on the "task at hand" leading some to choose not to focus on emotional needs at the time of crisis. Touching base with such persons is important for follow-up and offering assistance, but many find the return to work is a normal part of their focusing, processing, and normalizing processes. Additionally, others may be so consumed with surviving the present that they are not able to recognize their need for follow-up care. This is not to say they may not identify residual psychological symptoms and seek assistance at a later time. To this end, it is important to ensure that staff are aware of follow-up opportunities and that opportunities for contacting support programming are easily accessible to staff.

In summary, immediate BEST intervention provided in Stages 1 and 2 of Roberts's seven-stage crisis intervention model should provide information to:

- Assist in identifying and normalizing common reactions to potentially traumatizing situations
- Identify and improve upon individual coping mechanisms
- Identify significant symptoms associated with traumatic responses to crisis situations, including psychological trauma–based symptoms that include risk of harm to self or others
- Provide education related to normal symptoms and reactions to potentially traumatizing situations
- Increase awareness of and access to ongoing support services

The identification of alternative actions serves as the next logical step in the rebuilding process. Up to this point, interventions have been directed toward stabilization and restoration of cognitive functioning; from here, the intervenor is able to move the group and individuals within the group toward establishing the return to normal functioning.

## UNDERSTANDING AND COPING: APPLICATION OF ROBERTS'S SEVEN-STAGE CRISIS INTERVENTION MODEL

### Stages 3 and 4: Identify Major Problems and Deal With Feelings and Emotions

When addressing potentially traumatizing experiences, the identification of major problems is focusing on barriers to individual or group return to normal functioning. The basis of ASD and subsequent PTSD is an inability to return to baseline functioning or a failure to recover (Cougle et al., 2009). Barriers to recovery can be related to the event itself, or they can be driven by events outside of the work environment or a combination of several concurrent issues in the individual's life that become the focus for the intervention.

For example, a nurse who was involved in the operating room fire may state that she was not greatly impacted by the event itself. She reports that her back was turned when the incident occurred, and it was essentially over before she knew what was happening. Smiling politely, she reports in session that she is fine, and one could easily assume that she has no need for additional intervention. Suppose this nurse continues in her work in the operating room, but her supervisor indicates she is having interpersonal difficulties with peers, appears easily agitated, and is not acting like her normal positive, upbeat self. When the surgical team director expresses concern, this nurse shares:

> My elderly parents were involved in a car accident 4 weeks ago, and both were hospitalized. My mother is now in a skilled nursing facility, my father remains in the hospital with severe internal injuries, and his kidneys have now failed. I'm running between my parents' home, two healthcare facilities, work, and my home taking care of my two elementary-age kids. ... It's more than I can take. I've only been getting 3 to 4 hours of sleep a night, and it's just beginning to wear me down. Part of why I can't sleep is I keep thinking what if that fire was worse? I'm the only child ... who would be taking care of my kids and my parents if I had been injured ... don't you see it's just too much!

In this case, the major problem is more than just the incident. The combination of factors within and outside of work have caused a disruption in the life of this healthcare provider. More often than not, those who work in healthcare feel a responsibility to care for others. The desire to help and the reward that comes from accomplishing complex tasks in high-risk situations drives such individuals to excel in their work. Sadly, the same attributes frequently work against healthcare professionals. Their very desire to excel sets them up to question their ability. And when the desire to help is combined with the difficult physical, emotional, and moral distress encountered on a daily basis, the formula is complete for establishing a barrier to returning to normal functioning after one or a series of potentially traumatizing events.

Now that we have considered an example of the identifying major problems, let us turn our focus to how feelings and emotions come into play. Earlier in this chapter, the discussion of addressing thoughts, feelings, and behaviors emerged. In this case example, a nurse is having thoughts about other possible outcomes of the fire, based on her need to care for her injured elderly parents and her children. The baseline emotional state is one of feeling overwhelmed. Add the potential of injury to self, and the emotional state becomes one of fear added to already feeling overwhelmed.

The result is decreased sleep, as the nurse lies awake, her thoughts racing, as she thinks of the tasks that she need to complete for the next day. This lack of sleep increases the degree to which she is feeling overwhelmed to a point of discomfort. When she is asked to complete one additional task at work, she tells her supervisor, "Absolutely not ... I cannot take on a single additional task at this time." To the nursing supervisor, this appears to be out of the normal realm of response, and when the issue is pushed because staffing is short, there is an emotional confrontation in the workplace. It is not until the entire story is told that staff are able to comprehend what is driving the behavior of the individual. If not explored in the context of burnout or compassion fatigue, this interaction could have easily led to disciplinary actions, which would have further complicated matters. In the long run, this may have resulted in the nurse looking for a new job, one that is less stressful and with more understanding leadership.

## Stages 5 and 6: Generate and Explore Alternatives, and Develop and Formulate an Action Plan

In the initial stages of crisis intervention education, active supportive listening and assessment are the driving aspects of BEST intervention. In Steps 5 and 6 of Roberts's model, the process is one of reframing the cognitive distortions that are drivers of thoughts, feelings, and subsequent behavior (Roberts, 2000). Earlier in this chapter, it is suggested that it is appropriate and defensible to evaluate (when feasible) anyone who has been involved in potentially traumatizing events, regardless of work role or the severity of the experience. If the assessment indicates that any individuals require more focused intervention, those persons should proceed to multisession interventions that have empirical support. The reason for this step is because one-time debriefing approaches are frequently insufficient to process the full extent of traumatic exposure. A growing body of evidence suggests that CBT for recently traumatized individuals shows promising results in mitigating the long-term effects of exposure to potentially traumatizing events (Foa et al., 1995).

In the case of the RN, four 45-minute sessions were used to process the series of traumatic events she had experienced. The first session included a review of information provided in the initial debriefing session. Education was provided regarding the impact of events and how cognitive and physical factors combine to create the trauma response. This progressed to a discussion of the event or events and the nurse beginning to demonstrate behaviors of avoidance, procrastination, and resistance to certain interactions that served to remind her of the event and her subsequent response to the trauma. A list of avoidance behaviors, procrastination, and resistance behaviors was created, and the nurse was asked to keep track of each of these items during the week before the next session. This was followed by teaching of relaxation technique. A digital copy of the relaxation technique was provided and the nurse was encouraged to practice this technique daily between sessions, either at the end of her day or throughout the day when she is feeling stressed.

Each of the next three sessions involved imaginal exposure to the traumatic events. In the second session, cognitive restructuring was introduced when maladaptive beliefs emerged during the nurse's narrative accounts of each event. Examples of maladaptive beliefs included statements such as "I should have been paying more attention to the surgical procedure" and "I should have known my mother was going to wreck the car." Once the narrative reconstruction of the events was completed, the statements, which were digitally recorded, were played back, and the nurse was asked to reconsider what she had said. The session continued as follows:

Nurse:  I should have been paying more attention to the surgical procedure.

Question:  What were you doing?

Nurse:  I was prepping for the next step in the procedure.

Question:  Would you be looking at what was occurring in the surgery, or would you have your back to the procedure at this time?

Nurse:  I would be busy prepping, that's what I do, ... so I would have my back to the procedure.

Question:  If you were doing what you should be doing, why are you blaming yourself for not doing what you are supposed to be doing?

Nurse:  I don't know, I just feel I should be paying better attention.

Question:  So, what could you tell yourself about the event?

Nurse:  I guess, I was doing what I was supposed to be doing, and that I didn't play any role in causing the event?

Question:  So, then what is the issue?

Nurse:  I didn't feel safe?

Question:  What actions can be taken to help you feel safe in the future?

Nurse:  If we could turn the prep table, so it's not in the way, but I can work behind it, I could see what is happening, and I would also be right next to the phone, and in the event that something would occur, I could call for help.

The nurse was asked to review the session and to practice relaxation technique. She was also given worksheets to record additional maladaptive thoughts as they emerged throughout her day. This process was repeated for the following session. Out of these sessions, several actions were developed and implemented. The nurse was participating on the quality improvement team examining this event. She was able to make the recommendation to relocate the prep table to enable her and other nurses to be more aware of actions occurring within the operating room. She was also able to develop and implement plans for the care of her parents, moving them to a single long-term care facility, and to work out a schedule with her husband and others to make certain her children were able to attend all scheduled summer activities. The final session reviewed her plan and its implementation and summarized the progress she had made in resolving the crisis.

When considering the process experienced in second victim syndrome, the final stage is building resilience, which coincides with the proposed model of intervention. In this phase, according to Wu (2000), those who have been involved in potentially traumatizing events follow three paths: isolating or dropping out, surviving, or thriving. There may be many combinations of experiences as one progresses through Wu's final stage of building resilience. After the event, one may first experience isolation, as part of processing the event. Members may drop out of social activities or engage less in work activities, given the nature of the experience. Some may experience both of these simultaneously. However, the key to building resilience is working toward thriving through mastery and accomplishment. In the case presented here, the nurse was involved in the quality improvement process, which resulted in positive changes to the work environment (Pipe et al., 2012). Building resilience in healthcare workers requires providing opportunities not only to work to resolve the issue but also to find opportunities for them to contribute to their work environment, their peers, and the community at large.

At the heart of crisis is the overwhelming of previously held coping skills. When the ability to cope is overwhelmed, the result is anxiety and feelings of loss of control (Roberts & Yeager, 2005). Nothing in the environment makes sense. Frequently, crisis situations shake and challenge our very way of thinking. After all, we have been exposed to the "just world concept"— that is, if you work hard and treat others well, you will be rewarded. Working in healthcare provides ample opportunities for this belief to be challenged. On a daily basis, healthcare workers see things they should not have to see and do things that most people find difficult to comprehend. Healthcare workers are not alone in this; firefighters, police officers, first responders, and the military all have this in common, and it is the foundation of the early psychological debriefing models. The unique concept of trauma support services and BEST intervention is that these approaches take the model to the next level by providing empirically based interventions beyond the single debriefing; they add the concept of resilience building by guiding the individual to master the potentially traumatizing event and turn it into a contribution. The nurse in this example not only was able to contribute to the operating room's efficacy and safety but also was able to meet the very high standards she has set for herself in caring for her parents. Would this mastery have come on its own? In most cases, yes; however, this intervention accelerated and formalized the process. The next and final step was arranging follow-up.

## Stage 7: Follow-Up

In this case, information was provided about managing stress and methods to manage multiple stressors. The nurse was, at her request, linked with a health coach via the hospital's insurance plan to provide ongoing support and information on healthy diet, exercise, and stress management. Technology was applied, with several mobile apps recommended for relaxation, exercise tracking, and calendar and day planning options. Texted reminders regarding exercise and relaxation as positive methods of coping were sent on a weekly bases. When questions arose, they were texted to the provider, and resources for additional psychological support were provided as needed. Finally, as this discussion began the Stress, Trauma and Resilience (STAR) team and providers of BEST interventions visits units frequently to touch base with hospital staff who work in high-stress areas. It is important that the STAR team is consistently present to follow-up with all staff involved in potentially traumatic events to both provide support and to maintain contact in preparation for future unforeseen potentially traumatic events. At 6- and 9-month intervals, this nurse reported feeling better than ever and said that her parents were doing well and she was functioning at "the top of her game."

## SUMMARY

Few would question the importance of providing emotional support for healthcare workers in the aftermath of a potentially traumatizing event. There are in fact very good reasons for paying attention to the psychological well-being of healthcare providers. Studies have shown that addressing compassion fatigue, stress, and anxiety can reduce medical errors and improve levels of compassionate care, thus increasing both patient and staff satisfaction. Additionally, addressing healthcare worker stress, compassion fatigue, and burnout has significant financial advantages because this approach appears to reduce recidivism among healthcare providers. This chapter has outlined trauma support services using Roberts's seven-stage crisis intervention model, combined with BEST intervention, a therapeutic approach that combines elements of psychological debriefing with extended sessions of cognitive restructuring using CBT.

In their review of psychological debriefing literature, Rose et al. (2002) conclude that single-session intense exposure during most psychological debriefing might be countertherapeutic. For some individuals, such brief, emotionally intense exposures to traumatic memory may heighten arousal and distress without providing sufficient time for therapeutic processing of the event. Having insufficient time to process and challenge maladaptive thinking makes it more difficult to develop the necessary and sufficient skills to reduce, reframe, or resolve the intensely negative effects of the potentially traumatizing experience.

There is considerable evidence that the inclusion of cognitive restructuring over repeated sessions has greater efficacy in resolving potentially traumatizing events and functioning to mitigate the risk of developing ASD and

PTSD. Studies on the cognitive-behavioral approach by Foa et al. (1995) and Bryant (2000) suggest that the inclusion of cognitive restructuring is effective in reducing symptoms. The inclusion of CBT over a series of sessions in the early response to potentially traumatizing events is an important difference from current psychological debriefings, with improved outcome in approaches that include structured CBT.

The trauma support services model differs from the traditional psychological debriefing model with respect to the timing and duration of the intervention. In general, it has been suggested that debriefing staff who have been involved in potentially traumatizing events as soon as possible after the event will provide greater effectiveness. Although this recommendation appears logical, there is no clear evidence to suggest that early intervention is more effective. It appears that persons involved in potentially traumatizing events may be too distraught in the early aftermath to fully attend to or benefit from efforts to process the event. In the model presented in this chapter, early interventions occur within 24 to 72 hours of the event. Some intervention may occur as much as 5 to 7 days after the event to accommodate busy staff and procedure schedules. The trauma support services model emphasizes the importance of pre-incident unit visits referred to as rounding, keeping in touch with staff, so that when potentially traumatizing events occur, staff are familiar with and have established working relationships with the intervention team. In early BEST interventions the focus in initial sessions is on assessment, education, and efforts to stabilize and normalize responses following the event. In the assessment process, the focus is on both individual and unit functions, and individual functioning is assessed to determine stressors and supports within both the work and the home environment. Finally, the assessment will yield information on individuals who would most benefit from additional cognitive restructuring and attendance at additional sessions, with specific recommendations that build on existing unit and individual strengths.

Although a great deal of controversy has existed around the merits of early identification and intervention with recently traumatized individuals, the use of a well-organized, structured approach to debriefing combined with cognitive restructuring has provided support for those working within a healthcare environment. As with all approaches to managing psychological trauma, applying stricter scientific standards will enhance approaches to management of potentially traumatizing events. Using evidence-informed questions and approaches will ultimately improve outcomes and identify components of intervention that are most beneficial in assisting individuals and organizations in addressing both the short- and long-term aspects and consequences of exposure to potential traumatizing events.

REFERENCES

Aiken, L. H., Clarke, S. P., Sloane, D. M., Sochalski, J. A., Busse, R., Clarke, H., ... & Shamian, J. (2001). Nurses' reports on hospital care in five countries. *Health affairs, 20*(3), 43–53.

American Psychiatric Association. (APA). (2002). *Diagnostic and statistical manual of mental disorders* (4th ed., text rev.). Washington, DC: Author.

American Psychiatric Association. (2013). *Diagnostic and statistical manual of mental disorders* (5th ed.). Washington, DC: Author.

Baird, K., & Kracen, A. (2006). Vicarious traumatization and secondary traumatic stress: A research synthesis. *Counseling Psychology Quarterly, 19,* 181–188.

Balch, C. M., Shanafelt, T. D., Sloan, J., Satele, D. V., & Kuerer, H. M. (2011). Burnout and career satisfaction among surgical oncologists compared with other surgical specialties. *Annals of Surgical Oncology, 18*(1), 16–25.

Bride, B. (2007). Prevalence of secondary traumatic stress among social workers. *Social Work, 52*(1), 63–70.

Bryant, R. A. (2000). Cognitive behavior therapy of violence-related posttraumatic stress disorder. *Aggression and Violent Behavior, 5,* 79–97.

Campfield, K. M., & Hills, A. M. (2001). Effect of timing of critical incident stress debriefing (CISD) on posttraumatic symptoms. *Journal of Traumatic Stress, 14,* 327–340.

Clark, M., & Gioro, S. (1998). Nurses, indirect trauma, and prevention. *Image: Journal of Nursing Scholarship, 30,* 85–87.

Cougle, J. R., Resnick, H., & Kilpatrick, D. G. (2009). A prospective examination of PTSD symptoms as risk factors for subsequent exposure to potentially traumatic events among women. *Journal of Abnormal Psychology, 118* 405–411.

Dyrbye, L. N., Shanafelt, T. D., Thomas, M. R., & Durning, S. J. (2009). Brief observation: A national study of burnout among internal medicine clerkship directors. *American Journal of Medicine, 122,* 310–312.

Figley, C. (2002a). Compassion fatigue: Psychotherapists' chronic lack of self-care. *Journal of Clinical Psychology, 58,* 1433–1441.

Figley, C. (2002b). *Treating compassion fatigue.* New York: Brunner/ Routledge.

Foa, E. B., Hearst-Ikeda, D., & Perry, K. J. (1995). Evaluation of brief cognitive-behavioral program for the prevention of chronic PTSD in recent assault victims. *Journal of Counseling and Clinical Psychology, 63,* 948–955.

Green, B., Goodman, L., Krupnick, J., Corcoran, C., Petty, R., Stockton, P., & Stern, N. (2000). Outcomes of single versus multiple trauma exposure in a screening sample. *Journal of Traumatic Stress, 13,* 271–286.

Halpern, J., Maunder, R. G., Schwartz, B., & Gurevich, M. (2012). Attachment insecurity, responses to critical incident distress, and current emotional symptoms in ambulance workers. *Stress and Health, 28* (1), 51–60.

Hobfoll, S. E., Spielberger, C. D., Breznitz, S., Figley, C., & van der Kolk, B. (2001). War-related stress: Addressing the stress of war and other traumatic events. *American Psychologist, 46,* 848–855.

Jenkins, S., & Baird, S. (2002). Secondary traumatic stress and vicarious trauma: A validational study. *Journal of Traumatic Stress, 15,* 423–432.

Joinson, C. (1992). Coping with compassion fatigue. *Nursing, 22,* 116–122.

Jones, C. B., & Gates, M. (2007). The cost and benefits of nurse turnover: A business case for nurse retention. *OJIN: The Online Journal of Issues in Nursing, 12* (3), Manuscript 4. Retrieved from www.nursing-world.org/MainMenucategories/ANAmarketplace/ANAperiodicals/OJIN/TableofContents

Kessler, R., Sonnega, A., Bromet, E., & Nelson, C. (1997). Posttraumatic stress disorder in the National Comorbidity Study. *Archives of General Psychiatry, 52,* 1048–1060.

Letvak, S., Ruhm, C, J,, & McCoy, T. (2012). Depression in hospital-employed nurses. *Clinical Nurse Specialist., 26,* 177–182.

Litz, B. T., Gray, M. J., Bryant, R. A., & Adler, A. B. (2002). Early intervention for trauma: Current status and future directions. *Clinical Psychology: Science and Practice, 9,* 112–134.

Lyckholm, L. (2001). Dealing with stress, burnout, and grief in the practice of oncology. *The Lancet Oncology, 2*(12), 750–755.

Martin, L., Rosen, L. N., Durand, D. B., Knudson, K. H., & Stretch, R. H. (2000). Psychological and physical health effects of sexual assaults and nonsexual traumas among male and female United States Army soldiers. *Behavioral Medicine, 26* (1), 23–33.

Maslach, C., & Leiter, M. P. (1997). *The truth about burnout: How organizations cause personal stress and what to do about it.* San Francisco, CA: Jossey-Bass.

Maytum, J., Heiman, M., & Garwick, A. (2004). Compassion fatigue and burnout in nurses who work with children with chronic conditions and their families. *Journal of Pediatric Health Care, 18,* 171–179.

McNally, R. J., Bryant, R. A., & Ehlers, A. (2003). Does early psychological intervention promote recovery from posttraumatic stress? *Psychological Science in the Public Interest, 4* (2), 45–79.

Meadors, P., & Lamson, A. (2008). Compassion fatigue and secondary traumatization: Provider self-care on intensive care units for children. *Journal of Pediatric Healthcare, 22*(1), 24–34.

Nishith, P., Mechanic, M., & Resnick, P., (2000). Prior interpersonal trauma: The contribution to current PTSD symptoms in female rape victims. *Journal of Abnormal Psychology, 109,* 20–25.

Ortlepp, K., & Friedman, M. (2002). Prevalence and correlates of secondary traumatic stress in workplace lay trauma counselors. *Journal of Traumatic Stress, 15,* 213–222.

Peebles-Kleiger, M. (2000). Pediatric and neonatal intensive care hospitalization as traumatic stressor: Implications for intervention. *Bulletin of the Menninger Clinic, 64,* 257–280.

Pfifferling, J., & Gilley, K. (2000). Overcoming compassion fatigue. *Family Practice Management, 7,* 39–45.

Pipe, T. B., Buchda, V. L., Launder, S., Hudak, B., Hulvey, L., Karns, K. E., & Pendergast, D. (2012). Building personal and professional resources of resilience and agility in the healthcare workplace. *Stress and Health, 28* (1), 11–22.

Rama-Maceiras, P., Parente, S., & Kranke, P. (2012). Job satisfaction, stress and burnout in anaesthesia: Relevant topics for anaesthesiologists and healthcare managers? *European Journal of Anaesthesiology, 29,* 311–319.

Roberts, A. R. (1991). Conceptualizing crisis theory and crisis intervention model. In A. R. Roberts (Ed.), *Contemporary perspectives on crisis intervention and prevention* (pp. 3–17). Englewood Cliffs, NJ: Prentice-Hall.

Roberts, A. R. (Ed.). (2000). *Crisis intervention handbook: Assessment, treatment and research.* New York: Oxford University Press.

Roberts, A. R., & Yeager, K. (2009). *Pocket guide to crisis intervention.* Oxford: Oxford University Press.

Rose, S., Bisson, J., Churchill, R., & Wessely, S. (2002). Psychological debriefing for preventing post traumatic stress disorder (PTSD). *Cochrane Database Systematic Review, 2*(2).

Sabin-Farrell, R., & Turpin, G. (2003). Vicarious traumatization: Implications for the mental health of health workers? *Clinical Psychology Review, 23,* 449–480.

Sabo, B. (2006). Compassion fatigue and nursing work: Can we accurately capture the consequences of caring work? *International Journal of Nursing Practice, 12,* 136–142.

Salston, M., & Figley, C. (2003). Secondary traumatic stress effects of working with survivors of criminal victimization. *Journal of Traumatic Stress, 16,* 167–174.

Schwam, K. (1998). The phenomenon of compassion fatigue in perioperative nursing. *Association of Operating Room Nurses Journal, 68,* 642–645.

Shanafelt, T. D., Boone, S., Tan, L., Dyrbye, L. N., Sotile, W., Satele, D., West, C. P., ... Oreskovich, M. R. (2012). Burnout and satisfaction with work-life balance among US physicians relative to the general US population. *Archives of Internal Medicine, 172,* 1377–1385.

Thomas, R., & Wilson, J. (2004). Issues and controversies in the understanding and diagnosis of compassion fatigue, vicarious traumatization and secondary traumatic stress disorder. *International Journal of Emergency Mental Health, 6,* 81–92.

Van Servellen, G., & Leake, B. (1993). Burn-out in hospital nurses: A comparison of acquired immunodeficiency syndrome, oncology, general medical, and intensive care unit nurse samples. *Journal of Professional Nursing, 9,* 169–177.

West, C. P., Shanafelt, T. D., & Kolars, J. C. (2011). Quality of life, burnout, educational debt, and medical knowledge among internal medicine residents. *Journal of the American Medical Association, 306,* 952–960.

White, D. (2006). The hidden costs of caring: What managers need to know. *Health Care Manager, 25,* 341–347.

Wilson, J. P., Raphael, B., Meldrum, L., Bedosky, C., & Sigman, M. (2000). Preventing PTSD in trauma survivors. *Bulletin of the Menninger Clinic, 64,* 181–196.

Worley, C. A. (2005). The art of caring: Compassion fatigue. *Dermatology Nursing, 17*(6), 416.

Wu, A. W. (2000). Medical error: The second victim. *British Medical Journal* (international edition), *320,* 7237.

# 23

# *Crisis Intervention With Caregivers*

ALLEN J. OTTENS
DONNA KIRKPATRICK PINSON

There is no consensus on a definition of caregiving. A *caregiver* has been defined simply as "an individual who provides care for another person who, ordinarily, would not require care" (Ilardo & Rothman, 1999, p. 7). Caregivers can be defined more globally as "people who provide tangible, financial, emotional, or informational and coordination support to an impaired family member" (Argüelles, Klausner, Argüelles, & Coon, 2003, p. 101). However defined, family caregiving in the past two decades has become a prominent issue for researchers and clinicians in the field of geropsychology.

The graying of America is an established fact. More than 16% of the population is 62 or older, and within the past decade, the median age in the United States reached a new high of 37.2—up an astonishing 1.9 years from 2000 (US Census Bureau, 2011). Of course, there is a concomitant increase in the segment of this population requiring care and a burgeoning increase in the number of family caregivers who provide this care. A recent report found that there are 42.1 million caregivers in the United States who assist an adult who is limited in performing daily activities (Feinberg, Reinhard, Houser, & Choula, 2011). Rising up to address this healthcare challenge is a vast informal (i.e., unpaid) support system of friends and family, especially spouses or daughters or daughters-in-law. These caregivers assist their care recipients not only with the small necessities of life (e.g., shopping, house cleaning) and in strenuous activities of daily living (e.g., bathing, dressing, toileting) but often assume responsibility for delivering care previously provided by registered nurses (Hoffman & Mitchell, 1998). If there is such a person as an "average" US caregiver, it is a 49-year-old woman who spends 20 hours per week caring for her mother for almost 5 years (National Alliance for Caregiving, 2009).

Historically, families have been the primary source of support for aged adults. This continues to be so—but with a significant difference. Because adults are living longer lives, the responsibilities for providing care will be falling on more and more family caregivers. In one sense, Americans seem to be gearing up to assume such a role. Half of today's workforce expects to provide care for a friend or family members within the next 5 years (National Alliance for Caregiving, 2009). Eighty-three percent of Americans would feel highly obligated to care for parents if the need arose (Pew Research Center, 2010; www.pewsocialtrends.org/2010/11/18/iv-family/). Findings such as these suggest that caregiving has become a normative "lifespan experience" (Talley & Crews, 2007).

However, expecting to face the many intricacies of caregiving and being prepared to assume the role are two very different things. Almost every caregiver is forced to negotiate daunting legal, financial, emotional, and social challenges, and it is predicted that as the 21st century proceeds, the caregiving challenge will grow more complex due to the following factors:

- Long-distance caregiving.
- Blended families.
- Fewer adult children in the population to provide care.
- Continued increases in the number of working women.
- Caring for aged parents while having young children at home; 30% of caregivers occupy this "sandwich" position. (cited in Alzheimer's Association, 2013, p. 29)

Often literally overnight, a medical emergency can thrust spouses and adult children into complicated "uncharted territory." In today's complex environment, tending to disabled older persons may make heavy physical, emotional, social, and financial demands on caregivers. When caregivers are unprepared to negotiate these demands, they are likely to experience what has come to be known as *caregiver burden*. The stresses, for example, of caring for someone with Alzheimer's disease have been vividly chronicled in the popular book *The 36-Hour Day* (Mace & Rabins, 2011). As the burden saps the caregiver's capacity to cope, she or he teeters on the brink of crisis. In our experience of almost two decades working with dozens of caregivers, it is no exaggeration to say that many caregivers live day-to-day on the cusp of a crisis.

What we hope to accomplish in this chapter is to provide a context for understanding and a method for intervening with the crises encountered by caregivers of disabled older persons. Specifically, we begin with a description, in broad brushstrokes, of the caregiving experience. Next, we present a structure for pinpointing caregiver burden and for targeting possible interventions. The third section consists of a case description of a caregiver in crisis. We conclude with a section on the application of Roberts's (2005) seven-stage model to address this crisis.

## THE CAREGIVING EXPERIENCE

### Caregiving: Perhaps Fewer Untoward Effects

It is often assumed that caregivers of disabled older persons not only must bear up under dreary demands but do so while suffering the risks of declining physical and emotional health. However, research suggests that does not have to be the case. For example, Thompson, Gallagher-Thompson, and Haley (2003) pointed out that longitudinal studies of caregivers of persons with dementing disorders appear to contradict the conventional wisdom that caregiver stress increases as the care recipient's dementing disorder worsens and years of caregiving increase.

In truth, caregivers—and this includes caregivers of persons with dementia—often derive from the experience considerable satisfaction, renewed life purpose, and a closer relationship with the care recipient (e.g., Marks, Lambert, & Choi, 2002; Sanders, 2005; Tarlow et al., 2004). Moreover, when caregivers are able to identify positive aspects in the role they play, it may act as a buffer against perceived strain and burden (e.g., Cohen, Colantonio, & Vernich, 2002; Hilgeman, Allen, DeCoster, & Burgio, 2007; McLennon, Havermann, & Rice, 2011). In a similar vein, a caregiver's subjectively experienced burden may vary based on the type of relationship he or she has with the care recipient. Cicirelli (1993) found that caregivers who felt stronger attachments to their care recipients experienced less subjective burden, whereas stronger obligation to assume the caregiver role was related to greater burden.

There is also evidence that runs contrary to the conventional wisdom that caregiving takes a heavy toll on one's health. For example, Schulz et al. (1997) conducted a large and frequently cited study in which about one third of caregivers reported no strain or negative health effects. In a well-crafted study, Jenkins, Kabeto, and Langa (2009), comparing data from a longitudinal national survey of adults older than 50, concluded that caregiving did not have a deleterious effect on how these older caregivers perceived their health. Robison, Fortinsky, Kleppinger, Shugrue, and Porter (2009) collected data from more than 4,000 respondents and found that caregivers rated their health better than did the noncaregivers; the caregivers did not differ from noncaregivers on level of depression or degree of social isolation. Recently, Roth et al. (2013) reported findings from a 6-year longitudinal study of more than 3,500 family caregivers matched with noncaregivers, which included the intriguing finding that fewer of the caregivers died (7.5%) than did noncaregivers (9.0%).

A caregiver may be burdened but still experience an adequate or high level of well-being due to the presence of perceived social support (Chappell & Reid, 2002). Social support serves as a potent protective factor against distress among caregivers. It qualifies as the most effective moderator of caregiver stress (Logsdon & Robinson, 2000). In their review of culturally diverse caregivers, Gallagher-Thompson et al. (2000) suggested that compared with White caregivers, African American caregivers may exhibit less depression, stress, and burden as a result of the strengths of the African American community being brought to bear in support of caregivers and their care receivers.

The quality of the caregiving relationship can undergo a change for the better. King (1993), in a Canadian qualitative study of daughters caring for aging mothers, found that what began as an overinvolved, conflicted caregiving relationship often evolved over time into one in which the daughter learned to balance her mother's needs with her own. The caregiving relationship thus became healthier as the daughters were able to

(a) make contextual caregiving decisions; (b) set realistic limits on their caregiving activities; (c) accept responsibility for the outcomes of their care decisions; (d) be sensitive to situations that might pose threats to their own needs; (e) deal rationally with the guilt that necessarily accompanies contextual decisions. (p. 424)

A feeling of attachment to and positive relationship with the care recipient, perceived social support, and deriving meaning from the caregiver role all may serve to obviate experiencing excessive burden. Nonetheless, caregiving, with its unpredictable and uncontrollable course, fits the formula for a chronic stress experience and is recognized as a public health issue (Schulz & Sherwood, 2008). However, there is a host of risk factors for caregiver burden that will sorely test the potency of the protective factors and can impact caregivers' health. These issues will be touched upon in the following.

## Impacts on Caregivers' Health

In their reviews, Adelman, Tmanova, Delgado, Dion, and Lachs (2014) and Schulz and Sherwood (2008) have specified factors that are particularly troubling and that have higher probability of contributing to caregiver burden; they include:

- Residing with the care recipient
- High number of hours spent caregiving

- Lack of choice in assuming caregiver role
- Social isolation
- Scant financial resources
- Higher levels of care recipients' cognitive impairment and functional disabilities
- Challenging behavior problems manifested by the care recipient such as agitation and lack of cooperation

Older caregivers and those with lower socioeconomic statuses or barren social support networks appear more vulnerable for both poorer physical and psychological health (Schulz & Sherwood, 2008).

When laboring under these challenging and stressful conditions, caregivers may experience a variety of deleterious *physical, social,* and *psychological* impacts. The connection between caregiving and poorer physical health is weaker than the link between caregiving and poorer mental health (Bookwala, Yee, & Schulz, 2000). This may result from the different ways that physical health can be operationalized. Nevertheless, a burgeoning literature provides compelling testimony to the health risks and conditions that chronically stressed caregivers face all too frequently.

## Physical Health

Chronic stress can disrupt proper immune system functioning. Gouin, Hantsoo, and Kiecolt-Glaser (2008) have reviewed studies that find stressed caregivers to suffer from immune system dysregulation and poorer responses to immunization. Recent research has suggested that multiple daily stressors, such as those experienced by caregivers, may elevate the levels of inflammatory markers, not seen in noncaregiving peers (Gouin, Glaser, Malarkey, Beversdorf, & Kiecolt-Glaser, 2012). Kiecolt-Glaser and Glaser (2001) noted that chronic stress may accelerate the rate of normal, age-related immune system dysregulation. This health concern must be considered as the population of caregivers continues to age.

Schubert et al. (2008) found that 24% of a sample of 153 dementia caregivers were hospitalized or had an emergency room visit in the previous 6 months. These findings find support in a more recent study of Alzheimer's caregivers by Schulz and Cook (2011). They reported that caregivers evidenced a 25% increase in all types of healthcare services (e.g., emergency room visits, hospital use, physician visits) over the 18-month duration of the study.

There are studies conveying the sober message that caregivers' lives are at stake. Haley, Roth, Howard, and Stafford (2010) found that caregiving strain is associated with higher stroke risk, especially for African American men caring for their wives. In a study of a cohort of registered nurses followed for 4 years, caring for a disabled or ill spouse for 9 or more hours per week was found to be associated with increased risk of coronary heart disease (Lee, Colditz, Berkman, & Kawachi, 2003). The average coronary heart disease risk score was found to be higher in dementia caregivers than in noncaregiving controls, even when controlling for socioeconomic status, health habits, and psychological distress (von Känel et al., 2008). Perhaps most disconcerting are findings from an often-cited study by Schulz and Beach (1999), who conducted a prospective population-based cohort study with an average of 4.5 years of follow-up. After adjusting for sociodemographic and certain health factors, they found that those who were providing care and experiencing strain (i.e., mental or emotional strain associated with helping or getting help for each caregiving activity) had mortality risks that were 63% higher than those for a control group of noncaregivers.

## Impact on Social Functioning

With regard to social impacts of caregiving, dementia caregivers report less time for leisure, more employment complications, and more family conflict than nondementia caregivers (Ory, Hoffman, Yee, Tennstedt, & Shulz, 1999). The term *role captivity* used to describe caregivers' feeling of being trapped in their role and tethered to the caregiving site. This point is exemplified by recent findings in which more than half (53%) of family caregivers report reduced contact with friends and family (National Alliance for Caregiving, 2009; http://www.caregiving.org/pdf/research/FINALRegularExSum50plus.pdf). Moreover, role captivity has been identified as a factor predicting burden in dementia caregivers (Campbell et al., 2008).

## Psychological Impact

In their exhaustive review of research on the effects of caregiving on health, Bookwala et al. (2000) noted that the stresses of caregiving had become solidly linked to detrimental mental health outcomes. One of those outcomes, depression, is commonly reported by overburdened family caregivers. For example, in one review of previous studies, Zarit (2006) found that between 40% and 70% of family caregivers of older persons display clinically significant symptoms of depression. A longitudinal study on caregiving stressors indicated that caregiver depression may have a negative effect on quality of care (Smith, Williamson, Miller, & Schulz, 2011). Moreover, depressed caregivers, when also feeling high levels of anger or resentment toward the care recipient, are at risk of becoming abusive (MacNeil et al., 2010).

Women appear to be particularly vulnerable. For example, Yee and Schulz (2000) found that compared with men caregivers, women caregivers reported more psychiatric symptomatology (e.g., higher levels of depression and anxiety and lower life satisfaction). Yee and Schulz described a variety of factors that presumably place women at greater risk for psychiatric morbidity. Two such factors are that women are less likely to obtain either formal or informal assistance, and they tend to assume more hands-on roles in personal care tasks.

In another representative study, Haug, Ford, Stange, Noelker, and Gaines (1999) followed a random sample of caregivers over a 2-year period. This study is notable in that it utilized a longitudinal design and was not focused only on dementia caregivers. Haug et al. found that at the outset of their study, 40.5% of the caregivers assessed their mental/emotional states as "excellent." At the study's third and final assessment point, only 24.8% made that same claim. Haug et al. noted that a possible factor in this decline was the substantial increase in the mean number of instrumental activities of daily living (IADLs) and activities of daily living (ADLs) performed by the caregivers over the course of the study. In a sadly ironical twist of fate, dementia caregivers have been found to experience little psychological relief even after their care recipients have transitioned to long-term care. Schulz, Belle, Czaja, McGinnis, & Stevens (2004) found the caregivers at the same levels of depression and distress after placement.

It is not only dementia caregivers who feel the emotional impact. Caregivers of cancer patients often display symptoms of anxiety and depression—and find themselves socially isolated as well (Stenburg, Ruland, & Miaskowski, 2010). One sobering finding is that the level of psychological distress reported by caregivers of cancer patients meets or exceeds that actually reported by the patients (Hodges, Humphris, & Macfarlane, 2005).

## Summary Comments on the Caregiving Experience

Although the social, emotional, and physical impacts of caregiving are not necessarily negative, problems encountered and responsibilities assumed in caregiving can adversely stress the caregiver. The results of that stress are succinctly stated by Bookwala et al. (2000):

> In summary, based on the studies that we have reviewed here, we can conclude that caregivers of both dementia and nondementia patient groups evidence significant psychiatric morbidity compared to noncaregivers or community norms. Caregivers also consistently rate their physical health to be poorer than do noncaregivers and, in some cases, exhibit poorer health-related behaviors, physical disability, and immune and physiological functioning. (p. 127)

Where does caregiver distress come from? What is it about the caregiving experience that can strain the caregivers' capacities to cope? These questions lead us to consider the issue of caregiver burden.

## CAREGIVER BURDEN

Montgomery (1989) selected several terms from the literature that target what is meant by burden: stress effects, caregiving consequences, and care-giving impact. For Gottlieb, Thompson, and Bourgeois (2003), burden refers to "the extent to which problems commonly seen in caregiving situations are rated as distressing or troublesome to the caregiver" (p. 42).

A number of instruments have been developed to assess caregiver burden. One commonly used instrument, with reportedly good psychometric properties (Caserta, Lund, & Wright, 1996), is the 24-item Caregiver Burden Inventory (CBI; Novak & Guest, 1989). The CBI consists of five subscales measuring different aspects of caregiver burden: time dependence, developmental, physical, social, and emotional.

The CBI has been factor analyzed on a US sample by Schwiebert, Giordano, Zhang, and Sealander (1998). The resulting six factors provide compass points for where to locate burden and where to target crisis interventions. Each factor is discussed in the following, and examples are provided from our counseling experience with caregivers that illustrate specific sources of burden.

### Factor 1: Time-Dependence Burden

Time-dependence burden results from the caregiver's perceived restriction on time. It is commonly experienced by dementia caregivers who are involved in almost continuous and vigilant care. Caregivers' crises may be precipitated by a variety of time-dependence issues.

For example, crises can emanate from a feeling of *role captivity* (Campbell et al., 2008; Givens, Mezzacappa, Heeren, Yaffe, & Fredman, 2014). This term aptly captures the demoralizing sense of being tethered to the caregiving site as well as the constant monitoring performed by the caregiver. In our work, we have seen how a sense of role captivity will feed on itself. We recently heard one spouse caregiver's dilemma arising from attending the out-of-town first communion of a granddaughter: "I want to go so bad, but I won't. If I do step out, I'll enjoy the freedom too much, and coming back to this house and him will be more pain than I can bear." Similarly, we have heard a caregiver lament that just a few minutes' trip to the supermarket aroused great agitation in her care receiver: "He panics if I even go to the mailbox!" Moreover, time-dependence burden, not surprisingly, is associated in our experience with an extreme reluctance on the part of caregivers to request in-home care assistance: nobody, these caregivers believe, is able to provide the prompt or attentive care that they can.

As caregivers' time and space shrink, social isolation and resentment toward the care recipient increase. Because social isolation is a risk factor for elder abuse (Cooney & Mortimer, 1995), we recommend that crisis workers be on the alert for that possibility.

## Factor 2: Developmental Burden

This burden arises due to caregivers' feelings of being "off-time" developmentally in comparison to peers. There is a strong sense of being left behind, of missing out on life, and of wishing that current circumstances were different.

For caregivers, developmental burden can be linked with the sacrifices made (e.g., placing career, hobby, or friendships on hold) on behalf of the care recipient. It can be experienced by the daughter who expected that demands on her attention and affection would be coming from adolescent children and husband rather than from a cognitively impaired uncle.

Developmental burden can be experienced in many ways. Caregiver goals, dreams, and lifestyles may be derailed by the time and energy devoted to the caregiving experience (Zegwaard, Aartsen, Cuijpers, & Grypdonck, 2011). For one client of ours, a woman of financial means, it came in the form of an existential crisis. As she cared for a husband who was left permanently paralyzed by a stroke, she realized that her image of aging gracefully into a comfortable retirement would never materialize. How often she had pictured herself and her husband outside their opulent desert retirement home, bathed in the glow of a southwestern sunset, toasting their love and good fortune as they sat poolside in the company of their old country club friends! It's a picture she would never pose for.

## Factor 3: Physical Burden

Schwiebert, Giordano, Zhang, and Sealander (1998) found that three CBI items pertaining to fatigue and care recipient dependence constitute the physical burden factor. With this factor, stress arises due to a feeling that one is on a grueling treadmill: one is exhausted, but the pace never slackens.

"I'm exhausted, but the person is dependent on me" is a caregiver's stance that has crisis potential because it allows neither for easy negotiation nor for a way out. We recommend assessing the caregiver for other rule-bound thinking that closes off his or her options. For example, it is common to hear caregivers claim, "I'm exhausted, but we must stick to our routine."

## Factor 4: Social Burden

Feelings of social burden derive from perceived role conflict. Crises are often precipitated by conflicted relationships with other family members. Consider how the role of primary family caregiver devolves on one of several siblings: She or he may be regarded as father's "favorite," resides closest to parents, has a nursing background, and so forth. When the caregiver is chosen in this manner, it can lead to resentment and a sense of being obliged to take on the responsibilities. Caregivers may lash out angrily against the family member who needs to be reminded constantly about the money she or he grudgingly promised to chip in to cover caregiving expenses. We recall the caregiver who endured frequent, intrusive long-distance phone calls from a brother who was highly critical of financial decisions being made in his absence. However, much more common are caregivers' remarks about how little appreciation they receive from family for the work they do.

The conflict is compounded by its emotional aftereffects. Caregivers may consequently worry that their anger drove away potentially valuable support. Or, they may feel shame for saying things in anger that cannot be taken back.

## Factor 5: Emotional Burden

The burden caregivers perceive to be due to negative feelings toward their care receivers is termed *emotional burden*. This type of burden can lead to a crisis when the caregiver's resentment threatens the caregiving relationship. An overly strained and fatigued caregiver may express her or his resentment as "If it weren't for you, my life would not be a living hell."

Resentment can also run high if there has been a history of abuse in the family. For example, a wife who had endured chronic verbal abuse from her husband might feel especially strained by the demands of caring for him, and we should be alert to any signs of abuse being perpetrated or threatened against the husband. Likewise, caregiving daughters may be emotionally strained in circumstances where their care receiver is a mother who, years earlier, failed to provide protection against a father's abusive advances. In this regard, an underappreciated issue is how transference may complicate the issues of caregivers' emotional well-being. As the care receiver interacts with the caregiver, angry or hurtful emotions may reconstitute unresolved past conflicts. The caregiver may view the care receiver as a mother, aunt, or father. This may be healthy for the care receiver if that transference was positive, or negative if the mother was seen as a "bad mother" (Berman & Bezkor, 2010).

Emotional burden arises also out of feeling embarrassed by the behavior of the care receiver. Should the care recipient become incontinent, the caregiver is often doubly strained due to a reluctance to invite others into the home and by the great difficulty posed by coping with incontinence, an event that often leads to the wrenching decision of nursing home placement (Mittelman, Zeiss, Davies, & Guy, 2003).

With regard to emotional burden, we also need to mention the exasperation that many caregivers feel when assisting an "uncooperative" care receiver with his or her ADLs. Bathing, toileting, and physician visits can become tests of whose will shall prevail.

Despite the fact that their emotional burdens fairly cry out for assistance, caregivers increase their risks of experiencing crisis because they are among the most resistant or cautious about seeking support from the social service system. Toseland (1995) commented on the difficulty of recruiting a critical mass of caregivers for a support group:

> Making initial contact with a sufficient number of caregivers to begin a group can be difficult. Caregivers tend to be reluctant to ask for help. Seeking help is sometimes perceived as abandoning their responsibility and the person for whom they are caring. (p. 232)

## Factor 6: Health Burden

Schwiebert et al. (1998) identified a sixth factor from the CBI that did not appear in Novak and Guest's (1989) original analysis. Schwiebert et al. referred to this factor, which consists of three items, as *health burden*. These items appear to be reflective of caregivers' perceptions of their own diminishing health.

In our counseling work with caregivers, we have found that they tend to neglect their physical needs. One caregiver living with her 100-year-old mother said to us that she had relied on gardening for her exercise and that now she and her garden were both "going to pot." Studies bear out that caregivers report getting less physical activity and rest. For example, in one national survey almost 60% of the caregivers reported that their eating and exercise habits had worsened, whereas 82% reported sleep had been negatively affected (*Evercare*, 2006)

Self-care, exercise, good nutrition, and stress management are all components of a wellness-oriented intervention focus for caregivers (Myers, 2003). Yet, as Ilardo and Rothman (1999) point out, caregivers operate out of imperatives that militate against their performing essential self-care. One of these (and the one we most often hear) is "I shouldn't need to take a break. I'm strong" (p. 78). Caregivers continue to put themselves at risk of strain and crisis until such an imperative becomes tempered with a competing awareness: "Good caregiving starts with myself. If I don't look out for me, my care receiver suffers."

---

### Case Study: "Meet Millie"

Millie F. was an 83-year-old living at home with Frank, 84, her spouse of 57 years. They married on November 17, 1953, only a few weeks after he had been discharged from the navy. A childless couple, they often talked about how they had "adopted" all the kids on their block and how theirs was the house where all the youngsters liked to hang out. Both maintained lengthy careers, he as a mail fraud investigator with the postal service and she as an interior designer with a large department store chain. With her eye for decoration and color, she always favored splashy, coordinated clothing with jewelry and accessories to match. Frank loved to introduce his vivacious wife at any opportunity. "Here she is. *Meet Millie!*" he would say, beaming. Over the years, fewer and fewer people would catch Frank's little play on words—how he was also referring to *Meet Millie*, a popular TV show of the 1950s that starred Elena Verdugo.

About a year and a half before Millie found herself on the brink of crisis, she had noticed some subtle changes in Frank. For example, he seemed to be repeating the same question he had asked just minutes earlier. Then, there was the problem with his temper. He had always been an "ornery cuss," as she described him, but now his orneriness was becoming more intense and personal. Millie was not sure what to make of her observations. After all, Frank seemed his usual self most of the time. However, after an incident with the newspaper delivery boy, she decided to mention the situation to their primary care physician. "Why, he just cursed the boy out because the paper was a little ways down the driveway. I mean, he used language that would have made a sailor blush!"

After a few trips back to the physician with Frank in tow, they received some complicated information, a diagnosis of sorts of Frank's condition, and a prescription for medication that he at first refused to take. "I thought he told us that Frank had 'old-timers' disease," was how Millie summarized these visits.

As weeks went by, Millie was becoming increasingly exasperated, angry, and even fearful of Frank. She suspected something was wrong, but she was not quite sure to what she should attribute Frank's unpredictable, touchy, and hurtful behavior. Slowly, surely, and almost imperceptibly the situation deteriorated. Millie was beginning to feel like a prisoner in her own home as Frank alienated old friends. Fellowship visits from their church fell off. Frank's outbursts took the forms of personal criticism bordering on abuse and demands for obedience to his dictates. With the former came a growing depression that began to gnaw at Millie. With the latter came a growing resentment against Frank. His demands failed to take into consideration the fact that Millie was struggling with painful osteoarthritis in her knees and back. He lacked empathy for the efforts she was making to care for him.

The depression and resentment were joined by anxiety. About a week and a half before her referral to a community mental health center (CMHC), Millie witnessed two events in one day that brought home to her the precarious nature of the situation with Frank. Late that morning Frank had gone out to the mailbox at the end of the driveway. Some minutes later, Millie noticed that Frank had not yet returned inside. After a quick search, she found him in the backyard with a confused look on his face. He made up some excuse to explain why he was standing in the tulip bed. A few hours later, Frank forgot that he had turned on the faucet in a basement washtub. The overflow took 2 hours to mop up.

Perhaps it was more than coincidence that just two days later Millie made an appointment to speak with a services specialist at the Area Agency on Aging (AAA) in her community. She wanted information about a prescription drug program that she might qualify for. Besides giving Millie the prescription plan information, the services specialist noticed her fatigue and depression. The specialist inquired and learned that Millie was the sole caregiver for an older spouse with suspected Alzheimer's disease and that she had only a tenuous supportive network: a few diehard friends and some nieces and nephews who made irregular phone calls from the East Coast. Considering Millie's strained self-presentation, the specialist tactfully broached the topic of a referral to the local CMHC. Fortunately, the AAA and the CMHC had established a good collaborative arrangement (Lebowitz, Light, & Bailey, 1987) so that the referral could be made swiftly given the risk inherent in this caregiving situation.

Although the offer of a counseling referral took Millie by surprise ("He's the one with the screw loose, and you want *me* to get *my* head examined?"), she agreed to it, and the next day she had a walk-in appointment with the CMHC's on-call crisis counselor. With the referral secured, the AAA's services specialist had done well to apprehend Millie's signs of emotional difficulty and to inquire about her caregiving strain. Furthermore, the specialist was wise to initiate discussion of a referral, as caregivers are notoriously loath to refer themselves to programs that would alleviate their depression (Gottlieb et al., 2003).

## CRISIS INTERVENTION: THE SEVEN-STAGE MODEL

Millie's situation is not yet one in imminent crisis, but there is potential for crisis. One risk is possible mistreatment of the care recipient at the hands of a burdened caregiver, as discussed earlier. A second risk is to the caregiver's own health and emotional well-being. Without self-care, caregivers may jeopardize their health, which leads to an earlier and perhaps less appropriate long-term care placement for the care recipient. Roberts's (2000) model has applicability to caregiving situations that are crises in the offing.

### Stage 1: Conduct a Crisis Assessment (Including Lethality)

The crisis counselor noted that Millie had very limited social support. She had not accessed any resources in the community for day care or respite services. Informal support in the form of friends and family came sporadically. Low social support fed into Millie's isolation. She felt, she said, like the Lone Ranger.

Millie's emotional profile was that of someone experiencing depression and anxiety. Certainly her depression was exacerbated by the personal nature of the criticism she received from Frank, by her chronic fatigue and arthritis pain, and by a growing pessimism about how this caregiving situation would resolve. Worries about her health (arthritis and hypertension) featured prominently in her anxiety, and lack of sound information about the disease and what it was doing to Frank added to her uncertainty. There was no indication that Millie had been mistreating Frank, although she was worried that one day he might physically strike out at her.

Administration of the CBI found Millie highest on developmental and emotional burdens. The developmental burden resulted from a combination of a wish to escape her caregiving situation, the emotional drain attached to caregiving, and the role captivity and social isolation into which she felt she was sinking deeper. The emotional burden resulted from the embarrassment she felt when Frank attacked visitors, anger at his verbal criticism of her, and smoldering resentment for performing a difficult yet unappreciated caregiving role.

After the initial walk-in session, the crisis counselor began to conceptualize this caregiving situation. Besides the evident anxiety and depression, the crisis counselor singled out other issues for further exploration:

- Millie failed to request more information and explanations about Frank's dementing condition from their physician.
- Her attempts to reason, argue, or rationalize with Frank over his demands might actually stoke his anger and agitation.
- She eventually bowed to these demands, even when there was no evidence of their reasonableness.
- She neglected her own health needs.
- She lacked knowledge about her community's formal support and assistance programs.

## Stage 2: Establish Rapport

After providing a few of the elements of good listening (eye contact, undivided attention, reflecting feelings), the counselor found that Millie was hungry for social contact. Somewhat to Millie's surprise, she was really taking to this counselor who had the capacity to understand her point of view.

Initially, the crisis counselor suggested that she and Millie address her obvious stress and exhaustion. Because Millie is from a generation that might be suspicious of counseling, stress and exhaustion, which seem to have a physical basis, were "safer" topics than anxiety and depression. Millie agreed to this, and that served as the second step toward building a relationship.

The counselor established rapport in several other ways. For example, she was sensitive to some of the jargon and colloquialisms older persons might use. Thus, when Millie got off the elevator for her appointment and promptly got lost trying to find the counselor's office, both could chuckle at Millie's description of herself as a "Wrong-Way Corrigan." If the counselor did not understand Millie's slang, she asked for clarification, as when Millie described feeling the "heebie-jeebies" the day Frank was lost in the tulips.

Many older clients have a capacity for humor, and this can be used in the service of relationship building. It can even be used as a springboard to address counseling topics of substance, as this snippet of dialogue illustrates:

> Millie:      (laughing) Frank always liked to brag about his boxing exploits while in the navy. I guess he won a few fights as a welterweight, but he's really embellished that record quite a bit over the years. Now, to hear him tell it, he practically defeated everyone in the Pacific Fleet with one arm tied behind his back!
>
> Counselor:   (laughing along, but then becoming serious) Like the story about the fish that got away that gets bigger and bigger after every retelling! But let me ask you this: Is there anything else that he claims that *you* know isn't quite the case?
>
> Millie:      Well, come to think of it, a couple of weeks ago my friend Helen came to visit. He told her flat out, and used a few choice words in the process, that he didn't want her coming over anymore, because he said we make too much noise that disturbs him. But he plays the TV so darn loud, he couldn't have heard us over it!
>
> Counselor:   So, his reason for forbidding Helen to come over to visit really doesn't hold together. But you abide by it—mainly to keep the peace—and the result is that you feel more isolated. Is that right?

From the very first, it is essential for the counselor to foster a climate of collaboration with the client. By encouraging working *together*, the counselor strongly suggests that something good can be accomplished, and that builds a sense of hope in the client.

Finally, self-disclosure, at the right time, in the right amount, and of an appropriate content, can also help to establish rapport. In a second counseling visit, the counselor disclosed that she had had some deeply personal experience with caregiving herself. The counselor briefly talked about how she had been part of an extended family effort several years earlier on behalf of a physically disabled grandmother.

## Stage 3: Identify Major Problems or Crisis Precipitants

Roberts (2000) has pointed out the usefulness of identifying the "last straw" (p. 18), or precipitating event, as well as the client's previous coping methods. In Millie's case, two events—finding Frank in the backyard and the overflowing washtub—seemed to be the turning points in how she viewed her situation. These events could not be easily explained away, and they came to represent the hard truth that something was definitely wrong. They clashed with Millie's wish that all was well and that Frank's old self would prevail.

These two events fit into the counselor's evolving conceptualization of Millie's modal coping style. When faced with threat, especially threat that could overwhelm, Millie's tendency is to cope by using avoidance or hoping that things will get better. This is how she had reacted to evidence of Frank's cognitive slippage. When confronted with threat that is less easily bypassed, such as Frank's barrage of verbal criticism or demands for care, Millie adopted an *argue–acquiesce–blame self* coping pattern. That is, she would make a noisy but feeble attempt to argue or reason with him, give in to his demand so as to keep the peace, and then come around to blaming herself for having set him off.

Millie's passive, avoidant, and reactive (as opposed to proactive) coping styles explained her surprising lack of knowledge about Alzheimer's disease and lack of awareness of support services in the community. One question that the counselor posed piqued Millie's curiosity in such a way that she was motivated to learn more about the effect of Alzheimer's disease. At one point, the counselor asked offhandedly, "Frank's anger and cursing at you—do you wonder if this is Frank or the disease doing the talking?"

## Stage 4: Encourage Exploration of Feelings

There are two important objectives at Stage 4, as we have found from our work with older clients. One objective is for the client's "story" to be heard. As Mittelman et al. (2003) put it, "We have found that most AD [Alzheimer's disease] caregivers want to tell their stories and they more readily identify problems and solutions when they have been active participants in that process" (p. 79). When clients tell their stories and give us their slant on what the problem is, we listen for an overarching theme or title that could be given to that story. In Millie's case, the title that came to the counselor's mind was "I'm a Prisoner in My Own Home." When the counselor shared that title with Millie, her nonverbal reaction was such that the counselor knew it struck a chord. With regard to identifying problems and solutions from the story, the counselor suggested, "If that's what the title of the story is, could we put our heads together to come up with a workable 'escape plan'?" Put that way, Millie was intrigued to hear more.

A second objective is to validate the client's feelings. Millie's exhaustion, which Frank minimized, was validated: She *is* exhausted, she really is tired. That she felt anger and resentment was understandable. Her perception of the situation was validated. "Maybe," the counselor allowed, "the rules that Frank lays down and his angry outbursts, which you take exception to but then cave in to, are not as sound as your perception of the situation." From the extraction of the story title and the validation of feelings and perceptions come possibilities and alternatives.

## Stage 5: Generate and Explore Alternatives

The counselor is advised to collaborate, go slowly, and work with a manageable few, but relevant, behavioral alternatives. After putting their heads together and brainstorming, the counselor and Millie came up with these alternatives:

*The need for more information:* Information about dementia helps reduce the burden of informal family caregivers of dementia patients (Schindler, Engel, & Rupprecht, 2012). Information needs to be obtained from Frank's physician. What information the physician cannot supply, given his limited time, can be obtained from other sources, such as the local chapter of the Alzheimer's Association.

*The need for skills and support:* Certainly, it is important for Millie to reconnect with old friends. The counselor also planted the seed for another source of support by saying in a neutral way, "I don't know if you've ever considered becoming a part of a group that consists of other caregivers who are going through many of the same things you are. I know of a group that combines support with information and important new skills. It often helps to be with others in the same boat because they can supply an understanding perspective that our well-meaning regular friends just don't have."

The counselor knew that a group would be useful for Millie, especially one that (a) employed psychoeducational and psychotherapeutic approaches to allow caregivers to practice new skills and make behavioral changes; (b) utilized group processes (e.g., providing feedback, sharing similar concerns, group cohesion); and (c) is multidimensional (i.e., deals with multiple issues that are apt to be stressful such as managing fatigue, communicating with one's healthcare providers, obtaining tips for assisting the care recipients with daily activities; Zarit & Femia, 2008). Moreover, the counselor wanted an evidence-based group intervention—one that had a track record for actually increasing a sense of self-efficacy in its participants. Self-efficacy may act as a buffer against some of the negative physical and psychological consequences of caregiving (Semiatin & O'Connor, 2012).

A psychoeducational intervention that fits this bill is Powerful Tools for Caregivers™ (PTC), a 6-week class experience designed to promote self-efficacy for caregivers by also improving caregiver emotions and self-care behaviors (Clelland, Schmall, & Sturdevant, 2006; www. powerfultoolsforcaregivers.org/). A study conducted in Oregon in 2002 exhibited a significant improvement in caregiver self-care behaviors, self-efficacy, emotional well-being, and knowledge and utilization of community resources (Boise, Congleton, & Shannon, 2005). A more recent study demonstrated that PTC reduced stress burden (tension and anxiety resulting from caregiving) and reduced objective burden (intrusiveness on the caregiver life roles) compared with a control group. PTC appears to be a strong combatant against some of the common stressors typically associated with caregiving (Savundranayagam, Montgomery, Kosloski, & Little, 2011).

*The need for respite:* Millie and the counselor agreed that both she and Frank could benefit from some time away from each other, although Millie was very skeptical of how Frank would tolerate that. Part of respite also involved some necessary self-care on Millie's own behalf, which could include some recreation and even long-neglected physical therapy for her ailing knee.

*The need to resolutely confront the issues:* This is a behavioral alternative that was suggested by the counselor. She understood Millie's tendencies to avoid facing issues and to fail to persevere and see a solution through. As this alternative was discussed, Millie saw the importance of "taking the bull by the horns" and not backing off even when the bull began to charge.

## Stage 6: Develop and Formulate an Action Plan

The counselor and Millie took each of the preceding alternatives and worked them into an action plan. To obtain more information, Millie and the counselor role-played how to assertively request information from the physician. Millie learned to write down questions for the physician so she would not forget them in the rush and crush to get Frank to the clinic. Millie was encouraged to make another appointment with the services specialist at AAA to learn about community services and how to join an upcoming PTC class.

At the AAA, Millie learned about a respite program funded by the federal Older Americans Act to pay for a number of respite care hours each year. She learned how to apply and qualify for this service. Perhaps more important, she found out about places offering adult day care in her community where individuals with Alzheimer's disease could socialize and even have lunch. The counselor suggested that Frank attend day care at least twice a week for Millie to derive beneficial respite from it (Zarit, Stephens, Townsend, & Greene, 1998). While Frank was at day care or while the respite worker was in her home, Millie could use this time to visit friends or get therapy for her arthritic knee.

Resolutely confronting the issue was perhaps Millie's toughest challenge. "He's not going to like going to a day care center. It'll be like moving heaven and earth to get him there." In the past, Frank's protestations were too much for her to bear, and she would back down. This time she promised she would stick to her guns and give the day care and respite care "experiments" a chance to work. To her surprise, Frank began to look forward to day care, which he associated with going to a part-time job. He warmed up to the staff, flirted innocently with a couple of the women who attended, and found another Korean War veteran with whom he could share stories.

## Stage 7: Follow-Up

The counselor and Millie agreed that follow-up (or booster) appointments be scheduled for about 3 weeks and then stretched to every 6 weeks. The purpose of these check-in visits would be to take a measure of Millie's current stress level, and the counselor planned to re-administer the CBI at each follow-up session. The counselor also looked at these follow-up sessions as an opportunity to assess how well Millie was maintaining her active coping style, as opposed to avoidance. This would come into play over the developmental course of Millie and Frank's caregiving experience, as when, for example, the time came for Millie to consider and research long-term care placement for Frank.

## CONCLUSION

The typical challenges of caregiving for an older disabled adult often become burdens that strain the caregiver's capacities to cope. Caregiving can be a rewarding, even a spiritually deep, experience, certainly insofar as there is adequate support for the caregiver and a positive attachment to the care recipient. When burden takes a toll, however, there can be numerous untoward emotional and physical effects on the caregivers, and care recipients can experience the rebound effect of these, as in the case of elder abuse.

The caregiver in crisis resorts to maladaptive coping behaviors that often exacerbate an already difficult situation. Also, caregivers feel out of balance socially, emotionally, and physically. This is true for both dementia and nondementia caregivers. It is important to restore a sense of balance in the lives of caregivers because their focus can be solely on the care recipient to the exclusion of themselves. In this chapter, we illustrated how the stages of a widely adopted crisis intervention model can be utilized to address the burdens of a caregiver and help her find relief from their strain.

REFERENCES

Adelman, R. D., Tmanova, L. L., Delgado, D., Dion, S., & Lachs, M. S. (2014). Caregiver burden: A clinical review. *Journal of the American Medical Association, 311*, 1052–1060.

Alzheimer's Association. (2013). 2013 Alzheimer's disease facts and figures. *Alzheimer's & Dementia, 9*(2).

Argüelles, S., Klausner, E. J., Argüelles, T., & Coon, D. W. (2003). Family interventions to address the needs of the caregiving system. In D. W. Coon, D. Gallagher-Thompson, & L. W. Thompson (Eds.), *Innovative interventions to reduce dementia caregiver distress* (pp. 99–118). New York: Springer.

Berman, C. W., & Bezkor, M. F. (2010). Transference in patients and caregivers. *American Journal of Psychotherapy, 64*, 107–114.

Boise, L., Congleton, L., & Shannon, K. (2005). Empowering family caregivers: The tools for caregiving program. *Educational Gerontology, 31*, 573–586.

Bookwala, J., Yee, J. L., & Schulz, R. (2000). Caregiving and detrimental mental and physical health outcomes. In G. M. Williamson, D. R. Shaffer, & P. A. Parmlee (Eds.), *Physical illness and depression in older adults: A handbook of theory, research, and practice* (pp. 93–131). New York: Kluwer Academic/Plenum.

Campbell, P., Wright, J., Oyebode, J., Job, D., Crome, P., Bentham, P., . . . Lendon, C. (2008). Determinants of burden in those who care for someone with dementia. *International Journal of Geriatric Psychiatry, 23*, 1078–1085.

Caserta, M. S., Lund, D. A., & Wright, S. D. (1996). Exploring the Caregiver Burden Inventory (CBI): Further evidence for a multidimensional view of burden. *International Journal of Aging and Human Development, 43*, 21–34.

Chappell, N. L., & Reid, R. C. (2002). Burden and well-being among caregivers: Examining the distinction. *Gerontologist, 42*, 772–780.

Cicirelli, V. G. (1993). Attachment and obligation as daughters' motives for caregiving behavior and subsequent effect on subjective burden. *Psychology and Aging, 8*, 144–155.

Clelland, M., Schmall, V. L., & Sturdevant, M. (2006). *The caregiver helpbook: Powerful tools for caregiving* (2nd ed.). Portland OR: Legacy Caregiver Services.

Cohen, C. A., Colantonio, A., & Vernich, L. (2002). Positive aspects of caregiving: Rounding out the caregiver experience. *International Journal of Geriatric Psychiatry, 17*, 184–188.

Cooney, C., & Mortimer, A. (1995). Elder abuse and dementia: A pilot study. *International Journal of Social Psychiatry, 41*, 276–283.

*Evercare study of caregivers in decline: Findings from a national survey.* (2006, September). Minnetonka, MN: Evercare; Bethesda MD: National Alliance for Caregiving.

Feinberg, L., Reinhard, S. C., Houser, A., & Choula, R. (2011, July). *Valuing the invaluable: 2011 update: The growing contributions and costs of family caregiving.* Washington, DC: AARP Public Policy Institute.

Gallagher-Thompson, D., Arean, P., Coon, D., Menendez, A., Takagi, K., Haley, W. E., . . . Szapocznik, J. (2000). Development and implementation of intervention strategies for culturally diverse caregiving populations. In R. Schulz (Ed.), *Handbook on dementia caregiving: Evidence-based interventions for family caregivers* (pp. 151–185). New York: Springer.

Givens, J. L., Mezzacappa, C., Heeren, T., Yaffe, K., & Fredman, L. (2014). Depressive symptoms among dementia caregivers: Role of mediating factors. *American Journal of Geriatric Psychiatry, 22,* 481–488.

Gottlieb, B. H., Thompson, L. W., & Bourgeois, M. (2003). Monitoring and evaluating interventions. In D. W. Coon, D. Gallagher-Thompson, & L. W. Thompson (Eds.), *Innovative interventions to reduce dementia caregivers distress* (pp. 28–49). New York: Springer.

Gouin, J.-P., Glaser, R., Malarkey, W. B., Beversdorf, D., & Kiecolt-Glaser, J. (2012). Chronic stress, daily stressors, and circulating inflammatory markers. *Health Psychology, 31,* 264–268.

Gouin, J.-P., Hantsoo, L., & Kiecolt-Glaser, J. K. (2008). Immune dysregulation and chronic stress among older adults: A review. *Neuroimmunomodulation, 15,* 251–259.

Haley, W. E., Roth, D. L., Howard, G., & Stafford, M. M. (2010). Caregiving strain estimated risk for stroke and coronary heart disease among spouse caregivers: Differential effects by race and sex. *Stroke, 41,* 331–336.

Haug, M. R., Ford, A. B., Stange, K. C., Noelker, L. S., & Gaines, A. D. (1999). Effects of giving care on caregivers' health. *Research on Aging, 21,* 515–538.

Hilgeman, M. M., Allen, R. S., DeCoster, J., & Burgio, L. D. (2007). Positive aspects of caregiving as a moderator of treatment outcome over 12 months. *Psychology and Aging, 22,* 361–371.

Hodges, L. J., Humphris, G. M., & Macfarlane, G. (2005). A meta-analytic investigation of the relationship between the psychological distress of cancer patients and their careers. *Social Science and Medicine, 60,* 1–12.

Hoffman, R. L., & Mitchell, A. M. (1998). Caregiver burden: Historical development. *Nursing Forum, 33,* 5–111.

Ilardo, J. A., & Rothman, C. R. (1999). *I'll take care of you: A practical guide for family caregivers.* Oakland, CA: New Harbinger.

Jenkins, K. R., Kabeto, M. U., & Langa, K. M. (2009). Does caring for your spouse harm one's health? Evidence from a United States nationally-represented sample of older adults. *Ageing and Society, 29,* 277–293.

Kiecolt-Glaser, J. K., & Glaser, R. (2001). Stress and immunity: Age enhances the risks. *Current Directions in Psychological Science, 10,* 18–21.

King, T. (1993). The experiences of midlife daughters who are caregivers for their mothers. *Health Care for Women International, 14,* 419–426.

Lebowitz, B. D., Light, E., & Bailey, F. (1987). Mental health center services for the elderly: The impact of coordination with area agencies on aging. *Gerontologist, 27,* 699–702.

Lee, S., Colditz, G. A., Berkman, L. F., & Kawachi, I. (2003). Caregiving and risk of coronary heart disease in U.S. women: A prospective study. *American Journal of Preventive Medicine, 24,* 113–119.

Logsdon, M. C., & Robinson, K. (2000). Helping women caregivers obtain support: Barriers and recommendations. *Archives of Psychiatric Nursing, 14,* 244–248.

Mace, N. L., & Rabins, P. V. (2011). *The 36-hour day* (5th ed.). Baltimore: Johns Hopkins University Press.

MacNeil, G., Kosberg, J. I., Durkin, D. W., Dooley, W. K., DeCoster, J., & Williamson, G. M. (2010). Caregiver mental health and potentially harmful caregiving behavior: The central role of caregiver anger. *Gerontologist, 50,* 76–86.

Marks, N. F., Lambert, J. D., & Choi, H. (2002). Transitions to caregiving, gender, and psychological well-being: A prospective U.S. national study. *Journal of Marriage and the Family, 64,* 657–667.

McLennon, S. M., Havermann, B., & Rice, M. (2011). Finding meaning as a mediator of burden on the health of caregivers of spouses with dementia. *Aging and Mental Health, 15,* 522–530.

Mittelman, M., Zeiss, A., Davies, H., & Guy, D. (2003). Specific stressors of spousal caregivers: Difficult behaviors, loss of sexual intimacy, and incontinence. In D. W. Coon, D. Gallagher-Thompson, & L. W. Thompson (Eds.), *Innovative interventions to reduce caregiver distress* (pp. 77–98). New York: Springer.

Montgomery, R. J. V. (1989). Investigating caregiver burden. In K. S. Markides & C. L. Cooper (Eds.), *Aging, stress, and health* (pp. 201–218). New York: Wiley.

Myers, J. E. (2003). Coping with care-giving stress: A wellness-oriented, strengths-based approach for family counselors. *Family Journal: Counseling and Therapy for Couples and Families, 11,* 153–161.

National Alliance for Caregiving (NAC) and the American Association of Retired Persons (AARP). (2009, November). *Caregiving in the U.S. 2009.* Bethesda, MD: NAC; Washington, DC: AARP.

Novak, M., & Guest, C. (1989). Application of a multidimensional caregiver burden inventory. *Gerontologist, 29,* 798–802.

Ory, M. G., Hoffman, R. R., Yee, J. L., Tennstedt, S., & Schulz, R. (1999). Prevalence and impact of caregiving: A detailed comparison between dementia and nondementia caregivers. *Gerontologist, 39,* 177–185.

Pew Research Center. (2010, November). *Social and demographic trends: The decline of marriage and rise of new families.* Washington, DC: Author.

Roberts, A. R. (2000). An overview of crisis theory and crisis intervention. In A. R. Roberts (Ed.), *Crisis intervention handbook* (2nd ed., pp. 2–30). New York: Oxford University Press.

Roberts, A. R. (2005). Bridging the past and present to the future of crisis intervention and crisis management. In A. R. Roberts (Ed.), *Crisis intervention handbook; Assessment, treatment, and research* (3rd ed., pp. 3–34). New York: Oxford University Press.

Robison, J., Fortinsky, R., Kleppinger, A., Shugrue, N., & Porter, M. (2009). A broader view of caregiving: Effects of caregiving and caregiver conditions on depressive symptoms, health, work, and social isolation. *Journals of Gerontology, Series B: Psychological Sciences and Social Sciences, 64B*, 788–798.

Roth, D. L., Haley, W. E., Hovater, M., Perkinds, M., Wadley, V. G., & Judd, S. (2013). Family caregiving and all-cause mortality: Findings from a population-based propensity-matched analysis. *American Journal of Epidemiology, 178*, 1571–1578.

Sanders, S. (2005). Is the glass half empty or half full? Reflections on strain and gain in caregivers of individuals with Alzheimer's disease. *Social Work in Health Care, 40*(3), 57–73.

Savundranayagam, M. Y., Montgomery, R. J. V., Kosloski, K., & Little, T. D. (2011). Impact of a psychoeducational program on three types of caregiver burden among spouses. *International Journal of Geriatric Psychiatry, 26*, 388–396.

Schindler, M., Engel, S., & Rupprecht, R. (2012). The impact of perceived knowledge of dementia on caregiver burden. *GeroPsych, 25*, 127–134.

Schubert, C. C., Boustani, M., Callahan, C. M., Perkins, A. J., Hui, S., & Hendric, H. C. (2008). Acute care utilization by dementia caregivers within urban primary care practices. *Journal of General Internal Medicine, 23*, 1736–1740.

Schulz, R., & Beach, S. R. (1999). Caregiving as a risk factor for mortality: The caregiver effects study. *Journal of the American Medical Association, 282*, 2215–2219.

Schulz, R., Belle, S. H., Czaja, S. J., McGinnis, K. A., & Stevens, A. (2004). Long-term care placement of dementia patients and caregiver health and well-being. *Journal of the American Medical Association, 292*, 961–967.

Schulz, R., & Cook, T. (2011, November). *Caregiving costs: Declining health in the Alzheimer's caregivers as dementia increases in the care recipient.* Bethesda, MD: National Alliance for Caregiving.

Schulz, R., Newsom, J., Mittelmark, M., Burton, L., Hirsch, C., & Jackson, S. (1997). Health effects of caregiving: The Caregiver Health Effects Study: An ancillary study of the Cardiovascular Health Study. *Annals of Behavioral Medicine, 19*, 110–116.

Schulz, R., & Sherwood, P. R. (2008). Physical and mental health effects of family caregiving. *American Journal of Nursing, 108* (9 suppl.), 23–27.

Schwiebert, V. L., Giordano, F. G., Zhang, G., & Sealander, K. A. (1998). Multidimensional measures of caregiver burden: A replication and extension of the Caregiver Burden Inventory. *Journal of Mental Health and Aging, 4*, 47–57.

Semiatin, A. M., & O'Connor, M. K. (2012). The relationship between self-efficacy and positive aspects of caregiving in Alzheimer's disease caregivers. *Aging and Mental Health, 16*, 683–688.

Smith, G. R., Williamson, G. M., Miller, L. S., & Schulz, R. (2011). Depression and quality of informal care: A longitudinal investigation of caregiving stressors. *Psychology and Aging, 26,* 584–591.

Stenburg, U., Ruland, C. M., & Miaskowski, C. (2010). Review of the literature on the effects of caring for a patient with cancer. *Psycho-Oncology, 19,* 1013–1025.

Talley, R. C., & Crews, J. E. (2007). Reframing the public health of caregiving. *American Journal of Public Health, 97,* 224–228.

Tarlow, B. J., Wisniewski, S. R., Belle, S. H., Rupert, M., Ory, M., & Gallagher-Thompson, D. (2004). Positive aspects of caregiving: Contributions of the REACH project to the development of new measures for Alzheimer's caregiving. *Research on Aging, 26,* 429–453.

Thompson, L. W., Gallagher-Thompson, D., & Haley, W. E. (2003). Future directions in dementia care-giving intervention research and practice. In D. W. Coon, D. Gallagher-Thompson, & L. W. Thompson (Eds.), *Innovative interventions to reduce dementia caregiver distress* (pp. 299–311). New York: Springer.

Toseland, R. W. (1995). *Group work with the elderly and family caregivers.* New York: Springer.

US Census Bureau. (2011, May). *Age and sex composition: 2010.* U.US Department of Commerce. Washington, DC: Author.

von Känel, R., Mausbach, B. T., Patterson, T. L., Dimsdale, J. E., Aschbacher, K., Mills, P. J., . . . Grant, I. (2008). Increased Framingham Coronary Heart Disease Score in dementia caregivers relative to non-caregiving controls. *Gerontology, 54,* 131–137.

Yee, J. L., & Schulz, R. (2000). Gender differences in psychiatric morbidity among family caregivers: A review and analysis. *Gerontologist, 40,* 147–164.

Zarit, S. H. (2006). Assessment of family caregivers: A research perspective. In *Caregiver assessment: Voices and views from the field: Report from a national consensus development conference* (Vol. 2, pp. 113–137). San Francisco, CA: Family Caregiver Alliance.

Zarit, S. H., & Femia, E. (2008). Behavioral and psychosocial interventions for family caregivers. *Journal of Social Work Education, 44*(3), 47–53.

Zarit, S. H., Stephens, M. A. P., Townsend, A., & Greene, R. (1998). Stress reduction for family caregivers: Effects of adult day care use. *Journals of Gerontology, Series B: Psychological Sciences and Social Sciences, 53B,* S267–S277.

Zegwaard, M. I., Aartsen, M. J., Cuipers, P., & Grypdonck, M. H. F. (2011). Review: A conceptual model of perceived burden of informal caregivers for older persons with a severe functional psychiatric syndrome and concomitant problematic behaviour. *Journal of Clinical Nursing, 20,* 2233–2258.

# 24

# A Model of Crisis Intervention in Critical and Intensive Care Units of General Hospitals

NORMAN M. SHULMAN

Historically, when a patient in a medical-surgical hospital is recognized as having a need for psychological support as a result of a medical crisis, the attending physician requests a consultation from a psychiatrist, psychologist, or other mental health professional. Although this professional can provide important diagnostic information on the immediate mental status of the patient, usually little, if any, consideration is given to the patient's ongoing emotional needs. Typically, directives for medication and possibly a referral to another mental health or social service professional are given. Generally, only if a patient becomes a behavior management problem will daily psychological intervention be ordered. When such services are not available, behavior management is frequently left up to nursing, case management, or clerical staff, who often do not have the time or training to attend to these problems, which can be very disruptive. It is thus my assertion that this lack of proper attention to a patient's psychological needs results in an unnecessary burden for the immediate staff and frequently leads to an exacerbation of the patient's crisis. A standing psychological consult available to critical care and other areas of a general hospital would provide the means for giving proper attention to the patients' mind-body experience, while alleviating stressors that the staff is neither trained nor compensated to address. As a result, potential crisis situations can be minimized and in some cases prevented. Since the prior publications of this chapter in 1990, 2000, and 2005, respectively, a substantial body of research has been collated that supports the original contention that early, systematic psychological intervention on critical care units is beneficial to patients and family members alike.

## DEFINITION AND SCOPE OF MEDICAL CRISIS

Medical crises are an inevitable part of the human experience. Although the definition of a medical crisis is subjective, the drastic change in life-style resulting from the crisis is a common theme. Pollin and Kanaan (1995) defined a medical crisis as "a time of unusual emotional distress or disorientation caused by the onset of, or a major change in, the medical condition" (p. 15). Another definition of a medical crisis is the reaction of a person resulting from a substantial variation in experiences differing from the person's usual view of the world. These emergencies create such instability and chaos in the person's life that normality, as the patient previously experienced it, ceases to exist. People in a crisis state demonstrate the following identifiable characteristics (Roberts, 1990):

1. Perception of a meaningful and threatening event
2. Inability to cope with the impact of the event
3. Increased fear, tension, or confusion
4. Subjective discomfort
5. Rapid progression to a state of crisis or disequilibrium

The stress involved with medical crises is typically temporary, yet it can have lifelong effects. The individual's coping skills, cognitive processes, typical affective processes, and history of psychopathology not only determine the degree to which life is affected but also define the medical crisis itself (Roberts, 1996).

The medical crisis generates stress that is universal to all persons in crisis regardless of age, gender, race, and so on. Situational factors, including medical emergencies, life-threatening and chronic illnesses, family health problems, crime, and natural disasters, often incite a medical crisis (Roberts, 1996). Roberts (1996) cites valuable statistics provided by the US Department of Justice establishing the prevalence of medical crises as initiated by medical emergencies. For example, as a result of acute psychiatric or medical emergencies in 2007 4.1 million people visited emergency rooms (Owens, Mutter, & Stocks, 2010). Regarding life-threatening disease, medical professionals diagnose 1,660,290 new cancer cases in the year 2012 (American Cancer Society, 2013). More than 1.2 million people in the United States are living with HIV infection, and almost 1 in 7 (14%) are unaware of their condition. In 2012 an estimated 47,989 people were diagnosed with HIV infection (CDC, 2014). Chronic illnesses also account for a great deal of the medical problems experienced by persons in crisis. For instance, Owens, Mutter, and stocks (2010) report concluded that some 129.8 million Americans visited emergency departments in 2012. Of this number it estimated that 2.1% of the population is transferred to a psychiatric or other hospital (Owens, Mutter, & Stocks, 2010). In addition, 26.5 million individuals suffer problems caused by heart disease; other chronic illnesses that contribute to the high incidence of medical crises include arthritis, cystic fibrosis, multiple sclerosis, and diabetes mellitus ( Blackwell, Lucas, & Clark, 2014). Family health problems, consisting of child abuse, drug abuse, domestic violence, and so on, relate directly to the origin of medical crises (as cited in Roberts, 1996). Finally, violent crime estimates also illustrate the high incidence of crises in society today. Data based on statistics from the Bureau of Justice indicate that 357 persons are victims of forcible rape every day of the year (Roberts, 1996). Medical crises arbitrarily affect all humans, thus creating a scope of immense proportions.

What were once common-sense predictors of the negative impact of the intensive care unit (ICU) experience on patients have been confirmed by a myriad of studies that emphasize the essential health-promoting nature of integrated psychomedical care. Castillo, Aitken, and Cooke (2013) found that specific emotional symptoms, namely, post-traumatic stress disorder (PTSD), anxiety, and depression, have been clearly identified as requiring psychological and/or psychiatric intervention while patients are hospitalized on various ICUs. Myhren et al. (2010) confirmed these findings and learned that PTSD symptoms in patients even a year after ICU treatment were relatively common symptoms. .

More generally, Wade et al. (2012) discovered that acute psychological reactions in the ICU were the strongest risk factors for developing mental illness in the future. In fact, the ICU experience itself can contribute to PTSD development.

At the same time, abundant evidence has been reported establishing the efficacy of early psychological intervention on such symptoms. Zugli et al.(2011) learned that early intra-ICU psychological intervention promotes recovery from PTSD, anxiety, and depression in critically ill patients. O'Donnell et al. (2010) posited that mental health services such as screening and early intervention may be particularly useful for PTSD patients on ICUs.

These studies continue to provide new evidence of the psychopathological sequelae of trauma and how improved psychological care during critical illness reduces unnecessary suffering, promotes comfort, and improves long-term recovery for patients and loved ones alike.

# DIAGNOSTIC DESCRIPTORS OF PATIENTS AND FAMILY

Persons in a crisis state frequently experience similar emotions, reactions, and periods of vulnerability. The medical crisis produces stress for the patient and family. Furthermore, examination of patients in specialized hospital units indicates the same characteristics identifying persons in medical crisis.

Certain characteristics and vulnerabilities identify the patient in crisis. High-risk patients often have suppressed or agitated affect, or "frozen fright," which describes the complete inability to react (Pollin & Kanaan, 1995). Suicidal ideation combined with depressive symptoms clearly indicates a person with high-risk qualities. Depression is among the most prevalent psychological responses among patients in medical crisis. Goldman and Kimball (1987) report that 25% of patients admitted to critical care units experience symptoms of depression. Four common types of depressed states among special risk patients are (a) major depressive illness, (b) adjustment disorder, (c) dysthymic disorder, and (d) organic affective disorder (Goldman & Kimball, 1987). A contributory factor to the depression is low self-esteem. Patients report feeling dehumanized by the lack of privacy during treatment times (Rice & Williams, 1997).

Additional common concerns of the patient include quality of life, death, and dying. Other traits of crisis patients consist of inadequate communication with caregivers and inadequate cognitive assimilation of the crisis (Pollin & Kanaan, 1995). Control, self-image, dependency, abandonment, anger, and so on are issues that must be dealt with by the patient in crisis. These descriptors contribute to a patient's vulnerability during the traumatic event. At a time of extreme stress as produced by a medical crisis, patients are susceptible to emotional changes. The degree of vulnerability depends on the "newness, intensity, and duration of the stressful event" (Roberts, 1996, p. 26). Physical and emotional exhaustion, previous crisis experience, and available material resources are important considerations when determining the risk of the patient in medical crisis (Roberts, 1996).

The family of a person in medical crisis cannot be disregarded when considering the effect on lifestyle change. Family members frequently deny the severity of the situation (Pollin & Kanaan, 1995). A new role as the primary caregiver during hospitalization and after discharge can be an overwhelming responsibility for a family member who is not properly prepared emotionally. Daily care for people with chronic illness occurs in informal, noninstitutional settings in 70% to 95% of the situations necessitating such activities (as cited in Pollin & Kanaan, 1995, p. 123). Difficulty with living arrangements and financial commitments create a new burden for all persons involved.

Changes in the family dynamic resulting from differing coping styles in response to the crisis provide an additional stress. Tension between family members can escalate, introducing another problem for the family and patient in crisis that must be resolved. The unpredictability and obscurity of the medical problem are perhaps most difficult for the family. Rice and Williams (1997) describe the exacerbation of family members' fears and anxieties caused by the presence of intimidating equipment and the proximity of critically ill patients. Furthermore, emergency and intensive medical treatment is typically swift and may appear impersonal to a concerned family member. Dealing with life-sustaining issues, life-or-death decisions, and the possibility of death elicits familial emotional complications (Rice & Williams, 1997). The psychological distress of families may also include guilt as a result of the medical crisis.

## Specific Intensive Care Unit Symptoms

Patients of specialized ICUs experience similar symptoms; for example, rehabilitation hospitals provide services for patients with injuries that embody great potential for psychological distress (Bleiberg & Katz, 1991). As a result of medical problems with varying degrees of impairment, disability, and handicap, patients must cope with issues of autonomy, loss, self-concept, and cognitive capacity. Medical intensive care unit (MICU) patients exhibit symptoms of the high-risk patient. Patients diagnosed with cancer experience psychological distress involving matters regarding quality of life, possibilities of disfigurement or disability, pain, and changes in personal relationships (Rozensky, Sweet, & Tovian, 1991). Matus (as cited in Creer, Kotses, & Reynolds, 1991) attests that psychological precipitants (emotional arousal), psychological symptoms (panic), and psychological factors (secondary gain, low self-esteem, etc.) are operants with asthma patients. End-stage renal disease patients, whose treatment often requires up to 12 to 21 hours of dialysis per week, are disturbed by the constant threat of death and increasing dependency.

MICUs are treating increasing numbers of patients with human immunodeficiency virus (HIV) who require psychosocial services for themselves as well as their families and loved ones. Cardiac intensive care units (CICUs) also provide an arena for crisis patients in need of psychological treatment. Thompson (1990) indicates a reduction of anxiety and depression in crisis patients being treated for coronary disease who receive psychological services. Finally, pediatric intensive care units (PICUs) are the domain of children in crisis coping with a traumatic event. A sense of desperation involved with treating a sick child elicits heartfelt stressors for the staff and families (DeMaso, Koocher, & Meyer, 1996).

## A MODEL OF COMPREHENSIVE CARE

This section focuses on how an already established program in a general hospital increases the resilience of and reduces the impact of risk factors on patients suffering from a medical crisis. The section will examine how the traditional consult system has proved to be ineffective in helping a patient recover from a crisis. The rationale for a more effective and accessible system will be proposed, followed by a detailed description of the model, including how it interfaces with the rest of the hospital and the social support network.

### The Failure of the Traditional Consult System

The traditional consult system continues to fail within most hospitals, and therefore many medical crises that could be prevented are not. For example, in teaching hospitals, where psychiatric residents depend on mental health consults to gain experience, all too frequently several unprepared students respond to a consult and overwhelm an already vulnerable patient. A balance of the patient's emotional needs and the residents' educational needs can be effected with a modicum of sensitivity and forethought, but, unfortunately, this scenario is more the exception than the norm.

The stigma attached to the public's perception of mental illness continues to pervade the general society, and hospitals are no exception. This prejudice creates an indirect negative impact on patient care because hospital staffs often feel that suggesting psychological consultation may be interpreted as an insult by the patient. In fact, this perspective affects staff to the degree that the patient's emotional needs may never be considered. The social stigma attached to mental illness, coupled with the reality of an intense medical perspective of doctors and nurses, facilitates the psychological neglect of patients with psychological needs, especially those in critical care. This phenomenon occurs even when medical conditions are affected by a patient's mental and emotional status. Depression of the chronic type (e.g., dysthymic disorder) can contribute to hostility and behavioral management problems in critical patients.

Finally, physicians' inclinations to divert immediate attention from psychological treatment adversely affect the consult system in a variety of ways. Because physicians in critical care areas are trained specifically to identify and treat medical conditions, a patient's total care tends to remain unaddressed. A physician's professional agenda may also be threatened by a mental health clinician's involvement in the case, especially if it is not asked for, thus resulting in rejection of a psychological consultation. The end result is that all too many patients spend their hospital days without proper psychological help even in ICUs. This neglect often complicates and exacerbates a patient's existing medical problems to crisis proportions.

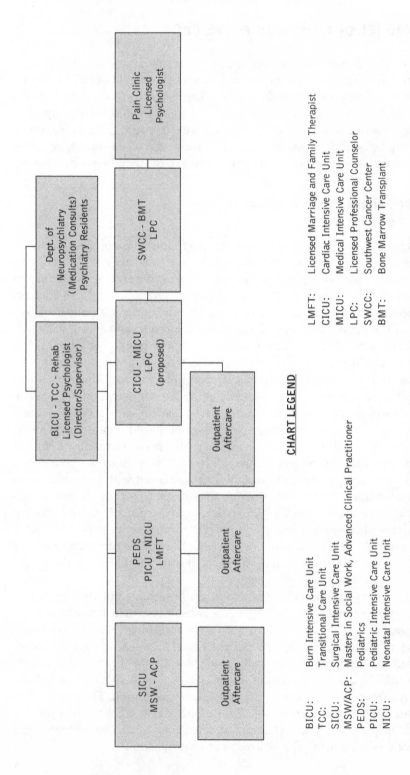

**CHART LEGEND**

| | |
|---|---|
| BICU: | Burn Intensive Care Unit |
| TCC: | Transitional Care Unit |
| SICU: | Surgical Intensive Care Unit |
| MSW/ACP: | Masters in Social Work, Advanced Clinical Practitioner |
| PEDS: | Pediatrics |
| PICU: | Pediatric Intensive Care Unit |
| NICU: | Neonatal Intensive Care Unit |

| | |
|---|---|
| LMFT: | Licensed Marriage and Family Therapist |
| CICU: | Cardiac Intensive Care Unit |
| MICU: | Medical Intensive Care Unit |
| LPC: | Licensed Professional Counselor |
| SWCC: | Southwest Cancer Center |
| BMT: | Bone Marrow Transplant |

Figure 24.1  Organizational Chart of Model of Comprehensive Health Care at Texas Tech University Medical Center

## Rationale for the Standing Consult

Increasing volumes of evidence demonstrate the efficacy of mental health interventions during a patient's hospital stay for medical or surgical crises. For example, MICUs employ mental health consultants in cancer treatment centers. Rozensky, Sweet, and Tovian (1991) describe the therapeutic efficacy of psychological consultation for cancer patients. Assessment of the patient's physical and social environments, psychological strengths and weaknesses, and response to the diagnosis and treatment of cancer, as well as assessment of the patient's personality and coping styles, provide a unique perspective that is integrated into individualized treatment strategies. It is essential that medical professionals realize the value of a holistic approach to treatment as essential within critical care areas, including psychological consultation and ongoing treatment. Such intervention during the patient's hospital stay defies the standard of the "one time only" consult and includes the provision of ongoing supportive and adjustment psychotherapy. This trend to consider a patient's continuing needs includes family therapy, particularly when treatment is compromised by unhealthy family interactions. Additional services include arranging for psychological testing and referrals to related specialists (e.g., neuropsychologists and outpatient aftercare community medical professionals).

Given the traumatic nature of a serious or critical illness or injury and the treatment necessary for patients in these conditions, it seems appropriate to adhere to a comprehensive approach to recovery. The vision of a standing psychological consult embodies the perspective of the mind-body interaction—specifically, that a patient's mental health directly correlates to length of stay and potential for recovery. The model proposed here includes ongoing attention to fluctuations in mental stability as a result of traumatic injury or severe medical conditions.

The preceding model (Figure 24.1) has been established at the Texas Tech University Medical Center in Lubbock, Texas. It includes the 14-bed burn intensive care and stepdown units. (The Southwest Cancer Center and the bone marrow transplant unit are covered in a similar fashion by an independent clinician.) The standing consult was approved on these units with the authorization of the acting chief of surgery, John T. Griswold, MD, of the Texas Tech University Medical School after the model was proposed to him in 1992.

Dr. Griswold had been thinking at the time the proposal was made that only half of a patient's needs were attended to at discharge from critical care areas. The Department of Psychiatry, the likely option to turn to regarding the provision of psychological support on these units, did not consider this to be part of its curriculum agenda. Its consultation role had been narrowly defined to include assessment and pharmacotherapy only. On rare occasions, a patient would be followed a few times until discharge, but usually the extent of the consultation ended after one interaction, if a consultation was requested at all. There was also a problem of responsiveness in that frequently a patient would be discharged before a psychiatric resident saw the patient. Unfortunately, when this problem was added to the understandable lack of attention to psychological issues by hospital staff, an inordinate number of patients never had an essential aspect of their treatment attended to.

Traditionally, automatic consults in general hospitals have been limited. Once the resistance to the standing psychological consult was overcome by Dr. Griswold's insistence to the staff of the importance of the program, it was instituted as a component of overall health care. The mental health professional, in this case a licensed psychologist, was able to systematically evaluate every patient admitted to the 14-bed burn ICU, the first unit on which it was tried.

The initial assessment included the patient's mental status, internal and external coping resources, degree of family support, and premorbid mental health history. The evaluation included a determination not only of the patient's need for services but also of whether the patient and family would accept those services. Psychological interventions were never imposed on a patient (or family), and it was the patient's (or family's) prerogative to terminate the relationship at any time. The attending physician always retained power over the course of treatment, including the option to cancel the intervention.

Rounds were made daily on the burn unit and on weekends when indicated. In addition, the attending physician or staff would call in the clinician at any other time if the situation warranted it. Deference to medical personnel was always given if a procedure was in process or needed to be done at the time of the session. The patient's condition was also taken into consideration in the sense that the patient was never pushed to tolerate more than he or she could handle. As it turned out, the length of the sessions increased as the patient's condition improved. Once a patient stabilized, less time was then required until discharge.

Patient needs were also informally determined by any physician, resident, intern, nurse, therapist, or aide who detected and then passed on important information to the psychologist. Formally, his attendance at weekly staffings provided input regarding the degree and type of interventions. Frequently, the psychologist, with and without his colleagues, would consult with other professionals who might shed more light on a patient's status. The psychologist was in a unique position to subsequently consult a psychiatrist for medication issues, a neuropsychologist, a substance abuse expert, or any other professional who could contribute to the comprehensive care of a patient.

Because a systems approach is utilized, family support was also given on a regular basis, particularly when a patient could not be communicated with directly. The psychologist made it a priority to either convey information himself or encourage physicians working on the case to keep a patient's family updated with concrete and realistic information, even if it was less than positive. Anecdotally, it is safe to say that the overwhelming majority of critical care patients and their families appreciate the consistent presence of a caring mental health professional on an ICU—even in cases where death is imminent. This professional can help a patient maintain dignity with a sense of purpose while facing death. Patients and families were also satisfied with the continuity of psychotherapeutic care made available. They realized that there were times when a patient needed to talk to a neutral party about issues that may not be easily shared with significant others, even clergy.

The unit psychologist was clearly in a unique position to prevent problems from occurring and to be available to respond to occasional conflicts among patients, family members, and professional caregivers, including physicians. Physicians open to the psychologist's role with the treatment team benefited from input not normally made available, as well as from not having to commit valuable time and energy to nonmedical issues. In general, the entire scope of a patient's needs was treated more effectively and efficiently.

Although a hospital nonaffiliated psychiatrist was used as a consultant on medication issues, this model suggests the ideal arrangement of pairing a psychiatrist with a psychologist to work in tandem on critical care units. Questions regarding psychiatric medications and follow-up maintenance need not be the concern of the attending and resident physicians alone.

As opposed to the limited consultation offered by existing models, a psychiatric counterpart to the psychologist can also follow a medicated patient daily. Such a professional liaison proves to be efficient for all members of the treatment team. For example, many times issues of drug interactions and the psychological effects of medication routinely administered to critical care patients can be handled by the specialist most uniquely qualified to address these issues. A psychiatrist experienced in the area of critical care is an invaluable member of the team, allowing other physicians to be free to concentrate on their specific areas of expertise.

At the Texas Tech University Medical Center intensive care and rehabilitation units, the psychological needs of patients are no longer neglected as a result of the absence of integrated treatment. Treatment is now more comprehensive, with issues of compliance, treatment interference, and patient-family-staff conflicts being dealt with quickly and as a function of overall care, since the psychologist is already involved. In this manner, demands on the staff to perform duties outside of their job description are minimized. After discharge, another advantage to the patient is the increased tendency to follow through with outpatient aftercare either with the unit psychologist or with another professional in the community.

The psychologist is also available to staff members whose equilibrium may be disturbed by the extraordinary demands of critical care. Individual and group interventions are useful either for ongoing support or in response to a traumatic event on the unit. As a result, the staff gains a measure of solidarity and security with the knowledge that a trusted professional is readily available to respond to their professional and personal needs.

## CASE ILLUSTRATIONS

### Case 1

T. is a 35-year-old Hispanic female who is being seen to evaluate her emotional response to traumatic double leg amputations. The patient was injured in an automobile accident, which also involved her 16-year-old son, who was driving and had fallen asleep at the wheel. The patient's son had informed her prior to the accident that he was very tired and that he wanted her to drive. Shortly thereafter, the accident occurred, and the patient's legs were crushed beyond repair. The boy suffered only minor injuries.

The first intervention was agreed to by the patient's husband, who wanted his son seen. This was to allow the boy to see his mother and determine that she was going to live, and to give her an early opportunity to absolve him of any guilt. Once this was accomplished, the patient was talked to daily and encouraged not to give up because her prognosis was good, given current rehabilitation capabilities. These interventions constituted the initial cognitive reframing efforts.

The importance of employing a systems approach is exemplified in this case. As the inpatient psychotherapy progressed (eventually over a course of 65 sessions covering two admissions, over a 5-month period), it came to the therapist's attention that the patient's husband and other son (aged 17) were in the midst of their own crises. This information necessitated that family and individual therapy be done with various combinations of family members collaterally with the treatment of the identified patient.

Adjustments and readjustments of coping styles have had to be made over the past several months as minor crises have erupted. For example, the father and one of the sons began drinking more to numb their pain over their loved one's condition. Second, the patient became recurrently depressed during the difficult physical rehabilitation she had to endure. In addition, she was forced to face the hard reality that an above-the-knee amputation posed extremely difficult prosthetic complications. Third, the other son considered dropping out of college, against his mother's wishes, because of his inability to concentrate.

At the time of this writing, the family members are still struggling to balance their respective means of coping. Overall, the situation has been partially reframed successfully in that some positive adaptations have been made. For example, T. returned to graduate school to get a master's degree in counseling so that she can help others. Her husband has stopped drinking, and the sons are being seen individually to facilitate their resolving any residual guilt, resentment, and substance abuse issues.

In the best of all possible circumstances, the family would have accepted the assistance of antidepressant medication, but the patient and her family wanted to work without its potential benefits. They remain committed to working together to complete their collective resolutions and should continue their treatment as outpatients until it is no longer indicated. It is important to note that much of the success of therapy was attributed to the early and consistent interventions provided by the standing consult in place at the time in the surgical ICU where the patient was initially treated. She was then able to be seen subsequently on the regular floor and later as an outpatient, thus ensuring an essential continuity of care.

## Case 2

N. is a 43-year-old White male referred for a mental status exam pursuant to several days of unconsciousness caused by a propane explosion. When he was initially seen, the patient had only a sketchy memory of the incident and could remember no details. He was oriented to person but not to place or time. Because one suspected cause of the explosion was a suicide attempt by purposely igniting the propane tank, an assessment of suicidal risk had to be done. However, because of the nature of his mental status, a risk assessment had to be done frequently during the first 2 weeks of his stay in the burn ICU. The patient vehemently denied that he was trying to kill himself, and he never changed his response.

It became imperative that the patient be seen frequently (a total of 32 sessions over a 4-month period) because of his mental health history. Shortly after admission, it became clear from the medications he was taking that he had a premorbid condition of bipolar disorder (depressed). Upon intubation, the patient was unable to receive his psychotropic medications, which included Serzone and Restoril. Therefore, it was feared that when he regained consciousness, he could present behavioral management problems and potential suicide risk, of which he did have a history.

During the course of N.'s hospitalization, rapport was developed and maintained as a hedge against any disruptive behavior on the floor or suicidal ideation. At times the patient did become agitated and difficult to manage, but with the assistance of psychiatry, a proper administration of his psychotropics restored him to stability. Prior to discharge, contact was made with a physician in his hometown, where treatment (pharmacotherapy and psychotherapy) could continue without interruption.

The standing consult again proved to be invaluable in preventing a crisis from evolving as the patient was seen shortly after admission and regularly after that until discharge. Rather than being treated with heavy sedation alone after becoming a behavior management problem, the patient did not fall between the cracks, and his psychological needs were consistently attended to. His mental illness was quickly and properly addressed, and he passed through the hospital with only minimal disturbance to the patient and staff.

## APPLICATION OF ROBERTS'S SEVEN-STAGE CRISIS INTERVENTION MODEL IN CRITICAL CARE AREAS

Roberts's (1996) seven-stage crisis intervention model can be applied in hospital settings where initial intervention with health emergencies and other traumatic events naturally occur. However, performing crisis intervention in critical care areas of general hospitals poses unique problems that must be considered. For example, in Case 2, a thorough assessment, including an assessment of lethality, could not be done until well after admission. Because a suicide attempt was suspected, close contact with the medical staff had to be maintained so that this critical assessment could be made as soon after extubation as possible. At this point, if suicidal ideation persisted, the proper suicide prevention protocol could be implemented on the unit, in this case, burn intensive care.

Regarding Case 1, in spite of the fact that a suicide attempt was not the cause of the accident, the patient's despondence in the aftermath of the double amputation had to be considered and a lethality assessment done until it was determined beyond any doubt that T. posed no threat to herself. The "captive audience" reality of the inpatient setting allows for lethality assessments to be made at least daily or, if necessary, multiple times daily by different staff members. Any change in the degree of the lethality is reported to the unit mental health clinician, who would alter the treatment plan as indicated.

Another distinguishing feature of the inpatient crisis intervention is the necessity of establishing rapport (Roberts's Stage 2) with a patient over a sometimes inordinate extended period. Mind-altering pain medications, pain itself, disorientation caused by ICU isolation (resulting in a phenomenon known as *ICU psychosis*), and the difficulty of determining staff identity due to masks and gowns all contribute to a difficult period of rapport building. In addition, frequent interruptions from medical staff for the application of intensive care procedures necessarily shorten time with the patient and interrupt the therapeutic flow.

Both N. and T. were unable to communicate until well after admission. Once the interventions began, rapport was established with both patients piecemeal and over several days. At times, information had to be repeated because of the patients' relatively incoherent mental status early in their medical care. In time (longer with N. than with T. because of mental illness), rapport was successfully established.

In both case examples, identification of the crisis precipitant (Stage 3) was readily apparent (i.e., the accidents). Although premorbid issues with both N. and T. certainly affected their individual responses to crisis, it is clear that the interventions were necessitated by the patients' misfortunes. In the cases of most ICU patients, the crisis begins and continues to resolve as their physical condition improves. However, in the case of T., who would suffer numerous physical and family-related emotional setbacks, each new precipitant had to be dealt with aggressively and in a timely manner. The already established rapport with her made subsequent interventions that much easier for her to take advantage of.

The majority of time with both patients was spent dealing with their various feelings about what had happened to them (Stage 4). Active listening techniques, as well as conveyance of validation, empathy, warmth, and reassurance, were used to help the patients understand that they were being heard by a caring professional. Basic counseling skills were employed in the course of the supportive psychotherapy to foster the patients' exploration of their emotions about what had happened to them and the potential consequences that awaited them during and after their recoveries. T. required more and longer sessions because of her many concerns about her husband and two sons, who complicated her recovery. Their difficulties coping with T.'s amputations and its meaning to them initially created secondary crisis precipitants for her, such as reactive drinking and depression. N.'s adaptations were relatively straightforward and uncomplicated.

In the course of helping T. and N. explore their feelings, various alternatives were generated and explored (Stage 5). T. benefited greatly from being aware of the resources available to amputees that would allow her to resume a relatively normal life. The physical rehabilitation protocol for amputees was reviewed with her shortly after she was able to communicate her feelings about the loss of her legs. She received much reassurance from knowing what to expect regarding her physical recovery (which would be done in her hometown), the fitting of prostheses, learning how to walk again, and gradually being able to resume her teaching career. She was also greatly relieved that her family members would be worked with individually and collectively to focus on their various problems. This allowed her to focus on her rehabilitation and to spend less time and energy on issues over which she had no control.

N. received comfort from learning that the unit was aware of his history of mental illness, was in contact with his treating doctors and family, and therefore would be able to maintain his medication schedule and his stable mental status. In addition, contact with his ex-wife, who remained a valuable source of support in his life, was encouraged and facilitated. This person was especially important because she was N's only nonprofessional support, whereas T. had a multitude of supportive family, friends, and well-wishers.

As a result of the extended stays of both patients, ample time was available for the development and formulation of their respective action plans (Stage 6). Prior to discharge, the hospital assisted in setting up the medical and psychiatric resources that would ensure cognitive and affective stability. With N., several conversations were held with his treating professionals and his ex-wife, who had an investment in assuring that N. would be referred back to his mental health providers upon his return home. The patient participated in developing the discharge plan and knew exactly what was expected of him (i.e., compliance), and what resources were available to him.

T. also had a clear idea of the postdischarge phase of her recovery. The mental health phase was offered to her in the form of aftercare psychotherapy for her and her family members in various combinations. She was pleased with the predictability and availability of the discharge plan and knew she could inquire about it with several different professionals and receive a straight answer.

Both patients agreed to follow-up plans (Stage 7). Because T. and her family would return to the hospital where the initial crisis was treated for medical and psychological care, follow-up was easily confirmed. At these times the progress of her medical and emotional rehabilitation was discussed, as well as what she could next expect and have to cope with. N.'s follow-up care, in contrast, was arranged where he was currently being treated. Phone calls to his providers near his home were made shortly after discharge to ensure follow-through.

Roberts's seven-stage model is well adapted to serving the psychological needs of patients in critical care areas. One can safely assume that crisis intervention with most of these patients is indicated by virtue of their need for intensive care. Although the model's application has to be tempered by the specific demands on units of this kind, the essential elements of the seven stages have universal utility. As a result, patients' crises are alleviated by timely intervention (i.e., as close to the time of the precipitating event as possible). In addition, future crises can be prevented because of the adaptive learning that takes place during the daily, intensive interventions.

## CLINICAL CONSIDERATIONS AND IMPLICATIONS

Several special direct service intervention considerations must be taken into account when working with patients in crisis in critical care areas. First, deference to medical staff has to be a priority. Because of the nature of intensive care medical services, there may never be a convenient time for a proper assessment or intervention. It is commonplace for several interruptions to occur during the course of as little as 10 to 15 minutes, making the atmosphere less than conducive for crisis management.

At times the therapist has to do his or her best to prioritize the treatment issues and address them in the time available. This becomes especially important when assessing suicidal risk or any other self-destructive behavior that may complicate treatment. In practical terms, this may mean that several brief interventions have to be done before a clear picture of the patient's functioning can be ascertained. The patient's tenuous condition, which can limit the effectiveness of a session, is frequently more of a reason for brief intervention than procedural interruptions.

A second consideration is the indicated emphasis on performing the initial crisis intervention as close to the time of the crisis as possible. As with any crisis, a medical crisis, especially a traumatic event, needs to be processed as early as possible before defenses have the opportunity of reconstituting. This issue becomes most relevant with PTSD, which if not treated early can fester and manifest its myriad symptoms months or even years later. Therefore, if possible, it is recommended that the patient be seen as soon after admission as possible—for example, shortly after extubation or after regaining consciousness.

Another advantage of early intervention is the forging of relationships even when a patient may be initially asymptomatic. Once a bond has been established, the patient will be far more inclined to talk about an emergence of symptoms when they do occur, sometimes well after discharge. It is not unusual for a patient to contact a therapist for issues of PTSD or depression months after the first contact and to request outpatient therapy. This, of course, is not as likely to occur without the initial formation of the therapeutic relationship. Creation of this early tie is particularly essential when the impact of heavy sedation, which has the capacity of masking psychopathological symptoms, is considered.

A third consideration is the importance of integrating a family systems model into one's crisis intervention techniques. A critical illness or accident affects an entire family or extended family because these relatives become victims as well. Effective crisis intervention considers the needs of the overall family, which can be used to further the emotional healing of a patient if correctly directed.

When doing critical care crisis intervention, much of the work takes place in the waiting areas or in the corridors of the hospital, talking to family members forced to cope with the consequences of a serious illness or accident. Frequently, they become as much or even more in need of crisis services as the patient. Therefore, time and attention should be focused on them in order to maintain family equilibrium for its own sake, as well as for the ultimate recovery of the patient.

A fourth consideration is the potential for burnout of the crisis intervenor performing daily crisis intervention services in repeated life-and-death situations, not to mention with patients who are severely maimed or disfigured. It is imperative that the demands placed on the crisis professional are not excessive and that the intervenor has adequate supervision and emotional support. A high tolerance for stress and multiple available coping resources are prime factors for the crisis professional to have access to while working in a critical care area.

The two case studies presented earlier are informative for crisis intervenors because they are reflective of the ICU patients who are seen as a matter of course. They represent more the rule than the exception. All four of the clinical considerations (i.e., treatment priority given to medical issues, early intervention, a family focus, and staff burnout potential) had to be taken into consideration when working with both patients. In fact, it is unusual to have a patient in critical care when less than all of these intervention themes are present. Occasionally, lack of family involvement becomes a problem. However, the absence of this coping resource usually exacerbates the potential for burnout because the intervenor's role becomes more demanding as involvement with the patient necessarily increases.

## Managed Care

Managed care poses unique problems regarding insurance reimbursement for the work performed on the ICUs described earlier. The brunt of inpatient care must be precertified before an insurance carrier is willing to pay for psychotherapeutic services. Unfortunately, the precertification process is often cumbersome, and several days may pass before permission is given. One would think that any patient suffering from severe illness or injury would be automatically certifiable for at least an initial assessment, but this is not the case.

All too often, billing for time spent doing crisis intervention is nonreimbursable because the sessions were not precertified. However, waiting for precertification would be anathema to the maximum efficacy of crisis intervention. Although there is no pat resolution to this issue, professional ethics dictate that the patient must be seen as soon as medically feasible. Hopefully, efforts to retrocertify will be successful on the basis of the logic of the argument. Perhaps someday a limited number of diagnostic evaluation sessions will be automatically precertified for patients victimized by accidents or some other trauma, but until that time comes, struggles with managed care will continue.

Two potential means of reimbursement may be explored to compensate for the denied sessions. One is for the hospital to provide a supplementary stipend to a clinician working in critical care areas. The amount could be based on the average number of nonreimbursable sessions combined with the average number of sessions spent with nonfunded patients. The second alternative is for the facility to apply for grants to foundations specializing in funding innovative medical programs. In fact, both of these options are being explored at the University Medical Center in Lubbock, Texas, where the comprehensive, integrated psychological support program mentioned earlier is in the process of being developed in all of its critical care units.

## CONCLUSION

It only makes sense for the psychological needs of patients in general hospitals to be attended to along with their physical problems. The general trend in medicine is to recognize this logical, inseparable connection in patients. Although individual physicians and, on a larger scale, certain critical care units integrate treatment successfully, the premise of this chapter is that the successful integration of treatment can be effected in an entire hospital.

If such treatment is properly implemented, patients, families, staff, and the facility should benefit in a variety of ways, not the least important of which is the predicted reduced length of stay (and reduced associated costs). Research should validate this hypothesis, among others, such as the predicted use of less medication, fewer psychological problems, and reduced stress on staff.

Common sense dictates that an essential aspect of health care is the prevention and minimization of potential psychological crises, which complicate and exacerbate ongoing and later treatment. A comprehensive model of crisis intervention in critical care units and ICUs is a sensible means of bringing about this necessary improvement in overall health care.

Unfortunately, in spite of overwhelming evidence, psychological care for intensive care patients has lagged behind care for physical problems (Rattray, Hull, & Alastan, 2008). This chapter has focused on the development of one intervention modification (i.e., the open consult system), which has proved to be extremely successful in identifying and improving the psychological outcomes of trauma patients.

It is the hope of this author that the underutilized open mental health consultation policy in critical care areas will be more widely adopted by hospitals committed to the comprehensive integrated treatment of the majority of trauma patients. By doing so, fewer trauma victims will fall through the cracks in the system; thus, overall, this consistently underserved population can have their complete treatment needs met. Additional research should validate this hypothesis, as well as the predicted use of less medication, fewer psychological problems, and reduced stress on staff.

## REFERENCES

American Cancer Society. (2013). *Cancer Facts & Figures 2013.* Atlanta: American Cancer Society.

Blackwell, D. L., Lucas, J. W., Clarke, T. C. (2014). Summary health statistics for U.S. adults: National Health Interview Survey, 2012. National Center for Health Statistics. *Vital Health Statistics* 10(260).

Bleiberg, R. C., & Katz, B. L. (1991). Psychological components of rehabilitation programs for brain-injured and spinal-cord injured patients. In R. H. Rozensky, J. J. Sweet, & S. M. Tovin (Eds.), *Handbook of clinical psychology in medical settings* (pp. 375–400). New York: Plenum.

Castillo, M. I., Aitken, L. M., & Cooke, M. L. (2013). Study protocol: Intensive care anxiety and emotional recovery (i care)—a prospective study. *Australian Critical Care: Official Journal of the Confederation of Australian Critical care Nurses, 26,* 142–147.

CDC. (2014). Monitoring selected national HIV prevention and care objectives by using HIV surveillance data—United States and 6 dependent areas—2012. *HIV Surveillance Supplemental Report,* 19(3).

Creer, T. L., Kotses, H., & Reynolds, R. V. (1991). Psychological theory, assessment, and interventions for adult and childhood asthma. In R. H. Rozensky, J. J. Sweet, & S. M. Tovin (Eds.), *Handbook of clinical psychology in medical settings* (pp. 497–516). New York: Plenum.

DeMaso, D. R., Koocher, G. P., & Meyer, E. C. (1996). Mental health consultation in the pediatric intensive care unit. *Professional Psychology: Research and Practice, 27,* 130–136.

Goldman, L. S., & Kimball, C. P. (1987). Depression in intensive care units. *International Journal of Psychiatry in Medicine, 17,* 201–212.

Myhren, H., Ekeberg, O., Toien, K., Karlsson, S., & Stockland, O. (2010). Post-traumatic stress, anxiety and depression symptoms in patients during the first year post intensive care unit discharge. *Critical Care (London, England), 14* (1).

O'Donnell, M. L., Creamer, M., Holmes, A. C., Ellen, S., McFarlane, A. C., Judson, R., Silove, D., & Bryant, R. A. (2010). Post-traumatic stress disorder after injury: Does admission to intensive care units increase risk? *Journal of Trauma 69,* 627–632.

Owens, P. L., Mutter, R., & Stocks, C. Mental health and substance abuse-related emergency department visits among adults, 2007. HCUP Statistical Brief #92. July 2010. Agency for Healthcare Research and Quality, Rockville, MD. http://www.hcup-us.ahrq.gov/reports/statbriefs/sb92.pdf

Pollin, I., & Kanaan, S. B. (1995). *Medical crisis counseling.* New York: Norton.

Rattray, J. E., & Hull, A. M. (2008). Emotional outcome after intensive care: Literature review. *Journal of Advanced Nursing,* 64(1), 2–13.

Rice, D. G., & Williams, C. C. (1997). The intensive care unit: Social work intervention with the families of critically ill patients. *Social Work in Health Care, 2,* 391–398.

Roberts, A. R. (1990). *Assessment and treatment research. Crisis intervention handbook*. Belmont, CA: Wadsworth.

Roberts, A. R. (1996). Epidemiology and definitions of acute crisis in American society. In A. R. Roberts (Ed.), *Crisis management and brief treatment: Theory, technique and application* (pp. 16–31). Belmont, CA: Brooks/Cole.

Rozensky, R. H., Sweet, J. J., & Tovian, S. M. (1991). *Handbook of clinical psychology in medical settings*. New York: Plenum.

Thompson, D. R. (1990 *Counselling the coronary patient and partner*. London: Scutari.

Wade, D. M., Howell, D. C., Weinman, J. A., Hardy, R.,

Mythen, M. G., Brewin, C. R., Borja-Boluda, S., Matejowsky, C. F., & Raine, R. (2012). Investigating risk factors for psychological morbidity three months after intensive care: A prospective cohort study. *Critical Care, 16* (5), 1–16.

Zugli, G., Bacchereti, A., Debolini, M., Vamini, E., Massimo, S., Balzi, H., Giovanni, V., & Belloni, L. (2011). Early intra-intensive care unit psychological intervention promotes recovery from post-traumatic stress disorders, anxiety and depression symptoms in critically ill patients. *Critical Care, 15* (1), 1–8.

# VI

**BEST PRACTICE OUTCOMES**

# 25

# Models for Effective Crisis Intervention

YVONNE EATON-STULL
MICHELLE MILLER

Responding to a suicidal individual, walking into a volatile domestic situation, or dealing with the intense emotions of grief are all crises that may cause anxiety for the responder. Many people can be taught the necessary skills to intervene in a crisis situation, and certain traits combined with these skills will increase the likelihood that the intervenor will be well received and the situation successfully de-escalated. Many counselor traits have been found to be positive factors for successful crisis intervention, and these traits can be further developed with determination and practice.

## TRAITS OF EFFECTIVE RESPONDERS

Self-awareness of one's own nature will offer perspective and foster patience during crisis intervention. Stanley (2006) asserts the importance of self-examination related to cultural competency by suggesting that by being curious and reflecting on one's own discomfort and dissimilarities between oneself and the client, the worker will foster the ability to view the situation from a multicultural perspective. Stanley (2006) suggests that self-awareness will relieve feelings of countertransference and increase the worker's ability to respond with a "culturally sensitive and relevant" approach. Wampold (n.d.) states that effective workers engage in self-reflection during interventions to minimize the effects of "countertransference" on the helping relationship. Countertransference is a common phenomenon in crisis work and must be managed through self-awareness. Self-awareness can be incredibly useful when gaining understanding of a client's crisis and collaborating with the client on identifying reasonable solutions.

Three traits that are frequently mentioned in the helping profession are empathy, genuineness, and warmth. *Empathy* is defined by Hohman (2012) as "understanding the world or problem as the client sees it" and communicating to the client that the worker understands his or her perspective. Empathy is a central quality in successful crisis intervenors because it helps to build trust and rapport with the client. Many studies support the finding that empathic providers have "higher success rates regardless of their theoretical orientation" (Moyers & Miller, 2013, p. 1). Qualities and actions of effective responders are available at https://www.apa.org/education/ce/effective-therapists.pdf. *Genuineness* means being your true self within your professional relationship. A genuine responder will naturally act spontaneously and with consistency; genuineness aids in showing the client that that the worker is authentic (Kirst-Ashman & Hull, 2008). A genuine crisis worker will connect with the client on a human level, as everyone experiences difficulties and needs support throughout their life. *Warmth* is defined as being an open-minded, caring person who is willing to actively listen to and suspend judgment of a client (Walsh et al., 2003). Clients feel comfortable sharing their feelings when they are interacting with a warm responder (Walsh et al., 2003). Warmth, genuineness, and empathy are three of the most important counselor traits for predicting positive therapeutic outcomes.

Effective crisis workers will further develop their skills and potential if they have determination to grow as a crisis intervenor. Wampold (n.d.) asserts that effective counselors regularly pursue professional growth because they desire to improve in their practice. Considering that crisis intervention is always changing (James & Gilliland, 2005), motivated crisis intervenors will regularly seek out current information and adapt their interventions to encompass evidence-based practices. The crisis worker who is determined to grow both personally and professionally will likely do well at facilitating growth with his or her clients and effectively managing work stress. Free online continuing education on various crisis topics can be accessed at http://www.treatmentsolutions.com/education/.

There are many traits that in combination will increase the likelihood of success with clients in crisis. These traits, paired with crisis intervention skills, will foster the development and growth of a crisis worker. A skilled crisis worker not only possesses the traits necessary to be successful but also has the knowledge and ability to utilize techniques to de-escalate a crisis situation. Various crisis intervention models offer frameworks for practitioners to follow when responding to crises. Three commonly utilized models will be described and applied to case examples to provide crisis responders with practical steps and skills for implementation.

During crises, time is of the essence, so workers must directly inquire about various factors. A thorough assessment of risk is a critical component and standard of crisis intervention (Joiner et al., 2007). According to the National Suicide Prevention Lifeline [NSPL] (2007), assessment must include inquiries into desire, capability, intent, and buffers. Desire explores ideation and emotional state; capability looks at prior history, means, and factors such as mental health history or substance use; intent considers active attempts, plans, and preparation; and buffers refers to the protective support factors. Readers are encouraged to visit the NSPL website for more details at http://www.suicidepreventionlifeline.org/media/5388/Suicide-R isk-Assessment-Standards.pdf. Sample triage questions that explore each of these standards are provided in the following form (Eaton, 2005, p. 622):

---

*Suicide risk assessment* should include obtaining answers to the following questions:

1. Are you/client having thoughts of self-harm? Yes ( ) No ( ) Unknown ( )
2. Have you/client done anything to intentionally hurt yourself? Yes ( ) No ( )
   If yes, describe _____
3. How long have you/client had thoughts to hurt yourself? _____
4. How might you/client hurt yourself? _____
5. Have you/client made any preparations to hurt yourself? Yes ( ) No ( ) Unknown ( )
   If yes, describe _____
6. Has there been a recent stressful or traumatic event in your life? Yes ( ) No ( )
   If yes, describe _____
7. Do you feel there is hope that things can improve? Yes ( ) No ( )
   If yes, describe _____
8. What keeps you/client from hurting self? _____

*Homicide/violence risk assessment* should include obtaining answers to the following questions:

1. Are you/client having thoughts to hurt others? Yes ( ) No ( ) Unknown ( )
   If yes, who do you/client think about hurting? _____
2. Have you verbally made any threats to hurt someone else? Yes ( ) No ( )
   If yes, please indicate what you said _____
3. Have you/client hurt anyone already? Yes ( ) No ( ) Unknown ( )
   If yes, describe what happened _____
   Whom did you hurt? _____
   What were the person's physical injuries? _____
4. How long have you/client had thoughts to hurt others? _____
5. How might you/client hurt others? _____
6. Do you have any weapons in your home? Yes ( ) No ( ) Unknown ( )
   If yes, what weapons? _____

7. Have you/client made any preparations to hurt others? Yes ( ) No ( ) Unknown ( )
   If yes, describe _____
8. What keeps you/client from hurting others? _____
9. Did the police ever arrest you? Yes ( ) No ( )
   If yes, please explain what the charges were and the outcome _____

Roberts's (2005) seven-stage crisis intervention model offers an invaluable framework for intervening in crises.

## APPLICATION OF ROBERTS SEVEN-STAGE CRISIS INTERVENTION MODEL

### Stage 1: Plan and Conduct a Crisis Assessment

Stage 1 should include a thorough assessment of stressors, coping skills, and available resources. This ongoing assessment should include the provoking event, responses, and both risk and protective factors (Jackson-Cherry & Erford, 2014). Dangerousness to self or others is a key component of this step, and responders must be sure to learn if the individual has attempted to harm him- or herself or others or has a plan, method, or intent to do so. The utilization of a thorough triage as seen in Table 25.1 is indicated during this step. Medical issues and any substance use should also be ascertained during this stage. This stage is intertwined with stage 2.

### Stage 2: Establish Rapport

The crisis worker attempts to establish a supportive relationship with the client while gaining critical information (Roberts & Yeager, 2009). A calm, patient style is the most effective approach to gaining trust and establishing rapport.

### Stage 3: Identify Pertinent Issues

This stage involves attempting to gain information about what has led to the current crisis state. Perhaps there was a major life event that impacted the client's social supports, or the client does not know how to cope effectively. Conferring with other collateral persons may also be needed during this step (Jackson-Cherry & Erford, 2014). Information gained in this stage will assist the worker in future steps.

## Stage 4: Deal With Feelings/Emotions

This stage involves letting the client vent his or her emotions while the crisis worker validates and listens. James and Gilliland (2005) define *active listening* as "attending, observing, understanding and responding with empathy, genuineness, respect, acceptance, non-judgment, and caring" (p. 20). Stages 1 through 4 involve the provision of a lot of supportive listening as the worker attempts to gather a thorough evaluation of the crisis. Information gained in the first four stages helps to inform the final three steps.

## Stage 5: Generate and Explore Alternatives

This stage involves a more active approach by the worker to explore options. Using information previously gained, the worker can potentially encourage the client to utilize prior coping strategies or resources. This stage also includes presenting various options to the client, so knowledge of community resources is an essential element during this process. Roberts and Yeager (20059) suggest that brainstorming options together may be an effective collaborative strategy that contributes to an increased feeling of control for the client.

## Stage 6: Implement a Concrete Action Plan

This stage includes initiating the necessary steps to assure client safety or implementing a plan for obtaining further assistance. This stage may include actions such as safeguarding the environment, linking the client with resources, obtaining medication, decreasing isolation, or hospitalizing (Roberts & Yeager, 2005).

## Stage 7: Follow Up

This final step should include planning follow-up, for example, it is essential to check in with a client or provider to ascertain his or her postcrisis status. The following case example illustrates these seven stages.

---

### Case Example

The on-call counselor was contacted by residence life staff. They had received a call from friends of a student who was "acting weird." Residence life staff were informed that the student had been trying to get into cars and buildings for some unknown reason. The student was walking around campus when residence life staff found him. He verbalized feeling confused and believed people were laughing at him and mocking him. He reported that he was in search of an "idol" to stop this behavior.

Upon arrival to campus, the worker began to talk with the student about recent events. During the assessment (Stage 1), it was determined that the student had been to a party the prior night and consumed alcohol. There were no prior medical or mental health conditions. The student was not voicing any suicidal ideation but was feeling agitated at those he believed were mocking him. He was a first-year student who reportedly had difficulty adjusting to college, and his home was across the country. We discussed his decision to attend college, his declared major, and his current living situation. As rapport increased, the student was more forthcoming about his thoughts (Stage 2). He shared that he was hearing voices at times telling him to look in various places for the "idol," which he was then acting on. He also endorsed delusions that this idol would not only stop the mocking behavior but also give him special powers to change others' behavior. The main problem at this time was that the student appeared to be experiencing a thought disturbance (Stage 3). We talked about his feelings, in particular the confusion and dissatisfaction of being so far from home (Stage 4). The worker gently began to discuss concerns about the student's behaviors as voiced by others, and how the confusion could be uncomfortable. The student was presented with the possibility that perhaps something had been put into his drink the night before. We discussed options, including having an evaluation at the emergency room or considering an admission to a local crisis residential unit (Stage 5). The student, with the added persuasion of the residence life staff, agreed to go to the hospital. The action plan was implemented, and ultimately the student was admitted to the inpatient mental health unit based on the level of thought disturbance (Stage 6). Throughout the hospitalization, the counselor followed up with the inpatient social worker to assist in discharge planning and communication with the student's family (Stage 7).

## GREENSTONE AND LEVITON CRISIS MODEL

According to Greenstone and Leviton (2011), the goal of crisis intervention is to help the client transition from a state of crisis back to his or her baseline level of functioning. Crises are unpredictable, so it is helpful to utilize a step-by-step method for a more successful intervention. Greenstone and Leviton describe their intervention model as being applicable to most crisis situations and advise intervenors to incorporate their personal skills and use their own knowledge about crises when intervening. The six steps of this model are as follows: immediacy, control, assessment, disposition, referral, and follow-up (Greenstone & Leviton, 2011, pp. 7–14).

*Immediacy* refers to responding quickly to relieve emotional distress. To accomplish this, the responder aims at decreasing anxiety that the client is experiencing and preventing harm to self or others.

*Control* is accomplished by first identifying yourself and your role in the crisis intervention while also providing structure until the client can regain self-control. Responders should use caution when entering a crisis situation by tuning into their senses, which will help the worker assess and approach the situation safely. It is important to appear calm, confident, and supportive to provide reassurance to clients. If possible, relocate the person away from the crisis situation or vice versa. Responders should be genuine in their approach because this will aid in gaining the client's trust and directing the intervention.

The *assessment* stage is when the responder attempts to gain a complete understanding of the situation. Responders should attempt to find out what the person's point of view is on the crisis and what the crisis means to him or her, as well as the facts about the crisis. While gathering information, focus on the present moment and the last 2 days. Ask short, straightforward questions, one at a time, and allow the person time to answer so that he or she does not feel overwhelmed by the assessment. The client may be feeling distressed, so allow for silence, ask for clarification when needed, and interrupt only when needed. Allow the person to vent his or her feelings and communicate openly by utilizing active listening skills. It is critical that the responder not pass judgment on the person or the crisis. The client needs to be empowered at this time, not chastised or reprimanded for his or her experience.

*Disposition* is the decision-making stage, which is the point of the intervention when the responder helps the client consider possible options for resolution. The intervenor will collaborate with the client to explore personal and social resource options that can be utilized to resolve the crisis. The intervenor will also provide hope that a resolution is possible and then create a plan with the client.

The fifth step of the model, *referral*, is the point at which the client is connected with necessary services. It is helpful to have access to updated resources so that the intervenor is prepared when entering the crisis situation. In the final step, *follow-up*, the intervenor follows up with the client to make sure that he or she made contact with the agency. The following case example demonstrates this model.

---

## Case Example

The on-call counselor was contacted by campus security. Security reported that a student by the name of Dawn was asking to speak to a counselor because she has been feeling depressed since her grandmother passed away.

No further information was provided by security. Immediacy: Immediately after receiving the call from security, the counselor phoned Dawn and introduced herself and defined her role. Safety was assessed, and the student denied suicidal ideation and reported that she had only thought about what happens to people after they die. The counselor normalized Dawn's thought processes and validated her feelings of sadness and loneliness. Control: The counselor determined that structuring of Dawn's experience and grief process needed to be provided for Dawn in order to help her regain control of her emotional state. Assessment: During the assessment stage, Dawn identified frequent crying spells, oversleeping, and a lack of energy as her primary concerns. She reported that she had to excuse herself from class today because she began crying, which is why she decided to seek help. The student shared that these symptoms emerged approximately 3 days after her grandmother died. The counselor allowed the student time to express her feelings related to the loss as the counselor utilized active listening skills. Disposition: The counselor and Dawn collaborated on considering different options to help her cope during her period of grief. The student identified her sister as a support. She also believed that meeting with a therapist on a regular basis would be helpful to work through her experience of loss. Dawn agreed to call her sister that night at 6:00 p.m. to share her feelings related to the loss of her grandmother. Refer: Dawn also scheduled an appointment with the counselor during office hours the following day. Follow up: The next day, Dawn arrived for her appointment at the counseling center.

---

## SAFER-R MODEL

A final model of intervention for responding to individuals in crisis consists of five steps. This SAFER-R model (Everly & Mitchell, 2008, p. 174) consists of the following stages:

1. Stabilize
2. Acknowledge
3. Facilitate understanding
4. Encourage adaptive coping
5. Restore functioning or refer

Stabilizing a potentially volatile situation is a critical first step to lessen the likelihood of further escalation or harm to the client or others. This stage may include removing any stressors that are exacerbating the crisis, such as separating disputants or relocating to an area without an audience. Steps that may be needed during this stage also include utilizing the assistance of other resources when necessary, such as emergency medical personnel or law enforcement.

Acknowledging the crisis is the second stage. According to Everly and Mitchell (2008), during this stage, the worker utilizes his or her listening and communication skills to ascertain what has happened and how the person is reacting to the situation. Hopefully this process supports clients in feeling heard and validated as they share their experience.

Third, the worker and the client gain an increased understanding of the crisis. Everly and Mitchell (2008) indicate that the worker begins to actively respond to what they have learned. Both the worker and the client gain information about what is needed. Necessary resources and coping strategies can be identified, which can then be used in the fourth stage.

The fourth stage, encouraging adaptive coping, is the active stage of intervention. This involves the facilitation of various interventions and coping strategies (Everly & Mitchell, 2008). For example, if a worker learned that the client had a former therapist, that person could assist in making a reconnection for the client. Additionally, active utilization of stress management or relaxation may be implemented at this point. However, if the crisis is acute and life-threatening, the worker may need to take another course of action.

The final stage, restoring adaptive functioning, occurs when the individual has successfully resolved the crisis or has a plan for resolution. Ideally, the client has become less emotional and feels more in control of the situation. At times, however, a client may need a higher level of care. At this time, a referral may be indicated to a hospital or other resource. The following case example illustrates the application of the SAFER-R model (Everly & Mitchell, 2008).

---

### Case Example

The on-call counselor received a call from campus security, which had been called by a male student who had had an altercation with his now ex-girlfriend. The student reported that he had attempted to end the relationship, and his girlfriend became distraught and tried to stab herself and overdose on a bottle of pills. He physically removed these items from her and then left her with her roommate. When the counselor arrived, the female student was crying hysterically in a lounge area, and the roommate was attempting to comfort her.

The counselor introduced herself and stated, "It seems like you are going through a difficult time right now. I'd like to see if I could help. Could we go to your room, or would you like to go to my office?" (stabilize). The counselor tried to separate this distraught student from others in the residence hall. Giving the student a choice helps her experience a sense of control in this situation. The student elected to talk in the counseling office. Upon arrival, the counselor acknowledged the crisis by stating, "Security shared that your boyfriend broke up with you tonight. Can you tell me what happened?" (acknowledge). The student shared the events of the evening and prior history of altercations with her boyfriend. Through active listening, the counselor was also able to learn of prior coping strategies that were helpful to this student. The student also shared that she was not suicidal, but that her actions were an attempt to stop him from leaving her (facilitate understanding). The student identified a close relationship with her mother, so this was incorporated into the plan. Her mother was contacted, and she agreed to come to campus and take the student home for the weekend. The student agreed to see the counselor on Monday, and she was provided with contact information for the mobile crisis service near her home should she need assistance prior to Monday (encourage adaptive coping). The counselor then maintained a supportive presence with the student while the mother drove to campus. The student was very goal oriented and futuristic, planning what she needed to take with her for the weekend to complete her schoolwork (restore functioning).

---

## TECHNOLOGY

Technology is an ever-growing field that significantly impacts youth in their daily lives and certainly during crises. The Pew Internet American Life Project reported that more than 93% of youth have access to the Internet, and more than 75% of youth have cellphones (DeAngellis, 2011). Most people are aware of telephone hotlines, but some providers also connect to their clients through video conferencing or the use of hyperlinks to connect with other service providers. Some responders are attempting to keep up with current trends by offering advanced means of crisis intervention.

One technological tool that is available by download is MY3, an app developed by the California Mental Health Services Authority, National Suicide Prevention Hotline, and Link2Health Solutions to provide easily accessible suicide prevention resources and safety plans to people who experience suicidal thoughts (MY3, n.d.). MY3 refers to the three support people who can be contacted when a person is struggling with suicidality. The app allows a person to add three support persons and their contact information so that they are already programmed into the phone when the person needs to reach out for support. The National Suicide Prevention Hotline number and 911 also are programmed into the phone so that the person has easy access to these supports as well. Another option of the app details the person's safety plan, which ideally is created with a mental health professional and includes an individual's warning signs, coping skills, distractions, support network, and ways to keep him or her safe (MY3, n.d.). Additional resources can be added that accommodate associations or groups that can offer further support, such as resources for veterans or mobile crisis organizations. MY3 is not a substitute for a mental health professional or physician; however, it is a resource that has incorporated technology in a way that is accessible and user-friendly for a person experiencing suicidal thoughts.

Technology has to be used judiciously in the crisis intervention field because of liability concerns and the need for providing appropriate services to clients. However, MY3 is one example of a resource that incorporates technological advances with crisis intervention techniques.

## CONCLUSION

Crises are inevitable situations that most practitioners will encounter multiple times during their careers. Fostering certain personal traits will assist the responder in being more effective when providing crisis intervention. Developing self-awareness, conveying empathy, genuineness, and warmth, and seeking continual professional growth are beneficial qualities. Additionally, utilizing Roberts's seven-stage crisis intervention model, Greenstone and Leviton's model, or the SAFER-R model provides crisis responders with valuable frameworks to guide their interventions.

REFERENCES

DeAngellis, T. (2011). Is technology ruining our kids? *Monitor on Psychology, 42* (9), 63–64. Retrieved from https://www.apa.org/monitor/2011/10/technology.aspx

Eaton, Y. (2005). The comprehensive crisis intervention model of Safe Harbor Behavioral Health Crisis Services. In A. R. Roberts (Ed.), *Crisis intervention handbook* (3rd ed., pp. 619–631). New York: Oxford University Press.

Everly, G. S., & Mitchell, J. T. (2008). *Integrative crisis intervention and disaster mental health.* Ellicott City, MD: Chevron.

Greenstone, J. L., & Leviton, S. C. (2011). *Elements of crisis intervention* (3rd ed.). Belmont, CA: Cengage Learning.

Hohman, M. (2012). *Motivational interviewing in social work practice.* New York: Guilford Press.

Jackson-Cherry, L. R., & Erford, B. T. (2014) *Crisis assessment, intervention, and prevention.* Upper Saddle River, NJ: Pearson Education.

James, R. K., & Gilliland, B. E. (2005). *Crisis intervention strategies* (5th ed.). Belmont, CA: Thomson Brooks/Cole.

Joiner, T., Kalafat, J., Draper, J., Stokes, H., Knudson, M., Berman, A. L., & McKeon, R. (2007). Establishing standards for the assessment of suicide risk among callers to the National Suicide Prevention Lifeline. *Suicide and Life-Threatening Behavior, 37,* 353–365.

Kirst-Ashman, K. K., & Hull, G. H. (2008). *Generalist practice with organizations and communities* (4th ed.). Belmont, CA: Cengage Learning.

Moyers, T. B., & Miller, W. R. (2013). Is low therapist empathy toxic? *Psychology of Addictive Behaviors, 27,* 878–884. doi:http://dx.doi.org/10.1037/a0030274

MY3. (n.d.). Help your clients stay connected to their network when they are having thoughts of suicide. Retrieved from http://www.my3app.org/get-involved/

National Suicide Prevention Lifeline. (2007). Suicide risk assessment standards. Retrieved from http://www.suicidepreventionlifeline.org/media/5388/Suicide-Risk-Assessment-Standards.pdf

Roberts, A. R. (2005). Bridging the past and present to the future of crisis intervention and crisis management. In A. R. Roberts (Ed.), *Crisis intervention handbook* (3rd ed., pp. 3–34). New York: Oxford University Press.

Roberts, A. R., & Yeager, K. R. (2009). *Pocket guide to crisis intervention.* New York: Oxford University Press.

Stanley, S. A. (2006). Cultural competency: From philosophy to research and practice. *Journal of Community Psychology, 34,* 237–245. doi:10.1002/jcop.20095

Walsh, M., Stretch, B., Moonie, N., Millar, E., Herne, D., & Webb, D. (2003). *BTEC national: Care.* Oxford: Heinemann Educational Publishers.

Wampold, B. E. (n.d.). Qualities and actions of effective therapists. American Psychological Association. Retrieved from https://www.apa.org/education/ce/effective-therapists.pdf

# 26

# The Crisis State Assessment
# Scale: Development and Psychometrics

SARAH J. LEWIS

Men are disturbed, not by things, but by the principles and notions
which they form concerning things.

—Epictetus (c. 55–c. 135), *The Enchiridion*

## STATEMENT OF THE PROBLEM

Crisis intervention, based on crisis theory, is one of the most widely used
types of brief treatment employed by counselors, social workers, and other
mental health professionals working in community settings (Roberts &
Everly, 2006). There is a large body of literature on crisis intervention models and techniques, and a recurring theme in this literature is the importance
placed on assessment (Adesanya, 2005; Myer & Conte, 2006; Roberts &
Everly, 2006). The question is—assessment of what? A number of instruments are available for measuring lethality, anxiety, stress, depression, and
global functioning. There are also a number of instruments to measure symptoms of post-traumatic stress disorder (PTSD) such as the PTSD Checklist
(PCL), Primary Care-PTSD (PC-PTSD), and the Clinician-Administered
PTSD Scale (CAPS; Tiet, Schutte, & Leyva, 2013). There are few instruments, however, that are designed to objectively assess the degree of an individual's crisis state.

The purpose of this study was to design and test a rapid assessment
instrument that measures two constructs: perceived psychological trauma
and perceived problems in coping efficacy. These two constructs predict or
indicate the magnitude of a crisis state.

## Rationale for Measurement

Clinicians generally justify treatment for one client and not another by applying a formula to calculate risks and benefits. This formula may be guided by practice wisdom garnered through years of experience or codified through instrumentation. Instrumentation can help a clinician to focus, stay on task, and be acutely attuned to the constructs that he or she is attempting to assess. It is important to stress that measurement tools in a clinical setting are not meant to replace the practice wisdom and professional judgment of the clinician, but to enhance them.

*Measurement* can be defined as the "systematic process of assigning a number to something" (Nunnally, 1978, p. 176). These variables are the client's thoughts or cognitions, behaviors, affect, feelings, or perceptions. The assignment of a number, or the quantification of the variable, allows clinicians to monitor change using a mathematical model. Standardized measurement is important to the field of crisis intervention because it allows clinicians to understand the comprehensive nature of the client's crisis state with greater accuracy (Roberts & Everly, 2006).

Accurate measurement is also necessary for gauging the magnitude of the crisis state and for monitoring progress from an objective standpoint. Accurately measuring the severity of different aspects of a crisis state permits the clinician to intervene in the area that is most germane to the current crisis and to use the appropriate degree of intervention. In this way, standardized measures can be used to triangulate: to provide additional information in which to look for congruence of assessment (Nurius & Hudson, 1993; Roberts & Everly, 2006).

## Focus of This Research

The purpose of this research was the development and validation of a multidimensional rapid assessment instrument (RAI) to assess two constructs associated with a crisis state. The primary goals of the instrument are (a) standardized measurement of two factors, perceived trauma and perceived ability to cope with said trauma; and (b) rapid clinical assessment. The underlying assumptions on which the scale is based are derived from interactional stress theory and crisis theory (Folkman, Lazarus, Dunkel-Schetter, DeLongis, & Gruen, 1986; Lazarus & Smith, 1988). These assumptions are as follows:

- A crisis state is a response to a new and intense event that is perceived through primary appraisal to pose a serious threat to either emotional or physical safety (considered to be perceived psychological trauma).
- An individual's crisis response is characterized by the perception through secondary appraisal that he or she is unable to resolve the event due to a dearth of prior experience, lack of resources, and physical and/or emotional turmoil (considered to be perceived problems in coping efficacy).

## LITERATURE REVIEW

### Primary Assumptions of Crisis Theory

One confusing aspect of crisis theory is the lexicon used to describe its features. It is often challenging to discern the difference in the literature between discussions of theory and method and between crisis intervention and other approaches.

There is not one crisis theory that encompasses what defines a crisis event (the phenomenon), a crisis response (human response to the phenomenon), or a crisis intervention (the helping process). Instead, there exists a body of literature grounded in the seminal work of Lindemann (1963), Caplan, (1964), and Roberts and Grau, (1970). A synthesis of ego and cognitive psychology and individual stress theories is also incorporated into crisis theory. A compilation of all of these theories contains the following primary assumptions:

- Everyone, at some point in his or her life, will experience acute stress that is not necessarily pathological. Whether or not the stressor is a crisis event is determined by its position in the overall context of the person's life.
- Homeostasis, or balance, is a natural state that all people seek, and when an individual is in a state of emotional disequilibrium, he or she strives to regain emotional balance.
- A period of disequilibrium in which the individual (or family) is vulnerable to further deterioration is present when a stressful event becomes a crisis.
- This disequilibrium makes the individual more amenable to intervention.
- New coping mechanisms are needed to deal with the crisis event.
- The dearth of prior experience with the crisis event creates increased anxiety and struggle, during which the individual often discovers hidden resources.
- The duration of the crisis is somewhat limited, depending on the precipitating event, response patterns, and available resources.
- Certain affective, cognitive, and behavioral tasks must be mastered throughout the crisis phase in order to move to resolution, regardless of the stressor.

The underlying theme here is that a noncrisis state is a state of inner balance, and when that balance is thrown off, the individual strives to regain the balance. Crisis occurs when the individual perceives that he or she does not have the resources necessary to regain balance.

Crisis is aptly defined by Roberts (2000) as follows:

An acute disruption of psychological homeostasis in which one's usual coping mechanisms fail and there exists evidence of distress and functional impairment. The subjective reaction to a stressful life experience that compromises the individual's stability and ability to cope or function. The main cause of a crisis is an intensely stressful, traumatic, or hazardous event, but two other conditions are also necessary: (1) the individual's perception of the event as the cause of considerable upset and/or disruption; and (2) the individual's inability to resolve the disruption by previously used coping methods. (p. 516)

## Measurement in Crisis Assessment

A major dilemma with the readily available, standardized instruments categorized under crisis assessment is that most focus on the potentiality of suicide, on the psychological effects of the trauma such as anxiety or depression, or on buffers against suicide. The problem is that although lethality assessment is an absolutely critical component of crisis assessment, it is not the only part of the assessment process. That is, not all individuals who are in crisis are either suicidal or homicidal—and yet they are still in crisis.

To assess aspects of a crisis state other than lethality, clinicians generally measure the severity of the event that precipitates the crisis, the stress caused by that event, or the emotional consequences of an unresolved crisis such as depression or anxiety (Roberts & Everly, 2006). However, measuring the magnitude of a crisis state or the resolution of a crisis state using these variables (precipitating event, stress caused by the event, or emotional consequences of the event) raises several dilemmas. It is the context in which someone experiences an event and his or her subjective response to the event that determine whether or not an event is a crisis (Berjot & Gillet, 2011; Kuppens, 2010). If this assumption is correct, any event may or may not be experienced as a crisis. More important, it is the subjective response to the event, and not necessarily the event itself, that defines a crisis. In other words, it is the individual who determines whether or not an event or situation is a crisis/tragedy/trauma in his or her subjective experience.

Experts in stress theory such as Lazarus and Folkman (1984), in addition to the previously mentioned experts in crisis theory, claim that stressors are natural. They claim that it is the subjective context of an individual's life circumstances and perception of resources that determine whether or not the stressor induces a crisis state. Here again, it is the individual's perception of his or her available resources in relation to the stressor that leads to a crisis, not the stressor itself. Finally, a crisis state does not equate with pathology but is instead best viewed as a problem in personal functioning (James & Gilliland, 2011; Kanel, 2015).

According to Hudson, Mathiesen, and Lewis (2002), "Personal functioning represents the internal events, processes, and experiences of an individual... [and] is problematic when an individual's level of distress become[s] large enough to be clinically significant" (p. 76). To better understand the crisis state as a personal problem, the microtheory of personal and social problems can be employed (Faul & Hudson, 1997). This theory has two fundamental axioms: "Human problems do not exist until someone defines them... [and] all human problems are defined in terms of a value base" (p. 49). The first step has already been discussed here: defining a crisis state. The value base has been established in that a crisis state is defined as a problem.

## Crisis/Stress Definitions

Working in the 1950s, Lazarus and his colleagues discovered that the effects of stress were not generalizable or universal; rather, the effects were dependent on individual differences in how people thought about, or appraised, the stressor, and in their motivation to relieve the stress (Lazarus & Eriksen, 1952). The contributions of Lazarus and Folkman (1984) to the study of stress primarily have to do with conceptualizing stress and coping as processes with mediating individual variables. They defined what is now commonly known as the stress process in the following terms: the event (stressor); the cognitions of the event, both primary and secondary (appraisal); and the behaviors that are used to deal with the event (coping).

Social cognitive theory posits that stress is a function of a cognitive appraisal process, or the evaluation of coping self-efficacy in a given situation (Bandura, 1986). When the demands of a situation outweigh an individual's perceived ability to cope, stress is the result (Bandura, 1986; Berjot & Gillet, 2011; Hill, 1949).

This is where a clarification of terminology becomes imperative. Authors in many fields have defined stress in many different ways; there is no universal definition for stress. Lazarus and Folkman (1984) define *psychological stress* as "a relationship between the person and the environment that is appraised by the person as taxing or exceeding his or her resources and endangering his or her well-being" (p. 21). This definition of psychological stress closely resembles Roberts's (2000) definition of a crisis: "The subjective reaction to a stressful life experience that compromises the individual's stability and ability to cope or function" (p. 516). This research relates the two concepts of stress and crisis by contending that the degree of a crisis, which is a psychological state, is mediated by thoughts about the magnitude of a stressful life experience (event or situation) and thoughts about whether or not a person can cope with the stressful life event. These thoughts are referred to in stress theory as primary and secondary appraisal.

### Primary Appraisal

*Primary appraisal* is the process of evaluating the threat or strain of an event or situation (Lazarus & Folkman, 1984). During the primary appraisal process, cognitions are concentrated on the magnitude of the threat or strain. According to Lazarus and Folkman, there are three kinds of primary appraisal: irrelevant, benign-positive, and stressful. If an event or situation is appraised as irrelevant, there is "no investment" (p. 32) in the outcome on the part of the individual. When a situation is appraised as benign-positive, it is believed to be solely positive, with no potential negative consequences. This study is concerned with the third type of primary appraisal: stressful. Stress appraisals include harm/loss, threat, and challenge.

Harm/loss appraisals are when the individual believes that he or she has sustained some physical or emotional harm or loss. Examples of this are the death of a loved one, physical injury, financial loss, loss of friendship, diminished self-esteem or sense of worth, and loss of a commitment such as marriage or a business partner. In this type of appraisal, the harm or loss has already happened.

Threat, a form of primary appraisal, is concerned with anticipated harm or loss. Even though an event or situation may have already happened, the individual may anticipate future harm or loss as a result of the event. For example, if a student fails a test, the event has happened (failure of the test). However, the student may still fear the loss of financial support from his or her parents when they find out about the failure.

Challenge appraisals may include threats. These appraisals tend to focus on positive events that contain within them the risk of future negative outcomes. The challenge has to do with mastery of an event or situation; however, there is risk inherent in challenge. For example, a new marriage may be seen as an exciting new challenge: it represents an opportunity to be successful in a relationship. However, it also represents the potential for failure.

## Secondary Appraisal

*Secondary appraisal* is the process of evaluating one's ability to deal with threat or strain. Lazarus and Folkman (1984) claim:

> Secondary appraisal is more than a mere intellectual exercise in spotting what must be done. It is a complex evaluative process that takes into account which coping options are available, the likelihood that a given coping option will accomplish what it is supposed to, and the likelihood that one can apply a particular strategy or set of strategies effectively. (p. 35)

Bandura (1977) further refined Lazarus and Folkman's (1984) theoretical model by adding the important variables of outcome expectancy and efficacy expectations to the concept of secondary appraisal. *Outcome expectancy* is an individual's belief that certain behaviors will lead to certain outcomes. *Efficacy expectation* refers to an individual's belief that he or she can effectively carry out the action or behavior necessary to produce the expected outcome.

Basically, Bandura, (1977) hypothesized that an individual's belief in his or her ability to handle an event (coping efficacy) mediates his or her stress reaction to that event. Individuals' belief that they can cause a positive outcome is based on their own personal repertoire, or menu, of past successes in similarly stressful situations, rather than on their belief in positive outcomes in general.

### Gaps in the Literature

There are currently few scales that measure the perceived magnitude of a stressor and situation-specific coping efficacy (Almeida, Wethington, & Kessler, 2002; Ellsworth, 2013; Ising, Weyers, Reuter, & Janke, 2006). In addition, most studies use a single-item indicator to measure coping efficacy, which creates serious limitations in validity claims (Rowley, Roesch, Jurica, & Vaughn, 2005). Many of the scales available do not measure the subjective state of the individual but instead are objective behavioral checklists completed by a clinician. The researchers who created those crisis instruments claim that because an individual is in crisis, he or she is not capable of completing a paper-and-pencil test (Bengelsdorf, Levy, Emerson, & Barile, 1984; Myer & Conte, 2006). This may be true in extreme cases; however, it is not true in all cases. There is no way to determine that an individual is not capable of filling out a paper-and-pencil test until an assessment has been made. To remove the possibility of a standardized objective assessment of a subjective state without any attempt may in fact be a disservice to the individual seeking assistance.

## CONCEPTUAL FRAMEWORK FOR THIS RESEARCH

This research focused on the subjective state that a person may experience as a result of a stressor. This state, termed here a *crisis state*, is an imbalance of internal equilibrium that is the result of a subjective response to a stressor. Internal equilibrium is mental or emotional stability. A stressor can be any event or situation. Coping efficacy is an individual's belief that he or she is capable of dealing with the event or situation considered to be the stressor. Coping efficacy is not equivalent to coping: coping is an action or set of actions that is employed to deal with a stressor.

Lazarus and Folkman (1984) proposed that reactions to a stressor are mediated by cognitive appraisals by the individual. Appraisals, primary and secondary, are simply beliefs about the magnitude of the event or situation, as well as beliefs about whether one can handle the event or situation. In primary appraisal, the individual assesses the magnitude of the event or situation considered to be a stressor. For example, he or she may think, "Oh, my gosh, this car accident is really bad, the car is not drivable." This perception of the stressor is termed *perceived psychological trauma*. Perceived psychological trauma is operationalized as an individual's unique perception of an event or enduring condition that leads the individual to believe that his or her physical life, way of life, or sanity is in jeopardy. This example relates to financial distress, which potentially jeopardizes way of life.

Secondary appraisal happens immediately following the initial cognition, if not simultaneously, and concerns the individual's thoughts about whether he or she can deal with the situation or event (Lazarus & Folkman, 1984). An example of secondary appraisal that corresponds with the prior example of primary appraisal is "I can handle this because my insurance will cover the cost to fix the car and a rental car." Or, "I can't handle this because I have no insurance." Coping is the actual action. In this example, coping would be the action of calling the insurance company. Coping efficacy, by contrast, is the belief that one can cope by calling the insurance agency.

These concepts constitute a crisis state. The state is internal and cannot necessarily be determined by indicators such as coping actions. In other words, an individual can be in a crisis state even while using healthy coping behaviors.

There are two main reasons why behavior cannot be used as an indicator of crisis. The first reason is that what may be unhealthy coping in one situation may be healthy coping in another. For example, using denial of imminent death from a terminal disease because one has a project that one wants to continue to work on is beneficial, even though denial is more typically perceived to be a negative coping response. The second reason is that even though a person may appear, through behavioral indicators, to be coping very well, he or she may have the perception of an inability to cope and therefore still have a disruption of equilibrium.

Internal equilibrium (a noncrisis state), referred to in the crisis literature as *homeostasis*, can be thought of as a playground seesaw that is perfectly balanced. On one side of the fulcrum is one's perception of situations or events (perceived psychological trauma); on the other is one's perception of ability to cope (coping efficacy) with those situations or events. When the perception of the psychological trauma is greater than the perception of coping efficacy, the seesaw is off balance. The key to determining if an individual is in a crisis state is to measure both sides of the seesaw and compare the two scores: perception of the gravity of the situation and perception of ability to cope in relation to a specific event or situation.

When perceived coping efficacy is viewed from the vantage point of perceived problems in coping efficacy, then both perceived psychological trauma and perceived problems in coping efficacy contribute to disruption in internal equilibrium. One important reason for measuring perceived problems in coping efficacy, as opposed to just perceived coping efficacy, is that clinicians generally focus on problem solving in a therapeutic interaction. The reason for this is that it is not possible to define health except through the relation between healthy and unhealthy. Thus, what indicates health is the lack of markers of ill health. A higher score on either factor indicates a greater problem and will be targeted as the focal point of clinical therapy.

The Crisis State Assessment Scale (CSAS) measures a crisis state defined as perceived psychological trauma and perceived problems in coping efficacy. The scale focuses the respondent on a specific event by having him or her specify the event or situation at the top of the instrument. The purpose of this is to help the respondent focus on that event when responding to each item. In this way, the instrument relies on Bandura's (1997) argument for situation-specific coping efficacy. This idea carries over to perceived psychological trauma. In other words, the scale is also sensitive to an identified problem area.

## SCALE PSYCHOMETRICS

### Scale Construction

The phenomenon that this scale attempts to capture is a crisis state, defined as an internal disequilibrium resulting from perceived psychological trauma and perceived problems in coping efficacy. These two factors are defined as follows:

*Perceived psychological trauma* is an individual's unique perception of an event or enduring condition that leads the individual to believe that his or her physical life, way of life, or sanity is in jeopardy.

*Perceived problems in coping efficacy* are an individual's belief that he or she cannot effectively master the demands of a traumatic condition, threat, or challenge because it exceeds his or her resources.

The tool developed in this study uses a 7-point Likert scale based on presence or absence of the item. The scaling is as follows: 1 = never, 2 = very rarely, 3 = rarely, 4 = sometimes, 5 = often, 6 = almost always, and 7 = always. A single-item indicator of subjective units of psychological distress is also present on the instrument and is scaled with a category partition.

Table 26.1   Data Collection Sites and Participant Rates

| Location | Packets Distributed | Packets Returned | Percentage Returned | CSAS Completed | Returned CSAS Completed |
|---|---|---|---|---|---|
| University 1 | 125 | 114 | 91 | 110 | 88 |
| University 2 | 350 | 298 | 85 | 292 | 83 |
| Total | 475 | 412 | 87 | 402 | 85 |

The category partition is broken up into equal parts ranging from 1 to 10 in terms of difficulty of the current situation. The partition is anchored with the terms *easy* and *most difficult*.

## Subjects

In this study, a convenience sample was used of students 18 years old and older enrolled at two universities, one in the South (University 1) and one in the Northeast (University 2). A total of 475 data packets were distributed. The return rate at the school in the South was 91.2%, and the return rate at the school in the Northeast was 85.14% (Table 26.1).

## RESULTS

### Demographics of Subjects

The sample from University 1 ($n = 114$) was predominantly female (87%), and the sample from University 2 ($n = 297$) was 50% female. The racial/ethnic makeup of the University 1 sample was as follows: 19% African American, 2% Asian, 67% White, 7% Hispanic, and 5% other. The racial/ethnic makeup of University 2 was 9% African American, 8% Asian, 69% White, 7% Hispanic, 1% Native American, and 6% other.

The mean age of the sample from University 1 was 26.68, with a standard deviation of 8.02. Because of the outliers in this sample, it is important to report that the inner quartile of this sample was between the ages of 21 and 28. The sample from University 2 was younger, with a mean age of 20.72 and a standard deviation of 2.34. The inner quartile for this sample was between the ages of 19 and 21.5.

### Reported Crisis Event(s)/Situation(s) on the CSAS

Respondents were asked to write a short description of the crisis event(s) and/or situation(s) to which they would refer while completing the CSAS

(Figure 26.1). The form provided space for three separate events or situations. Table 26.2 describes the crisis event(s) and/or situation(s) and the frequency with which they were reported. Sixteen respondents did not report a crisis event or situation, yet they still completed the CSAS. Of those reporting an event, 403 reported one event, 69 reported two events, and 37 reported three events.

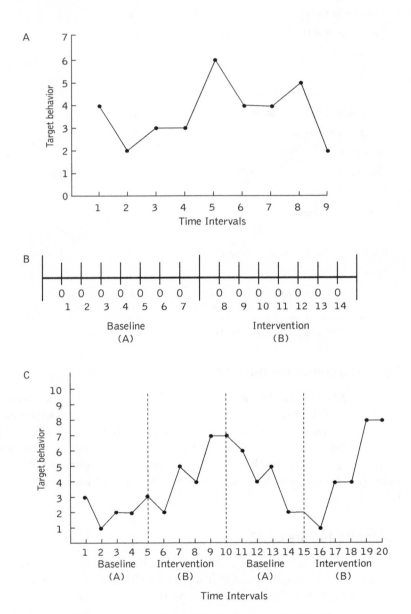

Figure 26.1   Crisis State Assessment Scale

Table 26.2    Crisis Event(s)/Situation(s)

| Event | Frequency | Percentage |
|---|---|---|
| Trouble with significant other | 86 | 21 |
| Problems with grades/school | 53 | 13 |
| Death of a loved one | 48 | 12 |
| Trouble with parents | 36 | 9 |
| Parents' or grandparents' health problems | 30 | 7 |
| Happy event | 30 | 7 |
| Accident | 28 | 7 |
| Problems with job | 25 | 6 |
| Problems with housing/moving | 26 | 4 |
| Problems with friends | 21 | 5 |
| Personal health | 21 | 5 |
| Graduation | 19 | 5 |
| Financial problems | 19 | 5 |
| Problems with siblings | 15 | 4 |
| Friend's tragedy | 10 | 2 |
| Know or saw someone who died violently | 9 | 2 |
| Rape | 7 | 2 |
| Other (baby, divorce, auto trouble, coming out, happy/sad anniversary, pet, know/saw suicide) | 60 | 15 |

Respondents could report up to three events, so percentages do not add up to 100.

## Content Validity for the CSAS

Content validity was established via the method purported recommended by Nunnally and Bernstein (1994), in which competent judges determined whether or not each item was a member of the population of items that composed each domain. Three experts in crisis theory judged each item and were in agreement on all items. The original CSAS consisted of 10 to 12 items per domain and had an overall Fleisch-Kincaid grade level index of 5.3.

## Reliability for the CSAS

There are two distinct scales in the CSAS: perceived psychological trauma and perceived problems in coping efficacy. The alpha and reliability for each of these scales were calculated, as well as the global reliability. Listwise deletion was used to remove cases with missing data. Thus, the reliability analyses for the CSAS was 403 ($n$ = 403). The alpha and reliability for each of these scales were found to be good to excellent at 0.85, 0.84, and 0.92, respectively.

## Factorial Validity

Because each of the subscales in the CSAS was developed according to theoretical propositions, multiple groups confirmatory factor analysis (CFA) was used to establish factorial validity. Correlations between subscale scores and item responses were computed. These correlations were then examined to determine whether items had the highest correlations with their intended subscale.

The CSAS has a strong factor structure, which suggests the presence of distinct factors. The strong correlations observed between the two factors of perceived psychological trauma and perceived problems in coping efficacy are consistent with the theory that these two factors compose another factor, a crisis state. This is also indicated by the strong global reliability coefficient.

## Convergent Validity

To establish convergent validity, correlations were found between factors on the CSAS and other indicators of those factors. First, the perceived psychological trauma mean scale score was compared to the mean score of the Index of Clinical Stress. With a sample size of 393, the Pearson's $r$ was .536 and was significant at the $p$ = .001 level.

Item number CSAS22 was used as the single-item indicator for perceived problems in coping efficacy. The item states: "I am confident that I can cope with the event/situation." Reverse-scoring this item demonstrates problems in perceived coping efficacy. Because the indicator was a member of the final scale item grouping, its influence had to be removed before the correlation was found. The correlation for the four remaining items on problems with perceived coping, and the single-item indicator, was .296 and was significant at the $p$ = .001 level with a sample size of 403.

## Discriminant Validity

Discriminant validity of the CSAS was tested using the background variables ethnicity, age, and academic standing. Table 26.3 illustrates the correlations between mean scale scores for both factors on the CSAS and the background variables.

Table 26.3    Discriminant Validity Correlation Coefficients

|  | Ethnicity | Age | Academic Standing |
| --- | --- | --- | --- |
| Perceived psychological trauma | .079 | −.013 | .059* |
| Perceived problems in coping efficacy | .031 | −.093 | −.035 |

*Significant at the $p = .01$ level (two-tailed).

## Criterion Validity

Criterion (concurrent) validity was established for perceived psychological trauma by creating two groups, low psychological trauma and high psychological trauma, from the single-item indicator for perceived psychological trauma. Subjects scoring 0 through 3 ($n = 87$) on the single-item indicator were placed in the low psychological trauma group, and subjects scoring 4 through 10 ($n = 304$) were placed in the high psychological trauma group. Logistic regression was computed to demonstrate the ability of perceived psychological trauma to predict group membership.

There were 389 cases included in the analysis, and after five iterations, the −2 log likelihood was 320.116. The Cox and Snell $R$ square was 0.208, and the Nagelkerke $R$ square was 0.319. Perceived psychological trauma was able to correctly predict group membership into the low psychological trauma group with 41.9% accuracy, and into the high psychological trauma group with 93.1% accuracy. The overall percentage correct was 81.7. The weighting value of B was 1.060, and the standard error was 0.137. The Wald test coefficient was 59.669 and was significant at the $p = .001$ level.

## DISCUSSION AND CONCLUSIONS

Crisis intervention has flourished as a therapeutic technique in the helping professions; however, no matter the novelty or the history, it is important to determine whether or not the techniques employed are efficacious. The clinician needs to know the degree of crisis state when the client enters the therapeutic encounter and the magnitude of the client's crisis state upon exit. The CSAS is a short, rapid assessment of the subjective state of an individual's perceived crisis state. It is currently in use in several mental health and crisis intervention organizations around the globe from South Africa to Australia.

### Crisis Theory

An interesting finding of this research is that relationships between perceived psychological trauma and specific crisis events were found (chi-square = 0.006); however, perceived problems in coping efficacy and crisis events were independent of one another (chi-square = 0.261). This finding is consistent with the guiding theory that coping efficacy is independent of the traumatic event and mediates the magnitude of a crisis state. It can be inferred from this finding that some individuals feel they can handle a specific difficult event, and some believe they cannot handle that same event. It is the individual's subjective belief about his or her ability to cope with the event that determines whether or not the individual will enter into a state of crisis.

## Clinical Implications

One of the purposes for which the CSAS was developed was to aid clinicians in the assessment of individuals presenting in a crisis state. The CSAS should not be used as the sole determinant of a crisis state but as an adjunct to other clinical assessment strategies.

No instrument until now has attempted to capture the magnitude of a crisis state in this configuration. Although the CSAS has limitations, such as its correlated measurement error, it is an important first step toward the measurement of the degree to which an individual is in crisis. Crisis intervention has become an increasingly popular therapeutic modality. One of the main reasons for this popularity is that managed care organizations and other insurers will often pay for only a few sessions, which is making longer therapies a thing of the past for all but the affluent. This means that crisis intervention is often used with the most marginalized individuals, those without many health care choices. Mental health clinicians have an obligation to ensure that available services to these vulnerable individuals are as efficient and effective as possible.

A unique feature of the CSAS is that it allows the client to identify the event or situation that he or she believes is the precipitant of the crisis. The client then has to focus on his or her feelings regarding the magnitude of the event, as well as feelings about whether or not he or she can cope with the event. By requiring the client to focus and complete a pencil-and-paper test, the instrument itself is a part of the intervention because it begins the process of de-escalation. The CSAS also provides talking points to which the clinician can refer to keep the intervention focused on problem solving in relation to the crisis state (Lewis & Roberts, 2002).

The CSAS can be used in college counseling centers for emergency/crisis sessions, as well as in other facilities. One strategy could be to give the client the scale along with other paperwork that must be completed before the session. Because the CSAS has only five items for each of the two factors, the client burden is not significant. The CSAS is easy to score: The clinician can calculate and interpret the instrument in less than 2 minutes. The ease of administration and scoring makes it possible to administer the scale at both the beginning and the end of the emergency session to quantify improvement. This suggestion is made with the caution that the score should not be the only indicator of a successful or unsuccessful therapeutic outcome, and that the clinician should be cognizant of the measurement error potential of the scale. In other words, there may be something other than perceived psychological trauma and perceived problems in coping efficacy that is causing the variation in the scale score.

## Scoring Instructions

Both factors on the final version of the CSAS consist of five items and are based on a 7-point scale. This makes summing and interpreting the scores quick and easy. There are two steps in the scoring process: finding each subscale score and calculating the global score.

To find subscale scores, reverse-score item 10 by replacing scores as follows: 1 with 7, 2 with 6, 3 with 5, 4 with 4, 5 with 3, 6 with 2, and 7 with 1. Then find the mean of each subscale by adding all item responses in that subscale and dividing by 5. To find the CSAS global score, add each of the subscale scores (mean scores) together and divide by 2.

## Interpretation

The same 7-point Likert scale that is used when responding to CSAS items is used to decipher the scores. If, for example, a person received a 6 on the perceived problems in coping subscale, it can be surmised that he or she "almost always" perceives that he or she is experiencing problems in coping. This may indicate that an intervention is called for to assist the client in finding alternative coping strategies. The global score is meant to be an indicator of the magnitude of a crisis state. Higher scores mean that the individual is in a greater state of crisis.

REFERENCES

Adesanya, A. (2005). Impact of a crisis assessment and treatment service on admissions into an acute psychiatric unit. *Australasian Psychiatry*, 13, 135–139. doi:10.1111/j.1440-1665.2005.02176.x

Almeida, D. M., Wethington, E., & Kessler, R. C. (2002). The daily inventory of stressful events: An interview-based approach for measuring daily stressors. *Assessment*, 9 (1), 41–55. Retrieved from http://www.ncbi.nlm.nih.gov/pubmed/11911234

Bandura, A. (1977). Self-efficacy: Toward a unifying theory of behavioral change. *Psychological Review, 84*, 191–215. doi:10.1037/0033-295X.84.2.191

Bandura, A. (1986). *Social foundations of thought and action: A social cognitive theory* (Vol. 1).

Bengelsdorf, H., Levy, L. E., Emerson, R. L., & Barile, F. A. (1984). A crisis triage rating scale: Brief dispositional assessment of patients at risk for hospitalization. *Journal of Nervous and Mental Disease, 172,* 424–430. doi:10.1097/00005053-198407000-00009

Berjot, S., & Gillet, N. (2011). Stress and coping with discrimination and stigmatization. *Frontiers in Psychology, 2,* 33. doi:10.3389/fpsyg.2011.00033

Caplan, G. (1964). *Principles of preventive psychiatry.* New York: Basic Books.

Ellsworth, P. C. (2013). Appraisal theory: Old and new questions. *Emotion Review, 5,* 125–131. doi:10.1177/1754073912463617

Faul, A. C., & Hudson, W. W. (1997). The Index of Drug Involvement: A partial validation. *Social Worker, 42,* 565–572.

Folkman, S., Lazarus, R. S., Dunkel-Schetter, C., DeLongis, A., & Gruen, R. J. (1986). Dynamics of a stressful encounter: Cognitive appraisal, coping, and encounter outcomes. *Journal of Personality and Social Psychology, 50,* 992–1003. doi:10.1037/0022-3514.50.5.992

Hill, R. (1949). *Families under stress: Adjustment to the crisis of war, separation, and reunion.* New York: Harper.

Hudson, W. W., Mathiesen, S. G., & Lewis, S. J. (2000). Personal and social functioning: A pilot study. *Social Service Review, 74* (4), 76–102.

Ising, M., Weyers, P., Reuter, M., & Janke, W. (2006). Comparing two approaches for the assessment of coping. *Journal of Individual Differences, 27* (1), 15–19. doi:10.1027/1614-0001.27.1.15

James, R. K., & Gilliland, B. E. (2011). *Crisis intervention strategies* (7th ed.). Belmont: CA: Brooks/Cole, Cengage Learning.

Kanel, K. (2015). *A guide to crisis intervention* (5th ed.). Stamford, CT: Cengage Learning.

Kuppens, P. (2010). From appraisal to emotion. *Emotion Review, 2*(2), 157–158. doi:10.1177/1754073909355010

Lazarus, R. S., & Eriksen, C. (1952). Effects of failure stress upon skilled performance. *Journal of Experimental Psychology, 43,* 100–105.

Lazarus, R. S., & Folkman, S. (1984). *Stress, appraisal and coping.* New York: Springer.

Lazarus, R. S., & Smith, C. A. (1988). Knowledge and appraisal in the cognition-emotion relationship. *Cognition and Emotion, 2*(4), 281–300. doi:10.1080/02699938808412701

Lindemann, E. (1963). Symptomatology and management of acute grief. *Pastoral Psychology, 14,* 8–18. doi:10.1007/BF01770375

Myer, R. A., & Conte, C. (2006). Assessment for crisis intervention. *Journal of Clinical Psychology, 62,* 959–970). doi:10.1002/jclp.20282

Nunnally, J. (1978). *Psychometric theory.* New York: McGraw-Hill.

Nunnally, J., & Bernstein, I. (1994) *Psychometric theory* (3rd ed.). New York: McGraw Hill.

Nurius, P., & Hudson, W. W. (1993). *Human services: Practice, evaluation, and computers.* Pacific Grove, CA: Brooks/Cole.

Roberts, A. R. (2000). An overview of crisis theory and crisis intervention. In A. R. Roberts (Ed.), *Crisis intervention handbook: Assessment treatment, and research* (2nd ed., pp. 3–30). New York: Oxford Univeristy Press.

Roberts, A. R., & Everly, G. S. (2006). A meta-analysis of 36 crisis intervention studies. *Brief Treatment and Crisis Intervention*, 6, 10–21. doi:10.1093/brief-treatment/mhj006

Roberts, A. R., & Grau, J. J. (1970). Procedures used in crisis intervention by suicide prevention agencies. *Public Health Reports, 85*, 691–698.

Rowley, A. A, Roesch, S. C., Jurica, B. J., & Vaughn, A. A. (2005). Developing and validating a stress appraisal measure for minority adolescents. *Journal of Adolescence, 28*, 547–57. doi:10.1016/j.adolescence.2004.10.010

Tiet, Q. Q., Schutte, K. K., & Leyva, Y. E. (2013). Diagnostic accuracy of brief PTSD screening instruments in military veterans. *Journal of Substance Abuse Treatment, 45*, 134–142. doi:10.1016/j.jsat.2013.01.010

# 27

## Designs and Procedures for Evaluating Crisis Intervention

SOPHIA F. DZIEGIELEWSKI
GEORGE A. JACINTO

The overall efficacy, popularity, and necessity of time-limited therapeutic encounters, including crisis intervention approaches used with various types of clients should always focus on clearly ascertaining the variables that can be linked directly to client change (Dziegielewski, 2013; Dziegielewski & Roberts, 2004). To date, however, methodological limitations inherent in most forms of time-limited intervention remain, placing an emphasis on deliberate attempts for inclusion of evidence-based practice approaches that support the overall effectiveness of and between competing intervention approaches (Monette, Sullivan, & DeJong, 2005; Nugent, Sieppert, & Hudson, 2001). Regardless, providing a firm basis for empirical support is considered the cornerstone of the services provided (Lambert, 2013). Historically, establishing treatment effectiveness in all areas of counseling has often been met with resistance, especially because client change behavior and the resulting therapeutic gains can be seen as subjective. In fact, Bergin and Suinn (1975) originally suggested that clients are likely to change over time even without any therapeutic intervention.

Over the years, it has become clear that all practitioners need to make a commitment to utilizing best practices that are evidence-based. In other words, all crisis workers and counselors need to thoroughly prepare for intervening on behalf of many types of persons in crisis. This can be done effectively only if practitioners develop the knowledge base to find out which crisis intervention protocol is most likely to lead to positive outcomes and crisis resolution among clients in crisis (Roberts & Yeager, 2004).

Evidence-based practice places necessary emphasis on the crisis clinician's use of empirically validated lethality assessments, intervention protocols, and program evaluation procedures, as well as the use of critical thinking in making decisions (Roberts & Yeager, 2004). Professional judgments should be systematically grounded in empirical research, and each client should be carefully assessed to determine the degree to which predicted outcomes have been attained. This needs to be accomplished in the preferred practice setting while taking into account the relevant technology such as utilizing the Internet. The expectation for evidence-based practice needs to be combined with maximizing client independence such as honoring requests to die in the most natural setting possible, the home (Jack et al., 2013). In a crisis situation, when assessing and treating suicidality in acute care settings such as the emergency room, the provision of brief treatment, especially involving the family, is best practice (Wharff, Ginnis, & Ross, 2012). A number of challenges can occur when practitioners utilize the Internet, and addressing these challenges requires a new skill set with regard to crisis intervention best practices. In order to clearly assist the client and his or her family, synchronous modes of assessment are necessary. In addition, assessing lethality and other types of assessment will always require constant updating reflective of the latest research in order to determine the optimum evidence-based approaches (National Association of Social Workers [NASW], 2007).

This subjectivity makes the task of establishing therapeutic effectiveness and efficiency a complicated one (Dziegielewski, 2014; Dziegielewski & Roberts, 2004). In an effort to formulate the evaluation process, it is useful to first identify two basic assumptions that underlie counseling efforts in the area of crisis management and intervention, and then discuss why they can complicate the measurement of intervention outcomes.

First, in time-limited intervention of any type, most practitioners agree that the main effect of therapy is not curative but rather one that directs, facilitates, and accelerates the pace of client progress toward change. Not only is the experience considered noncurative, but it must also be focused on a homeostatic balance that may or may not result in profound changes. When this is coupled with the requirement of an immediate response, time-limited service delivery becomes the primary mode for engaging best practices. This makes early and brief intervention a consistent requirement, especially because clients typically remain in treatment fewer than six sessions (Dziegielewski, 2013). Therefore, crisis intervention strategies need to create a homeostatic balance that supports and stabilizes clients, as well as helping them develop new coping strategies that allow for adjustment to the situational experience.

Second, crisis is itself a multifaceted phenomenon that does not respond readily to traditional forms of therapeutic measurement and evaluation. In addition, those who encounter extremely stressful life circumstances do not uniformly experience crisis situations in the same way. The nature, extent, and intensity of any given crisis are, in large measure, products of the individual's construction of the social reality. The intervention and the methods used to evaluate it often constitute the blueprint that guides the data collection efforts and must vary accordingly. In the absence of any compelling evidence in support of long-term therapy as a more effective mode of practice, crisis intervention as a unique form of brief, time-limited intervention is often preferred (Ghahramanlou-Holloway, Cox, & Greene, 2012). Crisis intervention as a time-limited therapy may actually accelerate treatment efficacy as time frames are clearly and openly established and agreed upon between the client and the counselor.

## THE IMPORTANCE OF INTEGRATING RESEARCH AND PRACTICE

Helping professionals who routinely work with victims (or survivors) of crises report that there are several factors that seem to be common to virtually all crisis situations. The first of these factors is the acknowledgment that the crisis situation often brings about a time-limited disequilibrium that must be addressed in order for the client to reach a homeostatic balance (Roberts & Dziegielewski, 1995). This perceived disequilibrium associated with crisis can serve as a powerful motivational force where the individual becomes open and ready for change. When faced with a crisis, the client is often more willing to question previous ways of coping, and thus to explore new or alternative ways of addressing situations that prior to the crisis would not have been considered acceptable. This renders the client more open to trying new courses of action for therapeutic intervention that can facilitate the planning of concrete goals and objectives. All of this is entirely consistent with a strengths perspective in which clients are believed to already possess the resources necessary to address stressful situations. They simply are not using them, are underutilizing them, or are currently unaware of how to best use them on their own behalf.

By nature, a crisis situation and the attendant reactions are self-limiting. Beginning with Lindemann's (1944) initial formulation of crisis intervention in his now classic study of the Coconut Grove Nightclub disaster, crises have been characterized as time-limited phenomena that inevitably get resolved one way or another (with or without professional help) in a relatively brief period. It is the client's desire to resolve the crisis by moving forward as a way to avoid the pain he or she is feeling. This uncomfortable state pushes the client forward heightening his/her motivation for change thereby creating an environment supportive of positive and sometimes dramatic therapeutic results.

Given this narrow window of vulnerability to change, it is considered essential that clients who experience crisis must be provided immediate assistance to maximize the potential for constructive growth. The intervention process includes ongoing tasks (assessment, safety, and support) that are monitored throughout the intervention and must be monitored by therapists working with clients in crisis. The tasks include assisting the client to regain control of the circumstances, defining the problem, and following up with the therapist to monitor progress. In light of the disorganized nature of a crisis, the client may make progress and then experience regression due to the existential angst endemic in crisis situations (Myer, Lewis, & James, 2013).

According to Gilliland and James (2013) and other professionals in the area, positive life changes can be achieved following a crisis. Furthermore, the way a client handles a present crisis may have a profound and lasting impact not only on the individual's current adjustment but also on his or her capacity to cope with future crisis situations. From a research perspective, this suggests that practitioners should seek to understand and accurately explain the intervention approach being implemented. In addition, it is important to accurately identify the expected impact of the intervention and the anticipated adaptive responses. Unless outcome measures are clearly defined in operational terms, it is difficult to determine whether the intervention goals and objectives have been attained. The goals and objectives, in turn, must clearly be linked to positive life changes and methods of coping that enhance continued client functioning. Consequently, the central task of outcome-based research is to measure the presence and magnitude of both immediate and long-term changes that result from the counseling process.

## THE ROLE OF THE PRACTITIONER IN EVIDENCE-BASED PRACTICE

From a clinical perspective, some of the important limitations associated with many of the studies that have traditionally compared short- and long-term intervention methods remain. In establishing an evidence-based basis for crisis intervention, similar to other forms of practice, one primary limitation rests in the fact that the independent variable cannot be adequately addressed in a clear, homogeneous fashion. Furthermore, although a variety of suicide interventions have been assessed, there are few systematic reviews outlining their effectiveness in the literature (HEN Synthesis Report, 2012). Without clear comparisons, the lack of information related to the particulars of a study sample such as information related to individual differences among clinicians and their treatment approaches, will go undocumented. Limited attention is given to ensuring that those who provide crisis intervention services have been adequately trained. It is assumed that all practitioners have the same effect on client progress. This lack of attention to measuring the relative effectiveness of the social worker can lead to myths that support some sort of global and homogeneous index of client improvement.

These "uniformity myths," as Kiesler (1966) originally coined them, deflect attention from possible important individual differences both within and between groups of clients and therapists who treat them. In 2006, Roberts and Everly, after completing a meta-analysis of 36 studies related to the effectiveness of crisis intervention strategy, found that when including critical incident stress management debriefing, improvement for individuals and families was noted, yet no direct connection was made to the influence that the therapist may have had on the process. When reporting effectiveness of treatments, there still appears to be an emphasis on providing information related to the long-term or continuous impact on which method works better than another, with limited information related to individual differences. The question remains, in determining treatment effectiveness and best practices, is it really possible for "one size to fit all" or in this case "one method to fit all." Simply stated, the critical issues to be addressed are essentially no different now than they were when Paul (1966) first issued his now famous dictum: "What treatment, by whom, is most effective for this individual with that specific problem, and under which set of circumstances?" (p. 111).

The purpose of this chapter is to present clinically grounded research models that are relevant for those in crisis situations and that remain sensitive to the three major variables of the therapeutic paradigm: the client, the social worker as a researcher/practitioner, and the outcome. Against a general background of group design, or nomothetic, research, we consider several evaluation models, all of which Chassan (1967) described in his classic work and others have referred to as "intensive" or "idiographic" designs. When used alone, none of these methods are foolproof. Together, however, they provide a useful set of assessment tools that can help social workers evaluate the efficacy of their practice and improve the quality of the services they provide. Once this background is provided, the other chapters in this text will clearly relate it to crisis intervention strategy outlining the use of Roberts's (1991, 1995) seven-stage crisis intervention model.

## MACRO AND MICRO ANALYSES IN CRISIS INTERVENTION

Over the years, a variety of measurement strategies have been employed in an effort to assess various dimensions of the crisis intervention process. When viewed as a whole, they provide an intriguing array of designs ranging from macro to micro levels of analysis. When effectiveness was measured from a macro perspective, these methods focused primarily on epidemiological data collected by local, regional, and national organizations. From this perspective, studies can compare suicide rates before and after the implementation of a particular intervention program. Other studies employed quasi-experimental designs in which similar populations of treated and untreated suicide attempters were compared. In still other studies, cohorts of treated clients were compared with population parameters based on data derived from the National Center for Health and Statistics in the United States. There are serious methodological problems inherent in the use of extant data, however, especially with respect to threats to internal validity as well as comparability across idiosyncratic samples. In an effort to address some of these apparent weaknesses, client or caller satisfaction methods are sometimes used to help validate client perceptions and support the intrinsic worth of the study. Based on these macro types of analyses, many suicide programs and crisis intervention services have failed to gather the kinds of information necessary to adequately establish program effectiveness (HEN Synthesis Report, 2012). Without such information, it is impossible to determine whether negative findings are the result of inadequacies in the practice theory or liabilities in the research methodology. For questions like this, there are no easy answers.

Because crisis is by nature a dynamic and multifaceted phenomenon, the measurement process can be complicated, particularly when it is done on an aggregate basis or when relying primarily on secondary sources. Studies that rely exclusively on self-report can also be problematic. Therefore, regardless of how data are collected (via a database, support lines, or self-report), crisis intervention strategies represent multifaceted perspectives that consistently pose challenging assessment problems for the professional practitioner.

Some practitioners have argued that the most effective way to assess the efficacy of practice interventions at the micro level is to focus the evaluation lens on the idiosyncratic interactions that take place between the worker and the client (Bloom, Fischer, & Orme, 2009). This approach typically combines both quantitative and qualitative methods that rely heavily on the client's personal constructions of the crisis experience. Such methods tend to minimize threats to internal validity, but they raise serious questions with respect to generalizability. In focusing on the rich detail of the client-worker transactions and subsequent outcomes, the search for scientifically objective generalizations is abandoned in favor of in-depth insights that can be attained only by exploring the individual case as it is subjectively experienced. Toward this end, the worker can employ a variety of evaluation strategies. It is generally agreed that no single measure can adequately capture all the relevant subtleties of the crisis intervention process. As a result, Denzin (2012) and others clearly outline the controversies in using multiple measures and ultimately encourage their use. Through an evaluation strategy referred to as *triangulation*, it is believed workers can arrive at a reasonably accurate approximation of what is actually going on in the intervention process.

When addressing service effectiveness on a much smaller scale or with a more individualized focus, the micro level of *intervention* becomes the primary locus of attention. For example, from a micro perspective, issues such as individual worker influences and the subsequent treatment effectiveness that results become paramount. To highlight this perspective, skills are sometimes measured through simulated calling experiences or formalized role-plays. In an attempt to quantify this more micro perspective, using specific measurement instruments designed to directly measure the skill of the worker is essential. When dealing with suicide prevention, these authors also suggest that one such instrument that may be utilized is the Suicide Intervention Response Inventory (SIRI-2), designed to measure forced responses of the professional helper in the crisis intervention setting. In fact, a variety of useful rapid assessment instruments have been designed and tested for use in crisis situations, including indices that measure life stress, negative expectations, depression, problem-solving behaviors and attitudes, personality characteristics, and other, similar traits associated with psychiatric conditions, as well as other relevant crisis-related phenomena (see Fischer & Corcoran, 2007a, 2007b). The micro approach not only invites the use of these indices for the measurement of crisis behaviors but virtually mandates it. However, the authors of these instruments recommend caution in their use. They recognize that the evaluation of a crisis situation is a multifaceted undertaking that cannot be adequately assessed if one relies solely on a single instrument or focuses on a single dimension such as the worker's effectiveness. Overall, these authors warn that there is a paucity of literature from both a macro and a micro perspective. Very few systematic reviews address outcome-based measurement involving the evaluation of crisis intervention in general or suicide prevention services (HEN Synthesis Report, 2012).

## PREREQUISITES TO EFFECTIVE EVALUATION

Each of the chapters in this handbook discusses the application of crisis intervention strategies utilizing Robert's (1991) seven-stage crisis intervention model with a different population at risk. Although treatment strategies can have much in common with respect to many of the technical characteristics of the crisis intervention process, it is clear that there is wide variability regarding various dimensions of the short-term therapeutic experience. Crisis experiences can vary in terms of the identified problem, the client's reaction, the social worker's handling of the situation, the surrounding circumstances, and the expected outcome. Although some researchers have historically utilized the classical pretest-posttest design to measure practice effectiveness (Dziegielewski, 1991), the challenges in utilizing such complicated designs can be problematic. Similarly, when utilizing single-subject designs, so much of the information related to the success of the design is related to visualization (Nugent, 2010). Therefore, all designs can be considered somewhat flawed in reaching conclusions that clearly outline performance, leading to either misrepresentation or under- or overrepresentation of the actual effect of the study and the subsequent conclusions drawn.

In discussing the need for specificity in conducting outcome research and thereby measuring best practices, it is essential to break down problems into specific sets of measures and operations that clearly outline the specific indicators and the progress made (Dziegielewski, 2013). With crisis intervention, identifying progress indicators must always remain situation specific. This makes measuring this concept complicated because techniques that evaluate crisis situations require an intimate understanding of the crisis counselor's interpretations, the client's perception, the stage of the crisis, and so on. This requires that the resulting assessment must also reflect the multifaceted aspects of the identified problem behaviors. In viewing crisis intervention from an empirical standpoint, the various dimensions of the intervention experience need to be treated as a complex network of functional relationships within which there occurs a series of interactions among the primary factors (i.e., the independent and dependent variables). Simply stated, in any functional relationship, the independent variables operate as the presumed causes, and the dependent variables operate as the presumed effects. Therefore, in crisis intervention, an important first step in the evaluation process is to sort out what are believed to be the causal connections operating in any given crisis situation. This involves identifying a series of interdependent and crisis-period-specific problem-solving steps that logically flow from the presenting problem. Embedded in the logic of this problem-solving process is an implied hypothesis, the calculus of which can be stated as follows:

> In crisis situations, if X (e.g., suicide prevention service) is employed as an intervention strategy (i.e., the independent variable), then it is expected that Y (i.e., a return to previous functioning level) will be the predicted outcome (i.e., the dependent variable).

Crisis intervention is no different from any other form of intervention. Inevitably, it involves, in one way or another, the testing of this implied hypothesis. For example, when residential crisis services can serve as a preventive measure for those in crisis, limiting hospitalization and increasing stabilization would constitute specific steps to outline a plan of action. Teague, Trabin, and Ray (2004) identified and discussed key concepts and common performance indicators and measures that should lead to accountability in behavioral health care. The Adult Mental Health Workgroup (AMHW) is a nationally representative group jointly sponsored by the Carter Center in Atlanta and the Substance Abuse and Mental Health Services Administration's Center for Mental Health Services and Center for

Substance Abuse treatment. Based on the consensus of five work groups, AMHW recently developed measures and outcomes for key aspects of quality and appropriate behavioral treatment. Examples of performance indicators are as follows:

> Treatment duration—Mean length of service during the reporting period for persons receiving services in each of three levels of care: inpatient/24-hour, day/night structured outpatient programs, and ambulatory; and

> Follow-up after hospitalization—Percent of persons discharged from 24-hour mental health inpatient care who receive follow-up ambulatory or day/night mental health treatment within 7 days. (Teague et al., 2004, p. 59)

Evidence-based practice requires that the clinician-researcher specify clearly what it is he or she intends to do with or on behalf of the client, as well as the expected consequences of those actions. To do this, both the intervention and the outcome must be defined in operational or measurable terms. To say that emotional support will result in enhanced client self-esteem, or that ventilation will reduce depression, although on the surface both may appear very important in practice, simply is not an adequate statement of a testable hypothesis. As is true in all time-limited interventions, practitioners need to continue to state clearly what is meant by concepts such as "emotional support" and "ventilation" and must relate these directly to how improvement or at least some degree of relief will be noted.

Based on this premise, Hartman and Sullivan (1996) were among the first to outline specific objectives for center staff working in residential crisis services. They maintain that the key objectives include stabilizing crisis situations efficiently by reducing presenting symptoms; maintaining or reducing the frequency of hospitalizations or preadmission levels; helping consumers return to previous levels of satisfaction and service, such as housing and vocational status; and attaining high levels of consumer satisfaction with services.

Although the task of operationally defining concepts is not an easy one, most researchers concur that it is essential to the effective evaluation of empirically based practice, regardless of one's theoretical orientation (Monette et al., 2005). Furthermore, the value and subsequent recognition of our clinical practice efforts will prove to be only as good as the empirical observations on which they are based.

## MEASURING GOALS AND OBJECTIVES

The time-limited nature of crisis intervention services presents some interesting challenges for the clinician who wishes to evaluate his or her practice. From the very outset, clients in crisis need to be convinced that change is possible and that they are capable of contributing to the change process. In so doing, they gain confidence and competence, attributes that should be mirrored in the behavior of the helping professional. The development of this mutual respect and confidence in one another's abilities provides the necessary foundation for both practice and its evaluation. Basically, no matter what evaluation strategy one employs, it is likely to be meaningful only if it is initiated early and brought to closure fairly quickly. In addition, the methodology itself should not be experienced by the client as being in any way intrusive to the helping process. Ideally, the purposes of both the intervention and the evaluation should be compatible and mutually supportive.

This mutuality of purpose can be facilitated by the social work professional not only by helping the client to participate in the development of appropriate treatment goals but also by enabling the client to stay task oriented in regard to pursuing them. The social work professional can facilitate this process by helping the client establish specific and limited goals (Dziegielewski, 2013). Simply stated, a *goal* may be defined as the desirable objective that is to be achieved as a result of treatment. Well-stated goals permit the practitioner to determine whether he or she has the skills and desire to work with the client (Cormier, Nurius, & Osborn, 2013).

To be effective, intervention goals need to be as behaviorally specific as possible. The more precisely they are defined in measurable terms, the easier it is to verify if and when they are achieved. Once defined, the goals may be further refined in terms of more specific immediate, intermediate, and long-term objectives. Second, both the helping professional and the client should mutually agree on all goals and objectives. This may seem difficult during times of crisis, particularly when the helping professional is required to assume a very active role to help the client meet his or her own needs. This role, however, should always be one of facilitation in which the client is helped to achieve what he or she has deemed essential to regain an enhanced homeostatic balance (Dziegielewski, 2013). Only the client can determine whether the goals and objectives sought are consistent with his or her own culture and values. It is up to the social worker to help the client structure and establish the intervention strategy; however, emphasis on mutuality is central to the development of goals and objectives.

Social workers have long realized the value of goal setting as a means of facilitating the intervention process. With the advent of managed care, however, pressures from both within and outside the profession have heightened awareness of the importance of documenting outcomes. A new performance standard has been established, one that requires practitioners to have mastered the technical skills necessary to evaluate the efficacy of their intervention strategies. For empirically based practice to be meaningful, social workers must be capable of establishing the kind of practice climate in which programmatic goals, and the specific objectives designed to meet them, are viewed as realistic, obtainable, and measurable. Given the complexities of contemporary practice, however, no one methodological approach is likely to prove appropriate for all types of crisis situations. The research challenge for crisis workers, as it is inevitably for practice in general, is to fit the method to the problem, and not vice versa. This requires a thoughtful selection of research strategies, the various threads of which can be creatively woven throughout the broader fabric of the overall intervention plan.

## Goal Attainment Scaling

One evaluation model that has historically gained attention and can continue to be utilized is Goal Attainment Scaling (GAS; McDougall & Wright, 2009). This type of scaling was originally introduced by Kiresuk and Sherman (1968) as a way of measuring programmatic outcomes for community mental health services and remains adaptable to a wide range of crisis intervention situations. It is discussed here as an example of an evaluation model that combines a number of very useful idiographic as well as nomothetic methodological features.

GAS employs a client-specific technique designed to provide outcome information regarding the attainment of individualized clinical and social goals. In today's practice environment, insight-oriented intervention strategy remains limited. Therefore, these types of highly structured scaling methods, with their clear conceptualization and methodology, will continue to be needed for practice survival in today's coordinated care environment (Simmons & Lehmann, 2013). The structured nature of crisis intervention, organized around the attainment of limited goals with concretely specified objectives, articulates especially well with the methodological requisites of standardized measures such as GAS.

GAS requires that a number of individually tailored intervention goals and objectives be specified in relation to a set of graded scale points ranging from the *least* to the *most* favorable outcomes considered likely. It is suggested that at least 2 of the 5 points composing the Likert-type scale be defined with sufficient specificity to permit reliable judgments with respect to whether the client's behavior falls at, above, or below a given point. Numerical values are then assigned to each point, with the least favorable outcome scored –2, the most favorable outcome scored +2, and the outcome considered most likely assigned a value of 0. The net result of this scaling procedure is a transformation of each outcome into an approximate random variable, thus allowing the overall attainment of specific goals to be treated as standard scores, a feature that becomes important when GAS is used for program evaluation purposes.

This process is operationalized in the form of goal attainment. For example, the intervention objectives for a particular suicidal client may include (a) the elimination of suicidal ideation, (b) the alleviation of depression, and

(c) the enhancement of self-esteem. Table 27.1 illustrates how these goals might be defined in terms of expected outcomes that are relevant to a specific client. Although goals can be tailored to each client's needs, Garwick and Lampman's *Dictionary of Goal Attainment Scaling* (1973) is available to assist clinicians in their efforts to operationally define goals and construct Goal Attainment Guides.

Although dated, the definitions contained in the *Goal Attainment Guide* continue to be relevant to today's behavioral-based, outcome-focused practice environment, structured as it is with a specific time frame in mind. It can also be used with other measures such as the International Classification of Functioning Disability and Health-Child and Youth (ICF-CY) to work with pediatric clients (McDougall & Wright, 2009) or the World Health

Table 27.1   Sample Goal Attainment Guide Illustrating Scaling Procedure for Hypothetical Suicidal Client

| Levels of Expected Attainment | Goals | | |
|---|---|---|---|
| | Suicide Weight: 40 | Depression Weight: 20 | Self-Esteem Weight: 10 |
| Least favorable outcome thought likely (−2) | Commits suicide or makes additional suicidal attempt(s). | | |
| Less than expected success (−1) | Preoccupied with thoughts of suicide as a possible solution to personal problems; says "life is not worth living." | Complains of being very depressed all the time; eating and sleeping patterns irregular; cries daily; not working. | Considers self a "bad person"; criticizes self; feels people would be better off without him or her. |
| Expected level of success (0) | Occasionally thinks about suicide but is able to consider alternative solutions to personal problems. | Complains of being depressed all the time; eats at least two meals a day; sleeps at least 6 hours a night; cries occasionally; misses work occasionally. | Does not verbally criticize self but says he or she is not very happy. |
| More than expected success (+1) | | Only occasional feelings of depression; eating and sleeping regularly; no longer crying; working regularly. | |
| Most favorable outcome thought likely (+2) | No longer considers suicide a viable solution to personal problems; talks of future plans. | | Reports he or she likes self and way of living and/or reports being "reasonably happy." |

Organization, Disability Assessment Scale (WHO-DAS) outlined in the fifth edition of the *Diagnostic and Statistical Manual of Mental Disorders* (*DSM-5*; American Psychiatric Association, 2013). The definitions for the expected level of success (i.e., the midpoint of the 5-point scale) represent clinical predictions concerning client performance at some predetermined future date (e.g., 4 or 6 weeks after the formulation of the goals; Lambert & Hill, 1994). The amount and direction of goal attainment can then be measured by comparing baseline functioning with the level of functioning recorded on the identified target date. A check mark is used to record the initial performance level, and an asterisk is used to record performance at the point of follow-up. The guide can be revised at follow-up to reflect new goals or anticipated changes in the performance levels of existing goals. Although goals and objectives are sometimes used synonymously in treatment records, in the context of GAS, they function as benchmarks in relation to which the outcome variables are identified and measured. Specific weights can also be assigned to each goal or objective as a way of reflecting its relative importance or priority in the overall intervention plan. Because weighting represents a relative rather than an absolute indicator of importance, however, the sum need not equal 100 or any other fixed total. The actual numerical value of the assigned weight is of significance only when GAS is used as a basis for comparing the relative effectiveness of alternative intervention approaches within or between programs.

The computing of GAS scores can be a simple or a complex matter, depending on the purposes for which the evaluation methodology is to be used. When employed as a program evaluation technique, which relies on the availability of aggregate data, it is appropriate that composite standardized scores be derived. This is a fairly complex process requiring some statistical sophistication. When used as a framework for the evaluation of a single case (e.g., individual, family, or group), however, the process is much less complicated. In fact, the only meaningful determination is whether or to what extent the predicted goals have been attained. For those who prefer to quantify such judgments, it is possible to derive a composite score by determining the amount and direction of change occurring in relation to each goal and then summing their respective contributions. An average attainment score can be calculated simply by dividing the composite score by the total number of goals. This makes it possible to compare attainment levels across clients while controlling for the number of goals.

Any number of goals may be specified for a particular client, and any subject area may be included as an appropriate goal. Even the same goal can be defined in more than one way. For example, the goal of alleviating depression may be scaled in relation to self-report or in relation to specific cutoff points on a standardized instrument such as the Beck Depression Inventory (Beck, 1967). It is essential, however, that all goals be defined in terms of a graded series of verifiable expectations in ways that are relevant to the idiosyncrasies of the particular case.

It should be emphasized that the use of GAS as a framework for the intensive study of a single case does not warrant inferences concerning causal relationships between intervention and outcome. In fact, by stressing the importance of outcome factors, it tends to deflect attention away from concern for issues directly involving interventions. Although it cannot be concluded that the identified intervention is necessarily responsible for the attainment of goals, when expected goals are not realized, it does raise serious questions concerning the efficacy of the intervention strategy. In addition, the construction of a Goal Attainment Guide can serve as a useful rallying point around which practitioners and clients can negotiate the particulars of an intervention contract, including the formulation of objectives, the establishment of priorities, and the assignment of responsibilities. In summary, GAS is an example of how goal and objective attainment can be specified in order to monitor, organize, and aid as a means for collecting information on the assessment process to establish empirically based practice (Hart, 1978).

GAS suffers from many of the same limitations as other systems of measurement that are designed to treat data that are inherently ordinal in nature as if they possessed the characteristics of an interval or ratio scale. Researchers have modified the original version of GAS to fit local conditions. Therefore, any consideration of it as a single system of measurement would be misleading (Lambert & Hill, 1994). Nevertheless, measurement vehicles such as GAS can provide a systematic yet flexible practice evaluation model that can help bridge the methodological gap between clinical and administrative interests.

## USING MEASUREMENT INSTRUMENTS

Once the goals and objectives of intervention have been established, the difficult task of evaluating the clinical intervention in standardized or operationally based terms can be addressed. This task is simplified greatly when problems are articulated in terms of realistic goals and operationally defined objectives rather than in vague and nebulous language. Terms such as *stress, anxiety,* and *depression* are often used to describe important facets of a client's social-psychological functioning. Although commonplace in our professional jargon, such terms tend to carry rather subjective connotations. This semantic elusiveness makes it very difficult to establish reliable measures of change.

Measuring practice effectiveness, as stated earlier, typically involves a process designed to determine whether or to what extent mutually negotiated goals and objectives have been met. Change is documented through some type of concrete measurement that is indicative of client progress. Dziegielewski (2013, 2014) suggests that this process can be greatly facilitated by establishing clear-cut contracts with clients, who, in turn, provide a viable foundation for a variety of individual or group evaluation designs. Once the contract is in place, standardized instruments can be used as repeated measures to gather consistent data from baseline through termination and follow-up. It is the responsibility of the social work professional, of course, to select, implement, and evaluate the appropriateness of the measurement instruments. Most professionals agree that standardized scales (i.e., those that have been assessed for reliability and validity) are generally preferred.

In recent years, social workers have begun to rely more heavily on standardized instruments in an effort to achieve greater accuracy and objectivity in their attempts to measure some of the more commonly encountered clinical problems. The most notable development in this regard has been the emergence of numerous brief pencil-and-paper assessment devices known as rapid assessment instruments (RAIs). As standardized measures, RAIs share a number of characteristics. They are brief; they are relatively easy to administer, score, and interpret; and they require very little knowledge of testing procedures on the part of the clinician. For the most part, they are self-report measures that can be completed by the client, usually within 15 minutes. They are independent of any particular theoretical orientation and as such can be used with a variety of intervention methods. Because they provide a systematic overview of the client's problem, they often tend to stimulate discussion related to the information elicited by the instrument itself. The score that is generated provides an operational index of the frequency, duration, or intensity of the problem. Most RAIs can be used as repeated measures and thus are adaptable to the methodological requirements of both research design and goal assessment purposes. In addition to providing a standardized means by which change can be monitored over time with a single client, RAIs can also be used to make equivalent comparisons across clients experiencing a common problem (e.g., marital conflict).

One of the major advantages of standardized RAIs is the availability of information concerning reliability and validity. *Reliability* refers to the stability of a measure; in other words, do the questions that compose the instrument mean the same thing to the individual answering them at different times, and would different individuals interpret those same questions in a similar manner? Unless an instrument yields consistent data, it is impossible for it to be valid. But even highly reliable instruments are of little value unless their validity can also be demonstrated. *Validity* speaks to the general question of whether an instrument does in fact measure what it purports to measure.

There are several approaches to establishing validity, each of which is designed to provide information regarding how much confidence we can have in the instrument as an accurate indicator of the problem under consideration. Levels of reliability and validity vary greatly among available instruments, and it is very helpful to the practitioner to know in advance the extent to which these issues have been addressed. Information concerning reliability and validity, as well as other factors related to the standardization process (e.g., the procedures for administering, scoring, and interpreting the instrument), can help the professional make informed judgments concerning the appropriateness of any given instrument (Cook, 2006).

The key to selecting the best instrument for the intervention is knowing where and how to access the relevant information concerning potentially useful measures. Fortunately, a number of excellent sources are available to the clinician to help facilitate this process. One such compilation of standardized measures is *Measures of Clinical Practice* by Fischer and Corcoran (2007a, 2007b). These reference texts can serve as valuable resources for identifying useful RAIs suited for the kinds of problems most commonly encountered in clinical social work practice. Fischer and Corcoran continue to do an excellent job not only in identifying and evaluating a viable cross section of useful clinically grounded instruments but also in discussing a number of issues critical to their use. In addition to an introduction to the basic principles of measurement, these books discuss various types of measurement tools, including the advantages and disadvantages of RAIs. Fischer and Corcoran also provide some useful guidelines for locating, selecting, evaluating, and administering prospective measures. Further, the instruments are provided in two volumes in relation to their appropriateness for use with one of three target populations: adults, children, or couples and families. They are also cross-indexed by problem area, which makes the selection process very easy. The availability of these as well as numerous other similar references related to special interest areas greatly enhances the social work professional's options with respect to monitoring and evaluation practice.

The RAIs can serve as valuable adjuncts for the social worker's evaluation efforts. In crisis intervention, however, more emphasis on their utility is needed. To date, the reviews and acceptance of this type of assessment tool have been mixed. For example, in the area of suicide risk, Joiner, Van Orden, Witte, and Rudd (2009) suggest that professionals familiar with such instruments tended to use them only infrequently. Many of these same professionals believed that, when RAIs were used specifically to quantify behaviors and feelings in times of crisis, their utility was limited. Until these perceived shortcomings have been resolved, RAIs should probably be employed only as one aspect of a more comprehensively triangulated evaluation strategy.

One of the more notable deficits cited in the evaluation literature related to crisis intervention is the paucity of studies that look directly at social work practitioner effectiveness. This type of introspective practice assessment is intentionally designed to provide social workers with the kinds of timely feedback they need to enable them to modify and refine their techniques and strategies for future use in similar cases. Several scales and other concrete measurement indices have been designed to assist the social worker to do this (Fischer & Corcoran, 2007a, 2007b).

Last, to further enhance the measurement of practice effectiveness, many social workers are feeling pressured to incorporate additional forms of measurement as part of the treatment plan (Dziegielewski, 2013, 2014). The pressure to incorporate individual, family, and social rankings is becoming more common. This requires a procedure capable of monitoring a client's functioning level that can be clearly measured and documented. To provide this additional form of measurement, an increasing number of professionals when utilizing the *DSM-IV* and the *DSM-IV-TR* turned to the Generalized Assessment of Functioning (GAF) rating scores for each client served (American Psychiatric Association, 1995, 2000). In using this method, ratings of a client's functioning were assigned at the outset of therapy and again on discharge. The scale allowed for the assignment of a number that represents a client's behaviors. The scales are designed to enable the worker to differentially rank identified behaviors from 0 to 100, with higher ratings indicating higher overall functioning and coping levels. By rating the highest level of functioning a client has attained over the past year and then comparing it to his or her current level of functioning, helpful comparisons can be made. Although this measurement scale is not offered in the latest version of the DSM [*DSM-5*], it can still be of help to both quantify client problems and document observable changes that may be attributable to the counseling relationship. This measurement instrument allows the worker to track performance variations across behaviors relative to client functioning.

In addition, *DSM-IV/DSM-IV-TR* introduced two modified version of the GAF listed in the section titled "Criteria Sets and Axes Provided for Further Study." Although these two scales were never required to complete the diagnosis they can still provide a format for ranking function that might be particularly helpful to social work professionals. The first of these is the relational functioning scale termed the Global Assessment of Relational Functioning (GARF). This index is used to address the status of family or other ongoing relationships on a hypothetical continuum from *competent* to *dysfunctional* (American Psychiatric Association, 2000). The second index is the Social and Occupational Functioning Assessment Scale (SOFAS). With this scale, the individual's level of social and occupational functioning can be addressed (American Psychiatric Association, 2000). The complementary nature of these scales in identifying and assessing client problems is evident in the fact that all three scales (GARF, GAF, and SOFAS) use the same rating system. The rankings for each scale range from 0 to 100, with the lower numbers representing more severe problems. The use of all three of these tools has been encouraging for obvious reasons. Collectively, they provide a viable framework within which social workers can apply concrete measures to a wide variety of practice situations. They also provide a multidimensional perspective that permits workers to document variations in levels of functioning across system sizes, including the individual (GAF), family (GARF), and social (SOFAS) perspectives.

In *DSM-5*, published in May 2013, measurement, particularly in the area of reliability, is placed at the forefront (American Psychiatric Association, 2013). For this reason and due to the lack of reliability information available, the three scales mentioned earlier (GAF, GARF, and SOFAS) were not included in *DSM-5*. In DSM-5, the importance of specificity with a clear explanation of how the criteria for a diagnosis is met is highlighted. In this latest edition, identifying and measuring mental health–related behaviors is coupled with the cross-cutting of symptoms. This type of symptom measurement is designed provide a bridge from the primarily categorical assessment system of its predecessor (*DSM-IV-TR*) to a more dimensional one (Dziegielewski, 2015). From this perspective, the practitioner is encouraged to acknowledge the diagnostic criteria while documenting the cross-cutting or overlapping of symptoms. This emphasis allows for explication of the relationship between symptom characteristics of more than one disorder without the creation or addition of a second disorder. Assessing symptoms that can occur across diagnoses, referred to as the *cross-cutting* of symptoms, allows for the measurement of two levels of symptom assessment and rating. The first level involves a brief survey of 13 domains for measuring symptomology in adult patients and 12 domains for child and adolescent patients. The second level provides a more in-depth level of assessment of certain domains. To supplement the written text, *DSM-5* also offers some aspects of this second level of assessment for cross-cutting online at www.psychiatry.org/dsm5. The use of this measurement scale allows the practitioner to document all symptoms related to a primary diagnosis and any secondary symptoms, allowing for a stronger diagnostic assessment while avoiding an unnecessary label indicative of a second diagnosis (Dziegielewski, 2015).

In summary, it is obvious that the helping relationship is a complex one that cannot be measured completely through the use of standardized scales or social worker assessment measures. To facilitate measurement of effectiveness, specific concrete goals and objectives must incorporate a number of direct behavioral observation techniques, self-anchored rating scales, client logs, projective tests, Q-sort techniques, unobtrusive measures, and personality tests, as well as a variety of mechanical devices for monitoring physiological functioning. Together, these methods can provide a range of qualitative and quantitative measures for evaluating practice. Several of them are especially well suited for the assessment of practice based on the more phenomenological and existentially grounded theories. Space limitations do not permit a discussion of these methods in this chapter; however, there are a number of excellent sources that discuss in detail the kinds of information one would need to make informed decisions regarding their selection and application to specific cases (Rubin & Babbie, 2011).

## CASE-RELATED OR MICRO DESIGNS IN
## CRISIS INTERVENTION

As a specific type of micro-level design, intensive models are distinguished from extensive models of research because intensive models are primarily concerned with the study of single cases (i.e., $N = 1$). In this chapter, intensive models are referred to as *single-system* (Bloom et al., 2009), *single-subject*, and *single-case designs* (Nugent, 2010) and these terms are used more or less interchangeably. Preference is noted, however, for the terms *single-system* and *single-case designs* because they allow for a broader definition of the case under study rather than simply referring directly to one specific client as a subject.

We have chosen to highlight the single-system or single-case designs in crisis intervention, even though it has been argued that they add little to the confirmatory process that leads to scientific generalizations. The reason for this focus is simple: They are of enormous value to the scientifically oriented clinician interested in evaluating the effectiveness of his or her own practice interventions (Bloom et al., 2009). These intensive designs provide the means by which clinicians can evaluate the idiosyncratic aspects of their practice, while at the same time allowing for the generation of practice-relevant hypotheses suitable for testing via the more traditional extensive research approaches.

Further, it is important to note that the distinction between extensive and intensive models of research relate directly to the long-standing controversy regarding the relative merits of nomothetic versus idiographic research as originally differentiated by Allport (1962). Advocates of the nomothetic approaches emphasize the primacy of the confirmatory aspect of scientific activity, in which the ultimate goal is to discover the laws that apply to individuals in general. These researchers believe that the aggregate is of greater importance than are the individuals who compose it. As a result, nomothetists devote their time to the study of groups in an effort to confirm or disprove hypothetical statements and thus arrive at scientific generalizations concerning some aspect of the empirical world. In contrast, advocates of the idiographic approach tend to be more interested in the study of individuals as individuals. Rather than focusing their attention on the discovery of general propositions, they prefer to investigate the rich and intricate details of specific cases, including the deviant cases that prove to be exceptions to the rule. In crisis intervention, the acknowledgment of both approaches appears relevant, and both contribute to the cushion of knowledge that informs our practice. One should not be seen as superior to the other, and with some overlap they can prove to be complementary.

The intensive or idiographic models of research are emphasized here simply because they lend themselves more directly to the primary purposes of the clinician, that is, the assessment of the social worker's own practice on a case-by-case basis. There is no intent to discount the importance of the extensive or nomothetic approaches. In fact, the probability of success in practice is likely to increase to the extent that more social workers can participate in studies that involve controlled observation and systematic verification. In this sense, the two approaches are indeed complementary, one generating scientific generalizations under controlled circumstances and the other applying and evaluating their utility in the idiosyncratic crucible of practice.

Ideally, in measuring the effectiveness of any time-limited crisis situation, the clinician-researcher needs to be able to identify with confidence a causal relationship between the independent variable (i.e., the intervention) and the dependent variable (i.e., the target behavior). For the social worker it is problematic when extraneous variables (those not directly related to the intervention) occur and cannot be clearly identified and controlled during the therapeutic process. These extraneous variables represent competing hypotheses that could be conceived as possible causes of change in the target behavior. To the extent that this occurs, it raises serious questions with respect to the internal validity of the intervention, thus reducing the level of confidence warranted by any causal inferences that might be drawn.

The classic work by Campbell and Stanley (1966) clearly describes a number of possible design weaknesses that pose threats to internal validity. For social workers engaging in empirically based practice, knowledge of these factors is essential for measuring effective and efficient services. It is important to remember that when a practice design can effectively control the influences and subsequent contamination from outside (extraneous) variables, it is said to be valid. Single-case designs can offer the practitioner a means for measuring practice effectiveness and can vary widely with respect to their ability to accomplish this goal (Richards, Taylor, & Ramasamy, 2014).

## TIME-SERIES DESIGNS

The prototype for the intensive/idiographic model of practice research is the time-series design (Fischer, 1976). The process involves the measurement of change in some target behavior (usually the identified problem) at given intervals over a more or less extended period (Bloom et al., 2009). In this case, the successive observations made during the course of therapeutic intervention enable the clinician to systematically monitor the nature and extent of change in a target behavior. The actual observations and the recording of those observations may be done by the social worker, the client, or any other willing mediator with whom the client interacts on a regular basis, including, for instance, a family member, a friend, or a teacher.

Once a target behavior has been identified and an appropriate observational approach selected, it is a relatively simple matter to record any changes that occur during the course of intervention. The amount and direction of changes are usually portrayed in the form of a two-dimensional graph, as illustrated in Figure 27.1.

Basically, the practitioner identifies the target behavior and plots it in relation to gradations (in frequency, duration, or intensity) arranged along the vertical axis. Successive observations are similarly recorded at regular time intervals, as indicated along the horizontal axis. The points are then joined in a continuous line that reflects the pattern of behavioral change that has occurred over the intervention time period.

This type of graph creates a visual presentation of information that facilitates the display of client behavior change (Nugent, 2010). For example, if a client reports an inability or lack of desire to handle his or her own affairs after the death of a loved one it responses can be graphed providing a visual representation of the problem. When one is charting client responses, it would be expected that frustration and the inability to handle everyday affairs would decrease when given a subsequent intervention and this would be visually displayed on the graph. Conversely, if the intent were to increase activities of daily living and eventually eliminate any dysfunctional crisis-related behaviors, a visual display could also assist to show that the observed pattern was going in the opposite direction helping to show the changes as they occur in response to the intervention.

In all single-subject designs, the pre-intervention observation phase is referred to as the *baseline period* and generally labeled "A." The intent of the baseline is to determine whether the pattern of behavior observed during the baseline (i.e., Phase A) changes in the expected direction after the introduction of treatment (Phase B). If changes occur during intervention, then the social worker has some basis on which to infer that the treatment may have had something to do with it.

In working with clients in crisis, however, collecting baseline data in advance of treatment may not be practical because the necessity of an immediate intervention may negate the luxury of advance data collection. Furthermore, to delay initiation of treatment not only is likely to be viewed as theoretically questionable but also may pose serious ethical implications. In crisis, often the best one can expect with respect to the collection of baseline information may be a retrospective reconstruction of relevant data as reported by the client or some other available informant.

In some instances, as in the case of a suicidal individual, reliable pre-intervention data concerning the target behavior (i.e., desire to commit suicide) may not be possible. In such cases, pre-intervention data of a historical nature may be available from family members or friends or from archival records. In other instances, such as those involving work with AIDS patients and their families, the use of available data can prove to be a potentially

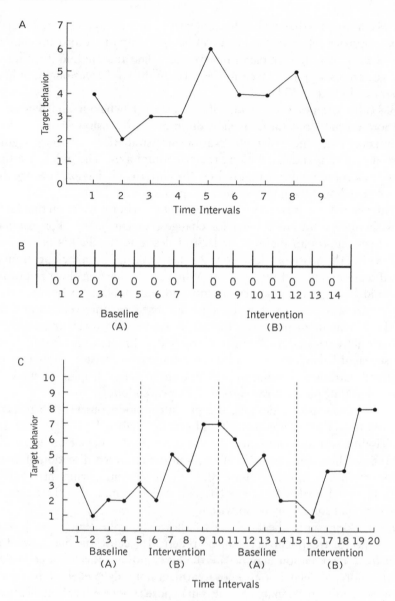

Figure 27.1    Changes in Target Behavior

valuable and reliable resource for the systematic reconstruction of important baseline information concerning the history of prior difficulties.

For example, Christ, Moynihan, and Gallo-Silver (1995) described the assessment process with someone who has recently been diagnosed with HIV infection. They defined a specific protocol to assist in gathering an expeditious and comprehensive assessment. The purpose of such a protocol is intended, in part, to document the incidences of current sexual activities and relationships as well as to use the information gathered to address past, current, or future potential for high-risk behaviors. To the extent that such "hard data" are systematically gathered and recorded in relation to specific high-risk behaviors, it may be possible to selectively exploit such information to create useful baseline measures. With some modifications, this strategy for collecting baseline information can be adopted by virtually any service delivery system that regularly interacts with clients who may subsequently be seen in a crisis situation.

It is apparent that the more rigorous the design, the more confidence one can have that threats to internal validity can be effectively ruled out. Unfortunately, the most rigorous designs require the use of baseline measures. Despite the limitations already noted, it is useful to understand some of the more sophisticated derivations of the time-series design. Although they may not always prove to be of practical value in the evaluation of particular crisis situations, they do provide useful models against which to compare the rigor of alternative approaches.

Two of the most commonly encountered variants of the basic time-series design are the reversal design and the multiple baseline approach (Bloom et al., 2009). In the reversal design, intervention is introduced for a prescribed period of time and then abruptly withdrawn, with the resulting circumstances essentially approximating pre-intervention or baseline conditions. In the absence of intervention, certain types of client behaviors might be expected to move in the direction of pre-intervention levels. When this occurs, it is generally considered to support a causal relationship, especially when treatment is subsequently reinstated $(A_1\text{-}B_1\text{-}A_2\text{-}B_2)$ with concomitant improvements in the client's functioning.

Suppose, for example, a clinician were employing cognitive therapy as a means of reducing anxiety associated with the inability to control violent tendencies. The theory supporting the use of this intervention assumes that the inability to control one's temper is escalated by irrational thoughts, which in turn inhibit self-control and justify violence as a course of action. The clinician employs cognitive techniques and observes an improvement in the client's self-control during the intervention phase $(B_1)$. The techniques are subsequently withdrawn, and the client returns to his or her former state of irrational thinking during the second baseline period $(A_2)$, with a concomitant increase in anxiety and potential fear over loss of control. This return to baseline conditions and ultimately to a second intervention phase provides the rationale for naming the process a reversal design. As can be seen by this example, reversal designs can be problematic, especially when the behavior one is exhibiting is dangerous to self or others. In this case, once the client's locus of control becomes questionable, immediate reinitiation of the treatment phase is warranted.

In a second type of design, the multiple baseline approach, like its A-B-A-B counterpart, is also used to minimize the possibility of behavior change due to chance. Unlike the reversal design, however, there is no withdrawal of intervention. Instead, baseline data are collected either on more than one target behavior, on the same target behavior but in more than one setting, or on more than one but similar clients. Intervention techniques are applied in a sequential manner so that once a change in the initial target behavior is observed, the intervention is systematically introduced with the next target behavior or in an alternative setting (Hardcastle, 2011; Bloom et al., 2009; Fischer, 1976).

The sequential nature of the multiple baseline approach is especially useful in client interventions where more than one problem must be addressed or there is more than one target behavior that is expected to be affected by the intervention. This is true in most crisis situations, where the precipitating events typically affect various aspects of the client's overall social-psychological functioning. It is important to keep in mind, however, that the validity of any multiple baseline approach is based on the assumption that the selected target behaviors are themselves independent of one another. If changes in one behavior were somehow functionally interdependent, use of the multiple baseline approach would be discouraged.

Both the A-B-A-B design and the multiple baseline approach begin to approximate the level of confidence achieved in what Campbell and Stanley (1966) refer to as "true experiments." However, they are the most difficult to implement and, with respect to the evaluation of crisis intervention, have only limited utility for the practical, ethical, and methodological reasons cited earlier.

A final note is in order before we conclude our discussion of the time-series designs. In most instances, it is possible to determine whether meaningful change has occurred by means of simple visual inspection of the two-dimensional graph. Sometimes, however, it is impossible to determine from visual inspection alone whether the shift that occurs between the baseline and the intervention phases is dramatic enough to constitute a significant change. Therefore, special attention needs to be given to whether the time-series data are serially dependent (Nugent, 2010). In cases in which the observed changes may be due to serial dependence, the worker can apply some fairly simple statistical procedures (referred to as *autocorrelation*) to help resolve the issue (Bloom et al., 2009).

## ALTERNATIVE MODELS

Thus far, we have discussed a number of basic time-series designs as prototype examples of intensive, idiographic, or micro-based models of practice research in crisis situations. In light of the identified limitations, a number of recommendations have emerged recently involving adaptations of the single-system model. When viewed collectively, they provide added flexibility with respect to the evaluation process. When used alone, they are not as methodologically rigorous as some of the more controlled designs. However, they do represent marked improvements over the methodologically soft or vague assessment techniques that typically characterize most efforts to evaluate social work practice. Most of the research strategies discussed here can be used in conjunction with various components of the more rigorous designs, thus providing a repertoire of techniques that can be used selectively in response to the idiosyncratic demands of a particular case. In addition, it is sometimes possible to employ several of the proposed evaluation strategies simultaneously within or across client systems. When this is done intentionally, it is referred to as *triangulation*, a process that enables the clinician to use each strategy as a means of cross-validating the findings generated by alternative strategies (Denzin, 2012; Howe, 2012).

In most crisis situations, there is a need for immediate clinical intervention. This inevitably makes the task of gathering relevant baseline data and the application of empirically based measures very difficult. Although direct observations of the client's pre-intervention or baseline functioning can be very useful, caution needs to be exercised to avoid the drawing of unwarranted conclusions (Hardcastle, 2011). Therefore, it is inappropriate to infer that any observed changes, which rely solely on the sample recording of repeated measures, are necessarily attributable to the social worker's intervention. Although positive (or negative) changes may occur concurrently with intervention, this approach does not permit us to rule out the possibility that other factors may be responsible for the observed change.

To address this limitation, a number of useful suggestions appear in the literature, including careful replication as a means of increasing causal validity utilizing geo-referencing technology with qualitative software (Fielding, 2012) and variations on the basic time-series design, including the use of baseline measures (Richards, Taylor, & Ramasamy, 2014). In such models, the series of observations used to monitor change in the target behavior begins prior to the introduction of any formal treatment and relies on an extended baseline with continuous measurements of the target behavior. It is worth noting, however, that extended baselines should not be relied on to control for many of the threats to causal validity. Only careful replication under controlled conditions can adequately address this limitation.

## INTERVENTION AND EVALUATION: INTEGRATING THE TWO

The process of integrating our social work interventions with appropriate evaluation strategies requires that the two functions complement one another in a seamless and synergistic manner. For many social workers, this

requirement has been both frustrating and confusing. Social work practitioners are increasingly being expected to operationalize the target behaviors
they wish to change in clients as part of the assessment process (Dziegielewski,
2013, 2014). Yet the link between their actual practice behaviors and the
strategies required to effectively assess them has proved to be elusive.

For example, in case planning, evidence-based practice dictates that the
problem statement, the behaviorally based goals and objectives, and the
accompanying intervention plan be clearly identified. To effectively implement
such a plan in an informed and sensitive manner, the social worker should be
well versed in the following procedures. Initially, it is essential that the worker
create a positive and supportive relationship with the client. This process is
greatly facilitated by the articulation of a set of mutually negotiated, realistic, and specific time-limited goals and objectives. These goals and objectives
should be clearly outlined in relation to the client's identified needs and capacities. Further, the social worker must be well aware of the personal, cultural,
and environmental dynamics that surround the crisis situation, as well as how
these dynamics may impact the problem-solving process. The social worker's
role is one of action and direction, particularly when individuals are in the
early phases of the crisis experience. It is essential to realize that for individuals in crisis, the usual methods of coping do not always appear to be working.
At times, clients may feel as though they are losing control and, as a result,
seek the active direction and involvement of the social worker.

Second, the social worker must also be aware of the unique set of characteristics embedded in the crisis situation and how those characteristics can
personally affect the social worker. The use of standardized methods, such
as RAIs, is essential in helping to quantify subjective aspects of the intervention; however, they should not be viewed as all-inclusive. They are often limited in utility by the very nature of the crisis situation itself. For example, an
RAI designed to measure depression may in fact prove quite reliable in measuring the symptoms associated with chronic depression. In crisis situations,
however, the development of depressive symptomology might indeed be
functional for a grieving widower or widow. The most appropriate approach
may be to allow the experience of losing a loved one to progress naturally.
In this instance, the dynamics that surround the crisis situation are somewhat atypical. Stated simply, the person who is depressed after a crisis (e.g.,
the loss of a loved one) may need to be treated very differently from the
individual who is experiencing depression based on a specific mental health
problem. As a situational factor, a reactive depression might actually prove
to be a positive step in the client's overall adjustment to the crisis situation.
Issues such as these, which are somewhat unique to crisis situations, can
complicate the use of RAIs. This ambiguity has encouraged social workers
to strive for other modes of formalized measurement. This has increased the
use of methods that require the client to rate stress and feelings of discontent
on instruments such as self-anchored rating scales. To further supplement

these efforts, scales such as the GAF, GARF, and SOFAS have also been used to assist in behaviorally based outcome measures. Overall, social workers are well advised to develop a range of measurement techniques that will enable them to operationally define the various dimensions of their practice.

Finally, if our goal is one of establishing empirically based practice, the importance of applying practice wisdom that is informed by theory cannot be overestimated. This requires not only that social workers be aware of what is likely to work for a particular client but also that they possess the theoretical knowledge necessary to justify the selection and application of appropriate intervention techniques. Theory informs practice by providing a plausible framework within which critical intervention and evaluation issues can be simultaneously raised and interpreted. The more we know about the theoretical underpinnings of any given problem-solving-focused counseling strategy, the better informed we will be in our efforts to predict and explain the possible consequences of the entire intervention process. As stated earlier, practice wisdom often dictates how best to proceed in helping a client, given the specific nature of the crisis situation and the surrounding circumstances. It can also help the practitioner decide when to apply or withdraw the various components of the treatment package throughout the course of the intervention process. Counseling and social work professionals are increasingly being called on to balance practice skills with empirical techniques, techniques that in the end will yield more efficient and effective modes of service. For the crisis intervention worker, the use of measurement devices, such as structured questionnaires and psychometric instruments, needs to be supplemented with practice wisdom, theory, and, in the final analysis, life experience (Fischer & Corcoran, 2007a). Although past approaches to crisis intervention have been evaluated, the increased range of services on the Internet provides many options that are difficult to evaluate. For instance, there are Internet therapies that include both synchronous and asynchronous modes of delivery. Some examples of asynchronous modes include e-mail exchanges between client and practitioner, journal writing, and blogs. Synchronous modes may include the use of webcams and Internet sources such as Skype, text chat, and virtual reality interventions that may include the use of avatars. There are self-diagnostic Internet sites that provide measurement and scaling tools. Social media provides social support through self-help and psychoeducational materials, and telemedicine interventions are available in rural and other areas.

## NEW SHIFTS WITHIN THE SERVICE DELIVERY SYSTEM

With the development of new technology, consumers of crisis mental health services have a number of options for intervention. Until the recent era,

most crisis intervention services were offered face-to-face, often with a practitioner meeting with an individual, family, or group at the same location.
With the development of the Internet, a range of communications methods
have emerged that many individuals have access to use during a crisis. The
literature related to evaluating crisis interventions through the wide range of
online services is in its infancy. This section of the chapter will present the
various features of online approaches and services to clients who might seek
Internet services.

Some choose to embrace their social support network using a range of
Internet technologies, including text messages, instant messaging, videoconferencing, and e-mail support. There are also a growing number
of online mental health practitioners who provide therapy over the web
(refer to Table 27.2 for some examples). Online mental health professionals offer a number of methods for treatment as well. Some of the therapeutic techniques include e-mail communication, videoconferencing,
asynchronous communication, instant messaging, and other forms of
telemedicine. The next sections of this chapter will address implications
of Internet therapy models, electronic medical documentation, online
measurement and scaling tools, social media, and web-based telemedicine interventions.

Table 27.2    Psychotherapy Online

| Website Title | Internet Address |
| --- | --- |
| ABC's of Internet Psychotherapy | http://www.metanoia.org/imhs/directry.htm |
| DMOZ Mental Health Directory (28 Directories) | http://www.dmoz.org/Health/Mental_Health/ Counseling_Services/Directories/ |
| eCounseling Websites | http://www.adca-online.org/links.htm |
| e Mental Health Center | http://www.e-mhc.com/ |
| Mental Health & Psychology Resources Online | http://psychcentral.com/resources/ |
| National Directory of Online Counselors | www.etherapyweb.com |
| Psychotherapy Online | http://psychology.about.com/od/ psychotherapy/a/onlinepsych.htm |
| Telemental Health Therapy Comparisons | http://www.telementalhealthcomparisons. com/?login=provider-networks |
| YAHOO Directory of Mental Health Resources | https://dir.yahoo.com/health/mental_health/ |
| Psychology.com Direction for How You Live | http://www.psychology.com/ |
| Psychology Today Mental Health Assessment | http://psychologytoday.tests.psychtests.com/ take_test.php?idRegTest=3040 |

## Implications of Internet Therapy

There are many interpretations as to what constitutes online or Internet therapy. One definition of online therapy that seems relevant to this discussion was developed by Rochlen, Zack, and Speyer (2004), who describe it as "any type of professional therapeutic interaction that makes use of the Internet to connect qualified mental health professionals and their clients" (p. 270). As technology has improved, there has been an increased use of synchronous modes using a webcam and an Internet source such as Skype. Initially, e-mail was the main modality, but currently numerous other delivery methods are available, including virtual reality, the use of avatars, Second Life (a three-dimensional virtual world), and text chat, to name a few (Barak & Grohol, 2011; Grohol, 2001, 2005, 2011.

Benefits of online work include convenience, disinhibition, reflection, and therapeutic writing (Rochlen, Zack & Speyer, 2004). Obstacles include missing visual cues if the therapist does not use teleconferencing tools, a response delay if one is using e-mail, not having direct personal contact if a client is in crisis and authenticating the client's identity (Rochlen, Zack & Speyer, 2004).

A paper by NASW (2007) titled Social Workers and e-Therapy provides a discussion on the implications of online therapy and social work practice. It discusses the possible use of telemedicine which allows a client, for example, located in a rural area to go to a local site to engage electronically with a therapist who is not at the same location. Other types of on-line therapy use telemedicine communications can include self-help groups and other types of psychoeducational services.

The NASW paper cites best practice requirements that include (a) submission of a pre-session information form, filled out by the client, that includes personal history and the client's treatment needs; (b) evidence that the practitioner is licensed; (c) the client's identifying information; (d) listing of the client's emergency contacts; (e) a directory of hyperlinks to a wide range of supportive Internet resources; and (f) the therapist's expectations regarding payment and treatment outcomes and limitations; and (g) privacy policies regarding the therapist's website. These important practice elements will make the experience more salubrious for both client and therapist. Lastly, the therapist would not characteristically provide services to a client who does not live in the state where the therapist is licensed to practice.

The preferred method of eTherapy, developed by Grohol (20114), is the exchange of e-mail between therapist and client. eTherapy, which is useful when working within a solution-focused model and is a method that assists persons in working through current issues of concern. eTherapy is not designed to provide a diagnosis of a mental disorder or treat a diagnosed mental or medical illness, rather, it is analogous to *coaching.* In coaching the emphasis is on working on the client's future and on the development of coping and other skills to enhance the client well-being. This method of therapy seems to have potential in working with people in crisis because it focuses on improved functioning for the present and the future by assisting clients to clarify their life situation and planning measurable and attainable goals. There are alternative interventions to eTherapy that include virtual reality, the use of avatars, e-mail, and text chat, to name a few (Grohol, 1999, 2011). A number of practitioners who practice online have a psycho-therapy focus (refer to Table 27.3 for a few examples of Internet resources).

## Electronic Medical Documentation

Over the past two decades, there has been increasing activity through the electronic media that is associated with medical documentation and crisis intervention. In addition, the growing use of electronic medical records has impacted how health providers document services (Jha, DesRoches, Kralovec, & Joshi, 2010). The use of basic or comprehensive electronic med-ical records in the industry has increased from 8.7% in 2008 to 11.9% in 2009 (Jha et al., 2010). Tsai and Bond (2008) reported that electronic medi-cal records reflected more complete medication documentation and were quicker to retrieve.

Although the use of electronic records may improve medication manage-ment for many patients, those diagnosed with schizophrenia were found to be lacking important information in all documentation formats. The use of forms with listings of items that the practitioner checks to indicate the client's symptoms has replaced past narrative forms of documentation, and although this trend began with paper documents, it has become standard in electronic medical documentation (e.g., Clements & Jacinto, 2014). Many practitioners use this format with brief notes at the bottom of the form to indicate diagnostic impression, recommended interventions, and client progress toward treatment goals.

With the introduction of encrypted medical records, confidentiality and the protection of sensitive information is increased (Jha et al., 2010; Tsai & Bond, 2008). Although electronic medical documentation has improved the delivery of services and the protection of client information, measurement and scaling tools produce a different challenge.

## Measurement or Scaling Tools

Prior to the introduction of the Internet, measurement and scaling tools were usually completed by using paper-and-pencil instruments or interview approaches. A number of online methods have been introduced in recent years (Metanoia.org, 2014; Patrick, 2011), and a growing number of online mental health therapy practitioners provide services, including counseling, psychotherapy, and crisis intervention, that offer assessment using diagnostic

Table 27.3    Internet Resources

| URL Site Name | Internet Address |
|---|---|
| American Association of Suicidology (Accredited Centers) | http://www.suicidology.org/crisis-centers |
| Big White Wall (Support Network) | http://www.bigwhitewall.com/landing-pages/default.aspx?ReturnUrl=%2f |
| Care Crisis Chat | http://www.crisischat.org/ |
| Common Ground | http://www.commonground.org/our-programs#.U2FviVcXLXx |
| Contra Costa Crisis Chat (California) | http://www.crisis-center.org/crisis-lines-chat-program/ |
| CrisisChat | http://www.crisischat.org/chat |
| Crisis Intervention Resources DHHS (Federal Resources) | http://healthfinder.gov/FindServcies/SearchContexst.aspx?topic=213&branch=6&show=1 |
| Crisisline Online (New York) | http://211lifeline.org/about-2-1-1life-line/ |
| Didi Hirsch Mental Health Services | http://www.didihirsch.org/chat |
| GLBT National Help Center Peer Support Chat | http://www.glnh.org/chat/index.html |
| TheHopeLine Live Coach Chat | http://unsuicide.wikispaces.com/The+HopeLine+Live+HopeCoach+Chat |
| IM Alive | https://www.imalive.org/ |
| Iowa Crisis Chat (English and Mandarin) | http://iowacrisischat.org/ |
| Mental Health Counselors Assn. (Resources) | http://www.amhca.org/public_resources/client_resources.aspx |
| Montana Warmline Chat | http://www.montanawarmline.org/Support.html |
| National Suicide Prevention Lifeline | http://www.suicidepreventionlifeline.org/ |
| RAINN Online Hotline (Rape, Abuse, Incest) | http://www.rainn.org/get-help/national-sexual-assault-online-hotline |
| Scarleteen (Online Sex Education Site) | http://www.scarleteen.com/ |
| Veteran's live Chat | http://veteranscrisisline.net/ChatTermsOfService.aspx |
| San Francisco Suicide Prevention | http://betterlifebayarea.org/live-chat |
| Suicide Forum (Chat Room) | http://www.suicideforum.com/ |
| Teen line Online | https://teenlineonline.org/ |
| 866 Teenlink | http://866teenlink.org/ |
| TrevorChat (LGBT) | http://www.thetrevorproject.org/pages/get-help-now |
| Warmline Chats (National Directory Listed By State) | http://www.warmline.org/ |
| Your Life, Your Voice (Youth) | http://www.yourlifeyourvoice.org/Pages/default.aspx |

instruments (About.com, 2014; Patrick, 2011). In addition to pathways that link clients to practitioners online, a number of self-diagnostic sites provide measurement instruments that are available online, such as an online mental health assessment tool that is provided through the *Psychology Today* website (*Psychology Today*, 2014). The instrument consists of 16 items that are focused on various mental health symptoms. Because there is limited opportunity for the person taking the test to selectively respond it may not be a good measure for an individual in an active crisis state.

A more useful instrument for those in an active crisis state is the Crisis Assessment Tool (CAT) Indiana Version (2002). This instrument is in the open domain and is used for the assessment of the mental health of children, adolescents, and their family members. The CAT is a comprehensive assessment that includes the most recent 24-hour period. It uses a Lickert-type scale ranging from 0 to 3, with 0 indicating that there is no reason to require action, and 3 indicating a need for immediate or intense action. The CAT is divided into the following categories: Risk Behaviors (10 items), Behavioral/Emotional Symptoms (9 items), Functioning Problems (7 items), Juvenile Justice (3 items), Child Protection (2 items), and Caregiver Needs and Strengths (7 items). The CAT corresponds to the Indiana Version of the Children and Adolescent Needs and Strengths (CANS) tool (Crisis Assessment Tool, 2002). Although the instrument was developed around the turn of the century, it remains the most relevant for use today.

## Social Media

Additional support for those experiencing crisis is available through a range of social media sites. *Social media* is defined as "forms of electronic communication (as websites for social networking and microblogging) through which users create online communities to share information, ideas, personal messages, and other content (as videos)" (Merriam-Webster, 2014). Social media covers many areas of concern for individuals based on their life circumstances and is also helpful to those experiencing a range of crisis experiences. Numerous online support groups and resources are available.

The selection of sites requires discernment to understand the focus and intent of a given site and to distinguish between sites with prosocial and antisocial content. Prosocial support for individuals in crisis can provide help for individuals who are facing difficult life circumstances by providing individual and group support, mentoring, and psychoeducational services. It must be noted that there are many antisocial websites that can potentially lead to psychological, spiritual, emotional, and physical harm.

When working with individuals in crisis, it is important to ask what social media sites they frequent. Working from the person-in-online-environment perspective requires one to discern how the use of the Internet will benefit the client given his or her current circumstances. If the person derives social support primarily through the Internet in text-based or virtual methods, this has implications for intervention strategies. The use of prosocial and antisocial Internet content will have an impact on therapeutic outcomes. The mental health practitioner may be of assistance in suggesting the use of online websites and support communities that will complement the therapeutic experience.

Social media resources are used to provide social support to prevent those who are considering committing suicide from doing so. At the same time, a growing number of suicide pacts have been established online. Japan has been the leader in *suicide clubs* through which individuals meet online to plan their suicide (referred to as *netto shinju*; BBC News, 2004; Wikipedia, 2014). When using social media, it is important to know if sites are legitimate in regard to suicide prevention. Under the umbrella of social media there are many resources that provide preventive assistance using e-mail, text services such as instant messaging, online self-help groups, tools to assist with self-assessment and goal setting, various kinds of chat rooms, video interaction, various forms of virtual reality formats, online psychotherapy, online crisis intervention, and telemedicine, to name a few options (Patrick, 2011). A number of Internet resources offer toll-free telephone numbers, online chat with a counselor 24 hours a day, and online support groups (see Table 27.1).

Some promising examples of social media include: creating a two-way avenue for the public to interact with government agencies; provides updated and immediate information for 18- to 25-year-olds who tend to access their news predominantly from social media; supports the use of cell phones to quickly disseminate breaking news; and. the linked-in communication network Amber Art system has assisted in the recovery of more than 660 abducted children (Office of Justice Programs, 2014). In 2012, use of this communication network alone helped the National Center for Missing and Exploited Children (NCMEC) to provide case related information from 52 Amber Alerts that assisted in the led to the recovery of 68 children. Twenty-six children (38%) representing 42% of the cases, were recovered within 3 hours of when the Amber Alert was issued (NCMEC, 2014).

## Web-Based or Telemedicine Interventions

Telemedicine had its origin in the 1970s, when Thomas Bird coined the phrase in reference to the use of telecommunications for health care delivery by physicians (Turnock, Mastouri, & Jivraj, 2008). There are several definitions of *telemedicine*; for the purposes of this chapter, the most useful definition is one provided by Medline Plus (2012): "the practice of medicine when the doctor and patient are widely separated using two-way voice and visual communication (as by satellite, computer, or closed-circuit television)."

Telemedicine is delivered using two modes: synchronous and asynchronous. The synchronous mode includes the two participants meeting at the same time using a communication technology that allows for real-time interface (Turnock, Mastouri, & Jivraj, 2008). Videophone calls and videoconferencing are two methods used in synchronous telemedicine. In addition to providing a visual image of the client, videoconferencing technology allows for devices (e.g., glucometers, ophthalmoscopes, stethoscopes) to be attached to the equipment, which may assist in examining and observing the client (Turnock, Mastouri, & Jivraj, 2008).

Asynchronous technology stores images, videos, audio recordings, and other clinical data on a client's computer. These stored records can be transferred to other locations at a later time. The e-mail communication between client and practitioner is another asynchronous method of communication in which the practitioner or client may send a message that might not be accessed for several hours or days. One potential barrier to telemedicine would be a breakdown in the telecommunication infrastructure resulting from a disaster, which could lead to a significant period without access to the Internet or other forms of electronic or digital communication (Turnock, Mastouri, & Jivraj, 2008). Another concern may be difficulties in providing necessary communication equipment during a disaster.

## SUMMARY

The efficacy of crisis intervention as a viable alternative to the more traditional long-term models of therapy continues to increase. The question is no longer whether crisis intervention or short-term therapeutic measures work, but rather, which techniques work best with what kinds of clients and problems and under what set of circumstances (Dziegielewski, 2014). Coordinated health care is presenting a new type of service delivery in which many of the formerly uninsured now have insurance coverage. Therefore, the pressure is great for social workers to show that show that time-limited services continue to provide the necessary and effective services, whether in the traditional medical setting or in the home or community, the natural settings in which crisis often occurs. This challenge has been a particularly vigorous one for crisis intervention advocates because of the fluctuating nature of any crisis response. In this arena, however, effectiveness must extend beyond merely helping the client. With increasing use of the Internet, the simple fact that many Internet providers do not accept insurance reimbursement will clearly affect the kind and quality of services provided to clients. Ultimately, the process of validating the effectiveness of current practice dictates that we be able to demonstrate that the greatest concrete and identifiable therapeutic gain has been achieved, in the quickest amount of time, and with the least expenditure of financial and professional resources. This means not only that the treatment that social workers provide should be therapeutically necessary and effective, but also that it should be delivered in a manner that is professionally competitive with other disciplines that offer similar treatment strategies and techniques.

Professional interest in the various forms of time-limited therapy has increased greatly, and the desire to increase data-based best practices will probably continue to grow in the coming years. Social work practice that operates within a framework of a planned, time-limited intervention format appears to be both a viable and an essential practice modality, especially in today's managed care environment. Health maintenance organizations and employee assistance programs generally favor highly structured, brief forms of therapy; as these programs continue to grow, so, too, will use of the time-limited models they support (Dziegielewski, 2013). Further, insight-oriented intervention strategies and cure-focused therapeutic approaches seem to have given way to more pragmatically grounded practice strategies.

Social workers, like their physician counterparts, rarely "cure" client problems; nor should they be expected to do so. What should be expected, however, is that all therapeutic efforts help clients utilize their own potential to diminish or alleviate symptoms and states of being that cause discomfort. The prevailing emphasis on client individuality and time-limited, concrete changes not only is accepted as a reasonable professional expectation but now is generally recognized as essential to state-of-the-art practice (Dziegielewski, 2013).

Throughout this chapter, it has been argued that the best way to evaluate the relative effectiveness of current crisis intervention strategies is through the creative use of various intensive research designs. In recent years, a range of quantitative and qualitative research methods have has evolved (Dziegielewski & Roberts, 2004). These idiographically grounded methods are of particular value to the social work and counseling professional because they are specially designed for use in clinical practice situations where the primary unit of attention is a single-client system (i.e., an individual, a family, a couple, or a group). For the most part, these are relatively simple, straightforward evaluation strategies that can be unobtrusively incorporated into the helping professional's daily practice routines. When used appropriately, they not only provide useful evaluative feedback but also enhance the overall quality of the intervention itself. Over time, these types of behavioral-based crisis intervention strategies are becoming incorporated into our community health centers and outreach facilities (Wells, Morrissey, Lee, & Radford, 2010).

The micro or intensive designs of research make no pretense with respect to their contribution to scientific generalizations (Baumgartner, Strong, & Hensley, 2002). They do, however, enable the crisis clinician to test the utility of scientific generalizations in the crucible of practice. The time-limited nature of most crises is such that both the intervention and the evaluation must be initiated quickly. In many instances, it is necessary to proceed under less than optimal circumstances. The clinician is inescapably faced with the issue of somehow balancing the requirements of evaluation with those of practice, and of course, in any apparent conflict between the two, the interests of the latter must always be accorded primary consideration. It is not surprising, therefore, that methodological purists may at times be critical of our evaluation efforts. But the methodological rigor of any research endeavor is inevitably a relative rather than an absolute condition. Each evaluation effort represents an imperfect attempt to arrive at a closer approximation of the truth. As such, research provides no guarantee of certitude. It simply helps us reduce the probability of error in the face of uncertainty. If we can tolerate its limitations and exploit its possibilities, we can almost certainly improve the quality of the services we provide our clients.

One final observation before concluding this discussion rests is the simple fact that the delivery of any human service, regardless of its form, never takes place in an ethical and political vacuum. Professional actions should always be guided by an unequivocal set of professional values. All professional codes of ethics speak to the paramount importance of client rights, including self-determination and confidentiality—rights that are believed to play a critical role in the helping process. However, practice also takes place in an administrative context that is driven by cost containment, as well as accountability to the agencies that deliver services and to the vendors that reimburse them (Dziegielewski, 2013). These opposing forces may, at times, cause tension between ideological and administrative considerations, particularly as the worker struggles to satisfy the conflicting expectations of multiple constituencies.

Issues of this type are never easily resolved. They require an uncanny ability to understand and balance multiple personal and organizational demands in ways that ultimately serve the best interests of our clients. Assuming that we are not immobilized by the magnitude of such moral and political dilemmas, we can take some solace in the words of the late John Cardinal Newman (1902): "Nothing would ever be accomplished if a person waited so long as to do it so well that no other person could find fault with it" (John Cardinal Newman quoted in Brainy.Quotes.com, n.d.,quote # 2).

ACKNOWLEDGMENTS    Special thanks to Gerald Powers for his contributions to the previous version of this chapter.

REFERENCES

About.com. (2014). *Better Help*. Retrieved from https://www. betterhelp.com/go/?utm_ source=AdWords&utm_ medium=Search_ PPC&utm_term=online%20 therapy&utm_content=2485898 6050&network=s&placement= &target=&matchtype=e&utm_ campaign=online_counseling&ad_

type=text&adposition=1t1target=&gclid=COqo09bXl74CFWIF7AodlmEAFw

Allport, G. W. (1962). The general and the unique in psychological science. *Journal of Personality, 30,* 405–422.

American Psychiatric Association. (2000). *Diagnostic and statistical manual of mental disorders—text revision* (4th ed.). Washington, DC: Author.

American Psychiatric Association. (2013). *Diagnostic and statistical manual of mental disorders* (5th ed.). Washington, DC: Author.

Barak, A., & Grohol, J. M. (2011). Current and future trends in internet-supported mental health interventions. *Journal of Technology and Human Services, 29,* 155–196.

Baumgartner, T. A., Strong, C. H., & Hensley, L. D. (2002). *Conducting and reading research in health performance* (3rd ed.). New York: McGraw-Hill.

BBC News. (2004, December 7). Japan's Internet suicide clubs. Author.

Beck, A. T. (1967). *Depression: Clinical, experimental and theoretical aspects.* New York: Harper and Row.

Bergin, A. E., & Suinn, R. M. (1975). Individual psychotherapy and behavior therapy. *Annual Review of Psychology, 26,* 509–555.

Bloom, M., Fischer, J., & Orme, J. G. (2009). *Evaluating practice: Guidelines for the accountable professional* (6th ed.). Boston: Pearson.

Campbell, D. T., & Stanley, J. C. (1966). *Experimental and quasi-experimental designs for research and teaching.* Chicago: Rand McNally.

Chassan, J. B. (1967). *Research designs in clinical psychology and psychiatry.* New York: Appleton-Century-Crofts.

Christ, G. H., Moynihan, R. T., & Gallo-Silver, L. (1995). Crisis intervention with AIDS patients and their families. In A. R. Roberts (Ed.), *Crisis intervention and time-limited cognitive treatment.* Thousand Oaks, CA: Sage.

Clements, P. R., & Jacinto, G. A. (2014). *Long term care geropsychiatric-maladaptive behavior record.* Belleair Beach, FL: Neuropsychiatric Guidance Press.

Cook, D. A., & Beckman. T. J. (2006). Current concepts in validity and reliability for psychometric instruments: Theory and application. *American Journal of Medicine, 119,* 166.e7–166.e16.

Cormier, S., Nurius, P. S., & Osborn. C. J. (2013). *Interviewing and change strategies for helpers* (7th ed.). Belmont, CA: Brooks/Cole

Crisis Assessment Tool. (2002). CAT Indiana Version. Winnetka, IL: Buddin Praed Foundation. Retrieved from www.buddinmpraed.org

Denzin, N. K. (2012). Triangulation 2.0. *Journal of Mixed Methods Research, 6,* 80–88. doi:10.1177/1558689812437186

Dziegielewski, S. F. (1991). Social group work with family members who have a relative suffering from dementia: A controlled evaluation. *Research on Social Work Practice, 1,* 358–370.

Dziegielewski, S. F. (2013). *The changing face of health care social work: Opportunities and challenges for professional practice* (3rd ed.). New York: Springer.

Dziegielewski, S. F. (2014). *DSM-IV-TR™ in action* (2nd ed., *DSM-5* update). Hoboken, NJ: Wiley.

Dziegielewski, S. F. (in press). *DSM-5™ in action*. Hoboken, NJ: Wiley.

Dziegielewski, S. F., & Roberts, A. R. (2004). Health care evidence-based practice: A product of political and cultural times. In A. R. Roberts & K. R. Yeager (Eds.), *Handbook of practice-focused research and evaluation* (pp. 200–204). New York: Oxford University Press.

Fielding, N. G. (2012). Triangulation and mixed methods designs: Data integration with new research technologies. *Journal of Mixed Methods Research, 6*, 124–136.

Fischer, J. (1976). *Effective casework practice: An eclectic approach.* New York: McGraw-Hill.

Fischer, J., & Corcoran, K. (2007a). *Measures of clinical practice: A sourcebook. Vol. 1. Couples, families, and children* (4th ed.). New York: Free Press.

Fischer, J., & Corcoran, K. (2007b). *Measures of clinical practice: A sourcebook. Vol. 2. Adults* (4th ed.). New York: Free Press.

Garwick, G., & Lampman, S. (1973). *Dictionary of goal attainment scaling.* Minneapolis, MN: Program Evaluation Project.

Ghahramanlou-Holloway, M., Cox, D. W., & Greene, F. N. (2012). Post-admission cognitive therapy: A brief intervention for psychiatric inpatients admitted after a suicide attempt. *Cognitive and Behavioral Practice, 19*, 233–244.

Gilliland, B. E., & James, R. K. (2013). *Crisis intervention strategies* (7th ed.). Pacific Grove, CA: Brooks/Cole.

Grohol, J. M. (2001). *Best practices in eTherapy: Clarifying the definition of eTherapy.* Retrieved from http://psychcentral.com/best/best5.htm

Grohol, J. M. (2005). *Best practices in eTherapy: Confidentiality and privacy.* Retrieved from http://psychcentral.com/best/best2.htm

Grohol, J. M. (2011). Wait, there's online therapy? PsychCentral. Retrieved from http://psychcentral.com/blog/archives/2011/07/14/telehealth-wait-theres-online-therapy/

Hardcastle, D. A. (2011). *Community practice: Theories and skills for social workers.* New York: Oxford University Press.

Hart, R. R. (1978). Therapeutic effectiveness of setting and monitoring goals. *Journal of Consulting and Clinical Psychology, 46*, 1242–1245.

Hartman, D. J., & Sullivan, W. P. (1996). Residential crisis services as an alternative to inpatient care. *Families in Society: The Journal of Contemporary Human Services, 77*(8), 496–501.

HEN Synthesis Report. (2012). *For which strategies of suicide prevention is there evidence of effectiveness?* Copenhagen, Denmark: WHO, Health Evidence Network.

Howe, K. R. (2012). Mixed methods, triangulation, and causal explanation. *Journal of Mixed Methods Research, 6*, 89–96. doi:10.1177/1558689812437187

Jack, B. A., Baldry, C. R., Groves, K. E., Whelan, A., Sephton, J., & Gaunt, K. (2013). Supporting home care for the dying: An evaluation of healthcare professionals' perspectives of an individually tailored hospice at home service. *Journal of Clinical Nursing, 22*, 2778–2786. doi:10.1111/j.1365-2702.2012.04301.x

Jha, A. K., DesRoches, C. M., Kralovec, P. D., & Joshi, M. S. (2010). A progress report on electronic health records in U.S. hospitals. *Health Affairs, 29*, 1951–1957.

Joiner, T. E., Jr., Van Orden, K. A., Witte, T. K., & Rudd, M. D. (2009). *The interpersonal theory of suicide: Guidance for working with suicidal clients.* Washington, D.C.: American Psychological Association.

Kiesler, D. J. (1966). Some myths of psychotherapy research and the search for a paradigm. *Psychological Bulletin, 65,* 110–136.

Kiresuk, T. J., & Sherman, R. E. (1968). Goal attainment scaling: A general method for evaluating comprehensive community mental health programs. *Community Mental Health Journal, 4,* 443–453.

Lambert, M. J. (Ed.). (2013). *Bergin and Garfield's handbook of psychotherapy and behavior change* (6th ed.). Hoboken, NJ: Wiley.

Lambert, M. J., & Hill, C. E. (1994). Assessing psychotherapy outcomes and process. In S. L. Garfield & A. E. Bergin (Eds.), *Handbook of psychotherapy and behavior change* (4th ed., pp. 72–113). Hoboken, NJ: Wiley.

Lindemann, E. (1944). Symptomatology and management of acute grief. *American Journal of Psychiatry, 101,* 141–148.

McDougall, J., & Wright, V. (2009). The ICF-CY and Goal Attainment Scaling: Benefits of their combined use for pediatric practice. *Disability and Rehabilitation, 31,* 1362–1372. doi:10.1080/09638280802572973

Medline Plus. (2012). Telemedicine. A service of the U.S. National Library of Medicine. Retrieved from http://www.nlm.nih.gov/medlineplus/mplusdictionary.html

Merriam-Webster. (2014). Social media. Retrieved from http://www.merriam-webster.com/

Metanoia.org. (2014) What can I do to help someone who is suicidal? Retrieved from http://www.metanoia.org/suicide/whattodo.htm

Monette, D. R., Sullivan, T. J., & DeJong, C. R. (2005). *Applied social research: A tool for human services.* Belmont, CA: Books/Cole–Thompson Learning.

Myer, R. A., Lewis, J. S., & James, R. K. (2013). The introduction of a task model for crisis intervention. *Journal of Mental Health Counseling, 35,* 95–107.

National Association of Social Workers (NASW). (2007). Social workers and e-therapy. Retrieved from http://www.socialworkers.org/ldf/legal_issue/2007/200704.sap

National Center for Missing and Exploited Children (NCMEC). (2014). *National Center for Missing and Exploited Children 2012 Amber Alert report.* Retrieved from http://www.missingkids.com/en_US/documents/2012AMBERAlertReport.pdf#page=22

Newman, J.H. (n.d.). BrainyQuote.com. Retrieved November 30, 2014, from BrainyQuote.com Website: http://www.brainyquote.com/quotes/quotes/j/johnhenryn126383.html

Nugent, W. R. (2010). *Analyzing single system design data.* New York: Oxford University Press.

Nugent, W. R., Sieppert, J. D., & Hudson, W. W. (2001). *Practice evaluation for the 21st century.* Belmont, CA: Brooks/Cole–Thomson Learning.

Office of Justice Programs. (2014). Amber Alert. Retrieved from http://www.amberalert.gov/statistics.htm

Patrick, R. G. (2011, April). *Using the Internet to provide crisis intervention services.* Paper presented at the 44th annual meeting of the American Association of Suicidology, Houston, TX.

Paul, G. L. (1966). *Insight versus de-sensitization in*

*psychotherapy*. Stanford, CA: Stanford University Press.

*Psychology Today*. (2014). Mental health assessment. Retrieved from http://psychologytoday. tests.psychtests.com/take_test. php?idRegTest=3040

Richards, S. B., Taylor, R. L., & Ramasamy, R. (2014). *Single subject research: Applications in educational and clinical settings*. Belmont, CA: Wadsworth.

Roberts, A. R. (1991). *Contemporary perspectives on crisis intervention and prevention*. Englewood Cliffs, NJ: Prentice-Hall.

Roberts, A. R. (2005). *Crisis intervention handbook: Assessment, treatment and research* (3rd ed.). New York: Oxford University Press.

Roberts, A. R., & Dziegielewski, S. F. (1995). Foundation skills and applications of crisis intervention and cognitive therapy. In A. R. Roberts (Ed.), *Crisis intervention and time-limited cognitive treatment* (pp. 3–27). Thousand Oaks, CA: Sage.

Roberts, A. R., & Everly, G. S. (2006). A meta-analysis of 36 crisis intervention studies. *Brief Treatment and Crisis Intervention*, 6 (1), 10–21.

Roberts, A. R., & Yeager, K. (2004). Systematic reviews of evidence-based studies and practice-based research: How to search for, develop, and use them. In A. R. Roberts & K. R. Yeager (Eds.), *Evidence-based practice manual: Research and outcome measures in health and human services* (pp. 3–14). New York: Oxford University Press.

Rochlen, A. B., Zack, J. S., & Speyer, C. (2004). Online therapy: Review of relevant definitions, debates, and current empirical support. *Journal of Clinical Psychology*, 60, 269–283.

Rubin, A., & Babbie, E. (2011). *Research methods for social work* (7th ed.). Pacific Grove, CA: Brooks/Cole.

Simmons, C. A., & Lehmann, P. (2013). *Tools for strengths-based assessment and evaluation*. New York: Springer.

Teague, G. B., Trabin, T., & Ray, C. (2004). Toward common performance indicators and measures for accountability in behavioral health care. In A. R. Roberts & K. R. Yeager (Eds.), *Evidence-based practice manual: Research and outcome measures in health and human services* (pp. 46–61). New York: Oxford University Press.

Tsai, J., & Bond, G. (2008). A comparison of electronic records to paper records in mental health centers. *International Journal for Quality in Health Care*, 20, 136–143.

Turnock, M., Mastouri, N., & Jivraj, A. (2008, December). Pre-hospital application of telemedicine in acute-onset disaster situations. Retrieved from http://www. un-spider.org/sites/default/files/ Prehospital%20telemedicine%20 in%20disasters.pdf

Wells, R., Morrissey, J. P., Lee, I., & Radford, A. (2010). Trends in behavioral health care service provision by community health centers, 1998–2007. *Psychiatric Services*, 61, 759–764.

Wharff, E. A., Ginnis, K. M., & Ross, A. M. (2012). Family-based crisis intervention with suicidal adolescents in the emergency room: A pilot study. *Social Work*, 57, 133–143.

Wikipedia. (2014, February). Internet suicide pact. Retrieved from http://en.wikipedia.org/wiki/ Internet_suicide_pact.

# Glossary

**24-hour hotlines:** Telephone services, often staffed by volunteers, that provide information, crisis assessments, crisis counseling, and referrals for callers with various problems, such as depression, suicide ideation, alcoholism, chemical dependency, impotence, domestic violence, and crime victimization. Because of their 24-hour availability, they can provide immediate, though temporary, intervention. (See Chapters 1 and 2.)

**A-B-C model of crisis management:** A three-stage sequential model for intervening with persons in crisis. The "A" refers to "achieving contact," the "B" to "boiling down the problem," and the "C" to "coping." (See Chapter 16.)

**Acquaintance rape:** Nonconsensual sex between adults who know each other. (See Chapter 13.)

**Adolescence:** Transitional period between childhood and adulthood, typically commencing with the onset of puberty, during which youth develop the physical, social, emotional, and intellectual skills necessary for adult functioning. (See chapter 12.)

**Adolescent school subgroups:** Naturally formed groups within school populations, commonly identified by ethnicity, activity, or year in school. Individuals may be associated with multiple groups. Examples include "jocks," "brains," "druggies," "homeboys," or "seniors." (See Chapter 15.)

**Adult day care:** Community-based programs that provide therapeutic activities and individualized services for older adults with disabilities, thus allowing family caregivers of persons with dementia, for example, an opportunity for respite. (See Chapter 23.)

**Affective disorders:** Affective disorders affect moods and are commonly called *mood disorders*. They comprise a wide spectrum of emotions, from elation to depression to mania, with depression dominating the clinical picture. Affective disorders also manifest themselves in physical symptoms, self-destructive behavior, loss of social functioning, and impaired reality testing. The frequency, intensity, and duration of the moods distinguish affective disorders from common, everyday moods. (See Chapter 19.)

**Aggression:** Acting with intent to dominate or behave destructively; physical or verbal force directed toward the environment, another person, or oneself. (See Chapter 16.)

**AIDS service organization (ASO):** A not-for-profit or for-profit community organization that may or may not provide health services. ASOs are generally funded through federal, state, and/or local dollars to provide psychosocial services to people with HIV and/or AIDS. (See Chapter 17.)

**Anticholinergic:** An agent that blocks parasympathetic nerve impulses. Associated with medications utilized to minimize the discomfort associated with opioid withdrawal. (See Chapter 18.)

**Anticomplementary counselor responses:** Counselor responses such as interpretations, reframes, and probes that are designed to "loosen" client's maladaptive cognitions or challenge dysfunctional behavioral choices. (See Chapter 8.)

**Assumptive world :** A system of core or fundamental beliefs that constitute what an individual knows to be true about his or her world. This belief system provides stability, predictability, and a sense of grounding to one's life. (See Chapter 13.)

**Baseline period:** The period during a pre-intervention phase when a series of observations are made to monitor subsequent changes in the client's target behavior. It provides a basis on which to determine whether the behavior observed during baseline (i.e., Phase A) changes in the expected direction following the introduction of treatment (i.e., Phase B). (See Chapters 14 and 17.)

**Battered women's hotlines and shelters:** The primary focus of these services is to ensure women's safety through crisis telephone counseling or provision of short-term housing at a safe residential shelter. Many shelters provide not only safe lodging but also peer counseling, support groups, information on women's legal rights, and referral to social service agencies. In some communities, emergency services for battered women have expanded further to include parenting education workshops, assistance in finding transitional and permanent housing, employment counseling and job placement, and group counseling for batterers. These crisis intervention and housing placements for battered women and their children exist in every state and in many large metropolitan areas in the United States. (See Chapter 1 and 16.)

**Bereavement:** See "Normal bereavement" and "Uncomplicated bereavement."

**Binge:** A prolonged episode of continuous alcohol or drug use extending over a period greater than 24 hours. (See Chapter 18.)

**Bioterrorism:** The use of biological weapons by terrorists that produce pathogens, organic biocides, and/or disease-producing microorganisms that inflict death, disease outbreaks, and injuries. (See Chapter 9.)

**Boundary spanning:** Collaborative professional teamwork that attempts to engage and employ the combined talents of individuals who previously operated independently due to perceived systemic, cultural, or institutional divisions. (See Chapter 10.)

**Brief therapy:** A type of intervention based on the premise that a system in crisis is more open to change, and that certain and often brief intervention into the unstable system can result in lasting changes in how the system functions. (See Chapters 1, 3, and 18.)

**Buprinex:** A medication used in opioid detoxification that binds with opiate receptors in the central nervous system, altering both perception of and emotional response to pain through an unknown mechanism. (See Chapter 18.)

**Caregiver Burden Inventory:** A short (24-item) but comprehensive and easily administered instrument for measuring five common dimensions of caregiver burden. (See Chapter 23.)

**Catastrophic events:** Acute, localized violent occurrences producing widespread trauma in those experiencing or exposed to the event. These incidents commonly directly victimize groups of people and frequently include multiple fatal assaults. (See Chapters 5, 7–9, 12, and 15.)

**Code:** Word used to alert the medical team to start resuscitation efforts (CPR) to revive a victim of cardiac and pulmonary arrest. Combined with different words to designate different types of emergencies at hospitals and broadcast over the PA system. Examples: Code Blue for victim of cardiac arrest; Code Red for fire. (See Chapter 22.)

**Completed suicide:** See "Suicide." *Suicide* and *completed suicide* are interchangeable terms. (See Chapter 2.)

**Coping questions:** Coping questions ask clients to talk about how they manage to survive and endure their problems. Coping questions help clients to notice their resources and strengths despite adversities. (See Chapters 1–4.)

**Counterterrorism:** This is a diplomatic, strategic, law enforcement intelligence offensive operation that uses specially trained personnel and resources to discover, disrupt, or destroy terrorist capabilities, plans, and networks. (See Chapters 8 and 9.)

**Cravings:** A term defined in various ways related to drug use. Typically it refers to an intense desire to obtain and use a drug. (See Chapter 18.)

**Crisis:** An acute disruption of psychological homeostasis in which one's usual coping mechanisms fail and there exists evidence of distress and functional impairment. The subjective reaction to a stressful life experience that compromises the individual's stability and ability to cope or function. The main cause of a crisis is an intensely stressful, traumatic, or hazardous event, but two other conditions are also necessary: (a) the individual's perception of the event as the cause of considerable upset and/or disruption; and (b) the individual's inability to resolve the disruption by previously used coping methods. *Crisis* also refers to "an upset in the steady state." It often has five components: a hazardous or traumatic event, a vulnerable state, a precipitating factor, an active crisis state, and the resolution of the crisis. (See Chapters 1–4.)

**Crisis call to domestic violence hotline:** A telephone call to a hotline in which the caller is in imminent danger or has just been abused or battered by an intimate partner. (See Chapters 1 and 16.)

**Crisis intervention:** The first stage of crisis intervention, also known as emotional "first aid," focuses on establishing rapport, making a rapid assessment, and stabilizing and reducing the person's symptoms of distress and the impact of a crisis. The next stages utilize crisis intervention strategies (e.g., active listening, ventilation, reflection of feeling, storytelling, reframing, and exploring alternative solutions) while assisting the individual in crisis to return to a state of adaptive functioning, crisis resolution, and cognitive mastery. This type of timely intervention focuses on helping to mobilize the resources of those differentially affected. Crisis intervention may be given over the telephone or in person. (See Chapters 1 and 2.) For in-depth case applications of Roberts's seven-stage crisis intervention model to a range of urgent and acute crisis episodes, See Chapters 1–5 and 12–23.)

**Crisis intervention service:** These services provide a person in crisis with the phone numbers of local hotlines, community crisis centers, crisis intervention units at the local community mental health center, rape crisis centers, battered women's shelters, and family crisis intervention programs, which then provide follow-up and home-based crisis services. Crisis intervention services are available 24 hours a day, seven days a week, and are usually staffed by crisis clinicians, counselors, social workers, hospital emergency room staff, and trained volunteers. (See Chapters 1, 2, and 18–20, 23.)

**Crisis intervention team (CIT):** A police-based mental health response model designed to pair specially trained law enforcement officers to assist individuals experiencing a mental health crisis. (See Chapter 10.)

**Crisis-oriented treatments:** Treatment approaches that apply to all practice models and techniques, which are focused on resolving immediate crisis situations and emotionally volatile conflicts with a minimum number of contacts (usually one to six) and are characterized as time limited and goal directed. (See Chapter 1.)

**Crisis residential unit:** A 24-hour supervised setting for individuals experiencing any type of crisis who are 18 years of age or older, medically stable, and no overt threat to themselves or others. This brief stay (up to 5 days) focuses on problem solving and crisis management through individual supportive counseling, group treatment, psychiatric and nursing services, and appropriate referrals. (See Chapter 17.)

**Crisis resolution:** The goal of interventions given by trained volunteers and professionals to persons in crisis. Resolution involves the restoration of equilibrium, cognitive mastery of the situation, and the development of new coping methods. An effective crisis resolution removes vulnerabilities from the individual's past and bolsters the individual with an increased repertoire of coping skills that serve as a buffer against similar situations in the future. (See Chapters 1–5.)

**Critical incident:** An event that has the potential to overwhelm one's usual coping mechanisms, resulting in psychological distress and an impairment of normal adaptive functioning. (See Chapter 7.)

**Critical Incident Stress Management (CISM):** An integrated and comprehensive multicomponent program for providing crisis and disaster mental health services. A variety of stress management techniques/ interventions provided to emergency services personnel, police, and/or firefighters who are exposed to life-threatening or traumatic incidents. (See Chapter 22.)

**Cyberstalking:** Repeated threats or harassment through e-mails or other computer-based communications. (See Chapter 16.)

**Date rape:** Nonconsensual sex between partners who date or are on a date. (See Chapter 13.)

**Date rape drugs:** Sedative-type drugs, some of which are illegal substances, that render victims unable to defend themselves against sexual exploitation; alcohol, Rohypnol, and Ectasy are three of the most common date rape drugs. (See Chapter 13.)

**Debriefing at school:** A meeting held soon after a crisis event to review the activities of a school crisis intervention team during a recent crisis response with the primary goal of supporting team members and ultimately improving the future functioning of the team as a whole and the quality of the interventions offered. (See Chapter 14.)

**Decompensation:** A person having a chronic mental condition may periodically experience worsening symptoms such as depression or psychosis. This general decline in condition is called *decompensation*. (See Chapters 11 and 19.)

**Deinstitutionalization:** The Community Mental Health Centers Act of 1963 required that mental health services be moved from inpatient institutions to community-based services. This transition is referred to as *deinstitutionalization*, and one of the services mandated by the act is crisis services. (See Chapter 19.)

**Dependent variables:** Variables that represent the presumed effect in any functional relationship. (See Chapter 27.)

**Disequilibrium:** An emotional state that may be characterized by confusing emotions, somatic complaints, and erratic behavior. The severe emotional discomfort experienced by the person in crisis propels him or her toward action that will reduce the subjective discomfort. Crisis intervention usually alleviates the early symptoms of disequilibrium within the first 6 weeks of treatment and hopefully soon restores equilibrium. (See Chapters 1, 2, and 5.)

**Dismantling treatment strategy:** A strategy involving the orderly removal of one or more components of the treatment package, accompanied by careful recording of the apparent effects. This systematic elimination, or isolation, enables the clinician to "determine the necessary and sufficient components for therapeutic change." (See Chapter 32.)

**District-level crisis intervention team:** A school crisis intervention team composed of staff from the school district's central office to provide oversight, resources, and administrative support to school-based crisis intervention teams. (See Chapter 14.)

**Ego fragmentation:** Ego fragmentations, sometimes referred to as *dissociative disorders*, are characterized by disturbances in normally integrated functions of memory, identity, or consciousness. They are found in diagnoses such as post-traumatic stress disorder, acute stress disorder, and somatization disorder. Harsh psychosocial stressors such as physical threat, wartime, and disasters predispose susceptible persons to ego fragmentations. (See Chapter 5.)

**Emergency room:** A department in a hospital open 24 hours a day to victims of emergent and urgent situations. Treatment is provided by a medical team of doctors, nurses, respiratory therapists, lab technicians, and social workers. (See Chapter 22.)

**Exception questions:** Questions that inquire about times when the problem is either absent, less intense, or dealt with in a manner that is acceptable to the client. (See Chapter 3.)

**Excitatory toxicity:** Massive release of neurotransmitters that in high enough concentrations may damage or destroy the neural substrates they serve. (See Chapter 5.)

**Extensive designs of research:** Designs that emphasize the primacy of the confirmatory aspect of scientific activity. The goal of these designs is to discover laws that apply to aggregates of individuals rather than to the individuals who constitute the aggregate. In this approach, the ultimate goal is to discover scientific generalization under controlled circumstances. (See Chapter 27.)

**First responder:** A public safety professional initially dispatched to or arriving at the scene of a crisis or emergency; often a police officer, firefighter, or paramedic. (See Chapter 10.)

**Frozen fright:** The inability of a high-risk patient to react due to a medical crisis. (See Chapter 22.)

**Goal Attainment Scaling (GAS):** This evaluation method measures intervention outcomes in which a number of individually tailored treatment goals are specified in relation to a set of graded scale points ranging from the least favorable to the most favorable outcomes considered likely. It is suggested that at least 5 points comprising a Likert-type scale be assigned, with the "least favorable outcome" scored -2, the "most favorable outcome" scored +2, and the "most likely outcome" assigned a value of 0. (See Chapter 27.)

**HIV trajectory:** The stages of HIV infection and the symptoms that accompany those stages. (See Chapter 20.)

**HIV viral load:** The amount of viral particles per milliliter of blood (scientifically *quantitative plasma HIV RNA*). The viral load is an indication of prognosis, with a high load indicating that the virus is progressing rapidly. (See Chapter 20.)

**Idiographic research:** This approach focuses on the study of individuals as individuals, rather than on the discovery of general propositions. Idiographic research investigates the rich and intricate detail of specific cases, including deviant cases that prove to be exceptions to the general rule. (See Chapter 27.)

**Imposter phenomenon (IP) :** A persistent belief, despite evidence to the contrary, that one's intellect or academic competence has been gotten through fraud or phoniness; once thought to be more prevalent among high-achieving women. (See Chapter 13.)

**Incident Command System (ICS) :** An all-hazards incident management system to make certain that standardized integration of multiple systems, capacities, and personnel. The ICS ensures that necessary services are being provided with a minimum of risk to survivors and responders while maintaining a reliable chain of command, and that there are appropriate levels of supervision to maintain oversight of all operations. Initially derived from operations of fire personnel, the practices have been adapted to address all potential scenarios of crisis and disaster relief. (See Chapter 8.)

**Independent variables:** Variables that represent the presumed cause of any functional relationship. (See Chapter 27.)

**Information and referral (I and R) services:** The goals of I and R services are to facilitate access to community human services and to overcome the many barriers that may obstruct a person's entry to needed community resources. (See Chapter 1.)

**Intensive designs of research:** Designs primarily concerned with the study of single cases. They provide the means by which clinicians can evaluate the idiosyncratic aspects of their practice. Intensive research models can serve to generate relevant hypotheses suitable for testing by the more traditional extensive research approaches. (See Chapter 27.)

**Internal validity:** The level of confidence warranted by any causal inference. The designs that effectively control contamination from outside variables are said to be internally valid. (See Chapter 27.)

**Intervention period:** The period of time, typically referred to as the B phase, in any time-series design during which treatment is purposefully administered. (See Chapter 27.)

**Intervention priority code:** Method of prioritizing crisis requests on a clinical basis. Priorities range from I to IV, depending on clinical symptoms and presenting problems of the individual. These priorities dictate in which order cases should be responded to and in what time frame. (See Chapter 7.)

**Intensive outpatient program (IOP):** Outpatient substance dependence treatment, usually offered three evenings per week, 3 hours each evening. (See Chapter 18.)

**Lethality:** Measure of the degree to which a person is capable of causing death. Assessing for lethality entails asking about suicidal ideation, prior suicide attempts, homicidal thoughts, and feasibility of carrying out suicidal ideation or homicide. (See Chapters 1, 2, and 227.)

**LSD (lysergic acid diethylamide):** A class of drugs referred to as the *serotonergic hallucinogens*. (See Chapter 18.)

**Maladaptive reaction:** A codependent's tendency to continue investing time and energy to control a substance abuser's actions and behaviors despite repetitive adverse consequences. (See Chapter 18.)

**Managed care:** A health care services delivery model that attempts to control the cost of services in two ways: first, by restricting services to approved providers who accept reduced payment levels; second, by restricting access to higher-cost services such as specialists or inpatient services by requiring referrals from primary care physicians and precertifications for certain services. (See Chapters 5 and 24.)

**Maslow's hierarchy of needs:** A continuum of needs continually experienced by humans, as identified by Abraham Maslow. These hierarchically ordered needs include (from lowest to highest level) physiological needs, safety needs, belongingness and love needs, esteem needs, aesthetic and cognitive needs, and self-actualization needs. Lower-level needs must be satisfied before the next level of need can be addressed. (See Chapter 15.)

**Medical crisis:** A time of unusual emotional distress or disorientation caused by the onset of, or a major change in, a medical condition. (See Chapter 24.)

**Memorialization:** Activities of grieving individuals and groups to remember and honor those who have died. (See Chapter 12.)

**Methamphetamine (Methedrine, Desoxyn):** Synthetic stimulant drug. Acts to stimulate or mimic activity in the sympathetic branch of the autonomic nervous system. (See Chapter 18.)

**Miracle question:** A question that helps clients to construct a vision of life without the presenting complaint. A widely used format is: "Suppose that after our meeting today you go home and go to bed. While you are sleeping, a miracle happens, and your problem is suddenly solved, like magic. The problem is gone. How will you know a miracle happened? What will be the first sign that tells you that a miracle has happened and the problem is resolved?" (See Chapter 3.)

**Mobile crisis services:** Crisis counseling, assessment, and intervention provided at the scene of the crisis (someone's home, other agencies, community, prison, etc.). (See Chapter 19.)

**Mobile crisis unit:** A self-contained team of mental health and law enforcement professionals trained to respond to a crisis anywhere in the community, including residences, public places, and schools. (See Chapter 19.)

**Multiple baseline approach:** A crisis intervention approach designed to minimize the possibility of behavior change due to chance. Baseline data are collected either (a) on more than one target behavior, (b) on the same target behavior but in more than one setting, or (c) on more than one but similar clients. Intervention techniques are then applied sequentially so that once a change in the initial target behavior is observed, the intervention is systematically introduced with the next target behavior or in an alternate setting. (See Chapter 27.)

**National Incident Management System (NIMS)** : A system that identifies the concepts and practices necessary to ensure consistent and practical delivery of services in response to crises or disasters regardless of scope, location, or existing infrastructure. Relying on the Incident Command System to oversee direct operations, NIMS provides for the identification of needs, resources, deployment, and response throughout the United States. (See Chapter 14.)

**Net Nanny:** A brand-name computer software system for blocking access to certain Internet websites. (See Chapter 18.)

**Nonurgent:** Problems that need to be treated sometime today and not necessarily in the emergency room (e.g., sore throat or simple laceration). (See Chapter 24.)

**Nonviolent crisis intervention:** Variety of prevention and intervention techniques proven effective in resolving potentially violent crises. This model is taught by the CPI Crisis Prevention Institute, Inc. (See Chapter 15.)

**Normal bereavement:** The reactions to loss of a significant person, which may not be immediate but rarely occurs after the first 2 to 3 months after the loss. Normal bereavement involves feelings of depression that the person regards as "normal," although professional help may be sought for associated symptoms, such as insomnia or weight loss. Bereavement varies considerably among people of different ages and cultural groups. (See Chapter 1.)

**Objectified case studies:** Studies that attempt to relate the process of intervention (what the worker does) to the outcome of that intervention (whether what the worker does can be concluded to be effective). (See Chapter 27.)

**Obsessional relationship intrusion:** Stalking that emerges from a desired or previous relationship with attempts to initiate or re-establish the relationship despite opposition and other attempts on the target's part to disengage from unwanted pursuit behaviors. (See Chapter 17.)

**Open psychological consultation** : A standing order on a critical care unit. It mandates that a mental health professional systematically provide an initial screening and the indicated follow-up care without a direct intervention order. (See Chapter 24.)

**Outcome evaluation:** A process aimed at establishing whether a program or intervention is achieving its objectives and whether the results are due to the interventions provided. (See Chapter 27.)

**Parametric treatment strategies:** Strategies that attempt to determine in what quantity and/or in what sequence the components of a treatment package are likely to have their most beneficial impact. By systematically manipulating one or more of the components of a treatment package, it is possible to monitor the differential effects. (See Chapter 27.)

**Perturbation:** A state of system disequilibrium characterized by disorganization and distress, resulting in adaptation and emerging complexity and differentiation. (See Chapter 26.)

**Postmodernism:** Refers to philosophical reflection in which a conception of reality independent of the observer is replaced with notions of language actually constituting the structures of a perspectival social reality. (See Chapter 3.)

**Post-traumatic stress disorder (PTSD):** A diagnosis given to people who experience symptoms of intrusion, avoidance, or hyperarousal after experiencing or observing serious injury, threat, or death of a close associate. PTSD occurs when a person perceives an event as life-threatening and/or when the experience challenges his or her notions of fairness and justice. (See Chapters 4 and 7.)

**Postvention :** Typically provided to surviving friends and family members of victims of suicide, postvention can also include services that assist individuals' return to precrisis functioning through environmental, climate, and social-oriented supports. Less structured than intervention services, these supports are commonly provided after the direct impact of a crisis or disaster has taken place and the individual is able to once again assimilate new perspectives and understanding. (See Chapter 14.)

**Prevention:** Efforts designed to avert inappropriate and antisocial behaviors prior to their occurrence. (See Chapter 14.)

**Powerful Tools for Caregiving :** An evidence-based self-care education program for caregivers designed to improve their self-care behaviors, management of emotions, self-efficacy, and use of community resources. (See Chapter 23.)

**Primary adolescent suicide prevention:** Programs offered in schools, churches, and recreational and social organizations, designed to serve as a deterrent to a suicidal crisis. These programs focus on education, peer counseling, and other prevention methods. Teaching about the prevention and identification of possible suicide attempters may be part of these programs. (See Chapter 13.)

**Protocol:** The step-by-step or sequential plan of a treatment. (See Chapters 20 and 27.)

**Psychosocial crises:** Crises that are characterized primarily by psychosocial problems such as homelessness, extreme social isolation, and unmet primary care needs, and that may contribute to physical and psychological trauma and illness. (See Chapter 1.)

**Rape crisis programs:** Programs that include specialized protocols for rape victims and that have been established by medical centers, community mental health centers, women's counseling centers, crisis clinics, and victim assistance centers. The protocol in these crisis intervention services generally begins with an initial visit from a social worker, victim advocate, or nurse while the victim is being examined in the hospital emergency room. Follow-up is often handled through telephone contact and in-person counseling sessions for 1 to 10 weeks after the rape. (See Chapters 1 and 5.)

**Rape-supportive attitudes:** Stereotypic beliefs or societal "myths" about rape that result in the following: women being portrayed as sexual objects, discounting the impact of rape as a traumatically violent act, and absolving the perpetrator of full responsibility for committing rape. (See Chapter 13.)

**Rape victim:** A person who reports having experienced a sexual assault that meets the legal criteria for rape. Forcible rape is unwanted and coerced sexual penetration of another person. (See Chapters 13 and 17.)

**Rapid assessment instruments (RAIs):** Evaluation instruments that refer to any one of numerous assessment devices that are relatively easy to administer, score, and interpret and can be used to measure one or more dimensions of a client's target behavior. RAIs require very little knowledge of testing procedures on the part of the practitioner. The score that is generated provides an operational index of the frequency, duration, or intensity of the problem or target behavior. (See Chapters 1, 7, 26, and 27.)

**Regional resource team:** A group of professionals representing a range of allied disciplines (e.g., educational, emergency response, law enforcement, medical, mental health) that meet on an ongoing basis and provide consultation and technical assistance to district-level crisis intervention teams in the development and implementation of school crisis intervention responses. (See Chapter 14.)

**Relapse prevention:** A set of procedures designed to maintain therapeutic change and to facilitate accommodation of trauma with limited long-term negative effects. (See Chapter 18.)

**Relationship questions:** Relationship questions ask clients how their significant others are reacting to their problem situation and their progress in finding solutions. The establishment of multiple indicators of change helps clients develop a clear vision of a desired future appropriate to their real-life context. (See Chapter 3.)

**Reliability:** An evaluation term that refers to the stability of a measure. One aspect of reliability is whether the questions that constitute an instrument mean the same thing to one or more individuals answering them at different times. (See Chapter 27.)

**Reversal designs:** Designs that involve a process in which an intervention is introduced for a time and then abruptly withdrawn, with the resulting circumstances essentially approximating pre-intervention or baseline conditions. In the absence of intervention, certain types of client behaviors might be expected to move in the direction of the pre-intervention levels. (See Chapter 27.)

**Revictimization:** Victims may experience this process when counselors, police officers, or prosecutors place themselves in the role of judging whether a reported rape or incest experience was "real," or whether they think the client "provoked" the attack. (See Chapters 1, 3, 4, and 17.)

**Safety contract:** Written agreement between the crisis worker and client that acknowledges that the client has agreed not to harm him- or herself or anyone else; if the client is unable to resist that urge, he or she will call for help first. (See Chapter 16.)

**Scaling questions:** Question that ask clients to rank their situation and/or goal on a scale of 1 to 10. Scaling questions provide a simple tool for clients to quantify and evaluate their situation and progress so that they establish clear indicators of progress for themselves. (See Chapter 3.)

**School-based crisis intervention team:** A team composed of school staff from one school to provide direct services to student and staff within that particular school. (See Chapters 14 and 15.)

**School crisis intervention team:** A group of individuals formed, outside the context of a particular crisis event, with the purpose of developing plans and protocols to meet the needs of students and school staff in the event of a crisis affecting the school community. (See Chapters 14 and 15.)

**School violence:** Aggression against property or persons within a school context. Against persons, the term denotes an intentional verbal or physical act that produces pain, either physical or emotional, in the recipient of that act while the recipient is under the supervision of the school. Similarly, this operational definition is concerned primarily with violence that occurs within the school environment and not with general violent incidents involving adolescents. (See Chapters 14 and 15.)

**Secondary trauma responses:** (Also known as *secondary victimization* or *compassion fatigue*.) Psychological aftereffects of traumatic victimization experienced by those who assist victims of violence. This vicarious traumatization commonly occurs in mental health workers who assist or treat victims of traumatic events. These responses can occur as reactions to short-term interactions with specific clients or as alterations of long-held beliefs that are challenged by interactions with multiple clients over time. (See Chapters 4 and 7.)

**Self-efficacy:** The conviction that one can successfully execute the behavior required to produce desired outcomes. (See Chapter 27.)

**Single-system design:** Crisis intervention approaches that focus on the study of individuals as individuals. These designs investigate the rich and intricate details of specific cases, including the deviant cases that prove to be exceptions to the general rule. (See Chapter 27.)

**Solution-focused approach:** A solution-focused therapy is a time-limited treatment model aiming at assisting people to find solutions to their concerns in as few sessions as needed. Rather than focusing on the history of the problems, such an approach emphasizes an individual's strengths and resources. (See Chapter 3.)

**Somatization:** This term is synonymous with *somatic distress*. Somatization involves experiencing physical symptoms that suggest a medical condition whose physiological causes are undetermined. It is usually assumed that psychological factors are connected to the multiple, recurring medical complaints. Somatization manifests itself in tension headaches, gastrointestinal problems, back pain, tremors, choking sensations, and sexual complaints. (See Chapters 4 and 5.)

**Stalking:** A pattern of willful, malicious, and repeated behavioral intrusion on another person that is clearly unwanted and unwelcome, and has an implicit or explicit threat that causes the victim fear. (See Chapters 16 and 17.)

**Steady state:** A total condition of the system in which it is in balance both internally and with its environment, but is in change; a moving balance or dynamic homeostasis. (See Chapter 9.)

**Strengths perspective:** A practice perspective that looks at individuals, families, and communities in light of their capacities, strengths, talents, competencies, possibilities, and resources. (See Chapter 3.)

**Stress inoculation training (SIT):** A useful treatment package for clients who have resolved many assault-related problems but continue to exhibit severe fear responses. A cognitively and behaviorally based anxiety management approach, SIT is designed to assist the client in actively coping with target-specific, assault-related anxiety. (See Chapters 1, 8, and 17.)

**Student developmental tasks:** Predictable challenges facing late adolescent college students that require some measure of successful resolution or adaptation. Typical age-related tasks include coordinating apparent contradictory aspects of self, managing emotions, achieving greater cognitive complexity, and forming mutually satisfying relationships characterized by autonomous interdependence. (See Chapter 14.)

**Suicidal behavior:** Potentially self-injurious behavior for which there is evidence that the person intended at some level to kill him- or herself or wished to use the appearance of such an intention to obtain some other end. (See Chapter 2.)

**Suicidal ideation:** Any self-reported thoughts of engaging in suicidal behavior. (See Chapter 2.)

**Suicidal intent:** One's motive for engaging in suicidal behavior. (See Chapters 4 and 5.)

**Suicide:** Death where there is evidence that the injury was self-inflicted and that the person intended to kill him- or herself. (See Chapter 2 and 12.)

**Suicide attempt:** A potentially self-injurious behavior with a nonfatal outcome, for which there is evidence that the person intended at some level to kill him- or herself. (See Chapter 2.)

**Suicide prevention and crisis centers:** Centers that provide immediate assessment and crisis intervention to suicidal and depressed callers. The first prototype for these centers was established in London in 1906 when the Salvation Army opened an antisuicide bureau aimed at helping suicide attempters. The first federally funded suicide prevention center was established in 1958 in Los Angeles. The Los Angeles Suicide Prevention Center, codirected by Edwin Schneidman and Norman Farberow, provided comprehensive training to medical interns, psychiatric residents, and graduate students in psychology, social work, and counseling. (See Chapters 1 and 7.)

**Suicidologists:** Researchers who study suicidal behavior and suicide-related phenomena. The term *suicidology* was introduced by Edwin Schneidman. (See Chapters 1, 2, and 5.)

**Surveillance report:** Reports produced by the Centers for Disease Control and Prevention (CDC) or state departments of health on the number of HIV and/or AIDS cases and the routes of transmission, age, race, and gender of those cases. (See Chapter 20.)

**SWAT team:** Special weapons and tactics teams are units based within police departments that receive focused training to deal with hostage situations. SWAT teams usually use state-of-the art equipment and communications technology, and team members are trained in hostage negotiation skills. (See Chapters 16 and 17.)

**Targeted violence :** A violent incident perpetrated by a known attacker who has preselected a particular location or person(s) to attack. (See Chapter 13.)

**Telephone crisis services:** Crisis counseling, crisis stabilization, screening, information, and referrals provided to any individual calling in crisis or any significant other calling for someone else. (See Chapters 1 and 19.)

**Time-series designs:** Research designs that involve the measurement of change in some target behavior (usually the identified problem) at given intervals over a more or less extended period of time. Successive observations made during the course of therapeutic intervention enable the practitioner to systematically monitor the nature and extent of change in a target behavior. Typically, the phases of the time series are referred to as baseline (A) and intervention (B). (See Chapter 27.)

**Transdermal infusion system:** A method of delivering medicine by placing it in a special gel-like matrix "patch" that is applied to the skin. The medicine is absorbed through the skin at a fixed rate. (See Chapter 20.)

**Treatment package strategy:** A treatment evaluation strategy in which the impact of intervention is assessed as a total entity. In order to rule out potential threats to internal validity, such as changes attributable to motivation, spontaneous remission, intervening historical events, and the like, some sort of control or comparison condition must be incorporated into the research design. (See Chapter 27.)

**Triangulation:** A process involving the use of several evaluation strategies simultaneously within or across client systems. When done intentionally, triangulation enables the clinician to use each strategy as a means of cross-validating the findings generated by alternative strategies. (See Chapter 27.)

**Trigger:** A term used to describe environmental cues that lead the substance-dependent person to crave his or her drug of choice. (See Chapter 18.) (See Chapter 27.)

**Unwanted pursuit behaviors:** Hyperintimacy behaviors exhibited in attempts to develop a relationship or to reconcile or stay involved in a relationship with the target that are intrusive, unwanted, and invasive. (See Chapter 17.)

**Urgent:** Urgent conditions are those requiring immediate attention within a few hours; there is possible danger to the patient if medically unattended and the disorder is acute. Problem should be treated as soon as possible—generally within 1 to 2 hours. (See Chapters 2, 5, and 7.)

**Validity:** An evaluation term that refers to the question of whether an instrument measures what it purports to measure. (See Chapter 27.)

**Vertical transmission:** The transmission of HIV from mother to fetus. (See Chapter 20.)

**Viability:** The evaluation of a construct on the basis of its consequences to the individual and society, as well as its coherence with prevailing personal and social beliefs. (See Chapter 19.)

**Victim:** An innocent person, such as someone who suffers as a result of a violent crime or a disaster, and who encounters physical injury, trauma, fear, acute anxiety, and/or loss of belongings. (See Chapter 8.)

**Violence risk factors:** Biological, social, and familial characteristics or phenomena that have been shown to contribute to participation in adolescent aggression and delinquency. Although numerous risk factors have been identified, associating with negative peer groups; overly lax, inconsistent, or harsh parenting styles; and involvement with illegal substance use are among the most powerful factors associated with aggressive and violent behavior by adolescents. It is believed that increasing numbers of risk factors are associated with an increased likelihood of association with aggressive acts. (See Chapters 7 and 12.)

**Viral mutation:** A change in the genetic structure of the viral particle. Mutation is a naturally occurring process in all living organisms and is dangerous in HIV when the new or mutated viruses are the only ones to survive and thrive, rendering the antiretroviral therapy ineffective. (See Chapter 20.)

**Walk-in crisis services:** Crisis counseling, assessment, and intervention provided at the crisis services office. (See Chapter 19.)

**Weapons of mass destruction (WMDs):** Refers to the most destructive weapons, including nuclear and radioactive, chemical, or biological weapons, used by terrorist or paramilitary groups with the purpose of inflicting fear and causing evacuation and cleanup, economic disruption, and large numbers of casualties. (See introduction and Chapters 8 and 9.)

**Weltanschauung:** An individual's worldview regarding safety, security, or sense of self. (See Chapter 5.)

**Withdrawal:** A definable illness that occurs with a cessation or decrease in use of alcohol or a drug. (See Chapter 18.)

# Directory of Suicide Prevention and Crisis Intervention Internet Resources and 24-Hour Hotlines

PREPARED BY
DAVID AURISANO
JONATHON SINGER
KENNETH R. YEAGER

## SUICIDE PREVENTION WEBSITES

### Organizations

- *American Association of Suicidology (AAS)*: The American Association of Suicidology is a national organization devoted to understanding and preventing suicide through promoting research, training professionals and volunteers, and working to raise public awareness. AAS offers a credentialing program both for crisis centers and for individual crisis workers. http://www.suicidology.org
- *American Foundation for Suicide Prevention*: This organization is committed to advancing knowledge and prevention of suicide. It provides statistics, articles on suicide, and information and services for survivors. http://www.afsp.org/
- *Befrienders International*: Befrienders International provides free, nonjudgmental counseling services for people in crisis. The website contains statistics and articles on suicide, and information on depression, self-harm, homosexuality, and antibullying. http://www.befrienders.org
- *Kristin Brooks Hope Center*: The Kristin Brooks Hope Center runs the international 1-800-SUICIDE hotline system. The website provides information on crisis centers and hotlines, suicide, and advocacy. http://www.hopeline.com
- *LivingWorks Education—Applied Suicide Intervention Training*: LivingWorks Education provides training on suicide intervention and prevention. https://www.livingworks.net/
- *National Suicide Prevention Lifeline* consists of a network of more than 100 24-hour crisis centers in 43 states throughout the United States. The network and telephone hotline routing system are operated by the Mental Health Association of New York City with funding from the Substance Abuse and Mental Health Services Administration

(SAMHSA) of the US Department of Health and Human Services. For callers in crisis, the 24-hour hotline number is 1-800-273-TALK (8255). http://www.suicidepreventionlifeline.org

- *Suicide Prevention Action Network USA (SPAN USA)*: SPAN USA promotes suicide prevention through community organizing to raise awareness in local communities, as well as among federal, state, and local policymakers. http://www.spanusa.org
- *Suicide Prevention Resource Center*: The Suicide Prevention Resource Center aims to advance the national strategy for suicide prevention by providing prevention support, training, and informational materials. http://www.sprc.org
- *Yellow Ribbon Suicide Prevention Program*: This multidimensional program provides both a forum for youth, and education for parents, teachers, and clergy. http://www.yellowribbon.org

## Government Websites

- *Suicide Prevention—A Resource Manual for the U.S. Army*: This manual covers primary, secondary, and tertiary prevention of suicide, including training on providing support to the suicidal person and screening. It also covers dealing with the chain of command and the use of critical incident stress debriefing after a suicide. http://www.armyg1.army.mil/dcs/docs/Suicide%20Prevention%20Manual.pdf
- *Marine Corps Suicide Prevention website*: The Marine Corps suicide prevention website is a part of Marine Corps Community Services. It contains information on risk factors and protective factors, frequently asked questions, and resources in suicide prevention specific to the Marine Corps.    http://www.med.navy.mil/sites/nmcphc/health-promotion/psychological-emotional-wellbeing/Pages/suicide-prevention.aspx
- *Taking Action, Saving Lives—U.S. Navy Suicide Prevention Training Manual*: This is a suicide prevention training manual for the U.S. Navy. It contains an overview of suicide and its warning signs, as well as protective factors. It also identifies local resources and describes how to access them through the military chain of command. http://www.med.navy.mil/sites/nmcphc/health-promotion/Pages/Test-page.aspx
- *National Strategy for Suicide Prevention*: This website is a collaborative effort of SAMHSA, CDC, NIH, HRSA, and IHS and presents the national strategy for reducing suicide. http://www.surgeongeneral.gov/library/reports/national-strategy-suicide-prevention/full-report.pdf
- *Surgeon General's Suicide Prevention Call to Action*: This surgeon general's report addresses suicide statistics, suicide among special populations, and the surgeon general's recommendations for suicide prevention. http://www.surgeongeneral.gov/library/calltoaction/default.htm

## WEB-BASED RESOURCES

- Solution-Focused Brief Therapy Association in North American: http://www.sfbta.org/Default.aspx
- Partners for Collaborative Solutions: http://www.partners4change.net/
- International Journal of Solution-Focused Practices: http://www.ijsfp.com/index.php/ijsfp
- European Brief Therapy Association: http://ebta.eu/

## ELECTRONIC RESOURCES: BEST PRACTICES AND RESOURCES FOR PRACTITIONERS, ADOLESCENTS, AND THEIR FAMILIES

- *Children and Trauma: Update for Mental Health Professionals*: Information provided by the American Psychological Association's Task Force on Posttraumatic Stress Disorder and Trauma in Children and Adolescents regarding what is known about child and adolescent PTSD and trauma. https://www.apa.org/pi/families/resources/children-trauma-update.aspx
- *National Child Traumatic Stress Network Empirically Supported Treatments and Promising Practices*: Fact sheets describing clinical treatment and trauma-informed service approaches for children and adolescents implemented by National Child Traumatic Stress Network centers. Resources for parents and caregivers are also provided on the website. http://www.nctsn.org/resources/topics/treatments-that-work/promising-practices
- *US Department of Health and Human Services Administration for Children and Families: Treatment for Traumatized Children, Youth, and Families*: Resources to help professionals identify and implement treatment programs to meet the needs of children, youth, and families affected by trauma. https://www.childwelfare.gov/responding/treatment.cfm
- *US Department of Health and Human Services: Office of Adolescent Health*: Provides resources on adolescent health, including webinars, a list of evidence-based programs, and an e-learning module on adolescent trauma. http://www.hhs.gov/ash/oah
- *National Institute of Mental Health: Helping Children and Adolescents Cope With Violence and Disasters: What Parents Can Do*: Provides information on common responses in children and adolescents exposed to trauma and what can be done to help. Also provides resources on trauma. http://www.nimh.nih.gov/health/publications/helping-children-and-adolescents-cope-with-violence-and-disasters-parents/index.shtml

- *Center for the Study of Traumatic Stress*: Resources and research addressing US Department of Defense concerns on the psychological impact and health consequences resulting from the impact of traumatic events. Includes information on children and families. http://www.cstsonline.org
- *Medical University of South Caroline (MUSC) Trauma-Focused Cognitive Behavioral Therapy Web-Based Learning Course*: TF-CBT Web educates mental health professionals about trauma-focused cognitive-behavioral therapy (TF-CBT). Also provides resources for therapists, children, and parents, including evidence-based practices. http://tfcbt.musc.edu
- *National Registry of Evidence-Based Programs and Practices (NREPP)*: The NREPP is an online registry of numerous substance abuse and mental health interventions. http://www.nrepp.samhsa.gov/
- *American Academy of Child and Adolescent Psychiatry*: Provides resources for families regarding children and adolescents. Some covered topics include disasters, military concerns, bullying, violence, and grief. http://www.aacap.org
- *Child Trauma Academy*: Provides information and resources for both practitioners and caregivers on child and adolescent trauma and PTSD, violence, abuse, and neglect, as well as interventions. http://childtrauma.org
- *US Department of Veterans Affairs: National Center for PTSD*: Provides information for the public and professionals about PTSD in children and adolescents, including assessment, treatment, and research. http://www.ptsd.va.gov/professional/treatment/children/ptsd_in_children_and_adolescents_overview_for_professionals.asp
- Online training in core competencies is available through the FEMA Emergency Management Institute at http://training.fema.gov/IS/crslist.aspx
- The Office of Victims of Crime published a bulletin describing the basic structure of the program elements: http://www.ovc.gov/publications/bulletins/schoolcrisis/welcome.html
- Report of the Connecticut School Safety Infrastructure Council, February 2014: http://das.ct.gov/images/1090/SSIC_Final_Draft_Report.pdf
- The National Center for Victims of Crime: Stalking Resource Center: www.victimsofcrime.org
- Crime Victim Services: http://www.crimevictimservices.org/
- Office on Women's Health: Violence Against Women: http://www.womenshealth.gov/violence-against-women/types-of-violence/stalking.html
- Office on Violence Against Women: http://www.ovw.usdoj.gov/about-stalking.htm
- American Psychological Association: Information about bullying: http://www.apa.org/topics/bullying/

- Centers for Disease Control and Prevention: Information about school violence: http://www.cdc.gov/VIOLENCEPREVENTION/youthviolence/schoolviolence/index.html
- National Organization of Victim Assistance (NOVA): http://www.trynova.org
- Stop Bullying: www.stopbullying.gov
- US Department of Education School Violence Factsheet: http://nces.ed.gov/fastfacts/display.asp?id=49
- American Association of Suicidology (Accredited Centers): http://www.suicidology.org/crisis-centers
- Big White Wall (support network): http://www.bigwhitewall.com/landing-pages/default.aspx?ReturnUrl=%2f
- Care Crisis Chat: http://www.crisischat.org/
- Common Ground: http://www.commonground.org/our-programs#.U2FviVcXLXx
- Contra Costa Crisis Chat (California): http://www.crisis-center.org/crisis-lines-chat-program/
- CrisisChat: http://www.crisischat.org/chat
- Crisisline Online (New York): http://211lifeline.org/about-2-1-1life-line/
- Didi Hirsch Mental Health Services: http://www.didihirsch.org/chat
- GLBT National Help Center Peer Support Chat: http://www.glnh.org/chat/index.html
- TheHopeLine Live Coach Chat: http://unsuicide.wikispaces.com/The+HopeLine+Live+HopeCoach+Chat
- IM Alive: https://www.imalive.org/
- Iowa Crisis Chat (English and Mandarin): http://iowacrisischat.org/
- Mental Health Counselors Assn. (Resources): http://www.amhca.org/public_resources/client_resources.aspx
- Montana Warmline Chat: http://www.montanawarmline.org/Support.html
- National Suicide Prevention Lifeline: http://www.suicidepreventionlifeline.org/
- RAINN Online Hotline (Rape, Abuse, Incest): http://www.rainn.org/get-help/national-sexual-assault-online-hotline
- Scarleteen (online sex education): http://www.scarleteen.com/
- Veterans' Live Chat: http://veteranscrisisline.net/ChatTermsOfService.aspx
- San Francisco Suicide Prevention: http://betterlifebayarea.org/live-chat
- Suicide Forum (chat room): http://www.suicideforum.com/
- 866 Teenlink: http://866teenlink.org/
- TrevorChat (LGBT): http://www.thetrevorproject.org/pages/get-help-now
- Warmline Chats (national directory listed by state): http://www.warmline.org/

- Your Life, Your Voice (youth): http://www.yourlifeyourvoice.org/ Pages/default.aspx
- University of Memphis CIT Center: http://cit.memphis.edu
- CIT International: http://www.citinternational.org
- NAMI CIT Resource Center: http://www.nami.org/template. cfm?section=CIT2
- NAMI Georgia CIT: http://www.namiga.org/CIT/
- Florida CIT: http://www.floridacit.org/
- Ohio Criminal Justice Coordinating Center of Excellence: http://www. neomed.edu/academics/criminal-justice-coordinating-center-of-excellence/
- Houston, Texas Police Department Mental Health Division: http:// www.houstoncit.org/
- ABCs of Internet Psychotherapy: http://www.metanoia.org/imhs/ directry.htm
- DMOZ Mental Health Directory (28 directories): http://www.dmoz. org/Health/Mental_Health/Counseling_Services/Directories/
- eCounseling websites: http://www.adca-online.org/links.htm
- eMental Health Center: http://www.e-mhc.com/
- Mental Health and Psychology Resources Online: http://psychcentral. com/resources/
- National Directory of Online Counselors: www.etherapyweb.com
- Psychotherapy Online: http://psychology.about.com/od/ psychotherapy/a/onlinepsych.htm
- Telemental Health Therapy Comparisons: http://www.telemental-healthcomparisons.com/?login=provider-networks
- YAHOO Directory of Mental Health Resource: https://dir.yahoo.com/ health/mental_health/
- Psychology.com Direction for How You Live: http://www.psychology. com/
- Psychology Today Mental Health Assessment: http://psychologytoday. tests.psychtests.com/take_test.php?idRegTest=3040

## Mobile Applications

- *ASK & Prevent Suicide*: App that helps users recognize the warning signs for suicide, ask about suicidal thoughts, and find help for people at risk (part of the Texas state GLS grant). http://itunes.apple.com/us/ app/ask-prevent-suicide/id419595716?mt=8
- *Suicide Crisis Support*: A free app for Android phones from the QPR Institute that provides an electronic version of the booklet "The Tender Leaves of Hope, Helping Someone Survive a Suicide Crisis." https:// play.google.com/store/apps/details?id=qprinstitute.crisis&hl=en
- *safeTALK Wallet Card*: A free iOS app for participants of the safe-TALK program, providing an interactive version of the wallet card that allows users to add "KeepSafe Connections." http://www.livingworks. net/page/safeTALK%20Wallet%20Card%20App%20for%20iOS

- *Wingman Project*: An app that teaches the Air National Guard's ACE suicide intervention method—Ask, Care, Escort. http://www.livingworks. net/page/safeTALK%20Wallet%20Card%20App%20for%20iOS

## Resources on Youth Suicide

- *Youth Suicide Prevention Program*: This website provides information on preventing suicide and self harm, as well as public awareness and training. http://www.yspp.org/
- *Youth Suicide Problems: Gay, Bisexual Male Focus*: This website focuses on information about and prevention of suicide among the highly neglected population of gay and bisexual adolescents. http:// www.youthsuicide.com/gay-bisexual

## CRISIS INTERVENTION WEBSITES

- *Brief Treatment and Crisis Intervention*: The quarterly peer-reviewed international journal *Brief Treatment and Crisis Intervention: A Journal of Evidence-Based Practice* is dedicated to advancing clinical practice, mental health policy, and knowledge building related to behavioral health, crisis assessment and crisis intervention, trauma treatment, and forensic studies. Dr. Albert R. Roberts is the editor-in-chief, and it is published by Oxford University Press journals division. http://www.oxfordjournals.org/our_journals/btcint/
- *Crisis Intervention Network*: This website provides information about crisis intervention strategies and protocols, as well as the latest books and journal articles focusing on evidence-based crisis intervention and time-limited treatment. It also includes news alerts on recent empirically based step-by-step crisis intervention protocols, the continuum of the duration and severity of woman battering, domestic violence safety protocols, and links to other suicide prevention and social work websites. The website was developed by Dr. Albert R. Roberts, with sections added on crisis intervention with substance abusers by Dr. Kenneth R. Yeager. http://www.crisisinterventionnetwork.com
- *Crisis Prevention Institute*: The Crisis Prevention Institute trains professionals in working with potentially violent individuals through a behavior management program called Nonviolent Crisis Intervention. http://www.crisisprevention.com
- *The American Academy of Experts in Traumatic Stress (AAETS)*: The American Academy of Experts in Traumatic Stress is a multidisciplinary organization of professionals that aims to advance the treatment of trauma, emergency services, and forensic mental health. This organization works to identify expertise and provide standards and training for professionals who provide trauma services. It publishes and disseminates to its members monographs and information sheets on traumatic

stress response protocols for emergency responders and violence prevention protocols. The 10-step Trauma Response Protocol developed by
Dr. Mark D. Lerner and Dr. Raymond Sheltonand their associates is
highlighted in Chapter 7 in this book. http://www.aaets.org

- *National Organization for Victim Assistance (NOVA)*: This professional organization is devoted to the recognition of victims' rights and
the delivery of victim services. NOVA offers training in group crisis
intervention throughout North America and maintains a national crisis response team. http://www.trynova.org

- *National Domestic Violence Hotline*: The National Domestic Violence
Hotline is a national hotline provided for by the Violence Against
Women Act of 1994. In addition to information about the hotline, the
website contains information on domestic violence, teens and dating
violence, domestic violence in the workplace, information for victims
and survivors of domestic violence, and information for abusers. http://
www.ndvh.org/.

## CHILD ABUSE AND NEGLECT

- *ChildhelpUSA: Treatment and Prevention of Child Abuse*: Childhelp-
USA is a private nonprofit organization founded in 1959. ChildhelpUSA
services include counseling, residential treatment, group homes,
foster care, professional training, educational programs, community outreach, and public awareness. ChildhelpUSA sponsors the
ChildhelpUSA® National Child Abuse Hotline, 1-800-4-A-CHILD®,
which provides toll-free 24-hour crisis counseling and referrals to local
agencies and adult survivor groups throughout the United States and
Canada. http://www.childhelpusa.org/

- *National Data Archive on Child Abuse and Neglect (NDACAN)*: The
purpose of NDACAN is to improve and expand the use of data collected by researchers. Based out of Cornell University, NDACAN
acquires microdata from researchers and national data collection
efforts and makes these data sets available to the research community
for secondary analysis. http://www.ndacan.cornell.edu/

- *The Child Abuse Prevention Network (CAPN)*: The target audience of
CAPN is professionals in the field of child abuse and neglect. CAPN
serves as a clearinghouse of websites related to child abuse prevention.
http://child-abuse.com/

## DEATH OF A LOVED ONE

- *HealthyPlace.com*: Provides basic information about grief and loss.
Three online videos discuss how to prepare for the death of a loved
one, how to cope with the loss of a parent, and how to help your child

through a death in the family. http://www.healthyplace.com/communities/depression/related/ loss_grief_3.asp

- *AARP*: A clearinghouse of resources on grief and loss, including links to community resources, articles on grief and loss over the life span, financial preparation, and remembrance rituals. http://www.aarp.org/life/griefandloss/
- *Alive Alone, Inc.*: Resources for parents who have lost a child. Includes a bimonthly newsletter and information on self-help support groups. http://www.alivealone.org
- *Bereaved Parents of the USA*: Nonprofit self-help group for parents who have lost a loved one, including children, pets, parents, and so on. Includes an excellent resource page with information on grief and loss, medical information, and financial resources. http://www.bereaved-parentsusa.org/
- *Parents of Murdered Children (PMOC)*: The PMOC, originally only for parents of murdered children, has an expanded focus to include support for all survivors of loved ones who have been murdered. Services include monthly meetings at local chapters, training for service providers, and a national crisis hotline at 1-800-818-POMC. http://www.pomc.com/
- *The National SIDS/Infant Death Resource Center*: Provides free online publications regarding SIDS and infant death. Useful resource page with links to related website. http://www.sidscenter.org/

## PERSONS WITH LIFE-THREATENING ILLNESS

- *AIDS Info*: This National Institutes of Health website provides information on treatment guidelines, clinical trials, and vaccines and answers to frequently asked questions. http://www.aidsinfo.nih.gov
- *CDC Division of HIV/AIDS Prevention*: This website provides information on the National CDC STD/HIV/AIDS/TB Hotline, which is open 24/7 (call 1-800-342-2437). This website also provides information on testing, transmission, symptoms, and HIV/AIDS in special populations. http://www.cdc.gov/hiv/dhap.htm
- *National Ovarian Cancer Coalition*: The National Ovarian Cancer Coalition is a clearinghouse for information on ovarian cancer and provides information on symptoms, diagnosis, treatment, and coping with the disease. http://www.ovarian.org/
- *Ovarian Cancer National Alliance*: The Ovarian Cancer National Alliance provides information and support for women with ovarian cancer, survivors, and family members. http://www.ovariancancer.org/
- *Colorectal Cancer Network*: The Colorectal Cancer Network provides information on colon cancer and treatment options. It also provides

support groups for people suffering from colorectal cancer. http://www.colorectal-cancer.net/

- *The Leukemia and Lymphoma Society*: The Leukemia and Lymphoma Society provides information on leukemia, lymphoma, myeloma, and other blood cancers. It provides free educational material and information on support groups for people with blood cancer. http://www.lls.org/

## SELF-HELP GROUPS/SUPPORT GROUPS CLEARINGHOUSE

- *American Self-Help Group Clearinghouse*: Located at the Graduate Center of the City University of New York, this clearinghouse provides research reports and information on how to set up a peer support group. Information is available to member agencies on more 1,100 national, international, local, and online support groups for addictions, bereavement, health, mental health, disabilities, abuse, parenting, caregiver concerns, and other possible crisis-inducing situations. Call 1-212-817-1822. http://www.selfhelpgroup.org
- *New Jersey Self-Help Group Clearinghouse*: This is a nonprofit service of Saint Claire's Health System and is funded by the New Jersey Division of Mental Health Services. It provides information by phone on more than 4,500 local self-help groups throughout the state of New Jersey, as well as affiliates of national support groups. In New Jersey, call 1-800-367-6274; outside New Jersey, call 973-326-6789. http://www.njgroups.org/

## SEVERELY MENTALLY ILL ADULTS

- *National Alliance for Mental Illness (NAMI)*: NAMI is a self-help, support, and advocacy group for consumers, friends, and families living with mental illness. The website includes online information regarding mental illness, education and training, and local support groups and resources. National information hotline (not crisis): 1-800-950-NAMI (6264). http://www.nami.org
- *National Resource and Training Center on Homeless and Mental Illness*: A service of SAMHSA, the website provides information on effective delivery of services to people with mental illness or substance abuse problems who are homeless. http://www.nrchmi.samhsa.gov/
- *National Alliance for Research on Schizophrenia and Depression (NARSAD)*: This organization provides up-to-date information on research on schizophrenia, depression, bipolar disorder, and anxiety disorders. It also provides information on evidence-based treatment options and best practices. http://www.narsad.org

## SUBSTANCE ABUSE AND OTHER ADDICTIONS

- *National Council on Alcoholism and Drug Dependence, Inc. (NCADD)*: The NCADD lists local resources, provides free publications, and sponsors a national alcoholism hotline: 1-800-622-2255. http://www.ncadd.org/
- *Substance Abuse and Mental Health Services Administration (SAMHSA)*: SAMHSA provides the most current and comprehensive information on substance abuse information for service providers, consumers, and researchers. Free publications. National Hotline for Alcohol and Drug Information: 1-800-729-6686. http://www.samhsa. gov/treatment
- *Focus Adolescent Services*: Designed for consumers, this website has links to US-specific and international resources, describes different types of drugs, and identifies slang terms associated with them. The substance abuse section is part of a more comprehensive website that addresses many of the issues faced by adolescents. http://www.focusas.org/
- *Al-Anon/Alateen*: One of the largest and oldest support groups for people who live with alcoholics. National hotline: 1-800-344-2666. http://www.al-anon.org/
- *American Council on Alcoholism*: Resource for the public on the effects of alcoholism. Provides information about treatment resources. National hotline: 1-800-527-5344. http://www.aca-usa.org/

## RUNAWAY YOUTH

- *National Runaway Switchboard (NRS)*: A service of the Family and Youth Service Bureaus, the NRS provides a 24-hour hotline for runaway youth. State-sponsored hotlines (e.g., Texas and Florida) are connected to the NRS's national hotline. The hotline provides crisis intervention, referrals to local services, and education on ways to return home. The site also provides information for parents, educators, social service providers, and law enforcement officials. 1-800-RUNAWAY. http://www.nrscrisisline.org/ kids.asp

## ADOLESCENT AND YOUNG ADULT MENTAL ILLNESS

- *Substance Abuse and Mental Health Services Administration (SAMHSA)*: SAMHSA provides information on child and adolescent mental health for consumers, service providers, and researchers. The child and adolescent section provides information on national

programs that address the various issues associated with children's mental health. http://www.samhsa.gov/
- *Youth and Mental Illness*: A self-help booklet produced by the Canadian Psychiatric Association. http://www.cpa-apc.org/browse/documents/46

## SEPARATION AND DIVORCE

- *Canadian Mental Health Association*: Provides information for consumers on separation and divorce. http://www.cmha.ca/english/info_centre/mh_pamphlets/mh_pamphlet_08.htm

# *Index*

Page numbers followed by "f" and "t" indicate figures and tables.